America

The Essential Learning Edition

America
The Essential Learning Edition

VOLUME TWO

DAVID EMORY SHI

GEORGE BROWN TINDALL

W. W. Norton & Company, Inc.

New York • London

W. W. Norton & Company has been independent since its founding in 1923, when William Warder Norton and Mary D. Herter Norton first published lectures delivered at the People's Institute, the adult education division of New York City's Cooper Union. The firm soon expanded its program beyond the Institute, publishing books by celebrated academics from America and abroad. By mid-century, the two major pillars of Norton's publishing program—trade books and college texts— were firmly established. In the 1950s, the Norton family transferred control of the company to its employees, and today—with a staff of four hundred and a comparable number of trade, college, and professional titles published each year—W. W. Norton & Company stands as the largest and oldest publishing house owned wholly by its employees.

Editor: Jon Durbin
Developmental Editors: Lisa Moore and John Elliott
Associate Editor: Justin Cahill
Project Editor: Melissa Atkin
Editorial Assistant: Penelope Lin
Marketing Manager, History: Sarah England
Manuscript Editor: Mike Fleming
Managing Editor, College: Marian Johnson
Managing Editor, College Digital Media: Kim Yi
Production Manager: Andy Ensor
Media Editor: Lisa Moore
Media Project Editor: Penelope Lin
Media Editorial Assistant: Chris Hillyer
Design Director: Hope Miller Goodell
Photo Editor: Nelson Colón
Permissions Manager: Megan Jackson
Composition: Graphic World, Inc.
Manufacturing: LSC Communications, Kendallville

The Library of Congress has cataloged the full edition as follows:

Tindall, George Brown.
    America : a narrative history / George Brown Tindall,
David Emory Shi.—9th ed.
        p.   cm.
    Includes bibliographical references and index.
    ISBN 978-0-393-91262-3 (hardcover)
        1. United States—History—Textbooks.   I. Shi, David E.   II. Title.
    E178.1.T55 2013   2012034504
    973—dc23
        This edition:
        ISBN 978-0-393-93803-6

W. W. Norton & Company, Inc., 500 Fifth Avenue, New York, NY 10110-0017
wwnorton.com
W. W. Norton & Company Ltd., 15 Carlisle Street, London W1D 3BS
2 3 4 5 6 7 8 9 0

For Jon Durbin, editor and friend

About the Authors

DAVID SHI is a professor of history and the president emeritus of Furman University. He is the author of several books on American cultural history, including the award-winning *The Simple Life: Plain Living and High Thinking in American Culture* and *Facing Facts: Realism in American Thought and Culture, 1850–1920*.

GEORGE TINDALL recently of the University of North Carolina, Chapel Hill, was an award-winning historian of the South with a number of major books to his credit, including *The Emergence of the New South, 1913–1945* and *The Disruption of the Solid South*.

Lead authors for media and pedagogy

JON LEE (San Antonio College, Texas) served on the American Historical Association/Lumina Tuning Project and educational commissions in the state of Texas to establish discipline-wide historical learning outcomes. He received the "Most Inspirational Professor" award from Phi Theta Kappa Beta Nu. He is the coordinator of the Honors Academy at San Antonio College.

ERIK ANDERSON (San Antonio College, Texas) teaches American history and is involved with the Honors Academy. He also serves as the academic liaison with the Travis Early College High School program at San Antonio College. Anderson earned his doctorate at Brown University.

Contents
in Brief

Contents

Maps

What's It All About?

Thinking Like A Historian

Preface

The Essential Learning Edition builds upon *America*'s long-established emphasis on history as a storytelling art. It features colorful characters and anecdotes informed by balanced analysis and social texture, all guided by the unfolding of key events. But this Essential Learning Edition, a new addition to the *America* family, includes innovative pedagogical features and tools to help students better understand the most important aspects of American history, to learn how historians study, interpret, and debate the past, and to assess their own progress.

To guide my efforts in crafting the Essential Learning Edition, I asked students and professors at a variety of colleges what they most needed in an introductory survey textbook. Their answers varied, but overall there was a strong consensus on several key points: students want a manageable, inexpensive textbook that focuses on the essentials of American history while telling the dramatic story of the nation's past in vivid but simple language. They stressed that many textbooks overwhelm them, either by flooding them with too much information or by taking too much for granted in terms of the knowledge that students bring to the introductory course. Students also asked for a textbook that would help them more easily identify the most important developments or issues to focus on (and remember) as they read.

To address these student concerns, I have streamlined and compressed the Brief Ninth Edition of *America* to build the Essential Learning Edition. It has 30 chapters as compared to 34 in the Brief Ninth Edition, which means that it nicely fits the chapter per week model for most courses. Moreover, I have trimmed the narrative text of the Brief Ninth Edition by about fifteen percent to focus on the most essential elements of *America*'s past. Finally, because I assumed little or no background knowledge on the part of the student reader, I sought to ensure that the major topics in each chapter are easily grasped and all key terms are clearly identified.

When asked about their needs in a survey text, instructors said much the same as their students, but they also asked for a textbook that introduced students to the nature of historical research, analysis, and debate. Many professors also mentioned the growing importance to them and their institutions of assessing the success of their classes in meeting the learning goals established by their department. Accordingly, I have aligned the Essential Learning Edition with specific learning outcomes for the introductory American history survey course approved by various state and national organizations, including the American Historical Association. To help me make those changes, my innovative editor, Jon Durbin, recruited a talented multi-disciplinary group of professors, pedagogical specialists, developmental editors, instructional designers, reviewers, and copy editors. In particular, Erik Anderson and Jon Lee of San Antonio College in Texas served as the pedagogical specialists and lead media authors for this project. They are both widely recognized as superb teachers and innovative leaders in assessment and community-college instruction. The new pedagogical features in the Essential Learning Edition were a direct outgrowth of their efforts teaching the survey course and working closely with students in a dynamic, collaborative, community-based learning environment in the Honors College at San Antonio College. Moreover, the new pedagogical features of this book and its accompanying media components—including the new Norton InQuizitive program, an adaptive online tool designed to guide student learning—make it much easier for professors to assess their students' performance on a variety of learning levels.

These and other suggestions from students and professors have shaped this Essential Learning Edition. Each of the 30 chapters begins with a list of five or six Core Objectives, carefully designed to help students understand—and remember—the major developments in each period. To make it easier for students to grasp the major developments, I have reorganized every chapter to ensure that the narrative aligns sequentially with the objectives. Each Core Objective appears at the beginning of each major section in the chapter for which it is relevant. Core Objective Flags, unique to this edition, appear in the page margins to highlight topics in the narrative that are essential to understanding the broader Core Objective. Key terms, chosen to reinforce the major concepts, are bolded in the text and defined in the margin, helping students appreciate and remember their significance. At the end of each chapter, new review features are designed to reinforce the Core Objectives, including clear chapter summaries, lists of key terms, and chapter chronologies.

This book breaks new ground by incorporating several new instructional features designed to improve student learning. Maps, for example, are essential to history textbooks, but in this version I have taken the additional step of listing questions underneath each map to help students analyze the implications embedded in maps in a way that promotes active learning.

Interactive maps are but just one example of the innovative elements in this book designed to deepen student learning. Each chapter in the Essential Learning Edition also includes a **What It's All About** feature, which visually summarizes in a graphical format major issues such as:

- Chapter 3: Comparative examination of how different regions of the English colonies were settled and developed.
- Chapter 9: Analyzes sectional conflicts and the role the economic policies of Henry Clay and Andrew Jackson played in those conflicts.

- Chapter 12: Abolitionist versus pro-slavery arguments on slavery.

- Chapter 15: Tracing the legal and legislative road from slavery to freedom for African Americans in the former Confederate States.

- Chapter 23: The First New Deal compared to the Second New Deal.

Another unique new feature, called **Thinking Like a Historian**, helps students better understand—and apply—the research techniques and interpretive skills used by historians. Through carefully selected examples the Thinking Like a Historian feature highlights the essential role of primary and secondary sources as the building blocks of history and illustrates the ways in which historians have differed in their interpretations of the past. There is one Thinking Like a Historian feature for each major period of American history; each feature takes on a major interpretive issue in that era. In Part I of the activity, students first read excerpts from two original secondary sources that offer competing interpretive views framing that period. In Part II, students then read some of the original primary sources that those same historians used to develop their arguments. Finally, students are asked to answer a series of questions that guide their reading and analysis of the sources.

As always, this new edition also includes new content. As I created the Essential Learning Edition, I have complemented the political narrative by incorporating more social and cultural history into the text. Key new discussions include:

- Chapter 3, Colonial Ways of Life, 1607–1750, includes a new portrait of Antonio, an enslaved African brutalized by his Dutch owner in Maryland in the mid-seventeenth century. There is also new material on the competition among American colonists for British luxury goods in the 1760s and 1770s.

- Chapter 4, From Colonies to States, 1607–1776, has enriched material on the non-importation efforts (boycotts of British goods) led by grassroots Americans prior to the Revolutionary War. It also includes new material about the conversion of American farmers into soldiers after the clash of arms at Lexington and Concord.

- Chapter 5, The American Revolution, 1776–1783, includes more material about slaves who took advantage of the war to escape or join the British forces, and about the ways in which women, Native Americans, and slaves became engaged in the war effort.

- Chapter 6, Creating a "More Perfect Union," 1783–1800, elaborates on Shays's Rebellion and other expressions of agrarian discontent across the nation after the Revolution, and there is also more discussion about how women, Native Americans, and slaves figured into the thinking of the Founding Fathers during the Constitutional Convention in 1787.

- Chapter 7, The Early Republic, 1800–1815, has new material on the way in which the War of 1812 affected slavery/blacks.

- Chapter 8, The Emergence of a Market Economy, 1815–1850, offers new discussions of the emergence of the cotton culture in the South and the plight of the Irish fleeing the famine at home and heading to America.

- Chapter 9, Nationalism and Sectionalism, 1815–1828, more fully discusses the role of labor advocates and unions in forging what would become the Jacksonian movement.

- Chapter 10, The Jacksonian Era, 1828–1840, describes the effect of the Panic of 1837 and the ensuing depression on the working poor.

- Chapter 11, The South and Slavery, 1800–1860, boasts substantial new material related to slavery and African American culture. There is also a new discussion of a New Orleans slave revolt led by Charles Deslondes in 1811, the largest slave revolt in American history.

- Chapter 12, Religion, Romanticism, and Reform, 1800–1860, includes enriched treatment of the revivalism of the Second Great Awakening, and a completely rewritten discussion of Mormonism.

- Chapter 14, The War of the Union, 1861–1865, adds new material about the social history of the Civil War, including more material on common soldiers, rioting in opposition to the military draft, and backwoods violence rarely included in discussions of the war, such as the summary of the execution of thirteen Unionists in Madison County, North Carolina.

- Chapter 15, Reconstruction, 1865–1877, highlights the circumstances of former slaves—from their perspective. It also includes new examples of the ways in which the Freedmen's Bureau helped negotiate labor contracts between white planters and freedmen.

- Chapter 16, Big Business and Organized Labor, 1860–1900, discusses the emergence of a new middle class during the Gilded Age, and includes substantially revised material on women's and labor history.

- Chapter 17, The South and the West Transformed, 1865–1900, offers a newly rewritten section on the emergence of new racial segregation in the South, and also new material about the everyday realities of Western expansion.

- Chapter 20, The Progressive Era, 1890–1920, provides new sections the attitudes of Theodore Roosevelt and Woodrow Wilson's attitudes and policies concerning race.

- Chapter 21, America and the Great War, 1914–1920, now highlights the war's social effects in the United States, with special attention to women, blacks, and Mexican Americans.

- Chapter 22, A Clash of Cultures, 1920–1929, incorporates new material on the consumer culture, women's history, and revised material on the Harlem Renaissance with a new profile of Zora Neale Hurston.

- Chapter 24, The Second World War, 1933–1945, includes new material about the wartime experience of Mexican Americans.

- Chapter 25, The Cold War and the Fair Deal, 1945–1952, benefits from new coverage of women industrial workers, and also the efforts of Latinos to gain equal rights in the aftermath of World War II.

- Chapter 27, New Frontiers, 1960–1968, showcases a new portrait of Fannie Lou Hamer, a black Mississippi activist, in the section on the early civil rights movements.

- Chapter 28, Rebellion and Reaction, the 1960s and 1970's, includes new material on the women's movement, Mexican Americans, and Native Americans.

In sum, this new *Essential Learning Edition* includes the most dramatic changes ever made in a resilient book that is celebrating its thirtieth year in print.

Media Tools for Students and Instructors

New lead authors for media and pedagogy Jon Lee and Erik Anderson have ensured that the Essential Learning Edition of *America* is supported by an array of digital media with tools faculty need to meet course goals—in the classroom and online—and activities for students to develop core skills in reading comprehension, writing, and analysis.

The Essential Learning Edition Team

I have already introduced you to Erik Anderson and Jon Lee, but our talented team of innovative support authors also includes Brandon Franke (Blinn College), Cathy Parzynski (Montgomery County Community College), Melissa Weinbrenner (Northeast Texas Community College), Brian Cervantez (Tarrant County College), and Laura Farkas (Ivy Tech College–West Lafayette), who have contributed to all of the enriching learning materials we can offer students and instructors for support:

⟨⟨⟩ INQUIZITIVE
Quizzing to Learn

InQuizitive, Norton's new adaptive quizzing platform, uses interactive questions and guided feedback to motivate students to read and understand the text. Varied question types—featuring images, maps, and sources—prompt critical and analytical thinking on each of the chapter's Core Objectives. Robust grading functionality helps instructors track their students' progress on learning outcomes.

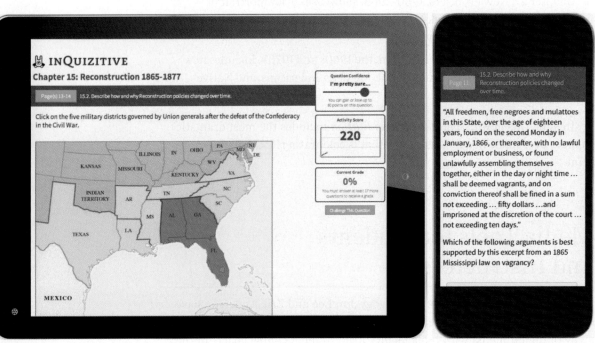

Student Site

This free site offers students access to additional primary source documents and images, Office Hour videos with author David Shi, and iMaps. It is ideal for instructors interested in granting students access to additional material without creating or administering online assignments.

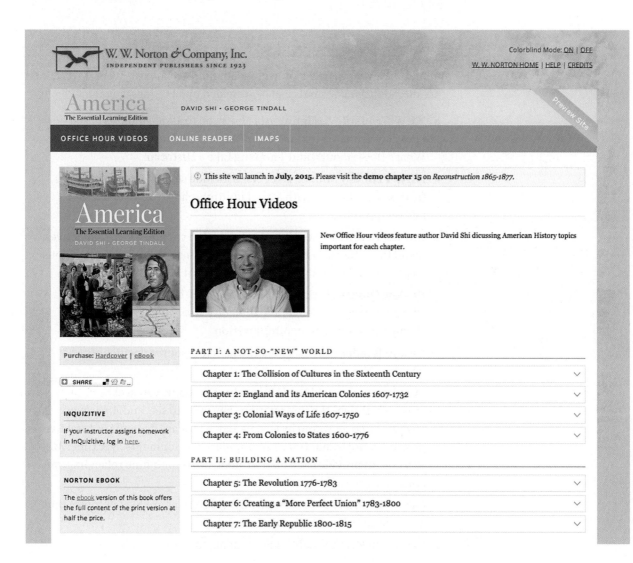

Norton Ebooks

Norton Ebooks let students access the entire book and much more: they can search, highlight, and take notes with ease, as well as collaborate and share their notes with instructors and classmates. Ebooks can be viewed on any device—laptop, tablet, phone, even a public computer—and will stay synced between devices.

Norton Coursepacks

Free Norton Coursepacks (downloadable in Blackboard, WebCT, D2L, and Moodle; additional formats can be provided upon request), include:

- **NEW Gradable Assignments** allow you to assign quizzes based on questions from the text including Assessing the Core Objectives, What's It All About?, and Thinking Like a Historian.
- **NEW Primary Source Exercises** include several primary sources from across cultures with a brief multiple choice exam and a short answer question.
- **Guided Reading Exercises,** keyed to each chapter's Core Objectives, instill the three-step Note-Summarize-Assess pedagogy. Each chapter has one exercise built around passages from the text.
- **Review Quizzes** include targeted feedback that highlights Core Objective, page reference, and difficulty. *Chrono-Quizzes* end each chapter quiz with a matching question.
- **Online Reader** provides over 100 primary-source documents and images.
- **Map Resources** include *iMaps*, where students can peel back each layer to highlight the information they want to see, and *American History Tours*, powered by Google Earth that are dynamic, interactive primary sources that trace geographical developments over time. *Map Worksheets* provide each map without labels for offline relabeling and quizzing.
- **Forum Prompts** for online and hybrid courses are a set of topics that can be used to launch discussions.
- **Key Term Flash Cards** allow students to self-study historical vocabulary.
- Links to **InQuizitive** for each chapter.

Classroom Presentation Tools

- **Lecture PowerPoints** and **Art PowerPoints** feature photographs and maps from the book, retouched for in-class presentation.

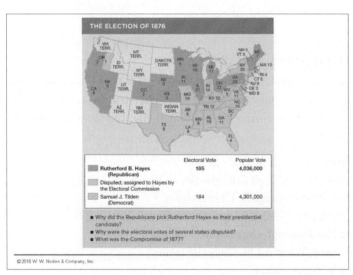

- The **Norton American History Digital Archive** includes over 1,700 images, audio and video files that are arranged chronologically and by theme, available online or on DVD.

Instructor's Manual (Melissa Weinbrenner, Northeast Texas Community College)

The Instructor's Manual for The Essential Learning Edition has everything instructors need to prepare lectures and classroom activities: chapter summaries, suggestions for teaching Core Objectives, as well as lecture ideas, classroom activities, and lists of recommended books, films, and websites.

Test Bank (Brandon Franke, Blinn College; Cathy Parzynski, Montgomery County Community College; and Melissa Weinbrenner, Northeast Texas Community College)

The Test Bank features multiple-choice, true/false, and essay questions aligned with the chapter's Core Objectives and classified according to level of difficulty, Bloom's Taxonomy, and the American Historical Association's guidelines for student learning outcomes, offering multiple avenues for content and skill assessment. All Norton test banks are available with Exam-View Test Generator software, allowing instructors to easily create, administer, and manage assessments.

Acknowledgments

The quality and range of reviews on this project were truly exceptional. The book and its accompanying media components benefited from the insights of numerous instructors.

Erik Anderson, San Antonio College
Milan Andrejevich, Ivy Tech College–South Bend
Evan Bennett, Florida Atlantic University
Laura Bergstrom, Ivy Tech College–Sellersburg
Keith Berry, Hillsborough Community College
Albert Broussard, Texas A&M, College Station
Blanche Brick, Blinn College
Cory Burger, Ivy Tech College–Terre Haute
Brian Cervantez, Tarrant County College–Northwest Campus
Michael L. Collins, Midwestern State University
Lee Cowan, Tarrant County College
Thomas A. DeBlack, Arkansas Tech University
Scott Derr, Ivy Tech College–Bloomington
S. Matthew DeSpain, Rose State College

Michael Downs, Tarrant County College–Northeast Campus
Shannon Duffy, Southwest Texas State University
Karen Dunn-Haley, University of California, Davis
Stephen D. Engle, Florida Atlantic University
Laura Farkas, Ivy Tech College–West Lafayette
David Haney, Austin Community College
Andrew Hollinger, Tarrant County College–Southeast Campus
Frances Jacobson, Tidewater Community College
Jon Lee, San Antonio College
Robert MacDonald, Ivy Tech College–Lafayette
Richard McCaslin, University of North Texas–Denton
Suzanne McFadden, Austin Community College
Joel McMahon, Kennesaw State University
Greg Miller, Hillsborough Community College
Catherine Parzynski, Montgomery Community College
R. Lynn Rainard, Tidewater Community College
Hazel Ramos, Glendale Community College
Nicole Ribianszky, Georgia Gwinnett College
Allen Smith, Ivy Tech College–Indianapolis
Bruce Solheim, Citrus College
Mark Stanley, University of North Texas–Denton
Melissa Weinbrenner, Northeast Texas Community College

Once again, I thank my friends and colleagues at W. W. Norton for their consummate professionalism and good cheer, especially Jon Durbin, Justin Cahill, Penelope Lin, Lisa Moore, Chris Hillyer, Melissa Atkin, John Elliott, Mike Fleming, Nelson Colón, Hope Miller Goodell, Debra Morton-Hoyt, Andy Ensor, and Sarah England. In addition, my talented friends Charles Cornwell and Jim Stewart read drafts of numerous chapters, helping me to clarify my descriptions and prune my prose.

Finally, I have dedicated this new version of *America* to Jon Durbin, my tireless editor at W. W. Norton, who is a marketing genius and so much more.

America

The Essential Learning Edition

A VISIT FROM THE OLD MISTRESS **(1876)** This powerful painting by Winslow Homer depicts a plantation mistress visiting her former slaves in the postwar South. Although their living conditions are humble, these freedwomen stand firmly and eye-to-eye with the woman who kept them in bondage.

Reconstruction

1865–1877

I n the spring of 1865, the Civil War was finally over. The United States was a "new nation," said an Illinois congressman, because it was now "wholly free." At a frightful cost of over 700,000 lives and the destruction of the southern economy, the Union had won the terrible war, and some 4 million enslaved Americans in the South and border states had seized their freedom. This was the most dramatic social change in the history of the nation. No longer would enslaved workers be whipped by their white owners, nor sold and separated from their families, nor prevented from learning to read and write or attending church. "I felt like a bird out of a cage," said former slave Houston Holloway from Georgia. "Amen. Amen. Amen. I could hardly ask to feel any better than I did that day."

In some places it took longer for freedom to be recognized and enforced. In 1865, Henry Adams left the Louisiana plantation where he had been enslaved "to see whether I am free by going without a pass." A group of whites confronted him on the road, asked the name of his owner, and beat him when he declared that "I now belong to no one." Some slaves rushed to give themselves new names to symbolize their new status. Other slaves left plantations and farms for cities, where, as one of them said, "freedom was free-er."

The ratification of the Thirteenth Amendment to the U.S. Constitution in December 1865 was intended to end all doubt about the status of former slaves by abolishing slavery everywhere. Now the nation faced the huge task of "reconstructing" and reuniting a ravaged South while helping to transform ex-slaves into free workers and equal citizens. It would not be easy. As

CORE OBJECTIVES INQUIZITIVE

1. Identify the federal government's major challenges in reconstructing the South after the Civil War during the period from 1865 to 1877.
2. Describe how and why Reconstruction policies changed over time.
3. Assess the attitudes of white and black southerners toward Reconstruction.
4. Analyze the political and economic factors that helped lead to the end of Reconstruction in 1877.
5. Explain the significance of Reconstruction for the nation's future.

a South Carolina planter threatened a federal official in the fall of 1865, "The war is not over."

The postwar Reconstruction Era, from 1865 to 1877, was a period during which former slaves became citizens. In addition, political leaders of the Reconstruction Era wrestled with how best to bring the Confederate states back into the Union. Those years witnessed a complex debate about the role of the federal government in ensuring civil rights. Some northerners wanted the former Confederate states returned to the Union with little or no changes in the South's social, political, and economic life. Others wanted the former Confederate political and military leaders imprisoned or executed and the South rebuilt in the image of the rest of the nation. Still others wanted the federal government to spend less time focused on the defeated South and more time promoting northern economic growth and westward expansion. Although the Reconstruction Era lasted only twelve years, it was one of the most significant periods in U.S. history. The decisions that were made and the policies enacted are still shaping American life nearly a hundred and fifty years later.

CORE **OBJECTIVE**

1. Identify the federal government's major challenges in reconstructing the South after the Civil War during the period from 1865 to 1877.

The War's Aftermath in the South

The former Confederacy presented a sharp contrast to the victorious North. Throughout the South, people were emotionally exhausted; many lives had been shattered. In 1866, the state of Mississippi spent a fifth of its annual budget on artificial limbs for Confederate soldiers. Property values had collapsed. In the year after the war ended, eighty-one plantations in Mississippi were sold for less than a tenth of what they had been worth in 1860. Confederate money was worthless; personal savings had vanished. Confederate general Braxton Bragg returned to his "once prosperous" Alabama home to find "all, all was lost, except my debts."

Many of the largest southern cities—Richmond, Atlanta, Columbia—were in ruins; most railroads were damaged or destroyed; many southerners, white and black, were homeless and hungry. Emancipation wiped out $4 billion invested in slavery, which had enabled the explosive growth of the cotton culture. But the expansion in the cotton market was over. Not until 1879 would the cotton crop again equal the record harvest of 1860; tobacco production did not regain its prewar level until 1880; the sugar crop of Louisiana did not recover until 1893; and the old rice industry along the coast of South Carolina and Georgia never regained its prewar levels of production or profit. In 1860, just before the Civil War, the South generated 30 percent of the nation's wealth; in 1870, only ten years later, it produced but 12 percent.

The process of forming new state governments in the South first required deciding the official status of the seceded states: Were they now conquered

Deciding the status of Confederate states and freed slaves

Richmond after the Civil War Before evacuating the capital of the Confederacy, Richmond, Virginia, local mobs set fire to warehouses and factories to prevent their falling into Union hands. Pictured here is one of Richmond's burnt districts in April 1865. Women in mourning attire walk among the shambles.

territories? If so, then the Constitution assigned Congress authority to re-create their state governments. But what if, as Abraham Lincoln had argued, the Confederate states had never officially left the Union because the act of secession was itself illegal? In that circumstance, the president would be responsible for re-forming state governments. Whichever branch of government—Congress or the President—directed the reconstruction of the South, it would have to address the most complicated and controversial is-sue: What would be the political, social, and economic status of the freed slaves? Were they citizens? If not, what was their status as Americans?

The Battle over Political Reconstruction

CORE **OBJECTIVE**
2. Describe how and why Reconstruction policies changed over time.

The reconstruction of former Confederate states actually began during the war and went through several phases, the first of which was Presidential Reconstruction. With Union forces advancing into the South during the fighting, President Lincoln in 1862 had named army generals to serve as temporary military governors for conquered Confederate areas. By the end of 1863, he had formulated a plan for regular governments in those states liberated from Confederate rule.

Lincoln's Wartime Reconstruction Plan

Presidential Reconstruction:
Lincoln's Proclamation of
Amnesty and Reconstruction

In late 1863, President Lincoln issued a Proclamation of Amnesty and Reconstruction, under which any former Rebel state could form a Union government whenever a number equal to 10 percent of those who had voted in 1860 took an oath of allegiance to the Constitution and the Union and received a presidential pardon acquitting them from treason charges. Certain groups, however, were excluded from the pardon: Confederate government officials; senior officers of the Confederate army and navy; judges, congressmen, and military officers of the United States who had left their federal posts to aid the rebellion; and those who had abused captured African American soldiers.

But northern politicians disagreed over who had the authority to restore Rebel states to the Union. Many Republicans, especially the so-called Radicals, who were most committed to black civil rights, argued that Congress, not the president, should supervise Reconstruction. By contrast, a few conservative and most moderate Republicans supported Lincoln's program that immediately restored pro-Union southern governments. The **Radical Republicans**, however, favored a drastic transformation of southern society through which freed slaves would be granted full citizenship rights. Many Radical Republican leaders, motivated primarily by strongly felt religious values and moral ideals, believed that all people, regardless of race, were equal in God's eyes. They wanted no compromise with the "sin" of racism.

The Radicals also hoped to reconstruct southern society by replacing the white, Democratic planter elite with a new generation of small farmers, along with wage-earning and middle-class Republicans, both black and white, who would help replace the all-white Democratic party in the South. "The middling classes who own the soil, and work it with their own hands," explained Radical leader Thaddeus Stevens, "are the main support of every free government."

In 1864, with the war still raging, the Radical Republicans tried to take charge of Reconstruction by passing the Wade-Davis Bill, sponsored by Senator Benjamin Franklin Wade of Ohio and Representative Henry Winter Davis of Maryland. In contrast to Lincoln's 10 percent plan, the Wade-Davis Bill required that a *majority* of white male citizens declare their allegiance to the Union before a Confederate state could be re-admitted.

Lincoln vetoes Wade-Davis Bill

But the Wade-Davis Bill never became law: Lincoln vetoed it as being too harsh. In retaliation, Republicans issued the Wade-Davis Manifesto, a public statement that accused Lincoln of exceeding his constitutional authority. Unfazed by the criticism, Lincoln moved ahead with his efforts to restore the Confederate states to the Union. He also rushed to provide assistance to the freed slaves in the South.

The Freedmen's Bureau

Radical Republicans
Congressmen who identified
with the abolitionist cause and
sought swift emancipation of
the slaves, punishment of the
Rebels, and tight controls over
former Confederate states.

In early 1865, Congress approved the Thirteenth Amendment to the Constitution, officially abolishing slavery everywhere in the United States. The amendment, and the war that enabled it, liberated 4 million slaves, but what did freedom mean for the former slaves, most of whom had no land, no home, no food, and no education? Throughout the major northern cities, people concerned about the plight of the former slaves had formed Freedmen's Aid Societies to raise funds and recruit volunteers to help the African Americans in the South. Many churches did the same. But the needs far exceeded such grassroots efforts.

It soon fell to the federal government to take charge of coordinating efforts to address the desperate plight of the former slaves. On March 3, 1865, Congress created the **Freedmen's Bureau** (within the War Department) to assist the suffering "freedmen and their wives and children." It was the first federal experiment in providing assistance directly to people rather than to states. In May 1865, General Oliver O. Howard, commissioner of the Freedmen's Bureau, declared that freed slaves "must be free to choose their own employers, and be paid for their labor." He sent Freedmen's Bureau agents to the South to negotiate labor contracts between blacks and white landowners, many of whom resisted. The agents also provided the former slaves with medical care, food and clothing, and helped set up schools and pay teachers. By 1870, the Bureau was supervising over 4,000 new schools in the South serving almost 250,000 students, many of whose teachers were initially women volunteers from the North. The Freedmen's Bureau also helped former slaves reestablish connection with their family members. Marriages that had been prohibited during slavery were now made legal through the assistance of the Freedmen's Bureau.

Freedmen's Bureau (1865)

Freedmen's Bureau Federal Reconstruction agency established to protect the legal rights of former slaves and to assist with their education, jobs, health care, and land ownership.

Freedmen's school in Virginia Throughout the former Confederate states, the Freedmen's Bureau set up schools for former slaves, such as this one.

The Assassination of Lincoln

Lincoln assassinated
(April 14, 1865)

Abraham Lincoln offered his last view of Reconstruction in the final speech of his life. On April 11, 1865, he rejected calls by Radicals for a vengeful Reconstruction. He wanted "no persecution, no bloody work," no hangings of Confederate leaders nor any extreme efforts to restructure southern social and economic life. Three days later, on April 14, 1865, the president and his wife Mary went to see a play at Ford's Theatre in Washington, D.C. Lincoln was sitting defenseless as John Wilkes Booth slipped into the unguarded presidential box. Booth, a famous actor and a rabid Confederate, fired his small pistol point-blank at the president's head. As Lincoln slumped forward, Booth pulled out a knife, stabbed Lincoln's aide, and jumped from the box to the stage, breaking his leg in the process. He then mounted a waiting horse and fled the city. The president died nine hours later. Eleven days later, Booth was found hiding in a barn in Virginia, where he was shot and killed.

Johnson's Plan

Lincoln's murder shocked and saddened the nation and propelled into the White House Vice President Andrew Johnson of Tennessee, a combative man with a quick temper and fierce prejudices (he hated both the white southern elite and the idea of racial equality). Johnson was a pro-Union Democrat who had joined Lincoln's National Union ticket in 1864 as a gesture of wartime bipartisan unity. Like Lincoln, he was a self-made man.

Born in poverty in Raleigh, North Carolina, Johnson never attended school. At age thirteen he relocated to Greeneville, in the mountains of east Tennessee, where

Paying respect The only photograph of Lincoln in his coffin, displayed here in New York's City Hall rotunda.

he became a tailor and eventually served as the mayor, a state legislator, governor, congressional representative, and U.S. senator.

Johnson's supporters were primarily the small farmers and working poor across the state. He called himself a Jacksonian Democrat "in the strictest meaning of the term. I am for putting down the [Confederate] rebellion, because it is a war [of wealthy plantation owners] against democracy." He had long disliked the planter elite, whom he dismissed as "a bloated, corrupted, damnable aristocracy." But Johnson shared the racist attitudes of most southern whites, rich and poor. "Damn the negroes," he exclaimed to a friend during the war. "I am fighting those traitorous aristocrats, their masters."

Johnson's plan to restore the Confederate states to the Union closely resembled Lincoln's lenient plan. In May 1865, the president issued a new Proclamation of Amnesty that excluded not only those ex-Confederates whom Lincoln had barred from a presidential pardon but also banned anyone with property worth more than $20,000. Johnson was determined to keep the wealthiest southerners from regaining political power in the former Confederate states. Surprisingly, however, he eventually gave pardons to most of the white "aristocrats" he claimed to despise. What brought about this change of heart? Johnson had apparently decided that he could buy the political support of prominent southerners by pardoning them, improving his own chances of reelection.

Johnson's "Restoration" Plan included the appointment of a Unionist as provisional governor in each southern state, with authority to call a convention of men elected by "loyal" (that is, not Confederate) voters. Each state convention had to ratify the Thirteenth Amendment ending slavery before it could be readmitted to the Union. Johnson also encouraged the state conventions to consider giving a few blacks voting rights, especially those with some education or with military service so as to "disarm" the "radicals who are wild upon" giving *all* African Americans the right to vote. Except for uncompromising Mississippi, each state of the former Confederacy held a convention that met Johnson's requirements but ignored his suggestion about giving voting rights to a few blacks.

> Presidential Reconstruction: Johnson's "Restoration" Plan

Andrew Johnson A pro-Union Democrat from Tennessee.

The Radical Republicans

Johnson's initial assault on the southern planter elite won him the support of the Radical Republicans, but not for long. Many Radicals who wanted "Reconstruction" to provide social and political equality for blacks were frustrated by Johnson's efforts to bring the South back into the Union as quickly as possible. The leading Radical Republicans, such as Thaddeus Stevens of Pennsylvania and Charles Sumner of Massachusetts, wanted to deny former Confederates the right to vote in order to keep them from electing the old planter elite and to enable the Republican party to gain a foothold in the Democratic region. Stevens argued that the Civil War was a *radical* revolution: the "whole fabric of southern society must be changed" in order to "revolutionize southern institutions, habits, and manners." Stevens and other Radicals wanted the federal government to confiscate the largest southern plantations, divide them into small farms, and give them to former slaves. And the Radicals claimed they had the authority to do so. The iron-willed Stevens, for example, viewed the Confederate states as "conquered provinces," subject to the absolute will of the U.S. Congress, not the president. Andrew Johnson, however, balked at such an expansion of federal authority. At base, he was committed to the states' rights to control their affairs rather than to an intrusive federal government. "White men alone must manage the South," Johnson told a visitor.

Unreconstructed Southerners

After the war most white southerners found their lives in turmoil. And it was only natural that former Confederates nursed bitter grievances against the North and the federal government. Many shared the attitude expressed by a North Carolinian in 1866 who said he felt the "bitterest hatred toward the North." He and others wanted to rebuild the new South as it had been before the war, the fabled "Old South," and they were determined to do so in their own way and under their own leadership. They saw no need for their beloved region to be "reconstructed" by outsiders.

Johnson's "Restoration" Plan Plan to require southern states to ratify the Thirteenth Amendment, disqualify wealthy ex-Confederates from voting, and appoint a Unionist governor.

So when the U.S. Congress met in December 1865, for the first time since the end of the war, the new state governments in the postwar South looked remarkably like the former Confederate governments. Southern voters had refused to extend voting rights to the newly freed slaves. Instead, they had elected as new U.S. senators and congressmen Georgia's Alexander Stephens, former vice president of the Confederacy, and four Confederate generals, eight colonels, and six Confederate cabinet members. The outraged Republicans in Congress denied seats to all such "Rebel" officials.

Then in May and July of 1866, white mobs murdered African Americans in Memphis and New Orleans. The massacres, Radical Republicans argued, resulted from Andrew Johnson's lenient policy toward white supremacists. "Witness Memphis, witness New Orleans," Massachusetts senator Charles Sumner cried. "Who can doubt that the President is the author of these tragedies?" The riots against blacks helped motivate Congress to pass the Fourteenth Amendment that year, extending federal civil rights protections to blacks.

Black codes

The violence directed against southern blacks was partly sparked by black protests over restrictive laws being passed by the new all-white southern state legislatures. These "**black codes**," as a white southerner explained, were intended to make sure "the ex-slave was not a free man; he was a free Negro." A northerner visiting the South said the black codes in each state were intended to enforce a widespread insistence that "the blacks at large belong to the whites at large."

The black codes varied from state to state, but some provisions were common in many of them. While black marriages were recognized, blacks could not vote or serve on juries or testify against whites. They could own property, but they could not own farmland in Mississippi or city property in South Carolina. In Mississippi, every black male over the age of eighteen had to be apprenticed to a white, preferably a former slave owner. Any blacks not apprenticed or employed by January 1866 would be jailed as "vagrants." If they could not pay the vagrancy fine—and most of them could not—they were forced to work as convict laborers for whites. In other words, aspects of slavery were simply being restored in new ways. As a reporter observed, southern whites never agreed that "freedom for the negro means the same thing as freedom for them." The black codes infuriated Republicans. "We [Republicans] must see to it," Senator William Stewart of Nevada resolved, "that the man made free by the Constitution of the United States is a freeman indeed." And that is what they set out to do.

Johnson's Battle with Congress

The Civil Rights Act (1866)

Largely because of southern whites' resistance to Reconstruction, by the end of 1865, the Radical Republicans had gained a majority in Congress and were warring with Andrew Johnson over the control of Reconstruction. Johnson started the fight when he vetoed a bill renewing funding for the Freedmen's Bureau. On February 22, three days after the veto vote, Johnson criticized the Radical Republicans for promoting black civil rights. Moderate Republi-

black codes Laws passed in southern states to restrict the rights of former slaves.

cans thereafter deserted the president and supported the Radicals. President Johnson had become in their eyes "an alien enemy of a foreign state," Thaddeus Stevens declared. In mid-March 1866, the Radical-led Congress passed the pathbreaking Civil Rights Act, which declared that "all persons born in the United States" (except Indians) were citizens entitled to "full and equal benefit of all laws."

The new legislation enraged President Johnson. Congress, he fumed, had no authority to grant citizenship to blacks, who did not deserve it. The Civil Rights Act discriminated against the "white race." Johnson vetoed the bill, but this time, on April 9, 1866, Congress overrode the presidential veto. It was the first time in history that Congress had overturned a presidential veto of a major bill. From that point on, President Johnson, a stubborn loner unable to accept criticism or compromise, steadily lost both public and political support in the fight over Reconstruction.

Congressional Reconstruction

To remove all doubt about the legality of the new Civil Rights Act, Congress passed the **Fourteenth Amendment** to the U.S. Constitution on June 16, 1866. It went far beyond the Civil Rights Act by guaranteeing citizenship to anyone born in the United States, except Native Americans. It also prohibited any efforts to violate the civil rights of "citizens," black or white; to deprive any person "of life, liberty, or property, without due process of law"; or to "deny any person . . . the equal protection of the laws." With the Fourteenth Amendment, the federal government was assuming responsibility for protecting the civil rights of Americans.

As 1866 drew to an end, the fall congressional elections revealed the growing split between President Andrew Johnson and the Radical Republicans. To win votes for his favored candidates, Johnson went on a speaking tour of the Midwest. But his efforts backfired when several of his speeches turned into ugly shouting contests between him and his critics. In Cleveland, Ohio, Johnson described the Radical Republicans as "factious, domineering, tyrannical" men, and he exchanged hot-tempered insults with a heckler. Radical Republicans claimed that Johnson was behaving like a "drunken imbecile."

The 1866 congressional elections were a devastating defeat for Johnson and the Democrats; in each house, Radical Republican candidates won more than a two-thirds majority, the margin required to override presidential vetoes. On March 2, 1867, Congress passed, over President Johnson's

"(?) Slavery Is Dead (?)" (1867) Thomas Nast's cartoon argues that blacks were still being treated as slaves despite the passage of the Fourteenth Amendment. This detail illustrates a case in Raleigh, North Carolina: a black man was whipped for a crime despite federal orders specifically prohibiting such forms of punishment.

Passage of the Fourteenth Amendment (1866)

Fourteenth Amendment (1866) Amendment to the U.S. Constitution guaranteeing equal protection under the law to all U.S. citizens, including former slaves.

vetoes, three crucial laws creating what came to be called **Congressional Reconstruction**: the Military Reconstruction Act, the Command of the Army Act, and the Tenure of Office Act.

The Military Reconstruction Act was the capstone of the Congressional Reconstruction plan. It abolished all of the new governments "in the rebel States" established under President Johnson's lenient reconstruction policies. In their place, Congress established military control over the defeated South. One state, Tennessee, was exempted because it had already ratified the Fourteenth Amendment. The other ten ex-Confederate states were divided into five military districts, each commanded by a general who acted as governor.

The Military Reconstruction Act required each state to create a new constitution that guaranteed the right of African American males to vote. (Women—black or white—did not yet have the vote and were not included in the discussions. The Radical Republicans were not so radical when it came to promoting the equality of women.) Once the new state constitution was ratified by a majority of voters in that state and accepted by Congress, a newly elected state legislature had to ratify the Fourteenth Amendment before regaining its state's representation in Congress.

The Command of the Army Act directed that all army orders from the president go through the army's commanding general, Ulysses S. Grant. The Radical Republicans feared that, to manage Reconstruction in the South, President Johnson would appoint generals who would be too lenient. So they bypassed the president and entrusted General Grant to enforce Congressional Reconstruction in the South.

The Tenure of Office Act required Senate permission for the president to remove any federal official whose appointment the Senate had confirmed. This act was intended to prevent Andrew Johnson from firing Secretary of War Edwin Stanton, the president's most outspoken critic in the cabinet. Stanton had openly criticized Johnson's lenient approach to the South and had allied himself with the Radicals.

Congressional Reconstruction thus sought to ensure that the freed slaves could participate in the creation of new state governments in the former Confederacy. As Thaddeus Stevens explained, the Congressional Reconstruction plan was designed to create a "perfect republic" based on the principle of *equal rights* for all citizens. "This is the promise of America," he insisted. "No More. No Less."

Impeaching the President

The first two years of Congressional Reconstruction saw dramatic changes in the South. One by one, a new set of southern state legislatures rewrote their constitutions and ratified the Fourteenth Amendment. Radical Republicans now seemed fully in control of Reconstruction, but one person still stood in their way—Andrew Johnson. During 1867 and early 1868, more and more Radicals decided that the defiant Democratic president must be removed from office.

Congressional Reconstruction
Phase of Reconstruction directed by Radical Republicans through the passage of three laws: the Military Reconstruction Act, the Command of the Army Act, and the Tenure of Office Act.

Johnson himself opened the door to impeachment (the formal process by which Congress charges the president with "high crimes and misdemeanors") when he tried to fire Secretary of War Edwin Stanton. The sharp-tongued Stanton had exasperated Johnson by refusing to resign from the cabinet despite his harsh criticism of the president's Reconstruction policy. Radical Republicans had passed the Tenure of Office Act in 1866 to make it illegal for Johnson to remove Stanton for championing their cause. Johnson, who considered the Tenure of Office Act an illegal restriction of presidential power, fired Stanton on August 12, 1867, appointing General Ulysses S. Grant in his place. To the Republicans, this was a declaration of war. John F. Farnsworth, an Illinois Congressman, denounced the president as an "ungrateful, despicable, besotted, traitorous man."

The Radical Republicans now saw their chance. By removing Stanton   **Johnson's presidency in crisis** without congressional approval, Johnson had violated the law. On February 24, 1868, the Republican-dominated House passed eleven articles of impeachment (that is, specific charges against the president), most of which dealt with Stanton's firing, and all of which were flimsy. In reality, the essential grievance against the president was that he had opposed the policies of the dominant Radical Republicans. According to Secretary of the Navy Gideon Welles, Radical Republicans were so angry at Johnson that they would have tried to remove him had he been accused of stepping on a dog's tail.

The first Senate trial of a sitting president began on March 5, 1868, and continued until May 26, with Chief Justice Salmon P. Chase presiding. It was a dramatic spectacle before a packed gallery of journalists, foreign dignitaries, corporate executives, and political leaders, all eager to watch the first effort to impeach a president. Thaddeus Stevens, the Radical leader, did not need to be convinced that Johnson should be removed. As the trial began, he warned the president: "Unfortunate, unhappy man, behold your doom!"

Trial of Andrew Johnson In this *Harper's Weekly* illustration, Johnson is seated at the center of the foreground among his defense committee. The galleries of the Senate are packed with men and women watching the proceedings.

The five-week impeachment trial ended in May 1868 in stunning fashion, but not as the Radicals had hoped. In the end, the Senate voted 35 to 19 for conviction, only *one* vote short of the two-thirds needed for removal from office. Senator Edmund G. Ross, a young Radical from Kansas, cast the deciding vote in favor of acquittal, knowing that his vote would ruin his political career. "I almost literally looked down into my open grave," Ross explained afterwards. "Friendships, position, fortune, everything that makes life desirable . . . were about to be swept away by the breath of my mouth." Ross was thereafter shunned by the Republicans. He lost his reelection campaign and died in near poverty.

The effort by Radicals to remove Johnson was in the end a grave political mistake, for it ended up weakening public support for Congressional Reconstruction. Nevertheless, the Radical cause did gain something: to avoid being convicted, President Johnson had privately agreed to stop obstructing Congressional Reconstruction.

Republican Rule in the South

In June 1868, Congressional Republicans agreed that eight former Confederate states—all but Virginia, Mississippi, and Texas—had met the tough new conditions for readmission to the Union. Virginia, Mississippi, and Texas were readmitted in 1870, with the added requirement that they ratify the **Fifteenth Amendment**, which gave voting rights to African American men. As the prominent black leader Frederick Douglass, himself a former slave, had declared in 1865, "slavery is not abolished until the black man has the ballot."

The Fifteenth Amendment, submitted to the states in 1869 and ratified in 1870, prohibited states from denying any person the vote on grounds of "race, color, or previous condition of servitude." Susan B. Anthony and Elizabeth Cady Stanton, leaders of the movement to secure voting rights for women, demanded that the Fifteenth Amendment be revised to include women as well as black men. As Anthony stressed in a famous speech, the U.S. Constitution says: "we, the people; not we, the white male citizens; nor yet we, the male citizens; but we, the whole people, who formed the Union— women as well as men." But most men remained unreconstructed when it came to female voting rights. Radical Republicans tried to deflect the issue by declaring that it was the "Negro's hour," and women would have to wait— another fifty years, as it turned out.

> Passage of the Fifteenth Amendment (1870)

Reconstruction in Practice

CORE **OBJECTIVE**
3. Assess the attitudes of white and black southerners toward Reconstruction.

When a federal official asked Garrison Frazier, a former slave in Georgia, if he and others wanted to live among whites or among themselves, he said that they preferred "to live by ourselves, for there is a prejudice against us in the South that will take years to get over." In forging new lives in freedom, Frazier and many other former slaves then set about creating their own social institutions.

The Reconstruction of Black Social Life

Fifteenth Amendment (1870) Amendment to the U.S. Constitution forbidding states to deny any male citizen the right to vote on grounds of "race, color or previous condition of servitude."

The northern victory in the Civil War led to a striking transformation of African American religious life in the South. Many former slaves identified their struggle for freedom with the biblical Hebrews, who were led out of slavery into the "promised land." Emancipation demonstrated to them that God was on *their* side. Before the war, slaves who were allowed to attend white churches were forced to sit in the back. After the war, with the help of many northern Christian missionaries, both black and white, ex-slaves eagerly established their own African American churches.

The black churches were the first social institution the former slaves could control, and they quickly became the crossroads for African American community life. Black ministers emerged as social and political leaders as well as preachers. One could not be a real minister, one of them claimed, without looking "out for the political interests of his people."

Many African Americans became Baptists or Methodists, in part because these were already the largest denominations in the South and in part because they reached out to the working poor. In 1866 alone, the African Methodist Episcopal (AME) Church gained 50,000 members. By 1890, over 1.3 million African Americans in the South had become Baptists, nearly three times as many as had joined any other denomination.

> African American churches

African American communities in the postwar South also rushed to establish schools. Starting schools, said one former slave, was the "first proof" of freedom. Most plantation owners had denied education to blacks in part because they feared that literate slaves would read abolitionist literature and organize uprisings. After the war, the white elite worried that formal education would encourage poor whites and poor blacks to leave the South in search of better social and economic opportunities. "They didn't want us to learn nothin'," one former slave recalled. "The only thing we had to learn was how to work."

> African American schools

White opposition to education for blacks made education all the more important to African Americans. South Carolina's Mary McLeod Bethune, the fifteenth child of former slaves, rejoiced in the opportunity to gain an education: "The whole world opened to me when I learned to read." She walked five miles to school as a child, then earned a scholarship to college, and went on to become the first black woman to found a school that became a four-year college: what is today known as Bethune-Cookman University, in Daytona Beach, Florida.

African Americans in Southern Politics

Participation in the Union army or navy had given many former slaves their first opportunity to express their loyalty to the American nation. A Virginia freedman explained that the United States was "now *our* country," paid for "by the blood of our brethren" who died while serving in the Union military during the Civil War. Serving in the military enabled many former slaves to learn to read and write. Black veterans would also form the core of the first generation of African American political leaders in the postwar South.

Any African American participation in southern political life was a first. With many ex-Confederates denied voting rights, new African American voters helped elect some six hundred blacks—most of them former slaves— as Republican state legislators under Congressional Reconstruction. In

> African American vote

African American political figures of Reconstruction
Blanche K. Bruce (left) and Hiram Revels (right) served in the U.S. Senate. Frederick Douglass (center) was a major figure in the abolitionist movement.

African American elected officials

Louisiana, Pinckney Pinchback, a northern free black and former Union soldier, was elected lieutenant governor. Several other African Americans were elected lieutenant governor, state treasurer, or secretary of state. There were two black senators in Congress, Hiram Revels and Blanche K. Bruce, both Mississippi natives who had been educated in the North, as well as fourteen black members of the U.S. House of Representatives during Reconstruction.

White southern Democrats were appalled at the election of black Republican politicians. They complained that freed slaves were illiterate and had no civic experience or appreciation of political issues and processes. In this regard, of course, blacks were no different from millions of poor or immigrant white males who had been allowed to vote for years. Some freedmen frankly confessed their disadvantages. Beverly Nash, an African American delegate to the South Carolina convention of 1868, told his colleagues: "I believe, my friends and fellow-citizens, we are not prepared for this suffrage [the vote]. But we can learn. Give a man tools and let him commence to use them, and in time he will learn a trade. So it is with voting."

Land, Labor, and Disappointment

A few northerners argued that what the former slaves needed most was neither the right to vote nor the opportunity to be paid laborers on plantations but their own land, where they could gain economic self-sufficiency. "What is freedom," Ohio Congressman James A. Garfield, a former general and future president, asked in 1865. "Is it the bare privilege of not being chained? If this is all, then freedom is a bitter mockery, a cruel delusion." Freed slaves felt the same way. Freedom, explained a black minister from Georgia, meant

Freedmen Voting in New Orleans The Fifteenth Amendment, ratified in 1870, guaranteed at the federal level the right of citizens to vote regardless of "race, color, or previous condition of servitude." But former slaves had been registering to vote—and voting in large numbers—in some state elections since 1867, as in this scene.

the freedom for blacks to "reap the fruit of our own labor, and take care of ourselves."

In several southern states, former slaves had been "given" land by Union armies after they had taken control of Confederate areas during the war. But such transfers of white-owned property to former slaves were reversed during 1865 by President Andrew Johnson. In South Carolina, the Union general responsible for evicting former slaves urged them to "lay aside their bitter feelings, and become reconciled to their old masters." But the assembled freedmen shouted "No, never!" and "Can't do it!" They knew that ownership of land was the foundation of their freedom. Yes, they had no deeds or titles for the land they now worked, but it had been "earned by the sweat of *our* brows," said a group of Alabama freedmen.

President Johnson, however, was insistent that the federal government had no right to take land from former Confederates. Tens of thousands of former slaves were forced to return their farms to the white owners. In addition, it was virtually impossible for former slaves to get loans to buy farm land because there were so few banks in the postwar South, and few of these were willing to lend to blacks. The sense of betrayal among the former slaves was profound. An ex-slave in Mississippi whose farm was returned to its white owner said the former slaves were left with nothing: "no *land*, no *house*, not so much as a place to lay our head."

Sharecropping replaces slavery

The intensity of racial prejudice in the South often blocked the efforts of federal troops and officials to protect the former slaves. In late June 1865, for example, Thomas Ferguson, a white plantation owner near Charleston, South Carolina, signed a contract with sixty-five of his former slaves. It called for them to "cultivate" his fields in exchange for "half of the crop raised after having deducted the seed of rice, corn, peas & potatoes." This labor system of **sharecropping**—where the landowner provided land, seed, and tools to a poor farmer in exchange for a *share* of the crop—essentially re-enslaved the workers because, as a federal army officer objected, no matter "how much they are abused, they cannot leave without permission of the owner." If they chose to leave, they would forfeit any right to a portion of the crop, and any workers who violated the terms of the contract could be evicted from the plantation, leaving them jobless and homeless—and subject to arrest. Across the former Confederacy, most white plantation owners and small farmers were determined to continue to control the lives of African Americans.

Sharecroppers A family is shown outside their Virginia home in this 1899 photograph, taken by Frances Benjamin Johnston, one of the earliest American female photojournalists.

With little money or technical training, many freed blacks preferred sharecropping over working for wages, since it freed them from day-to-day supervision by white landowners. But over time, most sharecroppers, black and white, found themselves deeper in debt to the landowner, with little choice but to remain tied to the same discouraging system of dependence that, over the years, felt much like slavery. As a former slave acknowledged, he and others had discovered that "freedom could make folks proud but it didn't make 'em rich."

"Carpetbaggers" and "Scalawags"

Most of the top positions in the new Republican southern state governments went to whites, who were dismissed as "carpetbaggers" and "scalawags" by their critics. Carpetbaggers were allegedly opportunistic northerners who rushed South with all their belongings in cheap suitcases made of carpeting ("carpetbags") to grab political power. Some northerners were indeed corrupt opportunists. However, most of the northerners in the postwar South were Union military veterans who had arrived as early as 1865 or 1866, drawn back to the South by the desire to rebuild the region's devastated economy. Others were Union soldiers who never returned home after fighting in the South. New Yorker George Spencer, for example, arrived in

sharecropping A farming system developed after the Civil War by which landless workers farmed land in exchange with the landowner for farm supplies and a share of the crop.

Alabama with the Union army during the war and decided to pursue his "chances of making a fortune" in selling cotton and building railroads. He eventually was elected to the U.S. Senate.

Many other so-called carpetbaggers were teachers, social workers, or ministers motivated by a genuine desire to help free blacks and poor whites improve the quality of their lives. Union general Adelbert Ames stayed in the South after the war because he felt a "sense of Mission with a large M" to help the former slaves develop healthy communities. He served as the military governor of Mississippi before being elected as a Republican U.S. senator in 1870. In 1873 Ames ran for governor of Mississippi in a bitter campaign against another white Republican, a "scalawag" named James Lusk Alcorn, a former Confederate general who owned the largest plantation in the Mississippi Delta and had served as Mississippi's governor from 1870 to 1871. Alcorn wrote his wife that "southerners must make the Negro their friend or the path ahead will be red with blood and damp with tears." Ames won the gubernatorial contest in 1873 and served as governor from 1874 to 1876 before resigning in the face of a resurgent white Democratic party.

Carpetbagger The cartoonist's caption to this critique of carpetbaggers reads: "The bag in front of him, filled with others' faults, he always sees. The one behind him, filled with his own faults, he never sees."

Most so-called scalawags were southerners who had opposed secession but supported the Confederacy once the war started, and then became Republicans after the war was over. Several distinguished figures became scalawags, including the former Confederate general James Longstreet, who decided after the war that the Old South must change its ways. He became a successful cotton broker in New Orleans, joined the Republican party, and supported the Congressional Reconstruction program. Another unlikely scalawag was Joseph E. Brown, the former Confederate governor of Georgia, who urged southerners to support Republicans because they were the only source of economic investment in the devastated region.

Southern Resistance and White "Redemption"

The scalawags, or southern white Republicans, were especially hated by southern Democrats, who often called them traitors. A Nashville, Tennessee, newspaper editor dismissed them as the "merest trash." Most southern whites viewed secession not as a mistake but as a noble "lost cause." At the same time, they viewed federal efforts at reconstruction as a tragedy. And they used all means possible—legal and illegal—to "redeem" their beloved South from northern control, Republican rule, and black assertiveness. An Alabama planter admitted that southern whites simply "can't learn to treat the freedmen like human beings." White southern ministers, for example, assured their congregations that God endorsed white supremacy. In an attempt to reunite the Protestant denominations of the north and south, many northern religionists became "apostles of forgiveness" for their southern

Reconstruction's final phase: Southern white resistance and "redemption"

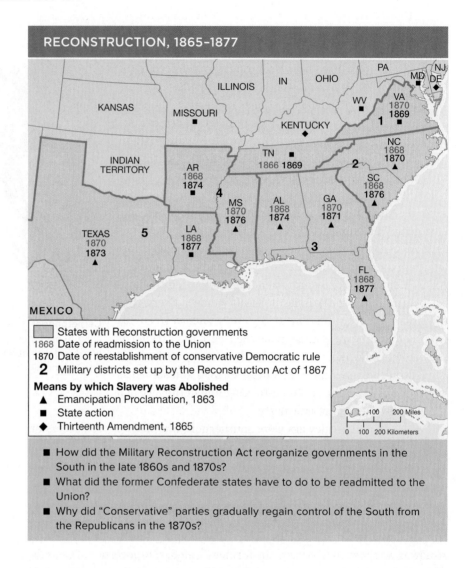

RECONSTRUCTION, 1865–1877

Legend:
- States with Reconstruction governments
- 1868 Date of readmission to the Union
- 1870 Date of reestablishment of conservative Democratic rule
- **2** Military districts set up by the Reconstruction Act of 1867

Means by which Slavery was Abolished
- ▲ Emancipation Proclamation, 1863
- ■ State action
- ◆ Thirteenth Amendment, 1865

- How did the Military Reconstruction Act reorganize governments in the South in the late 1860s and 1870s?
- What did the former Confederate states have to do to be readmitted to the Union?
- Why did "Conservative" parties gradually regain control of the South from the Republicans in the 1870s?

white brethren. Even abolitionists such as the Reverend Henry Ward Beecher, whose sister Harriet Beecher Stowe had written *Uncle Tom's Cabin* (1857), called for southern whites—rather than federal officials or African Americans themselves—to govern the South after the war.

The Civil War had brought freedom to enslaved African Americans, but it did not bring them protection against exploitation or abuse. The "black codes" created by white state governments in 1865 and 1866 were the first of many continuing efforts to deny equality to African Americans. With each passing year, southern whites used terror, intimidation, and violence to prevent blacks from exercising their political rights. Hundreds were killed across the South and many more injured in systematic efforts to "keep blacks in their place." In Texas a white farmer, D. B. Whitesides, told a former slave named Charles Brown that his newfound freedom would do him "damned little good . . . as I intend to shoot you"—and he did, shooting Brown in the chest as he tried to flee. Whitesides then rode his horse beside the wounded

> White violence against black political participation

Brown and asked, "I got you, did I Brown?" "Yes," a bleeding Brown replied. "You've got me good." Whitesides yelled that the wound would teach "niggers [like you] to put on airs because you are free."

Such ugly incidents revealed a harsh truth: the death of slavery did not mean the birth of true freedom for many African Americans. For a growing number of southern whites, resistance to Congressional Reconstruction and "Radical rule" became more and more violent. Several secret terrorist groups emerged to harass, intimidate, and even kill scalawags, carpetbaggers, and African Americans. The **Ku Klux Klan** (KKK), for instance, was formed in 1866 in Pulaski, Tennessee. The name *Ku Klux* was derived from the Greek word *kuklos* meaning "circle" or "band" (and *Klan* comes from the English word *clan*, or family). The Klan, and other groups like it, began initially as a social club, with costumes and secret rituals. At first a group of pranksters, its members soon turned to intimidation of blacks and white Republicans throughout the South. Their motives were varied—anger over the Confederate defeat, resentment

"Worse Than Slavery" This Thomas Nast cartoon condemns the Ku Klux Klan for promoting conditions "worse than slavery" for southern blacks after the Civil War.

against federal soldiers occupying the South, complaints about having to pay black workers, and an almost paranoid fear that former slaves might seek violent revenge against whites. Klansmen rode about at night in white sheets and masks spreading horrendous rumors, issuing threats, burning schools and churches. "We are going to kill all the Negroes," a white supremacist declared during one massacre.

The Legacy of Republican Rule

Yet for all of the violent opposition directed against the Republican state governments, the new constitutions they created remained in effect for some years after the end of Radical Republican control, and later constitutions incorporated many of their most progressive features. Among the most significant innovations brought about by the Republican state governments were those intended to increase the participation of the common people in the political process: protecting black voting rights, restructuring legislatures to reflect shifting populations, and making more state offices elective to weaken the "good old boy" tradition of rewarding political supporters with state government jobs. In South Carolina, former Confederate leaders opposed the Republican state legislature not simply because of its black members but because poor whites were also enjoying political clout for the first time, thereby threatening the traditional power of wealthy white plantation owners and merchants.

Given the hostile circumstances under which the Republican state governments operated in the South, their achievements were remarkable. They constructed an extensive railroad network and established public, though racially segregated, school systems—schools funded by state governments

Radical Republican achievements

Ku Klux Klan A secret terrorist organization founded in Pulaski, Tennessee, in 1866 targeting former slaves who voted and held political offices, as well as people the KKK labeled as carpetbaggers and scalawags.

and open to all children. Some six hundred thousand black pupils were enrolled in southern schools by 1877. State governments under the Radicals also gave more attention to the poor and to orphanages, asylums, and institutions for the deaf and the blind of both races. Public roads, bridges, and buildings were repaired or rebuilt. African Americans achieved rights and opportunities that would repeatedly be violated in coming decades but never completely taken away, at least in principle: equality before the law and the rights to own property, attend schools, learn to read and write, enter professions, and carry on business.

Yet several of the Republican state governments also engaged in corrupt practices. Bribes and kickbacks, whereby companies were awarded government contracts and then secretly rewarded officials with cash or stock, were commonplace. In Louisiana, the twenty-six-year-old Illinois carpetbagger, Henry Clay Warmoth, a Union war veteran and attorney, somehow turned an annual salary of $8,000 into a million-dollar fortune over four years serving as governor (he was impeached and removed from office). "I don't pretend to be honest," he admitted. "I only pretend to be as honest as anybody in politics." As was true in the North and the Midwest at the time, southern state governments awarded money to corporations, notably railroads, under conditions that invited shady dealings. In fact, some railroads were funded but never built at all. Republican state legislators doubled and even tripled their salaries. Bribery was rampant. Such corruption was not invented by the Radical Republican regimes, nor did it die with them. Governor Warmoth recognized as much: "Corruption is the fashion" in Louisiana, he explained.

CORE **OBJECTIVE**

4. Analyze the political and economic factors that helped lead to the end of Reconstruction in 1877.

The Grant Years and Northern Disillusionment

Democrat Andrew Johnson's crippled presidency created an opportunity for Republicans to elect one of their own in 1868. Both parties wooed Ulysses S. Grant, the "Lion of Vicksburg" credited by most Americans with the Union victory in the Civil War. His falling-out with President Johnson, however, had pushed him toward the Republicans.

The Election of 1868

The Republican party platform of 1868 endorsed Congressional Reconstruction. More important than the party platform, however, were the public expectations driving the election of Ulysses S. Grant, a heroic soldier whose campaign slogan was "Let us have peace."

African American votes help elect President Grant (1868)

The Democrats, not surprisingly, charged the Republican Congress with subjecting the South "to military despotism and Negro supremacy." They nominated Horatio Seymour, the wartime governor of New York and a passionate critic of Congressional Reconstruction. His vice-presidential running mate, Francis P. Blair Jr., a former Union general from Missouri who had served in Congress, appealed directly to white bigotry when he denounced Republicans for promoting equality for "a semi-barbarous race" of black men who sought to "subject the white women to their unbridled lust." A Democrat later said that Blair's egregiously "stupid and indefensible" remarks cost Seymour a close election. Grant swept the Electoral College, 214 to 80, but his popular majority was only 307,000 out of a total of almost 6 million votes. More than 500,000 African American voters accounted for Grant's margin of victory. The efforts of Radical Republicans to ensure that southern blacks had voting rights had paid off. When Grant was inaugurated in March 1869, a sullen Andrew Johnson refused to attend.

Grant had proved himself a great military leader, but as the youngest president ever (forty-six years old at the time of his inauguration), he was not nearly as bold a politician as he had been a general. He passively followed the lead of Congress and was often blind to the political forces and self-serving influence peddlers around him. A failure as a storekeeper before the Civil War, he was awestruck by men of wealth who lavished gifts on him, including houses. He also showed poor judgment in his selection of cabinet members. During Grant's two terms in office, his seven cabinet officers changed a total of twenty-four times. Some of them were out-and-out crooks who betrayed his trust and engaged in criminal behavior. His former comrade-in-arms, General William T. Sherman, said he felt sorry for his former commander because so many supposedly "loyal" Republicans used him for their own selfish gains.

Scandals

President Grant's new administration soon fell into a cesspool of scandal. In the summer of 1869, two unprincipled financial schemers, Jay Gould and James Fisk Jr. (known as "Jubilee Jim"), infamous for their bribing of politicians and judges, plotted with the president's brother-in-law to create a public craze for gold by purchasing massive quantities of the precious yellow metal to drive up its value. The only danger to the scheme lay in the possibility that the federal Treasury would burst the bubble by selling large amounts of its gold supply, which would deflate the value of gold by putting more in circulation. When President Grant was seen in public with Gould and Fisk, people assumed that he supported their gold scheme. As the rumor spread in New York City's financial district that the president endorsed the run-up in gold, its value soared.

> Corruption in the Grant administration

On September 24, 1869—soon to be remembered as "Black Friday"—the scheme of Gould and Fisk to drive up the price of gold worked to perfection. Starting at a price of $150 an ounce, the bidding on Wall Street in New York City started rising, first to $160, then $165, leading more and more investors across the nation and around the world to join the stampede. Then, around noon, President Grant and his Treasury secretary realized what was happening and began selling huge amounts of government gold. Within fifteen minutes, the bubble created by Fisk and Gould burst, and the price of gold plummeted to $138. People who had bought gold in large amounts lost fortunes.

Their agony, said a New Yorker, "made one feel as if the Battle of Gettysburg had been lost and the Rebels were marching down Broadway." Soon, the turmoil spread to the entire stock market, claiming thousands of victims. As Fisk noted, "It was each man drag out his own corpse." For weeks after the gold bubble collapsed, the financial markets were paralyzed and business confidence was rudely shaken. Congressman James Garfield wrote privately to a friend that President Grant had compromised his presidential integrity by his "indiscreet acceptance" of gifts from Fisk and Gould and that any investigation of "Black Friday" would lead "into the parlor of the President."

The plot to corner the gold market was only the first of several scandals that rocked the Grant administration. More disclosures of corruption followed, some involving members of the president's cabinet. The secretary of war, it turned out, had accepted bribes from merchants who traded with Indians at army posts in the West. In St. Louis, whiskey distillers—dubbed the "whiskey ring" in the press—bribed federal agents to avoid taxes, bilking the government out of millions of dollars in revenue. Grant's personal secretary was enmeshed in that scheme, taking large sums of money and other valuables in return for inside information.

There is no evidence that Grant himself was ever involved in any of the frauds, but his poor choice of associates earned him widespread criticism. Democrats scolded Republicans for their "monstrous corruption and extravagance" and launched thirty-six investigations into supposedly corrupt acts during Grant's administration.

The Money Supply

> Greenbacks vs. gold coins

Complex financial issues—especially monetary policy—dominated Grant's presidency. Prior to the Civil War, the economy operated on a gold standard. That is, state banks issued paper money which could be exchanged for an equal value of gold coins. So both gold coins and state bank notes circulated as the nation's currency. **Greenbacks** (because of the dye color used on the printed dollars) were issued during the Civil War to help pay for the war.

When a nation's supply of money grows faster than the economy itself, prices for goods and services increase (inflation). This is what happened during the Civil War when the greenbacks were issued. After the Civil War, the U.S. Treasury assumed that the greenbacks issued during the conflict would be recalled from circulation so that consumer prices would decline and the nation could return to a "hard-money" currency—gold, silver, and copper coins—which had always been viewed as more reliable in value than paper currency. The most vocal supporters of a return to "hard money" were eastern creditors (mostly bankers and merchants to whom others owed money) who did not want their debtors to pay them in paper currency. Critics of the gold standard tended to be farmers and other debtors. These so-called soft-money advocates opposed taking greenbacks out of circulation because shrinking the supply of money would bring lower prices (deflation) for their crops and livestock, thereby reducing their income and making it harder for

greenbacks Paper money, issued during the Civil War, that sparked currency debates after the war.

them to pay their long-term debts. In 1868 congressional supporters of such a "soft-money" policy—mostly Democrats—had forced the Treasury to stop the withdrawal of greenbacks from circulation.

President Grant sided with the "hard-money" camp. On March 18, 1869, he signed the Public Credit Act, which said that the investors who purchased government bonds to help finance the war effort must be paid back in gold coins rather than paper currency. It was the first act of Congress that Grant signed, and it soon generated a decline in consumer prices (deflation) that hurt debtors, helped creditors, and in the process ignited a ferocious political debate over the merits of "hard" and "soft" money that would last throughout the nineteenth century—and beyond.

| Public Credit Act (1869) |

Financial Panic

Grant's effort to withdraw the greenbacks from circulation unintentionally helped cause a major economic collapse. During 1873, some twenty-five railroads stopped paying their bills, leading Jay Cooke and Company, the nation's leading business lender, to go bankrupt on September 18, 1873. The resulting financial **Panic of 1873** triggered a deep economic depression. Thousands of businesses closed, and three million people lost their jobs. Those with jobs saw their wages slashed. In the major cities, unemployed, homeless Americans roamed the streets and formed long lines at charity soup kitchens.

| Panic of 1873 |

The terrible contraction of the economy led the U.S. Treasury to reverse course and begin printing more greenbacks. For a time, the supporters of paper money celebrated, but in 1874, President Grant vetoed a bill to issue even more greenbacks. His efforts to remove paper money from circulation pleased his supporters but only prolonged what was then the nation's worst economic depression in its history.

Liberal Republicans

The sudden collapse of the nation's economy in 1873 also contributed to northerners' losing interest in Reconstruction. Liberal Republicans, a new faction in the Republican party, called for ending federal Reconstruction efforts in the South and promoted "civil service reforms" designed to end the "patronage system" whereby new presidents rewarded political supporters with federal government jobs. In 1872 the Liberal Republicans held their own national convention, at which they accused the Grant administration of corruption, incompetence, and "despotism." They nominated an unlikely presidential candidate: Horace Greeley, the prominent editor of the *New York Tribune* and a longtime champion of a variety of causes: abolitionism, socialism, vegetarianism, and spiritualism. His image as an eccentric was complemented by his record of hostility to the Democrats, whose support the Liberal Republicans needed if they were going to win the election. The Democrats nevertheless gave their nomination to Greeley as the only hope of beating Grant.

| Reconstruction loses support |

Panic of 1873 Financial collapse triggered by President Grant's efforts to withdraw greenbacks from circulation and transition the economy back to hard currency.

The result was predictable. Greeley, the shared candidate of the Liberal Republicans and Democrats, carried only six southern states and none in the North. Grant won thirty-one states and carried the national election by 3,598,235 votes to Greeley's 2,834,761. An exhausted Greeley confessed that he was "the worst beaten man who ever ran for high office." He died three weeks later.

White Terror

Violence against blacks escalates

President Grant initially fought hard to enforce federal efforts to reconstruct the postwar South. But southern resistance to "Radical rule" increased and turned brutally violent. In Grayson County, Texas, a white man and two friends murdered three former slaves because they wanted to "thin the niggers out and drive them to their holes."

Klansmen focused their terror on prominent Republicans, black and white. In Mississippi they killed a black Republican leader in front of his family. Three white "scalawag" Republicans were murdered in Georgia in 1870. That same year an armed mob of whites assaulted a Republican political rally in Alabama, killing four blacks and wounding fifty-four. In South Carolina white supremacists were especially active—and violent. In 1871, some five hundred masked men laid siege to South Carolina's Union County jail and eventually lynched eight black prisoners. In March 1871, the Klan killed thirty African Americans in Meridian, Mississippi.

Enforcement Acts (1870–1871)

At the urging of President Grant, Republicans in Congress struck back at such racial violence with three Enforcement Acts (1870–1871). The first of these measures imposed penalties on anyone who interfered with any citizen's right to vote. A second measure dispatched federal election supervisors and marshals to monitor elections in southern districts where political terrorism flourished. The third, called the Ku Klux Klan Act, outlawed the main activities of the KKK—forming conspiracies, wearing disguises, resisting officers, and intimidating officials. In 1871, the federal government singled out nine counties in upcountry South Carolina as a center of Klan-instigated violence and jailed several hundred people. In general, however, the Enforcement Acts were not consistently applied. As a result, the efforts of southern whites to use violence to thwart Reconstruction escalated in the 1870s. On Easter Sunday in 1873 in Colfax, Louisiana, a mob of white vigilantes disappointed by local election results attacked a group of black Republicans, slaughtering eighty-one. It was the bloodiest racial incident during the Reconstruction period.

Southern "Redeemers"

The Ku Klux Klan's impact on southern politics varied from state to state. In the Upper South, it played only a modest role in helping Democrats win local elections. But in the Lower South, Klan violence and intimidation had more serious effects. In overwhelmingly black Yazoo County, Mississippi, vengeful whites used terrorism to reverse the political balance of power. In the 1873 elections, for example, the Republicans cast 2,449 votes and the Democrats 638; two years later the Democrats polled 4,049 votes, the Republicans 7. Throughout the South, the activities of the Klan and other white supremacists disheartened black and white Republicans alike. "We are helpless and unable to organize," wrote a Mississippi scalawag. We "dare not attempt to canvass [campaign for candidates], or make public speeches." At the same time, during the 1870s northerners displayed a growing weariness with efforts to use federal troops to reconstruct the South and protect civil rights. "The plain truth is," noted the *New York Herald*, "the North has got tired of the Negro."

The erosion of northern interest in civil rights resulted from more than weariness, however. Western expansion, Indian wars, and political controversy over economic issues distracted attention from southern resistance to Republican rule and black rights. Given the violent intensity of diehard former Confederates' efforts to resist Reconstruction, it would have required far more patience, conviction, and resources for the federal government to protect the civil rights of blacks in the South. Republican political control in the South gradually loosened as all-white "Conservative" parties mobilized the anti-Reconstruction vote. White Democrats—the so-called **redeemers** who supposedly "saved" the South from Republican control and "black rule"—emotionalized the race issue to excite the white electorate and intimidate black voters. Where persuasion failed to work, Democrats were willing to use trickery. As one enthusiastic Democrat boasted, "The white and black Republicans may outvote us, but we can outcount them."

> Resurgence of the southern white elite

Republican political control collapsed in Virginia and Tennessee as early as 1869; in Georgia and North Carolina it ended in 1870, although North Carolina had a Republican governor until 1876. Reconstruction lasted longest in the Deep South states with the largest black population; there, whites abandoned Klan masks for barefaced intimidation in paramilitary groups such as the Mississippi Rifle Club and the South Carolina Red Shirts. By 1876, Radical Republican regimes survived only in Louisiana, South Carolina, and Florida, and those collapsed after the elections of that year.

The return to power of the old white political elite in the South undermined the country's commitment to Congressional Reconstruction. The collapse of the economy and the much-publicized political scandals hurt Republicans in the 1874 congressional elections, in which the Democrats won control of the House of Representatives and gained seats in the Senate.

> Democrats win control of Congress (1874)

The Compromise of 1877

President Grant, despite the controversies swirling around him, wanted to run again in 1876, but many Republicans had lost confidence in his leadership and opposed the idea of his becoming the nation's first three-term president. In the summer of 1875, Grant acknowledged defeat and announced his retirement, admitting that he had entered the White House

redeemers Postwar white Democratic leaders in the South who supposedly saved the region from political, economic, and social domination by northerners and blacks.

with "no political training" and had made "errors in judgment." James Gillespie Blaine of Maine, former Speaker of the House, emerged as the Republican front-runner to succeed Grant, but he, too, bore the taint of scandal when it was revealed that he had promised political favors to railroad executives in exchange for shares of stock in the company.

The scandal led the Republican Convention to pass over Blaine in favor of Ohio's favorite son, Rutherford B. Hayes. Elected governor of Ohio three times, most recently as a "hard money" advocate of gold rather than greenbacks, Hayes had also made a name for himself as a civil service reformer by trying to reduce the number of government jobs subject to political appointment. But his chief virtue was that he offended neither Radicals nor reformers. As a journalist put it, he was "obnoxious to no one."

The Democratic Convention was uncharacteristically harmonious from the start. The nomination went on the second ballot to Samuel J. Tilden, a wealthy corporate lawyer and reform governor of New York.

The 1876 campaign raised no burning issues. Both candidates favored the trend toward relaxing federal authority in the South. As Hayes said privately, he did not approve of "bayonet rule" by federal troops in the South. In the absence of strong ideological differences, Democrats aired the Republicans' dirty linen. In response, Republicans waved "the bloody shirt," whereby they linked the Democratic party to secession, civil war, and the outrages committed against Republicans in the South. As Robert G. Ingersoll, the most celebrated Republican public speaker of the time, insisted: "The man that assassinated Abraham Lincoln was a Democrat. . . . Soldiers, every scar you have on your heroic bodies was given you by a Democrat!"

Disputed election of 1876

Despite the lack of major issues, the 1876 election generated the most votes of any national election in U.S. history up to that point. Early election returns pointed to a victory for the Democrat Tilden. Nationwide, he outpolled Hayes by almost 300,000 votes. By midnight following Election Day, Tilden had won 184 electoral votes—just one vote short of victory. Hayes went to bed that night convinced that he had lost. But overnight, Republican activists realized that the election hinged on nineteen disputed electoral votes from Florida, Louisiana, and South Carolina. The Democrats needed only one of the challenged votes to claim victory; the Republicans needed all nineteen. Republicans in those key states had engaged in election fraud while Democrats had used physical intimidation to keep black voters at home. But each of the three states was then governed by a Republican who appointed the election boards, each of which reported narrow victories for Hayes. The Democrats immediately challenged the results.

In all three of the disputed southern states, rival election boards sent in conflicting counts. The nation watched and wondered as the politicians bickered about the contested election. The Constitution offered no guidance in this unprecedented situation. Days, then weeks, passed with no solution. Finally, on January 29, 1877, the Congress set up a special Electoral Commission to settle the dispute. It met daily for weeks trying to verify the disputed vote counts in the three contested southern states. Finally, on March 1, 1877, the commission voted 8 to 7 along party lines in favor of Hayes. On March 2, 1877, the House of Representatives declared Hayes president by an electoral vote of 185 to 184. Tilden decided not to protest the decision. His campaign manager explained that they preferred "four years of Hayes's administration to four years of civil war."

Hayes's victory hinged on the defection of key southern Democrats, who, it turned out, had made a number of secret deals with the Republicans. On February 26, 1877, prominent Ohio Republicans (including future president James A. Garfield) and powerful southern Democrats struck a private bargain—the **Compromise of 1877**—at Wormley's Hotel in Washington, D.C. The Republicans promised that if Hayes were named president, he would remove the last federal troops from the South, letting the state Republican governments there collapse.

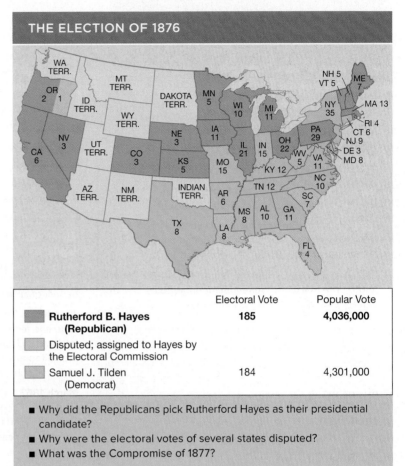

THE ELECTION OF 1876

	Electoral Vote	Popular Vote
Rutherford B. Hayes (Republican)	**185**	**4,036,000**
Disputed; assigned to Hayes by the Electoral Commission		
Samuel J. Tilden (Democrat)	184	4,301,000

- Why did the Republicans pick Rutherford Hayes as their presidential candidate?
- Why were the electoral votes of several states disputed?
- What was the Compromise of 1877?

The End of Reconstruction

In 1877, newly inaugurated President Hayes fulfilled his pledge: he withdrew federal troops from Louisiana and South Carolina, whose Republican governments collapsed soon thereafter. Hayes insisted that it was not his fault. "The practical destruction of the Republican organization in the South was accomplished before my southern policy was announced." Over the next thirty years, the protection of black civil rights in the South crumbled under the pressure of restored white Democratic rule. As Henry Adams, a former Louisiana slave, observed in 1877, "The whole South—every state in the South—has got [back] into the hands of the very men that held us as slaves." New white state governments in the South rewrote their constitutions, rid their administrations of "carpetbaggers, scalawags, and blacks," and cut back spending. "The Yankees helped free us, so they

Compromise of 1877 Secret deal forged by congressional leaders to resolve disputed election of 1876; Republican Rutherford B. Hayes, who had lost the popular vote, was declared the winner in exchange for his pledge to remove federal troops from the South, marking the end of Reconstruction.

From Slave to Citizen

The following timeline highlights important developments in the legal status of African Americans during the Civil War and Reconstruction. The timeline breaks the legal status of African Americans into three phases:

PHASE I From Slaves to Freedmen

1857 Supreme Court's *Dred Scott* decision ruled that African Americans were not citizens.

1863 Lincoln's **Emancipation Proclamation** freed slaves in areas still under rebellion during the Civil War, but their citizenship status remained unresolved.

1865 The **Thirteenth Amendment** abolished slavery throughout the United States.

PHASE II From Freedmen to Citizen

Summer 1865 As the war ended, southern states in the former Confederacy adopted a series of **black codes** to restrict the freedom of African Americans and to preserve many aspects of slavery.

March 1866 Republicans in Congress passed a **Civil Rights Act** that declared all persons born in the United States (except Native Americans) and not subject to any foreign power, were citizens entitled to full and equal benefit of all laws.

June 1866 The **Fourteenth Amendment** reaffirmed the state and federal citizenship of anyone born or naturalized in the United States (except Native Americans) and prohibited any state from allowing any citizen to be denied civil rights and equal protection of the laws.

March 1867 The **Military Reconstruction Act** called for new state constitutions in former Confederate states that had to guarantee the voting rights of African Americans (males) and to ratify the Fourteenth Amendment.

1869–1870 The **Fifteenth Amendment** to the U.S. Constitution prohibited states from denying the vote on the basis of "race, color, or previous condition of servitude."

PHASE III Full Citizenship Denied

1866–1870 African American men in southern states participated in elections at high rates. Six hundred were elected to office. Most African American voters and office holders supported the Republican Party.

1870–1877 White terrorist organizations such as the Ku Klux Klan used violence to suppress African American voting and other forms of political participation. Over time, northern voters lost interest in the process of Reconstruction.

1877 President Hayes withdrew the last federal troops from the South. Over the next several decades, southern states severely curtailed the civil rights of African Americans, including their political participation.

QUESTIONS FOR ANALYSIS

1. What events and movements prompted the federal government to redefine the standing of African Americans in American society between 1857 and 1877?

2. Which of these reforms were widely accepted and which were strongly resisted?

3. How did the Thirteenth, Fourteenth, and Fifteenth Amendments to the U.S. Constitution affect the nation's politics?

4. Why did the federal government abandon its pursuit of racial equality?

say," a former North Carolina slave named Thomas Hall remembered, "but [in 1877] they let us be put back in slavery again."

Reconstruction's Significance

After the Civil War, Congressional Reconstruction gave African Americans an opportunity to experience freedom—but not security or equality. As Thomas Hall noted in acknowledging the end of Reconstruction, African Americans were no longer slaves but they remained dependent "on the southern white man for work, food, and clothing," and most southern whites remained hostile to the notion of civil rights and social equality. The collapse of Congressional Reconstruction in 1877 had tragic consequences, for it allowed the South to renew long-standing patterns of discrimination against African Americans.

Yet for all of the unfulfilled promises of Congressional Reconstruction, it left an enduring legacy—the Thirteenth, Fourteenth, and Fifteenth Amendments—not dead in 1877 but dormant, waiting to be reawakened during the second reconstruction of civil rights in the 1950s and 1960s. If Reconstruction's experiment in interracial democracy did not provide true social equality or substantial economic opportunities for African Americans, it did create the essential constitutional foundation for future advances in the quest for equality and civil rights—not just for African Americans but for women and other minority groups as well. Until the pivotal Reconstruction Era, the states were responsible for protecting citizens' rights. Thereafter, thanks to the Fourteenth and Fifteenth Amendments, blacks had gained equal rights (in theory), and the federal government assumed responsibility for ensuring that states treated blacks equally in terms of their basic civil rights. Congressional Reconstruction was a half-way revolution, sighed the former governor of North Carolina Jonathan Worth, and "nobody can anticipate the action of revolutions." A hundred years later, the cause of civil rights would be embraced again by the federal government—this time permanently.

CORE **OBJECTIVE**

5. Explain the impact of Reconstruction on the nation's future.

Racial discrimination continues

Thirteenth, Fourteenth, and Fifteenth Amendments lay groundwork for future civil rights movements

Reviewing the
CORE OBJECTIVES | INQUIZITIVE

■ **Reconstruction Challenges** With the defeat of the Confederacy and the passage of the Thirteenth Amendment, the federal government had to develop policies and procedures to address a number of difficult questions: What was the status of the defeated states and how would they be reintegrated into the nation's political life? What would be the political status of the former slaves and what would the federal government do to integrate them into the nation's social and economic fabric?

■ **Reconstruction over Time** Abraham Lincoln and his successor, southerner Andrew Johnson, wanted a lenient and quick plan for Reconstruction. The *Freedmen's Bureau* attempted to educate and aid freed slaves, negotiate labor contracts, and reunite families. Lincoln's assassination led many northerners to favor the *Radical Republicans*, who wanted a more transformative plan designed to end the grasp of the old plantation elite on the South's society and economy. Southern whites resisted and established *black codes* to restrict the lives of blacks. *Congressional Reconstruction* responded by stipulating that to reenter the Union, former Confederate states had to ratify the *Fourteenth* and *Fifteenth Amendments* to the U.S. Constitution in order to expand and protect the rights of African Americans. Congress also passed the Military Reconstruction Act, which used federal troops to protect the voting rights and civil rights of African Americans.

■ **Views of Reconstruction** Many former slaves found comfort in their families and the independent churches they established, but land ownership reverted to the old white elite, reducing newly freed black farmers to *sharecropping*. African Americans enthusiastically participated in politics, with many serving as elected officials.

Along with white southern Republicans (scalawags) and northern carpetbaggers, they worked to rebuild the southern economy. Many white southerners, however, blamed their poverty on freed slaves and Republicans, and they supported the *Ku Klux Klan*'s violent intimidation of the supporters of these Reconstruction efforts and the goal of "redemption," or white Democratic control of Southern state governments.

■ **Political and Economic Developments and the End of Reconstruction** Scandals during the Grant administration involved an attempt to corner the gold market and the "whiskey ring's" plan to steal millions of dollars in tax revenue. In the face of these troubles and the economic downturn caused by both the *Panic of 1873* over railroad defaults and disagreement over whether to continue the use of *greenbacks* or return to the gold standard, northern support for Reconstruction eroded. Southern white *redeemers* were elected in 1874, successfully reversing the political progress of Republicans and blacks. In the *Compromise of 1877*, Democrats agreed to the election of Republican Rutherford B. Hayes, who put an end to the Radical Republican administrations in the southern states.

■ **The Significance of Reconstruction** Southern state governments quickly renewed long-standing patterns of discrimination against African Americans, but the Fourteenth and Fifteenth Amendments remained enshrined in the Constitution, creating the essential constitutional foundation for future advances in civil rights. These amendments give the federal government responsibility for ensuring equal treatment and political equality within the states, a role it would increasingly assume in the twentieth century.

KEY TERMS

CHRONOLOGY

1865	Congress sets up the Freedmen's Bureau
April 14, 1865	Lincoln assassinated
1865	Johnson issues Proclamation of Amnesty
	All-white southern state legislatures pass "black codes"
1866	Ku Klux Klan organized
	Congress passes the Civil Rights Act
1867	Congress passes the Military Reconstruction Act
	Freedmen begin participating in elections
1868	Fourteenth Amendment is ratified
	The U.S. House of Representatives impeaches President Andrew Johnson; the Senate fails to convict him
1868	Grant elected President
	Six former Confederate states readmitted to the Union
1869	Reestablishment of white conservative rule ("redeemers") in some former Confederate states
1870	Fifteenth Amendment ratified
1870	First Enforcement Acts passed in response to white terror in the South
1872	Grant wins reelection
1873	Panic of 1873 triggers depression
1877	Compromise of 1877 ends Reconstruction

INQUIZITIVE

Go to InQuizitive to see what you've learned—and learn what you've missed—with personalized feedback along the way.

DEBATING Reconstruction

Historians' interpretations of the past change over time. This happens for many reasons. Historians can revise their thinking in light of information from newly discovered *primary sources*. They can also interpret previously examined sources in new ways by applying new methodologies and theories. Finally, historians themselves are influenced by the values of their own society and times. Present-day events or particular personal interests can influence how historians think about the past. The study of how interpretations of history have changed is called *historiography*. It is the history of the field of history. For Part 4, *A House Divided,* the case study of Debating Reconstruction demonstrates how the views of historians have changed dramatically over time.

For this exercise you have two tasks:

PART 1: Compare the two secondary sources on Reconstruction.

PART 2: Using primary sources, evaluate the arguments of the two secondary sources.

PART I Comparing and Contrasting Secondary Sources

Two *secondary sources,* the work of prominent historians from different eras, are included below for you to review. The first selection comes from William Dunning's (1857–1922) *Reconstruction, Political and Economic, 1865–1877,* written in 1907. Dunning was born on the eve of the Civil War to a well-to-do New Jersey family and began his studies at Columbia University soon after the end of Reconstruction. He lived during a time when racial segregation and white supremacy were the unchallenged law of the land, and he wrote some of the first academic texts on Reconstruction. Dunning was such a compelling force in the first half of the twentieth century that the many historians trained and influenced by him are referred to as the "Dunning School." He was particularly hostile to political idealists, a group which, in his mind, included abolitionists and Radical Republicans. Like many historians of his day, Dunning never questioned his own objectivity. However, later academics and activists have noted that his writings reflect the political beliefs and prejudices of his generation.

Interpretations of Reconstruction have undergone many changes since Dunning's time. The second excerpt, written 101 years later, is from Eric Foner's *The Story of American Freedom.* Born in 1943, Foner is the son of civil rights activists (one of them a historian) deeply concerned with the plight of African Americans. Foner completed his Ph.D. in 1969 during the height of the civil rights movement. Widely regarded as a leading contemporary historian of Reconstruction, Foner's writing on the period brings together much of the scholarship that has revised "Dunning School" interpretations of Reconstruction, particularly as they described the role of African Americans in American society.

Before you begin reading these excerpts, it may be helpful to review Chapter 15 on the transition from President Andrew Johnson's Restoration Plan to Congressional Reconstruction.

Compare the work of these two historians by answering the following questions. Be sure to support your answers with specific examples drawn from the selections by Dunning and Foner.

■ What is the topic of each excerpt? What period of Reconstruction is the author writing about? What groups are examined in American society?

■ Generally, how does each author portray the Reconstruction process? What in each author's writing leads you to believe that this is how the author feels about Reconstruction? How do those feelings—whether positive or negative—affect each author's point of view?

■ How would you describe the similarities between these two excerpts?

■ What are the major differences in interpretation between the excerpts?

- What is the main argument each historian makes about the topic?

- How do these interpretations compare to that presented in Chapter 15?

- These two excerpts were written 101 years apart. How might this have influenced the development of their arguments?

Secondary Source 1

William Dunning, from *Reconstruction, Political and Economic, 1865–1877*

It was, indeed, no novelty for the people of the South to be subject to government by the United States army. . . . The reasoning by which the policy of Congress was justified in the North was regarded in the South as founded on false-hood and malice. So far as the "black codes" were con-cerned, it was pointed out that they could not be alleged as evidences of a tendency to restore slavery or introduce peonage [dependence], since the offensive acts had in many of the states been repealed by the legislatures them-selves, and in all had been duly superseded by the civil rights act. The much-exploited outrages on freedmen and Unionists were declared to be exaggerated or distorted reports of incidents which any time of social tension must produce among the criminal classes. The rejection of the Fourteenth Amendment was considered as merely a dig-nified refusal by honorable men to be the instruments of their own humiliation and shame.

Under all these circumstances the southerners felt that the policy of Congress had no real cause save the pur-pose of radical politicians to prolong and extend their party power by means of negro suffrage [voting rights]. This and this alone was the purpose for which major-generals had been empowered to remodel the state gov-ernments at their will, to exercise through general orders the functions of executive, legislature, and courts, and to compel the white people to recognize the blacks as their equals wherever the stern word of military command could reach. It was as inconceivable to the southerners that rational men of the North should seriously approve of negro suffrage per se as it had been in 1860 to the north-erners that rational men of the South should approve of secession per se. Hence, in the one case as in the other, a craving for political power was assumed to be the only ex-planation of an otherwise unintelligible proceeding.

Source: Dunning, William. *Reconstruction, Political and Economic, 1865–1877.* New York: Harper & Bros., 1907. 109–12.

Secondary Source 2

Eric Foner, from *The Story of American Freedom*

Rejecting the idea that emancipation implied civil or po-litical equality or opportunities to acquire property or advance economically, rights northerners deemed essen-tial to a free society, most white southerners insisted that blacks must remain a dependent plantation workforce in a laboring situation not very different from slavery. During Presidential Reconstruction—the period from 1865 to 1867 when Lincoln's successor, Andrew Johnson, gave the white South a free hand in determining the contours of Reconstruction—southern state governments enforced this view of black freedom by enacting the notorious Black Codes, which denied blacks equality before the law and political rights and imposed on them mandatory year-long labor contracts, coercive apprenticeship regulations, and criminal penalties for breach of contract. Through these laws, the South's white leadership sought to ensure that plantation agriculture survived emancipation.

Thus, the death of slavery did not automatically mean the birth of freedom. But the Black Codes so flagrantly vio-lated free labor principles that they invoked the wrath of the Republican North. Southern reluctance to accept the reality of emancipation resulted in a monumental struggle between President Andrew Johnson and the Republican Congress over the legacy of the Civil War. The result was the enactment of laws and constitutional amendments that redrew the boundaries of citizenship and expanded the definition of freedom for all Americans. . . .

Much of the ensuing conflict over Reconstruction re-volved around the problem, as Senator Lyman Trumbull of Illinois put it, of defining "what slavery is and what lib-erty is." . . . By 1866, a consensus had emerged within the Republican Party that civil equality was an essential at-tribute of freedom. The Civil War had elevated "equality" to a status in the vocabulary of freedom it had not enjoyed since the Revolution. . . . In a remarkable, if temporary, reversal of political traditions, the newly empowered na-tional state now sought to identify and protect the rights of all Americans.

Source: Foner, Eric. *The Story of American Freedom.* New York: W. W. Norton & Company, 1998. 103–105.

PART II Using Primary Sources to Evaluate Secondary Sources

When historians are faced with competing interpretations of the past, they often look at primary source material as part of the process of evaluating the different arguments. In the following selections, you'll find *primary sources* relating to the period of Reconstruction.

Carefully read each of the following primary sources and answer the following questions. Decide how the primary source documents support or refute Dunning's and Foner's arguments about this period. You may find that some documents do both, but for different parts of each historian's interpretation. Be sure to identify which specific components of each historian's argument the documents support or refute.

■ Which of the two historian's arguments is best supported by the primary source documents? Or if you find that both arguments are well supported by the evidence, why do you think the two historians had such different interpretations about the period?

■ Based on your comparison of the two arguments and your analysis of the primary sources, how has the interpretation of Reconstruction by historians shifted over time? What can you conclude about historiography from the work of these two historians?

Primary Source 1

Union Army General Carl Schurz, from *Report on the Condition of the South*

A belief, conviction, or prejudice, or whatever you may call it, so widely spread and apparently so deeply rooted as this, that the negro will not work without physical compulsion, is certainly calculated to have a very serious influence upon the conduct of the people entertaining it. It naturally produced a desire to preserve slavery in its original form as much and as long as possible—and you may, perhaps, remember the admission made by one of the provisional governors, over two months after the close of the war, that the people of his State still indulged in a lingering hope slavery might yet be preserved—or to introduce into the new system that element of physical compulsion which would make the negro work. Efforts were, indeed, made to hold the negro in his old state of subjection, especially in such localities where our military forces had not yet penetrated, or where the country was not garrisoned in detail. Here and there planters

succeeded for a limited period to keep their former slaves in ignorance, or at least doubt, about their new rights; but the main agency employed for that purpose was force and intimidation. In many instances negroes who walked away from the plantations, or were found upon the roads, were shot or otherwise severely punished, which was calculated to produce the impression among those remaining with their masters that an attempt to escape from slavery would result in certain destruction. A large proportion of the many acts of violence committed is undoubtedly attributable to this motive.

Source: Schurz, Carl. *Report on the Condition of the South*, 1865, 39TH CONGRESS, SENATE. Ex. Doc., 1st Session, No. 2, p. 19.

Primary Source 2

Mississippi Vagrant Law, 1865

All freedmen, free negroes and mulattoes in this State, over the age of eighteen years, found on the second Monday in January, 1866, or thereafter, with no lawful employment or business, or found unlawfully assembling themselves together, either in the day or night time, and all white persons so assembling themselves with freedmen, free negroes or mulattoes, or usually associating with freedmen, free negroes or mulattoes, on terms of equality, or living in adultery or fornication with a freed woman, free negro or mulatto, shall be deemed vagrants, and on conviction thereof shall be fined in a sum not exceeding, in the case of a freedman, free negro, or mulatto, fifty dollars, and a white man two hundred dollars, and imprisoned at the discretion of the court, the free negro not exceeding ten days, and the white man not exceeding six months. . . . All fines and forfeitures collected under the provisions of this act shall be paid into the county treasury for general county purposes, and in case any freedman, free negro or mulatto shall fail for five days after the imposition of any fine or forfeiture upon him or her for violation of any of the provisions of this act to pay the same, that it shall be, and is hereby, made the duty of the sheriff of the proper county to hire out said freedman, free negro or mulatto, to any person who will, for the shortest period of service, pay said fine and forfeiture and all costs. . . .

Source: Mississippi Vagrant Law, *Laws of Mississippi, 1865*, 90 in *Documentary History of Reconstruction: Political, Military, Social, Religious, Educational & Industrial, 1865 to the Present Time*. Ed. Walter Lynwood Fleming. Cleveland, Oh.: The Arthur H. Clark Company, 1906. 283–86.

Primary Source 3

Civil Rights Act of 1866

Be it enacted, . . . That all persons born in the United States and not subject to any foreign power, excluding Indians not taxed, are hereby declared to be citizens of the United States; and such citizens, of every race and color, without regard to any previous condition of slavery or involuntary servitude, except as a punishment for crime whereof the party shall have been duly convicted, shall have the same right, in every State and Territory in the United States, to make and enforce contracts, to sue, be parties, and give evidence, to inherit, purchase, lease, sell, hold, and convey real and personal property, and to full and equal benefit of all laws and proceedings for the security of person and property, as is enjoyed by white citizens, and shall be subject to like punishment, pains and penalties, and to none other, any law, statute, ordinance, regulation, or custom, to the contrary notwithstanding.

Source: Civil Rights Act of 1866, *United States Statutes at Large*, vol. xiv, 27 [April 9, 1866].

Primary Source 4

Radical Republican Thaddeus Stevens, from "The Advantages of Negro Suffrage"

Unless the rebel States, before admission, should be made republican in spirit, and placed under the guardianship of loyal men, all our blood and treasure will have been spent in vain. . . . There is more reason why colored voters should be admitted in the rebel States than in the Territories. In the States they form the great mass of the loyal men. Possibly with their aid loyal governments may be established in most of those States. Without it all are sure to be ruled by traitors; and loyal men, black and white, will be oppressed, exiled, or murdered. . . . Have not loyal blacks quite as good a right to choose rulers and make laws as rebel whites? In the second place, it is a necessity in order to protect the loyal white men in the seceded States. The white Union men are in a great minority in each of those States. With them the blacks would act in a body; and it is believed that in each of said States, except one, the two united would form a majority, control the States, and protect themselves. Now they are the victims of daily murder. They must suffer constant persecution or be exiled. . . . Another good reason is, it would insure the ascendency of the Union party. . . . I believe . . . that on the continued ascendency of that party depends the safety of this great nation. If impartial suffrage is excluded in the rebel States, then every one of them is sure to send a solid rebel representative delegation to Congress, and cast a solid rebel electoral vote. . . . I am for negro suffrage in every rebel State. If it be just, it should not be denied; if it be necessary, it should be adopted; if it be a punishment to traitors, they deserve it.

Source: Stevens, Thaddeus. *Congressional Globe*, January 3, 1867, 252. In *Documentary History of Reconstruction: Political, Military, Social, Religious, Educational & Industrial, 1865 to the Present Time.* Ed. Walter Lynwood Fleming. Cleveland, Oh.: The Arthur H. Clark Company, 1906. 149–50.

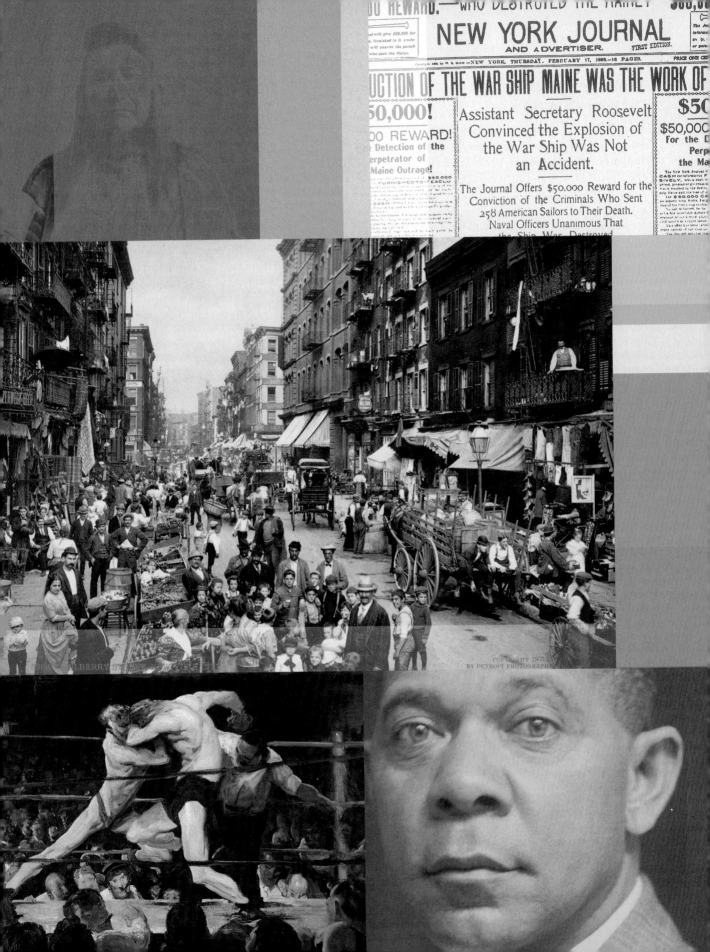

Growing Pains

The defeat of the Confederacy in 1865 restored the Union and in the process helped accelerate America's transformation into an agricultural empire and an industrial powerhouse. A stronger sense of nationalism began to replace the regional conflicts of the prewar era. During and after the Civil War, the Republican-led Congress pushed through legislation to promote industrial and commercial development as well as western expansion at the same time that it was "reconstructing" the former Confederate states. In the process of settling the rest of the continent, ruthlessly forcing Indians onto reservations, and exploiting the continent's natural resources, the United States forged a dynamic new industrial economy serving an increasingly national and even international market for American goods.

Fueled by innovations in mass production and mass marketing as well as advances in transportation and communications such as transcontinental railroads and transatlantic telegraph systems, huge corporations began to dominate the economy by the end of the nineteenth century. As the prominent social theorist William Graham Sumner remarked, the relentless process of industrial development "controls us all because we are all in it. It creates the conditions of our own existence, sets the limits of our social activity, and regulates the bonds of our social relations."

Late-nineteenth-century American life drew much of its energy from the mushrooming industrial cities. "This is the age of cities," declared Midwestern writer Hamlin Garland. "We are now predominantly urban." But the transition from an economy made up of mostly small local and regional businesses to one dominated by large-scale national and international corporations affected rural life as well. As early as 1869, novelist Harriet Beecher Stowe reported that the "simple, pastoral" America "is a thing forever gone. The hurry of railroads, and the rush and roar of business" had displaced the Jeffersonian ideal of America remaining a nation of small farms and few cities. For more and more Americans, their work day began with the shriek of a factory whistle rather than a crowing rooster. She exaggerated, of course. Small farms and small towns survived the impact of the Industrial Revolution, but farm folk, as one New Englander stressed, must now "understand farming as a business; if they do not it will go hard with them." The friction between the new forces of the national marketplace and the traditional folkways of small-scale family farming generated social unrest and political revolts (what one writer called "a seismic shock, a cyclonic violence") during the last quarter of the nineteenth century.

The clash between tradition and modernity, sleepy farm villages and bustling cities, peaked during the 1890s, one of the most strife-ridden decades in American history. A deep economic depression, political activism by farmers, and violent conflicts between industrial workers and employers transformed the presidential campaign of 1896 into a clash between rival visions of America's future. The Republican candidate, William McKinley, campaigned on modern urban and industrial values. By contrast, William Jennings Bryan, the nominee of both the Democratic and the Populist parties, was an eloquent defender of America's rural past. McKinley's victory proved to be a turning point in the nation's political and social history. By 1900 the United States had emerged as one of the world's greatest industrial powers, and it would thereafter assume a new leadership role in world affairs—for good and for ill.

CARNEGIE STEEL COMPANY Steelworkers operate the dangerous and magnificent Bessemer converters at Andrew Carnegie's huge steel mill in Pittsburgh, Pennsylvania.

Big Business and Organized Labor

1860-1900

After the Civil War, America witnessed a wild scramble for wealth and an epidemic of political corruption as people rushed to take advantage of boundless economic possibilities. The massive production of supplies for the war effort stimulated a dramatic expansion of the economy that quickened in the years after the war. From 1865 to 1900, the United States experienced the highest rate of economic growth in the world, more than double that of its closest rival, Great Britain. By 1900, American industries and farms dominated global markets in textiles, steel, and oil, wheat and cotton, timber and meat packing.

Such phenomenal economic growth generated profound social changes. Millions of young adults left farms and villages to work in factories, mines, and mills in the fast-growing cities. Women entered the workplace in growing numbers, mostly as clerks, typists, secretaries, teachers, nurses, and seamstresses. And workers in many industries, especially railroads, coal mines, and steel mills, joined unions in an effort to gain better working conditions and higher wages. Strikes—often accompanied by violence—became commonplace during the late nineteenth century as wage laborers sought economic justice.

Rapid industrialization resulted from many factors, not the least of which was the emergence of remarkable and often ruthless business titans who took full advantage of new opportunities, innovative

CORE
OBJECTIVES INQUIZITIVE

1. Explain the primary factors that stimulated unprecedented industrial and agricultural growth in the late nineteenth century.

2. Describe the entrepreneurs who pioneered the growth of Big Business, the goals they aimed to achieve, and the strategies they used to dominate their industries.

3. Evaluate the role of the federal government in the nation's economic development during this period.

4. Analyze the ways in which the social class structure and the lives of women changed in the late nineteenth century.

5. Evaluate the efforts of workers to organize unions to promote their interests during this era.

technologies, and political lobbying (including bribery) to grow huge businesses (called *trusts*) that dominated their respective industries. While amassing phenomenal personal wealth and exercising disproportionate political influence, the post–Civil War business leaders also aroused intense criticism. Slowly but insistently, reformers emerged to demand that the government step in to regulate the freewheeling entrepreneurs. By the end of the century, a massive reform movement would force all levels of government—local, state, and federal—to restrain the excesses of the nation's largest businesses to preserve social stability.

CORE **OBJECTIVE**

1. Explain the primary factors that stimulated | unprecedented industrial and agricultural growth in the late nineteenth century.

The Causes of Industrial Growth

Several factors converged after the Civil War to accelerate economic growth and industrial development. America's vast natural resources—land, rivers, forests, oil, coal, water, iron ore—created a huge advantage over other nations. At the same time, a flood of immigrants provided an army of new low-wage workers and also expanded the national market of consumers. Between 1865 and 1900, over 15 million newcomers arrived in the United States. In addition, inventors, research laboratories, and business owners developed labor-saving machinery and mass-production techniques that spurred dramatic advances in efficiency and productivity. Farms, canneries, factories, slaughterhouses, mines, mills, refineries, and other businesses turned out more products more cheaply, enabling more people to buy more of them. These technological advances created *economies of scale*, whereby larger business enterprises, including commercial farms, were able to afford expensive new machinery and large workforces that made them more productive than smaller enterprises.

Causes of industrial growth:
1) vast natural resources,
2) flood of immigrants,
3) technological innovations

Innovative business leadership also spurred economic growth. A group of shrewd, determined entrepreneurs created huge new national corporations, some of which became virtual monopolies in industries like oil, steel, sugar, and meatpacking. As one wealthy investor said, a new breed of ruthlessly focused capitalists had emerged after the Civil War, driven by the "same all-pervading, all-engrossing anxiety to grow rich."

The Second Industrial Revolution

Second Industrial Revolution
Beginning in the late nineteenth century, a wave of technological innovations, especially in iron and steel production, steam and electrical power, and telegraphic communications, all of which spurred industrial development and urban growth.

The dramatic increases in economic productivity were spurred by the **Second Industrial Revolution**, which began in the mid–nineteenth century and was centered in the United States and Germany. This revolution resulted from three related developments. The first was the creation of modern transportation and communication systems that gave farmers and factory owners access to national and international markets. The completion of transcontinental railroads and the development of larger, faster steamships helped expand markets worldwide, as did the laying of the telegraph cable under the Atlantic Ocean to connect the United States with Europe.

During the 1880s, a second major breakthrough—the creation of electrical power—accelerated the pace of change in industrial and urban development. Electricity dramatically increased the power, speed, and efficiency of machinery. It also spurred urban growth by making possible trolley and subway systems as well as elevators that enabled the construction of taller buildings.

> The Second Industrial Revolution: Modern transportation systems and electrical power

The third major catalyst for the Second Industrial Revolution was the systematic application of scientific research to industrial processes. In new laboratories staffed by graduates of new research universities and often funded by corporations or wealthy business owners, scientists (mostly chemists) and engineers discovered dramatic new ways to improve industrial processes. Researchers figured out, for example, how to refine kerosene and gasoline from crude oil, and how to make steel more efficiently and in much larger quantities.

> The Second Industrial Revolution: Improvement of industrial processes

Using these improved processes, inventors developed new products—telephones, typewriters, phonographs (record players), adding machines, sewing machines, cameras, zippers, farm machinery—that resulted in lower prices for an array of consumer items. These advances, in turn, expanded the scope and scale of industrial organizations. Capital-intensive industries, those requiring massive investments in specialized equipment, such as steel and oil, as well as processed food and tobacco, began emphasizing mass production and distribution across national and international markets. Serving customers across the nation and around the world required more sophisticated strategies of marketing and advertising, thus expanding those industries. Between 1870 and 1900, expenditures on advertising increased more than tenfold. As early as 1867, a journalist complained that advertisements were invading "every department of life."

Corporate Farming

At the same time that the industrial sector of the economy was experiencing rapid growth and an ever-increasing concentration of ownership and production into huge companies, the agricultural sector was also shifting quickly to a large-scale market model of operation. Corporations developed huge "bonanza" farms (growing mostly wheat and corn) that defied the nation's tradition of small-scale family farming. Bonanza farms appeared first in the Dakotas and Minnesota before spreading across the West. They were run like factories by professional, college-educated managers, who during harvest season would hire hundreds of migrant workers to bring in the crop. Bonanza farms using the latest machinery and scientific techniques became internationally famous for their productivity and efficiency. By 1870, America had become the world's leading agricultural producer, sending massive amounts of grain to foreign markets abroad. In addition, with the start of the

> Large-scale farming: "Bonanza farms"

commercial cattle industry, the processes of slaughtering and packing meat became major industries too. So the farm sector directly stimulated the industrial sector of the economy.

Technological Innovations

Technological innovations spur productivity

After the Civil War, technological innovations spurred phenomenal increases in industrial productivity. The U.S. Patent Office, which had recorded only 276 inventions during the 1790s, registered almost 235,000 new patents a century later, in the 1890s. The list of commercial innovations after the Civil War was lengthy: barbed wire; mechanical harvesters, reapers, and combines; refrigerated rail cars; air brakes for trains; machine tools; steam turbines; typewriters; sewing machines; vacuum cleaners; and countless others. Few, if any, inventions of the time could rival the importance of the telephone, which twenty-nine-year-old Alexander Graham Bell, a Scottish immigrant, patented in 1876. Four years later, Bell perfected the long-distance telephone lines that revolutionized communication. By 1895, there were over 300,000 telephones in use. Before the end of the century, the internal-combustion engine, motion picture, and automobile were stimulating new industries that would flourish in the twentieth century.

New job options for women: Office work and sweatshops

New inventions changed the nature of work. The development of typewriters, for example, brought a flood of women workers into business offices, which had been mostly all male. Because women were presumed to have greater dexterity in their fingers, owners hired them to operate typewriters, in part because they could be paid much less than men. Clerical positions soon became the fastest-growing job category for women. Likewise, the

Office typists Newly entrusted with typewriters, women occupied the secretarial positions at many offices, such as the Remington Typewriter Company, pictured here.

introduction of sewing machines for the mass production of clothing and linens opened new doors to women—if not usually pleasant ones to walk through. So-called sweatshops emerged in the major cities, where large numbers of mostly young women worked long hours stitching textiles in cramped, stifling conditions.

Technological discoveries transformed daily life, none more so than the creations of inventor Thomas Alva Edison. In the laboratory at his "science village" in Menlo Park, New Jersey, Edison promised to produce "a minor invention every ten days and a big thing every six months or so." He invented the phonograph in 1877 and the electric light bulb in 1879. Altogether he created or perfected hundreds of new devices and processes, including the storage battery, dictaphone, mimeograph copier, electric motor, and motion picture camera and projector.

Until the 1880s the United States was lit mostly by flickering kerosene or gas lamps. In 1882 the Edison Electric Illuminating Company, later renamed General Electric, supplied electrical current to eighty-five customers in New York City, launching the electric utility industry. The invention of electric motors enabled factories to locate wherever owners wished; they no longer had to cluster around waterfalls and coal deposits for a ready supply of energy.

| Edison and electricity |

Railroads Leading the Way

More than any other industry, the railroads symbolized the impact of innovative technologies on the economic revolution during the second half of the nineteenth century. No other form of transportation played so large a role in the development of the interconnected national marketplace. Railroads moved people and goods faster and farther than anything else could, and they did so in any weather. Towns that had rail stations thrived; those that did not died. A town's connection to a railroad, observed Anthony Trollope, a celebrated British writer touring the United States, was "the first necessity of life, and gives the only hope of wealth."

Although the first great wave of railroad building had occurred in the 1850s, the most spectacular growth took place during the quarter century after the Civil War. Between 1865 and 1873, 35,000 miles of new track were laid across the nation, as much as had been built in the previous thirty years. The national rail network grew to nearly 200,000 miles by 1897, more than all of Europe combined.

| Railroads' contributions to the economic boom |

The transcontinental rail lines led the way, helping to populate the Great Plains and the Far West by enabling more people to move west and ship their farm products back east. Railroads were expensive enterprises that required huge capital investments to purchase engines and cars and construct track, trestles, and bridges. The financing of railroads also involved complex transactions. Railroads became the first industry to contract with "investment banks" to raise capital by selling shares of stock to investors

Chinese railroad workers Using horse-drawn carts, picks, shovels, and dynamite, Chinese laborers played a large role in constructing the Transcontinental Railroad's Central Pacific track.

around the world. They were also the largest consumers in the economy, stimulating other industries through their vast purchases of iron and steel, coal, timber, leather (for seats), and glass. In addition, railroad companies were the nation's largest employers. By the 1870s, the Pennsylvania Railroad alone had 55,000 employees.

But the railroads also brought problems. Many freewheeling developers cared more about making money than building good railroads. In their race to build new lines, companies overlooked dangerous working conditions that caused thousands of laborers to be killed or injured. Too many unneeded railroads were built; by the 1880s, there were twice as many railroad companies as the economy could support. Some railroads were poorly or even criminally managed and went bankrupt. Railroad lobbyists helped to corrupt state and federal legislators, as the votes of politicians were "bought" with cash or shares of stock in the new railroad companies. As the head of the Union Pacific Railroad admitted, "Our method of doing business is founded upon lying, cheating, and stealing—all bad things."

Building the Transcontinentals

After the Civil War, railroad tracks in the South were gradually rebuilt and expanded. But the most spectacular achievements were the transcontinental lines built west of the Mississippi River across plains and deserts, over roaring rivers and deep canyons, and around and through the nation's tallest mountains, all the way to the Pacific coast. The Pacific Railway Act (1862) authorized the construction of a rail line to be built by the Union Pacific Railroad Company westward from Omaha, Nebraska, and by the Central Pacific Railroad Company eastward from Sacramento, California. Both companies began construction during the war, but most of the work was done after 1865.

By connecting the nation from ocean to ocean, the transcontinental railroads enabled the creation of a truly national market for goods and services, including tourism. In 1872 Congress created Yellowstone, the first national park, and railroads began bringing tourists to the park in northwest Wyoming ten years later. Furthermore, as they pushed into sparsely populated western states and territories, the railroad companies became

The Union Pacific meets the Central Pacific The celebration of the first transcontinental railroad's completion took place in Promontory, Utah, on May 10, 1869.

the region's primary real estate developers. They transported millions of settlers from the East, many of them immigrants who were eager to buy land. The railroads changed the economic and political as well as physical landscape, and enabled the United States to emerge as a world power.

The first transcontinental railroads were extremely expensive to build compared with lines in the East. Because the routes passed through long stretches of unpopulated desert areas, construction materials as well as workers and their food and water had to be hauled long distances. Camps had to be built for housing. Crossing high mountains required extensive use of dynamite and costly tunnels and bridges. Harsh weather caused frequent work disruptions. The high costs made the railroad owners dependent on government financial support, which came in the form of substantial loans and cash subsidies as well as massive grants of "public" land taken from the Indians. The owners also relied on federal troops to crush the Native Americans whose ancestral lands were along the rail route.

The transcontinental railroads were, in the words of General William Tecumseh Sherman, the "work of giants." Their construction required heroic feats by workers and engineers who laid the rails, built the bridges, and

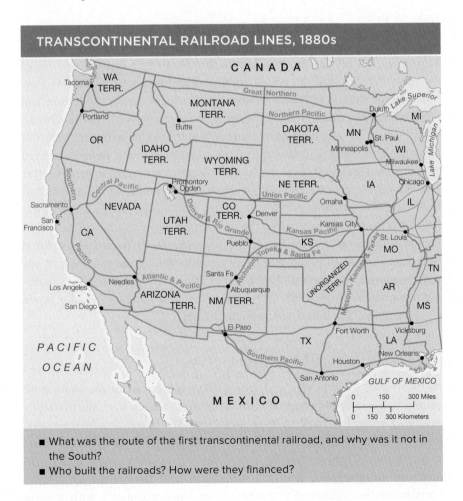

TRANSCONTINENTAL RAILROAD LINES, 1880s

- What was the route of the first transcontinental railroad, and why was it not in the South?
- Who built the railroads? How were they financed?

gouged out the tunnels amid dangerous working conditions and severe weather. Some 10,000 men worked on the two railroads as they raced to connect with one another. The Union Pacific crews were composed largely of young, unmarried former Civil War soldiers, both Union and Confederate, along with ex-slaves and Irish and German immigrants. The Central Pacific crews were mainly Chinese workers lured to America either earlier by the California gold rush or more recently by railroad jobs. Most of these "coolie" laborers were single men eager to make money to take back to their homeland, where they could then afford to marry and buy a parcel of land. Their temporary status and dreams of a good life back in China made them more willing than American laborers to endure the low pay and dangerous working conditions.

The Union Pacific had built 1,086 miles of track compared with the Central Pacific's 689 when the race ended at Promontory Summit in the Utah Territory. There, on May 10, 1869, president of the Central Pacific, Leland Stanford, drove a gold spike symbolizing the completion of the first transcontinental railroad. Others soon followed along routes to the north and south.

CORE OBJECTIVE

2. Describe the entrepreneurs who pioneered the growth of Big Business, the goals they aimed to achieve, and the strategies they used to dominate their industries.

The Rise of Big Business

The emergence of "Big Business" in the late nineteenth century was one of the most significant developments in American history. Corporations grew much larger than ever before, transacting business across the nation and often around the world. They were also much more powerful politically and socially, forming a web of interconnected relationships with each other to influence governors, legislators, Congress, and presidents. Before the Civil War, most businesses were small, local enterprises run by their owners. After 1865, much of America suddenly got bigger—towns and cities, ships, locomotives, factories, machines, mines, and mills—and business organizations followed the same path in creating the most sweeping economic revolution in history. But the rapid expansion in the size and power of businesses created problems along with prosperity. "The growing wealth and influence of our large corporations," warned the *New York Times*, "is one of the most alarming phenomena of our time. Our public companies already wield gigantic power, and they use it like unscrupulous giants."

The Growth of Corporations

Rise of limited liability corporations and elimination of competition

As businesses grew in size and scope, they took many forms. Some were owned by an individual, usually their founder; others were partnerships involving several owners. Increasingly during the late nineteenth century, however, large companies that served national and international markets were converted into "corporations"—legal entities that separate the *ownership* of an enterprise from the *management* of its operations. Once a corporation is registered ("chartered" or "incorporated") with a state government, it can raise money to operate ("capital") by selling shares of stock—representing partial ownership of the company—to people not otherwise involved with it, although those who found and manage a corporation usually own stock in it as well. Shareholders elect a board of directors who appoint and evaluate the corporation's executives ("management") and can replace them. One of the most important benefits of a corporation is "limited liability": stockholders share in the profits generated by a corporation, but they cannot be held personally liable for its debts if it fails.

Competition is supposed to be the great virtue of capitalism, since it forces businesses to produce better products and lower prices. But as many American businesses grew larger and became giant corporations, some of them came to view competition as a burden. To try to eliminate it, competing companies selling similar products often formed secret "pools" whereby they agreed to keep their prices the same. Pools rarely lasted, however, because one or more of the participants usually violated the agreement by cutting prices. The more effective strategy for the most aggressive companies was to drive out or buy out their weaker competitors.

Strategies like these, as well as the specific methods used to carry them out, aroused considerable controversy. In the process of forming huge companies and eliminating competition, many business leaders cut ethical corners, bribed politicians, exploited workers, and broke laws. When asked how people might react to the shady methods he used to build his network of railroads, William Henry Vanderbilt famously replied: "The public be damned!"

The Barons of Business

Most of the men (few women had such opportunities) who created big businesses and huge fortunes in the late nineteenth century were driven by a compulsive desire to become rich and influential. From the first days of the Jamestown colony in Virginia during the early seventeenth century, the drive to build a fortune has been one of the most powerful forces shaping American life. During and after the Civil War, becoming rich became a dominant ideal for many Americans. "To secure wealth is an honorable ambition," stressed Russell Conwell, a prominent Baptist minister from Philadelphia who crisscrossed the nation preaching the benefits of hard work and its just rewards. "Money is power," he explained, and "every good man and woman ought to strive for power, to do good with it when obtained. I say, get rich! get rich!"

The richly varied industrial and financial giants who emerged after the Civil War personified the values celebrated in Conwell's speech. They were outsized men of grit and genius who found innovative—and occasionally illegal—ways to increase production, create efficiencies, and eliminate competition. Three entrepreneurs, in particular, stand out in this period for their shrewdness, ruthlessness, and remarkable achievements: John D. Rockefeller, Andrew Carnegie, and John Pierpont Morgan.

> Rise of industrial and financial giants

John D. Rockefeller Co-founder of Standard Oil Company.

John D. Rockefeller

Born in New York in 1839, John D. Rockefeller moved as a youth to Cleveland, Ohio. Soon thereafter, his father abandoned the family. Raised by his mother, a devout Baptist, Rockefeller developed a single-minded passion for systematic organization and self-discipline, and as a young man in the 1860s, he decided to bring order and rationality to the chaotic new boom-and-bust oil industry. Fiercely ambitious and a hard bargainer, he was obsessed with precision, efficiency, tidiness, and money. (A childhood friend recalled that he was "mad about money, though sane about everything else.") He said little, rarely smiled, and hardly ever laughed.

The railroad and shipping connections around Cleveland made it a strategic location for serving the booming oil fields of nearby western Pennsylvania. The first oil well in the United States began producing in 1859 in Titusville, Pennsylvania, and led to the Pennsylvania oil rush of the 1860s. Because oil could be refined into kerosene, then widely used for lighting, heating, and cooking, the economic importance of the oil rush soon outstripped that of the California Gold Rush ten years earlier. Well before the end of the Civil War, oil refineries sprang up in Pittsburgh and Cleveland. Of the two cities, Cleveland had better rail service, so Rockefeller focused his energies there.

> Strategy: Horizontal and vertical integration

In 1870, Rockefeller teamed up with Henry M. Flagler, Samuel Andrews (inventor of an inexpensive means of refining crude oil), and his brother William Rockefeller to establish the **Standard Oil Company** of Ohio. Although the company quickly became the largest oil refiner in the nation, Rockefeller wanted more. His goal was to eliminate his competitors and win control of the entire oil industry, for once he gained a near monopoly, he could raise oil prices as he saw fit. During the 1870s, Rockefeller pursued a strategy of consolidating control called horizontal integration, in which a dominant corporation in a particular industry buys or forces out most of its competitors. In a few cases, Rockefeller hired former competitors as executives, but only "the big ones," he said, "those who have already proved they can do a big business. As for the others, unfortunately they will have to die." By 1879, Standard Oil controlled more than 90 percent of the oil refining in the nation. Still, that was not enough for Rockefeller, who intended "to secure the entire refining business of the world." His goal was a **monopoly**, a business that grows so large that it effectively controls an entire industry.

Rockefeller was ruthlessly efficient in his efforts to dominate the oil industry. He was adept at reducing expenses, incorporating the latest technologies, and eliminating waste while paying "nobody a profit." Because he shipped so much oil by rail, for example, he forced railroads to pay him secret "rebates" on his oil shipments, enabling him to pay less for shipping than his competitors paid. Most important, instead of depending upon the products or services of other firms, known as middlemen, Standard Oil eventually owned everything needed to produce, refine and deliver oil, from wells to the finished product. The company had its own pipelines, built factories to make

Standard Oil Company Corporation under the leadership of John D. Rockefeller that attempted to dominate the entire oil industry through horizontal and vertical integration.

monopoly Corporation so large that it effectively controls the entire market for its products or services.

The rise of oil Crowding this Pennsylvania farm are wooden derricks that extracted crude oil.

its own wagons and storage barrels, did its own hauling, owned storage tanks and tanker ships, and did whatever else it needed to produce crude oil, refine it into kerosene, gasoline, and lubricants, and then sell it. In economic terms, this business strategy is called vertical integration. A vertically integrated corporation owns all of the different businesses needed to produce and sell its product.

During the 1870s, Standard Oil bought so many of its competitors that, in an effort to limit its economic power, many state legislatures outlawed the practice of one corporation owning stock in competing ones. In 1882, Rockefeller tried to get around such laws by organizing the Standard Oil Trust, a new way of merging businesses. A **trust** is an arrangement that gives a person or corporation (the "trustee") the legal power to manage another person's money or another company. Instead of owning other companies outright, the Standard Oil Trust controlled more than thirty companies spread across several states by having their stockholders transfer their shares "in trust" to Rockefeller and eight other trustees. In return, the stockholders received "trust certificates," which paid them annual dividends from the Trust's earnings. The Standard Oil Trust gave Rockefeller a virtual monopoly over the American oil industry.

> Strategy: Corporate trusts, e.g., the Standard Oil Trust

But the formation of huge corporate trusts, a practice widely copied by the cattle, liquor, sugar, tobacco, salt, and leather industries, among others, generated intense criticism. In 1890, Congress responded by passing the Sherman Anti-Trust Act, which declared that efforts to monopolize industries and thereby "restrain" competition were illegal. Its language was so vague and unclear, however, that it proved to be virtually toothless.

> Sherman Anti-Trust Act

State laws against monopolies were initially more effective than the Sherman Act in controlling trusts. In 1892, Ohio's Supreme Court ordered the Standard Oil Trust dissolved because it was behaving like a monopoly. A furious Rockefeller then found another way of keeping control of his

trust Business arrangement that gives a person or corporation (the "trustee") the legal power to manage another person's money or another company without owning those entities outright.

numerous companies: creating a **holding company**, a huge corporation that controls other companies by "holding" most or all of their stock certificates. A holding company produces nothing itself; it simply owns a majority of the stock in other companies.

Rockefeller was convinced that ending competition among companies by creating a near monopoly was a good thing for the nation. Monopolies, he insisted, were the natural result of capitalism at work. "It is too late," he declared in 1899, "to argue about the advantages of [huge] industrial combinations. They are a necessity. The day of individualism is gone. Never to return." That year, Rockefeller brought his entire industrial empire under the direction of the Standard Oil Company of New Jersey, a gigantic holding company. By 1904, 318 holding companies in the United States controlled more than 5,300 factories.

Andrew Carnegie

Like Rockefeller, Andrew Carnegie, who created the largest steel company in the world during the late nineteenth century, rose from boyhood poverty to fabulous riches in his adult life. Born in Scotland, he migrated with his family in 1848 to Allegheny County, Pennsylvania. At age thirteen, he went to work in a textile mill. In 1853 he became personal secretary to Thomas Scott, then district superintendent of the Pennsylvania Railroad and later its president. When Scott moved up, Carnegie, bright and competitive, shrewd and charming, and driven by a fierce desire to succeed, took his place as superintendent. During the Civil War, when Scott became assistant secretary of war in charge of transportation, Carnegie went with him to Washington, D.C., and helped develop a military telegraph system.

Carnegie kept on moving—from telegraphy to railroading to bridge building and then to steelmaking and investments. In the early 1870s, he decided "to concentrate on the manufacture of iron and steel and be master in that." A tiny man (barely five feet tall) with giant ambitions, Carnegie wanted not simply to excel in the steel industry; he wanted to dominate it, just as John D. Rockefeller was doing with oil. Like Rockefeller, Carnegie accumulated vast wealth for the pure pleasure of the pursuit of it, and he often treated his workers ruthlessly.

Until the mid–nineteenth century, steel, which is stronger and more flexible than iron, could be made only from wrought iron—itself expensive since it had to be imported from Sweden—and only in small quantities. Bars of wrought iron were heated with charcoal over days to add carbon to carbon-free wrought iron. It took three tons of coke, a high-burning fuel derived from coal, to produce one ton of steel. As a result, steel was too costly to make in large quantities.

That changed in the 1850s, when England's Sir Henry Bessemer invented what became known as the Bessemer converter, a process by which high-quality steel could be produced more quickly by blasting air (oxygen) through the molten iron in the furnace. In the early 1870s, Carnegie

Andrew Carnegie Established the Carnegie Steel Company.

Strategy: Continuous innovation, e.g., the Bessemer converter

holding company Corporation established to own and manage other companies' stock rather than to produce goods and services itself.

decided to concentrate his operations on steel because Bessemer's process had made it so inexpensive to produce and the railroad industry needed massive amounts of it. As more steel was produced, its price dropped and its industrial uses soared. In 1860, the United States produced only 13,000 tons of steel. By 1880, production had reached 1.4 million tons annually. Between 1880 and 1900, Carnegie dominated the steel industry, expanding his own business by acquiring competitors or driving them out of business by cutting prices and taking their customers.

Carnegie was never a technical expert on steel. But he was a quick-witted and resilient promoter, salesman, and organizer—and a ferocious competitor. He insisted upon up-to-date machinery and equipment and, like Rockefeller, he expanded quickly and cheaply by purchasing struggling competitors. He also preached a philosophy of continuous innovation to reduce operating costs: "Cut the prices, scoop the market, run the mills full; watch the costs, and profits will take care of themselves."

Like Rockefeller, Carnegie sought to expand his industry by vertical integration, gaining control of every phase of the steel-making business, including the raw materials needed to make steel. He owned coal mines in West Virginia, bought huge deposits of iron ore in Michigan and Wisconsin, and transported the ore in his own ships across the Great Lakes and then by rail to his steel mills in Pittsburgh. The result was phenomenal. By 1900, the **Carnegie Steel Company** produced more steel each year than was produced in all of Great Britain. With 20,000 employees, it was the largest industrial company in the world. And Carnegie worked his people hard. His mills operated nonstop, with two twelve-hour shifts every day and night, the only exception being the Fourth of July.

Carnegie insisted that what he, Rockefeller, and other titans of industry were doing was simply the wave of the future. Rockefeller agreed, saying that the formation of huge trusts was simply "the working out of a law of nature and a law of God."

J. Pierpont Morgan

Unlike Rockefeller and Carnegie, J. Pierpont Morgan was born to wealth. His father was a partner in a large English bank. After attending school in Switzerland and university in Germany, the younger Morgan was sent in 1857 to work in New York City for a new enterprise, **J. Pierpont Morgan and Company**. The firm, under various names, invested European money into American businesses and grew into a financial power by helping competing corporations merge and by purchasing massive amounts of stock in American companies and selling them at a profit.

Morgan took over poorly run companies, appointed new executives, and supervised operations. Like Rockefeller and Carnegie, he believed in capitalism but hated the chaos of competition with other companies. In his view, high profits required order and stability, and stability required consolidating competitors into trusts that he would own and manipulate.

J. Pierpont Morgan Despite his privileged upbringing and financial success, he was self-conscious about his deformed nose, caused by chronic skin diseases.

Carnegie Steel Company Corporation under the leadership of Andrew Carnegie that came to dominate the American steel industry.

J. Pierpont Morgan and Company An investment bank under the leadership of J. Pierpont Morgan that bought or merged unrelated American companies, often using capital acquired from European investors.

Strategy: Mergers to eliminate competition, e.g., United States Steel Corporation

Morgan recognized early on the importance of railroads, and he acquired and reorganized one struggling rail line after another. By the 1890s, he controlled a sixth of the nation's railway system. But his crowning triumph was the consolidation of the steel industry. After a rapid series of mergers, he bought out Carnegie's huge steel and iron holdings in 1901. Morgan added scores of related companies to form the new United States Steel Corporation, the world's first billion-dollar corporation, employing 168,000 people. It was the climactic event in the efforts of the great financial capitalists to reduce industrial competition.

The "Gospel of Wealth"

However harsh the methods employed by the "captains of industry"—a term favored by their supporters—these men were convinced that they benefited the general public by accelerating the Industrial Revolution, creating jobs, and growing the economy. In his essay "The Gospel of Wealth" (1889), Carnegie argued that "not evil, but good, has come to the [Anglo-Saxon] race from the accumulation of wealth by those who have the ability and energy that produces it." But he also felt the need to justify his incredible wealth and denounced the "worship of money." Like other business barons, he and Rockefeller made colossal personal fortunes, but they gave much of their money away, mostly to support education and medicine.

Philanthropy

By 1900, Rockefeller had become the world's leading philanthropist. "I have always regarded it as a religious duty," he said late in life, "to get all I could honorably and to give all I could." He donated more than $500 million during his lifetime, including tens of millions to fund Baptist causes and $35 million to found the University of Chicago. His philanthropic influence continues today through the Rockefeller Foundation. As for Carnegie, after retiring from business at age sixty-five, he declared that the "man who dies rich dies disgraced" and devoted himself to dispensing his $400 million fortune for the public good. Calling himself a "distributor" of wealth (he disliked the term *philanthropy*), he gave huge sums to numerous universities, built 2,500 public libraries around the country, and helped fund churches, hospitals, parks, and halls for meetings and concerts, including New York City's Carnegie Hall.

CORE **OBJECTIVE**
3. Evaluate the role of government in the nation's economic development during this period.

The Alliance of Business and Politics

The building of big businesses by Rockefeller, Carnegie, Morgan, and others depended on more than just their skills as entrepreneurs. Such corporations also developed cozy relationships with local, state, and federal officials, a process of buying influence ("lobbying") that continues to this day. Big Business has legitimate political interests, but, because of its size and resources, it also sometimes exercises a corrupt influence on government. Never was

Celebrating Big Business
A lavish dinner celebrated the merger of the Carnegie and Morgan interests in 1901. The shape of the banquet table is meant to symbolize a rail.

this conflicting role more evident than during the decades after the Civil War. The *New York Times* noted that the largest corporations "control the Legislatures."

Federal and Republican Support for Business

During and after the Civil War, the Republican party and the U.S. government grew increasingly allied with Big Business. A key element of this alliance was tariff policy, one of the most important political issues throughout the nineteenth century. Since 1789, the federal government had imposed tariffs—taxes on imported goods—both to raise revenue and to benefit American manufacturers, by forcing their foreign competitors to raise the prices of their products. In 1861, as the Civil War was starting, the Republican-dominated Congress enacted the Morrill Tariff, which doubled the tax rates on hundreds of imported items as a means of raising money for the war and of rewarding the businesses that supported Abraham Lincoln and the Republican party.

After the war, President Ulysses S. Grant and later Republican presidents and Congresses continued the party's commitment to high tariffs despite complaints that the tariffs increased consumer prices by restricting foreign imports and thereby relieving American manufacturers of the need to keep their prices down to be competitive. Farmers in the South and Midwest resented federal tariffs because they had to sell their crops in an open world market but had to buy manufactured goods whose prices were artificially high because of tariffs. Farmers and other advocates of "free world trade," including most southern Democrats, generally wanted Congress to lower or eliminate tariffs.

High tariffs on imported goods

Introduction of national paper currency and land grants for homesteads and technical colleges

During the Civil War, the Republican-dominated Congress also passed other key pieces of legislation related to the economy. The Legal Tender Act of 1862 for the first time authorized the federal government to issue paper money to help pay for the war. The new national currency was called "greenbacks" because of its green color. Having a uniform paper currency rather than a hodgepodge of paper money issued by numerous state banks was essential to a modern national economy. To that end, the National Banking Act (1863) created new national banks authorized to issue greenbacks, which discouraged state banks from continuing to issue their own paper money.

At the same time, Congress also took steps to tie the new states and territories of the West into the national economy. The U.S. government owned vast amounts of western land, most of it acquired from the Louisiana Purchase of 1803 and the Oregon Treaty with Britain in 1846. In the Homestead Act of 1862, Congress provided free 160-acre homesteads to settlers on this land. By encouraging widespread western settlement, the Homestead Act promoted economic growth by creating new markets for goods and services and spurring railroad construction to connect frontier communities with major cities. The Morrill Land Grant Act of the same year transferred to each state 30,000 acres of federal land for each member of Congress the state had. The sale of those lands provided funds for states to create colleges of "agriculture and mechanic arts," such as Iowa State University and Kansas State University. The new "land grant" universities were created specifically to support economic growth by providing technical training needed by farmers as well as by rapidly growing industries such as mining, steel, petroleum, transportation, forestry, and construction (engineering). As already noted, Congressional authorization for construction

Homesteaders An African American family poses outside of their log and sod cabin in 1889.

of the first transcontinental railroad and generous federal subsidies, loans, and land grants for the project provided additional boosts to the nation's economic development.

Laissez-Faire Theory and Corrupt Practices

Equally important in propelling the postwar economic boom was what government did *not* do. It did not regulate the activities of big businesses in any significant way or impose high corporate taxes, nor did it provide any meaningful oversight of business operations or working conditions for wage earners. In general, both Congress and the presidents in this period accepted the economic doctrine of **laissez-faire**, a French phrase meaning "let them do as they will," which opposed government interference in the economy. Business leaders spent time—and money—ensuring that government officials did not regulate their businesses. For their part, members of Congress as well as state legislators were usually eager to help the new titans of industry and finance in exchange for campaign contributions and, often, direct bribes for looking the other way.

> Government's *laissez-faire* approach to business

A Changed Social Order

During the late nineteenth century, industrialization transformed not only the economy and the workplace; it also transformed social life. Class divisions became more visible. The growing gap between rich and poor was like "social dynamite," said the Reverend Josiah Strong in 1885. The Massachusetts reformer Lydia Maria Child noticed with alarm the growing class consciousness in America. The rich, she reported, "do not intermarry with the middle classes; the middle classes do not intermarry with the laboring class," nor did different classes "mix socially."

> CORE **OBJECTIVE**
> **4.** Analyze the ways in which the social class structure and the lives of women changed in the late nineteenth century.

The Ways of the Wealthy

The financiers and industrialists who dominated social, economic, and political life in post–Civil War America amassed such fabulous wealth and showed it off so publicly that the period is still called "the Gilded Age." The name came from a popular novel by Mark Twain and Charles Dudley Warner, *The Gilded Age: A Tale of Today* (1872), which mocked the crooked dealing and lavish wealth of political leaders and of the business elite, often called "robber barons" by their critics. During the Gilded Age, the share of the nation's wealth owned by the richest 10 percent of families tripled, to more than three-fourths in 1900. In 1861, there were only a few dozen millionaires in the United States. By 1900, there were over 4,000. Most of them were white Protestants who voted Republican, except for the small number of wealthy southern Democrats.

> "The Gilded Age"

> **laissez-faire** An economic doctrine holding that businesses and individuals should be able to pursue their economic interests without government interference.

Many of the *nouveaux riches* (French for "newly rich") indulged in what came to be called "conspicuous consumption," competing with each other to host the fanciest parties and live in the largest and most extravagantly furnished houses. In 1869, E. L. Godkin, the editor of the *Nation* magazine, wrote that New York City was being flooded by rich "barbarians"—and the following years provided considerable evidence for his accusation. One tycoon gave a lavish dinner honoring his dog and presented it with a $15,000 diamond necklace. At a party at New York's Delmonico's restaurant, the guests smoked cigarettes wrapped in $100 bills. Mrs. Bradley Martin received such a torrent of criticism after spending $368,000 on a banquet that she and her husband fled to England. When the rich were not attending such excessive parties, they were relaxing in monumental mansions overlooking the cliffs at Newport, Rhode Island, atop Nob Hill in San Francisco, along Chicago's Lake Shore Drive and New York City's Fifth Avenue, and down the "Main Line" in suburban Philadelphia.

"Who knows how to be rich in America?" Godkin asked. "Plenty of people know how to get money, but . . . to be rich properly is, indeed, a fine art. It requires culture, imagination, and character."

A Growing Middle Class

Rise of white middle-class professionals

It was left to the fast-growing middle class to display such "character" by practicing its traditional virtues of self-discipline and restraint, simplicity and frugality. The term "middle class" had first appeared in the 1830s and had become commonplace by the 1870s, as more and more Americans came to view themselves as members of a distinct social class between the ragged and the rich. The middle class, explained the Chicago writer George Ade in an 1895 essay, "The Advantage of Being 'Middle Class,'" meant those people who "work either with hand or brain, who are neither poverty-stricken nor offensively rich."

Accompanying the spread of huge corporations after the Civil War was a rising standard of living for many people. While the rich were getting much richer, a lot of other people were also becoming better off. Most middle-class Americans working outside the home were salaried employees of large businesses, people making up a new class of "white-collar" professionals: editors, engineers, accountants, supervisors, managers, marketers, and realtors. Others, with women a growing share of the total, were clerks, secretaries, salespeople, and government employees, including teachers and librarians. At the same time, the number of attorneys, physicians, professors, journalists, nurses, and social workers rose dramatically.

Middle-Class Women

Women admitted to colleges and professional jobs

The growing middle-class female presence in the workforce partly reflected the increasing number of women who were gaining access to higher education. Dozens of women's colleges were founded after the Civil War, and many

College women By the end of the century, women made up more than a third of all college students. Here, an astronomy class at New York's Vassar College is underway in 1880.

formerly all-male colleges began admitting women. By 1900, in fact, a third of college students were women. "After a struggle of many years," a New York woman boasted, "it is now pretty generally admitted that women possess the capacity to swallow intellectual food that was formerly considered the diet of men exclusively." To be sure, college women were often steered into home economics classes and "finishing" courses intended to perfect their house-keeping or social skills. Still, the doors of the professions—law, medicine, science, and the arts—were at least partially opened.

In this context, then, the "woman question" that created so much public discussion and controversy in the second half of the nineteenth century involved far more than the issue of voting rights; it also concerned the liberation of at least some women from the home and from longstanding limits on their social roles and even character traits. In addition to new jobs and professions, middle-class women took advantage of other, often new public venues for female interaction: charitable associations, women's clubs, literary societies, and church work. "If there is one thing that pervades and characterizes what is called the 'woman's movement,'" E. L. Youmans, a prominent science writer, remarked, "it is the spirit of revolt against the home, and the determination to escape from it into the outer spheres of activity."

The "woman question"

Neurasthenia

Yet such determination to escape the "cult of domesticity" often came at a high price. Many women who wanted to play a more active role in the public world contracted a peculiar affliction called neurasthenia, a draining psychological and physical disorder whose symptoms usually included insomnia, hysteria, headaches, depression, and a general state of fatigue. Although neurasthenia plagued both sexes, it most often affected college-educated middle-class women. Some prominent men tried to use this finding to force women back into the "cult of domesticity." George M. Beard, a neurologist who popularized the term *neurasthenia,* concluded—incorrectly—that women were "more nervous, immeasurably, than men," and that female neurasthenics tended to be women who had become "overly active" outside the home. This association of neurasthenia with independence led one doctor to insist that the malady provided the best "argument against higher education of women."

Many prominent women understandably objected to such self-serving male arguments. Charlotte Perkins Gilman, for instance, intended her short story "The Yellow Wallpaper" as a piece of "pure propaganda" to expose the horrors of the "rest cure" she was subjected to at age twenty-seven. A doctor had ordered her to "live as domestic a life as possible; have your child with you all the time; lie down an hour after each meal; have but two hours intellectual life a day; and *never touch pencil, brush, or pen as long as you live.*" This regimen, Gilman explained, took her "as near lunacy as one can, and come back."

Social worker Jane Addams also struggled with neurasthenia. After graduating in 1881 from Rockford College in Illinois, she found few opportunities to use her degree and lapsed into a state of depression during which she developed an intense "desire to live in a really *living* world." Middle-class women, she charged, were "so besotted with our [sentimental] novel reading that we have lost the power of seeing certain aspects of life with any sense of reality because we are continually looking for the possible romance." Addams's intense desire to engage "real life" eventually led her to found Hull House, the famous "settlement house" in Chicago. There, she and other social workers helped immigrants make the transition to American life, and young women like herself "could learn of life from life itself" rather than from books.

The examples of Addams and others helped convince many other middle-class women to enter the "real" world. By 1890, a magazine called *The Arena* could urge progressive-minded people to recognize the traditional view of women as homebodies for what it was: "hollow, false, and unreal." More and more people did just that. Upon returning from England to America in 1904, the illustrious writer Henry James reported that the predominance of "new" women and their struggle for autonomy had become "the sentence written largest in the American sky." Several years later he applauded the shifting emphasis "from the idea of woman's weakness to the idea of her strength."

Jane Addams She believed that social service requires a "scientific" observation of one's community in order to "see the needs" and provide "data for legislation" reform.

The Ladies' Home Journal

Middle-class women and domestic life

Not all middle-class women, however, wanted to venture out into the public world long dominated by men. Many of them identified more with the domestic life that was the focus of numerous mass-circulation magazines for women, the most popular of which was the *Ladies' Home Journal.* By 1892, it had 700,000 subscribers; in 1910 the number reached almost 2 million, the largest circulation of any magazine in the world.

Edward Bok, a Dutch immigrant raised in Brooklyn, New York, became editor of *Ladies' Home Journal* in 1889 at the age of twenty-six. For the next thirty years, he used the magazine as a means of providing a "great clearing house of information" to the large and rapidly growing urban middle class. The *Journal* included departments focused on sewing, cooking, religion, politics, and fiction. Bok was no feminist; "my idea," he stressed, "is to keep women in the home." There, he believed, they would maintain a high moral tone for society, for women were "better, purer, conscientious, and morally stronger than men." In particular, Bok saw the middle-class woman as the crucial "steadying influence" between the "unrest among the lower classes and [the] rottenness among the upper classes."

Bok's view of the ideal life for a woman was a far cry from the extravagant spending of the super-rich. It included "a healthful diet, simple, serviceable clothing, a clean, healthy dwelling-place, open-air exercise, and good reading." Bok preached contentment rather than conspicuous consumption, a message directed not just to his middle-class readers but also to the growing class of working poor. In a Christmas editorial, though, he recognized that "it is a hard thing for those who have little to believe that the greatest happiness of life is with them: that it is not with those who have abundance."

Mennen's Toilet Powder This advertisement appeared in the Independence Day edition of *Ladies' Home Journal* in 1908, suggesting that a homemaker's ability to protect her family from skin discomforts was her own declaration of independence.

The Working Class

The continuing demand for unskilled workers by railroads, factories, mills, mines, slaughterhouses, and sweatshops attracted new groups to the workforce: immigrants above all, but also growing numbers of women and children. In addition, millions of rural folk, especially young people, gave up farming and formed a migratory stream from the agricultural regions of the South and Midwest to the cities.

Although wage levels rose overall during the Gilded Age, there was a great disparity between the pay for skilled and unskilled workers. During the recessions and depressions that occurred about every six years on average, the unskilled workers were the first to be laid off or to have their wages slashed. In addition, working conditions were difficult and often dangerous for those at the bottom of the occupational scale. The average workweek during the late nineteenth century was fifty-nine hours, or nearly six ten-hour days. Most steelworkers put in a twelve-hour day. The death rate in the crowded working-class neighborhoods of major cities was much higher than in the countryside. American industry had the highest rate of workplace accidents and deaths in the world, and there were virtually no safety regulations or government inspections. Few machines had safety devices; few factories or mills had fire escapes. Respiratory diseases were common in mines and unventilated buildings. In the seven years between 1888 and 1894,

16,000 railroad workers were killed and 170,000 maimed in on-the-job accidents. The United States was the only industrial nation with no insurance program to cover medical expenses for on-the-job injuries.

Working Women

> Difficult, "unskilled" labor for working-class women

The Second Industrial Revolution transformed the nature of the workplace in ways that meant that mills, mines, factories, and large businesses needed far more unskilled workers than skilled ones. To fill these jobs, employers recruited women and children for many of the unskilled jobs because they were willing to work for lower wages than men. In addition to those laboring over typewriters, sewing machines, or textile looms, millions of women worked as maids, cooks, or other domestic laborers. In the manufacturing sector, women's wages averaged $7 a week, compared to $10 for unskilled men. A social worker sent to investigate working conditions for women reported that it was widely assumed in many factory settings that a married woman would accept lower wages because she "has a man to support her" (which was by no means always true). The number of women working for wages outside the home tripled between 1870 and 1900, when 5 million women (17 percent of all women) held full-time jobs. This development led one male editor to joke that he was being drowned "by the rising tide of femininity" in the workplace.

In a letter to the editor of the *Nation* in 1867, a "working woman" described the changing nature of gender roles in American life. Most middle-class women, she acknowledged, still lived in a "world of love, of a sweet and guarded domesticity, of drawing-rooms and boudoirs, of dainty coquetries, of quiet graces, where they flourish like fair flowers in a south window." But each year "thousands of women" were entering a different world "of mud, carts, ledgers, packing-boxes, counting-houses, paste, oils, leather, iron, boards, committees, big boots, and men who . . . meet women on a cool, business level of dollars and cents."

Child Labor

> Child labor

After the Civil War, a growing number of wage laborers were children who worked full time for meager wages under unhealthy conditions. Most young people had always worked in America; farms required everyone to pitch in. After the Civil War, however, millions of children took up work outside the home or off the farm, sorting coal, stitching clothes, shucking oysters, peeling shrimp, canning food, blowing glass, tending looms in textile mills, and operating other kinds of machinery. Parents desperate for income felt forced to put their children to work. By 1880, one of every six children under age fourteen in the nation was working full time; by 1900, the United States had almost 2 million child laborers. In Pennsylvania, West Virginia, and eastern Kentucky, soot-smeared boys worked in the coal mines. In New England and the South, thousands of children worked in dusty textile mills where, during the night shift, they had water thrown in their faces to keep them awake. In the southern mills, a fourth of the employees were below

Children in industry These four young boys performed the dangerous work of mine helpers in West Virginia around 1900.

the age of fifteen, and children as young as eight were laboring alongside adults twelve hours a day, six days a week. As a result, they received little or no education. Factories, mills, mines, and canneries were especially dangerous places for children, who suffered three times as many accidents as adult workers and higher rates of respiratory diseases as well. A child working in a southern textile mill was only half as likely to reach the age of twenty as a child who did not work in a mill.

The "Dreadful Chill of Change"

When the famous writer Henry James returned to the United States in the first decade of the twentieth century after a long stay in England, he was shocked by the "dreadful chill of change" transforming American social life. Urban-industrial development and western expansion had generated unparalleled prosperity, but the United States, he feared, had lost much of its social stability and cohesion. In 1885, one writer said that wage workers, by attempting to organize unions in order to improve their leverage with management, were unleashing "a seismic shock, a cyclonic violence" that threatened to tear society apart.

Organized Labor

During the Gilded Age, thousands of wage workers struggled to organize in an effort to force employers to recognize their needs and concerns. Yet the working poor who tried to form unions to improve their pay and working conditions faced huge obstacles. Most elected officials sided with business owners rather than workers. Another factor impeding the growth of labor

CORE **OBJECTIVE**
5. Assess the efforts of workers to organize unions in order to promote their interests during this era.

unions was that much of the workforce was made up of immigrants who spoke different languages and often distrusted those from other ethnic groups. Nonetheless, with or without unions, workers during the Gilded Age began to stage frequent strikes in response to wage cuts and other grievances. Strikes often led to violence. Perhaps at no time before or since have class tensions—both social and cultural—been as bitter as they were during the last quarter of the nineteenth century.

The Great Railroad Strike of 1877

> **The Great Railroad Strike of 1877**

After the financial panic of 1873, the major rail lines in the East cut the wages of their workers. In 1877, the companies announced another 10 percent wage cut, which led most of the railroad workers at Martinsburg, West Virginia, to walk off the job and block the tracks in order to shut down all traffic. The Great Railroad Strike of 1877 spread quickly to hundreds of other cities and towns, and the resulting violence left more than 100 people dead and millions of dollars in damaged property. In Pittsburgh, thousands of striking workers burned thirty-nine buildings and destroyed more than 1,000 rail cars and locomotives. State militiamen called in from Philadelphia dispersed a crowd at the cost of twenty-six lives, but looting and burning continued until federal troops finally ended it. A reporter described the scene as "the most horrible ever witnessed, except in the carnage of war. There were fifty miles of hot rails, ten tracks side by side, with as many miles of ties turned into glowing coals and tons on tons of iron car skeletons and wheels almost at white heat." Eventually the disgruntled workers, lacking organized bargaining power, had little choice but to drift back to work. The strike failed.

For many Americans, the Great Railroad Strike raised the possibility of what a Pittsburgh newspaper saw as "a great civil war in this country between labor and capital." Equally disturbing to those in positions of corporate and political power was the presence of many women among the protesters. A Baltimore journalist noted that the "singular part of the disturbances is the very active part taken by the women, who are the wives and mothers of the [railroad] firemen."

The Sandlot Incident

> **The Sandlot Incident**

In California the national railroad strike indirectly gave rise to a working-class political movement. In 1877, a meeting held in a sandy San Francisco lot to express sympathy for the railroad strikers ended with attacks on passing Chinese workers. In the aftermath of the so-called Sandlot Incident, white mobs attacked Chinatown, home to 25,000 Chinese, mostly males, who experienced the worst forms of discrimination and segregation. The depression of the 1870s had hit the West Coast especially hard, and the Chinese were handy scapegoats for frustrated white laborers who believed the Asians

"The Chinese Must Go" In this advertisement for the Missouri Steam Washer, the American-made machine drives the stereotype of the Chinese laundryman back to China, playing on the growing anti-Chinese sentiments in the 1880s.

had taken their jobs. Soon an Irish immigrant, Denis Kearney, had organized the Workingmen's Party of California, whose platform called for the United States to stop Chinese immigration. A gifted agitator who had only recently become a naturalized American, Kearney lectured the "sand-lotters" about the "foreign peril" and blasted the rich railroad barons for exploiting the poor. The Workingmen's movement peaked in 1879, when its candidates were elected as state legislators and as mayor of San Francisco. Although Kearney failed to build a lasting movement, his anti-Chinese theme became a national issue. In 1882, Congress voted to prohibit Chinese immigration for ten years.

The Workingmen's Party of California

Toward Permanent Unions

As the size and power of corporations increased during the second half of the nineteenth century, efforts to build a national labor union movement gained momentum. During the Civil War, because of the increased demand for skilled labor, so-called "craft unions" made up of workers skilled in a particular handicraft grew in strength and number. Yet there was no overall connection among such groups until 1866, when the National Labor Union (NLU) convened in Baltimore.

The NLU was more interested in advocating for new state and local laws to improve workplace conditions than in bargaining with employers about wages and hours. It advocated improvements such as the eight-hour workday, workers' cooperatives (in which workers, collectively, would create and own their own large-scale manufacturing and mining operations), "greenbackism" (the printing of paper money to inflate the currency and thereby relieve debtors), and equal voting rights for women and African Americans. Like most such organizations in the nineteenth century, however, the NLU did not allow women as members. As one official explained the attitude of male unionists, "Woman was created to be man's companion," not his competitor in the workplace who would cause his wages to fall.

After William Sylvis, the head of the NLU, died suddenly in 1869 at the age of forty-one, its support fell away, and by 1872 the union had disbanded. The NLU was not a total failure, however. It was influential in persuading Congress to enact an eight-hour workday for federal employees and to repeal the 1864 Contract Labor Act, which was passed during the Civil War to encourage the importation of laborers through an arrangement, similar to the indentured servitude of colonial times, that allowed employers to pay for the passage of foreign workers to America; in exchange, the workers were committed to work for a specified number of years. Employers had taken advantage of the Contract Labor Act to recruit foreign laborers willing to work for lower wages than their American counterparts.

The Knights of Labor

In 1869, another labor group of national standing had emerged: the Noble Order of the **Knights of Labor**. The union grew slowly at first, but even as other unions collapsed during the depression of the 1870s, it spread more rapidly. The Knights of Labor endorsed the reforms advanced by previous workingmen's groups, including the creation of a bureau of labor statistics and mechanics' lien laws (to ensure payment of wages), the elimination of convict-labor competition, the establishment of the eight-hour work day and worker cooperatives, and the use of paper currency. One plank in the platform, far ahead of the times, called for equal pay for equal work by men and women. Throughout its existence, the Knights of Labor condemned violence, class warfare, and socialism; they preferred boycotts to strikes as a

Knights of Labor A national labor organization with a broad reform platform; reached peak membership in the 1880s.

Knights of Labor This national union was the most egalitarian union during the Gilded Age.

way to pressure employers. The Knights allowed as members all who had ever worked for wages, except lawyers, doctors, bankers, and those who sold liquor. Theoretically, it was one big union of all workers, skilled and unskilled, men and women, immigrants and African Americans.

In 1879, Terence V. Powderly, the thirty-year-old mayor of Scranton, Pennsylvania, became head of the Knights of Labor. Born of Irish immigrant parents, Powderly had started working for a railroad at age sixteen. Frail, sensitive to criticism, and indecisive at critical moments, he was in many ways unsuited to his new job. He was temperamentally opposed to strikes, and when they did occur, he did not always support the local groups involved. Yet the Knights owed their greatest growth to strikes that occurred under his leadership. In the early 1880s the Knights increased their membership from about 100,000 to more than 700,000.

> Rise of the Knights of Labor and Terence V. Powderly

Anarchism

One of the many challenges facing the labor union movement was growing hostility from middle-class Americans who came to view unionized workers, especially those involved in clashes with police, as "radicals" or "anarchists." Anarchists believed that government—any government—was a device used by powerful capitalists to oppress and exploit the working poor. They dreamed of the eventual disappearance of government altogether, and some were willing to use bombs and bullets to achieve their revolutionary goal. Many European anarchists immigrated to the United States during the last quarter of the nineteenth century. Although most anarchists disavowed violence, the terrorists among them ensured that the label "anarchist" provoked frightening images in the minds of many Americans.

Labor-related violence increased during the 1880s as the gap between the rich and working poor widened. Between 1880 and 1900, 6.6 million hourly workers participated in more than 23,000 strikes nationwide. Chicago, the fastest-growing city in the nation, was a hotbed of labor unrest and a magnet for immigrants, especially German and Irish laborers, some of whom were socialists or anarchists who endorsed violence as a means of transforming the capitalist system. The Chicago labor movement's foremost demand was for an eight-hour workday, and what came to be called the **Haymarket Riot** grew indirectly out of prolonged agitation for this goal.

The Haymarket Riot

In May 1886, some 40,000 Chicago workers went on strike in support of an eight-hour workday. On May 3, violent clashes between strikers and "scabs" (nonunion workers who defied the strike) erupted outside the McCormick Harvesting Machine plant, where farm equipment was made. The police arrived, shots rang out, and two strikers were killed. The killings infuriated the

Haymarket Riot (1886) Violent uprising in Haymarket Square, Chicago, where police clashed with labor demonstrators in the aftermath of a bombing.

leaders of the tiny anarchist movement in Chicago, which included many women. They printed leaflets demanding "Revenge!" and "Workingmen, to Arms!" Calls went out for a mass protest the following night at Haymarket Square.

On the evening of May 4, after listening to long speeches complaining about low wages and long working hours, the crowd in Haymarket Square was beginning to break up when policemen arrived and ordered the people to disperse. At that point, someone threw a bomb toward the police. The police then fired into the crowd, killing and wounding people, including other policemen. Throughout the night, police arrested scores of people. The next day, all labor meetings were banned in the city, and newspapers across the nation printed sensational headlines about anarchists terrorizing Chicago. One New York paper demanded stern punishment for "the few long-haired, wild-eyed, bad-smelling, atheistic, reckless foreign wretches" who promoted such unrest.

At trials during the summer of 1886, seven anarchist leaders, all but one of them German speakers, were sentenced to death despite the lack of any evidence linking them to the bomb thrower, whose identity was never established. In a statement to the court after being sentenced to be hanged, Louis Lingg declared that he was innocent of the bombing but was proud to be an anarchist who was "in favor of using force" to attack the abuses of the capitalist system. Lawyers for the anarchists appealed the convictions to the Illinois Supreme Court. Meanwhile, petitions from around the world arrived at the Illinois governor's office appealing for clemency. One of the petitioners was Samuel Gompers, the founding president of the American Federation of Labor (AFL), which would soon replace the faltering Knights of Labor as the nation's leading union. "I abhor anarchy," Gompers stressed, "but I also abhor injustice when meted out even to the most despicable being on earth."

On November 10, 1887, Louis Lingg committed suicide in his cell. That same day, the governor commuted the sentences of two of the convicted conspirators to life imprisonment. The next day the four remaining condemned men were hanged. Two hundred thousand people lined the streets of Chicago as their caskets were taken for burial. To labor militants around the world, the executed anarchists were working-class martyrs; to the police and the economic elite in Chicago, they were demonic assassins. In his novel *The Titan*, Theodore Dreiser wrote that the Haymarket Riot "had brought to the fore, once and for all, as by a flash of lightning, the whole problem of mass against class."

Samuel Gompers The head of the American Federation of Labor strikes an assertive pose.

The Decline of the Knights of Labor

After the Haymarket Riot, tensions between workers and management reached a fever pitch. In 1886 alone there were 1,400 strikes across the country involving 700,000 workers. But the violence in Chicago had triggered widespread public hostility to the Knights of Labor and labor groups in general. Despite his best efforts, Terence Powderly could never separate in the public mind the Knights from the anarchists, since one of those convicted of conspiracy in the bombing was a member of the union. Powderly clung to leadership until 1893, but after that the union evaporated. Besides fear of its supposed radicalism and the failure of a railroad strike in 1886, membership in the Knights also declined because its leaders spent more time promoting national reforms than focusing on better wages and working conditions.

The Knights nevertheless attained some lasting achievements, among them an 1880 federal law providing for the arbitration of labor disputes and the creation of the federal Bureau of Labor Statistics in 1884 as well as several state labor bureaus. Another of their successes was the Foran Act of 1885, which, though poorly enforced, penalized employers who imported immigrant workers so that they could pay lower wages. And by their example, the Knights also spread the idea of unionism and initiated a new type of union organization: the industrial union, which included all skilled and unskilled workers within a particular industry, such as railroad workers or miners.

Gompers and the AFL

The craft unions, representing skilled workers, generally opposed efforts to unite with industrial unionism. Leaders of the craft unions feared that joining with unskilled laborers would mean a loss of their craft's identity and a loss of skilled workers' greater bargaining power. Thus, in 1886, delegates from twenty-five craft unions meeting in Columbus, Ohio, organized the **American Federation of Labor** (AFL). Its structure differed from that of the Knights of Labor in that it was a federation of many separate national unions, each of which was largely free to act on its own in dealing with business owners.

Samuel Gompers served as president of the AFL from its founding until his death, in 1924, with only one year's interruption. Born in England of Dutch Jewish ancestry, Gompers came to the United States as a teenager, joined the Cigarmakers' Union in 1864, and became president of his New York City local union in 1877. Unlike Terence Powderly and the Knights of Labor, Gompers focused on concrete economic gains—higher wages, shorter hours, better working conditions—and avoided utopian ideas or politics.

The AFL at first grew slowly, but by 1890 it had surpassed the Knights of Labor in membership. By the turn of the century, it claimed 500,000 members in affiliated unions; in 1914, on the eve of World War I, it had 2 million; and in 1920 it reached a peak of 4 million. But even then the AFL embraced less than 15 percent of the nation's nonagricultural workers. In fact, all unions, including the railroad brotherhoods unaffiliated with the AFL,

> Formation of the American Federation of Labor (AFL)

American Federation of Labor Founded in 1886 as a national federation of trade unions made up of skilled workers.

accounted for little more than 18 percent of those workers. Organized labor's strongholds were in transportation and the building trades. Most of the larger manufacturing industries—including steel, textiles, tobacco, and meatpacking—remained almost untouched. Gompers never opposed industrial unions, and several became important affiliates of the AFL: the United Mine Workers, the International Ladies Garment Workers, and the Amalgamated Clothing Workers. But the AFL had its greatest success in organizing skilled workers.

Two incidents in the 1890s stalled the emerging industrial-union movement: the **Homestead Steel Strike** of 1892 and the **Pullman Strike** of 1894. These violent labor conflicts represented the climactic economic events of the Gilded Age. Each pitted workers in a bitter contest against one of the nation's largest and most influential corporations. The two strikes not only represented a test of strength for the organized labor movement but also served to reshape the political landscape.

The Homestead Steel Strike

The Homestead Steel Strike

The Amalgamated Association of Iron and Steel Workers, founded in 1876, was the largest craft union. At the massive iron and steel mill at Homestead, Pennsylvania, near Pittsburgh, the union had enjoyed friendly relations with Andrew Carnegie's company until the stern Henry Clay Frick became company chairman and chief executive in 1889. A showdown was delayed until 1892, however, when the union contract came up for renewal. Carnegie, who had previously expressed sympathy for unions, went on a lengthy hunting trip in his native Scotland, leaving the rigid Frick to handle the difficult negotiations. Yet Carnegie knew what was in the works: a cost-cutting reduction in the number of highly paid skilled workers through the use of labor-saving machinery. It was a deliberate attempt to smash the union. "Am with you to the end," he wrote to Frick after leaving for Scotland.

As negotiations dragged on, the company announced on June 25 that it would stop negotiating with the union on June 29 unless an agreement was reached. A strike—or, more properly, a lockout of unionists, in which management closed down the mill to try to force the union to make concessions—began on that date. Frick told journalists that he was determined to have "absolute control of our plant and business." To that end, he built a twelve-foot-high fence around the plant and equipped it with watchtowers, searchlights, barbed wire, and high-pressure water cannons. He also hired a private army of 316 men from the Pinkerton Detective Agency to protect what was soon dubbed Fort Frick. Before dawn on July 6, 1892, the "Pinkertons" floated up the Monongahela River on two barges pulled by a tugboat.

Thousands of unionists and supporters, many of them armed, were waiting on shore. A fourteen-hour battle broke out in which seven workers and three Pinkertons were killed and dozens wounded. Hundreds of women on

Homestead Steel Strike (1892) Labor conflict at the Homestead steel mill near Pittsburgh, Pennsylvania, culminating in a battle between strikers and private security agents hired by the factory's management.

Pullman Strike (1894) A national strike by the American Railway Union, whose members shut down major railways in sympathy with striking workers in Pullman, Illinois; ended with intervention of federal troops.

shore shouted, "Kill the Pinkertons!" In the end, the Pinkertons surrendered, having agreed to be tried for murder, and were marched away to taunts from crowds lining the streets. A week later, the Pennsylvania governor dispatched 4,000 state militiamen to Homestead, where they surrounded the steel mill and dispersed the picketing workers. Frick then hired strikebreakers to operate the mill. He refused to resume negotiations: "I will never recognize the union, never, never!"

The strike dragged on until November, but by then the union was dead and its leaders had been charged with murder and treason. The union cause was not helped when Alexander Berkman, a Lithuanian anarchist, tried to assassinate Frick on July 23, shooting him twice in the neck and stabbing him three times. Despite his wounds, Frick fought back fiercely and, with the help of staff members, subdued the would-be assassin. Much of the local sympathy for the strikers evaporated. As a union leader explained, Berkman's bullets "went straight through the heart of the Homestead strike." Penniless and demoralized, the defeated workers ended their walkout on November 20 and accepted the company's harsh wage cuts. Only a fifth of the strikers were hired back; the rest were "blacklisted" to prevent other steel mills from hiring them. Carnegie and Frick, with the support of local, state, and national government officials, had eliminated the union.

The Pullman Strike

The Pullman Strike of 1894 was an even more notable confrontation between workers and management, as it paralyzed the economies of the twenty-seven states and territories making up the western half of the nation. It involved a dispute at Pullman, Illinois, a "model" industrial suburb of Chicago owned by the Pullman Palace Car Company, which made passenger train cars (called "Pullmans" or "sleeping cars"). Employees who built rail cars were required to live in the town's 1,400 cottages, which had been built to high standards, with gas heat and indoor plumbing. With 12,000 residents, the town of Pullman also boasted a library, a theater, a school, a church (without a congregation), parks and playgrounds, and a glass-roofed shopping mall owned by the company. There were no saloons, however, nor any social clubs, newspapers, or private property not owned by the company. No political activities, including election of local officials, were allowed.

As a "company town," Pullman was of much higher quality than the many villages in the South owned by textile mills, and the death rate there was less than half of that in neighboring communities. Yet over time, many workers complained that they did not like living under the thumb of the company's owner, George Pullman.

During the terrible depression of 1893, George Pullman laid off 3,000 of his 5,800 employees and cut wages 25 to 40 percent for the rest, but did not lower rents for housing or the price of food in the company store. In the spring of 1894, desperate workers joined the American Railway Union,

The Pullman Strike

The Growth of Big Business and Its Impact on Late-19th-Century America

The growth of Big Business in the late nineteenth century dramatically reshaped the lives of millions of Americans. Large corporations led the way in making the United States into the world's leading nation in manufacturing and the majority of the American labor force into factory workers and miners rather than farmers. The growth of Big Business made manufactured products and industrial resources like electricity widely available to Americans and enriched the nation as a whole. But the concentration of wealth in the hands of a relatively few corporate leaders and wealthy investors provoked profound discontent among millions of Americans frustrated by low wages and harsh working conditions.

Entrepreneurs of Big Business

- John D. Rockefeller, Standard Oil
- Andrew Carnegie, Carnegie Steel
- J. Pierpont Morgan, J. Pierpont Morgan and Company

Goals of Big Business

- Bring order and stability to various sectors of the economy
- Increase profits and destroy competitors

Strategies Pursued by Big Business

. . . to become a monopoly:

- **Horizontal integration:** A dominant corporation within an industry buys or forces out its competition to become a monopoly.

- **Vertical integration:** A corporation owns all the different businesses needed to produce and sell its products to become a monopoly.

. . . to avoid government regulation:

- **Limited liability corporations:** Ownership and management are separated, and stockholders share in the corporation's profits but are not liable for its debts.

- **Trusts:** Granted authority to manage people's investments or companies, for an annual dividend.

- **Holding companies:** Producing nothing but controlling a majority of stock in other companies.

. . . to maintain a monopoly:

- Continuous innovation, cost reduction, investment in technology, elimination of waste.

- At times, exploitation of workers, illegal activity, bribery and/or control of public officials through campaign funding and other contributions.

Consequences of Big Business

. . . for better:

- Created jobs, reduced unemployment
- Increase in supply of affordable products improved quality of life for many

. . . for worse:

- Increased economic inequality, with 10% of Americans controlling 75% of the nation's wealth by 1900
- American economy dominated by Big Business, with 318 holding companies controlling more than 5,300 factories by 1904
- Increased corruption in all major political parties and levels of government

Reactions to Big Business

General public
- Appreciated the technological innovations, increased access to new goods and services, employment opportunities, and other benefits
- Disturbed many who believed competition was great virtue of capitalism

Federal and state governments and courts
- Attempted to outlaw corrupt Big Business practices, though corporations found ways around legislation, which was often vague and hard to enforce
- Officials usually supported rights of corporations over its workers, even sending in federal troops to suppress strikes, e.g., the Homestead Strike of 1892 and the Pullman Strike of 1894

Labor unions and workers
- Combated exploitation, poor working conditions, lowered wages, and layoffs by negotiating with corporation owners, lobbying for pro-worker legislation, and striking
- Lost public support when violence resulted from their efforts
- Involvement of socialists and anarchists, in addition to the violence, led many to see labor activism as radical and frightening

QUESTIONS FOR ANALYSIS

1. What were the overall goals of Big Business?
2. What strategies were used to pursue these goals?
3. What were the consequences of the rise of Big Business?
4. How did the government and the public react to the growth of Big Business?

Eugene V. Debs Founder of the American Railway Union, and later the presidential candidate for the Socialist Party of America.

founded the previous year by Eugene V. Debs. The charismatic Debs was a child of working-class immigrants who had quit school at age fourteen to work for an Indiana railroad. By the early 1890s, he had become a tireless spokesman for labor radicalism, and he strove to organize all railway workers—skilled or unskilled—into the American Railway Union, which soon became a powerful labor organization. He quickly turned his attention to the Pullman controversy, urging the workers to obey the laws and avoid violence. After George Pullman fired three members of a workers' grievance committee, the workers went on strike on May 11, 1894.

In June, after Pullman refused Debs's plea for a negotiated settlement, the Railway Union workers stopped handling trains containing Pullman rail cars. By the end of July, they had shut down most of the railroads in the Midwest, cutting off all traffic through Chicago. To keep the trains running, railroad executives hired strikebreakers, and the U.S. attorney general, a former lawyer for railroad companies, swore in 3,400 special deputies to protect them. Angry workers assaulted strikebreakers and destroyed property.

Finally, on July 3, President Grover Cleveland sent 2,000 federal troops into the Chicago area, claiming it was his duty to ensure delivery of the mail. Meanwhile, the attorney general convinced a federal judge to sign an "injunction," an official court decree, prohibiting the labor union from interfering with the delivery of mail and interstate commerce. On July 13, the union called off the strike. A few days later, a judge cited Debs for violating the injunction, and he served six months in jail. The Supreme Court upheld the decree in the case of *In re Debs* (1895) on broad grounds of national sovereignty: "The strong arm of the national government may be put forth to

The Pullman Strike Federal troops guarding the railroads, 1894.

brush away all obstructions to the freedom of interstate commerce or the transportation of the mails." Debs emerged from jail as a socialist who would later run for president. In 1897, George Pullman died of a heart attack, and the following year, the city of Chicago annexed the town of Pullman. A reporter for the *Nation* noted that despite the town's attractive features, what the workers wanted most was the chance to own a house of their own. "Mr. Pullman," he explained, "overlooked this peculiar American characteristic."

Economic Success and Excess

For all of the stress and strain caused by the industrialization of the American economy, the nation's productivity soared in the late nineteenth century. By 1900, the United States was producing a third of the world's goods. The corporate empires created by a generation of outsized business leaders created enormous fortunes for a few and real improvements in the quality of life of the many. The majority of American workers for the first time now labored in factories and mines rather than on farms. "One can hardly believe," observed the philosopher John Dewey, "there has been a revolution in history so rapid, so extensive, so complete." The urban-industrial revolution and gigantic new corporations had transformed the size, scope, and power of the American economy, for good and for ill. As the twentieth century dawned, an unregulated capitalist economy had gotten recklessly out of balance—and only government intervention could restore economic fairness and social stability.

■ **The Causes of Industrial Growth** During the late nineteenth century, agricultural and industrial production increased sharply. The national railroad network increased to nearly 200,000 miles, the most of any nation in the world. Farmers and industrialists expanded their production for both national and international markets. The *Second Industrial Revolution* saw the expanded use of electrical power, the application of scientific research to industrial processes, and other commercial innovations that brought new products to market and improved methods for producing and distributing them.

■ **The Rise of Big Business** Many businesses transformed themselves into limited-liability corporations and grew to enormous size and power in this period, often ignoring ethics and the law in doing so. Leading entrepreneurs like John D. Rockefeller, Andrew Carnegie, and J. Pierpont Morgan were extraordinarily skilled at organizing and gaining control of particular industries. Companies such as Rockefeller's *Standard Oil* and *Carnegie Steel* practiced both vertical integration, through which they controlled all the various enterprises needed to produce and distribute their products, and horizontal integration, in which they absorbed or eliminated their competitors. To consolidate their holdings and get around laws prohibiting *monopolies,* they created *trusts* and eventually *holding companies* in an effort to bring "order and stability" to the marketplace.

■ **The Alliance of Business and Politics** The federal government encouraged economic growth after the Civil War by imposing high tariffs on imported products, granting public land to railroad companies and settlers in the West, establishing a stable currency, and encouraging the creation of "land grant" universities to spur technical innovation and research. Equally important, local, state, and federal governments made little effort to regulate the activities of businesses. This *laissez-faire* policy allowed entrepreneurs to experiment with new methods of organization, but also created the conditions for rampant corruption and abuses.

■ **A Changed Social Order** The huge fortunes of the "Gilded Age" flowed to a few prominent families, and social class tensions worsened as productivity increased. While the business and financial elite showed off their new wealth with extravagant homes and parties, the urban and industrial workforce was largely composed of unskilled workers, including recent immigrants, former farmers, and growing numbers of women and children. Business owners and managers showed little concern for workplace safety, and accidents and work-related diseases were common. Industrialization and the rise of Big Business also increased the number of people considering themselves part of the middle class. Middle-class women increasingly went to college, took business and professional jobs, and participated in other public activities despite male resistance.

■ **Organized Labor** It was difficult for unskilled workers to organize effectively into unions, in part because of racial and ethnic tensions among laborers, language barriers, and the efforts of owners and supervisors to undermine unionizing efforts. Business owners often hired "strikebreakers," usually immigrant workers who were willing to take jobs at the prevailing wage because they were so desperate for a job. Business owners often relied on the support of political leaders, who would mobilize state and local militias and federal troops against strikers. Nevertheless, several unions did organize and advocate for workers' rights at a national level, including the National Labor Union and the *Knights of Labor.* After the violence associated with the *Haymarket*

Riot and the *Homestead Steel Strike* and *Pullman Strike*, many Americans grew fearful of unions and viewed them as politically radical. Craft unions made up solely of skilled workers became more successful at organizing, such as the *American Federation of Labor*.

KEY TERMS

laissez-faire p. 567
Second Industrial Revolution
   p. 552
monopoly p. 560
Standard Oil Company p. 560

trust p. 561
holding company p. 562
Carnegie Steel Company p. 563
J. Pierpont Morgan and
   Company p. 563

Knights of Labor p. 576
Haymarket Riot (1886) p. 577
American Federation of Labor p. 579
Homestead Steel Strike (1892) p. 580
Pullman Strike (1894) p. 580

CHRONOLOGY

1859	First oil well is struck in Titusville, Pennsylvania
1861	Congress creates the Morrill Tariff
1869	First transcontinental railroad is completed
1876	Alexander Graham Bell patents his telephone
1876	Thomas A. Edison invents incandescent lightbulb
1880s	Widespread use of electrical power begins
1882	John D. Rockefeller organizes the Standard Oil Trust
1886	Haymarket Riot
1886	American Federation of Labor is organized
1892	Homestead Steel Strike
1894	Pullman Strike
1901	J. Pierpont Morgan creates the U.S. Steel Corporation

INQUIZITIVE

Go to InQuizitive to see what you've learned—and learn what you've missed—with personalized feedback along the way.

MINING ON THE COMSTOCK (1877) The Comstock Lode was one of the largest gold and silver mines to be discovered in America, yielding over $300 million over two decades. This illustration shows a cutaway of the Comstock Lode, revealing the complex network of shafts and supports, as well as the various tasks of miners within its tunnels.

The South and the West Transformed

1865–1900

After the Civil War, the devastated South and the untamed West provided two frontiers of enticing opportunities for economic enterprise. The war-devastated South had to be rebuilt; the sparsely settled territories and states west of the Mississippi River were ripe for the development of farms, businesses, railroads, and towns. Banks and financiers in America and Europe took advantage of these conditions to invest heavily in both regions. While both the South and West offered huge forests, valuable minerals, and plentiful opportunities for industrial projects, this was particularly true of the western region between the Mississippi River and California.

Throughout the first half of the nineteenth century, the Great Plains had been viewed as a barren landscape suitable only for Indians and animals. Half the state of Texas, for instance, was still not settled at the end of the Civil War. After 1865, however, the federal government encouraged western settlement and economic development. The construction of transcontinental railroads, the military conquest of the Indians, and the policy of distributing government-owned lands at low cost to settlers, ranchers, miners, and railroads combined to lure millions of pioneers and enterprising capitalists westward. Charles Goodnight, a Texas cattle rancher, recalled that "we were adventurers in a great land . . . fresh and full of the zest of darers." By 1900, a New West and a New South

CORE
OBJECTIVES INQUIZITIVE

1. Analyze the ways in which a "New South" emerged economically in the late nineteenth century.

2. Describe the crop-lien system that emerged in the South and explain how it shaped the region after the Civil War.

3. Explain how and why white southerners took away African Americans' right to vote and adopted "Jim Crow" segregation laws at the end of the nineteenth century.

4. Identify the various groups of migrants to the West after the Civil War and the reasons they went there.

5. Describe the experiences of miners, farmers, ranchers, and women in the West in the late nineteenth century.

6. Evaluate the impact on Native Americans of the federal government's policies in the West after the Civil War.

7. Describe how the South and West had changed by 1900.

had emerged, and eleven new states had been created out of the western territories.

CORE **OBJECTIVE**

1. Analyze the ways in which a "New South" emerged economically in the late nineteenth century.

The Myth of the New South

After the Civil War, the South fought an inner civil war over the future of the region. Many white southerners embraced the "Lost Cause," a romanticized interpretation of the war that pictured the Confederates as noble, chivalrous defenders of the distinctive southern way of life against a tyrannical federal government headed by Abraham Lincoln. Southerners devastated by defeat were haunted by a lingering nostalgia for the mythic Old South of white-columned plantations, white supremacy, and cotton-generated wealth produced by armies of enslaved blacks. As one southerner said, his native region remained "old-fashioned, medieval, provincial, worshipping the dead."

At the same time, no region has inspired a more tenacious *pride of place*, a localism anchored in family life enlivened by visions of a mythic past. The Mississippi writer Eudora Welty once explained that in the South, "feelings are bound up with place." *Home* and *history* are two of the most revered words in southern life. Nineteenth-century southerners did not simply live in the present and dream of the future. They were forever glancing backward in the process of moving forward. Their romanticized common history provided much of the script for the ongoing drama of their lives. As William Faulkner recognized in his novel *Intruder in the Dust*, "The past isn't dead. It's not even past."

A "New South"

Other prominent southerners, however, looked more to the future, a future much different than the Old South. They called for a New South where the region's predominantly agricultural economy would be diversified by an expanded industrial sector.

The tireless champion of the New South ideal during the 1880s was Henry Woodfin Grady (1850–1889), the powerful managing editor of the *Atlanta Constitution*. In 1886, he told a New York City audience that there had been an Old South "of slavery and secession—that South is dead. There is now a New South of union and freedom—that South, thank God, is living, breathing, and growing every hour." The Old South, he added, "rested everything on slavery and agriculture, unconscious that these could neither give nor maintain healthy growth."

Grady saw the New South becoming "a perfect democracy" of small farms growing varied crops. This healthy agricultural sector would be complemented by new mills, factories, and cities. The postwar South, Grady claimed, held the promise of a real democracy, one no longer run by the planter aristocracy and no longer dependent upon slave labor. He imagined a New South with "a hundred farms for every plantation, fifty homes for every palace—and a diversified industry that meets the complex needs of this complex age."

Many southerners shared Henry Grady's vision of a New South dotted with new industries. The Confederacy, they concluded, had lost the war because it had relied too much upon King Cotton—and slavery. In the future, the New South must follow the North's example ("out-Yankee the Yankees") and develop a strong industrial sector to go along with its agricultural foundation. Promoters of a New South also stressed that more-efficient farming, using the latest machinery and technical expertise, was essential in the still-backward South; that more-widespread vocational training was urgently needed; and that racial harmony built upon the acceptance by blacks of white supremacy would provide a stable social environment for economic growth.

Developing a Textile Industry

The chief accomplishment of the New South was a dramatic expansion of the region's textile industry, which produced thread and cotton-based bedding and clothing. From 1880 to 1900, the number of cotton mills in the South grew from 161 to 400, the number of mill workers (most of whom were white, with women and children outnumbering men) increased fivefold, and the demand for cotton products went up eightfold. Tens of thousands of dirt-poor farm folk—many of them children—rushed to take jobs in the new textile mills that blossomed after the war. Seventy percent of southern textile mill workers were under the age of twenty-one, and many were under the age of fourteen. A dawn-to-dusk job in a mill paying fifty cents a day "was much more interesting than one-horse farming," noted one worker, "because you can meet your bills." Those bills were usually paid to the mill owner, who provided ramshackle housing and basic supplies to the workers in his company village—for a fee. By 1900, the South had surpassed New England as the largest producer of cotton fabric in the nation.

| Cotton fabrics |

The Tobacco Industry

Tobacco growing and cigarette production also increased significantly in the New South. Essential to the rise of the tobacco industry was the Duke family of Durham, North Carolina. At the end of the Civil War, the story goes, Washington Duke took a barnload of tobacco, dried it, and, with the help of his two sons, hitched two mules to his wagon, and set out across the state, selling tobacco in small pouches as he went. By 1872 the Dukes had a factory producing 125,000 pounds of tobacco annually, and Washington Duke prepared to settle down and enjoy success.

| Tobacco and cigarettes |

His son James Buchanan "Buck" Duke wanted even greater success, however. He poured large sums into advertising schemes and perfected the mechanized mass production of cigarettes. Duke also undersold competitors in their own markets and cornered the supply of ingredients needed to make cigarettes. Eventually his primary competitors agreed to join forces

Southern smokes Allen & Ginter was a major tobacco manufacturer that joined the American Tobacco Company. This advertisement, featuring black laborers in the tobacco fields, plays to the southern nostalgia for the "Old Dominion" before the Civil War.

American Tobacco Company Business founded in 1890 by North Carolina's James Buchanan Duke, who combined the major tobacco manufacturers of the time, controlling 90 percent of the country's booming cigarette production.

Redeemers Post–Civil War Democratic leaders who supposedly saved the South from Yankee domination and preserved the primarily rural economy.

with him, and in 1890 Duke brought most of them into the **American Tobacco Company**, which controlled nine tenths of the nation's cigarette production. A ferociously hard worker, Duke was well on his way to becoming one of the wealthiest and most powerful men in the nation. "I needed no vacation or time off," Duke explained. "There ain't a thrill in the world to compare with building a business and watching it grow before your eyes."

Other New South Industries

Effective use of other abundant natural resources helped revitalize the South along the Appalachian Mountain chain from West Virginia to Alabama. Coal production in the South (including West Virginia) grew from 5 million tons in 1875 to 49 million tons by 1900. At the southern end of the mountains, Birmingham, Alabama, sprang up during the 1870s in the shadow of Red Mountain, so named for its iron ore, and boosters soon tagged the steelmaking city the "Pittsburgh of the South."

Urban and industrial expansion as well as rapid population growth created a need for housing, and after 1870 lumbering became a thriving industry in the South, as housing required wood. Northern investors bought up vast pine forests throughout the region and set about clear-cutting them. By 1900, lumber had surpassed textiles in annual economic value.

The Redeemers

Henry Grady's vision of a New South celebrated the heroic **Redeemers**, the conservative, pro-business politicians in the Democratic Party who had supposedly rescued the white South from the hell of federally imposed Reconstruction and embraced a new vision of industrial progress grounded in white supremacy. The supporters of these white Democratic leaders referred to them as Redeemers because they supposedly saved the South from Yankee domination and "black rule" during the Reconstruction Era.

The Redeemers included a rising class of lawyers, merchants, railroad executives, mill owners, and entrepreneurs who wanted a more diversified economy based upon industrial development and railroad expansion along with cuts in state taxes and expenditures, including those for the public-school systems started after the war. "Schools are not a necessity," claimed a Virginia governor. Louisiana cut back so much on school funding that the percentage of residents unable to read and write actually increased between 1880 and 1900. Black children in particular suffered from such cutbacks. But the Redeemers did not want educated African Americans. "What I want here is Negroes who can make cotton," explained a white planter, "and they don't need education to help them make cotton."

The Failings of the New South

CORE **OBJECTIVE**

2. Describe the crop-lien system that emerged in the South and explain how it shaped the region after the Civil War.

Despite the development of some mills and factories, by the end of the nineteenth century the South had fallen far short of the diversified economy that Henry Grady and others had envisioned in the mid-1880s. The South in 1900 remained the least industrial, least urban, least educated, and least prosperous region in the nation. Per capita income in the South in 1900 was only 60 percent that of the national average. The typical southerner was less likely to be tending a textile loom or a steel furnace than, as the saying went, facing the eastern end of a westbound mule or risking his life in an Appalachian coal mine. The postwar South remained dependent on the North for investment capital and for manufactured goods.

Henry Grady had also called for more diversified agriculture, but cotton remained king after the Civil War, even though it never regained the huge profitability it had generated in the 1850s. By the 1880s, southern farmers were producing as much cotton as they had before the war, but were earning far less money because the world price for cotton declined throughout the decade. "Cotton planting has been a mania," one observer noted. "The neglected corn field with all its consequences is a part of southern history."

Southern Poverty

Grady also hoped that growing numbers of southern farmers would own their own land by the end of the nineteenth century. But the opposite occurred. The majority of southern farmers struggled merely to survive after the Civil War, and many of them actually lost ownership of the land that they worked each year. A prolonged decline in crop prices that affected the entire economy during the last third of the nineteenth century made it more difficult than ever to own farm land. By 1890, falling rates of farm ownership in the Lower South dispelled Grady's dream as the region sank deeper and deeper into poverty. By 1900, 70 percent of farmers did not own the land they worked, and in no southern state were more than half of farmers landowners.

Because most southern communities had no banks after the Civil War, people had to find ways to operate with little or no cash. Many rural areas adopted a barter economy in which a local "crossroads" or "furnishing" merchant would provide food, clothing, seed, fertilizer, and other items to poor farmers "on credit" in exchange for a share (or "lien") of their crops when harvested.

Origins of the crop-lien system

The Crop-Lien System

The southern farmers, white and black, who participated in the **crop-lien system** fell into three distinct categories: small farm owners, sharecroppers, and tenants. The farms owned by most southerners were small and financially fragile; they did not generate much cash income. As a result, even

crop-lien system Credit system used by sharecroppers and share tenants who pledged a portion ("share") of their future crop to local merchants or land owners in exchange for farming supplies, food, and clothing.

"Free slaves" Sharecroppers painstakingly pick cotton while their white overseer observes them from atop his horse.

Tenant farmers and sharecroppers

owners had to pledge a portion of their future crop to the local merchant in return for supplies purchased "on credit."

Sharecroppers, mostly blacks who had nothing to offer but their labor, worked 20–40 acres of an owner's land in return for shelter, seed, fertilizer, mules, supplies, and food—as well as a share of the crop, generally about half. Share tenants, mostly white farmers who were barely better off, might have their own mule or horse, a plow and tools, and a line of credit with the nearby country store, but they still needed to rent land to farm. A few paid their rent in cash, but most, like sharecroppers, pledged a share of the harvested crops to the landowner. Usually, the tenant farmers were able to keep a larger share of the crop (about 60 percent) than the sharecroppers, which meant that landowners often preferred to rent acreage to "croppers" rather than tenants. And many African American sharecroppers worked for the same planter who had earlier owned them as slaves. "The colored folks," said a black Alabama sharecropper, "stayed with the old boss man and farmed and worked on the plantations. They were still slaves, but they were free slaves." Eighty percent of southern blacks lived on farms in the late nineteenth century. African American Ned Cobb, an Alabama sharecropper, recalled that his father "put me to plown' the first time at nine years old, right after my mother died." He plowed "barefoot" on rocky land.

The crop-lien system was terribly inefficient and even corrupting. The overwhelming focus on planting cotton or tobacco year after year stripped the soil of its fertility and stability, causing disastrous erosion as topsoil during storms washed into nearby creeks and rivers whose banks caved in, creating ever-deepening gullies. In addition, landowners required croppers and tenants to grow only a "cash crop," usually cotton or tobacco. This meant that the landless farmers could not grow their own vegetable gardens; they had to get their food from the local merchant in exchange for promised cotton. And because most farmers did not own the land they worked, the cabins they lived in, or the tools they used, they had little incentive to enrich the soil or maintain buildings and equipment owned by the

sharecroppers Poor, mostly black farmers who would work an owner's land in return for shelter, seed, fertilizer, mules, supplies, and food, as well as a substantial share of the crop produced.

landlord. "The tenant," explained a South Carolina–born economist, Matthew B. Hammond, "is interested only in the crop he is raising, and makes no effort to keep up the fertility of the land." The tenant system of farming, he concluded, had been "more wasteful and destructive than slavery was anywhere."

The crop-lien system was in essence a post–Civil War version of economic slavery for poor whites as well as blacks. Georgia's Tom Watson said that the masses of landless farmers were "like victims of some horrid nightmare . . . powerless—oppressed—shackled." The landowner or merchant (often the same person) decided what crop would be planted and how it would be cultivated, harvested, and sold. The landowner could enter a tenant or cropper's cabin whenever he pleased. In good times, croppers and tenants barely broke even; in bad times, they struggled to survive. Sharecroppers and share tenants were among the poorest people in the nation—for three generations. Most of them lived in poor health in rude shacks; they had little or no education, rarely enough healthy food, and little hope for a better future.

Those who worked the farms of large landowners developed an intense suspicion of them, for landlords often swindled the workers by not giving them their fair share of the crops. Landlords kept the books, handled the sale of the crops, and gave the cropper or tenant his share of the proceeds after deducting for all the items supplied during the year, plus interest that

> Crop-lien system: Inefficient, corrupt, a form of slavery, and self-defeating

> Economic stagnation

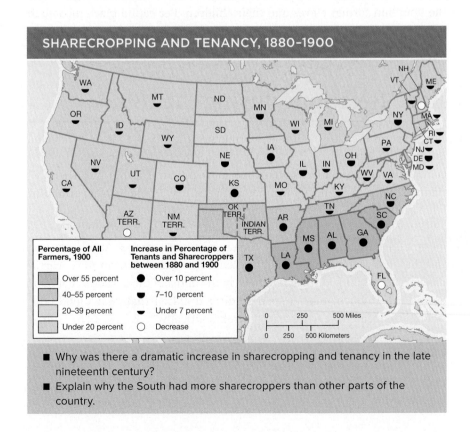

SHARECROPPING AND TENANCY, 1880–1900

Percentage of All Farmers, 1900

- Over 55 percent
- 40–55 percent
- 20–39 percent
- Under 20 percent

Increase in Percentage of Tenants and Sharecroppers between 1880 and 1900

- ● Over 10 percent
- ◗ 7–10 percent
- ◞ Under 7 percent
- ○ Decrease

0   250   500 Miles
0   250   500 Kilometers

■ Why was there a dramatic increase in sharecropping and tenancy in the late nineteenth century?

■ Explain why the South had more sharecroppers than other parts of the country.

ranged, according to one newspaper, "from 24 percent to grand larceny." Often, the cropper or tenant received nothing at the end of a harvest but a larger debt to be rolled over to next year's crop. Over time, the high interest charged on the credit offered by the local store or landowner, coupled with sagging prices for cotton and other crops, created a hopeless cycle of perennial debt among small farmers, sharecroppers, and share tenants.

Falling Cotton Prices

The one-crop system of southern agriculture was self-defeating. As cotton production soared during the last quarter of the nineteenth century, largely because of dramatic growth in Texas cultivation, the price paid for raw cotton fell steadily. "Have you all felt the effects of the low price of cotton," Mary Parham of Amite, Louisiana, wrote to her father in 1892. "It nearly ruined us. I did not get my house built. The farmers are very blue here. But [they are] getting ready to plant cotton again." As the price declined, desperate farmers planted even more cotton, which only accelerated the decline in price.

In the 1870s, annual production of cotton was about 2.6 billion pounds, which brought an average price of 11.77 cents per pound. In the 1880s, the average annual production was 3 billion pounds at 10.44 cents per pound. By 1896, the average price of cotton was down to 7.72 cents. The average annual income of white southerners in 1900 was about half that of Americans outside the South. Eleven percent of whites in the South were illiterate, twice the national average. The poorest people in the nation's poorest region were the 9 million former slaves and their children. Per capita black income in 1900 was a third of that of southern whites, and the black illiteracy rate in the South was nearly 50 percent, almost five times higher than that of whites.

CORE **OBJECTIVE**

3. Explain how and why white southerners took away African Americans' right to vote and adopted "Jim Crow" segregation laws at the end of the nineteenth century.

Race Relations during the 1890s

The desperate plight of southern farmers in the 1880s and 1890s affected race relations—for the worse. During the 1890s, white farmers and politicians demanded that blacks be stripped of their voting rights and other civil rights as well. At the end of the nineteenth century, a violent "**Negrophobia**" swept across the South and much of the nation. In part, the new wave of racism was spurred by the revival in the United States and Europe of the old idea that the Anglo-Saxon "race" was superior to other races. Another reason was that many whites had come to resent any signs of African American financial success and political influence in the midst of the decade's economic downturn. An Alabama newspaper editor declared that "our blood boils when the educated Negro asserts himself politically."

Disenfranchising African Americans

Negrophobia A violent new wave of racism that spread in the late nineteenth century largely spurred by white resentment for African American financial success and growing political influence.

By the 1890s, a new generation of African Americans born and educated since the end of the Civil War was determined to gain true equality. They were more assertive and less patient than their parents. "We are not the

Negro from whom the chains of slavery fell a quarter century ago, most assuredly not," a black editor announced. A growing number of young white adults, however, were equally determined to keep "Negroes in their place."

Mississippi led the way to the near-total loss of voting rights by blacks—and many poor whites as well. The so-called **Mississippi Plan**, a series of state constitutional amendments in 1890, set the pattern of disenfranchisement that nine more states would follow over the next twenty years. First, a residence requirement for voting—two years in the state, one year in an election district—struck at African American tenant farmers who were in the habit of moving yearly in search of better economic opportunities. Second, voters were disqualified if convicted of certain crimes that disproportionately involved blacks. Third, all taxes, including a so-called poll tax specifically for voting, had to be paid before a person could vote—a restriction that hurt both poor blacks and poor whites. Finally, all voters had to be literate, and white registrars decided who could read and who could not.

> The Mississippi Plan

Other states added variations on the Mississippi Plan. In 1898, Louisiana invented the "grandfather clause," which allowed illiterate whites to vote if their fathers or grandfathers had been eligible to vote on January 1, 1867, when African Americans were still disenfranchised. By 1910, Georgia, North Carolina, Virginia, Alabama, and Oklahoma had adopted the grandfather clause. Every southern state, moreover, adopted a statewide Democratic primary between 1896 and 1915, and most of these primaries excluded African American voters.

> Voter intimidation and suppression

When such "legal" means were not enough to ensure their political dominance, white candidates used fraud and violence to eliminate the black vote. Benjamin Tillman, the white male supremacist who served as governor of South Carolina from 1890 to 1894, provides a good example of the transformation in southern politics during the 1890s.

Tillman's election resulted from his effective use of the state's class divisions and racial tensions. Declaring that South Carolina's farm problems were caused by white farmers renting their land to "ignorant lazy negroes," he and other political rebels gained the support of poor whites across the state to oust the Redeemers, whom he claimed had failed to help the poor whites. Tillman claimed that "I organized the majority [of voters] and put the old families out of business, and we became and are the rulers of the state." To ensure his election, Tillman and his followers eliminated the black vote. He admitted that "we have done our level best [to prevent blacks from voting]. . . . We stuffed ballot boxes. We shot them. We are not ashamed of it." The whites had gained control of the state government, he concluded, "and we intend at any and all hazards to retain it."

By the end of the nineteenth century, widespread racial discrimination—segregation of public facilities, political disenfranchisement, and vigilante justice—had elevated government-sanctioned bigotry to an official way of life in the South. Benjamin Tillman bluntly declared in 1892 that blacks "must remain subordinate or be exterminated."

Mississippi Plan (1890) Series of state constitutional amendments that sought to disenfranchise black voters and was quickly adopted by nine other southern states.

The efforts to suppress the black vote quickly succeeded. In 1896, Louisiana had 130,000 registered black voters. By 1900, it had only 5,320. In Alabama in 1900, 121,159 black men over twenty-one were literate, according to the census; only 3,742, however, were registered to vote. By 1900, black voting across the southern states had declined by 62 percent, the white vote by 26 percent.

The Spread of Racial Segregation

At the same time that southern blacks were being shoved out of the political arena, they were also being segregated socially. The symbolic first target was the railroad passenger car. In 1885, novelist George Washington Cable noted that in South Carolina, blacks "ride in first-class [rail] cars as a right" and "their presence excites no comment." From 1875 to 1883, in fact, any local or state law requiring racial segregation violated the federal Civil Rights Act (1875). By 1883, however, many northern whites endorsed the resegregation of southern life. In that year, the U.S. Supreme Court ruled that the Civil Rights Act of 1875 was unconstitutional. The judges explained that private individuals and organizations could engage in acts of racial discrimination because the Fourteenth Amendment specified only that "no State" could deny citizens equal protection of the law.

The Court's interpretation of what came to be called the Civil Rights Cases (1883) left as an open question the validity of various state laws requiring racially segregated public facilities under the principle of "separate but equal," a slogan popular in the South in the late nineteenth century. In the 1880s, Tennessee and Mississippi required railroad passengers to ride in racially segregated cars.

When Louisiana followed suit in 1890, blacks challenged the law in the case of *Plessy v. Ferguson* (1896). The case originated in New Orleans when Homer Plessy, an octoroon (a person having one-eighth African ancestry), refused to leave a whites-only railroad car and was convicted of violating the law. In 1896, the Supreme Court ruled that states had a right to create laws segregating public places such as schools, hotels, and restaurants. Justice John Marshall Harlan, a Kentuckian who had once owned slaves, was the only member of the Court to dissent. He stressed that the Constitution is "color-blind, and neither knows nor tolerates classes among citizens. In respect of civil rights, all citizens are equal before the law." He feared that the Court's ruling would plant the "seeds of race hate" under "the sanction of law."

That is precisely what happened. The Court's ruling in the *Plessy* case legitimized the practice of racially **"separate but equal"** facilities in virtually every area of southern life, including streetcars, hotels, restaurants, hospitals, parks, sports stadiums, and places of employment. In 1900, the editor of the *Richmond Times* expressed the prevailing view throughout the white South when he insisted that racial segregation "be applied in every relation of Southern life. God Almighty drew the color line, and it cannot be

Civil Rights Act of 1875 declared unconstitutional

***Plessy v. Ferguson* (1896): "separate but equal"**

"separate but equal"
Underlying principle behind segregation that was legitimized by the Supreme Court ruling in *Plessy v. Ferguson* (1896).

obliterated. The negro must stay on his side of the line, and the white man must stay on his side, and the sooner both races recognize this fact and accept it, the better it will be for both."

The new regulations requiring racial segregation came to be called "Jim Crow" laws. The name derived from "Jump Jim Crow," an old song-and-dance caricature of African Americans performed by white actor Thomas D. Rice in blackface makeup during the 1830s. During the 1890s, the term "Jim Crow" became a satirical expression meaning "Negro." Signs reading "white only" or "colored only" above restrooms and water fountains emerged throughout the South as hallmarks of the "Jim Crow" system. Old racist customs dating back before the Civil War were revived. If whites walked along a sidewalk, blacks were expected to step aside and let them pass. There were even racially separate funeral homes, cemeteries, and churches. When a white deacon in a Mississippi Baptist church saw a black man in the sanctuary, he asked: "Boy, what you doin' in there? Don't you know this is a white church?" The black man replied: "Boss, I'm here to mop the floor." The white man paused and said, "Well, that's all right then, but don't let me catch you prayin'."

"Jim Crow" laws

As with disenfranchisement of black voters, widespread violence accompanied the creation of Jim Crow laws. From 1890 to 1899, the United States averaged 188 lynchings per year, 82 percent of which occurred in the South. Lynchings usually involved a black man (or men) accused of a crime, often rape. White mobs would seize, torture, and kill the accused, always in ghastly ways. Racial lynchings became so common that participating whites viewed them as forms of outdoor entertainment. Large crowds, including women and children, would watch the grisly event amid a carnival-like

Lynching

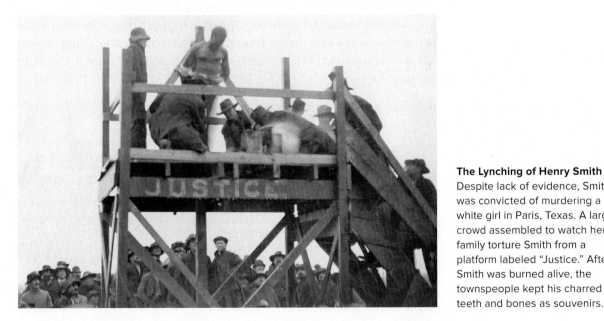

The Lynching of Henry Smith Despite lack of evidence, Smith was convicted of murdering a white girl in Paris, Texas. A large crowd assembled to watch her family torture Smith from a platform labeled "Justice." After Smith was burned alive, the townspeople kept his charred teeth and bones as souvenirs.

atmosphere. Photographs of gruesome lynchings surrounded by crowds of laughing and smiling whites were reproduced on postcards mailed across the nation. The governor of Mississippi declared that "if it is necessary that every Negro in the state will be lynched, it will be done to maintain white supremacy."

Mob Rule in North Carolina

White supremacy was violently imposed in the thriving coastal port of Wilmington, North Carolina, then the largest city in the state, with about twenty thousand residents. In 1894 and 1896, black voters, by then a majority in the city, elected blacks to various municipal offices, infuriating the city's white elite. "We will never surrender to a ragged raffle of Negroes," warned a former congressman and Confederate colonel named Alfred Waddell, "even if we have to choke the Cape Fear River with [black] carcasses." It was not an idle threat.

> Wilmington Insurrection

On the morning of November 10, 1898, some two thousand well-armed white men and teens rampaged through the streets of Wilmington. They first destroyed the offices of the *Daily Record*, the city's black-owned newspaper, then moved into the black neighborhoods, shooting African Americans and destroying homes and businesses. Almost a hundred blacks were killed. The mob then stormed the city hall, declared that Colonel Waddell was the new mayor, and forced the African American business leaders and elected officials to board northbound trains. The new self-appointed all-white city government issued a "Declaration of White Independence" that stripped blacks of their voting rights and their jobs. Desperate black residents appealed for help to the governor as well as President William McKinley, but received none.

The Wilmington Insurrection marked the first time in history that a lawfully elected municipal government had been overthrown in the United States. Two years later, in the 1900 statewide elections, white supremacist Democrats vowed to cement their control of the political process. The night

Wilmington Insurrection A mob of white supremacists pose with their rifles before the demolished printing press of the *Daily Record*, an African American newspaper.

before the election, Colonel Waddell urged supporters to use any means necessary to suppress black voting: "You are Anglo-Saxons. You are armed and prepared and you will do your duty. . . . Go to the polls tomorrow, and if you find the negro out voting, tell him to leave the polls, and if he refuses, kill him, shoot him down in his tracks. We shall win tomorrow if we have to do it with guns." The Democratic party won by a landslide.

The Black Response

African Americans responded to the resurgence of racism in various ways. Some left the South in search of greater safety, equality, and opportunity, but the vast majority stayed in their native region and tried to adjust to the brutal realities of white supremacy. "Had to walk a quiet life," explained James Plunkett, a Virginia African American. "The least little thing you would do, they [whites] would kill ya."

Yet accommodation did not mean submission. Black southerners nurtured their own culture and racial pride. A young white visitor to Mississippi in 1910 noticed that nearly every black person he met had "two distinct social selves, the one he reveals to his own people, the other he assumes among the whites."

African American churches continued to serve as hubs for black community life. Churches were used not only for worship but for social gatherings, club meetings, and political rallies. Churches enabled African Americans of all classes to interact and exercise roles denied them in the larger society. For men especially, churches offered leadership roles and political status. Serving as a deacon was often one of the most prestigious positions for an African American man.

African American churches

Booker T. Washington

By the 1890s, Booker T. Washington, born a slave in Virginia, in 1856, the son of a black mother and a white father, had become the foremost African American orator and educator in the nation. At sixteen, he had enrolled at Hampton Normal and Agricultural Institute, one of several colleges for former slaves created during Reconstruction. Nine years later, the founder of Hampton Institute, Samuel Armstrong, a former Union general, received a request from a group in northern Alabama starting a black college called Tuskegee Institute. They needed a president of the new school. Armstrong urged them to hire Washington. Although only twenty-five, he was, according to Armstrong, "a very capable mulatto, clear headed, modest, sensible, polite, and a thorough teacher and superior man."

Young Washington was selected, and he quickly went to creating a school on a vacant lot. The first students had to help construct the first buildings, making the bricks themselves. Washington became a skilled

Booker T. Washington Founder of the Tuskegee Institute, a historically black university. He went on to become the nation's most prominent African American leader.

fundraiser, gathering substantial gifts from wealthy whites, most of them northerners. As the years passed, bustling Tuskegee Institute became celebrated as a college dedicated to discipline and vocational training. Washington's recurring message to students was the importance of "practical knowledge." In part to please his white donors, he argued that blacks should not focus on fighting racial segregation. They should instead work hard, don't complain, and don't stir up trouble. At the same time that white southerners were preventing blacks from voting and imposing Jim Crow laws, Washington was urging African Americans to begin "at the bottom," as well-educated farmers, not as social activists.

Yet Washington's conservative approach emphasizing economic self-sufficiency did not satisfy many white racists. Thomas Dixon, a prominent North Carolina Baptist minister, state legislator, and novelist, complained that Washington was teaching his students "to be masters of men, to be independent, to own and operate their own industries," all of which would "destroy the last vestige of dependence on the white man for anything."

In a famous speech in Atlanta in 1895, Washington told the African Americans in the segregated audience that fighting for "social equality" would be a huge mistake ("the extremest folly"). Instead he emphasized that they should "cast down your bucket where you are—cast it down in making friends . . . of the people of all races by whom we are surrounded. Cast it down in agriculture, mechanics, in commerce, in domestic service, and in the professions." He insisted that black southerners could succeed economically while accepting the new Jim Crow laws segregating them from whites. "In all things that are purely social," he explained, "we can be as separate as the five fingers, yet one as the hand in all things essential to mutual progress." In sum, Washington wanted to build a prosperous black community and a thriving Tuskegee Institute, and to do so he became skilled at saying what whites wanted to hear. Civil rights for blacks would have to wait. Any effort at "agitation" in the white-dominant South would, he warned, backfire on the black community. The region's heritage of racial hatred would have to subside over time.

W. E. B. Du Bois

By the start of the twentieth century, Booker T. Washington had become the most influential African American leader in the nation. Some younger black leaders, however, criticized him for sacrificing civil and political rights in his crusade for vocational education. W. E. B. Du Bois led this criticism. A native of Massachusetts, Du Bois first experienced racial prejudice as a student at Fisk University in Nashville, Tennessee. Later he became the first African American to earn a doctoral degree from Harvard (in history and sociology). In addition to promoting civil rights, he left a distinguished record as a scholar, authoring more than twenty books. Trim and dapper, Du Bois had a flamboyant personality and a combative spirit. Not long after he

W. E. B. Du Bois A fierce advocate for black education and civil rights.

began teaching at Atlanta University in 1897, he launched a public assault on Booker T. Washington's strategy for improving the quality of life for African Americans.

Du Bois called Washington's 1895 speech "the **Atlanta Compromise**" and the name stuck. Du Bois refused to "surrender the leadership of this race to cowards." Washington, he argued, was so determined to please powerful whites that he "accepted the alleged inferiority of the Negro" so blacks could "concentrate all their energies on industrial education, the accumulation of wealth, and the conciliation of the South." Du Bois stressed that the priorities should be reversed—that African American leaders should adopt a strategy of "ceaseless agitation" directed at ensuring the right to vote and winning civil equality. The education of blacks, Du Bois maintained, should not be merely vocational but should develop bold leaders willing to challenge segregation and discrimination. He demanded that disenfranchisement and legalized segregation cease immediately and that the laws of the land be enforced.

For his part, Washington stressed that Du Bois never truly understood the brutal dynamics of southern racism. His militant strategy, if enacted in the South, would only have gotten more blacks lynched. Nor did Du Bois or other critics know that Washington secretly financed legal efforts to oppose the Jim Crow laws. Such "quiet efforts," he noted, were more successful and realistic than the "brass band" approach championed by Du Bois.

The dispute between Washington and Du Bois came to define the tensions that would divide the twentieth-century civil rights movement: militancy versus conciliation, separatism versus assimilation, social justice versus economic opportunities. By 1915, when Washington died, the leadership of the nation's black community was passing to Du Bois and others whose principled, yet uncompromising effort to gain true equality signaled the beginning of the civil-rights century.

The Settling of the New West

Like the South, the West is a region wrapped in myths and stereotypes. The vast land west of the Mississippi River contains remarkable geographic extremes: majestic mountains, roaring rivers, deep-sculpted canyons, blistering deserts, wide and grassy plains, and dense forests. For most western Americans, the great epics of the Civil War and Reconstruction were remote events hardly touching the lives of the Indians, Mexicans, Asians, farmers, ranchers, trappers, miners, and Mormons scattered through the plains, valleys, and mountains. There the relentless march of settlement and exploitation continued, propelled by a lust for land, a passion for profit, and a restless desire to improve one's lot in life. Between 1870 and 1900, Americans settled more land in the West than had been occupied

CORE **OBJECTIVE**

4. Describe the various groups of migrants to the West after the Civil War and the reasons they went there.

Atlanta Compromise (1895) Speech by Booker T. Washington that called for the black community to strive for economic prosperity before demanding political and social equality.

before 1870. The post–Civil War West symbolized the American emphasis on economic opportunity and personal freedom. On another level, however, the economic development of the West was a tragedy of shortsighted greed and irresponsible behavior, a story of reckless exploitation that scarred the land, decimated its wildlife, and nearly exterminated Native American culture.

The Western Landscape

After mid-century, farmers and their families began spreading west across Iowa and Kansas to the Great Plains—western Kansas, Nebraska, and Oklahoma, northern Texas, the Dakotas, and eastern Colorado, Wyoming, and Montana. From California, miners moved eastward through the mountains to Utah and Nevada, drawn by one new strike after another. From Texas, nomadic cowboys migrated northward onto the plains and across the Rocky Mountains, into the Great Basin of Utah.

The settlers in the West encountered climates and landscapes markedly different from those they had left behind. The Great Plains were dry, and the scarcity of water and timber rendered useless the familiar trappings of the pioneer—the ax, the log cabin, the rail fence—as well as the accustomed methods of tilling the soil. For a long time, the region between the Mississippi River and California had been called the Great American Desert, unfit for human habitation and therefore, in the minds of white Americans, the perfect refuge for Indians. But that view changed in the last half of the nineteenth century. The discovery of large deposits of gold, silver, copper, iron, and coal, the completion of the transcontinental railroads, the collapse of Indian resistance, and the rise of the range-cattle industry convinced many Americans that there were huge profits to be made in the West. With the use of what water was available, new techniques of "dry farming" and irrigation could make the land fruitful after all.

The Migratory Stream

During the second half of the nineteenth century, an unrelenting stream of migrants flowed into what had been the largely Indian and Hispanic West. Millions of Anglo-Americans, African Americans, Mexicans, South Americans, and European and Chinese immigrants transformed the patterns of western society and culture. Most of the settlers were relatively prosperous white, native-born farm folk. Because of the expense of transportation, land, and supplies, the very poor could not afford to relocate. Three quarters of the western migrants were men.

Canadian, Northern European, and Chinese immigrants

The largest number of foreign immigrants came from northern Europe and Canada. In the northern plains, Germans, Scandinavians, and Irish were especially numerous. In the new state of Nebraska in 1870, a quarter of the 123,000 residents were foreign born. In North Dakota in 1890, 45 percent of the residents were immigrants. Compared with European

THE NEW WEST

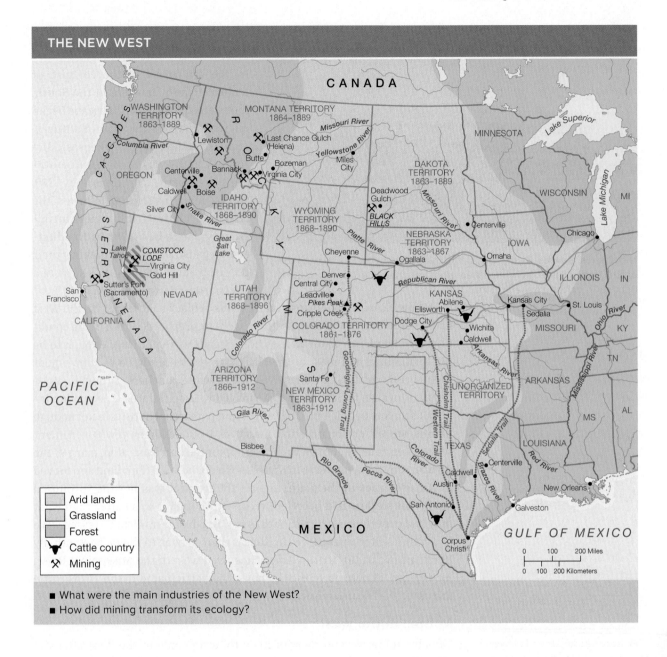

- What were the main industries of the New West?
- How did mining transform its ecology?

immigrants, those from China and Mexico were much less numerous but nonetheless significant. More than 200,000 Chinese arrived in California between 1876 and 1890, joining some seventy thousand others who had earlier come to the state to build railroads and work in the mining communities. The Chinese were frequently discriminated against and denied citizenship rights. As perpetual outsiders, they became scapegoats whenever there was an economic downturn. In 1882, Congress passed the Chinese Exclusion Act, effectively banning further immigration from China.

Nicodemus, Kansas By the 1880s, this colony had become a thriving town of Exodusters. Here, its residents are photographed in front of their First Baptist Church and general store.

The African American Migration

In the aftermath of the collapse of Radical Republican rule in the South, thousands of African Americans began migrating westward from Kentucky, Tennessee, Louisiana, Arkansas, Mississippi, and Texas. Some 6,000 southern blacks arrived in Kansas in 1879, and as many as 20,000 followed the next year. These African American migrants came to be known as **Exodusters**, because they were making their exodus from the South—in search of a haven from racism and poverty.

By the early 1880s, however, the exodus of black southerners to the West had petered out. Many of the settlers were unprepared for the living conditions on the plains. Their Kansas homesteads were not large enough to be self-sustaining, and most of the black farmers were forced to supplement their income by hiring themselves out to white ranchers. Drought, grasshoppers, prairie fires, and dust storms led to crop failures. The sudden influx of so many people taxed resources and patience. There were not enough houses, stores, or construction materials to build them, few government services, and rarely enough water. Disappointed and frustrated, many of the African American pioneers in Kansas soon abandoned their land and moved to the few cities in the state. Life on the frontier was not the "promised land" that settlers had been led to expect, though it was better than what they had experienced in the South. As an Exoduster minister stressed, "We had rather suffer and be free" in Kansas than go back to the racist South. By 1890 some 520,000 African Americans lived west of the Mississippi River. As many as 25 percent of the cowboys who participated in the Texas cattle drives were African Americans.

Mining in the West

Prospectors and their followers

Valuable mineral deposits continued to lure people to the West after the Civil War. Every territory and state in the Far West developed a mining industry and mining culture during the second half of the nineteenth century. The miners of the 1849 California gold rush (the forty-niners) set the typical pattern, in which mobs of prospectors rushed to a new find, followed quickly by camp followers—a motley crew of peddlers, saloon keepers, prostitutes, gamblers, hustlers, and assorted desperadoes eager to "mine the miners." Lawlessness gave way first to vigilante rule as groups of miners created their own informal legal codes for the community and enforced penalties, including hangings, and, finally, to stable communities with municipal governments, sanitation, and law enforcement.

Exodusters African Americans who migrated west from the South in search of a haven from racism and poverty after the collapse of Radical Republican rule.

The drama of the 1849 gold rush was reenacted time and again in the following three decades. Along the South Platte River, not far from Pikes Peak in Colorado, a prospecting party found gold in 1858, and stories of success brought perhaps 100,000 "fifty-niners" into the area by the next year. New discoveries in Colorado kept occurring: near Central City in 1859, at Leadville in the 1870s, and at Cripple Creek in 1891 and 1894—the last important strikes in the West, again gold and silver. During those years, farming and grazing had given the economy a stable base, and Colorado, the Centennial State, entered the union in 1876.

While the early miners were crowding around Pikes Peak in Colorado, the **Comstock Lode** was discovered near Gold Hill, Nevada, on the eastern slope of the Sierra Nevada Mountains near the California border. Henry Comstock, a Canadian-born fur trapper, had drifted to the Carson River diggings, which opened in 1856. He talked his way into a share of a new discovery made by two other prospectors in 1859 and gave it his own name. The lode produced massive amounts of gold and silver. Within twenty years, it had yielded more than $300 million from shafts that reached thousands of feet into the mountainside.

The growing demand for orderly government in the West led to the hasty designation of new territories and eventually the admission of a host of new states. After Colorado's admission in 1876, however, there was a long pause because of party divisions in Congress: Democrats were reluctant to create states out of territories that were heavily Republican. After the sweeping Republican victory in the 1888 legislative races, however, Congress admitted the Dakotas, Montana, and Washington in 1889 and Idaho and Wyoming in 1890. Utah entered the Union in 1896 (after the Mormons agreed to abandon the practice of polygamy) and Oklahoma in 1907, and in 1912 Arizona and New Mexico rounded out the forty-eight contiguous states. (The final two states, Alaska and Hawaii, were added fifty years later.)

> New western states

Life in the New West

The surge of western migration had many of the romantic qualities so often depicted in novels, films, and television shows. The people who braved harsh conditions to begin new lives in the West were indeed courageous and tenacious. Cowboys and Indians, outlaws and vigilantes, farmers, ranchers, and herders, populated the plains, while miners and trappers led nomadic lives in the hills and backwoods.

But these familiar images of western life tell only part of the story. Drudgery and tragedy were as commonplace as adventure and success. Droughts, locusts, disease, tornadoes, and the erratic fluctuations of commodities markets made life relentlessly precarious. The people who settled the trans-Mississippi frontier were in fact a diverse lot: they included women as well as men, African Americans, Hispanics, Asians, and European

> CORE **OBJECTIVE**
> **5.** Explain the experiences of miners, ranchers, farmers, and women in the West.

Comstock Lode Mine in eastern Nevada acquired by Canadian fur trapper Henry Comstock that between 1860 and 1880 yielded almost $1 billion worth of gold and silver.

The original cowboys Cowboys on horseback herd cattle into a corral beside the Cimarron River in 1905.

immigrants. The feverish quest for quick profits also helped fuel a boom/bust economic cycle that injected a chronic instability into the society and politics of the region. Ultimately, the massive western migrations would take a huge toll on the Native American tribes in the region.

The Cattle Boom

When ranchers began herding cattle into the grasslands where the buffalo had roamed, the western landscape was changed forever. For many years, wild cattle had competed with buffalo in the Spanish borderlands of Texas and Arizona. Interbreeding them with Anglo-American domesticated cattle produced the Texas longhorns: lean and rangy, they were noted more for speed and endurance than for yielding a choice steak. They had little marginal value, moreover, because the largest markets for beef were too far away.

> The cattle industry

That situation changed after the Civil War as railroads pushed farther west, where cattle could be driven through mostly vacant lands. Once the rail lines reached Kansas, Joseph G. McCoy, an Illinois livestock dealer, recognized the possibilities of moving Texas cattle northward to Kansas and then to the rest of the nation by rail. In 1867 in tiny Abilene, Kansas, he bought 250 acres for a stockyard and built a barn, an office building, livestock scales, a hotel, and a bank. He then sent an agent into Indian-owned areas to recruit the owners of herds bound north to go through Abilene. Once the Texas herds reached Kansas, the cattle were loaded onto rail cars and shipped to the Chicago stockyards and then (as beef) to the East Coast.

Abilene flourished as the first successful Kansas cow town. By 1871, 700,000 steers passed through it every year. The ability to ship huge numbers of western cattle by rail transformed ranching into a major national industry. Soon, other western territories and states—Colorado, Wyoming, Dakota, and Montana—followed the Kansas example and had cattle drives and railheads of their own.

The thriving cattle industry spurred rapid population growth. The population of Kansas increased from 107,000 in 1860 to 365,000 ten years later and reached almost 1 million by 1880. Nebraska witnessed similar increases. The flush times of the cow town soon passed, however, and the long cattle drives played out too, because they were economically unsound. The dangers of the trail, the wear and tear on men and cattle, the charges levied on drives across Indian territory, and the advance of farms across the trails combined to persuade cattlemen that they could function best near railroads. As railroads spread out into Texas and across the plains, the cattle business spread with them over the High Plains as far as Montana and on into Canada.

In the absence of laws governing the open range, cattle ranchers at first worked out a code of behavior largely dictated by circumstances. As cattle often wandered onto other ranchers' land, cowboys would "ride the line" to keep the animals off the adjoining ranches. In the spring they would "round up" the herds, which invariably got mixed up, and sort out ownership by identifying the distinctive ranch symbols "branded," or burned, into the cattle.

All that changed in 1873, when Joseph Glidden, an Illinois farmer, invented the first effective form of barbed wire, which ranchers used to fence off their lands at relatively low cost. People rushed to buy the new wire fencing, and soon the open range—owned by all, where a small rancher could graze his cattle anywhere—was no more. Barbed-wire fences triggered "range wars," where small ranchers, called fence cutters, fought with large ranchers to retain the open range. Fencing put a lot of ranchers out of business, and many of them became cowboys working for wages. Cattle raising, like mining, evolved from a romantic adventure into a big business dominated by large corporations. As one cowboy lamented, "times have changed."

> The end of the open range

Farming on the Plains

Farming has always been a hard life, and it was made more so on the Great Plains by the region's unforgiving environment and harsh weather. A New York newspaper publisher traveling to California described the Great Plains as a "land of starvation," "a treeless desert," scorching during daylight and "chill and piercing" cold at night. Still, people made the dangerous trek, lured by the inexpensive federal land and misleading advertisements celebrating life on the plains. One woman said she was "glad to be leaving" her

Innovative farming Powered by over a dozen horses and driven by two men, this early nineteenth-century machine boasted the ability of cutting, threshing, bagging, and weighing wheat all at the same time.

farm in Missouri: "We were going to a new land and get rich." Few did get rich, however. "In plain language," concluded a study by the Department of Agriculture: "a farmer's wife, as a general rule, is a laboring drudge."

Homesteaders

The first homesteaders in the Great Plains faced a grim struggle against danger, adversity, monotony, and loneliness. Though land was essentially free as a result of the Homestead Act (1862), horses, livestock, wagons, wells, lumber, fencing, seed, machinery, and fertilizer were not. Freight rates and interest rates on loans seemed criminally high. As in the South, declining crop prices produced chronic indebtedness, leading strapped western farmers to embrace virtually any plan to increase the money supply and thus pay off their debts with inflated currency. The virgin land itself, although fertile, resisted planting; the heavy sod woven with tough grass roots broke many a plow. Since wood and coal were rare on the prairie, pioneer families initially had to use buffalo chips (dried dung from buffaloes and cattle) for fuel.

Farm families also fought a constant battle with the elements: tornadoes, hailstorms, droughts, prairie fires, blizzards, and pests. Swarms of locusts often clouded the horizon, occasionally covering the ground six inches deep. A Wichita newspaper reported in 1878 that the grasshoppers devoured "everything green, stripping the foliage off the bark and from the tender twigs of the fruit trees, destroying every plant that is good for food or pleasant to the eyes, that man has planted." In the late 1880s, a prolonged drought forced many homesteaders on the plains to give up. Thousands left, some in wagons whose canvas coverings read: "In God we trusted, In Kansas we busted."

Commercial Farming

Eventually, as the railroads brought piles of lumber from the East, farmers could leave their houses built of sod for more comfortable frame dwellings. New farm equipment, for those who could afford to buy it, greatly improved productivity. In 1868, James Oliver, a Scottish immigrant living in Indiana, made a successful chilled-iron "sodbuster" plow that greatly eased the task of plowing the plains. Improvements and new inventions in threshing machines, hay mowers, planters, manure spreaders, cream separators, and other devices lightened the burden of farm labor but added to the farmers' capital outlay. By 1880, a steam-powered combine could do the work of twenty men. In Minnesota, the Dakotas, and central California, wealthy capitalists who could afford machinery for mass production created gigantic "bonanza farms" that became the marvels of the age. On one | Bonanza farms | farm in North Dakota, 13,000 acres of wheat made a single field. Another bonanza farm employed over 1,000 migrant workers to tend 34,000 acres. Such agribusinesses were the wave of the future. Jefferson's dream of an America primarily made up of small farmers gave way to industrial agriculture.

While the overall value of farmland and farm products increased in the late nineteenth century, small farmers did not keep up with the march of progress. Their numbers grew in size but decreased in proportion to the population at large. Wheat in the Western states, like cotton in the South, was the great export crop that spurred economic growth. For a variety of reasons, however, including an inability to afford the new machinery, few small farmers prospered. By the 1890s they were in open revolt against the "system" of corrupt processors (middlemen) and "greedy" bankers who they believed conspired against them.

Miners in the West

As ranchers and farmers settled the plains, miners played a crucial role in the economic and social development of the Far West. Throughout the region, mining camps and towns sprouted like mushrooms in the second half of the century. Initially, the miners lived in crude tents and shacks they built themselves. They worked a nine- to ten-hour day, six days a week, and usually took Sunday off. As a camp grew, it became a town with cabins, stores, and saloons providing modern services and conveniences.

The first wave of prospectors focused on "placer" (surface) mining, us- | Effects of large-scale mining | ing iron or tin pans to sift gold dust and nuggets out of riverbeds. But once the placer deposits were exhausted, miners had to use other methods, all of which required much larger operations and investments. As mining shifted from surface digging and panning to hydraulic mining, dredging,

Small Farmers and Independence in the Coming of the Modern Age

The South and the West both underwent major changes in the late nineteenth century. Neither experienced industrialization at the rate that states in the North and Midwest did. But the economic transformation brought about by the growth of industry and Big Business reached deep into each region, profoundly affecting the lives of ordinary men and women. Both regions remained more rural and agricultural than the rest of the nation, and a large proportion of the population dreamed of sustaining an agrarian lifestyle of landownership and economic independence. But by the 1890s, these goals were harder to achieve than ever before.

Challenges	Southern Farmers	Western Farmers
Farming models	Sharecroppers or tenant farmers rented land from landowners through the **crop-lien system**, usually for the planting of cotton	**Large-scale wheat farms**, or bonanza farms, were successful, taking advantage of the cheap land, while investing in new machinery (see below)
Overproduction	Pressure to pay off debts to landowners led to excessive cotton production, which led to **lower prices and profit margins**	Pressure to pay off debts for high costs (see below) led to overproduction of wheat and **lower prices and profit margins**
High costs	■ Most farmers could not pay off debts or **high interest loans** after landowners took their share of the crops ■ Decreasing profits caused growing indebtedness, a general **decline in land ownership**, and **cash shortage**	■ Large farms often required **hired labor** ■ Farmers borrowed money at **high interest** to pay for expensive plows, threshers, and other **equipment** ■ Limited grain storage and railway transportation resulted in **high shipping costs**
Environment	■ **Infertile soil** from long-term overproduction ■ Pressure to continuously plant cotton **discouraged farming technology innovation** and **diversification of crops**	■ **Unpredictable, harsh weather** ■ **Pests, e.g., locusts** ■ **Few banks made loans more expensive**

QUESTIONS FOR ANALYSIS

1. Why was it so hard for small farmers in the South and West to profit from farming?

2. How similar was the situation of small farmers in the South and in the West?

3. What options did small farmers have for responding to the challenges they faced?

and deep-shaft "hard-rock" tunneling, mining ceased being an individual pursuit and became a big business. Only large-scale mining corporations financed by American and European investors could afford the expensive specialized power equipment and blasting dynamite needed for such operations. Many prospectors who had hoped to "strike it rich" turned into wage laborers working for mining corporations. Eventually, many of those mine workers formed unions to represent their interests in negotiations with mine owners, in part because of low pay ($3 a day) and in part because deep-shaft mining was so dangerous. In the western hard-rock mines, on-the-job accidents disabled one out of every thirty miners and killed one out of eighty. Overall, some 7,500 workers were killed and 20,000 maimed in mine accidents during the late nineteenth century.

Mining and the Environment

Hydraulicking, dredging, and shaft mining transformed vast areas of landscape and vegetation. Massive stamping mills driven by steam engines crushed enormous mountains of rock. Huge hydraulic cannons shot enormous streams of water under high pressure, stripping the topsoil and gravel from hillsides and creating steep-sloped barren canyons that could not sustain plant life. The massive amounts of dirt and debris unearthed by the water cannons covered rich farmland downstream and created sandbars that clogged rivers and killed fish. All told, some 12 billion tons of earth were blasted out of the Sierra Nevada Mountains in California and washed into local rivers.

Mining Boomtowns

Tombstone, Arizona, only thirty miles from the Mexican border, was the site of substantial silver mining in the 1870s. By only its fourth year of existence, it was the fastest-growing boomtown in the Southwest. It boasted a bowling alley, four churches, an icehouse, a school, two banks, three newspapers, and an ice cream parlor, alongside 110 saloons, 14 gambling halls, and numerous dance halls and brothels. Miners and cowboys especially enjoyed shows at the Bird Cage Theatre, the "wildest, wickedest night spot between Basin Street [in New Orleans] and the Barbary Coast [in North Africa]," open twenty-four hours a day, 365 days a year.

Some of the other largest and most famous of the mining boomtowns | Life in boomtowns
included Virginia City in Nevada, Cripple Creek and Leadville in Colorado, and Deadwood in the Dakota Territory. They were male-dominated communities with a substantial population of immigrants: Chinese, Chileans, Peruvians, Mexicans, French, Germans, Scots, Welsh, Irish, and English. In terms of ethnic diversity, the western mining cities were the most cosmopolitan communities in America.

Mining towns were also violent places. The small gold-mining town of Belleville, California, had 50 murders in one year. In 1871 a visitor to Corinne, Utah, a town only four years old with 2,000 residents, noted that the streets "are full of white men armed to the teeth, miserable-looking Indians dressed in the ragged shirts and trousers furnished by the federal government, and yellow Chinese with a business-like air and hard, intelligent faces." Ethnic prejudice was as common as violence in mining towns. The Chinese, for example, were usually prohibited from working in the mines but were allowed to operate laundries and work in boarding houses. Mexicans were often treated the worst. "Mexicans have no business in this country," a Californian insisted. "The men were made to be shot at, and the women were made for our purposes. I'm a white man—I am! A Mexican is pretty near black. I hate all Mexicans."

Most of the boomtowns, many of which were in remote mountainous areas, lasted only a few years. Once the mines played out, the people moved on, leaving ghost towns behind. In 1870, Virginia City, then called the richest city in America, hosted a population of 20,000. Today, it has fewer than 1,000 residents.

Women in the West

Pioneer Women: Greater Equality and Independence

The West remained a largely male society throughout the nineteenth century. Women in mining towns, most of whom worked as house cleaners, were as valued as gold. Many mining towns had a male-to-female ratio as high as 9 to 1. When four "respectable" women arrived in Nevada City, one of them reported that the men stood and gazed "at us with mouth and eyes wide open, every time we go out" in the streets.

In both mining towns and farming communities, women were prized as spouses, in part because farming required help. In 1900, 98 percent of the women in Nebraska were married. The women pioneers continued to face the traditional legal barriers and social prejudices prevalent in the East. A

Gathering "meadow muffins"
A pioneer woman collects dried buffalo dung to be used as fuel for cooking and warmth in the cold prairie nights.

wife could not sell property without her husband's approval, for example. Texas women could not sue except for divorce, nor could they serve on juries, act as lawyers, or witness a will.

But the constant fight for survival west of the Mississippi made men and women more equal partners than in the East. Many women who lost their mates to the deadly toil of "sod busting" thereafter assumed complete responsibility for their farms. In general, women on the prairie became more independent than women leading domestic lives back East. A Kansas woman explained "that the environment was such as to bring out and develop the dominant qualities of individual character. Kansas women of that day learned at an early age to depend on themselves—to do whatever work there was to be done, and to face danger when it must be faced, as calmly as they were able."

It was not coincidental, then, that the new western territories and states were among the first to allow women to vote in local elections and hold office. Western territories and states also hoped that by allowing women to vote they would attract more women settlers. In 1890, Wyoming was admitted to the Union as the first state that allowed women to vote in all elections. Utah, Colorado, and Idaho followed soon thereafter.

The Fate of Western Indians

> **CORE OBJECTIVE**
> **6.** Evaluate the impact on Native Americans of the federal government's policies in the West after the Civil War.

As settlers spread across the continent from east and west, some 250,000 Native Americans were forced into what was supposed to be their last refuge, the Great Plains and the mountain regions of the Far West. The 1851 Fort Laramie Treaty, in which the chiefs of the Plains tribes agreed to accept definite tribal borders and allow white emigrants to travel across them on wagon trails, worked for a while. Fighting resumed, however, as the emigrants began to settle upon Indian lands rather than merely pass through them.

The Indian Wars

> Sand Creek Massacre

From the early 1860s until the late 1870s, the frontier raged with the so-called **Indian wars**. In the summer of 1862, during the Civil War, an uprising of hungry Sioux warriors killed 644 white traders, settlers, government officials, and soldiers in the Minnesota Valley. Two years later, another horrible incident occurred in Colorado, when the territorial governor persuaded Indians (mostly Cheyenne and Arapaho people) in his territory to gather at Fort Lyon, on Sand Creek in southeastern Colorado near the Kansas border, where they were promised protection. Despite that promise, at dawn on November 29, 1864, Colonel John M. Chivington's untrained militia attacked an Indian camp flying a white flag of truce, slaughtering and then mutilating 165 peaceful Indians—men, women, children, and the elderly—in what one general called the "foulest and most unjustifiable crime

Indian wars Bloody conflicts between U.S. soldiers and Native Americans that raged in the West from the early 1860s to the late 1870s, sparked by American settlers moving into ancestral Indian lands.

in the annals of America." Chivington had told his men to "kill all the Indians you come across." They did. But instead of pacifying the Indians, the Sand Creek Massacre led them to seek revenge. More massacres were to come, on both sides.

Further Indian Relocation

1867 Peace Commission

With other scattered battles erupting, a congressional committee in 1865 gathered evidence on the grisly Indian wars and massacres. Its 1867 "Report on the Condition of the Indian Tribes" led to the creation of an Indian Peace Commission charged with removing the causes of the Indian wars. Congress decided that this would be best accomplished by persuading Indians to move to out-of-the-way federal reservations. The Native Americans were to give up their ancestral lands, in return for peace, so that the whites could move in. In 1870, Indians outnumbered whites in the Dakota Territory by two to one; in 1880, whites outnumbered Indians by more than six to one.

In 1867, a conference at Medicine Lodge, Kansas, ended with the Kiowas, Comanches, Arapahos, and Cheyennes reluctantly accepting land in western Oklahoma. The following spring the Sioux agreed to settle within the Black Hills Reservation in Dakota Territory. But Indian resistance in the southern plains continued until the Red River War of 1874–1875, when General Philip Sheridan forced the Indians to disband in the spring of 1875. Seventy-two Indian chiefs were imprisoned for three years.

Custer and the Sioux

George A. Custer Reckless and glory-seeking Lieutenant Colonel of the U.S. Army.

Meanwhile, trouble was brewing again to the north. White prospectors searching for gold were soon filtering onto the Sioux hunting grounds despite promises that the army would keep them out. In 1874, Lieutenant Colonel George Armstrong Custer, a superb horseman but a reckless, ruthless, glory-seeking officer hated by many of his men, one of whom called him a "petty tyrant," led a thousand soldiers into the Black Hills. His mission was to find the roving bands of Sioux and Cheyenne warriors and force them back onto reservations. If they resisted, his orders were to kill them. The colorful Custer stood out among his men, with long golden hair, a red kerchief around his neck, and a velveteen uniform decorated with golden braid. In 1867 he had been court-martialed for "deserting his command" and was suspended from duty for a year. Now he was in charge of an expedition to attack the wandering bands of Sioux hunting parties, even though he recognized that the Americans had caused the renewal of warfare. As Custer told newspaper reporters, "We are goading the Indians to madness by invading their hallowed [hunting] grounds."

Great Sioux War Conflict between Sioux and Cheyenne Indians and federal troops over lands in the Dakotas in the mid-1870s.

What became the **Great Sioux War** was the largest military campaign since the end of the Civil War. The war lasted fifteen months and entailed fifteen battles in present-day Wyoming, Montana, South Dakota, and Nebraska.

Battle of Little Bighorn, 1876
Amos Bad Heart Bull, an Oglala Sioux artist and historian, painted this scene from the Battle of Little Bighorn.

In June 1876, after several indecisive encounters, the headstrong Custer found the main encampment of Sioux and their Northern Cheyenne and Arapaho allies on the Little Bighorn River in the Montana Territory. Against the advice of his experienced Indian scouts, Custer led his blue-coated men into a death trap on June 25. "Hurrah boys, we've got them," Custer shouted to his men. He assumed that Indians would always flee if confronted by a large, well-trained army unit. He was wrong. Separated from the main body of soldiers and surrounded by a thousand warriors led by the heroic chief Crazy Horse, Custer's detachment of 263 men, their ammunition exhausted, was annihilated. Afterwards, Cheyenne women pierced the dead Custer's eardrums with sewing needles because he had failed to listen to their warnings to stay out of their ancestral lands.

Instead of following up their victory, the Indians celebrated and renewed their hunting. President Ulysses Grant dispatched more troops ("Custer's Avengers") to find them. The army quickly regained the offensive. Warriors were slain, villages destroyed, and food supplies burned. Forced back onto reservations, the remaining Native Americans soon found themselves struggling to survive under harsh conditions. Many of them died of starvation or disease. When a peace commission imposed a settlement, Chief Spotted Tail said: "Tell your people that since the Great Father promised that we should never be removed, we have been moved five times. . . . I think you had better put the Indians on wheels and you can run them about wherever you wish."

The Last Resistance

In the Rocky Mountains and to the west, the same story of courageous yet hopeless resistance was repeated again and again. Indians were the last obstacle to white western expansion, and they suffered as a result. The

Chief Joseph Leader of the Nez Perce, he was widely recognized as a strong, eloquent voice against the injustices suffered by the Native Americans.

Blackfeet and Crows had to leave their homes in Montana. In a war along the California-Oregon boundary, the Modocs held out for six months in 1871–1872 before they were overwhelmed. In 1879 the Utes were forced to give up their vast territories in western Colorado. In Idaho the peaceful Nez Perce bands refused to surrender land along the Salmon River, and prolonged fighting erupted there and in eastern Oregon.

In 1877, Joseph, one of several Nez Perce chiefs, led some 650 of his people on a 1,300-mile journey through Montana in hopes of reaching safety in Canada. Just before reaching the border, they were caught by U.S. soldiers. Joseph delivered an eloquent speech of surrender that served as an epitaph to the Indians' efforts to withstand the march of American empire: "I am tired of fighting. Our chiefs are killed. . . . The old men are all dead. . . . I want to have time to look for my children, and see how many of them I can find. . . . Hear me, my chiefs! I am tired. My heart is sick and sad. From where the sun now stands I will fight no more forever." The Nez Perce asked to return to their ancestral lands in western Idaho, but they were forced to settle in the Indian Territory (Oklahoma), where many died of malaria.

A generation of Indian wars virtually ended in 1886 with the capture of Geronimo, a powerful chief of the Chiricahua Apaches, who had outridden, outwitted, and outfought the more numerous white soldiers in the Southwest for fifteen years. The fighting in Arizona and New Mexico was brutal. Once, the Apaches captured a group of settlers, tied them to their wagon wheels, and roasted them alive. U.S. Army units routinely lynched captured Apaches and treated women and children as combatants. The general in charge of the soldiers who captured Geronimo, exhausted and demoralized, called him "one of the brightest, most resolute, determined-looking men that I have ever encountered."

The Ghost Dance

Massacre at Wounded Knee

The last major clash between Indians and American soldiers occurred in 1890. Late in 1888, Wovoka (or Jack Wilson), a Paiute in western Nevada, fell ill and in a delirium imagined he had visited the spirit world, where he learned of a deliverer coming to rescue the Indians and restore their lands. To hasten their deliverance, he said, the Indians must perform a ceremonial dance that would make them bulletproof in battles with white soldiers. The Ghost Dance craze fed upon old legends of the dead reuniting with the living and bringing prosperity and peace.

The **Ghost Dance movement** spread rapidly. In 1890 the Lakota Sioux adopted it with such passion that it alarmed white authorities. They banned the Ghost Dance on Lakota reservations, but the Indians defied the order and a crisis erupted. On December 29, 1890, a bloodbath occurred at Wounded Knee, South Dakota, after nervous soldiers fired into a group of Indians who had come to surrender. Nearly two hundred Indians and twenty-five soldiers died in the Battle of Wounded Knee. The Indian wars had ended with characteristic brutality and misunderstanding. General

Ghost Dance movement
A spiritual and political movement among Native Americans whose followers performed a ceremonial "ghost dance" intended to connect the living with the dead and make the Native Americans bulletproof in battles intended to restore their homelands.

INDIAN WARS

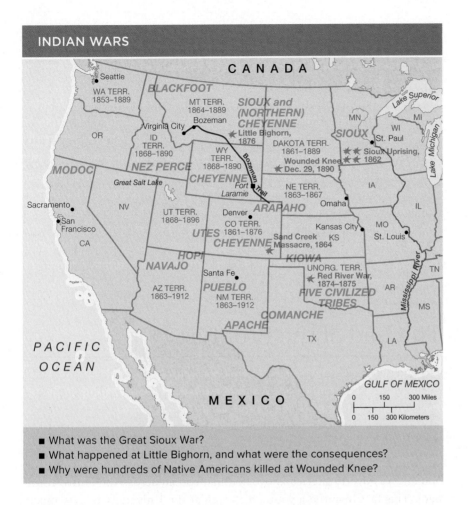

- What was the Great Sioux War?
- What happened at Little Bighorn, and what were the consequences?
- Why were hundreds of Native Americans killed at Wounded Knee?

Philip Sheridan, the commander of U.S. troops in these conflicts, was acidly candid in summarizing how whites had treated the Indians: "We took away their country and their means of support, broke up their mode of living, their habits of life, introduced disease and decay among them, and it was for this and against this that they made war. Could anyone expect less?"

Attempts to Aid Indians

Indeed, many politicians and religious leaders scolded government officials for the persistent mistreatment of Indians. In his annual message of 1877, President Rutherford B. Hayes joined the protest: "Many, if not most, of our Indian wars have had their origin in broken promises and acts of injustice on our part." Helen Hunt Jackson, a novelist and poet, focused attention on the Indian cause in *A Century of Dishonor* (1881), a book that powerfully detailed the sad history of America's exploitation of Native Americans over the centuries.

In part as a reaction to Jackson's book, U.S. policies regarding Indians gradually improved, but they did little to improve the Indians' difficult living conditions and actually helped destroy remnants of their culture. The reservation policy inaugurated by the Peace Commission in 1867 did little more than extend a practice that dated from colonial Virginia. Partly humanitarian in motive, it also saved money: housing and feeding Indians on reservations cost less than fighting them.

Well-intentioned reformers sought to "Americanize" Indians by forcing them to become individual farmers rather than members of bands or tribes. The fruition of such reform efforts came with the **Dawes Severalty Act of 1887**. Sponsored by Senator Henry L. Dawes of Massachusetts, the act divided tribal lands, granting 160 acres to each head of a family and lesser amounts to others. White Bear, a Kiowa chief, expressed a common complaint when he said that he did "not want to settle down in houses you [the federal government] would build for us. I love to roam over the wild prairie. There I am free and happy." But his preferences were not heeded. Between 1887 and 1934, Indians lost an estimated 86 million of their 130 million acres.

CORE **OBJECTIVE**

7. Describe how the South and West had changed by 1900.

The End of the Frontier

The end of Native American resistance was one of several developments at the end of the nineteenth century that marked a transformation in the nation's history. Another involved a historical turning point.

The End of the Frontier Era?

Turner's frontier thesis

The 1890 national census reported that the frontier era in American development was over; Americans by then had spread across the entire continent. This fact inspired a young historian at the University of Wisconsin, Frederick Jackson Turner, to develop his influential "frontier thesis" which argued in 1893 that "the existence of an area of free land, its continuous recession, and the advance of American settlement westward, explain American development."

The frontier, Turner added, had shaped the national character in fundamental ways. It was

> to the frontier [that] the American intellect owes its striking characteristics. That coarseness and strength combined with acuteness and acquisitiveness; that practical, inventive turn of mind, quick to find expedients; that masterful grasp of material things, lacking in the artistic but powerful to effect great ends; that restless, nervous energy; that dominant individualism, working for good and for evil, and withal that buoyancy and exuberance which comes with freedom—these are traits of the frontier, or traits called out elsewhere because of the existence of the frontier.

Dawes Severalty Act of 1887 Federal legislation that divided ancestral Native American lands among the heads of each Indian family in an attempt to "Americanize" Indians by forcing them to become farmers working individual plots of land.

Now, however, Turner stressed, "the frontier has gone and with its going has closed the first period of American history."

Turner's frontier thesis guided several generations of scholars and students in their understanding of the distinctive characteristics of American history. His view of the frontier—as the westward-moving source of the nation's democratic politics, open society, unfettered economy, and rugged individualism—gripped the popular imagination as well.

Turner's frontier was that usually depicted in novels and films. But it left out much of the story. The frontier experience that Turner described was in many respects a self-serving myth involving only Christian white men. He virtually ignored the role of diverse women, African Americans, Native Americans, Hispanics, and Asians in shaping the human geography of the western United States. Turner's frontier was always the site of heroism, triumph, and progress. He ignored the evidence of greed, exploitation, and failure. Turner also implied that the West would be fundamentally different after 1890 because the frontier experience was essentially over. But in many respects the West has retained the qualities associated with the rush for land, gold, timber, and water rights during the post–Civil War decades. The mining frontier, as one historian has recently written, "set a mood that has never disappeared from the West: the attitude of every extractive industry—get in, get rich, get out."

Discontented Farmers

By 1900, both the South and West were quite different places from what they had been in 1865. What they had in common were dramatically changed economic conditions. In the West, the emergence of highly mechanized commercial farming ("bonanza farms") changed the nature of farming. By the end of the nineteenth century, many homesteaders had been forced to abandon their farms and become wage-earning farm laborers, often moving with the seasons to different states to harvest different crops. These migrant workers were often treated as poorly as the sharecroppers in the South. One western worker complained that the landowner "looked at me, his hired hand, as if I was just another work horse."

As discontent rose among farmers and farm workers in the South and the West, a growing number of them joined the People's party, whose followers were known as Populists, a grassroots social and political movement that was sweeping the poorest rural regions of the nation. In 1892, a Minnesota Populist named Ignatius Donnelly told Populists at their national convention that "We meet in the midst of a nation brought to the verge of moral, political, and material ruin." He affirmed that Populism sought "to restore the Government of the Republic to the hands of the 'plain people' with whom it originated." It was the Populist movement that tied the South and West together in an effort to wrest control of the political and economic systems from the East. That struggle would come to define the 1890s and determine the shape of the new twentieth century.

The birth of the Populist party

■ **The New South** Many Southerners embraced the vision of the New South promoted by Henry Grady and others, which called for a more diverse economy with greater industrialization, wider distribution of wealth, and more vocational training. The cotton textile industry grew to surpass that of New England, iron and steel manufacturing increased, and the *American Tobacco Company* became the world's largest manufacturer of cigarettes. But agriculture—and especially the growing of cotton—still dominated the southern economy, much as it had before the Civil War. Land remained concentrated in few hands, and the crop-lien system left much of the population, both black and white, with little choice but to cultivate cotton for these large landholders.

■ **Jim Crow policies in the South** During the 1890s, Southern states disenfranchised the vast majority of African American voters and instituted a series of policies know as Jim Crow laws segregating blacks and whites in all public facilities. Starting with the *Mississippi Plan*, state governments passed a series of comprehensive measures making it impossible for most African Americans, and some poor whites, to vote through poll taxes, grandfather clauses, literacy tests, and residency requirements. Disenfranchisement was followed by legalized segregation, ruled constitutional by the Supreme Court in the 1896 *Plessy v. Ferguson* decision. African Americans who resisted were often the target of violence at the hands of whites, the worst form being organized *lynching*, or public torture, mutilation, and execution of African Americans, usually men. African Americans in the South responded by turning inward and strengthening their own social institutions, demanding the restoration of their civil rights.

■ **Western Migrants** Life in the West was often harsh and violent, but the promise of cheap land or wealth from mining drew settlers from the East.

Although most westerners were white Protestant Americans or immigrants from Germany and Scandinavia, Mexicans, African Americans (the *Exodusters*), and Chinese, as well as many other nationalities, contributed to the West's diversity. About three fourths of those who moved to the West were men.

■ **Miners, Farmers, Ranchers, and Women** Many migrants to the West were attracted to opportunities to mine, ranch, farm, or work on the railroads. Miners were drawn to the discovery of precious minerals such as silver at the *Comstock Lode* in Nevada in 1859. But most miners and cattle ranchers did not acquire wealth, because mining and raising cattle, particularly after the development of barbed wire and the end of the *open range*, became large-scale enterprises run by corporations. Because of the economic hardship and the rugged isolation of life in the West, women there achieved greater equality in everyday life, including voting rights, than did most women elsewhere in the country.

■ **Indian Wars and Policies** By 1900, Native Americans in the West were no longer free to roam the plains, as the influx of miners, ranchers, farmers, and soldiers had curtailed their traditional way of life. Instances of armed resistance, such as the *Great Sioux War*, were crushed. Initially, Indian tribes were forced to sign treaties and were confined to reservations. Beginning in 1887, with the *Dawes Severalty Act*, the American government's Indian policy shifted. It now forced Indians to relinquish their traditional culture and adopt the "American way" of individual landownership.

■ **The South and West in 1900.** In 1893, Frederick Jackson Turner, a prominent historian, declared that the frontier era was over. He argued that the western moving frontier of white settlement had been the nation's primary source of democratic politics and rugged individualism. To a certain extent, they were correct. By 1900, the West resembled the South where agricultural resources were concentrated in the hands of a few. In the 1890s, poor farmers in the West joined with tenant farmers in the South to support the People's Party or the Populist movement, which sought to wrest control of the political and economic system from the powerful East and return it to the "plain" folk. This contest would dominate the nation's politics in the 1890s and set its course for the twentieth century.

KEY TERMS

American Tobacco Company *p. 592*

Redeemers *p. 592*

crop-lien system *p. 593*

sharecroppers *p. 594*

Negrophobia *p. 596*

Mississippi Plan (1890) *p. 597*

"separate but equal" *p. 598*

Atlanta Compromise (1895) *p. 603*

Exodusters *p. 606*

Comstock Lode *p. 607*

Indian wars *p. 615*

Great Sioux War *p. 616*

Ghost Dance movement *p. 618*

Dawes Severalty Act of 1887 *p. 620*

CHRONOLOGY

1859	Comstock Lode is discovered
1862	Congress passes the Homestead Act
1864	Sand Creek Massacre in Colorado
1873	Joseph Glidden invents barbed wire
1876	Battle of Little Bighorn
1880s	Henry Grady spreads the New South idea
1886	Surrender of Geronimo marks the end of the Indian wars
1887	Congress passes the Dawes Severalty Act
1890	Battle of Wounded Knee
	James B. Duke forms the American Tobacco Company
1893	Frederick J. Turner outlines his "frontier thesis"
1900	South surpasses New England in production of cotton fabric

INQUIZITIVE

Go to InQuizitive to see what you've learned—and learn what you've missed—with personalized feedback along the way.

WET NIGHT ON THE BOWERY **(1911)** This scene of early twentieth-century life in New York City by John Sloan captures people of all walks of life converging on a rainy night: a smartly dressed society woman (left), a prostitute (center), and drunks stumbling about further down the block. Running overhead is the elevated train, while an electric trolley gleams from the wet street.

Society and Politics in the Gilded Age

1865–1900

Within three decades after the Civil War, American life experienced a stunning transformation. An agricultural society long rooted in the soil and little involved in global issues became an increasingly urban and industrialized nation deeply entwined in world markets and international politics. The period from the end of the Civil War to the beginning of the twentieth century was labeled the **Gilded Age** for its greed and vulgarity, as the newly rich showed off their enormous wealth that also financed widespread political and corporate corruption. Yet the Gilded Age also saw dramatic changes in other parts of society, including rural America, and in other aspects of social and cultural life.

Between 1865 and 1900, America's urban population skyrocketed from 8 million to 30 million. In 1865, there were fewer than twenty cities with populations over 50,000; by 1900 there were four times that many. Between 1865 and 1900, millions of European and Asian immigrants, as well as migrants from America's rural areas, streamed into cities, attracted by the jobs and excitements they offered. "We cannot all live in cities," cautioned Horace Greeley, the New York newspaper editor and Democratic presidential candidate in 1872, "yet nearly all seem determined to do so."

The populations of some of these cities, like Boston, New York, and Chicago, soared to sizes that many

CORE OBJECTIVES INQUIZITIVE

1. Understand the effects of urban growth during the Gilded Age, including the problems it created.

2. Describe the "new immigrants" of the late nineteenth century and how they were viewed by American society.

3. Explain how urban growth and the increasingly important role of science influenced leisure activities, cultural life, and social policy in the Gilded Age.

4. Assess how the nature of politics during the Gilded Age contributed to political corruption and stalemate.

5. Evaluate the effectiveness of politicians in developing responses to the major economic and social problems of the Gilded Age.

6. Analyze why the money supply became a major political issue during the Gilded Age and describe its impact on American politics.

Americans had never imagined, much less experienced. The growth of huge cities brought an array of problems, among them widespread poverty, unsanitary living conditions, and new forms of political corruption. How to feed, shelter, and educate the new city dwellers taxed the imaginations and resources of government officials. Even more challenging was the development of neighborhoods divided by racial and ethnic background as well as social class. By the 1890s, the largest cities had become explosive centers of unrest.

At the same time that cities were exercising a magnetic pull upon more and more people, scientific researchers were making a dazzling array of discoveries that improved human health, economic productivity, and communications. The advances of modern science stimulated public support for higher education at the graduate as well as the undergraduate level, but they also opened up a gulf of doubt about many long-accepted "truths" and religious beliefs, and led to conflicts over whether or how Charles Darwin's controversial theory of evolution could be applied to human society.

Political life during the Gilded Age was shaped by the close balance of power between Democrats and Republicans nationally and by enthusiastic public participation in politics locally, as well as the often corrupt alliance between industrial tycoons and political leaders in both parties and at all levels of government. The tradition of rewarding party supporters with government jobs drew criticism from reformers who pushed through legislation designed to limit such "patronage." Perhaps the most important underlying political issue of the Gilded Age, however, was the growing tension between city and country, industry and agriculture. In a still predominantly rural nation, millions of financially distressed farmers felt ignored or betrayed by the city-dominated political process. While industrialists and large commercial farmers prospered, small farmers in the South, Midwest, and West struggled with falling crop prices and growing indebtedness to banks, railroads, and what the farmers saw as other symbols of big-city greed and exploitation.

By the 1890s, discontented farmers had put their protest into political form and thrown themselves behind a growing movement seeking to expand ("inflate") the nation's money supply as a way to relieve economic distress. The climactic election of 1896 symbolized the central conflict of the Gilded Age: the clashing cultural and economic values of two Americas—one older, small-scale, and rural America, the other newer, bigger, and urban.

CORE **OBJECTIVE**

1. Understand the effects of urban growth during the Gilded Age, including the problems it created.

America's Move to Town

"The greater part of our population must live in cities," announced Josiah Strong, a prominent Congregationalist minister, in 1898. "There was no resisting the trend." After the Civil War, millions of Americans migrated from rural areas to cities. Many had been pushed off the land by new agricultural machinery that sharply reduced the need for farm workers. Four men could now perform the farm work that earlier had required fourteen. Others were drawn by jobs and other economic opportunities that were concentrated in cities, both old and new. By the end of the nineteenth century, much of the settlement of the West was taking an urban form, with new towns forming around mines and railroad junctions. Still other migrants, bored by rural or small-town life, moved to cities in search of a more exciting cultural life.

While the Far West had the greatest proportion of urban dwellers, concentrated in cities such as San Francisco and Denver, the Northeast and Midwest held far more people in huge cities—New York City, Boston, Philadelphia, Pittsburgh, Chicago, Cincinnati, St. Louis, and others. More and more of these city dwellers could not afford to buy a home; they had little or no money and had nothing but their labor to sell. By 1900, more than 90 percent of the residents of New York City's most densely populated borough, Manhattan, lived in rented houses or in congested, low-cost apartment buildings called **tenements**, where residents, many of them immigrants, were packed like sardines in poorly ventilated and poorly lit apartments.

Growth in All Directions

Several technological advances allowed city buildings to grow higher in order to house the surging populations. In the 1870s, heating innovations, such as steam radiators, enabled the construction of much larger apartment buildings, since coal-burning fireplaces and chimneys, expensive to build, were no longer needed in each apartment. In 1889, the Otis Elevator Company installed the first electric elevator, which made possible much taller buildings; before the 1860s, few structures had been taller than five or six stories. Now they could soar. During the 1880s, engineers developed cast-iron and steel-frame construction techniques that allowed for even taller structures—"skyscrapers."

Cities grew out as well as up, as transportation innovations like horse-drawn streetcars and commuter railways let people live at longer distances from their downtown workplaces. In 1873, San Francisco became the first city to use cable cars that clamped onto a moving underground cable driven by a central power source. Some cities ran steam-powered trains on elevated tracks, but by the 1890s electric trolleys were preferred. Mass transit received an added boost from underground subway trains built in Boston, New York City, and Philadelphia.

The new commuter trains and trolleys allowed a growing middle class of business executives and professionals (accountants, doctors, engineers, sales clerks, teachers, store managers, and attorneys) to retreat from crowded downtowns and live in quieter, tree-lined "streetcar suburbs." But the working poor, many of them immigrants or African Americans, could rarely afford to leave the inner cities. As their populations grew, cities

Skyscrapers and suburbs

Gilded Age (1860–1896) An era of dramatic industrial and urban growth characterized by widespread political corruption and loose government oversight of corporations.

tenements Shabby, low-cost inner-city apartment buildings that housed the urban poor in cramped, un-ventilated apartments.

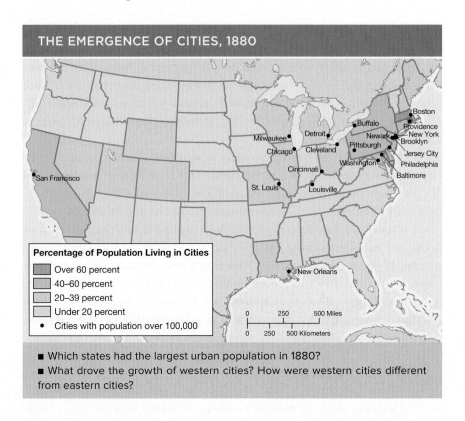

THE EMERGENCE OF CITIES, 1880

Percentage of Population Living in Cities

- Over 60 percent
- 40–60 percent
- 20–39 percent
- Under 20 percent
- • Cities with population over 100,000

■ Which states had the largest urban population in 1880?
■ What drove the growth of western cities? How were western cities different from eastern cities?

became dangerously congested and plagued with fires, violent crimes, and contagious diseases.

Crowds, Dirt, and Disease

Packed tenement housing

The wonders of big cities—their glittering new electric lights, streetcars, telephones, department stores, theaters, and many other attractions—were magnetic lures for rural youth bored by the routines of isolated farm life. In times of rural depression, thousands moved to the cities in search of economic opportunity and personal freedom. Yet in doing so they often traded one set of problems for another. In New York City in 1900, some 2.3 million people, two-thirds of the city's entire population, were living in overcrowded and often filthy tenement housing. Such rapid urban growth—much of it completely unregulated by municipal officials—affected sanitation, health, and morale. "The only trouble with New York City," said writer Mark Twain, "is that it is too large. You cannot accomplish anything in the way of business . . . without devoting a whole day to it. The distances are too great."

Tenement apartment buildings were usually six to eight stories tall, lacking elevators, and jammed so tightly against one another that most of the apartments had little or no natural light or fresh air. Such buildings

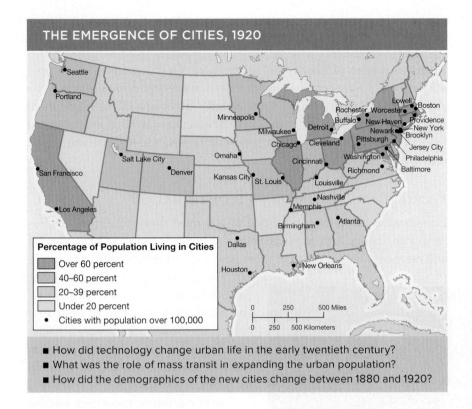

THE EMERGENCE OF CITIES, 1920

Percentage of Population Living in Cities
- Over 60 percent
- 40–60 percent
- 20–39 percent
- Under 20 percent
- Cities with population over 100,000

- How did technology change urban life in the early twentieth century?
- What was the role of mass transit in expanding the urban population?
- How did the demographics of the new cities change between 1880 and 1920?

typically housed twenty-four to thirty-two families, usually with lots of children who had few places to play except in the streets. On average, there was only one toilet (called a *privy*) for every twenty people. In one New York tenement apartment, twelve adults slept in a room only thirteen feet square.

Late-nineteenth-century cities were dirty, smelly, and disease-ridden. Streets were filled with contaminated water, horse urine and manure, and roaming pigs. Garbage and raw sewage were carelessly dumped into streets and waterways, causing epidemics of infectious diseases such as cholera, typhoid fever, and yellow fever. In one poor Chicago district at the end of the century, three of every five babies died before their first birthday.

So-called sanitary reformers—public health officials and engineers—eventually created cleaner conditions in tenements by creating regulations requiring more space per resident as well as more windows and plumbing facilities. Reformers also pushed successfully for new water and sewage systems and for regular trash collection, which by 1900 had been adopted in nearly all American cities. The many animals in cities were a huge sanitary challenge. Reformers lobbied to ban slaughterhouses as well as the raising of hogs and cattle within city limits, and to replace horse-drawn trolleys with electric-powered streetcars or trolleys.

> Unsanitary conditions and "sanitary reformers"

CORE **OBJECTIVE**

2. Describe the "new immigrants" of the late nineteenth century and how they were viewed by American society.

The New Immigration

America's roaring prosperity and the promise of political and religious freedom attracted waves of new immigrants from every part of the globe in the years after the Civil War. By 1900, nearly 30 percent of the residents of major cities were foreign-born. These newcomers provided much-needed labor, but their arrival in such huge numbers sparked racial and ethnic tensions.

A Surge of Newcomers from Europe

Immigration has always been one of the most powerful forces shaping American history. This was especially true between 1860 and 1920, as more and more immigrants, most of them poor, arrived from eastern and southern Europe in search of better living conditions and freedom from political and religious oppression. In 1890, four out of five New Yorkers were foreign-born, a higher proportion than in any other city in the world. Chicago was not far behind.

Rapidly growing industries seeking low-wage workers—including mines, railroads, mills, and factories—sent recruiting agents abroad to stir up interest in migration to the United States. Under the Contract Labor Act of 1864, the federal government helped pay for immigrants' travel expenses to America. The law was repealed in 1868, but not until 1885 did the government stop companies from importing foreign laborers, a practice that put immigrant workers under the control of their employers. The tide of immigration rose from just under 3 million annually in the 1870s to more than 5 million in the 1880s. It fell to a little over 3.5 million in the 1890s before rising to its record level of nearly 9 million per year in the first decade of the twentieth century.

Ellis Island To accommodate the soaring numbers of immigrants passing through New York, Congress built a reception center on Ellis Island, near the Statue of Liberty. Pictured here is its registry room, where immigrants awaited close questioning by officials.

The so-called old immigrants who came before 1880 were mainly Protestants and Roman Catholics from northern and western Europe. This pattern began to change, however, as the proportion of immigrants from southern and eastern Europe, especially Russia, Poland, Greece, and Italy, rose sharply. After 1890, these "**new immigrants**" made up a majority of the newcomers, and by the first decade of the new century, they formed 70 percent. Their languages and cultural backgrounds were markedly

new immigrants Wave of newcomers from southern and eastern Europe, including many Jews, who became a majority among immigrants to America after 1890.

different from those of most "old immigrants" as well as most native-born Americans. The dominant religions of the new immigrants, for example, were Judaism, Eastern Orthodox, and Roman Catholicism, whereas Protestants still formed a large majority of the total U.S. population.

In 1907 Congress appointed the bipartisan Dillingham Commission to examine the changes in immigration patterns to the United States. After four years of analysis and hearings, it released a 41-volume report in 1911. The Commission concluded that the "new" immigration that emerged in the 1880s and after involved dramatic differences from previous patterns. Most who had come under the "old" immigration had "mingled freely with . . . native Americans," and thus were assimilated. The new immigration that had begun around 1883, however, "was marked by an increase in transient, unskilled laborers who flocked to urban enclaves where they resisted assimilation." As a class of people, the "new" immigrants were "far less intelligent than the old, approximately one-third of all those over 14 years of age when admitted being illiterate. Racially, they are for the most part essentially unlike the British, German and other peoples who came during the prior period to 1880, and generally speaking they are actuated in coming by different ideals, for the old immigration came to be a part of the country, while the new in a large measure, comes with the intention of profiting, in a pecuniary way, by the superior advantages of the new world and then returning to the old country."

Strangers in a New Land

Once on American soil, immigrants who had not been brought over by an employer were usually desperately poor and needed to find jobs—quickly. Many were greeted at the docks by family and friends who had come over before them, others by representatives of immigrant-aid societies or by company agents offering low-paying and often dangerous jobs in mines, mills, or sweatshops and on railroads. Since most immigrants knew little if any English and nothing about American employment practices, they were easy targets for exploitation. Many unwittingly lost a healthy percentage of their wages to unscrupulous hiring agents in exchange for a bit of whiskey and a job. Other companies eager for workers gave immigrants train tickets to inland cities such as Buffalo, Pittsburgh, Cleveland, Chicago, Milwaukee, Cincinnati, and St. Louis.

Employer exploitation of immigrants

As strangers in America, most immigrants naturally wanted to live in neighborhoods populated by people from their homeland. The largest cities had vibrant immigrant districts with names such as Little Italy, Little Hungary, and Chinatown, which served as transitional communities between the newcomers' Old World past and their New World future. In these communities, immigrants practiced their native religions and customs, and spoke as well as read newspapers in their native languages. But they paid a price for such community solidarity. When "new immigrants" moved into

Immigrant neighborhoods

Mulberry Street, 1900 This photograph captures the many Italian immigrants who made Mulberry Street in downtown New York City their home at the turn of the century. Horse-drawn carts weave through people shopping, socializing, and people-gazing.

an area, the previous residents often moved out, taking with them whatever social prestige and political influence they had achieved. Living conditions in such neighborhoods often quickly deteriorated as housing and sanitation codes went unenforced.

The Nativist Response

Racism leads to restrictions on immigration

Then, as now, many native-born Americans saw the wave of "new immigrants" as a threat to their way of life and their jobs. Many of these "**nativists**" were also racists who believed that "Anglo-Saxon" Americans—people of British or Germanic background—were superior to the Slavic, Italian, Greek, and Jewish newcomers. A Stanford University professor, for instance, called the immigrants from southern and eastern Europe "illiterate, docile, lacking in self-reliance and initiative, and not possessing the Anglo-Teutonic conceptions of law, order, and government." Indeed, many of the new immigrants were illiterate, but others only appeared so because they could not speak or read English. Some desperate immigrants resorted to crime, encouraging suspicions that European nations were sending their criminals to America.

Throughout American history, Congress has passed laws regulating immigration that have been inconsistent in their goals and frequently rooted in racial and ethnic prejudice. During the late nineteenth century, such prejudice took an especially ugly turn against the Chinese, who suffered discrimination even beyond that leveled at the "new immigrants" from Europe. By 1880, some 75,000 Chinese formed about a ninth of the population of California. Their visible differences made them easy targets for

nativists Native-born Americans motivated by racial prejudice who blamed immigrants for social or economic problems and sought to restrict their access to America.

discrimination. They were not white, they were not Christian, and many could not read or write. Whites resented them for supposedly taking their jobs, although in many instances the Chinese were willing to do the menial work that whites refused to do. For these and other reasons, Congress in 1882 passed the **Chinese Exclusion Act**, the first federal law to restrict immigration on the basis of race. The act, which barred any more Chinese laborers from entering the country for the next ten years, was periodically renewed before being extended indefinitely in 1902. Not until 1943 were barriers to Chinese immigration finally removed.

But the Chinese were not the only group targeted. In 1891, nativists formed the Immigration Restriction League to save the Anglo-Saxon "race" from being "contaminated" by "alien" immigrants. The League sought to convince Congress to ban immigrants who were illiterate, even though illiterate immigrants from Britain and Germany had been allowed into the United States in the past. Three presidents vetoed bills banning illiterate immigrants: Grover Cleveland in 1897, William H. Taft in 1913, and Woodrow Wilson in 1915 and 1917. The last time, however, Congress overrode the veto.

Chinese Exclusion Act The Chinese caricature of John Chinaman is escorted out of America by Lady Liberty with his ironing board and opium pipe, while other accepted minorities look on.

Changes in Popular and Intellectual Culture

The flood of people into cities brought changes in patterns of recreation and leisure. Middle- and upper-class families, especially those who had moved to streetcar suburbs, often spent free time together at home, singing around a piano, reading novels, or playing games—cards, dominoes, backgammon, chess, and checkers. In congested urban areas, politics as a form of public entertainment attracted ever larger crowds, saloons became even more popular social centers for working-class men, and new forms of mass entertainment—movie theaters, music halls, vaudeville shows, art museums, symphony orchestras, and circuses—appealed to a broad cross-section of city residents.

Urbanization and technological progress also contributed to the prestige of modern science, which increased enormously during the second half of the nineteenth century. By encouraging what one writer called a "mania for facts," scientists generated changes throughout social, intellectual, and cultural life. "I tell you these are great times," the writer and social critic Henry Adams wrote to his brother in 1862. "Man has mounted science and is now run away." Scientific research led to transformational technologies

CORE **OBJECTIVE**

3. Explain how urban growth and the increasingly important role of science influenced leisure activities, cultural life, and social policy in the Gilded Age.

Chinese Exclusion Act (1882) Federal law that barred Chinese laborers from immigrating to America.

such as electrical power and lights, telephones, phonographs, motion pictures, bicycles, and automobiles.

Urban Leisure and Entertainment Options

Old and new forms of mass entertainment

Although only men could vote in most states, both men and women flocked to hear candidates speak at political party meetings. In the largest cities, membership in a political party offered many of the same benefits as belonging to a club or a college fraternity, as local political organizations provided lots of social activities in addition to promoting new candidates. As labor unions became increasingly common, they too took on social roles for working-class men.

The sheer number of city dwellers also helped generate new forms of mass entertainment, such as traveling Wild West shows, vaudeville shows featuring singers, dancers, and comedians, cycling, and spectator sports. In the last quarter of the nineteenth century, college football and basketball and professional baseball began attracting many fans. In large cities, the new streetcar transit systems helped people gather easily for sporting events, and rooting for the home team helped unify a city's ethnic and racial groups and social classes. By the end of the century, sports of all kinds had become a major part of American popular culture.

Vaudeville For as little as one cent for admission, vaudeville shows aimed to please the tastes of their wildly diverse audience with a great range of entertainment.

The popularity of saloons

Still, the most popular leisure destinations for the urban working class were not athletic stadiums but saloons, beer gardens, and dance halls. By 1900, the United States had more saloons (over 325,000) than grocery stores and meat markets. New York City alone had 10,000 saloons, or one for every 500 residents.

The saloon served as the workingman's social club, offering fellowship to men who often worked ten hours a day, six days a week. Saloons were especially popular among male immigrants seeking companionship. In cities such as New York, Boston, Philadelphia, and Chicago, the customers were disproportionately Irish, German, and Italian Catholics, who tended to vote Democratic partly because the "temperance" organizations that tried to close down saloons were led by Protestant Republicans. Politics was often the topic of discussion in saloons; in fact, in New York City in the 1880s, saloons doubled as polling places, where patrons could cast their votes in local elections. One journalist called the saloon "the social and intellectual center of the neighborhood."

Besides drinking, socializing, and talking politics, men also went to saloons to check job postings, engage in labor union activities, cash paychecks, mail letters, read newspapers, and gossip about neighborhood affairs. Because saloons were heated and offered public restrooms, they also served as places of refuge for the homeless, especially in the winter. Patrons could play chess, billiards, darts, cards, dice, or even handball, since many saloons included gymnasiums. Although the main bar room was for men only, women and children were allowed to enter a side door to buy a pail of beer to carry home (a task called "rushing the growler"). Some saloons also provided "snugs," separate rooms for women customers. About a third of saloons, called "stall saloons," included "wine rooms" where prostitutes worked.

Urban women and leisure

Married working-class women had even less leisure time than working-class men. Many of them were working for pay themselves, at least part-time, and even those who were not were frequently overwhelmed by housework and childrearing responsibilities. As a social worker noted, "The men have the saloons, political clubs, trade-unions or [fraternal] lodges for their recreation . . . while the mothers have almost no recreation, only a dreary round of work, day after day, with occasionally doorstep gossip to vary the monotony of their lives." Married working-class women often used the streets as their public space. Washing clothes, supervising children at play, or shopping at the local market provided opportunities for socializing with other women.

Single women, many of whom worked as domestic servants ("maids") who had more time than working mothers for leisure and recreation, flocked to dance halls, theaters, amusement parks, and picnic grounds. With the advent of movie theaters during the second decade of the twentieth century, the cinema became the most popular form of entertainment for working women. As an advertisement for a theater promised, "If you are tired of life, go to the movies. If you are sick of troubles rife, go to the picture show. You will forget your unpaid bills, rheumatism and other ills, if you stow your pills and go to the picture show."

The Impact of Darwinism

Virtually every field of thought during the Gilded Age felt the impact of English scientist Charles Darwin's controversial book *On the Origin of Species* (1859), whose first edition sold out in one day. Basing his conclusions on extensive research, Darwin argued that most organisms produce many more offspring than can survive. Those offspring with certain favorable characteristics tend to live while others die from disease or predators. This process of "natural selection" over many millions of years, Darwin said, had

Charles Darwin Darwin's scientific theories introduced and influenced more than a century of political and social debate.

led to the evolution of modern species from less complex forms of life; individuals and species that had characteristics advantageous for survival had successfully reproduced, while others fell by the wayside. Fossils revealed a natural history of conflict, pain, and species extinction. As Darwin wrote, "the vigorous, the healthy, and the happy survive and multiply."

The idea of biological evolution was shocking because most people in Europe and America still embraced a literal interpretation of the biblical creation story. Although Darwin himself had trained for the ministry and was reluctant to be drawn into religious controversy, his biological findings suggested to many, then and since, that there was no providential God controlling the universe and that people were no different from plants and animals, that they too evolved by trial and error rather than by God's purposeful hand.

These ideas—as well as the implications that people drew from them—generated heated arguments. Many Christians charged that Darwin's ideas led to atheism, a denial of the existence of God, while others found their faith severely shaken not only by evolutionary theory but also by new scientific standards of scholarly analysis that were being applied to the Bible itself. Most of the faithful, however, came to reconcile science and religion. They decided that the process of evolutionary change occurring in nature must be God's doing.

Social Darwinism

Although Darwin's complex theory of evolution applied only to biological phenomena, many drew broader implications from it, as the temptation to apply evolutionary theory to human society proved irresistible. Darwin's fellow Englishman Herbert Spencer, a leading social philosopher, was the first major prophet of what came to be called **Social Darwinism**. Spencer argued that human society and its institutions, like the organisms studied by Darwin, evolved through the same process of natural selection. The "survival of the fittest," in Spencer's chilling phrase, was the engine of social progress. By encouraging people, ideas, and nations to compete with one another for dominance, society, according to Spencer, would generate "the greatest perfection and the most complete happiness."

Darwin himself dismissed Spencer's social theories, objecting in particular to his assumption that the evolutionary process in the natural world had any relevance to human social institutions. Others, however, eagerly endorsed the notion of Social Darwinism. If, as Spencer believed, society naturally evolved for the better through "survival of the fittest," then government interference with human competition in the marketplace was a serious mistake because it would help "unfit" people survive and thereby hinder progress. Social Darwinism implied the need for hands-off, laissez-faire government policies; it argued against the regulation of business, for example, or of required minimum standards for sanitation and housing. To

Social Darwinism The application of Charles Darwin's theory of evolutionary natural selection to human society; Social Darwinists used the concept of "survival of the fittest" to justify class distinctions, explain poverty, and oppose government intervention in the economy.

Spencer and his many followers, the only acceptable charity was voluntary, and even that was of dubious value. Spencer warned that "fostering the good-for-nothing [people] at the expense of the good, is an extreme cruelty" to the health of civilization.

For Spencer and his many American supporters, successful business-men and corporations provided proof of the concept of "survival of the fit-test." If the unregulated process of capitalist development led to small businesses being destroyed or acquired by huge corporate monopolies, that too was simply a necessary phase of the evolutionary process. Oil tycoon John D. Rockefeller revealed his own embrace of Social Darwinism when he told his Baptist Sunday-school class that the "growth of a large business is merely a survival of the fittest.... This is not an evil tendency in business. It is merely the working-out of a law of nature and a law of God."

Popular Science Monthly, founded in 1872, became the chief magazine for promoting Social Darwinism in the United States. That year, Spencer's chief academic disciple, William Graham Sumner, began teaching at Yale University, where he preached the gospel of natural selection. Sumner's most lasting contribution, made in his book *Folkways* (1907), was to argue that it would be a mistake for government to try to promote equality, since doing so would interfere with the "survival of the fittest."

Reform Darwinism

Sumner's efforts to use Darwinism to promote "rugged individualism" and oppose government regulation of business and efforts at social reform pro-voked strong criticism and inspired an alternative use of Darwinism in the context of human society. What came to be called Reform Darwinism found its major advocate in Lester Frank Ward, a federal government em-ployee who fought his way up from poverty and never lost his empathy for the underdog. Ward's book *Dynamic Sociology* (1883) singled out one as-pect of evolution that both Darwin and Spencer had neglected: the human brain. True, as Sumner claimed, people, like animals, compete, but as Ward explained, people also collaborate; unlike animals, people can plan for a distant future; they have minds capable of shaping and directing social change. Far from being the helpless object of irresistible evolutionary forces, Ward argued, humanity could actively control the process of social evolution through long-range planning.

Ward's Reform Darwinism thus posed a direct challenge to Sumner's conservative Social Darwinism, holding that *cooperation*, not competition, would better promote social progress. Government, in Ward's view, could contribute to social progress by pursuing two main goals: alleviating pov-erty, which impeded the development of the mind, and promoting the edu-cation of the masses. "Intelligence, far more than necessity," Ward wrote, "is the mother of invention," and "the influence of knowledge as a social factor, like that of wealth, is proportional to the extent of its distribution."

Intellect, informed by science, could foster social improvement. As the intellectual justification for social progress, Ward's concept of Reform Darwinism would prove to be one of the pillars of the "progressive" movement that would improve the quality of life in modern America during the late nineteenth century and after.

Realism in Literature and Art

Before the Civil War, romanticism had dominated American literature and painting. Romantics such as the transcendentalists in New England believed that fundamental truths rested in the unseen world of ideas and spirit. The most prominent writers and artists before the Civil War were more concerned with romantic or biblical themes than with the everyday life around them.

During the second half of the nineteenth century, however, a new generation of writers and artists calling themselves "realists" began to challenge this romantic tradition. A writer in *Putnam's Monthly* noted in 1854 a growing emphasis in American life on "the real and the practical." This emphasis on "realism" matured into a full-fledged cultural force during the late nineteenth century as more and more writers and artists focused their attention on depicting the actual aspects of urban-industrial America: scientific research and technology, factories and railroads, cities and immigrants, labor unions and social tensions.

The rise of such cultural realism resulted from a transformed social, intellectual, and moral landscape. For many Americans, the horrors of the Civil War led to a less romanticized and more realistic view of life. An editor attending an art exhibition in 1865 sensed "the greater reality of feeling developed by the war. We have grown more sober, perhaps, and less patient of romantic idealism."

Another factor contributing to the rise of realism was the impact of modern science. "This is a world of reality," admitted a romantic writer, "and romance breaks against the many hard facts." The new "scientific age," she claimed, valued only "facts that can be seen or heard or weighed or measured." The "stupendous power of Science," announced one editor, will rid American thought of "every old-time idea, every trace of old romance and art, poetry and romantic or sentimental feeling" and wash away the "ideal . . . and visionary."

Realism, as writer Fanny Bates stressed, appealed especially to people living in the busy, swarming cities, people "whose lives are crowded with a variety of interests." Money was what attracted most people to the cities, and the worship of money was the most common theme in realistic novels and short stories during the Gilded Age. In William Dean Howells's *The Rise of Silas Lapham* (1885), for example, Bromfield Corey announces that money "is the romance, the poetry of our age." Lily Bart, the heroine of Edith Wharton's novel *The House of Mirth* (1905), declares that she

***Stag at Sharkey's* (1909)** New York painter George Bellows witnessed such explosive boxing matches across the street from his studio, at the saloon of retired heavyweight boxer, "Sailor" Sharkey. Bellows is one of the most famous artists from the Ashcan School, which was committed to capturing the gritty reality of the urban scene.

"must have a great deal of money" to be happy in the fashionable circles of a large city.

City streets and parks also provided countless scenes of *real* life to depict on canvas and in words. Realistic writers and artists loved to stroll city streets, window-shopping and people-watching, consuming what the magisterial novelist Henry James called the "spectacle of the world's presence." The daily urban scene, he said, unleashed a "flood of the real" for writers and artists to study and portray. The New York City painter John Sloan chose his subjects from his habit of spying on people from his Manhattan studio. He confided in his diary that he was addicted to *"watching every bit* of human life" through his windows and along the sidewalks. Others shared his "spectatorial" sensibility. "My favorite pastime," writer Theodore Dreiser remembered, "was to walk the city streets and view the lives and activities of others." His fictional characters did the same. In Dreiser's influential novel *Sister Carrie* (1900), Carrie Meeber uses her "gift of observation" to view strangers through the open windows of shops, offices, and factories, imagining what "they deal with, how they labored, to what end it all came."

The realists' emphasis on closely observing everyday reality grew out of the scientific spirit. Just as scientists observed visible and verifiable facts and transformed them into knowledge, cultural realists studied the world around them and made it into art and literature. Like a gust of fresh air, they made Americans aware of the significance of their everyday surroundings in all their beauty and ugliness.

CORE **OBJECTIVE**

4. Explain how the nature of politics during the Gilded Age contributed to political corruption and stalemate.

Gilded Age Politics

Like William Graham Sumner, many elected officials after the Civil War believed that governments should do as little as possible, so as to allow for the natural evolution of the economy and society. The Gilded Age was an era that saw more political corruption than political innovation. As a young college graduate in 1879, future president Woodrow Wilson described the state of the political system as "No leaders, no principles." The real movers and shakers of the Gilded Age were not the men who sat in the White House or Congress but those who owned the huge corporations. These "captains of industry," labeled "robber barons" by critics, regularly used their wealth to "buy" elections and favors from both major political parties and at all levels of government. Jay Gould, one of the most aggressive railroad giants, admitted that he elected "the [New York] legislature with my own money."

Corporate-funded corruption

The activities of "special interests," those businesses that bought favors from government officials, dominated Gilded Age politics. As President Rutherford B. Hayes confessed, the "real difficulty" with the political system of his time was "the vast wealth and power in the hands of the few and unscrupulous who represent or control capital." By the end of the nineteenth century, however, new political movements and parties were pushing reforms to deal with the many excesses and injustices created by a political system that had grown corrupt in its support for the "special interests" of Big Business.

Local Politics and Party Loyalties

A local rather than federal focus

Perhaps the most important feature of Gilded Age politics was its local focus. Americans of the time expected little direct support from the federal government, and most political activity occurred at the state and local levels. Unlike today, the federal government was an insignificant force in the daily lives of most Americans, in part because it was so small. In 1871 the entire federal civilian workforce totaled 51,000 (most of them postal workers), of whom only 6,000 actually worked in Washington, D.C. Not until the twentieth century did the importance of the federal government begin to surpass that of local and state governments. During the Gilded Age, in fact, large cities as a group spent far more on local services than did the federal government, and three-fourths of all public employees worked for state and local governments.

Political parties as social networks and forms of recreation

Americans during the Gilded Age were intensely loyal to their political party, which they joined as much for the social fellowship and networking connections as for its positions on issues. Attending political speeches and gatherings was a major form of public recreation, and party loyalists eagerly read newspaper coverage of political issues and joined in rallies, picnics, and parades.

Bribery, patronage, and boss rule

Party members paid dues to join, and party leaders were so powerful in promoting their "special interests" that they demanded campaign contributions from the most powerful captains of industry and finance. Collis Huntington, a California railroad tycoon, admitted that bribery in the form of campaign contributions was regularly expected in Congress: "If you have to pay money to have the right thing done, then it is only just and fair to do it." Roscoe Conkling, a powerful Republican senator from New York, was equally candid about the role of corruption: "Of course, we do rotten things in New York. . . . Politics is a rotten business." The Democrats were no better. Horatio Seymour, a Democratic governor of New York and a presidential candidate in 1868, explained that "our people want men in office who will not steal, but who will not interfere with those who do."

In cities crowded with new immigrant voters, politics was usually controlled by "rings"—small groups of powerful insiders who shaped policy and managed the nomination and election of candidates. Each ring typically had a powerful **party "boss,"** an absolute ruler who used his "machine"—a network of neighborhood activists and officials—to govern. Bosses staged election parades, fireworks displays, and free banquets—with alcoholic beverages—for voters. They helped settle local disputes, provided aid for the needy, and distributed government jobs and contracts to loyal followers and corporate donors. Throughout most of the nineteenth century, almost every government job—local, state, and federal—was subject to the latest election results. This meant that the party in power expected government employees to become campaign workers and to do the bidding of party bosses during elections.

Party bosses, often arrogant and dictatorial in their behavior, decided who the candidates would be, often determined the party's positions on significant issues, and commanded loyalty and obedience by rewarding and punishing their members. Once in power, the bosses excelled at **patronage**, the long-standing system whereby party leaders rewarded supporters with government jobs and contracts—the so-called spoils of office. It was—and remains—a system that invited abuse and corruption. As President Ulysses S. Grant's secretary told a Republican party boss, "I only hope you will distribute the patronage in such a manner as will help the Administration."

William "Boss" Tweed A larger-than-life political boss was New York City's William "Boss" Tweed, whose powerful connections made "no prison big enough to hold the Boss."

Partisan Politics at the National Level

Several factors gave national politics during the Gilded Age its distinctive texture. First, the national political parties were much more powerful forces than they are today. Party loyalty was intense, often extending over generations in many families. A second distinctive element of Gilded Age politics at the national level was the close division between Republicans and Democrats in Congress. Both parties avoided controversial issues or bold initiatives because neither was dominant. The third important aspect of post–Civil War politics was the intensity of voter involvement at all

party "boss" A powerful political leader who controlled a "machine" of associates and operatives to promote both individual and party interests, often using informal tactics such as intimidation or the patronage system.

patronage An informal system (sometimes called the "spoils system") used by politicians to reward their supporters with government appointments or contracts.

levels—local and state as well as national. Voter turnout during the Gilded Age was commonly about 70–80 percent. (By contrast, the turnout for the 2012 presidential election was 58 percent.)

Balanced national parties, evenly divided Congress, and intense voter involvement

During the Gilded Age, most voters cast their ballots for the same party year after year, generation after generation, regardless of the candidates. Party loyalty was often an emotional choice. In the 1870s and 1880s, for example, people north and south continued to fight the Civil War during political campaigns. Republican candidates regularly "waved the bloody shirt," encouraging war veterans to "vote like you shot," while accusing Democrats of having caused "secession and civil war." Democrats, especially in the South, responded to such attacks by reminding voters that they stood for limited government, states' rights, and white supremacy. Republicans tended to favor high tariffs on imports, but Democrats also supported tariffs if they benefited businesses in their districts. Third parties, such as the Greenbackers, Populists, and Prohibitionists, appealed to specific interests and issues, such as currency inflation, railroad regulations, or legislation to restrict alcohol consumption.

National politics and party loyalties: Regional, religious, and ethnic divisions

Party loyalties reflected religious and ethnic divisions as well as geographic ones. After the Civil War, the Republican party remained strongest in the North and West and weakest in the South. It attracted mainly Protestants of British descent. As the party of Abraham Lincoln (the "Great Emancipator") and Ulysses Grant, Republicans could also rely upon the votes of African Americans in the South (until their right to vote was taken away late in the century) and of a large bloc of Union veterans of the Civil War, who were organized into a powerful national fraternal group called the Grand Army of the Republic. The Democrats, by contrast, were a more diverse and often unruly coalition of southern whites, northern immigrants, Roman Catholics, Jews, freethinkers, and those repelled by the Protestant Republican "party of morality." As one Chicago Democrat explained, "A Republican is a man who wants you t' go t' church every Sunday. A Democrat says if a man wants to have a glass of beer on Sunday he can have it."

National politics with Congress evenly divided

As this quotation suggests, in the 1880s efforts to restrict or prohibit alcoholic beverages revived among Republicans, along with nativist policies designed to restrict immigration and the employment of foreigners. Among the immigrants crowded into the growing cities were many Irish, Germans, and Italians, all of whom had brought their robust drinking traditions with them into their new country. The mostly rural Republican Protestants considered saloons the central social evil around which all others revolved, and they associated these evils with the ethnic groups that frequented saloons. Carrie Nation, the most colorful member of the Women's Christian Temperance Union (WCTU), became nationally known for attacking saloons with a hatchet. Saloons, she argued, stripped a married woman of everything by turning working men into alcoholics, as had happened with Nation's first husband: "Her husband is torn from her, she is robbed of her sons, her home, her food, and her virtue."

Between 1869 and 1913, from the first term of President Ulysses S. Grant through the election of William Howard Taft, Republicans monopolized the White House except for the two nonconsecutive terms of New York Democrat Grover Cleveland. Otherwise, however, national politics was remarkably balanced between the two major parties. Between 1872 and 1896, their strength was so closely divided that, because of support for third party candidates, *no* president won a majority of the popular vote. In each of those presidential elections, sixteen states invariably voted Republican and fourteen voted Democratic, leaving six states whose results determined the outcome. The swing-vote role played by two of those states, New York and Ohio, decided the election of eight presidents from 1872 to 1908.

No chief executive between Abraham Lincoln and Theodore Roosevelt could be described as a "strong" president. All believed that Congress, not the White House, should formulate major policies. As Senator John Sherman of Ohio stressed, "the President should merely obey and enforce the law."

Corruption and Reform: Hayes to Harrison

> CORE **OBJECTIVE**
> **5.** Evaluate the effectiveness of politicians in developing responses to the major economic and social problems of the Gilded Age.

Both Republicans and Democrats had their share of corrupt officials willing to buy and sell government jobs or legislative votes, yet as early as the 1870s, in response to the corruption uncovered in the Grant administration, each party also developed factions promoting honesty in government. The struggle for "clean" government became one of the foremost issues of the Gilded Age.

Hayes and Civil Service Reform

President Rutherford B. Hayes brought to the White House in 1877 both a lingering controversy over the disputed election results (critics called him "His Fraudulency") and a new style of uprightness that was in sharp contrast to the barely concealed graft of the Grant era. The son of an Ohio farmer, Hayes was wounded four times in the Civil War. He went on to serve in Congress and as governor of Ohio. Stubbornly honest and conservative, he was, said a Republican journalist, a "third-rate nonentity" whose only virtue was that he was "obnoxious to no one."

Hayes had been the compromise presidential nominee of the two factions fighting for control of the Republican party, the so-called Stalwarts and Half-Breeds, led, respectively, by Senators Roscoe Conkling of New York and James G. Blaine of Maine. The Stalwarts had been "stalwart" in their support of President Grant during the furor over the misdeeds of his cabinet members. Further, they had mastered the "spoils system" of distributing political jobs to party loyalists. The Half-Breeds were called such because they supposedly were only half-loyal to Grant and half-committed to reform of the spoils system. But the two warring Republican factions existed primarily to advance the careers of Conkling and Blaine, who detested each other. Blaine once charged that Conkling and the Stalwarts were "all the desperate bad men, bent on loot and booty."

Republican resistance to Hayes's reform efforts

To his credit, President Hayes tried to stay above the petty political bickering. He joined the growing public outrage over political corruption, admitting that his party "must mend its ways" by focusing on Republican principles rather than fighting over the spoils of office. "He serves his party best who serves his country best," Hayes declared in announcing that it was time "for **civil service** [government jobs] **reform**." He appointed a committee to consider a "merit system" for hiring government employees, as used in some European countries, and a new practice in Britain in which civil service jobs were awarded on the basis of competitive written tests. In a dramatic gesture, Hayes also fired Chester A. Arthur, a Stalwart Republican who ran the New York Customs House, because Arthur had abused the patronage system in ways, according to Hayes, that promoted "ignorance, inefficiency, and corruption."

Hayes's commitment to cleaning up politics enraged Republican leaders. In 1879, Ohio Congressman James Garfield warned Hayes that "if he wishes to hold any influence" with fellow Republicans, he "must abandon some of his notions of Civil Service reform." For his part, Hayes confessed that he had little hope of success because he was "opposed by . . . the most powerful men in my party."

Conflict over expanding the money supply

On economic issues, Hayes held to a conservative line that would guide his successors—from both parties—for the rest of the century. His answer to the growing demands for expansion of the nation's money supply (which would become one of the leading political issues of the late nineteenth century) was to veto the Bland-Allison Act (1878), which provided for a slight increase in the supply of silver coins. (More money in circulation—inflation—was generally believed to raise farm prices and help those trying to pay off debts.) When Congress, including many Republicans, overturned Hayes's veto, the bruised president confided in his diary that he had become a president without a party. In 1879, with a year still left in his term, Hayes was ready to leave the White House. "I am now in my last year of the Presidency," he wrote a friend, "and look forward to its close as a schoolboy longs for the coming vacation."

civil service reform An extended effort led by political reformers to end the patronage system; led to the Pendleton Act (1883), which called for government jobs to be awarded based on merit rather than party loyalty.

Garfield, Arthur, and the Pendleton Act

With Hayes choosing not to pursue a second term, the Republican presidential nomination in 1880 was up for grabs. Former president Grant wanted the nomination but was unwilling to campaign for it. In the end, the party's squabbling factions selected a compromise candidate, Congressman James A. Garfield. An early foe of slavery, the tall Garfield had served as a

Union army general, like Grant and Hayes, before being elected to Congress in 1863. In an effort to please the Stalwarts and also win the crucial state of New York, Chester A. Arthur, whom Hayes had fired as head of the New York Customs House, was named the party's candidate for vice president.

The Democrats, as divided as the Republicans, selected their own compromise candidate: Winfield Scott Hancock, a retired Union general who had distinguished himself at the Battle of Gettysburg but had done little since. In large part, Hancock was chosen to help deflect the Republicans' "bloody-shirt" attacks on Democrats as the party of the Confederacy. In an election marked by widespread bribery, Garfield eked out a popular-vote plurality of only 39,000, or 48.5 percent. He won a more comfortable margin of 214 to 155 in the Electoral College.

A Presidency Cut Short

In his inaugural address, President Garfield gave an impassioned defense of civil rights, arguing that the "elevation of the negro race from slavery to the full rights of citizenship is the most important political change we have known since the adoption of the Constitution of 1787." The end of slavery, he said, "has added immensely to the moral and industrial forces of our people. It has liberated the master as well as the slave from a relation which wronged and enfeebled both." But he also confirmed that the Republicans had ended efforts to reconstruct the former Confederacy. Southern blacks were now on their own; they had been "surrendered to their own guardianship."

Garfield showed great potential as a president but had no chance to follow through. On July 2, 1881, after only four months in office, he was walking through the Washington, D.C., railroad station with James G. Blaine, now secretary of state, when he was shot twice by Charles Guiteau, a former Republican who had been turned down for a federal job. One bullet grazed the president's arm; the other went into his back. As a policeman wrestled the assassin to the ground, Guiteau shouted: "Yes! I have killed Garfield! [Chester] Arthur is President of the United States. I am a Stalwart!"—a declaration that would eventually destroy the Stalwart wing of the Republican Party. On September 19, after seventy-nine days, Garfield died of complications resulting from inept medical care. During a sensational ten-week trial, Guiteau explained that God had ordered him to kill the president. The jury refused to believe that he was insane and pronounced him guilty of murder. On June 30, 1882, Guiteau was hanged; an autopsy revealed that his brain was diseased.

The Civil Service Commission

In their grief over Garfield's death, Americans blamed Roscoe Conkling and the Stalwart Republicans for inciting Guiteau. One New York newspaper headline screamed: "MURDERED BY THE SPOILS SYSTEM!" The new president, Chester A. Arthur, who had been Conkling's trusted lieutenant,

Civil Service Commission: Merit system for government employees

surprised most political observers by distancing himself from the Stalwarts and even becoming a civil service reformer himself.

In 1883, the momentum against the "spoils system" generated by Garfield's assassination enabled George H. Pendleton, a Democratic senator from Ohio, to convince Congress to establish a Civil Service Commission, the first federal regulatory agency. Because of the Pendleton Civil Service Reform Act, a growing percentage of federal jobs would now be filled on the basis of competitive tests (the "merit system") rather than political favoritism. In addition, federal employees running for office were prohibited from receiving political contributions from other government workers.

The Pendleton Act was a limited first step in cleaning up the patronage process. It was sorely needed, in part because the federal government was expanding rapidly. By 1901, there would be 256,000 federal employees, five times the number in 1871. A growing number of these federal workers were women, who by 1890 held a third of the government's clerical jobs.

The Campaign of 1884

Chester Arthur's efforts to clean up the spoils system might have attracted voters, but they did not please Republican leaders. So in 1884 the Republicans dumped Arthur and chose as their presidential nominee James Gillespie Blaine of Maine, the handsome, colorful secretary of state, former senator, and longtime leader of the Half-Breeds, who had been at James Garfield's side three years earlier when the president was assassinated.

Corruption and a Sex Scandal

Blaine was the consummate politician. He inspired the party faithful with his electrifying speeches and knew how to wheel and deal in the backrooms, sometimes evading the law in the process. One critic charged that Blaine "wallowed in spoils like a rhinoceros in an African pool." Newspapers soon uncovered evidence of his corruption in the so-called Mulligan letters, which revealed that, as Speaker of the House, Blaine had secretly sold his votes on measures favorable to a railroad corporation. Nobody proved that he had committed any crimes, but the circumstantial evidence was powerful: his senatorial salary alone could not have built either his mansion in Washington, D.C. or his palatial home in Augusta, Maine (which has since become the state's governor's mansion). Former president Grant wrote a friend that he did not like Blaine and doubted his "reliability."

During the 1884 presidential campaign, more embarrassing letters surfaced linking Blaine to shady deal-making. For the reform element of the Republican party, this was too much, and many Republicans refused to endorse Blaine's candidacy. Party regulars scorned such critics as "goo-goos"—the good-government crowd. The editor of a New York newspaper jokingly called the anti-Blaine Republicans **Mugwumps**, after an Algonquian Indian word meaning "big chief." The Mugwumps, a self-appointed political

Mugwumps Reformers who bolted the Republican party in 1884 to support Democrat Grover Cleveland for president over Republican James G. Blaine, whose secret dealings on behalf of railroad companies had brought charges of corruption.

elite dedicated to promoting honest government, saw the election as "moral rather than political." Centered in the large cities and major universities of the northeast, they were mostly professors, editors, and writers who included in their number the most famous American of the time, Mark Twain. The Mugwumps generally opposed tariffs on imports and championed free trade. They opposed the regulation of railroads as well as efforts to inflate the money supply by coining more silver. Their foremost goal was to reform the process of appointing people to government jobs by making *all* federal jobs nonpartisan. Their break with the Republican party testified to the depth of their convictions.

The rise of the Mugwumps, as well as growing national concerns about political corruption, prompted the Democrats to nominate New Yorker Grover Cleveland, a minister's son, as a reform candidate. Cleveland had first attracted national attention in 1881, when he was elected the mayor of Buffalo on an anti-corruption platform. In 1882 he was elected governor of New York, and he continued to build a reform record by fighting New York City's corrupt Tammany Hall ring. As mayor and as governor, he repeatedly vetoed bills because in his view they served private interests at the expense of the public good. He supported civil service reform, opposed expanding the money supply, and preferred free trade to high tariffs, which tended to enrich big businesses at the expense of consumers.

Although Cleveland was known for his honesty and integrity, a juicy scandal erupted around him. A newspaper in Buffalo revealed that Cleveland, a bachelor, had befriended an attractive widow named Maria Halpin, who later named him the father of her baby born in 1874. Cleveland had discreetly provided financial support for the child.

The escapades of Blaine and Cleveland provided some of the most colorful battle cries in political history: "Blaine, Blaine, James G. Blaine, the continental liar from the state of Maine," Democrats chanted. Republicans countered with "Ma, ma, where's my pa?"

Grover Cleveland As president, Cleveland made the issue of tariff reform central to the politics of the late 1880s.

Blunders by the Blaine Campaign

Near the end of the nasty campaign, Blaine and his supporters committed two fateful blunders. The first occurred at New York City's fashionable Delmonico's restaurant, where Blaine went to a private dinner with 200 of the nation's wealthiest business leaders to ask them to help finance his campaign. Accounts of the unseemly event appeared in the newspapers for days afterwards. One headline blared: "Blaine Hobnobbing with the Mighty Money Kings!" The article explained that the banquet was intended to collect contributions for a "Republican corruption fund."

The second Blaine blunder occurred when a Protestant minister visiting Republican headquarters in New York referred to the Democrats as the party of "rum, Romanism, and rebellion [the Confederacy]." Blaine, who was present, let pass the implied insult to Catholics—a fatal oversight, since he had always cultivated Irish American support with his anti-English talk and repeated references to his mother being a Catholic. Democrats claimed that Blaine was, at heart, anti-Irish and anti-Catholic.

The two incidents may have tipped the close 1884 presidential election. The electoral vote came in at 219 to 182 in Cleveland's favor, but the popular vote ran far closer: Cleveland's plurality was fewer than 30,000 votes out of ten million cast. Cleveland won the key state of New York by only 1,149 votes out of 1,167,169 cast.

Cleveland's Reform Efforts

Democratic resistance to civil service reform

During his first few months in office, President Cleveland struggled to keep Democratic officials from reviving the patronage system. In a letter to a friend, the new president reported that he was living in a "nightmare," that "dreadful, damnable, office-seeking hangs over me and surrounds me" and that it made him "feel like resigning." Democratic newspapers heaped scorn on him for refusing to award federal jobs to his supporters. One accused Cleveland of "ingratitude" towards those who had "delivered the vote." Despite the president's best efforts to promote civil service reform, about two-thirds of the 120,000 federal jobs went to Democrats as patronage during his administration.

Cleveland also opposed federal favors to Big Business. "A public office is a public trust" was one of his favorite sayings. He held to a strictly limited view of government's role in both economic and social matters, a philosophy illustrated by his 1887 veto of a congressional effort to provide desperate Texas farmers with seeds in the aftermath of a drought. "Though the people support the government, the government should not support the people," Cleveland asserted. During his administration, he would veto more acts of Congress than any previous president.

Regulation of Railroad Rates

Creation of the Interstate Commerce Commission

For all of his genuine commitment to limited government intervention, Cleveland urged Congress to adopt an important new policy: federal regulation of the rates charged by interstate railroads (those whose tracks crossed state lines) to ship goods, crops, or livestock. He believed with many others that railroads were charging unfairly high freight rates, especially in communities served by only one railroad. States had adopted laws regulating railroads since the late 1860s, but in 1886 the Supreme Court declared in *Wabash, St. Louis, and Pacific Railroad Company v. Illinois* that no state could regulate the rates charged by railroads engaged in *interstate* traffic. Because most railroads did cross state lines, Cleveland urged Congress to close the loophole.

Congress followed through, and in 1887 Cleveland signed an act creating the **Interstate Commerce Commission** (ICC), a federal regulatory agency. The law empowered the ICC's five members to ensure that railroad

Interstate Commerce Commission An independent federal agency established in 1887 to oversee businesses engaged in interstate trade, especially railroads, but whose regulatory power was limited when tested in the courts.

freight rates were "reasonable and just." The commission's actual powers proved to be weak, however, when tested in the courts. Over time, the ICC came to be ignored, and the railroads continued their practice of charging high rates while making secret pricing deals with large shippers.

Tariff Reform and the Election of 1888

President Cleveland's most dramatic challenge to the power of Big Business focused on **tariff reform**. During the late nineteenth century, the government's high-tariff policies, shaped largely by the Republican party, had favored big businesses by effectively shutting out foreign imports, thereby enabling U.S. corporations to dominate their American markets and charge higher prices for their products. In 1887, Cleveland argued that Congress should reduce both the tariff rates ("the vicious, inequitable and illogical source of unnecessary taxation . . . [and] a burden upon the poor") and the number of imported goods subject to tariffs (over 4,000 items), so as to enable European companies to compete in the American marketplace. His outspoken stance against high tariffs set the stage for his reelection campaign in 1888.

> Cleveland's anti-tariff stance

To oppose Cleveland, the Republicans, now calling themselves the GOP (Grand Old Party) to emphasize their longevity, turned to the obscure Benjamin Harrison, a Civil War veteran whose greatest attributes were his availability and the fact that he was from Indiana, a pivotal state in presidential elections. The grandson of President William Henry Harrison, he had a modest political record; he had lost a race for governor and had served one term in the U.S. Senate (1881–1887).

The Republicans accepted Cleveland's challenge to make tariffs the chief issue in the campaign. As was often the case, they enjoyed a huge advantage in campaign funding and national organization; to fend off Cleveland's efforts to reduce the tariff, business executives contributed especially generously to the Republican cause. Still, the outcome was incredibly close. Cleveland won the popular vote by the thinnest of margins—5,540,329 to 5,439,853—but Harrison carried the Electoral College by 233 to 168. "Providence," said the new president, "has given us the victory." Matthew Quay, his campaign chairman, knew better. Harrison, he muttered, "ought to know that Providence hadn't a damned thing to do with it!" It was the distribution in key states of campaign money and promises of federal government jobs that won the election for Harrison.

Republican Activism under Harrison

Harrison owed a heavy debt to Civil War veterans, whose votes had been critical to his election, and he paid it by signing the Dependent Pension Act. As a result, the number of Union war veterans (and their family members) receiving federal pensions almost doubled between 1889 and 1893. In

tariff reform Effort led by the Democratic party to reduce taxes on imported goods, which Republicans argued were needed to protect American industries from foreign competition.

"King of the World" Reformers targeted the growing power of monopolies, such as that of John D. Rockefeller's Standard Oil.

addition, the Republicans took advantage of their control of the presidency and both houses of Congress to pass a cluster of other significant legislation in 1890: the Sherman Anti-Trust Act, the Sherman Silver Purchase Act, the McKinley Tariff Act, and the admission of Idaho and Wyoming as new states, which followed the admission of North and South Dakota, Montana, and Washington in 1889.

The Sherman Anti-Trust Act, named for Ohio senator John Sherman, was the first effort in the world to limit the size of businesses by prohibiting companies from "conspiring" to establish monopolies in their industries. Though badly needed, it was rarely enforced, in large part because of its vague definitions of "trusts" and "monopolies." From 1890 to 1901, only eighteen lawsuits were instituted, four of which were filed against labor unions rather than corporations.

As for tariff policy, Republicans viewed their victory over Cleveland in 1888 as a mandate not just to maintain the tariffs protecting American companies from foreign competition, but to raise the tariff rates even higher. Piloted through Congress by Ohio representative William McKinley, the McKinley Tariff Act of 1890 raised duties on imported manufactured goods to their highest level ever. Its passage encouraged many American businesses to raise prices for their own goods, since they had no need to worry about European competitors, who were now effectively shut out of the American market.

CORE **OBJECTIVE**

6. Analyze why the money supply became a major political issue during the Gilded Age and describe its impact on American politics.

A shrinking money supply in a growing economy

Inadequate Currency and Unhappy Farmers

Even more than tariffs, trusts, and efforts to clean up political corruption, national politics during the Gilded Age was preoccupied with complex monetary issues. In 1876, several farm organizations organized the independent "Greenback" party to promote the benefits of paper money over gold and silver coins; it won fifteen seats in Congress in 1878, illustrating the significance of currency issues to voters.

Behind many of these issues lay the fact that the nation's money supply had not grown along with the expanding economy of the late nineteenth century. From 1865 to 1890, the amount of money in circulation (both coins and paper currency) actually *decreased* about 10 percent at the same time that the economy was dramatically expanding. Such currency deflation raised the cost of borrowing money as the shrinking of the money supply enabled lenders to hike interest rates on loans. Creditors—bankers and others who loaned money—supported a "sound money" policy that limited the currency supply as a means of increasing their profits. By contrast, farmers, ranchers, and others who constantly had to borrow money to make ends meet claimed that the "sound money" policy had the deflationary effect of lowering prices for their crops and herds, driving them deeper into debt.

Increasing Unrest among Farmers

The 1890 congressional elections revealed a deep-seated unrest in the farming communities of the South and on the plains of Kansas and Nebraska, as well as in the mining towns of the Rocky Mountain region. People used the term "revolution" to describe the swelling grassroots support for the Populists, a new third party focused on the needs of miners and small farmers, many of whom did not own the land they worked. In drought-devastated Kansas, Populists won five congressional seats from Republicans. In early 1891, the newly elected Populists and Democrats took control of Congress just as an acute economic crisis appeared on the horizon: farmers' debts were mounting as crop prices plummeted.

A Vicious Cycle of Depressed Prices and Debt

Since the end of the Civil War, farmers in the South and the Great Plains had suffered from worsening economic conditions. The basic source of their problems was a decline in prices earned for their crops, a deflationary trend caused by overproduction and growing international competition in world food markets as well as the inadequate money supply. The vast new lands brought under cultivation in the plains poured an ever-increasing supply of farm products into world markets, driving prices down. Meanwhile, farmers, especially small farmers in the South and West, had become increasingly indebted to "greedy" local banks or merchants who loaned them money to buy seed, fertilizer, tools, and other supplies. As prices for wheat, cotton, and corn dropped, however, so did the income the farmers received, thus preventing them from paying their debts on time. In response, most farmers had no choice but to grow even more wheat, cotton, or corn, creating a vicious cycle: as still more grains and cotton were harvested and sold, the increased supply drove down prices and farmers' incomes even further. High tariffs on imported goods also hurt farmers because they blocked foreign competition, allowing U.S. companies to raise the prices of manufactured goods needed by farm families. Farmers, however, had to sell their crops in open world markets unprotected by tariffs, where competition lowered prices.

> Indebted farmers and falling crop prices

Besides bankers, merchants, and high tariffs, struggling farmers also blamed the railroads, warehouse owners, and food processors, the so-called middle men who helped get their products to market. They especially resented that railroads, most of which had a monopoly over the shipping of grains and livestock, charged such high rates to ship their farm products.

Silver and Inflation

Among all the factors distressing farmers, the nation's inadequate money supply emerged as the source of greatest frustration. In 1873, the Republican-controlled Congress had declared that silver could no longer be used for coins, only gold. This decision (called "the Crime of '73" by critics) occurred just when silver mines in the western states had begun to increase their production. Hard-pressed farmers in the West and South demanded increased coinage of silver, which would inflate the currency and thereby raise commodity prices, providing farmers with more income with which to pay their annual debts.

They found allies among legislators representing the new western states. All six states admitted to the Union in 1889 and 1890 had substantial silver mines, and their new congressional delegations—largely Republican—wanted the federal government to buy more silver for coins. The so-called silver delegates shifted the balance in Congress enough to pass the Sherman Silver Purchase Act (1890), which required the Treasury to purchase 4.5 million ounces of silver each month with new paper money. Such inflationary policies helped set the stage for the currency issue to eclipse all others during the financial panic that would sweep the country in 1893.

The Sherman Silver Purchase Act (1890)

In the 1890 midterm elections, voters rebelled not only against the McKinley Tariff but also in support of the militant new farm protests. The result was that Democrats outnumbered Republicans in the new House of Representatives by almost three to one; in the Senate the Republican majority was reduced to eight. One of the election casualties was Congressman McKinley himself.

The Granger Movement

When the Department of Agriculture sent Oliver H. Kelley on a tour of the South in 1866, he was struck most by the social isolation of people living on small farms. To address the problem, Kelley in 1867 helped found the National Grange of the Patrons of Husbandry, better known as the Grange (an old word for places where crops were stored). In the next few years, the Granger movement mushroomed, reaching a membership of 1.5 million by 1874. It started out by offering social and educational activities for isolated farmers and their families, but as it grew, it also began to promote "cooperatives" where farmers could join together to buy, store, and sell their crops to avoid the high fees charged by brokers and other middle-men.

"Granger laws"

In five Midwest states, Grangers persuaded legislatures to pass "Granger laws" to regulate the prices charged farmers by railroads and grain warehouses (called "elevators"). Railroads and warehouses challenged the new laws, but in *Munn v. Illinois* (1877), the Supreme Court ruled that states had the right to regulate property such as grain elevators and railroads that operated in a public interest. Nine years later, however, the Court threw out the *Munn* ruling, finding in *Wabash v. Illinois* (1886) that only Congress could regulate industries involved in interstate commerce.

Farmers' Alliances

The **Granger movement** gradually fizzled out as members directed their energies into political action. In the 1880s, **Farmers' Alliances** began growing in size and significance. Like the Grange, the Farmers' Alliances (divided at the national level into Northern, Southern, and Colored branches) organized social and recreational activities for farmers and their families, but they also emphasized political action. Struggling farmers throughout the South and Midwest, where most did not own their land, saw the Alliance movement as a way to address the hardships created by chronic indebtedness, declining crop prices, and devastating droughts.

"I Feed You All!" (1875) The farmer is the cornerstone of American society, according to this Granger-inspired poster. Without the food he produces, no man in any occupation can do his job—including the very railroad magnate (left) and warehouse owners who try to exploit him.

The Alliance movement swept across the South and established strong support in Kansas and the Dakotas. In 1886, a white minister in Texas responded to the appeals of African American farmers by organizing the Colored Farmers' National Alliance. By 1890, the white Alliance movement had about 1.5 million members from New York to California, and the Colored Farmers' National Alliance claimed more than 1 million members.

In the farm states west of the Mississippi River, political activism intensified after a winter of record blizzards in 1887, which killed most of the cattle and hogs across the northern plains, and a prolonged drought two years later that destroyed millions of acres of corn, wheat, and oats. Distressed farmers lashed out against what they considered to be a powerful conspiracy of eastern financial and industrial interests, which they variously called "monopolies," "the money power," "Wall Street," or "organized wealth." The Alliance movement sponsored more than 1,000 rural newspapers and 40,000 lecturers to spread the word about the "tyrannical" forces arrayed against farmers.

New Third Parties

The Alliances, frustrated that neither Democrats nor Republicans embraced their cause, called for third-party political action to address their economic concerns. In 1890, farm radicals in Colorado joined with miners and railroad workers to form the Independent party, and Nebraska farmers formed the People's Independent party. Across the South, however, white Alliance members hesitated to leave the Democratic party, seeking instead to influence or control it. Both the third-party and the southern approaches produced startling success.

Granger movement Began by offering social and educational activities for isolated farmers and their families and later started to promote "cooperatives" where farmers could join together to buy, store, and sell their crops to avoid the high fees charged by brokers and other middlemen.

Farmers' Alliances Like the Granger movement, these organizations sought to address the issues of small farming communities; however, Alliances emphasized more political action and called for the creation of a Third Party to advocate their concerns.

Populist successes in local and state elections, and formation of a national party

In the Midwest, new third parties elected a U.S. senator and almost elected a governor under the banner of the new **People's party (Populists)** in Kansas, where a Populist won the governor's race in 1892. The Populists supported increased government intervention in the economy, for only the U.S. Congress could expand the money supply, counterbalance the power of Big Business, and provide efficient national transportation networks to support the agricultural economy. Third parties also took control of one house of the Kansas legislature and both houses in Nebraska. In the South Dakota and Minnesota legislatures, Populists won enough seats to control the balance of power between Republicans and Democrats.

In the South, the Alliance movement forced Democrats to nominate candidates pledged to its farm program and succeeded in electing four of them as governors, forty-four as congressmen, and several as U.S. senators, as well as seven state legislatures controlled by Alliance supporters. Among the most respected of the southern Alliance leaders was red-haired Thomas E. Watson of Georgia. The son of prosperous slaveholders who had lost everything after the Civil War, Watson became a successful lawyer and speaker on behalf of the Alliance cause. He took the lead in urging African American tenant farmers and sharecroppers to join white farmers in ousting the political elite. "You are kept apart," he told black and white farmers, "that you may be separately fleeced of your earnings."

In Kansas, Mary Elizabeth Lease emerged as a fiery speaker for the farm protest movement. Born in Pennsylvania, Lease migrated to Kansas, taught school, raised a family, and failed at farming in the mid-1880s. She then studied law, "pinning sheets of notes above her wash tub," and became one of the state's first female attorneys. A proud, tall, and imposing woman, she began giving public speeches on behalf of struggling farmers that drew attentive audiences. "The people are at bay," she warned in 1894; "let the bloodhounds of money beware." She urged angry farmers to obtain their goals "with the ballot if possible, but if not that way then with the bayonet." Like so many Populists, Lease viewed the urban-industrial East as the enemy. "The great common people of this country are slaves," she shouted, "and monopoly is the master. The West and South are bound and prostrate before the manufacturing East."

The Election of 1892

People's party (Populists)
Political party formed in 1892 following the success of Farmers' Alliance candidates; Populists advocated a variety of reforms, including free coinage of silver, a progressive income tax, postal savings banks, regulation of railroads, and direct election of U.S. senators.

The success of the Farmer Alliance led to the formation of yet another new political party on the national level. In 1892, Alliance leaders organized a convention of the People's Party, which opened on July 4 in Omaha, Nebraska. Delegates drafted a platform that called for unlimited coinage of silver, a "progressive" income tax whose rates would rise with personal income levels, and federal control of the railroads. The Populists also endorsed the eight-hour workday and new laws restricting immigration, for fear that foreigners were taking Americans' jobs. The party's platform turned out to be more exciting than its presidential candidate: Iowa's James

B. Weaver, a former Union army officer who had headed the Greenback party ticket twelve years earlier. To attract southern voters, the Populists nominated a former Confederate general for vice president.

The major parties renominated the same candidates who had run in 1888: Democrat Grover Cleveland and Republican Benjamin Harrison. The tariff issue monopolized their attention. Each major candidate received more than 5 million votes, but Cleveland won a majority of the Electoral College. The Populists' Weaver received more than 1 million votes and carried Colorado, Kansas, Nevada, and Idaho. Alabama was the banner Populist state of the South, with 37 percent of its vote going to Weaver.

The Depression of 1893 and the "Free Silver" Crusade

While farmers were funneling their discontent into politics during the fall of 1892, a fundamental weakness in the economy was about to cause a major collapse and a social rebellion. Just ten days before Grover Cleveland started his second presidential term, in the winter of 1893, the Philadelphia and Reading Railroad declared bankruptcy, setting off a national financial crisis, now called the **Panic of 1893**, that grew into the worst depression the nation had ever experienced.

Other overextended railroads collapsed, taking many banks with them. A quarter of unskilled urban workers lost their jobs, and by the fall of 1893 more than 600 banks had closed and 15,000 businesses had failed. Farm foreclosures soared in the South and West; between 1890 and 1894, more than 11,000 farmers lost their farms in Kansas alone. By 1900, a third of all American farmers rented their land rather than owned it. Kansans grimly joked: "In God we trusted, in Kansas we busted." By 1894, the nation's economy had reached bottom. But the depression lasted another four years, with unemployment hovering at 20 percent. In New York City, the rate was close to 35 percent, and 20,000 homeless people camped out at police stations and other makeshift shelters.

President Cleveland's response to the economic catastrophe was to convince Congress to return the nation's money supply to a solely gold standard by repealing the Sherman Silver Purchase Act of 1890, a move that only made the depression worse. The weak economy needed more money in circulation, not less. Investors rushed to exchange their silver for gold, thus further constricting the nation's money supply. A wave of violent labor unrest symbolized the fracturing of the social order; in 1894, some 750,000 workers went on strike. The depression was reshaping America's economic and political landscape.

In this climate of turmoil and anxiety, the 1894 congressional elections devastated President Cleveland and the Democrats. The Republicans gained 121 seats in the House, the largest increase ever. Only in the "Solid South"

> Repeal of the Sherman Silver Purchase Act

Panic of 1893 A major collapse in the national economy after several major railroad companies declared bankruptcy, leading to a severe depression and several violent clashes between workers and management.

did the Democrats retain their advantage. The Populists emerged with six senators and seven representatives, and they expected the festering discontent in rural areas to carry them to national power in 1896. Their hopes would be dashed, however.

Silverites versus Goldbugs

Cleveland's decision to repeal the Sherman Silver Purchase Act had created an irreparable division in his own party. One embittered pro-silver Democrat labeled the president a traitor. Politicians from western states with large silver mines increased their demands for the "unlimited" coinage of silver, presenting a strategic dilemma for Populists: should the party promote the long list of varied reforms it had originally advocated, or should it try to ride the silver issue into power? The latter seemed more likely to succeed. Although flooding the economy with silver currency would probably not have provided the benefits its advocates claimed, the "free silver" crusade had taken on powerful symbolic overtones. Over the protests of more-radical members, Populist leaders decided to hold their 1896 nominating convention after the two major-party conventions, confident that the Republicans and Democrats would at best straddle the silver issue and enable the Populists to lure away pro-silver advocates from both.

Contrary to those expectations, the major parties took opposite positions on the currency issue. The Republicans, as expected, nominated William McKinley, a former congressman and governor of Ohio, on a platform committed to gold coins as the only form of currency. After the convention, a friend told McKinley that the **"money question"** would determine the election. He was right.

Bryan's "Cross of Gold" speech

The Democratic convention in the Chicago Coliseum, the largest building in the world, was one of the great turning points in American political history. The pro-silver, largely rural delegates surprised the party leadership and the "Gold Democrats" or "goldbugs" by capturing the convention for their inflationary crusade. Thirty-six-year-old William Jennings Bryan of Nebraska gave the final speech before the balloting began. A fiery evangelical moralist, Bryan was a two-term congressman who had lost a race for the Senate in 1894, when Democrats by the dozens were swept out of office. In the months before the convention, he had traveled throughout the South and West, speaking passionately for the unlimited coinage of silver and against Cleveland's "do-nothing" response to the depression.

"money question" Late-nineteenth-century national debate over the nature of U.S. currency; supporters of a fixed gold standard were generally money lenders, and thus preferred to keep the value of money high, while supporters of silver (and gold) coinage were debtors, they owed money, so they wanted to keep the value of money low by increasing the currency supply (inflation).

Bryan was a magnetic public speaker with a booming voice, a crusading preacher in the role of a politician. At the 1896 convention, he was only a "dark horse" candidate—that is, a little-known long shot—for the presidential nomination. So he chose to take a calculated risk: he would be intentionally provocative and disruptive. In his now famous speech, Bryan claimed to speak for the "producing masses of this nation" against the eastern "financial magnates" who had "enslaved" them by manipulating the money supply to ensure high interest rates for loans. He reminded the delegates that the "man who is employed for wages is as much a business man as his employer." As his melodramatic twenty-minute speech reached its peak, Bryan fused Christian imagery with Populist anger:

> I come to speak to you in defense of a cause as holy as the cause of liberty—the cause of humanity. . . . We have petitioned, and our petitions have been scorned. . . . We have begged, and they have mocked when our calamity came. We beg no longer; we entreat no more; we petition no more. We defy them!

Bryan then stretched his fingers across his forehead and reached his dramatic conclusion: "You shall not press down upon the brow of labor this crown of thorns. You shall not crucify mankind upon a cross of gold!"—at which point he extended his arms straight out from his sides, as if he were being crucified. It was a riveting performance that worked better than even Bryan himself had anticipated. As he walked triumphantly off the stage, the delegates erupted in wild applause. "Everybody seemed to go mad at once," reported the *New York World*. For their part, the Republicans were not at all amused by Bryan's antics. A Republican newspaper observed that no political movement had "ever before spawned such hideous and repulsive vipers."

William Jennings Bryan His "cross of gold" speech at the 1896 Democratic Convention roused the delegates and secured him the party's presidential nomination.

Pro-gold Democrats and pro-silver Populists

The day after his speech, Bryan won the presidential nomination on the fifth ballot, but in the process the Democratic party was fractured. Disappointed pro-gold, pro-Cleveland Democrats dismissed Bryan as a fanatic and a socialist. They were so alienated by both his positions and his rhetoric that they walked out of the convention and nominated their own candidate, Senator John M. Palmer of Illinois. "Fellow Democrats," Palmer announced, "I will not consider it any great fault if you decide to cast your vote for [the Republican] William McKinley."

When the Populists gathered in St. Louis for their presidential nominating convention two weeks later, they faced an impossible choice. They could name their own candidate and divide the pro-silver vote with the Democrats, or they could endorse Bryan and probably lose their identity as an independent party. In the end, they backed Bryan, but chose their own vice-presidential candidate, Thomas E. Watson, and invited the Democrats to drop their vice-presidential nominee. Bryan refused the offer.

The Election of 1896

The election of 1896 was one of the most dramatic in American history, in part because of the striking contrast between the candidates and in part because the terrible depression made the stakes so high. Bryan, the nominee of both the Democrats and the Populists, was the first major candidate since Andrew Jackson to champion the poor, the discontented, and the oppressed against the financial and industrial elite. And he was the first leader of a major party to call for the expansion of the federal government to help the working and middle classes.

National Issues of the Gilded Age

During the Gilded Age, politics was above all else a local affair. With a small federal government, an entrenched patronage system, and a highly partisan and closely divided electorate, there was little opportunity for effective national legislation. However, four issues of national political conflict did emerge: immigration, civil service and corporate reform, the "money question," and the tariff.

NATIONAL ISSUE 1 IMMIGRATION

	Supporters: Nonrestrictionists	Opponents: Nativists
Position	Few or no limits on immigration	Limit or ban on immigrants who were: ■ nonwhite (e.g., Chinese) ■ non-Anglo-Saxon (i.e., eastern and southern European) ■ non-English-speaking
Demographic	■ Democrat ■ Catholic or Jewish ■ Born outside of America	■ Republican ■ Protestant ■ Born in America
Success	President Cleveland's 1897 veto of law restricting immigration of non-English speakers	Chinese Exclusion Act of 1882 (repealed 61 years later by the Magnuson Act)

NATIONAL ISSUE 2 CIVIL SERVICE AND CORPORATE REFORM

	Supporters: Political Reformers	Opponents: Political Establishment
Position	Unskilled and semiskilled laborers had rights to safe working conditions, minimum wage, limited working day, etc.	Labor supply was a disposable commodity to be procured at the lowest possible price
Demographic	■ Democrat and Republican ■ Unskilled and semiskilled laborers ■ Female, African American, and child laborers	■ Democrat and Republican ■ Corporations ■ Political bosses and others receiving patronage from Big Businesses
Success	Pendleton Civil Service Reform Act (1883), Interstate Commerce Commission (1887), and Sherman Anti-Trust Act (1890)	Limited impact of regulatory legislation; military support in quelling strikes, e.g., the Great Railroad Strike (1877) and Haymarket Affair (1886)

NATIONAL ISSUE 3 THE "MONEY QUESTION"

	Supporters of "the Gold Standard"	Opponents: Proponents of Unlimited Silver Coinage
Position	■ Circulation of gold coinage only ■ Decrease money supply to cause deflation (lower consumer prices)	■ Circulation of silver and gold currency as well as paper money ■ Increase supply of money to cause inflation (higher prices for commodities like cotton and wheat)
Demographic	■ Creditors (money lenders), e.g., bankers ■ Veterans and others on a fixed pension ■ Primarily in North and East	■ Debtors (those who owe money) ■ Primary producers, e.g., farmers, ranchers, and miners ■ Primarily in South and West, where silver mines and/or farms were located
Success	Coinage Act (1873), Gold Standard Act (1900)	Bland-Allison Act (1878), Sherman Silver Purchase Act (1890)

NATIONAL ISSUE 4 THE TARIFF

	Supporters: Protectionists	Opponents: Proponents of Free Trade
Position	■ High tax on imported goods to benefit businesses by: 1. Protecting them from foreign competition 2. Allowing them to increase prices for their products	■ Little or no tax on imported goods to: 1. Benefit consumers by increasing price competition 2. Benefit small businesses dependent on foreign imports
Demographic	■ Majority of Republicans, some Democrats ■ Manufacturers	■ Mugwump Republicans ■ Majority of Democrats ■ Primary producers, e.g., farmers, ranchers, and miners
Success	McKinley Tariff (1890) raised rates	Wilson-Gorman Tariff (1894) lowered rates

QUESTIONS FOR ANALYSIS

1. Based on the demographic information in the tables above, which issues divided along political party lines? Which crossed them?

2. From your reading of the chapter and this feature, what role did socio-economic class and regionalism play in determining the supporters and opponents of a given issue? Explain.

3. Why did these four issues emerge at the national level, and what is the relationship among them?

Bryan's crusade for "the people"

Presidential campaign badges On the left wings of the "goldbug" and "silverite" badges are McKinley (top) and Bryan (bottom), with their running mates on the right.

McKinley defeats Bryan

Candidate Bryan crisscrossed the country like a man on a mission, delivering hundreds of impassioned speeches on behalf of the "producing masses"—workers, farmers, miners, and small-business owners. His populist crusade was for whites only, however. Like so many otherwise progressive Democratic leaders, Bryan never challenged the practices of racial segregation and violence against blacks in the solidly Democratic South.

McKinley, meanwhile, stayed at home. He knew he could not compete with Bryan as a speaker, so he conducted a "front-porch campaign," welcoming delegations of Republican supporters at his home in Canton, Ohio, and giving only prepared statements to the press. McKinley's brilliant campaign manager, Marcus "Mark" Hanna, a wealthy business executive, shrewdly portrayed Bryan as a "Popocrat," a radical whose "communistic spirit" would ruin the capitalist system and stir up a class war. Hanna convinced the Republican Party to declare that it was "unreservedly for sound money"—meaning gold coins. Theodore Roosevelt, a rising Republican star, was horrified by the thought of Bryan becoming president. "The silver craze surpasses belief," he wrote a friend. "Bryan's election would be a great calamity."

By appealing to such fears, the Republican campaign raised vast sums of money from corporations and wealthy donors to finance an army of 1,400 speakers who traveled the country in McKinley's support. It was the most sophisticated—and expensive—presidential campaign in history. McKinley promoted himself as the "advance agent of prosperity" who would provide workers with a "full dinner pail." In the end, Bryan was overwhelmed by the better-organized and better-financed Republicans. McKinley won the popular vote by 7.1 million to 6.5 million and the Electoral College vote by 271 to 176. Two million more voters cast ballots than in 1892.

Bryan carried most of the West and the South but found little support in the East. In the critical Midwest, from Minnesota and Iowa eastward to Ohio, he did not carry a single state. His evangelical Protestantism repelled many Roman Catholic voters, who were normally drawn to the Democrats. Farmers in the Northeast, moreover, were less attracted to radical reform than were farmers in the wheat and cotton belts of the West and South. In the cities, workers found it easier to identify with McKinley's focus on reviving the industrial economy than with Bryan's farm-based free-silver evangelism.

Although Bryan lost, he began the Democratic party's shift from pro-business conservatism to its eventual twentieth-century role as a party of liberal reform. The Populist party, however, virtually disintegrated. Having won a million votes in 1896, it collected only 50,000 in 1900. Conversely, McKinley's victory climaxed a generation-long struggle for the political control of an industrialized America. The Republicans would be dominant—for a while.

THE ELECTION OF 1896

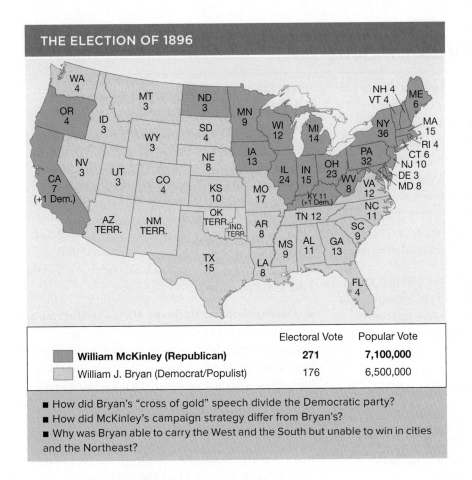

	Electoral Vote	Popular Vote
William McKinley (Republican)	**271**	**7,100,000**
William J. Bryan (Democrat/Populist)	176	6,500,000

- How did Bryan's "cross of gold" speech divide the Democratic party?
- How did McKinley's campaign strategy differ from Bryan's?
- Why was Bryan able to carry the West and the South but unable to win in cities and the Northeast?

By 1897, when McKinley was inaugurated as president, economic prosperity was returning. Part of the reason was inflation of the currency, which bore out the arguments of the Greenbackers and silverites that the money supply was inadequate. But the inflation came, in one of history's many ironies, not from more greenbacks or silver dollars issued by the federal government but from a flood of gold discovered in South Africa, northwest Canada, and Alaska. In 1900, Congress passed, and McKinley signed, a bill affirming that the United States money supply would be based only on gold.

> Economic recovery and new supplies of gold

Even though the Populist movement faded after William Jennings Bryan's defeat, most of the agenda promoted by Bryan Democrats and Populists, dismissed as too radical in 1896, would be implemented over the next two decades by a more diverse coalition of Democrats and Republicans who would call themselves "progressives."

- **America's Move to Town** America's cities grew in all directions during the *Gilded Age*. Electric elevators and new steel-frame construction allowed architects to extend buildings upward, and mass transit both above and below ground enabled the middle class to retreat to suburbs. Crowded *tenements* bred disease and crime and created an opportunity for urban political *party bosses* to gain power, in part by distributing to the poor the only relief that existed.

- **The New Immigration** By 1900, 30 percent of Americans living in major cities were foreign-born, with the majority of newcomers arriving from eastern and southern Europe rather than western and northern Europe, like most immigrants of generations past. Their languages, culture, and religion were quite different from those of native-born Americans. They tended to be Catholic, Eastern Orthodox, or Jewish rather than Protestant. Beginning in the 1880s, *nativists* advocated restrictive immigration laws and won passage of the *Chinese Exclusion Act.*

- **Changes in Culture and Thought** Many areas of American life underwent profound changes during the Gilded Age. The growth of large cities led to the popularity of vaudeville and Wild West shows and the emergence of football, baseball, and basketball as spectator sports. Saloons served as local social and political clubs for men, despite the disapproval of anti-liquor groups. Charles Darwin's *On the Origin of Species* shocked people who believed in a literal interpretation of the Bible's account of creation. Herbert Spencer and William Graham Sumner were proponents of *Social Darwinism*, which applied Darwin's theory of evolution to human society by equating economic and social success with the "survival of the fittest."

- **Gilded Age Politics** The politics of the time was dominated by huge corporations and the money they used to buy political influence. Political power was still concentrated at the state and local levels. Americans were intensely loyal to the two major parties, whose local "bosses" and "machines" won votes by distributing *patronage* jobs and contracts to members as well as charitable relief. Party loyalties reflected regional, ethnic, and religious differences. Though Republicans almost always held the presidency, the overall strength of the major parties was so closely balanced that neither party wanted to take bold stands for fear of alienating voters.

- **Corruption and Reform: Hayes to Harrison** In addition to the *"money question,"* national politics in this period focused on *tariff reform,* the regulation of corporations, and *civil service reform.* The passage of the Pendleton Civil Service Reform Act in 1883 began the professionalization of federal workers. In the 1884 presidential election, Republicans favoring reform, the *Mugwumps,* helped elect Democrat Grover Cleveland. Cleveland signed the 1887 act creating the *Interstate Commerce Commission (ICC)*, intended to regulate interstate railroads. In 1890, under President Benjamin Harrison, Republicans passed the Sherman Anti-Trust Act, the Sherman Silver Purchase Act, and the McKinley Tariff Act.

- **Inadequate Currency Supply and Unhappy Farmers** Over the course of the late nineteenth century, *the "money question"* had become a central political issue. The supply of money had not increased as the economy had grown. This deflationary trend increased the value of money, which was good for bankers and creditors who could charge higher interest rates on loans, but bad for farmers who faced both more expensive mortgages and declining prices for their products. Many farmers believed that the coinage of silver, rather than simply a gold standard system, would result in inflation which in turn would effectively increase the value of their products and reduce their debts. Farmers and others unsatisfied with the Republican and Democratic parties over a host of issues formed a series of political parties and alliances, one of which, the *People's party*, briefly operated as a national third party.

KEY TERMS

CHRONOLOGY

INQUIZITIVE

Go to InQuizitive to see what you've learned—and learn what you've missed—with personalized feedback along the way.

THE CHARGE OF THE ROUGH RIDERS ON SAN JUAN HILL (1898) Before Frederic Remington pursued art professionally, he had unsuccessful forays into hunting, ranching, and even the saloon business in the West. His intimacy with the Western way of life, along with his technical skill and keen sense of observation, were not lost on Theodore Roosevelt, who invited Remington to travel with the Rough Riders during the Spanish-American War.

Seizing an American Empire

1865–1913

Throughout the nineteenth century, Americans displayed little interest in foreign affairs. The overriding priorities were at home: industrial development, western settlement, and domestic politics. After the Civil War, a mood of isolationism—a desire to stay out of conflicts elsewhere in the world, especially those among powerful European nations—dominated public opinion. America's geographic advantages encouraged this isolationist attitude: wide oceans to the east and west, and militarily weak neighbors in the Western Hemisphere. That the powerful British navy protected the shipping lanes from the United States to the British Isles gave Americans a heightened sense of security.

Yet while wanting to stay out of conflicts in Europe, a growing number of Americans during the late nineteenth century urged U.S. officials to acquire additional territory outside North America. The old idea of "manifest destiny" from the 1840s—that the United States had been blessed by God ("destined") to expand its territory westward across the North American continent—evolved during the late nineteenth century to include expanding American control over other regions of the Western hemisphere and even in the Pacific and in Asia. Armed with this concept of a destiny made manifest (revealed) to people by what they saw as the obvious superiority of their way of life, Americans embraced a new form

CORE OBJECTIVES INQUIZITIVE

1. Describe the factors that motivated America's new imperialism after the Civil War.

2. Explain why and how America expanded its influence in the Pacific before the Spanish-American War (War of 1898).

3. Explain the causes of the Spanish-American War (War of 1898), and describe its major events.

4. Analyze the consequences of the Spanish-American War (War of 1898) for American foreign policy.

5. Describe the reasons for Theodore Roosevelt's rapid rise to the presidency, and evaluate the main elements of his foreign policies.

of expansionism that sought distant territories as "colonies" with no intention of their becoming equal states. The new manifest destiny, in other words, became a justification for imperialism. "Not to advance is to recede," wrote historian Brooks Adams in *The Law of Civilization and Decay* (1895). For the United States to survive and prosper, Adams and others argued, it had to keep pushing beyond its current borders; as historian Frederick Jackson Turner had proclaimed in 1893, the American "frontier" was gone, so Americans needed new frontiers in which to exercise their "expansive character" and to spread their democratic ideals and Christian beliefs. During the late nineteenth century, manifest destiny also took on racial meaning as many Americans agreed with Theodore Roosevelt that the United States needed to expand around the world "on behalf of the *destiny* of the [Anglo-Saxon] race."

In more practical terms, prominent political and business leaders argued that America's rapid industrial development required the fast-growing nation to acquire foreign territories—by conquest if necessary—in order to gain easier access to vital raw materials such as rubber, tin, copper, palm oil, and various dyes. At the same time, American manufacturers and commercial farmers had become increasingly dependent on international trade, a dependence that required an expanded naval force to protect its merchant vessels. And a modern, steam-powered navy needed ocean bases where its ships could replenish their supplies of coal and water.

For these and other reasons, the United States during the last quarter of the nineteenth century expanded its military presence and territorial possessions both within and beyond the Western Hemisphere. Within the span of a few months in 1898, a nation born in a revolution against British colonial rule would itself become an imperial ruler of colonies around the world. Motivated by a mixture of moral and religious idealism, assumptions of "Anglo-Saxon" racial superiority, and naked greed, the expansionist push also met with strong opposition. But most Americans sided with future president Theodore Roosevelt, who in his 1896 book *The Winning of the West* declared that the conquest of the "backward peoples" of the world, like the defeat of the Indians in the American West, benefited "civilization and the interests of mankind."

CORE **OBJECTIVE**

1. Describe the factors that motivated America's new imperialism after the Civil War.

Toward the New Imperialism

The United States was a latecomer to a new surge of **imperialism** by major Western nations. Beginning in the 1880s, the British, French, Belgians, Italians, Dutch, Spanish, and Germans had conquered most of Africa and Asia. Often competing with one another for particular territories, they had established colonial governments to rule over the native populations and exploited the colonies economically. Each of the imperial nations, including the United States, dispatched missionaries to convert conquered peoples to Christianity. By 1900, some 18,000 Protestant and Catholic missionaries were scattered around the world. Writing in 1902, the British economist J. A. Hobson declared that imperialism was "the most powerful factor in the current politics of the Western world."

During the late nineteenth century, a small yet influential group of American public officials aggressively encouraged the idea of expansion beyond North America. They included powerful senators Albert J. Beveridge of Indiana and Henry Cabot Lodge of Massachusetts, as well as Theodore Roosevelt and naval captain Alfred Thayer Mahan, president of the U.S. Naval War College in Rhode Island.

> Motives behind imperialism: Economic expansion, racial superiority, Christian evangelism

In 1890, Mahan published ***The Influence of Sea Power upon History, 1660–1783***, in which he argued that the modern history of Great Britain had demonstrated that national greatness flowed from naval power. Mahan insisted that modern economic development required a powerful navy centered on huge battleships, a strong merchant marine, foreign commerce, colonies to provide raw materials and new markets for American products, and global naval bases. A self-described imperialist, he urged American leaders to "look outward" beyond the continental United States. Mahan championed America's "destiny" to control the Caribbean Sea, build a Central American canal to connect the Atlantic and Pacific oceans, and spread Western civilization across the Pacific. His ideas were widely circulated within political and military circles in the United States as well as Great Britain and Germany, and by 1896 the U.S. had built eleven new steel battleships, making America's navy the third most powerful in the world behind Great Britain and Germany.

Claims of racial superiority reinforced the new imperialist spirit. During the late nineteenth century, many Americans readily assumed that some races were dominant (Anglo-Saxons) and some inferior (Indians, Africans). Such traditional notions justifying racism were given new "scientific" authority by researchers at universities throughout Europe and America. Scholars at times went to absurd lengths to make racial distinctions—measuring facial angles, skull size, and brain weight. At the Johns Hopkins University in Baltimore, Professor James K. Hosmer claimed that "the primacy of the world will lie with us" because of the superior qualities of the Anglo-Saxon race. Prominent Americans used the arguments of Social Darwinism to justify economic exploitation and territorial conquest abroad and racial segregation at home. Among nations as among individuals, they claimed, only the strongest survive. John Fiske, a Harvard historian and popular lecturer on Darwinism, proclaimed in 1885 the superior character of "Anglo-Saxon" institutions and peoples. The English-speaking "race," he argued, was destined to dominate the globe and transform the institutions, traditions, language—even the blood—of the world's "backward" races.

imperialism The use of diplomatic or military force to extend a nation's power and enhance its economic interests, often by acquiring territory or colonies and justifying such behavior with assumptions of racial superiority.

The Influence of Sea Power upon History, 1660–1783 **(1890)** Historical work in which Rear Admiral Alfred Thayer Mahan argues that a nation's greatness and prosperity comes from the power of its navy; the book helped bolster imperialist sentiment in the United States in the late nineteenth century.

CORE **OBJECTIVE**

2. Explain why and how America expanded its influence in the Pacific before the Spanish-American War (War of 1898).

The Alaska Purchase and annexation of Hawaii

Expansion in the Pacific

For John Fiske and other American imperialists, Asia offered an especially attractive target for expansion. In 1866, Secretary of State William H. Seward had predicted that the United States must inevitably impose its economic domination "on the Pacific Ocean, and its islands and continents." Eager for American manufacturers to take advantage of the huge Asian markets, Seward believed the United States first had to remove all foreign powers from the northern Pacific coast of North America and gain access to that region's valuable ports. To that end, he tried to acquire the British colony of British Columbia, sandwiched between Russian-owned Alaska and the Washington Territory.

Late in 1866, while encouraging business leaders and civil authorities in British Columbia to consider becoming a U.S. territory, Seward learned of Russia's desire to sell Alaska. He leaped at the opportunity, in part because the purchase might influence British Columbia to join the union. In 1867, the United States bought Alaska for $7.2 million, thus removing Russia from North America as an imperial power. Critics scoffed at "Seward's folly" of buying the Alaskan "icebox," but it proved to be the biggest bargain since the Louisiana Purchase, in part because of its vast deposits of gold and oil—as well as ice.

"Our New Senators" Mocking the Alaska Purchase, this political cartoon shows President Johnson and Seward welcoming two new senators from Alaska: an Eskimo and a penguin. That an Eskimo becoming senator is laughable reveals the racial discrimination of this period.

Hawaii

Seward and other Americans promoting expanded trade with Asia also wanted the Hawaiian islands. The islands, a unified kingdom since 1795, had a sizable population of American missionaries and a single profitable crop, sugar cane. In 1875, Hawaii had signed a reciprocal trade agreement with the United States, which agreed to allow Hawaiian sugar to enter the country duty-free in exchange for Hawaii's promise that none of its territory would be leased or granted to another nation. This agreement led to a boom in sugar production based on cheap immigrant labor, mainly Chinese and Japanese, and white American sugar planters soon formed an economic elite. By the 1890s, the native Hawaiian population had been reduced to a minority by smallpox and other foreign diseases, and Asians became the most numerous ethnic group.

Beginning in 1891, Queen Liliuokalani, the Hawaiian ruler, tried to restore "Hawaii for the Hawaiians" by restricting the growing political power exercised by U.S. planters in the islands. Two years later, however, Hawaii's white population (called *haoles*) revolted and overthrew the monarchy when John L. Stevens, the U.S. ambassador, brought in marines to support the coup in January 1893. The queen surrendered "to the superior force of the United States," leading Stevens to report to the secretary of state, "The Hawaiian pear is now fully ripe, and this is the golden hour for the United States to pluck it." Within a month, a committee representing the *haoles* came to Washington, D.C., to ask the United States to annex the islands, and President Benjamin Harrison sent an annexation treaty to the Senate just as he was leaving the presidency.

To investigate the situation, new president Grover Cleveland sent a special commissioner to Hawaii, who reported that the Americans there had acted improperly and that most native Hawaiians opposed annexation. Cleveland tried to restore the queen to power but met resistance from the *haoles*. On July 4, 1894, the government they controlled created the Republic of Hawaii, which included in its constitution a provision for American annexation.

In 1897, when William McKinley became president, he was looking for an excuse to annex the islands. "We need Hawaii," he claimed, "just as much and a good deal more than we did California. It is [America's] manifest destiny." The United States took control of Hawaii in the summer of 1898, over the protests of native Hawaiians who resented their nation being annexed "without reference to the consent of the people of the Hawaiian Islands." President McKinley explained that "We need Hawaii as much as in its day we needed California. It was Manifest Destiny."

Queen Liliuokalani
The Hawaiian queen sought to preserve her nation's independence.

The Spanish-American War (War of 1898)

> CORE **OBJECTIVE**
> **3.** Explain the causes of the Spanish-American War (War of 1898), and describe its major events.

The annexation of Hawaii set in motion a series of efforts to create an American presence in Asia. Ironically, this imperialist push originated not in Asia but in Cuba, a Spanish colony ninety miles south of Florida. Even more ironically, the chief motive for American intervention in Cuba was a sense of outrage at Spain's brutal imperialism.

"Free Cuba"

Throughout the second half of the nineteenth century, Cubans had repeatedly revolted against Spanish rule, only to be ruthlessly suppressed. As one of Spain's oldest colonies, Cuba was a major export market for Spanish goods. Yet American sugar and mining companies had also invested heavily in Cuba. In fact, the United States traded more with Cuba than Spain did, and the American owners of sugar plantations in Cuba grew increasingly concerned about the security of their investments amid the rebellions.

On February 24, 1895, Cubans began another guerrilla war against Spanish troops, when uprisings erupted throughout the island. During what became the Cuban War for Independence (1895–1898), 95,000 Cuban peasants died of combat wounds as well as disease and starvation in Spanish detention camps.

Americans followed the conflict each day through the newspapers, the only source for international news. Two newspapers locked in a fierce competition for readers, William Randolph Hearst's *New York Journal* and Joseph Pulitzer's *New York World*, strove to outdo each other with sensational headlines about every Spanish atrocity in Cuba, real or invented.

The newspapers' efforts to manipulate public opinion through sensationalist reporting came to be called **yellow journalism**. Editors sent their best reporters to Cuba and encouraged them to distort and exaggerate the facts in their stories to attract more readers. In addition to boosting the *Journal*'s circulation, Hearst wanted a war against Spain to propel the United States to world-power status. Once war was declared, he took credit for it; one of his headlines blared, "HOW DO YOU LIKE THE JOURNAL'S WAR?" Many Protestant ministers and publications also campaigned for war in Cuba, in part because of antagonism toward Catholic Spain. A Catholic official in New York City criticized such "bloodthirsty preachers."

The Political Path to War

At the outset of the Cuban War for Independence in 1895, President Grover Cleveland tried to protect U.S. business interests in Cuba while avoiding military involvement. Mounting public sympathy for the rebel cause prompted acute concern in Congress, however. By concurrent resolutions on April 6, 1896, the House and Senate endorsed granting official recognition to the Cuban rebels. After his inauguration in March 1897, President William McKinley continued the policy of official neutrality but took a sympathetic stance toward the rebels. Later that year, Spain offered Cubans autonomy (self-government without formal independence) in return for ending the rebellion, but the Cubans rejected the offer.

Early in 1898, events pushed Spain and the United States into a war that neither government wanted. On January 25, the **U.S. battleship *Maine*** docked in the harbor of Havana, the Cuban capital, supposedly on a courtesy call. On February 9, the *New York Journal* released the text of a letter from Depuy de Lôme, Spanish ambassador to the United States, to a friend in Havana. In the **de Lôme letter**, which had been stolen from the post office by a Cuban spy, de Lôme called McKinley "weak and a bidder for the admiration of the crowd, besides being a would-be politician who tries to leave a door open behind himself while keeping on good terms with

---

Yellow journalism, the de Lôme letter, and the sinking of the *Maine*

yellow journalism A type of news reporting, epitomized in the 1890s by the newspaper empires of William Randolph Hearst and Joseph Pulitzer, that intentionally manipulates public opinion through sensational headlines, illustrations, and articles about both real and invented events.

U.S. battleship *Maine* American warship that exploded in the Cuban port of Havana on January 25, 1898; though later discovered to be the result of an accident, the destruction of the *Maine* was attributed by war-hungry Americans to Spain, contributing to the onset of the Spanish-American War.

de Lôme letter (1898) Private correspondence written by the Spanish ambassador to the U.S., Depuy de Lôme, that described President McKinley as "weak"; the letter was stolen by Cuban revolutionaries and published in the *New York Journal*, deepening American resentment of Spain and moving the two countries closer to war in Cuba.

"$50,000 Reward!" As if the news of the *Maine* sinking were not disturbing enough, the *New York Journal* sought to sensationalize the incident by offering a $50,000 reward for the perpetrator—the equivalent of $1.3 million today.

the jingoes [aggressive nationalists] of his party." De Lôme resigned to prevent further embarrassment to his government.

Six days later, on February 15, the *Maine* exploded without warning and sank in Havana Harbor, with a loss of 266 men. Although years later the sinking was ruled an accident resulting from a coal explosion, those eager for a war with Spain in 1898 saw no need to delay judgment. The headline in the *New York Journal* screamed: "Whole Country Thrills with War Fever." The thirty-nine-year-old assistant secretary of the navy, Theodore Roosevelt, called the sinking "an act of dirty treachery on the part of the Spaniards" and told a friend that he "would give anything if President McKinley would order the fleet to Havana tomorrow." The United States, he claimed, "needs a war." But McKinley, who assumed that the sinking was an accident, refused to be rushed into war. As the days passed and war did not come, Roosevelt told his friends that the president was too timid; he "has no more backbone than a chocolate éclair." With Roosevelt's encouragement, the public's outcry against Spain grew behind the saying "Remember the *Maine!*"

In the weeks following the sinking, the Spanish government agreed to virtually every demand by the American government regarding its rule over Cuba. But the weight of outraged public opinion and the influence of Republican "jingoists" such as Roosevelt and the president's closest friend, Senator Henry Cabot Lodge, eroded McKinley's neutrality. On April 11, McKinley asked Congress for authority to use armed forces in Cuba to end the fighting there. On April 20, Congress declared Cuba independent and demanded the withdrawal of Spanish forces. Upon learning of the American actions, the Spanish government broke diplomatic ties with the United States and, after U.S. ships began blockading Cuban ports, declared war. Congress then passed its own declaration of war on April 25. The **Teller Amendment**, added on the Senate floor to the war resolution, denied any U.S. intention to annex Cuba.

A declaration of war and the Teller Amendment

Teller Amendment (1898) Addition to the congressional war resolution of April 20, 1898, which marked the U.S. entry into the war with Spain; the amendment declared that the United States' goal in entering the war was to ensure Cuba's independence, not to annex Cuba as a territory.

President McKinley signed the war resolution and called for 125,000 volunteers to supplement the 28,000 men already serving in the U.S. Army. Among the first to enlist was the man who most lusted for war: Theodore Roosevelt, who resigned from his government post and told his tailor to make him a dashing army uniform. His political opponent, Democrat William Jennings Bryan, joined the ranks as a colonel in the Third Nebraska Volunteers. Never has an American war, so casually begun and so enthusiastically supported, generated such unexpected and far-reaching consequences as did the conflict against Spain. Although McKinley had gone to war reluctantly, he soon saw it as an opportunity to acquire overseas territories. "While we are conducting war and until its conclusion," he wrote privately, "we must keep all we get; when the war is over we must keep what we want." A war to free Cuba thus became a way to gain an empire. (What had long been called the Spanish-American War has recently been renamed the War of 1898 because it involved not just Spanish and American combatants, but also Cubans, Filipinos, and Puerto Ricans.)

"A Splendid Little War"

The war with Spain lasted only 114 days. The conflict was barely underway before the U.S. Navy produced a spectacular victory in an unexpected location in the Pacific Ocean: Manila Bay in the Philippine Islands, a colony controlled by the Spanish for over 300 years. Just before war was declared, Roosevelt, who was still the assistant secretary of the navy, had ordered Commodore George Dewey, commander of the U.S. Asiatic Squadron, to engage Spanish forces in the Philippines in case of war on the other side of the world in Cuba. Dewey arrived in Manila Bay on April 30 with six modern warships, which quickly destroyed or captured the outdated Spanish vessels there. Almost 400 Spaniards were killed or wounded in the lopsided battle. One overweight American sailor died of heatstroke. An English reporter called it "a military execution rather than a real contest." However lopsided the battle, the news of Dewey's victory set off wild celebrations in the United States.

> Commodore Dewey's naval victory at Manila Bay

Commodore Dewey was now in awkward possession of Manila Bay but without any soldiers to go onshore. Promised reinforcements, he stayed while German and British warships cruised offshore like watchful vultures, ready to seize the Philippines if the United States did not do so. In the meantime, Emilio Aguinaldo, the leader of the Filipino nationalist movement, declared the Philippines independent from Spain on June 12. With Aguinaldo's help, Dewey's forces entered Manila on August 13 and accepted the surrender of the Spanish troops there, who had feared revenge if they surrendered to the Filipinos. News of the American victory sent President McKinley scurrying to find a map of Asia to locate "these darned islands" now occupied by U.S. soldiers and sailors. Dewey, the first hero of the war, was promoted to admiral. Senator Lodge was delighted with the news from the Philippines: "We hold the other side of the Pacific," he announced. "We

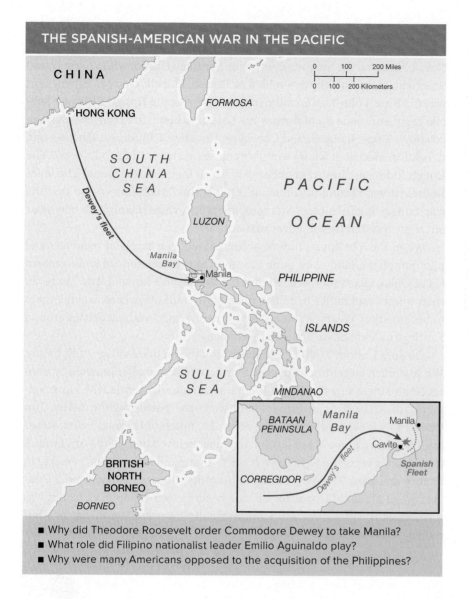

THE SPANISH-AMERICAN WAR IN THE PACIFIC

- Why did Theodore Roosevelt order Commodore Dewey to take Manila?
- What role did Filipino nationalist leader Emilio Aguinaldo play?
- Why were many Americans opposed to the acquisition of the Philippines?

must on no account let the [Philippine] Islands go." McKinley agreed, stressing that "we must keep all we get."

The Cuban Campaign

While these events were occurring halfway around the world, the fighting in Cuba reached a surprisingly quick climax. At the start of the war, the experienced Spanish army in Cuba was five times as large as the entire U.S. Army. But McKinley's call for volunteers inspired nearly a million men to enlist, far more than the military could absorb, leading to widespread

African American troops in Cuba
Soldiers stand in formation wearing old wool uniforms unsuited to Cuba's tropical heat.

Rough Riders The First Volunteer Cavalry, led in the Spanish-American War by Theodore Roosevelt; victorious in their only engagement, the Battle of San Juan Hill.

confusion and mismanagement. Those new recruits had to be equipped and trained before they would be ready for battle. In the meantime, the U.S. Navy blockaded the Spanish fleet inside Santiago Harbor while some 17,000 American troops hastily assembled at Tampa, Florida. One prominent unit was the First Volunteer Cavalry, better known as the **Rough Riders**, a special regiment made up of former Ivy League athletes, ex-convicts, western cowboys, Texas Rangers, and Cherokee, Choctaw, Chickasaw, Pawnee, and Creek Indians, all of whom were "young, good shots, and good riders." The Rough Riders are best remembered because Lieutenant Colonel Theodore Roosevelt was second in command. One of the Rough Riders said that the war-hungry Roosevelt was "nervous, energetic, virile [manly]. He may wear out some day, but he will never rust out."

When the 578 Rough Riders, accompanied by a gaggle of reporters and photographers, landed on June 22, 1898, at the undefended southeastern tip of Cuba, chaos followed. Except for Roosevelt's horse, Little Texas, all their horses and mules had been mistakenly sent elsewhere, leaving them to become the "Weary Walkers." Nevertheless, land and sea battles around Santiago quickly broke Spanish resistance.

On July 1, about 7,000 U.S. soldiers took the fortified village of El Caney. While a much larger force attacked San Juan Hill, a smaller unit, led by Roosevelt and including the Rough Riders, seized nearby Kettle Hill. Four regiments of African American soldiers were the heroes of the battle. But thanks to widespread newspaper coverage, much of it exaggerated, Roosevelt became a home-front legend, the most beloved hero of the brief war. A friend of his reported to Roosevelt's wife that her husband was "reveling in victory and gore." Never inclined to humility, Roosevelt requested a Congressional Medal of Honor for his much-publicized gallop in Cuba but was unsuccessful. (President Bill Clinton finally awarded the medal posthumously in 2001.)

Colonel Roosevelt With one hand on his hip, Roosevelt rides with the Rough Riders in Cuba. Most of this regiment was culled from Arizona, New Mexico, and Texas because the Southwestern climate resembled that of Cuba.

Spanish Defeat and Concessions

On July 3, the Spanish navy trapped at Santiago made a gallant run to evade the American fleet blockading the harbor. "The Spanish ships," reported Captain John Philip, commander of the U.S. warship *Texas*, "came out as gaily as brides to the altar." But the outdated, outgunned Spanish ships were quickly destroyed by the more modern American fleet. The casualties were as one-sided as those at Manila: 474 Spaniards were killed or wounded, while only one American was killed and one wounded. Spanish officials in Santiago surrendered on July 17. On July 25 an American force moved into Spanish-held Puerto Rico, meeting only minor resistance as it took control of the island.

> American victories in Santiago and Puerto Rico

The next day, July 26, the Spanish government sued for peace. A cease-fire agreement was signed on August 12, the day before Americans entered Manila. In Cuba, the Spanish forces formally surrendered to the U.S. commander and then sailed for home; excluded from the ceremony were the Cubans, for whom the war had supposedly been fought. On December 10, the United States and Spain signed the Treaty of Paris. Under its terms, Cuba was to become independent, and the United States was to annex Puerto Rico and continue to occupy Manila, pending a transfer of power in the Philippines. With the Treaty of Paris, the Spanish empire in the Americas, initiated by the voyages of Christopher Columbus some four centuries earlier, came to a humiliating end. Now the United States was ready to create its own empire.

> Terms of the peace treaty

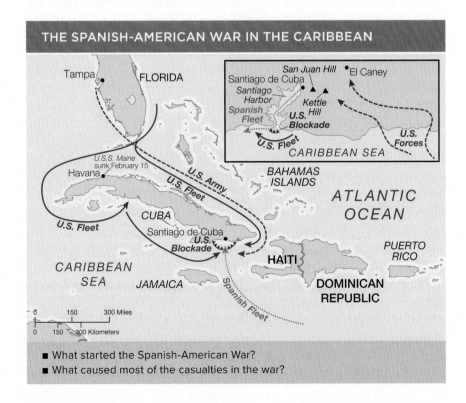

THE SPANISH-AMERICAN WAR IN THE CARIBBEAN

■ What started the Spanish-American War?
■ What caused most of the casualties in the war?

In all during the four-month Spanish-American War (War of 1898), more than 60,000 Spanish soldiers and sailors died of wounds or disease—mostly malaria, typhoid, dysentery, or yellow fever. Among the 274,000 Americans who served in the war, 5,462 died, but only 379 in battle; most of the rest died from unsanitary conditions in the army camps. At such a cost, the United States was launched onto the world scene as a great power, with all the benefits—and burdens—of a new colonial empire of its own.

Halfway through the conflict in Cuba, John Hay, the U.S. ambassador to Great Britain, who would soon become secretary of state, wrote a letter to Roosevelt, his close friend. In acknowledging Roosevelt's trial by fire, Hay called the conflict "a splendid little war, begun with the highest motives, carried on with magnificent intelligence and spirit, favored by that fortune which loves the brave."

CORE **OBJECTIVE**

4. Analyze the consequences of the Spanish-American War (War of 1898) for American foreign policy.

Consequences of Victory

John Hay's enthusiastic language suggests how the War of 1898 boosted American self-confidence and reinforced the self-serving belief, influenced by racism as well as Social Darwinism, that the United States had a "manifest destiny" to reshape the world in its own image. In 1885 the Reverend Josiah Strong wrote a best-selling book titled *Our Country* in which he used a Darwinian argument to strengthen the appeal of manifest destiny. The "wonderful progress of the United States," he boasted, was itself an illustration of Charles Darwin's concept of "natural selection," since Americans had demonstrated that they were the world's "superior" civilization, "a race of unequaled energy" who represented "the largest liberty, the purest Christianity, the highest civilization" in the world, a race of superior people destined to "spread itself over the earth," to Central and South America, and "out upon the islands" in the Pacific and beyond to Asia. Strong asserted that the United States had a Christian duty and economic opportunity to expand American influence around the world. A growing international trade, he noted, would grow directly out of America's missionary evangelism and racial superiority. "Can anyone doubt," he asked, "that this race . . . is destined to dispossess many weaker races, assimilate others, and mold the remainder until . . . it has Anglo-Saxonized mankind?"

America ascends to the world stage and redefines "manifest destiny"

Europeans agreed that the United States had now made an impressive entrance onto the world stage. The *Times* of London announced that the American victory over Spain must "effect a profound change in the whole attitude and policy of the United States. In the future America will play a part in the general affairs of the world such as she has never played before."

The United States had liberated most of Spain's remaining colonies, yet in some of them it would substitute its own imperialism for Spain's. If war with Spain had saved many lives by ending the insurrection in Cuba, it would also lead the United States to take many lives in suppressing another anti-colonial insurrection, in the Philippines. The acquisition of America's first imperial colonies created a host of long-lasting moral and practical problems, from the difficulties of imposing U.S. rule by force on native peoples to those of defending far-flung territories around the globe.

Annexation of the Philippines

The Treaty of Paris destroyed the Spanish empire. In Spain, the U.S. victory was called "The Disaster." But the treaty had left the political status of the Philippines unresolved. American business leaders wanted the United States to keep the islands so that they could more easily penetrate the vast markets of nearby China, with its huge population. American missionary organizations, mostly Protestant, also favored annexation, since they viewed the Philippines as a useful base from which to bring Protestant Christianity to "the little brown brother" throughout Asia.

"Well, I hardly know which to take first!" With a growing appetite for foreign territory, Uncle Sam browses his options: Cuba Steak, Puerto Rico Pig, Philippine Floating Islands, and others. An expectant President McKinley waits to take his order.

Not long after the United States took control of the Philippines, American authorities ended the Roman Catholic Church's status as the islands' official religion and made English the new official language, thus opening the door for Protestant missionaries to begin evangelical activities across the region.

These factors were among the considerations that convinced President McKinley of the need to annex "those darned islands" in the Philippines. He explained that

> American motives for annexation and further expansion in the Pacific

> . . . one night late it came to me this way—I don't know how it was, but it came: (1) that we could not give them back to Spain—that would be cowardly and dishonorable; (2) that we could not turn them over to France or Germany—our commercial rivals in the Orient—that would be bad business and discreditable; (3) that we could not leave them to themselves—they were unfit for self-government—and they would soon have anarchy and misrule over there worse than Spain's was; and (4) that there was nothing left for us to do but to take them all, and to educate the Filipinos, and uplift and civilize and Christianize them, and by God's grace do the very best we could by them, as our fellowmen for whom Christ also died. And then I went to bed, and went to sleep and slept soundly.

In this one brief statement, McKinley had summarized the motivating ideas of American imperialism: (1) national glory, (2) expanding commerce, (3) racial superiority, and (4) Christian evangelism. American negotiators in Paris finally offered Spain $20 million for the Philippines, Puerto Rico, and Guam, a Spanish-controlled island in the western Pacific between Hawaii and the Philippines.

Meanwhile, the United States took other giant steps toward imperial expansion in the Pacific. In addition to annexing Hawaii in 1898, the United States had also claimed Wake Island, between Guam and Hawaii, which would become a vital link in a future transpacific telegraph cable. Then, in 1899, Germany and the United States agreed to divide the Samoa Islands. The United States annexed the easternmost islands; Germany took the rest.

Philippines annexation

By early 1899, the Treaty of Paris ending the war with Spain had yet to be ratified in the Senate. Anti-imperialists argued that annexation of the Philippines would violate the longstanding American principle that people should be self-governing rather than colonial subjects. Opponents also noted the inconsistency of liberating Cuba and annexing the Philippines, as well as the danger that the Philippines would be impossible to defend if a foreign power such as Japan attacked. The opposition might have killed the treaty had not the most prominent national Democratic leader, William Jennings Bryan, argued that ending the war would open the way for the future independence of the Philippines. His support convinced enough Democrats to enable Senate approval of the treaty on February 6, 1899, by the narrowest of margins: only one vote more than the necessary two thirds.

President McKinley, however, had no intention of granting independence to the Philippines. Although he privately told a friend that "if old Dewey had just sailed away when he smashed that Spanish fleet, what a lot of trouble he would have saved us," he publicly insisted that the United States take control of the islands as an act of "benevolent assimilation" of the native population. But a California newspaper gave a more candid explanation. "Let us be frank," the editor exclaimed. "WE DO NOT WANT THE FILIPINOS. WE WANT THE PHILIPPINES."

Outbreak of war with Filipino nationalists

The Filipinos themselves had a different vision of their future. In January 1899, they declared their independence and named Emilio Aguinaldo the president of the first Philippine Republic. The following month, an American soldier outside Manila fired on soldiers in Aguinaldo's nationalist forces, called *insurrectos*, killing two. The next day, the U.S. army commander, without investigating the cause of the shooting, ordered his troops to assault the *insurrectos*, beginning a full-scale armed conflict that continued off and on for weeks. General Elwell S. Otis rejected Aguinaldo's proposals for a truce, saying that "fighting, having begun, must go on to the grim end." He would accept only the unconditional surrender of the Filipino forces.

On June 2, the Philippine Republic officially declared war against the United States, which now found itself in an even more costly conflict than

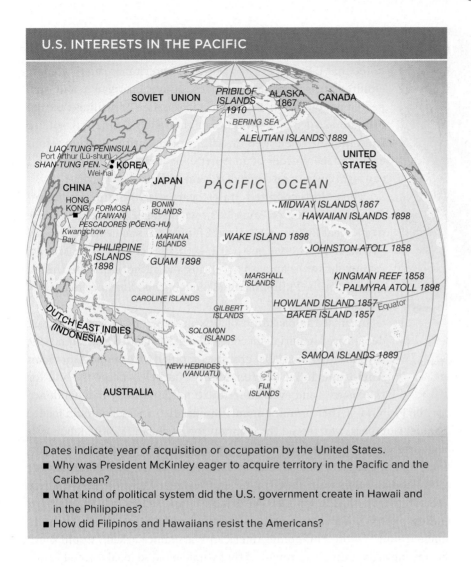

U.S. INTERESTS IN THE PACIFIC

Dates indicate year of acquisition or occupation by the United States.

■ Why was President McKinley eager to acquire territory in the Pacific and the Caribbean?

■ What kind of political system did the U.S. government create in Hawaii and in the Philippines?

■ How did Filipinos and Hawaiians resist the Americans?

the one with Spain, this one to suppress the Filipino independence movement. Since the *insurrectos* more or less controlled the Philippines outside Manila, what followed was largely an American war of conquest at odds with the founding principle of the United States: that people have the right to govern themselves.

The Philippine-American War

The American effort to crush Filipino nationalism lasted three years, involved some 126,000 U.S. troops, and took the lives of hundreds of thousands of Filipinos (most of them civilians) and 4,234 American soldiers. It was a brutal conflict, with massacres committed by both sides and racism contributing to numerous atrocities by the Americans, many of whom referred to the Filipinos as "niggers." U.S. troops burned villages, tortured and

"The water cure" American soldiers torture a Filipino prisoner during the Philippine-American War.

executed prisoners, and imprisoned civilians in overcrowded concentration camps. A reporter for the *Philadelphia Ledger* noted that U.S. soldiers had "killed to exterminate men, women, children, prisoners and captives, active insurgents and suspected people from lads of ten up, the idea prevailing that the Filipino as such was little better than a dog." One U.S. soldier from Indiana celebrated the killing of an entire village in retaliation for the murder of an American: "I am in my glory when I can sight my gun on some dark skin and pull the trigger."

Thus did the United States destroy a revolutionary movement modeled after America's own struggle for independence from Great Britain. Organized Filipino resistance had collapsed by the end of 1899. On April 1, 1901, at a ceremony in Manila, Aguinaldo swore an oath accepting the authority of the United States over the Philippines and pledging his allegiance to the U.S. government.

Against the backdrop of this nasty guerrilla war, the great debate over imperialism continued in the United States. In 1899, several anti-imperialist groups combined to form the **American Anti-Imperialist League**. Andrew Carnegie footed the bills for the League, and even offered $20 million to buy independence for the Filipinos. Other prominent anti-imperialists included union leader Samuel Gompers, who feared the competition of cheap Filipino labor, college presidents Charles Eliot of Harvard and David Starr Jordan of Stanford, and social reformer Jane Addams. Even former presidents Grover Cleveland and Benjamin Harrison urged President McKinley to withdraw U.S. forces from the Philippines. The drive for imperialism, said the Harvard philosopher William James, had caused the United States to "puke up its ancient soul." Of the Philippine-American War, James asked, "Could there be any more damning indictment of that whole bloated ideal termed 'modern civilization'?" Senator George Frisbie Hoar, one of the few surviving founders of the Republican party, led the opposition to annexation in the Senate. Under the Constitution, he pointed out, "no power is given the Federal government to acquire territory to be held and governed permanently as colonies" or "to conquer alien people and hold them in subjugation."

American Anti-Imperialist League Coalition of anti-imperialist groups united in 1899 to protest American territorial expansion, especially in the Philippine Islands; its membership included prominent politicians, industrialists, labor leaders, and social reformers.

Organizing the Former Spanish Territories

In the end, however, the imperialists won the debate over the status of the territories acquired from Spain. Senator Albert J. Beveridge boasted in 1900: "The Philippines are ours forever. And just beyond the Philippines are China's illimitable markets. We will not retreat from either. . . . The power that rules the Pacific is the power that rules the world." He added that the American economy was producing "more than we can consume, making more than we can use. Therefore we must find new markets for our produce." And American-controlled colonies would make the best new markets. Without acknowledging it, Beveridge and others were using many of the same arguments that England had used in founding the American colonies in the seventeenth century.

On July 4, 1901, the U.S. military government in the Philippines came to an end, and Judge William Howard Taft became the civil governor. In 1902 Congress passed the Philippine Government Act which declared the islands an "unorganized territory." In 1917, the Jones Act affirmed America's intention to grant the Philippines independence eventually, but that would not happen until 1946. Closer to home, Puerto Rico had been acquired in part to serve as a U.S. outpost guarding the Caribbean Sea. On April 12, 1900, the Foraker Act established a government on the island. The president appointed a governor and eleven members of an executive council, as well as an elected House of Delegates. Residents of the island were declared citizens of Puerto Rico; they were not made citizens of the United States until 1917.

In Cuba, the United States finally fulfilled the promise of independence after restoring order, organizing schools, and improving sanitary conditions. The problem of widespread disease in Cuba prompted the work of Dr. Walter Reed, who made an outstanding contribution to health in tropical regions around the world. Named head of the Army Yellow Fever Commission in 1900, he proved that mosquitoes carried yellow fever. The commission's experiments led the way to effective control of the disease worldwide.

In 1900, on President McKinley's order, Cubans drafted a constitution modeled on that of the United States. The Platt Amendment, added to an army appropriations bill in 1901, sharply restricted the Cuban government's independence, however. The amendment required that Cuba never impair its independence by signing a treaty with a third power, that it keep its debt within the government's power to repay it out of ordinary revenues, and that it acknowledge the right of the United States to intervene in Cuba whenever it saw fit. Finally, Cuba had to sell or lease to the United States lands to be used for coaling or naval stations, a stipulation that led to a U.S. naval base at Guantánamo Bay that still exists today. American troops remained in control of the rest of Cuba until 1902 and returned several times later to suppress insurrections.

Imperial Rivalries in East Asia

While the United States was conquering the Philippines, other nations were threatening to carve up China. After Japan defeated China in the First Sino-Japanese War (1894–1895), European nations set out to exploit the weakness of the huge, virtually defenseless nation. By the end of the century, Russia, Germany, France, and Great Britain had each established spheres of influence in China, territories within it that they (rather than the Chinese government) controlled but did not formally annex. In 1898 and again in 1899, the British asked the American government to join them in preserving the territorial integrity of China against further imperialist actions. Both times, however, the Senate rejected the request because the United States as yet had no strategic investment in the region.

"Open Door" policy

The American outlook toward Asia changed with the defeat of Spain and the acquisition of the Philippines. Instead of acting jointly with Great Britain, though, the U.S. government decided to act alone. What came to be known as the **Open Door policy** was outlined in Secretary of State John Hay's Open Door Note, dispatched in 1899 to his European counterparts. Without consulting the Chinese, Hay announced that China should remain an "Open Door" to European and American trade and that other nations should not try to take control of Chinese ports or territory. As it turned out, none of the European powers except Britain accepted Hay's principles, but none rejected them, either. So Hay simply announced that all the major powers involved in China had accepted the policy.

The Open Door policy was rooted in the desire of American businesses to dominate Chinese markets. However, it also appealed to those who opposed imperialism because it pledged to keep China from being carved up by powerful European nations. But the much-trumpeted policy had little legal standing. When the Japanese became concerned about growing Russian influence in the disputed region of Manchuria in northeast China and asked how the United States intended to enforce the Open Door policy, Hay replied that America was "not prepared . . . to enforce these views." So the situation would remain for forty years, until continued Japanese military expansion in China would bring about a diplomatic dispute with America that would ignite into war in December 1941.

Open Door policy (1899)
Official U.S. insistence that Chinese trade would be open to all nations; Secretary of State John Hay unilaterally announced the policy in 1899 in hopes of protecting the Chinese market for U.S. exports.

Intervention in China After quelling the Boxer Rebellion, U.S. troops march in the Forbidden Palace, the imperial palace in the Chinese capital of Beijing.

A new Asian crisis arose in 1900 when a group of Chinese nationalists known to the Western world as Boxers (they called themselves the "Fists of Righteous Harmony") rebelled against foreign involvement in China, especially Christian missionary efforts, and laid siege to foreign embassies in Peking (now known as Beijing). An international expedition of British, German, Russian, Japanese, and American soldiers rescued the international diplomats and their staffs. Hay, fearful that the intervention might become an excuse for other nations to dismember China, took the opportunity to refine the Open Door policy. The United States, he said in a letter of July 3, 1900, sought a solution that would "preserve Chinese territorial and administrative integrity" as well as "equal and impartial trade with all parts of the Chinese Empire." Six weeks later, the foreign military expedition reached Peking and ended the Boxer Rebellion.

Theodore Roosevelt and "Big-Stick" Diplomacy

CORE **OBJECTIVE**
5. Describe the reasons for Theodore Roosevelt's rapid rise to the presidency, evaluate the main elements of his foreign policies, and those of his successors in relation to Latin America.

More than any other American of his time, Theodore Roosevelt transformed the role of the United States in world affairs. The nation had emerged from the War of 1898 a world power with major new international responsibilities. To ensure that Americans accepted their new global role, Roosevelt stretched both the Constitution and executive power to the limit. In the process, he pushed a reluctant nation onto the center stage of world affairs.

Rise to National Prominence

Roosevelt's "strenuous life" and early political success

Born in 1858, Roosevelt had grown up in New York City in a cultured, wealthy family. He visited Europe as a child, spoke German fluently, and graduated from Harvard with honors in 1880. From a sickly, nearsighted boy with chronic asthma, he built himself into a physical and intellectual athlete, a man of almost superhuman energy and hyperactivity who for the rest of his days lived and championed the "strenuous life." A boxer, wrestler, mountain climber, hunter, and all-around outdoorsman, he also displayed extraordinary intellectual curiosity. He became a voracious reader, a natural scientist, a bird-watcher, a historian and essayist, and a zealous moralist. He wrote thirty-eight books on a wide variety of subjects. His boundless energy and fierce competitive spirit were contagious, and he was ever eager to express an opinion on any subject. Within two years of graduating from Harvard, Roosevelt won election to the New York legislature. "I rose like a rocket," he later observed.

But with the world seemingly at Roosevelt's feet, disaster struck. In 1884, his mother, Mittie, only forty-eight years old, died of typhoid fever.

Eleven hours later, in the same house, his twenty-two-year-old wife, Alice, died in his arms of kidney failure, having recently given birth to their only child just two days earlier. The double funeral service for his wife and mother was so emotional that the officiating minister wept throughout his prayer.

In an attempt to recover from this "strange and terrible fate," Roosevelt turned his newborn daughter over to his sister, quit his political career, sold the family house, and moved west to the Dakota Territory, where he threw himself into roping and branding steers, shooting buffalo and bears, punching out bullies, capturing outlaws, fighting Indians (whom he called a "lesser race"), and reading novels by the campfire. He was, by his own admission, a poor shot, a bad roper, and an average horseman, but he loved every minute of his western life. Although his time in the West lasted only two years, he never got over being a cowboy. "I owe more than I can express to the West," he emphasized in his memoirs.

Back in New York City, Roosevelt remarried and ran unsuccessfully for mayor in 1886. He later served six years as a federal civil service commissioner and two years as New York City's police commissioner. In 1896, Roosevelt campaigned energetically for William McKinley, and the new president was asked to reward him with the position of assistant secretary of the navy. McKinley resisted at first, saying that Roosevelt was too "hotheaded," but he eventually gave in.

Roosevelt took full advantage of the celebrity he had gained with the Rough Riders in Cuba to win the governorship of New York in 1898. By then, he had become the most prominent Republican in the nation. "I have played it in bull luck this summer," the governor-elect wrote a friend about his recent streak of successes. "First, to get into the war; then to get out of it; then to get elected." Two years later, Republican leaders were urging him to become the vice presidential running mate for William McKinley, who was hoping for a second term.

From Vice President to President

In the 1900 presidential contest, the Democrats turned once again to William Jennings Bryan, who wanted to make American imperialism the "paramount issue" of the campaign. The Democratic platform condemned the Philippine conflict as "an unnecessary war" that had placed the United States "in the false and un-American position of crushing with military force the efforts of our former allies to achieve liberty and self-government."

> Roosevelt's election as vice president and McKinley's assassination

The Republicans renominated McKinley and named Roosevelt, now known as "Mr. Imperialism," their candidate for vice president. Roosevelt, who despised Bryan as a dangerous "radical," criss-crossed the nation on behalf of McKinley, speaking in opposition to Bryan's "communistic and socialistic doctrines" promoting higher taxes and the unlimited coinage of silver. At one stop, Roosevelt claimed that Bryan's supporters were "all the lunatics, all the idiots, all the knaves, all the cowards." In the end, McKinley and Roosevelt won by 7.2 million to 6.4 million popular votes and 292 to 155 electoral votes. Bryan even lost Nebraska, his home state.

Less than a year later, however, McKinley's second term ended tragically. On September 6, 1901, while the president was shaking hands with well-wishers at the Pan-American Exposition in Buffalo, New York, a 28-year-old unemployed anarchist named Leon Czolgosz (pronounced *chol-gots*), the angry son of Polish immigrants, approached him with a gun concealed in a bandaged hand and fired twice at point-blank range. "I done my duty!" Czolgosz screamed. One bullet was deflected by the president's breastbone, but the other tore through his stomach and lodged in his back. As policemen wrestled the assassin to the ground, the wounded president urged them not to "hurt him."

For several days, the attending doctors issued optimistic reports about the president's condition, but after a week, McKinley knew he was dying. "It is useless, gentlemen," he told the doctors and nurses. "I think we ought to have a prayer." On September 14, McKinley died, and Theodore Roosevelt was elevated to the White House. "Now look," exclaimed Marcus "Mark" Hanna, the Ohio senator who had been McKinley's political manager, "that damned cowboy is President of the United States!" McKinley's assassination marked the end of one political era and the beginning of another.

Six weeks short of his forty-third birthday, Roosevelt was the youngest man ever to become president, but he had more experience in public affairs than most new presidents, and perhaps more vitality than any. One observer compared him to Niagara Falls—"both great wonders of nature." Even Woodrow Wilson, Roosevelt's main political opponent, described the former Rough Rider as "a great big boy" at heart, but, he added, "You can't resist the man." Roosevelt's glittering spectacles, glistening teeth, and overflowing enthusiasm were like divine gifts to political cartoonists, as was his famous motto, an old African proverb: "Speak softly, and carry a big stick."

"A great big boy" with a "bully pulpit"

Along with Roosevelt's boundless energy went an unshakable sense of self-righteousness, which led him to cast nearly every issue in moral and patriotic terms. He was the first truly activist president. The presidency was, as he put it, a "bully pulpit"—a wonderful platform for delivering fist-pumping speeches to the nation on the virtues of honesty, courage, and civic duty. Nowhere was President Roosevelt's forceful will more evident than in his handling of foreign affairs. Like many of his political friends and associates, he was convinced that the "civilized" and "barbarian" people of the world faced inevitable conflict, not unlike the fate of the Native Americans pushed off their ancestral lands by Americans. In 1899, Roosevelt argued that the United States, as a "great civilized power," needed to take control of other regions of the world so as to bring "law, order, and righteousness" to "backward peoples."

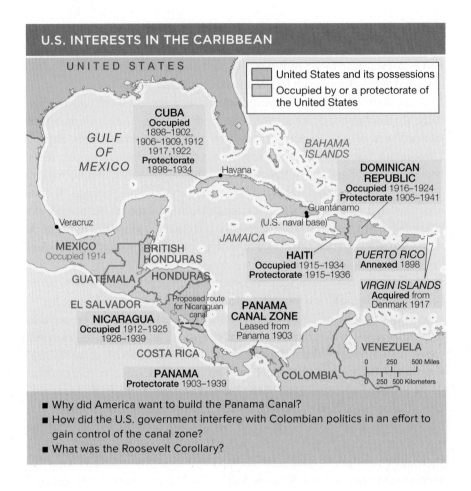

U.S. INTERESTS IN THE CARIBBEAN

- Why did America want to build the Panama Canal?
- How did the U.S. government interfere with Colombian politics in an effort to gain control of the canal zone?
- What was the Roosevelt Corollary?

The Panama Canal

After the War of 1898, the United States became more deeply involved in the Caribbean. One issue overshadowed every other in the region: the proposed Panama Canal. By enabling ships to travel from the Pacific Ocean to the Gulf of Mexico, such a canal would cut the travel distance between San Francisco and New York City by almost 8,000 miles. The narrow nation of Panama had first become a major concern of Americans in the late 1840s, when it became an important overland link in the sea route from the East coast to the California goldfields. Two treaties dating from that period loomed as obstacles to the construction of a canal, however. The Bidlack Treaty (1846) with Colombia (then called New Granada) guaranteed Colombia's control over Panama. In the Clayton-Bulwer Treaty (1850), the British agreed to acquire no more Central American territory, and the United States joined them in agreeing to build or fortify a canal only by mutual consent.

Taking the Panama Canal Zone

Secretary of State Hay asked the British ambassador for consent to build such a canal, and the outcome was the Hay-Pauncefote Treaty of 1901.

Other obstacles remained, however. From 1881 to 1887, a French company led by Ferdinand de Lesseps, who had engineered the Suez Canal in Egypt between 1859 and 1869, had spent nearly $300 million and some 20,000 lives to dig a canal a third of the way across Panama, which was still under the control of Colombia. The company asked that the United States purchase its partially-completed canal, which it did. Meanwhile, Secretary Hay had opened negotiations with Ambassador Tomás Herrán of Colombia. In return for acquiring a canal zone six miles wide, the United States agreed to pay $10 million. The U.S. Senate ratified the Hay-Herrán Treaty in 1903, but the Colombian senate held out for $25 million. As President Roosevelt raged against the "foolish and homicidal corruptionists in Bogotá," the Panamanians revolted against Colombian rule. Philippe Bunau-Varilla, an employee of the French canal company, assisted them and reported, after visiting Roosevelt and Hay in Washington, D.C., that U.S. warships would arrive at Colón, Panama, on November 2.

Colombian troops, who could not penetrate the overland jungle separating them from the Canal Zone, found the U.S. ships blocking the sealanes to the area. On November 13, the Roosevelt administration received its first ambassador from the newly independent Panama; he was Bunau-Varilla, who eagerly signed a treaty that extended the Canal Zone from six to ten miles wide. For a $10 million down payment and $250,000 a year, the United States received "in perpetuity the use, occupation and control" of the Canal Zone. The U.S. attorney general, asked to supply a legal opinion upholding Roosevelt's actions, responded wryly, "No, Mr. President, if I were you I would not have any taint of legality about it." Roosevelt later explained, "I took the Canal Zone and let Congress debate; and while the debate goes on the [construction of the] Canal does also." The Panama Canal opened on August 15, 1914, two weeks after the outbreak of the First World War in Europe.

The behavior of the United States in gaining control of the Panama Canal created ill will throughout Latin

THE BIG STICK IN THE CARIBBEAN SEA

Big Stick diplomacy President Theodore Roosevelt wields "the big stick," symbolizing his aggressive diplomacy. As he stomps through the Caribbean, he drags a string of American warships behind him.

America that would last for generations. Equally upsetting to Latin Americans was constant interference by both the United States and European countries in the internal affairs of various Latin American nations. A frequent excuse for intervention in the early twentieth century was the collection of debts owed to foreign banks. The Latin Americans responded to these actions with the Drago Doctrine (1902), named after the Argentinian foreign minister Luis María Drago, which prohibited armed intervention by other countries to collect debts.

In December 1902, however, German and British warships blockaded Venezuela to force repayment of debts owed to their nations' banks. Such an action defied not only the Drago Doctrine but also the Monroe Doctrine, the U.S. policy dating to 1823 that prohibited European intervention in the Western Hemisphere. Roosevelt decided that if the United States was going to keep European nations from intervening militarily in Latin America, "then sooner or later we must keep order [there] ourselves." In 1904, a crisis over the debts of the Dominican Republic prompted Roosevelt to issue what came to be known as the **Roosevelt Corollary** to the Monroe Doctrine: the principle, in short, that in certain circumstances the United States was justified in intervening in Latin American nations to prevent outsiders from doing so. "Chronic wrongdoing," Roosevelt asserted, would justify U.S. exercise of "an international police power" in the region. Thereafter, Roosevelt and other U.S. presidents repeatedly used military force to ensure that Latin American nations paid their debts to U.S. and European banks.

Relations with Japan

While wielding a "big stick" in Latin America, Roosevelt was playing the role of peacemaker in East Asia. The principle of equal trading rights in East Asia represented by the Open Door policy was tested further in 1904 when the long-standing rivalry between Russia and Japan flared into warfare. The Japanese had decided that the Russians threatened Japan's ambitions to expand its influence in China and Korea. On February 8, Japanese warships devastated the Russian fleet; the Japanese then occupied the Korean peninsula and drove the Russians back into Manchuria. When the Japanese signaled that they would welcome a negotiated settlement, Roosevelt sponsored a peace conference in Portsmouth, New Hampshire. In the Treaty of Portsmouth, signed on September 5, 1905, Russia acknowledged Japan's "predominant political, military, and economic interests in Korea" (Japan would annex the kingdom in 1910), and both powers agreed to leave Manchuria.

Japan's show of strength against Russia raised concerns among U.S. leaders about the security of the Philippines. During the Portsmouth talks, Roosevelt sent William Howard Taft to meet with the Japanese foreign minister in Tokyo. The two men negotiated the Taft-Katsura Agreement of July 29, 1905, in which the United States accepted Japanese control of Korea in exchange for Japan acknowledging U.S. control of the Philippines. Three years later, the Root-Takahira Agreement, negotiated by Secretary of State Elihu Root and the Japanese ambassador to the United States,

---

The Roosevelt Corollary to the Monroe Doctrine

Negotiating an end to the Russo-Japanese War

Roosevelt Corollary (1904) President Theodore Roosevelt's revision of the Monroe Doctrine (1823) in which he argued that the United States could use military force in Central and South America to prevent European nations from intervening in the Western Hemisphere.

The American Empire: Power and Consequences

By the early twentieth century, the United States had become one of the great powers on the international stage, able to project its power abroad and influence developments far from U.S. borders. The following chart lists the motives underlying American imperialism, the territories acquired in the late nineteenth and early twentieth centuries that made up America's empire, and the broader consequences of American imperialism.

MOTIVES FOR IMPERIALISM

"Manifest Destiny" and national glory

Racial superiority, fueled by Social Darwinism

Christian evangelism

Demand for raw materials and new markets

Access to naval bases and coaling stations

To prevent other nations from acquiring colonies

TERRITORIES ACQUIRED

Pacific Region	Latin America
Purchase	**War**
Alaska, 1867, from Russia	Puerto Rico, 1899 (Spanish-American War)
Annexation	
Hawaii, 1898	Guantanamo Bay, Cuba, 1901 (Spanish-American War)
Wake Island, 1898	
Eastern Samoa Islands, 1899	**Intervention**
War	Panama Canal Zone, 1903 (Hay–Bunau-Varilla Treaty)
Guam, 1899 (Spanish-American War)	
Philippines, 1899 (Philippine-American War)	

CONSEQUENCES OF IMPERIALISM

Spanish-American War (1899)

- End of Spain's New World empire
- Ill will between Latin American nationalists and U.S. troops

Philippine-American War (1899–1902)

- Exposed America's pro-colonialist leanings
- Formation of American Anti-Imperialist League (1899)

Open Door policy in China (1899)

- Established American presence in China

Roosevelt Corollary to the Monroe Doctrine (1904)

Taft-Katsura (1905) and Gentlemen's Agreements with Japan (1907)

Spread of American Protestant missionaries overseas

Medical breakthroughs in preventing tropical diseases

America emerges as a global power

QUESTIONS FOR ANALYSIS

1. What factors motivated American policy in creating this empire?

2. How did the United States acquire these territories?

3. What were the consequences of American imperialism?

Japanese immigration Japanese immigrants are vaccinated aboard a steamship on their way to Hawaii. By 1900, about 40 percent of Hawaii's population was Japanese.

The "Great White Fleet"

reinforced the Open Door policy by supporting "the independence and integrity of China" and "the principle of equal opportunity for commerce and industry in China."

Behind the outward appearances of goodwill, however, lay mutual distrust. For many Americans, the Russian threat in East Asia now gave way to concerns about the "yellow peril" (a term apparently coined by Kaiser Wilhelm II of Germany). Racial conflict on the West Coast, especially in California, helped sour relations with Japan. In 1906, San Francisco's school board ordered students of Asian descent to attend a separate public school. When the Japanese government sharply protested, President Roosevelt persuaded the school board to change its policy, but only after making sure that Japanese authorities would stop encouraging unemployed Japanese "laborers" to go to America. This "Gentlemen's Agreement" of 1907, the precise terms of which have never been revealed, halted what had become an influx of Japanese immigrants to California and brought some relief from racial tension there.

The Great White Fleet

After Roosevelt's election to a full term as president in 1904, he celebrated America's rise as a world power with a great flourish. In 1907, he sent the entire U.S. Navy, by then second in strength only to Britain's Royal Navy, on a grand fourteen-month tour around the world, announcing that he was ready for "a feast, a frolic, or a fight." At every port of call down the Atlantic coast of South America, up the Pacific coast, out to Hawaii, and down to New Zealand and Australia, the "Great White Fleet" of sixteen gleaming battleships received a rousing welcome. The triumphal procession continued to Japan, China, and the Philippines, then Egypt through the Suez Canal and across the Mediterranean Sea before steaming back to Virginia in early 1909, just in time to close Roosevelt's presidency on a note of triumph. No sooner had the "Great White Fleet" returned than the ships were all repainted in gray.

Roosevelt believed that the United States in the twentieth century must assume a much larger role in world affairs as a result of its own international economic interests and its growing military power. America had become, he noted, the "balance of power of the whole globe."

Yet Roosevelt's success in expanding U.S. power abroad would have mixed consequences, since underlying it was a militantly racist view of the world shared by many other imperialists of the time. In their view, the world was made up of "civilized" nations such as the United States, Japan, and the nations of Europe and those they described as "barbarous," "backward," or "impotent" peoples unable to meet their basic obligations as organized societies. It was the responsibility of the "civilized" nations to exercise control of the "barbarous" peoples, by force if necessary. Roosevelt once told the graduates of the Naval War College that all "the great masterful races have been fighting races, and the minute that a race loses the hard fighting virtues . . . it has lost the right to stand as equal to the best." On another occasion he called warfare the best way to promote "the clear instinct for race selfishness" and insisted that "the most ultimately righteous of all wars is a war with savages." Such belligerent, self-righteous bigotry defied American ideals of equality and would come back to haunt the United States in world affairs.

Taft's "Dollar Diplomacy"

Republican William Howard Taft, who succeeded Roosevelt as president in 1909, continued to promote America's economic interests abroad, practicing what Roosevelt called "**dollar diplomacy**." He used the State Department to help American companies and banks to invest in foreign countries, especially East Asia and the less developed nations of Latin America and the Caribbean. To ensure the stability of those investments, Taft, like Roosevelt, did not hesitate to intervene in nations experiencing political and economic turmoil. In 1909 Taft dispatched U.S. Marines to support a revolution in Nicaragua. Once the new government was formed, Secretary of State Philander C. Knox (a corporate attorney who had helped form the giant U.S. Steel Corporation) helped U.S. banks negotiate loans to prop it up. Two years later, he again sent American troops to restore political stability. This time the soldiers stayed for more than a decade.

> Taft's "dollar diplomacy"

Wilson's Interventionism

In 1913 the new Democratic president, Woodrow Wilson, attacked the "dollar diplomacy" practiced by Taft and Roosevelt, claiming that it was a form of economic imperialism. He promised to treat the Latin American nations "on terms of equality and honor." Yet Wilson, along with his secretary of state William Jennings Bryan, who called Latin Americans "our political children," dispatched American military forces to Latin America more often than Taft and Roosevelt.

> Wilson's Interventionism

Wilson argued that the United States must intervene to stabilize weak governments in the Western hemisphere in order to keep European nations from doing so. He said it was "reprehensible" to allow European governments to take control of these "weak and unfortunate republics."

During his two presidential terms, the idealistic Wilson sent U.S. troops into Cuba once, Panama twice, and Honduras five times. In 1915, when the Dominican Republic on the Caribbean island of Hispaniola refused to sign a treaty that would have given the United States a "special" role in governing the island nation, Wilson sent U.S. Marines, where they established a military government and fought a nasty guerrilla war against anti-American rebels. That same year, Wilson also intervened in Haiti, next door to the Dominican Republic. He admitted that his actions were "highhanded" but justified because the "necessity for exercising control there is immediate,

"dollar diplomacy" Practice advocated by President Theodore Roosevelt in which the U.S. government fostered American investments in less developed nations and then used U.S. military force to protect those investments.

urgent, imperative." Others disagreed. As the *New York Times* charged, Wilson's frequent interventions made Taft's dollar diplomacy look like "ten cent diplomacy."

The United States in Mexico

Mexico was a much thornier problem for President Wilson's well-intentioned but misguided meddling. In 1910, long-suffering Mexicans had revolted against the long-standing dictatorship of Porfirio Diaz, who had given foreign corporations a free rein in developing the nation's economy. After revolutionary armies occupied Mexico City in 1911, the victorious rebels began squabbling among themselves. The leader of the rebellion, Francisco Madero, was himself overthrown by his chief of staff, General Victoriano Huerta, who assumed power in early 1913 and then had Madero and thirty other political opponents murdered.

Pancho Villa

Shocked by Madero's murder, President Wilson refused to recognize "a government of butchers." It was vital, he insisted, for the Latin American nations to have "fairly decent rulers." Huerta ignored Wilson's criticism and established a dictatorship. Wilson decided that Huerta must be removed. To do so, he ordered U.S. warships to halt shipments of foreign weapons to Huerta's new government. "I am going to teach the South American republics to elect good men," Wilson vowed to a British diplomat. Meanwhile, several rival revolutionary Mexican armies, the largest of which was led by a charming but ruthless bandit named Francisco Pancho Villa, began trying to unseat Huerta.

Intervention in Mexico Marines enter Veracruz, Mexico, in 1914.

On April 9, 1914, nine American sailors were arrested in Tampico, Mexico, while trying to buy supplies. Mexican officials quickly released them and apologized to the U.S. naval commander. There the incident might have ended, but the imperious U.S. admiral demanded that the Mexicans fire a 21-gun salute to the American flag. After they refused, Wilson sent U.S. troops ashore at Veracruz on April 21, 1914. They occupied the city at a cost of nineteen American lives; at least 300 Mexicans were killed or wounded.

The use of military force in Mexico played out like many previous American interventions in the Caribbean and Central America. Congress readily supported the decision because American honor was supposedly at stake, and Wilson was sure that most Mexicans would welcome U.S. intervention since his intentions were so "unselfish." But the arrival of U.S. troops in Veracruz backfired. Instead of welcoming the Americans as liberators, Mexicans viewed them as invaders. Newspapers in Mexico shouted for "Vengeance! Vengeance! Vengeance!" For seven months, the Americans governed Veracruz. They left in late 1914 after Huerta was overthrown by Venustiano Carranza.

Still, the troubles south of the border continued as various factions engaged in ongoing civil wars. In 1916, the colorful rebel leader, "Pancho" Villa, launched raids into Texas and New Mexico in a deliberate attempt to trigger U.S. intervention and to reinforce his anti-American credentials. On March 9, he and his men attacked Columbus, New Mexico, just three miles across the border. With Villa shouting "Kill all the Gringos!" his army of 500 peasant revolutionaries looted stores, burned the town, and killed seventeen Americans, men and women.

A furious Woodrow Wilson sent General John J. Pershing to Mexico with 6,000 U.S. soldiers to capture Villa and destroy his army. For nearly a year, with little success, Pershing's troops chased Villa's army through the rugged mountains of northern Mexico. As Pershing muttered, "It's like trying to chase a rat in a cornfield." In 1917, the American troops were ordered home. The elusive Villa, meanwhile, named his mule "President Wilson." By then, however, Wilson paid little notice, for he was distracted by a much greater threat: war in Europe.

- **Toward the New Imperialism** Near the end of the nineteenth century, the popular idea that America had a "manifest destiny" to expand its territory abroad and industrialists' desire for new markets for their goods helped to fuel America's "new imperialism." The ideology of Social Darwinism was used to justify the colonization of less developed nations. American evangelical Protestants also thought they had a duty to Christianize and "uplift" people throughout the world.

- **Expansion in the Pacific** Business leaders hoped to extend America's commercial reach across the Pacific. The United States purchased the vast Alaska territory from Russia in 1867. American planters in the Kingdom of Hawaii developed a thriving sugar industry based on Asian immigrant labor. In 1894, Hawaii's minority white population, led by planters, overthrew the native Hawaiian queen, declared a republic, and requested that Hawaii be annexed by the United States.

- **The Spanish-American War (The War of 1898)** When Cubans revolted against Spanish colonial rule in 1895, many Americans supported their demand for independence. *Yellow journalism* publicizing the harsh Spanish suppression of the revolt, further aroused Americans' sympathy. Early in 1898, the publication of the *de Lôme letter*, in which Spain's ambassador to the United States criticized President McKinley, followed by the mysterious explosion sinking the *U.S. battleship Maine* in Havana Harbor, helped propel America into war with Spain. In its war resolution, Congress declared Cuba independent and, in the *Teller Amendment*, denied any plans to annex Cuba. Under the Treaty of Paris ending the war, Cuba became independent and the United States annexed Spain's other Caribbean possession, Puerto Rico, which it had occupied. In the Spanish colony of the Philippine Islands, America's Pacific naval fleet under Commodore George Dewey defeated the Spanish fleet in the Battle of Manila Bay at the beginning of the war and took control of the capital, Manila.

- **Consequences of Victory** A vicious guerrilla war followed in the Philippines when Filipinos who favored independence rebelled against American control. The rebellion was suppressed, and President McKinley announced that the U.S. would annex the Philippines. This prompted a significant debate in which the *Anti-Imperialist League* and others argued that acquiring overseas territories violated American principles of self-determination and independence. But the imperialists won the debate, and Congress set up a government in the Philippines as well as in Puerto Rico. In Cuba, the United States imposed significant restrictions on the new government after U.S. forces left the island. In the Pacific region, the United States also annexed Hawaii, Guam, Wake Island, and some of the Samoa Islands during or shortly after the War of 1898. In East Asia, Secretary of State John Hay promoted the *Open Door policy* of preserving China's territorial integrity and equal access by all nations to trade with China.

- **Theodore Roosevelt and Big-Stick Diplomacy** After succeeding to the presidency upon McKinley's assassination in 1901, Theodore Roosevelt pursued an imperialist foreign policy that confirmed the United States' new role as a world power. He helped negotiate the treaty that ended the Russo-Japanese War, oversaw diplomatic and military actions leading to the U.S. construction and control of the Panama Canal, and sent the navy's fleet of new battleships around the world as a symbol of American might. He also proclaimed the *Roosevelt Corollary* to the Monroe Doctrine, asserting that the United States would intervene in Latin America as necessary in order to prevent European intervention.

■ Taft and Wilson's Interventionism Abroad
William H. Taft and Woodrow Wilson, continued his pattern of intervening in the internal affairs of the other nations. What Roosevelt called *"dollar diplomacy"* involved the U.S. government fostering American investments in less developed nations, and then using U.S. military force to protect those investments.

KEY TERMS

imperialism *p. 667*
The Influence of Sea Power upon History, 1660–1783 (1890) *p. 667*
yellow journalism *p. 670*
U.S. battleship *Maine p. 670*

de Lôme letter (1898) *p. 670*
Teller Amendment (1898) *p. 671*
Rough Riders *p. 674*

American Anti-Imperialist League *p. 680*
Open Door policy (1899) *p. 682*
Roosevelt Corollary (1904) *p. 688*
"dollar diplomacy" *p. 691*

CHRONOLOGY

1867	The United States purchases Alaska from Russia
1880s	European nations create colonial empires in Asia and Africa
1890	Alfred Mahan publishes *The Influence of Sea Power upon History, 1660–1783*
1894	Republic of Hawaii is proclaimed
1895	Cuban insurrection breaks out against Spanish rule
1898	U.S. battleship *Maine* explodes in Havana Harbor
1898	The Spanish American War (War of 1898)
1898	United States annexes Hawaii
1899	U.S. Senate ratifies the Treaty of Paris, ending the Spanish-American War
1899–1902	Insurgents resist U.S. conquest of the Philippines
1903	Panamanians revolt against Colombia
1905	Russo-Japanese War
1907–1909	U.S. Great White Fleet circles the globe
1914	Panama Canal opens
1909–1917	U.S. military interventions in Mexico and Latin America

INQUIZITIVE

Go to InQuizitive to see what you've learned—and learn what you've missed—with personalized feedback along the way.

DEBATING the Annexation of the Philippines

Historians use different analytical methods to make sense of the past. Some historians focus on social and economic issues such as class conflict or who profits from a particular policy choice. Other historians focus more on culture to understand how ideas, values, and beliefs have shaped the actions of historical figures. For Part 5, *Growing Pains*, we will examine how different analytical methods result in contrasting explanations for why the United States annexed and retained the Philippines following the defeat of Spain in 1898.

For this exercise you have two tasks:

PART 1: Compare the two secondary sources on why the United States annexed the Philippines.

PART 2: Using primary sources, evaluate the arguments of the two secondary sources.

PART I Comparing Secondary Sources

Two secondary sources from very different analytical perspectives have been included for you to review. In *Standing at Armageddon: The United States, 1877–1919*, Nell Irvin Painter of Princeton University weaves together economic and foreign-policy concerns with the lives of ordinary Americans to explain the annexation of the Philippines. Kristin L. Hoganson of the University of Illinois, a gender historian, explores the question of why the United States annexed the Philippines in *Fighting for American Manhood: How Gender Politics Provoked the Spanish-American and Philippine-American Wars*. While both works contain elements of economic and cultural history, each historian emphasizes a particular analytical methodology.

Compare the views of these two scholars by answering the following questions. Be sure to find specific examples in the selections to support your answers.

■ According to each author, what problems in society did supporters of annexation think American control of the Philippines would solve?

■ Which author focuses on economic explanations, and which author focuses on cultural explanations, to explain imperialist support for annexation?

■ Do you think the authors' arguments are contradictory or complementary? In other words, can they both be correct?

Secondary Source 1

Nell Irvin Painter, "The White Man's Burden" (1989)

The foreign markets explanation sought the cause of depressions not in currency, distribution of wealth, or monopoly. The culprit, it seemed, was agricultural and industrial overproduction. Americans produced too much, it was said; it seemed to matter little that during the recent hard times thousands had run out of the very foodstuffs and manufactured goods reputedly overproduced. What was needed were new markets, especially in Asia, especially in the most populous country in the world, China. . . . While foreign markets had beckoned American businessmen for decades, this more urgent quest included the novel expectation that the government of the United States should play an active part in fostering exports. The Philippine Islands—like Hawaii—represented the perfect stepping-stones to China, stops along the way where coal burning ships bound for Asia could refuel. Expansionists saw the islands as the opportunity of the century. Manila might become an American version of Hong Kong, the British market city that tapped the markets and produce of South China. . . . For many Americans, expansion was the inevitable result of the machine age that had already filled up the continental United States and now seemed to demand the raw materials and foreign markets that overseas colonies promised. The vision of factories fuming nonstop and workers employed without interruption made this economic argument for annexation straightforward and persuasive.

Source: Painter, Nell Irvin. *Standing at Armageddon: The United States, 1877–1919.* New York: W. W. Norton & Company, 1989. 146–7.

Secondary Source 2

Kristin L. Hoganson, "The National Manhood Metaphor" (1998)

Whether they imagined the Filipinos as savages, children, or feminine figures, imperialists regarded them as a means for American men to develop their ability to govern. One adherent of imperialism summed up this belief when he averred that "the necessities involved in the unexpected annexation of strange dependencies will *call forth the governing faculty*." The savage, childlike, and feminine stereotypes appealed to imperialists because they not only suggested the Filipinos' incapacity for self-government, but also enabled imperialists to cast themselves as civilizers and authoritative heads of household—that is, as men who wielded power. Heedful of British imperialists' claims that empire made men and interpreting colonial endeavors as unparalleled challenges, imperialists looked to the Philippines to turn white, middle- and upper-class American men into what they considered to be ideal citizens—physically powerful men who would govern unmanly subordinates with a firm hand, men accustomed to wielding authority, men who had overcome the threat of degeneracy. . . . In response to the accusations that their Philippine policies violated the nation's deepest convictions, imperialists brandished a national manhood metaphor. The youthful republic had become an adult, they declared, and should assume the responsibilities of a mature man. Rather than dwelling on its childish past, the nation should manfully shoulder its new obligations. . . . Imperialists implied that failing to assume responsibility for dependents would reveal an unwillingness to advance from childlike dependency to paternalistic power. In short, it would reveal a lack of manhood in the nation.

Source: Hoganson, Kristin L. *Fighting for American Manhood: How Gender Politics Provoked the Spanish-American and Philippine-American Wars.* New Haven: Yale University Press, 1998. 155, 157.

PART II Using Primary Sources to Evaluate Secondary Sources

When historians are faced with competing interpretations of the past, they often look at primary source material as part of the process of evaluating the different arguments. Four speeches follow, each by an American politician who supported annexation and rule over the Philippines. The first is from President William McKinley's State of the Union speech following U.S. annexation of the Philippines and the start of the Philippine-American War. The second is from Henry Cabot Lodge, a Republican senator from Massachusetts who was a leading supporter of American imperialism. The third speech is from Albert Beveridge, senator from Indiana, who supported Lodge's imperialist policies. And the last speech, from Vice President Theodore Roosevelt, was delivered twelve days prior to assuming the presidency following McKinley's death. While these four politicians offer very different justifications for American annexation and rule over the Philippines, they were all prominent advocates of American imperialism. Your task is to understand their arguments and see how they might be used to support the analysis of the two historians.

Carefully read each of these primary sources and answer the following questions. Decide which of the primary source documents support or refute Painter and Hoganson's analysis of the annexation of the Philippines. You may find that some documents do both but for different parts of each historian's analysis. Be sure to specify which aspects of each historian's argument the documents support or refute.

■ What arguments for U.S. retention of the Philippines does each senator offer?

■ Which of these sources would either Painter or Hoganson (or both) find most useful, and how might they use them to support their argument?

■ What might be the limitations on the usefulness of the sources for supporting their arguments?

■ After looking at the primary sources about annexation, which historian's argument do you find more compelling and why do you find it so? If you find both arguments equally compelling, how could you combine the arguments?

Primary Source 1

William McKinley, "Annual Message of the President to Congress" (December 5, 1899)

The future government of the Philippines rests with the Congress of the United States. Few graver responsibilities have ever been confided to us. If we accept them in a spirit worthy of our race and our traditions, a great opportunity comes with them. The islands lie under the shelter of our flag. They are ours by every title of law and equity. They cannot be abandoned. If we desert them we leave them at once to anarchy and finally to barbarism. We fling them, a golden apple of discord, among the rival powers, no one of which could permit another to seize them unquestioned. . . . The suggestion has been made that we could renounce our authority over the islands and, giving them independence, could retain a protectorate over them. This proposition will not be found, I am sure, worthy of your serious attention. Such an arrangement would involve at the outset a cruel breach of faith. . . .

No effort will be spared to build up the waste places desolated by war and by long years of misgovernment. We shall not wait for the end of strife to begin the beneficent work. We shall continue, as we have begun, to open the schools and the churches, to set the courts in operation, to foster industry and trade and agriculture, and in every way in our power to make these people whom Providence has brought within our jurisdiction feel that it is their liberty and not our power, their welfare and not our gain, we are seeking to enhance. Our flag has never waved over any community but in blessing. I believe the Filipinos will soon recognize the fact that it has not lost its gift of benediction in its world-wide journey to their shores.

Source: McKinley, William. "Annual Message of the President to Congress, transmitted to Congress, December 5, 1899," in *Papers Relating to the Foreign Relations of the United States with Annual Message of the President to Congress, Transmitted to Congress, December 5, 1899.* Washington, D.C.: United States Government Printing Office, 1901. L–LII.

Primary Source 2

Henry Cabot Lodge, "The Retention of the Philippine Islands," Speech in the U.S. Senate (March 7, 1900)

I believe, we shall find arguments in favor of the retention of the Philippines as possessions of great value and a source of great profit to the people of the United States which cannot be overthrown. First, as to the islands themselves. They are over a hundred thousand square miles in extent, and are of the greatest richness and fertility. From these islands comes now the best hemp in the world, and there is no tropical product which cannot be raised there in abundance. Their forests are untouched, of great extent, and with a variety of hard woods of almost unexampled value. . . . It is sufficient for me to indicate these few elements of natural wealth in the islands which only await development. . . . A much more important point is to be found in the markets which they furnish. The total value of exports and imports for 1896 amounted in round numbers to $29,000,000, and this was below the average. . . .

The Philippine Islands took from us imports to the value of only $94,000. There can be no doubt that the islands in our peaceful possession would take from us a very large proportion of their imports. Even as the islands are to-day there is opportunity for a large absorption of products of the United States, but it must not be forgotten that the islands are entirely undeveloped. The people consume foreign imports at the rate of only a trifle more than $1 per capita. With the development of the islands and the increase of commerce and of business activity the consumption of foreign imports would rapidly advance, and of this increase we should reap the chief benefit. We shall also find great profit in the work of developing the islands. . . .

Manila, with its magnificent bay, is the prize and the pearl of the East. In our hands it will become one of the greatest distributing points, one of the richest emporiums of the world's commerce. Rich in itself, with all its fertile islands behind it, it will keep open to us the markets of China and enable American enterprise and intelligence to take a master share in all the trade of the Orient!

Source: Lodge, Henry Cabot. *The Retention of the Philippine Islands, Speech of Hon. Henry Cabot Lodge of Massachusetts, in the Senate of the United States, March 7, 1900.* Washington, D.C.: United States Government Printing Office, 1900. 37, 41.

Primary Source 3

Albert Beveridge, "Our Philippine Policy," Speech in the U.S. Senate (January 9, 1900)

But, Senators, it would be better to abandon the Philippines, and count our blood and treasure already spent a profitable loss, than to apply any academic arrangement of self-government to these children [the Filipino people]. They are not yet capable of self-government. How could they be? They are not a self-governing race; they are Orientals, Malays, instructed by Spaniards in the latter's worst estate. They know nothing of practical government, except as they have witnessed the weak, corrupt, cruel, and capricious rule of Spain. What magic will anyone employ to dissolve in their minds and characters those impressions of governors and governed which three centuries of misrule has created? What alchemy will change the oriental quality of their blood, in a year, and set the self-governing currents of the American pouring through their Malay veins? How shall they, in a decade, be exalted to the heights of self-governing peoples which required a thousand years for us to reach? . . .

Self-government is no cheap boon, to be bestowed on the merely audacious. It is the degree which crowns the graduate of liberty, not the reward of liberty's infant class, which has not yet mastered the alphabet of freedom. Savage blood, oriental blood, Malay blood, Spanish example—in these do we find the elements of self-government? . . .

The men we send to administer civilized government in the Philippines must be themselves the highest examples of our civilization. I use the word examples, for examples they must be in that word's most absolute sense. They must be men of the world and of affairs, students of their fellow-men, not theorists nor dreamers. They must be brave men, physically as well as morally. They must be men whom no force can frighten, no influence coerce, no money buy. Such men come high, even here in America. But they must be had. . . . Necessity will produce them. . . . Better abandon this priceless possession, admit ourselves incompetent to do our part in the world-redeeming work of our imperial race; better now haul down the flag than to apply academic notions of self-government to these children or attempt their government by any but the most perfect administrators our country can produce. I assert that such administrators can be found.

Source: Beveridge, Albert J. "Our Philippine Policy," in *The Meaning of the Times and Other Speeches*. Indianapolis: The Bobbs-Merrill Company, 1908. 71–6.

Primary Source 4

Theodore Roosevelt, "National Duties," Speech at Minnesota State Fair (September 2, 1901)

Let me insist again, for fear of possible misconstruction, upon the fact that our duty is twofold, and that we must raise others while we are benefiting ourselves. In bringing order to the Philippines, our soldiers added a new page to the honor-roll of American history, and they incalculably benefited the islanders themselves. Under the wise administration of Governor Taft the islands now enjoy a peace and liberty of which they have hitherto never even dreamed. But this peace and liberty under the law must be supplemented by material, by industrial development. Every encouragement should be given to their commercial development, to the introduction of American industries and products; not merely because this will be a good thing for our people, but infinitely more because it will be of incalculable benefit to the people in the Philippines. We shall make mistakes; and if we let these mistakes frighten us from our work we shall show ourselves weaklings. . . . We gird up our loins as a nation, with the stern purpose to play our part manfully in winning the ultimate triumph; and therefore we turn scornfully aside from the paths of mere ease and idleness and with unfaltering steps tread the rough road of endeavor. . . .

Source: Roosevelt, Theodore. "National Duties." In *The Strenuous Life: Essays and Addresses*. New York: The Century Company, 1902. 295–97.

Modern America

The United States entered the twentieth century on a wave of unrelenting change, not all of it beneficial. In 1800, America was a rural, agrarian, Christian society largely unconcerned with international affairs. By 1900, the United States had become the world's most powerful economy, a highly industrialized urban society with a growing involvement in world politics and international commerce. In other words, the nation was on the threshold of the modern era in which the United States emerged as a leading global power.

The prospect of modernity both excited and scared Americans. Old truths and beliefs clashed with unsettling new scientific discoveries and social practices. People debated the truth of Darwinism and the Bible, the existence of God, the dangers of jazz, and proposals to prohibit the sale of alcoholic beverages. The advent of automobiles and airplanes helped shrink distance between people, and communications innovations such as radio and film helped strengthen a sense of unity or national consciousness. In the process, the United States began to emerge from its isolationist shell. Throughout most of the nineteenth century, presidents and secretaries of state had sought to isolate America from the intrigues and conflicts of the great European powers. As early as 1780, in the midst of the Revolutionary War, future president John Adams had warned Congress against involving the United States in the affairs of Europe. "Our business with them, and theirs with us," he wrote, "is commerce, not politics, much less war."

With only a few exceptions, statesmen during the nineteenth century followed such advice. Non-involvement in foreign wars and non-intervention in the internal affairs of foreign governments formed the pillars of American foreign policy until the end of the century. During the 1890s, however, expanding commercial interests around the world led Americans to broaden the horizons of their concerns. Imperialism, the acquisition by force of foreign colonies, was considered essential among the great European powers, and a growing number of American expansionists demanded that the United States join in the hunt for new territories and markets. Such motives helped spark the Spanish-American War of 1898 and helped to justify the resulting acquisition of colonies outside the continental United States.

The outbreak of the Great War in Europe in 1914 posed an even greater challenge to the tradition of isolation and nonintervention. The prospect of a German victory over the French, the British, and the Russians threatened the European balance of power, which had long ensured the security of the United States. By 1917 it appeared that Germany might emerge triumphant and begin to menace the Western Hemisphere. Woodrow Wilson's crusade to transform international affairs in accordance with his idealistic principles during the Great War severed American foreign policy from its isolationist moorings. It also started a prolonged debate about the role of the United States in world affairs, a debate that World War II would resolve for a time on the side of internationalism.

While the United States was entering the world stage as a formidable military power, it was also settling into its role as a great industrial power. Cities and factories sprouted across the landscape. An abundance of new jobs and affordable farmland served as a magnet attracting millions of immigrants from nearly every region of the world. They were not always welcomed, nor did they readily fit into American society. Ethnic and racial conflict, as well as clashes between workers and owners, increased at the turn of the century. In the midst of such social turmoil and unparalleled economic development, reformers made their first serious attempts to adapt political and social institutions to the realities of the industrial age. The worst excesses and injustices of unregulated economic development—corporate monopolies, child labor, political corruption, hazardous working conditions, urban ghettos—were finally addressed in a comprehensive way. During the Progressive Era (1890–1917), local, state, and federal governments sought to rein in the excesses of industrial capitalism and develop more rational and efficient public policies.

A conservative Republican resurgence challenged the notion of the new regulatory approaches during the 1920s. Free enterprise and corporate capitalism witnessed a dramatic revival. But the stock market crash of 1929 helped propel the United States and the world into the worst economic downturn in history. The unprecedented severity of the Great Depression renewed public demands for federal programs to protect the general welfare. "This nation asks for action," declared President Franklin Delano Roosevelt in his 1933 inaugural address. The many New Deal initiatives and agencies instituted by Roosevelt and Congressional Democrats created the framework for a welfare state that has since served as the basis for public policy.

The New Deal helped revive public confidence and put people back to work, but it did not end the Great Depression. It took a second world war to restore full employment. The necessity of mobilizing the nation in support of the war against Germany and Japan also accelerated the growth of the federal government. And the vast scope of the war helped catapult the United States into a leadership role in world politics. The use of atomic bombs to end the war against Japan ushered in a new era of nuclear diplomacy that held the fate of the world in the balance. For all of the new creature comforts associated with modern life, Americans in 1945 found themselves living amid an array of new anxieties as a chilling cold war emerged out of the world war.

"VOTES FOR US WHEN WE ARE WOMEN!" Parades organized by women's suffrage groups brought together women of all ages and classes. Here, from a patriotically outfitted automobile, some very young suffragists ask their many spectators for "votes for us when we are women."

The Progressive Era

1890–1920

Theodore Roosevelt's emergence as a national political leader coincided with the onset of what historians have labelled the Progressive Era (1890–1920), an extraordinary period of intense social activism and dramatic political innovation. Millions of "progressives" believed that America was experiencing a "crisis of democracy" that required bold action by churches, charitable organizations, experts, individuals—and an expanded role for governments. "Our country is going through a terrific period of unrest," explained Amos Pinchot, a leading progressive attorney and reformer from New York City. "Something is wrong," he said. Corruption was "destroying our respect for government, uprooting faith in political parties, and causing every precedent and convention of the old order to strain at its moorings."

Pinchot and other progressives argued that the United States had been changing so rapidly since the end of the Civil War that the nation was at risk of imploding. America had quickly become the world's fastest growing industrial economy, but prosperity was not being evenly shared. The widening gap between the rich and poor during the Gilded Age had become a major concern. Walter Weyl, a progressive economist, insisted that "we shall not advance far in working out our American ideals without striking hard at . . . inequality." Political equality, he added, "is a farce and a peril unless there is at least some measure of economic equality." The growth of new industries

CORE
OBJECTIVES INQUIZITIVE

1. Explain the varied motives of progressive reformers.

2. Explain the various sources of thought and activism that contributed to the progressive movement.

3. Identify the specific goals of progressive reformers and the ways that they advanced these public goals.

4. Describe the contributions of Presidents Theodore Roosevelt and William Howard Taft to the progressive movement, and explain how and why the two men came to disagree.

5. Describe the progressive policies of President Woodrow Wilson, and explain why and how they differed from those of Presidents Roosevelt and Taft.

like railroading, steel, coal, and oil had attracted massive waves of poor farm folk and foreign immigrants to large cities whose basic social services—food, water, housing, education, sanitation, transportation, and medical care—could not keep pace with the rate of urban growth.

Between 1890 and 1920, progressive reformers attacked the pressing problems created by unregulated industrialization, unplanned urbanization, and the increasingly unequal distribution of wealth and power. But most of all, they insisted, something must be done to control the very large, very powerful corporations that dominated America's economic life and corrupted its political life. As Amos Pinchot said, "we have permitted an uncontrolled industrial oligarchy to assume . . . tremendous and arrogant power." By the beginning of the twentieth century, progressivism had become the most dynamic social and political force in the nation. In 1910, Woodrow Wilson, then serving as president of Princeton University, told a gathering of clergymen that progressivism had generated "an extraordinary awakening in civic consciousness" over the previous twenty years.

CORE **OBJECTIVE**

1. Explain the varied motives of progressive reformers.

Addressing problems created by rapid urban and industrial growth

The Progressive Impulse

Progressives were liberals not revolutionaries. They wanted to reform and regulate their capitalist society, not destroy it. Most of them were civic-minded Christian moralists who felt that politics had become a contest between good and evil, honesty and corruption. What they all shared was the assumption that governments—local, state, and national—must take a more active role in addressing the huge problems created by rapid urban and industrial growth. Chicago's Jane Addams, a leading progressive reformer, reported that charities and churches were "totally inadequate to deal with the vast numbers of the city's disinherited." The "real heart of the [progressive] movement," declared another reformer, was to expand the role of government "as an agency of human welfare."

Progressivism was more a widespread impulse supported by elements of both major political parties than it was a single movement with a common agenda. The Republican Roosevelt called it the "forward movement" because its emphasis was on positive changes in society led by people "who stand for the cause of progress, for the cause of the uplift of humanity and the betterment of mankind." Progressives, he stressed, "fight to make this country a better place to live in for those who have been harshly treated by fate." Many progressives disagreed bitterly with each other over tactics and goals.

Unlike Populism, whose grassroots appeal was largely confined to poor rural regions in the South and Midwest, progressivism was a wide-ranging national movement, centered in large cities but also popular in rural areas among what came to be called populist progressives. Progressive activists, though mostly white, urban, middle-class professionals, were so numerous that they came in all stripes: men and women; Democrats, Republicans, Populists, and Socialists; labor unionists and business executives; teachers and professors; social workers and journalists; farmers and homemakers; whites and blacks; clergymen, atheists, and agnostics. Whatever their motives and methods, their combined efforts led to significant improvements at all levels of government and across all levels of society.

To make governments more responsive and "efficient" and businesses more honest and safer for workers and consumers, progressives drew upon the new "social sciences"—sociology, political science, psychology, public health, and economics—being developed at new research universities. The progressive approach to social problems was to "investigate, educate, and legislate." Florence Kelley, a tireless activist who fought to improve living conditions for the poor and to end child labor, voiced the era's widespread belief that once people knew "the truth" about social ills, "they would act upon it."

Making government more responsive and efficient, and businesses more honest and safer places to work

Yet progressivism had its flaws and limitations, inconsistencies and hypocrisies. Progressives often armed themselves with Christian moralism, but their "do-good" perspective was limited by the racial and ethnic prejudices of the day as well as social and intellectual snobbery. The goals of white progressives rarely included racial equality; many otherwise "progressive" people, including Theodore Roosevelt and Woodrow Wilson, believed in the supremacy of the "Anglo-Saxon race." Many well-educated progressives also felt—and acted—superior to the working class they wanted to help. They assumed that modern society was too complicated for the uninformed masses to understand, much less improve, without direction by those who knew better—progressives.

The Varied Sources of Progressivism

CORE **OBJECTIVE**

2. Explain the various sources of thought and activism that contributed to the progressive movement.

During the last quarter of the nineteenth century, political progressives at the local and state levels began to attack corrupt political bosses and irresponsible corporate barons. Their goals were more honest and efficient government, more effective regulation of big businesses ("the trusts"), and better lives for the majority of Americans who worked with their hands for wages. Only by expanding the scope of local, state, and federal governments, they believed, could these goals be attained.

Depression and Populism

More than any other factor, the devastating depression of the 1890s ignited the progressive spirit of reform. The worst economic downturn in American history to that point brought massive layoffs in factories, mines, railroads,

The depression of the 1890s and the Populists

and mills. Nearly a quarter of the adults in the workforce lost their jobs. Although the United States boasted the highest per capita income in the world, it also contained some of the highest concentrations of poverty among the industrialized nations. In 1900, an estimated 10 million of the 82 million Americans lived in desperate poverty, with annual incomes barely adequate to provide the minimum necessities of life. The devastating effects of the depression prompted many upper-middle-class urban people—lawyers, doctors, executives, social workers, teachers, professors, journalists, and college-educated women—to organize efforts to reform society.

Populism, with its roots in the rural South and West, was another thread in the fabric of progressivism. The Populist platforms of 1892 and 1896 included political reforms intended to give more power to "the people," such as the "direct" election of U.S. senators by the voters rather than by state legislatures. Although the defeat of William Jennings Bryan in the 1896 presidential campaign ended the Populist party as a serious political force, many of the reforms pushed by the Populists were implemented by progressives during the early twentieth century.

"Honest Government" Activism and Socialism

The Mugwumps and the Socialist party

The Mugwumps—"gentlemen" reformers who had fought the patronage system and insisted that government jobs be awarded on the basis of merit—supplied progressivism with another important element of its thinking: the "honest government" ideal. Over the years, the good-government movement expanded to include efforts not only to end political corruption but also to address persistent urban issues such as rising crime; access to electricity, clean water, and sewers; mass transit; and garbage collection.

Another significant "progressive" force was the growing influence of socialist ideas. In 1902, a pamphlet promoting working-class reforms claimed that "socialism is coming . . . and nothing can stop it. You can feel it in the air." The Socialist Party of America, supported mostly by militant farmers and immigrant Germans and Jews, served as the radical wing of progressivism. But unlike European socialists, who followed the economic doctrines of Karl Marx, most American socialists did not call for the government to take ownership of large corporations. They focused instead on improving working conditions in factories and mills and on closing the widening income gap between rich and poor through "progressive" taxation. In any case, most progressives were capitalist reformers, not socialist radicals. They rejected the extremes of both socialism and laissez-faire individualism, preferring instead a regulated capitalism "softened" by humanitarianism. Labor leader Samuel Gompers, for example, dismissed socialists as unrealistic: "Economically you are unsound, socially you are wrong, industrially you are an impossibility!"

Muckraking Journalism

Progressivism depended upon newspapers and magazines to inform the public about political corruption and social problems. The so-called **muckrakers** were investigative journalists whose aggressive reporting played a crucial role in educating the upper and middle classes about political and corporate wrongdoing as well as about "how the other half lives"—the title of Jacob Riis's pioneering work of photojournalism about life in the slums of New York (1890). "The rich are farther from the poor than ever before," wrote a journalist in 1886, and muckrakers saw it as the responsibility of reporters to show people in comfortable circumstances the ugly realities of poverty.

The muckrakers, who in addition to Riis included Ida Tarbell, Ray Stannard Baker, Lincoln Steffens, and William Allen White, got their nickname from Theodore Roosevelt, who said that crusading journalists were "often indispensable to . . . society, but only if they know when to stop raking the muck." By uncovering political corruption and writing about social ills in newspapers and popular monthly magazines such as *McClure's*, *Munsey's*, and *Cosmopolitan*, the muckrakers changed the face of journalism and gave it a new political role. Muckrakers challenged readers to take action against political corruption and corporate wrongdoing. "For it is OUR business," Tarbell insisted, "we, the people of the United States, and nobody else, must cure whatever is wrong" with America. Roosevelt, both as governor of New York and as president, frequently used muckrakers to drum up support for his policies; he corresponded with them, invited them to the White House, asked their advice, and used their popularity with readers to help shape public opinion.

The golden age of muckraking is sometimes dated from 1902, when Samuel S. McClure, the owner of *McClure's*, began paying idealistic journalists to root out the rampant corruption in politics and corporations. McClure was determined to make his popular magazine a "power for good"; the "vitality of democracy," he insisted, depended upon journalists educating the public about "complex questions" involving the miserable conditions in which poor Americans lived and worked.

Ida Tarbell, one of the most dedicated muckrakers, loved "the sense of vitality, of adventure, of excitement" at *McClure's*. She spent years doggedly investigating the illegal means by which John D. Rockefeller had built his gigantic Standard Oil trust. At the end of her series of nineteen *McClure's* articles reporting the results of her research, she asked readers: "And what are we going to do about it?" She stressed that it was "the people of the United States, and nobody else, [who] must cure whatever is wrong in the industrial situation." McClure told Tarbell that her campaign against monopolies had made her "the most famous woman in America."

Without the muckrakers, progressivism would never have achieved widespread popular support. During the early twentieth century, investigative

Muckrakers

Cover of *McClure's* magazine, 1902 This issue features Ida Tarbell's muckraking series on the Standard Oil Company.

muckrakers Writers who exposed corruption and abuses in politics, business, consumer safety, working conditions, and more, spurring public interest in progressive reforms.

journalism became such a powerful force for change that one editor said that Americans now had "Government by Magazine."

Religious Activism

Still another of the streams flowing into progressivism was religious activism based on social justice, the idea that society had an ethical obligation to help its poorest and most vulnerable members. A related ideal was the **social gospel**, a newer, specifically Protestant belief that religious institutions and individual Christians had an obligation to lead this effort in order to bring about the "Kingdom of God" on earth. In many respects, in fact, the progressive movement as a whole formed a new phase of Christian spiritual revival, an energetic form of public outreach also incorporating other religious (and nonreligious) groups and focusing not so much on individual conversion and salvation as on social action. "We believe," as a social gospel organization explained, "that the age of sheer individualism is past, and the age of social responsibility has arrived."

The Social Gospel

The YMCA/YWCAs and the Salvation Army

During the last quarter of the nineteenth century, a growing number of churches and synagogues began emphasizing community service and the care of the unfortunate. New organizations also made key contributions to the movement. The Young Men's Christian Association (YMCA) and a similar group for women, the YWCA, both entered the United States from England in the 1850s and grew rapidly after 1870; the Salvation Army, founded in London in 1878, came to the United States a year later. During the late nineteenth century, the YMCA and YWCA—both known as "the Y"—combined nondenominational religious evangelism with social services and fitness training in centers, segregated by race as well as gender, that were built in cities across the country. Intended to provide low-cost housing and healthful exercise in a "safe Christian environment" for young men and women from rural areas or foreign countries, the YMCA/YWCA centers often also included libraries, classrooms, and kitchens. "Hebrew" counterparts—YMHAs and YWHAs—provided many of the same facilities in cities with large Jewish populations. Salvation Army centers offered "soup kitchens" to feed the poor and day nurseries for the children of working mothers.

The major forces behind the **social gospel** movement were Protestants and Catholics who feared that Christianity had become too closely associated with the upper and middle classes and was losing its appeal to the working poor. In 1875, Washington Gladden, a prominent pastor in Springfield, Massachusetts, invited striking workers at a shoe factory to attend his church, but they refused because the factory owners and managers were members of it. Their refusal shocked Gladden, who was heartbroken that Christianity was dividing along class lines. He then wrote a pathbreaking book, *Working People and Their Employers* (1876), which argued that true Christianity was based on the principle that "thou shalt love thy neighbor as

social gospel Mostly Protestant movement that stressed the Christian obligation to address the mounting social problems caused by urbanization and industrialization.

thyself." Rejecting the view of the social Darwinists that the poor deserved their fate and should not be helped, Gladden became the first prominent American religious leader to support the rights of workers to form unions. He also spoke out against racial segregation and efforts to discriminate against immigrants.

Gladden's efforts helped launch a new era in American religious life in which churches addressed the urgent problems created by a rapidly urbanizing and industrializing society. He and other "social gospelers" reached out to the working poor who labored long hours for low wages, lived in miserable slum housing, and lacked the legal right to form unions as well as insurance coverage for on-the-job accidents. Walter Rauschenbusch, a Baptist minister serving tenement dwellers in the Hell's Kitchen neighborhood of New York City, said churches should embrace "the social aims of Jesus," for Christianity was intended to be a "revolutionary" faith, and American religious life needed the social gospel to revitalize it and make it socially relevant. Rauschenbusch became extremely influential as a public figure, serving as a presidential adviser to both Theodore Roosevelt and Woodrow Wilson.

> Washington Gladden and Walter Rauschenbusch

Rauschenbusch, Gladden, and other preachers of the social gospel sought to expand the "Kingdom of God" not by giving fiery sermons but by following Christ's example and serving the poor and powerless in the streets. Rugged individualism may have been the path to wealth, they argued, but it was "Christian socialism" that offered hope for unity among all classes of Americans. "Every religious and political question," said George Herron, a religion professor at Grinnell College, "is fundamentally economic." And the solution to economic tensions was social solidarity. As the progressive economist Richard Ely put it, America could truly thrive only when it recognized that "our true welfare is not an individual matter purely, but likewise a social affair."

Settlement Houses

Among the most visible champions of the "social gospel" were those who volunteered in innovative community centers called settlement houses. At the Hull House settlement on Halsted Street in a working-class Chicago neighborhood, for instance, two women from privileged backgrounds, Jane Addams and Ellen Gates Starr, practiced social solidarity by addressing the everyday needs of the working poor, especially newly arrived European immigrants. In founding Hull House, Addams and Starr were driven by what Addams called an "impulse to share the lives of the poor" and to make social service "express the spirit of Christ." Their staff of two dozen women, most of whom lived at Hull House, served thousands of people each week. Besides a nursery for the infant children of working mothers, Hull House also sponsored health clinics, lectures, music lessons and art studios, men's clubs, an employment bureau, job training, a gymnasium, a coffeehouse, and a savings bank. By the early twentieth century, there were hundreds of settlement houses in cities across the United States, most of them in the Northeast and Midwest.

> Jane Addams, Ellen Gates Starr, and the settlement house movement

While working to improve the quality of life for the powerless, the mostly white, middle-class settlement house workers saw their own lives enriched. Addams said her work at Hull House gave her the "joy of finding Christ" by joining "in fellowship" with those in need in an America that had grown "divided into two nations"—rich and poor. To her, the social gospel driving progressive reformers reflected their "yearning sense of justice and compassion."

Addams and other settlement house leaders soon realized, however, that their charitable work in the rapidly spreading immigrant slums was like bailing out the ocean with a teaspoon. They thus added political reform to their already lengthy agenda and began lobbying for new laws and regulations to ameliorate the living conditions in poor neighborhoods. As her influence in Chicago grew, Addams was appointed to prominent governmental and community boards, where she focused on improving public health and food safety, pushing for better street lighting and police protection, and reducing the use of narcotics. An ardent pacifist and outspoken advocate for suffrage (voting rights) for women, Addams would become the first American woman to win the Nobel Peace Prize.

The Woman Suffrage Movement

Jane Addams and other settlement house workers made up only a small share of the growing numbers of women working outside the home by the early twentieth century. The number of employed women tripled from 2.6 million in 1880 to 7.8 million in 1910. As women, especially college-educated women, became more involved in the public world of work and wages, the women's rights movement also grew as it tirelessly pursued the right to vote. Immediately after the Civil War, women in the movement had hoped that the Fifteenth Amendment, which guaranteed voting rights for African American men, would aid their own efforts to gain the vote. Such arguments made little impression on the majority of men, however, who still insisted that women stay out of politics, often insisting that engaging in the rough-and-tumble world of politics would corrupt the moral purity expected of women during the late nineteenth century. A Mississippi Democrat was blunt about his opposition: "I would rather die and go to hell," he claimed, "than vote for woman's suffrage."

Western states' leadership on the suffrage issue

In 1869, the year the Wyoming Territory became the first place in the United States to extend equal voting rights to women, a divisive issue broke the unity of the women's rights movement: whether it should continue to concentrate on gaining the vote or adopt a broader agenda of women's issues. Susan B. Anthony and Elizabeth Cady Stanton founded the National Woman Suffrage Association (NWSA) to promote a **woman suffrage** amendment to the Constitution, but they considered the right to vote only one among many feminist causes to be championed. For example, they also campaigned for new laws requiring higher pay for women workers and

woman suffrage Movement to give women the right to vote through a constitutional amendment, spearheaded by Susan B. Anthony and Elizabeth Cady Stanton's National Woman Suffrage Association.

East meets West San Francisco suffragists marched across the country in 1915 to deliver an amendment petition with more than 500,000 signatures to Congress in Washington, D.C. Along the way, they were warmly received by other suffragists, like those of New Jersey, pictured here.

making it easier for abused wives to get divorces. Other suffrage activists insisted that pursuing multiple issues hurt their cause. In 1869, they formed the American Woman Suffrage Association (AWSA), which focused single-mindedly on voting rights.

In 1890, after three years of negotiation, the rival groups united as the National American Woman Suffrage Association (NAWSA), the same year Wyoming was admitted as a state, the first with full voting rights for women. It was in the territories and states west of the Mississippi River that the suffrage movement had its earliest successes. In those frontier areas, where Populism found its strongest support, women were more engaged in grassroots political activities than they were in the East. Suffrage activists in the West also emphasized getting working women engaged in the effort, and they adopted many of the tactics used by labor unions in the West. For these reasons and others, the West was more supportive of women's rights. Between 1890 and 1896, the suffrage movement won three more victories in western states—Utah, Colorado, and Idaho.

In the early twentieth century, however, the suffrage movement remained in the doldrums until proposals for voting rights at the state level easily won a Washington state referendum in 1910 and then carried California by a close majority in 1911. The following year three more western states—Arizona, Kansas, and Oregon—joined in to make a total of nine western states with full suffrage. In 1913, Illinois granted women voting rights in presidential and municipal elections. Yet not until New York acted in 1917 did a state east of the Mississippi River allow women to vote in all elections.

The advocates of women's suffrage put forth several arguments for their position. Many said that the right to vote and hold office was a matter of

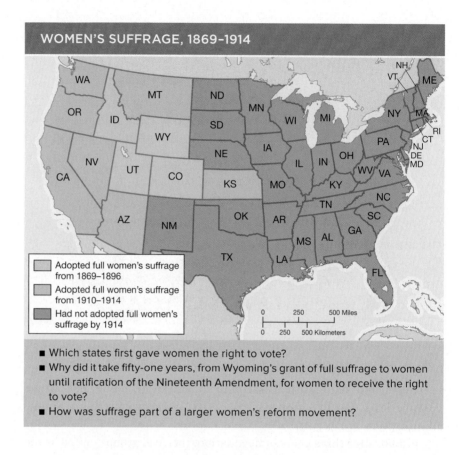

WOMEN'S SUFFRAGE, 1869–1914

Adopted full women's suffrage from 1869–1896

Adopted full women's suffrage from 1910–1914

Had not adopted full women's suffrage by 1914

■ Which states first gave women the right to vote?

■ Why did it take fifty-one years, from Wyoming's grant of full suffrage to women until ratification of the Nineteenth Amendment, for women to receive the right to vote?

■ How was suffrage part of a larger women's reform movement?

simple justice: women were just as capable as men of exercising the rights and responsibilities of citizenship. Others insisted that women were morally superior to men and therefore their participation would raise the quality of the political process and reduce the likelihood of future wars, corruption, and scandals. Women voters and politicians, advocates argued, would promote the welfare of society as a whole rather than partisan or selfish goals, so allowing women to participate in politics would create a great engine for progressive social change. One activist explicitly linked women's suffrage with the social gospel, declaring that women followed the teachings of Christ more faithfully than men; if they were elected to public office, they would "far more effectively guard the morals of society and the sanitary conditions of cities."

Yet the woman suffrage movement was not free from the social, ethnic, and racial prejudices of its time. Carrie Chapman Catt, who became president of the National American Woman Suffrage Association in 1900, echoed the fears of many middle- and upper-class women when she warned of the danger that "lies in the votes possessed by the males in the slums of the cities, and the ignorant foreign [immigrant] vote." She added that the nation with "ill-advised haste" had given "the foreigner, the Negro and the Indian" the vote but still withheld it from white women. In the South, one suffragist

The suffragists' arguments and prejudices

claimed that giving white women the vote would help "insure immediate and durable white supremacy." Throughout the country, most suffrage organizations excluded African American women.

Progressives' Aims and Achievements

CORE **OBJECTIVE**
3. Identify the specific goals of progressive reformers and the ways that they advanced toward these goals.

All of the impulses and groups comprising the progressive movement grew out of what Theodore Roosevelt called the "fierce discontent with evil" that many Americans felt at the turn of the nineteenth century. Given their great diversity, however, progressives focused on many specific goals and used many different methods. They assaulted a wide array of what they saw as social and political evils: from corrupt politicians to too-powerful corporations, from economic distress on small farms and in big cities to the general feeling that "the people" had lost control of the nation to what Roosevelt called "the special interests," selfish businesses and their leaders who were solely interested in "money-getting" at the expense of public welfare.

Reforms in the Political Process

Adoption of the direct primary, initiative, referendum, and recall

In his monthly articles in *McClure's* magazine, Lincoln Steffens, one of the leading muckrakers, regularly asked: "Will the people rule? Is democracy possible?" Steffens himself and other progressives often answered that the way to improve America's democracy was to make it even more democratic. To empower citizens to clean up a corrupt political system driven by backroom deals and rigged party conventions, Steffens and other progressives pushed for several reforms intended to make the political process more open and transparent. One was the direct primary, allowing all members of a political party to vote on the party's nominees for office, rather than the traditional practice in which an inner circle of party leaders chose the candidates. In 1896, South Carolina became the first state to adopt a statewide primary, and within twenty years nearly every state had done so.

While urging states to adopt party primaries, progressives developed other ways to increase participation in the political process. In 1898, South Dakota became the first state to adopt the *initiative* and *referendum*, procedures that allowed voters to create laws directly rather than having to wait for legislative action. Citizens could sign petitions to have a proposal put on the ballot (the initiative) and could then vote it up or down (the referendum). Still another progressive innovation was the *recall*, first adopted in Oregon in 1910, whereby corrupt or incompetent elected officials could be removed by a public petition and vote. By 1920, nearly twenty states had

The Seventeenth Amendment:
Direct election of U.S. senators

adopted the initiative and referendum, and nearly a dozen had added the recall procedure.

Progressives also fought to change the way that U.S. senators were elected. Under the Constitution, state legislatures elected senators, a process that was frequently corrupted by lobbyists and vote-buying. In 1900, for example, Senate investigators revealed that a Montana senator had given more than $100,000 in secret bribes to members of the legislature that chose him. In 1894, the House of Representatives passed a constitutional amendment to allow voters to elect senators directly, only to see it defeated in the Senate. In 1913, thanks to the efforts of progressives, the **Seventeenth Amendment**, providing for the direct election of senators, was ratified by enough states to become law.

Efficiency Movement in Business and Government

Taylorism in industrial
management

A second major theme of progressivism was called the "gospel of efficiency." Its champion was Frederick Winslow Taylor, a Philadelphia-born engineer who during the 1890s became a celebrated business consultant, helping mills and factories operate more efficiently by practicing "scientific management." A self-described progressive who became the nation's first "efficiency expert," Taylor showed employers how to cut waste and increase productivity. By breaking down work activities (filling a wheelbarrow, driving a nail, shoveling coal) into a sequence of mechanical steps and using stopwatches to measure the time it took each worker to perform each step in a task, Taylor established detailed performance standards (and cash rewards) for each job classification, specifying how fast people doing each job should work and when they should rest. The goal of what came to be called **Taylorism** was to improve both productivity and profits for employers and also raise pay for workers; as Taylor wrote, "Men will not do an extraordinary day's work for an ordinary day's pay." There would be no need for strikes by workers in such a system, he argued.

Many workers, however, resented Taylor's innovations, seeing them as just a tool to make people work faster. Yet Taylor's controversial system of industrial management became one of the most important contributions to capitalist economies in the twentieth century. It did bring concrete improvements in productivity. "In the future," Taylor predicted in 1911, "the system [rather than the individual workers] will be first."

Political progressives applied Taylorism to the operations of government by calling for the reorganization of state and federal agencies to eliminate overlap, the establishment of clear lines of authority, and the replacement of political appointees with trained specialists. By the early twentieth century, many complex functions of government had come to require specialists with technical expertise. As the young political scientist

Seventeenth Amendment (1913) Constitutional amendment that provided for the public election of senators rather than the traditional practice allowing state legislatures to name them.

Taylorism Labor system based on detailed study of work tasks, championed by Frederick Winslow Taylor, intended to maximize efficiency and profits for employers.

and future president Woodrow Wilson wrote, progressive ideals could be achieved only if government at all levels—local, state, and national—was "informed and administered by experts." Many cities set up "efficiency bureaus" to identify ways their governments were wasting money and to apply more cost-effective "best practices" from other cities.

Two Taylorist ideas for restructuring city and county governments also emerged in the first decade of the new century. One, the commission system, was first adopted in 1901 by Galveston, Texas, after the local government collapsed following a devastating hurricane and tidal wave that killed over 8,000 people, the greatest natural disaster in American history. The commission system placed ultimate authority in a board composed of a small group of commissioners who combined both legislative and executive powers in heading up city departments—commissioners of sanitation, police, utilities, and so on. Houston, Texas, created a commission system in 1906, Dallas and Des Moines, Iowa, in 1907, and Memphis in 1909.

> The commission system and the city-manager plan

Even more popular than the commission system was the city-manager plan, under which an appointed professional administrator ran a city or county government in accordance with policies set by the elected council and mayor. Staunton, Virginia, adopted the first city-manager plan in 1908. Five years later, the inadequate response of municipal officials to a flood led Dayton, Ohio, to become the first large city in the nation to adopt the plan.

Yet along with concrete benefits, the efforts to make local governments more "business-like" and professional had a downside. Shifting control from elected officials representing individual neighborhoods to at-large commissioners and nonpartisan specialists separated local government from party politics, which for many working-class voters had been the main way they could have a voice in how they were governed locally. In addition, running a city like a business led commissioners and managers to focus on reducing expenses rather than expanding services, even when such expansion was clearly needed.

> La Follette and the "Wisconsin idea"

At the statewide level, this ideal of efficient government run by nonpartisan experts was pursued most notably by progressive Republican governor Robert M. La Follette of Wisconsin between 1901 and 1906. A small, wiry man with a huge head, "Fighting Bob" La Follette declared war on "vast corporate combinations" and political corruption by creating a nonpartisan state government that would become a "laboratory for democracy." To do so, he worked closely with professors from the University of Wisconsin to establish a Legislative Reference Bureau, which provided elected officials across the state with nonpartisan research, advice, and help in the drafting of legislation. La Follette used the bureau's reports to enact such reforms as the direct primary, stronger railroad regulation, the conservation of natural resources, and workmen's compensation programs to support people injured on the job. The "Wisconsin idea" of more efficient government run by experts was widely publicized and copied by other

Friends of the working man
(*Left to right*) American labor leader Andrew Furuseth, Governor Robert M. La Follette, and muckraker Lincoln Steffens, c. 1915.

progressive governors. La Follette explained that the "Wisconsin idea" was a commitment to use government power to make "a happier and better state to live in, that its institutions are more democratic, that the opportunities of all its people are more equal, that social justice more nearly prevails."

Regulation of Business

Of all the problems facing American society at the turn of the century, one towered above all: the regulation of giant corporations, a third major theme of progressivism. The threat of corporate monopolies increased during the depression of the 1890s as struggling companies were gobbled up by larger ones. Between 1895 and 1904, 157 new holding companies gained control of 1,800 different businesses. Almost fifty of these giant holding companies controlled over 70 percent of the market in their respective industries. In 1896, fewer than a dozen companies other than railroads were worth $10 million or more. By 1903, that number had soared to 300. The explosive growth of big business changed the nature of business life. "We have come upon a very different age from any that preceded us," New Jersey governor Woodrow Wilson observed. People now worked "not for themselves" but "as employees of great corporations."

> Little success in regulating Big Business

Concerns over the concentration of economic power in "trusts" and other forms of monopolies had led Congress to pass the Sherman Anti-Trust Act in 1890, but its language about what constituted a monopoly was so vague that it proved ineffective. In addition, government agencies responsible for regulating businesses often came under the influence of those they were supposed to regulate. Retired railroad executives, for instance, were appointed to the Interstate Commerce Commission (ICC), which had been created to regulate railroads. The issue of regulating the regulators has never been fully resolved.

Promotion of Social Justice

A fourth important focus of the progressive movement was the effort to promote greater social justice for the working poor and for jobless and homeless people. In addition to their work in settlement houses and other religiously inspired efforts, many progressives formed new advocacy organizations such as the National Consumers' League, which educated consumers about harsh working conditions in factories and mills as well as companies' widespread use of child workers as a means of lowering labor costs.

Campaigns for social justice by advocacy organizations and women's clubs

Other grassroots progressive organizations such as the General Federation of Women's Clubs, founded in 1890, insisted that the nation's civic life needed the humanizing effect of female leadership. Caroline Brown started the Chicago Women's Club to help women address the "live issues of this world we live in." Women's clubs across the country sought to clean up filthy city slums by educating residents about personal and household hygiene ("municipal housekeeping"), urging construction of sewer systems, and launching public-awareness campaigns about the connection between unsanitary conditions and disease. Women's clubs also campaigned for child-care centers, kindergartens, government inspection of food processing plants, stricter housing codes, laws protecting women in the workplace, and more social services for the poor, sick, disabled, and abused. Still others addressed the widespread problems related to prostitution and alcohol abuse.

The Campaign against Drinking

Middle-class women reformers, most of them motivated by strong religious convictions, were the driving force behind grassroots progressivism. Among the most powerful campaigns organized by women to address social ills was that of the Women's Christian Temperance Union (WCTU). Founded in 1874 in Cleveland, Ohio, by 1900 the WCTU had grown into the largest women's group in the nation, boasting 300,000 members. By attacking drunkenness and closing saloons, such reformers hoped to accomplish three things: (1) prevent domestic violence by husbands and fathers, (2) reduce crime in the streets, and (3) remove one of the worst tools of corruption—free beer on election days—used by political bosses to "buy" votes among the working class. As a Boston sociologist concluded, the saloon had become "the enemy of society because of the evil results produced upon the individual."

Initially, WCTU members met in churches to pray and then marched to nearby saloons to try to convince their owners to shut them down, often using "pray-ins" to heighten the impact. As the organization's name suggests, the Women's Christian Temperance Union advocated *temperance*—the reduction of alcohol consumption. But along with other groups, the WCTU

Temperance, abstinence, and prohibition: The WCTU and the Anti-Saloon League also urged individuals to embrace *abstinence*, refusing to drink any alcoholic beverages. Members wore white ribbon bows to symbolize their commitment to the bodily purity associated with this goal.

Frances Willard, the dynamic president of the WCTU between 1879 and 1898, greatly expanded the goals and scope of the organization. Under her leadership, it moved beyond moral persuasion of saloonkeepers and drinkers and began promoting legislation to ban alcohol ("prohibition") at the local, state, and federal levels. Willard also pushed the WCTU to lobby for other progressive reforms important to women, including a nationwide eight-hour workday, the regulation of child labor, government-funded kindergartens, the right to vote for women, and federal inspections of the food industry. More than anything else, however, the WCTU stayed true to its original mission and continued to campaign against drinking.

Opposition to alcohol abuse was one of the most widely popular of the many progressive reforms. What came to be called the prohibition or temperance movement was national in scope but especially popular in the Midwest and South, where conservative Protestants were most numerous. The battle against alcoholic beverages took on new strength in 1893 with the formation of the Anti-Saloon League, an organization based in local churches that pioneered the strategy of the single-issue political pressure group. Describing itself as "the Protestant church in action against the saloon," the bipartisan League, like the WCTU, initially focused on closing down saloons rather than abolishing alcohol. Eventually, however, it decided to force the prohibition issue into the forefront of state and local elections. At its "Jubilee Convention" in 1913, the League endorsed the nineteenth amendment to the Constitution. It prohibited the manufacture, sale, and consumption of alcoholic beverages. Congress finally approved the Prohibition amendment in 1917.

Frances Willard Founder of the WCTU who lobbied for women's suffrage.

Labor Legislation

In addition to the efforts to reduce alcohol consumption, other progressive reformers pushed legislation to improve working conditions in mills, mines, and factories—and on railroads. In 1890, almost half of American wage workers toiled up to twelve hours a day—sometimes seven days a week—in unsafe, unsanitary, and unregulated conditions. Legislation to ensure better working conditions and limit child labor was perhaps the most significant reform to emerge from the drive for progressive social justice.

Efforts to regulate children's and women's work

At the end of the nineteenth century, fewer than half of working families lived solely on the husband's earnings. Everyone in the family who could work did so. Many married women engaged in "homework"—making clothes, selling flower arrangements, preparing food for others, and taking in boarders. Parents in poor families also frequently took their children out of school in order to put them to work outside the home—in factories, shops, mines, mills, and canneries, and on farms. In 1900, some 1.75 million children between the ages of 10 and 15 were working outside the home.

Child labor Children shuck oysters in 1913 at the Varn & Platt Canning Company in Bluffton, South Carolina.

Many progressives argued that children, too, had rights in a democracy. The National Child Labor Committee, organized in 1904, led a movement to prohibit the employment of young children. Within ten years, the committee lobbied successfully for legislation in most states banning the hiring of children below a certain age (varying by state from twelve to sixteen) and limiting the hours children might work. Progressives who focused on improving the lives of children also demanded that cities build more parks and playgrounds. Further, reformers made a concerted effort to regulate the length of the workday for women, in part because some of them were pregnant and others had children at home with inadequate supervision. Spearheaded by Florence Kelley, the first president of the National Consumers' League, progressives convinced many state governments to ban work by both women and children at night or in dangerous jobs.

It took a tragic disaster to spur meaningful government regulation of dangerous workplaces. On March 25, 1911, a fire broke out at the Triangle Shirtwaist factory (called a "sweatshop" because of its cramped and unventilated work areas) in New York City. Escape routes were limited because the owner kept the stairway door locked to prevent theft, and 146 workers trapped on the upper floors of the ten-story building died in the fire or leaped to their deaths. The victims of the Triangle Shirtwaist fire were mostly young, foreign-born women in their teens, almost all of whom were Jewish, Italian, or Russian immigrants. In the aftermath of the gruesome

Response to the Triangle Shirtwaist fire

PRODUCTS OF THE TENEMENT WORKSHO

Glove Finishing

Chiffon Applique

Infants Dress (D)

National Consumers' League exhibit To raise awareness about labor reform, everyday objects are displayed alongside descriptions of the poor working conditions and exploitation that went into their manufacture.

deaths, dozens of new city and state regulations dealing with fire hazards, dangerous working conditions, and child labor were enacted across the nation.

The Supreme Court followed an inconsistent course in its rulings on state labor laws. In *Lochner v. New York* (1905), the Court ruled that a ten-hour-workday law was unconstitutional because it violated workers' right to accept any jobs they wanted, no matter how bad the working conditions or how low the pay. Three years later, however, in *Muller v. Oregon* (1908), the Court upheld a ten-hour-workday law for women, largely on the basis of research showing the ill effects of long working hours on women's health. In *Bunting v. Oregon* (1917), the Court accepted a state law allowing no more than a ten-hour workday for both men and women. But for twenty more years, the nation's highest court held out against state laws requiring a minimum wage.

The "Progressive" Income Tax

Progressives also promoted social justice by addressing America's growing economic inequality. One way to redistribute wealth was through the creation of a "progressive" federal income tax—so called not because of the idea's association with the progressive movement, but because the tax rates are based on a sliding scale—that is, the rates "progress" or rise as income levels rise, thus forcing the rich to pay more. Such a "graduated" or "progressive" tax system was the climax of the progressive movement's commitment to a more equitable distribution of wealth.

The progressive income tax was an old idea. In 1894, William Jennings Bryan had persuaded Congress to create a 2 percent tax on annual incomes over $4,000. When millionaires responded by threatening to leave America, Bryan exclaimed, "If some of our 'best people' prefer to leave the country rather than pay the tax ... let them depart." Soon after the tax became law, however, the Supreme Court declared it unconstitutional on a technicality.

The idea of a "graduated" federal income tax refused to die, however. Progressives believed that such a tax would help slow the concentration of wealth in the hands of the richest Americans, who between 1890 and 1910 had nearly doubled their share of the national income, chiefly at the expense of the middle class. In 1907, President Theodore Roosevelt announced his support for the tax. Two years later, his successor, William Howard Taft, endorsed a constitutional amendment allowing such a tax, and Congress agreed. Finally, in 1913, this **Sixteenth Amendment** was ratified by enough states to become law.

The Sixteenth Amendment: Authorization of an income tax

Sixteenth Amendment (1913)
Constitutional amendment that authorized the federal income tax.

Progressivism under Roosevelt and Taft

CORE **OBJECTIVE**

4. Describe the contributions of Presidents Theodore Roosevelt and William Howard Taft to the progressive movement, and explain how and why the two men came to disagree.

In the late nineteenth century, most progressive policies originated at the state and local levels. Federal reform efforts began in earnest only when Theodore Roosevelt became president in 1901 after the assassination of William McKinley. During his rapid rise to national fame and leadership, Roosevelt had grown more progressive with each passing year. Unlike McKinley, who was patient and cautious, "T.R." was intensely energetic, and, in the words of one journalist, "impetuous, impatient, and wholly lacking in tact." He could not stand indecision or inaction. And he loved what he called "strenuosity." In the White House, the ever-boyish Roosevelt invited male guests to wrestle and box with him, or to fight with wooden swords or climb trees. "His personality," said a friend, "so crowds the room that the walls are worn thin and threaten to burst outward."

Like Andrew Jackson, Roosevelt greatly increased the power of the presidency in the process of enacting his progressive agenda. His friend and successor, William Howard Taft, continued Roosevelt's "progressive" effort to regulate corporate trusts, but he proved neither as energetic nor as wide-ranging in his role as a reformer president—a difference that led to a fateful break between the two men.

Roosevelt's Taming of Big Business

Roosevelt accomplished more by aggressive executive action than by convincing Congress to pass legislation. As president, he believed he could do anything not expressly forbidden by the Constitution. Mark Twain, the most popular writer in America, said that Roosevelt was willing to "kick the Constitution into the backyard whenever it gets in his way."

In outlining his progressive agenda, Roosevelt applauded the growth of industrial capitalism but declared war on corruption and on cronyism—the awarding of political appointments, government contracts, and other favors to politicians' personal friends and donors. He endorsed a "**Square Deal**" for "every man, great or small, rich or poor." The Square Deal program featured what was called the "Three Cs": greater government *control* of corporations; enhanced *conservation* of natural resources; and, new regulations to protect *consumers* against contaminated food and medicines. Roosevelt began by calling for more rigorous government enforcement of the Sherman Anti-Trust Act against huge corporations engaged in illegal activities. In his view, some big businesses were bad not because they were big but because their executives acted unethically or unfairly. From his youth, Roosevelt had developed a firm commitment to "fair play" in sports, in business, and in politics, and his version of progressivism centered on a commitment to equal opportunity. "A great democracy," he said, "has got to be *progressive* or it will soon cease to be great or a democracy."

Square Deal Roosevelt's progressive agenda of the "Three C's": *control* of corporations, *conservation* of natural resources, and *consumer* protection.

Square Deal This 1906 cartoon likens Roosevelt to the Greek legend Hercules, who as a baby strangled snakes sent from Hell to kill him. Here, the serpents are pro-corporation senator Nelson Aldrich and Standard Oil's John D. Rockefeller.

In 1902, only five months into his presidency, Roosevelt ordered the U.S. attorney general to break up the Northern Securities Company, a vast network of railroads and steamships run by J. Pierpont Morgan that monopolized transportation in several regions of the country. Shocked that Roosevelt would try to break up his corporation, Morgan rushed from New York to the White House and told the president: "If I have done anything wrong, send your man to my man and they can fix it up." But the attorney general, who was also at the meeting, told Morgan: "We don't want to 'fix it up.' We want to stop it." Turning to Roosevelt, Morgan then asked if the president planned to attack his other trusts, such as U.S. Steel and General Electric. "Certainly not," Roosevelt replied, "unless we find out that . . . they have done something wrong." In 1904, the Supreme Court ruled 5–4 that the Northern Securities Company was indeed a monopoly and must be dismantled.

Altogether, Roosevelt approved about twenty-five anti-trust suits against oversized corporations. He also sought stronger regulation of the railroads. In 1903, Congress passed the Elkins Act, making it illegal for railroads to give secret rebates (cash refunds) on freight charges to favored high-volume customers. That same year, Congress created a Bureau of Corporations to monitor the activities of big businesses. When the Standard Oil Company refused to turn over its records, the government brought an anti-trust suit that led to the breakup of the powerful company in 1911. The Supreme Court also ordered the American Tobacco Company dismantled because it had monopolized the cigarette industry.

The 1902 Coal Strike

> Roosevelt as a referee between management and labor

In everything he did, Roosevelt acted forcefully. On May 12, 1902, for example, some 150,000 members of the United Mine Workers (UMW) walked off the job at coal mines in Pennsylvania and West Virginia. The miners were seeking a 20 percent wage increase, a reduction in daily working hours from ten to nine, and official recognition of the union by the mine owners, who refused to negotiate. Instead, the owners shut down the mines to starve out the miners, many of whom were immigrants from eastern Europe. One owner expressed the ethnic prejudices shared by many other owners when he proclaimed, "The miners don't suffer—why, they can't even speak English."

By October, the lengthy shutdown had caused the price of coal to soar, and hospitals and schools reported empty coal bins as winter approached. In many northern cities, the poor had run out of coal for heating. "The country is on the verge of a vast public calamity," warned Walter Rauschenbusch. Washington Gladden led a petition drive urging Roosevelt to step in to mediate the strike. The president decided upon a bold move: he invited leaders of both sides to a conference in Washington, D.C., where he appealed to their "patriotism, to the spirit that sinks personal considerations and makes individual sacrifices for the public good." The mine owners in attendance, however, refused even to speak to the UMW leaders.

Roosevelt was infuriated by what he called the "extraordinary stupidity and temper" of the "wooden-headed" owners, saying he wanted to grab their spokesman "by the seat of his breeches" and "chuck him out" a window. Instead, he threatened to take over the mines and send in soldiers to run them. When a congressman questioned the constitutionality of such a move, Roosevelt roared, "To hell with the Constitution when the people want coal!" The threat worked: the strike ended on October 23. The miners won a reduction to a nine-hour workday and a 10 percent wage increase, but failed to gain union recognition by the owners. Roosevelt had become the first president to use his authority to referee a dispute between management and labor.

Roosevelt's Election to a Second Term

Roosevelt's forceful leadership won him the Republican nomination for election in his own right in 1904. The Democrats, having lost twice with William Jennings Bryan, turned to the more conservative and virtually unknown Alton B. Parker, chief justice of the New York Supreme Court. His only distinction was being the dullest—and most forgettable—presidential candidate in history. One journalist dubbed him "the enigma from New York." The most interesting item in Parker's official campaign biography was that he trained pigs to come when called by name.

A reelection mandate for Roosevelt and progressivism

In the election, the Democrats suffered their worst defeat in 32 years. After sweeping to victory by a popular vote of 7.6 million to 5.1 million and an electoral vote of 336 to 140, Roosevelt told his wife that he was "no longer a political accident." He now had a popular mandate to do great things. On the eve of his inauguration in March 1905, Roosevelt announced: "Tomorrow I shall come into office in my own right. Then watch out for me!" He was ready to become the leader of the progressive movement.

Regulation of the Railroad, Food, and Drug Industries

Roosevelt launched his second term with an even stronger commitment to regulating corporations and their corrupt owners (the "criminal rich") who exploited their workers and tried to eliminate competition. In his efforts to promote the "moral regeneration of business," he took aim at the railroads first. In 1906, he persuaded Congress to pass the Hepburn Act, which for the first time gave the federal Interstate Commerce Commission the power to set maximum freight rates for the railroad industry.

The Hepburn Act (1906) and the ICC

Under Roosevelt's Square Deal programs, the federal government also assumed oversight of key industries affecting public health: meat packers, food processors, and makers of drugs and patent medicines. Muckraking journalists had revealed all sorts of unsanitary and dangerous activities in the

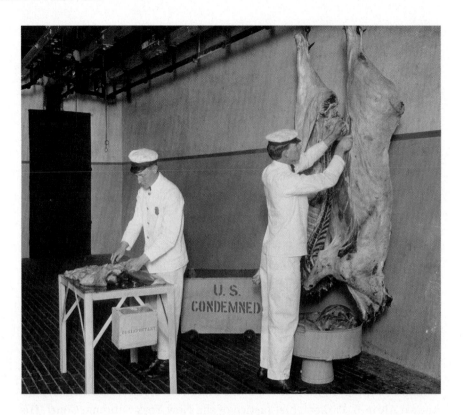

Bad meat Government inspectors closely examine tainted sides of beef at a meatpacking plant.

preparation of food and drug products by many companies. Perhaps the most powerful blow against these abuses was struck by Upton Sinclair's novel *The Jungle* (1906), which told the story of a Lithuanian immigrant working in a filthy Chicago meatpacking plant:

> It was too dark in these storage places to see well, but a man could run his hand over these piles of meat and sweep off handfuls of the dried dung of rats. These rats were nuisances, and the packers would put poisoned bread out for them, they would die, and then rats, bread, and meat would go into the hoppers [to be ground up] together.

The Meat Inspection Act and The Pure Food and Drug Act

After reading *The Jungle* Roosevelt urged Congress to pass the Meat Inspection Act of 1906. It required the Department of Agriculture to inspect every red-meat animal whose carcass crossed state lines—both before and after slaughter. The Pure Food and Drug Act (1906), enacted the same day, required producers of food and medicines to host government inspectors, too.

Environmental Conservation

One of the most enduring legacies of Roosevelt's leadership was his energetic support for environmental conservation, one of the pillars of his Square Deal programs. Roosevelt, an avid outdoorsman, naturalist, and amateur scientist, championed efforts to manage and preserve the nation's natural resources (which he called "wild places") for the benefit of future generations. He created fifty federal wildlife refuges, approved five new national parks and fifty-one federal bird sanctuaries, and designated eighteen national monuments, including the Grand Canyon.

In 1898, Roosevelt had endorsed the appointment of his friend Gifford Pinchot, Amos's brother and the nation's first professionally trained forest manager, as the head of the U.S. Department of Agriculture's Division of Forestry. A handsome, wealthy man who devoted his life to forestry, Pinchot, like Roosevelt, was a pragmatic conservationist; he believed in economic growth as well as environmental preservation. Pinchot said that the conservation movement promoted the "greatest good for the greatest number for the longest time." Roosevelt and Pinchot used the Forest Reserve Act (1891) to protect 172 million acres of federally owned forests from being logged. Lumber companies were furious, but Roosevelt held firm, declaring, "I hate a man who skins the land." Overall, Roosevelt set aside more than 234 million acres of federal land for conservation purposes and created 45 national forests in 11 western states. As Pinchot recalled late in life, "Launching the conservation movement was the most significant achievement of the T.R. Administration, as he himself believed."

> Roosevelt and Gifford Pinchot: Preserving natural resources

Roosevelt and Race

Roosevelt's most significant failure as a progressive was his refusal to confront the movement's major blind spot: racism. Like populists, progressives worked to empower "the people" against the entrenched "special interests." In the view of most of them, however, "the people" did not include African Americans, Native Americans, or some immigrant groups. Most white progressives shared the prevailing racist attitudes of the time. They ignored or even endorsed the passage of Jim Crow laws in the South that prevented blacks from voting and subjected them to rigid racial separation in schools, housing, parks, and playgrounds. By 1901, nearly every southern state had successfully prevented almost all African Americans from voting or holding political office by disqualifying or terrorizing them. During the Progressive Era, hundreds of African Americans were lynched each year across the South, where virtually no blacks were allowed to serve on juries or work as sheriffs or policemen. A white candidate for governor in Mississippi in 1903 announced that he believed "in the divine right of the white man to rule, to do all the voting, and to hold all the offices, both state and federal." The South, wrote W. E. B. Du Bois, then a young sociologist at Atlanta University, "is simply an armed camp for intimidating black folk."

At the same time, few progressives raised objections to the many informal and private patterns of segregation and prejudice in the North and West. "The plain fact is," the muckraking journalist Ray Stannard Baker admitted in 1909, "most of us in the North do not believe in any real democracy between white and colored men."

Theodore Roosevelt himself shared such prejudices. He confided to a friend in 1906 his belief that "as a race and in the mass" African Americans "are altogether inferior to whites." Yet on occasion the president made exceptions. On October 16, 1901, soon after becoming president, Roosevelt invited Booker T. Washington, then the nation's most prominent black leader, to the White House for dinner to discuss presidential appointments in the South. Upon learning of the meeting, white Southerners exploded with fury. The *Memphis Scimitar* newspaper screamed that Roosevelt's allowing a "nigger" to dine with him was "the most damnable outrage that has ever been perpetrated by a citizen of the United States." South Carolina senator Benjamin R. Tillman was even angrier. He threatened that "a thousand niggers in the South will have to be killed to teach them 'their place' again."

Theodore Roosevelt and Booker T. Washington
Roosevelt addresses the National Negro Business League in 1900 with Washington seated to his left.

Roosevelt was stunned by the violent reaction, saying he found it "inexplicable" and insisting that he had done nothing wrong. But in the end he gave in to the criticism. Never again would he host a black leader. During a tour of the southern states in 1905, he pandered to whites by highlighting his own southern ancestry (his mother was from Georgia) and expressing his admiration for the Confederacy and Robert E. Lee. His behavior, said a black leader, was "national treachery to the Negro."

But worse was to come. The following year, 1906, witnessed a violent racial incident in Brownsville, Texas, where a dozen or so members of an African American army regiment from a nearby fort got into a shootout with whites who had been harassing them outside a saloon. One white bartender was killed and a police officer seriously wounded. Both sides claimed the other started the shooting. An investigation concluded that the soldiers were at fault, but no one could identify any of the shooters and none of the soldiers was willing to talk about the incident.

Roosevelt responded to their silence by dishonorably discharging the entire regiment of 167 soldiers, several of whom (like the president himself) had been awarded the Congressional Medal of Honor for their service in Cuba during the War of 1898. None of them was given a hearing or a trial.

Critics of Roosevelt's harsh action flooded the White House with angry telegrams. "Once enshrined in our love as our Moses" for inviting Booker T. Washington to the White House, a black minister wrote, Roosevelt "is now enshrouded in our scorn as our Judas." Secretary of War William H. Taft urged the president to reconsider his decision, but Roosevelt refused to show any mercy to "murderers, assassins, cowards, and comrades of murderers." (Sixty years later, the U.S. Army "cleared the records" of all the black soldiers.) Disheartened black leaders predicted that Roosevelt's harsh language would ignite "race hatred and violence" against innocent African Americans. "We shall oppose the re-nomination of Theodore Roosevelt," said the *Washington Bee*, a black-owned newspaper.

The Transition from Roosevelt to Taft

In fact, after his 1904 victory Roosevelt had decided he would not run for president again, in part because he did not want to be the first president to serve the equivalent of a third term. It was a noble gesture but a political blunder he would later come to regret. His personal pledge to serve only four more years would have momentous political consequences. For now, however, he urged Republicans to nominate his long-time friend and secretary of war, William Howard Taft, whom the Republican Convention endorsed on its first ballot in 1908. The Democrats decided to give William Jennings Bryan one more chance. Although Roosevelt dismissed Bryan as a "quack," he retained a faithful following, especially in the South.

Taft promised to continue Roosevelt's policies, and the Republican platform endorsed the president's progressive program. The Democratic platform echoed the Republican emphasis on needed regulation of business but called for a lower tariff. Bryan struggled to attract national support and was defeated for a third time, as Taft swept the Electoral College, 321 to 162.

William Howard Taft had superb qualifications to be president. Born in Cincinnati in 1857, he was the son of a prominent attorney who had served in President Grant's cabinet. He had graduated second in his class at Yale, where he studied under the famous social Darwinist William Graham Sumner, and gone on to become a leading legal scholar, serving on the Ohio Supreme Court. In 1900, President McKinley had appointed him the first American governor-general of the Philippines, and three years later Roosevelt named him secretary of war.

Unlike the robust, athletic Roosevelt, Taft struggled most of his life with obesity, topping out at 332 pounds and earning the nickname "Big Bill." Roosevelt, he explained, "loves the woods, he loves hunting; he loves roughing it, and I don't." Although good-natured and easygoing, Taft as president never managed—even in his own mind—to escape the shadow of his charismatic predecessor. "When I hear someone say 'Mr. President,'" he confessed, "I look around expecting to see Roosevelt."

Taft was a cautious and conservative progressive who vowed to preserve capitalism by protecting "the right of property" and the "right of liberty." In practice, this meant that he was even more determined than Roosevelt to support "the spirit of commercial freedom" against monopolistic trusts, but he was not interested in pushing for additional reforms. Taft was no crusader; he viewed himself as a judge-like administrator, not an innovator. He said he "hated politics" and was reluctant to exercise presidential authority (after leaving the White House, he got the job he had always wanted most, chief justice of the U.S. Supreme Court).

William Howard Taft As the 27th president, Taft was the first president to throw the first pitch of the baseball season.

> Taft as president: Highly qualified, judge-like administrator

Taft and Tariffs

Taft's failure to gain real tariff reform

After taking office, Taft displayed his credentials as a progressive Republican by supporting lower tariffs on imports; he even called a special session of Congress to address the matter. But he proved less skillful than Roosevelt in dealing with Congress. He discontinued Roosevelt's practice of holding weekly press conferences at which the president tried to influence Congressmen by using his "big stick through the press." Taft confessed that he did not know how to use the "bully pulpit," which Roosevelt had perfected. In the end, the Payne-Aldrich Tariff (1909) made little change in federal tariff policies. Some rates went down while others went up, but overall, tariff policies continued to favor the industrial Northeast over the rest of the nation. Taft's failure to gain real reform and his lack of a "crusading spirit" like Roosevelt's angered the progressive, pro-Roosevelt wing of the Republican party, whom Taft dismissed as "assistant Democrats."

The Ballinger–Pinchot Controversy

Taft's commercial "giveaway" of federal lands

In 1910, the split between the conservative and progressive Republican factions was widened by what came to be called the Ballinger-Pinchot controversy, which made Taft appear to be abandoning Roosevelt's environmental conservation policies. Taft's new secretary of the interior, Richard A. Ballinger, threw open to commercial use millions of acres of federal lands that Roosevelt had ordered protected. As chief of forestry, Gifford Pinchot expressed concerns to Taft about the "giveaway," but the president refused to intervene. When Pinchot made his opposition public early in 1910, Taft fired him, labeling him a "fanatic." In doing so, Taft set in motion a feud with Roosevelt that would eventually end their friendship—and cost him his reelection.

The Taft–Roosevelt Feud

Taft's progressive record

In 1909, soon after Taft became president, Roosevelt and his son Kermit sailed to Africa, where they would spend nearly a year shooting big-game animals. (When he heard about the extended safari, J. Pierpont Morgan, still angry at Roosevelt for breaking up the Northern Securities Company, expressed the hope that "every lion would do its duty.") Roosevelt had left the White House assuming that his chosen successor would continue to pursue a progressive agenda. Instead, in his view, by filling the cabinet with corporate lawyers and firing Gifford Pinchot, Taft had failed to "carry out my work unbroken." Taft means well, Roosevelt would say, "but he means well *feebly*." He was "utterly helpless as a leader."

Roosevelt's rebuke of Taft was in many ways undeserved. Taft had at least attempted tariff reform, which Roosevelt had never dared. Yes, he had fired Pinchot, but he had replaced him with other conservationists. In the end, Taft's administration preserved more federal land in four years than Roosevelt's had in nearly eight. Taft's administration also filed twice as many anti-trust suits as did Roosevelt's, including the one that led to the breakup of the Standard Oil Company in 1911.

Taft advanced other progressive causes as well. He strengthened federal control over railroad freight rates, an issue long promoted by farmers and farm organizations. In 1910, with his support, Congress passed the Mann-Elkins Act, which extended the authority of the Interstate Commerce Commission beyond railroads to telephone and telegraph companies. Taft established a federal Children's Bureau (1912) to promote children's welfare and a Bureau of Mines (1910) to oversee that huge industry. Taft also supported giving women the right to vote and workers the right to join unions.

But none of that satisfied Roosevelt. During the fall of 1910, the former president, still furious at Taft and eager to return to the political spotlight, gave a speech at Osawatomie, a small town in eastern Kansas, in which he gave a catchy name to his latest progressive principles and proposals, calling his sweeping agenda the New Nationalism. Roosevelt explained that he wanted to go beyond ensuring a "Square Deal" in which corporations were forced to "play by the rules"; he now promised to "change the rules" to force large corporations to promote social welfare and to serve the needs of working people. To save capitalism from the threat of a working-class revolution, he called for tighter federal regulation of "arrogant" corporations ("the great special business interests") that too often tried to "control and corrupt" politics, for a federal income tax (the Sixteenth Amendment had still not been ratified by the states), and for federal laws regulating child labor. It was a sweeping agenda that would greatly expand the power of the federal government over economic and political life. "What I have advocated," he explained, "is not wild radicalism. It is the highest and wisest kind of conservatism."

Then, on February 24, 1912, Roosevelt abandoned his earlier pledge and announced his entry into the race for the 1912 Republican presidential nomination. He dismissed Taft as a "hopeless fathead" who had "sold the Square Deal down the river." Taft responded to his friend's attacks by calling Roosevelt a "dangerous egotist" and a "demagogue." The two former colleagues and friends now began a bitter war in which Roosevelt had the better weapons, not the least of which was his love of a good fight. Elihu Root, a Republican leader, described his friend Roosevelt as "essentially a fighter, and when he gets into a fight he is completely dominated by the desire to destroy" his opponent.

By 1912 a dozen or so "progressive" states were letting citizens vote for presidential candidates in party primaries rather than the traditional practice whereby a state's party leaders chose the nominee. Roosevelt decided that if he won big in the Republican primaries, he could claim to be "the people's choice" for the nomination. But even though he won all but two of the primaries, including the one in Taft's home state of Ohio, his personal popularity was no match for Taft's authority as party leader. In the 36 states that still chose candidates by conventions dominated by party bosses, the Taft Republicans prevailed, and at the Republican National Convention Taft was easily nominated for reelection.

| Roosevelt's New Nationalism |

Sideshow Ted This 1912 cartoon criticizes the Bull Moose Party for being just a sideshow (with suffragists selling lemonade outside) and points out the menacing ego of Roosevelt himself.

An outraged Roosevelt denounced Taft and his supporters as thieves and walked out of the convention along with his delegates—mostly social workers, teachers, professors, journalists, and crusaders for women's suffrage, along with a few wealthy business executives who loved Roosevelt. Six weeks later the breakaway faction reconvened in Chicago to create a **Progressive party** with Roosevelt as its candidate. In his appearance before the delegates, he assured them that he felt "fit as a bull moose," leading journalists to nickname the Progressives the "Bull Moose party." When Roosevelt closed his acceptance speech by saying that "We stand at Armageddon [the climactic encounter between Christ and Satan], and we battle for the Lord," the delegates began singing the hymn "Onward, Christian Soldiers." One reporter wrote that the "Bull Moose" movement was not so much a politcal party as it was a religion.

The Progressive party platform revealed Roosevelt's growing liberalism. It supported a minimum "living wage" for hourly workers, women's suffrage, campaign finance reform, and a federal system of social insurance to protect people against sickness, unemployment, and disabilities. It also pledged to end the "boss system" governing American politics. But honesty and integrity in government was the basic theme of the new party: "To dissolve the unholy alliance between corrupt business and corrupt politics is the first task of the statesmanship of the day." Conservative critics now called Roosevelt "a socialist," a "revolutionist," and "a virtual traitor to American institutions."

Once nominated, Roosevelt repeatedly declared that Taft was not a progressive because he had tried to "undo" efforts at environmental conservation and had failed to fight either for social justice or against the "special interests." Instead, the former president charged, Taft had aligned himself with the "privileged" political and business leaders who steadfastly opposed "the cause of justice for the helpless and the wronged."

CORE **OBJECTIVE**

5. Describe the progressive policies of President Woodrow Wilson, and explain why and how they differed from those of Presidents Roosevelt and Taft.

Woodrow Wilson's Progressivism

The Republican fight between Taft and Roosevelt gave hope to the Democrats, whose presidential nominee, New Jersey governor Woodrow Wilson, had enjoyed remarkable success in his brief political career. Until his nomination and election as governor in 1910, Wilson had been a college professor and then president of Princeton University; he had never run for any other political office or worked in business. Instead, he was a man of ideas with extraordinary abilities: a keen intellect, an analytical temperament, a fertile imagination, a tireless work ethic, and an inspiring speaking style. He was convinced that he knew what was best for the nation. People often "call me an idealist," Wilson explained. "Well, that is the way I know I am an American."

Wilson's Dramatic Rise

Born in Staunton, Virginia, in 1856, the son and grandson of Presbyterian ministers, Thomas Woodrow Wilson had grown up in Georgia and the Carolinas during the Civil War and Reconstruction. Tall and slender with a long, chiselled face, he developed an unquestioning religious faith. He prayed and read the Bible daily all his life. Driven by a consuming sense that God had destined him to "serve" humanity, he often displayed an unbending self-righteousness and a fiery temper, qualities that would prove to be his undoing as president. Over the course of his presidency, he would sometimes mutter, "God save us from compromise."

Woodrow Wilson The only president to hold a Ph.D. degree to date.

Wilson graduated from Princeton in 1879. After law school at the University of Virginia, he briefly practiced law in Atlanta, but he found legal work "dreadful drudgery" and soon enrolled at Johns Hopkins University to study history and political science, earning one of the nation's first doctoral degrees. He became an expert in constitutional government and preferred the British prime-minister system over the American presidential model because it enabled a leader to accomplish more. He then taught at several colleges before being named president of Princeton in 1902. Eight years later, New Jersey Democrats offered Wilson their support for the 1910 gubernatorial nomination. He accepted the offer but already harbored higher ambitions. If he could become governor, he reflected, "I stand a very good chance of being the next President of the United States." Like Theodore Roosevelt, Wilson was an intensely ambitious and idealistic man who felt destined to preside over America's emergence as the greatest world power.

Although Wilson called himself an "amateur" politician, he proved a surprisingly effective campaigner and won a landslide victory. The professor-turned-governor then persuaded the state legislature to adopt an array of progressive reforms to curb the power of political party bosses and corporate lobbyists. "After dealing with college politicians," Wilson joked, "I find that the men who I am dealing with now seem like amateurs."

Governor Wilson soon attracted the attention of national Democratic leaders. At the 1912 Democratic convention, less than two years after beginning his political career, he faced stiff competition from several veteran party leaders for the presidential nomination, but with the support of William Jennings Bryan, he won on the forty-sixth ballot. It was, Wilson said, a "political miracle."

The Election of 1912

The 1912 presidential campaign was one of the most exciting in history. It involved four distinguished candidates: Democrat Woodrow Wilson, Republican William Howard Taft, Socialist Eugene V. Debs, and Progressive

Progressive party Political party founded by Theodore Roosevelt to support his bid to regain the presidency in 1912 after his split from the Taft Republicans.

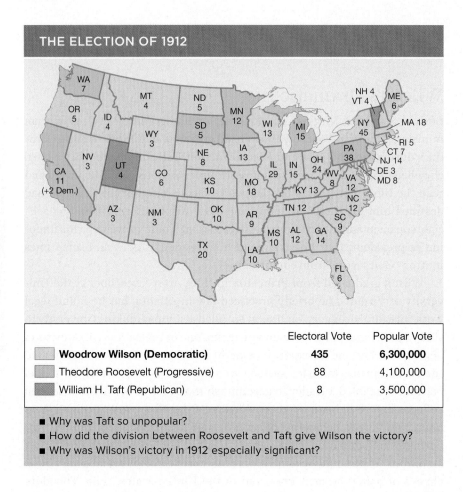

THE ELECTION OF 1912

	Electoral Vote	Popular Vote
Woodrow Wilson (Democratic)	**435**	**6,300,000**
Theodore Roosevelt (Progressive)	88	4,100,000
William H. Taft (Republican)	8	3,500,000

- Why was Taft so unpopular?
- How did the division between Roosevelt and Taft give Wilson the victory?
- Why was Wilson's victory in 1912 especially significant?

Theodore Roosevelt. For all of their differences in personality and temperament, the candidates shared a basic progressive assumption that modern social problems could be resolved only through active governmental intervention.

As the contest unfolded, it settled down to a running debate between Roosevelt's New Nationalism and Wilson's **New Freedom**, a program designed by Louis D. Brandeis, a progressive Boston lawyer and future justice of the U.S. Supreme Court. The New Freedom aimed to restore competition in the economy by eliminating all trusts rather than simply regulating them. Where Roosevelt admired the power and efficiency of law-abiding corporations, no matter how large, Brandeis and Wilson were convinced that huge, "heartless" industries needed to be broken up.

On election day, Wilson won handily in the Electoral College, collecting 435 votes to 88 for Roosevelt and only 8 for Taft, the only Republican nominee for president ever to finish third. After learning of his election, the self-righteous Wilson told the chairman of his campaign committee that "I owe you nothing. God ordained that I should be the next president of the United

> The New Freedom: Eliminating rather than regulating trusts

New Freedom Program championed in 1912 by the Woodrow Wilson campaign that aimed to restore competition in the economy by eliminating all trusts rather than simply regulating them.

States. Neither you nor any other mortal could have prevented that." Had the Republicans not divided their votes between Taft and Roosevelt, however, Wilson would have lost. His was the victory of a minority candidate over a divided opposition. Since all four candidates called themselves progressives, however, the president-elect expressed his hope "that the thoughtful progressive forces of the nation may now at last unite." The election of 1912 profoundly altered the character of the Republican party. The defection of the Bull Moose Progressives had weakened the party's progressive wing. As a result, when Republicans returned to power in the 1920s, they would be more conservative in tone and temperament than Roosevelt and his progressive supporters.

The real surprise of the 1912 election, however, was the strong showing of the Socialist party candidate, Eugene V. Debs, running for the fourth time. The tall, lanky, blue-eyed idealist had devoted his adult life to fighting against the "monstrous system of capitalism" on behalf of the working class, first as a labor union official, then as a socialist promoting government ownership of railroads and other key industries and the sharing of profits with workers. Debs voiced a brand of socialism that was flexible rather than rigid, Christian rather than Marxist, democratic rather than totalitarian. He believed in political transformation, not violent revolution. As one of his supporters said, "That old man with the burning eyes actually believes that there can be such a thing as the brotherhood of man. And that's not the funniest part of it. As long as he's around I believe it myself."

Debs had become the unifying symbol of a diverse American radical movement that united West Virginia coal miners, Oklahoma sharecroppers, Pacific Northwest lumberjacks, and immigrant workers in New York City sweatshops. One newspaper highlighted "The Rising Tide of Socialism" in 1912 as some 1,150 Socialists won election to local and state offices across the nation, including eighteen mayors. To many voters, the Socialists, whose 118,000 dues-paying members in 1912 were double the number compared with the year before, offered the only real alternative to a stalemated political system in which the two major parties had few real differences. A business executive in New York City explained that he had become a Socialist "because the old parties [Democrats and Republicans] were flimflamming us all the time." But fear of socialism was also widespread during the Progressive Era. Theodore Roosevelt warned that the rapid growth of the Socialist party was "far more ominous than any Populist or similar movement in the past."

Eugene V. Debs and the "Rising Tide of Socialism"

In 1912, with very few campaign funds, Debs crisscrossed the nation giving fiery speeches that frequently announced: "Comrades, this is our year!" He dismissed Roosevelt as "a fraud" whose progressive promises were nothing more than "the mouthings of a low and utterly unprincipled self-seeker and demagogue." Debs's untiring efforts brought him over 900,000 votes, an astonishing total for a Socialist, more than twice as many as he had received four years earlier.

A Burst of Reform Bills

On March 4, 1913, a huge crowd surrounded the Capitol in Washington, D.C., to watch Woodrow Wilson's inauguration. The new president with the long nose and spectacles declared that it was not "a day of triumph" but "a day of dedication." He promised to lower "the stiff and stupid" Republican tariffs, create a new national banking system, strengthen anti-trust laws, and establish an administration "more concerned about human rights than about property rights."

President Wilson: An expert on government, an activist, and a "fierce" reformer

Wilson worried about people comparing him to the colorful, hyperactive Roosevelt: "He appeals to their imagination; I do not. He is a real, vivid person. . . . I am a vague, conjectural [philosophical] personality, more made up of opinions and academic prepossessions than of human traits and red corpuscles." Roosevelt had been a strong president by force of personality; Wilson became a strong president by force of conviction.

For all of their differences, the two progressive presidents shared a belief that national problems demanded national solutions. Together they set in motion the modern presidency. They both shared Wilson's view that the U.S. president "is at liberty in both law and conscience to be as big as he can." Like Roosevelt, Wilson was an activist president; he was the first to speak to the nation over the radio and to host weekly press conferences. He was also unusual among presidents in that he frequently spoke to Congress and visited legislators in their offices in the Capitol. As a political scientist, Wilson was an expert at the processes of government. During his first two years, he pushed through Congress more new bills than any previous president. But like "most reformers," the president of Harvard University noted, Wilson "had a fierce and unlovely side." The new president found it hard to understand—much less work with—people who disagreed with him.

Wilson's victory, coupled with Democratic majorities in the House and Senate, gave his party effective national power for the first time since the Civil War. It also gave southerners a significant role in national politics for the first time since 1860. In addition to the president himself, five of Wilson's ten cabinet members were born in the South. At his right hand was "Colonel" Edward M. House of Texas, who held no official government position but was Wilson's most trusted adviser. The president described House as "my second personality. He is my independent self." House helped steer Wilson's proposals through a Congress in which southerners, by virtue of their seniority, held the lion's share of committee chairmanships. As a result, much of the progressive legislation of the Wilson era would bear the names of southern Democrats.

The Tariff and the Income Tax

Wilson's new administration faced its first big test on the complex issue of tariff reform. By 1913, the federal tariff included hundreds of taxes on different imported goods, from oil to nails, all designed to benefit American manufacturers. The president believed that U.S. corporations were misusing the tariff to keep out foreign competitors and create American monopolies that kept consumer prices artificially high. In order to attack high tariff rates, Wilson summoned Congress to a special session that lasted eighteen months, the longest in history, and he addressed its members in person—the first president to do so since John Adams. The new tariff bill passed the House easily. The crunch came in the Senate, the traditional graveyard of tariff reform, where swarms of industry lobbyists grew so thick, Wilson said, that "a brick couldn't be thrown without hitting one of them." The president finally won approval there by publicly criticizing the "industrious and insidious" tariff lobby.

The Underwood-Simmons Tariff (1913) lowered average tariff rates on imports—from about 40 percent to 25 percent—for the first time since the Civil War. To compensate for the government's reduced tariff revenue, the bill created the first income tax allowed under the newly ratified Sixteenth Amendment: the initial tax rates were 1 percent on income more than $3,000 ($4,000 for married couples) up to a top rate of 7 percent on annual income of $50,000 or more. Most Americans (99 percent) paid no income tax at all because they earned less than $3,000 a year.

> A lower tariff and a new income tax

The Federal Reserve Act

Before the new tariff had cleared the Senate, the administration proposed the first major banking reform since the Civil War. Ever since Andrew Jackson had killed the Second Bank of the United States in the 1830s, the nation had been without a central bank to manage its currency. Instead, the money supply was chaotically "managed" by thousands of local and state banks. Such a decentralized system produced instability and inefficiency because during financial panics fearful depositors, eager to get their money, would create "runs" that often led to the failure of smaller banks. In fact, the primary reason for a new central bank was to prevent more such panics, which had occurred five times since 1873. The most recent crisis, in 1907, had prompted the creation of a congressional commission to decide whether the United States needed a centralized banking system.

> Creation of the Federal Reserve System

By 1913, Wilson agreed that the nation's banking system needed a central reserve agency that, in a crisis, could distribute emergency cash to banks threatened by runs. But he insisted that any new national banking system must be overseen by the government rather than by bankers themselves (the "money power"). He wanted a new central bank that would benefit the entire economy, not just the large banks headquartered on Wall Street in New York City.

After much dickering, Congress finally passed the **Federal Reserve Act** on December 23, 1913. It created a new national banking system with twelve regional districts, each of which had its own Federal Reserve Bank that was owned by member banks in the district. Nationally chartered banks, which agreed to regulation by a Federal Reserve Bank in exchange for the right to issue money, had to be members of the Federal Reserve System. But state-chartered banks—essentially unregulated—did not (and, indeed, two-thirds

Federal Reserve Act (1913) Legislation passed by Congress to create a new national banking system in order to regulate the nation's currency supply and ensure the stability and integrity of member banks who made up the Federal Reserve System across the nation.

of the nation's banks chose not to become members of the Federal Reserve System). The twelve regional Federal Reserve banks were supervised by a central board of directors in Washington, D.C.

The purpose of the new Federal Reserve System was to adjust the nation's currency supply to match the needs of the economy and to ensure the stability and integrity of member banks. When banks were short of cash, they could borrow from the Federal Reserve, using their loans as collateral. Each of the new regional Federal Reserve banks issued Federal Reserve notes (currency) to member banks in exchange for their loans. By doing so, "the Fed," as the system came to be called, promoted economic growth and helped preserve the stability of banks during panics. The Federal Reserve board required member banks to have a certain percentage of their total deposits in cash on hand ("reserve") at all times.

A conservative Republican called the Federal Reserve Act "populistic, socialistic, half-baked, destructive, and unworkable." The new system soon proved its worth, however, and the criticism eased. The Federal Reserve Act was the most significant new program of Wilson's presidency.

Anti-Trust Actions

> A new Federal Trade Commission and Anti-Trust Act

While promoting tariff and banking reforms, Wilson made "trust-busting" the central focus of his New Freedom program. Giant corporations had continued to grow despite the Sherman Anti-Trust Act and the Bureau of Corporations, the federal watchdog agency created by Theodore Roosevelt. Wilson decided to make a strong **Federal Trade Commission** (FTC) the cornerstone of his anti-trust program. Created in 1914, the five-member FTC replaced the Bureau of Corporations and assumed new powers to define "unfair trade practices" and issue "cease and desist" orders when it found evidence of such practices.

Like Roosevelt, Wilson also supported efforts to strengthen and clarify the Sherman Anti-Trust Act. Henry D. Clayton, a Democrat from Alabama, drafted an anti-trust bill in 1914. The **Clayton Anti-Trust Act** declared that labor unions were not to be viewed as "monopolies in restraint of trade," as courts had done since 1890. It also prohibited directors from serving on the boards of competing companies and further clarified the meaning of various "monopolistic" activities.

Progressives' Disappointments with Wilson

In November 1914, just two years after his election, President Wilson announced that he had accomplished the major goals of progressivism. He had fulfilled his promises to lower the tariff, create a national banking system, and strengthen the anti-trust laws. The New Freedom was now complete, he wrote. But his announcement bewildered many progressives, especially those who had long advocated additional federal social-justice legislation that Wilson had earlier supported. Herbert Croly, the influential editor of the *New Republic* magazine, was dumbfounded by Wilson's conservative

Federal Trade Commission (1914) Independent agency created by the Wilson administration that replaced the Bureau of Corporations as an even more powerful tool to combat unfair trade practices and monopolies.

Clayton Anti-Trust Act (1914) Legislation that served to enhance the Sherman Anti-Trust Act (1890) by clarifying what constituted "monopolistic" activities and declaring that labor unions were not to be viewed as "monopolies in restraint of trade."

turn. He wondered how the president could assert "that the fundamental wrongs of a modern society can be easily and quickly righted as a consequence of [passing] a few laws." Wilson's about-face, he concluded, "casts suspicion upon his own sincerity [as a progressive] or upon his grasp of the realities of modern social and industrial life."

Progressivism for Whites Only

African Americans were also disappointed by Wilson's racial conservatism. Like many other progressives, Wilson showed little interest in addressing the discrimination and violence that African Americans faced. In fact, he shared many of the racist attitudes common at the time. As a student at Princeton, he had expressed his disgust at the guarantee of voting rights for black men after the Civil War, arguing that whites must always resist domination by "an ignorant and inferior race." Later, as a politician, Wilson did court African American voters, but he rarely consulted black leaders and largely avoided associating with them in public or expressing support for them. That he refused to create a National Race Commission was a great disappointment to the black community, as were his cabinet appointments of white southerners who were outspoken racists.

Josephus Daniels, a North Carolina newspaper editor who became Wilson's secretary of the navy, was a white supremacist who wrote that "the subjection of the negro, politically, and the separation of the negro, socially, are paramount to all other considerations in the South." For Daniels and other southern progressives, "progress" was possible only if blacks were "kept in their place." Daniels and other cabinet members racially segregated the employees in their agencies; Secretary of State William Jennings Bryan supported such efforts to create separate offices, dining facilities,

> Wilson's support for racial segregation

New freedom, old rules Wilson and the First Lady ride in a carriage with African American drivers.

restrooms, and water fountains. Wilson claimed that racial segregation "is not humiliating but a benefit." He was the first president since the Civil War who openly endorsed discrimination against African Americans, arguing that segregation in government buildings was in "their best interests." His administration also reduced the number of African American appointees to federal offices.

After visiting Washington, D.C., in 1913, Booker T. Washington reported that he had "never seen the colored people so discouraged and bitter." In November 1914, a delegation of African American leaders met with Wilson in the White House to ask how a "progressive" president could adopt such "regressive" racial policies. Wilson responded that both races benefited from the policies because they eliminated "the possibility of friction." William Trotter, a Harvard-educated African American newspaper editor who had helped found the National Association for the Advancement of Colored People (NAACP), scolded the president: "Have you a 'new freedom' for white Americans, and a new slavery for 'your Afro-American fellow citizens' [a phrase Wilson had used in a speech]? God forbid." A furious Wilson then told Trotter and the other visitors to leave, saying that their unchristian "tone offends me."

The Vote for Women

Activists for women's suffrage also were disappointed in President Wilson (as they had been in President Roosevelt). Despite having two daughters who were suffragists, he insisted that the issue of women's voting rights should be left to the states rather than embodied in a constitutional amendment.

Wilson's lack of support led some leaders of the suffrage movement to revise their tactics. In 1910, Alice Paul, a New Jersey–born Quaker social worker who had earned a doctoral degree in political science from the University of Pennsylvania, returned from an apprenticeship with the militant suffragists of England, who had developed effective forms of civil disobedience as a way of generating attention and support. After Paul joined the National American Woman Suffrage Association (NAWSA), she urged activists to picket state legislatures, target and "punish" politicians who failed to endorse suffrage, chain themselves to public buildings, incite police to arrest them, and undertake hunger strikes. In March 1913, Paul organized 5,000 suffragists to march in protest at Wilson's inauguration.

Four years later, Paul, having broken with NAWSA and formed the National Woman's Party, decided that suffragists must do something even more dramatic to force Wilson to support their cause: picket the White House. Beginning on January 11, 1917, Paul and her followers took turns carrying signs there all day, five days a week, for six months, until the president ordered their arrest. Some sixty suffragists were jailed. For her leadership role, Paul was sentenced to seven months in prison. She then went on a hunger strike, leading prison officials to force-feed her through a tube inserted in

Alice Paul Sewing a suffrage flag—orange and purple, with stars—that she and other suffragists often waved at strikes and protests.

The Expanding Role of the Federal Government

Progressive reformers wanted to improve the quality of life for all Americans and believed that government should play a crucial role in doing so. Their activities led to a significant expansion in the activity of the federal government in the first two decades of the twentieth century. After the presidencies of Theodore Roosevelt, William Taft, and Woodrow Wilson, the government had gained new powers to shape the direction of the nation's economic and social well-being. The following timeline reviews many important presidential actions, legislative developments, and constitutional amendments between 1901 and 1917.

PROGRESSIVE POLICIES AT THE FEDERAL LEVEL, 1901–1917

1901–1909
Presidency of Theodore Roosevelt

 1902

■ The Roosevelt Administration sues the Northern Securities Company for violating the Sherman Anti-Trust Act. The Supreme Court would dissolve the corporation in 1904.

■ Roosevelt intervenes in a major coal miners' strike, eventually threatening to send in federal troops to operate the mines if the owners did not negotiate with the striking workers. The owners conceded to a reduction in work hours and a 10 percent wage increase.

1903

■ Congress creates the Bureau of Corporations to monitor the activities of Big Business. The Roosevelt administration sued the Standard Oil Company for violation of the Sherman Anti-Trust Act, resulting in the Supreme Court's dissolving the corporation in 1911.

■ Congress passes the Elkins Act, outlawing secret rebates by railroad companies to favored customers.

1909–1913
Presidency of William Taft

1910

■ Congress passes the Mann-Elkins Act, giving the Interstate Commerce Commission the power to regulate telegraph and telephone companies.

 1913

■ Passage of the Sixteenth Amendment to the Constitution, authorizing a federal income tax, and the Seventeenth Amendment, allowing for the direct election of U.S. senators, are ratified.

1913–1921
Presidency of Woodrow Wilson

 1913

■ Congress passes the Underwood-Simmons Tariff, lowering tariffs on imports and creating the nation's first progressive income tax to make up for lost federal revenue.

■ Congress passes the Federal Reserve Act to oversee and regulate the nation's banking system and provide a stable currency.

 1914

■ Congress creates the Federal Trade Commission to replace the Bureau of Corporations in overseeing the behavior of Big Business and gives the new agency the ability to define unfair trade practices and issue cease and desist orders when it identified unfair trade practices.

■ Congress passes the Clayton Anti-Trust Act, which exempted labor unions from anti-trust prosecution, prohibited corporate directors from serving on boards of competing companies, and further defined various meanings of monopolistic practices.

QUESTIONS FOR ANALYSIS

1. What were some of the major progressive concerns that the federal government addressed in this era?

2. What generalizations can you make about the kinds of strategies used to address these concerns?

3. What were the limits of progressivism in this period?

her nose. Under an avalanche of press coverage and public criticism, Wilson finally pardoned her and the other jailed activists.

Progressive Resurgence

By 1916, the need to create a winning political coalition in the upcoming presidential election—which required courting Republican as well as Democratic progressives—had pushed Wilson back onto the road of reform. The president scored progressive points when he nominated Louis D. Brandeis to the Supreme Court, making him the Court's first Jewish member when he was confirmed by the Senate. Wilson also won congressional approval for a broad program of legislation to help farmers and workers.

Farm Legislation

Because farmers continued to suffer from a shortage of capital available for lending, Wilson supported a proposal to set up special rural banks to provide long-term farm loans. The Federal Farm Loan Act became law in 1916. Under the control of the Federal Farm Loan Board, twelve Federal Land banks offered loans to farmers for five to forty years at low interest rates. Under the act, farmers could borrow up to 50 percent of the value of their land. At about the same time, a dream long advocated by Populists—federal loans to farmers on the security of their crops stored in warehouses—finally came to fruition when Congress passed the Warehouse Act of 1916. These crop-security loans were available to sharecroppers and tenant farmers as well as to farmers who owned the land that they worked.

Farmers were also pleased by the passage of the Smith-Lever Act of 1914 and the Smith-Hughes Act of 1917. The Smith-Lever Act provided federal programs to educate farmers about new farm machinery and new ideas related to agricultural efficiency. The Smith-Hughes Act funded agricultural and mechanical education in high schools. Farmers with the newfangled automobiles had more than a passing interest as well in the Federal Highways Act of 1916, which helped finance new highways, especially in rural areas.

Labor Legislation

The progressive resurgence of 1916 broke the logjam on workplace reforms as well. One of the long-standing goals of many progressive Democrats was a federal child-labor law. When Congress passed the Keating-Owen Act in 1916, banning products made by child workers under fourteen from being shipped across state lines, Wilson expressed doubts about its constitutionality but eventually signed it. The act was later ruled unconstitutional by the Supreme Court on the grounds that child labor was outside the bounds of Congress's authority to regulate interstate commerce. Effective action against child labor abuses had to wait until the New Deal of the 1930s.

Another landmark law was the eight-hour workday for railroad workers, a measure that the Supreme Court upheld. The Adamson Act of 1916 resulted from a threatened strike by railroad unions demanding an eight-hour day and other concessions. Wilson, who objected to some of the unions' demands, nevertheless asked Congress to approve the Adamson Act. It required time-and-a-half pay for overtime work beyond eight hours and appointed a commission to study working conditions in the railroad industry.

The Limits of Progressivism

Progressivism reached its peak during Wilson's two terms as president. People grew optimistic about the economy and an improving society. After two decades of political upheaval and social reform (three if the Populists in the 1890s are counted), Progressivism had shattered the traditional "*laissez-faire*" notion that government had no role in regulating the economy. The courage and compassion displayed by progressives of all stripes demonstrated that people of good will could make a difference in improving the quality of life for all. Progressivism awoke people to the evils and possibilities of modern urban-industrial life. Most important, progressives established the principle that governments—local, state, and federal—had a responsibility to ensure that Americans were protected from abuse by powerful businesses and corrupt politicians. As a Texas progressive said in 1910, most Americans now acknowledged that governments must protect "the weak against the encroachments of the strong."

Yet even though it had succeeded in accomplishing most of its goals—and its racial, ethnic, and class biases are more obvious today than they were at the time—on several fronts progressivism still fell short of its supporters' hopes and ideals. Child labor would not be addressed on a national level until the Great Depression in the 1930s. It would also take the shock of the Depression to lead to the passage of a national minimum wage and the creation of a government-administered pension program for retirees and disabled workers (Social Security). Like all great historic movements, too, progressivism produced unexpected consequences. For all of its efforts to give more power to "the people," voter participation actually declined during the Progressive Era. Probably the main reason for the decline of party loyalty and voter turnout was that by the twentieth century people had many more activities to distract them from politics; new forms of recreation like movies, cycling, automobiles, and spectator sports competed with politics for time and attention. But people showed less interest in political parties and public issues in part because of the progressive emphasis on government by appointed specialists and experts rather than elected politicians.

Finally, progressivism faded because international relations pushed aside domestic concerns. By 1916, the optimism of a few years earlier was being challenged by the distressing slaughter occurring in Europe in the Great War. The twentieth century, which had dawned with such bright hopes for social progress, held in store episodes of unprecedented brutality that led people to question whether governments could be trusted to serve the "public interest" or that "progress" was even possible anymore.

■ **The Progressive Impulse** Progressives believed that industrialization and urbanization were negatively affecting American life. They were mostly middle-class idealists who promoted reform and government regulation in order to ensure social justice. They also called for legislation to end child labor, promote safety in the workplace, ban the sale of alcoholic beverages, regulate or eliminate trusts and other monopolies, and grant *woman suffrage.*

■ **The Varied Sources of Progressivism** Progressivism grew out of many sources going back several decades. The depression in the 1890s led many urban middle-class people to pursue reforms to aid the working class and the poor. Many religious reformers, such as those involved in the *social gospel* movement, had urged their fellow Christians to reject social Darwinism and do more to promote a better life for the urban poor. The settlement house movement spread through urban America as educated middle-class women formed community centers in poverty-stricken neighborhoods. *Muckrakers*—investigative journalists who exposed significant political and corporate corruption—further fueled the desire of progressive reformers to address abuses of power in American society.

■ **Progressives' Aims and Achievements** To address corruption in politics, they implemented political reforms such as the direct primary; initiative, referendum, and recall at the state level; and the direct election of senators through the *Seventeenth Amendment.* They also focused on incorporating new modes of efficiency into government administration through *Taylorism.*

Many middle-class women reformers targeted what they saw as the social evils of alcohol consumption, prostitution, and poor living and working conditions. Social justice reformers also fought successfully for a progressive income tax with the passage of the *Sixteenth Amendment.*

■ **Progressivism under Roosevelt and Taft** The administrations of Theodore Roosevelt and William H. Taft increased the power of the president and the federal government to regulate corporate power. Roosevelt promoted his progressive *Square Deal* program, which included the arbitration of the 1902 coal strike, and Pure Food and Drug Acts. After severe criticism of his White House meeting with Booker T. Washington, he made no further gestures toward racial harmony or equality.

Choosing not to seek reelection in 1908, Roosevelt endorsed Taft, who easily won the election. But Taft's inability to bring about major tariff reduction with the Payne-Aldrich Tariff Act, among other failings, led Roosevelt to run again for president, promoting his New Nationalism vision. Unable to defeat Taft for the Republican nomination, Roosevelt formed a *Progressive party.* This split the Republican vote, allowing Democrat Woodrow Wilson, another progressive reformer, to win the office.

■ **Woodrow Wilson's Progressivism** Wilson's *New Freedom* program promised less federal intervention in business and a return to traditional Democratic policies like low tariffs and anti-trust regulation. He followed through on his promises with the Underwood-Simmons Tariff Act, the *Federal Reserve Act,* and to begin a rigorous anti-trust program with the passage of the *Clayton Anti-Trust Act* and the creation of the *Federal Trade Commission.* To rally Republican progressives to his side for the 1916 reelection, he endorsed greater regulation of child labor and railroad corporations, particularly through the Adamson Act. He also successfully sponsored two bills to allow farmers to get federal loans, a longtime goal of the populist movement.

KEY TERMS

muckrakers *p. 709*
social gospel *p. 710*
woman suffrage *p. 712*
Seventeenth Amendment (1913)
   p. 716

Taylorism *p. 716*
Sixteenth Amendment (1913) *p. 722*
Square Deal *p. 723*
Progressive party *p. 733*
New Freedom *p. 734*

Federal Reserve Act (1913) *p. 737*
Federal Trade Commission (1914)
   p. 738
Clayton Anti-Trust Act (1914)
   p. 738

CHRONOLOGY

1889	Hull House, a settlement house, opens in Chicago
1901	William McKinley is assassinated; Theodore Roosevelt becomes president
	Governor of Wisconsin Robert La Follette creates the "Wisconsin idea"
	Galveston, Texas, adopts the commission system of city government
1902	Roosevelt attempts to arbitrate a strike by coal miners
1902	Justice Department breaks up Northern Securities Company
1903	Congress passes the Elkins Act and creates the Bureau of Corporations
1904	National Child Labor Committee formed
1906	Upton Sinclair's *The Jungle* is published
1906	Congress passes the Meat Inspection Act and the Pure Food and Drug Act
1909	William Howard Taft inaugurated
1911	Triangle Shirtwaist fire
1912	Woodrow Wilson wins four-way presidential election
1913	Alice Paul and 5,000 suffragists protest Wilson's inauguration
	Sixteenth and Seventeenth Amendments ratified
	Underwood-Simmons Tariff and Federal Reserve Act passed
1914	Congress passes the Clayton Anti-Trust Act
1916	Congress passes the Adamson Act and the Keating-Owen Act

INQUIZITIVE

Go to InQuizitive to see what you've learned—and learn what you've missed—with personalized feedback along the way.

THE NAVY NEEDS YOU! DON'T READ AMERICAN HISTORY— MAKE IT!

MAKE AMERICAN HISTORY In this poster for a U.S. Navy recruiting station in New York City, a sailor encourages a young man to play an active role in the Great War and gestures toward battleships in the distance.

America and the Great War

1914–1920

Throughout the nineteenth century, the Atlantic Ocean had protected America from the major land wars on the continent of Europe. During the early twentieth century, however, the nation's century-long isolation from European wars ended. Ever-expanding world trade meant that American interests were becoming deeply entwined with the economies of Europe. In addition, the development of steam-powered ships and submarines meant that foreign navies could directly threaten American security. At the same time, the election of Woodrow Wilson in 1912 brought to the White House a self-righteous moralist determined to impose his standards for proper conduct on what he saw as renegade nations. This combination of circumstances made the outbreak of the "Great War" in Europe in 1914 a profound crisis for the United States, a crisis that would become the defining event of the early twentieth century and force America to accept its role and responsibilities as a dominant world power.

Once America entered the war, mobilization called millions of men into active military duty and caused mass migrations of African Americans to northern cities and southern whites to urban centers in search of industrial work to support the war effort. With victory in hand in 1919, America would find itself as the reluctant leading world power divided over

CORE OBJECTIVES INQUIZITIVE

1. Describe the outbreak of the Great War and the distinctive nature of the fighting on the Western Front, and explain why the United States was drawn into the war.

2. Explain how the Wilson administration mobilized the home front, and analyze how mobilization efforts shaped American society.

3. Describe the major events of the war after U.S. entry, and explain the U.S. contribution to the defeat of the Central Powers.

4. Evaluate Wilson's efforts to promote his plans for a peaceful world order as outlined in his Fourteen Points.

5. Analyze the consequences of the war at home and abroad.

whether to approve the Treaty of Versailles while facing substantial social and economic challenges at home with the return of legions of soldiers entering the workforce.

CORE **OBJECTIVE**

1. Describe the outbreak of the Great War and the distinctive nature of the fighting on the Western Front, and explain why the United States was drawn into the war.

An Uneasy Neutrality

Woodrow Wilson once declared that he had "a first-class mind." Although lacking humility, he was indeed highly intelligent, thoughtful, principled, and courageous. Upon learning of death threats against him, for example, he refused to change his schedule of public appearances. "The country," he explained, "cannot afford to have a coward for President." For all of his accomplishments and abilities, however, Wilson had no experience or expertise in international relations before his election as president. The former college professor admitted before taking office that "it would be an irony of fate if my administration had to deal chiefly with foreign affairs"—a topic he did not even mention in his 1913 inaugural address. But from the summer of 1914, when a terrible war erupted in Europe, foreign relations increasingly overshadowed all else, including Wilson's ambitious New Freedom program of progressive reforms.

Although inexperienced in international affairs, Wilson did not lack ideas or convictions about global issues. "Sometimes people call me an idealist," he once told an audience in South Dakota. "Well, that is the way I know I'm an American." He fervently believed that the world should follow America's example of capitalist democracy and correct behavior: "America is an idea. America is an ideal, America is a vision." Wilson saw himself as directed by God to help create a new world order governed by morality and ideals rather than by selfish national interests. Both Wilson and William Jennings Bryan, his secretary of state, believed that America had a duty to promote democracy and Christianity around the world. "Every nation of the world," Wilson declared, "needs to be drawn into the tutelage [guidance] of America."

The Outbreak of War

Wilson was faced with his greatest challenge beginning in the summer of 1914, when war broke out in Europe. Most Americans were caught off guard by the news. The "dreadful conflict" erupted suddenly, like "lightning out of a clear sky," a North Carolina congressman said. And no one could have predicted the horrifying results. Lasting for more than four years, from 1914 to 1918, the conflict became known as the Great War because it would involve more nations and cause greater destruction than any previous war. The appalling slaughter would cost 20 million military and civilian deaths, and 21 million more people would be wounded. The Great War would topple monarchs and destroy empires, create new nations, and set in motion a series of events that would lead to an even greater war in 1939—one that led to the retroactive renaming of the Great War as the First World War, or World War I.

Wars are much easier to start than to control. The Great War resulted from long-simmering and extremely complex national rivalries and ethnic conflicts in central Europe that second-rate statesmen and war-hungry generals allowed to spin out of control. At the core of the tensions was the Austro-Hungarian Empire, a collection of eleven nationalities that was determined to stop the aggressive expansionism of its neighbor and long-standing enemy, Serbia, in the Balkan peninsula. At the same time, a recklessly militaristic Germany, led by Kaiser (Emperor) Wilhelm II, was eager to assert its dominance on the European continent against its old enemies, the Russian Empire and France, at the same time that it was expanding its navy to challenge the British Empire's supremacy on the seas.

War erupted just five weeks after Gavrilo Princip, a nineteen-year-old Serbian nationalist in Sarajevo (the capital of present-day Bosnia-Herzegovina), used a pistol to assassinate the heir to the Austro-Hungarian throne, 50-year-old Archduke Franz Ferdinand, and his pregnant wife Sophie, on June 28, 1914. It was a war that few wanted but nobody could stop.

To avenge the murders, Austria-Hungary, with Germany's approval, recklessly bullied and humiliated Serbia by demanding a say in its internal affairs. Serbia gave in to virtually all of the demands, but Austria-Hungary declared war anyway. In turn, Russia mobilized its army to defend Serbia, an action that triggered chain reactions by a complex system of European military alliances: the Triple Alliance, or **Central Powers** (Germany, Austria-Hungary, and Italy), and the Triple Entente, or **Allied Powers** (France, Great Britain, and Russia).

Germany declared war on Russia on August 1, 1914, and on France two days later. Germany, hoping to defeat France before Russia could mobilize its armies in the east, invaded neutral Belgium to get at France, murdering hundreds of civilians in the process. The "rape of Belgium" brought Great Britain into the war against Germany on August 4 on the **Western Front**, the line of fighting in northern France and Belgium. Despite being a member of the Triple Alliance, Italy at first declared its neutrality in the war and then joined the Allies in return for a promise of territory taken from Austria-Hungary. On the huge Eastern Front, Russian armies would clash with German and Austro-Hungarian forces as well as those of the Turkish (Ottoman) Empire. Within five weeks of the assassination in Sarajevo, a "great war" had erupted (it would not be called the First World War until the second one came along in 1939).

> Assassination in Sarajevo

Central Powers One of the two sides during the Great War, including Germany, Austria-Hungary, the Ottoman Empire, and Bulgaria.

Allied Powers Nations fighting the Central Powers during the Great War, including France, Great Britain, and Russia; later joined by Italy and, after Russia quit the war in 1917, the United States.

Western Front Contested frontier between the Central and Allied Powers that ran along northern France and across Belgium.

An Industrial War

What started as a local conflict in the Balkans became a catastrophic war that reshaped the world. By its end, in November 1918, more than forty nations had joined the fighting, in large part because most of the warring nations had far-flung colonies around the globe. The Great War was the first

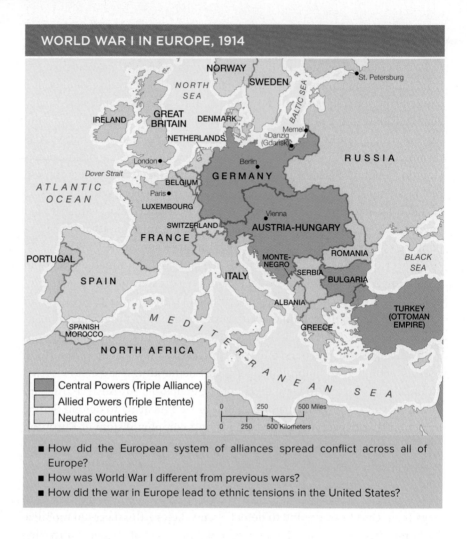

WORLD WAR I IN EUROPE, 1914

Central Powers (Triple Alliance)
Allied Powers (Triple Entente)
Neutral countries

- How did the European system of alliances spread conflict across all of Europe?
- How was World War I different from previous wars?
- How did the war in Europe lead to ethnic tensions in the United States?

industrial war, fought between nations using new weapons that dramatically increased the war's scope and destruction. Machine guns, submarines, aerial bombing, poison gas, flame throwers, land mines, mortars, long-range artillery, and armored tanks changed the nature of warfare and produced appalling casualties and widespread destruction, a slaughter on a scale unimaginable to this day. An average of 900 Frenchmen and 1,300 Germans died *every* day on the Western Front. It was the mechanized weaponry that made possible such mass killing on an "industrial" scale— the same scale on which items were mass-produced in an industrial economy.

Mechanized trench warfare

The early weeks of the war involved fast-moving assaults as German armies swept westward across Belgium and northeastern France. Then mistakes piled up on both sides. What began as a war of quick movement in August 1914 bogged down into a prolonged stalemate: nightmarish

Total ruin German soldiers stand before the French Fort Souville between the Battles of Verdun in September of 1916. The heavy and constant artillery fire dug craters into the land and destroyed all traces of the forest that stood there before.

trench warfare in which often inept generals sent masses of mud-streaked, steel-helmeted soldiers up and out of waterlogged, zigzagging trenches, some of them 40 feet deep and swarming with rats, that had been dug along the Western Front from the coast of Belgium some 450 miles across northeastern France to the border of Switzerland. On either side, the attackers were usually at a disadvantage as they slogged across a few muddy acres of devastated "no-man's-land" between the opposing entrenchments, soon running into webs of entangling barbed wire and fire from machine guns and high-powered rifles overlaid by constant artillery shelling. From 1914 to 1918, the opposing armies in northeastern France attacked and counterattacked, along the Western Front, hardly gaining any ground one way or another despite casualties in the millions.

It was not the kind of warfare anyone had expected or wanted. Words cannot convey the scale of the carnage. During the Battle of Verdun, in northeast France, which lasted from February to December 1916, some 32 million artillery shells streaked across the landscape—1,500 shells for *every* square yard of the battlefield. Thousands of soldiers on both sides fell victim to "shell shock," now known as post–traumatic stress disorder. "It was a horrible thing," explained a nurse. "They became quite unconscious, with violent shivering and shaking." The unprecedented firepower ravaged the land, obliterating nine villages and turning farmland and forests into cratered wastelands. Some 162,000 French soldiers died at Verdun; the Germans lost 143,000. Charles de Gaulle, a young French

trench warfare A form of prolonged combat between the entrenched positions of opposing armies, often with little tactical movement.

lieutenant who forty years later would become his nation's president, said the conflict had become a "war of extermination." Its horrific butchery seemed especially pointless, since neither side was capable of gaining the advantage. A British army chaplain described the war as a senseless "Waste of Muscle, Waste of Brain, Waste of Patience, Waste of Pain . . . Waste of Glory, Waste of God."

Muddy trench warfare in which soldiers fought, ate, slept, and often died in their dirt holes gave the Great War its lasting character. Most battles were won not by skillful maneuvers or superior generalship but by brute force. The object in such a war of attrition was not so much to gain ground as to keep inflicting death and destruction on the enemy until their manpower and resources were exhausted. In one attack at Ypres in Belgium, the British lost 13,000 men in three hours of fighting—during which time they gained 100 meaningless yards. As the war ground on, nations on both sides found themselves using up their available men, resources, courage, and cash.

An end to innocence about war

There was no precedent for such a ghastly war. Throughout 1914, both sides talked about the "glory" and "glamour" of war, notions that the British poet Wilfred Owen called "the old Lie." (Owen would be killed in action in 1918, just a week before the war ended.) The old-fashioned romantic concepts of war were forever changed as masses of soldiers died like cattle in a slaughterhouse, killed often at such long distances that they never saw their opponents. Amid the senseless killing in the mucky trenches, the innocence about the true nature of warfare died, too. "Never such innocence again," wrote the English poet Phillip Larkin. "I am cured of ever wishing to be a soldier again," wrote one young veteran.

In 1917, George Barnes, a British official whose son had been killed in the war, went to speak at a military hospital in London where injured soldiers were being fitted with artificial limbs. At the appointed hour, the wounded men, in wheelchairs and on crutches, all with empty sleeves or pants legs, arrived to hear the speaker. Yet when Barnes was introduced and rose to talk, he found himself speechless—literally. As the minutes passed in awkward silence, tears rolled down his cheeks. Finally, without having said a word, he simply sat down. What the mutilated soldiers heard was not a war-glorifying speech but the muted sound of grief. The war's mindless horrors had come home. Britain's King George V called it a "horrible and unnecessary war."

Initial American Reactions

Shock in the United States over the bloodbath in Europe mingled with gratitude that a wide ocean stood between America and the killing fields. "Our isolated position and freedom from entangling alliances," said the *Literary Digest*, ensure that "we are in no peril of being drawn into the European quarrel." President Wilson maintained that the United States "was too proud to fight" in Europe's war, "with which we have nothing to do, whose causes cannot touch us." He repeatedly urged Americans to remain "neutral in thought as well as in action." Privately, however, Wilson was not neutral. He sought to provide Great Britain and France as much financial assistance and supplies as possible.

That was more easily said than done. More than a third of the nation's citizens were "hyphenated Americans"—first- or second-generation immigrants who retained strong ties to their native countries. Eight million German Americans lived in the United States in 1914, and many among the 4 million Irish Americans felt a deep-rooted hatred toward Britain, which had ruled the Irish for centuries. These groups instinctively leaned toward the Central Powers. But most other white Americans, largely of British origin, supported Britain and France.

> Ethnic divisions in American public opinion

By the spring of 1915, the Allied Powers' desperate need for food and supplies had generated an economic boom for American businesses, bankers, and farmers. U.S. exports to France and Great Britain quadrupled from 1914 to 1916. To finance their record-breaking purchases of American supplies, the Allies, especially Britain and France, needed loans from U.S. banks and "credits" from the U.S. government that would allow the Allies to pay for their American purchases later. Early in the war, Secretary of State Bryan, a strict pacifist, took advantage of Wilson's absence from Washington after the death of his wife to declare that loans and credits to any warring nation were "inconsistent with the true spirit of neutrality." Upon his return, a furious Wilson reversed Bryan's policy by removing all restrictions on loans to the warring nations ("belligerents"). American banks and other investors would eventually advance more than $2 billion to the Allies before the United States entered the war, and only $27 million to Germany.

> Official U.S. neutrality and "freedom of the seas"

Despite the disproportionate financial assistance provided to the Allies, the Wilson administration clung to its official stance of neutrality through two and a half years of warfare. Wilson tried valiantly in particular to uphold the "freedom of the seas." As a neutral nation, the United States, according to international law, should have been able to continue its trade with all the belligerents. On August 6, 1914, Secretary of State Bryan called upon the warring nations to respect the rights of all neutral nations to ship goods across the Atlantic. The Central Powers promptly accepted, but the British refused. In November 1914, the British ordered the ships of neutral nations like the United States to submit to searches to discover if cargoes were bound for Germany. A few months later, they announced that they would seize any ships carrying goods to Germany.

"The Sandwich Man" To illustrate America's hypocritical brand of neutrality, this political cartoon shows Uncle Sam wearing a sandwich board that advertises its conflicting desires.

Neutral Rights and Submarine Attacks

With the German naval fleet bottled up by a British blockade of German ports, the German government proclaimed a war zone around the British Isles. All ships in those waters would be attacked by submarines, the Germans warned, and "it may not always be possible to save crews and passengers." The German decision, based on the fact that surprise was the chief advantage of the submarine or **U-boat** (*Unterseeboot* in German), violated the long-established wartime custom of stopping an enemy vessel and allowing the passengers and crew to board lifeboats before sinking it. During 1915, German U-boats sank 227 British ships in the Atlantic Ocean and the North Sea.

The United States called the German submarine policy "an indefensible violation of neutral rights," and Wilson warned that Germany would be held to "strict accountability" for any destruction of American lives and property. Then, on May 7, 1915, a German submarine sank an unarmed British luxury liner off the Irish coast. Only as it tipped into the waves was the German commander able to make out the name *Lusitania* on the ship's hull. Of the 1,198 persons on board who died, 128 were Americans.

Americans were outraged. The sinking of the *Lusitania*, asserted ex-president Theodore Roosevelt, was an act of piracy and mass murder that called for a declaration of war. Wilson at first urged patience: "There is such a thing as a man being too proud to fight. There is such a thing as a nation being so right that it does not need to convince others by force that it is right." Critics scolded Wilson for his bloodless response, with Roosevelt dismissing it as "unmanly," calling the president a "jackass," and threatening to "skin him alive if he doesn't go to war." Wilson himself privately admitted that he had misspoken. "I have a bad habit of thinking out loud," he confessed to a friend the day after his "too proud to fight" speech. The timid language, he said, had "occurred to me while I was speaking, and I let it out. I should have kept it in."

Wilson's previous demand for "strict accountability" now forced him to make a stronger response. On May 13, Secretary of State Bryan signed a letter demanding that the Germans abandon unrestricted submarine warfare and pay reparations to the families of those killed in the sinking of the *Lusitania*. The Germans responded that the ship was armed (which was false) and secretly carried a cargo of rifles and ammunition (which was true). A second letter, on June 9, repeated the American demands in stronger terms. The United States, Wilson asserted, was "contending for nothing less high and sacred than the rights of humanity."

Bryan, unwilling to risk war over the issue, resigned in protest of the president's pro-British stance, leading Edith Bolling Galt, soon to be Wilson's second wife, to shout: "Hurrah! Old Bryan is out!" She called the former secretary of state an "awful Deserter." The president confided that he, too, viewed Bryan as a "traitor." He complimented Edith on her vindictiveness: "What a dear partisan you are . . . and how you can hate, too!" Bryan's successor, Robert Lansing, signed the second "*Lusitania* Note."

German U-boats and the sinking of the *Lusitania*

U-boat German military submarine used during the Great War to attack enemy naval vessels as well as merchant ships of enemy and neutral nations.

Lusitania British ocean liner torpedoed and sunk by a German U-boat; the deaths of nearly 1,200 of its civilian passengers, including many Americans, caused international outrage.

In response to the uproar over the *Lusitania*, the German government ordered U-boat captains to avoid sinking any more passenger vessels. Despite the order, however, two Americans were killed in the sinking of the New York–bound British liner *Arabic*. The Germans paid a cash penalty to their families and offered a public assurance on September 1, 1915: "Liners will not be sunk by our submarines without warning and without safety of the lives of non-combatants, provided that the liners do not try to escape or offer resistance." This so-called *Arabic* Pledge enabled Wilson to claim victory for his neutrality policy.

During early 1916, Wilson's most trusted adviser, Colonel Edward M. House, visited London, Paris, and Berlin but found neither side ready to begin serious negotiations to end the war. On March 24, 1916, a U-boat torpedoed the French ferry *Sussex*, killing eighty passengers and injuring two Americans. When Wilson threatened to break off relations, Germany renewed its pledge that U-boats would not torpedo merchant and passenger ships. The *Sussex* Pledge was far stronger than the German promise after the *Arabic* sinking, the year before, and implied the virtual abandonment of submarine warfare.

The Debate over "Preparedness"

The sinking of the *Lusitania* and the quarrels over trading with a Europe at war contributed to a growing demand in the United States for a stronger army and navy. On December 1, 1914, champions of the "preparedness" movement, including Theodore Roosevelt, had organized the National Security League to promote more military spending. After the *Lusitania* sinking, Wilson asked the War and Navy Departments to develop plans for a $1-billion military expansion. Many Americans—pacifists, progressives, and Midwestern Republicans—opposed the "preparedness" effort, seeing it as simply a propaganda campaign to benefit businesses that made weapons and other military equipment. Some of them charged that Wilson was secretly plotting to get the nation into the war. A popular song in 1916 reflected such views: "I Didn't Raise My Boy to Be a Soldier."

Despite such opposition, Congress passed the National Defense Act in 1916, which provided for the expansion of the U.S. Army from 90,000 to 223,000 men over the next five years. While former secretary of state Bryan complained that Wilson wanted to "drag this nation into war," the reverse was actually true. Wilson told an aide that he was determined not to "be rushed into war, no matter if every damned congressman and senator stands up on his hind legs and proclaims me a coward."

> National Defense Act (1916) expands army

Opponents of "preparedness" insisted that the financial burden of military expansion should rest upon the wealthy people who they believed were promoting it in order to profit from trade with the Allies. The income tax became their weapon. Backed by a groundswell of popular support, the Revenue Act of 1916 doubled the basic income tax rate from 1 to 2 percent, levied a 12.5 percent tax on munitions makers, and added a new tax on "excessive" corporate profits. The new taxes were the capstone to the progressive legislation that Wilson supported in preparation for the upcoming presidential election.

The Election of 1916

As the 1916 election approached, Republicans hoped to reunify the party and regain the White House, and Theodore Roosevelt hoped to become their leader again. But he had committed the deadly political sin of abandoning his party to run as a Progressive in 1912. His eagerness for America to enter the European war also scared many voters. Needing a candidate who would draw Roosevelt progressives back into the fold, the Republicans turned to Supreme Court Justice Charles Evans Hughes, who had led New York as a progressive governor from 1907 to 1910.

Wilson's reelection slogan: "He kept us out of war"

The Democrats, staying with Wilson, adopted a platform that endorsed social-welfare legislation and prudent military preparedness. The peace theme, refined in the slogan "He kept us out of war," became the rallying cry of the Wilson campaign, although the president at the same time dismissed isolationism as outdated. The United States, he stressed, could no longer refuse to play the "great part in the world which was providentially cut out for her. . . . We have got to serve the world."

The candidates were remarkably similar. Both Wilson and Hughes were sons of preachers; both were attorneys and former professors; both had been progressive governors; both were known for their integrity. Roosevelt called the bearded Hughes a "whiskered Wilson." Wilson, however, proved to be the better campaigner—barely. By midnight on election night, Wilson went to bed assuming that he had lost. Roosevelt was so sure Hughes had won that he sent him a congratulatory telegram. At 4:00 A.M., however, the results from California were tallied, and Wilson had eked out a victory in that deciding state by only 4,000 votes, becoming the first Democrat to win a second consecutive term since Andrew Jackson in 1832.

America's Entry into the War

Unrestricted submarine warfare, the Zimmermann telegram, and the U.S. declaration of war

After his reelection, Wilson again urged the warring nations to stop fighting and negotiate a peace settlement, but to no avail. On January 31, 1917, desperate German military leaders announced the resumption of unrestricted submarine warfare in the Atlantic. All vessels from the United States headed for Britain, France, or Italy would be sunk without warning. "This was practically ordering the United States off the Atlantic," said an angry William McAdoo, Wilson's secretary of the treasury. "Freedom of the seas," said the *Brooklyn Eagle*, "will now be enjoyed [only] by icebergs and fish." The German decision, Colonel House wrote in his journal, left Wilson "sad and depressed," for the president knew it would mean war. For their part, the Germans greatly underestimated the American reaction. The United States, the German military newspaper proclaimed, "not only has no army, it has

Zimmermann telegram (1917) Message sent by a German official to the Mexican government urging an invasion of the United States; the telegram was intercepted by British intelligence agents and angered Americans, many of whom called for war against Germany.

no artillery, no means of transportation, no airplanes, and lacks all other instruments of modern warfare." When his advisers warned that German submarines might cause the United States to enter the war, Kaiser Wilhelm scoffed, "I don't care."

On February 3, President Wilson told a joint session of Congress that the United States had broken diplomatic relations with the German government. Three weeks later, on February 25, Wilson learned that the British had intercepted an important message from a German official, Arthur Zimmermann, to the Mexican government, urging the Mexicans to invade the United States. In exchange, Germany would give Mexico "lost territory in Texas, New Mexico, and Arizona." On March 1, news of the so-called **Zimmermann telegram** broke in the press, infuriating Americans and intensifying calls for war against the Germans, whose attacks on American vessels increased.

In March 1917, German submarines sank five U.S. ships in the North Atlantic. That was the last straw for President Wilson, who on April 2 asked Congress to declare war on Germany for its "cruel and unmanly" actions. He insisted that "the world must be made safe for democracy" and free from war. Wilson said the United States was entering the war, not so much to defend the nation or its honor as to lead a "great crusade" to end wars forever—an unattainable goal that would eventually lead to great disillusionment. For now, however, the Senate passed the war resolution by a vote of 82 to 6 on April 4. The House of Representatives followed, 373 to 50, and Wilson signed the measure on April 6.

Jeanette Rankin of Montana, the first woman elected to the House, was one of the members who voted against war. "You can no more win a war than you can win an earthquake," she explained. "I want to stand by my country, but I cannot vote for war." Wilson had doubts of his own. The president feared—accurately, as it turned out—that mobilizing the nation for war and stamping out dissent would destroy the ideals and momentum of progressivism: "Every reform we have made will be lost if we go into this war." Yet he saw no choice.

Mobilizing a Nation

In April 1917 the U.S. Army remained small and untested, armed with outdated weapons or none at all. With only 107,000 men, it was the seventeenth largest army in the world. Now the Wilson administration needed to recruit, equip, and train an army of millions and transport them across an ocean infested with German submarines. Mobilizing the nation for war led to an unprecedented expansion of federal government authority. The government drafted millions of men between the ages of 21 and 30 into the armed services, forced the conversion of industries and farms to wartime needs, took over the railroads, and in many other respects assumed control of national life.

CORE **OBJECTIVE**

2. Explain how the Wilson administration mobilized the home front, and analyze how mobilization efforts shaped American society.

Economic mobilization: The War Industries Board and the Food Administration

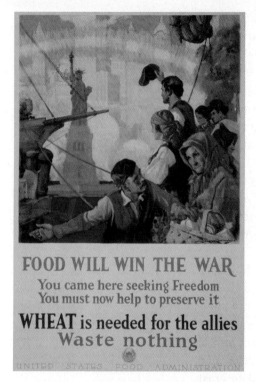

FOOD WILL WIN THE WAR
You came here seeking Freedom
You must now help to preserve it
WHEAT is needed for the allies
Waste nothing

UNITED STATES FOOD ADMINISTRATION

The immigrant effort This Food Administration poster emphasizes that "wheat is . . . for the allies," an important message to immigrants who hailed from Central Powers nations.

Soon after the U.S. declaration of war, President Wilson acknowledged that "it is not the army we must train and shape for war, it is a nation." He called for complete economic mobilization on the home front and created new federal agencies to coordinate this effort. The War Industries Board (WIB), established in 1917, soon became the most important of all the federal mobilization agencies. Bernard Baruch, a brilliant financier, headed the WIB, which had the authority to allocate raw materials, order construction of new factories, and set prices. Wilson appointed Republican Herbert Hoover, the celebrated engineer and business leader and future president, to head the new Food Administration, whose slogan was "Food will win the war." Its purpose was to increase agricultural production while reducing civilian food consumption, since Great Britain and France needed massive amounts of American corn and wheat. Hoover organized a huge group of volunteers who fanned out across the country to urge housewives and restaurants to participate in "Wheatless" Mondays, "Meatless" Tuesdays, and "Porkless" Thursdays and Saturdays.

Fighting in the Great War cost the U.S. government $30 billion, which was more than thirty times the entire federal budget in 1917. In addition to raising taxes to finance the war effort, the Wilson administration launched a campaign across the nation to sell "Liberty bonds," government securities in the form of paper certificates that guaranteed the purchaser a fixed rate of return. The government recruited dozens of celebrities to promote bond purchases, arguing that a Liberty bond was both a patriotic investment in the nation and a smart investment in one's own financial future. People who refused to buy bonds were branded as traitors. Even the Boy Scouts and Girl Scouts sold bonds, using advertising posters that said "Every Scout to Save a Soldier." By war's end, the government had sold over $20 billion in bonds, most of which were purchased by banks and investment houses rather than individuals.

A New Labor Force

Women's wartime work

Removing 4 million men from the workforce for service in the armed forces created an acute labor shortage across the United States during 1917. To meet it, women were encouraged to take jobs previously held mostly by men. One government poster shouted: "Women! Help America's Sons Win the War: Learn to Make Munitions." Another said, "For Every Fighter, a Woman Worker."

Initially, women had supported the war effort mostly in traditional ways. They helped organize fund-raising drives, donated canned food and war-related materials, volunteered for the Red Cross, and joined the army

At the munitions factory Women on both sides played crucial roles in the war effort, from building airplanes to cooking for soldiers overseas. Here, American women use welding torches to build bombs.

nurse corps. But as the scope of the war widened, both government and industry recruited women to work on farms, loading docks, and railway crews, as well as in the armaments industry, machine shops, steel and lumber mills, and chemical plants. "At last, after centuries of disabilities and discrimination," said a speaker at a Women's Trade Union League meeting in 1917, "women are coming into the labor [force] and festival of life on equal terms with men."

But the changes in female employment were limited and brief. About 1 million women participated in "war work," but most of them were young and single and already working outside the home, and most returned to their previous jobs once the war ended. In fact, male-dominated unions encouraged women to go back to domestic roles. The Central Federated Union of New York insisted that "the same patriotism which induced women to enter industry during the war should induce them to vacate their positions after the war."

The Great War also generated dramatic changes for many members of minority groups, both women and men. Hundreds of thousands of African American men joined or were drafted into the military, where they were required to serve in racially segregated units commanded by white officers, as in the Civil War half a century earlier. On the home front, northern businesses sent recruiting agents into the southern states, which were still largely rural and agricultural, to find workers for their factories and mills. For the first time, such efforts were directed at African Americans as well as whites. More than 400,000 southern blacks, mostly farmers, joined what came to be known as the **Great Migration** northward, a mass movement that would continue through the 1920s and change the political and social

Great Migration Mass exodus of African Americans from the rural South to the Northeast and Midwest during and after the Great War.

chemistry of northern cities such as St. Louis, Chicago, Detroit, New York, and Philadelphia. By 1930 the number of African Americans living in the North was triple that of 1910.

The Great Migration northward

Recruiting agents and newspaper editors, both black and white, portrayed the North as the "land of promise" for southern blacks suffering from their region's depressed agricultural economy and rising racial intimidation and violence. Northern factory jobs were plentiful and high-paying by southern standards, and racism was less obvious and violent—at least at first. A black migrant from Mississippi wrote home from Chicago in 1917 that he wished he had moved north twenty years earlier. "I just begin to feel like a man [here]," he explained. "It's a great deal of pleasure in knowing that you have some privilege. My children are going to the same school with the whites, and I don't have to be humble to no one."

Many Mexican Americans found similar opportunities to improve their status during the war and after. Some joined the military. David Barkley Hernandez had to drop his last name when he enlisted in San Antonio, Texas, because the local draft board was not accepting Mexicans. In 1918, just two days before the war ended, he died in France while returning from a dangerous mission behind German lines. Hernandez became the first person of Mexican descent in the U.S. Army to win the Congressional Medal of Honor.

Even more Latinos pursued economic opportunities created by the war effort. Between 1917 and 1920, some 100,000 Mexicans crossed the border into the United States. The economic expansion caused by the war enabled migrant farm workers already living in states such as Texas, New Mexico,

Segregation in the military Most black enlistees served in technical and supply units because whites believed them unfit for combat, despite black military contributions since the Revolution. Here, combat personnel of the 92nd (one of the few "colored" divisions sent overseas) march in Verdun, France.

Arizona, and California to take better jobs in factories and mills in rapidly growing cities such as Phoenix, Los Angeles, and Houston, where they moved into Spanish-speaking neighborhoods called *barrios*.

But the newcomers, whether Latinos or blacks, were often resented rather than welcomed. J. Luz Saenz, a Mexican American from Texas, noted in his diary that it took only three days after he was discharged from the army to have whites "throw us out from restaurants and deny us service as human beings." In 1917 more than forty African Americans and nine whites were killed during a riot in a weapons plant in East St. Louis, Illinois. Two years later, a Chicago race riot left twenty-three African Americans and fifteen whites dead.

A Loss of Civil Liberties

The Espionage and Sedition Acts (1917–1918)

Once war was declared, patriotic emotions often took a negative turn, as Americans equated anything German with disloyalty. Many Americans quit drinking beer because most of the breweries were owned by German Americans. Symphonies refused to perform classical music by Bach and Beethoven, schools dropped German language classes, and patriots renamed *sauerkraut* as "liberty cabbage," *German measles* as "liberty measles," and *dachshunds* as "liberty pups." President Wilson had predicted as much. "Once [we] lead this people into war," he said, "they'll forget there ever was such a thing as tolerance." What Wilson did not say was that he himself would lead the effort to suppress civil liberties, for, as he claimed, subversive forces in a nation at war must be "crushed out."

Under the Espionage and Sedition Acts, Congress outlawed criticism of government leaders and war policies. The Espionage Act of 1917 imposed penalties of up to $10,000 and twenty years in prison for anyone who gave aid to the enemy, tried to incite insubordination, disloyalty, or refusal of duty in the armed services, or tried to interfere with the war effort in other ways. To root out "vicious spies and conspirators," Wilson recruited 250,000 informers—the American Protective League—to turn in those suspected of treason. He was convinced that newly arrived immigrants had "poured the poison of disloyalty into the very arteries of our national life."

During the war, 1,055 people were convicted under the Espionage Act, not one of whom was a spy. Most of them were simply critics of the war. The Socialist leader Eugene V. Debs, a militant pacifist, was convicted under the Espionage Act simply for opposing the war and was sentenced to ten years in prison. He told the court he would always criticize wars imposed by the "master" class: "While there is a lower class, I am in it. While there is a criminal element, I am of it. While there is a soul in prison, I am not free."

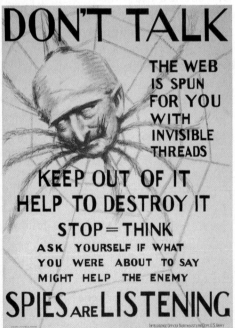

Keep out of it In this 1918 war poster, the Kaiser—with his famous moustache and spiked German helmet—is characterized as a spider, spinning an invisible web to catch the stray words of Allied civilians.

The Sedition Act of 1918 extended the penalties to those who did or said anything to obstruct government sales of war bonds or to advocate cutbacks in production, and—in case something had been overlooked—for saying, writing, or printing anything "disloyal, profane, scurrilous, or abusive" about the American form of government, the Constitution, or the army and navy.

In two important decisions just after the war, the Supreme Court upheld the Espionage and Sedition Acts. *Schenck v. United States* (1919) reaffirmed the conviction of Charles T. Schenck, the head of the Socialist party, for circulating anti-draft leaflets among members of the armed forces. Justice Oliver Wendell Holmes wrote the unanimous court opinion that freedom of speech did not apply to words that represented "a clear and present danger to the safety of the country." In *Abrams v. United States* (1919), the Court upheld the conviction of a man who had distributed pamphlets opposing American military intervention in Russia to remove the Bolsheviks who had seized power in 1917. Here, justices Holmes and Brandeis dissented from the majority view. The "surreptitious publishing of a silly leaflet by an unknown man," they argued, posed no danger to government policy.

CORE **OBJECTIVE**

3. Describe the major events of the war after U.S. entry, and explain the U.S. contribution to the defeat of the Central Powers.

The American Role in Fighting the War

In 1917, America's war strategy focused on helping the struggling French and British armies on the Western Front. The Allied leaders stressed that they needed at least a million American troops (called "doughboys") to defeat the Germans, but it would take months to recruit, equip, and train that many new soldiers. On December 21, 1917, French premier Georges Clemenceau urged the Americans to rush their army, called the American Expeditionary Force, to France. "A terrible blow is imminent," he told an American journalist about to leave Paris. "Tell your Americans to come quickly." Clemenceau was referring to the likelihood of a massive German attack, made more probable by the end of the fighting on the Eastern Front following the Bolshevik Revolution in Russia in November 1917.

The Bolshevik Revolution

Communist revolution in Russia

Among the many casualties of the Great War, none was greater in scale than the destruction of the Russian Empire and its monarchy. On March 15, 1917, bumbling Tsar Nicholas II, having presided over terrible losses in a war that also ruined the Russian economy, had turned the nation over to the "Provisional Government" of a new Russian republic committed to continuing the war. The fall of the tsar gave Americans the illusion that all the major Allied powers were now fighting for the ideals of constitutional democracy—an illusion that was shattered after the Germans in April helped exiled radical Vladimir Lenin return to Russia from Switzerland in a secret, sealed train, hoping that he would cause turmoil in his homeland. He did much more than that.

As Lenin observed, power in war-weary Russia was lying in the streets, waiting to be picked up. To do so, Lenin mobilized the Bolsheviks, a determined group of Communist revolutionaries, who during the night of November 6–7 seized power from the Provisional Government, established a dictatorship and called for a quick end to the European war. Lenin banned both political parties and organized religions (atheism became the official belief), eliminated civil liberties and the free press, and killed or imprisoned opposition leaders, including the tsar and his family. The Bolshevik Revolution triggered a prolonged civil war throughout Russia in which the United States and its allies worked to overthrow the Communists. Wilson sent 20,000 American soldiers to Siberia to support the anti-Communist Russian forces, an effort that proved unsuccessful.

Vladimir Lenin Russian communist revolutionary who led the Bolsheviks in overthrowing the monarchy and ultimately established the Soviet Union.

Lenin declared that the world would be freed from war only by a global revolution in which capitalism was replaced by communism. To that end, he wanted to get Russia out of the Great War as soon as possible. On March 3, 1918, Lenin signed a humiliating peace agreement with Germany, the Treaty of Brest-Litovsk. The treaty forced Russia to transfer vast territories to Germany and its ally Turkey and to recognize the independence of the Ukraine region. In addition, Russia had to pay $46 million to Germany. Lenin was willing to accept such a harsh peace because he needed to concentrate on his many internal enemies in the civil war.

Crucial U.S. Contribution on the Western Front

Less than three weeks later, on March 21, the Germans, now reinforced by units from the Eastern Front made available by Russia leaving the war, began the first of several spring offensives in France and Belgium designed to win the war before the Americans arrived in force. By May, the German armies had advanced to the Marne River, within fifty miles of Paris. That was as far as they got, for in June, at the month-long Battle of Belleau Wood, U.S. forces commanded by General John J. Pershing joined the French in driving the Germans back. During the ferocious fighting, a French officer urged an American unit to retreat. In a famous exchange, U.S. Marine Captain Lloyd W. Williams refused the order, saying: "Retreat? Hell, we just got here."

| American forces help repel the Germans in 1918 |

The crucial American role in the fighting occurred in a great Allied offensive, begun on September 26, 1918. With the French commander urging "everyone to battle," the American troops joined British and French armies in a drive toward Sedan, France, and its strategic railroad, which supplied

Meuse-Argonne Offensive
American soldiers of the 23rd Infantry, 2nd Division, fire machine guns at the Germans from what was left of the Argonne Forest in France.

the German army. With 1.2 million U.S. soldiers involved, including some 200,000 African Americans, it was the largest American action of the war, and it resulted in 117,000 U.S. casualties, including 26,000 dead. But along the entire French-Belgian front, the outnumbered Germans were in desperate retreat eastward across Belgium during the early fall of 1918. "America," wrote German General Erich Ludendorff, "became the decisive power in the war."

The End of the War

Wilson's Fourteen Points

Woodrow Wilson was determined to ensure that the Great War would be the last world war. During 1917, he appointed a group of American experts, called the Inquiry, to draft a peace plan. With their advice, Wilson developed what would come to be called the **Fourteen Points**, which he presented to a joint session of Congress on January 8, 1918, "as the only possible program" for peace. The first five points called for the open conduct of diplomacy, the recognition of neutral nations' right to continue maritime commerce in time of war ("freedom of the seas"), the removal of international trade barriers, the reduction of armaments, and the transformation of colonial empires.

Fourteen Points (1918)
President Woodrow Wilson's proposed plan for the peace agreement after the Great War that included the creation of a "league of nations" intended to keep the peace.

Most of the remaining points dealt with territorial claims: they called on the Central Powers to evacuate occupied lands and follow the difficult principle of "self-determination," allowing overlapping nationalities and ethnic groups to develop their own independent nations. Point 13 called for

THE GREAT WAR, THE WESTERN FRONT, 1918

- Why was the war on the western front a stalemate for most of World War I?
- What was the effect of the arrival of the American troops?
- Why was the Second Battle of the Marne the turning point of the war?

a new nation for the Poles, a people long dominated by the Russians on the east and the Germans on the west. Point 14, the capstone of Wilson's postwar scheme, called for the creation of a "league" of nations to preserve global peace. When the Fourteen Points were made public, African American leaders asked the president to add a fifteenth point: an end to racial discrimination. Wilson did not respond.

On October 3, 1918, a new German chancellor telegraphed President Wilson, asking for an end to the fighting on the basis of the Fourteen Points. British and French leaders accepted the Fourteen Points as a basis of negotiations, but with two significant reservations: the British insisted on the right to discuss limiting freedom of the seas, and the French demanded reparations (payments) from Germany and Austria for war damages.

Meanwhile, by the end of October 1918, Germany was on the verge of collapse. Revolutionaries rampaged through the streets. Sailors mutinied.

Armistice Night in New York **(1918)** George Luks, known for his vivid paintings of urban life, captured the unbridled outpouring of patriotism and joy that extended into the night of Germany's surrender.

Germany's allies dropped out of the war: Bulgaria on September 29, 1918, Turkey on October 30, and Austria-Hungary on November 3. On November 9, the German Kaiser resigned, and a republic was proclaimed. Then, on November 11 at 5:00 A.M., an armistice (cease-fire agreement) was signed by which the Germans were assured that Wilson's Fourteen Points would be the basis for the peace conference. Six hours later, at the eleventh hour of the eleventh day of the eleventh month, and after 1,563 days of terrible warfare, the guns fell silent. From Europe, Colonel House sent a telegram to President Wilson: "Autocracy [government by an individual with unlimited power] is dead; long live democracy and its immortal leader."

Cease-fire and celebrations

The end of fighting led to wild celebrations throughout the world as fear and grief gave way to hope. "The nightmare is over," wrote African American activist W. E. B. Du Bois. "The world awakes. The long, horrible years of dreadful night are passed. Behold the sun!" Wilson was not as joyful. The Great War, he said, had dealt a grievous injury to civilization "which can never be atoned for or repaired."

During its nineteen months in the Great War, the United States had lost 53,000 servicemen in combat. Another 63,000 died of various diseases, especially the influenza epidemic that swept through Europe and around the world in 1918. Germany's war dead totaled more than 2 million, including civilians; France lost nearly 1.4 million combatants, Great Britain 703,000, and Russia 1.7 million. The new Europe would be very different from the prewar version: much poorer, more violent, more polarized, more cynical, less sure of itself, and less capable of decisive action. The United States, for good or ill, emerged from the war as the world's dominant power.

The Fight for the Peace

CORE **OBJECTIVE**
4. Evaluate Wilson's efforts to promote his plans for a peaceful world order as outlined in his Fourteen Points.

In the making of a peace agreement, Woodrow Wilson showed himself both at his best and worst. His Fourteen Point peace program embodied his vision of a better world governed by fairer principles. For a glorious moment at the end of 1918, Wilson was the world's self-appointed prophet of peace. He felt guided "by the hand of God." Wilson's godlike vision of creating a peacekeeping "League of Nations" promised that henceforth all nations would live in harmony. If the diplomats gathering to draft the peace treaty failed to follow his ambitious plans to reshape the world in America's image, he warned, "there will be another world war" within a generation.

Wilson's Key Errors

Whatever the merits of Wilson's peace plan, his efforts to implement it proved clumsy. He made several key decisions at the war's end that would come back to haunt him. First, against the advice of his staff and of European leaders, he decided to attend the peace conference in Paris that opened on January 18, 1919. Never before had an American president visited Europe or left the nation for such a prolonged period (six months). During his months abroad, Wilson lost touch with political developments at home.

Second, in the congressional elections of November 1918, Wilson defied his advisers as well as political tradition by urging voters to elect a Democratic Congress to support his policies. Prior to that time, presidents had remained neutral during congressional elections. Republicans, who for the most part had backed Wilson's war measures, were not pleased. Nor were voters. In the elections, the Democrats lost control of both houses of Congress.

Wilson's mistakes: Prolonged absence in Europe, disregard for Republicans at home, self-image as messiah of peace

Wilson further weakened support for his peacemaking when, in a deliberate slight, he refused to appoint Senator Henry Cabot Lodge, his arch-enemy and the leading Republican in Congress, to the American delegation to the peace conference. As chairman of the Foreign Relations Committee, Lodge was the most appropriate senator to accompany Wilson to Paris, but the president instead appointed an ineffectual Republican to join the delegation. Former president William Howard Taft groused that Wilson's real intention in going to Paris was "to hog the whole show." He almost did.

When Wilson reached Europe in December 1918, the cheering crowds in London, Paris, and Rome verged on hysteria. Millions of grateful Europeans greeted him as a hero, even a savior. An Italian mayor described Wilson's visit as the "second coming of Christ." Others hailed him as the "God of peace." Wilson privately admitted that he was now "at the apex of my glory in the hearts of these people." From such a height, there could only be a fall. Although popular with the European people, Wilson had to deal at the

Fit for a messiah Wilson rode down the Champs Élysées as the crowds showered him with flower petals and cheered, "*Vive Wilson! Vive l'Amérique! Vive la liberté!*"

peace conference with tough-minded European statesmen who shared neither his lofty goals nor his American ideals. In fact, they resented his efforts to forge a peace settlement modeled on American values. In the end, the European leaders would force him to abandon many of his objectives and become a horse trader—not a messiah.

The Paris Peace Conference

The Paris Peace Conference lasted from January to June 1919. The participants had no time to waste. The German, Austro-Hungarian, and Ottoman empires were in ruins. Across much of the European continent, food was scarce and lawlessness flourished. The threat of revolution hung over central Europe as Communists in the defeated nations threatened to take control. As the most significant world event of the era, the peace conference dealt with immensely complex and controversial issues (including creating new nations, such as Yugoslavia and Iraq, and redrawing the maps of Europe and the Middle East) that required both political statesmanship and technical expertise. The British delegation alone included almost 400 members, many of them specialists in political geography or economics. The peacemakers met daily, debating, arguing, and compromising.

The Big Four: Wilsonian idealism vs. European realism

From the start, the Paris Peace Conference was controlled by the Big Four who met 140 times: the prime ministers of Britain, France, and Italy and the president of the United States. The seventy-seven-year-old French premier Georges Clemenceau, known as "The Tiger," was a stern realist who had little patience with President Wilson's preaching. In response to Wilson's declaration that "America is the only idealistic nation in the world,"

Clemenceau grumbled that talking with the American leader was like talking to Jesus Christ. "God gave us the Ten Commandments and we broke them," the French leader sneered. "Wilson gave us the Fourteen Points—we shall see." The Big Four fought not only in private but in public as well. The French and the British, led by Prime Minister David Lloyd George, insisted that Wilson agree to their harsh provisions to weaken Germany, while Vittorio Orlando, prime minister of Italy, focused on gaining territories from defeated Austria.

Wilson, suffering from poor health, lectured them all about the need to craft a peace treaty without revenge and to embrace his beloved **League of Nations**, which he insisted must be the "keystone" of any peace settlement. Whatever compromises he might have to make and whatever mistakes might result, Wilson believed that a world peace organization would abolish war. Article X of the League of Nations charter, which Wilson called "the heart of the League," pledged member nations to impose military and economic sanctions, or penalties, against those that engaged in military aggression. The League, Wilson assumed, would exercise enormous moral influence, making military action unnecessary. These unrealistic expectations became, for Wilson, a self-defeating crusade.

On February 14, 1919, Wilson presented the finished draft of the League covenant to the Allies and left Paris for a visit home, where he faced opposition among Republicans. The League of Nations, Theodore Roosevelt complained, would revive German militarism and undermine American morale. "To substitute internationalism for nationalism," Roosevelt argued, "means to do away with patriotism." His close friend Henry Cabot Lodge, chairman of the Senate Foreign Relations Committee, also scorned Wilson and his idealism. He told Roosevelt, "I never expected to hate anyone in politics with the hatred I feel toward Wilson." Lodge dismissed the League of Nations proposed in the treaty because, he claimed, it would allow the League to involve the U.S. military in foreign conflicts without Senate approval.

The Treaty of Versailles

Back in Paris in the spring of 1919, Wilson had lost his leverage with the British and French because it was increasingly uncertain that the U.S. Senate would approve any treaty he endorsed. Wilson also gave in on many controversial issues solely to ensure that the Europeans would approve his League of Nations. In Paris, Wilson yielded to French demands that Germany transfer vast territories to France on its west and to Poland on its east and north. In other territorial matters, Wilson had to abandon his lofty but impractical and ill-defined principle of national self-determination, whereby every ethnic group would be allowed to form its own nation. As Secretary of State Robert Lansing correctly predicted, trying to allow each ethnic group in Europe to determine its own fate "will raise hopes which can never be realized." (Wilson himself later told the Senate that he wished he had never said that "all nations have a right to self-determination.")

League of Nations Organization of nations formed in the aftermath of the Great War to mediate disputes and maintain international peace; despite President Wilson's intense lobbying for the League of Nations, Congress did not ratify the Versailles treaty and the United States failed to join.

In their efforts to allow for at least some degree of ethnic self-determination in multiethnic regions, the diplomats at Versailles created the independent countries of Austria, Hungary, Poland, Yugoslavia, and Czechoslovakia in central Europe and four new nations along the Baltic Sea: Finland, Estonia, Lithuania, and Latvia. But the victorious Allies did not create independent nations out of the colonies of the defeated and now defunct European empires. Instead, they assigned the former German colonies in Africa and the Turkish colonies in the Middle East to France and Great Britain to govern while the colonies prepared themselves for independence at some undesignated point in the future, while Japan took control of the former German colonies in east Asia.

> The Treaty of Versailles: Wilson's concessions on territory, reparations, and "war guilt"

The discussion of reparations triggered especially bitter arguments among the diplomats in Paris. The British and the French (on whose soil much of the war was fought) wanted Germany to pay the entire financial cost of the war, including their veterans' pensions. On this point, Wilson made perhaps his most fateful concessions. He agreed to a clause in the peace treaty by which Germany was forced to accept responsibility for the war and its entire expense. The "war guilt" clause, written by the young American John Foster Dulles, a future secretary of state, so offended Germans that it became a major factor in the rise of the Nazi party during the 1920s. Wilson himself privately admitted that if he were a German he would refuse to sign the treaty.

On May 7, 1919, the victorious powers presented the treaty to the German delegates, who returned three weeks later with 443 pages of criticism. A few changes were made, but when the Germans still refused to sign, the French threatened to launch a new military attack. Finally, on June 28, the Germans gave up and signed the treaty in the glittering Hall of Mirrors at Versailles, the magnificent palace built by King Louis XIV in the late seventeenth century. Thereafter, it was called the **Treaty of Versailles**. When Adolf Hitler, a young German soldier, learned of the treaty's provisions, he vowed revenge. "It cannot be that two million Germans have fallen in vain," he screamed during a speech in Munich in 1922. "We demand vengeance!" Wilson and the Allies were better at winning the war than making a lasting peace.

The Debate over Treaty Ratification

On July 8, 1919, Wilson returned home to advocate the approval of the treaty by the U.S. Senate, where the Republicans now outnumbered his Democrats. Before leaving Paris, he assured a French diplomat that he would not allow any changes to the treaty. "I shall consent to nothing," he vowed. "The Senate must take its medicine." Thus began one of the most brutally partisan and bitterly personal disputes in American political history. There was only one nation strong enough to reject Wilson's dream of a League of Nations: the United States.

On July 10, Wilson became the first president to enter the Senate and deliver a treaty to be voted on. He called upon senators to accept their "great

Treaty of Versailles (1919)
Peace treaty that ended the Great War, forcing Germany to dismantle its military, pay immense war reparations, and give up its colonies around the world.

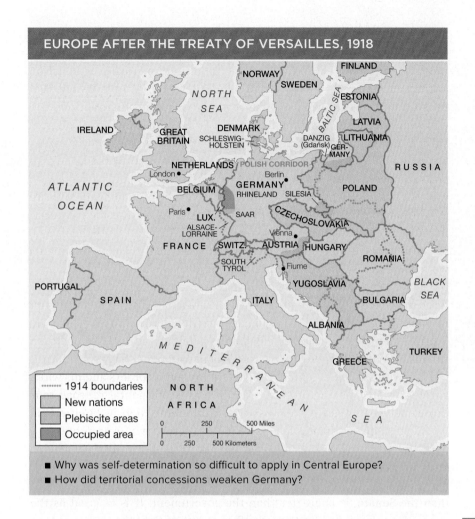

EUROPE AFTER THE TREATY OF VERSAILLES, 1918

- - - - 1914 boundaries
New nations
Plebiscite areas
Occupied area

■ Why was self-determination so difficult to apply in Central Europe?
■ How did territorial concessions weaken Germany?

duty" and ratify the treaty, which had been guided "by the hand of God."
Wilson then grew needlessly confrontational. He dismissed critics of the
League of Nations as "blind and little provincial people." The whole world,
Wilson claimed, was relying on the United States to sign the Versailles
Treaty: "Dare we reject it and break the heart of the world?"

Yes, answered Senate Republicans who had decided that Wilson's commitment to the League was a reckless threat to America's independence.
Henry Cabot Lodge denounced the treaty's "scheme of making mankind
suddenly virtuous by a statute or a written constitution." Lodge's strategy
was to stall approval of the treaty in hopes that public opposition to the
president would grow. He took six weeks simply reading aloud the lengthy
text of it to his Foreign Relations committee. He then organized a parade of
expert witnesses, most of them opposed to the treaty, to appear at the committee's hearings on ratification.

In the Senate, a group of "irreconcilables," fourteen Republicans and
two Democrats, refused to support U.S. membership in the League. They
were mainly western and midwestern progressives, isolationists who
feared that such sweeping foreign commitments would threaten

> The U.S. Senate debate over the
> Treaty of Versailles

domestic reforms. The irreconcilables would prove useful to Lodge's efforts to defeat the treaty, but he himself belonged to a larger group called the "reservationists," who insisted upon limiting American participation in the League in exchange for approving the treaty. The only way to get Senate approval was for Wilson to meet with Lodge and others and agree to revisions, the most important of which was the requirement that Congress authorize any American participation in a League-approved war.

As Republican senator Frank B. Kellogg of Minnesota noted, the proposed changes were crafted not by enemies of the treaty but by friends who wanted to save it. Republican senator James Watson of Indiana told Wilson that he had no choice but to accept some revisions: "Mr. President, you are licked. There is only one way you can take the United States into the League of Nations." The inflexible president, who assumed that his opponents were not just misguided but morally wrong, lashed back: "Lodge's reservations? Never!" Wilson was incapable of compromising with Lodge. He refused to negotiate or compromise, declaring that "if the Treaty is not ratified by the Senate, the War will have been fought in vain."

Wilson takes treaty to the American people

In September 1919, facing defeat after a summer of fruitless debate, an exhausted Wilson decided to bypass his Senate opponents by speaking directly to voters. On September 2, against his doctor's orders and his wife's advice, he left Washington for a grueling transcontinental railroad tour through the Midwest to the West Coast, intending to visit 29 cities. No president had ever made such a strenuous effort to win over public support. In St. Louis, Wilson said that he had returned from Paris "bringing one of the greatest documents of human history," which was now in danger of being rejected by the Senate. He pledged to "fight for a cause . . . greater than the Senate. It is greater than the government. It is as great as the cause of mankind, and I intend, in office or out, to fight that battle as long as I live."

Onward through Nebraska, South Dakota, Minnesota, North Dakota, Montana, Idaho, and Washington, Wilson traveled and spoke, sometimes as many as four times a day, despite suffering from pounding headaches. It did not help his morale to learn that his secretary of state, Robert Lansing, had said that the League of Nations was "entirely useless." By the time Wilson's train reached Spokane, Washington, the president was visibly fatigued. But he kept going, heading south through Oregon and California. Some 200,000 people greeted him in Los Angeles. In all, he had covered 10,000 miles in twenty-two days and given thirty-two major speeches.

Physical Breakdown and Political Failure

Then disaster struck. After delivering an emotional speech on September 25 in Pueblo, Colorado, Wilson collapsed from his headaches and had to admit that he could not finish the trip ("I am going to pieces"). With tears rolling down his cheeks as he looked out the train's window, he told his doctor that he had suffered the "greatest disappointment of [his] life." Back in

Washington, D.C., a week later, the president suffered a crushing stroke (cerebral hemorrhage) that almost killed him. The episode left him paralyzed on his left side; he could barely speak or see. Only his secretary, his doctor, and his wife, Edith, knew his true condition. For five months, Wilson lay flat on his back while his doctor issued reassuring medical bulletins to reporters. If a document needed Wilson's signature, his wife guided his trembling hand. Secretary of State Lansing urged the president's aides to declare him disabled and appoint the vice president in his place; they angrily refused. "I hate Lansing," Edith Wilson told Secretary of the Navy Josephus Daniels. Soon thereafter, Lansing was replaced.

The stroke made Wilson even more arrogant and stubborn. He became emotionally unstable, at times crying uncontrollably and behaving oddly. For the remaining seventeen months of his term, his protective wife, along with aides and trusted cabinet members, kept him isolated from all but the most essential business. When a group of Republican senators visited the White House, one of them said, "Well, Mr. President, we have all been praying for you." Wilson replied, "Which way, Senator?"

Wilson's stroke and the treaty's defeat

Such presidential humor was rare, however. Wilson's hardened arteries seemed to have hardened his political judgment as well. His outspoken wife reinforced his prejudices, calling Lodge a "stinking snake." For his part, Lodge pushed through the Senate fourteen changes (the number was not coincidental) in the draft of the Versailles Treaty. Wilson rejected the proposed changes, and as a result, his supporters in the Senate were thrown into an unlikely alliance with the irreconcilables, who opposed the treaty under any circumstances. The Senate vote on Lodge's revised treaty was 39 for and 55 against. On the question of approving the original treaty without changes, the irreconcilables and the reservationists, led by Lodge, combined to defeat ratification again, with 38 for and 53 against. Lodge said that if the president "had been a true idealist, in regard to the covenant of the League of Nations, he would have . . . secured its adoption by the Senate of the United States by accepting some modification of its terms."

Woodrow Wilson's grand effort at global peacemaking had failed miserably. After refusing to ratify the treaty, Congress tried to declare an official end to American involvement in the war by a joint resolution on May 20, 1920, which Wilson vetoed in a fit of spite. It was not until July 2, 1921, four months after he had left office and almost eighteen months after the fighting had stopped, that another joint resolution ended the state of war with Germany and Austria-Hungary. Separate peace treaties with Germany, Austria, and Hungary were ratified on October 18, 1921, but by then Warren G. Harding was president of the United States.

The failure of the United States to ratify the Versailles Treaty and exercise strong world leadership would have long-range consequences. With Great Britain and France too exhausted and too timid to keep Germany weak and isolated, a dangerous power vacuum would emerge in Europe during the 1920s which Adolf Hitler and the Nazis would fill.

CORE **OBJECTIVE**

5. Analyze the consequences of the war at home and abroad.

Lurching from War to Peace

The Versailles Treaty, for all the time the Senate spent on it, was but one of many issues demanding attention in the turbulent period after the war. The year 1919 began with joyous victory parades and congressional approval of women's suffrage, but celebration soon gave way to widespread labor unrest, socialist and Communist radicalism, race riots, terrorist bombings, and government crackdowns. With millions of servicemen returning to civilian life, war-related industries shutting down, and wartime price controls ending, unemployment and prices for consumer goods spiked. President Wilson's leadership was missing during the postwar crisis. Bedridden by his stroke, the president became increasingly grim, distant, and depressed. Wilson, observed David Lloyd George, the British prime minister, was "as much a victim of the war as any soldier who died in the trenches."

The Spanish Flu

Beginning in 1918, many Americans confronted an infectious enemy that produced far more casualties than the war itself. It became known as the Spanish flu (although its geographic origins are debated), and its contagion spread around the globe, transformed modern medicine, and altered the course of world history. The disease appeared suddenly in the spring of 1918, and its initial outbreak lasted a year and killed millions of people worldwide, twice as many as died in the war. In the United States alone it accounted for 675,000 deaths, over ten times the number of U.S. combat deaths in France. A fifth of the nation's population caught the flu, so many that the public health system was strained to the breaking point. Hospitals ran out of beds, and funeral homes ran out of coffins. By the spring of 1919, the pandemic had finally run its course, ending as suddenly—and as inexplicably—as it had begun. Although another outbreak occurred in the winter of 1920, people had grown more resistant to it. No disease in human history had killed so many people, and no war, famine, or natural catastrophe had killed so many people in such a short time.

Suffrage at Last

Women's suffrage: Ratification of the Nineteenth Amendment

As the first outbreak of the Spanish flu was ending, American women finally gained a Constitutional guarantee of their right to vote. After six months of delay, debate, and failed votes, Congress finally passed the **Nineteenth Amendment** in the spring of 1919 and sent it to the states for ratification. Tennessee's legislature was the last of thirty-six state assemblies to approve the amendment, and it did so in dramatic fashion. The initial vote was 48–48. Then a twenty-four-year-old Republican legislator named Harry T. Burn changed his vote to yes at the insistence of

Nineteenth Amendment (1920) Constitutional amendment that granted women the right to vote.

his mother. The Nineteenth Amendment became official on August 18, 1920, making the United States the twenty-second nation in the world to allow women's suffrage. It was a climactic achievement of the Progressive Era. Suddenly, 9.5 million women were eligible to vote in national elections; in the 1920 presidential election, they would make up 40 percent of the electorate.

The Economic Transition

As consumer prices continued to rise, discontented workers, released from wartime controls on wages, grew more willing to go out on strike for their demands.

Their first votes Women of New York City's East Side vote for the first time in the presidential election of 1920.

In 1919, more than 4 million hourly wage workers, 20 percent of the total in the U.S. workforce, participated in 3,600 strikes against management. Most of them wanted nothing more than higher wages and shorter workweeks, but their critics linked striking workers with the worldwide Communist movement. After a general strike in Seattle, the mayor, Ole Hanson, claimed the strikers were seeking a "revolution" under Bolshevik influence, and a Seattle newspaper declared that "this is America—not Russia." Such charges of a Communist conspiracy were greatly exaggerated. In 1919, fewer than 70,000 Americans nationwide belonged to the Communist party. The Seattle strike lasted only five days, but public resentment of the strikers damaged the cause and image of unions across the country.

> A surge of labor strikes and public reaction against them

The most controversial postwar labor dispute was in Boston, where most of the police went on strike on September 9, 1919. Massachusetts governor Calvin Coolidge was furious and mobilized the National Guard. After four days, the striking policemen offered to return, but instead they were all fired. When labor leaders appealed for their reinstatement, Coolidge responded in words that made him an instant national hero: "There is no right to strike against the public safety by anybody, anywhere, any time."

Racial Friction

The summer of 1919 also sparked a wave of deadly race riots across the nation. As more and more African Americans, including many of the 367,000 who were war veterans, moved out of the rural South to different parts of the country, developed successful careers, and asserted their civil

> "Red Summer" of race riots

Safe, briefly Escorted by a police officer, an African American family moves its belongings from their home, likely destroyed by white rioters, and into a protected area of Chicago.

rights in the face of deeply embedded segregationist practices, resentful whites reacted with an almost hysterical racism. One newspaper headline accused civil rights activists of being guided by Communists: "REDS TRY TO STIR NEGROES TO REVOLT!"

What African American leader James Weldon Johnson called the Red Summer (*red* signifying blood) began in July, when a mob of whites invaded the black neighborhood in Longview, Texas, angry over rumors of interracial dating. They burned shops and houses and ran several African Americans out of town. A week later, in Washington, D.C., exaggerated or even false reports of black assaults on white women stirred up white mobs, and gangs of white and black rioters waged a race war in the streets until soldiers and driving rains ended the fighting. The worst was yet to come. In late July, 38 people were killed and 537 injured in five days of race rioting in Chicago, where some 50,000 blacks, mostly from the rural South, had moved during the war, leading to tensions with local whites over jobs and housing. White unionized workers especially resented blacks who were hired as strikebreakers. Altogether, twenty-five race riots erupted in 1919, and there were eighty lynchings of African Americans, eleven of them war veterans.

The Red Scare

The Red Scare

With so much of the public convinced that the strikes and riots were inspired by Communists and anarchists (two very different groups who shared a hatred for capitalism), a New York journalist reported that Americans were "shivering in their boots over Bolshevism, and they are far more scared of Lenin than they ever were of the [German] Kaiser. We seem to be the most frightened victors the world ever saw." Fears of revolution in America were fueled by the violent actions of a few scattered militants. In early 1919, the Secret Service discovered a plot by Spanish anarchists to kill President Wilson and other government officials. In April 1919, postal workers intercepted nearly forty homemade mail bombs addressed to government officials. One slipped through and blew off the hands of a Georgia senator's maid. In June another bomb destroyed the front of U.S. Attorney General A. Mitchell Palmer's house in Washington, D.C. Palmer, who had ambitions to succeed Wilson as president, concluded that a "Red Menace," a Communist "blaze of revolution," was "sweeping over every American institution of law and order." In August 1919, Palmer appointed a twenty-four-year-old attorney named J. Edgar Hoover to lead a new government division created to collect information on radicals. Hoover and others in the Justice Department worked with a network of 250,000 informers in 600 cities, all of them members of the American Protective League, which was founded during the war to root out "traitors" and labor radicals.

On November 7, 1919, while Wilson lay incapacitated in the White House, federal agents rounded up 450 alien "radicals," most of whom were recent, law-abiding Russian immigrants looking for work. All were deported to Russia without a court hearing. On January 2, 1920, police raids in dozens of cities swept up 5,000 more suspects, many taken from their homes without arrest warrants.

J. Edgar Hoover Fresh out of law school, Hoover joined the Justice Department and rose the ranks to become the first director of the FBI.

What came to be called the **First Red Scare** (after another outbreak of anti-Communist hysteria occurred in the 1950s) represented one of the largest violations of civil liberties in American history. In 1919, novelist Katharine Fullerton Gerould announced in *Harper's Magazine* that, as a result of the government crackdown, America "is no longer a free country in the old sense." Civil liberties that had long been protected were being violated with abandon.

Panic about possible foreign terrorists erupted in communities across the nation as vigilantes took matters into their own hands. At a patriotic pageant in Washington, D.C., a sailor shot a spectator who refused to rise for "The Star-Spangled Banner"; the crowd cheered. In Hammond, Indiana, a jury took only two minutes to acquit a man who had murdered an immigrant for yelling "To hell with the U.S." In Waterbury, Connecticut, a salesman was sentenced to six months in jail for saying that Vladimir Lenin was "one of the brainiest" of the world's leaders.

By the summer of 1920, the Red Scare had begun to subside. Although Attorney General Palmer kept predicting more foreign-inspired terrorism, it never came. Bombings tapered off; the wave of strikes and race riots receded. By September 1920, when a bomb at the corner of Broad and Wall Streets in New York City killed thirty-eight people, Americans were ready to take it for what it was: the work of a crazed mind and not the start of a revolution. The Red Scare nonetheless left a lasting mark on American life. It strengthened the conservative crusade for "100 percent Americanism" and new restrictions on immigration.

Effects of the Great War

The extraordinary turbulence in 1919 and 1920 was an unmistakable indication of how the Great War had changed the shape of modern history: the world war was a turning point after which little was the same. It had destroyed old Europe—not only many of its cities, people, empires, and

First Red Scare Outbreak of anti-Communist hysteria that included the arrest without warrants of thousands of suspected radicals, most of whom (especially Russian immigrants) were deported.

The Great War

The Great War had a profound impact on the United States. Among other things, it significantly changed the nation's relationship with the rest of the world, the scale and scope of government involvement in the economy and society, the geographical and racial demographics of the population, the economic and political roles of women, and public attitudes toward the labor movement, African Americans, and immigrants. As you review the following list of facts, consider how participation in the war affected the role of the federal government in the United States; the position of women, African Americans, and immigrant communities in American society; and Americans' perceptions of themselves and their role in the world.

EFFECTS OF THE GREAT WAR ON THE UNITED STATES

FACT 1	FACT 2	FACT 3	FACT 4
The United States participated in a European war for the first time.	Millions of men were drafted into the military.	Industries and farms were converted to serve wartime needs through new federal agencies such as the War Industries Board and the Food Administration.	The Espionage and Sedition Acts severely curbed freedom of speech, making it a crime to speak out against American participation in the war or policies supporting the war effort.

FACT 5	FACT 6
Four hundred thousand African Americans migrated from the South to urban industrial centers in the North. Their arrival sparked racial tensions that often resulted in riots, particularly during the Red Summer of 1919. More African Americans would migrate in the next decade.	One million women participated in types of "war work" that had traditionally been reserved for men, particularly in industry. Most were young and single and, when the war ended, returned to previous jobs more commonly held by women at that time.

economies, but also its self-image as the admired center of civilized Western culture. Winston Churchill, the future British prime minister, called postwar Europe "a crippled, broken world." Peace did not bring stability; the trauma of the war lingered long after the shooting stopped. Most Germans and Austrians believed they were the victims of a harsh peace, and many wanted revenge, especially a hate-filled German war veteran named Adolf Hitler. At the same time, the war had hastened the already simmering Bolshevik Revolution that caused Russia to exit the war and abandon its western European allies and, in 1922, to reemerge on the world stage as the Union of Soviet Socialist Republics (USSR). Thereafter, Soviet communism would be one of the most powerful forces shaping the twentieth century.

FACT 7

Congress passed and President Wilson approved the Nineteenth Amendment to the Constitution, which gave women the right to vote. With the ratification of enough states, the amendment went into effect in time for the 1920 election.

FACT 8

To negotiate the Treaty of Versailles that officially ended the war, Wilson became the first president to travel overseas for a prolonged period while in office. At the Paris Peace Conference, he was unable to achieve many of his most important goals. Although the victorious Allies agreed to form a League of Nations, they imposed harsh reparations on Germany, stirring resentment in the defeated nation that would feed the growth of Nazism.

FACT 9

The U.S. Senate refused to ratify the Treaty of Versailles; and the United States, clearly the world's leading economic and military power after the war, did not join the new League of Nations.

FACT 10

During the summer of 1919, the nation experienced a red scare, a sudden fear that a radical revolution like the one in which communists had seized power in Russia during the war was sweeping across the nation. These fears were heightened by numerous strikes related to the difficult transition from the wartime to a peacetime economy and by incidents of domestic terrorism. The Justice Department responded by arresting and deporting many radicals, most of whom were recent immigrants.

QUESTIONS FOR ANALYSIS

1. How did participation in the war transform the role of the federal government in the United States?

2. How did participation in the war change the position of women, African Americans, and immigrant communities in American society?

3. How did the war affect Americans' perceptions of themselves and their role in the world?

Postwar America was a much different story. For the first time, the United States had decisively intervened in a major European war. The American economy had emerged from the conflict largely unscathed, and bankers and business executives were eager to fill the vacuum created by the destruction of the major European economies. The United States was now the world's dominant power. In 1928, ten years after the end of the Great War, a British official in London explained that Great Britain now faced "a phenomenon for which there is no parallel in our modern history." The United States, he added, was "twenty-five times as wealthy, three times as populous, twice as ambitious, almost invulnerable, and at least our equal in prosperity, vital energy, technical equipment, and industrial strength." What came to be called the "American Century" was at hand.

■ **An Uneasy Neutrality** In 1914, a system of military alliances divided Europe in two. Britain, France, and the Russian Empire had formed the Triple Entente, later called the *Allied Powers*. The Triple Alliance, later called the *Central Powers*, comprised Germany and Austria-Hungary along with Italy (which in 1915 would switch sides and join the Allied Powers). In the summer of 1914, the assassination of the heir to the Austro-Hungarian throne by a Serbian nationalist triggered a chain reaction involving these alliances that erupted into the Great War. On the *Western Front*, troops primarily engaged in *trench warfare*. New weapons such as machine guns, long-range artillery, and poison gas resulted in unprecedented casualties.

The Wilson administration declared the nation neutral but allowed American businesses to extend loans to the Allies. Americans were outraged by the German *U-boat* warfare, especially after the 1915 sinking of the British passenger liner *Lusitania*. In 1917, the publication of the *Zimmermann telegram* led the United States to enter the Great War.

■ **Mobilizing a Nation** The Wilson Administration drafted millions of young men and created new agencies, such as the War Industries Board and the Food Administration, to coordinate industrial and agricultural production. As white workers left their factory jobs to join the army, hundreds of thousands of African Americans migrated from the rural South to the urban North, known as the *Great Migration*. Many southern whites and Mexican Americans also migrated to industrial centers. One million women worked in defense industries. The federal government severely curtailed civil liberties during the war. The Espionage and Sedition Acts of 1917 and 1918 criminalized public opposition to the war.

■ **The American Role in Fighting the War** In 1918, the arrival of millions of fresh American troops turned the tide of the war, rolling back a final desperate German offensive. German leaders sued for peace, and an armistice was signed on November 11, 1918.

Woodrow Wilson insisted that the war aim of the United States was the emergence of a new, democratic Europe. His *Fourteen Points (1918)* speech outlined his ideas for smaller, ethnically based nation-states to replace the empires. A League of Nations would promote peaceful resolutions to future conflicts.

■ **The Fight for the Peace** At the Paris Peace Conference, Wilson was only partially successful in achieving his goals. The *Treaty of Versailles (1919)* did create the *League of Nations* but included a "war guilt" clause that forced Germany to pay massive reparations for war damages to France and Britain. In the United States, the fight for Senate ratification of the treaty pitted supporters and those who wanted certain revisions against those who feared that involvement in a league of nations would hinder domestic reforms and require U.S. participation in future wars. Wilson's refusal to compromise and alienation of Republican senators resulted in the failure of Senate ratification.

■ **Lurching from War to Peace** The Bolsheviks established a Communist regime in the old Russian Empire in 1917. The German and Austro-Hungarian empires were dismantled and replaced by smaller nation-states. The "war guilt" clause fostered German bitterness and contributed to the subsequent rise of the Nazis.

The United States struggled with its new status as the leading world power and with changes at home. As wartime industries shifted to peacetime production, wartime wage and price controls were ended, and millions of former soldiers reentered the workforce. Unemployment rose and consumer prices increased, provoking labor unrest in many cities. Many Americans believed the labor strikes were part of a Bolshevik plot to gain power in the United States. Several incidents of domestic terrorism fueled these fears and provoked the *First Red Scare*. Race riots broke out as resentful white mobs tried to stop African Americans from exercising their civil rights. The summer of 1919 also saw the ratification of the *Nineteenth Amendment*, which gave women throughout the country the right to vote.

KEY TERMS

Central Powers *p. 749*
Allied Powers *p. 749*
Western Front *p. 749*
trench warfare *p. 751*
U-boat *p. 754*

Lusitania *p. 754*
Zimmermann telegram (1917) *p. 756*
Great Migration *p. 759*
Fourteen Points (1918) *p. 764*

League of Nations *p. 769*
Treaty of Versailles (1919) *p. 770*
Nineteenth Amendment (1920) *p. 774*
First Red Scare (1919–1920) *p. 777*

CHRONOLOGY

1914	The Great War (World War I) begins in Europe
1915	The British liner *Lusitania* is torpedoed by a German U-boat; 128 Americans are killed
1916	Congress passes the National Defense Act and the Revenue Act
April 1917	United States enters the Great War
January 1918	Woodrow Wilson delivers his Fourteen Points
November 11, 1918	Representatives of warring nations sign armistice
1919	Paris Peace Conference convenes
	Germany signs the Treaty of Versailles
	Race riots break out across America during the Red Summer
	First Red Scare leads to arrests and deportations of suspected radicals
	Boston police strike ends with firing of all strikers
1920	Senate rejects the Treaty of Versailles
	Nineteenth Amendment is ratified

INQUIZITIVE

Go to InQuizitive to see what you've learned—and learn what you've missed—with personalized feedback along the way.

NIGHTCLUB (1933) With all its striking sights and sounds, the roar of the twenties subsided for some at the heart of it all. In this painting by American artist Guy Pène du Bois, flappers and their dates crowd into a fashionable nightclub, yet their loneliness amidst the excitement is utterly palpable.

A Clash of Cultures

1920–1929

The 1920s was perhaps the most dynamic decade in American history, a legendary era bounded on both ends by tragedies: the butchery of the Great War and the miseries of the Great Depression. It was a contradictory and conflict-ridden decade of rapid urbanization, technological innovation, widespread prosperity, unparalleled social freedom, cultural upheaval, and political conservatism. As the disruptive innovations associated with "modernism" clashed with the entrenched certainties of traditionalism, old and new values confronted each other in a cultural civil war that continues today. The decade's two most popular labels—the Jazz Age and the Roaring Twenties—describe a turbulent period that was, as a writer in the *New York Times* declared in 1923, "the greatest era of transition the human race has ever known. Old institutions are crumbling, old ideals are being battered into dust; the shock of the most cataclysmic war in history has left the world more disorganized than ever."

Among the most obvious changes during the twenties was an economic boom fueled by the spread of transformational new technologies (automobiles, trucks, tractors, airplanes, radios, movies, electrical appliances, indoor plumbing) that greatly reshaped and improved the standard of living for most Americans. At the same time, major social and political changes signaled what many people called a "New Era"

CORE
OBJECTIVES INQUIZITIVE

1. Describe the consumer culture that emerged in America during the 1920s, and explain the factors that contributed to its growth.

2. Describe other major new social and cultural trends and movements that became prominent during the twenties, and explain how they challenged traditional standards and customs.

3. Explain what "modernism" means in intellectual and artistic terms and how the modernist movement influenced American culture in the early twentieth century.

4. Identify important examples of reactionary conservatism in the decade, and analyze their impact on government policies.

5. Trace the Republican party's dominance of the federal government during the twenties, and analyze the extent to which its policies were a rejection of progressivism.

in American life. Women were at last allowed to vote in all states (although most African American women—and men—in the South were limited from doing so) and to experience many freedoms previously limited to men. The Eighteenth Amendment outlawed alcoholic beverages ("Prohibition"), setting off an epidemic of lawbreaking. Another disruptive force was growing public awareness of the scientific discoveries of Albert Einstein in physics and Sigmund Freud in psychology, findings that undermined many traditional assumptions about God, the universe, and human behavior while profoundly affecting social and cultural life. Such sweeping and speedy changes created what one historian called a "nervous generation" of Americans "groping for what certainty they could find."

Much of the cultural conflict during the 1920s grew out of tension between rural and urban ways of life. For the first time, more Americans lived in cities than in rural areas. While urban Americans generally prospered, farmers suffered from the end of the wartime boom in food exports to Europe. As the rural economy remained depressed throughout the twenties, 4 million people moved from farms to cities. Amid this population shift, bitter fights erupted between supporters and opponents of evolutionary theory, Prohibition, and the increasing ethnic and religious diversity of America, among other issues.

In the political arena, both major parties still included "progressive" wings, but they were shrinking. Woodrow Wilson's losing fight with the Republican-led Senate over the Treaty of Versailles, coupled with his administration's savage crackdown on dissenters and socialists during and after the war, had weakened an already fragmented progressive movement. As the tireless reformer Amos Pinchot bitterly observed, President Wilson had "put his enemies in office and his friends in jail." By 1920, many progressives had withdrawn from public life. The prominent reformer Jane Addams lamented that the twenties, dominated politically by a Republican party devoted to the interests of business, were "a period of political and social sag."

A "New Era" of Consumption

CORE **OBJECTIVE**

1. Describe the consumer culture that emerged in America during the 1920s, and explain the factors that contributed to its growth.

During the twenties, the U.S. economy became the envy of the world. Following the brief postwar recession in 1920–1921, Americans benefited from the fastest economic growth rate in history to that point. Jobs were plentiful, inflation was low, and income rose throughout the decade. The nation's total wealth almost doubled between 1920 and 1930, while wage workers enjoyed a whopping 30 percent increase in income, the sharpest rise in history to that point. By 1929, the United States had the highest standard of living in the world.

Construction led the way. The war had caused people to postpone building offices, plants, homes, and apartments. By 1921, however, a building boom was underway that would last the rest of the decade. At the same time, the remarkable growth of the automotive industry created an immediate need for roads and highways helped to stimulate other industries such as steel, concrete, and furniture. Technology also played a key role in the prosperity of the twenties by making manufacturing a more mechanical, assembly-line process. New machines (electric motors, steam turbines, dump trucks, tractors, bulldozers, steam shovels) and more efficient ways of operating farms, factories, plants, mines, and mills generated dramatic increases in production.

In the late nineteenth century, the U.S. economy had been driven by commercial agriculture and large-scale industrial production—the building of railroads and bridges, the manufacturing of steel, and the construction of housing and businesses in cities. During the twenties, such industrial production continued, but the dominant aspect of the economy involved an explosion of new consumer goods.

A Growing Consumer Culture

Perhaps the most visible change during the twenties was the emergence of a powerful, urban-dominated "**consumer culture**" in which the mass production and consumption of nationally advertised products came to dictate much of social life and social status. A 1920 newspaper editorial insisted that, with the war over, the American's "first importance to his country is no longer that of citizen but that of consumer. Consumption is a new necessity." The United States economy had entered what many called a "New Era" in which the consumption of goods became a national obsession. To keep factory production humming required converting people into carefree shoppers. "People may ruin themselves by saving instead of spending," warned one economist.

In the twenties, old virtues of hard work, plain living, and frugal money management were challenged by a new system of values celebrating leisure, self-expression, and self-indulgence, all achieved through the purchase of "name brand" products. "During the war," a journalist noted in 1920, "we accustomed ourselves to doing without, to buying carefully, to using economically. But with the close of the war came reaction. A veritable orgy of extravagant buying is going on. Reckless spending takes the place of saving, waste replaces conservation." Writing in *Nation's Business* in 1926, journalist William A. Feather proclaimed that the ideal American was unashamedly believed "in the doctrine of selfishness" and was proudly "rich, fat, arrogant, [and] superior."

To keep people buying, business executives focused their attention and resources on two crucial innovations: marketing and advertising campaigns to increase consumer demand and new ways for buyers to finance purchases over time ("layaway") rather than have to pay cash up front. Installment buying promised instant gratification for consumers ("Buy Now, Pay

> Rise of mass culture: New emphasis on spending, advertising, credit, and conveniences

consumer culture A society in which mass production and consumption of nationally advertised products comes to dictate much of social life and status.

Later"). As paying with cash and staying out of debt came to be seen as needlessly "old-fashioned" practices, consumer debt almost tripled during the twenties. By 1929, almost 60 percent of American purchases were made on the installment plan.

Mass advertising, first developed in the late nineteenth century, grew into a huge enterprise essential to the success of the mass-production/mass-consumption economy. Popular new weekday radio programs, for example, were often sponsored by national companies trying to sell laundry detergent and hand soap—hence the term "soap operas." Because women purchased two-thirds of consumer goods during the twenties, advertisers aimed at them especially. An ad in *Photoplay* magazine targeted the "woman of the house" because "she buys most of the things which go to make the home happy, healthful, and beautiful. Through her slim, safe fingers goes most of the family money."

A modern home This 1925 Westinghouse advertisement urges homemakers to buy its "Cozy Glow, Jr." heater and "Sol-Lux Luminaire" lamp, among other electrical appliances that would "do anything for you in return."

Zelda Sayre Fitzgerald, the writer and wife of the wildly popular young novelist F. Scott Fitzgerald, recalled that "we grew up founding our dreams on the infinite promises of American advertising." Men were by no means ignored by advertisers, however. In his best-selling novel *Babbitt* (1922), Sinclair Lewis described George F. Babbitt, a frustrated real estate salesman, as a true believer in the benefits of the new consumer culture: "Just as he was an Elk, a Booster, and a member of the chamber of commerce, just as the priests of the Presbyterian Church determined his every religious belief . . . so did the large national advertisers fix the surface of his life, fix what he believed to be his individuality."

Perhaps no decade in American history witnessed such dramatic changes in everyday life as a result of the consumer culture. The huge jump in the use of electricity during the twenties was a revolutionary new force. In 1920, only 35 percent of homes had electricity; by 1930 the number was 68 percent. Similar increases occurred in the number of households with indoor plumbing, washing machines, and automobiles. Moderately priced creature comforts and conveniences, such as flush toilets, electric irons and fans, handheld cameras, wristwatches, cigarette lighters, vacuum cleaners, and linoleum floors, became more widely available, especially among the urban middle class.

The Rise of Mass Culture

The powerful new consumer culture helped create a national marketplace of retail stores and brands in which local and regional businesses were squeezed out by giant "chain" corporations. By the 1920s, Woolworth's, for example, had 1,500 stores scattered across the country. Large national retailers bought goods in such large quantities that they were able to get discounted prices that they passed on to consumers. Mass advertising and marketing campaigns increasingly led to a mass culture: more and more Americans now not only saw and heard the same advertisements and shopped at the same companies' stores but also read the same magazines, listened to the same radio programs, and watched the same movies. Through these media, they could follow the lives and careers of the nation's first celebrities and superstars. At the same time, Americans were increasingly on the move: automobiles enabled more people to travel easily, exposing them to new values and different viewpoints. America in the twenties, explained the celebrated New York journalist Walter Lippmann, was experiencing "a vast dissolution of ancient habits" as more and more Americans embraced the "New Era."

A Love Affair with Movies

In 1896, a New York City audience viewed the first moving-picture show. By 1924, there were 20,000 movie theaters (the largest of which were called "motion picture palaces") across the nation, showing 700 new "silent" films a year that used captions to show the dialogue. Hollywood, California, became the international center of movie production, grinding out Westerns, crime dramas, and comedies. By 1930, even most small towns had theaters, and movies had become the nation's chief form of mass entertainment. Movie attendance during the 1920s averaged 80 million people a week, more than half the national population, and attendance surged even more after 1928, when "talking" movies appeared. Americans spent ten times as much on movies as they did on tickets to baseball and football games.

Charlie Chaplin An English-born actor who rose to international fame as the "Tramp," pictured above in the 1921 silent film *The Kid.*

The Effects of Radio

Radio broadcasting experienced even more spectacular growth. In 1920, station WWJ in Detroit began transmitting news bulletins, and KDKA in Pittsburgh began broadcasting regularly scheduled programs. The first radio commercial aired in New York in 1922. By the end of that year, there were 508 stations and some 3 million radios in use. In 1926, the National Broadcasting Company (NBC), a subsidiary of the Radio Corporation of America (RCA), began linking stations into a national network; the Columbia Broadcasting System (CBS) entered the field the next year.

The widespread ownership of radios changed the patterns of everyday life. At night after dinner, families gathered around the radio to listen to music, speeches, news broadcasts, weather forecasts, and comedy shows. One ad claimed that the radio "is your theater, your college, your newspaper, your library." Calvin Coolidge became the first president to address the nation by radio, and he did so monthly, paving the way for Franklin Delano Roosevelt's influential "fireside chats" a decade later.

Taking to the Air

> Charles Lindbergh's and Amelia Earhart's boost to the new aviation industry

Advances in transportation were as significant as the impact of radio and movies. In 1903, Wilbur and Orville Wright, owners of a bicycle shop in Dayton, Ohio, had built and flown the first airplane at Kitty Hawk, North Carolina. But airplane technology advanced slowly until the outbreak of war in 1914, after which Europeans rapidly adapted the airplane as a military weapon. When the United States entered the war, it had no combat planes—American pilots flew British or French planes. An American aircraft industry arose during the war but collapsed in the postwar demobilization. Under the Kelly Act of 1925, however, the federal government began to subsidize the industry through the awarding of airmail contracts. The Air Commerce Act of 1926 provided federal funds for the advancement of air transportation and navigation, including the construction of airports.

The aviation industry received a huge psychological boost in 1927 when twenty-six-year-old Charles A. Lindbergh Jr. made the first *solo* transatlantic flight, traveling from New York City to Paris in thirty-three and a half hours. The heroic feat, which won him $25,000 and a Congressional Medal of Honor, was truly dramatic: already exhausted from lack of sleep when he took off, Lindbergh flew through severe storms as well as a dense fog for part of the way that forced him to descend to within ten feet of the ocean's surface. When he landed in France, 100,000 people greeted him with thunderous cheers, and a New York City parade celebrating Lindbergh's accomplishment surpassed even the celebration of the armistice ending World War I. Youngsters developed a new dance step in his honor, called the Lindy Hop. Five years after Lindbergh's famous flight, New York City celebrated another pioneering aviator—Amelia Earhart, a former stunt pilot at air shows who became the first woman to fly solo across the Atlantic.

The Car Culture

Amelia Earhart The pioneering aviator would tragically disappear in her 1937 attempt to fly around the world.

By far the most significant economic and social development of the early twentieth century was the widespread ownership of automobiles. The first motorcar had been manufactured for sale in 1895, but the founding of the Ford Motor Company in 1903 revolutionized the infant industry. Henry Ford vowed "to democratize the automobile." "When I'm through," he predicted, "everybody will be able to afford one, and about everyone will have one." Ford's Model T, the celebrated "Tin Lizzie," cheap and long-lasting, came out in 1908 at a price of $850 (about $22,000 at today's prices). By

1924, as a result of Ford's increasingly efficient production techniques, the same car sold for $290 (less than $4000 today). The Model T changed little from year to year, and it came in only one color: black. Ford ads assured buyers that they "could have any color you want, as long as it is black."

In 1916, the total number of cars in the United States passed 1 million; by 1920 more than 8 million were registered, and in 1929 there were more than 23 million. The automobile revolution was in part propelled by the discovery of vast oil fields in Texas, Oklahoma, Wyoming, and California. By 1920, the United States produced two-thirds of the world's oil and gasoline.

The automobile industry became the leading example of modern mass-production techniques and efficiency. Ford's Highland Park plant outside Detroit was designed to increase output dramatically by creating a moving assembly line rather than having a crew of workers assemble each car in a fixed position. With conveyors pulling the parts along feeder lines and the chassis down an assembly line, each worker performed a single particular task, such as installing a fender or a wheel. This system could produce a new car in ninety-three minutes.

Such efficiency enabled Ford to lower the price of his cars, thereby increasing the number of people who could afford them and enabling him to pay his workers the highest wages in the industry. For the workers, however, producing cars this way made for a monotonous, mind-numbing experience, especially since Ford prohibited them from talking, sitting, smoking, or singing on the job. But his methods accomplished his goal. During the twenties, the United States built ten times more automobiles than all of Europe.

Just as the railroad helped transform the pace and scale of American life in the second half of the nineteenth century, the mass production of automobiles changed social life during the twentieth century. During the 1920s, Americans literally developed a love affair with cars. In the words of one man, young people viewed the car as "an incredible engine of escape" from parental control and a safe place to "take a girl and hold hands, neck,

Henry Ford and the automotive revolution

Ford Motor Company's Highland Park plant, 1913 Gravity slides and chain conveyors contributed to the mass production of automobiles.

pet, or . . . go the limit." In 1923–1924, nineteen women in Muncie, Indiana, were arrested for "sex crimes" in automobiles.

Cars enabled people to live farther away from their workplaces, thus encouraging suburban sprawl. Cars also helped fuel the economic boom of the 1920s by creating tens of thousands of new jobs and a huge demand for steel, rubber, leather, oil, and gasoline. The ever-expanding car culture stimulated road construction (financed in large part by a gasoline tax), sparked a real estate boom in Florida and California, and dotted the land-scape with gasoline stations, traffic lights, billboards, and motor hotels ("motels"). By 1929, the federal government was constructing 10,000 miles of paved highways each year.

Spectator Sports

Mass popularity of baseball, football, and boxing

The widespread ownership of automobiles as well as rising incomes changed the way people spent their leisure time. City dwellers could easily drive into the countryside, visit friends and relatives, and go to ballparks, stadiums, or boxing rings to see baseball or football games and prizefights. During the 1920s, Americans fell in love with mass spectator sports.

Created in the 1870s in rural areas, baseball had, by the 1920s, gone urban and earned its label of "the national pastime." With larger-than-life heroes such as New York Yankee stars George Herman "Babe" Ruth Jr. and Henry Louis "Lou" Gehrig, professional baseball teams attracted intense loyalties and huge crowds. In 1920, more than a million spectators attended Yankees' games. Two years later, the Yankees built a new stadium, called the "house that Ruth built," and they went on to win World Series championships in 1923, 1927, and 1928. More than 20 million people attended professional baseball games in 1927, the year that Ruth, the "Sultan of Swat," set a record by hitting sixty home runs. Because baseball was still a segregated sport, so-called Negro leagues were organized at the amateur, semiprofessional, and professional levels for African Americans to play in and watch.

Football, especially at the college level, also attracted huge crowds, usually more affluent than baseball spectators. It, too, benefited from superstars such as Harold Edward

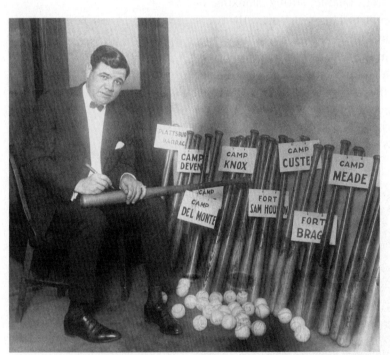

Babe Ruth This star pitcher and outfielder won the hearts of Americans with the Boston Red Sox, New York Yankees, and finally the Boston Braves. Here, he autographs bats and balls for military training camps.

"Red" Grange, the phenomenal running back for the University of Illinois and the first athlete to appear on the cover of *Time* magazine. In a game against the University of Michigan, the "Galloping Ghost" scored a touchdown each of the first four times he carried the ball; after Illinois won, students carried Grange on their shoulders for two miles across the campus. When Grange signed a contract with the Chicago Bears in 1926, he single-handedly made professional football competitive with baseball as a spectator sport.

What Ruth and Grange were to their sports, William Harrison "Jack" Dempsey was to boxing. In 1919, he won the world heavyweight title from Jess Willard, a giant of a man weighing 300 pounds and standing six and a half feet tall. Dempsey knocked him down seven times in the first round. After Willard, his face bruised and bloodied, threw in the towel in the fourth round, Dempsey became a national celebrity and a wealthy man. Like Babe Ruth, the brawling Dempsey was especially popular with working-class men, for he too had been born poor and had worked with his hands for wages. In 1927, when James Joseph "Gene" Tunney defeated Dempsey, more than 100,000 people attended, including a thousand reporters, ten state governors, and numerous Hollywood celebrities. Some 60 million people listened to the fight over the radio.

The "Jazz Age"

CORE **OBJECTIVE**
2. Describe other major new social and cultural trends and movements that became prominent during the twenties, and explain how they challenged traditional standards and customs.

While most Americans of all ages became devoted to spectator sports, radio programs, and movies during the twenties, many young people focused their energies on social and cultural rebellion. F. Scott Fitzgerald, a boyishly handsome Princeton University dropout, was labeled "the voice of his generation" after his first novel, *This Side of Paradise* (1920), became a best seller with its account of student life at Princeton. Fitzgerald fastened upon the "**Jazz Age**" as a label for the spirit of rebelliousness and spontaneity he saw welling up among many young Americans.

The Birth of Jazz

Fitzgerald's term referred to the raging popularity of jazz music, a dynamic blend of several musical traditions. It had first emerged as piano-based "ragtime" at the end of the nineteenth century. Thereafter, African American musicians such as Jelly Roll Morton, Duke Ellington, Louis Armstrong, and Bessie Smith (the "Empress of the Blues") combined the energies of ragtime with the emotions of the blues to create *jazz*, originally an African American slang term meaning sexual intercourse. With its constant improvisations and variations and its sensual spontaneity, jazz

The craze for jazz music and dancing

Jazz Age Term coined by writer F. Scott Fitzgerald to characterize the spirit of rebellion and spontaneity among young Americans in the 1920s, a spirit epitomized by the hugely popular jazz music of the era.

F. Scott Fitzgerald Author known for his depictions of the youthful, boisterous spirit of the roaring twenties in *This Side of Paradise* (1920) and *The Great Gatsby* (1925).

appealed to many people of all ethnicities and ages because it was all about pleasure and immediacy, letting go and enjoying the freedom of the moment. In 1925 an African American journalist announced that jazz had "absorbed the national spirit of go and nervousness, lack of conventionality and boisterous good nature characteristic of the American, black or white."

The culture of jazz quickly spread from its origins in New Orleans, Kansas City, Memphis, and St. Louis to the African American neighborhoods of Harlem in New York City and Chicago's South Side. Large dance halls were built to meet the swelling demand for jazz music and the dance craze that accompanied it, including new dances like the Charleston and the Black Bottom whose sexually provocative movements shocked traditionalists. Affluent whites flocked to dance halls as well as to "black" nightclubs and "jazz joints." During the 1920s, people commonly spoke of—"jazzing something up" (enlivening it) or "jazzing around" (acting youthfully and energetically).

Many Americans, however, were not fans of jazz. Several prominent women's rights leaders dismissed both ragtime and jazz as dangerously sensual music that encouraged rape. In 1921 the *Ladies' Home Journal* discouraged jazz dancing because of its "direct appeal to the body's sensory centers," and Princeton professor Henry van Dyke dismissed jazz as "merely an irritation of the nerves of hearing, a sensual teasing of the strings of physical passion." Such shortsighted criticism, however, failed to stem the frenzied popularity of jazz, which swept across Europe as well as America.

Duke Ellington and his band Jazz emerged in the 1920s as an especially American expression of the modernist spirit. African American artists bent musical conventions to give freer rein to improvisation and sensuality.

A Revolution in Manners and Morals

Much of the shock to old-timers during the Jazz Age came from the revolution in manners and morals among young people, especially those on college campuses. From novels such as *This Side of Paradise* as well as dozens of magazine articles, middle-class Americans learned about the hidden world of "flaming youth" (the title of another popular novel): wild parties, free love, speakeasies, skinny-dipping, and the uses to which automobiles were put on lovers' lanes. A promotional poster for the 1923 silent film *Flaming Youth* asked: "How Far Can a Girl Go?" Other ads claimed the movie appealed especially to "neckers, petters, white kisses, red kisses, pleasure-mad daughters, [and] sensation-craving mothers."

"Flaming youth," Freud, and flappers

The increasingly frank treatment of sex during the twenties resulted in part from the spreading influence of Sigmund Freud, the founder of modern psychoanalysis. Freud, an Austrian who was trained as a physician, changed the way people understood their behavior and feelings by insisting that the mind is essentially and mysteriously "conflicted" by often unconscious efforts to control or repress powerful irrational impulses and sexual desires ("libido"). In 1899, he had published his pathbreaking book *The Interpretation of Dreams*, which stressed the crucial role of the subconscious, that dark swamp of our irrational minds, in shaping behavior and moods. Dreams, he said, revealed "repressed" sexual yearnings deep in the psyche, many of which resulted from early childhood experiences.

Sigmund Freud Founder of modern psychoanalysis, in 1926.

By 1909, when Freud first visited the United States to lecture at Clark University in Massachusetts, he was surprised to find himself famous "even in prudish America." It did not take long for his ideas to penetrate society at large. Psychoanalysis soon became the most celebrated—and controversial—technique for helping troubled people come to grips with their demons. Through "talk therapy," patients discussed their inner frustrations and revealed their repressed fears and urges. By 1916, there were some 500 psychoanalysts in New York City alone.

Freud's emphasis on unruly sexual desires swirling about in the subconscious fascinated some people and scared others. For many young Americans especially, Freud seemed to provide scientific justification for rebelling against social conventions and indulging in sex. Some oversimplified his theories by claiming that sexual pleasure was essential for emotional health, that all forms of sexual activity were good, and that all inhibitions—feelings of restraint—about sex were bad. In his novel *Dark Laughter* (1925), Sherwood Anderson contrasted the sexual puritanism of white Americans with what he saw as the unrepressed sensuality of African Americans: "If there is anything that you do not understand in life," one of the characters advises, "consult the works of Dr. Freud." Traditionalists, on the other hand, were shocked at the behavior of rebellious young women who claimed to be acting out Freud's theories. "One hears it

The beautiful and the damned In an outfit typical of flappers, Zelda Fitzgerald poses with her husband on the Riviera in 1926.

flappers Young women of the 1920s whose rebellion against prewar standards of femininity included wearing shorter dresses, bobbing their hair, dancing to jazz music, driving cars, smoking cigarettes, and indulging in illegal drinking and gambling.

said," complained a Baptist magazine, "that the girls are actually tempting the boys more than the boys do the girls, by their dress and conversation."

As such remarks suggest, new fashions in clothing reflected the rebellion against traditional female roles. The emancipated "new woman" of the twenties eagerly discarded the confining wardrobe of the nineteenth and early twentieth centuries—pinched-in corsets, layers of petticoats, and floor-length dresses. In 1919 skirts were typically six inches above the ground; by 1927 they were at the knee. The shortest ones were worn by the so-called **flappers**, young women who—in defiance of proper prewar standards—drove automobiles, "bobbed" their hair (cut it short, requiring the invention of the "bobby pin"), and wore minimal underclothing, gauzy fabrics, sheer stockings, and plenty of makeup, especially rouge and lipstick. They also often joined young men in smoking cigarettes, (illegally) drinking and gambling, and dancing to jazz music—not to mention even more sensual activities.

Self-consciously outrageous and outlandish, flappers wanted more out of life than marriage and motherhood. Their carefree version of feminism was fun-loving, defiant, and self-indulgent. F. Scott Fitzgerald claimed that his rebellious wife, Zelda, was the "First American Flapper." The wayward daughter of a strict Alabama judge, Zelda was wild to the point of exhaustion. Emboldened by alcohol, she loved to do what she called "crazy things" such as dancing in New York City fountains and stripping off her clothes in the middle of Grand Central Station. Many were appalled by the flappers. A Catholic priest in Brooklyn complained that the feminism of the 1920s had provoked a "pandemonium of powder, a riot of rouge, and a moral anarchy of dress." In discussing the flapper phenomenon, a newspaper columnist reported that "the world is divided into those who delight in her, those who fear her, and those who try pathetically to take her as a matter of course."

Women in the 1920s

Most women in the 1920s, even most young, college-educated women, were not flappers, however. Lillian Symes, a longtime activist in the women's movement, stressed that her "generation of feminists" had little in common with the "spike-heeled, over-rouged flapper of today. We grew up before the postwar disillusionment engulfed the youth of the land." Although more middle-class women attended college in the 1920s than ever before, a higher percentage of them married soon after graduation than had been the case in the nineteenth century.

The conservative political mood of the twenties helped to steer women back into their traditional roles as homemakers, and college curricula began to shift accordingly. At Vassar College in New York, an all-women's school, students took courses such as "Husband and Wife," "Motherhood," and "The Family as an Economic Unit." At the same time, fewer college-educated women pursued careers: the proportion of physicians who were women fell from 6 to 4 percent during the twenties, with similar reductions among dentists, architects, and chemists. A student at all-female Smith College expressed frustration "that a woman must choose between a home and her work, when a man may have both. There must be a way out, and it is the problem of our generation to find the way."

> A return to more "traditional" domestic roles for most women

As before, most women who worked outside the home labored in un-skilled, low-wage jobs. Only 4 percent of working women in the 1920s were salaried professionals; the vast majority worked for hourly wages. Some women moved into new vocations created by the growing consumer culture, such as accounting assistants and department store clerks. The number of beauty shops soared from five thousand in 1920 to forty thousand in 1930, creating new jobs for hair stylists, manicurists, and cosmeticians.

The majority of women, however, were still either full-time wives and mothers or household servants. Fortunately, the advent of electricity and electrical appliances—vacuum cleaners, toasters, stoves, washing machines, irons—made housework quicker and easier than it had been for their mothers and grandmothers. African American and Mexican American women faced the greatest challenges. As a New York City newspaper observed, they were forced to do "work which white women will not do." Women of color usually worked as maids, laundresses, or seamstresses or on farms.

The Harlem Renaissance

As their Great Migration from the South continued into the twenties, African Americans found new freedom of speech and action in northern settings; they also gained leverage as voters by settling in states with many electoral votes. With these new opportunities came a bristling spirit of protest that became known as the **Harlem Renaissance**, the nation's first self-conscious black literary and artistic movement.

> The Harlem Renaissance

The movement started among the fast-growing African American community in the Harlem neighborhood of northern Manhattan in New York City. In 1890, one in seventy people in Manhattan had been African American; by 1930 it was one in nine. The "great, dark city" of Harlem, as poet Langston Hughes's called it, contained more blacks per square mile than any other urban neighborhood in the nation. Their dense concentration there generated a sense of common identity, growing power, and distinctive

Harlem Renaissance The nation's first self-conscious black literary and artistic movement; centered in New York City's Harlem district, which had a largely black population in the wake of the Great Migration from the South.

Augusta Savage The sculptor, shown with her statue *Realization* (1938), found success in America and abroad, though after much struggle with racism.

self-expression that soon made Harlem the cultural capital of African American life. Dotted with raucous nightclubs where writers and painters discussed literature and art while listening to jazz and drinking bootleg alcohol, Harlem became what journalists called the "Nightclub Capital of the World."

The Harlem Renaissance writers celebrated African Americans' heritage as well as their more recent contributions to American culture, including jazz and the blues. As Langston Hughes wrote, "I am a Negro—and beautiful. . . . The night is beautiful. So [are] the faces of my people." He loved Africa and its cultural heritage, but declared, "I was not Africa. I was Chicago and Kansas City and Broadway and Harlem." The Harlem group promoted a racially integrated society. James Weldon Johnson coined the term "Aframerican" to designate Americans with African ancestry, whom he called "conscious collaborators" in the creation of American society and culture. By 1930 the Harlem Renaissance writers had produced dozens of novels and volumes of poetry, several Broadway plays, and a flood of short stories, essays, and films. A people capable of producing such great art and literature, Johnson declared, should never again be "looked upon as inferior."

Garveyism

The celebration of black culture also found expression in what came to be called Negro nationalism, which promoted black separatism from mainstream American life. Its leading spokesman was the flamboyant Marcus Garvey. In 1916, Garvey brought to Harlem the headquarters of the Universal Negro Improvement Association (UNIA), which he had started in his native Jamaica two years before.

Garvey insisted that blacks had nothing in common with whites—and that was a good thing. He therefore called for racial separation to integration. In passionate speeches and in editorials in his newspaper, the *Negro World*, Garvey urged African Americans to separate themselves from the surrounding white culture. He saw every white person as a "potential Klansman" and endorsed the "social and political separation of all peoples to the extent that they promote their own ideals and civilization."

The UNIA grew rapidly amid the racial tensions of the postwar years. By 1923, Garvey claimed to have as many as 4 million UNIA members served by 800 offices. The UNIA became the largest black political organization in the twentieth century. Garvey's goal was to build an all-black empire in Africa: "We will let white men have America and Europe, but we are going to have Africa." To that end, he began calling himself the "Provisional President of Africa," raising funds to send Americans to Africa, and expelling any UNIA member who married a white.

Garvey's message of black nationalism and racial solidarity appealed to many African Americans living in slums in northern cities, but it appalled other black leaders. W. E. B. Du Bois, for example, labeled Garvey "the most dangerous enemy of the Negro race. . . . He is either a lunatic or a traitor." An African American newspaper pledged to help "drive Garvey and Garveyism in all its sinister viciousness from the American soil."

Garvey's crusade collapsed in 1923 when he was convicted of mail fraud related to overselling shares of stock in a steamship corporation intended to transport American blacks to Africa. Sentenced to five years in prison, in 1927 he was pardoned by President Calvin Coolidge on the condition that he be deported to Jamaica. One of the largest crowds in Jamaican history greeted him upon his return to his native country. Garvey died in obscurity in 1940, but the memory of his movement kept alive an undercurrent that would re-emerge in the 1960s under the slogan "black power."

Marcus Garvey Founder of the Universal Negro Improvement Association and leading spokesman for "Negro nationalism" in the 1920s.

The NAACP

A more lasting force for racial equality during the twenties was the **National Association for the Advancement of Colored People (NAACP)**, founded in 1910 by black activists and white progressives. Black NAACP leaders came mainly from the Niagara Movement, a group that had met each year since 1905 at places associated with the anti-slavery movement (Niagara Falls; Oberlin, Ohio; Boston; Harpers Ferry) and issued defiant statements against discrimination. Within a few years, the NAACP had become a broad-based national organization. It embraced the progressive idea that the solution to social problems begins with education, by informing people about social problems. W. E. B. Du Bois became the organization's director of publicity and research and the editor of its journal, *Crisis*.

Politically, the NAACP's main strategy focused on legal action to bring the Fourteenth and Fifteenth Amendments back to life. One early victory came with *Guinn v. United States* (1915), in which the Supreme Court struck down Oklahoma's efforts to deprive African Americans of the vote. In *Buchanan v. Warley* (1917) the Court invalidated a residential segregation ordinance in Louisville, Kentucky. In 1919, the NAACP launched a national campaign against lynching, still a common form of vigilante racist violence. An anti-lynching bill to make mob murder a federal crime passed the House in 1922 but lost to a filibuster by southerners in the Senate.

The NAACP: Progressive interracial activism on racial issues

National Association for the Advancement of Colored People (NAACP) Organization founded in 1910 by black activists and white progressives that promoted education as a means of combating social problems and focused on legal action to secure the civil rights supposedly guaranteed by the Fourteenth and Fifteenth Amendments.

CORE **OBJECTIVE**

3. Explain what "modernism" means in intellectual and artistic terms and how the modernist movement influenced American culture in the early twentieth century.

The Modernist Revolt

The dramatic changes in society and the economy during the twenties were spurred by transformations in science and the arts that marked the onset of a "modernist" sensibility. Modernists were rebellious intellectuals, writers, and artists who believed that the start of the twentieth century was a historical hinge opening the way for a new world view that rejected traditional notions of reality and values (progress, reason, and even God) and adopting radical new forms of artistic expression. As the celebrated American writer Willa Cather declared, "The world broke in two in 1922 or thereabouts." She meant that during the twenties a civil war erupted between cultural modernists and their traditionalist critics. In 1922 the Irish modernist James Joyce published his pathbreaking novel *Ulysses* and the Anglo-American poet T.S. Eliot wrote "The Waste Land." Critics charged that Eliot, Joyce, and others were "ruining" literature. One said that Eliot's impenetrable writing was "a gash at the root of our poetry." Modernists fought back, claiming that as apostles of radical change they were simply acknowledging the arrival of an unsettling new way of viewing life and expressing its raucous energies.

Of course, modernism, as much a state of mind as a movement, did not simply drop out of the sky in 1922. It had been years in the making. During the early twentieth century, people were both inspired and terrified by an explosion of new scientific and technical knowledge that unveiled troubling mysteries of the universe. Since the eighteenth-century Enlightenment, conventional wisdom had held that the universe was governed by basic underlying laws of time and energy, light and motion. This rational world of order and certainty disintegrated in the early twentieth century, thanks to the discoveries of European physicists.

Science and Modernism: Einstein and Relativity

In the first decade of the century, Albert Einstein, a young German physicist, published several research papers that changed science forever while at times defying common sense. The first paper, for which he was later awarded the Nobel Prize, described how light was not only a wave of energy but also a stream of particles, called quanta or photons. This wave-particle duality became the foundation of what is known as quantum physics and would later provide the theoretical basis for such developments as television, laser beams, and semiconductors used to make computers. The second paper confirmed the existence of molecules and atoms by showing statistically how their random collisions explained the jerky motion of tiny particles in water.

Important as both of these papers were, it was Einstein's third paper that truly upended traditional notions of the universe. It grew out of one of

Albert Einstein One of the most influential scientists of the twentieth century, Einstein was awarded a Nobel Prize in 1921.

his favorite thought experiments: if you could travel at the speed of light, what would a light wave look like? If you were in a train that neared the speed of light, would you see time and space differently? Einstein's conclusions to those questions led him to create the special theory of relativity (1905), which explains that no matter how fast one is moving toward or away from a source of light, the speed of that light beam will appear the same, a constant 186,000 miles per second. But space and time will appear relative. As a train accelerates to near the speed of light, time on the train will slow down from the perspective of a stationary observer, and the train will get shorter and heavier.

The most important of Einstein's ideas was his general theory of relativity (1916), which maintained that the fundamental concepts of space, time, matter, and energy were not distinct, independent things with continuous dimensions, as Sir Isaac Newton had assumed in the eighteenth century, but instead were interacting elements.

> Modernism and science: Einstein's breakthroughs and impact

Nothing is fixed or absolute in Einstein's bewildering universe; everything is *relative* to the location and motion of the observer and the effects of gravity, which warps space and time. Things are big or little, long or short, slow or fast, light or heavy only by comparison to something else. So, for example, the particular spot on earth on which we are positioned at any given moment is not fixed but is, relative to the sun, moving through space at 18.5 miles per second. Einstein also revealed that objects shrink as they approach the speed of light, that beams of light are bent by gravity, and that all matter is simply stored energy.

Einstein's new vision of the universe revolutionized the way people understood time, space, and light. Although few understood the details of his theories, many began to embrace the idea that there were no absolute standards or fixed points of reference in the world. During the twenties, the idea of "relativity" gradually emerged in popular discussions of decidedly nonscientific topics such as sexuality, the arts, and politics; there was less faith in absolutes, not only of time and space but also of truth and morality. Just as Darwinism became not just a biological theory but also a social, economic, and political one, so too did relativity shape many of the intellectual, cultural, and social currents of the twentieth century. In 1920, the year before Einstein was awarded the Nobel Prize, an American journalist said that his theories had moved physics into the region of "metaphysics, where paradox and magic take the place of solid fact . . . and common sense." The farther scientists reached out into the universe and into the microscopic world of the atom, the more Western certainty dissolved.

Modernist Art and Literature

The scientific breakthroughs associated with Freud, Einstein, and others helped to inspire a "modernist" cultural revolution among intellectuals and creative artists. **Modernism** as a recognizable movement in the arts and ideas had appeared first in the capitals of Europe—London, Paris,

modernism An early-twentieth-century cultural movement that rejected traditional notions of reality and adopted radical new forms of artistic expression.

Berlin, and Vienna—in the 1890s. By the second decade of the twentieth century, it had spread to the United States, especially New York City and Chicago. It arose out of a widespread recognition that Western civilization was entering an era of bewildering change as new technologies, modes of transportation and communication, and startling scientific discoveries combined to transform the nature of everyday life and the way people "saw" the world.

> Modernism as a cultural movement

The shocking horrors of the Great War accelerated and expanded the appeal of modernism—and helped explain why modernists cared little for established standards of good taste or for history. To be "modern" in the early twentieth century was to break free of tradition, by taking chances, violating artistic rules and moral restrictions, and behaving in deliberately shocking ways, including treating sexuality with a startling frankness. "Art," said a modernist painter, "is meant to disturb."

As an experimental cultural impulse, full of astonishing energy and contradictions, surprise and scandal, modernism was loosely based on three unsettling assumptions: (1) God did not exist; (2) "reality" was not rational, orderly, or obvious; and, in the aftermath of the Great War, (3) social progress could no longer be taken for granted. These modernist premises challenged writers, painters, musicians, dancers, and architects to risk poverty and humiliation by rudely rebelling against good taste, old-fashioned morals, and old-time religion. In its simplest sense, modernism was a disrespectful war of new values against old ones. Experimental poet Ezra Pound provided the slogan for modernism: "Make It New!"

Like many previous cultural movements, modernism also involved a new way of *seeing* the world by a new intellectual and cultural elite determined to capture and express the hidden realm of imagination and dreams. Doing so, however, often made their experimental writing, art, music, and dance vague and obscure, famously difficult to understand, interpret, or explain. "The pure modernist is merely a snob," explained a British writer. For many modernists, being misunderstood by the general public was a badge of honor. The American experimentalist writer Gertrude Stein, for example, declared that a novel "which tells about what happens is of no interest." Instead of depicting "real" life or telling recognizable stories, she was interested in playing with language. Words, not people, are the characters in her writings.

Much about modernism provoked, perplexed, and upset people. Until the twentieth century, most writers and artists had taken for granted an accessible "real" world that could be readily observed, scientifically explained, and accurately represented in words or paint or even music. The young generation of modernists, however, applied Einstein's ideas about relativity to a world in which "reality" no longer had an objective or recognizable basis. They agreed wholeheartedly with Freud that reality was something deeply personal and even unrecognizable by others, something to be imagined and expressed by one's innermost being rather than observed in and reproduced from the visible world. Walter Pach, an early

Russian Ballet **(1916)** Jewish American artist Max Weber's painting is a modernist take on a traditional subject. Splicing the scene of the performance into planes of jarring colors, this painting exemplifies the impact of psychoanalysis and the theory of relativity on the arts.

American champion of modern art, explained that modernism resulted from the discovery by Freud and others of "the role played by the unconscious in our lives."

For modernists such as the Spanish painter Pablo Picasso and the Irish writer James Joyce, then, their work required an unpredictable journey into the realm of individual fantasy and dreams, exploring and expressing the personal, the unknown, the primitive, the abstract. Paul Cezanne, one of the earliest French modernists, insisted that a painting "should represent nothing but color." American artist Marsden Hartley reported from Paris that his reading of Freud and other "new psychologists" had led him to quit painting objects from "real life" and instead paint "intuitive abstractions." In the early twentieth-century art world, modernists discarded literal representation of recognizable subjects in favor of vibrant color masses, simplified forms, or geometric shapes.

The Armory Show

The crusade to bring European-inspired modernism to the United States reached a climax in the Armory Show of 1913, the most scandalous event in the history of American art. Mabel Dodge, one of the organizers, wrote that the exhibition would cause "a riot and revolution and things will never be the same afterwards."

To house the 1,200 modernist works of art collected from more than 300 painters and sculptors in America and Europe, the two dozen young painters who organized the show leased the vast 69th Regiment Armory

Modernism and art: The Armory Show of 1913

in New York City. The Armory Show, officially known as the International Exhibition of Modern Art, opened on February 17, 1913. As Dodge had predicted, it created an immediate sensation. For many, modern art became the thing that they loved to hate. Modernism, growled a prominent art critic, "is nothing else than the total destruction of the art of painting." The *New York Times* warned visitors who shared the "old belief in reality" that they would enter "a stark region of abstractions" at the "lunatic asylum" show that was "hideous to our unaccustomed eyes." The experimentalist ("*avant-garde*") artists whose works were on display (including paintings by Vincent Van Gogh, Paul Gaugin, and Henri Matisse as well as Cezanne and Picasso) were "in love with science but not with objective reality," the *Times* critic complained, adding that they had produced paintings "revolting in their inhumanity." Former president Theodore Roosevelt dismissed the show as "repellent from every standpoint"—an indication of the gap separating political progressivism from artistic modernism.

Yet the Armory Show also generated excitement. "A new world has arisen before our eyes," announced an American art magazine. "To miss modern art," a critic stressed, "is to miss one of the few thrills that life holds." From New York, the show went on to Chicago and Boston, where it aroused similarly strong responses and attracted comparable crowds. A quarter million people viewed the exhibition in the three cities.

After the Avmovy Show, modern art became one of the nation's favorite topics of debate. Many adjusted to the shock of modernism and found a new faith in the disturbing powers of art. "America in its newness," predicted Walt Kuhn, a painter who helped organize the exhibition, "is destined to become the coming center" of modernism. Indeed, the Museum of Modern Art, founded in New York City in 1929, came to house the world's most celebrated collection of avant-garde paintings and sculpture.

The "Lost Generation"

Modernism and literature: The Lost Generation

In addition to modernism, the arts and literature of the twenties were also greatly influenced by the horrors of the Great War. F. Scott Fitzgerald wrote in *This Side of Paradise* that the younger generation of Americans, the "sad young men" who had fought in Europe to "make the world safe for democracy," had "grown up to find all Gods dead, all wars fought, all faiths in man shaken." Cynicism had displaced idealism in the wake of the war's horrific senselessness. As Fitzgerald asserted, "There's only one lesson to be learned from life anyway.... That there's no lesson to be learned from life." Frederic Henry, a character in Ernest Hemingway's novel *A Farewell to Arms* (1929), declares that "abstract words such as *glory, honor, courage* . . . were obscene" in the context of the war's colossal casualties.

Fitzgerald, Hemingway, and other self-conscious young modernists of the era came to be labeled the Lost Generation—those who had lost faith in the values and institutions of Western civilization and were frantically looking for new gods to worship. It was Gertrude Stein who in 1921 told

Hemingway that he and his friends who had served in the war were "a lost generation." When Hemingway objected, she held her ground. "You are [lost]. You have no respect for anything. You drink yourselves to death."

In his first novel, *The Sun Also Rises* (1926), Hemingway used the phrase "lost generation" as the book's opening quotation. The novel centers on Jake Barnes, a young American journalist castrated by a war injury. His despairing impotence leads him to wander the cafes and nightclubs of postwar Europe with his unhappy friends, who acknowledge that they are all wounded and sterile in their own way: they have lost their innocence, their illusions, and their motivation to do anything with their lives.

Fitzgerald, the earliest chronicler of the "lost generation," blazed up brilliantly and then quickly flickered out like many of the sad young characters in his novels. He wrote about self-indulgent and self-destructive people like him who drank and partied too much before zooming around in their sleek cars. In Fitzgerald's fiction, automobiles function not only as stylish symbols of wealth and power and freedom but also as modern engines of death and destruction. A friend and fellow writer called Fitzgerald "our darling, our genius, our fool." What gave depth to the best of his work was what a character in *The Great Gatsby* (1925), his finest novel, called "a sense of the fundamental decencies" amid all the surface gaiety—and almost always a sense of impending doom in a world that had lost its meaning through the disorienting discoveries of modern science and the horrors of world war.

The Reactionary Twenties

CORE **OBJECTIVE**

4. Identify important examples of reactionary conservatism in the decade, and analyze their impact on government policies.

The self-indulgent excesses of the "lost generation" made little sense to the vast majority of Americans during the twenties, many of whom aggressively defended established values, old certainties, and the comfort of past routines. The reactionary conservatism of the twenties fed on the energies provided by militant traditional Protestantism and a revival of **nativism**.

Nativism

The Red Scare of 1919 and a renewal of the large-scale immigration that had been cut off during the war helped generate a renewed surge of anti-immigrant hysteria. From June 1920 to June 1921, more than 800,000 people immigrated to the United States, 65 percent of them from southern and eastern Europe. In the early 1920s, more than half of the white men and a third of the white women working in mines, mills, and factories were European immigrants, some of whom had brought with them to America a passion for socialism or anarchism. The foreign connections of so many political radicals triggered efforts to close the door to immigrants. Many nativists also tried to stir up hatred of immigrants already in the United States and of their "un-American" religions and ideas.

nativism Reactionary conservative movement characterized by heightened nationalism, anti-immigrant sentiment, and laws setting stricter regulations on immigration.

The Sacco and Vanzetti case and new immigration limits

Sacco and Vanzetti

The most celebrated criminal case of the 1920s reinforced the connection between European immigrants and political radicalism. On May 5, 1920, two Italian immigrants who described themselves as revolutionary anarchists eager to topple the American government, shoemaker Nicola Sacco and fish peddler Bartolomeo Vanzetti, were arrested outside Boston, Massachusetts. They were charged with stealing $16,000 from a shoe factory payroll and killing the paymaster and a guard. Both men were armed with loaded pistols when arrested, both lied to police about their activities, and both were identified by eyewitnesses. But the stolen money was never found.

The **Sacco and Vanzetti case** occurred at the height of Italian immigration to the United States and against the backdrop of numerous terror attacks by anarchists, some of which Sacco and Vanzetti had participated in. Such a charged atmosphere ensured that their 1921 trial would become a huge public spectacle. The presiding judge was openly biased, referring to the defendants as "anarchist bastards." Sacco and Vanzetti were convicted and sentenced to death: their appeals lasted seven years before they were executed on August 23, 1927, still claiming their innocence. To millions around the world, Sacco and Vanzetti had become martyrs, victims of American injustice. The case remains passionately disputed today.

Immigration Restriction

Concerns about an invasion of foreign radicals led Congress to pass the Emergency Immigration Act of 1921, which restricted immigration from each European country each year to 3 percent of the total number of that nationality represented in the 1910 census. The **Immigration Act of 1924** reduced the number to 2 percent and changed the standard to the 1890 census, which had included fewer "new" immigrants from southern and eastern Europe. The law also set a permanent overall limitation, effective in 1929, of slightly over 150,000 new arrivals per year. The purpose of the new quotas was clear: to favor immigrants from northern and western Europe and reduce those from southern and eastern Europe. A Kansas congressman expressed the prejudices felt by many rural American Protestants: "On the one side is beer, bolshevism, unassimilating settlements and perhaps many flags—on the other side is constitutional government; one flag, stars and stripes."

The new immigration laws excluded anyone from Japan or China. On the other hand, the Immigration Act of 1924 left the gate open to new arrivals from countries in the Western Hemisphere, so that an unintended result of it was a substantial increase in the Hispanic Catholic population of the United States. People of Latin American descent (chiefly Mexicans, Puerto Ricans, and Cubans) became the fastest-growing ethnic minority in the country.

Sacco and Vanzetti case (1921) Trial of two Italian immigrants that occurred at the height of Italian immigration and against the backdrop of numerous terror attacks by anarchists; despite a lack of clear evidence, the two defendants, both self-professed anarchists, were convicted of murder and were executed.

Immigration Act of 1924 Federal legislation intended to favor northern and western European immigrants over those from southern and eastern Europe by restricting the number of immigrants from any one European country to 2 percent of the total number of immigrants per year, with an overall limit of slightly over 150,000 new arrivals per year.

The New Klan

The most violent of the reactionary movements during the twenties were the members of a revived Ku Klux Klan, the infamous post–Civil War group of anti-black racists that had recreated itself in 1915. The old Klan had died out in the 1870s once white Democrats regained control of the former Confederate states after Reconstruction. No longer simply a southern group intent on terrorizing African Americans, the new Klan was a nation-wide organization devoted to "100 percent Americanism"; only "natives"—white Protestants born in the United States—could be members.

With its secret signs and codes, weird rituals, and its costumes featuring white sheets and spooky hats, the Klan called for strict personal morality, opposed bootleg liquor, and preached hatred against not only African Americans but Roman Catholics, Jews, immigrants, Communists, atheists, prostitutes, and adulterers. The United States was no melting pot, shouted Imperial Wizard William J. Simmons, a traveling salesman turned Methodist preacher: "It is a garbage can! . . . When the hordes of aliens walk to the ballot box and their votes outnumber yours, then that alien horde has got you by the throat." The new Klan included a women's auxiliary group called the Kemellia, and whole families attended Klan gatherings, "klasping" hands while listening to inflammatory speeches, watching fireworks, and burning crosses.

The reborn Klan, headquartered in Atlanta and calling itself the "Invisible Empire," grew rapidly in cities and small towns across the nation. During the twenties, 40 percent of members were in three Midwestern states (Illinois, Indiana, and Ohio) and Connecticut had more Klan members than Mississippi. Recruiters, called Kleagles, were told to "play upon whatever prejudices were most acute in a particular area." In Texas, the Klan fed on prejudice against Mexicans. In California, it focused on Japanese

A revived Ku Klux Klan

Ku Klux Klan rally In 1925 the KKK held an expansive march down Pennsylvania Avenue in Washington, D.C.

Americans, and in New York, the enemy was primarily Jews and Catholics. Most Klan members were small farmers, sharecroppers, or wage workers, but the organization also attracted doctors, lawyers, accountants, business leaders, teachers, and even politicians. As a prominent southern journalist observed, the new Klan was "anti-Negro, anti-alien, anti-red, anti-Catholic, anti-Jew, anti-Darwin, anti-Modern, anti-Liberal; Fundamentalist, vastly Moral, militantly Protestant." African Americans grew increasingly concerned as the ranks of the new Klan mushroomed. The Chicago *Defender*, the black newspaper with the widest circulation in the nation, urged its readers to fight back against Klansmen trying to "win what their fathers [in the Civil War] lost by fire and sword."

By 1923, the Klan had more than 4 million members, including judges, mayors, sheriffs, state legislators, six governors, and three U.S. senators. The Grand Dragon of Indiana, a con man named David C. Stephenson, grew so influential in electing local and state officials (the "kluxing" of America, as he called it) that he boasted "I am the law in Indiana!" Klan-endorsed candidates won the Indiana governorship and controlled the state legislature. At the 1924 Republican State Convention, Stephenson patrolled the aisles with a pistol and later confessed that he "purchased the county and state officials." Stephenson, who had grown wealthy by skimming from the dues he collected from Klan members as well as selling robes and hoods, planned to run for president of the United States.

But the Klan's influence, both in Indiana and nationwide, crumbled after Stephenson was sentenced to life in prison in 1925 for kidnapping and raping a twenty-eight-year-old woman who then committed suicide. At the same time, several states passed anti-Klan laws and others banned the wearing of masks. By 1930, nationwide membership had dwindled to 100,000, mostly southerners. Yet the impulse underlying the Klan lived on, fed by deep-seated fears and hatreds that have yet to disappear.

Fundamentalism

While the Klan saw a threat mainly in the "alien menace," many defenders of "old-time religion" felt threatened by ideas circulating in "progressive" Protestant churches, especially the idea that the Bible should be studied in the light of modern scholarship (the "higher criticism") or that it should accommodate Darwinian theories of biological evolution. In response to such "modern" notions, conservative Protestants embraced a militant new fundamentalism, which was distinguished less by a shared faith than by a posture of hostility toward "liberal" beliefs and its insistence on the literal truth of the Bible.

| Fundamentalist hostility toward Darwinism: The Scopes trial |

Among national leaders, only the "Great Commoner," William Jennings Bryan, the former congressman, secretary of state, and three-time presidential candidate, had the support, prestige, and eloquence to transform fundamentalism into a popular crusade. Bryan remained a firm believer in the literal truth of the Bible, from the snake forced to spend eternity on its belly for tempting Eve to the looming Apocalypse predicted in the Book of Revelation. In 1921, Bryan backed new state laws banning the teaching of evolution in public schools. He passionately denounced Charles Darwin's theory of evolution, which suggested that human beings over millions of years had evolved from monkeys and apes. Anti-evolution bills were introduced in numerous state legislatures, but the only victories came in the South. Governor Miriam "Ma" Ferguson of Texas outlawed school textbooks that included sections on Darwinism. "I am a Christian mother," she declared, "and I am not going to let that kind of rot go into Texas schoolbooks."

The dramatic climax of the fundamentalist war on Darwinism came in Tennessee, where in 1925 the legislature outlawed the teaching of evolution in public schools and colleges. In the tiny mining town of Dayton, in eastern Tennessee, civic leaders eager for publicity persuaded John T. Scopes, a twenty-four-year-old high-school science teacher and part-time football coach, to become a test case against the new law. Scopes used a textbook that taught Darwinian evolution, and he was duly arrested for doing so. The town boosters succeeded beyond their wildest hopes: the **Scopes Trial** received worldwide publicity—but it was not flattering to Dayton.

Before the start of the twelve-day "monkey trial" on July 10, 1925, the streets of Dayton swarmed with evangelists, atheists, hot-dog and soda-pop peddlers, and hundreds of newspaper and radio reporters. A man tattooed with Bible verses preached on a street corner while a monkey was paraded about town.

The stars of the show pitting science against fundamentalism were both national celebrities: Bryan, who had offered his services to the prosecution, and Clarence Darrow, the nation's most famous trial lawyer, a tireless defender of hopeless causes who championed the rights of the working class, who had volunteered to defend Scopes and evolution.

Bryan insisted that the trial was not about Scopes but about a state's right to determine what was taught in the public schools, and he announced that the "contest between evolution and Christianity is a duel to the death." Darrow countered: "Scopes is not on trial. Civilization is on trial." His goal, Darrow thundered, was to prevent "bigots and ignoramuses from controlling the education of the United States" by proving that America was "founded on liberty and not on narrow, mean, intolerable and brainless prejudice of soulless religio-maniacs."

On July 20, the defense called Bryan as an "expert" witness on biblical interpretation. Under Darrow's aggressive cross-examination, Bryan repeatedly revealed his ignorance of biblical history and scholarship and gradually conceded that he had never worried that many of the Bible's stories conflicted with common sense and basic scientific truths. At one point, he claimed that Darrow was insulting Christians. Darrow, his thumbs clasping his colorful suspenders, shot back: "You insult every man of science and learning in the world because he does not believe in your fool religion." At one point, Darrow and Bryan, their patience exhausted in the broiling summer heat, lunged at each other, prompting the judge to adjourn court.

Scopes Trial (1925) Highly publicized trial of a high school teacher in Tennessee for violating a state law that prohibited the teaching of evolution; the trial was seen as the climax of the fundamentalist war on Darwinism.

Monkey trial In this snapshot of the courtroom, Scopes (*far left*) clasps his face in his hands and listens to his attorney (*second from right*). Darrow (*far right*), too, listens on, visibly affected by the sweltering weather.

As the trial ended, the judge ruled that the only issue before the jury was whether John T. Scopes had taught evolution, and no one had denied that he had done so. Eager to get on with their lives and get the peach harvest in, the jurors did not even sit down before deciding that Scopes was guilty. But the Tennessee Supreme Court, while upholding the anti-evolution law, waived Scopes's $100 fine on a technicality. Both sides claimed victory.

Five days after the trial ended, Bryan died of a heart condition aggravated by heat and fatigue. Scopes left Dayton to study geology at the University of Chicago; he became a petroleum engineer. Meanwhile, the Scopes Trial only sharpened the national debate between fundamentalism and evolution. The debate continues today.

Prohibition

Challenges and side effects of banning booze

William Jennings Bryan died knowing that one of his other crusades had succeeded: alcoholic beverages had been outlawed nationwide. The movement to prohibit beer, wine, and liquor forged an unusual alliance between rural and small-town Protestants and urban political progressives— between believers in "old-time religion," who considered drinking sinful, and social reformers, mostly women, who were convinced that **Prohibition** would reduce prostitution, spousal abuse, and other alcohol-related violence. What connected the two groups to each other and to nativist movements were the ethnic and social prejudices that many members shared. The head of the Anti-Saloon League, for example, declared that

Prohibition (1920–1933)
National ban on the manufacture and sale of alcohol, though the law was widely violated and proved too difficult to enforce effectively.

German Americans "eat like gluttons and drink like swine." For many anti-alcohol crusaders, in fact, the primary goal of Prohibition seemed to be policing the behavior of the foreign-born, the working class, and the poor.

During the Great War, both houses of Congress had finally responded to the efforts of the Anti-Saloon League and the Women's Christian Temperance Union. The wartime need to use grain for food rather than for making booze, combined with a grassroots backlash against beer brewers because of their German background, transformed the cause of Prohibition into a virtual test of American patriotism. On December 18, 1917, Congress sent to the states the Eighteenth Amendment. Ratified on January 16, 1919, it banned "the manufacture, sale, and transportation of intoxicating liquors," effective one year later.

Prohibition was thus the law—but it was not widely followed. As the most ambitious social reform ever attempted in the United States, it proved to be a colossal and costly failure. It was too sweeping for the government to enforce and too frustrating for most Americans to respect, and it had many consequences not widely foreseen. The loss of liquor taxes cost the federal government 10 percent of its annual revenue. The closing of breweries, distilleries, and saloons eliminated thousands of jobs. Even more troubling were the huge number of Americans who got into the habit of regular law-breaking and the huge boost that Prohibition during the twenties gave to police corruption and to organized crime.

The Volstead Act (1919), which outlined the rules and regulations needed to enforce the Eighteenth Amendment, had so many loopholes that it virtually guaranteed failure. For example, individuals and organizations were allowed to keep and use any liquor owned on January 16, 1919. Not surprisingly, people stocked up before the law took effect. The Yale Club in Manhattan stored enough liquor to supply itself for the entire thirteen years that Prohibition was enforced.

An even greater weakness of Prohibition was that Congress never supplied adequate funding to enforce it. In 1920, the United States had only 1,520 federal agents in the Prohibition Bureau. Given

All fair in drink and war Torpedoes filled with malt whiskey were discovered in the New York harbor in 1926, an elaborate attempt by bootleggers to smuggle alcohol during Prohibition. Each "torpedo" had an air compartment so it could be floated to shore.

the public thirst for alcohol and the profits to be made in making and selling it illegally, called "bootlegging," it would have taken armies of agents to police the nation. Even so, more than half a million people were jailed for violating

Cultural Clash in the 1920s

After the Great War, patterns of where and how Americans lived, how they entertained themselves, and how they saw their position in society changed dramatically. In many cases, these trends had begun before the war, but they exploded afterward, challenging traditional values and assumptions. During the 1920s, many Americans experimented with new kinds of freedom, new sources of information, and new forms of expression. But these new cultural patterns often clashed with older ones, provoking strong reactions from millions of Americans. The nation saw heated and sometimes violent debates emerge about what it meant to be American and "modern" and about what place racial and ethnic minorities and women should occupy within American society. Many aspects of this debate continued throughout the twentieth century and still have strong echoes today. After you read through the chart below of new developments in American culture after the Great War and the reactions to them, answer the Questions for Analysis that follow.

NEW CULTURAL DEVELOPMENTS AFTER WORLD WAR I

REACTIONS TO THESE CULTURAL DEVELOPMENTS

"The New Immigrants"
Until the 1950s, the immigration trends from the early twentieth century continued. Of the 800,000 immigrants who entered the country in 1920 and 1921, two thirds were from eastern and southern Europe. Two thirds of white workers in mines, mills, and factories were immigrants.

Nativism
Nativists associated the New Immigrants with radical ideas such as socialism, communism, and anarchism. Many political radicals did have foreign connections or came from regions in Europe where these ideas were popular. The Sacco and Vanzetti case reinforced these associations among millions of Americans. Congress severely reduced immigration from eastern and southern Europe through the Immigration Act of 1924.

The Great Migration and "the New Negro"
The migration of African Americans from the rural South to the urban North continued after the war. By 1930, roughly one million had migrated. In northern cities, African Americans developed a sense of common identity, growing political and economic power, and distinctive cultural expression, resulting in the coining of the phrase "the New Negro." Assertions of African American pride and influence on the broader society were seen in the Harlem Renaissance; the spreading popularity of jazz music beyond African American communities; the popularity of the Garveyism movement, which preached black nationalism and separatism; and the activism of the NAACP, which began organizing legal challenges to racial discrimination across the country.

The Klan
The Klan became a national organization that defined American identity as white and Protestant, anti-modern and anti-radical. The group's renewed popularity extended beyond the South. Membership soared in small towns and cities in the North, particularly the Midwest, including poorly educated farmers and middle-class professionals. The Klan continued its reign of terror against African Americans, and became highly influential in politics, electing numerous candidates to office.

New Technologies and the Growth of a Consumer Economy

During the 1920s, the mass production and consumption of automobiles, radios, motion pictures, and other new technologies produced unprecedented prosperity for much of the nation. Mass media and advertising created the world's first consumer culture, as millions of Americans indulged themselves with spectator sports, department-store shopping on installment plans, and media coverage of celebrities in the entertainment industry and elsewhere.

Modernism

Modernists were intellectuals, artists, and academics who called into question traditional notions of reality and human nature. They based their ideas and activities on new scientific discoveries and radical forms of artistic expression that had first appeared in 1900s–1910s.

Fundamentalists

Fundamentalists opposed applying modern scholarship to Biblical studies because they believed that every word in the Bible was literally true. In particular, they waged a campaign against biological theories of evolution and backed state laws that would ban the teaching of evolution in public schools. These efforts succeeded only in a few southern states. The movement lost its momentum after the nationwide coverage of the 1925 Scopes Trial that was largely unfavorable to the fundamentalists.

Flappers, or "the New Women"

Many women rebelled against traditional ideas about female sexuality and appropriate female behavior. They abandoned long skirts and corsets for loose-fitting clothing that showed their legs. They also cut their hair short, drank and smoked in public, and acted in a more brazen way than before the war. They were more likely to seek personal fulfillment outside marriage and motherhood.

Prohibition

By 1920, Prohibition—one of the great crusades of the Progressive Era—had become the law of the land. In banning the sale, manufacture, and transportation of almost all intoxicating beverages, the law united many social reformers who viewed alcohol as a major source of spousal abuse, crime, and prostitution with Protestants who considered its consumption immoral. The law proved tough to enforce, however, as Congress never provided enough funds to employ enough federal agents to police the nation. Prohibition was widely violated as millions of Americans found ways to consume alcohol, often provided to them through organized crime, which many Americans associated with new immigrant communities.

QUESTIONS FOR ANALYSIS

1. How did urbanization, new technologies, and the growth of a consumer-centered economy challenge older American values and ways of life? Why might some Americans have been disturbed by these changes?

2. How did the "new immigrants," "New Negro," "New Women," and modern artists and intellectuals challenge traditional assumptions about the American social order? What groups of Americans might have been most disturbed by these changes, and why?

3. How were nativism, the Klan, fundamentalism, and Prohibition related? What did they have in common, in terms of their causes, supporters, public expressions, and effects? What differences were there between them?

the Volstead Act. Many of the activities associated with the Roaring Twenties were fueled by bootleg liquor supplied by organized crime and sold in illegal saloons called "speakeasies," which were often ignored by local policemen corrupted by bribes. New York City's police commissioner estimated that there were 32,000 speakeasies in the city in 1929, compared to 15,000 saloons in 1919. President Harding regularly drank and served bootleg liquor in the White House, explaining that he was "unable to see this as a great moral issue," and the largest bootlegger in Washington, D.C., reported that "a majority of both houses" of Congress were regular customers. Although total national alcohol consumption did decrease, in many parts of the nation drinking actually *increased* during Prohibition. As the popular humorist Will Rogers quipped, "Prohibition is better than no liquor at all."

Prohibition supplied organized crime with a source of enormous new income. The most celebrated Prohibition-era gangster was "Scarface" Al Capone. In 1927, his Chicago-based bootlegging, prostitution, and gambling empire involved 700 gangsters and brought in $60 million. Capone insisted that he was merely giving the public the goods and services it demanded: "They say I violate the Prohibition law. Who doesn't?" He neglected to add that he had also beaten to death several police officers and ordered the execution of dozens of rival criminals. Law-enforcement officials led by FBI agent Eliot Ness began to smash Capone's bootlegging operations in 1929, but the charges finally pinned on him were for tax evasion. Tried in 1931, Capone was sentenced to eleven years in prison.

Republican Resurgence

CORE **OBJECTIVE**

5. Trace the Republican party's dominance of the federal government during the twenties, and analyze the extent to which its policies were a rejection of progressivism.

In national politics, the small-town backlash against modern city life—whether represented by immigrants plotting revolution, liberal churches accepting evolution, or jazzed-up flappers swilling cocktails—was mirrored by a Republican resurgence determined to reverse the progressivism of Theodore Roosevelt and Woodrow Wilson. By 1920, the progressive political coalition that had reelected Wilson in 1916 had fragmented. The growing middle class had become preoccupied less with reform than with enjoying the general prosperity based on mass production and consumption. Progressivism did not simply disappear, of course. The impulse for honest, efficient government and regulation of business remained strong, especially at the state and local levels, where movements for better roads, education, public health, and social-welfare programs gained momentum. At the national level, however, Republican conservatives returned to power.

Harding and "Normalcy"

After the Great War, most Americans had grown weary of Wilson's crusading idealism and were suspicious of any leader who promoted sweeping reforms. Wilson himself recognized the shifting public mood. "It is only once in a generation," he remarked, "that a people can be lifted above material things. That is why conservative government is in the saddle two-thirds of the time."

The Election of 1920

In 1920, Republican party leaders, unable to settle on a nationally prominent figure as their presidential candidate, turned in the end to Warren G. Harding, an easy-going, silver-haired senator from Ohio. Another Republican senator explained that Harding was selected not for his abilities or experience (which were not extensive) but because he was available and looked presidential. Harding, he said, was "the best of the second–raters."

Harding set the conservative tone of his campaign when he told a Boston audience that it was time to end Wilsonian progressivism: "America's present need is not heroics, but healing; not nostrums, but normalcy; not revolution, but restoration; not agitation, but adjustment; not surgery, but serenity; not the dramatic, but the dispassionate." In contrast to Wilson's grandiose internationalism, Harding promised to "safeguard America first . . . to exalt America first, to live for and revere America first."

Harding's vanilla promise of a **"return to normalcy"** reflected his unexceptional background and personality. A farmer's son and newspaper editor, he described himself as "just a plain fellow" who was "old-fashioned and even reactionary in matters of faith and morals." In his personal life, however, Harding secretly drank liquor in the White House, smoked and chewed tobacco, loved twice-weekly poker games with his buddies in the White House library, and had numerous extramarital affairs and even fathered children with women other than his austere wife, Florence, whom he called "the Duchess." One of the women tried to blackmail him, demanding money for her silence—which she received. The public, however, was unaware of Harding's escapades. Voters saw him as a handsome, charming politician who looked the part of a leader yet recognized his own limitations. "I am not fit for this office and should never have been here," he once admitted. "I cannot hope to be one of the great presidents, but perhaps I may be remembered as one of the best loved."

> Harding's victorious "return to normalcy"

The Democrats, meanwhile, had to contend with the breakup of the Wilsonian coalition and the conservative postwar mood. At the 1920 Democratic convention, another Ohioan, James Cox, a former newspaper publisher and former governor of the state, won the nomination of his increasingly divided party on the forty-fourth ballot. For vice president, the convention chose New Yorker Franklin Delano Roosevelt, only thirty-eight years old, who as assistant secretary of the navy occupied the same position his Republican cousin Theodore Roosevelt had once held.

The country voted overwhelmingly for Harding's promised "return to normalcy." Harding polled 16 million votes to 9 million for Cox, who won no state outside the South. The Republican majority in both houses of Congress increased. Franklin Roosevelt predicted that his party could not hope to return to national power until the Republicans led the nation "into a serious period of depression and unemployment." He was right.

"return to normalcy"
Campaign promise of Republican presidential candidate Warren G. Harding in 1920, meant to contrast with Woodrow Wilson's progressivism and internationalism.

Harding's Associates and Personality

Harding in office had much in common with Ulysses S. Grant. His cabinet, like Grant's, mixed some of the "best minds" in the party, whom he had promised to seek out, with some of its worst characters. Charles Evans Hughes, like Grant's Hamilton Fish, became a distinguished secretary of state. Herbert Hoover in the Commerce Department, Andrew W. Mellon in the Treasury Department, and Henry C. Wallace in the Agriculture Department were dedicated public servants. Other cabinet members and Harding appointees, however, were not so conscientious. The secretary of the interior landed in prison, and the attorney general narrowly escaped serving time.

Harding loved hobnobbing and "bloviating" (a favorite word of his, meaning "speaking in a pompous, long-winded way") at public events and joking around with his political buddies behind the scenes. As president, however, he was in over his head and knew it. "I don't think I'm big enough for the Presidency," he confided to a friend. He much preferred to relax with the "Ohio gang," his closest friends, who shared his taste for whiskey, poker, and women. Still, Harding and his social friends did have a political agenda.

Andrew Mellon and the Economy

The Harding administration inherited a slumping economy still burdened by high wartime taxes and a national debt that had ballooned from $1 billion in 1914 to $27 billion in 1920 because of the expenses associated with the war. Unemployment was at nearly 12 percent. To address these challenges, the new president established a pro-business tone, vetoing a bill to provide war veterans with a cash bonus, arguing that it would increase the federal budget deficit.

> The Mellon Plan: Economic growth through low taxes and spending and high tariffs

To generate economic growth, Secretary of the Treasury Andrew Mellon, the third richest man in the world behind John D. Rockefeller and Henry Ford, developed a plan to reduce federal spending and lower tax rates. Mellon persuaded Congress to pass the landmark Budget and Accounting Act of 1921, which created a Bureau of the Budget to streamline the process of preparing an annual federal budget. The bill also created a General Accounting Office to audit spending by federal agencies. This act fulfilled a long-held progressive desire to bring greater efficiency and nonpartisanship to the budget preparation process.

The brilliant but cold Mellon (his son described him as a "thin-voiced, thin-bodied, shy and uncommunicative man") also proposed a series of tax reductions. By 1918, the tax rate on the highest income bracket had risen to 73 percent because of the extraordinary expense of the war. Mellon believed that such high rates were pushing wealthy Americans to avoid paying taxes by investing their money in foreign countries or in tax-free government bonds. Throughout the twenties, with the support of Congress and

Presidents Harding and Coolidge, Mellon's policies systematically reduced tax rates while increasing tax revenues. The top tax rate was cut from 73 percent in 1921 to 24 percent in 1929. Rates for the people with the lowest annual incomes were also cut substantially, helping the working poor.

The Mellon Plan worked. By 1926, 65 percent of federal income tax revenue came from people with incomes of $300,000 or more. In 1921, less than 20 percent had come from this group. During this same period, the overall income tax burden on those with incomes of less than $10,000 dropped from $155 million to $32.5 million. By 1929, barely 2 percent of American workers had to pay any income tax at all.

At the same time, Mellon helped Harding reduce the federal budget. Government expenditures fell, as did the national debt, and the economy soared. Unemployment plummeted to 2.4 percent in 1923. Mellon's admirers tagged him the greatest secretary of the Treasury since Alexander Hamilton in the late eighteenth century. In addition to tax cuts, Mellon, who had earlier built huge empires in the steel, oil, shipbuilding, coal, banking, and aluminum industries, promoted the long-standing Republican policy of high tariffs on imported goods. The Fordney-McCumber Tariff of 1922 increased rates on chemical and metal products to help prevent the revival of German corporations that had dominated those industries before the Great War. To please commercial farmers, who historically had benefited little from tariffs, the new act further extended duties on agricultural imports.

Reduced Regulation and Racial Progressivism

The Republican economic program of the 1920s also featured reduced regulation of corporations. Neither Harding nor his successor, Calvin Coolidge, could dismantle the federal regulatory agencies created during the Progressive Era, but they named as commissioners of those agencies people who generally promoted regulation "friendly" to business interests. Progressive Republican senator George W. Norris characterized Harding's appointments as "the nullification of federal law by a process of boring from within." His conservative colleague Henry Cabot Lodge agreed, boasting that "we have torn up Wilsonism by the roots."

In addition, Harding's four Supreme Court appointments were all conservatives, including Chief Justice William Howard Taft, the former president, who announced that he had been "appointed to reverse a few decisions." During the 1920s, the Taft court struck down a federal child-labor law and a minimum-wage law for women and issued numerous injunctions against striking unions as well as rulings limiting the powers of federal regulatory agencies.

In one area, however, Harding proved to be more progressive than Woodrow Wilson. He reversed the Wilson administration's policy of excluding African Americans from federal government jobs and spoke out against the vigilante racism that had flared up across the country during

> Commission and court appointments friendly to business; policies and speeches opposed to racism

and after the war. In his first speech to Congress in 1921, Harding insisted that the nation deal with the "race question." He attacked the Ku Klux Klan for fomenting "hatred and prejudice and violence" and urged Congress "to wipe the stain of barbaric lynching from the banners of a free and orderly, representative democracy." Southern Democrats in the Senate, however, stopped an anti-lynching bill from becoming law.

Setbacks for Unions

> A corporate campaign against organized labor

Organized labor suffered under Republican rule in the 1920s. Although President Harding endorsed collective bargaining and tried to reduce the twelve-hour workday and the six-day workweek to give the working class "time for leisure and family life," he ran into stiff opposition in Congress. After the war, the Red Scare and strikes of 1919 had created fears that unions promoted radical socialism. The brief postwar depression further weakened the unions, and in 1921 business groups in Chicago designated the **open shop** to be the "American plan" of employment. Although the open shop in theory implied only an employer's right to hire anyone, whether a union member or not, in practice it meant discrimination against unionists and a refusal by companies to negotiate with unions even when most of the workers belonged to one. A labor organizer identified another reason for his movement's weakness: "The Ford car has done an awful lot of harm to the unions. . . . As long as men have enough money to buy a second-hand Ford and tires and gasoline, they'll be out on the road and paying no attention to union meetings."

To suppress unions, employers often required workers to sign "yellow-dog" contracts, which forced them to agree not to join a union. Owners also used labor spies, blacklists, and intimidation to keep their workers from organizing unions. Some employers, such as Henry Ford, tried to kill the unions with kindness by introducing programs of "industrial democracy" guided by company-sponsored unions or various schemes of "welfare capitalism," such as profit sharing, bonuses, pensions, health programs, recreational activities, and the like. All these efforts paid off. Union membership dropped from about 5 million in 1920 to 3.5 million in 1929. But the anti-union movement, led by businesses that wanted to keep wages low, helped to create a "purchasing crisis" whereby the working poor were not making enough money to buy the huge volume of goods being churned out by America's ever more productive industries.

Isolationism in Foreign Affairs

open shop Business policy of not requiring union membership as a condition of employment; such a policy, where legal, has the effect of weakening unions and diminishing workers' rights.

In addition to the Senate's rejection of American membership in the League of Nations, the postwar spirit of isolation from world affairs found other expressions: the Red Scare, the higher tariff rates on imports, and the restrictive immigration laws with which the nation all but shut the door to newcomers. George Jean Nathan, a drama critic, expressed the sentiments of many Americans when he announced that the "great problems of the world—social, political, economic and theological—do not concern me in the slightest. . . . What concerns me alone is myself, and the interests of a few close friends."

Yet the desire to stay out of foreign wars did not mean that the United States could ignore its own expanding global interests. American businesses now had worldwide connections. As a result of the Great War, the United States had become the world's chief banker, and American investments and loans enabled foreigners to purchase U.S. exports.

Probably nothing did more to heighten American isolationism—or anti-American feeling in Europe—than the complex challenge facing America's recent military allies: paying off their huge war debts to the United States. Beginning in 1917, when France and Great Britain ran out of money for military supplies, the U.S. government had advanced them massive loans, first for the war effort and then, after the war, for reconstruction projects. Most Americans, including Treasury Secretary Mellon, expected the debts to be repaid, but the Europeans thought otherwise. The British noted that after the American Revolution, the newly independent United States had refused to pay old debts to British merchants. The French likewise pointed out that they had never been repaid for helping the Americans win the Revolutionary War.

But the most difficult challenges in the 1920s were the practical problems of repayment. To get U.S. dollars to use to pay their war-related debts, European nations had to sell their goods to the United States. However, rising American tariff rates made imported European goods more expensive and less competitive with U.S. products, thus making it even harder for the Allies to repay their war-related debts. The French and British insisted that they could repay only by collecting the $33 billion in war reparations from defeated Germany, whose economy was devastated after the war by hyperinflation of consumer prices. Twice during the 1920s, the financial strain on the German economy forced American bankers to intervene with more loans so that Germany could pay its reparations to Britain and France, thereby enabling them to pay their debts to the United States.

> Isolationist foreign policy and expanding global economic interests

Attempts at Disarmament

After the Great War, many Americans decided that excessive armed forces and weaponry had been the principal causes of the terrible conflict. The best way to keep the peace, they argued, was to limit the size of armies and navies. The United States had no intention of maintaining a large army after 1920, but under the shipbuilding program begun in 1916, it had constructed a powerful navy second only to that of Great Britain. Although neither the British nor the Americans wanted a naval armaments race, both were worried about the growth of Japanese power.

To address the problem, President Harding in 1921 invited diplomats from eight nations to a conference in Washington, D.C., at which Secretary of State Charles Evans Hughes made a blockbuster proposal. The only way

> The Five-Power Treaty provides for naval disarmament

to avoid an expensive naval arms race, he declared, "is to end it now" by eliminating scores of existing warships and prohibiting the construction of new ones. It was one of the most dramatic moments in diplomatic history. In less than fifteen minutes, one journalist reported, Hughes had destroyed more warships "than all the admirals of the world have sunk in a cycle of centuries." His daring proposal was greeted by a "tornado of cheering" among the delegates.

Following Hughes's lead, delegates from the United States, Britain, Japan, France, and Italy signed the Five-Power Treaty (1922), which limited the size of their nations' navies. It was the first disarmament treaty in history. The five major powers also agreed to refrain from strengthening their military forces in the Pacific. The agreement in effect partitioned the world: U.S. naval power became supreme in the Western Hemisphere, Japanese power in the western Pacific, and British power from the North Sea to Singapore.

With these agreements in hand, Harding could boast of what seemed to be a brilliant diplomatic coup that relieved citizens of the need to pay for an enlarged navy and prevented potential conflicts in the Pacific. But the treaty set limits only on "capital" ships (battleships and aircraft carriers); the race to build cruisers, destroyers, submarines, and other smaller craft continued. Japan withdrew from the agreement in 1934, and by then the Soviet Union and Germany, which had been excluded from the conference, were building up their navies as well. Thus, twelve years after the Washington Naval Conference, the dream of naval disarmament died.

The Harding Scandals

Teapot Dome, other scandals, and Harding's death and historical reputation

Republican conservatives such as Henry Cabot Lodge, Andrew W. Mellon, Calvin Coolidge, and Herbert Hoover operated out of a philosophical conviction that was intended to benefit the nation. Members of Harding's Ohio gang, however, used their White House connections to line their own pockets. Early in 1923, for example, Harding learned that the head of the Veterans Bureau was systematically looting medical and hospital supplies. A few weeks later, the legal adviser to the bureau committed suicide. Not long afterward, a close friend of Attorney General Harry M. Daugherty, who had set up an office in the Justice Department from which he illegally sold paroles, pardons, and judgeships, was found shot dead in a hotel room after he had threatened to "quit the racket." Finally, the attorney general himself was implicated in the fraudulent handling of German assets seized after the war. These were but the most visible of the many scandals that touched federal agencies under Harding.

One major scandal rose above all, however. The "**Teapot Dome**," like "Watergate" fifty years later, would become the catchphrase for the climate of corruption surrounding a presidential administration. The Teapot Dome was a government-owned oil field in Wyoming that had been set aside as an oil reserve to ensure a supply of fuel for warships. After Harding moved administrative control of the field from the Department of the Navy to the

Teapot Dome (1923) Harding administration scandal in which Secretary of the Interior Albert B. Fall profited from secret leasing of government oil reserves in Wyoming to private oil companies.

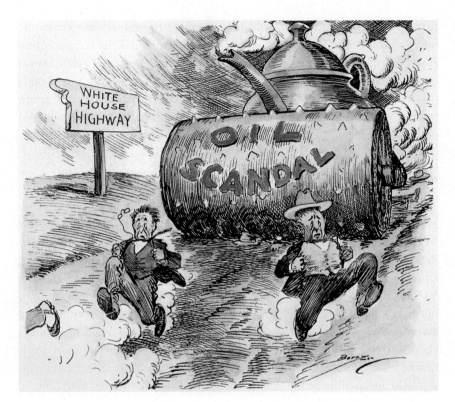

Department of the Interior, Interior Secretary Albert B. Fall, deeply in debt and eight years overdue in paying his taxes, began signing overly generous federal contracts with close friends who were executives of petroleum companies that wanted access to the field. It turned out that he had taken bribes of about $400,000 (which came in "a little black bag") from an oil tycoon. Fall was convicted of conspiracy and bribery and sentenced to a year in prison, the first former cabinet official to serve time as a result of misconduct in office.

How much Harding knew of the scandals was unclear, but he knew enough to be troubled. "My God, this is a hell of a job!" he confided to a journalist. "I have no trouble with my enemies; I can take care of my enemies all right. But my damn friends, my God-damn friends. . . . They're the ones that keep me walking the floor nights!" In 1923, Harding left on what would be his last journey, a speaking tour to the West Coast and a trip to the Alaska Territory. He suffered an attack of food poisoning in Seattle, recovered briefly, then died in a San Francisco hotel. He was fifty-seven years old.

Because of Harding's sexual misbehavior and his corrupt associates, his administration came to be viewed as one of the worst in history. Even Herbert Hoover, his loyal secretary of commerce, admitted that Harding was not "a man with either the experience or the intellectual quality that the position needed" and that he was unable to admit or resolve the "terrible corruption by his playmates." More recent assessments suggest, however, that the scandals obscured Harding's accomplishments. He led the nation out of the turmoil of the postwar years and helped create the remarkable economic boom of the 1920s. He also promoted diversity and civil rights, appointing Jews to key federal positions and becoming the first president to criticize racial segregation in a speech before a white audience in the South. No previous president had promoted women's rights as forcefully as he did. Like Hoover, though, even Harding's foremost scholarly defender admits that he lacked good judgment and "probably should never have been president."

Coolidge Conservatism

The news of Harding's death reached Vice President Calvin Coolidge when he was visiting his father in the isolated mountain village of Plymouth Notch, Vermont, his birthplace. There, at 2:47 A.M. on August 3, 1923, by the light of a kerosene lamp, Colonel John Coolidge, a farmer and merchant, administered the presidential oath of office to his son. Calvin Coolidge, born on the Fourth of July in 1872, was a throwback to an earlier era. A puritan in his personal life, he was, unlike Harding, horrified by the jazzed-up Roaring Twenties, whose rebellious social and cultural forces he could not understand. But he sincerely believed in the ideals of personal integrity and devotion to public service. He was also a virtuous evangelist for capitalism who would bring stability to the White House and prosperity to the economy.

A Modest, Upright, and Tight-Lipped Evangelist for Capitalism

Although Coolidge had won every political race he had entered, beginning in 1898, he had never loved the limelight. Shy and awkward, he was a man of famously few words—hence, his nickname, "Silent Cal." After being reelected president of the Massachusetts State Senate in 1916, he gave a four-sentence inaugural address that concluded with "above all things, be brief." Voters liked Coolidge's uprightness, his straight-talking style, and his personal humility. He was a simple, direct man of strong principles and intense patriotism who championed self-discipline and hard work.

As a Massachusetts state senator, Coolidge had often aligned himself with Republican progressives. He voted for women's suffrage, a state income tax, a minimum wage for female workers, and salary increases for public school teachers. By the time he entered the White House, however, he had abandoned most of those causes.

Coolidge was determined *not* to be an activist president. Unlike Theodore Roosevelt and Woodrow Wilson, he had no exaggerated sense of self-importance; he knew he was "not a great man." Nor did he have an ambitious program to push through Congress. "Four-fifths of our troubles," Coolidge believed, "would disappear if we would sit down and keep still." Following his own logic, he insisted on twelve hours of sleep *and* an afternoon nap. The irreverent journalist H. L. Mencken claimed that Coolidge "slept more than any other president."

Calvin Coolidge "Silent Cal" was so reticent that when he died in 1933, American humorist Dorothy Parker remarked, "How could they tell?"

Even more than Harding, Coolidge linked the nation's welfare with the success of big business. "The chief business of the American people is business," he preached. "The man who builds a factory builds a temple. The man who works there worships there." Where Harding had tried to balance the interests of labor, agriculture, and industry, Coolidge focused on promoting industrial development. He reduced federal regulations of business and, with the help of Treasury Secretary Mellon and Republican Congresses, continued to lower income tax rates.

Coolidge was also "obsessed" with reducing spending, even to the point of issuing government workers only one pencil at a time—and only after they turned in the stub of the old pencil. "I am for economy" in government spending, he stressed. "After that, I am for more economy." When a South African mayor sent the president two lion cubs as a present, Coolidge named them "Tax Reduction" and "Budget Bureau." His fiscal frugality and pro-corporate stance led the *Wall Street Journal* to rejoice: "Never before, here or anywhere else, has a government been so completely fused with business."

America also had too many laws, Coolidge insisted, and it was "much more important to kill bad bills than to pass good ones." True to his word, he vetoed fifty acts of Congress. As a journalist said, "In a great day of yes-men, Calvin Coolidge was a no-man."

> Coolidge: "The chief business of the American people is business."

The Election of 1924

A man of honesty, a good administrator who had restored the dignity of the presidency while speaking out against racial prejudice and capably managing the various Republican factions, Coolidge easily gained the party's 1924 presidential nomination. Meanwhile, the Democrats again fell to fighting among themselves, prompting humorist Will Rogers's classic statement that "I am a member of no organized political party. I am a Democrat." The party's fractiousness illustrated the deep divisions between urban and rural America during the 1920s. It took the Democrats 103 ballots to decide on a presidential candidate: John W. Davis, a corporate lawyer from West Virginia who could nearly outdo Coolidge in his conservatism.

While the Democrats bickered, rural populists and urban progressives again decided to abandon both major parties, as they had done in 1912. Reorganizing the old Progressive party, they nominated Robert M. "Fighting Bob" La Follette for president. The sixty-nine-year-old Republican Wisconsin senator (and former governor) had voted against the 1917 declaration of war against Germany. Now, in addition to the Progressives, he won the support of the Socialist party and the American Federation of Labor.

In the 1924 campaign, the voters preferred to "Keep Cool with Coolidge," who decisively swept both the popular and the electoral votes. Davis took only the solidly Democratic South, and La Follette carried only Wisconsin. The popular vote went 15.7 million for Coolidge, 8.4 million for Davis, and 4.8 million for La Follette—the largest vote ever for a third-party candidate up to that time.

> Coolidge landslide: The height of postwar conservatism

Coolidge's landslide victory represented the height of postwar political conservatism. The Democratic party was in disarray, and the Republicans were triumphant. Business executives interpreted the Republican victory as an endorsement of their leading influence on government, and Coolidge saw the economy's surging prosperity as confirmation of his aggressive support of the interests of business. In fact, the prosperity and technological achievements of the New Era did have much to do with Coolidge's victory.

The Rise of Herbert Hoover

Hoover and Republicans as champions of industrial efficiency

During the twenties, the drive for industrial efficiency, which had been a prominent theme among progressives, powered the wheels of mass production and consumption and became a cardinal belief of Republican leaders. Herbert Hoover, who served as secretary of commerce in the Harding and Coolidge cabinets, was himself a remarkable success story.

Born into an Iowa farm family in 1874, Hoover was a shy but industrious "loner" who had become a world-renowned mining engineer, oil tycoon, financial wizard, and multimillionaire before the age of forty. His meteoric success and genius for managing difficult tasks bred a self-confidence that bordered on conceit. Famously short-tempered and quick to take offense, Hoover had to have complete control of any project he managed. "I have insisted on having my own way," he admitted, and, in his twenties, he was already planning to be the president of the United States.

Hoover the "Wonder Boy"

After applying his managerial skills to the Food Administration during the Great War, Hoover served with the U.S. delegation at the Versailles peace conference. He idolized Woodrow Wilson and supported American membership in the League of Nations. A young Franklin Roosevelt, then assistant secretary of the navy, was dazzled by Hoover, the man he would eventually defeat in the presidential election of 1932. In 1920, Roosevelt said that Hoover was "certainly a wonder [boy], and I wish we could make him President of the United States."

Hoover soon disappointed Roosevelt, however, by declaring himself a Republican "progressive conservative." In a book entitled *American Individualism* (1922), Hoover promoted an "ideal of *service*" that went beyond "rugged individualism." He wanted government to encourage business leaders to forgo "cutthroat competition" and called instead for them to engage in "voluntary cooperation" by forming trade associations that would share information and promote standardization and efficiency.

As secretary of commerce during the 1920s, Hoover transformed the small Commerce Department into the government's most dynamic agency. He looked for new markets for business, created a Bureau of Aviation to promote the new airline industry, and established the Federal Radio Commission.

The 1928 Election: Hoover versus Smith

On August 2, 1927, while on vacation in the Black Hills of South Dakota, President Coolidge suddenly announced, "I do not choose to run for President in 1928." His choice surprised the nation and cleared the way for Hoover to win the 1928 Republican nomination. The party's platform took credit for the nation's longest period of sustained prosperity, the government's cost cutting, debt and tax reduction, and the high tariffs ("as vital to American agriculture as . . . to manufacturing") designed to "protect" American businesses from foreign competition.

The Democratic nomination went to four-term New York governor Alfred E. Smith, the "Happy Warrior." The two candidates presented sharply different images: Hoover, the successful businessman and bureaucratic manager from an Iowa farm, versus Smith, a professional politician from a Lower East Side neighborhood of New York City. To working-class Democrats in northern cities, Smith was a hero, the poor grandson of Irish immigrants who had worked himself up to being governor of the most populous state. His outspoken criticism of Prohibition also endeared him to the Irish, Italians, and others in the North.

> A third straight Republican presidential landslide

On the other hand, as the first Roman Catholic nominated for president by a major party, a product of big-city machine politics, and a "wet" on Prohibition (in direct opposition to his party's platform), Smith represented all that was hateful to southern and western rural Democrats—as well as most rural and small-town Republicans. A powerful Kansas newspaper editor declared that the "whole puritan civilization, which has built a sturdy, orderly nation, is threatened by Smith." The Ku Klux Klan issued a "Klarion Kall for a Krusade" against him, mailing thousands of postcards proclaiming that "Alcohol" Smith, the Catholic New Yorker, was the Antichrist. While Hoover stayed above the fray, reminding Americans of their unparalleled prosperity, Smith was forced to deal with constant criticism. He denounced his opponents for injecting "bigotry, hatred, intolerance and un-American sectarian division" into the campaign. But it did little good.

On Election Day, Hoover won in the third consecutive Republican presidential landslide, with 21 million popular votes to Smith's 15 million and an Electoral College majority of 444 to 87. Hoover even cracked the Democrats' Solid South, leaving Smith only six Deep South states plus Massachusetts and Rhode Island. Republicans kept control of both houses of Congress. The election was a clear indication that voters appreciated the prosperity generated during the Harding and Coolidge administrations. Coolidge, however, was skeptical that Hoover could sustain the good times. He quipped that the "Wonder Boy" had offered him "unsolicited advice for six years, all of it bad." Coolidge's skepticism about Hoover's political abilities would prove all too accurate, as the talented new president would soon be struck by an economic earthquake that would test all of his skills—and more.

- **A "New Era" of Consumption** During the 1920s, the American economy grew at the fastest rate in history, while consumer debt tripled. Innovations in production, advertising, and financing, combined with a jump in the use of electricity, enabled and encouraged millions of Americans to purchase automobiles, radios, and other electrical household appliances. The new *consumer culture,* valued leisure, self-expression, and self-indulgence. More and more Americans purchased national brand-name items from retail chain stores, listened to the same radio shows and watched the same movies.

- **The Jazz Age** New social and cultural movements challenged the traditional order. The carefree attitude of the 1920s, perhaps best represented by the frantic rhythms of jazz music, led writer F. Scott Fitzgerald to call the decade the *Jazz Age.* Though *flappers* emerged to challenge gender norms, the majority of women remained full-time housewives or domestic servants. As the Great Migration continued, African Americans in northern cities felt freer to speak out against racial injustice and express pride in their race. The *Harlem Renaissance* gave voice to African American literature and arts. Racial separatism and black nationalism grew popular under Marcus Garvey, while the *National Association for the Advancement of Colored People (NAACP)* made efforts to undo racism through education and legislation.

- **The Modernist Revolt** Many artists and intellectuals were attracted to *modernism*, which drew upon Einstein's theory of relativity and Freud's psychological explorations. For modernists, the world was no longer governed by reason, but rather something created and expressed through one's highly individual consciousness. To be "modern" meant to break free of tradition, to violate restrictions, and to shock and confuse the public.

- **The Reactionary Twenties** Retaliating against to these challenges to convention, various movements fought to uphold their traditional ideas of what America was and how it should remain. In reaction to a renewed surge of immigration after the Great War and the Red Scare, nativists persuaded Congress to restrict future immigration with the *Immigration Act of 1924.* A revived Ku Klux Klan gained a large membership and considerable political influence across the nation. Fundamentalist Protestants campaigned against teaching evolution in public schools, arguing instead for the literal truth of the Bible. Their efforts culminated in the 1925 *Scopes Trial.* Progressive reformers and conservative Protestants supported the nationwide *Prohibition* of alcoholic beverages that started in 1920. Union membership declined as businesses adopted new techniques like *open shop.*

- **Republican Resurgence** Disillusionment with the Great War turned the public against progressivism, and in favor of disarmament and isolationism. The Republican Party benefited from this shift in the public mood. Warren G. Harding's call for a *"return to normalcy"* brought about his landslide presidential victory in 1920. His administration followed the Mellon Plan, which succeeded in reviving the economy. The progressive goal of efficiency through better management remained a part of many Republican initiatives, such as the Budget and Accounting Act.

KEY TERMS

CHRONOLOGY

1903	Wright Brothers fly first motorized airplane
	Ford Motor Company is founded
1905	First movie house opens
1910	National Association for the Advancement of Colored People (NAACP) is founded
1913	Armory Show introduces Americans to modern art
1916	Marcus Garvey brings Universal Negro Improvement Association to New York
1920	Prohibition begins
	Warren G. Harding is elected president
1921	Sacco and Vanzetti Trial
	Washington Naval Conference and Five-Power Treaty
	Congress passes Emergency Immigration Act
1922	First radio commercial
1923	Teapot Dome scandal
1924	Congress passes Immigration Act
	Calvin Coolidge is reelected president
1925	Scopes "monkey trial"
1927	Charles A. Lindbergh Jr. makes first solo transatlantic airplane flight
	Sacco and Vanzetti are executed
1928	Herbert Hoover is elected president

INQUIZITIVE

Go to InQuizitive to see what you've learned—and learn what you've missed—with personalized feedback along the way.

***CONSTRUCTION OF A DAM* (1939), DETAIL** One of the most famous and controversial of the artists commissioned by the New Deal's Works Progress Administration was William Gropper, who painted this mural in the Department of the Interior building in Washington, D.C. Based on his observations of dam construction on the Columbia and Colorado Rivers, Gropper illustrates the triumph and brotherhood that emerged from America's grand undertakings during the Great Depression.

New Deal America

1929–1939

The milestone year 1929 dawned with high hopes. Rarely had a new president entered office with greater expectations. In fact, Herbert Hoover was worried that people viewed him as "a superman; that no problem is beyond my capacity." Hoover was right to be concerned. People did consider him a superman—"the man who had never failed"—a dedicated public servant whose engineering genius and business savvy would ensure continued prosperity. At the time, more Americans were working than ever before and earning record levels of income. But that was about to change.

The Great Depression, which began at the end of 1929, brought with it widespread human misery. No other business slump had been so deep, so long, or so painful. One out of four Americans in 1932 was unemployed; in many large cities, nearly half of the adults were out of work. Some 500,000 people had lost homes or farms because they could not pay their mortgages. Thousands of banks had failed; millions of people lost their life savings. What made the Great Depression so severe and so enduring was its global nature. In 1929, the economies of Europe were still reeling from the First World War. Once the American economy tumbled, it sent shock waves throughout Europe and elsewhere.

The suffering was worldwide when Franklin Delano Roosevelt was elected in 1932 to lead an anxious nation mired in the third year of an unprecedented economic downturn. Within days of becoming president,

Roosevelt took dramatic steps that forever transformed the scope and role of the federal government. He and a supportive Congress adopted bold measures to relieve the human suffering and promote economic recovery. Roosevelt was not an ideologue; rather, he was a pragmatist willing to try different approaches. As he once explained, "Take a method and try it. If it fails, admit it frankly and try another." Roosevelt's program for recovery, the New Deal, was therefore a series of trial-and-error actions rather than a comprehensive scheme. None of these well-intentioned but often poorly planned initiatives worked perfectly, and in fact some of them failed miserably. But their combined effect was to restore hope and energy to a nation paralyzed by fear and uncertainty.

CORE **OBJECTIVE**

1. Identify the major causes of the Great Depression.

The Causes of the Great Depression

Herbert Hoover's election in 1928 boosted the hopes of investors in what had come to be called "the Great Bull Market." Since 1924, the prices of stock shares invested in U.S. companies had steadily risen. Beginning in 1927, prices soared further on wings of reckless speculation. In 1929, President Hoover voiced concern about the "orgy of mad speculation" in the stock market, and he urged investors to be more cautious—but to no avail. Treasury Secretary Andrew W. Mellon's tax reductions had given people more money to spend or invest, much of which went into the stock market. The nation's foremost economist, Irving Fisher of Yale University, assured investors in 1929 that "stock prices have reached what looks like a permanently high plateau."

The Stock Market during the Twenties

Margin loans, reckless stock speculation, and slowing economy

What made it so easy for hundreds of thousands of people to invest in stocks during the twenties was the common practice of buying stock "on margin"—that is, an investor could make a small cash down payment (the "margin") on shares of stock and borrow the rest from a stockbroker, who held the stock certificates as security in case the stock price plummeted. If stock prices rose, as they did in 1927, 1928, and most of 1929, the investor made enough profits to pay for the "margin loan" and reinvest the rest. But if the stock price declined and the buyer failed to meet a "margin call" for cash to pay off the broker's loan, the broker could sell the stock at a much lower price to cover the loan. By August 1929, stockbrokers were lending investors more than two-thirds of the face value of the stocks they were buying. Yet few people seemed concerned, and stock prices kept rising.

But despite the soaring stock market, there were signs that the economy was weakening. By 1927, steel production, residential construction, and automobile sales were slowing, as was the rate of consumer spending. By mid-1929, industrial production, employment, and other measures of economic activity were also declining. Still, the stock market rose.

Then, in early September 1929, the speculative bubble burst when the stock market fell sharply. By the middle of October, world markets were in a steep decline. Still, most investors remained bullish. On October 22, 1929, a leading bank president assured reporters that there was "nothing fundamentally wrong with the stock market or with the underlying business and credit structure."

The Crash

The next week, however, stock market values tumbled, triggering a wild scramble as terrified investors tried to sell stocks whose values were falling. Then, on Black Tuesday, October 29—the worst day in the stock market's history to that point—widespread panic set in. Stock prices went into free fall. By the end of the month, stocks on the New York Stock Exchange had dropped an average of 37 percent. An atmosphere of gloom settled over the financial community. "Life would no longer be, ever again, all fun and games" the comedian Harpo Marx sighed, as he anticipated the onset of the worst depression in history.

> Black Tuesday

After the catastrophic drop in the stock market, fear and uncertainty spread like a virus across the nation and around the world. Investors who had borrowed heavily to buy stocks were now forced to sell their holdings at huge losses in order to pay their debts. Several stockbrokers and investors who had lost everything committed suicide. The president of a cigar company that had gone bankrupt jumped off the ledge of a New York hotel. A Seattle man shot himself. Two men, business partners, joined hands and jumped to their deaths from the Ritz Hotel in New York City. Room clerks in Manhattan hotels began asking guests at registration if they wanted a room for jumping or sleeping.

> Financial panic

During 1930, the national economy sputtered and stumbled. Some 26,355 businesses shut down; even more failed the following year. Half of the textile workers in New England mills were jobless. The resulting slowdown in economic growth, called a *recession*, became so severe and long-lasting that it came to be called the **Great Depression**. The collapse of the stock market did not *cause* the Great Depression. Rather, it revealed that the prosperity of the 1920s had been built on weak foundations.

Of course, the stock market crash had the added effect of creating a psychological panic that accelerated the economic decline. Frightened that they were at risk of losing everything, people rushed to get their money out of banks and out of the stock market. Such panicky behavior only made things worse. By 1932, more than 9,000 banks had closed their doors. The nation's formerly robust economy experienced a shocking collapse that would last over ten years.

Great Depression (1929–1941)
Worst economic downturn in American history; it was spurred by the stock market crash in the fall of 1929 and lasted until the Second World War.

Why the Economy Collapsed

Stagnant wages, slow consumer spending, drop in GDP, and widespread unemployment

What were the underlying *causes* of the Great Depression? Economists still debate the relative importance of the various factors, but most scholars emphasize a combination of interrelated elements that triggered the profound economic downturn. The economy had actually begun to fall into a recession in the summer of 1929, months *before* the stock market crash. Too many business owners during the twenties had taken large profits while denying wage increases to employees. And by plowing profits into business expansion, executive salaries, and stock dividends rather than wage increases for hourly workers, employers created a growing imbalance: factories and mills were producing more goods but the purchasing power of consumers was declining because of stagnant wages. During the twenties, industrial productivity had increased 43 percent, but the wages of factory workers had gone up only 11 percent, in part because labor unions had declined in power and had lost their ability to ensure that wages for their workers were fair. In 1920, there were 5 million union members in the United States; by 1929, there were only 3.4 million. Two-thirds of American families in 1929 earned less than $2,000 in annual income, an amount said by economists to provide "only basic necessities." In essence, the economy was producing more and more products that consumers could not afford to buy, and too many people had been borrowing too much money for unproductive purposes, such as speculating in the stock market.

Factories cut back production or shut down altogether. From 1929 to 1933, U.S. economic output (called *gross domestic product*, or GDP) dropped almost 27 percent. By 1932, one-quarter of the workforce was out of work. Businesses posted signs that read, "We are Firing, not Hiring."

Weak agricultural sector worsens

At the same time that the financial and industrial sectors were collapsing in the early 1930s, the farm sector remained feeble. Increasing production during the twenties had led to lower prices for grains and livestock, in part because the spreading use of tractors to replace horses and mules made farmers much more productive. As more corn and wheat were grown, however, the prices farmers earned for their crops began a relentless decline. To make matters worse, record harvests in the summer and fall of 1929 caused prices for corn, wheat, and cotton to fall even faster, pinching the income of struggling farmers. A bushel of wheat that brought a farmer $2.94 in 1920 brought only 30 cents by 1932.

Government Actions and the Economy

Government policies: High tariffs, shrinking trade, and an inadequate money supply

Government policies also contributed to the Depression. High tariffs hurt the economy by reducing foreign trade. Like most Republican presidents, Herbert Hoover supported Congressional efforts to raise tariffs on imported goods in order to keep out foreign competition. The Smoot-Hawley Tariff of 1930, authored by two leading Republicans, Reed Owen Smoot and Willis C. Hawley, was intended to help the farm sector by raising tariff barriers on farm products imported into the United States. But a swarm of corporate lobbyists convinced Congress to add hundreds of new imported manufactured items to the tariff bill. More than 1,000 economists urged Hoover to veto the tariff bill because its logic was flawed: by trying to "protect" American farmers from foreign competition, the bill would actually raise prices on most raw materials and consumer products by impeding imports. Hoover signed the bill anyway, causing another steep drop in the stock market. The new Smoot-Hawley Tariff also prompted other countries to retaliate by passing tariffs of their own, thereby making it more difficult for American farms and businesses to sell their products abroad. U.S. exports plummeted, worsening the depression.

Bank run As news of the Great Crash spread across the world, people rushed to their banks to withdraw their deposits. The line for this Millbury, Massachusetts, savings bank wraps around the building.

Another factor contributing to the Great Depression was the stance of the Federal Reserve (known as "the Fed"), the government agency responsible for serving as a "central bank" by managing the nation's money supply and interest rates. Instead of expanding the nation's money supply in an effort to generate growth, the Federal Reserve did the reverse, reducing the money supply out of concern for possible inflation in consumer prices. Between 1929 and 1932, the nation's money supply shrank by a third, leading almost 10,000 small banks to close their doors and, in turn, taking millions of their depositors with them into bankruptcy.

The Impact of Europe's Economy

A final cause of the Depression was the chaotic state of the European economy, which had never fully recovered from the shock of the Great War. During the late 1920s, nations such as Great Britain, France, Spain, and Italy slowed their purchases of American goods as their shattered economies, slowly recovering from the devastation of the war, were finally able to produce more goods of their own. Meanwhile, the important German economy continued to flounder. A related factor was the continuing inability of European nations to pay their debts to each other—and to the United States— that they had incurred during the war. The American government insisted that the $11 billion it loaned to the Allies be repaid, but nations such as Great Britain and France had no money to send to Washington, D.C. They were forced to borrow huge sums ($5 billion) from U.S. banks, which only increased their overall indebtedness. After the stock market crash in

> European nations default on paying war debts

October 1929, American banks could no longer prop up the European economies. The Federal Reserve's tighter monetary policy also drastically slowed the amount of American capital (money) going abroad. The economies of nations like Germany, which had grown dependent on loans from American banks during the twenties, were devastated as American money dried up. Then the Smoot-Hawley Tariff made it even more difficult for European nations to sell their products in the United States, which meant that those countries had less money with which to buy American goods. So as the European economy sputtered, it dragged the American economy deeper into depression.

<table>
<tr><td>CORE OBJECTIVE
2. Describe the impact of the Great Depression on the lives of the American people.</td></tr>
</table>

The Human Toll of the Depression

The Depression of the 1930s came to be called "Great" because its effects were so severe and long-lasting. It generated record levels of unemployment and widespread human distress. By 1932, perhaps a quarter of the entire population could not afford housing or adequate food. The carefree optimism of the twenties disappeared as the suffering spread. Grassroots protests erupted as the Depression worsened. In many cities, hungry people looted grocery stores. Angry mobs stopped local sheriffs from foreclosing on farms; others threatened to lynch judges at bankruptcy hearings. In Harlan, Kentucky, coal miners went on strike to protest a cut in their wages. The mine owners called in the National Guard, which routed the union. In 1931, Socialists recruited 45,000 people to join the Unemployed Citizens' League in Seattle, Washington, which helped people avoid eviction and bankruptcy, found them part-time jobs, and lobbied for more government assistance. Some people talked of revolution. "Folks are restless," Mississippi governor Theodore Bilbo told reporters in 1931. "Communism is gaining a foothold. . . . In fact, I'm getting a little pink myself." Yet for all the radical talk, few Americans embraced communism during the early 1930s. "There was anger and rebellion among a few," recounted an Iowa farmer but most people lived in "helpless despair and submission."

Unemployment and "Relief"

Soaring unemployment, spreading poverty, failure of local efforts at "relief"

As the economy spiraled downward between 1930 and 1933, growing numbers of workers were fired or saw their wages cut. National unemployment soared to 4 million in 1930, 8 million in 1931, and 12 million by 1932. Some 6,000 jobless New Yorkers sold apples on street corners.

Many struggling business executives and professionals—lawyers, doctors, dentists, accountants, stockbrokers, teachers, nurses, and engineers—

went without food and stopped going to doctors and dentists in order to save money and to avoid the humiliation of "going on relief." A dentist in New York City and his wife committed suicide, explaining in a note that "we want to get out of the way before we are forced to accept relief money." The sense of shame cut across class lines. In *The Grapes of Wrath* (1939), John Steinbeck's best-selling novel about the Depression, a poor but proud woman is disgraced by accepting "charity" from the Salvation Army: "We was hungry. They made us crawl for our dinner. They took our dignity."

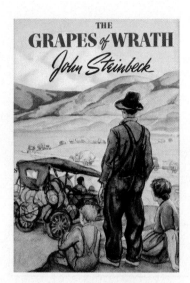

***The Grapes of Wrath* (1939)**
First edition of John Steinbeck's bestseller, adapted into an acclaimed film in 1940.

Hunger

Hard-pressed families went without fruit and most vegetables, eating mostly beans and soup. Surveys of children in the nation's public schools in 1932 showed that one quarter suffered from malnutrition. In a rural school in Appalachia, a teacher told a sickly child to go home and get something to eat. "I can't," she replied. "It's my sister's turn to eat." In 1931, New York City hospitals reported about 100 cases of actual starvation, where people died solely from the lack of food. Hungry people by the millions lined up at soup kitchens where minimal amounts of food and water were distributed; others rummaged through trash cans behind restaurants. In Detroit, "we saw the city at its worst," wrote Louise V. Armstrong. "One vivid, gruesome moment of those dark days we shall never forget. We saw a crowd of some fifty men fighting over a barrel of garbage which had been set outside the back door of a restaurant. American citizens fighting over scraps of food like animals!"

Homelessness

The contraction of the economy especially squeezed debtors, who had monthly mortgages or installment debts to pay. A thousand Americans per day lost their homes to foreclosure. At first, the poor made homeless by the Depression were usually placed in *poorhouses* or *workhouses*. By 1933, however, the numbers of homeless overwhelmed the small number of public facilities. People were forced to live under bridges, on park benches, and in doorways and police stations. To make matters worse, the poor were degraded as a class of outsiders and subject to frequent abuse and arrest. The constitutions of fourteen states even banned paupers from voting.

Millions of homeless people, mostly men, simply took to living on the road or the rails. These hobos, or tramps, as they were called, walked, hitchhiked in cars, or sneaked onto empty railway cars and rode from town to town. One railroad, the Missouri Pacific, counted 200,000 people living in its empty boxcars in 1931. The following year, the Southern Pacific Railroad reported that it had evicted 683,457 people from its freight trains. A black military veteran recalled life as a freight train hobo: "Black and white, it didn't make any difference who you were, 'cause everybody was poor. . . . They didn't have no mothers or sisters, they didn't have no home;

they were dirty, they had overalls on, they didn't have no food, they didn't have anything."

Desperate Responses

As always, those hardest hit were the most disadvantaged groups—immigrants, women, farmers, the urban unemployed, Native Americans, and African Americans. Desperate conditions did lead desperate people to do desperate things. Crime soared during the 1930s, as did street-corner begging, homelessness, and prostitution. A Pennsylvania man wrote the governor in 1931, explaining that he did not "want to steal, but I won't let my wife and boy cry for something to eat. . . . How long is this going to keep up? I cannot stand it any longer."

> **Families in distress: Crime, desertion, and declining birth rates**

Although the divorce rate dropped during the decade, in part because couples could not afford to live separately or pay the legal fees to obtain a divorce, many jobless husbands simply deserted their wives and children. Some 1.5 million husbands left home during the thirties. "You don't know what it's like when your husband's out of work," a woman told a reporter. "He's gloomy and unhappy all the time. Life is terrible. You must try all the time to keep him from going crazy." With their future so uncertain, married couples often decided not to have children; birth rates plummeted during the 1930s. Many struggling parents sent their children to live with relatives or friends. Some 900,000 children simply left home and joined the growing army of homeless tramps. During the Great Depression, for the first time ever, more people left the United States than arrived as immigrants.

The Plight of Married Working Women

Women were placed in a peculiar position by the Depression. By 1932, 20 percent of working women were unemployed, a slightly lower percentage than men. On the one hand, because women held a disproportionate number of the lowest-paying jobs, they were often able to keep their jobs as employers laid off the higher-paid men. Even if they kept their jobs, however, many women also had the added burden of keeping their families together emotionally when their husbands lost jobs. Many magazines during the thirties published articles about the challenge of maintaining households when the husband had been "unmanned" by losing his job as breadwinner. One of the most famous Broadway show tunes during the early thirties was "Remember My Forgotten Man."

> **Discrimination against married women and minorities in hiring and assistance**

As the Depression deepened, however, married women in the workforce became the primary targets of layoffs. Some 26 states passed laws prohibiting the employment of married women. The reasoning behind such laws was that a married woman—who presumably had a husband to take care of her—should not "steal" a job from a man. It was acceptable for single women to find jobs because these were usually lower-paying jobs considered "women's work": sales clerks, beauticians, schoolteachers, secretaries, and nurses. The job market for African American women was even more restricted, with most black women working as maids, cooks, or laundresses. In a desperate attempt to create jobs for unemployed men, many employers adopted policies barring married women from employment. For example, three-fourths of the public school systems across the nation during the Great Depression fired women teachers who got married. As a legislator commented, the working woman in Depression-era America was "the first orphan in the storm."

African Americans, Mexicans, and Asians

Most African Americans during the Depression still lived in the eleven southern states of the former Confederacy, where the southern economy, still farm-dominated, was already depressed. Most African Americans who lived in the South earned their livelihood from farming as tenants and sharecroppers. Pervasive racial discrimination kept blacks out of the few labor unions in the South and consigned them to the most-menial, lowest-paying jobs. Most blacks were still excluded from voting, segregated from whites in public places like hotels and trains, and limited mostly to farm work. Already living in poverty, they were among the hardest hit by the Depression. As a blues song called "Hard Times Ain't Gone Nowhere" revealed, "Hard times don't worry me; I was broke when it first started out." Some 3 million rural blacks in the South lived in cramped cabins without electricity, running water, or bathrooms.

Just dropping off a resume In October 1938, the government opened six custodian positions and 15,000 African American women started lining up overnight to turn in their applications. Pictured here is a policeman leaping over a hedge to administer some crowd control.

In many mills, factories, mines, and businesses, the philosophy of "last hired, first fired" meant that the people who could least afford to be jobless were fired first. Blacks who had left the poverty-stricken South to take factory jobs in the North were among the first to be laid off. Blacks across the nation had the highest rate of joblessness in the early years of the Great Depression. "At no time in the history of the Negro since slavery," reported the Urban League, "has his economic and social outlook seemed so discouraging." Churches and other charity organizations gave aid, but some only assisted whites and refused to provide support for blacks, Mexicans, and Asians.

Impoverished whites found themselves competing with local Hispanics and Asians for seasonal farm work in the cotton fields or orchards of large corporate farms. Many Chinese, Japanese, and Filipino farm laborers moved to cities. Mexicans were also mostly migrant farm workers, traveling from farm to farm to work during harvest and planting seasons of different crops. They settled in California, New Mexico, Arizona, Colorado, Texas, and the midwestern states. As economic conditions worsened, government

> Deportation of Mexican-born Americans

officials called for the deportation of Mexican-born Americans in order to avoid the cost of providing them with public services. By 1935, over 500,000 Mexican Americans and their American-born children were deported to Mexico. The state of Texas alone returned over 250,000 people.

Dust Bowl Migrants

Black blizzards and Dust Bowl refugees

In the southern plains of the Midwest and the Mississippi Valley, a terrible drought during the 1930s created a catastrophe known as the **Dust Bowl**. Colorado, New Mexico, Kansas, Nebraska, Texas, Arkansas, and Oklahoma were the states hardest hit. Crops withered and income plummeted. Strong winds swept across the treeless plains, scooping up millions of tons of parched topsoil into billowing dark clouds that floated east across entire states, engulfing farms and towns in what were called black blizzards. By 1938, over 25 million acres of prairie land had lost their topsoil.

Okies on the run A sharecropping family reaches its destination of Bakersfield, California, in 1935, after "we got blowed out in Oklahoma."

Human misery paralleled the environmental devastation. Parched farmers could not pay their debts, and banks foreclosed on their property. Suicides soared. With each year, millions of people abandoned their farms. Many uprooted farmers and their families from the South and the Midwest headed toward California, where jobs were said to be plentiful. So off they went on a cross-country trek in pursuit of new opportunities. Frequently lumped together as "Okies" or "Arkies," most of the dust bowl refugees were from cotton belt communities in Arkansas, Texas, Missouri, and Oklahoma. During the 1930s and 1940s, some 800,000 people, mostly whites, left those four states and headed to the Far West in a migration powerfully described in Steinbeck's *The Grapes of Wrath* as well as in the folk songs of Woody Guthrie, a musician who traveled the nation during the thirties, singing about people down on their luck.

Most people uprooted by the dust bowl went to California's urban areas—Los Angeles, San Diego, or San Francisco. Others moved into the San Joaquin Valley, the agricultural heartland of California. There they discovered that rural California was no paradise. Only a few of the dust bowl migrants could afford to buy land. Living in tents or crude cabins and frequently on the move, the migrant workers suffered from exposure to the elements, poor sanitation, and social abuse. As an Okie reported, when the big farmers "need us they call us *migrants*, and when we've picked their crop, we're *bums* and we got to get out."

Dust Bowl Vast area of the Midwest where windstorms blew away millions of tons of topsoil from parched farmland after a long drought in the 1930s, causing great social distress and a massive migration of farm families.

From Hooverism to the New Deal

CORE **OBJECTIVE**

3. Explain the response of the Hoover administration to the Great Depression.

The initial response of government officials to the Great Depression was denial: there was no crisis, they insisted. All that was needed, President Hoover and others argued, was to let the sick economy cure itself. The best policy, Treasury Secretary Andrew Mellon advised, would be to "liquidate labor, liquidate stocks, liquidate the farmers, liquidate real estate." Letting events run their course, he insisted, would "purge the rottenness out of the system. High costs of living and high living will come down. People will work harder, live a more moral life." Mellon's do-nothing approach did not work, however. Falling wages and declining land and home values made it harder for farmers, businesses, and households to pay their debts. With so many people losing jobs and income, consumers and businesses simply could not buy enough goods and services to get the economy growing again.

Hoover's Efforts at Recovery

President Hoover was less willing than Andrew Mellon to sit by and let events take their course. As the "Great Engineer," he in fact did more than any president had ever done before in such dire economic circumstances. Hoover, for example, invited business, labor, government, and agricultural leaders to a series of White House conferences in which the president urged companies to maintain employment and wage levels, asked union leaders to end strikes, and pleaded with states to follow through on planned construction projects. None of these efforts worked. Unemployment continued to rise, and wage levels continued to fall.

Hoover's efforts to end the Depression: Government construction projects and private cooperation

In speech after speech, Hoover became a cheerleader for American capitalism. He asked people to keep up hope. In early May 1930, the president told the U.S. Chamber of Commerce that he was "convinced we have passed the worst and with continued effort we shall rapidly recover." A few weeks later, Hoover assured a group of bankers that the "depression is over." The Hoover administration also circulated upbeat slogans such as "Business IS Better" and "Keep Smiling." But uplifting words were not enough. More and more people kept losing their jobs and homes.

Short-Sighted Tax Increases

The Great Depression was the greatest national emergency since the Civil War, and the nation was woefully unprepared to deal with it. As personal income plummeted, so too did government tax revenues. Despite the Depression, President Hoover insisted on trying to balance the federal budget. To do so, he pushed through Congress the Revenue Act of 1932, the largest—and most poorly timed—peacetime tax increase in American history. By taking money out of consumers' pockets, the higher taxes accelerated the economic slowdown. People had less money to spend when what the depressed economy most needed was increased consumer spending.

The Revenue Act of 1932

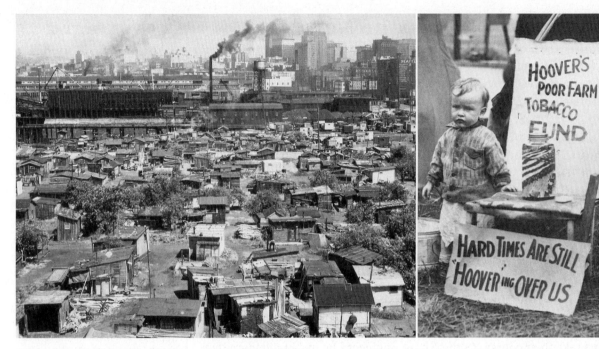

Hooverville *Left*: Of the many Hoovervilles set up in Seattle alone, this particular shantytown near the shipyards was the largest and lasted nine years. *Right*: A toddler begs for change in one of the Bonus Army camps.

Hoover's Reaction to the Social Crisis

By the fall of 1930, many city governments were buckling under the strain of lost revenue and growing human distress. The federal government had no programs to deal with homelessness and joblessness. State and local governments cut spending, worsening the economic situation. All across the country, shantytowns sprouted in vacant lots where people erected shacks out of cardboard and scrap wood and metal. There they shivered and suffered, calling their makeshift villages *Hoovervilles* in criticism of the president. To keep warm during the winter, the homeless wrapped themselves in newspapers, calling them *Hoover blankets*. As the numbers rose, more and more people called for governments to step in to deal with the emergency of homeless, starving people. Frustrated by his critics, Hoover dismissed the concerns of "calamity mongers and weeping men."

Hoover rejects federal intervention

President Hoover refused to provide any federal programs to help the needy for fear that the nation would be "plunged into socialism" if the government provided direct support to the poor. His governing philosophy, rooted in America's mythic commitment to rugged individualism, self-reliance, and free enterprise, set firm limits on emergency government action, and he was unwilling to set that philosophy aside even to meet an unprecedented national emergency. The president still trumpeted the virtues of "self-reliance" and individual initiative, claiming that government assistance would be the very worst thing for a nation in crisis, for it would rob people of the desire to help themselves.

Voluntarism

Hoover hoped that the "natural generosity" of the American people and local charitable organizations would be sufficient to handle the crisis, and he believed that volunteers (the backbone of local charity organizations) would relieve the social distress caused by the Depression. But Hoover's faith in traditional "voluntarism" was misplaced. Although most Americans tried to get jobs to earn a living, there simply were no jobs, even for industrious people. The local and state relief agencies were overwhelmed by the magnitude of the social crisis. Churches and charitable organizations like the Salvation Army and the Red Cross were also swamped with needy people.

Rising Criticism of Hoover

As always, a depressed economy hurt the political party in power—and its president. The *New York Times* reported in the summer of 1930 that public opinion "is turning rather heavily against the Hoover administration." The Democrats shrewdly exploited Hoover's predicament. In November 1930, the Democrats gained their first national election victory since 1916, winning a majority in the House and a near majority in the Senate. Hoover refused to see the elections as a warning signal. Instead, he grew more resistant to calls for federal intervention in the struggling economy. By 1932, almost 25 percent of the workforce—15 million people—were unemployed. Still, Hoover resisted calls for federal assistance. The *New York Times* concluded that Hoover had "failed as a party leader. He has failed as an economist. . . . He has failed as a business leader. . . . He has failed as a personality because of [his] awkwardness of manner and speech and lack of mass magnetism."

Congressional Initiatives

With a new Congress in session in 1932, demands for federal action forced Hoover to do more. That year, the new Congress set up the **Reconstruction Finance Corporation** (RFC) to make emergency loans to struggling banks, life-insurance companies, and railroads. Yet if the federal government could help huge banks and railroads, asked New York Democratic senator Robert F. Wagner, why not "extend a helping hand to that forlorn American, in every village and every city of the United States, who has been without wages since 1929?" Democrats like Wagner called for federal help for the people hit hardest by the economic collapse. But Hoover held back and only signed the Emergency Relief Act (1932), which authorized the RFC to make loans to the states for construction projects.

> Reconstruction Finance Corporation (RFC)

Farmers and Veterans in Protest

Meanwhile, desperate farmers across the nation took matters into their own hands. The average *annual* income of families working the land during the early 1930s was $240. Prices for agricultural products fell so low that farmers lost money if they took them to market. Thousands of Midwestern farmers joined the Farmers' Holiday Association to protest the low prices by dumping milk, vegetables, and fruits on the highways.

Reconstruction Finance Corporation (1932) Federal program established under President Hoover to loan money to banks and other corporations to help them avoid bankruptcy.

Fears of organized revolt arose when thousands of unemployed military veterans converged on the nation's capital in the spring of 1932. The **Bonus Expeditionary Force**, made up of veterans of the American Expeditionary Force (AEF) that fought in Europe in the Great War, pressed Congress to pay the cash bonus owed to nearly 4 million veterans. The House passed a bonus bill, but when the Senate voted it down to avoid a tax increase, most of the veterans went home. The rest, along with their wives and children, having no place to go, camped in vacant federal buildings and in a shantytown at Anacostia Flats, within sight of the nation's Capitol building.

Eager to remove the homeless veterans, Hoover persuaded Congress to pay for their train tickets home. More left, but others stayed even after Congress adjourned, hoping at least to meet with the president. Late in July, President Hoover ordered the government buildings cleared. In doing so, a policeman panicked, fired into the crowd, and killed two veterans. The secretary of war then dispatched seven hundred soldiers to remove the "Bonus Army." Using horses, tanks, tear gas, and bayonets, the soldiers dispersed the unarmed veterans and their families and burned their makeshift camp. Fifty-five veterans were injured and 135 arrested. The Democratic governor of New York was horrified as he read newspaper accounts of the army's violent assault on the unemployed military veterans. "Well," Franklin Roosevelt told an aide, "this elects me" as the next president. (The military veterans of the war were finally paid their "bonus" in 1936).

The disheartened, angry mood of the Bonus Army matched the sour mood of the country, as well as that of President Hoover himself. He worked hard, seven days a week, but the stress of dealing with the Great Depression sapped his health and morale. "I am so tired," he said, "that every bone in my body aches." When aides urged Hoover to be more of a public leader, he replied, "I have no Wilsonian qualities." The man who in 1928 had seemed to be an organizational genius and had promised Americans "permanent prosperity" was now the laughingstock of the nation. *Time* magazine reported that "two years have destroyed the Hoover legend." In the end, Hoover's efforts to restore prosperity were simply not enough, in large part because he never understood or acknowledged the seriousness of the economic problems that he and the nation faced.

The 1932 Election

In June 1932, glum Republicans gathered in Chicago to nominate Hoover for a second presidential term. The delegates went through the motions in a mood of defeat but felt they had no choice. By contrast, the Democrats arrived in Chicago for their nominating convention a few weeks later confident that they would nominate the next president. Fifty-year-old New York governor Franklin Delano Roosevelt won the nomination on the fourth ballot. In a bold gesture, Roosevelt flew for nine hours to Chicago to accept the nomination in person instead of awaiting formal notification. No nominee had ever done so. Roosevelt had broken with tradition, he told the delegates, because the stakes were so high. Hoover and the Republicans, he

Bonus Expeditionary Force (1932) Protest march on Washington, D.C. by thousands of military veterans and their families, calling for immediate payment of their service bonus certificates; violence ensued when President Herbert Hoover ordered their tent villages cleared.

stressed, had failed to address the terrible economic disaster. "I pledge you, I pledge myself to a *new deal* for the American people" that would "break foolish traditions" and create a new government "of competence and courage." But first he would have to defeat Herbert Hoover. His race against the Republican president would be "more than a political campaign; it is a call to arms." It was a vague but self-assured and uplifting message of hope at a time when many people were slipping into despair. Roosevelt's upbeat personality communicated joy, energy, and confidence. His campaign song was "Happy Days Are Here Again."

Throughout the campaign, Roosevelt blamed the Great Depression on the Republicans. He attacked Hoover for his "extravagant government spending," and repeatedly promised a "New Deal" for the American

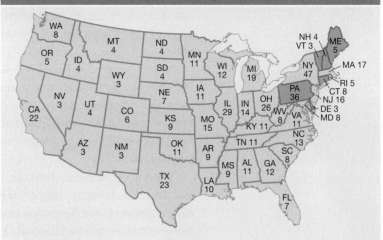

THE ELECTION OF 1932

	Electoral Vote	Popular Vote
Franklin D. Roosevelt (Democratic)	472	22,800,000
Herbert Hoover (Republican)	59	15,800,000

- Why did Roosevelt appeal to voters struggling during the Depression?
- What were Hoover's criticisms of Roosevelt's New Deal?
- What policies defined Roosevelt's New Deal during the presidential campaign?

people. Like Hoover, Roosevelt pledged to balance the federal budget, but he was willing to create short-term deficits to prevent starvation and revive the economy. Perhaps most important, he recognized that a revitalized economy would require new ideas and aggressive action. "The country needs, and, unless I mistake its temper, the country demands bold, persistent experimentation," he said. "Above all, try something."

In contrast to Roosevelt, the bewildered Hoover lacked vitality and vision. Roosevelt's proposals, he warned, "would destroy the very foundations of our American system." The election, he stressed, was a battle "between two philosophies of government" that would decide "the direction our nation will take over a century to come." On Election Day, Hoover lost that battle. Voters swept Roosevelt into office with 23 million votes to Hoover's 16 million.

Roosevelt's New Deal

Roosevelt had promised voters a "New Deal," and within hours of being inaugurated he and his aides set about changing the role of government in American life. The new president had seemingly been in a hurry all his life.

Born in 1882, the adored only child of wealthy, aristocratic parents, young Franklin Roosevelt had enjoyed a pampered life. He was educated by

CORE OBJECTIVE

4. Assess the goals and accomplishments of the early New Deal.

tutors at Hyde Park, his father's Hudson River estate north of New York City. Young Roosevelt attended Harvard College and Columbia University Law School. While a law student, he married Anna Eleanor Roosevelt, a niece of his fifth cousin, Theodore Roosevelt, then president of the United States.

In 1910, Franklin Roosevelt won a Democratic seat in the New York State Senate. Tall, handsome, and athletic, blessed with a sparkling personality and infectious smile, Roosevelt seemed destined for greatness. In 1913, Woodrow Wilson appointed him assistant secretary of the navy. In 1920, Roosevelt became James Cox's vice presidential running mate on the Democratic ticket.

Then a tragedy occurred. In 1921, at age thirty-nine, Roosevelt contracted polio, leaving him permanently disabled, unable to stand or walk without braces. For seven years, aided by his remarkable wife, Eleanor, Roosevelt strengthened his body to compensate for his disability. The long battle for recovery transformed the young aristocrat. He became less arrogant, less superficial, more focused, and more interesting. A friend recalled that Roosevelt emerged from his struggle with polio "completely warm-hearted, with a new humility of spirit" that led him to identify with the poor and the suffering. In 1928 and 1930, Roosevelt won the governorship of New York. The aristocrat had developed the common touch as well as a great talent for public relations, but he also was vain and calculating, a clever manipulator of others. In other words, he was a master politician.

Launching the New Deal

Roosevelt was neither an efficient administrator nor a deep thinker. One of his closest aides said the president never "read a serious book." But Roosevelt had courage, a charming personality, strong instincts, unrelenting optimism, and a willingness to experiment with different ways to address problems. He would support a balanced budget and complain about a "bloated bureaucracy," for example, only to incur more budget deficits than all his predecessors combined and dramatically expand the scope of federal government. His inconsistencies reflected his distinctively flexible personality as he launched his presidency and the New Deal.

The 1933 Inauguration

Inaugurated as president in March 1933, Franklin Delano Roosevelt assumed leadership during one of the greatest crises in modern history, a crisis that threatened the very fabric of American capitalism. No other business slump had been so deep, so long, or so painful as the Great Depression. "The situation is critical, Franklin," the prominent journalist Walter Lippmann warned President-elect Roosevelt. "You may have to assume dictatorial powers"—as had already happened in Germany, Italy, and the Soviet Union.

Roosevelt did not become a dictator, but he did take extraordinary steps to address the Depression while assuring Americans "that the only thing we have to fear is fear itself." Roosevelt confessed in his inaugural address that he did not have all the answers, but he did know that "this nation asks for action, and action now." To deal with the crisis, he asked Congress for "a broad Executive power to wage a war against the emergency" just as "if we were in fact invaded by a foreign foe." Roosevelt's uplifting speech won rave reviews. Nearly 500,000 Americans wrote letters to the new president after his inauguration.

The First Hundred Days

In March 1933, President Roosevelt confronted four major challenges: reviving the industrial economy, relieving the widespread human misery, rescuing the ravaged farm sector and its desperate families, and reforming those aspects of the capitalist system that had helped cause the Depression. His goal in providing "relief, recovery, and reform" was to save the nation's capitalist system, not destroy it, while also providing help to those in great distress. The new president admitted that he planned to try several different "experiments" to solve the Great Depression. Eleanor Roosevelt said her husband and his top advisers were "going at it blindly, because we're in a tremendous stream, and none of us knows where we are going to land." To advise him about options, the new president assembled a "brain trust" of brilliant specialists, many of them college professors, who feverishly developed fresh ideas to address the nation's urgent problems.

> New Deal goals: Relief, recovery, and reform

Roosevelt and his advisers initially settled on a three-pronged strategy to revive the economy. First, they addressed the immediate money crisis and provided short-term emergency relief for the jobless. Second, the New Dealers encouraged agreements between management and unions. Third, they attempted to raise depressed commodity prices by paying farmers "subsidies" to shrink the size of their crops and herds. By reducing the supply of grain, cattle, and pigs, prices would rise and thereby increase farm income. From March 9 to June 16, the so-called First Hundred Days, a cooperative Congress approved fifteen major pieces of legislation proposed by the president. Several of these programs comprised what came to be called the **First New Deal** (1933–1935).

Shoring Up the Financial System

Money is the lubricant of capitalism, and money was fast disappearing from circulation by 1933. Ever since the stock market crash of 1929, panicky depositors had been withdrawing their money from banks and the stock market for fear that the banks and corporations would fail. Taking so much money out of circulation, however, worsened the Depression and brought the banking system to the brink of collapse.

First New Deal (1933–1935) Franklin D. Roosevelt's ambitious first-term cluster of economic and social programs designed to combat the Great Depression.

Emergency Banking Relief Act and "fireside chats"

Banking Regulation

On his second day in office, March 9, 1933, Roosevelt called Congress into special session to pass the Emergency Banking Relief Act, which declared a four-day bank holiday to allow the financial panic to subside. (Herbert Hoover called it a "move to gigantic socialism.") For the first time in history, all banks closed their doors to stop the panic. "All business came to a complete halt," an Ohio woman reported. Roosevelt's financial experts worked all night drafting a bill to restore confidence in the nation's banks. On March 12, in the first of his radio-broadcast "fireside chats" to the American people, the president assured the 60 million listeners that it was safer to "keep your money in a reopened bank than under the mattress." His reassurances soothed a nervous nation. The following day, people took their money back to their banks. "Capitalism was saved in eight days," said one of Roosevelt's advisers.

A few weeks later, on June 16, 1933, Roosevelt signed the Banking Act of 1933, part of which created the **Federal Deposit Insurance Corporation** (FDIC), which guaranteed customer saving accounts in banks up to $2,500, thus reducing the likelihood of future panics. In addition to insuring savings accounts, the Glass-Steagall Act, which was actually another section of the Banking Act of 1933, called for the separation of commercial banking from investment banking in order to prevent conventional banks from investing the savings of depositors in the risky stock market; only banks that specialized in investment could invest in the stock market after 1933. In addition, the Federal Reserve Board was given more authority to intervene in future financial emergencies. The banking crisis had ended, and the new administration was ready to get on with a broader program of economic recovery.

Regulating Wall Street

Before the Great Crash in 1929, there was very little government oversight of the securities (stocks and bonds) industry, popularly known as "Wall Street," the financial district in Manhattan where the largest banks and brokerage houses were centered. In 1933, the Roosevelt administration developed two important pieces of legislation intended to regulate the operations of the stock market to eliminate fraud and abuses. The first, the Securities Exchange Act of 1933, was the first major federal legislation to regulate the sale of stocks and bonds. It required corporations that issued stock for public sale to "disclose" all relevant information about the operations and management of the company so that purchasers could know what they were buying. The second bill, the Securities Exchange Act of 1934, established the **Securities and Exchange Commission**, a federal agency created to enforce the new laws and regulations governing the issuance and trading of stocks and bonds. The Act also required that all stock brokers be licensed.

Franklin Delano Roosevelt Preparing to deliver the first of his popular "fireside chats." This message focused on measures to reform the American banking system.

Federal Deposit Insurance Corporation (1933) Independent government agency, established to prevent bank panics, that guarantees the safety of deposits in citizens' savings accounts.

Securities and Exchange Commission (1934) Federal agency established to regulate the issuance and trading of stocks and bonds in an effort to avoid financial panics and stock market "crashes."

The Federal Budget

Roosevelt next convinced Congress to pass an Economy Act (1933) allowing him to cut government workers' salaries, reduce payments to military veterans for non-service-connected disabilities, and reorganize federal agencies in order to reduce government expenses. Roosevelt then took the dramatic step of ending Prohibition, in part because it was being so widely violated, in part because most Democrats wanted it ended, and in part because he wanted to regain the federal tax revenues from the sale of alcoholic beverages. The Twenty-First Amendment was ratified on December 5, 1933. The "noble experiment" of Prohibition was over.

Economy Act and end of Prohibition

Helping the Unemployed and Homeless

Another urgent priority in 1933 was relieving the widespread human distress caused by the Great Depression. Herbert Hoover had stubbornly refused to help the unemployed and homeless, since he assumed that individual acts of charity (what he called *voluntarism*) and the efforts of local organizations (churches and charities) would be sufficient to get people clothed, fed, and housed. In dealing with the needs of millions of jobless and homeless Americans, the Roosevelt administration had a much greater sense of urgency than Hoover had displayed. As Roosevelt's aide Harry Hopkins said, "Hunger is not debatable." He and Roosevelt, from their experiences in New York state government, knew that the scope of the problem greatly exceeded the "voluntarism" that Hoover promoted. The new president was much more flexible, pushing through a series of new programs that created what came to be called the "welfare state." He did not believe that individuals should be given cash by the government (called a "dole"), but he did want the government to help people get jobs. For the first time, the federal government took primary responsibility for assisting the most desperate Americans, because the number of people in need far exceeded the capacity of charitable organizations and local government agencies.

Creation of the welfare state

Putting People to Work

The Federal Emergency Relief Administration (FERA), headed by Harry Hopkins, was Roosevelt's first major effort to deal with unemployment. It sent money to the states to spend on the unemployed and homeless. After the state-sponsored programs funded by the FERA proved inadequate, Congress created the Civil Works Administration (CWA) in November 1933. It was the first large-scale *federal* experiment with work relief, hiring people directly on the government payroll at competitive wages. Several states had done so before, but never the national government. The CWA provided 4 million federal jobs to those unable to find work during the winter of 1933–1934. The agency organized a variety of useful projects:

Federal work relief

repairing 500,000 miles of roads, laying sewer lines, constructing or improving more than a thousand airports and 40,000 public schools, and providing 50,000 teaching jobs that helped keep small rural public schools open. As the number of people employed by the CWA soared, however, the program's costs skyrocketed to over $1 billion. Roosevelt balked at such high costs and worried that the people hired would become dependent upon federal jobs. So in the spring of 1934, he ordered the CWA dissolved. By April, some 4 million workers were again unemployed.

The CCC

The most successful of the New Deal programs to provide jobs to the unemployed was the Civilian Conservation Corps (CCC), managed by the War Department. It built 2,500 camps around the nation to house 3 million unemployed, unmarried young men aged eighteen to twenty-five to work as "soil soldiers" in national forests, parks, and recreational areas and on soil-conservation projects. The CCC also recruited 150,000 unemployed military veterans and 85,000 Native Americans, housing them in separate camps. CCC workers built roads, bridges, campgrounds, fire towers, fish hatcheries, and 800 parks; planted 3 *billion* trees; taught farmers how to control soil erosion; and fought fires. The enrolees, who were supervised by soldiers, were given shelter, clothing, and food, as well as a small wage of $30 a month ($25 of which had to be sent home to their families). The CCC workers could also earn high-school diplomas at their camps.

Saving Homes

Federal Housing Administration (FHA) and the National Industrial Recovery Act (NIRA)

During 1933, a thousand homes or farms were being foreclosed upon each day. Roosevelt's Home Owners' Loan Act established the Home Owners' Loan Corporation, which helped home owners refinance their mortgages at lower interest rates and avoid bankruptcy. In 1934, Roosevelt created the Federal Housing Administration (FHA), which offered Americans much longer home mortgages (twenty years) in order to reduce their monthly payments.

Reviving the Industrial Sector

The centerpiece of the New Deal's efforts to revive the industrial economy was the National Industrial Recovery Act (NIRA) of 1933. One of its two major sections dealt with economic recovery by creating massive public-works construction projects funded by the federal government. The NIRA created the Public Works Administration (PWA), granting $3.3 billion for the construction of government buildings, highways, bridges, dams, port facilities, and sewage plants.

National Recovery Administration (1933) Controversial federal agency that brought together business and labor leaders to create "codes of fair competition" and "fair labor" policies, including a national minimum wage.

The second, and more controversial, part of the NIRA created the **National Recovery Administration** (NRA), headed by Hugh S. Johnson, a retired army general. Its primary purpose was to promote economic growth by temporarily waiving the anti-trust laws and allowing large corporations to create detailed "codes of fair competition" among themselves for 500 different industries, including the setting of prices on an array of products. At the same time, the NRA codes also included "fair labor" policies long sought by unions and social progressives: a national forty-hour work week, minimum weekly wages of $13 ($12 in the South, where living costs were lower), and a ban on the employment of children under the age of sixteen. The NRA also included a provision (Section 7a) that guaranteed the right of workers to organize unions.

These were landmark changes in working conditions and union rights, and, for a time, the downward spiral of wages and prices subsided. But as soon as economic recovery began, small business owners complained that the larger corporations dominated the NRA, whose price-fixing robbed small producers of the chance to compete. And because the NRA wage codes excluded agricultural and domestic workers (at the insistence of southern Democrats), three out of every four African Americans derived no direct benefit from the program. By 1935, the NRA had developed more critics than friends. When it died, in May 1935, struck down by the Supreme Court as unconstitutional, few paused to mourn.

Yet the NRA experiment had left an enduring mark. The NRA codes set new workplace standards, such as the forty-hour workweek, a minimum wage, and the abolition of child labor. The NRA's endorsement of collective bargaining between workers and owners spurred the growth of unions. Yet as 1934 ended, economic recovery was still nowhere in sight.

> The National Recovery Act (NRA): Creation of fair labor standards and recognition of the right to unionize

Agricultural Assistance

In addition to rescuing the banks and providing jobs to the unemployed, Roosevelt and his advisers promoted the long-term recovery of agriculture during the Hundred Days in the spring of 1933. Roosevelt created the Farm Credit Administration to help farmers deal with their crushing debts. Like the Home Owners' Loan Corporation, the Farm Credit Administration helped farmers lower their mortgage payments to avoid bankruptcy.

> Farm Credit Association and the Agricultural Adjustment Act (1933)

The **Agricultural Adjustment Act** of 1933 created a new federal agency, the Agricultural Adjustment Administration (AAA), which sought to raise prices for crops and herds by paying farmers to cut back production. The money for such payments came from a tax levied on the "processors" of certain basic commodities—cotton gins, flour mills, and slaughterhouses. By the time the AAA was created, however, the spring growing season was already under way. The prospect of another bumper cotton crop forced the AAA to sponsor a "plow-under" program in which farmers were paid to kill the sprouting seeds in their fields. To destroy a growing crop was a "shocking commentary on our civilization," Agriculture Secretary Henry A. Wallace admitted. "I could tolerate it only as a cleaning up of the wreckage from the old days of unbalanced production."

Agricultural Adjustment Act (1933) Legislation that paid farmers to produce less in order to raise crop prices for all; the AAA was later declared unconstitutional by the U.S. Supreme Court in the case of *United States v. Butler* (1936).

Norris Dam The massive dam in Tennessee, completed in 1936, was essential to creating jobs and expanding power production under the TVA.

Moreover, in an effort to raise pork prices, some 6 million baby pigs were slaughtered and buried. By the end of 1934, the AAA efforts had worked: wheat, cotton, and corn production had declined and prices for those commodities had risen. Farm income increased by 58 percent between 1932 and 1935.

Regional Planning: The TVA

One of the most innovative programs of the First New Deal created the Tennessee Valley Authority (TVA), an ambitious venture designed to bring electrical power, flood control efforts, and jobs to Appalachia, the desperately poor mountainous region including West Virginia, western Virginia and North Carolina, Kentucky, eastern Tennessee, and northern Georgia and Alabama. By 1940, the TVA, a multipurpose public corporation, had constructed twenty-one electricity-generating dams which created the "Great Lakes of the South." The agency, moreover, dredged rivers to allow for boat and barge traffic, promoted soil conservation and scientific forestry management, experimented with fertilizers, drew new industries to the region, encouraged the formation of labor unions, improved schools and libraries, and provided electricity to the depressed region. The TVA provided 1.5 million farms with access to electricity and indoor plumbing for the first time.

During Roosevelt's first year in office, his programs and his personal charm generated widespread support. A former CCC worker remembered that Roosevelt "restored a sense of confidence and morale and hope—hope being the greatest of all." The First New Deal programs—as well as Roosevelt's leadership—had given Americans a sense of renewed faith in the future. Voters showed their appreciation in the congressional elections of 1934: the Democrats increased their dominance in Congress with an almost unprecedented midterm victory for a party in power.

Eleanor Roosevelt

One of the reasons for Franklin Roosevelt's popularity was his energetic wife, Eleanor Roosevelt, who had become an enormous political asset and would prove to be one of the most influential leaders of the time. Born in 1884 in New York City, the niece of Theodore Roosevelt, Eleanor married her distant cousin Franklin in 1905. During the 1920s, Eleanor Roosevelt began a lifelong crusade on behalf of women, blacks, and youth. Her tireless compassion resulted in part from the loneliness she had experienced as she was growing up and in part from the sense of betrayal she felt upon learning in 1918 that her husband had fallen in love with Lucy Mercer, her personal secretary. "The bottom dropped out of my own particular world," she recalled. Eleanor and Franklin decided to maintain their marriage, but as their son James said, it became an "armed truce." Eleanor later observed that she could "forgive, but never forget." Alice Roosevelt Longworth—the daughter of Theodore Roosevelt, and a cousin of Eleanor's—actually nurtured the affair, hosting Mercer and Franklin for dinner several times. She later explained that Roosevelt "deserved a good time . . . he was married to Eleanor."

Eleanor Roosevelt redefined the role of the First Lady. She was not content just to host social events in the White House. Instead, she became an outspoken activist: the first woman to address a national political convention, to write a nationally-syndicated newspaper column, and to hold regular press conferences. The tireless Eleanor crisscrossed the nation, speaking in support of the New Deal, meeting with African American leaders, supporting women's causes and organized labor, and urging Americans to live up to their humanitarian ideals. In 1933, she convened a White House conference on the emergency needs of women which urged the Federal Emergency Relief Administration (FERA) to ensure that it "pay particular attention to see that women are employed wherever possible." Within six months, some 300,000 women were at work on various federal government projects.

A popular joke in Washington claimed that President Roosevelt's nightly prayer was: "Dear God, please make Eleanor a little tired." But he was in fact deeply dependent on his industrious wife. She was the agitator dedicated to what *should* be done; he was the practical politician concerned with what *could* be done.

Eleanor Roosevelt Intelligent, principled, and a political figure in her own right, she is pictured here addressing the Red Cross Convention in 1934.

The New Deal under Fire

CORE **OBJECTIVE**
5. Analyze the major criticisms of the early New Deal.

By 1934, Franklin Roosevelt had become the best loved and most hated president of the twentieth century. Although a child of wealth and prestige, he was loved because he believed in and fought for the common people, for the "forgotten man" (and woman). And he was loved for what one French leader called his "glittering personality." Roosevelt radiated personal charm, joy in his work, courage in a crisis, and optimism for the future. "Meeting him," said the British prime minister Winston Churchill, "was like uncorking a bottle of champagne."

But Roosevelt was hated too, especially by business leaders and political conservatives who believed the New Deal and the higher taxes it required were moving America toward socialism. Others, on the Left, hated Roosevelt for not doing enough to end the Depression. By the mid-1930s, the early New Deal programs had helped stop the economy's downward slide, but prosperity remained elusive. "We have been patient and long suffering," said a farm leader. "We were promised a New Deal. . . . Instead, we have the same old stacked deck."

New Deal criticized by those on the Left and Right

Continuing Hardships

Although the programs making up the so-called First New Deal helped ease the devastation caused by the Depression, they did not restore prosperity or end the widespread human suffering. The Depression continued to exact a terrible toll on Americans as the shattered economy slowly worked its way back to health. As late as 1939, some 9.5 million workers (17 percent of the labor force) remained unemployed. Critics stressed that the economy, while stabilized, remained mired in the Depression.

African Americans and the New Deal

However progressive Franklin Delano Roosevelt was on social issues, he showed little interest in the plight of African Americans, even as black voters, by 1936, were shifting from the Republicans (the "party of Lincoln") to the Democrats. President Roosevelt, like Woodrow Wilson before him, failed to address long-standing patterns of racism and segregation in the South for fear of angering conservative southern Democrats in Congress.

> New Deal discrimination, the NAACP, and the "Black Cabinet"

As a result, many of the New Deal programs discriminated against blacks. As Mary White Ovington, the treasurer of the National Association for the Advancement of Colored People (NAACP), stressed, the racism in any agency "varies according to the white people chosen to administer it, but always there is discrimination." For example, the payments from the AAA to farm owners to take land *out* of production in an effort to raise the prices for farm products forced hundreds of thousands of tenant farmers and sharecroppers, both blacks and whites, off the land. Meanwhile, the FHA refused to guarantee mortgages on houses purchased by blacks in white neighborhoods. In addition, both the CCC and the TVA practiced racial segregation. The NAACP waged an energetic legal campaign against racial prejudice throughout the 1930s, but a major setback occurred in the Supreme Court ruling on *Grovey v. Townsend* (1935), which upheld the Texas Democrats' whites-only election primary.

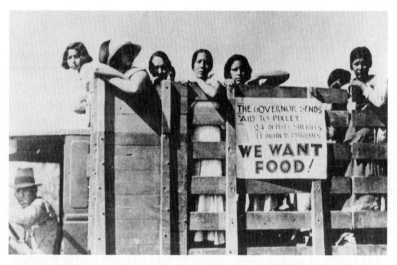

Latinos and the New Deal When Mexican migrant workers went on strike against California cotton growers in 1933, local authorities prohibited relief agencies from giving food to strikers and their families. Here, Mexican women and children picket for government aid in Pixley, California.

Thanks to relentless pressure from Eleanor Roosevelt, the president did appoint more African Americans to government positions than ever before. One of the most visible of the new appointees was Mary McLeod Bethune, the child of former slaves from South Carolina, who had founded

Bethune-Cookman College in Florida and had served as the head of the NAACP in the 1920s. In 1935, Roosevelt approved her appointment as the director of the Division of Negro Affairs within the National Youth Administration, an agency that provided jobs to unemployed young Americans. Bethune worked with other blacks in New Deal agencies to form an informal "Black Cabinet" to ensure that African Americans across the country had equal access to federal programs.

Court Cases and Civil Liberties

The continuing prejudice against blacks in the South was vividly revealed in a controversial case in Alabama. In 1931, an all-white jury, on flimsy evidence, hastily convicted nine black boys, ranging in age from thirteen to twenty-one, of raping two young white women while riding a freight train. Eight of the "Scottsboro Boys" were sentenced to death before cheering whites who packed the courtroom. In his award-winning novel *Native Son* (1940), the African American writer Richard Wright recalled the "mob who surrounded the Scottsboro jail with rope and kerosene" after the Scottsboro boys' initial conviction.

The "Scottsboro boys"

The injustice of the Scottsboro case sparked protests throughout the nation and around the world. The two white girls, it turned out, had been selling sex to white and black boys on the train. One of the girls eventually recanted the rape charges and began appearing at rallies on behalf of the black defendants.

No case in American legal history had ever produced as many trials, appeals, reversals, and retrials as the much-publicized Scottsboro case. Further, it prompted two important legal interpretations. In *Powell v. Alabama* (1932), the U.S. Supreme Court overturned the original convictions in the case because the judge had not ensured that the accused were provided adequate defense attorneys. The Court ordered new trials. In another case, *Norris v. Alabama* (1935), the Court ruled that the systematic

Scottsboro case Heywood Patterson (center), one of the defendants in the case, is seen here with his attorney, Samuel Liebowitz (left) in Decatur, Alabama, in 1933.

exclusion of African Americans from Alabama juries had denied the Scottsboro defendants equal protection under the law—a principle that had widespread impact on state courts by opening up juries to blacks. Eventually, but too late to help the defendants, whose lives were ruined, the state of Alabama dropped the charges against the four youngest of the "Scottsboro boys" and granted paroles to the others; the last one was released from prison in 1950.

Native Americans and the Depression

The "Indian New Deal"

The Great Depression also ravaged Native Americans. They were initially encouraged by Roosevelt's appointment of John Collier as the commissioner of the Bureau of Indian Affairs (BIA). Collier steadily increased the number of Native Americans employed by the BIA and ensured that Native Americans gained access to the various federal relief programs. Collier's primary objective, however, was passage of the Indian Reorganization Act. Designed to reinvigorate Native American cultural traditions by restoring land to tribes, the proposed law would grant them the right to start businesses and establish self-governing constitutions, and provide federal funds for vocational training and economic development. The act that Congress finally passed, however, was a much-diluted version of Collier's original proposal, and the "Indian New Deal" brought only a partial improvement to the lives of Native Americans. Yet it did spur the various tribes to revise their constitutions so as to give women the right to vote and hold office.

Critics Assault the New Deal

For all of their criticisms of the inadequacy of New Deal programs, Native Americans and African Americans still voted in large majorities for Franklin Roosevelt. Other New Deal critics, however, hated Roosevelt as much as his policies.

Huey Long

Huey Long As the powerful governor of Louisiana, Long was a shrewd lawyer and consummate politician.

The most potent threat to Roosevelt came from Louisiana's Democratic senator Huey P. Long. A short, colorful man with wild curly hair, Long, known as the "Kingfish," was a theatrical political performer (a demagogue) who appealed to the raw emotions of the masses. The swaggering son of a backwoods farmer, he sported pink suits and pastel shirts, red ties, and two-toned shoes. He claimed to serve the poor, arguing that his Louisiana would be a place where "every man [is] a king, but no one wears a crown." First as Louisiana's governor, then as its most powerful U.S. senator, Long viewed the state as his personal empire. Reporters called him the "dictator of Louisiana." True, he reduced state taxes, improved roads and schools, built charity hospitals, and provided better public services, but in the process, he became a bullying dictator who used bribery, intimidation, and blackmail to get his way.

In 1933, Senator Long arrived in Washington as a supporter of Roosevelt and the New Deal, but he quickly grew suspicious of the NRA's efforts to cooperate with big business. Having developed his own presidential aspirations, he had also grown jealous of "Prince Franklin" Roosevelt's popularity. To launch his own presidential candidacy, Long devised a simplistic plan for dealing with the Great Depression that he called the Share-the-Wealth Society. Long wanted to raise taxes on the wealthiest Americans and redistribute the money to "the people"—giving every poor family $5,000 and every worker an annual income of $2,500, providing pensions to retirees, reducing working hours, paying bonuses to military veterans, and enabling every qualified student to attend college.

> Huey Long's Share-the-Wealth Society

It did not matter that Long's plan would have spent far more dollars than would have been raised by his proposed taxes. As he told a group of Iowa farmers, "Maybe somebody says I don't understand it [government finance]. Well, you don't have to. Just shut your damn eyes and believe it. That's all." By early 1935, the outspoken Long claimed to have enough support to unseat Roosevelt. "I can take him," he bragged. "He's a phony. . . . He's scared of me. I can outpromise him, and he knows it. People will believe me, and they won't believe him."

The Townsend Plan

Another popular critic of Roosevelt was a retired California doctor, Francis E. Townsend. Outraged by the sight of three elderly women digging through garbage cans for food scraps, Townsend began promoting the Townsend Recovery Plan in 1934. It called for the federal government to pay $200 a month to every American over sixty who agreed to quit working. The recipients had to spend the money each month; it could not be saved. Townsend claimed that his plan would create new jobs for young people by forcing older people to retire, and it would energize the economy by enabling retirees to buy more products every month.

> The Townsend Plan and Father Coughlin

Like Huey Long's "Share Our Wealth" scheme, the numbers in Townsend's crackpot scheme did not add up: the Townsend Plan, which would serve only 9 percent of the population, would have paid those retirees more than half the total national income. Yet Townsend, like Long, didn't care about the numbers adding up. "I'm not in the least interested in the cost of the plan," he blandly told a Congressional committee. Not surprisingly, however, the Townsend Plan attracted great support among Americans 60 years of age and older. Thousands of Townsend Clubs sprang up across the nation, and advocates of the plan flooded the White House with letters urging Roosevelt to enact it.

Father Coughlin

A third outspoken critic of Roosevelt was Father Charles E. Coughlin, the Roman Catholic "radio priest" in Detroit who founded the National Union for Social Justice in 1935. In fiery weekly broadcasts over the CBS radio network that attracted as many as 40 million listeners, he assailed Roosevelt as "anti-God" and claimed that the New Deal was a Communist conspiracy. During the 1930s, Coughlin became increasingly anti-Semitic, claiming that Roosevelt was a tool of "international Jewish bankers" and relabeling the New Deal the "Jew Deal." He praised Hitler and the Nazis for killing Jews because he believed that all Jews were Communists who must be hunted down. "When we get through with the Jews in America," the thuggish Coughlin bragged, "they'll think the treatment they received in Germany was nothing."

Coughlin, Townsend, and Long were Roosevelt's most prominent critics. Of the three, Long had the largest political following. A 1935 survey showed that he could draw over 5 million votes as a third-party candidate for president in 1936, perhaps enough to prevent Roosevelt's reelection. Roosevelt decided to "steal the thunder" from his most vocal critics by instituting an array of new programs. "I'm fighting Communism, Huey Longism, Coughlinism, Townsendism," Roosevelt told a reporter in early 1935. He needed to fight even harder "to save our system, the capitalist system," from such "crackpot ideas."

Opposition from the Court

The opposition to the New Deal came from all directions. Among the most powerful was the Supreme Court. By the mid-1930s, businesses were filing law suits against various elements of the New Deal, and some of them made their way to the Supreme Court.

The Supreme Court vs. The New Deal

Supreme Court overturns some New Deal programs

On May 27, 1935, the U.S. Supreme Court killed the National Industrial Recovery Act (NIRA) by a unanimous vote. In *Schechter Poultry Corporation v. United States*, the justices ruled that Congress had given too much of its authority to the president when the NIRA created the National Recovery Administration and gave it the power to bring business and labor leaders together to create "codes of fair competition" for their industries. In a press conference soon after the Court announced its decision, Roosevelt fumed: "We have been relegated to the horse-and-buggy definition of interstate commerce."

But by 1935, the NRA had developed more critics than friends. While the NRA had worked for a time, and the downward spiral of wages and prices subsided, as soon as economic recovery began, small business owners complained that the larger corporations dominated the NRA, whose price-fixing robbed small producers of the chance to compete. And because the NRA wage codes excluded agricultural and domestic workers (at the insistence of southern Democrats), three out of every four African Americans derived no direct benefit from the program.

Then, on January 6, 1936, in *United States v. Butler*, the Supreme Court declared the Agricultural Adjustment Act's tax on the companies that processed food crops and commodities like cotton, unconstitutional. In response to the Court's decision, the Roosevelt administration passed the Agricultural Adjustment Act of 1938, which reestablished the earlier crop-reduction payment programs but left out the tax on processors. Although the AAA helped boost the overall farm economy, conservatives criticized its sweeping powers. By the end of its 1936 term, the Supreme Court had ruled against New Deal programs in seven of nine major cases. The same line of conservative judicial reasoning, Roosevelt warned, might endanger other New Deal programs—if he did not act swiftly to prevent it.

The Second New Deal

To rescue his legislative program from such judicial and political challenges, Roosevelt in January 1935 launched the second, more radical phase of the New Deal, explaining that "social justice, no longer a distant ideal, has become a definite goal" of his administration. In his effort "to steal Huey Long's thunder," the president called on Congress to pass a cluster of what he designated as his "must" legislation that included a new federal construction program to employ the jobless, banking reforms, increased taxes on the wealthy, and programs to protect people during unemployment, old age, and illness. Roosevelt's closest aide, Harry L. Hopkins, told the cabinet: "Boys—this is our hour. We've got to get everything we want—a [public] works program, social security, wages and hours, everything—now or never."

The WPA

In the first three months of 1935, dubbed the Second Hundred Days, Roosevelt used all of his considerable political skills to convince the Democratic-controlled Congress to pass most of the **Second New Deal**'s "must" legislation. The results changed the face of American life. The first major initiative, the $4.8-billion Emergency Relief Appropriation Act, sailed through the new Congress. Roosevelt called it the "Big Bill" because it was the largest peacetime spending bill in history up to that point. It included an array of federal job programs managed by a new government agency, the **Works Progress Administration** (WPA).

The WPA quickly became the nation's largest employer, hiring an average of 2 million people annually over four years. Federal WPA workers built New York's LaGuardia Airport, restored the St. Louis riverfront, and managed the bankrupt city of Key West, Florida. The WPA also employed a wide range of talented writers, artists, actors, and musicians in new cultural programs: the Federal Theatre Project, the Federal Art Project, the Federal Music Project, and the Federal Writers' Project. The National

CORE OBJECTIVE

6. Evaluate the ways the New Deal changed and how it transformed the role of federal government.

Second New Deal: Works Progress Administration (WPA)

Second New Deal (1935–1938) Expansive cluster of legislation proposed by President Roosevelt that established new regulatory agencies, strengthened the rights of workers to organize unions, and laid the foundation of a federal social welfare system through the creation of Social Security.

Works Progress Administration (1935) Government agency established to manage several federal job programs created under the New Deal; it became the largest employer in the nation.

Federal Art Project A group of WPA artists at work on *Building the Transcontinental Railroad*, a mural celebrating the contributions of immigrants that appears in the immigrants' dining hall on Ellis Island.

Youth Administration (NYA), also under the WPA, provided part-time employment to students and aided jobless youths. Twenty-seven-year-old Lyndon B. Johnson directed an NYA program in Texas, and Richard M. Nixon, a struggling Duke University law student, found work through the NYA at 35¢ an hour. Although the WPA took care of only 3 million of some 10 million jobless at any one time, in all it helped some 9 million people weather desperate circumstances before it expired in 1943.

The Wagner Act

Second New Deal: Wagner Act and unions

Another major element of the Second New Deal was the National Labor Relations Act, often called the **Wagner Act** in honor of the New York senator, Robert Wagner, who drafted it and convinced Roosevelt to support it. The Wagner Act was one of the most important pieces of labor legislation in history, guaranteeing workers the right to organize unions and bargain directly with management about wages and other issues. It also prohibited employers from interfering with union activities. The Wagner Act created a National Labor Relations Board to oversee union activities across the nation.

Wagner Act (1935) Legislation that guaranteed workers the right to organize unions, granted them direct bargaining power, and barred employers from interfering with union activities.

Social Security

Social Security Act (1935) Legislation enacted to provide federal assistance to retired workers through tax-funded pension payments and benefit payments to the unemployed and disabled.

As Francis Townsend stressed, the Great Depression hit the oldest Americans and those with disabilities especially hard. To address the problems faced by the old, blind, and disabled, Roosevelt proposed the **Social Security Act** of 1935. Social Security was, he announced, the "cornerstone" and "supreme achievement" of the New Deal. The basic concept of government assistance to the elderly was not new. Progressives during the early 1900s had proposed a federal system of social security for the aged, poor, disabled, and unemployed. Other nations had already enacted such programs, but not the United States. The hardships caused by the Great Depression revived the idea of a social security program, however, and Roosevelt masterfully guided the legislation through Congress.

The Social Security Act, designed by Secretary of Labor Frances Perkins, the first woman cabinet member in history, included three major provisions. Its centerpiece was a self-financed federal retirement fund for people over sixty-five. Beginning in 1937, workers and employers contributed payroll taxes to establish the fund. Most of the collected taxes were spent on pension payments to retirees; whatever was left over went into a trust fund for the future. Roosevelt stressed that Social Security was not intended to guarantee everyone a comfortable retirement. Rather, it was meant to supplement other sources of income and protect the elderly from some of the "hazards" of life. Only during the 1950s did voters and politicians come to view Social Security as the *primary* source of retirement income for working-class Americans.

The Social Security Act also set up a shared federal-state unemployment-insurance program, financed by a payroll tax on employers. In addition, the new legislation committed the national government to a broad range of social-welfare activities based upon the assumption that "unemployables"—people who were unable to work—would remain a state responsibility while the national government would provide work relief for the able-bodied. To that end, the Social Security Act provided federal funding for three state-administered public-assistance programs—old-age assistance, aid to dependent children, and aid for the blind—and further aid for maternal, child-welfare, and public health services.

When compared with similar programs in Europe, the new U.S. Social Security system was conservative. It was the only government-managed retirement program in the world financed by taxes on the earnings of workers; most other countries funded such programs out of general government revenues. The Social Security payroll tax was also a regressive tax because it used a single withholding tax *rate* for everyone, regardless of income level. It thus pinched the poor more than the rich, and it also hurt Roosevelt's efforts to revive the economy because it removed from circulation a significant amount of money: the new Social Security tax took money out of workers' pockets and placed it into a retirement fund, worsening the shrinking money supply that was one of the main causes of the Depression. In addition, the Social Security system, at the insistence of southern Democrats determined to maintain white supremacy in the region, excluded 9.5 million workers who most needed the new program: farm laborers, domestic workers (maids and cooks), and the self-employed, a disproportionate percentage of whom were African Americans.

Roosevelt regretted the limitations of the Social Security Act, but he knew that they were necessary compromises in order to gain Congressional approval and to withstand court challenges. As he replied to an aide who criticized funding the pension program out of employee contributions:

> I guess you're right on the economics, but those taxes were never a problem of economics. They are politics all the way through. We put those payroll contributions there so as to give the contributors a moral, legal, and political right to collect their pensions and their unemployment benefits. With those taxes in there, no damn politician can ever scrap my Social Security program.

> Second New Deal: Social Security and the Wealth-Tax Act

Roosevelt also preferred workers to fund their own Social Security pensions because he wanted Americans to view their retirement checks not as a welfare payment but as an *entitlement*—as something that they had paid for, something they deserved. On the other hand, conservatives condemned the Social Security Act as tyrannical. Former president Herbert Hoover was among a few Americans who refused to apply for a Social Security card because of his opposition to the "radical" program. He received a Social Security number anyway.

Taxing the Rich

Another major bill making up the second phase of the New Deal was the Revenue Act of 1935, sometimes called the "Wealth-Tax Act" but popularly known as the "soak-the-rich" tax. The Revenue Act raised tax rates on annual income above $50,000, in part because of stories that many wealthy Americans were not paying taxes. The powerful banker J. P. Morgan confessed to a Senate committee that he had created fictitious sales of stock to his wife that enabled him to pay no taxes. Morgan and other business leaders fumed over Roosevelt's tax and spending policies. The newspaper editor William Randolph Hearst growled that the wealth tax was "essentially communism." Roosevelt countered by stressing that "I am fighting communism. . . . I want to save our system, the capitalistic system." Yet he added that saving capitalism and "rebalancing" its essential elements required a more equal "distribution of wealth." Like his cousin Theodore, Franklin Roosevelt did not hate capitalism; he hated capitalists who engaged in "unfair" or illegal behavior.

A New Direction for Unions

The New Deal helped revive the labor union movement. When the National Industrial Recovery Act (NIRA) demanded that every industry code affirm workers' rights to organize, alert unionists quickly translated it to mean "the president wants you to join the union." John L. Lewis, head of the United Mine Workers (UMW), was among the first to capitalize upon the pro-union spirit of the NIRA. He rebuilt the UMW from 150,000 members to 500,000 within a year. Spurred by Lewis's success, Sidney Hillman of the Amalgamated Clothing Workers and David Dubinsky of the International Ladies Garment Workers organized workers in the clothing industry. As leaders of industrial unions (composed of all types of workers in a particular industry, skilled or unskilled), which were in the minority by far, they found the smaller, more restrictive craft unions (composed of skilled male workers only, with each union serving just one trade) to be obstacles to organizing workers in the country's basic industries.

In 1935, with the passage of the Wagner Act, industrial unionists formed a Committee for Industrial Organization (CIO), and craft unionists (skilled workers) began to fear submergence by the mass unions made up mainly of unskilled workers. Jurisdictional disputes divided them, and in 1936 the American Federation of Labor (AFL) expelled the CIO unions, which then formed a permanent structure, called after 1938 the Congress of Industrial Organizations (also known by the initials CIO). The rivalry spurred both groups to recruit more members.

The CIO's major organizing drives in the automobile and steel industries began in 1936, but until the Supreme Court upheld the Wagner Act in 1937, companies failed to cooperate with its pro-union provisions. Employers used various forms of intimidation to fight the efforts of workers to form unions. Early in 1937 automobile workers spontaneously adopted a new tactic, the "sit-down strike," in which workers refused to leave a workplace until employers had granted collective-bargaining rights to their union.

"Sit-down strikes"

Led by the fiery young autoworker and union organizer Walter Reuther, thousands of employees at the General Motors assembly plants in Flint, Michigan, occupied the factories and stopped all production. Female workers supported their male counterparts by picketing at the plant entrances. Company officials called in police to harass the strikers, sent spies to union meetings, and threatened to fire the workers. They also pleaded with President Roosevelt to dispatch federal troops. He refused,

Labor union violence This 1935 photograph captures unionized strikers fighting "scabs," or nonunion replacement employees, as the scabs attempt to pass the picket line and enter the factory.

while expressing his displeasure with the sit-down strike, which the courts later declared illegal. The standoff lasted over a month. Then, on February 11, 1937, the company relented and signed a contract recognizing the fledgling United Automobile Workers (UAW) as a legitimate union.

Combating the Great Depression

The federal government's efforts to combat the Great Depression changed over time. The following charts explore the first three phases of the federal government's response to the Great Depression, those of the Hoover administration (1929–1933), the Roosevelt administration during the First New Deal (1933–1935), and finally the Roosevelt administration during the Second New Deal (1935–1938). In each phase, the federal government had a particular strategy to end the Depression, each targeting a different set of problems to be solved, and each employing a different set of tactics and programs.

PHASE I Hoover Administration (1929–1933)

Overall Strategy to end the Depression: The economy will cure itself if left alone.

Problems the administration thought needed to be solved: "High costs of living and high living"; foreign competition; poor economic morale

Tactics and Programs:

- Increased taxes to balance the budget
- Smoot-Hawley Tariff of 1930 to keep out foreign goods
- Reconstruction Finance Corporation to make loans to major industries and to states for limited public works projects
- Upbeat slogans
- Dismissed critics as "calamity mongers and weeping men"

Results: The Great Depression worsened and spread globally.

PHASE II Roosevelt Administration during the First New Deal (1933–1935)

Overall Strategy to end the Depression: "Bold, persistent experimentation"

Problems the administration thought needed to be solved: Bank crisis; unemployment and homelessness; low wages and prices

Tactics and Programs:

- "Bank holiday," "fireside chats," and FDIC to insure deposits in order to stop bank runs
- Mortgage and foreclosure reform through Home Owners' Loan Corporation, and Federal Housing Administration
- Funding of state and federal work relief programs like the Civil Conservation Corps and Public Works Administration
- Agricultural Adjustment Administration (AAA) payments to farmers to cut production
- National Recovery Administration (NRA)–mandated increases of wages and prices
- Tennessee Valley Authority (TVA) development of the rural mountain South through flood control, electrification, and other projects

Results: In the First New Deal, FDR was able to use regulation to mitigate the banking crisis and begin resolving the housing crisis. Rural America received electricity and other regional improvements, but the work relief programs—many of which barred minorities from participation—failed to resolve the unemployment crisis, and the Great Depression continued.

Roosevelt's Second Term

On June 27, 1936, Franklin Delano Roosevelt accepted the Democratic Party's nomination for a second term. The Republicans chose Governor Alfred M. Landon of Kansas, a progressive Republican who had endorsed many New Deal programs. The Republicans hoped that the followers of Long, Coughlin, Townsend, and other Roosevelt critics would combine to

QUESTIONS FOR ANALYSIS

1. How and why did the overall approach employed by the federal government to combat the Depression change between the Hoover administration and the Roosevelt administration during the First New Deal?

2. What problems created by the Depression was the federal government able to resolve, and which problems continued?

3. How did the role of the federal government change as a result of these developments?

draw enough Democratic votes away from Roosevelt to throw the election to them. But that possibility faded when an assassin, the son-in-law of a Louisiana judge whom Huey Long had sought to remove, shot and killed the forty-two-year-old senator in 1935.

In the 1936 election, Roosevelt carried every state except Maine and Vermont, with a popular vote of 27.7 million to Landon's 16.7 million, the largest margin of victory up to that point. Democrats would also dominate Republicans in the new Congress, by 77 to 19 in the Senate and 328 to 107 in the House.

In winning another landslide election, Roosevelt forged in 1936 a new electoral coalition that would affect national politics for years to come. While holding the support of most traditional Democrats, North and South, the president made strong gains in the West among beneficiaries of New Deal agricultural programs. In the northern cities, he held on to the ethnic groups helped by New Deal welfare policies. Many middle-class voters whose property had been saved by New Deal measures flocked to support Roosevelt, as did intellectuals stirred by the ferment of new ideas coming from the government. The revived labor union movement threw its support to Roosevelt. And in the most profound departure of all, African American voters for the first time cast the majority of their ballots for a Democratic president. "My friends, go home and turn Lincoln's picture to the wall," a Pittsburgh journalist told black voters. "That debt has been paid in full."

The Court-Packing Plan

Roosevelt's landslide victory led him to bolder, and at times reckless, efforts to end the Great Depression. In his second inaugural address, delivered on January 20, 1937, he promised even greater reforms. The challenge to democracy, he maintained, was that millions lacked "the necessities of life. . . . I see one-third of a nation ill-housed, ill-clad, ill-nourished." Roosevelt argued that his re-election demonstrated that the nation wanted even more extensive government action to revive the economy. The three-to-one Democratic majorities in Congress ensured that he could pass new legislation. Yet one major roadblock stood in the way: the conservative Supreme Court.

Suits challenging the constitutionality of the Social Security and Wagner acts were pending. Given the conservative bent of the Court, the Second New Deal seemed in danger of being nullified by judges, just as much of the original New Deal had been.

For that reason, Roosevelt hatched a plan to change the Court's conservative stance by increasing its members. Congress, not the Constitution, determines the size of the Supreme Court, which over the years had numbered between six and ten justices. In 1937, the number was nine. On February 5, 1937, Roosevelt, without consulting Congressional leaders or even his own advisers, asked Congress to name up to six new Supreme Court justices, explaining that the aging justices then on the Court were falling behind in their work and needed help.

"Court-packing" plan

But the "Court-packing" plan, as opponents labeled the president's scheme, backfired. It was too manipulative and far too political. A leading journalist said that Roosevelt had become "drunk with power." Roosevelt's plan aroused fears even among Democrats that the president was seeking dangerous new powers.

As it turned out, unforeseen events blunted Roosevelt's clumsy effort to change the Court. A sequence of Court decisions during the spring of 1937 surprisingly upheld disputed provisions of the Wagner and Social Security acts. In addition, a conservative justice resigned, and Roosevelt replaced him with one of the most consistent New Dealers, Senator Hugo Black of Alabama. Despite criticism from both parties, however, Roosevelt insisted on forcing his Court-packing bill through the Congress. On July 22, 1937, the Senate overwhelmingly voted it down. It was the biggest political blunder and humiliation of Roosevelt's career. The episode fractured the Democratic party and damaged the president's prestige. For the first time, Democrats in large numbers, especially southerners, opposed him, and the momentum of his 1936 landslide victory was lost. As Secretary of Agriculture Henry A. Wallace later remarked, "The whole New Deal really went up in smoke as a result of the Supreme Court fight."

A Slumping Economy

During the years 1935 and 1936, the depressed economy was finally show- | "Roosevelt's recession" in 1937
ing signs of revival. By the spring of 1937, industrial output had moved above the 1929 level. In 1937, however, Roosevelt, worried about federal budget deficits and rising inflation, ordered sharp cuts in government spending. The result was that the economy suddenly stalled and then slid into a business slump deeper than that of 1929. In only three months, unemployment rose by 2 million people. When the spring of 1938 failed to bring economic recovery, Roosevelt asked Congress to adopt a new large-scale federal spending program, and Congress voted $3.3 billion in new expenditures. The increase in government spending reversed the economy's decline, but only during World War II would employment reach pre-1929 levels.

The Court-packing fight, the sit-down strikes, and the 1937 recession all undercut Roosevelt's prestige and power. When the 1937 congressional session ended, the only major New Deal initiatives were the Wagner-Steagall National Housing Act and the Bankhead-Jones Farm Tenant Act. The Housing Act, developed by Senator Robert F. Wagner, set up the federal Housing Authority which extended long-term loans to cities for public housing projects in blighted low-income neighborhoods. The agency also subsidized rents for poor people. Later, during World War II, it financed housing for workers in new defense plants.

The Farm Tenant Act addressed the epidemic of rural poverty. It created a new agency, the Farm Security Administration (FSA), which provided loans to keep farm owners from losing their land to bankruptcy. It also made loans to tenant farmers to enable them to purchase their own farms. In the end, however, the FSA proved to be little more than another relief operation that tided a few farmers over during difficult times. A more effective answer to the problem eventually arrived in the form of national mobilization for war, which landed many struggling tenant farmers in military service or the defense industry, broadened their horizons, and taught them new skills.

In 1938, the Democratic Congress also enacted the Fair Labor Standards Act. It replaced many of the provisions that had been in the NIRA, which had been declared unconstitutional. The federal government established a minimum wage of 40¢ an hour and a maximum workweek of forty hours. The act, which applied only to businesses engaged in *interstate* commerce, also prohibited the employment of children under the age of sixteen.

Setbacks for the President

> Democrats divided over New Deal

During the late 1930s, the Democrats in Congress increasingly split into two factions, with conservative southerners on one side and liberal northerners on the other. Many white southern Democrats balked at the national party's growing dependence on the votes of northern labor unions and African Americans. Senator Ellison "Cotton Ed" Smith of South Carolina, the powerful chair of the Committee on Agriculture, and several other southern delegates walked out of the 1936 Democratic party convention, with Smith declaring that he would not support any party that views "the Negro as a political and social equal." Other critics believed that Roosevelt was exercising too much power and spending too much money. Some disgruntled southern Democrats began to work with conservative Republicans to veto any additional New Deal programs.

Roosevelt now headed a divided party, and the congressional elections of November 1938 handed the administration another setback when the Democrats lost 7 seats in the Senate and 80 in the House. In his State of the Union message in 1939, Roosevelt for the first time proposed no new reforms but spoke of the need "to *preserve* our reforms." The conservative coalition of Republicans and southern Democrats had stalemated the once unstoppable Roosevelt. As one observer noted, the New Deal "has been reduced to a movement with no program, with no effective political organization, with no vast popular party strength behind it."

A Halfway Revolution

The New Deal's political momentum petered out in 1939 just as a new world war was erupting in Europe and Asia. Many of the New Deal programs had failed or were poorly conceived and implemented, victims of bureaucratic infighting and inefficient management, but others were changing American life for the better: Social Security, the federal regulation of stock markets and banks, minimum wage levels for workers, federally insured bank accounts, the right to join labor unions. Roosevelt had also transformed the nation's political dynamics, luring black voters in large numbers to the Democratic party. A self-proclaimed "preacher President," Roosevelt raised the nation's spirits through his relentless optimism.

In addition, Roosevelt changed the role of the federal government in national life. During the 1930s, for the first time, the federal government assumed responsibility for planning and managing the economy and intervening to ensure social stability. By the end of the 1930s, the power and scope of the national government were vastly larger than in 1932. Landmark laws expanded the powers of the national government by establishing regulatory agencies and laying the foundation of a social welfare system. Most important of all, however, the New Deal restored a sense of hope to many people who had grown discouraged and desperate. The enduring reforms of the New Deal entailed more than just a bigger federal government and revived public confidence; they also constituted a significant change from the progressivism of Theodore Roosevelt and Woodrow Wilson. Those reformers had assumed that the function of progressive government was to use aggressive *regulation* of industry and business to ensure that people had an equal opportunity to pursue the American Dream.

> Foundation for social welfare system

Franklin Roosevelt and the New Dealers went beyond the progressive concept of regulated capitalism by insisting that the government provide at least a minimal level of support for all Americans. The enduring protections afforded by bank-deposit insurance, unemployment benefits, a minimum hourly wage, the Wagner Act, and Social Security pensions provided people with a sense of security as well as a safeguard for the nation against future economic crises (there has not been a similar "depression" since the 1930s).

> Federal regulation of business and banking

The greatest failure of the New Deal was its inability to restore prosperity and end record levels of unemployment. In 1939, 10 million Americans—nearly 17 percent of the workforce—remained jobless. Only the prolonged crisis of the Second World War would finally produce full employment—in the military as well as in factories making things for the military.

Roosevelt's energetic pragmatism was his greatest strength—and weakness. He was flexible in developing new policies and programs; he kept what worked and discarded what failed. The result was both revolutionary and conservative. Roosevelt sharply increased the regulatory powers of the federal government and laid the foundation for what would become an expanding system of social welfare programs. Roosevelt, however, was no socialist, as Republican critics charged; he sought to preserve the basic capitalist economic structure while providing protection to the nation's most vulnerable people. In this sense, the New Deal represented a "halfway revolution" that permanently altered the nation's social and political landscape. In a time of peril, Roosevelt created for Americans a more secure future.

■ **The Great Depression** The 1929 stock market crash revealed the structural flaws in the economy, but it was not the only cause of the *Great Depression (1929–1941)*. During the twenties, business owners did not provide adequate wage increases for workers, resulting in the overproduction of many goods by the end of the decade. The nation's agricultural sector also suffered from overproduction. Government policies—such as high tariffs and the reduction of the nation's money supply as a means of dealing with the financial panic—further reduced the nation's overall consumption and exacerbated the emerging economic depression.

■ **The Human Toll of the Depression** Thousands of banks and businesses closed, while millions of homes and jobs were lost. By the early 1930s, many people were homeless and hopeless. The *Dust Bowl* of the 1930s compounded the hardship for rural Americans living on the southern Great Plains. Many state laws and business practices discouraged the employment of married women. Discrimination against African Americans, Native Americans, Hispanics, and Asian Americans in hiring was widespread.

■ **Hoover's Failure** The first phase of federal response to the Great Depression included President Hoover's attempts at increasing public works and exhorting unions, businesses, and farmers to revive economic growth. His philosophy of voluntary self-reliance prevented him from using federal intervention to relieve the human suffering. In March 1933, the economy was shattered. Millions more Americans were without jobs, basic necessities, and hope.

■ **The First New Deal** During his early months in office, Congress and President Roosevelt enacted the *First New Deal (1933–1935)*, which propped up the banking industry with the *Federal Deposit Insurance Corporation (1933)*, provided short-term emergency work relief promoted industrial recovery with the *National Recovery Administration (1933)*, and raised agricultural prices with the *Agricultural Adjustment Act (1933)*. In this second phase of the federal response, most of the early New Deal programs helped end the economy's downward spiral but still left millions unemployed and mired in poverty.

■ **New Deal under Fire** The Supreme Court ruled that several of the First New Deal programs were unconstitutional violations of private property and states' rights. Many conservatives criticized the New Deal for expanding the scope and reach of the federal government so much that it was steering the nation toward socialism. By contrast, other critics did not think the New Deal went far enough. African American critics decried the widespread discrimination in New Deal policies and agencies.

■ **The Second New Deal and the New Deal's Legacy** Roosevelt responded to the criticism and the continuing economic hardship with a third phase, the *Second New Deal (1935–1938)*, which sought to reshape the nation's social structure by expanding the role of the federal government. Many of its programs, such as the *Works Progress Administration (1935)*, *Social Security (1935)*, and the *Wagner Act (1935)*, aimed to achieve greater social justice by establishing new regulatory agencies and laying the foundation of a federal social welfare system. The Second New Deal reformed business, industry, and banking with provisions such as unemployment pay, a minimum hourly wage, old-age pensions, and bank-deposit insurance. The New Deal established the idea that the federal government should provide a baseline quality of life for all Americans.

KEY TERMS

CHRONOLOGY

1929	Hoover inaugurated as president in March, and stock market crashes in late October
1930	Congress passes the Hawley-Smoot Tariff
1932	Congress sets up the Reconstruction Finance Corporation
1932	Bonus Expeditionary Force heads to Washington, D.C.
1932	Franklin D. Roosevelt is elected President
March–June 1933	First One Hundred Days of Roosevelt's presidency
December 1933	Twenty-First Amendment repeals Prohibition
May 1935	Supreme Court finds National Industrial Recovery Act unconstitutional
1935	Roosevelt creates the Works Progress Administration
1935	Congress passes the Wagner Act
1936	President Roosevelt is reelected in a landslide
1937	Social Security goes into effect
1937	Roosevelt attempts Court-packing scheme

INQUIZITIVE

Go to InQuizitive to see what you've learned—and learn what you've missed—with personalized feedback along the way.

RAISING THE FLAG ON IWO JIMA (February 23, 1945) Five members of the United States Marine Corps raise the flag on Mount Suribachi, during the Battle of Iwo Jima. Three of these Marines would die within days of this photograph, which later earned photographer Joe Rosenthal the Pulitzer Prize. A bronze statue of this scene is the centerpiece of the Marine Corps War Memorial in Virginia.

The Second
World War

1933–1945

CHAPTER

24

W hen Franklin Roosevelt became president in 1933, he shared with most Americans a determination to stay out of international disputes. His focus was on combating the Great Depression. While the United States had become deeply involved in global trade during the twenties, it had remained aloof from global conflicts. So-called isolationists insisted that there was no justification for America to become embroiled in international affairs. With each passing year during the thirties, however, Germany, Italy, and Japan threatened the stability of Europe and Asia.

Roosevelt strove mightily to keep the United States out of what he called the "spreading epidemic of world lawlessness," as brutal fascist dictatorships in Germany and Italy and ultranationalist militarists in Japan violated international law by invading neighboring countries. By the end of the decade, Roosevelt had decided that the only way for the United States to avoid fighting in another war was to offer all possible assistance to its allies, Great Britain and France. His efforts to make the United States the "arsenal of democracy" ignited a fierce debate between isolationists and interventionists, a debate which ended with shocking suddenness on December 7, 1941, when Japan staged a surprise attack against U.S. military bases at Pearl Harbor in Hawaii. The second world war that Americans had struggled for years to avoid had arrived at last. It would become the most

CORE
OBJECTIVES InQuizitive

1. Assess how German and Japanese actions led to the outbreak of war in Europe and in Asia.

2. Evaluate how President Roosevelt and Congress responded to the outbreak of wars in Europe and Asia between 1933 and 1941.

3. Analyze the effects of the Second World War on American society.

4. Explain the major factors that enabled the United States and its allies to win the war in Europe.

5. Describe how the Japanese were defeated in the war in the Pacific.

6. Evaluate the efforts of President Roosevelt and the Allies to shape the postwar world.

869

significant event of the twentieth century, engulfing five continents and leaving few people untouched.

The Japanese attack unified the American people as never before. Men and women rushed to join the armed forces. Eventually, 16.4 million Americans would serve in the military during the war, including 350,000 women. To win the war against Japanese imperialism and German and Italian fascism, the United States would have to mobilize all of its economic resources; total war required massive government spending that boosted industrial production and wrenched the economy out of the Great Depression.

Four years after the Japanese attack on Pearl Harbor, the United States and its allies emerged victorious in the costliest and most destructive war in history. Whole cities were destroyed, nations dismembered, and societies transformed. More than 50 million people were killed in the war between 1939 and 1945—perhaps 60 percent of them civilians, including millions of Jews and other ethnic minorities murdered in Nazi death camps and Soviet concentration camps.

The global scope and scale of the Second World War transformed America's role in the world by ending the tradition of isolationism. By 1945 America was the world's most powerful nation, with new international interests and global responsibilities. The war left in its wake power vacuums in Europe and Asia that the Soviet Union and the United States sought to fill in order to protect their military, economic, and political interests. Instead of bringing peace, the end of the war led to a new "cold war" between two former allies, the United States and the Soviet Union. As the *New Yorker* magazine asked, "If you do not know that your country is now entangled beyond recall with the rest of the world, what do you know?"

CORE **OBJECTIVE**

1. Assess how German and Japanese actions led to the outbreak of war in Europe and in Asia.

The Rise of Fascism in Europe

In 1917, Woodrow Wilson had led the United States into the First World War in order to make the world "safe for democracy." In fact, though, democracy was in retreat after 1919. Soviet Communism was on the march during the twenties and thirties. So, too, was its ideological opponent, **fascism**, a radical form of totalitarian government in which a dictator uses propaganda and brute force to seize absolute control of all aspects of national life—the economy, the armed forces, the legal and educational systems, and the press. Fascism in Germany and Italy thrived on a violent ultranationalist patriotism and almost hysterical emotionalism built upon claims of racial superiority and the simmering resentments that grew out of defeat in the First World War. At the same time, halfway around the world, the Japanese government fell under the control of militarist expansionists eager to conquer China and all of south Asia. Japanese leaders were convinced that they were a "master race" with a "mission" to conquer and lead a resurgent Asia, just as Hitler claimed that Germany's "mission" as home of the superior

fascism A radical form of totalitarian government that emerged in 1920s Italy and Germany in which a dictator uses propaganda and brute force to seize control of all aspects of national life.

"Aryan" race was to dominate Europe. By 1941, there would be only a dozen or so democratic nations left on earth.

Italy and Germany

In 1922, political journalist Benito Mussolini and his black-shirted supporters had seized control in Italy, taking advantage of a paralyzed political system incapable of dealing with widespread unemployment and runaway inflation. By 1925, he was wielding dictatorial power as "Il Duce" (the Leader). All opposition political parties were eliminated, and several political opponents were murdered. "Mussolini Is Always Right," screamed propaganda posters. Indeed, there was something comical about the strutting, chest-thumping Mussolini, who claimed that "my animal instincts are always right." Italy, after all, was a declining industrial power whose pitiful performance in the First World War was a national embarrassment.

Fascist propaganda Mussolini's headquarters in Rome's Palazzo Braschi, which bore an oversized reproduction of his leering face and 132 *si*'s (Italian for "yes") in 1934.

Germany was another matter, however. There was nothing amusing about Mussolini's German counterpart, the Austrian-born Adolf Hitler, whom Mussolini privately described as "an aggressive little man . . . probably a liar, and certainly mad." Hitler's remarkable transformation during the 1920s from social misfit to head of the National Socialist German Workers' (Nazi) party startled the world. Hitler and the Nazis claimed that they represented a German ("Aryan") master race whose "purity and strength" were threatened by liberals, Jews, Communists, homosexuals, Gypsies, and other "inferior" peoples. Hitler promised to make Germany strong again by uniting all the German-speaking peoples of Europe into a vast empire that would give fast-growing Germany "living space" to expand, dominate the "lesser" races, and rid the continent of Jews.

> Mussolini seizes power in Italy (1922); Hitler becomes head of Nazi party in Germany

Hitler had little patience with conventional political processes. He urged that "democracy must be destroyed." To enforce his rise to power, Hitler recruited 2 million street-brawling thugs called "storm troopers" to intimidate his opponents. "We are barbarians!" Hitler shouted. "We want to be barbarians! It is an honorable title. We shall rejuvenate the world!" Hitler also urged Germany to defy the restrictions on its armed forces imposed by the hated Versailles Peace Treaty after the First World War.

Hitler portrayed himself as Germany's savior from the humiliation of defeat in the First World War and the widespread suffering caused by the Great Depression. Appointed chancellor on January 30, 1933, five weeks before Franklin Roosevelt was first inaugurated, Hitler, like Mussolini, declared himself absolute leader, or *Führer*, banned all political parties except the Nazis, created a secret police force known as the *Gestapo*, and stripped people of voting rights. There would be no more elections, labor unions, or strikes. During the mid-1930s, Hitler's brutal Nazi police state cranked up the engines of tyranny and terrorism, propaganda and censorship. Brown-shirted Nazi "storm troopers" fanned out across the nation, burning books and persecuting, imprisoning, and murdering Communists, Jews, and their sympathizers.

> Hitler becomes German chancellor, creates Nazi police state (1933)

Adolf Hitler Hitler performs the Nazi salute at a rally. The majestic banners, triumphant music, powerful oratory, and expansive military parades were both hypnotic and alluring to the public.

The Expanding Axis

Japan occupies Manchuria (1932) and begins military build-up (1934)

As the 1930s unfolded, a catastrophic series of events in Asia and Europe sent the world hurtling toward disaster. In 1931–1932, some ten thousand Japanese troops had occupied Manchuria, a weakly defended province in northeast China blessed with valuable deposits of iron ore and coal. At the time, China was fragmented by civil war between Communists led by Mao Zedong and Nationalists led by Chiang Kai-shek. The Japanese took advantage of China's weakness to proclaim Manchuria's independence, renaming it "The Republic of Manchukuo." This was the first major step in Japan's eventual effort to control all of China. In 1934, Japan began an aggressive military buildup in anticipation of conquering all of East Asia.

Mussolini conquers Ethiopia (1935), German soldiers enter the Rhineland (1936) and the Spanish Civil War (1936)

The next year, Mussolini launched Italy's reconquest of Ethiopia, a weak nation in eastern Africa that Italy had controlled until 1896 (Mussolini dismissed it as "a country without a trace of civilization"). When the League of Nations branded Mussolini as an aggressor and imposed economic sanctions on Italy, the racist Italian leader expressed surprise that European leaders would prefer a "horde of barbarian Negroes" in Ethiopia over Italy, the "mother of civilization."

In 1935, Hitler, in flagrant violation of the Versailles Treaty, began rebuilding Germany's armed forces. The next year, 1936, he sent 35,000 soldiers into the Rhineland, the demilitarized buffer zone between France and Germany. In a staged vote, 99 percent of the Germans living in the Rhineland approved Hitler's action. The failure of France and Great Britain to enforce the Versailles Treaty convinced Hitler that the western democracies were weak and frightened.

The year 1936 also witnessed the outbreak of the Spanish Civil War, which began when Spanish troops loyal to General Francisco Franco, with the support of the Roman Catholic Church, revolted against the fragile new republican government. Hitler and Mussolini rushed troops ("volunteers"), warplanes, and massive amounts of military and financial aid to support Franco's fascist insurgency.

While peace in Europe was unraveling, the Japanese government fell under the control of aggressive militarists. In 1937, a government official announced that the "tide has turned against the liberalism and democracy that once swept over the nation." On July 7, 1937, Japanese and Chinese soldiers clashed at China's Marco Polo Bridge, west of Beijing. The incident quickly developed into a full-scale conflict, the Sino-Japanese War. From Beijing, the Japanese army swept northward toward Nanjing, home of the Nationalist Chinese government. In 1937, Japan joined Germany and Italy in establishing the Rome-Berlin-Tokyo **"Axis" alliance**. Hitler and Mussolini vowed to create a "new order in Europe" that would end the domination of Great Britain and France, while the Japanese imperialists pursued their "divine right" to control all of East Asia by creating what they called the Greater East Asia Co-Prosperity Sphere.

Anschluss and the Munich Pact (1938)

Hitler was equally aggressive. In March 1938, he forced the *Anschluss* (union) of Austria with Germany. German armies marched into Austria, followed by Hitler, whose triumphant return to his native Austria was greeted by pro-German crowds waving Nazi flags and tossing flowers. When Mussolini congratulated Hitler for his bold action, the German dictator told his Italian partner that he would "never forget him for this. Never, never, never—whatever happens." A month later, after arresting over 70,000 opponents of the Nazis, German leaders announced that a remarkable 99.75 percent of Austrian voters had "approved" the forced annexation by Hitler's Germany (in fact, some 400,000 Austrians, mostly liberals and Jews, were prevented from voting). Again, no nation stepped up to oppose Hitler's aggressive actions, and soon the new Nazi government in Austria began adopting Hitler's policies of arresting or murdering opponents and imprisoning or exiling Jews, including the famed psychiatrist Sigmund Freud.

Hitler then declared his intention to annex the Sudeten territory (or Sudetenland), a mountainous region in western Czechoslovakia along the German border where more than 3 million ethnic Germans lived. Paralyzed by fear of another world war, British and French leaders tried to "appease" Hitler, hoping that if they agreed to his demands for the Sudeten territory he would stop his aggressions. On September 30, 1938, the British prime minister, Neville Chamberlain, the French prime minister, Édouard Daladier, Italian dictator Benito Mussolini, and Hitler signed the notorious Munich Pact, which transferred the Sudetenland to Germany, leading the

Germany annexes Austria (1938) and takes control of Czechoslovakia (1938-1939)

"Axis" alliance Military alliance formed in 1937 by the three major fascist powers: Germany, Italy, and Japan.

Czechoslovakian president to resign in protest. Chamberlain returned to London claiming that the Munich treaty provided "peace for our time. Peace with honor." Winston Churchill, a member of the British Parliament who would himself become prime minister in May 1940, strongly disagreed. In a speech to the House of Commons, Churchill claimed that "England has been offered a choice between war and shame. She has chosen shame, and will get war." The Munich Pact, he predicted, would not end Hitler's advances. "This is only the beginning of the reckoning."

Churchill was right. Hitler, in fact, had already confided to aides that he had no intention of abiding by the Munich Pact: "That piece of paper is of no further significance whatever." Although Hitler had promised that the Sudetenland would be his last territorial demand, he violated his pledge in March 1939, when he sent German tanks and soldiers to conquer the remainder of the Czech Republic. The European democracies, having shrunk their armies after the First World War, continued to cower in the face of Hitler's ruthless behavior and seemingly unstoppable military forces.

After Hitler's troops seized all of Czechoslovakia on March 15, 1939, the German leader announced it was "the greatest day of my life." President Roosevelt was not amused. He decided that Hitler and Mussolini were "madmen" who "respect force and force alone." Throughout late 1938 and 1939, he tried to convince Americans, as well as British and French leaders, that the growing menace of fascism would only respond to force, not words. He also persuaded Congress to increase military spending in anticipation of a possible war.

The Conquest of Poland

Later in 1939, the insatiable Hitler turned his sights to Poland, Germany's eastern neighbor. In part he wanted to regain German territory taken to form Poland after the First World War, but he also wanted to conquer Poland so as to give the German army a clear path to invade the Soviet Union. To ensure that the Soviets did not interfere with his plans, Hitler camouflaged his virulent anticommunism on August 23, 1939, when he signed the Nazi-Soviet Non-Aggression Pact with the antifascist Soviet premier, Josef Stalin. The announcement of the treaty stunned a world that had understood fascism and communism to be eternal enemies. By the terms of the treaty, the two tyrants secretly agreed to divide northern and eastern Europe between them. Just nine days later, at dawn on September 1, 1939, 1.5 million German troops invaded Poland from the north, south, and west. Hitler ordered his armies "to kill without mercy men, women, and children of the Polish race or language." The German leader also ordered all terminally ill patients in German hospitals killed to make room for soldiers wounded in Poland.

This was the final straw for the western democracies. Having allowed Austria and Czechoslovakia to be seized by Hitler's war machine, the leaders of Great Britain and France now did an about-face. On September 3,

Josef Stalin Leader of the Soviet Union who rose to power in the mid-1920s after the death of Vladimir Lenin.

1939, they honored their commitment to defend Poland. Europe, the world's smallest continent, was again embroiled in what would soon become another world war. The nations making up the British Empire and Commonwealth around the world—Canada, India, Australia, New Zealand—joined the war against Nazi Germany.

Sixteen days after German troops stormed across the Polish border, the Soviet Union invaded Poland from the east. Pressed from all sides by its old enemies, 700,000 poorly equipped Polish soldiers (many Poles fought on horseback) surrendered, having suffered seventy thousand deaths and many more wounded. On October 6, 1939, the Nazis and Soviets divided conquered Poland between them and then set about systematically destroying it. Hitler's goal was to obliterate Polish civilization, especially the Jews, and Germanize the country. For his part, Stalin wanted to recapture Polish territory lost by Russia during the First World War. Over the next five years, the Nazis and Soviets arrested, deported, enslaved, or murdered millions of Poles.

In late November 1939, the Soviets invaded neighboring Finland, leading President Roosevelt to condemn Russia's "wanton disregard for law." Outnumbered five to one, Finnish troops held off the Soviet invaders for three months but were forced to negotiate a surrender in March 1940 that gave the Soviet Union a tenth of Finland.

The Outbreak of War in Europe

After the quick German conquest of Poland, the war on the ground in Europe settled into a three-month stalemate during early 1940 that was called "the phony war," as Hitler's generals waited out the winter. Then, in the early spring, Germany suddenly attacked again. At dawn on April 9, without warning, Nazi armies occupied Denmark and landed along the Norwegian coast. German paratroopers, the first ever used in warfare, seized Norway's airports. Denmark fell in a day, Norway within a few weeks. On May 10, German forces invaded the Low Countries—Belgium, Luxembourg, and the Netherlands (Holland). Luxembourg fell the first day, the Netherlands four days later. Belgium lasted until May 28.

A few days later, German tanks roared into northern France. "The fight beginning today," Hitler declared, "decides the fate of the German nation for the next thousand years!" Hitler's brilliant **blitzkrieg** ("lightning war") strategy centered on speed. Fast-moving columns of tanks, motorized artillery, and truck-borne infantry, all supported by warplanes and paratroopers, moved so fast that they paralyzed their stunned opponents.

A British army sent to help the Belgians and the French was forced along with French troops to make a frantic retreat to the English Channel coast, with the Germans in hot pursuit. On May 26, while the German *Panzer* divisions (made up of tanks and other armored vehicles) followed Hitler's surprising order to rest and refuel, Great Britain was able to organize a desperate week-long evacuation of battle-weary British and French soldiers

blitzkrieg (1940) The German "lightning war" strategy characterized by swift, well-organized attacks using infantry, tanks, and warplanes.

Winston Churchill Prime Minister of Great Britain who led the nation during the Second World War.

from the beaches at Dunkirk, on the northern French coast near the border with Belgium. Despite attacks from German warplanes, some 338,000 soldiers escaped to England on more than a thousand ships and small boats, barges, and ferries, leaving behind vast stockpiles of vehicles, weaponry, and ammunition. "Wars are not won by evacuations," observed Prime Minister Churchill, "but there was a victory inside this deliverance."

While the miraculous evacuation at Dunkirk was unfolding, German forces decimated the remaining French armies. The crumbling French war effort prompted Italy's dictator, Mussolini, to declare war on France and Great Britain, which he dismissed as "the reactionary democracies of the West." Roosevelt characterized Mussolini's action as a "stab in the back."

On June 14, 1940, German soldiers marched unopposed into the streets of Paris. Eight days later, French leaders surrendered the entire nation. The rapid fall of France stunned the world. The war was but ten months old, yet Germany ruled most of Europe. The Germans then established a puppet

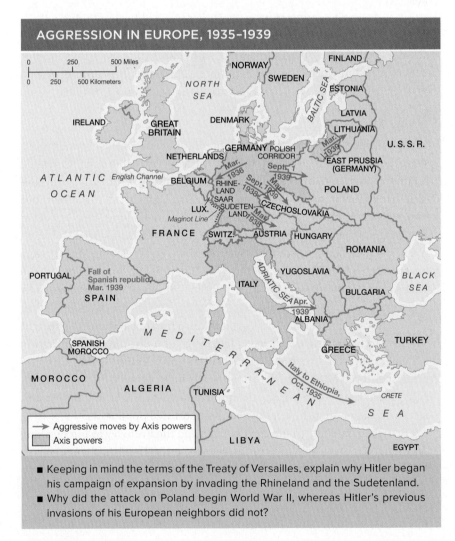

AGGRESSION IN EUROPE, 1935–1939

- Keeping in mind the terms of the Treaty of Versailles, explain why Hitler began his campaign of expansion by invading the Rhineland and the Sudetenland.
- Why did the attack on Poland begin World War II, whereas Hitler's previous invasions of his European neighbors did not?

French fascist government in the city of Vichy to manage the conquered nation and implement its own anti-Jewish policies. A Free French movement made up of exiles and soldiers rescued at Dunkirk organized in London to aid the Allies. Great Britain now stood alone facing Hitler's relentless military power. "The war is won," an ecstatic Hitler bragged to Mussolini. "The rest is only a matter of time." He spoke too soon.

The United States: From Isolationism to Intervention

During the 1930s, most Americans responded to the mounting crises in Europe and Asia by deepening their commitment to isolationism. In his 1933 inaugural address, President Roosevelt announced that he would continue the efforts of Herbert Hoover to promote what he called "the good neighbor policy" in the Western Hemisphere, declaring that no nation "has the right to intervene in the internal or external affairs of another." True to his word, he withdrew U.S. troops from Nicaragua and Haiti.

The nation's deeply rooted isolationist mood was reinforced by a prominent Senate inquiry into the role of bankers and businesses in the American decision to enter World War I. Chaired by Senator Gerald P. Nye of North Dakota, the "Nye Committee" began its hearings in 1934 and lasted until early 1936. The Committee concluded that weapons makers and bankers (the "merchants of death") had spurred U.S. intervention in the European conflict in 1917 and were continuing to "help frighten nations into military activity."

U.S. Neutrality

In 1935, in response to Italy's invasion of Ethiopia and the Nye Committee hearings, President Roosevelt signed the first of several "neutrality laws" intended to avoid the mistakes that had led the nation into the First World War. However, the president did not, as Woodrow Wilson had done in 1914, ask Americans to remain neutral in their hearts because "even a neutral has a right to take account of the facts," which in his view, unlike in 1914, made it clear to all that Germany was the aggressor. The Neutrality Act of 1935 prohibited Americans from selling weapons or traveling on ships owned by nations at war. Public opinion surveys showed that most Americans were determined to stay out of Europe's conflicts. As a Minnesota senator declared in 1935, "To hell with Europe and the rest of those nations!" In 1936, Congress revised the Neutrality Act by banning loans to warring nations.

Roosevelt, however, was not so sure that the United States could or should remain neutral in a world of growing conflict. In October 1937, he delivered a speech in Chicago, the heartland of isolationism, in which he

---

CORE **OBJECTIVE**
2. Explain how President Roosevelt and Congress responded to the outbreak of wars in Europe and Asia between 1933 and 1941.

1937 Neutrality Act: Nonmilitary goods for warring nations

called for international cooperation to "quarantine the aggressors," who were responsible for disturbing world peace, especially the Japanese who had assaulted China. But his appeal for a more active American role in world affairs fell flat in Congress and across the nation. The Neutrality Act of 1937 allowed the president to require that nonmilitary American goods bought by warring nations be sold on a cash-and-carry basis (that is, a nation would have to pay cash and then carry the American-made goods away in its own ships). This was intended to preserve America's profitable trade with warring nations without running the risk of being drawn into the fighting.

> 1939 Neutrality Act: Military supplies for Britain and France

In September 1939, Roosevelt decided that the United States must do more to help stop "aggressor" nations. He summoned Congress into special session to revise the Neutrality Act. "I regret the Congress passed the Act," the president said. "I regret equally that I signed the Act." After six weeks of debate, the Congress passed the Neutrality Act of 1939, which allowed Britain and France to send their own ships to the United States to bring back American military supplies. It was, said Roosevelt, the best way "to keep us out of war." Public opinion supported such measures as long as other nations did the actual fighting. "What the majority of the American people want," wrote the editors of the *Nation*, "is to be as un-neutral as possible without getting into war."

Preparing America for War

> U.S military buildup and increased aid to Great Britain and peacetime conscription

As Hitler's armies continued their conquest of Europe, the United States found itself in no condition to wage war. After the First World War, the U.S. Army was reduced to a small force; by 1939, it numbered only 175,000. By contrast, Germany had almost 5 million soldiers. In promoting "military preparedness," President Roosevelt in May 1940 called for increasing the size of the army and producing 50,000 combat planes in 1942, a seemingly outlandish goal, since Germany was producing only 15,000 warplanes that year. Roosevelt also increased military aid to Great Britain, promising to provide all possible "aid to the Allies short of war."

> The Manhattan Project

German submarines were now destroying many of the ships carrying desperately needed supplies from America to Great Britain. To address the challenge, Roosevelt and Prime Minister Churchill, whose mother was an American, negotiated a trade on September 2, 1940, called the Destroyers for Bases Agreement, by which fifty old U.S. warships went to the British Royal Navy in return for allowing the U.S. to build military bases on British island colonies in the Caribbean. Two weeks later, on September 16, 1940, Roosevelt made an even more controversial decision, opposed even by his wife Eleanor, by pushing through a reluctant Congress the first peacetime conscription (military draft) in American history, requiring the registration of all 16 million men aged twenty-one to thirty-five.

The world crisis transformed Roosevelt. Having been stalemated for much of his second term by congressional opposition to the New Deal, he was revitalized by the urgent need to stop the spread of Nazism across Europe. Adding to Roosevelt's concerns was the possibility that Germany might have a secret weapon. The famous physicist Albert Einstein, a Jewish Austrian refugee from Nazism, had alerted Roosevelt in the fall of 1939 that the Germans were trying to create atomic bombs. In June 1940, the president set up the National Defense Research Committee to coordinate military research, including a top-secret effort to develop an atomic bomb—the Manhattan Project—before the Germans did. Almost 200,000 people worked on the Manhattan Project, including Dr. J. Robert Oppenheimer, who led the team of distinguished scientists scat-

U-Boat After the Treaty of Versailles set limits on the size of the German navy, Germany developed military submarines of unprecedented size and power. Here, a row of Nazi U-boats are on display in the German port of Kiel in 1938.

tered among several secret facilities across the country. The Manhattan Project was so secret that Vice President Harry Truman knew nothing about it.

The Battle of Britain

Having conquered western Europe, Hitler began planning the invasion of Great Britain ("Operation Sea Lion"). The late summer of 1940 witnessed the desperate Battle of Britain, as the Germans first sought to destroy Britain's Royal Air Force (RAF) before invading the island nation. The Nazis deployed some 2,500 warplanes, outnumbering the RAF two to one. "Never has a nation been so naked before its foes," Prime Minister Winston Churchill admitted. Churchill became the symbol of Britain's determination to stop Hitler. With his bulldog face, ever-present cigar, and "V for Victory" gesture, he urged the British citizenry to make the war "their finest hour." He breathed defiance while preparing the nation for a German invasion. The British, he pledged, would confront Hitler's invaders with "blood, toil, tears, and sweat." They would "never surrender."

In July and August, 1940, the German air force (*Luftwaffe*) launched day and night bombing raids against military targets—ships and naval bases, warplanes and airfields—across southeast England. The Royal Air Force, with the benefit of radar, a secret new technology, surprised the world by fending off the German assault. Hitler then ordered his bombers to target civilians and cities (especially London) in nighttime raids designed to terrorize British civilians. In what came to be called "the Blitz" during September and October of 1940, the Germans caused massive destruction in Britain's major cities.

German bombers attack Great Britain: The Blitz

The London "Blitz" An aerial photograph of London set aflame by the heavy German bombing raids in 1940. Winston Churchill responded, "We shall never surrender."

The air raids killed some 43,000 British civilians, wounded thousands more, and left 2 million homeless. But the Blitz enraged rather than demoralized the British people. A London newspaper headline summarized the nation's defiant mood: "Is That the Best You Can Do, Adolf?" At the same time, British fighter pilots were destroying 1,300 German warplanes. The British success in the air proved to be a decisive turning point in the war, for in October 1940, Hitler gave up his planned invasion of the British Isles. It was the first battle he had lost.

Debate over America's Role

During 1940, Roosevelt began a long, urgent, and eloquent campaign to convince Americans that isolationism was impractical and even dangerous. His actions to aid Great Britain and prepare America for war outraged isolationists. A prominent Democrat remembered that the dispute between isolationists and so-called interventionists during the late 1930s was "the most savage political debate during my lifetime." Isolationists, mostly midwestern and western Republicans who believed that Roosevelt was systematically drawing the United States into another European war, formed the America First Committee to oppose "military preparedness." Charles Lindbergh, the first man to fly solo across the Atlantic ocean, led the isolationist effort. To Lindbergh, Roosevelt's efforts to help Britain were driven primarily by Jews who owned "our motion pictures, our press, our radio, and our government." Lindbergh assured Americans that Britain was doomed; they should join hands with Hitler.

Roosevelt's Third Term

Roosevelt reelected (1940)

Lindbergh and the other isolationists sought to make the 1940 presidential campaign a debate about the European war. In June, just as France was falling to Germany, the Republicans nominated a dark-horse candidate, Wendell L. Willkie of Indiana, a plainspoken corporate lawyer who as a former Democrat had voted for Roosevelt in 1932 and had remained registered as a Democrat until 1938. In his acceptance speech, Willkie clumsily referred to "you Republicans." Once the campaign started, Willkie warned that Roosevelt was a "warmonger" and predicted that "if you reelect him you may expect war in April, 1941." Roosevelt responded that he had "said this before, but I shall say it again and again and again: Your boys are not going to be sent into any foreign wars." In November 1940, Roosevelt won an unprecedented third term by a comfortable margin of 27 million votes to Willkie's 22 million and by an even more decisive margin, 449 to 82, in the Electoral College.

The Lend-Lease Bill

The Lend-Lease Bill (1941)

Once reelected, Roosevelt found an ingenious way to provide even more military aid to Britain, whose cash was running out. The **Lend-Lease Bill**, introduced in Congress on January 10, 1941, allowed the president to lend or lease military equipment to "any country whose defense the President deems vital to the defense of the United States." It was a bold challenge to the isolationists, prompted by Roosevelt's conviction that "no nation can appease the Nazis. No man can turn a tiger into a kitten by stroking it." The United States, he added, would provide everything the British needed to fend off a German invasion while doing the same for China in its war against Japan. "We must be the great arsenal of democracy," Roosevelt explained. Between 1941 and 1945, the Lend-Lease program would ship $50 billion worth of supplies to Great Britain, the Soviet Union, France, China, and other Allied nations. Lend-Lease was Roosevelt's most emphatic effort to move America from isolationism to interventionism in the growing wars in Europe and Asia. Winston Churchill called it the most generous "act in the history of any nation."

Germany Invades the Soviet Union

While Americans continued to debate Roosevelt's efforts to help Great Britain, the European war expanded. In the spring of 1941, German troops joined Italian forces in Libya, forcing the British army in North Africa to withdraw to Egypt. In April 1941, Nazi forces overwhelmed Yugoslavia and Greece. With Hungary, Romania, and Bulgaria also part of the Axis, Hitler controlled nearly all of Europe. But his ambition was unbounded. On June 22, 1941, without warning, massive German armies suddenly invaded their supposed ally, the Soviet Union, in "Operation Barbarossa." Hitler's objective in turning on Stalin was his long-standing dream to destroy communism, enslave the vast population of the Soviet Union, and exploit its considerable natural resources.

Hitler's decision to attack the Soviet Union was the defining moment of the European war, for the Germans would eventually be worn down and thrown back by the Soviets. At first, however, the largest invasion in history seemed a great success as the German armies raced across the vast plains of western Russia; entire Soviet armies and cities were surrounded and destroyed. During the second half of 1941, 3 million Soviet soldiers were captured, many of whom were then murdered or starved to death. For four months, the Soviet armies retreated in the face of the German blitzkrieg. By December, 1941, German units had reached the suburbs of Moscow, a thousand miles east of Berlin.

Lend-Lease Bill (1941)
Legislation that allowed the president to lend or lease military equipment to any country whose own defense was deemed vital to the defense of the United States.

To American isolationists, Germany's invasion of Russia confirmed that America should stay out of the war and let two dreadful dictatorships bleed each other to death. Roosevelt, however, insisted on including the Soviet Union in the Lend-Lease agreement, for, along with Winston Churchill, he was determined to keep the Soviets fighting Hitler rather than see them surrender. In 1941 alone, America sent thousands of trucks, tanks, guns, and warplanes to the Soviet Union, along with food (especially Spam), and enough cotton, blankets, shoes, and boots to clothe the entire Russian army.

Gradually, Stalin used his dictatorial powers to slow the Nazi advance by forcing people to fight—or be killed by their own Soviet troops. During the Battle of Moscow, Russian defenders showed their pitiless resolve by executing eight thousand civilians charged with "cowardice." Slowly, the tide started to turn against the once unbeatable Germans. By the winter of 1941–1942, Hitler's generals were learning the same bitter lesson that the Russians had taught Napoleon and the French army in 1812. Invading armies must contend not only with Russia's ferocious fighters and enormous population but also vast distances, deep snow, and subzero temperatures.

The Atlantic Charter

By the late summer of 1941, the United States was no longer a "neutral" nation. In August, Roosevelt and Churchill met on a U.S. warship off the Canadian coast, where they drew up a joint statement of "common principles" known as the **Atlantic Charter**. The agreement pledged that after the "final destruction of the Nazi tyranny" the victors would promote certain common values: the self-determination of all peoples, economic cooperation, freedom of the seas, and a new system of international security to be called the United Nations. Within weeks, eleven anti-Axis nations, including the Soviet Union, had endorsed the idealistic principles of the Atlantic Charter.

No sooner had Roosevelt signed the Atlantic Charter than U. S. ships in the North Atlantic were attacked. On October 17, 1941, a German submarine ("U-boat") sank the American warship *Kearny*. Eleven seamen were killed. Two weeks later, the destroyer *Reuben James* went down, with a loss of 115 seamen. The sinkings spurred Congress to change the 1939 Neutrality Act by allowing merchant vessels to be armed and to enter combat zones and the ports of nations at war ("belligerents"). Roosevelt ordered U.S. warships to "shoot on sight" any German submarines. Step by step, the United States had given up neutrality and begun to engage in naval warfare against Nazi Germany. Still, Americans hoped to avoid taking the final step into all-out war.

Atlantic Charter (1941) Joint statement crafted by Franklin D. Roosevelt and British prime minister Winston Churchill that listed the war goals of the Allied Powers.

The Storm in the Pacific

Hitler's efforts to conquer Great Britain and the Soviet Union had stalled by late 1941, but U.S. relations with Japan were worsening. In 1940, Japan and the United States began a series of moves that pushed them closer to war. Japan forced the helpless Vichy French government, under German

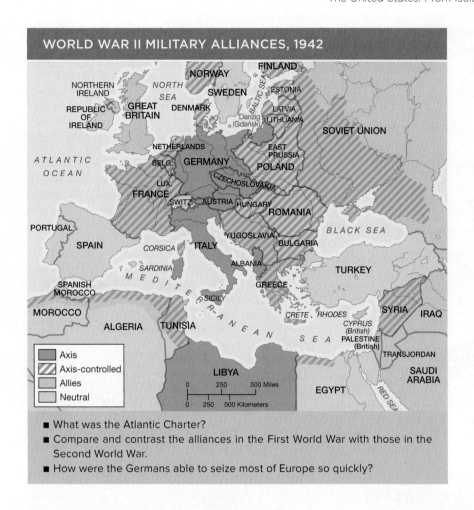

WORLD WAR II MILITARY ALLIANCES, 1942

Legend:
- Axis
- Axis-controlled
- Allies
- Neutral

■ What was the Atlantic Charter?
■ Compare and contrast the alliances in the First World War with those in the Second World War.
■ How were the Germans able to seize most of Europe so quickly?

control, to permit the construction of Japanese airfields in French-controlled northern Indochina and to cut off the railroad into south China. The United States responded with the Export Control Act of July 2, 1940, which authorized President Roosevelt to restrict the export of military supplies and other strategic materials crucial to Japan. By 1940, Japan was spending half of its annual government budget on military expansion.

> Japanese in Indochina and the Export Control Act (1940)

The Tripartite Pact

On September 27, 1940, the Tokyo government signed a Tripartite Pact with Germany and Italy, by which each pledged to declare war on any nation that attacked any of them. In July 1941, Japan announced that it was taking complete control of French Indochina in its effort to expand the "Empire of the Rising Sun." Roosevelt responded by freezing all Japanese financial assets in the United States and restricting oil exports to Japan (the United States was then producing half of the world's oil). He also closed the Panama Canal to Japanese shipping and merged the Filipino army with the U.S. Army. *Time* magazine claimed that Roosevelt was

> The Tripartite Pact (1940), Japan takes control of French Indochina, and United States freezes its assets

JAPANESE EXPANSION BEFORE THE ATTACK ON PEARL HARBOR

■ Why did the Japanese want to control French Indochina and the Dutch East Indies?
■ Why did Japan sign the Tripartite Pact with Germany and Italy?

"waging the first great undeclared war in U.S. history." Without access to American oil, iron, steel, and other products, Japan found that its expansionist plans were stalled, for Japan bought more than half its imports from the United States. Japanese military leaders responded to the American embargo by deciding to conquer areas in Southeast Asia such as French Indochina and the Dutch East Indies that could provide the much-needed strategic raw materials cut off by the United States.

The Attack on Pearl Harbor

On October 16, 1941, War Minister Hideki Tōjō became the Japanese prime minister. Viewing war with the United States as inevitable, he ordered a powerful fleet of Japanese warships to prepare for war. The Japanese naval commander, Admiral Isoroku Yamamoto, knew that his country could not defeat the United States in a long war; its only hope was "to decide the fate of the war on the very first day" by launching a "fatal attack" on the U.S. Navy.

On November 5, 1941, the Japanese asked the Roosevelt administration to end its embargo of oil and other products or "face conflict." The American secretary of state, Cordell Hull, responded on November 26 that Japan must remove all of its troops from China before the United States would lift its embargo. The Japanese had no intention of leaving China. Instead, they secretly ordered a fleet of warships to begin steaming toward Hawaii. By this time, political and military leaders on both sides considered war inevitable, and some even deemed it desirable.

The U.S. Navy Department in Washington, D.C., sent an urgent message to all of its commanders in the Pacific: "Negotiations with Japan . . . have ceased, and an aggressive move by Japan is expected within the next few days." For his part, Roosevelt staked his desperate hope for a peaceful solution on a last-minute message sent to Japan's emperor Hirohito. "Both of us," Roosevelt said, "have a sacred duty to restore traditional amity [cooperation] and prevent further death and destruction in the world."

By the time Roosevelt's message reached the emperor, Japanese warplanes were already in the air headed for U.S. bases in Hawaii. On the early morning of Sunday, December 7, 1941, 360 Japanese planes began bombing the unsuspecting U.S. fleet at **Pearl Harbor**. Of the eight American battleships, all were sunk or disabled, along with eleven other ships. Japanese bombers also destroyed 180 American warplanes. The raid, which lasted less than two hours, killed more than 2,400 American servicemen (mostly sailors) and civilians, and wounded nearly 1,200 more. At the same time that the Japanese were attacking Pearl Harbor, they were also assaulting U.S. military facilities in the Philippines and on Guam and Wake Islands in the Pacific, as well as British bases in Singapore, Hong Kong, and Malaysia.

The surprise attack fulfilled the dreams of its Japanese planners, but it fell short of military success in two important ways. First, the bombers ignored the maintenance facilities and oil storage tanks in Hawaii that supported the U.S. fleet, without which the surviving ships might have been forced back to the West Coast. Second, the Japanese bombers missed the U.S. aircraft carriers that had luckily left port a few days earlier. In the naval war to come, aircraft carriers, not battleships, would prove to be the decisive weapon. In a larger sense, the Japanese attack on Pearl Harbor was a spectacular miscalculation, for the surprise attack aroused the Americans to wage total, vengeful war and brought the isolationist movement to an abrupt end. "Lick the hell out of them," advised one formerly isolationist senator. Even the Japanese admiral who planned the attack had misgivings amid his officers' celebrations: "I fear that we have only succeeded in awakening a sleeping tiger."

On December 8, President Roosevelt, composed and determined, delivered his war message to Congress: "Yesterday, December 7, 1941—a date which will live in infamy—the United States of America was suddenly and

Hideki Tōjō Prime Minister and War Minister of Japan simultaneously until 1944, one year before Japan's unconditional surrender.

Pearl Harbor attacked, United States enters the war

Pearl Harbor (1941) Surprise Japanese attack on the U.S. fleet at Pearl Harbor on December 7, which prompted the immediate American entry into the war.

Explosion of the USS *Shaw*
The destroyer exploded after Japanese warplanes pummeled it with three bombs. The *Shaw* was repaired shortly thereafter and went on to earn eleven battle stars in the Pacific campaign.

deliberately attacked by naval and air forces of the Empire of Japan." Three days later, on December 11, Germany and Italy declared war on what Hitler called the "half Judaized and the other half Negrified" United States, which he insisted "was not dangerous to us." The separate wars raging in Asia, Europe, and Africa had now become one global conflict. President Roosevelt told the American people in a radio address that "We are going to win, and we are going to win the peace that follows."

Mobilization at Home

CORE **OBJECTIVE**
3. Analyze the effects of the Second World War on American society.

War Powers Act (1941)

Waging war against Germany and Japan required all of America's immense industrial capacity. On December 18, 1941, Congress passed the War Powers Act, which gave the president far-reaching authority to reorganize government agencies and create new ones, regulate business and industry, and even censor mail and other forms of communication. With the declaration of war, men between the ages of eighteen and forty-five were drafted. Some 16 million men and several hundred thousand women served in the military during the war. Many teens lied about their age in order to enlist. The average American soldier or sailor in the Second World War was 26 years old, stood five feet eight, and weighed 144 pounds, an inch taller and eight pounds heavier than the typical recruit in the First World War. Only one in ten had attended college and only one in four had graduated from high school.

Arsenal of Democracy

American industry shifts to the manufacture of armaments

In 1940, Adolf Hitler had scoffed at the idea that the United States could produce 50,000 warplanes a year, claiming that America was nothing but "beauty queens, millionaires, and Hollywood." His ignorance of America's industrial potential proved fatal to Germany's war plans. By the end of 1942, U.S. war production had already exceeded the *combined* output of Germany, Japan, and Italy. At an Allied planning conference in Iran in 1943, Josef Stalin raised a glass to toast "American production, without which this war would have been lost."

The **War Production Board**, created by Roosevelt in 1942, directed the conversion of industries to war production. In 1941, more than 3 million automobiles were manufactured in the United States; only 139 were built during the next four years. Instead of cars, automobile plants began making huge numbers of tanks, jeeps, trucks, and warplanes. "Something is happening that Hitler doesn't understand," announced *Time* magazine in 1942. "It is the miracle of production."

In making the United States the "great arsenal of democracy," the Roosevelt administration transformed the economy into the world's most efficient military machine. By 1945, the year the war ended, the United States would be manufacturing many of them running twenty-four hours a day, seven days a week, produced 300,000 warplanes, 89,000 tanks, 3 million machine guns, and 7 million rifles.

War Production Board This 1942 poster features caricatures of Mussolini, Hitler, and Tōjō, who—according to the poster—will fall on their "axis" if American civilians continue their relentless wartime production.

Financing the War

To cover the war's huge cost (some $3 trillion in today's values), Congress passed the Revenue Act of 1942 (also called the Victory Tax). It raised tax rates and increased the number of taxpayers. Where in 1939 only about 4 million people (about 5 percent of the workforce) filed tax returns, the new act made most workers (75 percent) taxpayers. By the end of war, 90 percent of workers were paying income tax. Tax revenues covered about 45 percent of military costs from 1939 to 1946; the government borrowed the rest, mostly through a massive promotional campaign that sold $185 billion worth of government war bonds, which paid interest to purchasers. In all, by the end of the war, the national debt was six times what it had been at the start.

The size of the federal government soared during the war. Over a dozen new federal agencies were created to manage the shift to a war economy. The number of civilian federal workers quadrupled, from 1 million to 4 million. Jobs were suddenly plentiful as millions of people quit work to join the military. The nation's unemployment rate plummeted from 14 percent in 1940 to 2 percent in 1943. People who had long lived on the margins of the economic system, especially women, were now brought fully into the labor

U.S. employment soars

War Production Board Federal agency created by Roosevelt in 1942 that converted America's industrial output to war production.

force. Stubborn pockets of poverty did not disappear, but for most civilians, especially those who had earlier lost their jobs and homes in the Depression, the war spelled a better life than ever before. Some 24 million Americans moved during the war to take advantage of new job opportunities. Many of them headed to the states along the West Coast, where shipyards and airplane factories were hiring nonstop.

Economic Controls

Office of Price Administration (1942)

The need for the United States not only to equip and feed its own military forces but also provide massive amounts of food, clothing, and weapons to its allies created shortages of many consumer goods. Such shortages caused sharp price increases for many items. In 1942, Congress responded to such price inflation by authorizing the Office of Price Administration to set price ceilings. With prices frozen, basic goods had to be allocated through rationing, with coupons doled out for limited amounts of sugar, coffee, gasoline, automobile tires, and meat. The government promoted patriotic conservation with a massive public relations campaign that circulated posters with slogans such as "Use it up, wear it out, make it do, or do without." Businesses and workers often grumbled about the wage and price controls. On occasion the government seized industries threatened by strikes. Despite these problems, however, the government effort to stabilize wages and prices succeeded. By the end of the war, consumer prices had risen about 31 percent, a record far better than the World War I rise of 62 percent.

A Conservative Backlash

Smith-Connally War Labor Disputes Act (1943)

For all of the patriotism inspired by the war effort, criticism of government actions such as rationing increased with each passing year. In the 1942 congressional elections, Republicans gained forty-six seats in the House and nine in the Senate. During the 1940s, a coalition of conservatives from both parties dismantled "nonessential" New Deal agencies such as the Work Projects Administration (originally the Works Progress Administration), the National Youth Administration, and the Civilian Conservation Corps. Organized labor, despite substantial gains in membership and power during the war, felt the impact of the conservative trend. In the spring of 1943, when 400,000 coal miners went on strike demanding a $2-a-day wage increase, conservatives in Congress passed, over Roosevelt's veto, the Smith-Connally War Labor Disputes Act, which authorized the government to seize plants and mines and keep them operating if workers went on strike.

The War at Home

As a total war, the Second World War transformed life at home as it was being fought abroad. The dramatic changes required by the conflict also caused unexpected changes in many areas of social life, the impact of which would last long after the war's end.

Women of the workforce, 1942 At the Douglas Aircraft Company in Long Beach, California, three women assemble the tail fuselage of a Boeing B-17 Flying Fortress bomber.

Women in the War

The war marked a watershed in the status of women. With millions of men going into military service, the demand for civilian workers shook up old prejudices about gender roles in the workplace—and in the military. During the war, nearly 200,000 women served in the **Women's Army Corps** (WAC) and the navy's equivalent, Women Accepted for Volunteer Emergency Service (WAVES). Others joined the Marine Corps, the Coast Guard, and the Army Air Force.

Sidney Hillman, appointed by Roosevelt to find workers for the defense plants, announced that "war is calling on the women of America for production skills." More than 6 million women entered the civilian workforce during the war, an increase of more than 50 percent overall (110 percent in manufacturing alone). To help recruit women to take traditionally male jobs in industry, the government launched a promotional campaign featuring the story of "Rosie the Riveter," a woman named Rosina Bonavita, who excelled as a riveter at an airplane factory.

Many men opposed the surge of women taking traditionally male jobs. A disgruntled male legislator asked who would handle traditional household tasks if women flocked to factories: "Who will do the cooking, the washing, the mending, the humble homey tasks to which every woman has devoted herself; who will rear and nurture the children?" Many women, however, were eager to escape the bland routines of domestic life and earn good wages. A female welder remembered that her wartime job "was the first time I had a chance to get out of the kitchen and work in industry and make a few bucks. This was something I had never dreamed would happen."

> Millions of women join workforce and the military

Women's Army Corps Women's branch of the United States Army; by the end of the Second World War, nearly 150,000 women had served in the WAC.

African Americans

While President Roosevelt focused on military strategy, his wife Eleanor focused on organizing the home front. She insisted that the government's wartime partnership with business not neglect the needs of workers, argued that America could not fight racism abroad while tolerating it at home, and championed the mass influx of women into the once-male workforce during the war.

African Americans move West

More than a half million African Americans left the South for better opportunities during the war years, and more than a million blacks nationwide joined the industrial workforce for the first time. Lured by jobs and higher wages in new military-related plants and factories, African Americans from Texas, Oklahoma, Arkansas, and Louisiana headed west, where the dramatic expansion of defense-related jobs had significant effects on the region's population. During the war years, the number of African Americans rose sharply in western cities such as Seattle, Portland, and Los Angeles.

Rural poor take manufacturing jobs

At the same time, the construction of military bases and the influx of new personnel provided a boon to southern textile mills responding to the war effort through the manufacture of military uniforms. Manufacturing jobs led tens of thousands of "dirt poor" sharecroppers and tenant farmers, many of them African Americans, to leave the land for steady work in new mills and factories. Sixty of the hundred new army camps created during the war were in southern states, further transforming local economies. Throughout the United States during the Second World War, the rural population decreased by 20 percent.

Racial Tension at Home

Racial discrimination and race riots at home

Although Americans found themselves fighting against the racial bigotry promoted by fascism and Nazism, the war did not end racism in the United States. The Red Cross, for example, initially refused to accept blood donated by blacks, and the president of North American Aviation announced that "we will not employ Negroes." Blacks who were hired were often limited to the lowest-paid, lowest-skilled jobs.

Some courageous black leaders refused to accept these racist practices. In 1941, A. Philip Randolph, head of the Brotherhood of Sleeping Car Porters, planned a march on Washington, D.C., to demand an end to racial discrimination in defense industries. To fend off the march, the Roosevelt administration struck a bargain. Randolph called off the demonstration in return for a presidential order calling for equal treatment in the hiring of workers.

Throughout the war, African Americans noted the irony of the United States fighting against racism abroad while tolerating it at home. "The army is about to take me to fight for democracy," a black Detroit draftee said, "but I would [rather] fight for democracy right here." During the summer of 1943 alone, there were 274 race-related incidents in almost 50

Home front versus frontlines *Left*: Though tasked with protecting the African American man from further violence in the Detroit Riots of 1943, the police officers do nothing when a member of the white mob reaches out to strike him. *Right*: The Tuskegee Airmen were the first African American military pilots. Here, the first graduates are reviewed at Tuskegee, Alabama, in 1941.

cities. In Detroit, growing racial tensions escalated into a full-fledged riot. Fighting raged for two days until federal troops arrived. By then, twenty-five blacks and nine whites had been killed, and more than 700 people had been injured.

African Americans in Uniform

The most volatile social issue ignited by the war was African American participation in the military. Although the armed forces were still racially segregated in 1941, African Americans rushed to enlist after the Japanese attack on Pearl Harbor. As African American Joe Louis, the world heavyweight boxing champion, put it, "Lots of things [are] wrong with America, but Hitler ain't going to fix them." Black soldiers and sailors, assigned to racially segregated units, were initially excluded from combat units. Black officers could not command white soldiers or sailors. Henry L. Stimson, the secretary of war, claimed that "leadership is not embedded in the negro race." Every army camp and navy base had segregated facilities—and experienced frequent racial "incidents."

Altogether, about a million African Americans—men and women—served in the armed forces during the war. Among the most famous African American servicemen were some 600 pilots trained in Tuskegee, Alabama. The so-called **Tuskegee Airmen** ended up flying more than 15,000 missions during the war. Their unquestionable excellence spurred military and civilian leaders to desegregate the armed forces after the war.

African Americans serve in segregated military units

Tuskegee Airmen U.S. Army Air Corps unit of African American pilots whose combat success spurred military and civilian leaders to desegregate the armed forces after the war.

Off to court Latinos dressed in zoot suits are chained and escorted onto a Los Angeles County Sheriff's bus for a court appearance in June of 1943.

Mexicans and Mexican Americans

As rural dwellers moved to western cities, many farm counties experienced a labor shortage. In an ironic about-face, local and federal government authorities who before the war had forced migrant laborers back across the Mexican border now recruited them to harvest crops on American farms. The Mexican government would not consent to provide the needed workers, however, until the United States promised to ensure decent working and living conditions for the migrant workers. The result was the creation of the **bracero program** in 1942, whereby Mexico agreed to provide seasonal farm workers on year-long contracts. Under the bracero program, some 200,000 Mexican farm workers entered the western United States. At least that many more crossed the border as undocumented workers.

The rising tide of Mexican Americans in Los Angeles prompted a stream of anti-Mexican editorials and ugly racial incidents. Even though some 300,000 Mexican Americans served in the war and earned a higher percentage of Congressional Medals of Honor than any other minority group, racial prejudices still prevailed. In southern California there was constant conflict between Anglo servicemen and Mexican American gang members and teenage "zoot-suiters" (zoot suits were flamboyant clothing worn by some young Mexican American men). In 1943 several thousand off-duty sailors and soldiers, joined by hundreds of local whites, rampaged through the streets of Los Angeles, assaulting Hispanics, African Americans, and Filipinos. The weeklong violence came to be called the "Zoot Suit Riots."

Native Americans in the Military

Indians supported the war effort more fully than any other group in American society. Almost a third of eligible Native American men served in the armed forces. Many others worked in defense-related industries, and thousands of Indian women volunteered as nurses or joined the WAVES.

bracero program (1942)
System that permitted seasonal farm workers from Mexico to work in the United States on year-long contracts.

"war relocation camps"
Detention camps housing thousands of Japanese Americans from the West Coast who were forcibly interned from 1942 until the end of the Second World War.

As was the case with African Americans, Indians benefited from the experiences afforded by the war. Those who left reservations to work in defense plants or to join the military gained new vocational skills as well as a greater awareness of mainstream society and how to succeed within it.

Why did so many Native Americans fight for a nation that had stripped them of their land and ravaged their heritage? Some felt that they had no choice. Mobilization for the war effort ended many New Deal programs that had provided Indians with jobs. At the same time, many viewed the Nazis and the Japanese warlords as threats to their own homeland. Whatever their motivations, Indians distinguished themselves in the military. Unlike their African American counterparts, Indian servicemen were integrated into regular units with whites. Perhaps their most distinctive role was serving as "code talkers": every military branch used Indians, especially Navajos, to encode and decipher messages using Indian languages unknown to the Germans and Japanese.

Navajo code talkers
The complex makeup of the Navajo language made it impossible for the Axis Powers to decode American messages. Here, a code talker relays messages for the Marines in the Battle of Bougainville in the South Pacific in 1943.

Discrimination against Japanese Americans

The attack on Pearl Harbor ignited a hunger for vengeance against the Nisei—people of Japanese descent living in the United States. As Idaho's governor declared, "A good solution to the Jap problem would be to send them all back to Japan, then sink the island." Such hysteria helps explain why the U.S. government sponsored one of the worst violations of civil liberties during the twentieth century when more than 112,000 Nisei were forcibly removed from their homes along the West Coast and transported to ten **"war relocation camps."**

President Roosevelt initiated the removal of Japanese Americans (whom he called "Japs") when he issued Executive Order 9066 on February 19, 1942. More than 60 percent of the internees were U.S. citizens; a third were under the age of nineteen. Forced to sell their farms and businesses at great loss within 48 hours, the internees lost not only their property but also their liberty. Few if any were disloyal (in fact, 39,000 Japanese-Americans served in the armed forces during the war), but all were victims of fear and racial prejudice. Not until 1983 did the government acknowledge the injustice of the internment policy. Five years later it granted those Nisei still living $20,000 each in compensation, a tiny amount relative to what they had lost during four years of confinement.

A farewell to civil rights American troops escorted Japanese Americans by gunpoint to remote internment camps, many of which were horse racing tracks, whose stables served as housing.

CORE **OBJECTIVE**

4. Explain the major factors that enabled the United States and its allies to win the war in Europe.

The Allied Drive toward Berlin

By mid-1942, the "home front" was hearing good news from the war in Europe. U.S. naval forces had been increasingly successful at destroying German U-boats off the Atlantic coast. This was all the more important because the Grand Alliance—Great Britain, United States, and the Soviet Union—called for the defeat of Germany first. Defeating the Japanese in the Pacific could wait.

War Aims and Strategy

The Russian Front

A major consideration for Allied military strategy was the fighting on the vast Eastern Front in the Soviet Union, where, in fact, the outcome of the war against Hitler was largely decided. During 1941–1942, the Nazis and the Soviets waged colossal battles against each other. The Soviet population—by far—bore the brunt of the war against the Nazis, leading Josef Stalin to insist that the Americans and British relieve the pressure on his troops by attacking the Germans in western Europe, thereby forcing Hitler to pull units away from the Russian Front.

Meanwhile, with most of the German army deployed on the Russian Front, the British and American air forces, flying from bases in England, would bomb military and industrial targets in German-occupied western Europe, and especially in Germany itself, while American and British generals prepared plans to attack Nazi troops in North Africa, Italy, and France.

Roosevelt and Churchill agreed that they needed to create a second front in western Europe, but they could not agree on the timing or the location of an attack on German forces. U.S. military planners wanted to attack the Germans in France before the end of 1942. The British, however, were wary of moving too fast. An Allied defeat on the French coast, Churchill warned, was "the only way in which we could possibly lose this war." Finally, Roosevelt told U.S. military planners to accept Churchill's compromise proposal for a joint Anglo-American invasion of North Africa, which was occupied by German and Italian armies.

The North Africa Campaign

Allied armies take North Africa

On November 8, 1942, British and American forces landed in Morocco and Algeria on the North African coast ("Operation Torch"). They were led by a little-known U.S. general, Dwight D. Eisenhower, who was as untested in battle as were his troops. Farther east, British armies were pushing the Germans and Italians back across Libya. The American soldiers and their commanders were beaten badly in early battles. During the winter and spring of 1943, however, Eisenhower, soon known universally by his nickname, "Ike," found a brilliant field commander in General George Patton. Armed with ivory-handled pistols and brimming with bravado, he showed American troops how to fight a war of speed and daring in an exotic landscape. Corporal Morris Zimmerman wrote his mother from North Africa, "This is your son reporting from the land of Arabs and wine, sticky flies and red sand. I have always wanted to cross an ocean to see what was on the other side and darned if I didn't." Hammered from all sides and unable to retreat, some 250,000 Germans and Italians surrendered on May 12, 1943, leaving all of North Africa in Allied control.

The Casablanca Conference

Five months earlier, in January 1943, Roosevelt, Churchill, and the Anglo-American military chiefs met at Casablanca, the largest city in Morocco. It was a historic occasion. No U.S. president had ever flown abroad while in office, and none had ever visited Africa. Stalin chose to stay in the Soviet Union, but he sent a message which again urged the Allies to invade Nazi-controlled western Europe in order to relieve the pressure on the Russians.

At the Casablanca Conference, Churchill and Roosevelt made several key decisions. After intense debates, the British convinced the Americans that they should follow up the anticipated victory in North Africa with an assault on German and Italian forces on the Italian island of Sicily before then attacking Italy itself. Roosevelt and Churchill also decided to step up the bombing of Germany and to increase shipments of military supplies to the Soviet Union and the Nationalist Chinese forces fighting the Japanese.

Before leaving the Casablanca conference, Roosevelt announced, with Churchill's blessing, that the war would end only with the "unconditional surrender" of all enemy nations. This decision was designed to quiet Soviet suspicions that the Western Allies might negotiate separately with Hitler to end the war in western Europe. The announcement also reflected Roosevelt's determination that "every person in Germany should realize that this time Germany is a defeated nation."

The Battle of the Atlantic

While fighting raged in North Africa, the Battle of the Atlantic reached its climax. Great Britain desperately needed more food and military supplies from the United States, but German submarines were sinking the British vessels transporting American goods faster than British shipyards could replace them. Also, there could be no invasion of German-occupied France until the U-boat menace was defeated. By July 1942, some 230 Allied ships and almost 5 million tons of war supplies had been lost. "The only thing that ever frightened me during the war," recalled Churchill, "was the U-boat peril."

By the end of 1942, however, the British and Americans discovered ways to defeat the U-boats. A key breakthrough occurred when British experts cracked the German naval radio codes, enabling Allied convoys to steer clear of U-boats or to hunt them down with long-range warplanes (called "subchasers") and new anti-submarine weapons deployed on warships. New technology also helped. Sonar and radar allowed Allied ships to track submarines. Yet the best tactic against U-boats was to group cargo vessels

> New military technologies: Sonar and radar

Contributions and Impacts of World War II

World War II had a profound impact on American society. Women, African Americans, Mexican Americans, Japanese Americans, and Native Americans were just some of the groups whose wartime experiences were both essential to Allied victory and transformative at home. The chart below outlines some of the contributions that these groups made toward the American war effort, and some of the ways the war impacted them.

WOMEN

Contributions to the War	Impacts from the War
Hundreds of thousands of women volunteered to serve in the Women's Army Corps (WAC), Women Accepted for Volunteer Emergency Service (WAVES), and other service branches. Millions of women worked in war-related industries or for the federal government.	6 million more women entered the civilian workforce during the war. The valuable experience, education, and income from women's exposure to nontraditional roles set the stage for the women's movements of the 1960s and 1970s.

AFRICAN AMERICANS

Contributions to the War	Impacts from the War
Approximately 1 million African Americans served in the armed forces in segregated units, including 600 fighter pilots who served as Tuskegee Airmen. Millions of African Americans worked in industries to produce materials for the war effort.	Forced de-segregation of defense industries. About 500,000 more African Americans left the South. Almost 1 million more African Americans joined the industrial workforce; African American migration to cities increased. African American population of the West Coast increased greatly. African Americans faced increasing racial violence. Laid the foundation for the desegregation of the armed forces and civil rights movement of the fifties and sixties.

MEXICAN AMERICANS AND MEXICAN IMMIGRANTS

Contributions to the War	Impacts from the War
About 300,000 Mexican Americans served in the military. Mexicans and Mexican Americans worked in war industries and in production of needed food, having been recruited as farm laborers through the bracero program.	Hundreds of thousands of Mexican farm workers came to the United States through the bracero program. Mexican Americans faced increased racial violence in cities like Los Angeles. Set the stage for the Mexican American civil rights movement following the war.

JAPANESE AMERICANS

Contributions to the War	Impacts from the War
Large numbers of Japanese Americans served in the U.S. military during the war, including many who had faced internment.	Over 112,000 Japanese Americans living on the West Coast were forcibly placed in "war relocation camps." Many internees had to sell their property, such as farms and businesses.

NATIVE AMERICANS

Contributions to the War	Impacts from the War
One-third of all eligible Native Americans served in the armed forces. "Code talkers" sent and received encoded messages for the military using Native American languages. Many Native Americans left reservations to work in war industries.	Some Native Americans gained new skills and greater exposure to American society outside of Indian reservations. Set the stage for the "red power" movement of the 1960s and 1970s.

QUESTIONS FOR ANALYSIS

1. What were some of the ways that these groups contributed to the American war effort?

2. How did the war shape the way different groups of people lived? Do any patterns emerge?

3. How did the war impact these groups economically?

together into tightly bunched convoys so that warships could protect them more effectively. In May 1943, the Allies destroyed forty-one U-boats. Thereafter, the U-boats were on the defensive, and Allied shipping losses fell significantly.

Sicily and Italy

Allied forces reclaim Sicily and Italy: Mussolini flees

On July 10, 1943, following the Allied victory in North Africa, about 250,000 British and American troops landed on the coast of Sicily in the first effort to reclaim European territory since the war began. The entire island was in Allied hands by August 17, bringing to an end Benito Mussolini's twenty years of fascist rule in Italy. On July 25, 1943, the Italian king had dismissed Mussolini as prime minister and had him arrested. The new Italian government startled the Allies when it offered not only to surrender but also to switch sides in the war. To prevent them from doing so, Hitler sent German armies into Italy. Mussolini, plucked from prison by a daring German airborne raid, became head of a puppet fascist government in northern Italy as Allied forces took control of the rest of the country. On June 4, 1944, the U.S. Fifth Army entered Rome.

The Tehran Conference

Late in the fall of 1943, in Tehran, Iran, Churchill and Roosevelt had their first joint meeting with Josef Stalin. Their discussions focused on the planned invasion of Nazi-controlled France and a simultaneous Russian offensive westward across eastern Europe. The three leaders agreed to create an international organization—the United Nations—to maintain peace after the war. Upon arriving back in the United States, Roosevelt confided to Churchill his distrust of Stalin, stressing that it was a "ticklish" business keeping the "Russians cozy with us" because of the tension between communism and capitalism. As General Eisenhower stressed, however, the fate of Britain and the U.S. depended on the Soviets' survival as an ally against Nazi Germany. "The prize we seek," he said in 1942, "is to keep 8 million Russians [soldiers] in the war."

The Strategic Bombing of Europe

Allied air supremacy over Europe

Behind the long-anticipated Allied invasion of German-occupied France lay months of preparation. While waiting for D-day (the day the invasion would begin), the U.S. Army Air Force tried to pound Germany into submission with long-range bombers such as the B-17 "Flying Fortress" and the B-24 "Liberator." The American and British air campaign against Germany, carried out night and day, killed some 350,000 civilians (by comparison, the entire Blitz on Britain cost 43,000 lives) and frightened many others. A German girl in Berlin reported that "bombs belonged to my life." Yet the strategic air offensive failed to shatter either German morale or war production; many bombs missed their targets because of thick clouds, high winds, and inaccurate navigational systems, and many Allied planes were shot down by German fighter planes and anti-aircraft batteries. The massive Allied bombing campaign, however, did force the Germans to commit precious resources to air-raid defense and eventually wore down their air force. With Allied air supremacy over Europe assured by 1944, the much-anticipated invasion of Hitler's "Fortress Europe" could move forward.

Planning an Invasion

In early 1944, General Dwight D. Eisenhower arrived in London with a new title: Supreme Commander of the Allied Expeditionary Force (AEF) that would invade Nazi-controlled western Europe. Eisenhower faced enormous challenges. Not only did he have to create an effective command structure for the combined U.S. and British armed services, but he was also forced to handle disagreements between President Roosevelt and Prime Minister Churchill. He also faced the daunting task of planning Operation Overlord, the daring assault on Hitler's "Atlantic Wall," a formidable array of fortifications, mines, machine guns, barbed wire, and jagged beach obstacles along the French coastline. An attack by sea against heavily fortified defenders was the toughest of military operations. The planned invasion of France gave Churchill nightmares: "When I think of the beaches . . . choked with the flower of American and British youth . . . I see the tides running red with their blood. I have my doubts. I have my doubts."

For months, Eisenhower dedicated himself to planning the risky invasion and managing the complex political and military rivalries among the Allied leaders. He was a perfectionist, impatient with his staff, and at times unleashing a volcanic temper. Awake before dawn and asleep only after midnight, he drank fifteen cups of coffee and smoked four packs of cigarettes a day as he attended to every detail.

As D-day approached in early June 1944, Eisenhower's chief of staff predicted only a 50–50 chance of success. The seaborne invasion was the greatest gamble and most complex military operation in history. "I am very uneasy about the whole operation," admitted Sir Alan Brooke, the head of British forces. "It may well be the most ghastly disaster of the whole war." Eisenhower was so concerned about the invasion that he carried in his wallet a note which was to be circulated if the Allies failed. It read: "If any blame or fault attaches to the attempt, it is mine alone."

D-day and After

Operation Overlord succeeded in part because it surprised the German defenders. The Allies made elaborate efforts—including the positioning of British decoy troops and making misleading public statements—to fool the Nazis into believing that the invasion would come at Pas-de-Calais, on the French-Belgian border, where the English Channel was narrowest. Instead, the landings would occur along fifty miles of shoreline in northern Normandy, a French coastal region almost 200 miles south.

On the evening of June 5, General Eisenhower visited some of the 16,000 American paratroopers preparing to drop behind the German lines in France at night to seize key bridges and roads. The tough soldiers, many of

General Dwight D. Eisenhower
Eisenhower instructing paratroopers before they launch the D-day assault in Operation Overlord.

Operation Overlord

their faces blackened by burnt cork and heads shaved to resemble Indian warriors, noticed Eisenhower's concern and tried to lift his spirits. "Now quit worrying, General," one of them said, "we'll take care of this thing for you." Another said, "We ain't worried. It's Hitler's turn to worry." After the planes took off, Eisenhower returned to his car with tears in his eyes. "Well," he said quietly to his driver, "it's on."

As the planes carrying the paratroopers arrived over France, thick clouds and German anti-aircraft fire disrupted the formations. Some soldiers were dropped miles from their landing sites, some were dropped far out at sea, some were dropped so low that their parachutes never opened. Yet the U.S. 82nd and 101st Airborne Divisions, although badly scattered, outfought three German divisions during the chaotic night and prepared the way for the main invasion by destroying bridges and capturing artillery positions and key road junctions.

The Normandy Landings

D-day: The Normandy Landings

As the gray, misty light of dawn broke on D-day morning, June 6, 1944, the biggest invasion fleet in history—some 5,300 Allied ships carrying 370,000 soldiers and sailors—filled the horizon off the Normandy coast. Sleepy German soldiers guarding the beaches awoke to see Allied ships of every size. A French boy said he saw "more ships than sea."

Major battles often depend on luck. For several hours on D-day, the local German commanders misinterpreted the Normandy landings as merely a diversion for the "real" attack at Pas-de-Calais. (It helped that the German commander, Field Marshal Erwin Rommel, assuming that the weather was too foul for an invasion, had gone home to Germany to celebrate his wife's birthday.) "How stupid of me," Rommel said when he heard the news. "How stupid of me!"

When Hitler learned of the Allied landings, he boasted that "the news couldn't be better. As long as they [the Allied armies] were in Britain, we couldn't get at them. Now we have them where we can destroy them." In the United States, word that the long-anticipated liberation of Nazi Europe had begun captured the nation's attention. Businesses closed, church bells tolled, and traffic was stopped so that people could pray in the streets. Churchill called the D-day invasion "undoubtedly the most complicated and difficult" military operation in history.

Resilience and creativity are crucial virtues amid the confusion of battles (the "fog of war"), which rarely go according to plan, and despite Eisenhower's meticulous preparations, the huge operation almost failed. During the first day of the Normandy landings, many Allied planes dropped their bombs too far inland, often on Allied troops as they moved off the beaches. Rough seas caused injuries and nausea and capsized dozens of landing craft. Indeed, many of them never managed to land at all, and over a thousand men, weighed down by their packs and equipment, drowned as they stepped off landing craft into water over their heads. Some of the landing craft delivered their often seasick troops to the wrong locations. "We

The landing at Normandy D-day, June 6, 1944. Before they could huddle under a seawall and begin to root out the region's Nazi defenders, soldiers on Omaha Beach had to cross a fifty-yard stretch that exposed them to machine guns housed in concrete bunkers.

have landed in the wrong place," shouted Brigadier General Theodore Roosevelt Jr. (son of the former president), who would receive the Medal of Honor for his courage that day. "But we will start the war from here." The noise was deafening as shells exploded across the beach and in the surf. The bodies of the killed, wounded, and drowned piled up amid wrenching cries for help. "As our boat touched sand and the ramp went down," Private Harry Parley remembered, "I became a visitor to Hell."

The first U.S. units ashore at Omaha Beach, beneath 130-foot-tall cliffs defended by German machine guns and mortars, lost more than 90 percent of their men. In one company, 197 of the 205 men were killed or wounded within ten minutes. Officers struggled to rally the exhausted, bewildered men pinned down on the beach. "Two kinds of men are staying on this beach," shouted Colonel George Taylor on Omaha Beach. "The dead and those who are going to die. Get up! Move in! Goddammit! Move in and die!" Inch by inch, backed up by waves of reinforcements, the U.S. soldiers pushed across the beach and up the cliffs. By nightfall, 156,000 Allied soldiers—57,000 of them Americans—were scattered across fifty miles of Normandy coastline. So too were the bodies of some 5,000 dead or wounded Allied soldiers.

On June 13, a week after the Normandy landings, Erwin Rommel, the German commander, told his wife that the "battle is not going at all well for us." Within three weeks, the Allies had landed more than 1 million troops, 566,000 tons of supplies, and 171,000 vehicles. "Whether the enemy can still be stopped at this point is questionable," German headquarters near Paris warned Hitler. "The enemy air superiority is terrific and smothers almost every one of our movements. . . . Losses in men and equipment are extraordinary."

Operation Overlord was the greatest seaborne invasion in the annals of warfare, but it was small when compared with the offensive launched by the Soviets in Russia a few weeks after D-day. Between June and August 1944, the Soviet Army killed, wounded, or captured more German soldiers (350,000) than were stationed in all of western Europe.

Still, the Normandy invasion was a turning point in the war. With the beachhead secured, the Allied leaders knew that victory was in their grasp. "What a plan!" Churchill exclaimed to the British Parliament. For all of the Allied success, however, Eisenhower privately struggled with the daily casualty reports. "How I wish this cruel business of war could be completed quickly," he wrote his wife. "War demands real toughness of fiber—not only in the soldiers [who] must endure, but in the homes that must sacrifice their best."

The Liberation of Paris

It would take seven more weeks and 37,000 more lives for the Allied troops to gain control of Normandy; the Germans lost more than twice as many. Some 19,000 French civilians were killed in the carnage. Then, on July 25, 1944, American armies broke out from Normandy and headed east toward Paris. On August 15, a joint American-French invasion force landed on the French Mediterranean coast and raced up the Rhone Valley in eastern France.

The path to victory in France was anything but smooth; German resistance collapsed only after ten weeks of ferocious fighting. A division of the Free French Resistance, aided by American units, had the honor of liberating Paris on August 25. As American soldiers marched through the city's cheering crowds, a reporter said that he had never "seen in any place such joy as radiated from the people of Paris this morning." One American soldier wrote home: "I was kissed at least by five million girls—and I mean beautiful girls."

By mid-September, most of France and Belgium had been cleared of German troops; meanwhile, the Soviet army moved relentlessly westward along a twelve-hundred-mile front, pushing the fleeing Germans out of Russia. Between D-day until the end of the war in Europe a year later, 1.2 million Germans were killed and wounded on the western and eastern fronts. Only 572 German warplanes were still operable, compared to 14,000 planes flown by American and British pilots.

Roosevelt's Fourth Term

Roosevelt elected to fourth term (1944)

In 1944, war or no war, the calendar required another presidential election. This time the Republicans turned to New York governor Thomas E. Dewey as their candidate. Dewey did not propose to dismantle Roosevelt's popular

WORLD WAR II IN EUROPE AND AFRICA 1942–1945

Legend:
- ★ Major battle
- Axis Powers at outbreak of the war
- Maximum extent of Axis military power
- → Allied offensives
- ⇢ Heaviest Allied aerial bombing
- ⋯ Inside limit of German U-boat operations

0   250   500 Miles
0   250   500 Kilometers

- What was the Allies' strategy in North Africa, and why was it important for the invasion of Italy?
- Why did Eisenhower's plan on D-day succeed?
- What was the role of strategic bombing in the war? Was it effective?

New Deal programs but argued that it was time for a younger man to replace the "tired" Democratic leader. Nevertheless, on November 7, 1944, Franklin Roosevelt was elected yet again, this time by a popular vote of 25.6 million to 22 million and an electoral vote of 432 to 99.

The End of the War in the European Theatre

By the time Roosevelt was reelected, Allied armies were approaching the German border from the east and west. Churchill worried that if the Soviets arrived first in shattered Berlin, the German capital, Stalin would control the postwar map of Europe. He urged Eisenhower to beat the Soviets to Berlin. But Eisenhower decided it was not worth the estimated 100,000 Americans who would be killed or wounded to liberate Berlin before the Soviets did.

The Yalta Conference

Anticipating victory in Germany, the Soviets hosted the "Big Three" Allied leaders at a seaside resort on the Black Sea for the **Yalta Conference** (February 4–11, 1945). The leaders agreed that, once Germany surrendered, the Soviets would control eastern Germany, and the Americans and British would control the industrial areas of the west. Berlin, the German capital within the Soviet zone, would be subject to joint occupation. The Americans and British later created a fourth occupation zone for the French to administer.

Stalin's goals at Yalta were both defensive and expansive: he wanted to retrieve former Russian territory ceded to Poland after World War I and to impose Soviet control over the countries of eastern and central Europe. Roosevelt, exhausted and in failing health, was cooperative because he needed the Soviets to help defeat Japan in northeast Asia. Military analysts estimated that Japan could hold out for eighteen months after the defeat of Germany.

The Collapse of Nazi Germany

By early 1945, Nazi Germany was on the verge of defeat. But President Roosevelt would not live to join the victory celebrations. In the spring of 1945, he went to the "Little White House" in Warm Springs, Georgia, to rest up for the conference that would create the United Nations. On the morning of April 12, 1945, he complained of a headache but seemed to be in good spirits, pleasantly distracted by his beloved stamp collection. It was nearly lunchtime when he said to an artist painting his portrait, "Now we've got just about 15 minutes more to work." Then, as she watched him reading some documents, he groaned, saying that he had "terrific pain" in the back of his head. Suddenly he slumped over and fell into a coma. He died two hours later.

On hand to witness the president's death was Lucy Mercer Rutherford, the woman with whom Roosevelt had had an affair in 1916–1918. Eleanor Roosevelt was in Washington, D.C. when Franklin died, unaware of the president's guest. Although Franklin had promised in 1918 to end all communications with Mercer, he had in fact secretly stayed in touch, even enabling her to attend his presidential inauguration in 1933.

Roosevelt's death shocked and saddened people all over the world. Even his sharpest critics were devastated. Ohio Senator Robert Taft, known as "Mr. Republican," called Roosevelt's death one of the worst tragedies in American history. "The President's death removes the greatest figure of our time at the very climax of his career. . . . He dies a hero of the war, for he

The Yalta Conference Churchill, Roosevelt, and Stalin (with their respective foreign ministers behind them) confer on plans for the postwar world in February 1945.

Yalta Conference (1945) Meeting of the "Big Three" Allied leaders, Franklin D. Roosevelt, Winston Churchill, and Joseph Stalin, to discuss how to divide control of postwar Germany and eastern Europe.

literally worked himself to death in the service of the American people." By contrast, a desperate Adolf Hitler saw in Roosevelt's death a "great miracle" for the besieged Germans. "The war is not lost," he told an aide. "Read it. Roosevelt is dead!"

Hitler's shrinking Nazi empire collapsed less than a month later. In Berlin, as Soviet troops prepared to enter the city, Adolf Hitler married his mistress, Eva Braun, in an underground bunker on the last day of April. She then poisoned herself, and he killed himself with a pistol shot. On May 2, Berlin fell. Five days later, on May 7, the chief of staff of the German armed forces signed a treaty agreeing to unconditional surrender. So ended Nazi domination of Europe, little more than twelve years after Hitler had come to power proclaiming his "Thousand-Year Reich."

On May 8, V-E Day (Victory in Europe) generated massive celebrations. In Paris, an American bomber pilot flew his plane through the Eiffel Tower. In New York City, 500,000 people celebrated in the streets. But the elation was tempered by the ongoing war against Japan and the immense challenges of helping war-torn Europe rebuild. The German economy had to be revived, a new democratic government had to be formed, and the Germans and millions of other Europeans had to be clothed, housed, and fed.

> Soviet troops enter Berlin; Germany surrenders

The Holocaust

The end of the war in Europe revealed the horrific extent of the **Holocaust**, Hitler's systematic efforts to destroy the Jews of Europe. Reports of the Nazis' methodical slaughter of Jews had appeared as early as 1942, but the ghastly stories seemed beyond belief until the Allied armies liberated the death camps in central and eastern Europe where the Germans had imposed their "Final Solution" to what Hitler called the "Jewish problem": the wholesale extermination of some 6 million Jews, along with more than 1 million other captured peoples.

Holocaust survivors American troops encounter survivors of the Mauthausen concentration camp in their barracks in May of 1945. The Nazis tattooed their prisoners with identification numbers on their wrists or chests, as seen on the man at left.

In 1945, the Allied troops were horrified at what they discovered in the concentration camps. Bodies were piled as high as buildings; survivors were virtually skeletons. General Eisenhower reported to his wife that the evidence of "starvation, cruelty, and bestiality were so overpowering as to leave me a bit sick."

American officials, even some Jewish leaders, had dragged their feet in acknowledging the Holocaust during the war for fear that relief efforts for

Holocaust Systematic efforts by the Nazis to exterminate the Jews of Europe, resulting in the murder of over 6 million Jews and more than a million other "undesirables."

Jewish refugees might stir up anti-Semitism at home. Under pressure, President Roosevelt had set up a War Refugee Board early in 1944. It managed to rescue about 200,000 European Jews and some 20,000 others. Overall, however, the Allied response to the Nazi atrocities was inept at best and disgraceful at worst. In 1944, Churchill called the Holocaust the "most horrible crime ever committed in the history of the world."

CORE **OBJECTIVE**

5. Describe how the Japanese were defeated in the war in the Pacific.

Fighting in the Pacific

For months after the attack on Pearl Harbor, the news from the Pacific was "all bad," as President Roosevelt confessed. The Japanese captured numerous territories in Asia, including the British colonies of Hong Kong, Burma, Malaysia, and Singapore, as well as the French colony of Indochina. "Everywhere in the Pacific," said Winston Churchill, "we were weak and naked." In the Philippines, U.S. forces and their Filipino allies, outmanned, outgunned, and malnourished, surrendered in the early spring of 1942. Soon, Japan had seized control of a vast new Pacific empire and was on the verge of assaulting Australia.

Coral Sea and Midway

Battles of Coral Sea and Midway (1942)

During the spring of 1942, U.S. forces finally had some success in two key naval battles. The Battle of the Coral Sea (May 7–8, 1942) stopped a Japanese fleet headed toward the enormous island of New Guinea. Planes from the *Lexington* and the *Yorktown* sank one Japanese carrier, damaged another, and destroyed several smaller ships. American losses were greater, but the Japanese threat against Australia was stopped.

Less than a month later, Admiral Yamamoto steered his main Japanese battle fleet toward Midway, the westernmost of Hawaii's inhabited islands, from which he hoped to strike again at Pearl Harbor. This time it was the Japanese who were taken by surprise. Americans had broken the Japanese military radio code, allowing Admiral Chester Nimitz, commander of the U.S. central Pacific fleet, to learn where Yamamoto's fleet was heading. Nimitz was able to reinforce the American air base at tiny Midway Island with planes and aircraft carriers.

The first Japanese attack against Midway, on June 4, 1942, severely damaged the island's defenses, but at the cost of about a third of the Japanese planes. American bombers then struck back. In the strategic Battle of Midway, U.S. warplanes sank three Japanese aircraft carriers and crippled a fourth that was later sunk by a torpedo; it was the first major defeat for the Japanese navy in 350 years and the turning point of the Pacific war. The American victory at Midway blunted Japan's military momentum, eliminated the threat to Hawaii, and bought time for the United States to organize its massive industrial productivity for a wider war. Japanese hopes for a short, decisive war were dashed.

MacArthur's Pacific Strategy

American and Australian forces were under the command of General Douglas MacArthur, a self-infatuated military genius who constantly irritated his superiors in Washington with his "unpleasant personality" and his relentless efforts to embellish his image as a hero. Yet MacArthur was indeed a brilliant strategist. In 1942, his forces began to dislodge the Japanese from islands in the southwest Pacific.

After first pushing the Japanese back in New Guinea, on August 7, 1942, 19,000 U.S. Marines landed on Guadalcanal Island, only 1,200 miles from Australia, where the Japanese had built an air base. The American commander was optimistic that his undersupplied troops could defeat the entrenched Japanese even though, he said, there were "a hundred reasons why this operation should fail." But it did not fail. The savage fighting on Guadalcanal lasted through February 1943, but resulted in the Japanese army's first defeat, a loss of 20,000 men compared to 1,752 Americans.

The Japanese were skilled defensive fighters who rarely surrendered, and they controlled most of the islands in the Pacific. Their suicidal intensity in battles in New Guinea and on Guadalcanal led MacArthur and American military planners to adopt a brilliant "leapfrogging" strategy whereby they focused on the most important islands and used airpower and seapower to bypass the others, leaving the isolated Japanese bases to "wither on the vine," as Admiral Nimitz put it. For example, when U.S. warplanes destroyed the Japanese airfield at Rabaul in eastern New Guinea, 135,000 Japanese troops were left stranded on the island, cut off from resupply by air or by sea. What the Allies did to the Japanese garrison on Rabaul set the pattern for the remainder of the "island-hopping" war in the Pacific.

> Guadalcanal (1943) and Pacific Leapfrogging

Battles in the Central Pacific

On June 15, 1944, just days after the D-day invasion, U.S. forces liberated Tinian, Guam, and Saipan, three Japanese-controlled islands in the Mariana Islands. Saipan was strategically important because it allowed the new American B-29 "Superfortress" bombers to strike Japan itself. With New Guinea and the Mariana Islands all but liberated, General MacArthur's forces invaded the Japanese-held Philippines on October 20. The Japanese, knowing that the loss of the Philippines would cut them off from essential raw materials, brought in warships from three directions to battle the U.S. fleet.

The four sea battles that were fought in the Philippine Sea from October 23 to October 26, 1944, came to be known collectively as the Battle of Leyte Gulf, the largest naval engagement in history and the worst Japanese defeat of the war. By the end of the day, thirty-six Japanese warships, including four aircraft carriers, had been destroyed. The battle included the first Japanese *kamikaze* ("divine wind") attacks—suicide pilots deliberately crashing their bomb-laden planes into American warships.

> Battle of Leyte Gulf (1944)

General Douglas MacArthur
MacArthur theatrically coming ashore at the island of Leyte in the Philippines, October 1944.

As General MacArthur waded ashore with the U.S. troops liberating the Philippines, he reminded reporters of his 1942 pledge to return when he was evacuated from the islands in the face of the Japanese invasion. Now the U.S. commander announced with great fanfare: "People of the Philippines, I have returned! The hour of your redemption is here. . . . Rally to me."

A Grinding War against Japan

Iwo Jima (1945)

The closer the Allied forces got to Japan itself, the fiercer the resistance they encountered. While fighting continued in the Philippines, 30,000 U.S. Marines landed on Japanese-held Iwo Jima island, a speck of volcanic rock 760 miles from Tokyo that the Americans needed as a base for fighter planes to escort bombers over Japan. It took nearly six weeks to secure the tiny island at a cost of nearly 7,000 American lives.

Battle of Okinawa

Battle of Okinawa (1945)

The fight for the Japanese island of Okinawa, which began on Easter Sunday, April 1, was even bloodier. Okinawa was strategically important because it would serve as the staging area for the planned Allied invasion of Japan. The conquest of Okinawa was the largest amphibious operation of the Pacific war, involving some 300,000 troops, and almost three months of brutal fighting. More than 110,000 Japanese were killed; the remaining 7,871 were either captured or surrendered.

WORLD WAR II IN THE PACIFIC, 1942–1945

Areas controlled by Japan, 1942
Major Allied naval offensives
Major Allied air offensives
Japanese advances
Limit of Japanese control
Major battle

- What was "leapfrogging"? Why were the battles in the Marianas a major turning point in the war?
- What was the significance of the Battle of Leyte Gulf?
- How did the battle at Okinawa affect the way both sides proceeded in the war?

Preparations for the Invasion of Japan

Even as the fighting still raged on Okinawa, Allied commanders began planning Operation Downfall—the invasion of Japan itself. To weaken the Japanese defenses, destroy many of their war-related industries, and erode civilian morale, the Allied command launched massive bombing raids over Japan in the summer of 1944. In early 1945, General Curtis Lemay, head of the U.S. Bomber Command, ordered devastating "firebomb" raids over Japan upon Japanese cities. On March 9, for example, some 300 B-29 bombers dropped napalm bombs on Tokyo, incinerating sixteen square miles of the city and killing 85,000 people.

Allies firebomb Tokyo

The Atomic Bomb

Atomic bomb dropped on Hiroshima

Still, the Japanese showed no willingness to surrender. In early 1945, new president Harry S. Truman learned of the first successful test explosion of an atomic bomb in New Mexico. Now that military planners knew the bomb would work, they selected two Japanese cities as targets. The first was **Hiroshima**, a port city and army headquarters in southern Japan, on the island of Honshu. On July 25, 1945, Truman ordered that the atomic bomb be used if Japan did not surrender before August 3. Although an intense debate has emerged over the decision to drop the bomb, Truman said that he "never had any doubt that it should be used." He later recalled that "we faced half a million casualties trying to take Japan by land. It was either that or the atom bomb, and I didn't hesitate a minute, and I've never lost any sleep over it since."

To Truman and others, the use of atomic bombs seemed a logical next step to end the war. As it turned out, scientists greatly underestimated the physical effects of the bomb. They predicted that 20,000 people would be killed, an estimate that proved much too low.

In mid-July 1945, the Allied leaders met in Potsdam, Germany, near Berlin. There they issued the Potsdam Declaration. In addition to outlawing Nazism, it demanded that Japan surrender or face "prompt and utter destruction."

The aftermath of Little Boy This image shows the wasteland that remained after the atomic bomb "Little Boy" decimated Hiroshima, Japan, on August 6, 1945.

The deadline passed, and on August 6, 1945, a B-29 bomber named the *Enola Gay* (after the pilot's mother) took off at 2:00 A.M. from the island of Tinian and headed for Hiroshima. At 8:15 A.M., flying at 31,600 feet, the *Enola Gay* released the five-ton, ten-foot-long uranium bomb nicknamed "Little Boy." Forty-three seconds later, as the *Enola Gay* turned sharply to avoid the blast, the bomb tumbled to an altitude of 1,900 feet where it exploded, creating a blinding flash of light followed by a fireball towering to 40,000 feet. The tail gunner on the *Enola Gay* described the scene: "It's like bubbling molasses down there . . . the mushroom is spreading out . . . fires are springing up everywhere . . . it's like a peep into hell."

Hiroshima (1945) Japanese port city that was the first target of the newly developed atomic bomb on August 6, 1945. Most of the city was destroyed.

The powerful bomb's shock wave and firestorm killed some 78,000 people, including thousands of Japanese soldiers and twenty-three American prisoners of war housed in the city. By the end of the year, the death toll would reach 140,000, as more people died of injuries or radiation poisoning. In addition, 70,000 buildings were destroyed, and four square miles of the city turned to rubble.

President Truman was aboard the battleship *Augusta* returning from the Potsdam Conference when news arrived that the atomic bomb had been dropped. "This is the greatest thing in history!" he exclaimed. In the United States, Americans greeted the news with similar joy. To them, the atomic bomb promised a quick end to the long nightmare of war. "No tears of sympathy will be shed in America for the Japanese people," the *Omaha World-Herald* predicted. "Had they possessed a comparable weapon at Pearl Harbor, would they have hesitated to use it?" Others reacted more soberly when they considered the implications of atomic warfare. "Yesterday," journalist Hanson Baldwin wrote in the *New York Times,* "we clinched victory in the Pacific, but we sowed the whirlwind."

Two days after the Hiroshima bombing, an opportunistic Soviet Union, hoping to share in the spoils of victory, hastened to enter the war in the Pacific by sending Russian troops into Japanese-occupied Manchuria along the border between China and the Soviet Union. Truman and his aides, frustrated by the stubborn refusal of Japanese leaders to surrender and fearful that the Soviet Union's entry would complicate negotiations, ordered a second atomic bomb ("Fat Man") to be dropped on Japan. On August 9, the city of Nagasaki, a shipbuilding center on the island of Kyushu, experienced the same nuclear devastation that had destroyed Hiroshima. Five days later, on August 14, 1945, the Japanese emperor finally accepted the terms of surrender.

Bombing of Nagasaki A 20,000-foot tall mushroom cloud swallowed the city of Nagasaki after the atomic bombing on August 9, 1945

A New Age Is Born

Thus ended the largest and costliest war in human history. The Soviet Union suffered 20 million deaths, China 10 million, Germany 5.6 million, and Japan 2.3 million. The Second World War (1939–1945) was more costly for the United States than any other foreign war: 292,000 battle deaths and 114,000 noncombat deaths; a million Americans were wounded, half of them seriously disabled. But in proportion to its population, the United States suffered far fewer losses than did the other major Allies or their enemies, and American territory escaped the devastation suffered in so many other parts of the world. For every American killed in the Second World War, for example, some 59 Soviets died.

The Second World War was the pivotal event of the twentieth century; it reshaped entire societies and transformed international relations. German and Italian fascism as well as Japanese militarism were destroyed. The colonial empires in Africa and Asia governed by European nations rapidly crumbled as the changes wrought by the war unleashed independence

CORE **OBJECTIVE**

6. Evaluate the efforts of President Roosevelt and the Allies to shape the postwar world.

The end of colonial empires and the emergence of the Soviet Union as a global power movements. In 1947, for example, the new nations of India and Pakistan liberated themselves from British control. The Soviet Union emerged from the war as a new global superpower, while the United States, as Winston Churchill told the House of Commons, stood "at the summit of the world."

Why Did the Allies Win?

Many factors contributed to the Allied victory in the Second World War. The American and British leaders—Roosevelt and Churchill—were better at coordinating military efforts and maintaining national morale than were Hitler, Mussolini, and the Japanese emperor, Hirohito. By 1944, Hitler had grown increasingly unstable and unpredictable in his decision making and more withdrawn from the German people, especially after a failed attempt by high-ranking officers to assassinate him in July.

In the end, however, what turned the tide of war was the awesome productivity of American industry and the ability of the Soviet Union to absorb the massive German invasion and then push back all the way to Berlin. By the end of the war, Japan had run out of food and Germany had run out of fuel. By contrast, the United States was churning out more of everything at war's end. As early as 1942, just a few weeks after the Japanese attack on Pearl Harbor, Fritz Todt, a Nazi engineer, told Hitler that the war against the United States was already lost because of America's ability to out-produce all the other warring nations combined.

Yalta's Legacy and the Postwar World

The United Nations (1945)

Franklin Roosevelt viewed the Yalta meeting as a test of whether the wartime alliance between the United States and the Soviet Union would survive once the conflict ended. Roosevelt staked his hopes for postwar cooperation on the creation of a new international peacekeeping organization, the United Nations. At Yalta, the "Big Three" agreed to hold organizational meetings in the United States beginning on April 25, 1945. Like Woodrow Wilson before him, Roosevelt was determined to replace America's "outdated" isolationism of the 1920s and 1930s with an engaged internationalism. But the creation of the United Nations came at a high price. In order to get Stalin's approval of the United Nations, Roosevelt gave in to Stalin's demands for territory held by Japan in northeast Asia.

Soviet domination of eastern Europe

Stalin also signed the Yalta Declaration of Liberated Europe, which called for free and open elections in the liberated nations of eastern Europe. Nevertheless, the wily Stalin would fail to live up to the promises he made at Yalta. When the Red Army "liberated" Hungary, Romania, Bulgaria, Czechoslovakia, Poland, and eastern Germany, it plundered and sent back to Russia anything of economic value, dismantling thousands of factories and mills and rebuilding them in the Soviet Union. To ensure control over the nations of eastern Europe, the Soviets shipped off to prisons anyone who questioned the new communist governments they created.

Republicans later savagely attacked Roosevelt for "giving" eastern Europe over to Soviet domination at Yalta. Some blamed his behavior on his declining health (he would die in a few weeks). But even a robust Roosevelt could not have dislodged the Soviet army from its control of eastern Europe. The course of the war shaped the outcome at Yalta, not Roosevelt's failed diplomacy. The United States had no real leverage when it came to eastern Europe; the huge Soviet army controlled Poland and its neighbors. As a U.S. diplomat admitted, "Stalin held all the cards" at Yalta.

The Transformation of American Life

Wars often have far-reaching societal effects. This was especially true of the Second World War. The war changed many Americans from being isolationists, often proudly ignorant of and indifferent to the rest of the world, into internationalists aware that they now had profound responsibilities for the stability and security of the entire world.

The war also transformed American life by ending the Great Depression and launching a period of unprecedented prosperity. Big businesses during the war grew into gigantic corporations as a result of huge government contracts for military weapons and supplies. New technologies and products developed for military purposes—radar, computers, electronics, plastics and synthetics, jet engines, rockets, atomic energy—began to transform the private sector, as did new consumer products that were generated from war-related innovations. And new opportunities for women as well as for African Americans, Mexican Americans, and other minorities set in motion major social changes that would culminate in the civil rights movement of the 1960s and the feminist movement of the 1970s.

> The post-war United States: New technologies, bustling industries, social change, and opportunities for women and minorities

The expansion of the federal government spurred by the war effort continued after 1945. Presidential authority increased enormously at the expense of congressional and state power. The isolationist sentiment in foreign relations that had been so powerful in the 1920s and 1930s evaporated, as the United States assumed new global responsibilities and economic interests.

> The post-war United States: Global superpower

In August 1945, President Truman told the nation that the United States had "emerged from this war the most powerful nation in this world—the most powerful nation, perhaps, in all history." But the Soviet Union, despite its profound human losses and physical destruction, had gained much new territory, built massive armed forces, and enhanced its international influence, making it the greatest power in Europe and Asia. A little over a century after Frenchman Alexis de Tocqueville had predicted that Europe would eventually be overshadowed by the United States and Russia, his prophecy had come to pass.

■ **Fascism and the Start of the War** In Italy, Benito Mussolini assumed control by promising law and order. Adolf Hitler rearmed Germany in defiance of the Treaty of Versailles and aimed to unite all German speakers in a "Greater Germany." Civil war in Spain and the growth of the Soviet Union under Josef Stalin contributed to a precarious balance of power in Europe. By March 1939, Nazi Germany had annexed Austria and seized Czechoslovakia. Hitler then sent troops to invade Poland with the *blitzkrieg* strategy in September 1939, after signing a non-aggression pact with the Soviet Union. At last, the British and French governments declared war.

■ **America Goes to War** The United States issued "neutrality laws" to keep it out of war, but with the fall of France, Roosevelt accelerated military aid to Great Britain through the *Lend-Lease Bill*. In 1941, the United States and Great Britain signed the *Atlantic Charter*, announcing their aims in the war. After Japan joined with Germany and Italy to form the *"Axis" alliance* and Japan announced its intention to take control of French Indochina, President Roosevelt froze Japanese assets in the United States and restricted oil exports to Japan. The frustrated Japanese decided to launch a surprise attack at *Pearl Harbor*, Hawaii, in hopes of destroying the U.S. Pacific Fleet.

■ **The Second World War and American Society** The war had profound effects on American society. Americans migrated west to take jobs in defense factories, making unemployment a thing of the past. Farmers, too, recovered from hard times, supported by Mexican labor through the *bracero program*. The federal government, through agencies like the *War Production Board*, took control of managing the economy for the war effort. Many women took nontraditional jobs, some in the *Women's Army Corps*. About 1 million African Americans served in the military in segregated units such as the *Tuskegee Airmen*. More than 100,000 Japanese Americans were forcibly interned in "*war relocation camps.*"

■ **Road to Allied Victory in Europe** By 1943, the Allies had defeated the German and Italian armies occupying North Africa then launched attacks on Sicily and the mainland of Italy. Stalin demanded an Allied attack on the Atlantic coast of France, but Operation Overlord was delayed until 1944. Invaded from the west and the east, German resistance slowly crumbled. Allied leaders Roosevelt, Churchill, and Stalin met at the *Yalta Conference* in February 1945, where they decided to divide a conquered Germany into four occupation zones. In May, Soviet forces captured Berlin and Germany surrendered. After the war, Allied forces discovered the extent of the *Holocaust*—the Nazis' systematic attempt to exterminate the Jews.

■ **The Pacific War** The Japanese advance across the Pacific was halted in June 1942 when the U.S. Navy destroyed much of the Japenese fleet in the Battle of Midway. The United States fought costly battles in New Guinea and Guadalcanal before dislodging the Japanese from the Philippines in 1944. Fierce Japanese resistance at Iwo Jima and Okinawa and refusal to surrender led the new president, Harry S. Truman, to drop atomic bombs on the Japanese cities of *Hiroshima* and Nagasaki.

■ **Postwar World** The Soviet Union and the United States emerged from the war as global superpowers. The United States possessed the world's strongest economy. Military production had brought America out of the Great Depression, and new military technologies changed industrial and private life. The opportunities for women and minorities during the war also increased their aspirations and would contribute to the emergence of the civil rights and feminist movements.

KEY TERMS

fascism *p. 870*
"Axis" alliance *p. 873*
blitzkrieg (1940) *p. 875*
Lend-Lease Bill (1941) *p. 881*
Atlantic Charter (1941) *p. 882*

Pearl Harbor (1941) *p. 885*
War Production Board *p. 887*
Women's Army Corps *p. 889*
Tuskegee Airmen *p. 891*
bracero program (1942) *p. 892*

"war relocation camps" *p. 892*
Yalta Conference (1945) *p. 904*
Holocaust *p. 905*
Hiroshima (1945) *p. 910*

CHRONOLOGY

1933	Hitler becomes chancellor of Germany
1935	Italy invades Ethiopia
1936–1939	Spanish Civil War
1937	War between China and Japan begins
1938	Hitler forces the *Anschluss* (union) of Austria and Germany
1939	Soviet Union agrees to a non-aggression pact with Germany
September 1939	German troops invade Poland
1940	Battle of Britain
September 1940	Germany, Italy, and Japan sign the Tripartite Pact
June 1941	Germany invades Soviet Union
August 1941	United States and Great Britain sign the Atlantic Charter
December 7, 1941	Japanese launch surprise attack at Pearl Harbor, Hawaii
June 1942	Battle of Midway
July 1943	Allied forces land on Sicily
June 6, 1944	D-day
February 1945	Yalta Conference
May 8, 1945	Nazi Germany surrenders unconditionally; V-E Day
August 1945	Atomic bombs dropped on Hiroshima and Nagasaki
September 2, 1945	Japan surrenders; V-J Day

INQUIZITIVE

Go to InQuizitive to see what you've learned—and learn what you've missed—with personalized feedback along the way.

DEBATING the United States' Response to the Holocaust

One of the more difficult tasks that historians face is assessing the actions and beliefs of historical figures within an ethical framework. Should individuals be judged by the standards of their own time or by those of today? Should we hold celebrated historical figures to a higher ethical standard? How should we assess a nation's priorities in a time of crisis and war? For Part 6, *Modern America*, President Franklin D. Roosevelt's and the U.S. government's response to the Holocaust during the Second World War demonstrate how historians can disagree when they attempt to evaluate historic individuals from an ethical perspective.

For this exercise you have two tasks:

PART 1: Compare the two secondary sources on the United States and Holocaust.
PART 2: Using primary sources, evaluate the arguments of the two secondary sources.

PART I Comparing Secondary Sources

Secondary sources from two scholars are included for you to review. The first is from David Wyman, formerly of the University of Massachusetts at Amherst and currently chairman of the David S. Wyman Institute of Holocaust Studies. Wyman is one of the most influential historians on the American response to the Holocaust. The second is from Holocaust historian Richard Breitman, editor of the scholarly journal *Holocaust and Genocide Studies*, and historian Allan J. Lichtman. Both teach at American University. In the following selections, these scholars explore President Franklin Delano Roosevelt's response to the challenges posed by the Holocaust.

Compare the views of these two scholars by answering the following questions. Be sure to find specific examples in the selections to support your answers.

■ How do the authors characterize the American response to the Holocaust, and what explanation(s) do they give for that conduct?

■ What role in America's response to the Holocaust does each author ascribe to Franklin D. Roosevelt?

■ How does each author assess the morality of the response to the Holocaust of both the U.S. government and President Roosevelt? What ethical standards do the authors use in making their assessments?

■ What ethical standard would you use to evaluate the conduct of President Roosevelt and the U.S. government?

Secondary Source 1

David S. Wyman, *The Abandonment of the Jews* (1985)

Why did America fail to carry out the kind of rescue effort that it could have?

The American State Department . . . had no intention of rescuing large numbers of European Jews. On the contrary, they continually feared that Germany or other Axis nations might release tens of thousands of Jews into Allied hands. Any such exodus would have placed intense pressure on Britain to open Palestine and on the United States to take in more Jewish refugees, a situation the two great powers did not want to face. Consequently, their policies aimed at obstructing rescue possibilities and dampening public pressures for government action.

Authenticated information that the Nazis were systematically exterminating European Jewry was made public in the United States in November 1942. President Roosevelt did nothing about the mass murder for fourteen months, then moved only because he was confronted with political pressures he could not avoid and because his administration stood on the brink of a nasty scandal over its rescue policies. The War Refugee Board, which the President then established to save Jews and other victims of the Nazis, received little power, almost no cooperation from Roosevelt or his administration, and grossly inadequate government funding.

Strong popular pressure for action would have brought a much fuller government commitment to rescue and would have produced it sooner. Several factors hampered the growth of public pressure. Among them were anti-Semitism and anti-immigration attitudes, both widespread in American society in that era. . . . In 1944 the United States War Department rejected several appeals to bomb the Auschwitz gas chambers and the railroads leading to Auschwitz, claiming that such actions would divert essential airpower from decisive operations elsewhere. . . . Franklin Roosevelt's indifference to so momentous an historical event as the systematic annihilation of European Jewry emerges as the worst failure of his presidency.

Source: Wyman, David S. *The Abandonment of the Jews: America and the Holocaust, 1941–1945.* New York: The New Press, 1985. xiv–xv.

Secondary Source 2

Richard Breitman and Allan J. Lichtman, *FDR and the Jews* (2013)

Some scholars have condemned Franklin Delano Roosevelt, the president of the United States from 1933 to 1945, for callously standing by while Hitler persecuted German Jewry and then exterminated nearly two-thirds of Europe's Jews. . . . Others claim that Roosevelt did everything feasible to rescue European Jews and saved millions of potential victims by orchestrating the defeat of Nazi Germany in World War II. . . . For most of his presidency Roosevelt did little to aid the imperiled Jews of Germany and Europe. He put other policy priorities well ahead of saving Jews and deferred to fears of an anti-Semitic backlash at home. He worried that measures to assist European Jews might endanger his political coalition at home and then a wartime alliance abroad. FDR usually avoided singling out the Jews in public. When he engaged Jewish issues, he maneuvered, often behind the scenes. When he hesitated, other American officials with far less sympathy for Jews set or carried out policies. Still, at times Roosevelt acted decisively to rescue Jews, often withstanding contrary pressures from the American public, Congress, and his own State Department. Oddly enough, he did more for the Jews than any other world figure, even if his efforts seem deficient in retrospect. He was a far better president for Jews than any of his political adversaries would have been. Roosevelt defied most Republican opponents and some isolationist Democrats to lead political and military opposition to Nazi Germany's plans for expansion and world domination. . . . Unlike other authors, we examine FDR's decision-making as president from the perspective of his life experiences and full political career. Roosevelt's handling of the crisis of European Jewry may offer the best opportunity to understand the political dynamics of American responses to persecution and genocide in foreign lands. FDR was a man of faith. He recognized both moral issues across the globe and the practical concerns of governing a great nation. . . . How he responded, and why, reveals much about the strengths and limitations of the American presidency. The story of FDR and the Jews is ultimately a tragic one that transcends the achievements and failures of any one leader. Even if FDR had been more willing to override domestic opposition and twist arms abroad, he could not have stopped the Nazis' mass murder of some six million Jews. For Hitler and his followers, the annihilation of Jews was not a diversion from the war effort, but integral to its purpose. For America and Britain, the rescue of Jews, even if practical, was ultimately subordinate to the overriding priorities of total war and unconditional surrender of the enemy. "Action expresses priorities," Mahatma Gandhi said while engaged in a freedom struggle of his own.

Source: Breitman, Richard, and Allan J. Lichtman. *FDR and the Jews.* Cambridge, Mass.: The Belknap Press of Harvard University Press, 2013. 2, 6–7.

PART II Using Primary Sources to Evaluate Secondary Sources

When historians are faced with competing interpretations of the past, they often look at primary source material as part of the process of evaluating the different arguments. A selection of primary source materials relating to the United States and the Holocaust follows. The first document is a 1942 letter to the president from the leaders of the American Jewish community soon after the public revelation of the holocaust. The second selection comes from a State Department memorandum to the British government regarding refugees from Nazi-occupied territories. The third document is from a letter from Secretary of State Cordell Hull to the president regarding the Bermuda conference of April 1943, in which the United States and Great Britain discuss the issue of Jewish refugees. The fourth document is a 1944 memorandum written by John Pehle, an assistant to Treasury Secretary Henry Morgenthau Jr., following a meeting with President Roosevelt. Morgenthau was the highest-ranking Jewish member of FDR's cabinet and the leading advocate for U.S. intervention in stopping the Holocaust. The fifth document is a draft of a statement by FDR regarding crimes against humanity that was distributed to Axis forces in Europe in 1944. The final document is a July 4, 1944, letter from Assistant Secretary of War John J. McCloy to John W. Pehle outlining reasons why the War Department rejected Pehle's request to bomb the rail lines used to transport Jews and other prisoners to the Nazi death camps.

Carefully read each of the primary sources and answer the following questions. Which of the primary source documents support or refute Wyman's or Breitman and Lichtman's arguments about the U.S. response to the Holocaust. You may find that some documents do both, but for different parts of each historian's interpretation. Be sure to identify which specific components of each historian's argument the documents support or refute.

■ Based on these primary sources, how would you characterize the U.S. government's response to the Holocaust?

■ Judging from these primary sources, what role did FDR play in formulating U.S. policy toward the Holocaust?

■ Which of the primary sources do you think Wyman or Breitman and Lichtman would find most useful, and how might they use them to support their argument?

■ Which of the secondary sources do you think is best supported by the primary source evidence?

■ Based on the ethical standard you would use to evaluate the conduct of President Roosevelt and the U.S. government (see the previous questions for comparing secondary sources), how do you assess what these primary sources reveal about the U.S. government's and FDR's response to the Holocaust?

Primary Source 1

Representatives of the Jewish Community of the United States, "Letter to the President" (December 8, 1942)

Dear Mr. President:

We come to you as representatives of all sections of the Jewish community of the United States. Within recent months all Americans have been horrified by the verification of reports concerning the barbarities against the inhabitants of countries over-run by Hitler's forces. To these

horrors has now been added the news of Hitler's edict calling for the extermination of all Jews in the subjugated lands.

Already almost two million Jews, men, women and children, have been cruelly done to death, and five million more Jews live under the threat of a similar doom.

The record of these heinous crimes against the Jews in East Europe is detailed in the attached memorandum.

. . .

In the midst of their suffering, however, the peoples of Europe are sustained by a hope that the victory of the Democracies will destroy the Nazi scourge and restore freedom to the world. European Jews share that hope. But will they live to see the dawn of this day of freedom? Unless action is taken immediately, the Jews of Hitler's Europe are doomed.

In this hour of deepest anguish and despair we turn to you, Mr. President. . . .

We ask you now once again to raise your voice—in behalf of the Jews of Europe. We ask you once again to warn the Nazis that they will be held to strict accountability for their crimes. We ask you to employ every available means to bring solemn protest and warning to the peoples of the Axis countries so that they may be deterred from acting as the instruments of the monstrous designs of their mad leaders.

Maurice Wertheim, President, American Jewish Committee
Dr. Stephen Wise, President, American Jewish Congress
Adolph Held, President, American Jewish Labor Committee
Henry Monsky, President, B'nai B'rith
Israel Goldstein, President, Synagogue Council of America
Rabbi Israel Rosenberg, Chairman, Union of Orthodox Rabbis in the United States

---

Source: Wertheim, Maurice, Adolph Held, Israel Goldstein, Stephen Wise, Henry Honsky, and Rabbi Israel Rosenberg. "Letter to the President, December 8, 1942." Selected Digitized Documents Related to the Holocaust and Refugees, 1933–1945. Official File 76—Church Matters: 76c—Jewish, October–December 1942. Franklin D. Roosevelt Presidential Library & Museum. Accessed at the *FRANKLIN, FDR Library's Digital Collections*: www.fdrlibrary.marist.edu/_resources/images/hol/hol00023.pdf#search=>.

Primary Source 2

U.S. Department of State, Response to British Embassy on Assisting Jewish refugees (February 25, 1943)

Since the entry of the United States into the war, there have been no new restrictions placed by the Government of the United States upon the number of aliens of any nationality permitted to proceed to this country under existing laws, except for the more intensive examination of aliens required for security reasons. . . . In affording asylum to refugees, however, it is and must be bound by legislation enacted by Congress [in] determining the immigration policy of the United States.

Source: United States Department of State. "Refugees from Nazi-Occupied Territory: Reception in the United Kingdom and British Colonial Territory [February 25, 1943]." President's Secretary's File, Box 71, State Department—Summary of Consular Reports Relating to Conditions in Occupied Countries, January 1942–May 1943, July 8, 1941. Franklin D. Roosevelt, Papers as President: The President's Secretary's File (PSF), 1933–1945. Franklin D. Roosevelt Presidential Library & Museum. Accessed at *FRANKLIN, FDR Library's Digital Collections*: <http://www.fdrlibrary.marist.edu/_resources/images/psf/b-psfc000198.pdf#search=>.

Primary Source 3

Secretary of State and the President's Correspondence, Abstract (May 7, 1943)

Writes at length to the President re the recent Bermuda Conference on Refugees, and in this connection encloses a copy of the summary or outline of the recommendations, which have been unanimously made by the American and British Delegates. . . . the most important of the items recommended at Bermuda concerns the evacuation of some 5,000 persons from Bulgaria via Turkey to Palestine, another important recommendation requires action by the U.S. Government as well as by the British Government relates to the movement of some 20,000 refugees from Spain to North Africa, "not only to relieve the Spanish authorities of the present burden, but also to make it possible for Spain to receive more and more refugees who in turn may be evacuated to North Africa." . . . The President made certain suggestions . . . as follows: that we do not give unlimited promise but that we undertake with Britain to share the cost of financing from time to time any specific cases—in connection with the providing for refugees; that we can do nothing but comply strictly with the present immigration laws. . . . he agrees that we cannot open the question of our immigration laws, and he agrees with Sec'y. Hull as to bringing in temporary visitors, stating: "We have already brought in a large number." The President returned the above-mentioned cablegram with his O.K.

Source: "Abstract, Letter to President Franklin Delano Roosevelt from Secretary of State Cordell Hull, May 7, 1943." Selected Digital Documents Related to the Holocaust and Refugees, 1933–1945. Series 1, Official File 76—Church Matters: 76c—Jewish—Abstracts, 1943–1945. Franklin D. Roosevelt Presidential Library & Museum. Accessed at *FRANKLIN, FDR Library's Digital Collections*: <http://www.fdrlibrary.marist.edu/_resources/images/hol/hol00029.pdf#search=>.

Primary Source 4

U.S. State Department's Efforts to Rescue European Jews, Memorandum (January 16, 1944)

Secretary Morgenthau advised the President that he was deeply disturbed about the failure of the State Department to take any effective action to save the remaining Jews in Europe. He explained that the Treasury Department . . . had uncovered evidence indicating that not only were the people in the State Department inefficient in dealing with this problem, but that they were actually taking action to prevent the rescue of the Jews. . . . The President listened attentively and seemed to grasp the significance of the various points. . . . The President said he agreed that some effective action could be taken. . . . The President seemed disinclined to believe that Long [Assistant Secretary of State Breckinridge Long] wanted to stop effective action from being taken, but said that Long had been somewhat soured on the problem when Rabbi Wise got Long to approve a long list of people being brought into this country, many of whom turned out to be bad people. Secretary Morgenthau reminded the President that at a Cabinet meeting Biddle [identify] had indicated that only three Jews of those entering the United States during the war had turned out to be undesirable. The President said that he had been advised that the figure was considerably larger. In any event he felt that Long was inclined to be soured on the situation. . . . The Secretary told Mr. Stettinius in plain words that he was convinced that people in the State Department, particularly Breckinridge Long, were deliberately obstructing the execution of any plan to save the Jews and that forthright immediate action was necessary if this Government was not going to be placed in the same position as Hitler and share the responsibility for exterminating all the Jews of Europe. . . .

Source: Pehle, John. "Memorandum for the Secretary's Files, January 16, 1944." Eleanor Roosevelt Papers—Henry Morgenthau Jr. Diary, Vol. 694: Acquiescence Memo, Personal Report to the President, and related documents, January 13–16, 1944. Selected Digitized Documents Related to the Holocaust and Refugees, 1933–1945. Franklin D. Roosevelt Presidential Library & Museum. Accessed at *FRANKLIN, FDR Library's Digital Collections*: <http://www.fdrlibrary.marist.edu/_resources/images/hol/hol00521.pdf#search=morgenthau>.

Primary Source 5

Franklin D. Roosevelt, "The Blackest Crimes of All History" (April 3, 1944)

[O]ne of the blackest crimes of all history—begun by the Nazis in the days of peace, and multiplied by them a hundred fold in time of war—the wholesale systematic murder of the Jews of Europe—goes on unabated every hour.

It is therefore fitting that we should again proclaim our determination that none who participate in any of these acts of savagery shall go unpunished. The United Nations have made it clear that they will pursue the guilty and deliver them up in order that justice be done. That warning applies not only to the leaders but also to their functionaries and subordinates in Germany and in the satellite countries. All who knowingly take part in the deportation of Jews to their death in Poland, or Norwegians and French to their death in Germany, are equally guilty with the executioner. All who share the guilt shall share the punishment.

Source: "Draft Press Release, Statement by the President re: the Holocaust, April 3, 1944." Series 1: Franklin D. Roosevelt Significant Documents, Box 1, FDR-63. Significant Documents Collection. Franklin D. Roosevelt Presidential Library & Museum. Accessed at *FRANKLIN, FDR Library's Digital Collections*: <http://www.fdrlibrary.marist.edu/_resources/images/sign/fdr_60.pdf#search=>.

Primary Source 6

U.S. War Department to Treasury Department, On Bombing Death Camp Railways (July 4, 1944)

I refer to your letter of June 29 . . . proposing that certain sections of railway lines between Hungary and Poland be bombed to interrupt the transportation of Jews from Hungary. The War Department is of the opinion that the suggested air operation is impracticable. It could be executed only by the diversion of considerable air support essential to the success of our forces now engaged in decisive operations and would in any case be of such very doubtful efficacy that it would not amount to a practical project. The War Department fully appreciates the humanitarian motives which prompted the suggested operation, but for the reasons stated above, the operation suggested does not appear justified.

Source: McCloy, John J. "Letter, John J. McCloy to John W. Pehle re: bombing of railway lines transporting Jews to death camps, July 4, 1944." Series 1: Franklin D. Roosevelt Significant Documents, Box 1, FDR-63. Significant Documents Collection. Franklin D. Roosevelt Presidential Library & Museum. Accessed at *FRANKLIN, FDR Library's Digital Collections*: <http://www.fdrlibrary.marist.edu/_resources/images/sign/fdr_63.pdf#search=john%20j.%20mccloy>.

The American Age

As the Second World War was coming to an end in 1945, President Franklin D. Roosevelt staked his hopes for a peaceful future on a new international organization, the United Nations. On April 25, 1945, two weeks after Roosevelt's death and two weeks before the German surrender, delegates from fifty nations at war with Germany and Japan met in San Francisco to draw up the Charter of the United Nations. The UN Security Council was given "primary responsibility for the maintenance of international peace and security." The Security Council included five *permanent* members: the United States, the Soviet Union (replaced by the Russian Federation in 1991), Great Britain, France, and the Republic of China (replaced by the People's Republic of China in 1971). Each permanent member could *veto* any proposed action by the United Nations. Not long after the United Nations was created, however, it became evident that two members of the Security Council, the United States and the Soviet Union, had such intense differences of opinion about international policies that the United Nations was largely impotent in dealing with the cold war that dominated postwar politics.

The United States emerged from the Second World War as the world's preeminent military and economic power, the only nation in possession of atomic weapons. While much of Europe and Asia struggled to recover from the human misery and physical devastation of the war, including an acute shortage of men, the United States was virtually unscathed, its economic infrastructure intact and operating at peak efficiency. Jobs that had been scarce in the 1930s were now available for the taking. By 1955 the United States, with only 6 percent of the world's population, was producing half of the world's goods. American capitalism became a dominant cultural force around the world, too. In Europe, Japan, South Korea, and elsewhere, American products, fashion, and forms of entertainment attracted excited attention. Henry Luce, the publisher of *Time* and *Life* magazines, proclaimed that the twentieth century had become the "American century."

Yet a deepening "cold war" between the democratic and Communist nations cast a cloud of concern over the postwar world. The tense ideological contest with the Soviet Union produced numerous foreign crises and sparked a domestic witch hunt for Communists in the United States. After 1945, Republican and Democratic presidents aggressively sought to "contain" the spread of communism around the world. This bedrock assumption embroiled the United States in costly wars in Korea and in Southeast Asia. A backlash against the Vietnam War (1964–1973) also inflamed a rebellious "countercultural" movement at home in which young idealists not only opposed the war but also provided much of the energy for many overdue social reforms, including racial equality, gay rights, feminism, and environmentalism. The anti-war movement destroyed Lyndon Johnson's presidency in 1968 and provoked a conservative counterattack. President Richard Nixon's paranoid reaction to his critics led to the Watergate affair and the destruction of his presidency.

Through all of this turmoil, however, the expanding role of the federal government that Franklin Roosevelt and his New Deal programs had initiated remained essentially intact. With only a few exceptions, both Republicans and Democrats after 1945 acknowledged that the federal government must assume greater responsibility for the welfare of individuals. Even President Ronald Reagan, a sharp critic of federal social-welfare programs during the 1980s, recognized the need for the government to provide a "safety net" for those who could not help themselves.

Yet this fragile consensus on public policy and the cold war had largely broken down by the late 1980s amid stunning international developments and social changes at home. The surprising collapse of the Soviet Union in 1989 and the disintegration of European communism left the United States the only superpower. After forty-five years, U.S. foreign policy was no longer focused on a single adversary. During the early 1990s, East and West Germany reunited, racial segregation (*apartheid*) in South Africa ended, and Israel and the Palestinians, long-standing foes, signed a treaty ending hostilities—at least for a while.

The end of the cold war and the dissolution of the Soviet Union into fifteen separate nations lowered the threat of nuclear war and reduced public interest in foreign affairs. Yet numerous ethnic, nationalist, and separatist conflicts brought constant tensions and in-stability at the end of the twentieth century and into the twenty-first. The United States found itself drawn into political and military crises in faraway lands such as Bosnia, Somalia, Afghanistan, Iraq, Ukraine, and Syria.

Throughout the 1990s, the United States waged a difficult struggle against many groups engaged in orga-nized terrorism. The challenges facing intelligence agencies in tracking the movements of foreign terror-ists became tragically evident in 2001. At 8:46 on the morning of September 11, 2001, the world watched in horror as a hijacked commercial airplane slammed into the North Tower of the World Trade Center in New York City. Seventeen minutes later, a second hijacked plane hit the South Tower. While the catastrophe was unfold-ing in New York City, a third hijacked airliner crashed into the Pentagon in Washington, D.C., while a fourth, headed for the White House, missed its mark when passengers assaulted the terrorists, sending the plane out of control and crashing to the ground near Shanksville, Pennsylvania, killing all on board.

Within hours of the hijackings, officials identified the nineteen hijackers as members of Al Qaeda (Arabic for "The Base"), a well-financed worldwide network of Islamic terrorists, led by a wealthy Saudi renegade, Osama bin

Laden. The new president, Republican George W. Bush, responded by declaring a "war on terror." With the passage of the so-called Patriot Act, Congress gave the president new authority to track down and imprison terrorists at home and abroad. The "war on terror" began with assaults first on terrorist bases in Afghanistan and then on Saddam Hussein's dictatorship in Iraq ("Operation Iraqi Freedom"). Yet terrorism proved to be an elusive and resilient foe, and the war in Iraq and the ensuing U.S. military occupation was much longer, more expensive, and less successful than Americans had expected.

The 9/11 terror attacks generated a wave of patriotism in the United States but divisive issues remained. A huge federal debt, rising annual budget deficits, and soaring health-care costs threatened to bankrupt an America that was becoming top-heavy with retirees as the baby boom generation born during and after the Second World War entered its sixties. The "graying of America" had profound social and political implications. It made the tone of political debate more conservative (because older people tend to be more conservative) and exerted increasing stress on health-care costs, nursing-home facilities, and the Social Security system.

The surprising victory of Barack Obama in the 2008 presidential election resulted from people embracing his theme of "hope and change." He pledged to end the wars in Iraq and Afghanistan, unite a divided nation, and provide jobs to the growing numbers of unemployed. As the first African American president, Obama symbolized the societal changes transforming national life in the twenty-first century. Yet no sooner was Obama inaugurated than he inherited the worst economic slowdown since the Great Depression of the 1930s. What came to be called the Great Recession has dominated the Obama presidency and, indeed, much of American life, bringing with it a prolonged sense of uncertainty and insecurity. For all of its economic power and military might, the United States in the twenty-first century has not eliminated the threat of terrorism or unlocked the mystery of sustaining prosperity in an era of globalization.

DUCK AND COVER The familiar duck-and-cover drill that is practiced in many schools across the country was first implemented in 1949, when the Soviet Union set off its first nuclear explosive and the cold war arms race. Pictured above are American schoolchildren practicing ducking and covering in February 1951.

The Cold War and the Fair Deal

1945–1952

No sooner did the Second World War end than a prolonged "cold war" began. The awkward wartime alliance between the capitalist United States and the communist Soviet Union collapsed during the spring and summer of 1945. With the elimination of their common enemy, Nazism, the two strongest nations to emerge from the war became intense rivals who could not bridge their ideological differences over basic issues such as human rights, individual liberties, democratic elections, and religious freedom. Mutual suspicion and a race to gain influence over the "nonaligned" nations of the world in Asia, Africa, the Middle East, and Central and South America further distanced the two former allies. The defeat of Japan and Germany had created power vacuums in Europe and Asia that sucked the Soviet Union and the United States into an unrelenting war of words fed by clashing strategic interests and political ideologies.

The postwar era also saw an eruption of anti-colonial liberation movements in Asia, Africa, and the Middle East that would soon strip Great Britain, France, the Netherlands, and the United States of their global empires. The Philippines, for example, gained its independence from America in 1946. The next year, Great Britain withdrew from Hindu-dominated India after carving out two new Islamic nations, Pakistan and

CORE OBJECTIVES INQUIZITIVE

1. Explain why and how the cold war between the United States and the Soviet Union developed after the Second World War.

2. Analyze the impact of American efforts to contain the Soviet Union and the expansion of communism during Truman's presidency.

3. Describe Truman's efforts to expand the New Deal, and evaluate the effectiveness of his own "Fair Deal" agenda.

4. Assess the major international developments during 1949–1950, including the outbreak of the Korean War, and explain how they altered U.S. foreign policy.

5. Examine the emergence of the Red Scare, after the Second World War, and explain its impact on American politics and society.

Bangladesh (originally called East Pakistan). The emergence of Communist China (the People's Republic) in 1949 further complicated global politics and the dynamics of the cold war.

The postwar world was thus an unstable one in which international tensions shaped domestic politics as well as foreign relations. The advent of atomic weapons was both a blessing and curse. Such weapons of mass destruction made the very idea of warfare unthinkably horrific, which in turn made national leaders more cautious to avoid letting disputes get out of hand. But even the mere possibility of nuclear holocaust cast a cloud of anxiety over the postwar era.

CORE **OBJECTIVE**

1. Explain why and how the cold war between the United States and the Soviet Union developed after the Second World War.

The Cold War

Less than three months after Harry S. Truman had begun his new role as vice president, Eleanor Roosevelt calmly told him, "Harry, the President is dead." When Truman asked what he could do to help her, the First Lady replied: "Is there anything we can do for *you*? For you are the one in trouble now."

Truman was a clumsy public speaker, frequently stumbling over big words and long sentences. He lacked Roosevelt's dash and charm, his brilliance and creativity. But the plain-speaking man from Missouri had virtues of his own. Truman resembled Andrew Jackson in his decisiveness, bluntness, folksy manner—and raw courage. A common man who became president at an uncommon time, Truman was a feisty leader who rose above his limitations to do extraordinary things. In his two presidential terms, Truman made many important decisions with long-term consequences. His challenges were enormous: he was expected to lead America out of the Second World War and into a postwar era complicated by the cold war against communism and the need to rebuild a devastated Europe and Asia. And Truman was supposed to do all of that while managing the complex conversion to peacetime at home. He ended up doing better than anyone expected. While visiting Truman at the end of his presidency in 1952, the British leader Winston Churchill confessed that he initially "held you in very low regard. I loathed your taking the place of Franklin Roosevelt. I misjudged you badly. Since that time, you, more than any other man, have saved Western civilization."

Origins of the Cold War

Historians have long debated the unanswerable question: Was the United States or the Soviet Union more responsible for the onset of the cold war? The conventional view argues that the Soviets, led by Josef Stalin, a ruthless Communist dictator ruling a traditionally insecure nation, set out to dominate the globe after 1945. The United States had no choice but to stand firm in defense of democratic capitalist values. By contrast, "revisionist" historians insist that President Truman was the primary culprit. Instead of

Harry S. Truman The successor to Franklin Roosevelt who led the United States out of World War II.

continuing Roosevelt's efforts to collaborate with Stalin and the Soviets, Truman's aggressive, confrontational foreign policy aggravated the tensions between the two countries. Yet such an interpretation fails to recognize that President Truman inherited a deteriorating relationship with the Soviets. East and West in the postwar world were captives of a nuclear nightmare of fear, suspicion, and posturing.

In retrospect, the onset of the cold war seems to have been inevitable. America's traditional commitment to capitalism, political self-determination, and religious freedom conflicted dramatically with the Soviet Union's preference for controlling its neighbors, enforcing ideological conformity, and prohibiting religions. Insecurity, as much as Communist ideology, drove much of Soviet behavior after the Second World War. Russia, after all, had been invaded by Germany twice in the first half of the twentieth century, and Soviet leaders wanted loyal nations on their borders for protection. As had often happened before, the peoples of Eastern Europe were caught in the middle.

> U.S.–Soviet fears and suspicions; conflicting visions for postwar Europe

Differences with the Soviets

The wartime military alliance against Nazism disintegrated after 1945 as the Soviet Union violated the promises it had made at the Yalta Conference and imposed its military control and Communist political system on the nations of Eastern Europe. On May 12, 1945, four days after victory in Europe, Winston Churchill asked Truman: "What is to happen about Europe? An **iron curtain** is drawn down upon [the Russian] front. We do not know what is going on behind [it]." Churchill and Truman wanted to lift the "iron curtain" created by Soviet military occupation in Eastern Europe and help those nations develop democratic governments. They still hoped that the Yalta agreements would be carried out, but events during the second half of 1945 dashed those expectations and made compromise and conciliation more difficult.

> Iron curtain

As early as the spring of 1945 and continuing for the next two years, the Soviet Union installed new "puppet" governments in Central and Eastern Europe (Bulgaria, Czechoslovakia, East Germany, Poland, Romania, and Yugoslavia). In each nation, one by one, the Soviets eliminated all political parties except the Communists, created secret police forces, took control of intellectual and cultural life, including the mass media (especially the radio networks), undermined the Roman Catholic Church, and organized a process of "ethnic cleansing" whereby millions of Germans, as well as Poles and Hungarians, were relocated from Eastern Europe, usually to West Germany or to prisons. Europeans who opposed the new Soviet regime were exiled, silenced, executed, or imprisoned. The postwar reign of terror unleashed by Stalin was intended to make people better Communists by locking up or killing the ones who refused to be Communists.

> Soviets establish Communist regimes in central and Eastern Europe

Stalin's promises at the Yalta Conference to allow open elections in the nations of Eastern Europe controlled by Soviet armies had turned out to be

iron curtain Term coined by Winston Churchill to describe the cold war divide between Western Europe and the Soviet Union's Eastern European satellite nations.

lies. U.S. secretary of state James F. Byrnes tried to use America's monopoly on atomic bombs as leverage to pressure the Soviets to abide by the Yalta accords. In April 1945, he had suggested to President Truman that nuclear weapons "might well put us in position to dictate our own terms [with the Soviets] at the end of the war." But the Soviets had paid little notice to such "atomic diplomacy," in part because their spies had kept them informed of what American scientists had been doing and in part because they were quickly developing their own atomic bombs.

Throughout the spring of 1945, the Soviets created new "friendly governments" in Eastern Europe, arguing that the United States had done the same in Italy and Japan after those nations had surrendered. The difference was the Soviets violated their pledges at the Yalta Conference by preventing noncommunists from participating in the political process in Poland and Bulgaria.

A few days before the opening of the San Francisco conference to organize the United Nations in April, Truman met with Soviet foreign minister Vyacheslav Molotov at the White House. The Soviets had just put in place a pro-Communist government in Poland in violation of Stalin's pledge at Yalta to allow free elections. Truman directed Molotov to tell Stalin that the United States expected the Soviet leader to live up to his agreements. "I have never been talked to like that in my life," Molotov angrily replied. "Carry out your agreements," Truman snapped, "and you won't get talked to like that."

Later, in July 1945, when President Truman first met Stalin at the Potsdam Conference, he wrote his mother that he had never seen "such pigheaded people as are the Russians." He described himself as "an innocent idealist" surrounded by wolves. He later acknowledged that the Soviets broke their promises to him "as soon as the unconscionable Russian Dictator [Stalin] returned to Moscow!" Truman added, with a note of embarrassment, "And I liked the little son of a bitch."

CORE **OBJECTIVE**

2. Analyze the impact of American efforts to contain the Soviet Union and the expansion of communism during Truman's presidency.

George Kennan's "Long Telegram" and containment policy

The Containment Policy

By the beginning of 1947, relations with the Soviet Union had grown ice cold. A year before, in February 1946, Stalin had declared that peace was impossible "under the present capitalist development of the world economy." His provocative statement led the State Department to ask for an analysis of Soviet communism from forty-two-year-old George F. Kennan, the best-informed expert on the Soviet Union working in the U.S. embassy in Moscow.

Kennan responded on February 22, 1946, with a famous 8,000-word "Long Telegram" in which he sketched the roots of Russian history, the pillars of Soviet policy, Stalin's "neurotic view of world affairs," and Russia's historic determination to protect its western border with Europe. In his extensive analysis, Kennan explained that the Soviet Union was founded on a rigid ideology (Marxism–Leninism) that saw a fundamental conflict between the communist and capitalist nations. Stalin and other Soviet leaders, he added, could not imagine "permanent peaceful coexistence" with the capitalist nations. The Soviet goal was to build military strength while promoting tensions between the capitalist democracies and subverting their stability by all possible means. The best way for the United States to deal with such an ideological foe, Kennan advised, was not military confrontation. Instead, he called for patient, persistent, and firm "strategic" efforts to "contain" Soviet expansionism over the long term, without resorting to war. Creating such "unalterable counterforce," he predicted, would eventually cause "either the breakup or the gradual mellowing of Soviet power" because communism, in Kennan's view, was an inherently unstable system that would eventually collapse if Americans were patient and helped postwar Europe rebuild its economies.

New secretary of state George C. Marshall, who had commanded all of America's military forces during the war, was so impressed by Kennan's analysis that he put him in charge of the State Department's Policy Planning office. No other American diplomat at the time forecast so accurately what would in fact happen to the Soviet Union some forty years later.

In its broadest dimensions, Kennan's call for the "firm and vigilant **containment** of Russian expansive tendencies" echoed the outlook of Truman and his advisers and would guide U.S. foreign policy for decades. Kennan's careful analysis, however, remained vague on several key issues: How exactly were the United States and its allies to "contain" the Soviet Union's expansionist tendencies? How should the United States respond to specific acts of Soviet aggression around the world?

Kennan was an analyst, not a policymaker. He left the task of "containing" communism to President Truman and his advisers, most of whom, unlike Kennan, viewed containment as a *military* doctrine rather than a *political* strategy. In 1946, civil war broke out in Greece between an undemocratic, authoritarian government backed by the British and a Communist-led insurgency supported by the Soviets that held the northern part of the nation.

> The Communist threat abroad: Civil war in Greece

On February 21, 1947, the British informed the U.S. government that they could no longer provide economic and military aid to Greece; they would withdraw in five weeks. Truman quickly conferred with congressional leaders, one of whom, Republican senator Arthur Vandenberg of Michigan, warned the president that he would need to "scare the hell out of the American people" about the urgent necessity to stop the menace of spreading communism in order to gain public support for his aid program. Truman was eager to do so, for he had grown tired of "babying the Russians."

containment U.S. cold war strategy to exert political, economic, and, if necessary, military pressure on global Soviet expansion as a means of combating the spread of communism.

The Truman Doctrine

On March 12, 1947, President Truman gave a national radio speech in which he asked Congress for $400 million to assist Greece and Turkey. More important, the president announced what came to be known as the **Truman Doctrine**. He declared that since the Communist challenge was worldwide, it had to be confronted everywhere around the globe. Like a row of dominoes, he predicted, the fall of Greece to communism would spread to the other nations of the Middle East, then to Western Europe. To prevent such a catastrophe, he said, the United States must "support free peoples who are resisting attempted subjugation by armed minorities or by outside pressures." In this single sentence, the president established the foundation of U.S. foreign policy for the next forty years. In Truman's view, shared by later presidents, the assumptions of the "domino theory" made an aggressive "containment" strategy against communism a necessity.

At the State Department, George Marshall thought the "flamboyant anticommunism" in Truman's speech was unnecessarily provocative, and George F. Kennan cringed at the president's "grandiose" commitment to "contain" communism *everywhere*. In his view, Truman's "militarized view of the cold war" was foolish. Efforts to "contain" communism needed to be selective rather than universal, political and economic rather than military in nature. All crises, Kennan insisted, were not equally significant. For all of its power, he noted, the United States could not intervene in every "hot spot" around the world. Kennan saw no need to provide military aid to Turkey, where no Communist threat existed. And he preferred that economic assistance, not weapons, be provided to Greece. In his view, the Soviet threat was primarily political, not military, in nature.

Truman and his advisers rejected Kennan's concerns. In 1947, Congress approved the president's request for economic and military assistance to Greece and neighboring Turkey. The Truman Doctrine marked the beginning of a contest that the former presidential adviser Bernard Baruch named in a 1947 speech to the legislature of South Carolina: "Let us not be deceived—today we are in the midst of a *cold war*." Only a few observers at the time questioned the implications of the Truman Doctrine. Walter Lippmann, the nation's leading political journalist, characterized Truman's new policy as a "strategic monstrosity" that would entangle the United States in endless international disputes and force it to partner with right-wing dictatorships—as turned out to be the case.

The Marshall Plan

In the spring of 1947, most of postwar Europe remained broke, shattered, and desperate. Factories had been bombed to rubble, railroads and bridges had been destroyed. People were starving for food and for jobs, and political unrest was growing. By 1947, socialist and communist parties were emerging in many European nations struggling to recover after the war,

The Truman Doctrine

Truman Doctrine (1947)
President Truman's program of "containing" communism in Eastern Europe and providing economic and military aid to any nations at risk of Communist takeover.

including Italy, France, and Belgium. The crisis in postwar Europe required bold action.

While giving a graduation speech at Harvard University in May, Secretary of State George C. Marshall, building upon suggestions given to him by George Kennan and other members of the State Department, called for massive financial and technical assistance to rescue war-ravaged Europe, including the Soviet Union. What came to be known as the **Marshall Plan** was "directed not against country or doctrine, but against hunger, poverty, desperation, and chaos." It was intended to reconstruct the European economy, neutralize communist insurgencies, and build up secure foreign markets for American products. As Truman said, "the American [capitalist] system can survive only if it is part of a world system." But the Marshall Plan was about more than economics. It was also part of Truman's effort to contain the expansionist tendencies of the Soviet Union by building up a strong Western Europe. The Americans, said a British official, "want an integrated Europe looking like the United States of America."

In December 1947, Truman submitted Marshall's proposal to a special session of Congress. Initially, Republican critics dismissed it as "New Dealism" for Europe. However, two months later, on February 25, 1948, a Communist-led coup in Czechoslovakia, the last nation in eastern Europe with a democratic government, ensured congressional passage of the Marshall Plan, for it seemed to confirm the immediate Communist threat to Western Europe.

From 1948 until 1951, the Marshall Plan provided $13 billion to sixteen European nations to help revive their war-ravaged economies. The Soviet Union, however, refused to participate, calling it "dollar imperialism."

The Marshall Plan worked as hoped; prosperity returned to Europe. The British foreign minister called the plan "a lifeline to sinking men." By 1951, Western Europe's industrial production had soared to 40 percent above prewar levels, and its farm output was larger than ever. The Marshall Plan also snatched the initiative in the cold war away from the Soviet Union. England's *Economist* magazine called the Marshall Plan "an act without peer in history."

Divided Germany

The Marshall Plan drew the nations of Western Europe closer together, but it increased tensions with the Soviet Union, for Stalin saw the American effort to rebuild the European economy as a way to weaken Soviet influence in the region. The breakdown of the wartime alliance between the United States and the Soviet Union also left the problem of postwar Germany unsettled. In 1945 Berlin, the German capital, had been divided into four sectors or zones, each governed by one of the four principal allied nations, the United States, France, Great Britain, and the Soviet Union. The German economy languished, requiring the U.S. Army to provide food and basic

The Marshall Plan

Marshall Plan (1948) Secretary of State George C. Marshall's post–World War II program providing massive U.S. financial and technical assistance to war-torn European countries.

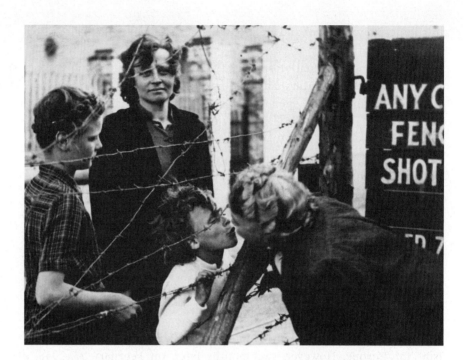

Family reunion A girl gives her grandmother a kiss through the barbed wire fence that divides the Dutch-German frontier in 1947, while the British border guards turn a blind eye.

necessities to millions of civilians. Slowly, the Allied occupation zones evolved into functioning governments. In 1948, the British, French, and Americans united their three administrative zones into one and developed a common currency to be used in West Germany as well as in West Berlin. The West Germans also organized state governments and began drafting a federal constitution.

> **Soviet blockade of Berlin and the Berlin Airlift**

The political unification of West Germany infuriated Stalin, who was determined to keep Germany weak. And the status of divided Berlin, located deep inside the Soviet occupation zone (East Germany), had become a powder keg. In March 1948, Stalin forced the issue of Berlin's status by preventing the new West German currency from being delivered into the city. Then, on June 23, Stalin decided that there was nothing to be gained by continuing to pretend that the Soviet Union and the United States were anything but enemies. He ordered the Soviet army occupying eastern Germany to stop all road and rail traffic into West Berlin, hoping the blockade would force the United States and its allies to leave the divided city.

The Americans interpreted Stalin's aggressive blockade as a tipping point in the cold war. "When Berlin falls," predicted General Lucius D. Clay, the iron-willed U.S. army commander in Germany, "western Germany will be next. Communism will run rampant." The United States thus faced a dilemma fraught with dangers: risk a third world war by using force to break the Soviet blockade or begin a humiliating retreat from West Berlin, leaving the residents to be swallowed up by communism.

Truman, who prided himself on his decisiveness, made clear his stance when he declared: "We stay in Berlin—period." In response to the Soviet blockade, the United States announced an embargo against all goods exported from Soviet-controlled eastern Germany, and it began organizing a massive airlift to provide needed food and supplies to West Berliners.

By October 1948, the U.S. and British air forces were landing cargo planes every few minutes at the Berlin airport, flying in 7,000 tons of food, fuel, medicine, coal, and equipment each day to keep the 2.25 million Berliners alive. To support the Berlin airlift and prepare for a possible war, thousands of former military pilots were called back into service, Truman revived the military draft, and Congress provided emergency funds to increase military spending.

Through the iron curtain German children greet a United States cargo plane with waves and cheers as it flies over West Berlin to drop off much-needed food and supplies.

At times it seemed that the two superpowers were on the verge of warfare in Berlin. President Truman confided in his diary that he had a "terrible feeling" that "we are very close to war." For all the threats and harsh words, however, the **Berlin airlift** went on daily for eleven months without any shots being fired. Finally, on May 12, 1949, the Soviets lifted the blockade, in part because bad Russian harvests made them desperate for food grown in western Germany.

The Berlin airlift was the first major "victory" for the West in the cold war. The unprecedented efforts of the United States and Great Britain to supply West Berliners transformed most of them from defeated adversaries into devoted allies. In May 1949, as the Soviet blockade was ending, the Federal Republic of Germany (West Germany) was founded. Six months later, in October, the German Democratic Republic (East Germany) came into being.

Forming Alliances

The Soviet blockade of Berlin convinced the United States and its allies that they needed to act together to stop further communist expansion into Western Europe. On April 4, 1949, a month before the Berlin Blockade ended, the North Atlantic Treaty was signed by twelve nations: the United States, Great Britain, France, Belgium, the Netherlands, Luxembourg, Canada, Denmark, Iceland, Italy, Norway, and Portugal. Greece and Turkey joined the alliance in 1952, West Germany in 1955, and Spain in 1982.

The **North Atlantic Treaty Organization (NATO)**, the largest collective defense alliance in the world, declared that an attack against any one of the members would be considered an attack against all. The creation of

Berlin airlift (1948) Effort by the United States and Great Britain to fly massive amounts of food and supplies into West Berlin in response to the Soviet land blockade of the city.

North Atlantic Treaty Organization (NATO) Defensive political and military alliance formed in 1949 by the United States, Canada, and ten Western European nations to deter Soviet expansion in Europe.

THE OCCUPATION OF GERMANY AND AUSTRIA

Legend:
- French zone
- British zone
- U.S. zone
- Soviet zone

■ How did the Allies divide Germany and Austria at the Yalta Conference?
■ What was the "iron curtain"?
■ Why did the Allies airlift supplies to Berlin?

NATO marked the high point of efforts to "contain" the Soviets from expanding into Western Europe. In 1949, Congress provided $1 billion in military equipment to NATO members. By joining NATO, the United States—for the first time since its alliance with France during the Revolutionary War—committed itself to go to war on behalf of its allies. Isolationism was dead.

Reorganizing the Military

The onset of the cold war and the emergence of nuclear weapons led Truman to restructure the way the U.S. armed forces were managed. In 1947, Congress passed the **National Security Act**, which centralized the National Military Establishment. It created a Department of Defense to oversee the three separate military branches—the Army, Navy, and Air Force—and the National Security Council (NSC), a group of the government's top specialists in international relations who advised the president. The act made

National Security Act (1947)
Congressional legislation that created the Department of Defense, the National Security Council, and the Central Intelligence Agency.

permanent the Joint Chiefs of Staff, a wartime innovation bringing together the leaders of the branches of the armed forces, and it established the Central Intelligence Agency (CIA) to coordinate global intelligence-gathering activities. In 1952 Truman created the National Security Agency (NSA) within the Defense Department, charged with the mission to "encrypt" government communications to ensure their privacy and to intercept the communications of other nations. The NSA also provided surveillance of individuals targeted by other agencies as potential threats.

A New Jewish Nation: Israel

At the same time that the United States was helping to form new alliances, it was also helping to form a new nation. Palestine, the biblical Holy Land, had been a British protectorate since 1919. For hundreds of years, Jews throughout the world had dreamed of returning to their ancestral homeland of Israel and its ancient capital Zion, a part of Jerusalem. Many Zionists, Jews who wanted a separate Jewish nation, had migrated there. More arrived during and after the Nazi persecution of European Jews, and they received energetic support from American Jews and worldwide Jewish organizations. Hitler's gruesome effort to kill millions of Jews convinced many that their only hope for a secure future was to create their own nation.

Late in 1947, the United Nations voted to divide ("partition") Palestine into separate Jewish and Arab states. The Jews readily agreed, but the Arabs fiercely opposed the UN partition. Palestine was their ancestral home, too. Jerusalem was as holy to Muslims as it was to Jews and Christians. Arabs viewed the creation of a Jewish nation in Palestine as an act of war, and they attacked Israelis in early 1948. Hundreds of people were killed before the Haganah (Jewish militia) won control of most of Palestine. When the British administration of Palestine officially expired on May 14, 1948, David Ben-Gurion, the Jewish leader in Palestine, soon to be elected prime minister, proclaimed the independence of Israel. President Truman, who had been in close touch with American Jewish leaders, officially recognized the new Israeli state within minutes, as did the Soviet Union.

One million Jews, most of them European immigrants, now had their own nation. Early the next morning, however, the Arab League nations—Lebanon, Syria, Iraq, Jordan, and Egypt—invaded Israel, beginning a period of nearly constant warfare in the Holy Land. UN mediators gradually worked out a truce agreement, restoring an uneasy peace by May 11, 1949, when Israel joined the United Nations. Israel got to keep all its conquered territories, including the whole Palestine coast. The Palestinian Arabs lost everything. Most of them became stateless refugees who scattered into the neighboring nations of Lebanon, Jordan, and Egypt. But stored-up resentments and sporadic warfare between Israel and the Arab states have festered ever since, complicating U.S. foreign policy, which has tried to maintain friendship with both sides but has usually tilted toward Israel.

Israel joins the United Nations

CORE **OBJECTIVE**

3. Describe Truman's efforts to expand the New Deal, and evaluate the effectiveness of his own "Fair Deal" agenda.

Expanding the New Deal

For the most part, Republicans and Democrats in Congress cooperated with President Truman on issues related to the cold war. They were not as unified in dealing with domestic policies. The cost-cutting Republicans in Congress hoped that they could end the New Deal as the war itself ended. As a brand-new president, Truman thought otherwise as he guided the nation's "complicated and difficult" transition from war to peace.

From War to Peace

Conversion to a peacetime economy

With the end of the wars in Europe and Asia, Truman in September 1945 called Congress into a special emergency session at which he presented a twenty-one-point program to guide the nation's "reconversion" effort from wartime back to peacetime. Massive government spending during the war had ended the Great Depression and brought about full employment, but Truman's postwar challenge was to ensure that the peacetime economy absorbed the millions of men and women who had served in the armed forces and were now seeking civilian jobs. During the second half of 1945 and throughout 1946, some 700,000 people in uniform, mostly men, returned to civilian life. By 1947, the total armed forces had shrunk from 12 million to 1.5 million.

Truman's program to ensure a smooth transition to a peacetime economy included proposals for unemployment insurance to cover more workers, a higher minimum wage, the construction of massive low-cost public housing projects, regional development projects modeled on the Tennessee Valley Authority to put military veterans to work, and much more. A powerful Republican congressman named Joseph W. Martin was stunned by the scope of Truman's proposals. "Not even President Roosevelt," he gasped, "ever asked for so much at one sitting."

Truman's primary goal was to "prevent prolonged unemployment" while avoiding the "bitter mistakes" made after the First World War that had produced a wild inflation in prices and a recession. To do so, he also wanted to retain, for a while, the wartime controls on wages, prices, and rents as well as the rationing of scarce food items. Most of all, Truman wanted to minimize unemployment as workers in defense plants were laid off and millions of military veterans went looking for civilian jobs.

Congress responded by approving the Employment Act of 1946, which authorized Truman and the federal government "to promote maximum employment, production, and purchasing power." But Republicans and conservative southern Democrats in Congress balked at most of Truman's efforts to revive or expand New Deal programs. One called Truman's proposals "creeping socialism." The Great Depression was over, critics stressed. Different times demanded different programs—or none at all.

Peacetime: Women return home, the GI Bill, and a "baby boom"

The end of the war caused short-term economic problems but not the postwar depression that many had feared. Many women who had been recruited to work in defense industries were shoved out as men took off uniforms and looked for jobs. At a shipyard in California, the foreman gathered all the women workers and told them to go welcome the troop ships as they pulled into port. "We were thrilled. We all waved," recalled one of the women. Then, the next day, all of the women working at the shipyard were let go to make room for male veterans.

Still, several shock absorbers cushioned the economic impact of demobilization: federal unemployment insurance and other Social Security benefits; the Servicemen's Readjustment Act of 1944, known as the GI Bill of Rights, under which the federal government spent $13 billion on military veterans for education, vocational training, medical treatment, unemployment insurance, and loans for building houses and starting new businesses.

With the war over, military veterans eagerly returned to schools, jobs, wives, and babies. Marriage rates soared at war's end. So, too, did population growth, which had dropped off sharply in the 1930s. Americans born during this postwar period (roughly 1946–1964) composed what came to be known as the "baby-boom generation," a disproportionately large group that would shape the nation's social and cultural life throughout the second half of the twentieth century and after.

Wages, Prices, and Labor Unrest

The most acute economic problem Truman faced was the postwar spike in prices for consumer goods. During the war, the government had frozen all wages and prices—and banned strikes by labor unions. When wartime economic controls on the economy were removed, prices for high-demand consumer items shot up, which led labor unions to demand pay increases for workers. When such raises were not given, a series of postwar strikes erupted across the nation in 1945–1946.

> Inflation spikes after the war

Major labor disputes developed in the coal and railroad industries. Like Theodore Roosevelt before him, Truman grew frustrated with the stubbornness of both management and labor leaders. He took federal control of the coal mines, whereupon the mine owners agreed to union demands. Truman also seized control of the railroads and won a five-day postponement of a strike. But when the union leaders refused to make further concessions, the president lashed out against their "obstinate arrogance" and threatened to draft striking railroad workers into the armed forces. A few weeks later, the unions backed down and returned to work, having won healthy improvements in wages and benefits. But by taking such a hard line, Truman had damaged his relationship with a key constituency within the Democratic party coalition: unionists.

> Widespread union strikes

Political Cooperation and Conflict

As Congressional elections approached in the fall of 1946, Republicans used a simple campaign slogan: "Had Enough? Vote Republican!" Public discontent ran high, especially among the 5 million workers who had gone out on strike during that single year. A union leader tagged Truman "the No. 1 Strikebreaker," while much of the public, upset at the unions, price increases, and food shortages, blamed the strikes on the White House. Labor unions emerged from the war with more power than ever before. Some 14.5 million workers, over a third of the workforce, were unionized. Members had tended to vote Democratic, but not in the 1946 elections, which gave Republicans majorities in both houses of Congress for the first time since 1928. "The New Deal is kaput," one newspaper editor crowed—prematurely, as it turned out.

The new Republican Congress reflected the discontent of middle-class Americans and business executives with striking unions. It curbed the power of unions by passing the **Taft-Hartley Labor Act** of 1947 (officially called the Labor-Management Relations Act), which prohibited "unfair labor practices" such as the "closed shop" (in which nonunion workers could not be hired by a unionized company). The Taft-Hartley Act also required union leaders to take "loyalty oaths" declaring that they were not members of the Communist party. The Taft-Hartley act also banned strikes by federal employees and imposed a "cooling-off" period of eighty days on any strike that the president deemed dangerous to the public welfare. Yet the most troubling element of the new bill was a provision that allowed state legislatures to pass "right-to-work" laws which ended the practice of forcing all wage workers at a company to join a union once a majority voted to unionize.

In a show of support for organized labor, whose members tended to vote Democratic, Truman vetoed the Taft-Hartley bill, which unions called "the slave-labor act." He denounced the "shocking" bill as "unworkable," "burdensome," and "disruptive." Working-class Democrats were delighted. Many blue-collar unionists who had gone over to the Republicans in 1946 returned to the Democrats as a result of Truman's stance. Congress, however, overturned the president's veto of the Taft-Hartley Act, and it became law. By 1954, fifteen states, mainly in the South and West, had used the Taft-Hartley Act to enact "right-to-work" laws forbidding union shops. Those states thereafter recruited industries to relocate because of their low wages and "nonunion" policies.

Civil Rights during the 1940s

Another of Truman's challenges in postwar labor relations was the bigotry faced by returning African American soldiers. When one black soldier arrived home in a uniform decorated with combat medals, he was welcomed by a white neighbor who said: "Don't you forget . . . that you're still a nigger."

But the Second World War had changed America's racial landscape. As a *New York Times* editorial explained in early 1946, "This is a particularly good time to campaign against the evils of bigotry, prejudice, and race

Taft-Hartley Labor Act (1947)

Taft-Hartley Labor Act (1947) Congressional legislation that banned "unfair labor practices" by unions, required union leaders to sign anti-Communist "loyalty oaths," and prohibited federal employees from going on strike.

Truman appoints Committee on Civil Rights and desegregates the military

hatred because we have witnessed the defeat of enemies who tried to found a mastery of the world upon such cruel and fallacious policy." African American veterans had fought in large numbers to overthrow the Nazi regime of government-sponsored racism, and returning veterans were unwilling to put up with continuing racial abuse at home. The cold war confrontation with the Soviet Union also gave political leaders added incentive to improve race relations. In the ideological contest with communism for influence among the newly emerging nations of Africa, the Soviets often compared racism in the South to the Nazis' treatment of the Jews.

Black veterans who spoke out against racial bigotry often risked their lives. In 1946, two African American couples in rural Georgia were gunned down by a white mob. One of the murderers explained that George Dorsey, one of the victims, was "a good nigger" until he went into the army. "But when he came out, he thought he was as good as any white people."

In the fall of 1946, a delegation of civil rights activists urged President Truman to condemn the Ku Klux Klan and the lynching of African Americans. The delegation graphically described incidents of torture and intimidation against blacks in the South.

Such horrific racial incidents so shocked Truman that he appointed a Committee on Civil Rights to investigate violence against African Americans. On July 26, 1948, Truman took a bolder step when he banned racial discrimination in the federal government. Four days later, he issued an executive order ending racial segregation in the armed forces. The air force and navy quickly complied, but the army dragged its feet until the early 1950s. By 1960, however, the armed forces were the most racially integrated of all national organizations. Desegregating the military was, Truman claimed, "the greatest thing that ever happened to America.

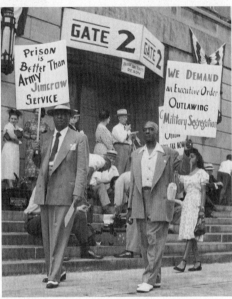

Fight for desegregation Demonstrators led by activist A. Philip Randolph (left) picket the Democratic National Convention on July 12, 1948, calling for racial integration of the armed forces.

Jackie Robinson

Meanwhile, racial segregation was being dismantled in a much more public field of endeavor: professional baseball. In April 1947, as the baseball season opened, the Brooklyn Dodger roster included the first African American to play major league baseball: Jackie Robinson. He was selected in part because of his baseball abilities and in part because of his personality: he was a strong, quiet warrior of incomparable courage who was capable of not fighting back when provoked. And he was often provoked. During his first season with the Dodgers, teammates and opposing players viciously baited Robinson, pitchers threw at him, base runners spiked him, and spectators booed him, even as he led the team to win the National League championship. Hotels refused him rooms, and restaurants denied him service. Hate mail arrived by the bucketful. One sportswriter called the trailblazing

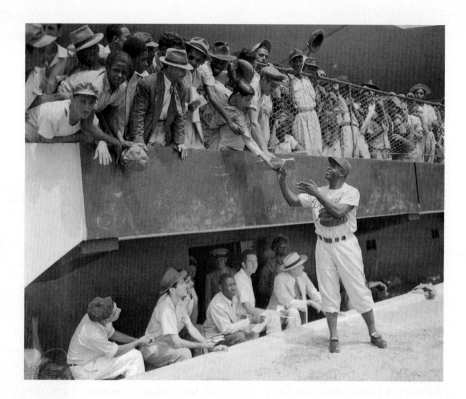

Jackie Robinson Robinson's unfaltering courage and skill diversified the baseball stands, drawing African American and Latino spectators to the games. Here, he greets his Dominican fans at Trujillo High School in Santo Domingo.

Robinson "the loneliest man I have ever seen in sports." On the other hand, black spectators were electrified by Robinson's courageous example; they turned out in droves to watch him play. As time passed, Robinson won over many fans and players with his courage, wit, and talent. Other teams soon began signing black players. Racial attitudes were changing—slowly.

Mexican Americans

In the Far West, Mexican Americans (often grouped together with other Spanish-speaking immigrants as *Hispanics* or *Latinos*) continued to experience ethnic prejudice after the war. Schools in Arizona, New Mexico, Texas, and California routinely segregated Mexican American children from whites. After the war, the 500,000 Latino veterans were especially frustrated that their efforts in the armed forces were not rewarded with equality at home. "We had paid our dues," said one war veteran, yet nothing had changed. Latinos were frequently denied access to the educational, medical, and housing benefits made available to white servicemen. In fact, some mortuaries even denied funeral services to Mexican Americans killed in combat. As a funeral director in Texas explained, "the Anglo people would not stand for it."

To fight such prejudicial treatment, Mexican American war veterans led by Dr. Hector Perez Garcia, a decorated U.S. Army major who had served as a combat surgeon, organized the American GI Forum in Texas in 1948. Soon there were branches throughout Texas and across the nation. Garcia, born in Mexico in 1914 and raised in Texas, stressed the importance of formal education to Mexican Americans. The new organization's motto read: "Education Is Our Freedom and Freedom Should Be Everybody's Business." At a time when Mexican Americans in Texas averaged no more than a third-grade education, Garcia and five of his siblings were exceptional, each having completed medical school and become physicians. Yet upon Major Garcia's return from the war, he encountered "discrimination everywhere. We had no opportunities. We had to pay [poll taxes] to vote. We had segregated schools. We were not allowed to go into public places."

Garcia and the GI Forum initially focused on veterans' issues but soon expanded the organization's scope to include fostering equal opportunities and equal treatment for all people. The GI Forum lobbied to end poll taxes, sued for the right of Latinos to serve on juries, and developed schools for jobless veterans. In 1984, President Ronald Reagan presented Garcia with the Presidential Medal of Freedom, the nation's highest civilian honor.

Shaping the Fair Deal

By early 1948, after three years in the White House, Truman had yet to shake the widespread impression that he was not up to the job. Most political analysts assumed that the president would lose his reelection effort in November. The Democratic party was about to split in two: southern conservatives resented Truman's outspoken support of civil rights, while the left wing of the party resented his firing of Secretary of Commerce Henry A. Wallace in September 1946 for openly criticizing the administration's anti-Soviet policies in a speech at Madison Square Garden in New York City. "Getting tough [with the Soviet Union]," Wallace argued, "never brought anything real and lasting—whether for schoolyard bullies or world powers. The tougher we get, the tougher the Russians will get." Wallace added that the United States had "no more business in the *political affairs* of Eastern Europe than Russia has in the *political affairs* of Latin America." The secretary of state and other leaders of the State Department were so outraged by Wallace's comments that Truman felt he had no choice but to get rid of him.

The gloomy predictions of a Truman defeat in 1948 did not faze the combative president, however. He mounted an intense reelection campaign. His first step was to shore up the major elements of the New Deal coalition of working-class voters: farmers, labor unionists, and African Americans. In his 1948 State of the Union message, Truman announced that the programs that he would later call his "**Fair Deal**" (to distinguish his new domestic program from Roosevelt's New Deal) would build upon the New Deal by offering something to nearly every group the Democrats hoped to attract as voters. The first goal, Truman said, was to ensure civil rights for all Americans. He added proposals to increase federal aid to education, expand

Truman's "Fair Deal"

Fair Deal (1949) President Truman's proposals to build upon the New Deal with national health insurance, the repeal of the Taft-Hartley Act, new civil rights legislation, and other initiatives; most were rejected by the Republican-controlled Congress.

unemployment and retirement benefits, create a comprehensive system of national health insurance, enable more rural people to connect to electricity, and increase the minimum wage.

The Election of 1948

Upset victory: Truman reelected (1948)

The Republican-controlled Congress dismissed Truman's proposals, an action it would later regret. At the Republican Convention, New York governor Thomas E. Dewey won the presidential nomination on the third ballot. The platform endorsed most of the New Deal reforms and approved the administration's bipartisan foreign policy; Dewey promised to run things more efficiently, however. In July, a glum Democratic Convention gathered in Philadelphia. But delegates who expected to do little more than go through the motions were doubly surprised: first by the battle on the convention floor over civil rights and then by President Truman's acceptance speech. Liberal Democrats called on Congress to take more aggressive steps to end segregation in the South and commended Truman "for his courageous stand on the issue of civil rights." White segregationist delegates from Alabama and Mississippi walked out of the convention in protest.

Birth of the Dixiecrats Alabama delegates stand to boo Truman's announcement of his civil rights platform before walking out of the 1948 Democratic National Convention.

On July 17, a group of rebellious southern Democrats met in Birmingham, Alabama. While waving Confederate flags and singing "Dixie," they nominated South Carolina's segregationist governor, Strom Thurmond, on a States' Rights Democratic ticket, quickly dubbed the "Dixiecrat party." The **Dixiecrats** denounced Truman's "infamous" civil rights initiatives and championed states' rights against any federal efforts to change the tradition of white supremacy in the South.

A few days later, on July 23, the left wing of the Democratic party gathered in Philadelphia to form a new Progressive party and nominate for president Henry A. Wallace, Roosevelt's former secretary of agriculture and vice president—whom Truman had fired as secretary of commerce. One Democratic leader asked Truman to withdraw from the race to help the party's chances. He replied: "I was not brought up to run from a fight."

The splits in the Democratic ranks seemed to spell the final blow to Truman, but the feisty president pledged to "win this election and make the Republicans like it!" He then set out on a 31,000-mile "whistle-stop" train tour, making ten speeches a day scolding the "do-nothing" Eightieth Congress. Friendly audiences loved his fighting spirit and dogged courage, shouting, "Pour it on, Harry!" and "Give 'em hell, Harry." Truman responded: "I don't give 'em hell. I just tell the truth and they think it's hell."

Dixiecrats Breakaway faction of white southern Democrats who defected from the national Democratic party in 1948 to protest the party's increased support for black civil rights and to nominate their own segregationist candidates for elective office.

The polls predicted a sure win for Dewey and the Republicans, but on election day Truman won the biggest upset in history, taking 24.2 million votes (49.5 percent) to Dewey's 22 million (45.1 percent) and winning a thumping margin of 303 to 189 in the Electoral College. Thurmond and Wallace each received more than 1 million votes, but the revolt of right and left had worked to Truman's advantage. The Dixiecrat rebellion backfired by angering black voters, who turned out in droves to support Truman, while the Progressive party's radicalism made it hard for Republicans to tag Truman as soft on communism. Thurmond carried four southern states (South Carolina, Mississippi, Alabama, and Louisiana).

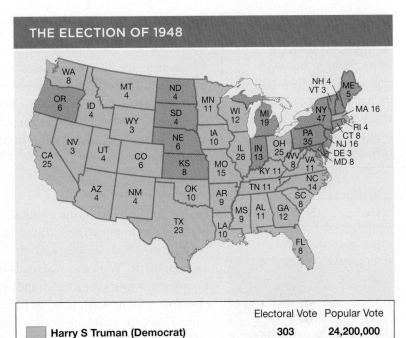

THE ELECTION OF 1948

	Electoral Vote	Popular Vote
Harry S Truman (Democrat)	303	24,200,000
Thomas E. Dewey (Republican)	189	22,000,000
J. Strom Thurmond (States' Rights Democrat)	39	1,200,000

■ Why did the political pundits predict a Dewey victory?
■ Why was civil rights a divisive issue at the Democratic Convention?
■ How did the candidacies of Thurmond and Wallace help Truman?

The Fair Deal Rejected

Truman viewed his surprising victory as a mandate for expanding the social welfare programs established by Franklin Roosevelt. His State of the Union message in early 1949 repeated the agenda he had set forth the year before. "Every segment of our population and every individual," he declared, "has a right to expect from our government a *fair deal*." Truman's Fair Deal proposals promised "greater economic opportunity for the mass of the people."

Most of Truman's Fair Deal proposals that gained Congressional approval were extensions or enlargements of earlier New Deal programs: a higher minimum hourly wage, expansion of Social Security coverage to 10 million workers not included in the original 1935 bill, and a sizable slum-clearance and public-housing program for 800,000 poor Americans. Despite enjoying Democratic majorities in Congress, however, Truman ran up against the same alliance of conservative southern Democrats and Republicans who had allied against Roosevelt in the late 1930s. The bipartisan conservative coalition nixed most of Truman's new Fair Deal programs. Congress rejected several civil rights bills, national health insurance, federal aid to education, and a new approach to subsidizing farmers. Congress also turned down Truman's requested repeal of the anti-union Taft-Hartley Act. Yet the Fair Deal was not a complete failure. It laid the foundation for programs that the next generation of reformers would promote in the sixties and after.

> Congress rejects Fair Deal legislation

CORE **OBJECTIVE**

4. Assess the major international developments during 1949–1950, including the outbreak of the Korean War, and explain how they altered U.S. foreign policy.

The Cold War Heats Up

As was true during Truman's first term, global concerns during his second term would again distract the president's attention from domestic issues. In his 1949 inaugural address, President Truman called for a vigilant anti-Communist foreign policy resting on three pillars: the United Nations, the Marshall Plan, and NATO. None of those pillars could help resolve the civil war in China, however.

"Losing" China

Communist victory in China

One of the thorniest postwar problems, the Chinese civil war, was fast coming to a head in 1949. The Chinese Nationalists, led by Chiang Kai-shek, had been fighting Mao Zedong and the Communists since the 1920s. After the Second World War, the Nationalists were put on the defensive as the Communists won over most of the peasants. By the end of 1949, the Nationalist government was forced to flee to the island of Formosa, which it renamed Taiwan. Truman's critics—mostly Republicans—now asked bitterly, "Who lost China to communism?" What they did not explain in attacking Truman was how he could have prevented a Communist victory without a massive U.S. military intervention, which would have been risky, unpopular, and expensive. After 1949, the United States continued to recognize the Nationalist government on Taiwan as the official government of China, delaying formal relations with "Red China" (the People's Republic of China) for thirty years.

Mao Zedong Chairman of the Chinese Communist Party and founder of the People's Republic of China.

The Soviets Develop Atomic Bombs

H-bomb

As the Communists were gaining control of China, the Soviets were heightening American concerns by developing atomic bombs of their own. News that the Soviets had detonated a nuclear weapon in 1949 frightened people around the world and led Truman to speed up the construction of a hydrogen "superbomb," a weapon far more powerful than the atomic bombs dropped on Japan. That the Soviets now possessed atomic weapons greatly heightened every cold war confrontation between East and West. "There is only one thing worse than one nation having an atomic bomb," said Nobel Prize–winning physicist Harold C. Urey. "That's two nations having it." Now, the fear of nuclear annihilation joined the fear of communism in deepening the Red Scare.

NSC-68

NSC-68 (1950) Top-secret policy paper approved by President Truman that outlined a militaristic approach to combating the spread of global communism.

In January 1950 President Truman, concerned about the Soviets possessing atomic weapons, asked the National Security Council to assess America's changing role in the cold war world. Four months later, the Council submitted to the president a top-secret report called **NSC-68**. The document, officially approved by Truman in September, laid out in alarmist tones the major assumptions of U.S. foreign policy for the next twenty years: "The

Shelter for sale On display in a 1950s showroom is a basement bomb fallout shelter, complete with a television, library, and exercise bike.

issues that face us are momentous, involving the fulfillment or destruction not only of this Republic but of civilization itself." NSC-68 endorsed George Kennan's "containment" strategy, but where he had focused on political and economic counterpressure against the Soviets, its tone was global and militaristic, calling for "a policy of calculated and gradual coercion" against Soviet expansionism—everywhere.

Hawkish Paul Nitze, Kennan's successor as director of policy planning for the State Department, was the NSC-68's primary author. He claimed that the Soviets, driven by their "fanatical faith" in their destiny to impose their will "on the rest of the world," were becoming increasingly "reckless" in their international behavior and would invade Western Europe by 1954, by which time they would have enough nuclear weapons to destroy the United States.

By signing NSC-68, Truman endorsed its assumptions about a perpetual struggle with Soviet communism in which there could be only victory or defeat. "It meant," he said, "doubling or tripling the budget, increasing taxes heavily, and imposing various kinds of economic controls. It meant a great change in our normal peacetime way of doing things." NSC-68 became the guidebook for future American policy, especially as the United States became involved in an unexpected war in Korea that ignited into open combat the smoldering animosity between East and West, communism and capitalism.

War in Korea

By mid-1950, tensions between the United States and the Soviet Union in Europe had temporarily eased into a stalemate as a result of the "balance of terror" created by both sides having atomic weapons. In Asia, however, the situation remained turbulent. The Communists had gained control of mainland China and were threatening to destroy the Chinese Nationalists, who had taken refuge on the island of Taiwan. Japan, meanwhile, was

Fight and flight American soldiers brush shoulders with Korean refugees as they march into the Nakdong River region in the south.

experiencing a dramatic recovery from the devastation of defeat and the destruction caused by U.S. bombing raids during the Second World War. Douglas MacArthur showed deft leadership as the consul in charge of U.S.-occupied Japan. He oversaw the disarming of the Japanese military, the drafting of a democratic constitution, and the nation's economic recovery, all of which were turning Japan into America's friend.

To the east of Japan, however, tensions between North Korea and South Korea threatened to erupt into civil war. The Japanese had occupied the Korean peninsula since 1910, and after their defeat and withdrawal in 1945 the victorious Allies had faced the difficult task of creating a new independent Korean nation. Complicating that effort was the presence of Soviet troops in northern Korea. They had accepted the surrender of Japanese forces above the 38th parallel, which divides the Korean peninsula, while U.S. forces had overseen the Japanese surrender south of that line. The Soviets quickly organized a Communist government, the Democratic People's Republic of Korea (North Korea) in the industrial north, just as they were doing in eastern Europe. The Americans countered by helping to establish a democratic government in the agricultural and more populous south, the Republic of Korea (South Korea). By the end of 1948, separate regimes had appeared in the two sectors, Soviet and American forces had withdrawn, and some 2 million North Koreans had fled to South Korea.

On June 25, 1950, with the encouragement of the Soviet Union and Communist China, the Soviet-equipped North Korean People's Army invaded the Republic of South Korea and drove the South Korean army down the peninsula in a headlong retreat. Within three days of fighting, Seoul, the South Korean capital, was captured and only 22,000 of the 100,000 South Korean soldiers were still capable of combat. When asked how he would respond to the invasion, President Truman declared: "By God, I'm going to let them have it!" He assumed, correctly, that the North Korean attack had been encouraged by the Soviets. "There's no telling what they'll do if we don't put up a fight right now," Truman predicted. He then made a critical decision: without consulting the Joint Chiefs of Staff or Congress, he decided to wage war through the backing of the United Nations rather than seeking a declaration of war from Congress.

An emergency meeting of the UN Security Council in New York City in late June 1950 quickly censured the North Korean "breach of peace." By sheer coincidence, the Soviet delegate, who held a veto power, was at the time boycotting the council because it would not seat Communist China in place of Nationalist China. On June 27, the Security Council took advantage of his absence to call on UN members to "furnish such assistance to the Republic of Korea as may be necessary to repel the armed attack and to restore international peace and security in the area." Truman ordered U.S. air, naval, and ground forces into action. He then appointed 70-year-old Douglas MacArthur as the supreme commander of the UN forces.

The Korean conflict was the first military action authorized by the United Nations, only five years old, and some twenty other nations participated. The United States provided the largest contingent of non-Korean forces by far, some 330,000 troops. The American military defense of South Korea set a worrisome precedent: war by order of a president rather than by a vote of Congress, which the U.S. Constitution requires. Truman dodged the constitutional issue by officially calling the conflict in Korea a "police action" rather than a war. Critics labeled it "Mr. Truman's War."

> U.S. "police action" in Korea

Turning the Tables

For the first three months, the fighting in Korea went badly for the Republic of Korea (ROK) and the UN forces. By September 1950, the decimated South Korean troops were barely hanging on to the southeast corner of the Korean peninsula. Then, in a brilliant maneuver on September 15, General MacArthur staged a surprise amphibious landing behind the North Korean lines at Inchon, the port city for Seoul. UN troops drove a wedge through the North Korean army; only a quarter of the North Koreans, some 25,000 soldiers, managed to flee across the border. Days later, South Korean troops recaptured Seoul.

At that point, MacArthur became overconfident and persuaded Truman to allow the U.S. troops to push north into North Korea and seek to reunify Korea. Containment of communism was no longer enough; MacArthur now hatched a grandiose plan to rid North Korea of the "red menace," even if this meant expanding the war into China in order to prevent the Chinese from resupplying their North Korean allies.

The Chinese Intervene

By October 1950, UN forces were about to capture the North Korean capital, Pyongyang. President Truman, concerned that MacArthur's move into North Korea would provoke Communist China to enter the war, flew seven

> Chinese intervention in Korea

thousand miles to Wake Island for a conference with MacArthur on October 15 (the haughty general had refused to travel to the United States). At his meeting with Truman, MacArthur dismissed Chinese threats to intervene, even though they had massed troops on the Korean border. That same day, the Communist government in Beijing announced that China "cannot stand idly by" as their North Korean allies were humiliated. On October 20, UN forces entered the North Korean capital, and on October 26, advance units had reached Ch'osan, on the Yalu River, North Korea's border with China.

MacArthur predicted total victory by Christmas. On the night of November 25, however, some 300,000 Chinese "volunteers" vowing to "liberate Korea" and drive "warmonger MacArthur into the sea" counterattacked, sending the U.S. forces in desperate retreat just at the onset of winter. By January 15, the Communist Chinese and North Koreans had recaptured Seoul, the South Korean capital. "We ran like antelopes," said one American soldier. "We lost everything we had."

MacArthur Pushes the Limit

The Chinese intervention caught MacArthur wholly unprepared. It had become "an entirely new war," he said. The U.S. commander of UN forces asked for thirty-four atomic bombs and proposed air raids on China. MacArthur's plans to use nuclear weapons and attack China horrified the military leadership in Washington, D.C. It would be, explained General Omar Bradley, chairman of the Joint Chiefs of Staff, "the wrong war at the wrong place at the wrong time with the wrong enemy." Truman agreed, saying that MacArthur's plan would lead the United States into the "gigantic booby trap" of war with China.

In late 1950, the UN forces rallied. By January 1951, they finally secured their lines below Seoul and then launched a counterattack. When Truman began negotiations with the North Koreans to restore the prewar boundary, General MacArthur undermined the president by issuing an ultimatum for China to make peace or suffer an attack on their own country. On April 5, on the floor of Congress, the Republican minority leader read a letter from General MacArthur that criticized the president and said that "there is no substitute for victory." Such a reckless act of open insubordination left Truman only two choices: he could either accept MacArthur's aggressive demands or fire him.

Sacking a Hero

MacArthur controversy

On April 11, 1951, with civilian control of the military at stake, Truman removed the brilliant but bullheaded MacArthur (Truman called him "Mr. Prima Donna") and replaced him with jut-jawed General Matthew B. Ridgway. "I believe that we must try to limit the war to Korea," Truman explained. "A number of events have made it evident that General MacArthur did not agree with that policy. I have therefore considered it essential to

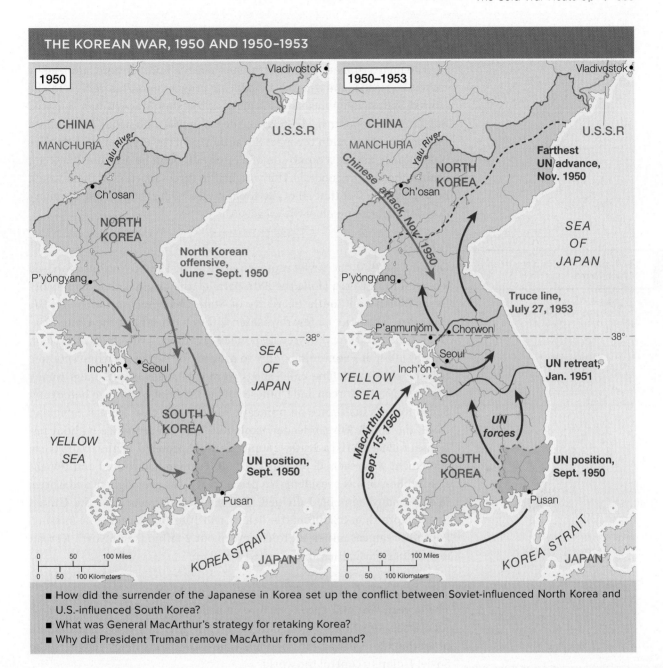

THE KOREAN WAR, 1950 AND 1950–1953

1950

Vladivostok

CHINA
MANCHURIA
Yalu River
Ch'osan
NORTH KOREA
P'yŏngyang

U.S.S.R

North Korean offensive, June – Sept. 1950

Inch'ŏn • Seoul
SEA OF JAPAN

SOUTH KOREA

YELLOW SEA

UN position, Sept. 1950

Pusan

0   50   100 Miles
0   50   100 Kilometers

KOREA STRAIT   JAPAN

1950–1953

Vladivostok

CHINA
MANCHURIA
Yalu River
Chinese attack, Nov. 1950
Ch'osan
NORTH KOREA

Farthest UN advance, Nov. 1950

SEA OF JAPAN

P'yŏngyang

P'anmunjŏm • Chorwon

Truce line, July 27, 1953

Seoul
Inch'ŏn
YELLOW SEA

MacArthur Sept. 15, 1950

UN retreat, Jan. 1951

UN forces

SOUTH KOREA

UN position, Sept. 1950

Pusan

0   50   100 Miles
0   50   100 Kilometers

KOREA STRAIT   JAPAN

- How did the surrender of the Japanese in Korea set up the conflict between Soviet-influenced North Korea and U.S.-influenced South Korea?
- What was General MacArthur's strategy for retaking Korea?
- Why did President Truman remove MacArthur from command?

relieve General MacArthur so that there would be no doubt or confusion as to the real purpose and aim of our policy."

Truman's sacking of MacArthur, the Army's only five-star general, divided a shocked nation into two emotional camps. *Time* magazine reported that "seldom had a more unpopular man fired a more popular one." Senator Joseph McCarthy called the president a "son of a bitch" for sacking MacArthur. In his diary, Truman noted the ferocious backlash against him: "Quite an explosion. . . . Letters of abuse by the dozens." Sixty-six percent of Americans initially opposed Truman's relieving MacArthur of command.

The man Truman fired was a larger-than-life military hero, idolized by most Americans, and greeted by adoring crowds upon his return to the United States. Republicans in Congress protested MacArthur's removal, but Truman stood firm, claiming the decision was an obvious one: "I fired him because he wouldn't respect the authority of the President. I didn't fire him because he was a dumb son of a bitch, although he was, but that's not against the law for generals. If it was, half to three-quarters of them would be in jail." The fact that all of the top military leaders supported Truman's decision deflated much of the criticism.

A Cease-Fire

> 38th parallel divided North and South Korea

On June 24, 1951, the Soviet representative at the United Nations proposed a cease-fire in Korea along the 38th parallel, the original dividing line between North and South. Secretary of State Dean Acheson accepted the cease-fire (armistice) a few days later with the consent of the United Nations. China and North Korea responded favorably. Truce talks started on July 10, 1951, at Panmunjom, only to drag on for two years while sporadic fighting continued. The chief snags were exchanges of prisoners (many captured North Korean and Chinese soldiers did not want to go home) and South Korea's insistence on unification of the two rival Koreas. Syngman Rhee, the South Korean leader, explained that "an armistice without national unification [is] a death sentence without protest." By the time a truce agreement was reached, on July 27, 1953, Truman had retired and Dwight D. Eisenhower was president. No peace treaty was ever signed, and Korea, like Germany, remained divided. The inconclusive war cost the United States more than 33,000 battle deaths and 103,000 wounded or missing. South Korean casualties, all told, were about 2 million, and North Korean and Chinese casualties an estimated 3 million.

The Impact of the Korean War

The Korean War influenced U.S. foreign policy in significant ways. To most Americans, the North Korean attack on South Korea provided concrete proof that there was an international Communist conspiracy guided by the Soviet Union to control the world.

> U.S. military buildup worldwide

Truman's assumption that Stalin and the Soviets were behind the invasion of South Korea prompted three far-reaching decisions. First, Truman mistakenly viewed the Korean conflict as actually a diversion for a Soviet invasion of Western Europe, so he ordered a major expansion of U.S. military forces in Europe—and around the world. Second, the president increased assistance to French troops fighting a Communist independence movement in the French colony of Indochina (which included Vietnam), starting America's deepening military involvement in Southeast Asia. Third, the Korean War demonstrated how important a role Japan would play in America's military presence in Asia.

Another Red Scare

The Korean War excited another Red Scare at home, as in 1919, as people grew fearful that Soviet-directed Communists were infiltrating American society. Since 1938 the **House Committee on Un-American Activities (HUAC)** had kept up a drumbeat of accusations about supposed Communist agents in the federal government. On March 21, 1947, just nine days after he announced the Truman Doctrine, the president signed an executive order (also known as the Loyalty Order) requiring federal government workers to go through a background investigation to ensure they were not Communists or even associated with Communists (as well as other "subversive" groups).

The president knew that the "loyalty program" violated the civil liberties of government workers, but he felt he had no choice. He was responding to pressure from FBI director J. Edgar Hoover and Attorney General Tom Clark, both of whom were convinced that there were numerous spies working inside the federal government. Truman was also eager to blunt criticism by Republicans that he was not doing enough to ensure that Soviet sympathizers were working in government.

The president himself thought that all of the fear about Communist subversives was misplaced. "People are very much wrought up about the communist 'bugaboo,'" he wrote to Pennsylvania governor George Earle, "but I am of the opinion that the country is perfectly safe so far as Communism is concerned." By early 1951, the federal Civil Service Commission had cleared over 3 million people, while only 378 had been dismissed for doubtful loyalty. Others, however, had resigned for fear they would be dismissed. In 1953, President Dwight D. Eisenhower revoked the Loyalty Order.

The Hollywood Ten

In May 1947, charges that Hollywood was a "hotbed of communism" led the House Committee on Un-American Activities to launch a full-blown investigation of the motion-picture industry. The HUAC subpoenaed dozens of prominent actors, producers, and directors to testify at its hearings, held in Los Angeles in October. Ten witnesses refused to answer questions about their political activities, arguing that such questions violated their First Amendment rights. When asked if he were a member of the Communist party, screenwriter Ring Lardner Jr. replied: "I could answer, but I would hate myself in the morning." Another member of the so-called Hollywood Ten, screenwriter Dalton Trumbo, shouted as he left the hearings, "This is the beginning of an American concentration camp." All ten were cited for contempt, given prison terms, and blacklisted (banned) from the film industry.

The witch hunt launched by the HUAC inspired playwright Arthur Miller, who himself was blacklisted, to write *The Crucible* (1953), a dramatic

> **CORE OBJECTIVE**
>
> **5.** Examine the emergence of the Red Scare after the Second World War and explain its impact on American politics and society.

House Committee on Un-American Activities (HUAC) Committee of the U.S. House of Representatives formed in 1938; originally tasked with investigating Nazi subversion during the Second World War and later focused on rooting out Communists in the government and the motion-picture industry.

The verge of verdict A few courageous movie stars attended the HUAC hearings to support their friends and colleagues who were accused of being Communists. *Left to right*: Danny Kaye, June Havoc, Humphrey Bogart, and Lauren Bacall (seated).

account of the notorious witch trials in Salem, Massachusetts, at the end of the seventeenth century, intended to alert readers about the dangers of the anti-Communist hysteria.

Alger Hiss

The spy case most damaging to the Truman administration involved Alger Hiss, president of the Carnegie Endowment for International Peace, who had earlier served in several government agencies, including the State Department. Whittaker Chambers, a former Soviet spy and later an editor of *Time* magazine, told the HUAC in 1948 that Hiss had given him secret documents ten years earlier, when Chambers was spying for the Soviets and Hiss was working in the State Department. Hiss sued for libel, and Chambers produced microfilms of the State Department documents that he said Hiss had passed to him. Hiss denied the accusation, whereupon he was indicted and, after one mistrial, convicted in 1950. The charge was perjury, but he was convicted of lying about espionage, for which he could not be tried because the statute of limitations on that crime had expired.

More cases of Communist infiltration surfaced. In 1949, eleven top leaders of the Communist party of the United States were convicted under the Smith Act of 1940, which outlawed any conspiracy to advocate the overthrow of the government. The Supreme Court upheld the law under the doctrine of a "clear and present danger," which overrode the right to free speech.

Atomic Spying

Julius and Ethel Rosenberg

In 1950, the F.B.I. unearthed the existence of a British-American spy network that had secretly passed information about the development of the atomic bomb to the Soviet Union. These disclosures led to the widely publicized arrest of Klaus Fuchs, a German-born English nuclear physicist who had worked in the United States during the war, helping to develop the atomic bomb.

As it turned out, a New York couple, former Communists Julius and Ethel Rosenberg, were part of the same Soviet spy ring. Their claims of innocence were undercut by the confession of Ethel's brother, who admitted he was a spy along with his sister and brother-in-law.

The convictions of Fuchs and the Rosenbergs fueled Republican charges that Truman's administration was not doing enough to hunt down Communist agents who were stealing American military secrets. The Rosenberg case, called the crime of the century by J. Edgar Hoover, also served to heighten American fears that a vast Soviet network of spies and sympathizers was operating in the United States—and now had "given" Stalin the secret of building atomic weapons. Irving Kaufman, the federal judge who sentenced the Rosenbergs to death in the electric chair, explained that "plain, deliberate murder is dwarfed . . . by comparison with the crime you have committed." They were the first Americans ever executed for spying.

McCarthy's Witch Hunt

Evidence of Soviet spying in the United States encouraged politicians to exploit the public's fears of the Communist menace at home. Early in 1950, a little-known Republican senator, Joseph R. McCarthy of Wisconsin, suddenly surfaced as the most ruthless manipulator of the nation's anti-Communist anxieties.

An intelligent, determined, but unethical man eager to attract media attention, McCarthy took up the cause of anti-Communism with a fiery speech to a women's Republican club in Wheeling, West Virginia, on February 9, 1950, in which he charged that the State Department was infested with Communists—and he claimed to have their names, although he never provided them.

"Joe" McCarthy's reckless charges created a media sensation and, over the next four years, led the senator to make more reckless accusations, initially against Democrats, whom he attacked as "dupes" or "fellow travelers" of the "Commies," then against just about everyone, including the U.S. Army.

Truman privately denounced McCarthy as "just a ballyhoo artist who has to cover up his shortcomings with wild charges," but McCarthy was not so easily dismissed. He enjoyed the backing of fellow Republicans eager to hurt Democrats in the 1950 Congressional elections by claiming they were "soft on Communism." Senator Lyndon B. Johnson of Texas said McCarthy was "the sorriest senator" in Washington. "But he's riding high now, he's got people scared to death. . . ."

By the summer of 1951, what had come to be called **McCarthyism** had gotten out of control. McCarthy's excesses were revealed for all to see when he outrageously accused George Marshall, the former secretary of state and war hero, of making "common cause with Stalin." Concerns about the truth or fair play did not faze him. He refused to answer critics or provide evidence; his focus was on creating a reign of terror by groundless accusations.

Despite his outlandish claims and boorish bullying, McCarthy's witch hunt for Communists never uncovered a single Communist agent in the government. But his smear campaign, which tarnished many lives and

Joseph R. McCarthy The senator with a mission to sweep the Communists from the government and beyond, 1954.

McCarthyism Anti-Communist hysteria led by Senator Joseph McCarthy's "witch hunts" attacking the loyalty of politicians, federal employees, and public figures, despite a lack of evidence.

The Cold War and the Rise of the National Security State

The federal government had assumed a commitment to improving the lives of millions of Americans through the New Deal during the Great Depression, and continued to do so after World War II. The demands of the war effort further expanded the role of the federal government in the nation's life. Immediately after World War II, President Truman worked to demilitarize the nation but soon reversed course as he became alarmed at the Soviet threat around the world, developing an aggressive policy to "contain" the Soviets in both Europe and Asia. The emergence of the cold war—an intense, bitter, and all-consuming rivalry between the Soviet Union and the United States—fundamentally altered the federal government and laid the foundation for a National Security State. After you review the historical developments, consider the questions further below.

FEBRUARY 1946

Kennan's "Long Telegram"

After witnessing Soviet-U.S. tensions in Germany, Korea, and East Europe, state official George Kennan declares in his famous telegram that Marxist-Leninist philosophy presumed a fundamental conflict between the communist and capitalist worlds. Kennan urged persistent and firm containment of Soviet expansion.

MARCH 1947

Truman Doctrine

Truman announces the U.S. commitment to "support free peoples who are resisting subjugation . . . by outside pressures." Congress approved U.S. economic and military assistance to non-communist forces in the Greek civil war and the Turkish government.

MARCH 1947

Loyalty Order

Truman orders all federal government employees to undergo background checks in response to growing fears that communists had infiltrated the U.S. government.

MAY 1947

Marshall Plan

Secretary of State George Marshall announces the program that would ultimately provide $13 billion in financial assistance to European nations struggling to restore their economies and to fend off communism.

JULY 1947

National Security Act

Congress authorizes the creation of a Department of Defense, a National Security Council, and a Central Intelligence Agency.

OCTOBER 1948–MAY 1949

Berlin airlift

The United States organizes an airlift of supplies to the Western-controlled sections of Berlin in response to the Soviet blockade.

APRIL 1949	1949–1950	JANUARY–APRIL 1950
North Atlantic Treaty Organization (NATO)	**Hydrogen bomb (H-bomb)**	**NSC-68 Report**
The United States and 12 other North American and Western European nations form a defensive political and military alliance.	The Soviet Union detonates a nuclear weapon. In response, Truman speeds up the development of an H-bomb, far more powerful than the atomic bomb.	The National Security Council report calls for "a policy of calculated and gradual coercion against Soviet expansionism—everywhere." This promotion of struggle against communism, according to Truman, would require "doubling or tripling the budget" and "a great change in our normal peacetime way of doing things."

EARLY 1950s	JUNE 1950	SEPTEMBER 1950	1950–1952
McCarthy's Second Red Scare	**"Police Action" in Korea**	**McCarran International Security Act**	**United States expands involvement to global scale**
Senator Joseph McCarthy takes up the anti-communist cause with a series of charges accusing many U.S. government officials of being Soviet spies or covering up for alleged spies within the U.S. government.	The United States receives the United Nations Security Council's blessing to lead a "police action" to combat North Korean aggression.	The act made it unlawful "to conspire . . . to perform any act which would substantially contribute to . . . the establishment of a totalitarian dictatorship."	In response to the Korean War, Truman orders the expansion of U.S. military presence in Western Europe and increases U.S. assistance of French troops fighting a communist insurgency in Vietnam, a French colony in Southeast Asia.

QUESTIONS FOR ANALYSIS

1. What new policies and institutions did Truman and Congress initiate to contain Soviet expansion?

2. Why did Truman build a stronger military presence in Europe and Asia?

3. How did cold war tensions affect U.S. military spending?

4. In what ways did the cold war affect civil liberties in the United States?

5. How did the emergence of the cold war shape the size and role of the federal government?

reputations, went largely unchallenged until the end of the Korean War. During the Red Scare, thousands of left-wing Americans were "blacklisted" from employment because of past political associations, real or rumored. Movies with titles like "I Married a Communist" fed the hysteria, and stories in popular magazines warned of "a Red under every bed."

McCarran Internal Security Act

Fears of Soviet spies in the United States working with American sympathizers led Congress in 1950 to pass the McCarran Internal Security Act over President Truman's veto, making it unlawful "to combine, conspire, or agree with any other person to perform any act which would substantially contribute to . . . the establishment of a totalitarian dictatorship." Communist organizations had to register with the attorney general. Would-be immigrants who had belonged to totalitarian parties in their home countries were barred from admission to the United States. And during any future national emergencies, American Communists were to be herded into concentration camps. The McCarran Internal Security Act, Truman said in his veto message, would "put the government into the business of thought control."

Assessing the Red Scare and the Cold War

Violations of civil liberties and overstretched foreign policy

Playing upon the fears of the American public did not make for good policy in 1919, nor did it work well in the early fifties. Both Red Scares ended up violating the civil liberties of innocent people. If international events had set the stage for the cold war and the Red Scare, the actions of political leaders and thinkers set events in motion. Hindsight is always clearer than foresight, and President Truman may have erred in 1947 by creating a government loyalty program that aggravated the anti-Communist hysteria. Truman's own attorney general, Tom Clark, contended that there were "so many Communists in America" that they "were everywhere—in factories, offices, butcher shops, on street corners, in private businesses—and each carries with him the germs of death for society." Truman also overstretched American resources when he pledged to "contain" communism everywhere. Containment itself proved hard to contain amid the ideological posturing of Soviet and American leaders. Its chief theorist, George F. Kennan, later confessed that he was partly to blame because he had failed at the outset to spell out the limits of the containment policy and to stress that the United States needed to prioritize its responses to Soviet adventurism.

The years after the Second World War were unlike any other postwar period in American history. Having taken on global burdens, the nation became committed to a permanently large national military establishment, along with the attendant creation of shadowy new government agencies such as the National Security Council (NSC), the National Security Agency (NSA), and the Central Intelligence Agency (CIA). The federal government—and the presidency—continued to grow larger, more powerful, and more secretive during the cold war, fueled by the actions of both major political parties as well as by the intense lobbying efforts of what Dwight D. Eisenhower would later call the *military-industrial complex.*

Creation of the "military-industrial complex"

Fears of communism at home grew out of legitimate concerns about a Soviet spy network in the United States but mushroomed into politically motivated paranoia. As had been true during the First Red Scare, after the First World War, long-standing prejudices against Jews fed the anti-Communist hysteria; indeed, many Communist sympathizers were Jews from eastern Europe. The Red Scare also provided a powerful tool for Republicans eager to attack the Truman administration and the Democratic party, claiming that the Democrats were "soft on Communism." One of the worst effects of the Red Scare was to encourage widespread conformity of thought and behavior in the United States. By 1950, it had become dangerous to criticize anything associated with the American way of life.

On March 30, 1952, Harry Truman announced he would not seek another presidential term, in part because it was unlikely he could win. Less than 25 percent of voters surveyed said that he was doing a good job, the lowest presidential approval rating in history. Although Americans applauded Truman's integrity and courage, they were disheartened that members of his administration were inept and even corrupt. The unrelenting war against communism, at home and abroad, led people to question Truman's strategy. Negotiations to end the war in Korea had bogged down for many months, the "red-baiting" of McCarthyism was expanding across the nation, and conservative southern Democrats, members of Truman's own party, had defeated most of the president's Fair Deal proposals in Congress. The war in Korea had brought higher taxes and higher prices for American consumers, many of whom blamed Truman for their frustrations. Only years later would people (and historians) fully appreciate how effective Truman had been in dealing with so many complex problems.

To the end of his presidency, Truman, a plainspoken man who made decisions based on his "gut-feeling" about what was "right," viewed himself as an ordinary person who had been given opportunities to do extraordinary things. "I have tried my best to give the nation everything I have in me," Truman told reporters at one of his last press conferences. "There are a great many people . . . who could have done the job better than I did it. But I had the job and had to do it." And it was not a simple job, by any means. At the end of one difficult day in the White House, Truman growled while sipping a bourbon and water: "They [his critics] talk about the power of the President, how I can just push a button to get things done. Why, I spend most of my time kissing somebody's . . . [butt]."

By the time a frustrated Truman left the White House in early 1953, the cold war against Communism had become an accepted part of the American way of life. But fears of Soviet and Chinese communism on the march around the world were counterbalanced by the joys of unexpected prosperity. Toward the end of Truman's presidency, during the early fifties, the economy began to grow at what would become the fastest rate in history, transforming social and cultural life, and becoming the marvel of the world. The booming economy brought with it the "nifty" fifties.

■ **The Cold War** The cold war was an ideological contest between the Western democracies (especially the United States) and the Communist countries (especially the Soviet Union). At the end of the Second World War, the Soviet Union established "friendly" governments in the Eastern European countries it occupied behind an *iron curtain*, violating promises that Stalin had made at the Yalta Conference. The United States and the Soviet Union, former allies, came to differ openly on issues of human rights, individual liberties, self-determination, and religious freedoms. As mutual hostility emerged, the two nations and their allies competed to shape the postwar order around the globe.

■ **Containment** President Truman responded to the Soviet occupation of Eastern Europe with *containment*, a policy to halt the spread of communism by opposing it wherever it emerged around the world. With the *Truman Doctrine (1947)*, he proposed giving economic and military aid to countries facing Communist insurgencies, such as Greece and Turkey. The *National Security Act* reorganized the U.S. armed forces and created the Central Intelligence Agency. The *Marshall Plan* offered postwar redevelopment aid to all European nations. In 1948, the United States withstood a Soviet blockade of supplies to West Berlin with the *Berlin airlift and,* in 1949, became a founding member of the *North Atlantic Treaty Organization (NATO)*.

■ **Truman's Fair Deal** The *Fair Deal* proposed to preserve and expand the New Deal in the face of intense Republican opposition in Congress. While he could not stop the Republican-backed, anti-union *Taft-Hartley Labor Act*. Truman successfully expanded Social Security, desegregated the military, and banned racial discrimination in the hiring of federal employees. In his second term, he proposed new laws such as a civil rights bill, national health insurance, federal aid to education, and new farm subsidies. However, conservative majorities of Republicans and southern Democrats (*Dixiecrats*) were able to defeat these initiatives in domestic policy.

■ **The Korean War** While containment policies halted Soviet expansion in Europe, they proved less effective in East Asia as Communists won a long civil war in China in 1949 and ignited a war in Korea. In response, Truman authorized *NSC-68*, which called for a dramatic increase in military spending and nuclear arms. When North Korean troops invaded South Korea in June 1950, Truman considered this an attempt by the Soviet Union to distract the U.S. from Western Europe, so he quickly decided to go to war under the auspices of the United Nations, thus bypassing Congress's authority to declare war. After three years of war, a truce established a demilitarized zone in Korea on either side of the 38th parallel. Truman also began assisting French efforts to subdue a Communist insurgency in its Southeast Asian colony of Indochina.

■ **The Red Scare** The onset of the cold war inflamed another Red Scare. After the Second World War, investigations by the *House Committee on Un-American Activities (HUAC)* sought to find "subversives" within the federal government. Starting in 1950, Senator Joseph R. McCarthy exploited American fears of Soviet infiltration of the U.S. government. *McCarthyism* flourished in the short term because the threat of a world dominated by Communist governments seemed all too real to many Americans.

KEY TERMS

CHRONOLOGY

1944	Congress passes the GI Bill of Rights
April 1945	Fifty Allied nations sign the United Nations Charter
	Soviet Union begins installing "puppet" Communist regimes in Eastern Europe
February 1946	State Department official George Kennan issues his "Long Telegram"
March 1947	President Truman announces the Truman Doctrine
May 1947	Secretary of State George Marshall proposes the Marshall Plan
June 1947	Congress passes the Taft-Hartley Labor Act
July 1947	National Security Council (NSC) is established
May 1948	Israel is proclaimed an independent nation
July 1948	Truman issues an executive order ending segregation in the U.S. armed forces
August 1948	Alger Hiss accused of having been a Soviet spy before the HUAC
October 1948	Berlin airlift
April 1949	NATO is created
October 1949	China "falls" to communism
	Soviet Union tests an atomic bomb
February 1950	Second Red Scare begins
June 1950–July 1953	The Korean War

INQUIZITIVE

Go to InQuizitive to see what you've learned—and learn what you've missed—with personalized feedback along the way.

THE ART OF CONSUMERISM   The United States experienced tremendous prosperity after the Second World War, giving many Americans the unprecedented opportunity of carefree consumption in the 1950s—and personal indebtedness. The Pop Art movement tapped into this era's affluence and anxiety. Its artists made use of the newly mass-produced and advertised American landscape to comment on consumer culture. One such artist was Tom Wesselman, a detail of whose 1962 collage *Untitled* (*Still-Life No. 22*) is shown above.

Affluence and Anxiety in the Atomic Age

1950–1959

In the summer of 1959, two newlyweds spent their honeymoon in an underground bomb shelter in the backyard of their home. *Life* magazine showed the couple in their twenty-ton, steel and concrete bunker stocked with enough food and water to survive an atomic attack. The image of the newlyweds seeking sheltered security in a new age of nuclear terror symbolized how America in the 1950s was awash in contrasting emotions. The deepening cold war with the Soviet Union cast a frightening shadow over the nation's traditional sunny optimism. In 1959, two out of three Americans listed the possibility of atomic war as the nation's most urgent threat. Despite the fears of nuclear destruction, however, Americans emerged from the Second World War proud of their military strength, international stature, and industrial might. It was a time rich with possibilities, and people were eager to seize their destinies. As the editors of *Fortune* magazine proclaimed in 1946, "This is a dream era . . . The Great American Boom is on."

So it was, at least for the growing number of white middle-class Americans. During the late 1940s and throughout the 1950s, the United States enjoyed unprecedented economic growth that created a dazzling array of new consumer products. Amid the insecurities of the cold war, most Americans were remarkably content with the improving quality of their lives. Divorce

CORE
OBJECTIVES INQUIZITIVE

1. Explain President Eisenhower's political philosophy and priorities.

2. Identify the factors that contributed to postwar prosperity, and analyze to what extent all Americans benefited from it.

3. Examine the criticism of postwar American society and culture, and describe the various forms of dissent and anxiety.

4. Evaluate the goals, strategies, and impact of the civil rights movement that emerged in the 1950s.

5. Assess President Eisenhower's priorities in conducting the nation's foreign policy and his influence on global affairs.

and homicide rates fell and people lived longer, on average, thanks in part to miraculous medical breakthroughs such as new antibiotics and the vaccine invented by Dr. Jonas Salk that ended the menace of polio. The "happy days" image of America in the fifties as an innocent, prosperous nation awash in good times and enlivened by teenage energies has a kernel of truth, but life in the fifties was much more complicated than that, hugely varied and even contradictory and hypocritical at times, with many Americans worried about an uncontrollable future.

CORE **OBJECTIVE**

1. Explain President Eisenhower's political philosophy and priorities.

Moderate Republicanism—The Eisenhower Years

Dwight David Eisenhower dominated the political landscape during the 1950s. The military hero of World War II was a model of moderation, stability, and optimism. Eisenhower's commitment to what he called **moderate Republicanism** promised to restore the authority of state and local governments, and restrain the federal government from engaging in any more political and social "engineering." In the process, he sought to renew traditional virtues and inspire Americans with a vision of a brighter future despite the continuing cold war.

"Time for a Change"

By 1952, the Truman administration had piled up a heavy burden of political liabilities. Its bold stand in Korea had resulted in a bloody stalemate in the war, renewed wage and price controls at home, and the embarrassing exposure of corrupt lobbyists who rigged military contracts. The disclosure of corruption within several federal agencies led Truman to fire nearly 250 employees of the Internal Revenue Service, but doubts lingered that the president would ever finish the housecleaning.

It was, Republicans claimed, "time for a change," and public sentiment turned their way as the 1952 election approached. Beginning in the late 1940s, both Republican and Democratic leaders, including President Truman, recruited General Eisenhower to be their presidential candidate. Born in Texas but raised in Kansas, the affable Eisenhower, known as "Ike," had displayed remarkable organizational and diplomatic abilities in coordinating the Allied invasion of Nazi-controlled Europe. In 1952, after serving as president of Columbia University, he had moved to Paris to become the supreme commander of NATO forces in Europe. His decision to run for president as a Republican was wildly popular. Bumper stickers announced simply: "I Like Ike."

Eisenhower won the nomination on the first ballot. Republican leaders then tried to reassure conservatives by balancing the ticket with a youthful, fiercely ambitious running mate: Richard M. Nixon, a thirty-nine-year-old California senator whose dogged insistence on pursuing the Alger Hiss

Dwight D. Eisenhower His many supporters wore "I Like Ike" hats, pins, and even nylon stockings, speaking to consumer culture's impact on politics.

moderate Republicanism Promise to curb federal government and restore state and local government authority, spearheaded by President Eisenhower.

spying case in Congressional hearings had brought him national promi- ⟨ Rolling back communism
nence. Nixon built his early political career as an anti-Communist bent on
exposing left-wing "subversives" holding government posts in the Truman
administration. The Republican party platform declared that the Democratic emphasis on "containing" communism was a "negative, futile, and
misguided" form of appeasement. The Eisenhower administration, if
elected, would roll back the Communist threat by bringing "genuine independence" to the "captive peoples" of Eastern Europe.

The Election of 1952

The 1952 presidential campaign matched two contrasting personalities. ⟨ An end to the Korean War
Eisenhower, though a political amateur, had been in the public eye for a
decade. Illinois governor Adlai Stevenson, the Democratic candidate, was
hardly known outside his home state. Eisenhower pledged to clean up "the
mess in Washington." To this he added a promise to secure "an early and
honorable" end to the conflict in Korea.

Stevenson was outmatched. Although a brilliant man whose witty
speeches charmed liberals, he came across to most voters as too aloof and
intellectual. The Republicans labeled him an "egghead" (meant to suggest
a balding professor with more intellect than common sense). Even Truman questioned Stevenson's decisiveness, grumbling that the Democratic
candidate "was too busy making up his mind whether he had to go to the
bathroom or not."

On election night, Eisenhower
triumphed in a landslide, gathering
nearly 34 million votes to Stevenson's
27 million. The electoral vote was
much more lopsided: 442 to 89. The
hapless Stevenson even failed to win
his home state of Illinois.

More important, the election
marked a turning point in Republican
fortunes in the South. For the first
time in more than a century, the Democratic "Solid South" was moving toward a two-party system. By winning
four Democratic southern states,
Eisenhower had made it respectable,
even fashionable, to vote for a Republican presidential candidate in the
South.

Voters liked Eisenhower's folksy
charm and battle-tested poise better
than they liked his political party.
In the 1952 election, Democrats retained most of the governorships,

THE ELECTION OF 1952

	Electoral Vote	Popular Vote
Dwight D. Eisenhower (Republican)	**442**	**33,900,000**
Adlai E. Stevenson (Democrat)	89	27,300,000

■ Why was the contest between Adlai Stevenson and Dwight D. Eisenhower lopsided?
■ Why was Eisenhower's victory in the South remarkable?

lost control of the House by only eight seats, and broke even in the Senate, where only the vote of the vice president gave Republicans the slimmest possible majority. The congressional elections two years later would further weaken the Republican grip on Congress, and Eisenhower would have to work with a Democratic Congress throughout his second term.

A "Middle Way" Presidency

Consensus and compromise

Eisenhower was the first professional soldier elected president since Ulysses S. Grant in 1868, and the last president born in the nineteenth century. He promised to pursue a "middle way between untrammelled freedom of the individual and the demands of the welfare of the whole nation." He saw no need to dismantle all of the Democrats' New Deal and Fair Deal programs. Instead, he wanted to end the "excesses" that had resulted from twenty years of Democratic control of the White House. He pledged to reduce the federal bureaucracy and make it more efficient while restoring the balance between the executive and legislative branches of government. Eisenhower's cautious personality and genial public face fit perfectly with the prevailing mood of most voters. He was a unifier, not a divider; he inspired trust and sought consensus and compromise; he avoided confrontation. Eisenhower also championed the nineteenth-century view that Congress should make policy and the president should carry it out. A journalist noted in 1959 that "the public loves Ike. The less he does, the more they love him."

"Dynamic Conservatism" at Home

"Dynamic conservatism"

Eisenhower called his domestic program "dynamic conservatism," by which he meant being "conservative when it comes to money and liberal when it comes to human beings." His administration set out to reduce defense spending, lower tax rates, weaken government regulation of business, and restore power to the states. The new president warned repeatedly against the dangers of "creeping socialism," "huge bureaucracies," and budget deficits.

In the end, however, Eisenhower kept intact the basic structure of the New Deal, much to the chagrin of conservative Republicans. He told his brother Edgar in 1954 that if the "stupid" right wing of the Republican party tried "to abolish Social Security and eliminate labor laws and farm programs, you would not hear of that party again in our political history." In some ways, Eisenhower's administration actually expanded New Deal programs, especially after 1954, when it had the help of Democratic majorities in Congress. Amendments to the Social Security Act in 1954 and 1956 extended the retirement program to millions of workers formerly excluded: white-collar professionals, maids and sales clerks, farm workers, and members of the armed forces. Eisenhower also approved increases in the minimum wage and additional public housing projects for low-income occupants.

Under Eisenhower, the federal government launched two massive construction projects: the St. Lawrence Seaway and the Interstate Highway System, both of which resembled the huge public works projects constructed under the New Deal during the 1930s. The St. Lawrence Seaway project (in partnership with Canada) opened the Great Lakes to oceangoing ships.

The **Federal-Aid Highway Act** (1956) created a national network of interstate highways to serve the needs of commerce and defense, as well as the convenience of citizens. The interstate highway system, funded by gasoline taxes, took twenty-five years to construct and was the largest federal project in history. It stretched for 47,000 miles and required 55,512 bridges. The vast project created jobs, stimulated the economy, and spurred the tourism, motor hotel ("motel"), and long-haul trucking industries. Interstate highways transformed the way people traveled and where they lived, and it even created a new form of middle-class leisure, the family vacation by car.

Drive in, cash in Founded by brothers Maurice and Richard McDonald in southern California, this hugely successful fast food chain started as a carhop drive-in and did not have customer seating until the 1960s.

> The Federal-Aid Highway Act (1956)

The second great age of the automobile had arrived after the war. In 1948, only 60 percent of families owned a car; by 1955, 90 percent owned a car and many households had two. "The American," the Mississippi writer William Faulkner observed in 1948, "really loves nothing but his automobile." Americans had always cherished personal freedom and mobility, rugged individualism and masculine force, and automobiles embodied all these qualities and more. Thanks to the new highway system, explained President Eisenhower, cars would provide "greater convenience, greater happiness, and greater standards of living." Cars in the fifties were much more than a form of transportation; they provided social status and personal freedom. They were the means of personal democracy, acting as a social leveling force, granting more and more people a wider range of personal choices—where to travel, where to work and live, where to seek personal pleasure and social recreation. The "car culture" soon transformed social behavior, prompting the creation of "convenience stores," drive-in movies, and fast-food restaurants.

The End of McCarthyism

Republicans thought their presidential victory in 1952 would curb the often unscrupulous efforts of Wisconsin senator Joseph R. McCarthy to ferret out Communist spies in the federal government. Instead, the

Federal-Aid Highway Act (1956) Largest federal project in U.S. history that created a national network of interstate highways.

publicity-seeking senator grew even more outlandish in his behavior. McCarthy finally overreached when he made the absurd charge that the U.S. Army itself was "soft" on communism. On December 2, 1954, the Senate voted 67 to 22 to "condemn" the crusading senator for his reckless tactics. Soon thereafter, his political influence collapsed. His savage crusade against Communists in government had catapulted him into the limelight and captured the nation's attention, but in the process he had trampled upon civil liberties. McCarthy's political demise helped the Democrats capture control of both houses of Congress in the 1954 elections. In 1957, at the age of forty-eight, he died of a liver inflammation brought on by years of alcohol abuse.

A People of Plenty

CORE **OBJECTIVE**

2. Identify the factors that contributed to post-war prosperity, and analyze to what extent all Americans benefited from it.

What most distinguished the United States from the rest of the world after the Second World War was what one journalist called America's "screwball materialism." After a brief postwar recession in 1945–1946, the economy soared to record heights as businesses shifted from wartime production to the construction of new housing and the manufacture of an array of mass-produced consumer goods. In 1953, Eisenhower's first year in office, the United States, with 6 percent of the world's population, was producing two-thirds of the world's manufactured goods. In 1957, *U.S. News and World Report* magazine declared that "never had so many people, anywhere, been so well off." By 1960, over 75 percent of American families owned a car and 87 percent had a television set.

Postwar Prosperity

Global arms race

Several factors created the nation's tremendous prosperity. First, huge federal expenditures during the Second World War and the Korean War catapulted the economy out of the Great Depression. High government spending at all levels—federal, state, and local—continued in the 1950s, thanks to the global arms race unleashed by the cold war and the relentless construction of new highways, bridges, airports, and ports. The still-large military budget after 1945 represented the single most important stimulant to the economy.

Robust manufacturing and dramatic new technologies

The superior productivity of American industries also contributed to dramatic economic growth. No sooner was the war over than the federal government turned over to civilian owners many of its war-related plants, giving them a boost as they retooled for peacetime manufacturing. Military-related research also helped stimulate new glamour industries: chemicals (including plastics), electronics, and aviation. By 1957, the aircraft industry was the nation's largest employer. The extraordinary increase in productivity benefited from new technologies, including the first generation of computers. Factories and industries became increasingly "automated." At the same time, the oil boom in Texas, Wyoming, and Oklahoma continued to provide the United States with low-cost fuel to heat buildings and drive cars and trucks.

Another reason for the record-breaking growth of the U.S. economy was the lack of foreign competition. Most of the other major industrial nations—Great Britain, France, Germany, Japan, and the Soviet Union—had been physically devastated during the Second World War, leaving American manufacturers with a virtual monopoly on international trade that lasted well into the 1950s.

U.S. dominance in international trade

The Consumer Culture

The major catalyst in promoting economic expansion after 1945, however, was the unleashing of pent-up consumer demand from the Depression and the war years, when civilians had been forced to conserve and do without. What differentiated the postwar era from earlier periods of prosperity was the large number of people who shared in the rising standard of living—not just corporate executives and salaried managers but also hourly wage workers. Between 1947 and 1960, the average income for the working class increased by as much as it had in the previous *fifty* years. More and more blue-collar Americans, especially automotive and steel workers, moved into the middle class. George Meany, the leading union spokesman during the 1950s, declared in 1955 that his members "never had it so good." That same year, three out of every four American adults categorized themselves as "middle class."

Increased income across classes

Americans had money to spend during the fifties, and they did so with gusto, becoming famous around the world for their carefree consumption. In 1955, a marketing consultant stressed that the nation's "enormously productive economy demands that we make *consumption* a way of life, that we convert the buying and use of goods into [religious] rituals, that we seek our spiritual satisfaction, our ego satisfaction, in consumption." The consumer culture, he explained, demanded that things be "consumed, burned up, worn out, replaced, and discarded at an ever-increasing rate."

Americans engaged in a prolonged buying spree aided by financing innovations that made it easier to buy things. The first credit card appeared in 1949; by the end of the decade, "buying with plastic" had become the new norm for tens of millions of people. Personal indebtedness doubled during the fifties, in part because people were so confident about their economic future. Frugality became unpatriotic. As television personality Hugh Downs remembered, "those were exciting days . . . of hope and optimism . . . when the sky was the limit."

Increased consumer spending: Credit cards, home ownership, and television

A Buying Spree

What most Americans wanted to buy after the Second World War was a new house. In 1945, only 40 percent of Americans owned homes; by 1960, the number had increased to 60 percent. And those new homes featured the latest electrical appliances—refrigerators, dishwashers, washing machines, vacuum cleaners, electric mixers, carving knives, even shoe polishers.

Family, modified The fantasy of the American family changed with the onslaught of new, affordable products. In this 1959 advertisement for TV dinners, the family eats out of disposable containers in front of the television.

The use of electricity tripled during the decade, in part because of the popularity of television. Watching television quickly displaced listening to the radio or going to the movies as the most popular way to spend free time. Between 1948 and 1952, the number of homes with TV sets jumped from 172,000 to 15.3 million. In 1954, grocery stores began selling frozen "TV dinners" to be heated and consumed while watching popular shows such as *Father Knows Best, I Love Lucy,* and *The Adventures of Ozzie and Harriet,* all of which idealized the child-centered world of suburban white families. In 1955, *U.S. News and World Report* magazine noted that the "biggest of the new forces in American life today is television. There has been nothing like it in the postwar decade, or in many decades before that—perhaps not since the invention of the printing press. Even radio, by contrast, was a placid experience."

The popularity of television provided a powerful new medium for advertisers to promote a powerful new phase of the consumer culture that reshaped the contours of postwar life: the nature of work, where people lived and traveled, how they interacted, and what they valued. It also affected class structure, race relations, and gender roles. Jack Metzgar, the son of a Pennsylvania steelworker, remembered that in 1946 "we did not have a car, a television set, or a refrigerator. By 1952, we had all those things."

The GI Bill of Rights

GI Bill of Rights (1944) Provided unemployment, education, and financial benefits for World War II veterans to ease their transition back to the civilian world.

In 1944, as Americans grew confident that the war would soon be won, fears that the sudden influx of war veterans into the civilian workforce would disrupt the economy and produce widespread unemployment led Congress to pass the Servicemen's Readjustment Act of 1944, nicknamed the **GI Bill of Rights** ("GI" meaning "government issue," a phrase stamped on military uniforms and equipment that became slang for "serviceman").

Between 1944 and 1956, the GI Bill boosted upward social mobility in postwar America. It included a package of crucial benefits to veterans: unemployment pay for one year, preference to those applying for federal government jobs, loans for home construction or starting a business, access to government hospitals, and generous subsidies for education. Some 5 million veterans bought new homes with the assistance of GI Bill mortgage loans, which required no down payment. Almost 8 million veterans took advantage of $14.5 billion in GI Bill benefits to attend college or enroll in job-training programs. Before the Second World War, approximately 160,000 Americans had graduated from college each year. By 1950, the figure had risen to 500,000. In 1949, veterans accounted for 40 percent of college enrollments, and the United States could boast the world's best-educated workforce, largely because of the GI Bill. To cite but one example: Joe Shi, a decorated Army veteran from Macon, Georgia, was able to attend graduate school in business at the University of Pennsylvania because of the financial aid provided by the GI Bill.

> GI Bill

Overall, the GI Bill was one of the most successful federal programs in history. Many African American veterans, however, could not take advantage of many of its benefits. Most colleges and universities remained racially segregated and refused to admit blacks. Those that enrolled blacks often discriminated against them. African Americans attending white colleges or universities were barred from playing on athletic teams, attending social events, and joining fraternities or sororities. Black veterans were also often prevented from buying homes in white neighborhoods. Although women veterans were eligible for GI Bill benefits, there were so few of them that the program had the unintended effect of widening the income gap between men and women.

The Suburban Frontier

The second half of the twentieth century witnessed a mass migration to a new frontier—the suburbs. The acute housing shortage after the war (98 percent of cities reported shortages of houses and apartments in 1945) sparked the suburban revolution. Of the 13 million homes built between 1948 and 1958, 11 million were in suburbs. Rural America continued to lose population during the 1950s (and after), as many among the exploding middle-class white population moved to what were called the Sunbelt states—California, Arizona, Florida, Texas, and the southeast region, where rapid population growth generated an economic boom. As air conditioning became a common household fixture in the Sunbelt states, it greatly enhanced the appeal of living in warmer climates.

> Sunbelt migration, suburban development, and the car culture

Suburbia met an acute need—affordable housing—and fulfilled a common dream—personal freedom and familial security within commuting distance of cities. In the half century after the Second World War, the suburban good life for middle-class white families included a big home with a big yard on a big lot accessed by a big car—or two. The widespread

suburbia Communities formed from mass migration of middle-class whites from urban centers.

Levittown Identical mass-produced houses in Levittown, New York, and other suburbs across the country provided veterans and their families with affordable homes.

Suburbia, Levittowns, and racial segregation

ownership of cars enabled the suburban revolution during the fifties. Nine of ten suburban families in the 1950s owned a car, compared to six of ten urban households. During the 1950s, suburbs grew six times as fast as cities, and by 1970 more people lived in suburbs than in cities.

A brassy New York real estate developer, William Levitt, led the suburban revolution. Between 1947 and 1951, on 6,000 acres of Long Island farmland near New York City, he built 17,447 small, look-alike homes (essentially identical in design) to house more than 82,000 people. The planned community, called Levittown, included schools, swimming pools, shopping centers, and playing fields. Levitt encouraged and even enforced uniformity and conformity in Levittown. The houses all sold for the same price—$6,900, with no down payments for veterans—and featured the same floor plan and accessories. Each had a picture window, a living room, a bathroom, a kitchen, and two bedrooms. Trees were planted every twenty-eight feet in the former potato fields, and homeowners were required to cut their grass once a week.

Levitt soon built three more Levittowns in Pennsylvania, New Jersey, and Puerto Rico. They and other planned suburban communities benefited greatly from government assistance. Federal and state tax codes favored homeowners over renters, and local governments paid for the infrastructure required by new Levittown-style suburban subdivisions: roads, water and sewer lines, fire and police protection. By insuring loans for up to 95 percent of the value of a house, the Federal Housing Administration (FHA) made it easy for builders to construct low-cost homes and for people to buy them.

Levitt and other suburban developers created lily-white communities. Initially, the contracts for houses in Levittown specifically excluded "members of other than the Caucasian race," since Levitt believed that whites would not want to buy a house in Levittown if blacks were living there. As he explained, "We can solve a housing problem or we can try to solve a racial problem. But we can't combine the two." A year later, however, the U.S. Supreme Court ruled in *Shelley v. Kraemer* (1948) that such racial restrictions were illegal. The court ruling, however, did not end segregated housing practices; it simply made them more discreet. In 1953, when Levittown's population reached 70,000, it was the largest community in the nation without a single African American resident. Although Jewish himself, Levitt also discouraged Jews from living in his communities. "As a Jew," he explained, "I have no room in my heart for racial prejudice. But the plain fact is that most whites prefer not to live in mixed communities. This attitude may be wrong morally, and someday it may change. I hope it will."

Other developers across the country soon mimicked Levitt's efforts, building suburban communities with rustic names such as Lakewood, Streamwood, Elmwood, Cedar Hill, Park Forest, and Deer Park. In 1955, *House and Garden* magazine could declare that suburbia had become the "national way of life." By 1960, however, only 5 percent of African Americans lived in suburbs.

Minorities on the Move

African Americans were not part of the initial wave of suburban development, but they began moving in large numbers after 1945. The mass migration of rural southern blacks to the urban North, Midwest, and West after the Second World War was much larger than the similar trend after the First World War, and its social consequences were even more dramatic. After 1945, more than 5 million southern blacks formed a new "great migration" out of the South in search of better jobs, higher wages, decent housing, and greater civil rights.

A new "great migration"

By 1960, for the first time in history, more African Americans were living in urban areas than in rural areas. As blacks moved into northern cities, many white residents moved to the suburbs, leaving behind racial ghettos. Nine of the nation's ten largest cities lost population to the suburbs during the 1950s. Between 1950 and 1960, some 3.6 million whites left the nation's largest cities for new suburban neighborhoods while 4.5 million blacks moved into those same cities, most of them coming from the rural South.

Deeply entrenched racial attitudes outside the South forced blacks to organize their own efforts to counter the hostility they confronted in communities across the nation. Through organizations such as the National Association for the Advancement of Colored People (NAACP), the Congress of Racial Equality (CORE), and the National Urban League, they sought to change the hearts and minds of their white neighbors. However, for all of the varied forms of racism that black migrants to the North and West encountered, most of them found their new lives preferable to the enforced segregation and often violent racism that they had left behind in the South. Southern blacks still faced voting discrimination and segregation in theaters, parks, schools, colleges, hospitals, buses, cinemas, libraries, restrooms, beaches, bars, and prisons. By the late 1950s, local black leaders had convinced most northern states to adopt some form of anti-discrimination legislation.

Anti-discrimination legislation in the North

Just as African Americans were on the move, so, too, were Mexicans and Puerto Ricans. Congress renewed the bracero program, begun during the Second World War, which enabled Mexicans to work as wage laborers in the United States, often as migrant workers moving from farm to farm as needed for the planting and harvest seasons. Mexicans streamed across the nation's southwest border, and by 1960 Los Angeles had the largest concentration of Mexican Americans in the nation. Like African Americans who served in the war, Mexican Americans, Puerto Ricans, and other Hispanic/Latino minorities benefited from the GI Bill. Between 1940 and 1960, nearly a million Puerto Ricans, mostly small farmers and agricultural workers, moved into mainland American cities, especially New York City. In fact, by

Hispanic migration to the United States

Fountains of truth An Alabama day-hotel offers its white clientele chilled water from a cooler, while its African American guests must use a rudimentary drinking fountain.

the late 1960s more Puerto Ricans lived in New York City than in San Juan, the capital of Puerto Rico. The popular Broadway musical drama *West Side Story* (1957) highlighted the tensions generated by the influx of Puerto Ricans into traditionally white neighborhoods.

Shifting Women's Roles

During the Second World War, millions of women had responded to patriotic appeals and assumed traditionally male jobs in factories and mills to help the war effort. After the war, those same working women were encouraged to return to their traditional roles as loving wives, caring mothers, and happy homemakers. A 1945 article in *House Beautiful* magazine lectured women on their domestic duties. The returning war veteran, it said, was "head man again. . . . Your part in the remaking of this man is to fit his home to him, understanding why he wants it this way, forgetting your own preferences."

"The happy homemaker"

Advertisements in popular magazines often targeted middle-class women, depicting them happily bound to the house, at work in the kitchen in dresses adorned with jewelry (usually pearl necklaces) and high heels, conversing with children, serving dinner, cleaning, and otherwise displaying the joy of a clean home or the latest kitchen appliance. The prevailing images of middle-class life in the fifties featured tree-lined suburban streets, kids riding their bikes through beautiful neighborhoods, and women as devoted servants to their husbands. Idealized images of "the happy homemaker" and middle-class suburban life in popular television programs like *The Donna Reed Show* or *Leave It to Beaver* also supported the cold war campaign to portray the superiority of capitalism, democracy, freedom, and religion over life under Soviet communism; Russian women, by contrast, were depicted toiling in drudgery as manual laborers in drab factories or on government farms.

During the fifties, the U.S. marriage rate reached an all-time high, and the average age of marriage for women plummeted to nineteen. There was enormous social pressure on teen-aged girls to get married quickly; if a woman wasn't engaged or married by her early twenties, she was in danger of becoming an "old maid." Getting married during high school or while in college became the norm. In 1956, one-fourth of all white college women wed while still enrolled in school, and most dropped out before receiving a degree. A common joke of the time was that women went to college to get an "M.R.S. degree"—that is, a husband.

Female college students were encouraged to take courses to prepare them for home life—home economics, interior decoration, and family finance. Lynn White, president of Mills College, argued that "the curriculum for female students should prepare women to foster the intellectual and emotional life of her family and community." Although women had other aspirations in life, the celebration of marriage and motherhood in the culture and media promoted the idea that getting a husband was far more important for a young woman than earning a college degree.

Despite this modern version of the nineteenth century's "cult of domesticity," in which women's roles were largely confined to the home and family duties, many women did work outside the home during the fifties, usually out of necessity. In 1950, women comprised 29 percent of the work force, and that percentage rose steadily throughout the decade. Some 70 percent of employed women worked in clerical positions—secretaries, bank tellers, or sales clerks—or worked on assembly lines in factories or in the service industry (waitresses, laundresses, maids). Less than 15 percent of women were employed in a professional capacity (teachers, nurses, accountants, social workers). Women represented only 3.5 percent of attorneys and 6 percent of physicians. African American and other minority women had even fewer vocational choices, mostly low-paying domestic service jobs as maids and cooks.

The Child-Centered Fifties

The fifties witnessed a record number of marriages—and births. The decade was an ideal time to be a child. The horrors of the Second World War were over, the economy was surging, and social life became centered on the needs of children—because there were so many of them. Between 1946 and 1964, the birth of 76 million Americans reversed a century-long decline in the nation's birth rate and created a demographic upheaval whose

Hollywood homemakers TV shows and films were outlets for homemakers' anxieties and fantasies. *Top: Bewitched* was a popular comedy about a witch-turned-homemaker even though her family has bigger dreams for her. *Bottom:* Domestic bliss was never in reach for African American female characters. In *Porgy and Bess* (1959), Dorothy Dandridge plays an addict so lost in the vice of New Orleans that even her self-sacrificing disabled lover (Sidney Poitier) cannot save her.

repercussions are still being felt. The "**baby boom**" peaked in 1957, when a record 4.3 million births occurred, one every seven seconds. A majority of brides during the fifties were pregnant within seven months of their wedding, and they didn't just stop at one child. Large families were typical. From 1940 to 1960, the number of families with three children doubled and the number of families having a fourth child quadrupled. Dr. Benjamin Spock's *The Common Sense Book of Baby and Child Care* sold more than a million copies a year during the fifties.

Demands of a "baby boom"

The unusually large baby boom generation has since shaped social history and economic development. Postwar babies initially created a surge in demand for diapers, washing machines, and baby food, then required the construction of thousands of new schools—and the hiring of teachers to staff them. As the so-called baby boomers became children and then adolescents, their needs drove much of the economy's growth, creating a huge market for toys, candy, gum, records, clothes, and other items. In 1958, *Life* magazine reported that the nation's four-year-olds were creating a "backlog of business orders that will take two decades to fulfill."

The powerful forces promoting conformity in American social life during the cold war influenced the role of women. A special issue of *Life* magazine in 1956 featured the "ideal" middle-class woman: a thirty-two-year-old "pretty and popular" white suburban housewife, mother of four, who had married at age sixteen. She was described as an excellent wife, mother, volunteer, and "home manager" who preferred marriage and childrearing to a career outside the home. She made her own clothes, hosted dozens of dinner parties each year, sang in her church choir, and was devoted to her husband. "In her daily round," *Life* reported, "she attends club or charity meetings, drives the children to school, does the weekly grocery shopping, makes ceramics, and is planning to study French." The soaring birth rate reinforced the deeply embedded notion that a woman's place was in the home. "Of all the accomplishments of the American woman," the *Life* cover story proclaimed, "the one she brings off with the most spectacular success is having babies."

A Religious Nation

After the Second World War, Americans, unlike Europeans, joined churches and synagogues in record numbers. In 1940, less than half the adult population belonged to a church; by 1960, over 65 percent were members of churches or synagogues. Sales of Bibles soared, as did the demand for books, movies, and songs with religious themes. The cold war provided a direct stimulant to Christian evangelism. Communism, explained the Reverend Billy Graham, the most famous evangelist of the fifties, was "a great sinister anti-Christian movement masterminded by Satan" that must be fought wherever it emerged around the world.

President Eisenhower promoted a patriotic religious crusade during the fifties. "Recognition of the Supreme Being," he declared, "is the first, the

baby boom Markedly high birth rate in the years following World War II, leading to the biggest demographic "bubble" in U.S. history.

most basic, expression of Americanism. Without God, there could be no American form of government, nor an American way of life." In 1954, Congress added the phrase "one nation under God" to the Pledge of Allegiance and in 1956 made the statement "In God We Trust" the nation's official motto. Eisenhower ordered that the motto be displayed on all currency. A godly nation, it was widely assumed, would better withstand the march of "godless" communism.

The prevailing tone of the popular religious revival of the 1950s was upbeat and soothing. As the Protestant Council of New York City explained to its radio and television presenters, their on-air broadcasts "should project love, joy, courage, hope, faith, trust in God, goodwill. Generally avoid condemnation, criticism, controversy. In a very real sense we are 'selling' religion, the good news of the Gospel."

The best salesman for this gospel of reassuring "good news" was the Reverend Norman Vincent Peale, the champion of feel-good religion. No speaker was more in demand during the 1950s, and no writer was more widely read. Peale's book *The Power of Positive Thinking* (1952) was a phenomenal best

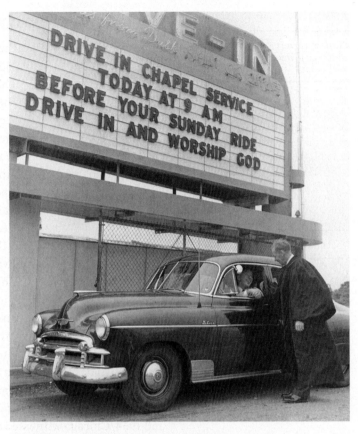

Roadside service Drive-in churches offered its members the comfort of listening to Sunday Mass from their cars. Here, the pastor of New York's Tremont Methodist Church greets a member of his car-centered congregation.

seller throughout the decade—and for good reason. It offered a simple how-to course in personal happiness. "Flush out all depressing, negative, and tired thoughts," Peale advised. "Start thinking faith, enthusiasm, and joy." By following this simple formula for success, he pledged, each American could become "a more popular, esteemed, and well-liked individual."

Cracks in the Picture Window

CORE **OBJECTIVE**

3. Examine the criticism of postwar American society and culture, and describe the various forms of dissent and anxiety.

In contrast to Peale's feel-good religion, the fifties also experienced growing anxiety, dissent, and diversity. In *The Affluent Society* (1958), for example, economist John Kenneth Galbraith attacked the prevailing notion that sustained economic growth was solving chronic social problems. He reminded readers that for all of America's vaunted prosperity, the nation had yet to eradicate poverty, especially among minorities in inner cities, female-led households, Mexican American migrant farm workers, Native Americans, and rural southerners, both black and white.

Poverty amid Prosperity

Chronic poverty; income gap widens between whites and minorities

Uncritical praise for the "throwaway" culture of consumption during the 1950s masked the chronic poverty amid America's mythic plenty. In 1959, a quarter of the population had *no* financial assets, and more than half had no savings accounts or credit cards. Poverty afflicted nearly half of the African American population, compared to only a quarter of whites. True, by 1950 blacks were earning on average more than four times their 1940 wages. But African Americans and members of other minority groups lagged well behind whites in their *rate* of improvement, and the gap between the average yearly income of whites and minorities widened. At least 40 million people remained "poor" during the 1950s, but their plight was largely ignored amid the wave of middle-class white consumerism.

Racial tensions

The "promised land" in the North where many minorities moved was not perfect. Because those who moved out of the South were often undereducated, poor, and black, they were regularly denied access to good jobs, good schools, and good housing. Although states in the North, Midwest, and Far West did not have the same blatant forms of racial discrimination as the South, African Americans still encountered racial prejudice and discrimination in workplace hiring, in housing, in schools, and in social life. Outside the South, blacks and whites typically lived in separate neighborhoods and led unequal lives. When a black family tried to move into Levittown, Pennsylvania, white residents greeted them by throwing rocks. Between 1945 and 1954, Chicago witnessed nine race riots.

Literature

Many social critics, writers, and artists were alarmed by America's worship of consumerism during the fifties. One of the most striking aspects of the decade was the sharp contrast between the happy public mood and the increasingly bitter social criticism coming from intellectuals, theologians, novelists, playwrights, poets, and artists. A growing number of writers and artists questioned the prevailing complacency about the goodness and superiority of the American way of life. Writer Norman Mailer, for instance, said the 1950s was "one of the worst decades in the history of man."

Mailer was one of many social critics who challenged what they viewed as the decade's moral complacency and bland conformity. For all of America's mythic devotion to rugged individualism, the nation during the cold war celebrated conformity. As novelist John Updike observed, he and other writers felt estranged "from a government that extolled business and mediocrity." The most enduring novels of the postwar period emphasized the individual's struggle for survival amid the smothering forces of mass society. The characters in books such as James Jones's *From Here to Eternity* (1951), Ralph Ellison's *Invisible Man* (1952), Saul Bellow's *Seize the Day* (1956), J. D. Salinger's *Catcher in the Rye* (1951), William Styron's *Lie Down in Darkness* (1951), and Updike's *Rabbit, Run* (1961) are restless, tormented souls who can find neither contentment nor respect in an uninterested world.

The upper-middle-class white suburbs and the culture of comfortable conformity they created were frequent literary targets during the fifties. Writer John Cheever located most of his often brilliant short stories in suburban neighborhoods outside of New York City—"cesspools of conformity" where life was mindless and hollow. The typical suburban dweller, as one critic charged in 1956, did everything like the neighbors: "buys the right car, keeps his lawn like his neighbor's, eats crunchy breakfast cereal, and votes Republican."

In his vicious satire of affluent suburbia, *The Crack in the Picture Window* (1956), John Keats charged that "miles of identical boxes are spreading like gangrene" across the nation, producing a runaway consumerism, "haggard" businessmen, "tense and anxious" housewives, and "the gimme kids" who, after unwrapping the last Christmas gift, "look up and ask whether that is all." He dismissed the Levittowns of America as residential "developments conceived in error, nurtured by greed, corroding everything they touch. They destroy established cities and trade patterns, pose dangerous problems for the areas they invade, and actually drive mad myriads of housewives shut up in them."

> Social criticism: Complacency and conformity in the suburbs

The Beats

A small but highly visible and controversial group of young writers, poets, painters, and musicians rejected the materialism of the consumer culture as well as the traditional expectations and responsibilities of middle-class life. They were known as the **Beats**, a term with multiple meanings: to be "beat" was likened to being "upbeat" and even "beatific," as well as being "on the beat" in "real cool" jazz music. But the rebellious Beats also liked the name because it implied "weariness," being "exhausted" or "beaten down," qualities which none of them actually exhibited.

> The Beats (bohemians) reject middle-class values

Jack Kerouac, Allen Ginsberg, William Burroughs, Neal Cassady, Gary Snyder, and other Beats were cultural outlaws who rebelled against conventional literary and artistic expression and excelled at outrageous behavior. Intensely self-absorbed, they celebrated, even embodied, lives of breathtaking risk and originality, fueled by spontaneity and energy. They pursued rebellious and reckless lives of alcohol- and drug-induced ecstasies and sexual excesses (many of them were gay or bi-sexual during an era when homosexuality was viewed as a form of deviance requiring psychotherapy). The mostly male Beats viewed women as second-class accessories; Carolyn Cassady said her husband Neal's approach to making love was "rape." She added that Neal and the "boys didn't know where they were going. . . . They just knew they wanted to *go*."

Beats Group of bohemian writers, artists, and musicians who flouted convention in favor of liberated forms of self-expression.

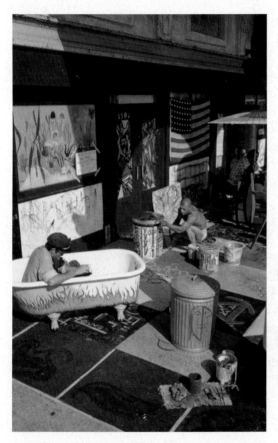

Art ache The Beat community fostered in its members a frenzied desire to create. In this 1959 photograph, poet Tex Kleen reads in a bathtub at Venice Beach, California, while artist Mad Mike paints trash cans.

The Beat hipsters grew out of the bohemian underground in New York City's Greenwich Village. Undisciplined and often unkempt, they were essentially apolitical and more interested in transforming themselves than in reforming the world. They sought personal rather than social solutions to their needs and anxieties; they wanted their art and literature to change consciousness rather than address social ills. As Kerouac insisted in his remarkable novel *On the Road* (1957), the first draft of which was typed almost nonstop onto a continuous roll of butcher paper during three feverish weeks, his rootless, reckless friends were not beat in the sense of beaten down; they were "mad to live, mad to talk, mad to be saved, desirous of everything at the same time, the ones who never yawn or say a commonplace thing, but burn, burn, burn like fabulous yellow roman candles exploding like spiders across the stars."

The Beats nursed an urge to "go, go, go" and not stop until they got there, wherever "there" might be. Their road to salvation lay in hallucinogenic drugs and lots of alcohol, casual sex, petty crime, gratuitous violence, a passion for up-tempo jazz ("bebop"), fast cars, the street life of urban ghettos, an affinity for Buddhism, and a restless, vagabond spirit that took them racing back and forth across the country between San Francisco and New York. At heart, the Beats were romantics searching for an authentic sense of self in a nation absorbed in consumerism, conformism, and anti-communism. The tortured rebelliousness of the Beats set the stage for the more widespread youth revolt of the 1960s.

Rock 'n' Roll

Youth culture and juvenile delinquency

The millions of children making up the first wave of the baby boomers born during and just after the Second World War became adolescents in the 1950s. A distinctive teen subculture began to emerge, and a wave of juvenile delinquency swept across middle-class society. By 1956, over a million teens were being arrested each year. One contributing factor was access to automobiles, which enabled teens to escape parental control and, in the words of one journalist, provided "a private lounge for drinking and for petting [embracing and kissing] or sex episodes."

Rebellion, sexual suggestion, and new forms of music

Many concerned observers blamed teen delinquency on rock 'n' roll, a new form of music that emerged during the 1950s. Alan Freed, a Cleveland disc jockey, coined the term rock 'n' roll in 1951. He had noticed that white teenagers buying rhythm and blues (R&B) records preferred the livelier recordings by African Americans and Hispanic Americans. Freed began playing R&B records on his radio show, but he called the music "rock 'n' roll" (a phrase used in African American communities to refer to dancing and sex). Freed's popular program helped bridge the gap between "white" and "black" music. African American singers such as Chuck Berry, Little Richard, and Ray Charles, as well as Hispanic American performers such as Ritchie Valens (Richard Valenzuela), captivated young, white, middle-class audiences eager to claim their own cultural style.

At the same time, Elvis Presley, the lanky son of a poor Mississippi farm family who moved to a public housing project in Memphis, Tennessee, began experimenting with "rockabilly" music, a unique blend of gospel, country-and-western, and R&B. At the same time, Sam Phillips, a local radio disk jockey, was searching for a particular type of pop singer. "If I could find a white man with a Negro sound," Phillips said, "I could make a billion dollars."

Then he found Elvis. In 1956, the twenty-one-year-old Presley, by then a

Elvis Presley Hysterical girls grab at him from all angles, but the "King of Rock and Roll" stays cool, crooning into the camera while performing in Miami, 1956.

regional star famous for his long, unruly hair, his sensual sneer, and his wildly swiveling hips, released his smash-hit recording "Heartbreak Hotel." Over the next two years, he emerged as the most popular musician in American history. Presley's gyrating, sensual stage performances (his nickname was "Elvis the Pelvis") and his incomparably rich and raw baritone voice drove teenagers (a word that came into use during the fifties) wild and earned him millions of fans around the world. His movements, said one music critic, "suggest, in a word, sex."

Cultural conservatives were outraged by Presley's antics. Critics urged parents to destroy his records because they promoted "a pagan concept of life." A Roman Catholic official denounced Presley as a vile symptom of a teenage "creed of dishonesty, violence, lust and degeneration." Patriotic groups claimed that rock 'n' roll music was part of a Communist plot to corrupt America's youth. Writing in the *New York Times*, a psychiatrist characterized rock 'n' roll as a "communicable disease." A U.S. Senate subcommittee investigating juvenile delinquency warned that Elvis was threatening "to rock-n-roll the juvenile world into open revolt against society. The gangster of tomorrow is the Elvis Presley type of today."

Yet rock 'n' roll flourished amid such opposition, in part because it was so controversial. It gave teenagers a self-conscious sense of belonging to a tribal social group. More important, it brought together, on equal terms, musicians (and their audiences) of varied races and backgrounds. In doing so, it helped dispel the racial prejudices that conflicted with the nation's ideals.

CORE **OBJECTIVE**

4. Evaluate the goals, strategies, and impact of the civil rights movement that emerged in the 1950s.

The Early Years of the Civil Rights Movement

Soon after the cold war began, Soviet diplomats began to use America's racial discrimination against African Americans as a propaganda tool to illustrate the supposed defects of the American way of life. Under the Jim Crow system in the southern states, blacks still risked being lynched if they registered to vote. They were forced to use separate facilities in public—water fountains, restrooms, hotels, theaters, parks—and to attend segregated schools. In the North, discrimination was not as "official," but it was equally real, especially in housing and employment. During the mid-1950s, the ongoing tragedy of race relations in the United States offered President Eisenhower an opportunity to exercise transformational leadership; his unwillingness to do so was his greatest failure. As *Time* magazine noted in 1958, Eisenhower "overlooked the fact that the U.S. needed [his] moral leadership in fighting segregation."

Eisenhower and Race

Eisenhower had entered the White House committed to civil rights in principle, and he pushed for improvements in some areas. During his first three years as president, for example, public facilities (parks, playgrounds, libraries, restaurants) in Washington, D.C., were desegregated, and he intervened to end discrimination at military bases in Virginia and South Carolina. The president also appointed the first African American to an executive office: E. Frederic Morrow, who was named Administrative Officer for Special Projects. Beyond that, however, Eisenhower refused to make civil rights for African Americans a moral crusade. Pushing too hard against segregation in the South, he believed, would "raise tempers and increase prejudices," doing more harm than good.

Eisenhower's civil rights record

Two aspects of Eisenhower's political philosophy limited his commitment to racial equality: his preference for state or local action over federal involvement and his doubt that laws could change attitudes. "I don't believe you can change the hearts of men with laws or decisions," he insisted. His passive attitude toward racial issues meant that governmental leadership on civil rights would come from the judiciary more than from the executive or legislative branch.

In 1953, Eisenhower appointed former Republican governor Earl Warren of California as chief justice of the U.S. Supreme Court, a decision he later said was the "biggest damn fool mistake I ever made." Warren, who had seemed safely conservative while in elected office, displayed a social conscience and a streak of libertarianism that was shared by another Eisenhower appointee to the Court, William J. Brennan Jr. Under Warren's leadership (1953–1969), the Supreme Court became one of the most powerful forces for social and political change through the 1960s.

African American Activism

However, the most crucial leaders of the civil rights movement came from the long-suffering people whose rights were most often violated: African Americans, Hispanic Americans, Asian Americans, and other minorities. Rural and urban, young and old, male and female, courageous blacks led what would become the most important social movement in twentieth-century American history. With brilliance, bravery, and dignity, they fought on all fronts—in the courts, at the ballot box, and in the streets—against the deeply entrenched system of racial segregation and discrimination. Although many African Americans moved to the North and West during and after the Second World War, a majority remained in the South, where they were forced to attend segregated public schools, to accept the least desirable jobs, and to operate within a rigidly segregated society that restricted their civil rights. In the 1952 presidential election, for example, only 20 percent of eligible African Americans were registered to vote.

NAACP's legal efforts

In the mid-1930s, the National Association for the Advancement of Colored People (NAACP) challenged the **separate-but-equal** judicial doctrine that had upheld racial segregation since the *Plessy* decision by the Supreme Court in 1896. Yet it took almost fifteen years to convince the courts that racial segregation must end. Finally, in *Sweatt v. Painter* (1950), the Supreme Court ruled that a separate black law school in Texas was *not* equal in quality to the state's whites-only schools. The Court ordered the state to remedy the situation. It was the first step toward dismantling America's tradition of racial segregation.

The *Brown* Decision

By the early 1950s, challenges to state laws mandating racial segregation in the public schools were rising through the court system. Five such cases, from Kansas, Delaware, South Carolina, Virginia, and the District of Columbia—usually cited by reference to the first, ***Brown v. Board of Education*** of *Topeka, Kansas*—came to the Supreme Court for joint argument by NAACP attorneys in 1952. President Eisenhower told the attorney general that he hoped the justices would postpone dealing with the explosive case "until the next Administration took over." When it became obvious that the Court was moving forward, Eisenhower invited Earl Warren to a White House dinner during which he urged the chief justice to side with segregationists. Warren was not swayed: "You mind your business," he told the president, "and I'll mind mine."

Brown v. Board of Education: The separate-but-equal doctrine overturned

Warren himself wrote the pathbreaking opinion, handed down on May 17, 1954, in which a unanimous Court declared that "in the field of public education the doctrine of 'separate but equal' has no place." In support of its opinion, the Court cited sociological and psychological findings demonstrating that even if racially separate schools were equal in quality, the very practice of separating students by race caused feelings of inferiority among

separate-but-equal Principle that formed the basis for legal racial segregation.

Brown v. Board of Education **(1952)** Landmark Supreme Court case that struck down racial segregation in public schools and declared "separate-but-equal" unconstitutional.

black children. A year later, the Court directed that the process of racial *integration* should move "with all deliberate speed."

Eisenhower refused to endorse or enforce the Court's ruling. Privately, he grumbled "that the Supreme Court decision set back progress in the South at least fifteen years." Anyone who thinks "you can do these things by force is just plain nuts," he said. While token racial integration began as early as 1954 in Kentucky and Missouri, hostility mounted in the Lower South and Virginia. The Alabama State Senate and the Virginia legislature both passed resolutions "nullifying" the Supreme Court's decision.

Opponents of court-ordered integration of schools and other public places were defiant. In 1956, 101 members of Congress signed a Declaration of Constitutional Principles ("Southern Manifesto") denouncing the Supreme Court's decision in the *Brown* case as "a clear abuse of judicial power" that had created an "explosive and dangerous condition" in the South. Only three southern Democrats in Congress refused to sign. One of them, Senator Lyndon B. Johnson of Texas, would become president seven years later. In six southern states at the end of 1956, two years after the *Brown* ruling, not a single black child attended school with whites.

The Montgomery Bus Boycott

The *Brown* case did much more than mobilize white resistance in the South. It inspired many blacks (and white activists) by suggesting that the federal government was finally beginning to confront racial discrimination. Yet the essential role played by the NAACP and the courts in providing a legal lever for the civil rights movement often overshadows the courageous contributions of individual African Americans who took great personal risks to challenge segregation in their communities.

For example, in Montgomery, Alabama, on December 1, 1955, Mrs. Rosa Parks, a forty-two-year-old black seamstress, civil rights activist, and secretary of the local NAACP chapter, refused to give up her seat on a city bus to a white man. Like many southern communities, Montgomery, the "Cradle of the Confederacy," required blacks to sit in the rear seats of buses or trains. They could sit in the front seats designated for whites only if there were empty seats. If a white rider asked for a black to move, they were expected to go "to the back of the bus." Parks, however, was "tired of giving in" to the humiliating practice. When the bus driver told her that "niggers must move back" or he would have her arrested, she replied, with quiet courage and fierce determination, "You may do that." Police then arrested her. The next night, black community leaders met in the Dexter Avenue Baptist Church to organize a long-planned boycott of the city's bus system, 75 percent of whose riders were African Americans. Student and faculty volunteers from Alabama State University stayed up all night to distribute 35,000 flyers denouncing the arrest of Rosa Parks and urging support for the **Montgomery bus boycott**.

Montgomery bus boycott

Montgomery bus boycott
Boycott of bus system in Montgomery, Alabama, organized by civil rights activists after the arrest of Rosa Parks in 1955.

Civil disobedience *Left*: Rosa Parks is fingerprinted by a Montgomery policeman on February 22, 1956, along with about 100 others who joined the bus boycott. *Right*: Martin Luther King, Jr. is roughly arrested for loitering in 1958. He would be arrested 30 times in his life for defying racist laws.

In the Dexter Avenue church's twenty-six-year-old pastor, Martin Luther King Jr., the boycott movement found a brave and charismatic leader. Born in Atlanta, the grandson of a slave and son of a prominent minister, the short, stocky King was intelligent and courageous. He also was an eloquent and passionate speaker. "We must use the weapon of love," King told his supporters. "We must realize so many people are taught to hate us that they are not totally responsible for their hate." To his foes, the self-controlled King warned, "We will soon wear you down by our capacity to suffer, and in winning our freedom we will so appeal to your heart and conscience that we will win you in the process." King preached **nonviolent civil disobedience**, the tactic of defying unjust laws through peaceful actions, but he also valued militancy, for without confrontation with those in power there would be no negotiation or progress.

The Montgomery bus boycott achieved remarkable unity. For 381 days, African Americans, women and men, used carpools, called black-owned taxis, hitchhiked, or simply walked. White supporters also provided rides. A few boycotters rode horses or mules to work. The unprecedented mass protest infuriated many whites; police harassed and ticketed black carpools, and white thugs attacked black pedestrians. Ku Klux Klan members burned black churches and bombed houses owned by King and other boycott leaders. King himself was arrested twice. In trying to calm an angry black crowd eager for revenge against their white tormentors, he urged restraint: "Don't get panicky. Don't get your weapons. We want to love our enemies."

On December 20, 1956, the Montgomery boycotters won a federal case they had initiated against racial segregation on public buses. The Supreme Court affirmed that "the separate but equal doctrine can no longer be safely followed as a correct statement of the law." The next day, King and other African Americans boarded the buses. The success of the boycott showed

Martin Luther King's nonviolent resistance

nonviolent civil disobedience Tactic of defying unjust laws through peaceful actions championed by Dr. Martin Luther King, Jr.

that well-coordinated, nonviolent black activism could trigger major changes in public policy. Among African Americans, hope replaced resignation during the bus boycott, and action supplanted passivity. The boycott also catapulted King into the national spotlight. And what of Rosa Parks? She and her husband lost their jobs, and hate mail as well as death threats forced them to leave Alabama. They moved to Detroit, where they remained fully engaged in the evolving civil rights movement.

The Civil Rights Acts of 1957 and 1960

Civil Rights Acts (1957, 1960)

President Eisenhower's timidity in the field of race relations emerged again when he was asked to protect the right of African Americans to vote. In 1956, hoping to exploit divisions between northern and southern Democrats and to reclaim some of the black vote for Republicans, congressional leaders agreed to support what became the Civil Rights Act of 1957. The first civil rights law passed since 1875, it finally got through the Senate, after a year's delay, with the help of majority leader Lyndon B. Johnson, a Texas Democrat who knew that he could never be elected president if he was viewed as just another racist white southerner. The bill was intended to ensure that all Americans, regardless of their race or ethnicity, were allowed to vote. Although Johnson believed that the civil rights bill was just and necessary, he won southern acceptance of the bill by watering down its enforcement provisions. Eisenhower reassured Johnson that the final version represented "the mildest civil rights bill possible."

The Civil Rights Act established the Civil Rights Commission and a new Civil Rights Division in the Justice Department intended to prevent interference with the right to vote. Yet by 1959, the Civil Rights Act had not resulted in a single southern black voter being added to the rolls. Neither did the Civil Rights Act of 1960, which provided for federal courts to register African Americans to vote in districts around the country where there was a "pattern and practice" of racial discrimination. This bill, too, lacked teeth and depended upon vigorous presidential enforcement to achieve any tangible results.

Desegregation in Little Rock

Eisenhower sends federal troops to Little Rock

A few weeks after the Civil Rights Act of 1957 was passed, Arkansas's Democratic governor, Orval Faubus, a rabid segregationist eager to win a third term, called out the state's National Guard to prevent nine black students from entering Little Rock's Central High School under a federal court order. The National Guard commander's orders were explicit: "No niggers in the building." When one of the students, fifteen-year-old Elizabeth Eckford, tried to enter the school, a surging mob of jeering whites shrieked, "Lynch her! Lynch her!" Local authorities removed the students from the school in an effort to protect them, and the mayor frantically called the White House to request federal troops to stop the violence. At that point, President Eisenhower reluctantly dispatched a thousand Army paratroopers to

Little Rock to protect the brave black students as they entered the school. It was the first time since the 1870s that federal troops had been sent to the South to protect the rights of African Americans. Dunbar Ogden, a Presbyterian minister in Little Rock, found a ray of hope in the ugly confrontation: "This may be looked back upon by future historians as the turning point—for good—of race relations in this country."

The soldiers stayed in Little Rock through the school year. Unyielding southern segregationists lashed out at the president, charging that Eisenhower was violating states' rights. In 1954 Virginia senator and former governor, Harry F. Byrd, supplied a rallying cry for white diehards when he called for "**massive resistance**" against federal efforts to enforce integration in the South. Senator Richard Russell of Georgia said the paratroopers in Little Rock were be-

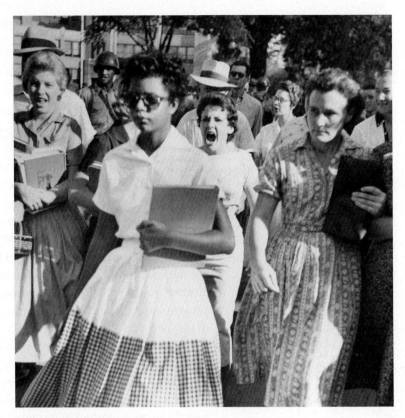

"Lynch her!" Fifteen-year-old Elizabeth Eckford endures the hostile screams of future classmates as she enters Central High School in Little Rock.

having like "Hitler's storm troopers." Eisenhower was quick to deny that he was making any moral judgment about the situation in Little Rock. He stressed that his use of federal troops had little to do with "the integration or segregation question" and everything to do with maintaining law and order. Martin Luther King Jr., who had earlier criticized Eisenhower's tepid support of civil rights, now told the president that the "overwhelming majority of southerners, Negro and white, stand behind your resolute action to restore law and order in Little Rock." Southern politicians had a different view. Many called for the president's impeachment and removal.

In the summer of 1958, Governor Faubus, supported by the state legislature, closed the Little Rock high schools rather than allow racial integration. The governor of Virginia did the same in his state. Their actions led Jonathan Daniels, editor of the Raleigh, North Carolina, *News & Observer*, to write that closing public schools is "something beyond secession from the Union; [it] is secession from civilization." Court proceedings in Arkansas dragged into 1959 before the schools were reopened. Resistance to integration in Virginia collapsed when both state and federal courts struck down state laws that had cut off funds to integrated public schools. Thereafter, massive resistance to racial integration was confined mostly to the Lower South, where five states—from South Carolina westward through

massive resistance White rallying cry for disrupting federal efforts to enforce racial integration in the South.

Louisiana—still opposed even token integration. Faubus went on to serve six terms as governor of Arkansas.

Southern Christian Leadership Conference

After the confrontation at Little Rock, progress toward greater civil rights seemed agonizingly slow. Frustrated African Americans began blaming the NAACP for relying too much on the courts to end segregation. "The Negro masses are angry and restless, tired of prolonged legal battles that end in paper decrees," reported black journalist Louis Lomax. "The organizations that understand this unrest and rise to lead it will survive; those that do not will perish."

The widespread sense of disappointment after the Little Rock incident gave Martin Luther King's nonviolent civil rights movement even greater visibility. As King explained, "We were confronted with blasted hopes, and the dark shadow of a deep disappointment settled upon us. So we had no alternative except that of preparing for direct action, whereby we would present our very bodies as a means of laying our case before the conscience of the local and national community."

Southern Christian Leadership Conference (SCLC)

On January 10, 1957, following the Montgomery bus boycott victory and consultations with Bayard Rustin, Ella Baker, and others, Dr. King invited about 60 black ministers and leaders to Ebenezer Church in Atlanta. Their goal was to form an organization to coordinate and support nonviolent direct action as a method of desegregating bus systems across the South. In addition to Rustin and Baker, the Reverend Fred Shuttlesworth of Birmingham, the Reverend Joseph Lowery of Mobile, the Reverend Ralph Abernathy of Montgomery, and the Reverend C. K. Steele of Tallahassee all played key roles in this meeting.

On February 15, a follow-up meeting was held in New Orleans. Out of these two meetings came the creation of a new organization called the **Southern Christian Leadership Conference (SCLC)**, with Dr. King as its president. Unlike the NAACP, which recruited individual members, SCLC coordinated activities on behalf of a cluster of organizations, mostly individual churches or community groups such as the Montgomery Improvement Association. Because Dr. King pushed SCLC and its member churches to take direct action against the segregated white South, only a few African American ministers were initially willing to affiliate with SCLC, for fear of a white backlash.

Southern Christian Leadership Conference (SCLC) Civil rights organization formed by Dr. Martin Luther King, Jr., that championed nonviolent direct action as a means of ending segregation.

King persisted, however, and over time SCLC grew into a powerful organization at the center of the growing civil rights movement. The civil rights activists knew that violence awaited them. Roy Wilkins, the head of the NAACP, noted that "the Negro citizen has come to the point where he is not afraid of violence. He no longer shrinks back. He will assert himself, and if violence comes, so be it." Thus began the second phase of the civil rights movement, a phase that would come to fruition in the 1960s as King and other African American activists showed the nation the courage to resist injustice, the power to love everyone, and the strength to endure discouragement and opposition.

Foreign Policy in the 1950s

CORE OBJECTIVE
5. Assess President Eisenhower's priorities in conducting the nation's foreign policy and his influence on global affairs.

The Truman administration's commitment to "contain" communism focused on the Soviet threat to Western Europe. During the 1950s, the Eisenhower administration, especially Secretary of State John Foster Dulles, expanded America's objective in the cold war. "Containment" was no longer enough; communism must be "rolled back" around the world. The Eisenhower administration soon discovered, however, that the complexities of world affairs and the realities of Soviet and Communist Chinese power made the commitment to manage the destiny of the world unrealistic—and costly.

Concluding an Armistice

A truce in Korea (1953)

To break the stalemate in the Korean peace talks, Eisenhower took the bold step in mid-May 1953 of intensifying the aerial bombardment of North Korea. The president let it be known that he would use nuclear weapons if a truce were not forthcoming. Thereafter, negotiations moved quickly toward a ceasefire agreement (called an armistice) on July 26, 1953, affirming the established border between the two Koreas just above the 38th parallel. Other factors in bringing about the armistice were China's rising military losses in the conflict and the spirit of uncertainty and caution felt by the Soviet Communists after the death of Joseph Stalin on March 5, 1953, six weeks after Eisenhower's inauguration.

Dulles and Massive Retaliation

The architect of the Eisenhower administration's efforts to "roll back" communism was Secretary of State John Foster Dulles. Like Woodrow Wilson, Dulles was a minister's son, a self-righteous and humorless statesman, and a man of immense energy and intelligence who believed that the United States was "born with a sense of destiny and mission" to lead the world. His British counterparts, however, were not impressed with his sermonizing speeches, calling them "dull, duller, Dulles."

Eisenhower's "liberation" doctrine

Dulles insisted that the Democratic policy of "containing" communism was "immoral" because it did nothing to free people from oppression. America, he argued, should instead work toward the "liberation" of the "captive peoples" of Eastern Europe and China. When George F. Kennan, the leading Soviet analyst in the State Department who had first suggested the containment doctrine, dismissed such hollow rhetoric as lunacy, Dulles fired him. Eisenhower was quick to explain that the "liberation" doctrine would not involve military force. He would promote the removal of Communist control "by every peaceful means, but only by peaceful means."

The threat of nuclear war and brinkmanship

Dulles and Eisenhower knew that the United States could not win a ground war against the Soviet Union or Communist China, both of whose armies had millions more soldiers than the United States. Nor could the administration afford—politically or financially—to sustain military expenditures at the levels required during the Korean War. So in an effort to get "more bang for the buck," Dulles and Eisenhower crafted a new strategy growing out of the Korean experience. It came to be called "**massive retaliation**," which meant using the threat of nuclear warfare ("massive retaliatory power") to prevent Communist aggression. The massive retaliation strategy, Eisenhower, Dulles, and the military chiefs argued, would provide a "maximum deterrent at bearable cost."

The strategy of promising "massive retaliation" had major weaknesses, however. By the mid-1950s, both the United States and the Soviet Union had developed hydrogen bombs, which were 750 times as powerful as the atomic bombs dropped on Japan in 1945. A single hydrogen bomb would have a devastating global impact, yet war planners envisioned using hundreds of them. "The necessary art," Dulles explained, was in the brinksmanship, "the ability to get to the verge without getting into war. . . . If you are scared to go to the brink, you are lost."

The CIA and Foreign Interventions

At the same time that Eisenhower and Dulles were publicly promoting the "liberation" of Communist nations in Europe and Asia and "massive retaliation" as a strategy against the Soviets, they were secretly using the new **Central Intelligence Agency (CIA)** to influence world politics.

CIA intervention in the Middle East and Latin America

The anti-colonial independence movements unleashed by the Second World War placed the United States in the awkward position of watching nationalist groups around the globe revolt against British and French rule. In Iran in May 1951, the parliament seized control of the nation's British-run oil industry. The following year, a newly elected prime minister, European-educated Mohammed Mossadegh, cut all diplomatic ties with Great Britain. Dulles predicted that Iran was on the verge of falling under Communist control. The CIA and the British intelligence service, MI6, then launched Operation Ajax, designed, in the words of the agency's head, Allen Dulles (the secretary of state's brother), to "bring about the fall of Mossadegh."

massive retaliation Strategy that used the threat of nuclear warfare as a means of combating the global spread of communism.

Central Intelligence Agency (CIA) Intelligence-gathering government agency founded in 1947; under President Eisenhower's orders, secretly undermined elected governments deemed susceptible to communism.

The CIA bribed Iranian army officers and hired Iranian agents to arrest Mossadegh, who was convicted of high treason. He was imprisoned for three years, then put under house arrest until his death in 1967. In return for access to Iranian oil, the U.S. government thereafter provided massive support for the anti-Communist and increasingly authoritarian regime of the shah (king) of Iran, Mohammad Reza Pahlavi, who was able to consolidate power after the removal of Mossadegh.

The success of the CIA-engineered coup in Iran emboldened Eisenhower to authorize other secret operations designed to undermine "unfriendly" government regimes. In 1954, the target was Guatemala, a desperately poor Central American country led by Colonel Jacobo Arbenz Guzman. Arbenz's decision to take over U.S.-owned property and industries in Guatemala convinced John Foster Dulles that Guatemala was falling victim to "international communism." He persuaded Eisenhower to approve a CIA operation to organize a secret Guatemalan army in Honduras. On June 18, 1954, aided by CIA-piloted warplanes, the 150 paid "liberators" crossed the border into Guatemala and forced Arbenz Guzman into exile in Mexico. The United States then installed a new ruler in Guatemala who eliminated all political opposition.

The CIA operations revealed that the United States was secretly overthrowing elected governments around the world to ensure that they did not join the Soviet bloc. The illegal operations succeeded in toppling rulers, but in doing so they destabilized Iran and Guatemala and created problems in the Middle East and Central America that would come back to haunt the United States decades later.

Indochina: Background to America's Longest War

During the fifties, the United States also became embroiled in the complex region of Southeast Asia. Indochina, created by French imperialists in the nineteenth century out of the old kingdoms of Cambodia, Laos, and Vietnam, offered a distinctive case of anti-colonial nationalism. During the Second World War, after Japanese troops occupied the region, the Viet Minh (League for the Independence of Vietnam) waged a guerrilla resistance movement. They were led by Ho Chi Minh, a seasoned revolutionary and passionate nationalist. Mild-mannered and soft-spoken, "Uncle Ho," a wispy man weighing barely a hundred pounds, worked sixteen hours each day toward a single goal: independence for his country. "You must give the people an example of poverty, misery, and denial," he explained. At the end of the war against Japan, the Viet Minh controlled part of northern Vietnam. On September 2, 1945, Ho Chi Minh proclaimed the creation of a Democratic Republic of Vietnam, with its capital in Hanoi.

The French, like the Americans would later, underestimated the determination of Ho and the Vietnamese nationalists to maintain their independence. In 1946, the First Indochina War began when Ho's fighters resisted French efforts to restore the colonial regime. French forces quickly regained control of the cities, while the Viet Minh controlled the countryside. When the Korean War ended, the United States continued its efforts to strengthen French control of Vietnam. By the end of 1953, the Eisenhower administration was paying nearly 80 percent of the cost of the French military effort, and the United States found itself at the brink of military intervention.

In December 1953, some 12,000 French soldiers parachuted into **Dien Bien Phu**, a cluster of villages in a valley ringed by mountains in northern Vietnam near the Laotian border. The French military plan, which

Ho Chi Minh Though a ruthless leader, he cultivated a humble, proletarian version of himself as Uncle Ho, a man of the people.

Dien Bien Phu Cluster of Vietnamese villages and site of a major Vietnamese victory over the French in the First Indochina War.

Dien Bien Phu Viet Minh soldiers march French captives to a prisoner camp in Dien Bien Phu on May 7, 1954.

Eisenhower deemed foolish, was to build a well-fortified base to lure Viet Minh guerrillas into the open and then overwhelm them with superior fire-power. The French assumed that the surrounding forested hills were impassable. But slowly, in single file, over 55,000 Viet Minh fighters equipped with Chinese Communist weapons took up positions atop the ridges over-looking the French military base. They laboriously dismantled cannons and carried them in pieces up the hills, then dug trenches and tunnels down into the valley. By March 1954, the French found themselves surrounded.

As the weeks passed, the French government pleaded with the United States to use its warplanes to relieve the pressure on Dien Bien Phu, which a French journalist called "Hell in a very small place." The National Security Council—Dulles, Vice President Nixon, and the chairman of the Joint Chiefs of Staff—urged Eisenhower to use atomic bombs to aid the trapped French force. Eisenhower snapped back: "You boys must be crazy. We can't use those awful things against Asians for the second time in less than ten years. My God!" The president opposed any U.S. intervention unless the British joined the effort. When they refused, Eisenhower told the French that U.S. military action in Vietnam was "politically impossible." As Eisenhower stressed, "No one could be more bitterly opposed to ever getting the U.S. involved in a hot war in that region than I am." On May 7, 1954, the Viet Minh fighters overwhelmed the last French resistance at Dien Bien Phu. The catastrophic defeat signaled the end of French colonial rule in Asia.

On July 20, 1954, representatives of France, Britain, the Soviet Union, the People's Republic of China, and the Viet Minh signed the Geneva Accords. The complex agreement gave Laos and Cambodia their independence and divided Vietnam in two at the 17th parallel. The Geneva Accords gave the Viet Minh Communists control in the North; the French would remain south of the line until nationwide elections in 1956 reunified all of Vietnam. American and South Vietnamese representatives refused to sign the Geneva Accords, arguing that the treaties legitimized the Communist victory. After 1954 Ho Chi Minh took complete control of the government in North Vietnam, executing thousands of Vietnamese he deemed opponents.

The Geneva Accords, South Vietnam, and the Viet Cong

In South Vietnam, power gravitated to a new premier chosen by the French at American urging: Ngo Dinh Diem, a Catholic nationalist who had opposed both the French and the Viet Minh. In 1954, Eisenhower began

POSTWAR ALLIANCES: THE FAR EAST

- How did the United States become increasingly involved in Vietnam?
- Why did the installation of Ngo Dinh Diem by the French and the Americans backfire and generate more conflict in Vietnam?
- Why was the protection of Taiwan important to the United States?

providing military and economic aid to Diem. The president remained opposed to the use of U.S. combat troops, believing that military intervention would lead to a costly stalemate—as indeed it eventually did. Diem's autocratic efforts to eliminate all opposition played into the hands of the Communists, who found eager recruits among the discontented South Vietnamese. By 1957, Communist guerrillas known as the **Viet Cong** were launching attacks on the Diem government. As the warfare intensified, the Eisenhower administration concluded that its only option was to "sink or swim with Diem."

Viet Cong Communist guerrillas in South Vietnam who launched attacks on the Diem government.

In 1954, Eisenhower had used what he called the "**falling domino**" **theory** to explain why the United States needed to fight communism in Vietnam: "You have a row of dominos set up, you knock over the first one, and what will happen to the last one is the certainty that it will go over very quickly." If South Vietnam were to fall to communism, he predicted, the rest of Southeast Asia would soon follow.

The domino analogy, originally used by President Truman and echoed by presidents Eisenhower, Kennedy, Johnson, and Nixon, assumed that communism was a monolithic global movement directed by Soviet leaders in Moscow. Yet anti-colonial insurgencies such as those in Southeast Asia were animated as much by nationalist motives as by ideology. The domino analogy also meant that the United States was assuming that it must police the entire world to ensure that the dominoes, no matter how small, did not begin falling. As a consequence, every insurgency around the world mushroomed into a strategic crisis.

Reelection and Foreign Crises

While Secretary of State John Foster Dulles was trying to intimidate communist governments, a new presidential campaign unfolded in 1956. Eisenhower still enjoyed widespread public support. James Reston, a political reporter for the *New York Times*, noted that the president's popularity "has got beyond the bounds of reasonable calculation and will have to be put down as a national phenomenon, like baseball." Americans had developed a "love affair" with Eisenhower. But the president's health was beginning to deteriorate. In September 1955, he suffered a heart attack, the first of three major illnesses that would affect the rest of his presidency.

In 1956, the Republicans eagerly renominated Eisenhower and Nixon. The party platform endorsed Eisenhower's "Moderate Republicanism," meaning balanced budgets, reduced government intervention in the economy, and an internationalist rather than an isolationist foreign policy. The Republicans promised "peace, progress, and prosperity," crowing that "everything's booming but the guns." The Democrats turned again to the liberal Illinois leader, Adlai Stevenson. During the last week of the campaign, fighting erupted along the Suez Canal in Egypt and in the streets of Budapest, Hungary, events that caused major international crises.

Repression in Hungary

Soviets crush Hungarian revolt

On October 23, 1956, Hungarian nationalists, encouraged by American propaganda broadcasts through Radio Free Europe, revolted against Communist troops in Budapest. The Soviets responded by sending 500,000 soldiers and 4,000 tanks into Hungary, where they killed thousands of Hungarian "freedom fighters" before installing a new puppet government.

Eisenhower offered his sympathy for the Hungarian people, but nothing more. His strategy in dealing with such crises was, as he later said, "Take a hard line—and bluff." Although he avoided war over the Soviet

falling domino theory Theory that if one country fell to communism, its neighboring countries would necessarily follow suit.

suppression of democracy in Hungary, Eisenhower had allowed administration officials, especially Secretary of State Dulles, to make reckless pledges about "rolling back" communism and "liberating" the nations of Eastern Europe. "To all those suffering under Communist slavery," Dulles promised, "let us say you can count on us."

In Hungary, the Soviets called the Eisenhower administration's bluff. The Hungarian freedom fighters, having been led to expect U.S. support, paid with their lives. Vice President Richard Nixon cynically reassured Eisenhower that the Soviet crackdown on the rebellion would be beneficial in showing the world the ruthlessness of communism. The president, however, felt pangs of guilt, telling Dulles that "we have excited Hungarians for all these years," and are "now turning our backs on them when they are in a jam." Dulles showed little concern, reminding the president that "we always have been against violent rebellion."

The Suez War

Eisenhower was more successful in handling an unexpected international crisis in Egypt, which occurred at the same time as the revolt in Hungary. In 1952, an Egyptian army officer, Gamal Abdel Nasser, had overthrown King Farouk. Once in power, Nasser set out to become the leader of the entire Arab world. To do so, he promised to destroy the new Israeli nation, created in 1948. Nasser, with Soviet support, first sought control of the Suez Canal, the crucial international waterway in Egypt connecting the Mediterranean and Red Seas. The canal had opened in 1869 as a joint French-Egyptian venture, and from 1882 on, British troops protected the canal as the British Empire's "lifeline" to India and its other Asian colonies. When Nasser's nationalist regime pressed for the withdrawal of the British forces, Eisenhower and Dulles supported the demand. In 1954, an Anglo-Egyptian treaty provided for British withdrawal within twenty months.

In 1955, Nasser, adept at playing both sides in the cold war, announced a huge arms deal with the Soviet Union. The United States countered by offering to help Egypt finance a massive hydroelectric dam at Aswan on the Nile River. In 1956, when Nasser increased trade with the Soviet bloc and recognized the People's Republic of China, Dulles abruptly cancelled the offer to fund the Aswan Dam.

Unable to retaliate directly against the United States, Nasser seized control of the Suez Canal Company and denied access to Israel-bound ships. The British and French were furious. On October 29, 1956, while Hungarian rebels were battling Soviet tanks, Israeli, British, and French forces invaded Egypt. Nasser responded by sinking all forty of the international ships then in the Suez Canal. A few days later, Anglo-French commandos and paratroopers took control of the canal.

The attack on Egypt by Britain, France, and Israel almost destroyed the NATO alliance. Eisenhower saw the military action as a revival of the "old-fashioned gunboat diplomacy" associated with colonial imperialism: "How could we possibly support Britain and France," he asked, "if in doing so we

Cease-fire in Suez crisis

lose the whole Arab world?" Eisenhower adopted a bold stance. He demanded that the British and French withdraw from the Suez Canal and that the Israelis evacuate the Sinai peninsula—or face severe economic sanctions. That the three aggressor nations grudgingly complied with a cease-fire agreement on November 7 testified to Eisenhower's strength, influence, and savvy in dealing with military matters.

The **Suez crisis** and the Hungarian revolt led Adlai Stevenson to declare the administration's foreign policy "bankrupt." Most voters, however, reasoned that the foreign turmoil spelled a poor time to switch leaders, and they handed Eisenhower an even more lopsided victory than the one in 1952. In carrying Louisiana, Eisenhower became the first Republican to win a Lower South state since Reconstruction; nationally, he carried all but seven states and won the electoral vote by 457 to 73. Eisenhower's decisive victory, however, failed to swing a congressional majority for his party in either house.

Reactions to Sputnik

Sputnik (1957)

On October 4, 1957, the Soviets launched the first communications satellite, called *Sputnik 1*. NBC News reported that it was "the most important story of the century." Americans panicked at the news. The Soviet success in space dealt a severe blow to the prestige of American science and technology, which had seemed unquestionably preeminent since the Second World War. It also changed the military balance of power. If the Soviets were so advanced in rocketry, many people reasoned, then perhaps they could hit U.S. cities with nuclear missiles. Democrats charged that the Soviets had "humiliated" the United States; they launched a congressional investigation to assess the new threat to the nation's security.

"*Sputnik* mania" led the United States to increase defense spending and establish a crash program to enhance science education. In 1958, Congress created the National Aeronautics and Space Administration (NASA) to coordinate research and development related to outer space. The same year, Congress, with Eisenhower's support, enacted the National Defense Education Act (NDEA), which authorized massive federal grants to colleges and universities to enhance education and research in mathematics, science, and modern languages, as well as for student loans and fellowships. The NDEA provided more financial aid to higher education than any other previous legislation.

The Eisenhower Doctrine

Suez crisis (1956) British, French, and Israeli attack on Egypt after Nasser's seizure of the Suez Canal; President Eisenhower interceded to demand the withdrawal of the British, French, and Israeli forces from the Sinai peninsula and the strategic canal.

In the aftermath of the Suez crisis, Eisenhower decided that the United States must replace Great Britain and France as the guarantor of Western interests in the Middle East. In 1958, Congress approved what came to be called the Eisenhower Doctrine, a resolution that promised to extend economic and military aid to Arab nations and to use armed force if necessary to assist any such nation against Communist aggression. When

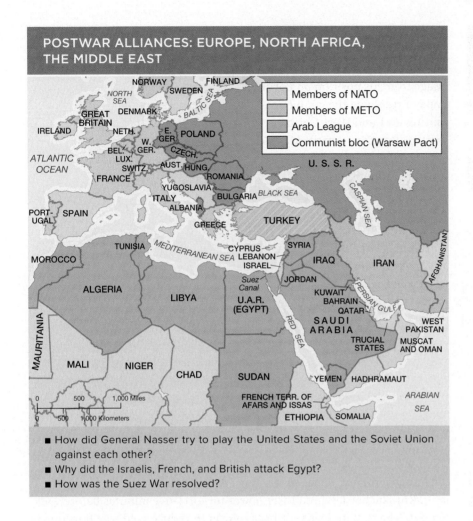

POSTWAR ALLIANCES: EUROPE, NORTH AFRICA, THE MIDDLE EAST

Legend:
- Members of NATO
- Members of METO
- Arab League
- Communist bloc (Warsaw Pact)

■ How did General Nasser try to play the United States and the Soviet Union against each other?

■ Why did the Israelis, French, and British attack Egypt?

■ How was the Suez War resolved?

Lebanon appealed to the United States to help fend off an insurgency, Eisenhower ordered 5,000 marines into the country. In October 1958, once the situation had stabilized, U.S. forces (up to 15,000 at one point) withdrew.

Crisis in Berlin

The unique problem of West Berlin, an island of Western capitalism deep in Soviet-controlled East Germany, boiled over in the late 1950s. Since the Second World War, West Berlin had served as a "showplace" of Western democracy and prosperity, a listening post for Western intelligence gathering, and a funnel through which news and propaganda from the West penetrated what British leader Winston Churchill had labeled "the iron curtain." Although East Germany had sealed its western frontiers, refugees could still pass from East to West Berlin. On November 10, 1958, however, Nikita Khrushchev, the unpredictable Soviet leader who had earlier boasted that "history is on our side. We will bury you," threatened to give East Germany control of East Berlin and of the air lanes into West Berlin. After the

Nikita Khrushchev The Soviet premier speaks on the problem of the divided city of Berlin, 1959.

U.S.–Soviet setback: The U-2 conflict; diplomatic relations with Cuba suspended

deadline he set (May 27, 1959), Western occupation authorities would have to deal with the Soviet-controlled East German government, in effect recognizing it, or face the possibility of another blockade. Eisenhower refused to budge from his position on Berlin but sought a settlement. There was little hope of resolving the conflicting views on Berlin and the possibility of reuniting East and West Germany into one nation, but the negotiations distracted attention from the May 27 deadline, which passed almost unnoticed. In September 1959, Khrushchev and Eisenhower agreed that the time was ripe for a summit meeting of the two leaders.

The U-2 Summit

The summit meeting blew up in Eisenhower's face, however. On Sunday morning, May 1, 1960, he learned that a Soviet rocket had brought down a U.S. spy plane (called the U-2) flying at 70,000 feet some 1,200 miles inside the Soviet border. Khrushchev, embarrassed by the ability of American spy planes to enter Soviet airspace, sprang a trap on Eisenhower. At first the Soviets announced only that the plane had been shot down. The U.S. government, not realizing that the Soviets had captured the downed pilot, lied by saying it was missing a weather plane over Turkey. Khrushchev then disclosed that the Soviets had American pilot Francis Gary Powers "alive and kicking" and also had the photographs he had taken of Soviet military installations. On May 11, Eisenhower abandoned U.S. efforts to cover up the incident, acknowledging that "we will now just have to endure the storm." Rather than blame others, Eisenhower took personal responsibility for the spying, explaining that such illegally obtained intelligence information was crucial to national security. At the testy summit meeting in Paris five days later, Khrushchev lectured Eisenhower for forty-five minutes before walking out. The U-2 incident set back efforts to reduce cold war tensions in Berlin and worldwide. Later, in 1962, Francis Gary Powers would be exchanged for a captured Soviet spy.

Castro's Cuba

Of all of Eisenhower's crises in foreign affairs, the greatest embarrassment was Fidel Castro's new communist regime in Cuba, which came to power on January 1, 1959, after two years of guerrilla warfare against the U.S.-supported dictator, Fulgencio Batista. Castro readily embraced Soviet support, leading a CIA agent to predict, "We're going to take care of Castro just like we took care of Arbenz [in Guatemala]." The Soviets warned that any American intervention in Cuba would trigger a military response. One of Eisenhower's last acts as president, on January 3, 1961, was to suspend diplomatic relations with Castro's Cuba. Eisenhower also authorized a secret CIA operation to train a force of Cuban refugees to oust Castro. But the final decision on the use of the anti-Castro invasion force would rest with the next president, John F. Kennedy.

Fidel Castro Castro (center) became Cuba's Communist premier in 1959 after three years of guerrilla warfare.

Assessing the Eisenhower Presidency

During President Eisenhower's second term, Congress added Alaska and Hawaii as the forty-ninth and fiftieth states (1959), while the nation experienced its worst economic slump since the Great Depression. Volatile issues such as civil rights, defense policy, and corrupt aides, including White House chief of staff Sherman Adams, Eisenhower's most trusted and influential adviser, compounded the administration's troubles. The president's desire to avoid divisive issues and maintain public goodwill led him at times to value harmony and popularity over justice. One observer called the Eisenhower years "the time of the great postponement," during which the president left domestic and foreign policies "about where he found them in 1953."

Opinion of Eisenhower's presidency has improved with time, however. After all, Eisenhower presided with steady self-confidence over a nation content with a leader whose essential virtue was prudence. He fulfilled his pledge to end the war in Korea, refused to intervene militarily in Indochina, and maintained the peace in the face of explosive global tensions. Eisenhower's greatest decisions were the wars he chose to avoid. After the truce in Korea, not a single American soldier died in combat during his two administrations, something no president since has achieved. For the most part, he acted with poise, restraint, and intelligence in managing an increasingly complex cold war that he predicted would last for decades. If Eisenhower did little to address social and racial problems, he did balance the budget while sustaining the major reforms of the New Deal. If he tolerated unemployment of as much as 7 percent, he saw to it that inflation remained minimal. Even Adlai Stevenson, defeated twice by Eisenhower, admitted that Ike's victory in 1952 had been good for America. "I like Ike, too," he said.

Eisenhower's January 17, 1961, farewell address to the American people focused on a topic never before addressed by a public official: the threat posed to government integrity by "an immense military establishment and a large arms industry." As a much-celebrated military leader, it was all the more striking for Eisenhower to highlight the dangers of a large "military-industrial complex" exerting "unwarranted influence" in Congress and the White House. "The potential for the disastrous rise of misplaced power exists and will persist," he warned. Eisenhower confessed that his greatest disappointment was that he could affirm only that "war has been avoided," not that "a lasting peace is in sight." Despite the combative language of Secretary of State John Foster Dulles, Eisenhower never promoted warfare as an instrument of foreign policy. Instead, he pledged to "do anything to achieve peace within honorable means. I'll travel anywhere. I'll talk to anyone." His successors were not as successful in keeping war at bay.

Political Consensus after World War II

President Dwight D. Eisenhower's policies and personality symbolized American politics in the 1950s. As the first Republican president since Herbert Hoover, he inherited a federal government whose roles, responsibilities, and institutions had expanded profoundly since the 1920s. An advocate of "moderate Republicanism," he did not seek to undo most of the programs created by the New Deal and Fair Deal of Presidents Roosevelt and Truman, although he complained about their expense. In comparing Eisenhower's policies and positions to those of his Democratic predecessor, Harry Truman, broad patterns of agreement are evident, reflecting a postwar consensus among the American electorate. As you review the following chart comparing the two presidents' positions on domestic policies, foreign affairs, and civil rights, consider the questions at the end of this exercise.

	Harry Truman, 1945–1953	Dwight Eisenhower, 1953–1961
Domestic Policy: "Expansion of the New Deal"	Truman's Fair Deal called for national health insurance and an expansion of many popular New Deal programs (however, most of his proposals were rejected by a conservative Congress): 1. expansion of social security coverage 2. farm subsidies 3. a higher minimum wage 4. federal aid to education 5. increased public housing 6. public works construction projects 7. opposition to the Taft-Hartley legislation	Eisenhower called for an end to "political and social engineering from the federal government" and opposed national health insurance, but he favored sustaining and expanding other popular New and Fair Deal programs: 1. expansion of social security coverage 2. support for existing farm programs 3. a higher minimum wage 4. increased spending on science education 5. increased public housing 6. major public works projects: St. Lawrence seaway and the interstate highway system 7. support for existing labor laws

	Harry Truman, 1945–1953	Dwight Eisenhower, 1953–1961
Foreign Affairs: "Policies and Strategies to Contain Communism"	**1.** Initiated a global containment strategy (the Truman Doctrine) to block Soviet expansionism after World War II. **2.** The United States joined NATO and began stationing troops in Western Europe. **3.** Committed U.S. military forces to defend noncommunist South Korea from communist North Korean aggression. **4.** Promoted military and financial assistance to nations resisting communism. Increased assistance to French forces fighting a communist independence movement in Vietnam. **5.** Sustained high defense spendings to wage the cold war and authorized the development of the hydrogen bomb.	**1.** Committed to containing the Soviet Union but also spoke of "rolling back" communism. **2.** Supported NATO and expanded American alliances to wage the cold war through covert C.I.A. operations rather than troops. **3.** Negotiated an end to the Korean War and resisted calls for military intervention in Vietnam. **4.** Empowered the CIA to covertly work to overthrow leftist regimes in Iran, Guatemala, and Cuba but did not use force to support the Hungarian revolt against Soviet Russia. Committed the United States to fighting communism in the Middle East (the Eisenhower Doctrine). Committed the United States to upholding an independent noncommunist South Vietnam. **5.** Reduced overall military spending, expanding the cold war instead through threats of nuclear retaliation.
Civil Rights: "Desegregation" and "Voting Rights"	**1.** Proposed a major civil rights bill to Congress. **2.** Through executive orders, desegregated the armed forces and banned racial discrimination in federal employment.	**1.** Supported Civil Rights Acts in 1957 and 1960 which committed the federal government to protect the voting rights of African Americans, but gave federal authorities no real power to enforce the commitment. **2.** Sent federal troops to enforce the desegregation of a high school in Little Rock in the *Brown* decision, but he never pushed Southern states to comply with the law.

QUESTIONS FOR ANALYSIS

1. How did each president view the reforms of the New Deal period and what did each believe was the role of the federal government in the nation's economic life?

2. How did Truman and Eisenhower differ in their strategies towards containing Soviet expansion abroad?

3. What role did Truman and Eisenhower believe they should play as president in addressing racial inequality?

4. In what areas do their presidencies suggest broad agreement among the American voters after World War II? Where was there less consensus?

Reviewing the
CORE OBJECTIVES | INQUIZITIVE

■ **Eisenhower's Dynamic Conservatism**
As president, Dwight Eisenhower promoted what he called *moderate Republicanism* or "dynamic conservatism." While critical of excessive government spending on social programs, he also expanded Social Security coverage and launched ambitious public works programs, such as the *Federal-Aid Highway Act* that constructed the Interstate Highway System. He opposed large budget deficits, however, and cut spending on national defense and an array of domestic programs.

■ **Growth of the U.S. Economy** High levels of federal government spending, begun before the war, continued during the postwar period. The *GI Bill of Rights* boosted home buying and helped many veterans attend college and enter the middle class. Consumer demand for homes, cars, and household goods that had been unavailable during the war fueled the economy, as did buying with new credit cards as well as demand created by the *baby boom*. After the Second World War, with the growth of *suburbia*, corporations, and advertising, America's mass culture displayed what critics called a bland sameness. A large majority of Americans, including many in the working class, experienced unprecedented rising living standards during the 1950s. But discrimination in the work force continued against African Americans, Hispanics, and women who were relegated to lower paying jobs. African Americans were largely excluded from the new suburbs, and women experienced enormous social pressure to marry and raise children as opposed to pursuing careers.

■ **Critics of Mainstream Culture**
The *Beats* rebelled against what they claimed was the suffocating conformity of middle-class life in the fifties, as did many other writers and artists. Adolescents rebelled through acts of juvenile delinquency and a new form of sexually provocative music called rock 'n' roll. Pockets of chronic poverty persisted despite record-breaking economic growth, and minorities did not prosper to the extent that white Americans did.

■ **Civil Rights Movement** During the early 1950s, the NAACP mounted legal challenges in federal courts to states requiring racially segregated public schools. In the most significant case, *Brown v. Board of Education (1954)*, the U.S. Supreme Court nullified the *separate-but-equal* doctrine. Many white southerners adopted a strategy of *massive resistance* against court-ordered desegregation. In response, civil rights activists, both blacks and whites, used *nonviolent civil disobedience* to force local and state officials to allow integration, as demonstrated in the *Montgomery bus boycott* in Alabama and the forced desegregation of public schools in Little Rock, Arkansas. Martin Luther King organized the *Southern Christian Leadership Conference (SCLC)* to rally civil rights opposition after white violence against activists in Little Rock. In 1957, the U.S. Congress passed a Civil Rights Act intended to stop discrimination against black voters in the South, but it was rarely enforced.

■ **American Foreign Policy in the 1950s**
Eisenhower's first major foreign-policy accomplishment was to end the fighting in Korea. Thereafter, Eisenhower kept the nation out of war. Instead, he relied on secret *Central Intelligence Agency (CIA)* intervention, financial and military aid, and threats of *massive retaliation* to stem the spread of communism. Though American aid was not enough to save the French at *Dien Bien Phu*, Eisenhower's belief in the *falling domino theory* deepened U.S. support for the government in South Vietnam in its war with North Vietnam and the communist *Viet Cong* insurgents. He came closest to ordering military intervention in the *Suez crisis*, but was able to mediate a solution. Closer to home, however, he approved a secret CIA operation to overthrow Fidel Castro, Cuba's communist leader.

KEY TERMS

CHRONOLOGY

1949	The first credit card is introduced
1952	Eisenhower wins the presidency
July 1953	Armistice is reached in Korea
	CIA organizes the overthrow of Mohammed Mossadegh in Iran and Jacobo Arbenz Guzman in Guatemala
1954	*Brown v. Board of Education*
July 1954	Geneva Accords adopted
December 1955	Montgomery, Alabama, bus boycott begins
1956	Elvis Presley releases "Heartbreak Hotel"
	Congress passes the Federal-Aid Highway Act
	Soviets suppress Hungarian revolt
	In Suez War, Israel, Britain, and France attack Egypt
1957	Desegregation of Central High School in Little Rock, Arkansas
	Soviet Union launches *Sputnik 1* satellite
	Baby boom peaks
1959	Fidel Castro seizes power in Cuba
1960	The U-2 incident

INQUIZITIVE

Go to InQuizitive to see what you've learned—and learn what you've missed—with personalized feedback along the way.

***SKYWAY* (1964)** With new frontiers came new fears. Artist Robert Rauschenberg's collage encapsulates the turbulence of the sixties: the stark collisions of the old and the new, and the total disorder of it all. John F. Kennedy, early manned space flights, and the Vietnam War are suspended within the childish form of the collage, making Rauschenberg's message all the more foreboding.

New Frontiers

1960-1968

For those who considered the social and political climate of the fifties dull, the following decade provided a striking contrast. The sixties were years of extraordinary social turbulence and liberal activism, tragic assassinations and painful trauma. Assassins killed four of the most important leaders of the time: John F. Kennedy, Malcolm X, Martin Luther King, and Robert F. Kennedy. The "politics of expectation" that a British journalist said shone brightly in Kennedy's short tenure as president did not die with the president in November 1963. Instead, Kennedy's idealistic commitment to improving America's quality of life—for everyone—was given new meaning and energy by his very different successor, Texan Lyndon B. Johnson, whose War on Poverty and Great Society programs outstripped Franklin Roosevelt's New Deal in their scope and promises.

Johnson's remarkable energy and legislative savvy resulted in a blizzard of new federal programs. At the same time, many social issues that had been ignored or postponed for decades—civil rights for minorities, equality for women, gay rights, federal aid to the poor—forced their way to the forefront of national concerns. In the end, however, Lyndon Johnson promised too much. The elaborate Great Society programs fell victim to unrealistic hopes, poor execution, and the nation's expanding involvement with the war in Vietnam. The deeply entrenched assumptions of the cold war against global communism led the nation into the longest, most controversial, and least successful war in its history to that point.

1. Assess President John F. Kennedy's efforts to contain communism abroad and pursue civil rights and other social programs at home.

2. Describe the strategies and achievements of the civil rights movement in the 1960s, and explain the divisions that emerged among its activists during the decade.

3. Analyze Lyndon B. Johnson's War on Poverty and Great Society initiatives, and evaluate their impact on American society.

4. Explain Presidents Kennedy and Johnson's motivations for deepening America's military involvement in the Vietnam War and appraise their efforts to preserve a noncommunist South Vietnam.

5. Examine the presidential election of 1968 and explain the issues that propelled Richard Nixon to victory.

CORE **OBJECTIVE**

1. Assess President John F. Kennedy's efforts to contain communism abroad and pursue civil rights and other social programs at home.

The New Frontier

In his 1960 speech accepting the Democratic presidential nomination, John F. Kennedy showcased the muscular language that would stamp the rest of his campaign and his presidency: "We stand today on the edge of a **New Frontier**—the frontier of unknown opportunities and perils—a frontier of unfulfilled hopes and threats." Kennedy and his staff fastened upon the frontier metaphor as the label for their proposed domestic program because they believed that Americans had always been adventurers, eager to conquer and exploit new frontiers. Kennedy promised that if elected he would get the country "moving again" and be a more aggressive cold warrior than Eisenhower.

Kennedy versus Nixon

In 1960, the presidential election pitted two candidates—Vice President Richard M. Nixon and Massachusetts senator John F. Kennedy (JFK)—of similar ages but contrasting personalities and backgrounds. As the popular Eisenhower's partner over successive terms, Nixon was assured the Republican nomination for president in 1960. A native of California, he had fought tenaciously to be a success, first as an attorney, then as a congressman. He had come to Washington eager to reverse the tide of New Deal liberalism. His visibility among Republicans benefited from his leadership of the anti-Communist hearings in Congress during the McCarthy hysteria.

New Frontier Proposed domestic program championed by the incoming Kennedy administration in 1961 that aimed to jump-start the economy and trigger social progress.

All his life, Nixon had had to claw and struggle to the top. Now he had the presidency within his grasp. But Nixon, graceless, awkward, and stiff, proved to be one of the most complicated and most interesting political figures in American history.

By 1960, Vice President Nixon had developed the reputation for being a cunning deceiver, the "Tricky Dick" who concealed his real ideas and bigoted attitudes. Kennedy told an aide that "Nixon doesn't know who he is . . . so every time he makes a speech he has to decide which Nixon he is, and that will be very exhausting."

The forty-three-year-old Kennedy had not distinguished himself in the House or the Senate, but he was handsome and charming, and he had the energy and wit to match his grace and ambition. He also had a bright, agile mind, a quick wit, a Harvard education, a record of heroism in the

The Kennedy–Nixon debates Nixon's decision to debate his less prominent opponent on television backfired.

Second World War, a rich and powerful Roman Catholic family, and a beautiful, accomplished, and young wife, only 32 years-old. In the words of a southern senator, Kennedy combined "the best qualities of Elvis Presley and Franklin D. Roosevelt"—a combination that played well in the first-ever televised presidential debate. Some 70 million people tuned in and saw an obviously uncomfortable Nixon, still weak from a recent illness, perspiring heavily and looking pale, haggard, and even sinister before the camera. Kennedy, on the other hand, appeared tanned and calm, projected a cool poise, and offered crisp answers that made him seem Nixon's equal, if not superior, in his fitness for the nation's highest office.

John Kennedy's political rise owed much to the effective public relations campaign engineered by his father, Joseph Kennedy, a self-made tycoon with a genius for promotion. "Can't you get it into your head," the elder Kennedy told John, "that it's not important what you *really* are? The only important thing is what people *think* you are." To ensure that people thought well of his son, the elder Kennedy hired writers to produce his son's two books, paid a publisher to print them, purchased thousands of copies to make them "best sellers," and helped engineer his son's elections to the Congress and Senate.

Yet much of the glamour surrounding Kennedy was cosmetic. Despite his athletic interests and robust appearance, he suffered from lifelong health problems: Addison's disease (a debilitating disorder of the adrenal glands), venereal disease, chronic back pain, and fierce fevers. He took powerful prescription medicines daily, sometimes hourly. Like Franklin D. Roosevelt, he and his aides and family members masked from the public his physical ailments—as well as his reckless sexual forays.

The momentum that Kennedy gained from the first debate with Nixon was not enough to ensure his victory. The Democratic candidate became a relentless campaigner—traveling 65,000 miles, visiting 25 states, and making over 350 speeches—including an address to Protestant ministers in Texas in which he neutralized concerns about his being a Roman Catholic by stressing that the pope in Rome would never "tell the President—should he be a Catholic—how to

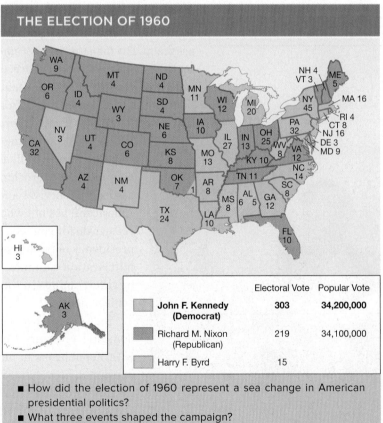

THE ELECTION OF 1960

		Electoral Vote	Popular Vote
	John F. Kennedy (Democrat)	**303**	**34,200,000**
	Richard M. Nixon (Republican)	219	34,100,000
	Harry F. Byrd	15	

■ How did the election of 1960 represent a sea change in American presidential politics?
■ What three events shaped the campaign?
■ How did John F. Kennedy win the election in spite of winning fewer states than Richard M. Nixon?

act." Kennedy also worked to increase the registration of African American voters across the nation, and he won the hearts of many black voters by helping to get Martin Luther King Jr. out of a Georgia jail after he had been convicted of "trespassing" in an all-white restaurant. "I've got a suitcase of votes," explained King's appreciative father, "and I'm going to take them to Mr. Kennedy and dump them in his lap." On the Sunday before election day, a million leaflets about Kennedy's enabling King's release from prison were distributed in African American churches across the nation.

When the votes were counted, Kennedy and his running mate, the powerful Texas senator Lyndon B. Johnson, had won the closest presidential election since 1888. The winning margin was only 118,574 votes out of more than 68 million cast. Nixon had carried more states than Kennedy, sweeping most of the West and holding four of the six southern states that Eisenhower had carried in 1956. But Kennedy won 70 percent of the black vote, which proved decisive in at least three key states.

A Vigorous New Administration

Kennedy's New Frontier

John F. Kennedy was the youngest person and first Roman Catholic elected president. His inauguration ceremony on a cold, clear, blustery January day set the tone of youthful elegance, charm, and energy that would come to be called the *Kennedy style*. In his inaugural speech, the president quite intentionally spoke as the leader of "a new generation of Americans," implying that Eisenhower had come to represent older Americans. Kennedy dazzled listeners with uplifting words: "Let every nation know, whether it wishes us well or ill, that we shall pay any price, bear any burden, meet any hardship, support any friend, oppose any foe, to assure the survival and success of liberty. And so, my fellow Americans: ask not what your country can do for you—ask what *you* can do for your country." Such inspiring language heralded a presidency of fresh promise and new beginnings, an activist administration committed to bringing together the "best and the brightest" minds in the nation to fashion a new era in political achievement.

Yet Kennedy had a difficult time launching his New Frontier domestic program. Conservative southern Democrats joined with Republicans to block his efforts to increase federal aid to education, provide medical insurance for the aged, and create a cabinet-level department of urban affairs and housing to address poverty in the inner cities. Legislators did approve the Peace Corps, created in 1961 to recruit idealistic young volunteers who would provide educational and technical service abroad, and also the Alliance for Progress, a financial assistance program to Latin American countries intended to blunt the appeal of communism in those nations. The Kennedy administration further persuaded Congress to increase the minimum wage

Jack and Jackie Young, refined, and fabulous, the Kennedys were instant celebrities. Women teased their hair into the First Lady's famous hairdo, while men craved JFK's effortless cool.

and pass a Housing Act that earmarked nearly $5 billion for new public housing projects in poverty-stricken inner-city areas. Kennedy also won support for an accelerated space program with the audacious goal of landing astronauts on the moon before the end of the decade.

Kennedy and Civil Rights

The most important development in domestic life during the sixties occurred in civil rights. Throughout the South, racial segregation remained firmly in place. Signs outside public restrooms distinguished between "Whites" and "Colored"; restaurants declared "Colored Not Allowed," or "Colored Served Only in Rear." Stores prohibited African Americans from trying on clothes before buying them. Witnesses in courtrooms were sworn in with their hands placed on different Bibles, depending on their race. Despite the *Brown v. Board of Education* ruling in 1954, many public schools across the South remained segregated and unequal in quality.

Like Franklin D. Roosevelt, John F. Kennedy celebrated racial equality but did little to promote it until events forced him to do so. He was reluctant to challenge conservative southern Democrats on the explosive issue of segregation. Both he and his brother Robert ("Bobby"), the attorney general as well as the president's closest adviser, had to be dragged unwillingly into actively supporting the civil rights movement.

Catastrophe in Cuba

Kennedy's record in foreign relations, as in domestic affairs, was mixed, but more spectacularly so. Although he had told a reporter that he wanted to "break out of the confines of the Cold War," he quickly found himself reinforcing its confining assumptions. While still a senator, Kennedy had blasted Eisenhower for not being tough enough with the Soviets and for allowing Fidel Castro and his Communist followers to take over Cuba in 1959.

Walk of shame Captured anti-Castro Cubans at the Bay of Pigs.

Soon after his inauguration, Kennedy learned that a secret CIA operation, approved by Eisenhower, was training 1,500 anti-Castro Cubans for an invasion of their homeland. U.S. military leaders assured Kennedy that the invasion plan (Operation Trinidad) was feasible; CIA analysts predicted that news of the invasion would inspire anti-Castro Cubans to rebel against their Communist dictator. In reality, the covert operation had little chance of succeeding. When the ragtag force, transported on American ships, landed at the **Bay of Pigs** on Cuba's south shore on April 17, 1961, it was

Bay of Pigs (1961) Failed CIA operation that deployed Cuban rebels to overthrow Fidel Castro's Communist regime.

Severed ties Two West Berliners climb the newly constructed Berlin Wall to communicate with a family member at an open window.

quickly defeated. Kennedy panicked when he realized the operation was failing and refused desperate pleas from the Cuban rebels for "promised" support from U.S. warplanes. A *New York Times* columnist reported that the Americans involved in the botched invasion "looked like fools to our friends, rascals to our enemies, and incompetents to the rest." The clumsy effort to overthrow the Cuban government humiliated the new American president. To his credit, Kennedy admitted that the Bay of Pigs invasion was a "colossal mistake" and "the worst experience of my life."

The Vienna Summit

Berlin Wall

Just six weeks after the Bay of Pigs fiasco, Kennedy, heavily medicated because of chronic back pain, met Soviet premier Nikita Khrushchev at a summit conference in Vienna, Austria. Khrushchev bullied the young president and threatened to limit American access to Berlin, the divided city inside Communist East Germany. Kennedy, desperate not to appear weak, responded by calling up Army Reserve and National Guard units to protect West Berlin. Then on August 13, 1961, the Soviets decided to stop all traffic between East and West Berlin by erecting the twenty-seven-mile-long **Berlin Wall**, made of concrete and topped with barbed wire. For the United States, the wall became a powerful propaganda weapon. As Kennedy said, "Freedom has many difficulties and democracy is not perfect, but we have never had to put up a wall to keep our people in."

The Berlin Wall demonstrated the Soviets' willingness to challenge American resolve in Europe. Kennedy and Secretary of Defense Robert McNamara responded by embarking upon the most intensive arms race in history, increasing the number of nuclear missiles fivefold, adding 300,000 men to the armed forces, and creating the U.S. Special Forces

Berlin Wall Twenty-seven-mile-long concrete wall constructed in 1961 by East German authorities to stop the flow of East Germans fleeing to West Berlin.

(Green Berets), an elite group of commandos specializing in guerrilla warfare who could provide a "more flexible response" than nuclear weapons to "hotspots" around the world and enable the United States to wage small wars in faraway lands.

| Green Berets |

The Cuban Missile Crisis

In the fall of 1962, Nikita Khrushchev and the Soviets posed another challenge to Kennedy, this time only ninety miles off the Florida coast. To protect Communist Cuba from another American-backed invasion, Khrushchev approved the secret installation of Soviet missiles on the island nation. The Soviets felt they were justified in doing so because the United States had earlier installed missiles with nuclear warheads in Turkey, along the Soviet border.

| Soviet missiles in Cuba |

On October 16, 1962, photos taken by U.S. spy planes revealed the Soviet missile sites in Cuba. Although the Soviet actions violated no law or treaty, Kennedy decided that the forty or so missiles had to be removed. But how? As the air force chief of staff told Kennedy, "You're in a pretty bad fix, Mr. President."

Over the next thirteen days, perhaps the most dangerous two weeks in history, Kennedy and the National Security Council (NSC) discussed several possible responses, ranging from doing nothing to invading Cuba. The commander of the Marines at one point reminded the group that the missiles in Cuba were not a true threat. The Soviet Union "has a hell of a lot better way to attack us than to attack us from Cuba." Yet the group insisted that the missiles be removed for symbolic reasons.

| Naval quarantine of Cuba |

At that point, the world came closer to a war involving the exchange of nuclear weapons than it ever has before or since. Kennedy and the NSC discussed in some detail the unthinkable possibility of a nuclear war, even estimating the damage that atomic bombs might inflict on major cities. Eventually, however, the group narrowed the options to a choice between a "surgical" air strike on the missiles and a naval blockade of Cuba. Although the military advisers urged bombing the missile sites followed by an invasion of the island, Kennedy chose the naval blockade, which was carefully disguised by calling it a *quarantine*, since a *blockade* is technically an act of war.

On Monday night, October 22, President Kennedy delivered a solemn speech to the world, announcing that the U.S. Navy was establishing a naval quarantine of Cuba to prevent Soviet ships from delivering the goods and weapons that the island nation depended on. He urged the Soviets to "move the world back from the abyss of destruction."

Tensions grew as Khrushchev replied that Soviet ships would ignore the quarantine. He accused Kennedy of "an act of aggression propelling humankind into the abyss of a world nuclear-missile war." Despite such rhetoric, however, on Wednesday, October 24, five Soviet ships, presumably with more missiles aboard, stopped well short of the quarantine line.

| Soviets remove missiles under nuclear threat |

Two days later, Khrushchev, knowing that the U.S. still enjoyed a 5 to 1 advantage in nuclear weapons, offered a deal. The Soviets would remove the missiles in return for a *public* pledge by the United States not to invade Cuba—and a *secret* agreement to remove U.S. missiles from Turkey. Kennedy agreed. Secretary of State Dean Rusk stressed to a newscaster, "Remember, when you report this, [say] that eyeball to eyeball, they [the Soviets] blinked first."

In the aftermath of the **Cuban missile crisis**, tensions between the United States and the Soviet Union subsided, in part because of several symbolic steps: an agreement to sell the Soviet Union surplus American wheat, the installation of a "hotline" telephone between Washington and Moscow to provide instant contact between the heads of government, and the removal of aging U.S. missiles from Turkey, Italy, and Britain.

Controlling Atomic Weapons

Test Ban Treaty: Bans testing of nuclear weapons in the atmosphere

Going to the edge of nuclear war over Soviet missiles in Cuba led Kennedy and others in the administration to soften their cold war rhetoric and pursue other ways to reduce the threat of atomic warfare. As Kennedy told his advisers at a White House meeting, "It is insane that two men, sitting on opposite sides of the world, should be able to decide to bring an end to civilization." In June 1963, the president began discussions with the Soviets to reduce the risk of nuclear war. "If we cannot end our differences," he said, "at least we can help make the world a safe place for diversity." After two months of difficult negotiations, those discussions resulted in the Test Ban Treaty with the Soviet Union and Great Britain, ratified in September 1963, which banned the testing of nuclear weapons in the atmosphere. It was an important move toward improved relations with the Soviet Union. As Kennedy put it, using an ancient Chinese proverb, "A journey of a thousand miles begins with one step."

Kennedy and Vietnam

Military advisers in Vietnam

As tensions with the Soviet Union eased, a new crisis was growing in Southeast Asia, where events were moving toward what would eventually become the greatest American foreign-policy calamity of the century. The situation in South Vietnam had worsened under the corrupt leadership of Premier Ngo Dinh Diem and his family. He had backed away from promised social and economic reforms, and his repressive tactics, directed not only against Communists but also against the Buddhist majority and other critics, played into the hands of his enemies. Kennedy continued to dispatch military "advisers" to South Vietnam in the hope of stabilizing the situation (they were called advisers to avoid the impression that U.S. troops were doing the fighting). When he took office, the United States had 2,000 troops in Vietnam; by the end of 1963, there were 16,000, all of whom were officially classified as advisers rather than combatants.

Cuban missile crisis (1962) Thirteen-day U.S.-Soviet standoff sparked by the discovery of Soviet missile sites in Cuba; closest the world has come to nuclear war since 1945.

United States backs coup in South Vietnam

By 1963, Kennedy was receiving sharply conflicting reports from South Vietnam. U.S. military analysts expressed confidence in the Army of the Republic of Vietnam. On-site journalists, however, predicted civil turmoil as long as Diem remained in power. By midyear, frequent Buddhist demonstrations against Diem ignited widespread discontent. The spectacle of Buddhist monks setting themselves on fire in public squares to protest government tyranny stunned Americans. By the fall of 1963, the Kennedy administration had decided that the autocratic Diem was "out of touch with his people" and had to go. On November 1, army generals seized the South Vietnamese government but then took a step that Kennedy had neither intended nor expected: they murdered Diem and his brother. The rebel generals, however, provided no more political stability than had Diem, and successive coups set the fragile country spinning from one military leader to another.

By September 1963, Kennedy seemed to have developed doubts about the ability of the United States to prop up the South Vietnamese government. When asked about the South Vietnamese effort to hold off Communist insurgents, he replied: "In the final analysis it's their war. They're the ones who have to win it or lose it. We can help them as advisers but they have to win it."

Kennedy's Assassination

By the fall of 1963, John F. Kennedy had matured a great deal as president. Not only had he come to understand the urgency and momentum of the civil rights movement, he also had come to see the cold war as a more complex issue than he had believed during his first year in office. In October 1963, he announced his intention to withdraw U.S. forces from South Vietnam by the end of 1965.

What Kennedy would have done thereafter in Vietnam has remained a matter of endless discussion, because on November 22, 1963, while riding in an open car through Dallas, Texas, he was shot and killed by Lee Harvey Oswald, a twenty-four-year-old ex-Marine turned Communist who worked in the Texas School Book Depository, from which he fired at Kennedy with a rifle. Debate still swirls about whether Oswald acted alone or was part of a conspiracy to assassinate the president, in part because Oswald did not live long enough to tell his story. As Oswald was being transported to a court hearing, Jack Ruby, a Dallas nightclub owner distraught over Kennedy's death, shot and killed a handcuffed Oswald as a nationwide television audience watched.

Kennedy's shocking assassination and his heartrending funeral enshrined the young president in the public imagination as a martyred leader cut down in the prime of his life. His short-lived but drama-filled presidency had flamed up and out like a comet hitting the earth's atmosphere. Americans wept in the streets, and the world was on edge as the wounded nation welcomed a new and very different president.

CORE **OBJECTIVE**

2. Describe the strategies and achievements of the civil rights movement in the 1960s, and explain the divisions that emerged among its activists during the decade.

Expansion of the Civil Rights Movement

After the Montgomery bus boycott of 1955–1956, Martin Luther King Jr.'s philosophy of militant nonviolence stirred others to challenge the deeply entrenched patterns of racial segregation in the South. The civil rights movement had challenged the complacent prosperity of the fifties, and many young adults were inspired by Kennedy's direct appeals to youthful idealism. Thousands enrolled in the Peace Corps and others joined African Americans in the fight for civil rights.

Sit-Ins

The Greensboro Four: Lunch counter "sit-ins"

The civil rights movement gained added momentum when four polite, well-dressed black college students sat down and ordered coffee and doughnuts at an "all-white" Woolworth's lunch counter in Greensboro, North Carolina, on February 1, 1960. The clerk refused to serve them, explaining that blacks had to eat standing up or take their food outside. The Greensboro Four, as the students came to be called, waited for forty-five minutes and then returned the next day with two dozen more students. Along with others, they returned every day for a week, patiently tolerating being jeered at, jostled, and spat upon by white hooligans.

The "sit-in" movement spread quickly to six more towns in the state, and within two months similar sit-ins—involving 50,000 blacks and whites, men and women, young and old—had occurred in over a hundred cities in thirteen states. Some 3,600 people had been arrested. By the end of July 1960, officials in Greensboro lifted the whites-only policy at the Woolworth's lunch counter. The civil rights movement had found an effective new tactic: nonviolent sit-ins against segregation.

In April 1960, some 200 college student activists, black and white, had converged in Raleigh, North Carolina, to form the **Student Nonviolent Coordinating Committee** (**SNCC**—pronounced "snick"). The goal of what they came to call "the movement" was to intensify the effort to dismantle segregation. SNCC broadened the sit-ins, which began at restaurants, to include "kneel-ins" at all-white churches and "wade-ins" at segregated public swimming pools. In many communities, demonstrators were pelted with rocks, burned with cigarettes, subjected to unending verbal abuse, and even killed by white racists. As a Florida hog farmer named Holstead "Hoss" Manucy explained to a journalist, "I ain't got no bad habits. Don't smoke. Don't cuss. My only bad habit is fightin' niggahs."

Freedom Rides

Student Nonviolent Coordinating Committee (SNCC) Interracial organization formed in 1960 with the goal of intensifying the effort to end racial segregation.

In 1961, civil rights leaders decided to put "the movement on wheels" by integrating public transportation: buses and trains. Their larger goal was to force the Kennedy administration to engage the cause of civil rights in the Democratic South. On May 4, the New York–based Congress of Racial

Civil rights and its peaceful warriors *Left*: The Greensboro Four—(*listed from left*) Joseph McNeil, Franklin McCain, Billy Smith, and Clarence Henderson—await service on day two of their sit-in at the Woolworth's. *Right*: On May 14, 1961, a white mob assaulted a Freedom Bus, flinging fire bombs into its windows and beating the activists as they emerged. Here, the surviving Freedom Riders sit outside the burnt shell of their bus.

Equality (CORE), led by James Farmer, sent a courageous group of eighteen black and white **Freedom Riders**, as they were called, on two public buses from Washington, D.C., through the Lower South to New Orleans. They wanted to test a federal court ruling that banned racial segregation on buses and trains, and in terminals. Farmer warned Attorney General Robert F. Kennedy that the bus riders would probably be attacked as they traveled through the South.

The warning was well founded, for on May 14, a mob of white racists in rural Alabama, many of them members of the Ku Klux Klan, surrounded the Greyhound bus carrying the Freedom Riders. After throwing a firebomb into the bus, angry whites barricaded the bus's door. "Burn them alive," one of them yelled. "Fry the damned niggers." After the gas tank exploded, the riders were able to escape the burning bus, only to be battered by metal pipes, chains, and clubs.

A few hours later, Freedom Riders on a second bus were beaten by whites armed with bats and chains after entering whites-only waiting rooms at the bus terminal in Birmingham. The police, as it turned out, had encouraged the beatings. Alabama's governor complained that the Freedom Riders were violating "our law and customs." The next day, the Freedom Riders wanted to continue their trip, but the bus drivers refused.

When Diane Nash, a fearless black college student and SNCC leader in Nashville, Tennessee, heard about the violence in Birmingham, she recruited new riders. On May 17, Nash and ten students took a bus to Birmingham, where they were arrested. While in jail, the students sang

| Freedom Riders |

Freedom Riders Activists who, beginning in 1961, traveled by bus through the South to test federal court rulings that banned segregation on buses and trains.

"freedom songs": "We'll Never Turn Back," "Ain't Gonna Let Nobody Turn Me Around," "We Shall Overcome." Eugene "Bull" Connor, the notoriously racist police chief, grew so frustrated at their joyous rebelliousness that he drove them in the middle of the night to the Tennessee state line and dropped them off to walk, saying, "I couldn't stand your singing." Instead of going to Nashville, however, the gutsy students returned to Birmingham.

President Kennedy was not inspired by the courageous Freedom Riders, in part because he was preoccupied with the crisis with the Soviet Union over Berlin. The president and his brother dismissed the Freedom Riders as "publicity seekers."

The demonstrators persisted, finally forcing the president to provide another bus which enabled them to renew the journey to New Orleans. When the new group of Freedom Riders reached Montgomery, the capital of Alabama, they were attacked. The next night, civil rights activists gathered at a Montgomery church to honor the Freedom Riders, but their meeting was interrupted by a rampaging mob of whites armed with rocks and fire bombs. Ministers made frantic appeals to the White House. President Kennedy responded by urging the Alabama governor to intervene. After midnight, National Guardsmen arrived to disperse the mob. The Freedom Riders continued into Mississippi, where they were imprisoned. They never made it to New Orleans.

Integration of interstate transportation facilities

Still, they succeeded in their larger goal. The courage and principled resistance of the Freedom Riders—and of federal judges across the nation whose rulings supported integration efforts—led the Interstate Commerce Commission (ICC) in September 1961 to order that all interstate transportation facilities be integrated. The Freedom Riders had worked and were a turning point in the civil rights movement. Widespread media coverage showed the nation that the nonviolent protesters were prepared to die for their rights rather than continue to endure racist assaults on their dignity.

James Meredith

Desegregating the University of Mississippi

In the fall of 1962, James Meredith, an African American student and Air Force veteran whose grandfather had been a slave, tried to enroll at the all-white University of Mississippi in Oxford. Ross Barnett, the governor of Mississippi, refused to allow Meredith to register for classes. Robert F. Kennedy then dispatched federal marshals to enforce the law. When the marshals were assaulted by a white mob shouting "Go to Hell, JFK," President Kennedy sent National Guard troops (all white). The arrival of soldiers on the campus ignited rioting that left two dead and dozens injured. Once the violence subsided, however, James Meredith was registered at the university. "Only in America," a reporter noted, "would the federal government send thousands of troops to enforce the right of an otherwise obscure citizen to attend a particular university."

Birmingham

Several months later, in early 1963, in conjunction with the celebration of the hundredth anniversary of Abraham Lincoln's Emancipation Proclamation, Martin Luther King Jr. announced that he and other civil rights activists were fed up "with tokenism and gradualism and see-how-far-you've-comeism. We can't wait any longer. Now is the time." He then defied the wishes of President Kennedy by organizing a massive series of demonstrations against segregation in Birmingham, Alabama, a state presided over by a feisty new racist governor—George Wallace—who had vowed to protect "segregation now, segregation tomorrow, segregation forever!" King knew that demonstrations in Birmingham would likely provoke violence, but a hard-won victory there, he felt, would build national support and "break the back of segregation all over the nation."

As King and other activists led demonstrations through Birmingham streets in April, the all-white police force led by Bull Connor used snarling dogs, tear gas, electric cattle prods, and fire hoses on the protesters. Millions of Americans across the nation were outraged when they saw the ugly confrontations on television. "The civil rights movement," President Kennedy observed, "owes Bull Connor as much as it owes Abraham Lincoln." It also owed a lot to the power of television, which brought the savagery of racism into millions of American homes.

> Nonviolent civil disobedience: King's "Letter from Birmingham City Jail"

More than 3,000 demonstrators were arrested in Birmingham, including Dr. King. While in jail, he wrote a "Letter from Birmingham City Jail," a stirring defense of "**nonviolent civil disobedience**" that has since become a classic document of the civil rights movement. "One who breaks an unjust law," King stressed, "must do so openly, lovingly, and with a willingness to *accept the penalty*." King's efforts prevailed when Birmingham

Bull's dogs Eugene "Bull" Connor ordered Birmingham police to unleash their dogs on civil rights demonstrators in May of 1963.

officials finally agreed to end their segregationist practices. White racists did not change overnight, however. One angry Alabaman sent a letter to King: "This isn't a threat but a promise—your head will be blown off as sure as Christ made green apples."

Throughout the Lower South, whites defied efforts at racial integration. On June 11, 1963, Alabama governor George Wallace personally blocked the door at the University of Alabama as African American students tried to register for classes. Wallace finally stepped aside in the face of insistent

nonviolent civil disobedience The principled tactic that Martin Luther King Jr. advocated: peaceful lawbreaking as a means of ending segregation.

federal marshals and army troops. That night President Kennedy told the nation that he was urging Congress to pass a major new civil rights bill. Four hours later, an African American civil rights activist, Medgar Evers, was shot to death in his driveway in Jackson, Mississippi. Such violence aroused the nation's indignation and elevated civil rights as America's most pressing social issue. Yet southern Democrats in Congress blocked Kennedy's civil rights bill.

"I Have a Dream!"

Nonviolent civil disobedience: March on Washington

The standoff in Congress led African American leaders to take a bold step. On August 28, some 250,000 blacks and whites of all ages, many of them schoolchildren brought on buses for the occasion, marched arm-in-arm down the Mall in Washington, D.C., chanting "Equality Now!" and singing "We Shall Overcome."

The **March on Washington** for Jobs and Freedom was the largest political demonstration in American history. The organizers, primarily civil rights veterans Bayard Rustin and A. Philip Randolph, never imagined that so many people would participate. "When you looked at the crowd," remembered a U.S. Park Service ranger, "you didn't see blacks or whites. You saw America." Prominent entertainers Mahalia Jackson, Marian Anderson, Joan Baez, Bob Dylan, Odetta, and Peter, Paul, and Mary sang protest songs, and civil rights activists gave speeches calling for racial justice.

Then something remarkable happened. Standing on the steps of the Lincoln Memorial, 34-year-old Martin Luther King Jr., who in recent years had been attacked four times, had seen his home bombed three times, and had been arrested fourteen times, spoke to the huge crowd. He began awkwardly. Noticing his nervousness, someone on stage urged him to "tell 'em about the dream." As if suddenly inspired, King set aside his prepared remarks and delivered an extraordinary speech. He started slowly and picked up speed, as if he were speaking at a revival, giving poetic voice to the hopes of millions as he stressed the "fierce urgency of now" and the unstoppable power of "meeting physical force with soul force." President Kennedy, who earlier had tried to convince organizers to call off the march, was watching King's speech on TV at the White House, just a mile away. As King spoke, the president told an aide that "he's damn good."

Dr. King then shared his dream of an America in which the ideal of equality would be realized:

> In spite of the difficulties and frustrations of the moment, I still have a *dream*. It is a *dream* deeply rooted in the American dream. I have a *dream* that one day this nation will rise up and live out the true meaning of its creed: 'We hold these truths to be self-evident; that all men are created equal.' I have a *dream* that one day . . . the sons of former slaves and the sons of former slaveowners will be able to sit together at the table of brotherhood.

March on Washington (1963)
Civil rights demonstration on the National Mall, where Martin Luther King, Jr. gave his famous "I Have a Dream" speech.

As if at a massive church service, many in the crowd began shouting "Amen!" as King summoned a flawed nation to justice: "So let freedom ring!" he shouted, for "when we allow freedom to ring from every town and every hamlet, from every state and every city, we will be able to speed up the day when *all* God's children—black men and white men, Jews and Gentiles, Protestants and Catholics—will be able to join hands and sing in the words of the old Negro spiritual, *"Free at last, free at last, thank God Almighty, we are free at last!"* As King finished, there was a startling hush, then a deafening ovation. The crowd spontaneously began singing "We Shall Overcome," holding hands and swaying as if at a prayer meeting.

King's dream of ending racial violence remained just that—a dream. Eighteen days after the March on Washington, four Klansmen in Birmingham detonated a bomb in a black church, killing four young girls. The awful murders sparked indignation across the country—and around the world. The editors of the *Milwaukee Sentinel* stressed that the Birmingham bombing "should serve to goad the conscience. The deaths . . . in a sense are on the hands of each of us."

The Warren Court

The civil rights movement depended as much on the courts as it did on the leadership of Dr. King and others, and federal judges kept forcing states and localities to integrate schools and other public places. Under Chief Justice Earl Warren, the U.S. Supreme Court also made landmark decisions in other areas of American life.

> Federal Courts force integration in schools and public places

In 1962, the Court ruled that a school prayer adopted by the New York State Board of Regents violated the constitutional prohibition against government-supported religion. In *Gideon v. Wainwright* (1963), the Court required that every felony defendant be provided a lawyer regardless of the defendant's ability to pay. In 1964, the Court ruled in *Escobedo v. Illinois* that a person accused of a crime must be allowed to consult a lawyer before being interrogated by police. Two years later, in *Miranda v. Arizona*, the Court issued a bitterly criticized ruling when it ordered that an accused person in police custody be informed of certain basic rights: the right to remain silent; the right to know that anything said to authorities can be used against the individual in court; and the right to have a defense attorney present during interrogation; since then, these requirements have been known as "Miranda rights." In addition, the Court established rules for police to follow in informing suspects of their legal rights before questioning could begin.

Freedom Summer

During late 1963 and throughout 1964, in the aftermath of President Kennedy's assassination, the civil rights movement grew in scope, visibility, and power. Racism, however, remained entrenched in the Lower South. Blacks continued to be excluded from the political process. For example, in

1963 only 6.7 percent of Mississippi blacks were registered to vote, the lowest percentage in the nation. White officials in the South kept African Americans from voting through a variety of means: charging them expensive poll taxes, forcing them to take difficult literacy tests, making the application process inconvenient, and intimidating them through the use of arson, beatings, and lynchings.

In early 1964, Harvard-educated Robert "Bob" Moses, a thin, bespectacled, black New Yorker who had resigned from Martin Luther King's SCLC to head up the Student Nonviolent Coordinating Committee (SNCC) office in Mississippi, decided it would take "an army" to force the state to give voting rights to blacks. So he set about recruiting an army of black and white volunteers who would live with rural African Americans, teach them in "freedom schools," and help them register to vote.

Most of the recruits for what came to be called "Freedom Summer" were idealistic white college students, and many were Jewish. Mississippi's white leaders prepared for "the nigger-communist invasion" by doubling the state police force and stockpiling tear gas, electric cattle prods, and shotguns. The famous writer Eudora Welty reported from her hometown of Jackson, Mississippi, that she had heard that "this summer all hell is going to break loose."

It did. In mid-June, the volunteer activists met at an Ohio college to learn about southern racial history, nonviolent civil disobedience, and the likely abuses they would suffer. On the final evening of the training session, Moses pleaded with anyone who feared heading to Mississippi to go home; several of them did. The next day, the remaining volunteers boarded buses and headed south, fanning out across the state. In all, forty-one "freedom schools" that summer taught thousands of children math, writing, and history. They also tutored black adults about the complicated process of voter registration.

Forty-six-year-old Fannie Lou Hamer was one of the local blacks who worked with the SNCC volunteers during Freedom Summer. The youngest in a household of twenty children, she had spent most of her life working on local cotton plantations. During the Freedom Summer of 1963 and after, she led gatherings of volunteers in freedom songs and excelled as a lay preacher. "God is not pleased," she said, "at all the murdering, and all of the brutality, and all the killings for no reason at all. God is not pleased at the Negro children in the State of Mississippi, suffering from malnutrition. God is not pleased because we have to go raggedy each day. God is not pleased because we have to go to the field and work from ten to eleven hours for three lousy dollars."

In response to Freedom Summer, the Ku Klux Klan, local police, and other white racists harassed, arrested, and assaulted many of the young volunteers. Hamer was brutally beaten by jail guards in Winona. Then, in June 1964, Klan members abducted and murdered three young civil rights workers: James Earl Chaney, Andrew Goodman, and Michael "Mickey" Schwerner. Their decomposed bodies were found two months later in a

African American voter registration drives

"Freedom schools"

cattle pond. In the process of searching for the missing men, authorities found the bodies of eight black males in rivers and swamps. The murders, said one volunteer, were "the end of innocence," after which "things could never be the same."

From Civil Rights to Black Power

Racism was never limited solely to the South. In retrospect, it was predictable that the civil rights movement would shift its focus from the rural South to the very different plight of urban blacks. By the mid-sixties, about 70 percent of the nation's African Americans were living in urban areas, most of them in central-city ghettos bypassed by prosperity. Though the majority of African Americans continued to identify with the nonviolent, Christian-centered integration movement promoted by Martin Luther King Jr. and organizations such as the NAACP, SCLC, CORE, and the Urban League, King and others acknowledged privately that many young blacks, especially those in large cities, were losing faith in the strategy of nonviolence.

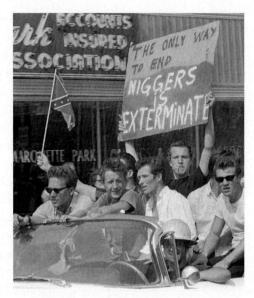

White terror Young men cruise through a riot zone in Chicago in 1966, brandishing a Confederate flag and racist signs.

The fragmentation of the civil rights movement was tragically evident on August 11, 1965, when Watts, the largest black ghetto in Los Angeles, exploded in a frenzy of rioting and looting. When the uprising ended, thirty-four were dead, almost 4,000 were in jail, and property damage exceeded $35 million. Chicago and Cleveland, along with forty other American cities, experienced similar race riots in the summer of 1966. The following summer, Newark, New Jersey, and Detroit, Michigan, burst into flames. Between 1965 and 1968, nearly 300 racial uprisings shattered the peace of urban America.

> Race riots

The racial violence in northern cities revealed the civil war within the civil rights movement. As Gil Scot-Heron, a black musician, sang: "We are tired of praying and marching and thinking and learning / Brothers want to start cutting and shooting and stealing and burning." What came to be called "Black Power" began to compete with the integrationist, nonviolent philosophy espoused by Dr. King and the SCLC.

> Black power movement

The most articulate spokesman for the **black power movement** was Malcolm X (formerly Malcolm Little, the X denoting his lost African family name). His parents were courageous supporters of Marcus Garvey's 1920s crusade for black nationalism, and his childhood home in Lansing, Michigan, was burned to the ground by white racists. Malcolm quit school during ninth grade and began to display what would become a lifelong ability to reinvent himself. By age nineteen, now known as Detroit Red, he had become a thief, drug dealer, and pimp. He spent seven years in Massachusetts prisons, where he experienced a conversion and joined a small Chicago-based religious sect, the Nation of Islam (NOI), whose members were called Black Muslims. The organization had little to do with Islam and everything to do with its domineering leader, Elijah Muhammad, and the cultlike devotion he required. Muhammad dismissed whites as "devils"

black power movement Militant form of civil rights protest focused on urban communities in the North that emerged as a response to impatience with the nonviolent tactics of Martin Luther King, Jr.

Malcolm X The black power movement's most influential spokesman.

Malcolm X assassinated; Black Panther party

and championed black nationalism, racial pride, self-respect, and self-discipline. By 1953, a year after leaving prison, Malcolm X was a full-time NOI minister famous for his electrifying speeches attacking white racism and black powerlessness.

Malcolm X dismissed mainstream civil rights leaders such as Martin Luther King Jr. as being "nothing but modern Uncle Toms" who "keep you and me in check, keep us under control, keep us passive and peaceful and nonviolent." His militant speeches inspired thousands of mostly urban blacks to join NOI. "Yes, I'm an extremist," Malcolm acknowledged in 1964. "The black race in the United States is in extremely bad shape. You show me a black man who isn't an extremist and I'll show you one who needs psychiatric attention." More than most black leaders, Malcolm X expressed the emotions and frustrations of the inner-city African American working poor. Yet at the peak of his influence, Malcolm X became embroiled in a conflict with Elijah Muhammad that proved fatal; NOI assassins killed Malcolm X in Manhattan on February 21, 1965.

Black militancy did not die with Malcolm X, however. By 1966, "black power" had become a rallying cry for young extremists. When Stokely Carmichael, a twenty-five-year-old graduate of Howard University, became head of the Student Nonviolent Coordinating Committee (SNCC), he enforced the separatist philosophy of black power by ousting whites from the organization. "When you talk of black power," Carmichael shouted, "you talk of bringing this country to its knees, of building a movement that will smash everything Western civilization has created."

Where Dr. King spoke to white America's moral conscience, Carmichael spoke to the seething rage of the young black underclass impatient with nonviolent protest. Soon he would move on to the Black Panther party, a group of leather-jacketed black revolutionaries founded in Oakland, California, attracting recruits with its incendiary strategies. H. Rap Brown, who succeeded Carmichael as head of SNCC in 1967, was equally committed to a strategy of violence. He urged blacks to "get you some guns" and "kill the honkies [whites]."

Black Power in Retrospect

Although widely covered in the media, the black power movement never attracted more than a small minority of African Americans. Dr. King dismissed black separatism and the promotion of violent social change, reminding his followers that "we can't win violently."

Still, the emphasis on black power had two positive effects upon the civil rights movement. First, black power advocates forced King and other mainstream black leaders and organizations to shift their focus from the rural South to poverty-stricken inner-city ghettos in the North and West. Legal access to restaurants, schools, and other public accommodations, King pointed out, meant little to people mired in chronic poverty. They needed jobs and decent housing as much as they needed access to all-white facilities. To this end, King began to emphasize the economic needs of the black urban underclass, launching his own war on poverty. The time had come, he declared while launching his "Poor People's Campaign" in December 1967, for radical new measures "to provide jobs and income for the poor." Yet as King and others stressed, the hugely expensive war in Vietnam was taking funds away from federal programs serving the poor, and black soldiers were dying in disproportionate numbers in Southeast Asia.

Second, the controversial black power movement also motivated African Americans to take greater pride in their racial heritage by pushing for black studies programs in schools and colleges, the celebration of African cultural and artistic traditions, the organizing of inner-city voters to elect black mayors, laws forcing landlords to

Panther power Black Panthers throw up the black power salute outside of a San Francisco Liberation School, where activists raised awareness and appreciation of African American history, a topic ignored by white, mainstream curriculum.

treat blacks fairly, and the creation of grassroots organizations and community centers in black neighborhoods. It was Malcolm X who insisted that blacks call themselves *African Americans* as a symbol of pride in their roots and as a spur to learn more about their history. As the popular singer James Brown urged, "Say it loud—I'm black and I'm proud."

Lyndon B. Johnson and the Great Society

CORE **OBJECTIVE**
3. Analyze Lyndon B. Johnson's War on Poverty and Great Society initiatives, and evaluate their impact on American society.

Growing federal support for civil rights came from an unlikely source: a drawling white Texan who succeeded John F. Kennedy in the White House. Lyndon B. Johnson, the towering Texan, took the presidential oath of office on board the plane that brought Kennedy's body back to Washington from Dallas. Fifty-five years old, six feet four inches tall, Johnson had spent twenty-six years in Washington and served nearly a decade as perhaps the most powerful Democratic leader ever in the Senate. Now he was the first southern president since Woodrow Wilson, a legislative magician who had excelled as Senate majority leader. His transition to the presidency was not easy. The Kennedy brothers despised Johnson, and he felt the same about them. They had excluded him from key decisions, often dismissing the rural Texan with the deep southern drawl as "Rufus Cornpone."

Johnson brought to the White House a dramatically different personality and style from that of his predecessor. Unlike Kennedy, who was born to

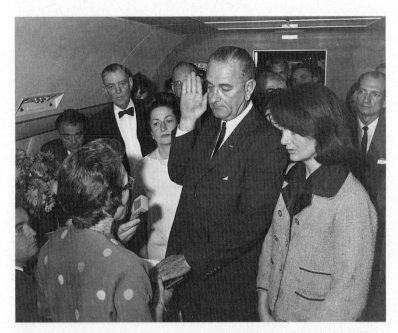

The oath of office Less than an hour and a half after Kennedy's death, Johnson took the presidential oath aboard Air Force One between his wife, Lady Bird (left), and Jacqueline Kennedy (right), before flying out of Dallas for Washington, D.C.

great wealth, Johnson was a rags-to-riches story. With almost superhuman energy and crushing ambition, he had worked his way out of poverty during the Great Depression to become one of the Senate's most dominating figures. LBJ had none of the Kennedy elegance. His ego and insecurities were as massive as his vanity and ambition; he insisted on being the center of attention wherever he went. Ruthless and often bullying, needy and warmhearted, he was a whirlwind of energy and dreams, a crude idealist and a brutal optimist. Yet he was also compassionate and generous toward the poor. Johnson yearned to be loved and respected as a transformational leader. Like Kennedy, he displayed a lifelong weakness for attractive women. (His wife, Lady Bird, acknowledged that "Lyndon loved the human race, and half of the human race are women.")

Those who viewed Johnson as a stereotypical southern conservative failed to appreciate his long-standing admiration for Franklin D. Roosevelt, the depth of his concern for the poor, and his bold support for the cause of civil rights (in part because he needed to win over the northern wing of the Democratic party). "I'm going to be the best friend the Negro ever had," Johnson bragged to a member of the White House staff soon after becoming president. His commitment to civil rights was in part motivated by politics and in part by his desire to bring the South into the mainstream of American life.

Unlike the politically cautious Kennedy, Johnson had Texas-sized ambitions. Few presidents had ever dreamed as big as Lyndon Johnson. He wanted to be the greatest American president, the one who did the most good for the most people. He promised to "help every child get an education, to help every Negro and every American citizen have an equal opportunity, to help every family get a decent home, and to help bring healing to the sick and dignity to the old."

Politics and Poverty

LBJ's first legislation: The Revenue Act (1964), Civil Rights Act (1964), and Economic Opportunity Act (1964)

Johnson managed legislation through Congress better than any president in history, including Franklin Roosevelt, his idol. He was the consummate wheeler-dealer. "It is the politician's task," Johnson asserted, "to pass legislation, not to sit around saying principled things." In 1964 he set about doing just that, taking advantage of widespread public support to push through Congress Kennedy's stalled measures for tax reductions and civil rights. He later said that he wanted to take Kennedy's incomplete program "and turn it into a martyr's cause." The Revenue Act of 1964 provided a 20 percent reduction in tax rates (the top rate was then a whopping 91 percent, compared to 39.6 today). It was intended to give consumers more money to spend so as to boost economic growth and create new jobs, and it worked as planned. Unemployment fell from 5.2 percent in 1964 to 4.5 percent in 1965, and 3.8 percent in 1966.

Civil Rights Act of 1964

Long thwarted by southern Democrats who had held it up in Congress, the **Civil Rights Act of 1964** finally became law on July 2 after eighty days of Congressional debate. President Johnson played a crucial role in its passage. A son of the South, he used his experience as a power broker in the Senate to launch his own risky crusade for racial justice as president. One senator who survived the "Johnson treatment," as it came to be called, said that the president would "twist your arm off at the shoulder and beat your head with it" if you did not agree to vote as he wanted.

Soon after becoming president, Johnson hosted his close friend and arch-segregationist, Senator Richard Russell of Georgia, for lunch at the White House and warned him that "you've got to get out of my way. I'm going to run over you" in order to pass the Civil Rights Act. "You may do that," Russell replied. "But by God, it's going to cost you the South and cost you the election of 1964." Johnson answered: "If that's the price I've got to pay, I'll pay it gladly." Soon thereafter, Johnson told Congress that "we have talked long enough in this country about equal rights. . . . It is time now to write the next chapter, and to write it in the book of law."

Many others (called the "coalition of conscience" by labor leader Walter Reuther) helped Johnson convince Congress to pass the Civil Rights Act—Congressional committee chairs, both Republicans and Democrats, labor unions, church leaders, and civil rights organizations. Their collective efforts produced what is arguably the single most important piece of legislation created in the twentieth century. The passage of the Civil Rights Act after more than a year of Congressional delays marked one of those extraordinary moments when the ideals of democracy, equal opportunity, and human dignity are affirmed by action.

Civil Rights Act of 1964 Legislation that outlawed discrimination in public accommodations and employment, passed at the urging of President Lyndon B. Johnson.

Down with segregation A worker removes a sign from a Greensboro, North Carolina bus that reads: "White Patrons Please Seat from Front. Colored Patrons Please Seat from Rear."

The Civil Rights Act of 1964 dealt a major blow to the deeply entrenched system of racial segregation. It banned racial segregation in public places such as bus terminals, restaurants, theaters, and hotels. It also gave new powers to the federal government to bring lawsuits against organizations or businesses that violated constitutional rights, and it established the Equal Employment Opportunities Commission to ensure that employers treated job applicants equally, regardless of race, gender, or national origin. On the night after signing the pathbreaking Civil Rights Act, Johnson knew that many conservative white southerners would be outraged. He correctly predicted that "we have just delivered the South to the Republican party for a long time to come."

The War on Poverty

Johnson's War on Poverty

In addition to fulfilling Kennedy's legislative priorities that had been stalled in Congress, Johnson launched a much more elaborate legislative program of his own by declaring "unconditional war on poverty in America." Americans had "rediscovered" poverty in 1962 when the social critic Michael Harrington published a powerful exposé, *The Other America*. Harrington revealed that more than 40 million people were mired in an invisible "culture of poverty" that held them hostage in a vicious cycle. Poverty led to poor housing conditions, which in turn led to poor health, poor attendance at school or work, alcohol and drug abuse, unwanted pregnancies, single-parent families, and so on. Harrington added that poverty was much more extensive in the United States than people realized because much of it was hidden from view in isolated rural areas or inner-city slums. He urged the United States to launch a "comprehensive assault on poverty."

President Kennedy had read Harrington's book and had asked his advisers in the fall of 1963, just before his assassination, to investigate the poverty problem and suggest solutions. Upon taking office as president, Johnson announced that he wanted an anti-poverty legislative package that was "big and bold, that would hit the nation with real impact." Money for the program would come from the tax revenues generated by corporate profits made possible by the tax reduction of 1964, which had led to one of the longest sustained economic booms in history. By the mid-sixties, unemployment had dropped, consumer spending had increased, and corporate profits were soaring.

Economic Opportunity Act of 1964

Economic Opportunity Act (1964) Key legislation in President Johnson's "War on Poverty" that created the Office of Economic Opportunity and programs like Head Start and the work-study financial-aid program for low-income college students.

The **Economic Opportunity Act of 1964** was the primary weapon in Johnson's much-trumpeted "War on Poverty." It created an Office of Economic Opportunity (OEO) to administer eleven new community-based programs, many of which still exist. They included a Job Corps training program for inner-city youths aged sixteen to twenty-one; a Head Start educational program for disadvantaged pre-schoolers; a Legal Services Corporation to provide legal assistance for low-income Americans;

work-study financial-aid programs for low-income college students; grants to small farmers and rural businesses; loans to businesses that hired the chronically unemployed; the Volunteers in Service to America program (VISTA) that recruited volunteers to combat inner-city poverty; and the Community Action Program, which would allow the poor "maximum feasible participation" in organizing and directing their own neighborhood programs designed for their benefit. In 1964, Congress also approved the Food Stamp Act, a program run by the Department of Agriculture to help poor people afford to buy groceries.

The Election of 1964

Johnson's successes in creating an array of new federal social-welfare programs triggered a Republican counterattack. Arizona senator Barry Goldwater, a wealthy department-store owner, emerged as the blunt-talking leader of the growing conservative wing of the Republican party. In his best-selling book *The Conscience of a Conservative* (1960), Goldwater had called for ending the income tax and drastically reducing federal entitlement programs such as Social Security. Conservatives controlled the Republican Convention when it gathered in San Francisco in the early summer of 1964, and they ensured Goldwater's nomination. "I would remind you," Goldwater told the delegates, "that extremism in the defense of liberty is no vice." He later explained that his objective was like that of Calvin Coolidge in the 1920s: "to reduce the size of government. Not to pass laws, but repeal them."

In his memoirs, Goldwater admitted that he knew he had no chance to win the presidency: "I just wanted the conservatives to have a real voice in the country." As a candidate, he frightened many voters when he urged wholesale bombing of North Vietnam and even suggested using atomic weapons. He criticized Johnson's War on Poverty as a waste of money, told students that the federal government should not provide any assistance for education, and opposed the nuclear test ban treaty and the Civil Rights Act of 1964, having been one of only six Republican senators to vote against it. To Republican campaign buttons that claimed, "In your heart, you know he's right," Democrats responded, "In your guts, you know he's nuts."

Johnson portrayed himself as a responsible centrist in contrast to Goldwater's "extreme" conservatism. He chose as his running mate Hubert H. Humphrey of Minnesota, a prominent liberal senator who had long promoted civil rights. In contrast to Goldwater's aggressive rhetoric on Vietnam, Johnson pledged that he was "not about to send American boys nine or ten thousand miles from home to do what Asian boys ought to be doing for themselves."

The result was a landslide. Johnson polled 61 percent of the vote; Goldwater carried only Arizona and five states in the Lower South. Johnson won the electoral vote by a whopping 486 to 52. In the Senate, the Democrats increased their majority by two (68 to 32) and in the House by thirty-seven (295 to 140). Goldwater's success in the Lower South, however, accelerated the region's shift to the Republican party, and his candidacy proved to be a turning point in the development of the national conservative movement, inspiring a generation of young activists and the formation of conservative organizations that would transform the dynamics of American politics during the 1970s and 1980s. Their success would culminate in the presidency of Ronald Reagan, the Hollywood actor who co-chaired the California for Goldwater campaign in 1964.

The Great Society

Johnson's Great Society program

Lyndon Johnson made a classical mistake by misreading his lopsided victory as a mandate for massive changes. He knew, however, that his popularity could quickly fade. "Every day I'm in office," he told his aides, "I'm going to lose votes. I'm going to alienate somebody. . . . We've got to get this legislation fast. You've got to get it during my honeymoon."

As Johnson's War on Poverty gathered momentum, his already-outsized ambitions grew even more. In May 1964, he announced his intention to create an array of new programs intended to create a "Great Society" that would end poverty and racial injustice and provide "abundance and liberty for all." That was a magisterial goal, but it "was just the beginning," Johnson insisted, given that the United States had the resources to do much more than assault poverty. "We have the opportunity to move not only toward the rich society and the powerful society, but upward to the Great Society." He did not explain precisely what he meant by a "great society," but it soon became clear that Johnson viewed the federal government as the magical lever for raising the quality of life for all Americans—rich and poor. He would surpass his hero Franklin Roosevelt in expanding the goals and scope of the federal government to ensure that Americans were a people of plenty.

When Johnson became president in November 1963, Social Security was America's only nationwide social program. That soon changed. In 1965, Johnson began flooding Congress with waves of Great Society legislation that he said would end poverty, revitalize decaying cities, provide every young person the chance to attend college, protect the health of the elderly, enhance the arts and humanities, clean up the nation's polluted air and water, and make the highways safer and prettier. The scope of Johnson's Great Society programs exceeded Franklin D. Roosevelt's New Deal, in part because of the nation's extraordinary prosperity during the mid-1960s. "This country," Johnson proclaimed, "is rich enough to do anything it has the guts to do and the vision to do and the will to do." That proved *not* to be the case, however.

Health Insurance, Housing, and Higher Education

Johnson's first priority was federal health insurance and aid to help young people pursue higher education, "liberal" proposals that had languished since President Truman had proposed them in 1945. For twenty years, the

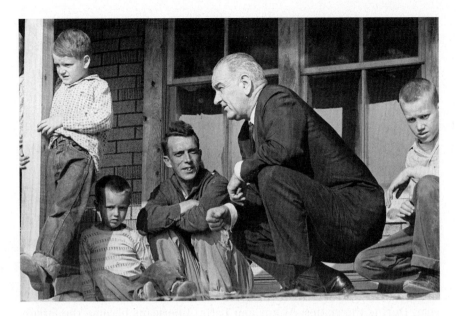

War on Poverty In 1964, Johnson visited Tom Fletcher, a father of eight children living in a tar-paper shack in rural Kentucky. Fletcher became a "poster father" for the War on Poverty, though, as it turned out, his life improved little from its programs.

steadfast opposition of the physicians making up the American Medical Association (AMA) had stalled a comprehensive medical-insurance program. Now that Johnson and the Democrats had the votes to pass the measure, however, the AMA joined Republicans in supporting a bill serving those over age sixty-five. The act that finally emerged went well beyond the original proposal. It created not just a **Medicare** health-insurance program for the elderly but also a **Medicaid** program of federal grants to states to help cover medical expenses for the poor. Johnson signed the bill on July 30, 1965, in Independence, Missouri, with eighty-one-year-old Harry Truman looking on.

The Higher Education Act of 1965 increased federal grants to universities, created scholarships for low-income students, provided low-interest loans for students, and established a National Teachers Corps. "Every child," Johnson asserted, "must be encouraged to get as much education as he has the ability to take."

The momentum generated by the Higher Education and Medicare acts helped carry 435 more Great Society bills through Congress. Among them was the Appalachian Regional Development Act of 1966, which allocated $1 billion for programs in remote mountain areas that had long been pockets of desperate poverty. The Housing and Urban Development Act of 1965 provided $3 billion for urban renewal projects. Funds to help low-income families pay their rent followed in 1966, and the same year a new Department of Housing and Urban Development appeared, headed by Robert C. Weaver, the first African American cabinet member.

In implementing his Great Society programs, Lyndon Johnson had, in the words of one Washington reporter, "brought to harvest a generation's backlog of ideas and social legislation." People were amazed by Johnson's

Johnson's Great Society: Medicare and Medicaid (1965), the Higher Education Act (1965), and the Housing and Urban Development Act (1965)

Medicare and Medicaid Health-care programs designed to aid the elderly and disadvantaged, respectively, as part of President Johnson's Great Society initiative.

energy, drive, and legislative skills. He never seemed to stop or slow down. A woman in Hawaii noted that Johnson "is a mover of men. Kennedy could inspire men, but he couldn't move them."

The Immigration Act

Johnson's Great Society: Immigration and Nationality Services Act (1965)

Little noticed in the stream of Great Society legislation was a major new immigration bill, the **Immigration and Nationality Services Act of 1965**, which Johnson signed in a ceremony held on Liberty Island in New York Harbor. In his speech, he stressed that the law would redress the wrong done to those "from southern and eastern Europe" and the "developing continents" of Asia, Africa, and Latin America. It abolished the discriminatory annual quotas based upon an immigrant's national origin and treated all nationalities and races equally. In place of nationality quotas, it created hemispheric ceilings on visas issued: 170,000 for persons from outside the Western Hemisphere, 120,000 for persons from within. It also stipulated that no more than 20,000 people could come from any one country each year. During the sixties, Asians and Latin Americans became the largest contingent of new Americans.

Voting Rights Legislation

Johnson's Great Society: Voting Rights Act (1965)

Building upon the successes of "Freedom Summer," Martin Luther King Jr. organized an effort in early 1965 to register the 3 million unregistered African American voters in the South. In Selma, Alabama, where only 250 of the 15,000 blacks of voting age were registered voters, 8,000 black and white civil rights protesters began a march to Montgomery, about forty miles away, only to be assaulted by 500 state troopers using clubs, tear gas, and bullwhips. A federal judge agreed to allow the marchers to continue, and President Johnson provided troops for their protection. Still, two white marchers—a mother of five from Detroit and a Boston minister—were murdered. By March 25, when the demonstrators reached Montgomery, some 25,000 people were with them, and Dr. King delivered a rousing address on the steps of the state capitol in which he said, "the battle is in our hands. And we can answer with creative nonviolence the call to higher ground to which the new directions of our struggle summons us."

Several days earlier, Johnson had urged Congress to "overcome the crippling legacy of bigotry and injustice" by making the cause of civil rights "our cause too." He then concluded by slowly speaking the words of the movement's hymn: "And we *shall* overcome."

Immigration and Nationality Services Act of 1965
Legislation that abolished discriminatory quotas based upon immigrants' national origin and treated all nationalities and races equally.

Voting Rights Act of 1965
Legislation ensuring that all Americans were able to vote; ended literacy tests and other means of restricting voting rights.

The resulting **Voting Rights Act of 1965** ensured all citizens the right to vote. It authorized the attorney general to send federal officials to register voters in areas that had long experienced racial discrimination. In states or counties where fewer than half the adults had voted in 1964, the act banned the various ways, like literacy tests, that local officials used to keep blacks and Hispanics from voting. By the end of the year, some 250,000 African Americans were newly registered to vote in several southern states. By

1968, 53 percent of blacks in Alabama were registered to vote compared to only 14 percent in 1960. In this respect, the Voting Rights Act was even more important than the Civil Rights Act because it empowered black voters in the South, thereby transforming the white-dominated politics in the region and enabling, for the first time, the election of black public officials.

Assessing the Great Society

As an accidental president following a tragic assassination, Lyndon B. Johnson sought to give Americans a sense of forward movement in troubled times and show them that he could overcome their fears of a divided America and create a "Great Society" whereby people would be "more concerned with the quality of their goals than the quantity of their goods."

Yet the Great Society and War on Poverty programs never lived up to Johnson's grandiose goals, in part because the Vietnam War soon took priority and siphoned away funding and in part because neither Johnson nor his Congressional supporters understood the stubborn complexity of chronic poverty. The Great Society did include several triumphs for low-income Americans, however. Infant mortality has dropped, college completion rates have soared, malnutrition has virtually disappeared, and far fewer elderly Americans are living below the poverty line. The federal guarantee of civil rights and voting rights remains in place to this day. Medicare and Medicaid have become two of the most appreciated government programs. Consumers now have a federal agency protecting them. Head Start programs providing preschool enrichment activities for poor students have produced long-term benefits. The federal food stamp program has improved the nutrition and health of children living in poverty. Finally, the scholarships provided to low-income college students have been immensely valuable in enabling young people to gain access to higher education.

Several of Johnson's most ambitious programs, however, were ill-conceived, others were vastly underfunded, and many were mismanaged and even corrupt. Some of the problems they were meant to address actually worsened. As Joseph Califano, one of Johnson's senior aides, confessed: "Did we legislate too much? Were mistakes made? Plenty of them." Medicare, for example, removed incentives for hospitals to control costs, so medical bills skyrocketed—for everyone. In addition, food stamp fraud soared as people took advantage of a program intended to ensure healthy nutrition.

Overall, Great Society programs helped reduce the percentage of people living in poverty from 19 in 1964 to 10 in 1973, but it did so largely by providing federal welfare payments, not by finding people decent jobs. By 1966, middle-class resentment over the cost and excesses of the Great Society programs had generated a conservative backlash that fueled a Republican resurgence in Congress. By then, however, the Great Society had transformed public expectations of the power and role of federal government. Its greatest successes were the civil rights acts of 1964 and 1965.

Conservative backlash

CORE **OBJECTIVE**

4. Explain Presidents Kennedy and Johnson's motivations for deepening America's military involvement in the Vietnam War and appraise their efforts to preserve a noncommunist South Vietnam.

The Tragedy of Vietnam

In foreign affairs, Lyndon Johnson was, like Woodrow Wilson, a novice. And, again like Wilson, his presidency would become a victim of his crusading idealism. As racial violence erupted in America's cities, the war in Vietnam reached new levels of intensity and destruction. With weapons supplied by China and the Soviet Union, North Vietnam provided massive support to the Viet Cong (VC), the Communist guerrillas fighting in South Vietnam to overthrow the U.S.-backed government and unify the divided nation under Communist control.

When he became president, Johnson inherited a long-standing U.S. commitment to prevent a Communist takeover in Vietnam. Beginning with Harry S. Truman, U.S. presidents had done just enough to avoid being charged with having "lost" Vietnam to communism. Johnson initially sought to do the same, fearing that any other course of action would undermine his political influence and jeopardize his Great Society programs in Congress. His path, however, took the United States into a deeper military commitment in Southeast Asia.

In November 1963, when President Kennedy was assassinated, there were 16,000 U.S. military "advisers" in South Vietnam. Early in his presidency, Johnson doubted that Vietnam was worth more extensive military involvement. In May 1964, he told his national security adviser, McGeorge Bundy, that he had spent a sleepless night worrying about Vietnam: "It looks to me like we are getting into another Korea. . . . I don't think it's worth fighting for. And I don't think we can get out. It's just the biggest damned mess that I ever saw."

Yet Johnson's fear of appearing weak abroad outweighed his misgivings. By the end of 1965, there were 184,000 U.S. troops in Vietnam; in 1966 there were 385,000; and by 1969, at the height of the American war effort, 542,000.

Escalation in Vietnam

The official justification for the military "escalation"—a Defense Department term favored in the Vietnam era—was the **Tonkin Gulf Resolution**, passed by the Senate on August 7, 1964. On that day, President Johnson told a national television audience that on August 2 and 4, North Vietnamese torpedo boats had attacked two destroyers, the U.S.S. *Maddox* and the U.S.S. *C. Turner Joy*, in the Gulf of Tonkin, off the coast of North Vietnam. Johnson's description was later shown to be false and misleading; the U.S. ships had actually fired first. They had been supporting South Vietnamese attacks against two North Vietnamese islands—attacks planned by American advisers.

The Tonkin Gulf Resolution authorized the president to "take all necessary measures to repel any armed attack against the forces of the United States and to prevent further aggression." Senator Wayne Morse of Oregon, who had learned that Johnson's account of the incident in the Tonkin Gulf

U.S. air strikes Sustained bombing of Vietnam left 30–50-foot wide craters that can still be seen today.

Tonkin Gulf Resolution (1964) Congressional action that granted the president unlimited authority to defend U.S. forces abroad, after an allegedly unprovoked attack on American warships off the coast of North Vietnam.

was false, argued that American warships were in fact engaged in "acts of war rather than acts of defense." His efforts to oppose Johnson failed, however. Only Morse and one other senator voted against the Tonkin Gulf Resolution, which Johnson thereafter interpreted as equivalent to a congressional declaration of war.

Soon after his landslide victory over Goldwater in November 1964, Johnson made the crucial decisions that committed the United States to a full-scale war in Vietnam. On February 5, 1965, Viet Cong (VC) guerrillas killed 8 and wounded 126 at a U.S. base near Pleiku, in South Vietnam. More attacks later that week led Johnson to order Operation Rolling Thunder, the first sustained bombing of North Vietnam, which was intended to stop the flow of soldiers and supplies into the south. Thereafter, there were essentially two fronts in the expanding war: one, in North Vietnam, where U.S. warplanes continued a massive bombing campaign, and the other, in South Vietnam, where nearly all the ground combat occurred.

In March 1965, the new U.S. commander in Vietnam, General William C. Westmoreland, greeted the first American combat troops in Vietnam. By the summer, U.S. forces were engaged in "search and destroy" opera-

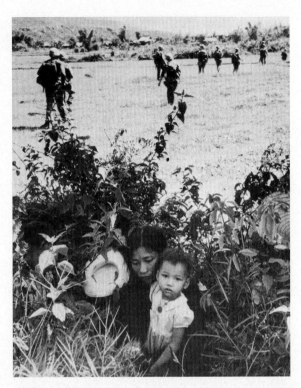

Hidden A Vietnamese mother hides her son and herself in the bushes near the village of Le My in 1965 after U.S. Marines clear the area of Viet Cong forces.

tions against VC guerrillas throughout South Vietnam. It was a frustrating war for the Americans. The Viet Cong, made up of both men and women, wore no uniforms and dissolved by day into the villages, hiding among Vietnamese civilians. Their elusiveness exasperated American soldiers, most of whom were not trained for such unconventional warfare in dense jungles and intense heat and humidity.

As combat operations increased, so did casualties (the number of killed, wounded, and missing) announced each week on the nightly television news, along with the "body count" of alleged VC dead. "Westy's war," although fought with helicopter gunships, chemical defoliants (Agent Orange), and highly flammable napalm, became like the trench warfare of World War I—a war of attrition, whereby each side hoped to outlast the other by causing so much loss of life as to force a surrender. "We will not be defeated," Johnson told the nation in April. "We will not grow tired. We will not withdraw."

The Context for Policy

President Johnson's decision to "Americanize" the Vietnam War, so mistaken in retrospect, was consistent with the foreign-policy principles pursued by all presidents after the Second World War. The idea of "containing" communism, articulated first in the Truman Doctrine, endorsed

Commitment to "containing" communism

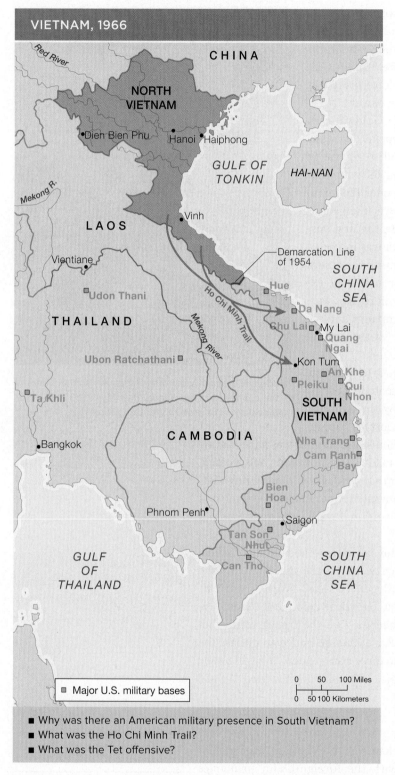

VIETNAM, 1966

- Major U.S. military bases

0   50   100 Miles

0   50 100 Kilometers

- Why was there an American military presence in South Vietnam?
- What was the Ho Chi Minh Trail?
- What was the Tet offensive?

by President Eisenhower, and reaffirmed by President Kennedy, included a pledge to oppose the advance of communism anywhere in the world. "Why are we in Vietnam?" Johnson asked during a speech at Johns Hopkins University in 1965. "We are there because we have a promise to keep. . . . To leave Vietnam to its fate would shake the confidence of all these people in the value of American commitment." Military intervention was thus a logical culmination of the assumptions that had long been shared by the foreign-policy establishment and the leaders of both political parties.

At the same time, Johnson and his advisers believed that military efforts in Vietnam must not reach levels that would cause the Chinese or Soviets to become involved—which meant, in effect, that a military victory was never possible. As a practical matter, the United States was not fighting to "win" the war, but to prevent the North Vietnamese and the Viet Cong from winning and, eventually, thereby, force them to sign a negotiated settlement. This meant that the United States would have to maintain a military presence as long as the enemy retained the will to fight.

The Vietnam War was the defining event for the baby boomers, the largest generation of Americans ever, and it divided that generation in lasting ways. As it turned out, American support for the war eroded faster than the will of the North Vietnamese leaders to tolerate devastating casualties and destruction.

Widespread opposition to the war on college campuses began in 1965 with "teach-ins" at the University of Michigan. The following year, Senator J. William Fulbright of Arkansas, chairman of the Senate Foreign

Relations Committee, began congressional investigations into American policy in Vietnam. George F. Kennan, the author of the containment doctrine, told the committee that the doctrine was appropriate for Europe but not for Southeast Asia, a region that was not essential to U.S. security. In addition, a respected military leader testified that America's strategy had no chance of achieving victory.

By 1967, anti-war demonstrations were attracting massive support, and Americans were dividing themselves into "hawks" who supported the war and "doves" who opposed it. Nightly television accounts of the fighting—Vietnam was the first war to receive extended television coverage and hence was dubbed the "living-room war"—called into question the accuracy of statements by military and government officials claiming the Americans were winning. By May 1967, even Secretary of Defense Robert McNamara was wavering: "The picture of the world's greatest superpower killing or injuring 1,000 civilians a week, while trying to pound a tiny backward nation into submission on an issue whose merits are hotly disputed, is not a pretty one." Between 1965 and 1968, U.S. warplanes dropped more bombs on Vietnam than had fallen on all enemy targets in the Second World War.

> Mounting opposition to the Vietnam War

Johnson and his advisers badly underestimated the strength of the North Vietnamese and Viet Cong commitment to unify Vietnam and expel American forces. While the United States fought a limited war for limited objectives, the Vietnamese Communists, aided by the Soviets and Chinese, fought an all-out war for their very survival. Just as General Westmoreland was assuring Johnson and the public in early 1968 that his troops were on the verge of gaining the upper hand, the Communists organized widespread assaults that jolted American confidence and resolve.

The Turning Point

On January 31, 1968, the first day of the Vietnamese New Year (Tet), the Viet Cong defied a holiday truce by launching well-coordinated assaults on American and South Vietnamese forces throughout South Vietnam. The old capital city of Hué fell to the Communists, and VC fighters temporarily occupied the U.S. embassy in Saigon, the capital of South Vietnam. Within a few days, however, superior American firepower turned the tables. General Westmoreland proclaimed the **Tet offensive** a major defeat for the Viet Cong, and most military strategists later agreed with him.

> Tet Offensive

The Viet Cong had hoped the Tet offensive would ignite a general uprising in the countryside. In that, they failed. Yet while VC casualties were enormous, the *political* impact of the surprise attack was dramatic, for it decisively turned Americans against the war. The scope and intensity of the Tet offensive contradicted upbeat claims by U.S. commanders that the war had been going well. "What the hell is going on?" CBS newscaster Walter Cronkite demanded when he heard about the offensive. "I thought we were

Tet offensive (1968) Surprise attack by Viet Cong guerrillas and the North Vietnamese army on U.S. and South Vietnamese forces that shocked the American public and led to widespread sentiment against the war.

winning this war." *Time* and *Newsweek* magazines soon ran anti-war editorials urging the withdrawal of U.S. forces. President Johnson's popularity plummeted.

Civil rights leaders and social activists felt betrayed as they saw federal funds earmarked for the War on Poverty gobbled up by the ever-expanding war. By 1967, the United States was spending some $2 billion each month in Vietnam, about $322,000 for every VC killed; anti-poverty programs at home received only $53 per person. As Martin Luther King Jr. pointed out, "the bombs in Vietnam explode at home—they destroy the hopes and possibilities for a decent America."

> Lyndon Johnson under siege

President Johnson, under constant assault by critics of "Johnson's War," grew increasingly embittered and isolated. He suffered from depression and bouts of paranoia as he realized that the Vietnam War ("that bitch of a war") was a never-ending stalemate dividing the nation and undermining his Great Society programs. Clark Clifford, Johnson's new secretary of defense, reported in early 1968 that a task force of prominent soldiers and civilians saw no prospect for a military victory.

Robert F. Kennedy, now a New York Senator, was considering a run for the presidency to challenge Johnson's Vietnam policy. Senator Eugene McCarthy of Minnesota had already decided to oppose Johnson. With anti-war students rallying to his "Dump Johnson" candidacy, McCarthy polled a stunning 42 percent of the vote to Johnson's 48 percent in New Hampshire's March Democratic primary. It was a remarkable showing for a little-known senator. Each presidential primary now promised to become a referendum on Johnson's Vietnam policy. In Wisconsin, the scene of the next primary, the president's political advisers forecast a humiliating defeat.

On March 31, 1968, Johnson appeared on national television to announce a limited halt to the bombing of North Vietnam and renewed efforts for a negotiated cease-fire. Then he added a shocking postscript: "I shall not seek, and I will not accept, the nomination of my party for another term as your President." As his daughter explained, the "agony of Vietnam" had engulfed her father.

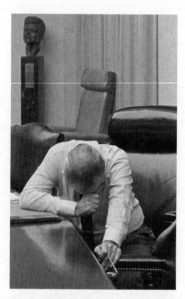

Whose war? Johnson lowers his head in disappointment as he listens to a commander's report from Vietnam in 1968.

Johnson, a flawed giant, had promised far more than he could accomplish, raising false hopes and stoking violent resentments. He ended up losing two wars—the one in Vietnam and the one against poverty. Although U.S. troops would remain in Vietnam for five more years, the quest for military victory ended with Johnson's presidency. America had tried to fight a "limited war" in Vietnam. The problem with such a strategy was that the Vietnamese Communists fought an absolute war. Among other things, Johnson's presidency revealed that the resources of the United States, including its military power, were limited; the nation could not do everything it wanted, which was a disheartening realization for many Americans used to getting their way.

Sixties Crescendo

CORE **OBJECTIVE**

5. Examine the presidential election of 1968 and explain the issues that propelled Richard Nixon to victory.

By the late 1960s, traditional notions of authority were everywhere under attack. An angry spirit of rebelliousness among disaffected youth who were "beyond your command," according to singer Bob Dylan, expanded into a multidimensional attack, not only on the Johnson administration and the war in Vietnam but on virtually every aspect of mainstream life, including the family, the middle-class work ethic, universities, religion, and the integrationist philosophy underpinning the nonviolent civil rights movement led by Martin Luther King Jr. Many alienated young Americans during the sixties, often lumped together as "hippies," felt that they were part of "the Revolution," a magical force of history that would overthrow a corrupt and outdated way of life.

A Traumatic Year

Change moved at a fearful pace throughout the sixties, but 1968, another election year, was the most traumatic year of all, filled with chaos punctuated by tragedy. As *Time* magazine reported, "Nineteen sixty-eight was a knife blade that severed past from future." On April 4, only four days after Lyndon Johnson's shocking withdrawal from the presidential race, a white racist named James Earl Ray shot and killed Martin Luther King Jr. as he stood on the second-floor balcony of the Lorraine Motel in a black neighborhood of Memphis, Tennessee.

Martin Luther King assassinated

King's murder set off a wave of violence. The prominent African American writer James Baldwin said that whites would never understand the depth of black grief. Riots occurred in over a hundred cities. Forty-six people died, all but five of them black. Some 20,000 Army troops and 34,000 National Guardsmen were mobilized to stop the violence across the country. On April 15 Chicago's Mayor Daley ordered his police to shoot to kill arsonists and to shoot to maim looters.

The night that Martin Luther King died, Senator Robert Kennedy was in Indianapolis, Indiana. Upon hearing the sad news, he stood on a flatbed truck to speak to a grieving crowd of African Americans. "Those of you who are black can be filled with hatred, with bitterness and a desire for revenge," he said. "We can move toward further polarization. Or we can make an effort, as Dr. King did, to understand, to reconcile ourselves and to love."

Love was hard to find in 1968. Two months after King's death, after midnight on June 6, 1968, Robert Kennedy appeared at the Ambassador Hotel in Los Angeles to celebrate his victory over Senator Eugene McCarthy in the California Democratic presidential primary. Kennedy closed his remarks by pledging that "we can end the divisions within the United States, end the violence."

Robert F. Kennedy assassinated

After the applause subsided, he walked through the kitchen on his way to the press room for interviews. Along the way, a Jordanian Arab named Sirhan Sirhan, resentful of the senator's strong support of Israel, shot Kennedy in the head. He died the next day.

Only forty-two years old, the father of ten children with another on the way, Kennedy was buried beside his brother John in Arlington National Cemetery outside of Washington, D.C. The assassinations of Robert Kennedy, Martin Luther King, Malcolm X, and John Kennedy came to frame the sixties. With their deaths, a wealth of idealism died too—the idealism that Bobby Kennedy had hoped would put a fragmented America back together again. A growing number of young people felt orphaned from the political system. Having lost the leading voices for real change in the political process, many of them lost hope in democracy and turned to radicalism and violence.

Chicago and Miami

Riots at the 1968 Democratic National Convention

In the summer of 1968, the social unrest in the nation came to a head at the Democratic National Convention. In August, delegates gathered inside a Chicago convention hall to nominate Johnson's faithful vice president, Hubert H. Humphrey, as the party's contender for the presidency.

Outside, almost 20,000 police officers, National Guard troops, and television reporters stood watch over a large gathering of scruffy, passionate anti-war protesters herded together miles away in a public park, their youthful energy having been converted to electrical fury as they taunted the police with obscenities. Richard J. Daley, Chicago's gruff Democratic mayor, warned that he would not tolerate disruptions. Nonetheless, ugly riots broke out and were televised nationwide. It was war in the streets. As police used tear gas and clubs to pummel anti-war demonstrators, others chanted, "The whole world is watching." As the *New York Times* reported, "Those were our children in the streets, and the Chicago police beat them up."

Nixon and the "silent majority"

Three weeks before the Chicago riots, the Republicans had gathered in Miami Beach to nominate Richard Nixon. Only six years earlier, after he had lost the California governor's race, Nixon had vowed never again to run for public office. By 1968, however, he had changed his mind and become a self-appointed spokesman for the values of "middle America." He and the Republicans offered a vision of stability ("law and order") that appealed to what Nixon called the "**silent majority**" of Americans. In accepting the nomination, Nixon promised to listen to "the voice of the great majority of Americans, the forgotten Americans, the non-shouters, the non-demonstrators, that are not racists or sick, that are not guilty of the crime that plagues the land."

silent majority Term popularized by President Richard Nixon to describe the great majority of American voters who did not express their political opinions publicly—"the non-demonstrators."

George Wallace, the governor of Alabama and an outspoken segregationist, dismissed both Democrats and Republicans as too liberal ("owned by the Eastern Establishment") and ran on the American Independent party ticket, a party he formed to defend racial segregation. Wallace promised to get tough on "scummy anarchists" and bring stability to the nation. He appealed even more forcefully than Nixon to voters' concerns about antiwar protesters, the mushrooming federal welfare system, the growth of the federal government, forced racial integration, and rioting in urban ghettos. He displayed a savage wit on the campaign trail, once saying that the "only four-letter words that hippies did not know were w-o-r-k and s-o-a-p." Wallace predicted that on Election Day, the nation would realize that "there are a lot of rednecks in this country." His candidacy generated considerable appeal outside his native South, especially among white working-class communities, where resentment of Johnson's Great Society liberalism flourished. Although never likely to win, Wallace hoped to deny Humphrey and Nixon an electoral majority and thereby throw the choice into the House of Representatives, which would have provided a fitting climax to a chaotic year.

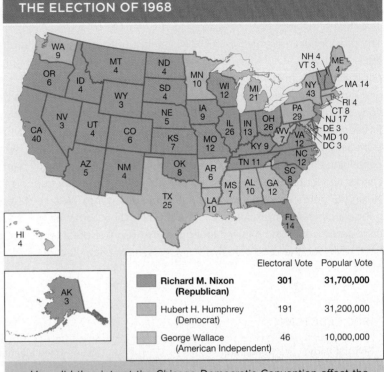

THE ELECTION OF 1968

	Electoral Vote	Popular Vote
Richard M. Nixon (Republican)	**301**	**31,700,000**
Hubert H. Humphrey (Democrat)	191	31,200,000
George Wallace (American Independent)	46	10,000,000

- How did the riots at the Chicago Democratic Convention affect the 1968 presidential campaign?
- What does the electoral map reveal about the support base for each of the three major candidates?
- How was Nixon able to win enough electoral votes in such a close, three-way presidential race?
- What was Wallace's appeal to 10 million voters?

Nixon Triumphant

It did not happen that way. Richard Nixon and Governor Spiro Agnew of Maryland, his acid-tongued running mate, eked out a narrow victory of about 500,000 votes, a margin of about 1 percentage point. The electoral vote was more decisive: 301 for Nixon, 191 for Hubert Humphrey. George Wallace received 10 million votes, 13.5 percent of the total, while all but one of Wallace's 46 electoral votes were from the Lower South. Nixon swept all but four of the states west of the Mississippi. By contrast, Humphrey's support came almost exclusively from the Northeast.

Nixon elected (1968)

So at the end of a turbulent year, near the end of a traumatic decade, a society divided between sharply hostile points of view on the right and left looked to combative Richard Nixon to bring "peace with honor" in Vietnam and to "bring us together" as a nation.

Presidential Elections in the Sixties

The presidential elections of 1960, 1964, and 1968 show the tumultuous 1960s through the eyes of American voters. Issues that divided the country—civil rights, the cold war, particularly U.S. military engagement in Vietnam and the continued growth of the federal government—were key factors in each election. Democrats won the first two elections, but faltered in the third. Democratic candidates Kennedy, Johnson, and Humphrey, to various degrees, supported expanding the role of the federal government at home, especially when it came to securing civil rights for all Americans, while aggressively containing communist expansion abroad. By 1968, voters strongly rejected Democratic candidate Hubert Humphrey, giving over 55 percent of their support to either Richard Nixon (43 percent), the Republican nominee, or George Wallace (13 percent), an independent candidate from Alabama. The 1968 election began an era in which Republican candidates would go on to win four out of the next five presidential contests. When you have reviewed the candidates and major issues in each election, answer the questions further below.

1960 ELECTION

Political Party	Candidate	Issues in the Election	Results
Democratic Party	Senator John F. Kennedy (Massachusetts)	■ Promised new domestic programs to get the country "moving again" and more aggressive cold war efforts than under Eisenhower ■ First Roman Catholic to run for president since Alfred E. Smith, the Democratic nominee in 1928 ■ Dynamic and comfortable in the nation's first televised presidential debates ■ Influenced the release of civil rights activist Martin Luther King Jr., in jail for "trespassing" on a whites-only restaurant	Kennedy won the closest election since 1888 by a margin of 118,574 votes out of 68 million cast. Kennedy's margin in the electoral college was 303 to 219, even though Nixon won more states. Kennedy won 70 percent of the African American vote.
Republican Party	Vice President Richard Nixon (California)	■ Popular with the Republican Party ■ Vice President for the previous eight years under Eisenhower ■ Cunning and deceptive reputation, earning him the nickname "Tricky Dick"	

1964 ELECTION

Political Party	Candidates	Issues in the Election	Results
Democratic Party	**President Lyndon Johnson (Texas)**	■ Touted his success at passing Kennedy's stalled legislation: the Civil Rights Act, major tax reduction, and the Economic Opportunity Act ("War on Poverty") ■ Pledged to build a "Great Society" to eradicate poverty and racial discrimination in America ■ Campaigning as a foreign policy centrist, pledged not to send U.S. troops to South Vietnam	Johnson won in a landslide, polling 61 percent of the votes. Johnson won the electoral college by 486 to 52. Goldwater won six states in the South, signaling the conservative region's continued shift to the Republican party.
Republican Party	**Senator Barry Goldwater (Arizona)**	■ Opposed the Civil Rights Act ■ Pledged to limit the federal government's size and reach by cutting income tax and federal entitlement programs ■ Urged a more aggressive foreign policy in Vietnam	Goldwater's candidacy inspired many young conservative activists to reshape the Republican party in the 1970s and 1980s.

1968 ELECTION

Political Party	Candidates	Issues in the Election	Results
Democratic Party	**Vice President Hubert Humphrey (Minnesota)**	■ Deeply divided over the Vietnam War ■ Promised to try new ways of ending the Vietnam War	Nixon won a narrow victory of 500,000 votes, a margin of only 1 percent of all votes cast.
Republican Party	**Former Vice President Richard Nixon (California)**	■ Self-appointed spokesman for "Middle America" ■ Promised to represent the majority of Americans disturbed by the lawlessness of antiwar protests and urban riots ■ Pledged to end the Vietnam War	Nixon won the electoral college 301 to 191.
American Independent Party	**Former Governor of Alabama George Wallace**	■ Savagely criticized antiwar protestors and "hippies" ■ Opposed the growth of the federal government and its welfare system ■ Denounced forced racial integration and rioting blacks in urban ghettos ■ Targeted white working-class communities outside of the South	Wallace received 13.5 percent of the vote and 46 electoral votes, all but one from the Lower South.

QUESTIONS FOR ANALYSIS

1. How did the issue of race influence the outcomes of these elections?

2. How did voters respond to Lyndon Johnson's term in office?

3. What kind of voter did George Wallace appeal to in 1968 and how did his successes challenge the Democratic party?

■ **Kennedy's New Frontier** President John F. Kennedy promised a *"New Frontier"* in 1961, but many of his domestic policies stalled in Congress. He inherited a CIA plan to topple Fidel Castro's regime in Cuba that resulted in the *Bay of Pigs* fiasco. Soviet premiered Nikita Khrushchev tested American resolve by erecting the *Berlin Wall* and installing missiles in Cuba, provoking the *Cuban missile crisis*. Determined to stand up to the Soviet Union, Kennedy ordered a naval "quarantine" of Cuba and succeeded in forcing Khrushchev to withdraw the missiles. During his presidency, Kennedy also deepened America's anticommunist commitment in Vietnam.

■ **Civil Rights' Achievements** At the beginning of the decade, growing numbers of African Americans and whites staged acts of *nonviolent civil disobedience* to protest discrimination in the South. In 1960, student activists formed the *Student Nonviolent Coordinating Committee (SNCC)* to intensify efforts to dismantle segregation. In 1961, courageous *Freedom Riders* attempted to integrate Southern bus and train stations. Martin Luther King, Jr. delivered his famous "I Have a Dream" speech at the *March on Washington* (1963). But King and other leaders did little to address the concerns of the inner cities, where 70 percent of the nation's African American population lived and experienced frequent discrimination in housing, education, and employment. The *black power movement*, emphasized militancy, black nationalism, separatism, and, often, violence.

■ **Johnson's Great Society** Early in his presidency, Johnson shepherded the *Civil Rights Act of 1964* and, as part of his "war" on poverty, the *Economic Opportunity Act* through Congress. After his resounding presidential victory in 1964, he pushed his vision for a Great Society through Congress—hundreds of initiatives that expanded federal social welfare programs, such as the *Voting Rights Act*, *Medicare*, and *Medicaid*. It also ended national quotas in immigration law through the *Immigration and Nationality Services Act of 1965*.

■ **1968 Presidential Election** Johnson shockingly chose not to seek reelection in early 1968. Anti-war Democrats rallied around Senators Eugene McCarthy and Robert Kennedy. In April, Martin Luther King Jr. was assassinated, setting off a series of violent riots in urban ghettos across the country. Robert Kennedy himself was assasinated in June. Ultimately, the Democrats selected Johnson's loyal vice president, Hubert Humphrey, as their nominee, provoking angry protests by anti-war demonstrators at the 1968 Chicago Democratic Party Convention. The Republicans nominated former candidate Richard Nixon who claimed to represent the *"silent majority."* The segregationist former governor of Alabama, George Wallace, ran as an independent candidate and also appealed to the "silent majority." In the end, Nixon narrowly beat Humphrey and Wallace who made one of the best showings ever by a third-party candidate.

KEY TERMS

New Frontier *p. 1008*
Bay of Pigs (1961) *p. 1011*
Berlin Wall *p. 1012*
Cuban missile crisis (1962)
  p. 1014
Student Nonviolent Coordinating
  Committee (SNCC) *p. 1016*
Freedom Riders *p. 1017*

nonviolent civil disobedience
  p. 1019
March on Washington (1963)
  p. 1020
black power movement *p. 1023*
Civil Rights Act of 1964 *p. 1027*
Economic Opportunity Act
  (1964) *p. 1028*

Medicare and Medicaid *p. 1031*
Immigration and Nationality
  Services Act of 1965 *p. 1032*
Voting Rights Act of 1965 *p. 1032*
Tonkin Gulf Resolution (1964)
  p. 1034
Tet offensive (1968) *p. 1037*
silent majority *p. 1040*

CHRONOLOGY

February 1960	Greensboro Four stage a sit-in
April 1960	Student Nonviolent Coordinating Committee (SNCC) formed
November 1960	John F. Kennedy elected president
April 1961	Bay of Pigs invasion fails
May 1961	Freedom Rides begin
August 1961	Soviets erect the Berlin Wall
October 1962	Cuban missile crisis
August 1963	March on Washington for Jobs and Freedom
November 1963	John F. Kennedy assassinated in Dallas, Texas
June 1964	Congress passes the Civil Rights Act
August 1964	Congress passes the Tonkin Gulf Resolution
November 1964	Lyndon B. Johnson elected to a full term
February 1965	Malcolm X assassinated
June–August 1965	Congress passes immigration reform, Medicare and Medicaid, the Voting Rights Act
August 1965	Race riots in Watts, California
January 1968	Viet Cong stage the Tet offensive
April 1968	Martin Luther King Jr. assassinated
June 1968	Robert Kennedy assassinated
November 1968	Richard Nixon elected president

INQUIZITIVE

Go to InQuizitive to see what you've learned—and learn what you've missed—with personalized feedback along the way.

REBELS WITH A CAUSE Established in 1967, the Vietnam Veterans Against the War (VVAW) grew quickly during the sixties and seventies. Here, a former Marine throws his service uniform jacket and medals onto the steps of the Capitol on April 23, 1971, as part of a five-day protest against the U.S. invasion of Laos.

Rebellion and Reaction

The 1960s and 1970s

A s Richard M. Nixon entered the White House in early 1969, he took charge of a nation whose social fabric was in tatters. Everywhere, it seemed, institutions and notions of authority were under attack. The traumatic events of 1968 had been like a knife blade cutting the past away from the future, revealing how deeply divided America had become and how difficult a task Nixon faced in carrying out his campaign pledge to restore social harmony.

In the end, the stability and harmony he promised proved elusive. His controversial policies and his combative temperament heightened rather than reduced societal tensions. Ironically, many of the same forces that had enabled the complacent prosperity of the fifties—the baby boom, the cold war, and the growing consumer culture—helped generate the social upheaval of the sixties and early seventies. The civil rights movement promoting equality for African Americans inspired efforts to ensure equal treatment for other minorities—women, gays, Native Americans, Hispanics, and others. It was one of the most turbulent and significant periods in American history—exciting, threatening, explosive, and transformative.

Despite President Nixon's promise to restore the public's faith in the integrity of government leaders, he ended up aggravating the growing cynicism about the motives and methods of government officials. During 1973 and 1974, the Watergate scandal resulted in the greatest constitutional crisis since the impeachment of President Andrew Johnson in 1868, and it ended with the first resignation in history of a U.S. president.

CORE OBJECTIVES InQuizitive

1. Analyze the origins of the youth revolt and compare the responses of the New Left and the counterculture.

2. Assess the influence of the youth revolt and the early civil rights movement on other protest movements and how new protest movements affected social attitudes and public policy.

3. Analyze how Richard Nixon's election strategy and domestic policies were affected by the political environment of the late sixties.

4. Analyze how and why Richard Nixon and Henry Kissinger changed military and political strategies to end America's involvement in the Vietnam War.

5. Examine the world order that evolved after the Vietnam War from Richard Nixon's and Henry Kissinger's diplomacy and foreign policies.

6. Explain how the Watergate scandal unfolded, and assess its political significance.

CORE **OBJECTIVE**

1. Analyze the origins of the youth revolt and compare the responses of the New Left and the counterculture.

"Forever Young": The Youth Revolt

The Greensboro sit-ins in 1960 not only launched a decade of civil rights activism but also signaled an end to the carefree inertia that had enveloped many college campuses and much of social life during the fifties. Rennie Davis, a sophomore at Ohio's Oberlin College in 1960, remembered that the young Greensboro civil rights advocates inspired him and many others to become political and social activists. "Here were four students from Greensboro who were suddenly all over *Life* magazine. There was a feeling that they were us and we were them, and a recognition that they were expressing something we were feeling as well."

Youth disillusionment with the U.S. government and "authority"

The sit-ins, marches, protests, ideals, and sacrifices associated with the civil rights movement inspired other minority groups—women, Native Americans, Hispanics, gays, and the disabled—to demand justice, freedom, and equality as well. As Bob Dylan sang in 1963, "How many times can a man turn his head / Pretending he just doesn't see." He and many other idealistic young people decided that they could no longer turn a blind eye to the growing evidence of injustice and inequality staining the American dream.

A full-fledged youth revolt erupted during the mid-sixties. "Your sons and your daughters are beyond your command," sang Dylan in "The Times They Are a-Changin'." By 1970, more than half of Americans were under thirty years of age, and almost 8 million of them were attending college. The baby boomers, who unlike their parents had experienced neither an economic depression nor a major war during their young lifetimes, were now attending colleges and universities in record numbers; enrollment quadrupled between 1945 and 1970. Many universities had become gigantic institutions dependent upon huge research contracts from corporations and the federal government, especially the Defense Department. As these "multiversities" grew larger and more bureaucratic, they became targets for a generation of students wary of involvement in what President Dwight D. Eisenhower had labeled "the military-industrial complex." As criticism of U.S. military involvement in Vietnam mounted, young people disillusioned with the government and "authority" of all kinds flowed into two distinct yet frequently overlapping movements: the New Left and the counterculture.

The New Left

Students for a Democratic Society (SDS)

The political arm of the youth revolt originated in 1960 when Tom Hayden and Alan Haber, two University of Michigan students, formed Students for a Democratic Society (SDS), a campus-based organization influenced by the tactics and successes of the civil rights movement. In 1962, Hayden and Haber called a meeting of sixty young men and women activists at Port

Huron, Michigan. Their goal was ambitious: to design a strategy to remake the United States into a more democratic society. Hayden drafted an impassioned document known as the Port Huron Statement. It began: "We are the people of this generation, bred in at least moderate comfort, housed in universities, looking uncomfortably to the world we inherit." Only by giving power to "the people," the manifesto insisted, could America restore its founding principles. Hayden called for political reforms, racial equality, and workers' rights. Inspired by the example of African American civil rights activists in the South, Hayden declared that college students should engage in "participatory democracy" by snatching "control of the educational process from the administrative bureaucracy."

Hayden and others adopted the term **New Left** to distinguish their efforts at grassroots democracy from those of the Old Left of the thirties, which had embraced an orthodox Marxism. "We have no sure formulas, no closed theories," Hayden explained. The New Left was determined to let the people decide what form the new society would take. SDS grew quickly during the sixties, forming chapters on over a thousand campuses.

In the fall of 1964, students at the University of California at Berkeley took Hayden's New Left program to heart. Several had returned to the campus after spending the summer working with the Student Nonviolent Coordinating Committee's (SNCC) voter-registration project in Mississippi, where three volunteers had been killed and many others arrested or harassed. Their idealism and activism had been aroused, and they were eager to bring changes to campus life as well. When the university's chancellor announced that political demonstrations would no longer be allowed on campus, thousands of students staged a sit-in. After a tense thirty-two-hour standoff, the administration relented. Student groups then formed the free-speech movement (FSM).

Led by Mario Savio, a philosophy major who had participated in Freedom Summer in Mississippi, the FSM initially protested on behalf of students' rights, but it quickly mounted a more general criticism of the university and what Savio called the "depersonalized, unresponsive bureaucracy" smothering American life. In 1964, Savio led hundreds of students into UC Berkeley's administration building and organized a sit-in. They were not welcomed by the president. In the early-morning hours, 600 policemen, dispatched by the governor, arrested the protesters. But their example lived on.

Student free-speech movement (FSM)

Anti-War Protests

The goals and tactics of FSM and SDS soon spread to colleges across the country. By 1965, however, the growing U.S. involvement in Vietnam changed the rebellious students' agenda. With the dramatic expansion of the war after 1965, millions of young men during the late sixties faced the grim prospect of being drafted to fight in an increasingly unpopular

New Left Term coined by the Students for a Democratic Society to distinguish their efforts at grassroots democracy from those of the 1930s Old Left, which had embraced orthodox Marxism and admired the Soviet Union under Stalin.

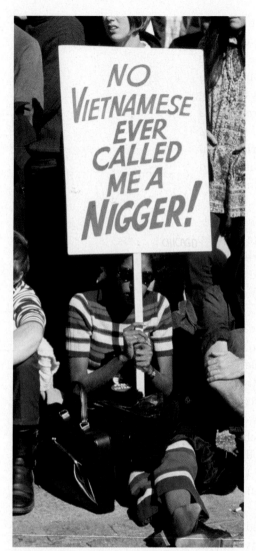

All that rises must converge This protester's sign at a Washington, D.C. demonstration bridged the civil rights and anti-war movements, which called for many of the same racial and political reforms.

conflict. In fact, however, the Vietnam War, like virtually every other, was primarily a poor man's fight. Most college students were able to postpone military service until they received their degree or reached the age of twenty-four; in 1965–1966, college students made up only 2 percent of all military inductees. African Americans and Hispanics were twice as likely to be drafted as whites.

As the war dragged on, Americans divided into two bitter factions, hawks and doves, those who supported the war and those who opposed it. Some 200,000 young men ignored their draft notices during the sixties, and some 4,000 served prison sentences for doing so. Another 56,000 qualified for conscientious objector status during the Vietnam War, compared with only 7,600 during the Korean conflict. Others ceremoniously burned their draft cards in front of television cameras. Still others fled the United States altogether—several thousand moved to Canada or Sweden—to avoid military service. The most popular way to escape the draft was to use a variety of creative ways to flunk the physical examination. Whatever the preferred method, many college students succeeded in avoiding military service. Of the 1,200 men in Harvard's class of 1970, only 56 served in the military, and just 2 of them went to Vietnam.

Rising Violence

Throughout 1967 and 1968, the anti-war movement grew more violent as inner-city ghettos in Cleveland, Detroit, Newark, and other large cities were exploding in flames fanned by racial injustice. Frustration over deeply entrenched patterns of discrimination in employment and housing, as well as staggering rates of joblessness among inner-city African American youths, ignited rage in scores of urban ghettos. "There was a sense everywhere, in 1968," journalist Garry Wills wrote, "that things were giving way. That man had not only lost control of his history, but might never regain it."

During the eventful spring of 1968—when Lyndon Johnson announced that he would not run for reelection and Martin Luther King Jr. and Robert F. Kennedy were assassinated—campus unrest boiled over across the country. The turmoil reached a climax at Columbia University, where SDS student radicals and black militants occupied the president's office and classroom buildings. The administration was forced to cancel classes and call in the New York City police.

The events at Columbia inspired similar clashes among students, administrators, and police at Harvard, Cornell, and San Francisco State, among others. Vice President Spiro Agnew dismissed the anti-war protesters as "impudent snobs who characterize themselves as intellectuals."

The Counterculture

Looking back over the 1960s, Tom Hayden, the founder of SDS, recalled that most rebellious young Americans did not join SDS. They "were not narrowly political. Most were not so interested in attaining [elected] office but in changing lifestyles. They were not interested in being opinion makers as in changing the climate of opinion." Hayden acknowledged that the shocking events of 1968 led disaffected young rebels—so-called hippies—to abandon conventional political activism and embrace the **counterculture**, an unorganized rebellion against mainstream institutions, values, and behavior that at times overlapped with the New Left but more often was focused on cultural rebellion rather than political activism. Hippies focused on changing lifestyles rather than changing political policies. In pursuing personal liberation, they rejected the pursuit of wealth and careers and instead embraced plain living, authenticity, friendship, peace, and, especially, *freedom*.

Counterculture: Hippies and Yippies and communes

Columbia riots Mark Rudd, leader of SDS at Columbia University, speaks to the media during student protests in April 1968.

The counterculture and the New Left both fiercely rejected the status quo in American society, but most of the hippies preferred to "drop out" rather than try to change the political system. Their preferred anti-war slogan was "Make Love, Not War." Like the Beats of the fifties, hippies celebrated personal freedom from virtually all traditional constraints. In all their technicolor variety, they were at once defiant, innocent, optimistic, and indulgent as they rejected the authority of the nation's core institutions: the family, government, political parties, corporations, the military, and colleges and universities.

The colorful lifestyle of those embracing the counterculture included an array of popular ideals and activities: peace, love, harmony, rock music, mystical religions, mind-altering drugs, casual sex, and communal living arrangements. Many hippies practiced meditation and yoga. Hippie fashion featured defiantly long hair for both women and men (prompting the label *long hairs*), flowing cotton dresses, ragged bell-bottom blue jeans, tie-dyed T-shirts, love beads, peace symbols, and sandals. Young men grew beards and women discarded makeup as badges of difference (or indifference, as it were).

The countercultural rebels were primarily middle-class whites alienated by the Vietnam War, racism, political corruption, and parental authority. In their view, a superficial materialism had settled over urban and suburban life, and they were determined to break out of conventional behavior by

counterculture Unorganized youth rebellion against mainstream institutions, values, and behavior that more often focused on cultural radicalism rather than political activism.

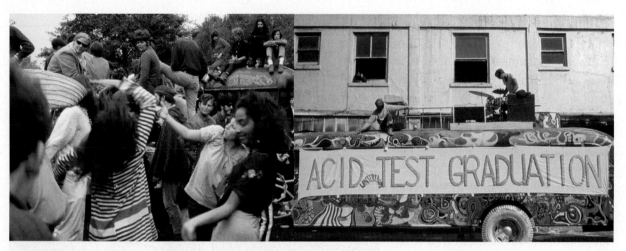

Flower power *Left*: Hippies let loose at a 1967 love-in, gatherings that celebrated peace, free love, and non-theological spirituality, often as a gesture of protest. *Right*: Author Ken Kesey and his posse, the Merry Pranksters, held Acid Test Graduation parties throughout the San Francisco, California, area that celebrated the psychedelic drug LSD (also known as "acid").

embracing the tactics recommended by the drug-promoting former Harvard psychology professor Timothy Leary: "Tune in, turn on, drop out." Illegal drugs—marijuana, amphetamines, cocaine, peyote, hashish, heroin, and LSD—were commonplace within the counterculture. Said Todd Gitlin, a former SDS president, "More and more, to get access to youth culture" in the late 1960s, "you had to get high." The Byrds sang about getting "Eight Miles High," and singer/songwriter Bob Dylan proclaimed that "everybody must get stoned!"

In fact, getting stoned was one of the principal purposes of the 1967 "Summer of Love" centered in San Francisco when over 100,000 hippies ("flower children") from around the country converged on the city's hip Haight-Ashbury district and other enclaves around northern California. The loosely organized "Council for the Summer of Love" intended the gathering to be the first step in a grassroots revolution celebrating alternative lifestyles, especially those "of compassion, awareness, and love, and the revelation of unity for all mankind." That same summer, the Beatles issued one of their all-time best-selling songs, "All You Need Is Love"—a number-one hit worldwide.

The countercultural alternative to SDS and the New Left was the zany Youth International Party, better known as the Yippie movement, founded by two irreverent pranksters, Jerry Rubin and Abbie Hoffman. Often calling themselves Groucho Marxists, the Yippies were countercultural comedians, wacky mischief-makers bent on thumbing their noses at conventional laws and behavior and mocking capitalism as well as the consumer culture. Abbie Hoffman, a founding Yippie, explained that their "conception of revolution is that it's fun." The Yippies were the jokesters in the generational revolution, a clownish force of history that, they believed, would overthrow the power structure. Rubin claimed that the widespread use of "psychedelic" drugs among young Americans "signifies the total end of the Protestant ethic: screw work, we want to know ourselves," and that meant rejecting America's "sick notion of work, success, reward, and status."

The anarchistic Yippies specialized in scandalous theatrical gestures and pranks intended to generate media coverage. They organized marijuana "smoke-ins," threw pies in the faces of political figures, nominated a pig named Pigasus for the presidency, urged voters to cast their ballots for "None of the Above," and threatened to put LSD in the city of Chicago's water supply during the Democratic National Convention in 1968. When asked what being a Yippie meant, Hoffman replied: "Energy–fun–fierceness–exclamation point!" He had no interest in making the Yippies a traditional political organization. "We shall not defeat *Amerika* by organizing a political party," he declared. "We shall do it by building a new nation—a nation as rugged as the marijuana leaf."

For some, the counterculture involved experimenting with alternative living arrangements, especially "intentional communities" or "communes." Communal living in urban areas such as San Francisco's Haight-Ashbury district, New York's Greenwich Village, Chicago's Uptown, and Atlanta's 14th Street neighborhood were popular for a time, as were rural communes. Thousands of inexperienced hippie romantics flocked to the countryside during the late 1960s, eager to liberate themselves from parental and institutional restraints, live in harmony with nature, and coexist in an atmosphere of love and openness.

The participants in the back-to-the-land movement, as it became known, were seeking a path to more authentic living that would deepen their sense of self and forge authentic community ties. "Out here," one of the rural communalists reflected, "we've got the earth and ourselves and God above. . . . We came for simplicity and to rediscover God."

Yet all but a handful of the back-to-the-land experiments collapsed within a few months or years. Almost none of those attracted by rural life actually knew how to farm. And in many cases they were not willing to do the hard work that living off the land required. "The hippies will not change America," a journalist predicted, "because change means pain, and the hippie subculture is rooted in the pleasure principle." In a candid reflection, a young hippie confessed that "we are so stupid, so unable to cope with anything practical." A resident of Paper Farm in northern California, which started in 1968 and collapsed a year later, said of its participants: "They had no commitment to the land—a big problem. All would take food from the land, but few would tend it. . . . We were entirely open. We did not say no [to anyone]. We felt this would make for a more dynamic group. But we got a lot of sick people."

The sixties counterculture thrived on music—initially folk "protest" songs and later psychedelic or "acid rock" music. During the early sixties, Pete Seeger, Joan Baez, Peter, Paul, and Mary, and Bob Dylan, among others, produced powerful songs of social reform. In Dylan's "The Times They Are A-Changin'," first sung in 1963, he warns: "There's a battle outside and

Bob Dylan Born Robert Allen Zimmerman, Dylan came to the New York folk music scene by way of northern Minnesota, penning the anti-war movement anthem "Blowin' in the Wind."

it's ragin' / It'll soon shake your windows and rattle your walls / For the times, they are a-changin'." Within a few years, however, the hippies' favorite performers were those under the influence of mind-altering drugs, especially the San Francisco–based "acid rock" bands: Jefferson Airplane, Big Brother and the Holding Company (Janis Joplin), and The Grateful Dead.

The Woodstock Festival (1969)

Huge outdoor music concerts were wildly popular events among the counterculture. The largest of these was the sprawling Woodstock Music and Art Fair ("Aquarian Exposition"). In mid-August 1969, more than 400,000 mostly young people converged on a 600-acre farm near the tiny rural town of Bethel, New York, for what was called the world's "largest happening," three days "of peace and music." The powerful lure of the festival was the all-star cast of musicians: Jimi Hendrix, the Jefferson Airplane, Janis Joplin, Santana, The Who, Joan Baez, and Crosby, Stills & Nash, among many others. For three days amid summer heat, rain storms, and rivers of mud, the assembled "flower children" "grooved" on good music, beer and booze, cheap marijuana, and casual sex. Drug use was rampant, but there were no robberies, assaults, or rapes. Reflecting on the scene, a long-haired teen said: "People are finally getting together."

The carefree "spirit of love" that blossomed at the Woodstock festival was short-lived, however. Just four months later, when other concert promoters tried to replicate the "Woodstock Nation" experience at the Altamont Speedway Free Festival near San Francisco, the counterculture fell victim to the criminal culture. The Rolling Stones hired the Hells Angels motorcycle gang to provide "security" for their show. During the band's performance of "Under My Thumb," a drunken Hells Angel stabbed to death an eighteen-year-old African American man wielding a gun in front of the stage. Three other spectators were accidentally killed that night, and much of the vitality and innocence of the counterculture died with them. After 1969, the hippie phenomenon began to fade as the counterculture became counterproductive. The spirit of liberation ran up against the hard realities of growing poverty, drug addiction, crime, and mental and physical illness among the "flower children."

Decline of the New Left

At the same time, the New Left was also self-destructing as an organized political movement. In large measure, SDS had committed suicide by abandoning the pacifist principles that had originally inspired participants and given the movement moral legitimacy. The Weathermen, a violent SDS splinter group named for a line in a Bob Dylan song, took to the streets of Chicago in October 1969 to assault police and trash the city. Almost 300 were arrested. During the so-called Days of Rage between September 1969 and May 1970, there were 250 bombings of draft board offices, ROTC buildings on university campuses, federal government facilities, and corporate headquarters. In March 1970, three Weathermen died when a bomb they were making in New York City exploded prematurely.

SDS and other radical groups were also plagued by internal disputes and were forced underground by the aggressive efforts of federal law enforcement agencies. The energy behind the youth revolt waned as the Vietnam War began to wind down. There would be a resurgent wave of student protests against the Nixon administration in 1970–1971, but thereafter campus unrest diminished as Nixon ended the military draft and withdrew U.S. troops from Vietnam, which greatly defused the resistance movement.

Social Activism Spreads

The same liberationist ideals that prompted young people to revolt against mainstream American values and to protest against the Vietnam War also led many of them to embrace other causes. The success of the civil rights movement inspired other groups to demand equal opportunities and equal rights as well—women; Mexican Americans, Native Americans, and other ethnic groups; gays; the elderly; and the physically and mentally disabled. Still others joined the emerging environmental movement or groups working on behalf of consumers, led by the crusading Ralph Nader.

The New Feminism

Like the New Left, the new feminism drew much of its inspiration and many of its tactics from the civil rights movement. The women's movement in the late nineteenth and early twentieth centuries had focused on gaining the right to vote. The feminist movement of the sixties and seventies was much more comprehensive in its goals, seeking equal rights in virtually every area of life. Its aim was to challenge the conventional ideal of female domesticity and ensure that women were treated equally in the workplace.

Most women in the early sixties, however, did not yet view gender equality as possible or even desirable. In 1962, more than two-thirds of women surveyed agreed that the most important family decisions "should be made by the man of the house." Although the Equal Pay Act of 1963 had made it illegal to pay women less than men for doing the same job, varied forms of discrimination and harassment continued in the workplace and throughout society. Women, who were 51 percent of the nation's population in the sixties and held 37 percent of the jobs, earned overall salaries that were 42 percent less than those for men.

Betty Friedan, a forty-two-year-old journalist and mother of three from Peoria, Illinois, emerged as the leader of the **women's movement** during the mid-sixties. Her influential book *The Feminine Mystique* (1963) helped launch the new phase of female protest. Friedan claimed that "something was very wrong with the way American women are trying to live their lives today." Her generation of white, college-educated women (she did not discuss working-class or African American women) had actually lost ground after the Second World War, when many left wartime employment and settled in suburbia as full-time wives and mothers, only to

CORE **OBJECTIVE**

2. Assess the influence of the youth revolt and the early civil rights movement on other protest movements and how new protest movements affected social attitudes and public policy.

The Feminine Mystique (1963)

women's movement Wave of activism sparked by Betty Friedan's *The Feminine Mystique* (1963); it argued for equal rights for women and fought against the cult of domesticity that limited women's roles to the home as wife, mother, and homemaker.

Betty Friedan Author of *The Feminine Mystique* and the first president of NOW.

National Organization for Women (NOW)

Roe v. Wade **(1973)** Landmark Supreme Court decision striking down state laws that banned abortions during the first trimester of pregnancy.

suffer from the "happy homemaker" syndrome which undermined their intellectual capacity and public aspirations while tying them to household duties. "A century earlier," she wrote, "women had fought for higher education; now girls went to college to get a husband." Friedan blamed a massive propaganda campaign by advertisers and women's magazines for brainwashing women to embrace the "feminine mystique" of blissful domesticity in which fulfillment came only with marriage and motherhood. Underemployed women, Friedan claimed, "were being duped into believing homemaking was their natural destiny."

The Feminine Mystique, an immediate best seller, forever changed American society by defining "the problem that has no name." Friedan's analysis of the "feminine mystique" that limited women's lives to being bored housewives and tired mothers inspired many well-educated, unfulfilled middle- and upper-class white women who felt trapped by a suffocating suburban ideal of household drudgery. Moreover, Friedan discovered that there were far more women working outside the home (a third of the workforce) than she had assumed. Many of these working women were frustrated by the demands of holding "two full-time jobs instead of just one—underpaid clerical worker and unpaid housekeeper." Perhaps most important, Friedan helped the emerging women's movement to focus on empowering women to achieve their "full human capacities"—in the home, in schools, in offices, on college campuses, and in politics.

In 1966, Friedan and other activists founded the National Organization for Women (NOW). They chose the acronym NOW because it was part of a popular civil rights chant: "What do you want?" protesters yelled. "FREEDOM!" "When do you want it?" "NOW!"

Initially, NOW sought to end gender discrimination in the workplace and went on to spearhead efforts to legalize abortion and obtain federal and state support for child-care centers. In August 1970, Friedan organized a march for women's equality in New York City that involved 50,000 people walking down Fifth Avenue. Change came slowly, however. By 1970, there was still only one woman in the U.S. Senate, ten in the House of Representatives, and none on the Supreme Court or in the president's cabinet.

In the early seventies, members of Congress, the Supreme Court, and NOW advanced the cause of gender equality. Title IX of the Educational Amendments of 1972 barred discrimination on the basis of sex in any "education program or activity receiving federal financial assistance." Most notably applied to athletics, Title IX has allowed for female participation in high school sports to increase nearly tenfold and almost double at the college level. Congress also overwhelmingly approved an equal-rights amendment (ERA) to the federal constitution, which, if ratified by the states, would have required equal treatment for women throughout society and politics. By mid-1973, twenty-eight states had approved the amendment, still ten short of the thirty-eight states needed for approval.

In 1973, the Supreme Court, in its ***Roe v. Wade*** decision, made history by striking down state laws forbidding abortions during the first three months of pregnancy. The majority on the Court ruled that women have a fundamental "right to choose" whether to bear a child or not, since pregnancy necessarily affects a woman's health and well-being. The *Roe v. Wade* decision and the ensuing success of NOW's efforts to liberalize local and state abortion laws generated a powerful conservative backlash, especially among Roman Catholics and evangelical Protestants, who mounted a potent "right-to-life" crusade that helped fuel the conservative political resurgence in the seventies and thereafter.

Meanwhile, all-male colleges, including Yale, Princeton, and the U.S. Military Academy, led a movement for coeducation that swept the country. "If the 1960s belonged to blacks," said one feminist, "the next ten years are ours."

Radical Feminism

During the late sixties, a new wave of younger and more radical feminists emerged to challenge everything from women's economic, political, and legal status to sexual double standards for men and women. They sought "women's liberation" from all forms of "sexism" (also called "male chauvinism" or "male oppression"), not simply equality in the workplace.

Radical feminism: Direct action and social transformation

The new generation of feminists, often called "women's libbers," was more militant than Betty Friedan and others who had established NOW. Many younger feminists were veterans of the civil rights movement and the anti-war crusade who had come to realize that male revolutionaries could be sexists too. They began meeting in small groups to discuss their opposition to the war and racism, only to discover at such "consciousness-raising" sessions that what bound them together were their shared grievances as women operating in a "man's world."

To gain true liberation, many of them decided, required exercising "sexual politics" whereby women would organize themselves into a political movement based on women's common problems and goals. The writer Robin Morgan captured this newly politicized feminism in the slogan, "The personal is political," a radical notion that Betty Friedan rejected. When lesbians demanded a public role in the women's movement, Friedan deplored the "lavender menace" of lesbianism as a divisive distraction that would only enrage their opponents. By 1973, however, NOW had endorsed gay rights.

Friedan, however, could not dampen or deflect the younger generation of women activists, just as Martin Luther King, Jr. had failed to control the Black Power movement. The goal of the women's liberation movement, said Susan Brownmiller, a self-described "radical feminist," was to "go beyond a simple concept of equality. NOW's emphasis on legislative change left the radicals cold." She dismissed Friedan as "hopelessly bourgeois." For women to be truly equal, Brownmiller and others believed, required transforming *every* aspect of society: child rearing, entertainment, domestic duties, business, and the arts. Lesbianism, she and others argued, should be celebrated rather than hidden.

What women want *Left*: The Women's Strike for Equality brought tens of thousands of women together on August 26, 1970 to march for gender equality and celebrate the 50th anniversary of the Nineteenth Amendment. *Right*: The antifeminist campaign, STOP ERA ("Stop Taking Our Privileges, Equal Rights Amendment"), found its most outspoken activist in Phyllis Schlafly, a constitutional lawyer and staunch conservative.

Like civil rights activists, feminists also demanded that their "hidden history," the story of women's rights advocates over the centuries, be taught in schools and colleges. Radical feminists also took direct action, such as picketing the 1968 Miss America Pageant, burning copies of *Playboy* and other men's magazines, tossing their bras and high-heeled shoes into "freedom cans," and assaulting gender-based discrimination in all of its forms. They also formed militant organizations like WITCH (Women's International Terrorist Conspiracy from Hell), WRAP (Women's Radical Action Project), Keep on Truckin' Sisters, and the Redstockings, whose manifesto proclaimed that they were tired of being exploited by men "as sex objects, breeders, domestic servants, and cheap labor." Members sported buttons proclaiming their collective nickname: "Uppity Women."

Fractured Feminism

Successes and failures of feminism: Gains in education, employment, and politics; conservative backlash; and failure of the ERA

By the end of the seventies, sharp disputes between moderate and radical feminists had fractured the women's movement in ways similar to the fragmentation experienced by civil rights organizations a decade earlier. The movement's failure to broaden its appeal much beyond the confines of the white middle class also caused reform efforts to stall. Ratification of the Equal Rights Amendment, which had once seemed a straightforward assertion of equal opportunity ("Equality of rights under the law shall not be denied or abridged by the United States or by any State on account of sex"), was stymied in several state legislatures by the organized opposition of conservative groups, many of which used the possibility of women having to serve in combat roles in the armed services as reason enough to oppose the ERA. By 1982, it had finally died, three states short of passage. The defeat of the ERA was seen as a triumph by the surging conservative movement that drew its strength, in part, from the backlash against changing social attitudes about women's roles.

Yet the successes of the women's movement endured. Whether young or old, conventional or radical, those women fighting for equal rights focused on several basic issues during the sixties and seventies: gender discrimination in the workplace, equal pay for equal work, an equal chance at jobs traditionally reserved for men, the availability of high-quality, government-subsidized child-care centers, and easier access to birth control devices, prenatal care, and abortion. Feminists helped win improvements in divorce laws and gained easier access for women seeking clinical abortions.

It was also the feminist movement that called attention to issues long hidden or ignored in American society. In 1970, for example, 36 percent of the nation's "poor" families were headed by women, as were most urban families dependent on federal welfare services. Nearly 3 million poor children needed access to day-care centers but there were only places for 530,000. It was the feminist movement that helped women achieve mass entry into the labor market and enjoy steady improvements towards equal pay and treatment in the workplace. In 1960, some 38 percent of women were working outside the home; by 1980, 52 percent were doing so.

A growing presence in the labor force brought women a greater share of economic and political influence. By 1976, more than half of married women, and nine of ten female college graduates, were employed outside the home, a development that one economist called "the single most outstanding phenomenon of this century." Women also enrolled in graduate and professional schools in record numbers. During the 1970s, women began winning elected offices at the local, state, and national levels.

The Sexual Revolution and the Pill

The feminist movement coincided with the so-called sexual revolution, a much-discussed loosening of traditional restrictions on social behavior. During the sixties and after, Americans became more tolerant of premarital sex, and women became more sexually active. Between 1960 and 1975, the number of college women engaging in sexual intercourse doubled, from 27 percent to 50 percent. Enabling this change, in large part, was a scientific breakthrough in contraception: the birth-control pill, approved for public use by the Food and Drug Administration in 1960.

Widespread access to the pill fundamentally changed social life by giving women a greater sense of sexual freedom. The pill also led to more open discussion of birth control, reproduction, and sexuality in general. By 1990, the world would have 400 million fewer people as a result of the pill. Although the birth control pill also contributed to a rise in sexually transmitted diseases, many women viewed it as a godsend—an inexpensive,

Birth control and changing sexual attitudes

nonintrusive way for them to gain better control over their bodies and their futures. "It was a savior," recalled Eleanor Smeal, president of the Feminist Majority Foundation. "The whole country was waiting for it. I can't even describe to you how excited people were."

Hispanic Rights

The activism of student revolts, the civil rights movement, and the crusade for women's rights soon spread to various ethnic minority groups. The word *Hispanic*, referring to people who trace their ancestry to Spanish-speaking Latin America or Spain, came into increasing use after 1945 in conjunction with growing efforts to promote economic and social justice. (Although frequently used as a synonym for Hispanic, the term *Latino* technically refers only to people of Latin American descent.) Labor shortages during the Second World War had led defense industries to offer Hispanic Americans their first significant access to skilled-labor jobs. And as was the case with African Americans, service in the military during the war years helped to heighten an American identity among Hispanic Americans, increasing their desire for equal rights and social opportunities.

Social equality, however, remained elusive for Hispanics who were wanted in the United States for their labor but not for their race and culture. After the Second World War, Hispanic Americans still faced widespread discrimination in hiring, housing, and education. Poverty was rampant. In 1960, for example, the median income of a Mexican American family was only 62 percent of the national average. Hispanic American activists denounced segregation, called for improved public schools serving their children, and struggled to increase Hispanic political influence, economic opportunities, and visibility in the curricula of schools and colleges.

Hispanic civil rights leaders faced an awkward dilemma: What should they do about the continuing stream of undocumented Mexican immigrants flowing across the border into the United States? Many Mexican Americans argued that their hopes for economic advancement and social equality were put at risk by the daily influx of Mexican laborers willing to accept low-paying jobs. Mexican American leaders thus helped end the bracero program in 1964 (which trucked in contract day-laborers from Mexico during harvest season).

United Farm Workers (UFW)

In the early sixties, Mexican American workers formed their own civil rights organization, the **United Farm Workers (UFW)**. The founder of the UFW was the charismatic Cesar Chavez. Born in 1927 in Yuma, Arizona, the son of Mexican immigrants, Chavez moved with his family to California in 1939. There they joined thousands of other poor migrant farmworkers moving from job to job, living in tents, cars, or ramshackle cabins. After serving in the U.S. Navy during the Second World War and then working as a migrant laborer, Chavez first became a community organizer focused on registering Latinos to vote.

United Farm Workers (UFW) Organization formed in 1962 to represent the interests of Mexican American migrant workers.

Cesar Chavez The usually energetic Chavez is visibly weakened from what would be a 25-day hunger strike in support of the United Farm Workers Union in March of 1968. Robert F. Kennedy, a great admirer of Chavez, is seated to his right.

Then, along with Dolores Huerta, a talented organizer, Chavez created UFW, a union for migrant lettuce workers and grape pickers, many of them undocumented immigrants who could be deported at any time. Up and down California, Chavez led nonviolent mass protest marches that had the energy of religious pilgrimages; he staged hunger strikes like those of his hero, India's Mahatma Gandhi; and he managed nationwide boycotts.

Nonviolent Protest: Marches, boycotts, and *la huelga* (strike against California grape growers)

The United Farm Workers gained national attention in September 1965 when the union organized a strike ("*la huelga*") against the corporate grape growers in California's San Joaquin Valley. As Huerta explained, "We have to get farmworkers the same type of benefits, the same type of wages, and the respect that they deserve because they do the most sacred work of all. They feed our nation every day."

Chavez's relentless energy and deep Catholic faith, his insistence upon nonviolent tactics, his reliance upon college-student volunteers, his skillful alliance with organized labor and religious groups, and the life of poverty he chose for himself—all combined to attract media interest and popular support.

However, the chief strength of the Hispanic rights movement lay less in the tactics of sit-ins and protest marches than in the rapid growth of the Hispanic American population. In 1970, Hispanics in the United States numbered 9 million (4.8 percent of the total population); by 2000 their numbers had increased to 35 million (12.5 percent); and in 2012, they numbered 53 million, making them the nation's largest minority group (17 percent). The voting power of Hispanics and their concentration in states with key electoral votes has helped give the Hispanic point of view significant political clout.

Native American Rights

American Indians—many of whom had begun calling themselves *Native Americans*—also emerged as a political force in the late sixties. Two conditions combined to make Indian rights a priority. First, many whites felt guilty for the destructive actions of their ancestors toward a people who had, after all, been here first. Second, the plight of Native Americans was more desperate than that of any other group in the country. Indian unemployment was ten times the national rate, life expectancy was twenty years lower than the national average, and the suicide rate was a hundred times higher than the rate for whites.

> "Red Power" and the occupation of Wounded Knee

Although President Lyndon Johnson attempted to funnel federal antipoverty-program funds into reservations, militants within the Indian community grew impatient with the pace of change. Those promoting "**Red Power**" organized protests and demonstrations against local, state, and federal agencies. On November 20, 1969, fourteen Red Power activists occupied Alcatraz Island near San Francisco, which until 1963 had hosted a federal prison. Over the next several months, they were joined by hundreds of others, mostly students. The Nixon administration responded by cutting off electrical service and telephone lines. Stranded without electrical power and fresh water, most of the protesters left the island. Finally, on June 11, 1971, the government removed the remaining fifteen Native Americans from the island.

Red Power Activism by militant Native American groups to protest living conditions on Indian reservations through demonstrations, legal action, and, at times, violence.

In 1968, the year before the Alcatraz occupation, two Chippewas (or Ojibwas) living in Minneapolis, George Mitchell and Dennis Banks, founded the American Indian Movement (AIM). In October 1972 AIM organized the Trail of Broke Treaties caravan which traveled by bus and car across the nation from the West coast to Washington, D.C., drawing attention to the history of the federal government's broken treaties and promises. When officials in the Nixon administration refused to meet with the protesters, they occupied the federal Bureau of Indian Affairs on November 3. The sit-in ended when federal negotiators agreed to renew discussions of Native American grievances about the administration of government programs intended to improve their quality of life.

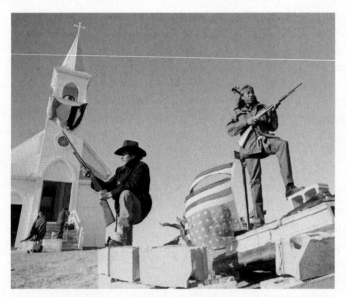

Standoff at Wounded Knee After occupying Wounded Knee and taking eleven hostages, members of the American Indian Movement and the Oglala Sioux stand guard outside of the town's Sacred Heart Catholic Church.

In 1973, AIM led 200 Sioux in the occupation of the tiny village of Wounded Knee, South Dakota, where the U.S. Seventh Cavalry had massacred a Sioux village in 1890. Outraged by the light sentences given a group of local whites who had killed a Sioux in 1972, the organizers sought to draw attention to the plight of the Indians living on the reservation there. After the militants took eleven hostages, federal marshals and FBI agents surrounded the encampment. The occupation at Wounded Knee captured more media attention in its first few days than the Indian rights movement had received in the decade up to that point. For ten weeks the two sides engaged in a tense standoff. When AIM leaders tried to bring in food and supplies, a shoot-out erupted, with one Indian killed and another wounded. Soon thereafter, the confrontation ended with a government promise to reexamine Indian treaty rights.

Indian protesters subsequently discovered a more effective tactic than direct action and sit-ins: they went into federal courts armed with copies of old treaties and demanded that the documents become the basis for financial restitution for the lands taken from them over the centuries. In Alaska, Maine, South Carolina, and Massachusetts, they won substantial settlements that officially recognized their tribal rights and awarded monetary compensation at levels that upgraded the standard of living on several reservations.

> Legal recognition of historic Native American treaties and tribal rights

Gay Rights

The liberationist impulses of the sixties also encouraged homosexuals to assert their right to equal treatment. Throughout the sixties, gay men and lesbians continued to be treated frequently with disgust, cruelty, and violence. On Saturday night, June 28, 1969, New York City vice police raided the Stonewall Inn, a popular gay bar in Greenwich Village, because it lacked a liquor license. Instead of dispersing, the diverse patrons fought back, and the struggle spilled into the streets. Hundreds of other gays and their supporters joined the fracas.

> Stonewall riots (1969)

The **Stonewall riots** lasted throughout the weekend, during which the Stonewall Inn caught fire and burned down. When the turmoil ended, gays had forged a new sense of solidarity embodied in two new organizations, the Gay Liberation Front and the Gay Activists' Alliance, both of which focused on ending discrimination and harassment against gays and transvestites. "Gay is good for all of us," proclaimed one of its members. "The artificial categories 'heterosexual' and 'homosexual' have been laid on us by a sexist society."

As news of the Stonewall rebellion spread, the gay rights movement grew in its numbers and its demands. By 1973, almost 800 gay organizations had been formed across the country, and every major city had a visible gay community and cultural life. That year, the American Psychiatric Association removed homosexuality from its official manual of "mental illnesses." Colleges and universities began offering courses and majors in "Gay Studies" (also called Queer Studies), and grassroots movements as well as national organizations began pushing for official government recognition of same-sex marriages. As was the case with the civil rights and women's movements, however, the campaign for gay rights soon suffered from internal divisions and a conservative counterattack.

Stonewall riots (1969) Violent clashes between police and gay patrons of New York City's Stonewall Inn, seen as the starting point of the modern gay rights movement.

The Movements of the 1960s and 1970s

The struggles and successes of the African American civil rights that began in the fifties and evolved into a powerful political force in the sixties inspired many other groups and individuals in American society. The 1950s also saw the beginning of a student movement and an emerging counterculture, but by the sixties and seventies these had grown into a more general youth rebellion that often focused on opposing the Vietnam War as well as promoting a more democratic society. Other civil rights movements also emerged. Marginalized Americans such as women, homosexuals, Hispanics, and Native Americans demanded a more equitable role in American society. The following chart describes some of these movements.

Movement	Causes	Main Organizations (year founded)	Origins & Influences	Significant Events
Student Movement	Create a more democratic society through political reforms, racial equality, and workers' rights; later, anti-war causes	Students for a Democratic Society (SDS) (1960), The Weathermen faction (1969)	Inspired by the civil rights movement Founded by Michigan students Tom Hayden and Alan Haber in 1960	■ Free Speech Movement (FSM) founded (1964) ■ Emergence of the New Left (1960s) ■ Columbia riots (1968) ■ Kent State and Jackson State anti-war protests and shootings (1970)
Counterculture Movement	Refusing conventional consumerism and embracing alternative, more authentic social arrangements	Hippies, Youth International Party (Yippie movement) (1967), back-to-land movement (1960s–1970s)	Associated with anti-war cause Music: rock, folk, psychedelic or "acid rock" Mysticism, mind-altering drugs, casual sex, communal living	■ Summer of Love (1967) ■ Woodstock Music and Art Fair (1969)
Women's Movement	Challenge social assumptions of women's domesticity Fight against gender discrimination and for reproductive rights	National Organization for Women (NOW) (1963), WITCH (1968) and other radical feminist organizations	*The Feminine Mystique* (1963) by Betty Freidan Inspired by the civil rights movement	■ Title IX of the Educational Amendments passed (1972) ■ *Roe v. Wade* (1973) ■ Failure of the Equal Rights Amendment (1982) ■ Internal divisions and conservative opposition slowed reforms (1970s)

Movement	Causes	Main Organizations (year founded)	Origins & Influences	Significant Events
Hispanic American Rights Movement	Combat racial segregation and lack of economic opportunity for Hispanic Americans	United Farm Workers (UFW) (1962)	World War II labor shortages and military service provided first significant access to skilled labor jobs and military service, increasing demand for equal rights Inspired by the civil rights movement	■ End of the bracero program (1964) ■ Increase in political power with dramatic population growth
Red Power Movement	Reform of state and federal Native American policies to improve conditions on reservations	American Indian Movement (AIM) (1963)	Lacking opportunities and funds from government agencies, as one of the nation's most disenfranchised groups Inspired by the civil rights movement	■ Occupation at Alcatraz Island (1963) ■ AIM's standoff at Wounded Knee (1972) ■ Native American enforcement of historic treaties in federal court
Gay Rights Movement	Equal treatment and social acceptance for homosexuals; gay solidarity	Gay Liberation Front (1969), Gay Activists' Alliance (1969)	Sparked by Stonewall riots in New York City (1969)	■ Stonewall riots (1969) ■ Removal of "homosexuality" from official U.S. mental illness manual (1973) ■ Internal divisions and conservative opposition slowed reforms (1970s)

QUESTIONS FOR ANALYSIS

1. What similarities were there in the origins and goals of these movements?

2. What patterns do you see among these movements' successes and failures?

3. What role did the African American civil rights movement play in the development of these other movements?

CORE **OBJECTIVE**

3. Analyze how Richard Nixon's election strategy and domestic policies were affected by the political environment of the late sixties.

Nixon and the Revival of Conservatism

By the end of the sixties, Americans were engaged in a cultural civil war. The turmoil of the sixties spawned a cultural backlash among what Richard Nixon called the "great silent majority" of middle-class Americans that propelled him to a narrow election victory in November 1968, in large part because he promised to bring "law and order" to a nation overflowing with "violence, lawlessness, and permissiveness." Nixon was no friend of the civil rights movement, the youth revolt, or spreading social activism. He had been elected president as the representative of middle America, those voters fed up with liberal politics, countercultural hippies, radical feminism, and **affirmative-action** programs giving preferential treatment to minorities and women to atone for past injustices.

The Conservative Backlash

Alabama's Democratic governor, George Wallace, led the conservative counterattack. "Liberals, intellectuals, and long hairs," he shouted, "have run the country for too long." Wallace repeatedly lashed out at "welfare queens," unmarried women who he claimed "were breeding children as a cash crop" in order to receive federal child-support checks. Wallace's support was not limited to the South. He became the popular voice for many working-class whites across the nation fed up with political liberalism and social radicalism.

All in the Family, the most popular TV show in the 1970s, was created to showcase the decade's cultural wars. In the much-celebrated sitcom (situation comedy), the Bunker family lived in a state of perpetual conflict in a working-class suburb outside of New York City. Semi-literate Archie Bunker (played by Carroll O'Connor), a Polish-American loading-dock worker, was the gruff but lovable head of the family, a proud Republican, Nixon supporter, and talkative member of the "silent majority" who was a bundle of racial, ethnic, and political prejudices. Enthroned in his easy chair, he railed each week against blacks, Jews, Italians, gays, feminists, hippies, and liberals (including his live-in daughter and her hippie husband, both "bleeding-heart" liberals). At one point, Archie says: "I ain't no bigot. I'm the first guy to say, 'It ain't your fault that youse are colored.'" The producer of the series, Norman Lear, intended Archie's raging intolerance as a satire to provoke viewers to question their own prejudices. In fact, however, many of the 50 million people watching each Saturday night identified *with* the narrow-minded values of Archie Bunker, who in 1973 was "the most recognized face in America."

At a grassroots level, conservatives in the early seventies fought back in the courts against preferential treatment for historically disadvantaged groups, arguing that government-mandated affirmative-action programs were neither fair nor efficient ways to address the problems of historic

The "silent majority"

affirmative action Programs designed to give preferential treatment to women and minorities as compensation for past injustices.

inequality. Others sought to combat the counterculture by creating new rules and regulations to enforce old values. In Louisville, Kentucky, for instance, the Fire Department announced that "beards, goatees, or any other extraneous facial hair will not be permitted." In supporting such efforts, Nixon appealed to the working- and middle-class whites who feared that America was being corrupted by permissiveness, anarchy, and the tyranny of the rebellious minority. He promised to return "law and order" to a nation on the verge of chaos.

In 1952, the powerful Senator Robert A. Taft of Ohio, known as "Mr. Republican," had characterized young Senator Richard Nixon as a "little man in a big hurry" with "a mean and vindictive streak." A grocer's son from Whittier, California, Nixon was a humorless man of fierce ambition and extraordinary perseverance. Raised in a family that struggled with poverty, he had to claw and struggle to the top his whole life, and he nursed a deep resentment of people who had an easier time of it (the "moneyed class").

Nixon was much more than persistent, however. He was also smart, shrewd, cunning, and doggedly determined to succeed in politics. Republican senator Barry Goldwater described Nixon as "the most complete loner I've ever known." Throughout his career, Nixon displayed violent mood swings punctuated by raging temper tantrums, vulgar profanity, and anti-Semitic outbursts. He was nicknamed "Tricky Dick" because he was a good liar. In his speech accepting the Republican nomination in 1968, Nixon pledged "to find the truth, to speak the truth, and live with the truth." In fact, however, he often did not speak the truth. One of his presidential aides admitted that "we did often lie, mislead, deceive, try to use [the media], and to con them."

Nixon's Appointments

In his first term, Nixon selected for his cabinet and White House staff only white men who would carry out his orders with blind obedience. John Mitchell, the gruff attorney general who had been a senior partner in Nixon's New York law firm, was the new president's closest confidant. H. R. (Bob) Haldeman, a former advertising executive, served as chief of staff. As Haldeman explained, "Every President needs a son of a bitch, and I'm Nixon's. I'm his buffer, I'm his bastard." John Ehrlichman, a Seattle attorney and college schoolmate of Haldeman, served as Nixon's chief domestic-policy adviser. John W. Dean III, an associate deputy in the office of the U.S. Attorney General, became the White House legal counsel.

Nixon tapped as secretary of state his old friend William Rogers, who had served as attorney general under Dwight D. Eisenhower, but Nixon had no intention of making Rogers the nation's chief diplomat. Instead, the president virtually ignored Rogers and the State Department in the process of forging an unlikely partnership with Dr. Henry Kissinger, a brilliant German-born Harvard political scientist who had become the nation's leading foreign-policy expert. His thick German accent, owlish appearance, and outsized ego had helped to make him an international celebrity, courted by presidents of both parties. In 1969 Nixon named Kissinger his National Security Advisor, and in 1973 Kissinger became secretary of state.

Nixon and Kissinger, the politician and the professor, formed an odd but effective diplomatic team. Both were loners and outsiders who preferred operating in secret; both were insecure and even paranoid at times; and both mistrusted and envied the other's power and prestige. Nixon would eventually grow tired of Kissinger's efforts at self-promotion and his frequent threats to resign if he did not get his way. For his part, Kissinger lavished praise on Nixon in public, while in private he was less supportive, dismissing the president's "meatball mind" and criticizing his excessive drinking. Yet for all of their differences, they worked well together, in part because they both loved secrecy and intrigue, power politics and diplomatic flexibility, and in part because of their shared vision of a new multipolar world order beginning to replace the bipolar cold war as the United States slowly withdrew its military forces from Vietnam.

The Southern Strategy

A major reason for Nixon's election victories in 1968 and 1972 was his shrewd southern strategy, designed to win over white southern Democrats upset by the civil rights revolution. Of all the nation's regions, the South had long been the most conservative. The majority of white southern voters were religious and patriotic, fervently anti-Communist and anti-union, and skeptical of social-welfare programs. For a century, whites in the "Solid South" had steadfastly voted for Democrats in national elections. Their doing so reflected lingering southern resentments, dating back to the Civil War and Reconstruction, that demonized Abraham Lincoln and his Republican successors for imposing northern ways of life on the South, including racial integration. During the late sixties and seventies, however, a surging economy and a spurt of population growth transformed the South. The region's warm climate, low cost of living, absence of labor unions, low taxes, and government incentives for economic development convinced waves of businesses, workers, professionals, and retirees to relocate to the region.

Between 1970 and 1990, the South's population grew by 40 percent, more than twice the national average. During the seventies, job growth in the South was seven times greater than in New York and Pennsylvania. In the sixties and seventies, southern "redneck" culture suddenly became all the rage, as people across the nation embraced stock car racing, cowboy boots, pickup trucks, barbecue, and country music. As Alabama's George Wallace had claimed while campaigning for president in 1968, "For 100 years, both parties have looked down their noses and called us rednecks down here in this part of the country. I'm sick and tired of it, and on November 5, they're goin' to find out there are a lot of rednecks in this country."

Rapid population growth—and the continuing spread of air-condition-ing—brought the Sunbelt states of the South, the Southwest, and California more congressional seats and more electoral votes. Every president elected between 1964 and 2008 had roots in the Sunbelt, the region that spear-headed the backlash against sixties radicalism. Nixon's favorite singer, country star Merle Haggard, crooned in his smash hit, "Okie from Musk-ogee": "We don't smoke marijuana in Muskogee / We don't take our trips on LSD / We don't burn our draft cards down on Main Street / We like livin' right and bein' free." Haggard's conservative working-class fans bristled at anti-war protesters, hippies, rising taxes, social-welfare programs, and civil rights activism. The alienation of many blue-collar whites from the liberal-ism of the Democratic party, as well as the demographic changes transform-ing Sunbelt states and the white backlash against court-ordered integration, created a welcome opportunity for the Republican party to exploit, which Richard Nixon eagerly seized.

In the 1968 presidential campaign, Nixon's southern strategy took ad-vantage of the backlash against liberalism and civil rights in the region to win over traditionally Democratic white voters. Nixon shrewdly "played the race card," assuring white conservatives that he would appoint justices to the Supreme Court who would undermine federal enforcement of civil rights laws such as mandatory school busing to achieve racial integration and affirmative action that gave minorities priority in hiring decisions and the awarding of government contracts. Nixon also appealed to the economic concerns of middle-class southern whites by promising lower tax rates and less government regulation. Finally, like George Wallace, he specialized in hard-hitting, polarizing rhetoric in which he pledged to restore "law and order" in the streets of America.

> Political realignment in a conservative South

In the 1972 election, it was Nixon's southern strategy that won the day: he carried every southern state by whopping majorities. The Republican takeover of the once "solid" Democratic South was the greatest realignment in American politics since Franklin D. Roosevelt's election in 1932.

Nixon's Domestic Agenda

As president, Nixon was less a rigid conservative ideologue than he was a crafty politician forced to deal with a Congress controlled by Democrats. He therefore chose his battles carefully and showed surprising flexibility, lead-ing political journalist Tom Wicker to describe him as "at once liberal and conservative, generous and begrudging, cynical and idealistic, choleric and calm, resentful and forgiving."

Nixon's focus during his first term was developing policies and programs that would gain him reelection in 1972. To please conservative Republicans and recruit conservative Democrats, he touted his New Federalism whereby he sent federal monies to the states and local governments for them to spend as they saw fit. He also disbanded the core agency of Lyndon John-son's War on Poverty program—the Office of Economic Opportunity—and

> New Federalism and Democratic legislation

cut funding to several Great Society programs. At the same time, the Democrats in Congress passed significant new legislation that Nixon did sign: the right of eighteen-year-olds to vote in national elections (1970) and in all elections under the Twenty-Sixth Amendment (1971); increases in Social Security benefits and food-stamp funding; the Occupational Safety and Health Act (1970) to ensure safer workplace environments; and the Federal Election Campaign Act (1971), which modified the rules governing corporate financial donations to political campaigns.

Nixon and Civil Rights

During his first term, President Nixon followed through on his campaign pledges to conservative white southerners to blunt the momentum of the civil rights movement. He appointed no African Americans to his cabinet, and refused even to meet with the all-Democratic Congressional Black Caucus. "We've had enough social programs: forced integration, education, housing," he told his chief of staff. "People don't want more [people] on welfare. They don't want to help the working poor, and our mood needs to be harder on this, not softer."

Nixon also launched a concerted effort to block congressional renewal of the Voting Rights Act of 1965 and to delay implementation of federal court orders requiring the racial desegregation of school districts in Mississippi. Sixty-five lawyers in the U.S. Justice Department signed a letter protesting Nixon's stance. The Democratic-controlled Congress then extended the Voting Rights Act over Nixon's veto.

The Supreme Court also thwarted Nixon's efforts to slow desegregation. Above the entrance to the Supreme Court building in Washington, D.C., are inscribed four words: "Equal justice under law." In its first decision under the new chief justice, Warren Burger—a Nixon appointee—the Court ordered the racial integration of the Mississippi public schools in *Alexander v. Holmes County Board of Education* (1969). During Nixon's first term, more schools were desegregated under court orders than in all the Kennedy-Johnson years combined.

Nixon's efforts to block desegregation in urban areas were also failures. The Burger Court ruled unanimously in *Swann v. Charlotte-Mecklenburg Board of Education* (1971) that school systems must bus students out of their neighborhoods if necessary to achieve racially integrated schools. Protests over busing desegregation thereafter erupted in the North, the Midwest, and the Southwest, as white families in Boston, Denver, and other cities denounced the destruction of "the neighborhood school." Angry white parents in Pontiac, Michigan, were so determined to stop mandatory busing to achieve racial integration that they firebombed empty school buses.

Off to school Because of violent protests against desegregation, school buses in South Boston are escorted by police in October of 1974.

Nixon and Environmental Protection

Dramatic increases in the price of oil and gasoline during the seventies fueled a major energy crisis in the United States. Natural resources grew limited—and increasingly precious. Bowing to pressure from both parties, as well as polls showing that 75 percent of voters supported stronger environmental protections, President Nixon told an aide to "keep me out of trouble on environmental issues"—he was "bored" by them. Yet he recognized that the public mood had shifted in favor of greater federal environmental protections, especially after two widely publicized environmental events in 1969.

The first was a massive oil spill off the coast of Santa Barbara, California. Within ten days, an enormous slick of crude oil contaminated 200 miles of California beaches, killing thousands of sea birds and marine animals. Six months later, on June 22, 1969, the Cuyahoga River, an 80-mile-long stream that slices through the center of Cleveland, Ohio, spontaneously caught fire. Fouled with oil and grease, bubbling with subsurface gases, and littered with debris, the chocolate-colored river ignited and burned for five days, its flames leaping fifty feet into the air. Like the Santa Barbara oil spill, the images of the burning river became an important catalyst in the raising of environmental awareness across the nation. A 1969 survey of college campuses by the *New York Times* revealed that many young people were transferring their attention and idealism from the anti-war movement to the environmental movement.

President Nixon knew that if he vetoed legislative efforts to improve environmental quality, the Democratic majorities in Congress would overrule him, so he chose not to stand in the way. In late 1969, Nixon signed the amended Endangered Species Preservation Act and the National Environmental Policy Act. The latter became effective on January 1, 1970, the year that environmental groups established an annual Earth Day celebration that would involve millions nationwide. In 1970, Nixon by executive order created two new federal environmental agencies, the **Environmental Protection Agency (EPA)** and the National Oceanic and Atmospheric Administration (NOAA). The same year, he signed the Clean Air Act to reduce air pollution on a national level. Two years later, however, Nixon vetoed a new clean water act, only to see Congress override his effort. He also undermined many of the new environmental laws by refusing to spend money appropriated by Congress to fund them.

> Nixon approves Environmental Protection Agency (EPA)

"Stagflation"

The major domestic development during the Nixon administration was a floundering economy. The accumulated expense of the Vietnam War and the Great Society programs helped quadruple the annual inflation rate from 3 percent in 1967 to 12 percent in 1974. Meanwhile, unemployment, at a low

Environmental Protection Agency (EPA) (1970) Federal environmental agency created by Nixon to appease the demands of congressional Democrats for a federal environmental watchdog agency.

of 3.3 percent when Nixon took office, nearly doubled to 6 percent by the end of 1970. Economists coined the term **stagflation** to describe the unprecedented situation of stalled economic growth (stagnation), rising inflation, and high unemployment all occurring at the same time. Consumer prices usually rose with a rapidly growing economy and rising employment. Now it was just the reverse, and there were no easy ways to fight the unusual combination of recession and inflation.

Stagflation had at least three deep-rooted causes. First, the Johnson administration had financed both the Great Society social-welfare programs and the Vietnam War without a major tax increase, thereby generating larger federal deficits, a major expansion of the money supply, and price inflation. Second, and more important, U.S. companies were now facing stiff international competition from West Germany, Japan, and other emerging industrial powers around the world. The technological and economic superiority that the U.S. had enjoyed since the Second World War was no longer unchallenged. Third, America's prosperity since 1945 had resulted in part from the ready availability of cheap sources of energy. No other nation was more dependent than the United States upon the automobile and the automobile industry, and no other nation was more wasteful in its use of fossil fuels in factories and homes. During the seventies, however, oil and gasoline became scarcer and costlier. High energy prices and oil shortages took their toll on the economy.

Just as domestic petroleum reserves began to dwindle and dependence upon foreign sources increased, the Organization of Petroleum Exporting Countries (OPEC) decided to use its huge oil supplies as a political and economic weapon. In 1973, the United States sent massive aid to Israel after a devastating Syrian-Egyptian attack that was launched on Yom Kippur, the holiest day on the Jewish calendar. OPEC responded by announcing that it would not sell oil to nations supporting Israel in the so-called Yom Kippur War and that it was raising its oil prices by 400 percent. The Arab oil embargo, called an "economic Pearl Harbor," caused gasoline shortages and skyrocketing prices. American motorists suddenly faced mile-long lines at gas stations, and factories cut production because of spiking energy costs. The environmental movement received a boost from the effects of the OPEC oil embargo as growing numbers of concerned Americans envisioned a future based on energy conservation, renewable energy, and simpler living.

Another condition leading to stagflation was the flood of new workers—mainly baby boomers and women—into the labor market. From 1965 to 1980, the workforce grew by almost 30 million workers, a number greater than the total labor force of France or West Germany. The number of new jobs could not keep up with the growth of the workforce, leaving many unemployed.

The Nixon administration responded erratically and ineffectively to stagflation, trying old remedies for a new problem. First, the president

"The Nixon Recession": Federal deficits, international competition, new workers, and an oil crisis

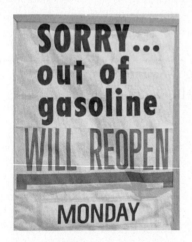

Oil crisis, 1973 The scarcity of oil forced the rationing of gasoline. Gas stations, such as this one in Colorado, closed on Sundays to conserve supplies.

stagflation Term coined by economists during the Nixon presidency to describe the unprecedented situation of stagnant economic growth and consumer price inflation occurring at the same time.

sought to reduce the federal deficit by raising taxes and cutting the budget. When the Democratic Congress refused to cooperate, he encouraged the Federal Reserve Board to reduce the nation's money supply by raising interest rates. The stock market immediately nose-dived, and the economy plunged into the "Nixon recession."

A sense of desperation about the stagnant economy seized the White House. In 1969, when asked about the possibility of imposing government caps on wages and prices, Nixon had been clear: "Controls. Oh, my God, no! . . . We'll never go to controls." In 1971, however, he reversed himself. He froze all wages and prices for ninety days. Still, the economy remained sluggish.

"Peace with Honor": Ending the Vietnam War

CORE **OBJECTIVE**

4. Analyze how and why Richard Nixon and Henry Kissinger changed military and political strategies to end America's involvement in the Vietnam War.

By the time Nixon entered the White House in January 1969, he and Henry Kissinger had developed a comprehensive vision of a new world order. The result of their collaboration was a dramatic transformation of U.S. foreign policy. Since 1945, the United States had lost its monopoly on nuclear weapons, its overwhelming economic dominance, and much of its geopolitical influence. The rapid rise of competing power centers in Europe, China, and Japan complicated the cold war as well as international relations in general.

Nixon and Kissinger envisioned defusing the cold war by pursuing peaceful coexistence with the Soviets and Chinese. After a "period of confrontation," Nixon explained in his 1969 inaugural address, "we are entering an era of negotiation." Preoccupied with secrecy, Nixon and Kissinger bypassed the State Department, including Secretary of State Rogers, and the Congress in their efforts to take advantage of quickly shifting world events.

The immediate task for Nixon and Kissinger was ending the war in Vietnam, which one presidential aide called a "bone in the nation's throat." Until the war was ended and all troops had returned home, the nation would find it difficult to achieve the social harmony that President Nixon had promised. Privately, he had decided that "there's no way to win the war" in Vietnam, so instead he sought what he called "peace with honor." That is, the United States could not simply cut and run; it needed to withdraw in a way that upheld the credibility of its military alliances around the world. Peace, however, was long in coming, not very honorable, and shockingly brief.

"Peace with honor"

Gradual Withdrawal

The Vietnam policy implemented by Nixon and his national security adviser Henry Kissinger moved along three fronts. First, U.S. negotiators in Paris demanded the withdrawal of Viet Cong forces from South Vietnam and the preservation of the U.S.-backed government of President Nguyen

Van Thieu. The North Vietnamese and Viet Cong negotiators, for their part, insisted on retaining a Communist military presence in the south and re-unifying the Vietnamese people under a government dominated by the Communists. There was no common ground. Hidden from public aware-ness and from America's South Vietnamese allies were secret meetings be-tween Kissinger and the North Vietnamese.

On the second front, Nixon tried to quell domestic unrest. He labeled the anti-war movement a "brotherhood of the misguided, the mistaken, the well-meaning, and the malevolent." He sought to defuse the anti-war move-ment by reducing the number of U.S. troops in Vietnam, justifying the re-duction as the natural result of "**Vietnamization**"—the equipping and training of South Vietnamese soldiers and pilots to assume the burden of combat. From a peak of 560,000 troops in 1969, U.S. combat forces were withdrawn by Nixon at a steady pace. By 1973, only 50,000 troops remained in Vietnam.

In 1969, Nixon also established a draft lottery whereby the birthdates of nineteen-year-old men were randomly selected and assigned a number be-tween 1 and 365 in order of their selection. Those with low lottery numbers would be the first drafted into military service. The lottery system elimi-nated many inequities and clarified the likelihood of being drafted. Four years later, in 1973, the president did away with the draft altogether by cre-ating an all-volunteer military. Those initiatives, coupled with the troop withdrawals from Vietnam, defused the anti-war movement. Opinion polls showed strong public support for Nixon's policies related to the Vietnam War. "We've got those liberal bastards on the run now," the president gloated, "and we're going to keep them on the run." Nixon had much less success in forcing concessions from the North Vietnamese negotiators.

On the third front, while steadily reducing the number of U.S. combat troops in Southeast Asia, Nixon and Kissinger greatly expanded the bomb-ing of North Vietnam in hopes of pressuring the Communist leaders to end the war. Kissinger felt that "a fourth-rate power" like North Vietnam must have a "breaking point" at which it would decide it was suffering too much damage. Nixon agreed, suggesting that they let the North Vietnamese lead-ers know that he was so "obsessed about Communism" that he might use the "nuclear button" if necessary.

In March 1969, the United States began a fourteen-month-long bombing campaign aimed at Communist forces that were using neighboring Cambo-dia as a base for raids into South Vietnam. Congress did not learn of the se-cret airstrikes until 1970, although the total tonnage of bombs dropped was four times that dropped on Japan during the Second World War. Still, Hanoi's leaders did not flinch; they decided to wait and let Nixon's domestic critics undermine his presidency. Then, on April 30, 1970, Nixon announced an "incursion" into "neutral" Cambodia by U.S. troops to "clean out" hidden Vietnamese Communist military bases. Privately, Nixon told Kissinger, who strongly endorsed the decision to extend the fighting into Cambodia, "If this doesn't work, it'll be your ass, Henry." Nixon knew that sending

"Vietnamization" and ending the military draft

Three fronts: Negotiation, troop reduction, and airstrikes

Vietnamization Nixon-era pol-icy of equipping and training South Vietnamese forces to take over the burden of combat from U.S. troops.

troops into Cambodia would reignite the anti-war movement. Secretary of State William Rogers predicted that "this will make the [anti-war] students puke."

Divisions at Home

Just as Nixon had expected, the escalation of the air war in Vietnam and the extension of the war into Cambodia triggered widespread anti-war demonstrations. In the fall of 1969, two massive day-long demonstrations in hundreds of cities across the nation and around the world brought millions of protesters into the streets. Nixon, however, was unmoved. "As far as this kind of activity is concerned," he gruffly explained, "we expect it; however, under no circumstances will I be affected whatever by it." Nixon later referred to student protesters as "bums."

Escalation of anti-war riots over the invasion of Cambodia

In the spring of 1970, news of the secret Cambodian "incursion" by U.S. forces breathed new life into the anti-war movement and set off explosive demonstrations on college campuses and across the nation. At Kent State University, the Ohio National Guard was called in to control campus rioting. The poorly trained guardsmen panicked and opened fire on the rock-throwing demonstrators, killing four student bystanders.

The killings at Kent State added new fury to the anti-war and anti-Nixon movement. That spring, demonstrations occurred on more than 350 campuses. A presidential commission charged with investigating the shootings concluded that they were "unnecessary and unwarranted." Eleven days after the Kent State tragedy, on May 15, Mississippi highway patrolmen riddled a dormitory at Jackson State College with bullets, killing two students who were protesting the war. In New York City, anti-war demonstrators who gathered to protest the student deaths and the invasion of Cambodia were attacked by conser-

Shooting at Kent State Mary Ann Vecchio, a teenage runaway participating in the anti-war demonstration, decries the murder of a Kent State student after the National Guard fired into the crowd.

vative "hard-hat" construction workers, who forced the protesters to disperse and then marched on City Hall to raise the U.S. flag, which had been lowered to half-staff in mourning for the Kent State victims.

The following year, in June 1971, the *New York Times* began publishing excerpts from *The History of the U.S. Decision-Making Process of Vietnam Policy*, a secret Defense Department study commissioned by Robert McNamara before his resignation as Lyndon Johnson's secretary of defense in 1968. The so-called Pentagon Papers, leaked to the press by Daniel Ellsberg, a former Defense Department official, confirmed what many critics of the war had long suspected: Congress and the public had not received the

The Pentagon Papers published (1971)

full story on the Gulf of Tonkin incident of 1964, and contingency plans for U.S. entry into the war were being drawn up even as President Johnson was promising that combat troops would never be sent to Vietnam. Although the Pentagon Papers dealt with events only up to 1965, the Nixon administration blocked their publication, arguing that release of the classified information would endanger national security and would prolong the war. By a vote of 6 to 3, the Supreme Court ruled against the government. Newspapers throughout the country began publishing the controversial documents the next day.

War without End

During 1972, mounting social divisions at home and the approach of the presidential election influenced the negotiations in Paris between the United States and representatives of North Vietnam. In the summer of 1972, Henry Kissinger renewed private meetings with the North Vietnamese negotiators, and he now dropped his insistence upon the removal of all North Vietnamese troops from South Vietnam before the withdrawal of the remaining U.S. troops. On October 26, only a week before the U.S. presidential election, Kissinger announced that "Peace is at hand."

Christmas bombings of North Vietnam (1972)

As it turned out, however, this was a cynical ploy to win votes. Several days earlier, the Thieu regime in South Vietnam had rejected the Kissinger plan for a cease-fire, fearful that allowing North Vietnamese troops to remain in the south would virtually guarantee a Communist victory. The Paris peace talks broke off on December 16, and two days later the newly reelected Nixon ordered massive bombings of Hanoi and Haiphong, the two largest cities in North Vietnam. "The bastards have never been bombed like they're going to be bombed this time," Nixon pledged. These so-called Christmas bombings and the simultaneous U.S. mining of North Vietnamese harbors aroused worldwide protest.

Paris Peace Accords (1973)

Yet the bombings also made the North Vietnamese more willing to negotiate. The air strikes stopped on December 29, and the talks in Paris soon resumed. On January 27, 1973, the United States, North and South Vietnam, and the Viet Cong signed an "agreement on ending the war and restoring peace in Vietnam," known as the Paris Peace Accords. In fact, it was a carefully disguised surrender that enabled the United States to end its combat role. While Nixon and Kissinger claimed that the bombings had brought North Vietnam to its senses, in truth the North Vietnamese never altered their basic stance; they kept 150,000 troops in South Vietnam and remained committed to the reunification of Vietnam under one government.

What had changed was the willingness of the South Vietnamese, who were never allowed to participate in the negotiations, to accept the agreement, however reluctantly, on the basis of Nixon's promise that the United States would respond "with full force" to any Communist violation of the agreement. Kissinger had little confidence that the treaty provisions would enable South Vietnam to survive on its own. He told a White House staffer, "If they're lucky, they can hold out for a year and a half."

By the time the Paris Peace Accords were signed in 1973, another 20,000 Americans had died since Nixon had taken office in 1969, the morale of the U.S. military had been shattered, millions of Southeast Asians had been killed or wounded, and fighting soon broke out again in both Vietnam and Cambodia. In the end, Nixon and Kissinger's diplomatic efforts gained nothing the president could not have accomplished in 1969 by ending the war on similar terms.

The Collapse of South Vietnam

On March 29, 1973, the last U.S. combat troops left Vietnam. The same day, almost 600 American prisoners of war, most of them downed pilots, were released from Hanoi. Within months of the U.S. withdrawal, however, the cease-fire in Vietnam collapsed, the war between North and South resumed, and the Communist forces gained the upper hand. In Cambodia (renamed the Khmer Republic after a 1970 military coup) and Laos, where fighting had been more sporadic, a Communist victory also seemed inevitable.

In 1975, the North Vietnamese launched a full-scale invasion, sending the South Vietnamese army into headlong panic, followed by ragged columns of terrified civilians. South Vietnamese president Nguyen Van Thieu desperately appealed to Washington for the promised U.S. assistance to which he was entitled by the Paris Peace Accords—and to which South Vietnam had grown addicted. But the U.S. Congress, long since weary of spending more dollars and lives in Vietnam, refused. On April 21, Thieu resigned and flew to Taiwan, carrying with him three and a half tons of gold to ease his sorrow.

"Peace with honor" had proven to be, in the words of one CIA official, only a "decent interval"—enough time for the United States to remove itself before the collapse of the South Vietnamese government. On April 30, 1975, Americans watched on television as North Vietnamese tanks rolled into Saigon, soon to be renamed Ho Chi Minh City, and military helicopters lifted desperate U.S. embassy and South Vietnamese officials and their families to warships waiting offshore.

The longest, most controversial, and least successful war in American history up to that point was finally over, leaving a bitter legacy. During the period of U.S. involvement, almost 2 million combatants and civilians were killed on both sides. North Vietnam absorbed incredible losses—some 600,000 soldiers and countless civilians killed. South Vietnam lost 240,000 soldiers, and over 500,000 Vietnamese became refugees in the United States. More than 58,000 Americans died in Vietnam, 300,000 were wounded, 2,500 were declared missing, and almost 100,000 returned missing one or more limbs. The United States spent over $158 billion on the war.

The Vietnam War was the defining life event for the "baby boomers," the largest generation of Americans ever, the generation that provided most of the U.S. troops in Vietnam as well as most of the anti-war protesters. The war divided that generation in ways that would be felt for years. The "loss"

Leave with honor Hundreds of thousands of South Vietnamese tried to flee the Communist forces with evacuating Americans. Here U.S. official punches a Vietnamese man attempting to join his family in an overflowing airplane at Nha Trang.

of the war, combined with news of atrocities committed by American soldiers, eroded respect for the military so thoroughly that many young people came to regard military service as corrupting and dishonorable.

The Vietnam combat veterans (average age 19, compared to 26, the average age of servicemen in the Second World War) faced a unique ordeal. They had "lost" a war in which their country had lost interest. When they returned to America, many of them found that even their families were unwilling to talk about what they had experienced, or were embarrassed about it. "I went over there thinking I was doing something right and came back a bum," said Larry Langowski from Illinois. "I came back decked with medals on my uniform, and I got spit on by a hippie girl."

The Vietnam War, initially described as a crusade on behalf of democratic ideals, instead revealed that democracy was not easily transferable to regions of the world that lacked any historical experience with democratic government. Fought to show that the United States would be steadfast in containing the spread of communism, the war instead sapped the national will and fragmented the national consensus that had governed foreign affairs since 1947, when President Truman developed policies to "contain" Communism around the world. It also changed the balance of power in domestic politics.

As opposition to the war undermined Lyndon B. Johnson's presidency, it also created enduring fractures within the Democratic party. Said George McGovern, the anti-war senator and 1972 Democratic presidential nominee, "The Vietnam tragedy is at the root of the confusion and division of the Democratic party. It tore up our souls."

Not only had a decade of American effort in Vietnam proved futile, but the Khmer Rouge, the insurgent Cambodian Communist movement, had also won a resounding victory over the government of the U.S.-backed Khmer Republic, plunging that country into a bloodbath. The maniacal Khmer Rouge leaders renamed the country Kampuchea and organized a genocidal campaign to destroy all of their opponents, killing almost a third of the total population.

The Nixon Doctrine and a Thawing Cold War

CORE **OBJECTIVE**
5. Examine the world order that evolved after the Vietnam War from Richard Nixon's and Henry Kissinger's diplomacy and foreign policies.

Despite the frustrations associated with his efforts to end the Vietnam War, Richard Nixon, like John F. Kennedy, greatly preferred foreign policy over domestic policy (which he compared to building "sewer projects"), and his greatest successes were in international relations. Nixon was an expert in foreign affairs and had traveled abroad frequently as Eisenhower's vice president during the 1950s, and he benefited greatly from the expertise and strategic vision of Henry Kissinger. Their grand design for U.S. foreign policy after the Vietnam War centered on developing friendly relations with the Soviet Union and Communist China. Kissinger said they wanted to "improve the possibilities of accommodations with each as we increase our options with both," enabling all three superpowers to reduce the cost of the arms race while minimizing the possibility of nuclear war. Kissinger pressed for a return to an Eisenhower-era approach to foreign policy that entailed using the Central Intelligence Agency (CIA) to pursue America's strategic interests covertly and reducing large-scale military interventions.

The CIA in Chile

Ever since Fidel Castro and his Communist supporters gained control of Cuba in 1959, American presidents had been determined to prevent any more Communist insurgencies in the Western Hemisphere. In 1970, Salvador Allende, a Marxist, a Socialist party leader, and a friend of Fidel Castro, was a leading presidential candidate in Chile, a thousand-mile-long nation on the southwest coast of South America. Allende's candidacy caused President Nixon and Henry Kissinger great concern, for they knew that, if elected, Allende planned to "nationalize" Chilean industries, including those owned by U.S. corporations. They did not want "another Castro" in Latin America.

In September 1970, Nixon told the head of the CIA that an Allende government in Chile was "unacceptable," and he authorized $10 million to prevent an Allende presidency, urging the CIA to do anything "your

U.S. foreign policy in Latin America: Anti-communism and the CIA imagination can conjure" up to stop Allende. Nevertheless, although CIA agents provided campaign funds to Allende's opponents, he was elected on October 24, 1970. The CIA then encouraged Chilean military leaders to oust him. In September 1973, the army took control, Allende either committed suicide or was murdered, and General Augusto Pinochet, a ruthless military dictator supposedly friendly to the United States, declared himself the head of the government.

After Pinochet assumed power, Kissinger, now secretary of state, told Nixon that the CIA "didn't do it," but "we helped them" by creating the conditions that made the coup possible. In consolidating control over Chile, Pinochet executed thousands of people. It was yet another example of the United States being so obsessed by anti-communism and protecting American business interests that it was willing to interfere in the democratic process of other nations and help remove elected officials through covert operations.

The Nixon Doctrine

The Nixon Doctrine and détente

In July 1969, while trying to get America out of the war in Vietnam, President Nixon revealed the negative effects of the lengthy war at a press conference on Guam island in the Pacific. There, while announcing the first U.S. troop withdrawals, he unveiled what came to be called the Nixon Doctrine, a new approach to America's handling of international crises. Unlike John F. Kennedy, who had declared that the United States would "pay any price, bear any burden" to win the cold war, Nixon explained that "America cannot—and will not—conceive *all* the plans, design *all* the programs, execute *all* the decisions, and undertake *all* the defense of the free nations of the world." Those nations experiencing Communist insurgencies must in the future assume primary responsibility for their own defense. The United States would provide weapons and money but not soldiers.

At the same time that Nixon was reducing the likelihood of U.S. military interventions, he announced that the United States would pursue partnerships with Communist countries in areas of mutual interest. That Nixon, a Republican with a history of rabid anti-communism, would pursue such a policy of **détente** (a French word meaning "easing of relations") with America's Communist archenemies shocked many observers and demonstrated yet again his pragmatic flexibility.

The People's Republic of China

Nixon had a genius for surprise, an exquisite gift for defying expectations. In 1971, without even informing Secretary of State Rogers, Nixon sent Henry Kissinger on a secret trip to Beijing to explore the possibility of U.S. recognition of Communist China. Since 1949, when Mao Zedong's revolutionary movement established control in China, the United States had refused to recognize the People's Republic of China, preferring to regard Chiang Kai-shek's exiled regime on the island of Taiwan as the legitimate Chinese

détente Period of improving relations between the United States and Communist nations, particularly China and the Soviet Union, during the Nixon administration.

government. But now the time seemed ripe for a bold renewal of ties. Both the United States and Communist China were exhausted from intense domestic strife (anti-war protests in America, the Cultural Revolution in China), and both were eager to resist Soviet expansionism.

Nixon's bombshell announcement on July 15, 1971, that Kissinger had just returned from Beijing and that the president himself would be going to China the following year sent shock waves around the world. Nixon became the first U.S. president to use the term *People's Republic of China*, an important symbolic step in his efforts to normalize relations with the most populous nation in the world. The Nationalist Chinese on Taiwan felt betrayed, and the Japanese, historic enemies of China, were furious at the American news. What they called "Nixon shock" was a major factor in the collapse of the Japanese government. In October 1971, the United Nations voted to admit the People's Republic of China and expel Taiwan.

On February 21, 1972, during the "week that changed the world," Americans who had lived amid the intense anti-Communist atmosphere of the cold war were stunned to turn on their televisions and see President Nixon shake hands and drink toasts in Beijing with Prime Minister Zhou Enlai and Communist Party Chairman Mao Zedong. In one simple but astonishing stroke, Nixon and Kissinger had ended two decades of diplomatic isolation of the People's Republic of China. They had seen a geopolitical opportunity and seized it.

During the president's week-long visit, the two nations agreed to scientific and cultural exchanges, steps toward the resumption of trade, and the eventual reunification of Taiwan with the mainland. A year after Nixon's visit, "liaison offices" that served as unofficial embassies were established in Washington and Beijing, and in 1979, diplomatic recognition was formalized. As a conservative anti-Communist, Nixon had accomplished a diplomatic feat that his Democratic predecessors could not have attempted for fear of being branded "soft on Communism." Nixon and Kissinger's bold move in China had the added benefit of giving them leverage with the Soviet Union, which was understandably nervous about a U.S.-Chinese alliance.

> Nixon recognizes Communist China (1972)

Nixon goes to China President Nixon and Chinese premier Zhou Enlai raise a toast to each other at the lavish farewell banquet in Shanghai that rounded off the historic visit.

Embracing the Soviet Union

In truth, China welcomed the breakthrough in relations with the United States because of tensions with its neighbor, the Soviet Union, with which it shared a long but contested border. By 1972, the Chinese leadership had become more fearful of the Soviet Union than the United States. The Soviet leaders, in turn troubled by the agreements between China and the United States, were also eager to ease tensions with the Americans. Once again, President Nixon surprised the world by announcing that he would visit

> The Moscow summit: Trade agreements, arms reductions, and the easing of cold war tensions

Moscow in 1972 for discussions with Leonid Brezhnev, the Soviet premier. The high drama of the China visit was repeated in Moscow, with toasts and elegant dinners attended by world leaders who had previously regarded each other as incarnations of evil.

What became known as détente with the Soviets offered the promise of less intense competition between the superpowers. Nixon and Brezhnev signed the pathbreaking **Strategic Arms Limitation Treaty (SALT I)**, which negotiators had been working on since 1969. The SALT agreement did not end the nuclear arms race, but it did limit the number of missiles with nuclear warheads and prohibited the construction of missile-defense systems. The Moscow summit also produced new trade agreements, including an arrangement whereby the United States sold almost a quarter of its wheat crop to the Soviets at a favorable price (critics called it the Great Grain Robbery).

The Moscow summit resulted in the dramatic easing of tensions between the two cold war superpowers. As Nixon told Congress upon his return, "never before have two adversaries, so deeply divided by conflicting ideologies and political rivalries, been able to limit the armaments upon which their survival depends." For Nixon and Kissinger, the agreements with China and the Soviet Union represented monumental changes in the global order that would have lasting consequences. Over time, the détente policy with the Soviet Union would help end the cold war altogether by lowering Soviet hostility to Western influences penetrating their closed society, which in turn slowly eroded Communist rule from the inside.

Shuttle Diplomacy

> U.S.-negotiated cease-fire in the Middle East

The Nixon-Kissinger initiatives in the Middle East were less dramatic and less conclusive than the agreements with China and the Soviet Union, but they did show that the United States at long last recognized the legitimacy of Arab interests in the region and its own dependence upon Middle Eastern oil, even though the Arab nations were adamantly opposed to the existence of Israel. In the Six-Day War of 1967, Israeli forces had routed the armies of Egypt, Syria, and Jordan, and seized territory from all three nations. Moreover, the number of Palestinian refugees, many of them homeless since the creation of Israel in 1948, increased after the Israeli victory.

The Middle East remained a tinderbox of tensions. On October 6, 1973, the Jewish holy day of Yom Kippur, Syria and Egypt, backed by money from Saudi Arabia and armed with Soviet weapons, attacked Israel, igniting what became the Yom Kippur War. It created the most dangerous confrontation between the United States and the Soviet Union since the Cuban missile crisis. When the Israeli army, with weapons supplied by the United States, launched a fierce counterattack that appeared likely to overwhelm Egypt, the Soviets threatened to intervene militarily. Nixon, whose presidency was at risk because of the ongoing Watergate investigations, was bedridden because he was drunk, according to Henry Kissinger and other aides, so

Strategic Arms Limitation Treaty (SALT I) (1972) Agreement signed by President Nixon and Secretary Brezhnev prohibiting the development of missile defense systems in the United States and Soviet Union and limiting the quantity of nuclear warheads for both.

Kissinger, as secretary of state, presided over a National Security Council meeting that placed America's military forces on full alert to keep the Soviets out of the Middle Eastern war. On October 20, Kissinger flew to Moscow to meet with Soviet premier Leonid Brezhnev. Kissinger skillfully negotiated a cease-fire agreement and exerted pressure on the Israelis to prevent them from taking additional Arab territory. In an attempt to broker a lasting settlement, Kissinger made numerous flights among the capitals of the Middle East. His "shuttle diplomacy" won acclaim from all sides, though he failed to find a comprehensive formula for peace. He did, however, lay the groundwork for an important treaty between Israel and Egypt in 1977.

Watergate

CORE **OBJECTIVE**

6. Explain how the Watergate scandal unfolded, and assess its political significance.

Nixon's foreign policy achievements allowed him to stage the presidential campaign of 1972 as a triumphal procession. Early on, the main threat to his reelection came from George Wallace, who had the potential as a third-party candidate to deprive the Republicans of conservative southern votes and thereby throw the election to the Democrats. That threat ended, however, on May 15, 1972, when Wallace was shot in an assassination attempt. Although he survived, he was left paralyzed below the waist and had to withdraw from the campaign.

Meanwhile, the Democrats nominated Senator George McGovern of South Dakota, an anti-war liberal. A poor campaigner who was viewed by many Americans as a left-wing extremist, he never had a chance of winning. In the 1972 election, Nixon won the greatest victory of any Republican presidential candidate in history, capturing 520 electoral votes to only 17 for McGovern. The popular vote was equally decisive: 46 million to 28 million, a proportion of the total vote (60.8 percent) that was second only to Lyndon Johnson's victory over Barry Goldwater in 1964. After his landslide victory, Nixon planned to promote the "more conservative values and beliefs of the New Majority throughout the country and use my power to put some teeth in my new American Revolution."

For all of his abilities and accomplishments, however, Nixon was a chronically insecure person. More than most presidents, he nursed grudges and took politics personally, and he could be ruthless in attacking his opponents. As president, he began keeping a secret "enemies list" and launched numerous efforts to embarrass and punish those on the list. Little did he know that such behavior would bring his second term crashing down around him.

"Dirty Tricks"

By the spring of 1972, senior Nixon aide John Ehrlichman was overseeing a secret team of agents who performed various acts of sabotage against leading Democrats, such as falsely accusing Senators Hubert H. Humphrey and

Henry Jackson of sexual improprieties, forging press releases, setting off stink bombs at Democratic campaign events, and planting spies on McGovern's campaign plane.

During the campaign, McGovern had complained about the numerous "dirty tricks" orchestrated by members of the Nixon administration. Nixon, it turned out, had ordered illegal wiretaps on his opponents (as well as on his own aides), tried to coerce the Internal Revenue Service to intimidate Democrats, and told his chief of staff, Bob Haldeman, to break into the safe at the Brookings Institution, a Washington research center with Democratic ties. "Goddamnit," he told Haldeman, "get in and get those files. Blow the safe and get it."

The Watergate break-in (1972)

McGovern was especially disturbed by an incident on June 17, 1972, when five burglars were caught breaking into the Democratic National Committee headquarters in the exclusive **Watergate** apartment and office complex in Washington, D.C. The burglars were former CIA agents, and one, James W. McCord, worked for the Nixon reelection campaign. At the time, McGovern's complaints about the Watergate break-in seemed like sour grapes from a candidate running far behind in the polls. Nixon and his staff ignored the news of the "third-rate burglary." The president said that no one cares "when somebody bugs somebody else," and he denied any involvement in this "very bizarre incident." Privately, however, he and his senior aides began feverish efforts to cover up the Watergate affair. They secretly provided $400,000 in "hush money" to the jailed burglars to buy their silence and tried to keep the FBI out of the investigation. They also discussed using the CIA to derail the Justice Department's investigation of the burglary.

Uncovering the Cover-up

CREEP: Committee to Re-Elect the President

During the trial of the accused Watergate burglars in January 1973, the relentless questioning of federal judge John J. Sirica led one of the accused to tell the full story of the Nixon administration's involvement. James W. McCord, security chief of the Committee to Re-Elect the President (CREEP), was the first in what would become a long line of informers to reveal the systematic efforts of Nixon and his aides to create an "imperial presidency" above the law. By the time of the Watergate break-in, the money to finance "dirty tricks" was being illegally collected through CREEP and controlled by the White House staff.

The Watergate cover-up

The trail of evidence pursued first by Judge Sirica, then by a grand jury, and then by a Senate committee headed by Democrat Samuel J. Ervin Jr. of North Carolina, led directly to what the White House legal counsel John Dean called a "cancer close to the Presidency." Nixon was personally involved in the cover-up of the Watergate incident, using his presidential powers to discredit and block the investigation. He ordered the CIA to keep the FBI off the case and even coached his aides how to lie under oath. Most alarming, as it turned out, the Watergate burglary was merely one small part

Watergate (1972–1974)
Scandal that exposed the criminality and corruption of the Nixon administration and ultimately led to President Nixon's resignation in 1974.

of a larger pattern of corruption and criminality sanctioned by the Nixon White House.

The Watergate cover-up crumbled as various people, including John Dean, began to cooperate with prosecutors. At the same time, two reporters for the *Washington Post*, Carl Bernstein and Bob Woodward, relentlessly pursued the story, eventually making it a compelling topic of national conversation.

The cover-up unraveled further in 1973 when L. Patrick Gray, acting director of the FBI, resigned after confessing that he had destroyed several incriminating documents. On April 30, Ehrlichman and Haldeman resigned (they would later serve time in prison), as did Attorney General Richard Kleindienst. A few days later, Nixon nervously assured the public in a television address, "I am not a crook." Then Dean, whom Nixon had dismissed because of his cooperation with prosecutors, shocked the nation by testifying before the Ervin committee that there had been a White House–led cover-up approved by the president.

Nixon thereafter became preoccupied with frantic efforts at self-defense and survival. He refused to provide Senator Ervin's committee with documents it requested, citing "executive privilege" to protect national security. In another shocking disclosure, a White House aide told the Ervin committee that Nixon had installed a secret taping system in the White House, and that many of the conversations about the Watergate burglary and cover-up had been recorded.

The bombshell news about the recording system in the Oval Office set off a yearlong legal battle for the "Nixon tapes." Harvard law professor Archibald Cox, whom Nixon's new attorney general, Elliot Richardson, had appointed as special prosecutor to investigate the Watergate case, took the president to court in October 1973 to obtain the tapes. Nixon refused to release the recordings and ordered Cox fired. On October 20, in what became known as the "Saturday Night Massacre," Richardson and Deputy Attorney General William Ruckelshaus resigned rather than fire the special prosecutor. (Solicitor General Robert Bork finally fired Cox.) Nixon's dismissal of Cox produced a firestorm of public indignation. Numerous newspaper and magazine editorials, as well as a growing chorus of legislators, called for the president to be impeached for obstructing justice. A Gallup poll revealed that Nixon's approval rating had plunged to 17 percent, the lowest level any president had ever received.

> The "Nixon tapes" and the Saturday Night Massacre

Cox's dismissal failed to end Nixon's legal troubles. The new special prosecutor, Leon Jaworski, also took the president to court. In March 1974, the Watergate grand jury indicted John Ehrlichman, Bob Haldeman, and former Attorney General John Mitchell for obstruction of justice and named Nixon an "unindicted co-conspirator." On April 30, Nixon, still refusing to turn over the actual tapes, released 1,254 pages of transcribed recordings that he had edited himself, often substituting the phrase "expletive deleted" for the vulgar language and anti-Semitic rants he had

> Calls for Nixon's impeachment

frequently unleashed ("People said my language was bad," Nixon later rationalized, "but Jesus, you should have heard LBJ!"). At one point in the transcripts, the president told his aides that they should have frequent memory lapses when testifying about the cover-up.

The transcripts provoked widespread anger and disgust, for they revealed a president who behaved in disgracefully unpresidential ways. His Oval Office conversations were so petty, self-serving, bigoted, and profane that they degraded the stature of the presidency—"shabby, disgusting, immoral," said Republican senator Hugh Scott. The transcripts only fueled the growing demands for Nixon to resign.

United States v. Richard M. Nixon (1974)

By the summer of 1974, Nixon was under intense pressure and in full retreat. He became alternately combative, melancholy, and petty. During White House visits, Henry Kissinger found him increasingly unstable and drinking heavily. Nixon's efforts to orchestrate the cover-up obsessed him, unbalanced him, and unhinged him. After meeting with the president, Senator Barry Goldwater reported that Nixon "jabbered incessantly, often incoherently." He seemed "to be cracking."

The Watergate drama transfixed Americans, who watched the daily Ervin committee hearings as if they were episodes in a soap opera. On July 24, 1974, the Supreme Court ruled unanimously, in *United States v. Richard M. Nixon*, that the president must surrender *all* of the tape recordings. A few days later, the House Judiciary Committee voted to recommend three articles of impeachment: obstruction of justice through the payment of "hush money" to witnesses and the withholding of evidence; abuse of power through the use of federal agencies to deprive citizens of their constitutional rights; and defiance of Congress by withholding the tapes.

Before the House of Representatives could meet to vote on impeachment, Nixon grudgingly handed over the complete set of White House tapes. The drama continued, however, when investigators learned that sections of certain recordings were missing, including eighteen minutes of a key conversation in June 1972 during which Nixon first mentioned the Watergate burglary. The president's loyal secretary took the blame for the erasure, claiming that she had accidentally pushed the wrong button, but technical experts later concluded that the missing segments had been intentionally deleted. The other White House tape recordings, however, provided more than enough evidence of Nixon's involvement in the cover-up. At one point, the same president who had been the architect of détente with the Soviet Union and the recognition of Communist China had yelled at aides who were asking what they and others should say to Watergate investigators, "I don't give a shit what happens. I want you all to stonewall it, let them plead the Fifth Amendment, cover up or anything else."

Nixon the first president to resign in office

The evidence in the tape recordings led Republican leaders to urge Nixon to quit rather than face an impeachment trial in the Senate. On August 9, 1974, the embattled president resigned from office, the only president ever to do so. In 1969, he had begun his presidency hoping to heal America, to "bring people together." Now he left the White House to begin a self-imposed exile at his home in San Clemente, California, having deeply wounded the nation. Nixon was one of the strangest, most complicated, and most interesting political figures in American history. He never understood why the Watergate affair could have ended his presidency; in his view, his only mistake was getting caught. Nixon claimed that a president's actions could not be "illegal." He was wrong. The Watergate affair's clearest lesson was that not even a president is above the law.

Watergate and the Presidency

If there was a silver lining in the dark cloud of Watergate, it was the vigor and resilience of the institutions that had brought a rogue president to justice—the press, Congress, the courts, and aroused public opinion.

Congress responded to the Watergate revelations with several pieces of legislation designed to curb executive power. Already nervous about possible efforts to renew American military assistance to South Vietnam, the Democratic Congress passed the **War Powers Act** (1973), which requires a president to inform Congress within forty-eight hours if U.S. troops are deployed in combat abroad and to withdraw troops after sixty days unless Congress specifically approves their stay. In an effort to correct abuses in the use of campaign funds, Congress enacted legislation in 1974 that set new ceilings on political contributions and expenditures. And in reaction to the Nixon claim of "executive privilege" as a means of withholding evidence, Congress strengthened the 1966 Freedom of Information Act to require prompt responses to requests for information from government files and to place on government agencies the burden of proof for classifying information as secret.

An Unelected President

During Richard Nixon's last year in office, the Watergate crisis so dominated national politics that major domestic and foreign problems received little attention. Vice President Spiro Agnew had himself been forced to resign in October 1973 for accepting bribes from contractors before and during his term in office. The vice president at the time of Nixon's resignation was Gerald Ford, a congenial former House minority leader from Michigan whom Nixon had appointed to succeed Agnew under the provisions of the Twenty-Fifth Amendment, which was ratified in 1967. On August 9, 1974, Ford was sworn in as the nation's first politically appointed chief executive, the only person in history to serve as both vice president and president without having been elected to those offices.

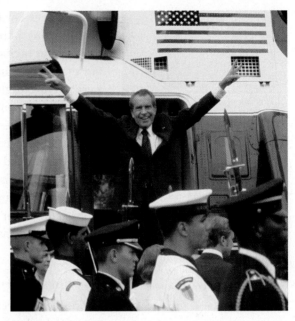

V for "victory" Before boarding the White House helicopter following his resignation, Nixon flashes a bright smile and his trademark V-sign to the world on August 9, 1974.

Gerald Ford assumes presidency (1974)

War Powers Act (1973) Legislation requiring the president to inform Congress within 48 hours of the deployment of U.S. troops abroad and to withdraw them after 60 days unless Congress approves their continued deployment.

Gerald Ford The 38th president listens apprehensively to news of rising rates of unemployment and inflation in 1974.

President Ford reassured the nation that "our long nightmare is over," but restoring public confidence in elected leaders was not easy. Only a month after taking office, Ford reopened the wounds of Watergate by issuing a "full, free, and absolute pardon" to Richard Nixon. Many Americans were not in a forgiving mood when it came to Nixon, and Ford's pardon unleashed a storm of controversy. "Jail Ford!" yelled many protesters outside the White House. Ford was grilled by a House subcommittee wanting to know whether Nixon had made a secret deal with Ford for the pardon. Ford vigorously denied the charge, adding that nothing was to be gained by putting Nixon in prison. But the pardon hobbled Ford's presidency. His approval rating plummeted from 71 percent to 49 percent in one day, the steepest drop ever recorded. Even Ford's press secretary resigned in protest of his boss's decision. The president never fully recovered the public's confidence.

The Ford Years

As president, Gerald Ford soon adopted the posture he had developed as the minority leader in the House of Representatives: naysaying leader of the opposition who believed that the federal government exercised too much power. In his first fifteen months as president, Ford vetoed thirty-nine bills passed by Congress, thereby outstripping Herbert Hoover's all-time veto record in less than half the time.

By far the most important development during Ford's brief presidency was the struggling economy. During the fall of 1974, the nation had entered the deepest recession since the Great Depression. Unemployment jumped to 9 percent in 1975, the annual rate of inflation reached double digits, and the federal deficit soon hit a record. President Ford announced that inflation had become "Public Enemy No. 1," but instead of taking bold action, he launched a timid public relations campaign featuring lapel buttons that simply read WIN, symbolizing the administration's determination to "Whip Inflation Now."

The WIN buttons became a national joke and a symbol of Ford's ineffectiveness in the fight against stagflation. He himself later admitted that it was a failed "gimmick." Ford initially supported increased taxes on corporations and individuals to fight inflation, only to reverse himself. By 1975, when Ford delivered his State of the Union address, he lamely conceded that "the state of the union is not good." In March 1975, Ford signed a tax reduction bill that failed in its goal of stimulating economic growth. Instead it was the federal budget deficit that grew from $53 billion in 1975 to $74 billion in 1976.

In foreign policy, Ford retained Henry Kissinger as secretary of state (while stripping him of his dual role as national security adviser) and pursued Nixon's goals of stability in the Middle East, friendly relations with China, and détente with the Soviet Union. In addition, Kissinger's tireless

Middle East diplomacy produced an important agreement: Israel promised to return to Egypt most of the Sinai territory captured in the 1967 War, and the two nations agreed to rely upon negotiations rather than force to settle future disagreements. These limited but significant achievements should have enhanced Ford's image, but they were drowned in the sea of criticism over the collapse of the South Vietnamese government in the face of the North Vietnamese invasion.

The Election of 1976

Both political parties were in disarray as they prepared for the 1976 presidential election. At the Republican Convention, Gerald Ford had to fend off a powerful challenge from the darling of the party's growing conservative wing, Ronald Reagan, a former two-term California governor and Hollywood actor.

The Democrats chose James Earl Carter Jr., who had served one term as governor of Georgia. A former naval officer and engineer turned peanut farmer, Carter was one of several Democratic southern governors who sought to move their party away from its traditional "tax and spend" liberalism. Carter insisted that he was neither a liberal nor a conservative but a pragmatic "engineer" who would be able to get the "right thing" done in the "right ways." He capitalized on post-Watergate cynicism by promising that he would "never tell a lie to the American people." He also trumpeted his status as a political "outsider" whose inexperience in Washington politics would be an asset. Carter was certainly different from conventional candidates. Political reporters covering the campaign marveled at a Southern Baptist candidate who was a "born again" Christian.

Ford made a crucial mistake during a televised debate with Carter when he mistakenly claimed that "there is no Soviet domination of Eastern Europe, and there never will be under a Ford administration." To the surprise of many, the little-known Carter revived the New Deal voting alliance of southern whites, blacks, urban labor unionists, and ethnic groups like Jews and Hispanics to eke out a narrow win, receiving 41 million votes to Ford's 39 million. A heavy turnout of African Americans in the South enabled Carter to sweep every state in the region except Virginia. He also benefited from the appeal of Walter F. Mondale, his liberal running mate and a favorite among blue-collar workers and the urban poor.

The significant story of the election was not so much Carter or Ford but the low voter turnout. "Neither Ford nor Carter won as many votes as Mr. Nobody," said one reporter, commenting on how almost half the eligible voters, apparently alienated by Watergate, the stagnant economy, and the two lackluster candidates, chose to sit out the election. It was not a good omen for a new Democratic president about to begin his term.

- **Youth Revolt** Civil rights activism inspired a heightened interest in a number of social causes during the sixties, especially among the youth. Students for a Democratic Society (SDS) embodied the *New Left* ideology, and helped spur the free-speech movement (FSM) starting at the University of California, Berkeley, and spreading to many campuses across the nation. By 1970, a distinctive *counterculture* also emerged among disaffected youth and attracted hippies many of whom used mind-altering drugs, lived on rural communes, and refused conventional life, which they viewed as corrupt and constricting.

- **The Inspirational Effects of the Civil Rights Movement** The energy, ideals, tactics, and courage of the civil rights movement inspired many other social reform movements, including the *women's movement*, the *"Red Power"* movement and the *United Farm Workers (UFW)*. The 1969 *Stonewall riots* marked a militant new era in the crusade for gay rights.

- **Reaction and Domestic Agenda** Richard Nixon took advantage of the backlash against these liberal politics and cultural movements to win election in 1968. His "southern strategy" drew large numbers of conservative southern white Democrats into the Republican party for the first time. As president, he sought to slow the momentum of the civil rights movement with *affirmative action* programs and vetoed the extension of the Voting Rights Act of 1968, though with no success. Nixon did grudgingly support important new federal environmental policies like the *Environmental Protection Agency (EPA)*. Both the Nixon and Ford administrations were unable to overcome *stagflation*.

- **End of the Vietnam War** In his 1968 campaign, Nixon pledged to secure "peace with honor" in Vietnam, but years would pass before the war ended. He did change the military strategy in Vietnam by implementing *Vietnamization:* increasing aid to South Vietnam and aggressively bombing North Vietnam, while attempting to negotiate a cease-fire with North Vietnam. The Pentagon Papers and the intense bombing of North Vietnam in December 1972 sparked worldwide protests. But a month into the bombings, North and South Vietnam agreed to a cease-fire called the Paris Peace Accords. In 1975 the South Vietnamese government collapsed after a massive North Vietnamese invasion. The Communist victors forcibly reunited the North and South.

- **Détente** Nixon's greatest accomplishments were in foreign policy. As an aggressive anti-Communist, he shocked the world by opening diplomatic relations with Communist China and pursuing *détente* with the Soviet Union, focusing on areas of shared agreement with SALT I. He and Henry Kissinger eased tensions in the Middle East, while aggravating anti-American feelings in countries like Chile with covert CIA operations to overthrow governments with Communist ties.

- **Watergate** During the 1972 presidential campaign, the Committee to Re-Elect the President (CREEP) was implicated in a break-in of the Democratic campaign's Watergate headquarters. In *United States v. Richard M. Nixon* (1974), the Supreme Court ruled that Nixon had to surrender the recordings of White House meetings dealing with the scandal. Nixon resigned in 1974 to avoid impeachment. He was succeeded by Vice President Gerald Ford, whose presidency was undermined by continued economic struggles, international incidents, and his controversial decision to pardon Nixon.

KEY TERMS

New Left *p. 1049*
counterculture *p. 1051*
women's movement *p. 1055*
Roe v. Wade (1973) *p. 1056*
United Farm Workers (UFW)
    p. 1060

Red Power *p. 1062*
Stonewall riots (1969) *p. 1063*
affirmative action *p. 1066*
Environmental Protection
    Agency (EPA) (1970) *p. 1071*
stagflation *p. 1072*

Vietnamization *p. 1074*
détente *p. 1080*
Strategic Arms Limitation Treaty
    (SALT I) (1972) *p. 1082*
Watergate (1972–1974) *p. 1084*
War Powers Act (1973) *p. 1087*

CHRONOLOGY

1960	Students for a Democratic Society (SDS) founded
1962	United Farm Workers (UFW) established
1963	Betty Friedan's *The Feminine Mystique* published
1965	Forced integration of Mississippi schools
1966	National Organization for Women (NOW) founded
1967–1968	Inner-city riots; student sit-ins on college campuses
1968	Riots at the Democratic National Convention
	American Indian Movement (AIM) founded
March 1969	U.S. warplanes bomb Cambodia
June 1969	Stonewall riots in New York City
August 1969	Woodstock music festival attracts 400,000 people
1970	Kent State and Jackson State shootings
1971	*Pentagon Papers* published
1972	Nixon visits China and U.S.S.R., signs SALT I
1972–1974	Watergate scandal unfolds
1973	Sioux occupation of Wounded Knee, South Dakota
	U.S. troop withdrawal from Vietnam begins
	Roe v. Wade
1974	Nixon resigns; Gerald Ford becomes president
April 1975	Saigon falls to the North Vietnamese

INQUIZITIVE

Go to InQuizitive to see what you've learned—and learn what you've missed—with personalized feedback along the way.

FEELS GOOD TO BE RIGHT This proud Republican and Reagan supporter lets his cowboy hat adorned with campaign buttons speak for him at the 1980 Republican National Convention. Held in Detroit, Michigan, the convention nominated former California governor Ronald Reagan, who promised to "make America great again."

Conservative Revival

1977–1990

During the seventies, the United States lost much of its self-confidence. The failed Vietnam War, the sordid revelations of the Watergate scandal, and the spike in oil prices, interest rates, and consumer prices revealed the limits of the nation's power, prosperity, and virtue. Surveys showed that Americans felt defensive and dispirited about their nation and its prospects in what journalists were calling an "age of limits." For a nation long accustomed to economic growth and spreading prosperity, the frustrating persistence of stagflation and gasoline shortages undermined national optimism. At the same time, a fast-growing environmental movement criticized the widespread pollution of the nation's air, water, and wetlands caused by unregulated economic development. Even in July 1976, as the United States celebrated the bicentennial of its independence, many people were downsizing their expectations of the American Dream.

Jimmy Carter took office promising a government that would be "competent" as well as "decent, open, fair, and compassionate." After four years as president, however, Carter had little to show for his efforts. The economy remained sluggish, consumer prices continued to increase at historic levels, and failed efforts to free Americans held hostage in Iran prompted critics, including Democrats, to denounce the administration as being indecisive and inept. In the end, Carter's inability to mobilize national support for his ill-fated energy program and his call for "a time of

CORE OBJECTIVES INQUIZITIVE

1. Analyze why Jimmy Carter had such limited success as America's thirty-ninth president.

2. Identify the factors that led to the election of Ronald Reagan, the rise of the conservative movement, and the resurgence of the Republican party.

3. Define "Reaganomics" and evaluate its effects on American society and economy.

4. Explain how Reagan's Soviet strategy helped end the Cold War .

5. Characterize the social and economic issues and innovations that emerged during the 1980s.

6. Appraise the impact of the end of the cold war and the efforts of President George H. W. Bush to create a post–cold war foreign policy.

national austerity" revealed both his ineffective legislative skills and his misreading of the public mood.

The Republicans capitalized on public frustration by electing Ronald Reagan president in 1980. Where Jimmy Carter had denounced the evils of unregulated capitalism, Reagan promised to unleash the capitalist spirit, restore national pride, and regain international respect. He did all of that and more. During his two-term presidency in the 1980s, he transformed the political landscape. Reagan accelerated the conservative resurgence in politics, helped restore prosperity, and set in motion the forces that would cause the collapse of the Soviet Union and the end of the Cold War.

CORE **OBJECTIVE**

1. Analyze why Jimmy Carter had such limited success as America's thirty-ninth president.

The Carter Presidency

James (Jimmy) Earl Carter Jr. won the close 1976 election because he convinced voters that he was an incorruptible political "outsider," a common man of pure motives who would restore integrity and honesty to the presidency in the aftermath of the Watergate scandal (his campaign slogan was "I'll never tell a lie"). He also promised that he was not a "tax and spend" liberal. Instead he represented a new generation of "moderate" southern Democratic leaders who were committed to restrain "big government" spending. In his 1977 inaugural address, Carter highlighted America's limitations rather than its power: "We have learned that 'more' is not necessarily 'better,' that even our great nation has its recognized limits, and that we can neither answer all questions nor solve all problems." That may have been true, but it was not what many Americans wanted to hear.

Jimmy Who?

Like Gerald Ford before him, Jimmy Carter was an honest, forthright man. Yet his charming modesty in public masked a complex and at times contradictory personality. "Jimmy's a hard person to get to know," admitted his top aide Hamilton Jordan. No modern president was as openly committed to his Christian faith as Carter was. At the same time, few other presidents were as tough on others as Carter, who once called the lovable Democratic leader Hubert Humphrey "a loser." The former governor of Georgia who came out of nowhere to win the presidential campaign ("Jimmy Who?") was both blessed and cursed by a surplus of self-confidence. All his life he had displayed a fierce determination to succeed and expected those around him to show the same tenacity. "I am pretty rigid," Carter admitted. As he entered the White House in early 1977, Carter, the former naval officer, nuclear engineer, efficiency expert, and business executive stressed that he wanted to be a "strong, aggressive president" who would reshape the federal government to run more smoothly at less expense to the taxpayers by eliminating waste and providing expert management.

In 1977 Carter needed to summon all of his intelligence and conviction ("I like to run things," he said), for he faced difficult economic problems and formidable international challenges. He was expected to cure the stubborn economic recession and reduce inflation at a time when all industrial economies around the world were struggling. Carter was also expected to restore U.S. stature abroad and lift the national spirit through a set of political institutions in which many people had lost faith as a result of the Watergate scandal.

Early Success

During the first two years of his presidency, Carter enjoyed several successes, both symbolic and real. In a sign of his commitment to efficiency, he reduced the size of the White House staff by a third and told cabinet officers to give up their government cars and drive their own. His new administration included more African Americans and women than any before. He fulfilled a controversial campaign pledge by offering amnesty (forgiveness) to the thousands of young men who had fled the country rather than serve with the U.S. military in Vietnam. He reorganized the executive branch and reduced government red tape by slowing burdensome new regulations and creating two new cabinet-level agencies, the Departments of Energy and Education. He also pushed through Congress several significant environmental initiatives, including stricter controls over the strip-mining of coal, the creation of a $1.6-billion "Superfund" to clean up toxic chemical waste sites, and a bill protecting more than 100 million acres of Alaskan land from development. At the end of his first hundred days in office, Carter enjoyed a 75 percent public approval rating.

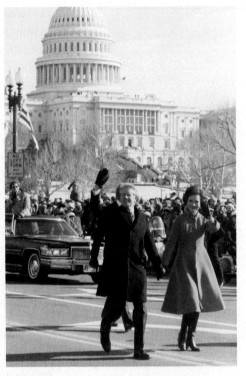

The Carters After his inauguration, President Jimmy Carter forgoes the traditional limousine and walks down Pennsylvania Avenue with his wife, Rosalynn.

Carter's Limitations

Carter's successes were short-lived, however. By nature, he was less a leader than a bureaucrat, a compulsive micromanager (he even insisted on scheduling the use of the White House tennis court) who failed to establish a compelling vision for the nation's future. Instead of focusing on a few priorities, Carter tried to do too much too fast, and his inexperienced team of senior aides, most of whom he had brought with him from Georgia, was often more a burden than a blessing. The "outsider" president saw little need to consult with Democratic leaders in Congress, which helps explain why many of his legislative requests were voted down.

Ultimately, however, it was Carter's mismanagement of the economy that crippled his presidency. Stagflation continued to defy easy solutions. Carter first tried to attack unemployment, authorizing some $14 billion in federal spending to trigger job growth while cutting taxes by $34 billion. His actions helped generate new jobs but in doing so caused a spike in inflation.

A deepening recession

Annual inflation (increases in consumer prices) jumped from 5 percent when he took office to as much as 13 percent during 1980. The result was a deepening recession, rising unemployment, and growing criticism of the president.

The "energy crisis"

What made Carter's efforts to restore prosperity more challenging was the worsening "energy crisis." Since the Arab oil embargo in 1973, the price of imported oil had doubled, while U.S. dependence on foreign oil had grown from 35 percent to 50 percent of its annual needs. In April 1977, Carter presented Congress with a comprehensive energy proposal designed to cut oil consumption, but legislators defeated most of the bill's specific measures, in part because of Carter's poor relationship with Democratic leaders. The final energy bill, the National Energy Act of 1978, was so gutted by oil, gas, and automobile industry lobbyists that one presidential aide said it looked like it had been "nibbled to death by ducks."

In 1979, the energy crisis grew even more troublesome when Islamic fundamentalists took over the government in oil-rich Iran. The revolution shut off the supply of Iranian oil to the United States, creating shortages of gasoline and much higher prices. Warning that the "growing scarcity in energy" would paralyze the U.S. economy, Carter asked Congress for a new and much more comprehensive energy bill, but again the legislators turned down its most important provisions for energy conservation intended to reduce America's dependence on foreign oil.

A "Crisis of Confidence"

Loss of congressional support and public confidence

By July 1979, Carter had grown so discouraged by his inability to lead the nation out of the doldrums that he took an unusual step: for two weeks he holed up at Camp David, the presidential retreat in the Maryland mountains. There he met privately with leaders from all walks of life—business, labor, education, religion, even psychiatry. Then, on July 15, the president returned to the White House and delivered a televised speech in which he claimed that a "crisis of confidence" was paralyzing the nation and that the people had lost confidence in his leadership. He then made a crucial mistake when he seemingly blamed the American people for the problems facing the nation. "All the legislation in the world can't fix what's wrong with America," Carter stressed in a tone more appropriate to an angry preacher than an uplifting president. People had become preoccupied with "owning and consuming things" at the expense of "hard work, strong families, close-knit communities, and our faith in God." The nation was at a crossroads, he concluded. Americans could choose continued self-indulgence and political stalemate, or they could revive traditional values such as thrift, mutual aid, simple living, and spirituality. "We can take the first step down that path as we begin to solve our energy problem. Energy will be the immediate test of our ability to unite this nation."

But Carter failed that test. Many Americans felt the president's "sad and worried" speech had blamed them for his own failures of leadership. An

Arizona newspaper said that "the nation did not tune in Carter to hear a sermon. It wanted answers. It did not get them." Carter's new energy proposals got nowhere in Congress, in part because many members resented the president's abrupt decision to fire half of his cabinet members and transfer several others. The sudden firings seemed an act of self-serving desperation. By the end of the summer of 1979, Carter's negative ratings in public polls were the highest in history.

Carter's Foreign Policy

Carter's crowning achievement, which even his most bitter critics applauded, was his dogged effort to work out a 1978 peace agreement between Prime Minister Menachem Begin of Israel and President Anwar Sadat of Egypt. It was the first time that an Arab nation (Egypt) had officially recognized the existence of Israel. However, this historic agreement, dubbed the **Camp David Accords** for the presidential retreat where the negotiations took place, created only a "framework for peace," not a true settlement of differences. In the wake of the Camp David Accords, most Arab nations condemned Sadat as a traitor, and Islamic extremists assassinated him in 1981. Still, Carter's high-level diplomacy made an all-out war between Israel and the Arab world less likely.

> Carter's foreign policy controversies: Human rights, the Panama Canal Treaty, responses to the Soviet invasion of Afghanistan

Human Rights

Carter also got caught in a political crossfire when he vowed that "the soul of our foreign policy" should be an absolute "commitment to human rights" abroad, drawing a direct contrast between his international "idealism" and the geopolitical "realism" practiced by Richard Nixon and Henry Kissinger. Carter created an Office of Human Rights within the State Department and selectively cut off financial assistance to some repressive governments around the world (Chile, El Salvador, Rhodesia, and South Africa) while maintaining support of brutal governments in places like Argentina, Ethiopia, Pakistan, and Uruguay. Carter's inconsistent moralism led critics on the right to argue that he was sacrificing America's national interests in order to promote an impossible standard of international moral purity, while critics on the left highlighted his seeming hypocrisy in pursuing human rights in a few nations but not everywhere.

Panama Canal

Similarly, Carter's controversial decision to turn over control of the Panama Canal Zone to the Panamanian government aroused intense criticism. The president argued that Panama's deep resentment of America's having taken control of the Canal Zone during the presidency of Theodore Roosevelt left him no choice but to transfer management of the canal to Panama. Conservatives blasted Carter for surrendering U.S. control of such a

Camp David Accords (1978) Peace agreement facilitated by President Carter between Prime Minister Menachem Begin of Israel and President Anwar Sadat of Egypt, the first Arab head of state to officially recognize the state of Israel.

strategic asset. Ronald Reagan claimed the canal was America's forever: "We bought it, we paid for it, it's ours."

Afghanistan

In 1979, Carter faced another crisis when the Soviet army invaded Afghanistan, where a faltering Communist government was being challenged by Islamist *jihadis* ("holy warriors") and ethnic warlords. Carter responded with a series of steps, some of which provoked intense criticism: he refused to sign a new Strategic Arms Limitation Talks treaty with the Soviets (SALT II), suspended grain shipments to the Soviet Union, began supplying Afghan "freedom fighters" with weapons smuggled through Pakistan, requested large increases in military spending, required all nineteen-year-old men to register for the military draft, and called for an international boycott of the 1980 Olympic Games, which were to be held that summer in Moscow.

The Soviet invasion of Afghanistan also prompted Carter to announce what came to be called the Carter Doctrine, in which the president threatened to use military force to prevent any nation from gaining control of the Persian Gulf waterways, through which most of the oil from the Middle East made its way to foreign ports, including American cities.

A king's ransom An Iranian militant holds a group of U.S. embassy staff members hostage in Tehran, Iran, in 1979.

Crisis in Iran

Then came the **Iranian hostage crisis**, a series of dramatic events that illustrated the inability of the United States to control world affairs. In January 1979, Islamic revolutionaries in Iran had ousted the pro-American government led by the shah of Iran, Mohammad Reza Pahlavi, who owed his rule to secret CIA intervention in 1953. The turmoil in Iran led to a sharp drop in oil production, driving gasoline prices up. By the spring of 1979, Americans were again waiting in long lines to pay record prices for limited amounts of gas.

In October, the United States allowed the deposed shah to receive medical treatment at an American hospital. This "humanitarian" decision enraged Iranian revolutionaries. On November 4, 1979, a frenzied mob of Iranian youths stormed the U.S. embassy in Tehran and seized sixty-six diplomats and staff, including fifty-two American citizens. The Iranian leader, Ayatollah Ruhollah Khomeini, endorsed the mob action and demanded the return of the hated shah of Iran from the United States (along with all his wealth) in exchange for the release of the hostages. Nightly

Iranian hostage crisis (1979) Storming of the U.S. embassy in Tehran by Iranian revolutionaries, who held fifty-two Americans hostage for 444 days, despite President Carter's appeals for their release and a botched rescue attempt.

television coverage of the taunting Iranian rebels generated among viewers a near obsession with the fate of the hostages and the falling stature of the United States.

Angry Americans, including many in Congress, demanded a military response to the kidnappings in Iran. Carter, however, believed his options were limited to avoid the hostages being killed. He appealed to the United Nations, but Khomeini scoffed at UN requests for release of the hostages. Carter then froze all Iranian financial assets in America and asked Europe to join the United States in a trade embargo of Iran, including its oil. The trade restrictions were only partially effective because America's allies were not willing to lose access to Iranian oil. As the hostage crisis continued and gasoline prices rose to record levels, a frustrated Carter authorized a risky rescue attempt by U.S. commandos on April 24, 1980 (his decision caused his secretary of state, Cyrus Vance, to resign in protest). The raid had to be cancelled when three of the eight helicopters developed mechanical problems; it ended with eight U.S. deaths when a helicopter collided with a transport plane at a remote staging site in the Iranian desert.

For fourteen months, the frustrating Iranian hostage crisis paralyzed Carter's ability to lead the nation. Like a black cloud, it loomed over every decision he made. For many, the prolonged standoff with Iran became a symbol of his failed presidency. "For the first time in its history," *Business Week* magazine's editors observed, "the United States is no longer growing in power and influence among the nations of the world." The hostage crisis finally ended after 444 days, on January 20, 1981, when Carter, just hours before leaving office, released several billion dollars of Iranian assets to ransom the hostages.

Ayatollah Khomeini Religious figure and leader of the Iranian Revolution that overthrew the Iranian monarchy in 1979.

The Rise of Ronald Reagan

No sooner had Carter been elected in 1976 than conservative Republicans (the "New Right") began working to ensure that he would not win a second term. Their plans for a Republican revival centered on the popularity of tall, square-shouldered, plain-speaking Ronald Reagan, the Hollywood actor, two-term California governor, and prominent political commentator. Reagan was not a deep thinker, but he was a superb reader of the public mood, an outspoken emotional patriot, and a committed champion of conservative principles.

The Actor Turned President

Born in the drab prairie town of Tampico, Illinois, in 1911, the son of an often-drunk shoe salesman and a devout, Bible-quoting mother, Ronald Reagan graduated from tiny Eureka College in 1932 during the depths of the Great Depression. He first worked as a radio sportscaster before starting a

Ronald Reagan The "Great Communicator" flashes his charming, trademark smile.

movie career in Hollywood in 1937. He served three years in the army during the Second World War, making training films. At that time, as Reagan recalled, he was a Democrat, "a New Dealer to the core" who voted for Franklin D. Roosevelt four times. After the war, Reagan became president of the acting profession's union, the Screen Actors Guild (SAG), where he honed his negotiating skills and fended off Communist efforts to infiltrate the union. Reagan supported Democrat Harry S. Truman in the 1948 presidential election, but during the fifties he decided that federal taxes were too high. In 1960 he campaigned as a Democrat for Richard Nixon, and two years later he abandoned the Democrats and joined the Republican party. Reagan achieved political stardom in 1964 when he delivered a rousing speech on national television on behalf of Barry Goldwater's presidential candidacy. Soon thereafter, wealthy admirers convinced him to run for governor of California in 1966, and he won by a landslide.

Now, as the Republican presidential nominee in 1980, Reagan set about drawing a vivid contrast between his optimistic vision of America's future and Jimmy Carter's bleak outlook. Unlike Carter, Reagan insisted that there was "nothing wrong with the American people" and that there were "simple answers" to the complex problems facing the United States, though they were not *easy* answers. He pledged to reverse the social-welfare programs that had grown so dramatically during and after Lyndon Johnson's presidency, increase military spending to "win" the Cold War, dismantle the "bloated" federal bureaucracy, restore states' rights, reduce taxes and government regulations of business ("get the government off our backs"), and appoint conservative judges to the Supreme Court and federal courts across the nation. He also promised to affirm old-time religious values by banning abortions and reinstituting prayer in public schools. (He ended up doing neither.)

Reagan's popularity resulted from his remarkable skill as a public speaker (journalists dubbed him the "Great Communicator") and his steadfast commitment to a few basic principles and simple themes. Blessed with a baritone voice and a wealth of entertaining stories, he charmed audiences. Reagan rejected Carter's assumption that Americans needed "to start getting along with less, to accept a decline in our standard of living." He instead promised boundless economic expansion. By reducing taxes and easing government regulations of businesses, he pledged, the engine of capitalism would spread prosperity to everyone.

The Rise of the "New Right"

Population growth in conservative Sunbelt states

By 1980, social developments had made Reagan's anti-liberal stance a major asset. An increase in the number of senior citizens, a group that tends to be more politically and socially conservative, and the steady migration of people—especially older Americans—to the conservative Sunbelt states was shifting the political balance of power toward Reagan's philosophy. Fully 90 percent of the nation's total population growth during the eighties occurred in southern or western Sunbelt states, while the Northeast and industrial states of the Midwest—Ohio, Michigan, and Illinois (called the "rust belt")—experienced economic decline and population losses. The population shifts forced a massive redistricting of the House of Representatives, with Florida, California, and Texas gaining seats and northern states such as New York losing them.

A related development during the seventies was a growing grassroots tax revolt spurred by prolonged inflation. As consumer prices and the value of houses rose, so too did property taxes. In California, Ronald Reagan's home state, skyrocketing property taxes threatened to force many working-class people from their homes. This led to grassroots efforts to cut back on the size and cost of state government to enable reductions in property taxes. In June 1978, tax rebels in California, with Reagan's support, succeeded in putting an initiative known as Proposition 13 on the state ballot. An overwhelming majority of voters—both Republicans and Democrats—approved the measure, which slashed property taxes by 57 percent and amended the state constitution to make it more difficult for local and state governments to raise taxes. The "Prop 13" tax revolt in California soon spread across the nation, leading the *New York Times* to call it a "modern Boston Tea Party."

| Tax revolts |

The Religious Right

The California tax revolt fed into a national conservative resurgence led by the rapidly growing "**religious right**." Religious conservatives pushing a faith-based political agenda formed the strongest grassroots movement of the late twentieth century. By the eighties, Catholic conservatives and Protestant evangelicals owned powerful television and radio stations, operated their own schools and universities, and organized "mega-churches" from which such "televangelists" as the Reverend Jerry Falwell launched a cultural crusade against the "demonic" forces of liberalism at home and communism abroad.

| A crusade against liberalism, feminism, and abortion |

In 1979, Falwell formed a group he called the Moral Majority (later renamed the Liberty Alliance) to campaign for the major political and social goals of the religious right: the economy should operate without "interference" by the government, which should be reduced in size; the Supreme Court decision in *Roe v. Wade* (1973) legalizing abortion should be reversed; Darwinian evolution should be replaced in school textbooks by the biblical story of creation; prayer should return to public schools; women should submit to their husbands; and Soviet communism should be opposed as a form of pagan totalitarianism.

That Ronald Reagan became the hero of the religious right was a tribute to the candidate's political skills, for he himself rarely attended church

religious right Christian conservatives with a faith-based political agenda that includes prohibition of abortion and allowing prayer in public schools.

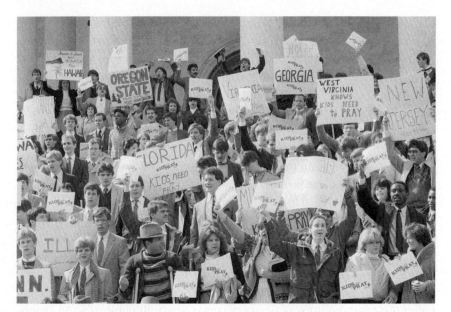

Look on the Right side The rise of the religious right saw protests against Supreme Court rulings that reinforced the separation of church and state. Here, in a 1984 protest organized by the Moral Majority, students chant "Kids want to pray!" in support of an amendment to reinstate prayer in public schools.

services and had no strong religious affiliations. However, white evangelical Christians—alienated by the liberal social agenda of the Democratic party, especially policies regarding abortions and endorsement of gay rights—became a crucial element in Reagan's electoral strategy.

Anti-Feminist Backlash

By the late seventies, a well-organized and well-financed backlash against the feminist movement reinforced the rise of the "New Right." Anti-feminist activists like Phyllis Schlafly, a conservative Catholic attorney and Republican activist from Alton, Illinois, campaigned successfully to keep the ERA from being ratified by the required thirty-eight states. Schlafly's STOP (Stop Taking Our Privileges) ERA organization, founded in 1972, warned that the ERA would allow husbands to abandon their wives, force women into military service, and give gay "perverts" the right to marry. She and others also stressed that the gender equality promised by the proposed amendment violated biblical teachings about women's "God-given" roles as nurturers and helpmates. By the late seventies, the national effort to gain ratification of the ERA had failed, largely because no states in the conservative South and West had ratified it.

Many of Schlafly's anti-ERA supporters also participated in the growing anti-abortion, or "pro-life," movement. The National Right to Life Committee, supported by the National Conference of Catholic Bishops, denounced abortion as murder, and the emotional intensity of the issue made it a powerful political force. Reagan highlighted his support for traditional "family values," gender roles, and the "rights" of the unborn, which helped persuade many northern Democrats—mostly working-class Catholics—to switch parties and support Reagan.

Financing Conservatism

The business community as well had become a source of revitalized conservative activism. In 1972, the leaders of the nation's largest corporations formed the Business Roundtable to promote business interests in Congress. Within a few years, many of those corporations had created political action committees (PACs) to distribute money to pro-business political candidates. Corporate donations also helped fund conservative "think tanks," such as the American Enterprise Institute, the Cato Institute, and the Heritage Foundation, all of which opposed "liberal" legislation. By 1980, the national conservative insurgency had become a powerful political force with substantial financial resources, carefully crafted ideas, and grassroots energy, all of which helped to explain Ronald Reagan's presidential victory.

The Election of 1980

Reagan's supporters during the 1980 campaign loved his simple solutions, upbeat personality, and folksy humor, and they responded passionately to his recurring question at campaign stops: "Are you better off than you were four years ago?" Their answer was a resounding "No!" On election day, Reagan swept to a lopsided victory, with 489 electoral votes to 49 for Carter, who carried only six states. The popular vote was 44 million (51 percent) for Reagan to Carter's 35 million (41 percent), with 7 percent going to John Anderson, a moderate Republican who ran on an independent ticket. Reagan's thumping of Carter signaled a major realignment of voters in which many so-called Reagan Democrats—conservative white southern Protestants and blue-collar northern Catholics crossed over to the Republican party.

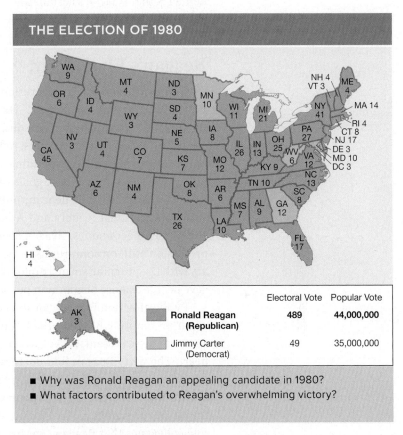

THE ELECTION OF 1980

	Electoral Vote	Popular Vote
Ronald Reagan (Republican)	489	44,000,000
Jimmy Carter (Democrat)	49	35,000,000

■ Why was Ronald Reagan an appealing candidate in 1980?
■ What factors contributed to Reagan's overwhelming victory?

The Reagan Revolution

Those Democrats who dismissed 69-year-old Ronald Reagan, the oldest man to assume the presidency, as a third-rate actor and mental lightweight famously inattentive to the details of policy and management, underrated his many virtues, including the importance of his years in front of a

CORE **OBJECTIVE**
3. Define "Reaganomics" and evaluate its effects on American society and economy.

camera. Politics is a performing art, all the more so in the age of television, and few people, if any, in public life had Reagan's stage presence—or confidence. He may have been a mediocre actor, but no one played the part of president better than Reagan. His remarkable ability to make Americans again believe in the greatness of their country won him two presidential elections, in 1980 and 1984, and ensured the victory of his chosen successor, Vice President George H. W. Bush, in 1988. Just how revolutionary the "Reagan Era" was remains a subject of intense debate, but what cannot be denied is that Reagan's actions and beliefs set the tone for the decade's political and economic life.

Reagan's First Term

"Fellow conservatives," new-president Ronald Reagan said in a speech in 1981, "Our moment has arrived." He succeeded as president where Jimmy Carter failed for three main reasons. First, Reagan focused on a few essential priorities (lowering tax rates, reducing the scope of the federal government, increasing military spending, and conducting an anti-Soviet foreign policy), and he pursued those goals with what an aide called a "warmly ruthless" intensity. Second, Reagan, unlike Carter, was skilled at negotiating with congressional leaders and foreign heads of state. A true believer in conservative economics, Reagan also recognized early on that politics is a profession built on compromises. He combined the passion of a revolutionary with the pragmatism of a diplomat. Third, Reagan's infectious optimism gave people a sense of common purpose and renewed confidence.

Public affection for Reagan spiked just two months into his presidency when an emotionally-disturbed young man eager for notoriety fired six shots at the president, one of which punctured a lung and lodged near his heart. The witty Reagan told doctors as they prepared for surgery: "Please tell me you're Republicans." Reagan's gritty response to the assassination and his injuries created an outpouring of support that gave added momentum to his presidency. The Democratic Speaker of the House, Tip O'Neill, told colleagues that Reagan "has become a hero. We can't argue with a man as popular as he is."

Reaganomics

Economic Recovery Tax Act (1981)

On August 1, 1981, the president signed the Economic Recovery Tax Act (ERTA), which cut personal income taxes by 25 percent, lowered the maximum rate from 70 to 50 percent for 1982, and offered a broad array of other tax concessions. The tax-cut bill was the centerpiece of what Reagan called his "common sense" economic plan. While theorists called the philosophy behind the plan "supply-side economics," journalists dubbed the president's proposals **Reaganomics**.

Simply put, Reaganomics argued that the stagflation of the seventies had resulted from excessive taxes, which weakened incentives for individuals and businesses to increase productivity, save money, and reinvest in

Reaganomics President Reagan's "supply-side" economic philosophy combining tax cuts with the goals of decreased government spending, reduced regulation of business, and a balanced budget.

economic expansion. The "supply-side" or Reaganomics solution to stagflation was to slash tax rates on companies and individuals, especially on the wealthy, in the belief that they would spend their tax savings on business expansion and consumer goods (the "supply side" of the economy). By generating economic growth, Reaganomics promised to generate enough new tax revenues from rising corporate profits and personal incomes to pay for the cuts in tax rates. In the short term, however, ERTA did not work as planned. The federal budget deficit grew rather than shrank. By November 1981, the economy was officially in recession, "a slight one," explained the president.

Budget Cuts

To offset the loss of government tax revenues, David Stockman, Reagan's budget director, proposed sharp reductions in federal spending, including Social Security and Medicare, the two most expensive—and most popular—federal social programs. Liberal Democrats howled at efforts to dismantle social-welfare programs. Reagan responded that he was committed to maintaining the "safety net" of government services for the "truly needy." When the president told Stockman that there would be no cuts to Social Security, the budget director knew that there was no hope to balance the federal budget.

Failure to curb "liberal" social-welfare programs

For all of Reagan's bold talk about shrinking the government, he was not a true revolutionary in that regard. It was much easier to promise to reduce the scope of federal government while a candidate than as president. In the end, the president and Congress agreed to cut "food stamps" (government subsidies to help poor people buy groceries) only 4 percent from what the Carter administration had planned to spend. The Reagan administration

A miss for Reaganomics
A throng of more than 5,000 senior citizens staged a demonstration in downtown Detroit against Reagan's decision to cut federal budgets for Social Security and other programs to aid the elderly in 1982.

also continued huge federal subsidies to corporations and agribusinesses—what critics called "welfare for the rich." In the end, Reagan never dismantled the major federal social programs that he savagely criticized.

Within a year, David Stockman realized that the cuts in domestic spending approved by Reagan had fallen far short of what would be needed to balance the budget in four years, as the president had promised. Massive increases in military spending greatly complicated the situation. In essence, Reagan gave the Defense Department a blank check, telling the secretary of defense to "spend what you need." Over the next five years, the administration would spend some $1.2 *trillion* on military expenses. Something had to give.

A growing federal deficit

In the summer of 1981, Stockman warned the president that "we're heading for a crash landing on the budget. We're facing potential deficit numbers so big that they could wreck the president's entire economic program." The fast-growing federal budget deficit, which helped trigger the worst economic recession since the 1930s, was Reagan's greatest failure, as he himself admitted. During 1982, there were 10 million Americans unable to find jobs. "The stench of failure hangs over Ronald Reagan's White House," declared the *New York Times*.

Stockman and other worried aides finally convinced the president that the government needed "revenue enhancements" (tax increases). With Reagan's support, Congress passed a tax increase bill in 1982 that would raise almost $100 billion, but the economic slump persisted for a time, with unemployment standing at 10.4 percent. In the 1982 Congressional midterm elections, Democrats picked up twenty-six seats in the House of Representatives.

Increased military spending, lower interest rates and lower tax rates

But Reagan's determination to "stay the course" in pursuing his economic program began to pay off. By the summer of 1983, a major economic recovery was under way, in part because of increased government spending and lower interest rates and in part because of lower tax rates. Inflation subsided along with unemployment and "deregulation" of business, as Reagan appointed pro-business conservatives to head regulatory agencies.

Reaganomics, however, was not helping to balance the budget: in fact, the annual federal deficits had grown larger—so much so that the president, who in 1980 had pledged to balance the federal budget by 1983, had in fact run up an accumulated federal debt larger than that of all his predecessors combined. Reagan was willing to tolerate the growing budget deficits in part because he believed that they would force more responsible spending behavior in Congress, and in part because he was so committed to increased military spending as a way to intimidate the Soviets.

Reagan's Anti-Liberalism

Setbacks for unions

During Reagan's presidency, organized labor suffered severe setbacks, even though Reagan himself had been a union leader. In 1981, Reagan fired members of the Professional Air Traffic Controllers Organization who had participated in an illegal strike intended to shut down air travel. Even more important, Reagan's actions broke the political power of the American Federation of Labor–Congress of Industrial Organizations (AFL-CIO), the national confederation of labor unions that traditionally supported Democratic candidates. His criticism of unions reflected a general trend in public opinion. Although record numbers of new jobs were created during the eighties, union membership steadily dropped. By 1987, unions represented only 17 percent of the nation's full-time workers, down from 24 percent in 1979.

Reagan also went on the offensive against feminism and the enforcement of civil rights. Echoing Phyllis Schlafly, he opposed the Equal Rights Amendment, legal abortion, and proposals to require equal pay for jobs of comparable worth. He did name Sandra Day O'Connor as the first woman Supreme Court justice, but critics labeled it a token gesture rather than a reflection of genuine commitment to gender equality. Reagan also cut funds for civil rights enforcement and the Equal Employment Opportunity Commission, and he opposed renewal of the Voting Rights Act of 1965 before being overruled by Congress.

Sandra Day O'Connor Her Supreme Court confirmation hearing in September 1981 was picketed by conservatives who decried her pro-abortion stance.

The Election of 1984

By 1983, prosperity had returned, the stock market was soaring, and Reagan's "supply-side" economic program was at last working as advertised—except for the growing budget deficits. By 1984, reporters had begun to speak of the "Reagan Revolution." The economy surged with new energy. The slogan at the Republican National Convention was "America is back and standing tall." The Democrats' presidential nominee, Jimmy Carter's vice president, Walter Mondale, struggled to present a competing vision. Endorsed by the AFL-CIO, the National Organization for Women (NOW), and many prominent African Americans, Mondale was viewed as the candidate of liberal special-interest groups. He set a precedent by choosing as his running mate Geraldine Ferraro, a New York congresswoman, who was quickly placed on the defensive by the need to explain her husband's complicated business dealings.

A bit of frankness in Mondale's acceptance speech ended up hurting his campaign. "Mr. Reagan will raise taxes, and so will I," he told the convention. "He won't tell you. I just did." Reagan responded by vowing never to approve another tax increase (a promise he could not keep) and by chiding Mondale for his stance. Reagan also repeated a theme he had used against Jimmy Carter: the future, according to Mondale and the Democrats, was "dark and getting darker." Reagan's vision of America's future, however, was bright with optimism and hope. As his campaign ads claimed, "It's morning again in America," and record numbers of Americans were headed to work. In the end, Reagan took 59 percent of the popular vote and lost only Minnesota (Mondale's home state) and the District of Columbia.

Reagan's Second Term

Tax Reform Act (1986)

Spurred by his overwhelming victory, Reagan called for "a Second American Revolution of hope and opportunity." He dared Democrats to raise taxes; his veto pen was ready. "Go ahead and make my day," he said, echoing a popular line from a Clint Eastwood movie. Through much of 1985, the president drummed up support for a tax-simplification plan. After vigorous debate that ran nearly two years, Congress passed a comprehensive Tax Reform Act that the president signed in 1986. The measure reduced the number of federal tax brackets from fourteen to two and reduced rates from the maximum of 50 percent to 15 and 28 percent—the lowest since Calvin Coolidge was president in the twenties.

Reagan's Half-Hearted Revolution

Ronald Wilson Reagan was the first president since Dwight Eisenhower to complete two full terms in office. Although in 1981 he had proclaimed his intention to "curb the size and influence of the federal establishment," he did not, in part because the Democrats controlled the House of Representatives throughout his presidency. The number of federal employees actually *grew* during the Reagan presidency. Neither the Social Security system nor Medicare, the two largest federal social programs, were overhauled during Reagan's two-term presidency. And the federal agencies that Reagan had threatened to abolish, such as the Department of Education, not only survived but saw their budgets grow. The federal budget deficit almost tripled during his two terms.

Reagan and his aides repeatedly blamed Congress for the problem, "since only Congress can spend money," but in fact the legislators essentially approved the budgets that Reagan had submitted to them (and he never submitted a balanced budget). The cost of Social Security, the most expensive government "entitlement" program, grew by 27 percent, as some 6,000 Americans each day turned 65. Moreover, Reagan failed to fulfill his campaign promises to the religious right, such as reinstituting daily prayer in public schools and a ban on abortions. But he did follow through on his pledge to reshape the federal court system. During his two terms, Reagan was much more successful in transforming the judicial system than in ending the welfare state. He appointed 368 mostly conservative judges, three of whom were added to the U.S. Supreme Court: Sandra Day O'Connor (the Court's first woman justice), Antonin Scalia, and Anthony Kennedy.

"The Great Expansion"

Martin Anderson, Reagan's domestic policy adviser, stressed that it was "a mistake to think that there ever was a Reagan Revolution, or that Reagan gave it life." It was the grassroots conservative revolution that "caused Reagan—and the same forces will continue to the end of the century." What Reagan, the half-hearted revolutionary on the right, did accomplish was to end the prolonged period of economic "stagflation" and set in motion what economists called "The Great Expansion," an unprecedented, twenty-year-long burst of productivity and prosperity. True, Reagan's presidency left the nation with a massive debt burden that would eventually cause major problems, but the "Great Communicator" who defined America as "a sunrise every day—fresh new opportunities, dreams to build," also renewed the nation's strength, self-confidence, and soaring sense of possibilities.

Over his two terms, Ronald Reagan became a transformational president. In the process of restoring the stature of the presidency and reviving the economy, he transformed political life by accelerating the nation's shift toward conservatism and by revitalizing the Republican party after the Watergate scandal. He put the Democratic party on the defensive and forced conventional New Deal "liberalism" into a panicked retreat. For the next twenty years or so, Reagan's anti-government, anti-tax conservative agenda would dominate the national political landscape.

An Anti-Communist Foreign Policy

> CORE **OBJECTIVE**
> **4.** Explain how Reagan's Soviet strategy helped end the Cold War.

On a flight to Detroit, Michigan, to accept the Republican party's presidential nomination in the summer of 1980, Ronald Reagan was asked why he wanted to be president. He answered: "To end the Cold War." A few years earlier, he had offered a simple formula for success against what he described as the international Communist conspiracy directed by the Soviet Union: "We win, they lose." As president, Reagan systematically worked to make that happen by promoting what he called his "peace through strength" strategy. Through a series of bold steps, he would build up U.S. military strength to the point it would overwhelm the Soviet Union, both financially and militarily. At the same time, Reagan launched a widespread "war of ideas" against communism by charging that the Soviet Union (the "evil empire") was "the focus of evil in the modern world."

> "War of ideas" and the Reagan Doctrine

What came to be called the Reagan Doctrine revived and expanded the old notion of "containment" by pledging to combat Soviet adventurism throughout the world, even if it meant partnering with brutal dictatorships to do so. Reagan believed that aggressive CIA-led efforts to stalemate Soviet expansionism would eventually cause the unstable Soviet system to implode "on the ash heap of history."

A Massive Defense Buildup

> The arms race and bankrupting the Soviet Union

Reagan's conduct of foreign policy reflected his belief that trouble in the world stemmed mainly from Moscow, the capital of what he called the "evil empire." Reagan had long believed that former Republican presidents Nixon and Ford—following the advice of Henry Kissinger—had been too soft on the Soviets. Kissinger's emphasis on détente, he said, had been a "one-way street" favoring the Soviets.

By contrast, Reagan first wanted to reduce the risk of nuclear war by convincing the Soviets that they could not win such a conflict. To do so, he and Secretary of Defense Caspar Weinberger embarked upon a major buildup of nuclear and conventional weapons. During Reagan's two presidential terms, defense spending came to represent a fourth of all federal government expenditures. Reagan claimed that such expensive defense allocations had another purpose: it was also intended to bankrupt the Soviets by forcing them to spend much more on their own military budgets. To critics who complained about the money being spent on expensive new U.S. weapons systems, Reagan replied, "It will break the Soviets first." It did.

In 1983, Reagan escalated the nuclear arms race by authorizing the Defense Department to develop the controversial **Strategic Defense Initiative (SDI)**, featuring a complex anti-missile defense system positioning satellites with laser weapons in outer space to "intercept and destroy" Soviet missiles in flight. Despite skepticism among the media, many scientists, and even government officials that such a defense system (dubbed "Star Wars" by the media) could ever be built (Secretary of State George Shultz called it "lunacy"), Congress approved the first stage of funding, which in turn forced the Soviets to launch an expensive research and development effort of their own to keep pace.

The Americas

Fighting the Communist threat in Central America

Reagan's foremost international concern, however, was Central America, where he detected the most serious Communist threat. The tiny nation of El Salvador, caught up since 1980 in a brutal struggle between Communist-supported revolutionaries and right-wing militants, received U.S. economic and military assistance. Critics argued that U.S. involvement ensured that the revolutionary forces would gain public support by capitalizing on "anti-Yankee" sentiment. Supporters countered that allowing a Communist victory in El Salvador would lead all of Central America into the Communist camp (a new "domino" theory). By 1984, however, the U.S.-backed government of President José Napoleón Duarte had brought some stability to El Salvador.

Even more troubling to Reagan was the situation in Nicaragua. The State Department claimed that the Cuban-sponsored Sandinista socialist government, which had seized power in 1979, was sending Soviet and Cuban arms to leftist Salvadoran rebels. In response, the Reagan administration ordered the CIA to train anti-Communist Nicaraguans, or Contras (short for *contrarevolucionarios*, or counterrevolutionaries), who staged attacks on Sandinista bases from sanctuaries in Honduras.

In supporting these "freedom fighters," Reagan sought not only to impede the traffic in arms to Salvadoran rebels but also to replace the Sandinistas with a democratic government in Nicaragua. Critics accused the Contras of being mostly right-wing fanatics who killed indiscriminately. They also feared that the United States might eventually commit its own combat forces, leading to a Vietnam-like intervention. Reagan warned that if the Communists prevailed in Central America, "our credibility would collapse, our alliances would crumble, and the safety of our homeland would be jeopardized."

Strategic Defense Initiative (SDI) (1983) Ronald Reagan's proposed space-based anti-missile defense system, dubbed "Star Wars" by the media, that aroused great controversy and escalated the arms race between the United States and the Soviet Union.

The Iran-Contra Affair

During the fall of 1986, Democrats regained control of the Senate with a 55 to 45 majority. They also picked up 6 seats in the House to increase their already comfortable margin to 259 to 176. Those results had less to do with Reagan's popularity than with the qualities of the particular candidates and local and state issues. Whatever the reason, the 1986 elections meant that Reagan would face an oppositional Congress during the last two years of his presidency.

What was worse, reports surfaced in late 1986 that the United States had been secretly selling arms to U.S.-hating Iran (which Reagan had called an "outlaw state") in the hope of securing the release of American hostages held in Lebanon by extremist groups sympathetic to Iran. Such action contradicted Reagan's repeated insistence that his administration would never negotiate with terrorists. The disclosures angered America's allies as well as many Americans who vividly remembered the 1979 Iranian takeover of the embassy in Tehran. Over the next several months, revelations reminiscent of the Watergate affair disclosed a complicated series of covert activities carried out by administration officials.

At the center of what came to be called the **Iran-Contra affair** was Marine lieutenant colonel Oliver North, a swashbuckling aide to the National Security Council who specialized in counterterrorism. Working from the basement of the White House, North had been secretly selling military supplies to Iran and using the proceeds to support the Contra rebels fighting in Nicaragua at a time when Congress had voted to ban such aid.

North's illegal activities, it turned out, had been approved by national security adviser Robert McFarlane; McFarlane's successor, Admiral John Poindexter; and CIA director William Casey. Both Secretary of State George Shultz and Secretary of Defense Caspar Weinberger criticized the arms sale to Iran, but their objections were ignored, and they were thereafter kept in the dark about what was going on. On three occasions, Shultz threatened to resign over the "pathetic" scheme. After information about the secret dealings surfaced in the press, North and others erased incriminating computer files and destroyed documents. McFarlane attempted suicide, Poindexter resigned, and North was fired. Casey, who denied any connection to the clumsy operation, left the CIA for health reasons and died shortly thereafter from a brain tumor.

Iran-Contra hearings Admiral John Poindexter listens to a question from the investigation committee with apprehension on July 21, 1987.

Under increasing criticism, Reagan appointed a three-member commission, led by former Republican senator John Tower, to investigate the scandal. The Tower Commission issued a devastating report early in 1987 that placed much of the responsibility for the bungled Iran-Contra affair on Reagan's loose management style. When asked if he had known of Colonel North's illegal actions, the president simply replied: "I don't remember." He was stunned that "for the first time in my life, people didn't believe me."

Iran-Contra affair (1987) Reagan administration scandal over the secret, unlawful U.S. sale of arms to Iran in partial exchange for the release of hostages in Lebanon; the arms money in turn was used illegally to aid Nicaraguan right-wing insurgents, the Contras.

During the spring and summer of 1987, a joint House-Senate committee began holding hearings into the Iran-Contra affair. The televised sessions revealed a tangled web of inept financial and diplomatic transactions, the illegal shredding of incriminating government documents, crass profiteering, and misguided patriotism.

The investigations of the independent counsel led to six indictments in 1988. A Washington jury found Oliver North guilty of three relatively minor charges but innocent of nine more serious counts, apparently reflecting the jury's reasoning that he acted as an agent of higher-ups. His conviction was later overturned on appeal. Of those involved in the affair, only John Poindexter received a jail sentence—six months for obstructing justice and lying to Congress.

A Historic Treaty

The most positive achievement at the end of Reagan's second term was a surprising arms-reduction agreement with the Soviet government. Under Mikhail Gorbachev, who came to power in 1985, the Soviets pursued renewed détente so that they could reduce military spending related to the Cold War and focus on more pressing problems, especially a notoriously inefficient economy and a losing war in Afghanistan.

In October 1986 Reagan and Gorbachev met in Reykjavik, Iceland, to discuss ways to reduce the threat of nuclear war. At one point during ten hours of intense negotiations, Reagan shocked the Soviets by saying, "It would be fine with me if we eliminated all nuclear weapons." Equally shocking was Gorbachev's reply: "We can do that." By the end of the meeting, however, the two sides remained so far apart on the details that they had given up.

The logjam in the disarmament negotiations with the Soviet Union suddenly broke in 1987, when Gorbachev announced that he was willing to consider mutually reducing nuclear weaponry. After nine months of strenuous negotiations, Reagan and Gorbachev met amid much fanfare in Washington, D.C., on December 9, 1987, and signed the **Intermediate-Range Nuclear Forces (INF) Treaty**, an agreement to eliminate intermediate-range (300- to 3,000-mile) missiles. Reagan's steadfast show of strength against the Soviets and a new kind of Soviet leader in Mikhail Gorbachev combined to produce the most sweeping reduction in nuclear weaponry in history.

The INF treaty marked the first time that the two nations had agreed to destroy a whole class of weapons systems. Under the terms of the treaty, the United States would destroy 859 missiles, and the Soviets would eliminate 1,752. Still, the reductions represented only 4 percent of the total nuclear-missile count on both sides.

Gorbachev's successful efforts to liberalize Soviet domestic life and improve East-West relations cheered Americans. The Soviets suddenly began stressing cooperation with the West in dealing with hot spots around

Mikhail Gorbachev Deputy Chairman, and later President, of the Soviet Union in 1988.

Intermediate-Range Nuclear Forces (INF) Treaty (1987) Agreement signed by U.S. president Ronald Reagan and Soviet premier Mikhail Gorbachev to eliminate the deployment of intermediate-range missiles with nuclear warheads.

the world. In the Middle East, they urged the Palestine Liberation Organization, founded in 1964 to represent the Palestinian people, to recognize Israel's right to exist and advocated a greater role for the United Nations in the volatile Persian Gulf. Perhaps the most dramatic symbol of a thawing cold war was the phased withdrawal of 115,000 Soviet troops from Afghanistan, which began in 1988.

Reagan's Global Legacy

Reagan achieved the unthinkable by helping to end the Cold War. Although his massive defense buildup almost bankrupted the United States, it did bankrupt the Soviet Union and force it to the bargaining table. By negotiating the nuclear disarmament treaty and lighting the fuse of democratic freedom in Soviet-controlled Eastern Europe, he set in motion events that would cause the collapse of the Soviet Union. In June 1987, Reagan visited the huge concrete and barbed wire Berlin Wall and, in a dramatic speech, called upon the Soviet Union to allow greater freedom within the countries under its control. "General Secretary Gorbachev, if you seek peace, if you seek prosperity for the Soviet Union and Eastern Europe, if you seek liberalization: Come here to this gate! Mr. Gorbachev, open this gate! Mr. Gorbachev, tear down this wall!"

The Changing Economic and Social Landscape

> CORE **OBJECTIVE**
> **5.** Characterize the social and economic issues and innovations that emerged during the 1980s.

During the eighties, profound changes transformed American life. The economy went through a wrenching transformation in adapting to an increasingly interconnected global marketplace. The nations that had been devastated by the Second World War—France, Germany, the Soviet Union, Japan, and China—had by the eighties developed formidable economies with higher levels of productivity than the United States. More and more American manufacturing companies shifted their production overseas, thereby accelerating the transition of the economy from its once-dominant industrial base to a more services-oriented economy. Driving all of these changes was the impact of the computer revolution and the development of the Internet.

The Computer Revolution

The idea of a programmable machine that would rapidly perform mental tasks had been around since the eighteenth century, but it took the Second World War to marshal the intellectual and financial resources needed to create such a "computer." In 1946, a team of engineers at the University of Pennsylvania created ENIAC (electronic numerical integrator and computer), the first all-purpose, all-electronic digital computer.

The Reagan Revolution

The election of Ronald Reagan in 1980 was a turning point in American political history—in many ways a reaction against the previous two decades in politics. Reagan and the "New Right" political movement he embodied helped shift the focus of American politics away from the New Deal "liberalism" that had dominated the domestic agenda since 1932. While Reagan did not put an end to the federal welfare state (as some of his supporters fervently hoped), he did slow its expansion. In foreign policy, Reagan also broke with past presidents by taking a more confrontational stance against the Soviet Union. As you examine the ways in which "The Reagan Revolution" reshaped the political landscape, consider the questions below.

FACTORS CONTRIBUTING TO REAGAN'S ELECTION	REAGAN'S GOVERNING PHILOSOPHY
Economic Distress of the 1970s: High inflation and economic stagnation increased the appeal of Reagan's "supply-side" economic message over the New Deal "liberalism" of Carter and other past presidents, spawning tax revolts among some working- and middle-class property owners, who joined anti-tax and anti–big government movements.	**"Supply-Side" Economics:** Cut taxes to incentivize individuals and businesses to increase productivity, invest, and spend.
Growth of the Sunbelt: Population growth of southern and western states increased the electoral influence of older and more conservative voters.	**Anti–Big Government:** Shrink the federal bureaucracy, empower states' rights, reduce regulation of business, and reduce the role of the federal government generally.
Rise of the Religious Right and Anti-Feminism: Religious conservatives mobilized against abortion rights and restrictions on school prayer, leading to greater organization and political power; anger at the feminist movement over abortion rights, as well as challenges to traditional gender roles, moved many culturally conservative Democrats, especially working-class Roman Catholics, toward Reagan.	**Social Conservatism:** Support traditional "family values," gender roles, and the "rights" of the unborn; oppose feminism, abortion rights, gay rights, and secularism.
Resentment of Protest Movements: Reagan attracted voters alienated by protests over the Vietnam War and civil rights, and promised a "renewed" America and a return to more traditional values.	**Hard-line Anti-Communism:** Take a tougher stance against communism and the Soviet Union, and support anti-Communist efforts across the globe.
Iran Hostage Crisis: The seizure of the American embassy in Tehran made President Carter appear weak and ineffective.	

The next major breakthrough was the invention in 1971 of the **microprocessor**—virtually a tiny computer on a silicon chip. The functions that had once been performed by huge computers that took up an entire room could now be performed by a microchip circuit the size of a postage stamp.

The microchip made possible the personal computer. In 1975, an engineer named Ed Roberts developed the Altair 8800, the prototype of the personal computer. Its potential excited a Harvard sophomore named Bill

microprocessor An electronic circuit printed on a tiny silicon chip; a major technological breakthrough in 1971, it paved the way for the development of the personal computer.

EFFECTS OF REAGAN'S DOMESTIC POLICIES

Tax Cuts for High Income Earners and Investors: Increased economic growth and consumerism; increased budget deficit and national debt.

Deregulation: Relaxed government price controls on oil and natural gas led to a decline in energy prices that helped stimulate economic growth.

Efforts to Weaken the Power of Labor Unions: Decline in union membership and the power of unions.

Slowed Growth of Social Welfare Programs: Slowed expansion of federal welfare state; increased income inequality.

Criticism of Feminist, Civil Rights, and Environmental Movements: Increased influence of the "New Right" conservative movement in American politics.

EFFECTS OF REAGAN'S FOREIGN POLICY

Increased Anti-Communist Rhetoric: Energized anti-Soviet movements in Eastern Europe.

Increased Anti-Communist Activities in Central America: Military assistance to anti-Communist forces; Iran-Contra affair.

Increased Military Spending: Increased budget deficit and national debt; economic pressure of arms race contributed to economic and political collapse of Soviet Union; arms-reduction treaty with Soviets.

QUESTIONS FOR ANALYSIS

1. How was Reagan's governing philosophy different from that of recent presidents?

2. How did the events and trends of the sixties and seventies help lead to Reagan's election in 1980?

3. What were the effects of Reagan's domestic policy?

4. How did Reagan's foreign policy reshape the Cold War?

Gates, who improved the software of the Altair 8800, dropped out of college, and formed a company called Microsoft to sell the new system. By 1977, Gates and others had helped transform the personal computer into a mass consumer product. The development of the Internet, electronic mail (e-mail), and cell-phone technology during the eighties and nineties allowed for instantaneous communication, thereby accelerating the globalization of the economy and dramatically increasing productivity in the workplace.

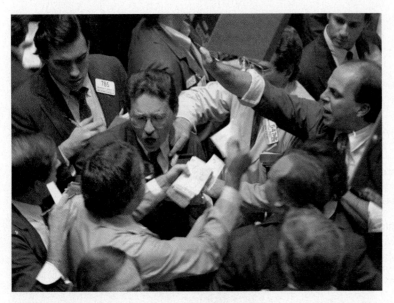

Black Monday A 508-point plunge devastated Wall Street on October 19, 1987 and sent traders on the floor of the New York Stock Exchange into a panic-selling frenzy.

Debt and the Stock Market Plunge

During the eighties, Ronald Reagan lowered tax rates so that people would have more money to spend and thereby accelerate the growth of the economy. Americans had little trouble going on a spending spree. During the "Reagan Era," marketers and advertisers celebrated instant gratification at the expense of the future. Michelob beer commercials promised that "you can have it all," and many people went on self-indulgent spending sprees. The more they bought, the more they wanted. Compulsive shoppers donned T-shirts proclaiming: "Born to Shop." Money—lots of it—came to define the American Dream. In the hit movie *Wall Street* (1987), the high-flying land developer and corporate raider Gordon Gekko, played by actor Michael Douglas, announced that "greed . . . is good. Greed is right."

The Poor

Increased homelessness

The eighties were years of vivid contrast. Despite unprecedented prosperity, growing numbers of underclass Americans were without hope. Widespread homelessness became the most acute social issue.

A variety of causes had led to a shortage of low-cost housing. The government had given up on building public housing, urban-renewal programs had demolished blighted residential areas but provided no housing for those who were displaced, and owners had abandoned unprofitable buildings in poor neighborhoods or converted them into expensive condominiums, a process called *gentrification*. In addition, after new medications allowed for the release of some mentally ill patients from institutions, many of them ended up on the streets because the promised mental-health services failed to materialize. Drug and alcohol abuse were rampant among the homeless, mostly unemployed single adults. A quarter of them had spent time in mental institutions; some 40 percent had spent time in jail; a third were delusional.

The AIDS Epidemic

HIV/AIDS Human immunodeficiency virus (HIV) transmitted via the bodily fluids of infected persons to cause acquired immunodeficiency syndrome (AIDS), an often-fatal disease of the immune system when it appeared in the 1980s.

Still another group of outcasts in the eighties included those suffering from a newly identified disease called AIDS (acquired immunodeficiency syndrome). At the beginning of the eighties, public health officials had reported that gay men and intravenous drug users were especially at risk for developing AIDS. People contracted the human immunodeficiency

AIDS Memorial Quilt Composed of more than 48,000 panels, the quilt was first conceptualized by gay rights and AIDS activist Cleve Jones to commemorate those who died of AIDS-related causes. It continues to grow to this day.

virus (HIV), by coming into contact with the blood or bodily fluids of an infected person. Those infected with the virus that causes AIDS showed signs of extreme fatigue, developed a strange combination of infections, and soon died.

The Reagan administration showed little interest in AIDS in part be- cause it was initially viewed as a "gay" disease. Patrick Buchanan, the con- servative spokesman who served as Reagan's director of communications, said that homosexuals had "declared war on nature, and now nature is extracting an awful retribution." Buchanan and others convinced Reagan not to engage the **HIV/AIDS** issue. By 2000, AIDS had claimed almost 300,000 American lives and was spreading among a larger segment of the population. Nearly 1 million Americans were carrying the deadly virus, and it had become the leading cause of death among men ages twenty-five to forty-four.

> AIDS becomes leading cause of death for young men

The Presidency of George H. W. Bush

Reagan's two-term vice president, George H. W. Bush, won the Republican presidential nomination in 1988. Born into a prominent New England fam- ily, the son of a U.S. senator, he enlisted at the age of eighteen in the U.S. Navy at the start of the Second World War, becoming America's youngest combat pilot. After his distinguished service in the war, Bush graduated

> CORE **OBJECTIVE**
> **6.** Appraise the impact of the end of the Cold War and the efforts of President George H. W. Bush to create a post- cold war foreign policy.

George H. W. Bush His son, George W. Bush, would also serve as president, making them the second father-son presidential duo in history (the first was John Adams and John Quincy Adams).

from Yale University, having also been captain of the baseball team. Bush and his family moved to west Texas, where he became a wealthy oil executive before entering government service, first as a member of the U.S. House of Representatives, then as U.S. ambassador to the UN, a diplomat in China, and head of the CIA before becoming vice president in 1981.

In all of those roles, Bush had displayed intelligence, integrity, and courage. But he lacked Reagan's charm and speaking skills. One Democrat described him as a man born "with a silver foot in his mouth." Bush was a centrist Republican who had never embraced right-wing conservatism. He promised to use the White House to fight bigotry, illiteracy, and homelessness. "I want a kinder, gentler nation," Bush said in his speech accepting the Republican nomination. His most memorable line in the speech, though, was a defiant statement ruling out any tax increases to deal with the massive budget deficits created during the Reagan years: "The Congress will push me to raise taxes, and I'll say no, and they'll push, and I'll say no, and they'll push again. And I'll say to them: Read my lips. No new taxes."

Meanwhile, Massachusetts governor Michael Dukakis won the Democratic nomination, but it did little good. In the end, Bush won a decisive victory. Dukakis carried only ten states plus the District of Columbia, with clusters of support in the Northeast, Midwest, and Northwest. Bush carried the rest, with a margin of about 54 percent to 46 percent in the popular vote and 426 to 111 in the Electoral College, but the Democrats retained control of the House and Senate.

George H. W. Bush sought to reinforce the initiatives that Reagan had put in place rather than launch his own array of programs and policies. "We don't need to remake society," he announced. As an example of his "gentler, kinder" conservatism, Bush supported the Democratic-proposed Americans with Disabilities Act (1990), which strengthened the civil rights of the physically or mentally disabled in areas such as employment, public transportation, and housing. The act also required organizations (for-profit, non-profit, and governmental) to ensure that people with disabilities could access facilities by providing mechanized doors, wheelchair ramps, and elevators.

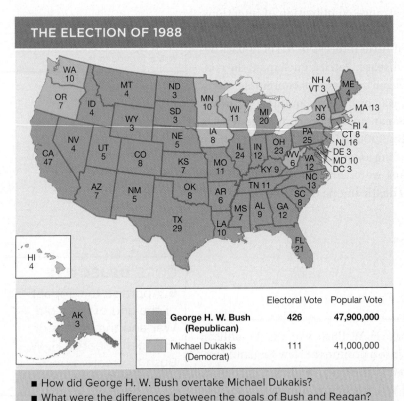

THE ELECTION OF 1988

	Electoral Vote	Popular Vote
George H. W. Bush (Republican)	**426**	**47,900,000**
Michael Dukakis (Democrat)	111	41,000,000

- How did George H. W. Bush overtake Michael Dukakis?
- What were the differences between the goals of Bush and Reagan?

The Federal Debt and Recession

The biggest problem facing the Bush administration was the huge national debt, which stood at $2.6 trillion in 1989, nearly three times its 1980 level. Bush's pledge not to increase taxes (especially income taxes) made it more difficult to reduce the annual deficit or trim the long-term debt. Likewise, Bush was not willing to make substantial cutbacks in spending on defense or social welfare programs like Social Security, Medicare, and food stamps. As a result, by 1990 the country faced "a fiscal mess."

During the summer of 1990, Bush agreed with Congressional Democrats to approve "tax revenue increases," which he had sworn to avoid. His decision to support tax increases set off a revolt among conservative Republicans, from which he never recovered. The increase in the top tax rate from 28 to 31 percent raised federal revenue but eroded Bush's political support among conservative Republicans. The economy barely grew at all during the first three years of the Bush administration—the worst record since the end of the Second World War.

The Democracy Movement Abroad

George H. W. Bush entered the White House with more foreign-policy experience than most presidents, and, like Nixon before him, preferred to deal with international relations rather than domestic issues such as the deficit, drug abuse, and the problems of the inner cities. In the Soviet Union, amazing changes were underway. With the economy failing, Mikhail Gorbachev responded with policies of **perestroika** (economic restructuring) and **glasnost** (openness), a loosening of centralized economic planning and censorship of the press. His foreign policy sought harmony and trade with the West. Early in 1989, Soviet troops left Afghanistan after nine years. Gorbachev then renounced the right of the Soviet Union to intervene in the internal affairs of other Communist countries. Soon thereafter, the old Communist regimes in Eastern Europe fell with surprisingly little bloodshed. Communist rule enforced by the Soviet Union ended first in Poland and Hungary, then in Czechoslovakia and Bulgaria. In Romania, the year of peaceful revolution ended in a bloodbath when the people joined the army in a bloody uprising against Nicolae Ceaușescu, the country's brutal dictator. He and his wife were captured, tried, and then executed on Christmas Day.

> The end of the Soviet empire; the reunification of East and West Germany

The End of the Berlin Wall

The most spectacular event in the collapse of the Soviet Empire came on November 9, 1989, when Germans—using hand tools and even their bare hands—tore down the Berlin Wall, the chief symbol of the Cold War. With the borders to the West now fully open, the Communist government of East Germany collapsed, and a freely elected government came to power. On October 3, 1990, the five states of East Germany were united with West

perestroika Russian term for "economic restructuring"; applied to Mikhail Gorbachev's series of political and economic reforms that included shifting a centrally planned Commmunist economy to a mixed economy allowing for capitalism.

glasnost Russian term for "openness"; applied to the loosening of censorship in the Soviet Union under Mikhail Gorbachev.

A hammer to the Soviet Empire A West German demonstrator pounds away at the Berlin Wall on November 11, 1989, while East Berlin border guards look on. Two days later, all the crossings between East and West Germany were opened.

Germany. The reform impulse that Gorbachev helped unleash in the Eastern-bloc countries sped out of control within the Soviet Union itself, however. Gorbachev had proven unusually adept at political restructuring, yielding the Communist monopoly of government but building a new presidential system that gave him, if anything, increased powers. His skills, however, could not salvage an antiquated economy that resisted change.

Communist Coup Fails

Gorbachev's popularity shrank in the Soviet Union even as it grew abroad. Communist hard-liners saw in his reforms the unraveling of their bureaucratic and political empire. Once the genie of freedom was released from the Communist lamp, however, it took on a momentum of its own. On August 18, 1991, a group of political and military leaders tried to seize the reins of power. They accosted Gorbachev at his vacation retreat in Crimea and demanded that he proclaim a state of emergency and transfer his powers to them. He replied, "Go to hell," whereupon he was placed under house arrest.

The coup was doomed from the start, however. Poorly planned and clumsily implemented, it lacked effective coordination. The plotters failed to arrest popular leaders such as Boris Yeltsin, the president of the Russian republic. They also neglected to close the airports or cut off telephone and television communications, and they were opposed by key elements of the military and KGB (the secret police).

> U.S. recognition of the new Soviet government and the independent Baltic republics

On August 20, President Bush responded favorably to Yeltsin's request for support and persuaded other world leaders to join him in refusing to recognize the legitimacy of the new Soviet government. The next day, word began to seep out that the plotters had given up and were fleeing. Several committed suicide, and a newly released Gorbachev ordered the others arrested.

Yet things did not go back to the way they had been. Although Gorbachev reclaimed the title of president, he was forced to resign as head of the Communist party and admit that he had made a grave mistake in appointing the men who had turned against him. Boris Yeltsin emerged as the most popular political figure in the country.

So what had begun as a reactionary coup turned into a powerful accelerant for astonishing changes in the Soviet Union, or the "Soviet Disunion," as one journalist termed it. Most of the fifteen republics proclaimed their independence from Russia, with the Baltic states of Latvia, Lithuania, and Estonia regaining the status of independent nations. The Communist party was dismantled, prompting celebrating crowds to topple statues of Lenin and other Communist heroes.

Reducing the Nuclear Threat

The collapse of the Soviet Union accelerated efforts to reduce their stockpiles of nuclear weapons. In late 1991, President Bush announced that the United States would destroy all its tactical nuclear weapons in Europe and Asia. Bush explained that the prospect of a Soviet invasion of Western Europe was "no longer a realistic threat," and that this transformation provided an unprecedented opportunity for reducing the threat of nuclear holocaust. President Gorbachev responded by announcing similar Soviet cutbacks. The sudden end of the Cold War led many to believe that the United States could greatly reduce the vast global military responsibilities it had developed over four decades of anti-Communism.

> The end of the Soviet "threat"

Panama

The end of the Cold War did not spell the end of international tensions and conflict, however. Indeed, before the end of 1989, U.S. troops were engaged in battle in Panama, where a petty tyrant provoked the first of America's military engagements under George H. W. Bush. In 1983, General Manuel Noriega had become leader of the Panamanian Defense Forces, which made him the head of the government in fact if not in title.

In 1988, federal grand juries in Miami and Tampa indicted Noriega and fifteen others on charges of drug trafficking. The next year, the Panamanian president tried to fire Noriega, but the National Assembly ousted the president instead and named Noriega "maximum leader." The legislators then declared Panama "in a state of war" with the United States. On December 16, 1989, a U.S. marine in Panama was killed, whereupon President Bush ordered an invasion of Panama to capture Noriega and install a government to be headed by Guillermo Endara, who had won the presidency in a recent election that was then nullified by Noriega.

> Panama–U.S. "war"

In the early morning of December 20, U.S. troops struck at strategic targets in the country. Within hours, Noriega had surrendered. Twenty-three U.S. servicemen were killed in the action, and estimates of Panamanian casualties, including many civilians, were as high as 4,000. In April 1992, Noriega was convicted in the United States on eight counts of racketeering and drug distribution.

The Gulf War

Months later, Saddam Hussein, dictator of Iraq, focused U.S. attention back upon the Middle East when his army suddenly invaded its tiny neighbor, Kuwait, on August 2, 1990. Kuwait had recently increased its production of oil, contrary to agreements with the Organization of the Petroleum Exporting Countries (OPEC). The resulting drop in global oil prices offended the Iraqi regime, which was deeply in debt and heavily dependent upon oil revenues.

> First Gulf War

President Bush condemned Iraq's "naked aggression" and dispatched planes and troops to Saudi Arabia on a "wholly defensive" mission: to protect

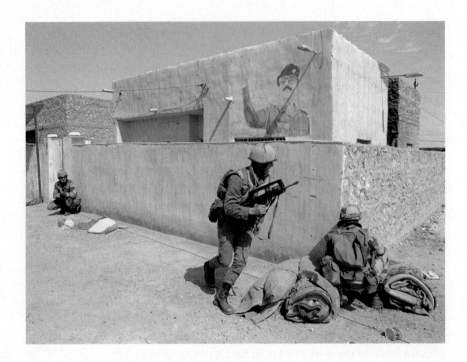

Operation Desert Storm Allied soldiers patrol the southern Iraqi town of Salman on February 27, 1991. On the side of a building is a propaganda mural of dictator Saddam Hussein in military uniform.

Operation Desert Storm (1991) Assault by American-led multinational forces that quickly defeated Iraqi forces under Saddam Hussein in the First Gulf War, ending the Iraqi occupation of Kuwait.

Saudi Arabia. British forces soon joined in, as did Arab units from Egypt, Morocco, Syria, Oman, the United Arab Emirates, and Qatar. A flurry of negotiations failed, as Iraq refused to yield, leading Congress on January 12, 1991, to authorize the use of U.S. armed forces. Four days later, more than thirty nations, including ten Islamic countries, launched **Operation Desert Storm** against Iraq. The swift-moving allied ground assault began on February 24 and lasted only four days. Iraqi soldiers surrendered by the thousands.

On February 28, six weeks after the fighting began, President Bush called for a cease-fire. The Iraqis accepted, and the shooting ended. There were 137 American fatalities. The lowest estimate of Iraqi deaths, civilian and military, was 100,000. The coalition forces occupied about a fifth of Iraq, but Hussein's tyrannical regime was intact. What came to be called the First Gulf War was thus a triumph without victory. Hussein had been defeated, but he was allowed to escape and foster greater mischief. The consequences of the brief but intense First Gulf War, the "mother of all battles," in Saddam Hussein's words, would be played out in the future in ways that no one had predicted. Arabs who felt humiliated by the lopsided American triumph began plotting revenge that would spiral into a new war of terrorism.

Bush's "New World Order"

For months after the First Gulf War in 1991, George H. W. Bush seemed unbeatable; his public approval rating soared to 91 percent. Yet the aftermath of Desert Storm was mixed, with Saddam Hussein's iron grip on Iraq still intact. The Soviet Union meanwhile stumbled on to its surprising end. On December 25, 1991, the Soviet flag over the Kremlin was replaced by the flag of the Russian Federation. The Cold War had ended with the dismemberment of the Soviet Union and its fifteen republics. As a result, the United States had become the world's only dominant military power.

"Containment" of the Soviet Union, the bedrock of U.S. foreign policy for more than four decades, had suddenly become irrelevant. For all of its potential horrors, the Cold War brought stability because the two superpowers, the United States and the Soviet Union, had restrained themselves from an all-out war that may well have involved the use of nuclear weapons. Now the world would witness a growing number of unresolved political crises and unstable regimes, some of which had access to weapons of mass destruction—nuclear as well as chemical and biological weapons. Bush struggled to interpret the fluid new international scene. He spoke of a "new world order" but never defined it, admitting that he had trouble with "the vision thing." By the end of 1991, the euphoria of the Gulf War victory had worn off and a listless Bush faced a challenge in the Republican primary from the feisty conservative commentator and former White House aide Patrick Buchanan, who adopted the slogan "America First" and called on Bush to "bring home the boys."

> Bush's "New World Order"

The excitement over the allied victory in the Gulf War quickly gave way to anxiety over the depressed economy. In addressing the recession, Bush tried a clumsy balancing act, on the one hand acknowledging that "people are hurting" while on the other telling Americans that "this is a good time to buy a car." By 1991, the public approval rating of his economic policy had plummeted to 18 percent.

The Election of 1992

At the 1992 Republican Convention, Patrick Buchanan, who had won about a third of the votes in the party's primaries, blasted Bush for breaking his pledge not to raise taxes and for becoming the "biggest spender in American history." As the 1992 election unfolded, Bush's real problem was not Pat Buchanan and the conservative wing of the Republican party, however. What threatened his reelection was his own failed effort to improve the economy. A popular bumper sticker reflected the growing public frustration with the economic policies of the Bush administration: "Saddam Hussein still has his job. What about you?"

In contrast to the divided Republicans, the Democrats at their 1992 convention presented an image of centrist or moderate forces in control. For several years, the Democratic Leadership Council, led by Arkansas governor William Jefferson Clinton, had been pushing the party from the liberal left to the center of the political spectrum. Clinton called for a "third way" positioned between conservatism and liberalism.

The 1992 campaign also featured a third-party candidate, Texan H. Ross Perot, a puckish billionaire who found a large audience for his criticism of

Reaganomics as "voodoo economics" (a phrase originally used in the 1980 Republican primary by then-contender George H. W. Bush before he was named the vice-presidential candidate on the Reagan presidential ticket) and his warnings about the impending crisis posed by the huge federal debt.

Born in 1946 in Hope, Arkansas, Bill Clinton never knew his biological father, a traveling salesman who died in a car crash a few months before his son was born. Even as a teen, Clinton yearned to be a political leader on a national scale. He attended Georgetown University in Washington, D.C., won a Rhodes Scholarship to Oxford University, and then earned a law degree from Yale University, where he met his future wife, Hillary Rodham. Clinton returned to Arkansas and won election as the state's attorney general. By 1979, at age thirty-two, Bill Clinton was the youngest governor in the country. He served three more terms as Arkansas governor and in the process emerged as a dynamic young leader of the "**New Democrats**" committed to winning back the middle-class whites ("Reagan Democrats") who had voted Republican during the 1980s.

A self-described moderate seeking the Democratic presidential nomination, Clinton promised to cut the defense budget, provide tax relief for the middle class, and create a massive economic aid package for the former republics of the Soviet Union to help them forge democratic societies. Witty, intelligent, and charismatic, with an in-depth knowledge of public policy, Clinton was a superb campaigner; he projected energy, youth, and optimism, reminding many political observers of John F. Kennedy, Clinton's boyhood hero.

But beneath Clinton's charisma and public-policy expertise lurked several flaws. Self-absorbed and self-indulgent, he, like Lyndon Johnson, yearned to be loved. The *New York Times* explained that Clinton was "emotionally needy, indecisive, and undisciplined." Even more enticing to the media were charges that Clinton was a chronic adulterer. Clinton's evasive denials of both allegations could not dispel a lingering mistrust of his character.

After a series of bruising party primaries, Clinton won the Democratic presidential nomination in the summer of 1992, promising to restore the "hopes of the forgotten middle class." He chose Senator Albert "Al" Gore Jr. of Tennessee as his running mate. Gore described himself as a "raging moderate." So the Democratic candidates were two Southern Baptists from adjoining states, Arkansas and Tennessee. Flushed with their convention victory and sporting a ten-point lead over Bush in the polls, the Clinton-Gore team hammered Bush on economic issues to win over working-class voters. Clinton pledged that, if elected, he would cut the federal budget deficit in half in four years while cutting taxes on middle-class Americans.

Bill Clinton and Al Gore The hopeful Democratic candidates round out their presidential campaign in Clinton's hometown of Little Rock, Arkansas on November 3, 1992.

New Democrats Centrist ("moderate") Democrats led by President Bill Clinton that emerged in the late 1980s and early 1990s to challenge the "liberal" direction of the party.

Such promises helped Clinton win the election with 370 electoral votes and about 43 percent of the vote; Bush received 168 electoral votes and 39 percent of the vote; and, Perot garnered 19 percent of the popular vote, more than any other third-party candidate since Theodore Roosevelt in 1912. As 1992 came to an end, Bill Clinton, the "New Democrat," prepared to lead the United States through the last decade of the twentieth century. "The urgent question of our time," he said, "is whether we can make change our friend and not our enemy." During his eight years as president, Clinton would embrace many unexpected changes while ushering America into the twenty-first century.

- **The Carter Presidency** Jimmy Carter had notable achievements, such as the *Camp David Accords*. Yet, his administration suffered from legislative inexperience, a deepening economic recession, soaring inflation, and the *Iranian hostage crisis*. His sermonizing about the need for Americans to lead simpler lives compounded the public's loss of faith in his presidency.

- **The Rise of Conservatism** Ronald Reagan's charm, coupled with the public's disillusionment over Carter's presidency, won Reagan the election in 1980. The Republican insurgency, characterized in part by a cultural backlash against the feminist movement, was dominated by the *religious right*. Sunbelt voters, many of whom were older transplants to southern and western states, were socially conservative and favored lower taxes and a smaller, less intrusive federal government. California passed a property-tax-lowering referendum, Proposition 13, which led to a nationwide tax revolt.

- **Reaganomics** Reagan introduced a "supply-side" economic philosophy, commonly called *Reaganomics*, that championed tax cuts for the rich, reduced government regulation, cuts to social-welfare programs, and increased defense spending. In practice, however, Reagan was unable to cut domestic spending significantly, and the tax cuts failed to pay for themselves as promised. The result was a dramatic increase in the national debt. Reagan also did much to weaken unions and the feminist movement, and to shift the political landscape away from the New Deal liberalism that had dominated American politics since 1932.

- **The End of the Cold War** Reagan's massive military buildup, including preliminary development of the *Strategic Defense Initiative*, brought the Soviets to agreement on the *Intermediate-Range Nuclear Forces (INF) Treaty*—the beginning of the end of the Cold War. But Reagan's foreign policy was badly tarnished by the *Iran-Contra affair*: members of his administration had illegally sold U.S. armaments to Iran to secure the release of American hostages. The proceeds were then secretly funneled to Nicaraguan Contras (despite a congressional ban on such aid). Reagan's loose management style, an independent commission determined, had allowed these illegal activities to flourish.

- **America in the 1980s** The eighties brought not only unprecedented prosperity but also rising poverty and homelessness. The prevailing conservative mood condemned *HIV/AIDS* as a "gay" disease. The *microprocessor* ignited the computer revolution, which dramatically increased productivity and communications while generating new industries. Consumerism flourished all too well, resulting in massive public and private debt as well as the stock market collapse of 1987.

- **A New World Order** In the late 1980s, democratic political movements erupted, failing in Communist China but succeeding in Eastern Europe. Gorbachev's steps to restructure the Soviet Union's economy (*perestroika*) and promote more open policies (*glasnost*) ultimately led to the collapse of the Soviet empire. Iraq, led by Saddam Hussein, invaded Kuwait in 1990. The U.S. led allied forces in *Operation Desert Storm*; the Iraqis soon surrendered. Despite the success of the first Gulf War, the sluggish economy led to Bush's defeat by the *"New Democrats"* under Bill Clinton.

KEY TERMS

CHRONOLOGY

1971	Microprocessor developed
1975	First personal computer, the Altair 8800, produced
1978	Camp David Accords
	Tax revolt in California leads to the passage of Proposition 13
1979	Jerry Falwell organizes the Moral Majority
November 1979	Iranian hostage crisis
1980	Ronald Reagan elected president
1981	Reagan enacts major tax cuts
1983	Strategic Defense Initiative (SDI) authorized
1987	Tower Commission issues report on Iran-Contra affair
	Reagan delivers Berlin Wall speech
October 1987	Stock market plunges 23 percent on "Black Monday"
1988	George H. W. Bush elected president
November 1989	Berlin Wall torn down
December 1989	U.S. troops invade Panama and capture Manuel Noriega
August 1990–1991	First Gulf War
	Soviet Union dissolves
1992	Bill Clinton elected president

INQUIZITIVE

Go to InQuizitive to see what you've learned—and learn what you've missed—with personalized feedback along the way.

YOUTH SPEAKS The Occupy Wall Street movement was born when thousands of protestors, many of them unemployed young adults, "occupied" Wall Street in downtown Manhattan to protest the "tyrannical" financial industry. The grassroots movement soon spread across the nation, then the world. Here, members of the movement stage a protest outside of the New York Stock Exchange in September 2011.

Twenty-First–Century America

1993–Present

The United States entered the final decade of the twentieth century triumphant. American persistence in fighting and financing the Cold War had contributed to the shocking collapse of the Soviet Union and the birth of democracy and capitalism in Eastern Europe. By the end of the twentieth century, the United States was the only superpower.

During the 1990s, the U.S. economy became the marvel of the world as remarkable gains in productivity enabled by new "digital" technologies created the greatest period of prosperity in modern history.

Yet no sooner did the century come to an end than America's sense of physical security and material comfort was shattered by surprise terrorist attacks in 2001 on New York City and Washington, D.C., attacks that killed thousands, plunged the economy into recession, and raised profound questions about national security and personal safety.

The United States led the fight against global terrorism, which embroiled the nation in long, costly, and controversial wars in Iraq and Afghanistan. Opposition to the conduct of those wars would provide much of the momentum for Democrat Barack Obama to win election in 2008 as the nation's first African American president. Obama entered the White House at the same time that the United States was experiencing the Great Recession, a sharp, prolonged economic downturn that almost destroyed the global banking system, caused widespread unemployment, and ignited growing social unrest and political tensions at home and abroad.

CORE OBJECTIVES INQUIZITIVE

1. Describe the major population trends (demographics) in the United States during the twenty-first century, and assess their impact on the nation's politics.

2. Evaluate the accomplishments and setbacks of Bill Clinton's presidency.

3. Summarize the impact of global terrorism on the United States during the presidency of George W. Bush, and evaluate the effectiveness of his "war on terror."

4. Assess the issues and developments during Bush's second term that helped lead to Barack Obama's historic victory in the 2008 presidential election.

5. Identify President Obama's priorities at home and abroad, and assess his efforts to pursue them.

CORE **OBJECTIVE**

1. Describe the major population trends (demographics) in the United States during the twenty-first century, and assess their impact on the nation's politics.

America's Changing Population

The United States at the end of the twentieth century and the beginning of the twenty-first century witnessed dramatic social changes. By the end of 2014, there were more than 320 million Americans, over 80 percent of whom lived in cities or suburbs.

Even more important, the nation's racial and ethnic composition was changing rapidly. The majority white population continued to decline as a proportion of the total population while the proportion represented by minority groups soared. Hispanics/Latinos represented 18 percent of the population, African Americans 13 percent, Asians about 5 percent, and Native Americans 1 percent. The rate of increase among those four groups was twice as fast as it had been during the 1980s. In 2005, Hispanics surpassed African Americans as the nation's largest minority group. Yet the fastest-growing group in the nation were the nearly 10 million who described themselves as "multiracial," representing over 3 percent of the entire population.

Population growth among Hispanics, African Americans, Asians, and Native Americans

The primary cause of this dramatic change in the nation's ethnic mix during the twenty-first century was a surge of immigration. In 1992, the Republican presidential candidate Pat Buchanan warned that the United States was experiencing "the greatest invasion in its history, a migration of millions of illegal aliens a year from Mexico." While Buchanan and others wanted to close the border with Mexico, many others believed that embracing immigrants remained one of the nation's essential ideals.

In 2014, the United States had more foreign-born residents than ever before, more than 45 million Americans, 11 million of whom were undocumented immigrants (formerly classified as "illegal aliens"). In the first decade of the twenty-first century, the United States became home to more than twice as many immigrants as *all* other countries in the world combined. For the first time in the nation's history, the majority of immigrants came not from Europe but from other parts of the world: Asia, Latin America, and Africa. Mexicans made up the largest share of Hispanics, followed by Puerto Ricans, and Cubans. (Americans now consume more salsa than ketchup each year.)

Rising immigration from Asia, Latin America, and Africa

The changing ethnic composition of American society has had an increasingly significant impact on social life. In 1980, Hispanic Americans lived mainly in five states: California, Arizona, New Mexico, Texas, and Florida. By 2014, *every* state had a rapidly growing Hispanic population. "These are big demographic changes," said Mark Mather, a population analyst. "There is going to be some culture shock, especially in communities that haven't had high numbers of immigrants or minorities in the past."

Immigration also had significant political effects. In 1980, there were six Hispanic Americans serving in the U.S. Congress. By 2010, there were more than five times as many. In 1992, Hispanics constituted only 2 percent of American voters; by 2014 they were 10 percent. Asian Americans increased

Over the quota, under the radar Increasing numbers of Chinese people were willing to risk their lives to gain entry to the United States. A freighter carrying undocumented immigrants ran aground near Rockaway Beach, New York, in June 1993, forcing its undocumented passengers to swim ashore.

their numbers at a faster rate than any other ethnic group, largely because of a surge in Chinese immigrants. Such new voters represented an increasing share of America's future, and politicians could no longer ignore them, as had often happened in the past.

Like Hispanics, African Americans and Asian Americans tend to vote for Democrats, in large part because minority groups benefit more from affirmative-action programs and government-funded social services frequently under attack from Republicans. As the population was becoming more racially and ethnically diverse, the Republican party nationwide was becoming a party dominated by white men. In 2012 the Pew Research Center reported that the Republican party was 87 percent white—virtually the same as it was thirty years before. That was not a problem in 1980, when 86 percent of the voters were white. By 2012, however, only 72 percent of voters were white. A Republican campaign consultant recognized that "we need to do better in minority communities." The rapidly changing ethnic and racial mix of the nation's population would become a major factor in the shifting social and political life of the twenty-first century.

The Clinton Presidency

Clinton's inexperience in international affairs and congressional maneuvering led to several missteps in his first year as president. Like George H. W. Bush before him, he reneged on several campaign promises. In a bruising battle with Congress, he was forced to abandon his proposed middle-class tax cut in order to keep another campaign promise, to reduce the federal

CORE **OBJECTIVE**
2. Evaluate the accomplishments and setbacks of Bill Clinton's presidency.

deficit. Then he dropped his promise to allow gays to serve in the armed forces after military commanders expressed strong opposition. Instead, he later announced an ambiguous new policy concerning gays in the military that came to be known as "don't ask, don't tell" (DADT), which allowed gays, lesbians, and bisexuals to serve in the military but only if they kept their sexual orientation secret. "I got the worst of both worlds," Clinton later confessed. "I lost the fight, and the gay community was highly critical of me for the compromise." In Clinton's first two weeks in office, his approval rating dropped 20 percent. Throughout his presidency, however, Clinton displayed a remarkable ability to manage crises and rebound from adversity.

> Early setbacks: "Don't ask, don't tell" (DADT) and abandonment of middle-class tax relief

The Economy

> Successes: NAFTA, higher taxes for the wealthy, and an economic stimulus package

As a candidate, Clinton had pledged to reduce the federal deficit without damaging the economy or hurting the nation's most vulnerable people. To this end, the new president proposed $241 billion in higher taxes for corporations and for the wealthiest individuals (the top rate rising from 33 to 39.6 percent) over four years and $255 billion in spending cuts over the same period. The hotly contested bill finally passed by 218 to 216 in the House and 51 to 50 in the Senate, with Vice President Al Gore providing the tie-breaking vote. For virtually the first time since 1945, Congress had passed a major bill without a single Republican vote, a troubling indication of the nation's growing partisan divide. Clinton's deficit-reduction effort worked as planned, however. It led to lower interest rates which, along with low energy prices, helped spur dramatic economic growth throughout the nineties.

Equally difficult was gaining congressional approval of the **North American Free Trade Agreement (NAFTA)**, which the Bush administration had already negotiated with Canada and Mexico. Clinton urged approval of NAFTA, which would make North America the largest free-trade zone in the world. Opponents of the bill favored tariffs to discourage the importation of cheaper foreign products, especially from Mexico. Yet Clinton prevailed with solid Republican support while losing a sizable minority of Democrats, mostly labor unionists and southerners, who feared that many textile mills would lose business (and millions of jobs) to "cheap labor" countries—as they did.

Health-Care Reform

> Failed health-care reform

North American Free Trade Agreement (NAFTA) (1994) Agreement eliminating trade barriers that was signed in 1994 by the United States, Canada, and Mexico, making North America the largest free-trade zone in the world.

Clinton's major public-policy initiative was an ambitious plan to overhaul the nation's health-care system. "If I don't get health care," he declared, "I'll wish I didn't run for president." Public support for government-administered health insurance spread as annual medical costs skyrocketed and some 37 million Americans, most of them poor or unemployed, went without any medical insurance at all. The Clinton administration argued that making medical insurance available to everyone, regardless of income, would reduce the costs of health care to the nation as a whole, but critics in Congress questioned the savings as well as the ability of the federal government to manage such a huge program efficiently. The plan called for all large businesses to pay for most of the medical insurance expenses of their employees, and required small businesses to form "health alliances" so that they, too, could provide subsidized health insurance to their workers. By the summer of 1994, Clinton's 1,364-page health-insurance plan, developed by a task force headed by the First Lady, Hillary Rodham Clinton, rather than congressional leaders, was doomed, in part because the president opposed any changes to his wife's plan and in part because the thousand-page report was impossibly complicated. Strenuously opposed by Republicans and health-care interest groups, especially the pharmaceutical and insurance industries, Clinton's prized health-care bill was voted down by Congress in August 1994.

Landslide Republican Victory

The health-care bill disaster influenced the 1994 midterm elections, when the Democrats, the world's oldest political party, suffered a humbling defeat. It was the first election since 1952 in which Republicans captured both houses of Congress at the same time. The Republicans also won 32 governorships, including the largest states of California, New York, and Texas, where George W. Bush, the son of the former president and a future president himself, won handily.

> Midterm Elections: Republicans win the majority in the House and the Senate

The Republican victory was led by a feisty Georgia conservative named Newton ("Newt") Leroy Gingrich. In early 1995, he became the first Republican Speaker of the House in forty-two years. Gingrich, a former history professor with a lust for controversy and an unruly ego, was a superb tactician who had helped mobilize religious and social conservatives associated with the Christian Coalition. The Christian Coalition, organized by television evangelist Pat Robertson in 1989 to replace Jerry Falwell's Moral Majority (which had disbanded that year), chose the Republican party as the best vehicle for promoting its pro–school prayer, anti-abortion, anti-feminist, and anti–gay rights positions. In addition to celebrating "traditional family values," it urged politicians to "radically downsize" government. Ralph Reed, a born-again Christian political activist who would head the Christian Coalition, declared that Christians needed "to take back this country." In many respects, the religious right did take control of the political and social landscape in the nineties.

> Republican opposition: Contract with America

In 1994, Gingrich and the Republican candidates for Congress rallied conservative voters by promising a **Contract with America**, a pledge to dismantle the "corrupt liberal welfare state" created by Democrats eager to serve the undeserving poor. The ten-point, anti-big-government "contract" featured less regulation of businesses, less environmental protection, term limits for members of Congress, reductions in social welfare programs, and a constitutional amendment requiring a balanced budget. As Texan Tom DeLay, a leading Republican in the House of Representatives, explained, "You've got to understand, we are ideologues. We have an agenda. We have a philosophy." Republicans were determined to change how America was governed.

Contract with America (1994) List of conservative promises in response to the supposed liberalism of the Clinton administration; drafted by Speaker of the House Newt Gingrich and other congressional Republicans as a campaign tactic for the 1994 midterm elections.

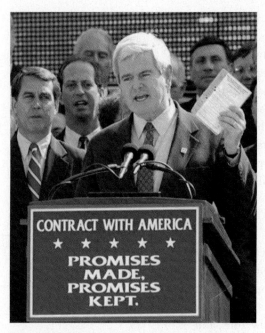

Newt Gingrich Joined by 160 of his fellow House Republicans, Gingrich promotes the Contract with America in April of 1995.

Yet the much-trumpeted Contract with America quickly fizzled. The conservatives pushed their agenda too hard and too fast, realizing only too late that their slim majority in Congress could not launch a Republican revolution. Even with their control of Congress, the Republicans were only able to pass four of the most minor elements of their "Contract." Gingrich's heavy-handed methods contributed to the disintegration of the Contract with America. Republican senator Bob Dole said Gingrich was "a one-man band who rarely took advice." He was too ambitious, too abrasive, too divisive. When Clinton refused to go along with Republican demands for a balanced-budget pledge, Gingrich twice shut down the federal government during the fall of 1995. The tactic backfired. By 1996, Gingrich had higher negative ratings in public surveys than the president.

The Supreme Court and Race

The conservative mood during the mid-nineties also revealed itself in Supreme Court rulings that undermined affirmative-action programs created by colleges in the sixties to give African American students special consideration in admissions and financial aid awards. Between 1970 and 1977, as a result of such programs, African American enrollment in colleges and universities doubled, even as white students and their parents complained about "reverse discrimination" against them.

In 1996, two major steps were taken against affirmative action in college admissions. In *Hopwood v. Texas*, a federal court ruled that race could not be used as a consideration for admission. Later that year, the state of California passed Proposition 209, an initiative that ruled out any preferential treatment based on race, sex, ethnicity, or national origin. Similar complaints were directed against affirmative-action programs that awarded government contracts to minority-owned businesses. In 1995, the Court in *Adarand Constructors v. Peña* declared that affirmative-action programs had to be "narrowly tailored" to serve a "compelling national interest." The implication of such vague language was clear: the Court had come to share the growing public suspicion of the value and legitimacy of race-based benefit programs.

Legislative Breakthrough

Welfare reform

After the surprising 1994 Republican takeover of Congress, Bill Clinton shrewdly resolved to save his presidency by reinforcing his claim that he was a "centrist," not a liberal. He co-opted much of the energy of the growing conservative movement by announcing that "the era of big government is over" and by reforming the federal system of welfare payments to the poor, created during the 1930s under the New Deal.

Late in the summer of 1996, the Republican Congress passed a comprehensive welfare-reform measure that Clinton signed after some revisions. The **Personal Responsibility and Work Opportunity Act of 1996 (PRWOA)** illustrated Clinton's efforts to move the Democratic party away from the old liberalism it had promoted since the 1930s. PRWOA abolished the Aid to Families with Dependent Children (AFDC) program, which provided poor families with almost $8,000 a year in support, and replaced it with the Temporary Assistance for Needy Families program, which limited the duration of welfare payments to two years in an effort to encourage unemployed people to get jobs. Liberal Democrats bitterly criticized Clinton's "welfare reform" deal with Republicans. Yet the new federal approach to supporting the poor was a statistical success. The number of welfare recipients and poverty rates both declined during the late nineties, leading the editors of the left-leaning *The New Republic* to report that the PRWOA had "worked much as its designers had hoped."

The 1996 Campaign

The Republican takeover of Congress in 1994 gave them hope that they could prevent Clinton's reelection. After clinching the Republican presidential nomination in 1996, Senate majority leader Bob Dole resigned his seat in order to devote his attention to defeating Bill Clinton. Clinton, however, maintained a large lead in the polls. With an improving economy and no major foreign-policy crises, cultural and personal issues again surged into prominence. Concern about Dole's age (seventy-three) and his gruff public personality, as well as tensions within the Republican party between economic conservatives and social conservatives over volatile issues such as abortion and gun control, hampered Dole's efforts to generate widespread support, especially among the growing number of independent voters who identified with neither party.

On November 5, 1996, Clinton won a second term as president, with an electoral vote victory of 379 to 159 and 49 percent of the popular vote. Dole received only 41 percent of the popular vote, and third-party candidate Ross Perot got 8 percent.

The "New Economy"

Bill Clinton's presidency benefited from a prolonged period of unprecedented prosperity. During his last three years in office (1998–2000), the federal government generated unheard-of budget *surpluses*. At the end of the twentieth century, what came to be called the **"new economy"** featured high-flying electronics, computer, software, telecommunications (cellular phones, cable TV, etc.), and e-commerce Internet firms called "dot-com" companies. These dynamic new enterprises helped the economy set records in every area: low inflation, low unemployment, and dizzying corporate profits and personal fortunes. The stock-market value of U.S. companies nearly tripled during the nineties. People began to claim that the new

Personal Responsibility and Work Opportunity Act of 1996 (PRWOA) Comprehensive welfare-reform measure aiming to decrease the size of the "welfare state" by limiting the amount of government unemployment aid to encourage its recipients to find jobs.

"new economy" Period of sustained economic prosperity during the nineties marked by federal budget surpluses, the explosion of dot-com industries, low inflation, and low unemployment.

economy defied the boom-and-bust cycles of the previous hundred years. Alan Greenspan, the Federal Reserve Board chairman, suggested "that we have moved 'beyond history'"—into an economy that seemed only to grow. He would be proven wrong.

Globalization

Another major feature of the new economy in the nineties was **globalization**. The end of the Cold War and the disintegration of the Soviet Union opened up many new opportunities for U.S. companies in international trade. In addition, new globe-spanning communication technologies and massive new container-carrying ships and cargo jets shortened time and distance, enabling United States–based multinational companies to conduct a growing business abroad as more and more nations lowered trade barriers.

Bill Clinton accelerated the process of globalization. "The global economy," he said, "is giving more of our own people, and billions around the world, the chance to work and live and raise their families with dignity." He especially welcomed the World Wide Web, which opened the Internet up not just to the elite community of scientists but to everyone, and, by doing so, greatly accelerated U.S. dominance of the international economy.

> "Outsourcing" jobs abroad and foreign manufacturers at home

By 2000, over a third of the production of U.S. multinational companies was occurring abroad, compared with only 9 percent in 1980. In 1970, there were 7,000 American multinational companies; by 2000, the number had soared to 63,000. Many U.S. multinational companies pursued controversial "outsourcing" strategies by which they moved their production "offshore" to nations such as Mexico and China to take advantage of lower labor costs and fewer workplace and environmental regulations. At the same time, many European and Asian companies, especially automobile manufacturers, built large plants in the United States to reduce the shipping expenses required to get their products to American markets. The U.S. economy had become internationalized to such a profound extent that global concerns exercised an ever-increasing influence on domestic and foreign policies.

Foreign Policy in the Nineties

Unlike his predecessor George H. W. Bush, Bill Clinton had little interest in global politics. "Foreign policy is not what I came here to do," he admitted. Untrained and inexperienced in international relations, he had hoped that the post–cold war era would be focused on creating opportunities around the world for U.S. business expansion. Yet as the international analyst Leslie Gelb cautioned the new president, "A foreign economic policy is not a foreign policy, and it is not a national security strategy."

Haiti

Events soon forced Clinton to intervene to help nations in crisis. In 1990, the politically unstable Caribbean island nation of Haiti, the hemisphere's poorest country, had installed its first democratically elected president, a

globalization An important and controversial transformation of the world economy led by the growing number of multinational companies and the Internet, whereby an international marketplace for goods and services was created.

popular Catholic priest named Jean-Bertrand Aristide. When Haitian army officers ousted Aristide the following year, he and thousands of his supporters took up exile in America, most of them settling in south Florida, which upset many Floridians.

In 1994 President Clinton announced his intention to restore Aristide to power, in part to return the exiled "boat people" to their homeland. With drawn-out negotiations leading nowhere, Clinton asked in July for a UN resolution authorizing military intervention in Haiti. At that juncture, former president Jimmy Carter volunteered to help negotiate a last-minute settlement, and he convinced the military leaders to relinquish their control of the government and leave the nation. Clinton sent 20,000 U.S. troops to ensure a peaceful transfer of power. Aristide returned to Haiti on October 15, and on March 31, 1995, the U.S. peacekeeping troops left as a UN force commanded by an American general took over. But neither Aristide nor his successors were able to generate prosperity or stability.

> Restoration of democratic rule in Haiti

The Middle East

President Clinton continued George H. W. Bush's policy of orchestrating patient negotiations between the Arabs and the Israelis. A new development was the inclusion of the Palestinian Liberation Organization (PLO) in the negotiations. In 1993, secret talks between Israeli and Palestinian representatives in Oslo, Norway, resulted in a draft agreement between Israel and the PLO. This agreement provided for the restoration of Palestinian self-rule in the occupied Gaza Strip and in Jericho, on the West Bank, in a "land for peace" exchange as provided in UN Security Council resolutions. A formal signing occurred at the White House on September 13, 1993. With President Clinton presiding, Israeli prime minister Yitzhak Rabin and PLO leader Yasir Arafat exchanged handshakes, and their foreign ministers signed the agreement.

> Arab-Israeli peace negotiations

The Middle East peace process suffered a terrible blow in early November 1995, however, when Prime Minister Rabin was assassinated by an Israeli zealot who resented Rabin's efforts to negotiate with the Palestinians. Some observers feared that the assassin had killed the peace process as well when seven months later conservative hard-liner Benjamin Netanyahu narrowly defeated the United States–backed Shimon Peres in the Israeli national elections. Yet in October 1998, Clinton brought Arafat, Netanyahu, and King Hussein of Jordan together at a conference in Maryland, where they reached an agreement. Under the Wye River Accords, Israel agreed to surrender land in return for security guarantees by the Palestinians.

The Balkans

Clinton also felt compelled to address violent turmoil in the Eastern European nations that had freed themselves from Soviet domination. In 1991, Yugoslavia had disintegrated into ethnic warfare as four of its six

> U.S.-NATO intervention in the Balkans

multiethnic republics declared their independence. Serb minorities, backed by the new Republic of Serbia, stirred up civil wars in neighboring Croatia and Bosnia. In Bosnia, the conflict involved systematic efforts to eliminate Muslims. Clinton decided that the situation was "intolerable" because the massacres of tens of thousands of people "tore at the very fabric" of human decency. He ordered food and medical supplies sent to besieged Bosnian Muslims and dispatched warplanes to stop the massacres.

In 1995, U.S. negotiators finally persuaded the foreign ministers of Croatia, Bosnia, and Yugoslavia (by then only a loose federation of the republics of Serbia and Montenegro) to agree to a comprehensive peace plan. Bosnia would remain a single nation but would be divided into two states: a Muslim-Croat federation controlling 51 percent of the territory and a Bosnian-Serb republic controlling the remaining 49 percent. Basic human rights would be restored and free elections would be held to appoint a parliament and joint president. To enforce the agreement, 60,000 NATO peace-keeping troops were dispatched to Bosnia.

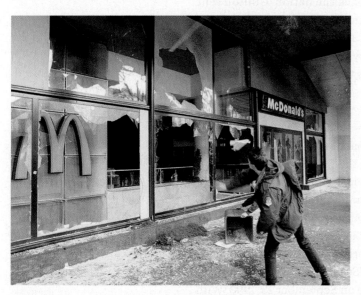

McRubble Pro-Milošević residents of Belgrade, Yugoslavia, destroy the storefront of a McDonald's fast-food restaurant in 1999 to protest NATO and the United States' airstrikes on their homeland.

In 1998, the Balkan tinderbox flared up again, this time in the Yugoslav province of Kosovo, which had long been considered sacred ground by Christian Serbs, although 90 percent of the 2 million Kosovars were in fact Albanian Muslims. In 1998, Yugoslav president Slobodan Milošević began a program of "**ethnic cleansing**," whereby Yugoslav forces burned Albanian villages, murdered men, raped women, and displaced hundreds of thousands of Muslim Kosovars.

On March 24, 1999, NATO, relying heavily upon U.S. military resources and leadership, launched air strikes against Yugoslavian military targets. "Ending this tragedy is a moral imperative," explained President Clinton. After seventy-two days of bombardment, Milošević sued for peace on NATO's terms, in part because his Russian allies had finally abandoned him. An agreement was reached on June 3, 1999. President Clinton pledged extensive U.S. aid in helping the Yugoslavs rebuild their war-torn economy.

ethnic cleansing Systematic removal of an ethnic group from a territory through violence or intimidation in order to create a homogeneous society; the term was popularized by the Yugoslav policy brutally targeting Albanian Muslims in Kosovo.

The Scandal Machine

For a time, Clinton's preoccupation with foreign crises helped deflect public attention from a growing number of investigations into his personal conduct. During his first term, the president was dogged by old charges revolving around investments that he and his wife Hillary had made in Whitewater, a planned resort development in Arkansas. The project turned out to be a fraud and a failure, and the Clintons were accused of conspiring with the developer. In 1994, Kenneth Starr, a former judge and a conservative Republican, was appointed as independent counsel to investigate the Whitewater case.

Starr did not uncover any evidence that the Clintons were directly involved in the Whitewater fraud, but in the course of another investigation he happened upon evidence of a White House sex scandal.

Between 1995 and 1997, Clinton had engaged in a sexual affair with a twenty-two-year-old White House intern, Monica Lewinsky. Even more disturbing, he had pressed her to lie about their relationship, even under oath. Clinton initially denied the charges, telling the nation in late January 1998 that "I did not have sexual relations with that woman, Miss Lewinsky." Yet the scandal would not disappear.

For the next thirteen months, the media circus surrounding the "Monicagate" or "Zippergate" affair captured public attention. In August, however, the bottom fell out of Clinton's denials when Lewinsky agreed to provide a federal grand jury with a detailed account of her relationship with the president.

Soon thereafter, Clinton became the first president in history to testify before a grand jury. On August 17, the self-pitying, defiant president admitted having had "inappropriate, intimate physical contact" with Lewinsky but insisted that he had done nothing illegal.

The Impeachment of President Clinton

On September 9, 1998, Starr, the special prosecutor, submitted to Congress thirty-six boxes of documents that included a lengthy, disturbingly graphic account of the Lewinsky episode, claiming that there was "substantial and creditable" evidence of presidential wrongdoing (committing perjury, obstructing justice, and abusing his presidential powers). The Starr Report led the Republican-dominated House of Representatives on October 8 to begin a wide-ranging impeachment inquiry of the president. Thirty-one Democrats joined the Republicans in supporting the investigation.

The Starr Report

On December 19, 1998, William Jefferson Clinton was impeached (charged with "high crimes and misdemeanors") by the House of Representatives. The House officially approved two articles of impeachment, charging Clinton with lying under oath to a federal grand jury and obstructing justice.

President Clinton impeached and acquitted

The Senate impeachment trial of President Clinton began on January 7, 1999. Five weeks later, on February 12, Clinton was acquitted, largely on a party-line vote. A majority of senators, both Democrats and a few Republicans (55–45), decided that Clinton's adultery and lies were not the "high crimes and misdemeanors" required to remove a president from office. The president was acquitted—much to the regret of many Republicans.

A New Century

The United States—and the world—greeted with great fanfare the new century, in a new millennium. Wild celebrations ushered in the year 2000, but the joyous mood did not last. Powerful new forces were emerging to destabilize the post–cold war world, the most dangerous of which were global networks of menacing high-tech terrorists eager to disrupt and destroy Western values and institutions. As Americans decided on a new president in the fall of 2000, none suspected that the United States would soon experience the first major foreign attack on American soil since the Japanese bombed Pearl Harbor in December 1941.

A Disputed Election

The presidential election of 2000 proved to be one of the closest and most controversial in history. The two major-party candidates for president, Vice President Albert Gore Jr., the Democrat, and Texas governor George W. Bush, the son of the former Republican president, offered contrasting views on the role of the federal government, tax cuts, environmental policies, and the best way to preserve Social Security and Medicare.

Gore, a Tennessee native and Harvard graduate whose father had been a prominent senator, favored an active federal government that would do much more to protect the environment.

Bush, on the other hand, campaigned on a theme of "compassionate conservatism" at home, promising to restore "honor and dignity" to the White House and proposing, as previous Republican presidents had done, to transfer power from the federal government to the states. A "born-again" Christian with degrees from Yale University and Harvard Business School, Bush also urged a more "humble" foreign policy, one that would end U.S. efforts to install democratic governments in undemocratic societies ("nation building").

The bitter tone of party politics (called *polarization*) continued to inspire candidates at the extremes to run as third-party candidates. Two independent candidates added zest to the 2000 presidential campaign: the colorful conservative commentator Patrick Buchanan, and the liberal consumer activist Ralph Nader, representing the Green party.

The November election created high drama. The television networks initially reported that Gore had narrowly won the state of Florida and its decisive twenty-five electoral votes. Later in the evening, however, the networks reversed themselves, saying that Florida was too close to call. In the chaotic early-morning hours, the networks declared that Bush had been elected president. The final tally in Florida showed Bush with a razor-thin lead, but state law required a recount. For the first time in 125 years, the results of a presidential election remained in doubt for weeks after the voting.

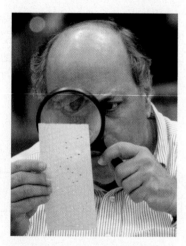

The recount In yet another recount on November 24, 2000, Judge Robert Rosenberg examines a ballot with a magnifying glass. That Florida's voting machines had limited accuracy introduced a great margin of doubt in a close election.

As a painstaking hand count of ballots proceeded in Florida, supporters of Bush and Gore sparred in the Florida courts and the U.S. Supreme Court; each side accused the other of trying to steal the election. The political drama lasted for five weeks. At last, on December 12, 2000, a bitterly divided Supreme Court handed down its decision in the case known as *Bush v. Gore*, with a bare 5–4 majority ruling that the recount in Florida was to be halted. Bush was declared the winner in Florida by only 537 votes. Although Gore had amassed a 540,000-vote lead nationwide, he lost in the Electoral College by two votes when he lost Florida. Although Al Gore "strongly disagreed" with the Supreme Court's decision, he asked voters to rally around President-elect Bush and move forward. "Partisan rancor," he urged, "must be put aside."

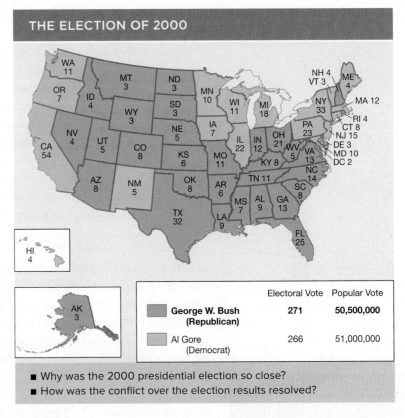

THE ELECTION OF 2000

	Electoral Vote	Popular Vote
George W. Bush (Republican)	271	50,500,000
Al Gore (Democrat)	266	51,000,000

■ Why was the 2000 presidential election so close?
■ How was the conflict over the election results resolved?

A Change of Direction

George W. Bush had promised during the campaign to cut taxes for the wealthy, increase military spending, oppose strict environmental regulations, and "privatize" Social Security by investing workers' retirement pension funds in the stock market.

First, however, the new president had to deal with a sputtering economy and a falling stock market. By March 2001, the economy was in recession for the first time in over a decade. Bush decided that cutting taxes was the best way to boost economic growth. On June 7, 2001, he signed the Economic Growth and Tax Relief Act, which cut $1.35 trillion in taxes—even more than the famous Reagan tax cuts. Instead of paying for themselves in renewed economic growth, however, the Bush tax cuts like those pushed by Ronald Reagan, led to a sharp drop in federal revenue, producing in turn a fast-growing budget deficit as the Clinton surpluses were quickly used up. Huge increases in the costs of Medicare and Medicaid, the federal health-care programs, resulting from the aging of the baby-boom generation, contributed to the soaring budget deficits, as did unexpected military expenditures resulting from an unexpected war.

As had happened so often with presidents during the twentieth century, President Bush soon found himself distracted by global issues and foreign crises. Islamic militants around the world bitterly resented what they viewed as the "imperial" globalization of U.S. culture and power. With increasing frequency, they used brutal terrorism, including suicide bombings, to gain notoriety, exact vengeance, and generate fear and insecurity, making the world vulnerable to chaos and violence. Throughout the nineties, the United States had fought a losing struggle against global terrorist groups, in part because terrorism thrives in impoverished nations with weak governments overwhelmed by rapid population growth, scarce resources, widespread poverty, and huge numbers of unemployed young men; there were lots of nations suffering from those symptoms around the world. The ineffectiveness of U.S. intelligence agencies in tracking the movements and intentions of militant extremists became tragically evident in the late summer of 2001.

9/11—A New Day of Infamy

9/11: Terrorist attacks

At 8:45 A.M. on sunny September 11, 2001, an airliner that had been hijacked by Islamist terrorists slammed into the north tower of the World Trade Center in New York City. Eighteen minutes later, a second hijacked jumbo jet crashed into the south tower. The twin towers, 110 stories tall and filled with offices employing 50,000 workers, burned fiercely, the inferno forcing hundreds of desperate people to jump to their deaths as thousands more, on floors below the points of impact, struggled to evacuate the skyscrapers. Quickly, though, the steel structures collapsed from the intense heat, destroying surrounding buildings and killing nearly 3,000 people, including more than 400 firefighters and police officers who had rushed into the burning towers. The southern end of Manhattan—"ground zero"—became a hellish scene of twisted steel, suffocating smoke, wailing sirens, and panicked people.

While the catastrophic drama in New York City was unfolding, a third hijacked plane crashed into the Pentagon in Washington, D.C. A fourth airliner, probably headed for the White House, missed its mark when passengers—who had heard reports of the earlier hijackings via their cell phones—assaulted the hijackers in order to prevent the plane from being used as a weapon. During the struggle in the cockpit, the plane went out of control and plummeted into the ground near Shanksville, Pennsylvania, killing all aboard.

Within hours of the hijackings, officials had identified the nineteen dead terrorists as members of al Qaeda (Arabic for "the Base"), a well-financed network of Islamic extremists led by a wealthy Saudi renegade, Osama bin Laden. Years before, bin Laden had declared *jihad* (holy war) on the United States, Israel, and the Saudi monarchy in his effort to create a single Islamist *caliphate* (global empire). To foster his clash of civilizations by organizing global Islamist terrorism, he used remote bases in Sudan and war-torn Afghanistan as training centers for *jihadist* fighters. Collaborating with bin Laden's terrorist network was Afghanistan's ruling Taliban, a coalition of ultraconservative Islamists who provided bin Laden with a safe haven.

September 11th Smoke pours out of the north tower of the World Trade Center as the south tower bursts into flames after being struck by a second hijacked airplane. Both would collapse within an hour.

The "War on Terror"

The 9/11 assault on the United States, like the Japanese attack on Pearl Harbor on December 7, 1941, changed the course of modern life. The falling World Trade Center towers symbolized the shocking collapse of one era and the start of a new one. Numbed by the terrible events, people were initially paralyzed by grief, fear, and anger. The U.S. economy, already in decline, went into free fall. President Bush was thrust into the role of commander in chief of a wounded nation eager for vengeance. The new president told the world that he was going to launch a global **war on terror** "to answer these attacks and rid the world of evil," as if he were launching a religious crusade, warning other nations that "either you are with us or you are with the terrorists." A wave of patriotic fervor rolled across the nation. "United We Stand"

War fever President George W. Bush addresses the Special Forces in July 2002 as part of an appeal to Congress to increase defense spending after the September 11th attacks.

became the motto for people determined to rebuild what had been lost in the rubble of the fallen towers and to defeat the heartless fanatics who had caused such destruction and suffering. People formed long lines to donate blood while others signed up for military service.

Bush demanded that Afghanistan's Taliban government surrender the al Qaeda terrorists or risk military attack. On October 7, 2001, after the Taliban refused to turn over bin Laden, the United States and its allies launched a military campaign—called Operation Enduring Freedom—to punish terrorists or "those harboring terrorists." American and British cruise missiles and bombers destroyed Afghan military installations and al Qaeda training camps, followed by an American-led invasion by ground troops from the United States and some of its NATO allies who, working with Afghan opponents of the Taliban, routed Taliban forces in just two months. On December 9, the Taliban regime collapsed. The war in Afghanistan then transitioned into a high-stakes manhunt for the elusive Osama bin Laden, who escaped into the mountains of Pakistan along with a large number of al Qaeda and Taliban fighters.

War on terror abroad: Operation Enduring Freedom in Afghanistan (2001)

The "War on Terror" at Home

While the military campaign continued in Afghanistan, officials in Washington worried that terrorists might attack the United States with biological, chemical, or even nuclear weapons. To address the threat and to help restore public confidence, President Bush created a new federal agency, the Office of Homeland Security. Another new federal agency, the Transportation Security Administration, assumed responsibility for screening airline passengers for weapons and bombs. At the same time, President Bush and a supportive Congress created the **USA Patriot Act**, which gave government

war on terror Global crusade to root out anti-Western and anti-American Islamist terrorist cells launched by President George W. Bush as a response to the 9/11 attacks.

USA Patriot Act (2001) Wide-reaching Congressional legislation, triggered by the War on Terror, which gave government agencies the right to eavesdrop on confidential conversations between prison inmates and their lawyers and permitted suspected terrorists to be tried in secret military courts.

War on terror at home: Homeland Security and the USA Patriot Act

agencies the right to eavesdrop on confidential conversations between prison inmates and their lawyers and permitted suspected terrorists to be tried in secret military courts. Civil liberties groups voiced grave concerns that the measures jeopardized constitutional rights and protections, but the superheated atmosphere after 9/11 led most people to support these extraordinary steps.

What the public did not know was that Vice President Cheney, Secretary of Defense Donald Rumsfeld, and others convinced the president to authorize the use of torture ("enhanced interrogation techniques") in the CIA and FBI's treatment of captured terrorist suspects, tactics that violated international law and compromised the human rights ideals that had always been America's greatest strength. When asked about such activities, the shadowy Cheney scoffed that America sometimes had to work "the dark side": "We've got to spend time in the shadows in the intelligence world...."

The Bush Doctrine

Bush Doctrine: Preemptive military action

In the fall of 2002, President Bush unveiled a dramatic new national security policy. The **Bush Doctrine** said that the growing menace posed by "shadowy networks" of terrorist groups and unstable rogue nations with "weapons of mass destruction" required that the United States at times must abandon diplomacy and use preemptive military action. "If we wait for threats to fully materialize," or wait for allies to join America, he explained, "we will have waited too long. In the world we have entered, the only path to safety is the path of action. And this nation will *act*."

The Second Iraq War

War on terror abroad: United States invades Iraq (2003)

During 2002 and 2003, Iraq emerged as the focus of the Bush administration's new policy of "preemptive" military action. Three of the president's most influential advisers, Vice President Cheney, Secretary of Defense Rumsfeld, and Deputy Defense Secretary Paul Wolfowitz convinced Bush that the dictatorial regime of Saddam Hussein and his loyal Sunni faction of Muslims, who lorded over the Shiite majority and the ethnic Kurds in the north, represented a "grave and gathering danger" because of its supposed possession of biological and chemical weapons of mass destruction.

On March 17, 2003, President Bush, eager to finish what his father had started, issued an ultimatum to Saddam Hussein: he and his sons must leave Iraq within forty-eight hours or face a United States–led invasion. Hussein refused. Two days later, on March 19, American and British forces attacked Iraq. Despite U.S. diplomatic attempts to assemble an international coalition similar to that of the First Gulf War a decade earlier, France and Germany refused to participate in what they viewed as unnecessary American aggression.

"Operation Iraqi Freedom" began with a massive bombing campaign intended to provoke "shock and awe," followed by a fast-moving invasion across the Iraqi desert from bases in Kuwait. Some 250,000 American

Bush Doctrine National security policy launched in 2002 by which the Bush administration claimed the right to launch preemptive military attacks against perceived enemies, particularly outlaw nations or terrorist organizations believed to possess weapons of mass destruction.

soldiers, sailors, and marines were joined by 50,000 British troops. On April 9, after three weeks of intense fighting amid sweltering heat and blinding sandstorms, U.S. forces captured Baghdad, the capital of Iraq. Saddam Hussein's regime and his inept, demoralized army collapsed a week later.

The six-week war came at a cost of fewer than 200 combat deaths among the 300,000 allied troops. Over 2,000 Iraqi soldiers were killed; civilian casualties numbered in the tens of thousands. President Bush donned a pilot's flight suit to stage a celebration on a U.S. aircraft carrier at which he announced victory in Iraq under a massive banner proclaiming "MISSION ACCOMPLISHED." But he declared victory much too soon; the initial military triumph carried with it the seeds of disappointment and disaster, for no weapons of mass destruction were to be found in Iraq. Bush later said that the absence of WMDs in Iraq left him with a "sickening feeling," for he knew that his primary justification for the war had evaporated.

Rebuilding Iraq

It proved far easier to win the brief war than to rebuild Iraq in America's image. Unprepared U.S. officials faced the daunting task of restoring order and installing a democratic government in an Iraq fractured by ancient religious feuds and ethnic tensions—made worse by the breakdown in law and order caused by the allied invasion. Looting and violence immediately engulfed the war-torn country, large parts of which fell under the control of local warlords and criminal gangs. Within weeks, vengeful Islamic radicals from around the world streamed into the crippled nation to wage a merciless campaign of terror, sabotage, and suicide bombings against the U.S. forces. Bush's macho reaction to the insurgency in Iraq—"Bring 'em on!"—revealed how uninformed he was about the fast-deteriorating situation. The leader of the new Iraqi government, Prime Minister Nouri al-Maliki, quickly imposed his own authoritarian, Shiite-dominated regime which discriminated against the Sunnis, the Kurds, and other ethnic and religious minorities.

> Growing insurgency in Iraq

Ignoring the advice of Defense Department analysts and some of his top generals, Secretary Rumsfeld greatly underestimated the difficulty and expense of occupying, pacifying, and reconstructing postwar Iraq. By the fall of 2003, President Bush admitted that substantial numbers of American troops (around 150,000) would have to remain in Iraq much longer than anticipated. He also said that rebuilding the splintered nation amid its religious and ethnic civil wars would take years and cost almost a *trillion* dollars. The investigative reporter James Fallows concluded that the U.S. "occupation in Iraq is a debacle not because the government did no planning but because a vast amount of expert planning was willfully ignored by the people in charge."

Victory on the battlefields of Iraq did not bring victory in the "war on terrorism." Militant Islamist groups seething with hatred towards the United States remained a constant global threat. Among Americans, the

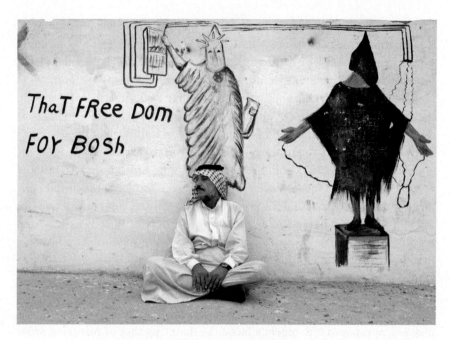

Freedom for whom? The American torture of Iraqi prisoners in Abu Ghraib only exacerbated the anger and humiliation that Iraqis experienced since the First Gulf War. In response to America's incessant promises of peace and autonomy, a Baghdad mural fires back: "That Freedom For B[u]sh."

thrill of a quick battlefield victory turned to dismay as the number of casualties and the expense of the military occupation in Iraq soared. Americans grew more alienated when journalists revealed graphic pictures of U.S. soldiers abusing and torturing Arab detainees in the infamous Abu Ghraib prison near Baghdad. "When you lose the moral high ground," an army general sadly observed, "you lose it all."

In the face of mounting criticism, President Bush urged Americans to "stay the course," insisting that a democratic Iraq would bring stability to the volatile Middle East and thereby blunt the momentum of Islamic terrorism. Although Saddam Hussein was captured in December 2003 and later hanged by the new Iraqi authorities, Iraq now seemed less secure than ever to anxious Americans worried about the rising cost of an unending occupation. By the beginning of 2004, a thousand Americans had died in the conflict and more than 10,000 had been wounded. And the ethnic and religious tensions embroiling Iraq only worsened as violent Sunni *jihadists* allied with al Qaeda to undermine the new Iraqi government and assault U.S. forces.

The Election of 2004

Growing public concern about Iraq complicated George W. Bush's campaign for a second presidential term in 2004. The Democratic nominee, Senator John Kerry of Massachusetts, condemned the Bush administration for misleading the nation about weapons of mass destruction in Iraq and for its slipshod handling of the reconstruction of postwar Iraq. Kerry also highlighted the record budget deficits occurring under the Republican administration. Bush countered that the tortuous efforts to create a democratic government in Iraq would enhance America's long-term security.

On election day, November 2, 2004, the exit polls suggested a Kerry victory, but in the end the election hinged on the crucial swing state of Ohio. No Republican had ever lost Ohio and still won the presidency. Despite early returns from Ohio indicating a Kerry victory there, late returns appeared to tip the balance slightly toward Bush, even as rumors of electoral "irregularities" began to circulate. Nevertheless, Kerry conceded the election. "The outcome," he stressed, "should be decided by voters, not a protracted legal battle."

By narrowly winning Ohio, Bush captured 286 electoral votes to Kerry's 251. Yet in some respects the close election was not so close. Bush received 3.5 million more votes nationwide than Kerry, and Republicans increased their majority control of both houses of Congress.

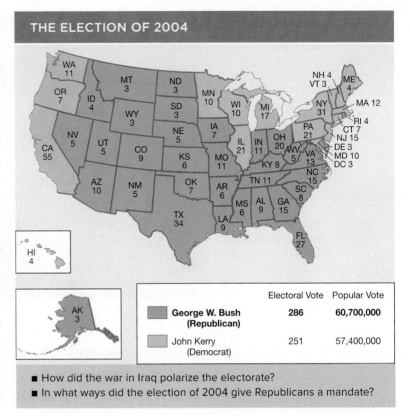

THE ELECTION OF 2004

	Electoral Vote	Popular Vote
George W. Bush (Republican)	286	60,700,000
John Kerry (Democrat)	251	57,400,000

■ How did the war in Iraq polarize the electorate?

■ In what ways did the election of 2004 give Republicans a mandate?

A Resurgent Democratic Party

George Bush stumbled in his second term as he was beset by thorny political problems, a sluggish economy, and continuing turmoil and violence in Iraq. In 2005, he pushed through Congress an energy bill and a Central American Free Trade Act. But his effort to privatize Social Security retirement accounts, enabling individuals to invest their accumulated pension dollars themselves, went nowhere, and soaring budget deficits made many fiscal conservatives feel betrayed by the supposedly "conservative" Bush. The editors of the *Economist*, an influential conservative newsmagazine, declared that Bush had become "the least popular re-elected president since Richard Nixon."

Hurricane Katrina

In 2005, President Bush's eroding public support suffered another blow, this time when a natural disaster turned into a political crisis. In late August, a killer hurricane named Katrina slammed into the Gulf coast, devastating large areas of Alabama, Mississippi, and Louisiana. Katrina's awful wake left over a thousand people dead in the three states and millions homeless and hopeless, especially in New Orleans. Local political officials and the Federal Emergency Management Agency (FEMA) were caught

> CORE **OBJECTIVE**
>
> **4.** Assess the issues and developments during Bush's second term that helped lead to Barack Obama's historic victory in the 2008 presidential election.

Bush's stalled presidency

Hurricane Katrina and Democrats win control of the House

The aftermath of Katrina Two men paddle through high water with wooden planks in a devastated New Orleans.

unprepared as the catastrophe unfolded. Disaster plans were incomplete; confusion and incompetence abounded. In the face of blistering criticism, President Bush accepted responsibility for the balky federal response to the disaster and accepted the resignation of the FEMA director. Rebuilding the Gulf coast would take a long time and a lot of money.

In the November 2006 congressional elections, the Democrats capitalized on widespread public disapproval of the Bush administration to win control of the House of Representatives, the Senate, and a majority of governorships and state legislatures. Former Texas Republican congressman Dick Armey said that "the Republican Revolution of 1994 officially ended" with the 2006 election. "It was a rout." The transformational election also included a significant milestone: Californian Nancy Pelosi, the leader of the Democrats in the House of Representatives, became the highest-ranking woman in the history of the U.S. Congress upon her election as House Speaker in January 2007.

Nancy Pelosi The Speaker of the House at a news conference on Capitol Hill.

The "Surge" in Iraq

George W. Bush bore the brunt of public indignation over the bungled federal response to the Katrina disaster and the continuing cost and casualties of the war in Iraq. Senator Chuck Hagel, a Nebraska Republican, declared in 2005 that "we're losing in Iraq." Throughout the fall of 2006, the violence in Iraq spiraled upward. Bush eventually responded to declining public and political support for the Iraq War by creating the Iraq Study Group, a bipartisan task force whose final report recommended that the United States withdraw its combat forces from a "grave and deteriorating Iraq" by the spring of 2008.

President Bush disagreed with the Study Group and others, including key military leaders, who urged a phased withdrawal. On January 10, 2007, he announced that he was sending a "surge" of 20,000 (eventually 30,000) additional troops to Iraq, bringing the total to almost 170,000. From a military perspective, the "surge" strategy succeeded. By the fall of 2008, the convulsive violence in Iraq had declined dramatically, and the United States–supported Iraqi government had grown in stature and confidence. Still, by 2008, over 60 percent of Americans said that the war in Iraq had been a mistake.

The "Surge" in Iraq

Economic Shock

After the intense but brief 2001 recession, the boom/bust capitalist economy had begun another period of prolonged expansion. Between 1997 and 2006, home prices in the United States, especially in the fast-growing Sunbelt states, rose 85 percent, leading to a frenzy of irresponsible mortgage lending for the purchase of homes—and a debt-financed consumer spending spree. Tens of millions of people bought houses they could not afford, refinanced their mortgages, or tapped home-equity loans to make discretionary purchases. The irrational confidence in soaring housing prices also led government regulatory agencies and mortgage lenders to ease credit restrictions so that unqualified people could buy homes.

Financial collapses typically follow real estate bubbles, rising indebtedness, and prolonged budget deficits. The housing bubble burst in 2007, when home values and housing sales began a sharp decline. During 2008, the loss of trillions of dollars in home values set off a seismic shock across the economy. Record numbers of borrowers defaulted on their mortgage payments. Foreclosures and bankruptcies soared. Banks lost billions, first on the shaky mortgages, then on most other categories of debt: credit cards, car loans, student loans, and an array of commercial mortgage-backed securities.

The sudden contraction of corporate spending and consumer purchases pushed the economy into a deepening recession in 2008. The scale and suddenness of the slump caught economic experts and business leaders by surprise. Some of the nation's most prestigious banks, investment firms, and insurance companies went belly-up. The price of

Rio Vista, California With an $816,000 deficit, this northern California city filed for bankruptcy and pulled the plug on its massive, 750-home housing development in November 2008. Here, model homes stand eerily in a blank landscape of sidewalks and cul-de-sacs.

food and gasoline spiked. Unemployment soared. What had begun as a sharp decline in home prices became a panicky global economic meltdown. No investment seemed safe.

The economic crisis demanded decisive action to stem the panic and restore confidence. On October 3, 2008, just before the presidential election, President Bush signed into law a bank bailout fund called the Troubled Asset Relief Program (TARP), which called for the Treasury Department to spend $700 billion to keep big banks and other large financial institutions from collapsing. Yet the passage of the bill did little to restore confidence. In early October, stock markets around the world began to crash with the onset of what came to be called the **Great Recession**, which technically lasted from December 2007 to January 2009, and forced almost 9 million people out of work. But its effects would last long thereafter. The economic recovery that began in June 2009 would be the weakest since the end of the Second World War. "The Age of Prosperity is over," announced the prominent Republican economist Arthur Laffer in 2008.

Great Recession (2007–2009)
Massive, prolonged economic downturn sparked by the collapse of the housing market and the financial institutions holding unpaid mortgages; resulted in 9 million Americans losing their jobs.

A Historic New Presidency

George Bush's unpopularity excited Democrats about regaining the White House in the 2008 election. The early front-runner for the Democratic nomination was New York senator Hillary Rodham Clinton, the spouse of ex-president Bill Clinton. Like her husband, she displayed an impressive command of policy issues and mobilized a well-funded campaign team. And, as the first woman with a serious chance of gaining the presidency, she had widespread support among voters eager for female leadership. In the end, however, an overconfident Clinton was upset in the Democratic primaries and caucuses by little-known first-term senator Barack Obama of Illinois. Young, handsome, and intelligent, Obama was an inspiring speaker who attracted huge crowds by promising a "politics of hope." He mounted an innovative Internet-based campaign directed at grassroots voters, donors, and volunteers. In early June 2008, he gained enough delegates to secure the Democratic nomination alongside Senator Joseph Biden of Delaware as his vice presidential running mate.

Obama was the first African American presidential nominee of either party, the gifted biracial son of a white mother from Kansas and a black Kenyan father who left the household and returned to Africa when Barack was a toddler. Obama made the most of his abilities, eventually graduating from Columbia University in New York before earning a law degree from Harvard. The forty-seven-year-old senator presented himself to voters as a deal-maker who could inspire and unite a diverse people and forge bipartisan collaborations. Obama radiated poise,

Barack Obama The president-elect and his family wave to the crowd of supporters in Chicago's Grant Park.

confidence, and energy. By contrast, his Republican opponent, seventy-two-year-old Arizona senator John McCain, was the oldest presidential candidate in history. As a twenty-five-year veteran of Congress, a leading Republican senator, and a candidate for the Republican presidential nomination in 2000, he had developed a reputation as a bipartisan "maverick" willing to work with Democrats to achieve key legislative goals.

On November 4, 2008, Barack Obama made history by becoming the nation's first person of color to be elected president. He won the popular vote by 53 percent to 46 percent. His margin in the Electoral College was even more impressive: 365 to 173. Obama also helped the Democrats win solid majorities in both houses of Congress. Within days of his victory, Obama adopted a bipartisan approach in selecting his new cabinet members.

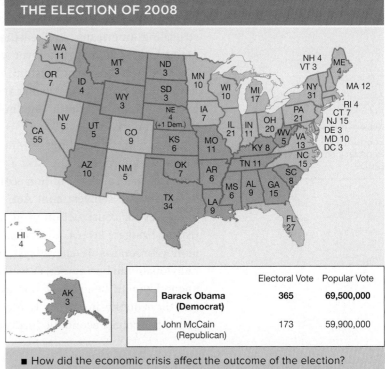

THE ELECTION OF 2008

	Electoral Vote	Popular Vote
Barack Obama (Democrat)	365	69,500,000
John McCain (Republican)	173	59,900,000

■ How did the economic crisis affect the outcome of the election?
■ What are the similarities and differences between the map of the 2004 election and the map of the 2008 election?

He appointed Hillary Clinton secretary of state, retained Republican Robert Gates as secretary of defense, selected retired general James Jones, who had campaigned for McCain, as his national security adviser, and appointed Eric Holder as the nation's first African American attorney general. But picking a bipartisan cabinet proved easier than forging a bipartisan presidency.

New Priorities at Home and Abroad

CORE **OBJECTIVE**
5. Identify President Obama's priorities at home and abroad, and assess his efforts to pursue them.

The new Obama administration inherited two unpopular wars, in Iraq and Afghanistan, and the worst economic stumble in eighty years. His most pressing challenge was to keep the Great Recession from becoming a prolonged depression. Unemployment in early 2009 had passed 8 percent and was still rising. The financial sector remained paralyzed. And public confidence plummeted.

Obama's First Term

To enable banks to start lending again, the new administration continued the implementation of the TARP program created by the outgoing Bush administration, providing massive government bailouts to save the largest

Wall Street bank bailouts

banks and financial institutions. The big bank bailouts were highly controversial, attacked by both the left and the right as deeply unfair to most struggling Americans. As Treasury secretary Timothy Geithner later explained, "We had to do whatever we could to help people feel their money was safe in the [banking] system, even if it made us unpopular." Had they not saved the big banks, Obama and Geithner argued, the whole economy would have crashed. Geithner admitted that we saved "the economy, but we lost the country doing it."

Preserving the banking system did not create new jobs, however. To do so, in mid-February 2009, after a prolonged debate, Congress passed, and Obama signed, an $832-billion economic stimulus bill called the American Recovery and Reinvestment Act. The bill included cash distributions to the states for construction projects to renew the nation's infrastructure (roads, bridges, levees, government buildings, and the electricity grid), money for renewable-energy systems, and $212 billion in tax reductions for individuals and businesses, as well as additional funds for food stamps and unemployment benefits. It was the largest government infusion of cash into the economy in history. In the end, however, it was not large enough to generate a robust economic recovery.

Health-Care Reform

The economic crisis merited Obama's full attention, but he chose as his top legislative priority a controversial federal health-insurance program that had been one of his key campaign pledges. From his first day in office, Obama stressed his intention to reform a health-care system so broken that it was "bankrupting families, bankrupting businesses, and bankrupting our government at the state and federal level." The United States, home to the world's costliest health system, was spending 18 percent of its total economic resources on health care. Great Britain, Norway, and Sweden each spent half as much, but their citizens lived longer. America was the only rich nation without a national health-care program. Since 1970, the proportion of uninsured people had been steadily rising along with health care costs. In 2010 roughly 50 million Americans, 16 percent of the population, had no health insurance, most of them being either poor or young, or people of color.

The president's goal in creating the Patient Protection and **Affordable Care Act (ACA)**, which many people refer to as "Obamacare," was to make health insurance more affordable and make health care accessible for everyone, regardless of income. The $940-billion health-care law, proposed in 2009 and debated bitterly for a year, centered on the so-called *individual mandate*, which required uninsured adults to purchase an approved *private* insurance policy made available through state-run exchanges (websites where people could shop for insurance) or pay a tax penalty. Lower-income Americans would be provided with federal subsidies to help pay for their coverage. Insurance companies could no longer deny coverage to people

Economic Stimulus: American Recovery and Reinvestment Act (2009)

A national health care program: The Affordable Care Act (2010)

Affordable Care Act (ACA) (2010) Vast health-care reform initiative championed by President Obama and widely criticized by Republicans that aimed to make health insurance more affordable and make health care accessible to everyone, regardless of income or prior medical conditions.

with pre-existing illnesses. Employers who did not offer health insurance would also have to pay higher taxes, and drug companies as well as manufacturers of medical devices would have to pay annual government fees. Everyone, but especially the wealthy, would pay higher Medicare payroll taxes to help fund the changes.

All of the many efforts at providing national health insurance over the previous sixty years had been controversial. The ACA was no exception. The individual mandate was designed to ensure that all Americans had health insurance so as to reduce the skyrocketing costs of hospitals providing "charity care" for the uninsured poor. The ACA did not change the American tradition of using employment-based health insurance provided by private companies as the basic vehicle for financing medical care. But the idea of forcing people to buy such insurance flew in the face of the principle of individual freedom and personal responsibility. Critics questioned not only the individual mandate but also the administration's projections that the new program would reduce federal expenditures over the long haul.

Republicans quickly mobilized to defeat the ACA. "If we're able to stop Obama on this it will be his Waterloo. It will break him," predicted South Carolina senator Jim DeMint. Despite heated Republican opposition, however, the ACA was passed with narrow party-line majorities in both houses of Congress and signed into law by President Obama on March 23, 2010. Its complex provisions, implemented over a four-year transition period, would bring health insurance to 32 million people, half of whom would be covered by expanded Medicaid, and the other half covered by the individual mandate. In its scope and goals, the ACA was a landmark law in the history of health and social welfare—as well as the expansion of the federal government.

Obamacare and the Courts

No sooner had Obama pushed his controversial health-care plan through Congress than Republican opponents began challenging its constitutionality. On June 28, 2012, the Supreme Court issued its much-awaited decision in the case of *National Federation of Independent Business v. Sebelius*. The landmark 5–4 ruling surprised Court observers by declaring most of the new federal law to be constitutional. Even more surprising was that the deciding vote was cast by the chief justice, John G. Roberts, a philosophical conservative who had never before voted with the four "liberal" justices on the Court. Roberts upheld the ACA's individual mandate that required people to buy private health insurance or else pay a tax, arguing that it was within the Congress's power to impose taxes as outlined in Article 1 of the Constitution. Many conservatives, including the four dissenting justices, felt betrayed by Roberts's unexpected decision. The unexpected verdict led the *New York Times* to predict that the ruling "may secure Obama's place in history."

Regulating Wall Street

Wall Street Reform and Consumer Protection Act (2010) ▷

The near collapse of the nation's financial system beginning in 2008 prompted calls for overhauling the financial regulatory system. On July 21, 2010, Obama signed the Wall Street Reform and Consumer Protection Act, also called the Dodd-Frank bill after its two congressional sponsors. It was the most comprehensive reform of the financial system since the New Deal in the thirties. The 2,319-page law required government agencies to exercise greater oversight over complex new financial transactions and protected consumers from unfair practices in loans and credit cards by establishing a new consumer financial-protection agency. President Obama predicted that the bill, despite its complexity, would "lift our economy," give "certainty to everybody" about the technical rules governing banking, and end "tax-funded bailouts—period." By 2010, however, the economy had not been "lifted" and many bankers remained confused about the new rules regulating the financial industry.

The Obama Doctrine and Iraq

The Obama Doctrine ▷

President Obama had more success in dealing with foreign affairs than in reviving the American economy. His foremost concern was the overextension of U.S. power abroad. What journalists came to call the Obama Doctrine was very much like the Nixon Doctrine (1970), stressing that the United States could not afford to continue to be the world's principal policeman. Yet it would not be easy to lower the nation's posture abroad, for the fate of America's economy and security was entangled more than ever with the fate of an unstable and often violent world.

The Obama Doctrine grew out of the fact that the president was trying to end two complex and expensive wars, one in Iraq and the other in Afghanistan. On February 27, 2009, Obama announced that all 142,000 U.S. troops would be withdrawn from Iraq by the end of 2011, as had been agreed to by the Iraqi government and the Bush administration in 2008. True to his word, the last U.S. combat troops left Iraq in December 2011. Their exit marked the end of a bitterly divisive war that had raged for nearly nine years.

The U.S. intervention in Iraq had cost over 4,500 American lives, 30,000 wounded (many grievously so), more than 110,000 Iraqi lives, and $2 trillion. Perhaps the greatest embarrassment was that the government that the U.S. left behind in Iraq was inept and not even friendly to American interests.

A "Surge" in Afghanistan

End of U.S. military presence in Iraq and Afghanistan ▷

At the same time that President Obama was reducing U.S. military involvement in Iraq, he dispatched 21,000 additional troops to Afghanistan in what was called a "surge." While doing so, however, he narrowed the focus of the U.S. mission to suppressing terrorists rather than "nation building"—the idea of transforming strife-torn Afghanistan into a stable capitalist democracy. The military surge worked as hoped. By the summer of 2011, President Obama announced that the "tide of war was receding" and that the United States had largely achieved its goals in Afghanistan, setting in motion a substantial withdrawal of forces beginning in 2011 and lasting until 2014. In April 2014, despite threats by the Taliban to kill voters, Afghans turned out in huge numbers to choose a new president to lead them into the post-American era. But it was an expensive outcome for America's longest war. In the thirteen years since the United States invaded Afghanistan in 2001, America had spent over a trillion dollars there and had lost 2,300 servicemen.

The Death of Osama Bin Laden

The crowning achievement of Obama's anti-terrorism efforts was the discovery, at long last, of Osama bin Laden's hideout. Ever since the attacks of 9/11, bin Laden had eluded an intensive manhunt after crossing the Afghan border into Pakistan. His luck ran out in August 2011, however, when U.S. intelligence analysts discovered his sanctuary in a walled residential compound outside of Abbottabad, Pakistan. On May 1, 2011, without alerting the Pakistani government, President Obama authorized a daring night raid by a U.S. Navy SEAL team of two dozen specially trained commandos transported by helicopters from Afghanistan. After a brief firefight, the Navy SEAL team killed bin Laden and then dropped his body into the sea. Bin Laden's death was a watershed moment, but it did not spell the end of Islamist terrorism.

Death of Osama bin Laden (2011)

The "Arab Awakening"

In late 2010 and early 2011, spontaneous democratic uprisings erupted throughout much of the Arab world, as long-oppressed peoples rose up against authoritarian regimes. One by one, corrupt Arab tyrants were forced out of power by a new generation of young activists inspired by democratic ideals and connected by social media on the Internet. What was soon dubbed "the Arab Awakening" sent waves of unrest rippling across Tunisia, Algeria, Bahrain, Jordan, Morocco, Egypt, Oman, Yemen, Libya, Saudi Arabia, and Syria during what came to be called the Arab Spring of 2011. The remarkable uprisings heralded a new era in the history of the Middle East struggling to be born.

For all the excitement about "people power" emerging in the Middle East, however, the work of building new democratic governments proved much harder than expected. Grassroots democratic movements in most Arab nations stumbled and stalled by 2014, lurching

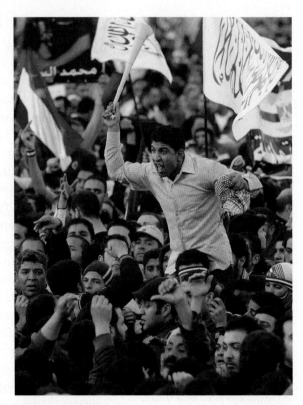

Arab Awakening Thousands of protesters converge in Cairo's Tahrir Square to call for an end to Moubarak's rule.

from crisis to crisis usually triggered by their unwillingness to allow for freedom of religion.

Libya Ousts Gaddafi

The pro-democracy turmoil in North Africa engulfed oil-rich Libya, long governed by the mercurial dictator Colonel Muammar Gaddafi, the Arab world's most violent despot. Anti-government demonstrations began on February 15, 2011, prompting Gaddafi to order Libyan soldiers and mercenaries (paid foreign soldiers) to suppress the rebellious "rats." By the end of February, what began as a peaceful pro-democratic uprising had turned into a full-scale civil war that provided the first real test of the Obama Doctrine. True to his word, the president refused to act alone in helping the Libyan rebels. Instead, he encouraged European allies to take the lead. On March 19, France and Great Britain, with American support, launched a bombing campaign against Gaddafi's military strongholds. In late August, rebel forces captured the capital of Tripoli, scattering Gaddafi's government and marking the end of his forty-two-year dictatorship. On October 20, rebel fighters captured and killed Gaddafi. But the rebel militias that removed Gaddafi soon started shooting at each other, and stability remained elusive by the end of 2014.

Polarized Politics

At the same time that Arabs were rebelling against entrenched political elites, grassroots rebellions were occurring in the United States as well. Barack Obama had campaigned in 2008 on the promise of bringing dramatic change to the federal government in an evenhanded way that would reduce the partisan warfare between the two national parties.

By the end of Obama's first year in office, however, a Gallup poll found that he had become the most polarizing president in modern history. It was not solely his fault. His Republican opponents had no interest in negotiating compromises with him. American political culture in the twenty-first century suffered from a crisis of mutual resentment, so polarized that it resembled two separate nations. Each had its own political party, its own cable-news station and rabidly partisan commentators, its own newspapers, its own think tanks, and its own billionaire activists.

And both "nations"—blue and red, liberal and conservative—had their own factions committed to a politics of rage. No sooner was Obama sworn in than anti-government conservatives mobilized against him and the "tax-and-spend" liberalism he represented in their eyes. In January 2009, a New York stock trader named Graham Makohoniuk sent an e-mail message urging people to send tea bags to their congressional representatives to symbolize the famous Boston Tea Party of 1773 when American colonists protested against British tax policies.

Within a year or so, the tax revolt had become a national **Tea Party** movement, with groups spread across the fifty states. The Tea Party is not

---

Polarized politics: Conservative resurgence (the Tea Party)

Tea Party Right-wing populist movement, largely made up of middle-class, white male conservatives, that emerged as a response to the expansion of the federal government under the Obama administration.

so much a cohesive political organization as it is a mood, an attitude, and an ideology, a diverse collection of self-described "disaffected," "angry," and "very conservative" activists, mostly white, male, married middle-class Republicans over forty-five, boiling mad at the massive government bailouts of huge banks and corporations that had come in the wake of the 2008 economic meltdown. To the grassroots anti-tax rebels, the federal bailouts ordered by Bush and Obama were a form of "crony capitalism" whereby elected officials of both parties (the "elite") rewarded the big companies that had funded their campaigns. Tea Party members demanded a radically smaller federal government (although most of them supported Social Security and Medicare, the two most expensive federal social programs). Democrats, including President Obama, initially dismissed the Tea Party as a fringe group of extremists, but the 2010 election results proved them wrong.

Democratic House and Senate candidates (as well as moderate Republicans), including many long-serving leaders, were defeated in droves when conservative Republicans, many of them aligned with the Tea Party, gained sixty-three seats to recapture control of the House of Representatives and won a near majority in the Senate as well. It was the most lopsided midterm election since 1938. "We've come to take our government back," declared one Republican congressional winner. Thereafter, Obama and the Republican-dominated House of Representatives engaged in a harsh sparring match. With each side refusing to negotiate or compromise, the bickering between both parties prevented meaningful action on the languishing economy, chronic joblessness, and the runaway federal budget deficit.

The emergence of the Tea Party was mirrored on the far left wing of the political spectrum by the Occupy Wall Street (OWS) movement, mobilized in the fall of 2011 when a call went out over the Internet to "Occupy Wall Street. Bring tent." Dozens, then hundreds, then thousands of people, mostly young adults, many of them unemployed, converged on Zuccotti Park in lower Manhattan. They formed tent villages and gathered in festive groups to "occupy" Wall Street, protesting the "tyrannical" power of Wall Street banks and investment companies. The protesters described themselves as the voice of the 99 percent of Americans who were being victimized by the 1 percent

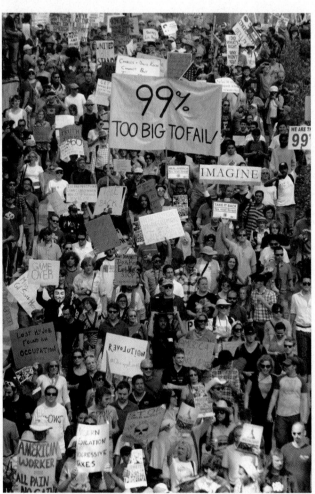

Occupy Wall Street The Manhattan-born grassroots movement grew rapidly from rallies to massive marches in financial districts nationwide, like this demonstration in downtown Los Angeles.

of the wealthiest and most politically connected Americans. Unlike the Tea Party, however, OWS did not have staying power. Within a year, its energies and visibility had waned, in part because of mass arrests, in part because it was an intentionally "leaderless" movement more interested in saying what it was *against* than explaining what it was *for*.

American politics has always been chaotic and combative; its raucous energy is one of the strengths of a democracy. But during Obama's presidency, the emergence of the Tea Party and Occupy Wall Street symbolized how political combat had become so fierce that *compromise* and *moderation* had become dirty words. Rarely before had Democrats and Republicans viewed each other with greater venom and less respect.

Bold Decisions

For all of the angry political sniping and Congressional stalemate, however, attitudes toward "hot-button" cultural values were slowly changing. In December 2010, Congress took a significant step toward equal treatment for gays when it repealed the "don't ask, don't tell" (DADT) military policy that, since 1993, had resulted in some 9,500 men and women being discharged from the armed forces. A year after the repeal was enacted, a report by army officers concluded that the repeal of DADT "has had no overall negative impact on military readiness or its component dimensions, including cohesion, recruitment, retention, assaults, harassment, or morale."

In May 2012 President Obama jumped headfirst into the nation's simmering cultural wars by announcing his support for the right of gay and lesbian couples to marry. That his statement came a day after the state of North Carolina legislature voted to ban all rights for gay couples illustrated how incendiary the issue was around the country. While asserting that it was the "right" thing to do, Obama also knew that endorsing **same-sex marriage** had powerful political implications. The gay community would play an energetic role in the 2012 presidential election, and the youth vote—the under-30 electorate who among all the voting-age groups most supported gay marriage—would be equally crucial to Obama's reelection chances. No sooner had Obama made his pathbreaking announcement than polls showed that American voters for the first time split half and half on the charged issue, with Democrats and independent voters providing the bulk of support for Obama's pro-same-sex-marriage position.

The following month, in June 2012, Obama again made waves by issuing an executive order (soon labeled the DREAM Act) that allowed 1.5 million undocumented immigrants who had been brought to the United States as children to remain in the country as citizens. His unanticipated decision thrilled Hispanic supporters who had lost heart over his failure to convince Congress to support a more comprehensive reform of immigration laws. Republicans in Congress steadfastly opposed giving the estimated 12 million undocumented immigrants, 80 percent of whom were Latinos, a "pathway

Failure of bipartisanship

same-sex marriage Legal right for gay and lesbian couples to marry; the most divisive issue in the culture wars of the early 2010s as increasing numbers of court rulings affirmed this right across the United States.

Refugees from gangland
Braving hundreds of miles on foot, Honduran and Salvadorian children are sent off by their parents for a better life in the United States, away from the drugs and violence of Central America. Here, border guards stop a group of child refugees in Granjeno, Texas.

to citizenship," as Obama proposed, without first ensuring that the U.S.-Mexican border was secured.

The DREAM Act, however, had unexpected consequences. It excited the dreams of masses of Central Americans willing to endure enormous risks to live in America. Panicked parents in El Salvador, Guatemala, and Honduras, worried about widespread drug-related gang violence, started sending their children on a dangerous journey through Mexico to the United States in hopes of connecting with relatives and being granted citizenship. During 2014, some 57,000 young migrants were caught along the nearly 2,000 mile-long border with Mexico, and communities across the United States rushed to find families to "sponsor" the unaccompanied children.

At the same time, the Obama administration was deporting record numbers of undocumented immigrants (over 2 million by the end of 2014), some of whom had been working in the nation for decades while others were Central American gang members, in what was called the "great expulsion." Obama, called the "Deporter in Chief" by critics, claimed that he was only following the laws written by anti-immigration Republicans. Others suggested that the president's harsh deportation policy was part of his "grand strategy" to force Congress to pass a comprehensive immigration reform bill. Either way, it was the immigrants who were caught in the middle.

The Supreme Court in the Twenty-First Century

The Supreme Court surprised observers in 2013 by overturning the Defense of Marriage Act (DOMA) of 1996, signed by President Bill Clinton, which had denied gay and lesbian couples who married in states allowing such unions the right to federal benefits. In *United States v. Windsor* (2013), the Court by a 5-4 vote ruled that the federal government could not withhold

Supreme Court overturns the Defense of Marriage Act (DOMA) (2013)

spousal benefits from same-sex couples who had been legally married. While restoring federal benefits, the Court did not rule that same-sex marriage is a *right* guaranteed under the U.S. Constitution. Each state, therefore, decided whether to allow such marriages. During 2014, however, federal courts repeatedly overturned state laws banning same-sex marriages, arguing that the right to marry was guaranteed by the Constitution.

Supreme Court dismantles the 1965 Voting Rights Act (2013)

While the Supreme Court disappointed social conservatives with its ruling in the *Windsor* case, the five conservatives on the Supreme Court continued to make rulings intended to restrict the powers of the federal government. In June 2013, in *Shelby County v. Holder* (2013), the Court gutted key provisions of the 1965 Voting Rights Act (VRA). The majority opinion declared that in five of the six southern states originally covered by the VRA, black voter turnout now exceeded white turnout. To the judges, this seemed to prove that there was no evidence of continuing racial discrimination. Soon after the Court's ruling, counties and states in the South pushed through new laws that had the effect of making it more difficult for minorities and poor people to vote by reducing voting hours or requiring that driver's licenses be shown on voting days.

The 2012 Election

As the November 2012 presidential election approached, one thing was certain: it would be the most expensive election ever, in part because the U.S. Supreme Court ruled in *Citizens United v. Federal Elections Committee* (2010) that corporations could spend as much as they wanted in support of candidates.

But if spending on the campaign was certain to be a record, it remained to be seen whether President Obama could shift the focus of voters from the sluggish economy to cultural politics and social issues. After a divisive battle in the primaries that included twenty televised debates with nearly a dozen other candidates, Mitt Romney won the Republican presidential nomination primarily because he promised, as a former corporate executive and Massachusetts governor, to accelerate economic growth.

Two things injured Romney's candidacy toward the end of the most expensive campaign in history ($6 billion). First was his decision to please right-wing voters by opposing immigration reforms that might allow undocumented immigrants a pathway to citizenship. The second was the disclosure late in the campaign that Romney had privately told a group of wealthy contributors that he "did not care" about the 47 percent of Americans who failed "to take personal responsibility and care for their lives." It was not his job "to worry about" those who did not pay federal income taxes because they were dependent on federal government programs. The Obama campaign seized on the impolitic statement, demonizing the wealthy Romney as an uncaring elitist. On Election Day, the president won with 66 million votes to Romney's 61 million, and 332 electoral votes to 206.

Embedded in the election returns were some striking statistics. Nearly 60 percent of white voters chose Romney. But the nation's fastest growing groups—Hispanics, Asian Americans, and African Americans—voted overwhelmingly for Obama, as did college-educated women, white and non-white. In the aftermath of Romney's defeat, David Frum, a prominent Republican speechwriter and columnist, confessed that his party was becoming "increasingly isolated and estranged from modern America."

Obama elected to a second term (2012)

Obamacare on the Defensive

President Obama's proudest achievement, the Affordable Care Act, was so massive in its scope and complicated in its implementation that it took four years of preparation before it was ready to "roll out." In the fall of 2013, the federal online health insurance "exchange" where people without insurance, mostly the working poor, could sign up, opened with great fanfare. Obama assured Americans that using the new online registration system would be "real simple." It was not. On October 1, millions tried to sign up for Obamacare online; few succeeded. As it turned out, the government website had never been properly tested, and it was hobbled with technical glitches. At the same time, it became evident that Obama had misled the nation about key elements of his health-care plan. In campaigning for its passage in 2010, he had repeatedly told voters that if they liked their current health insurance plan, they could, under Obamacare, "keep that insurance. Period. End of story." As it turned out, however, many saw their policies canceled by insurers.

Democrats had little time to celebrate, however. By November 2013, 57 percent of voters said they opposed Obamacare, in part because the program benefited only a quarter of the population, the uninsured and the underinsured, and Obama's job approval ratings had plunged. It had taken the president weeks to acknowledge the botched roll-out of Obamacare: "We created this problem we didn't need to create," he said to aides. "And it's our own doing, and it's our most important initiative," and "nobody is madder than me."

A frantic effort to repair the ACA website bore fruit. By August 2014, over 9 million people, well above the original target number, had signed up for the new health insurance. "The Affordable Care Act is here to stay," President Obama assured a nation still uncertain of its benefits. Yet Republican critics of Obamacare were so angry over its implementation that they filed a lawsuit against the president and some even talked of impeaching him.

New Global Challenges in an Age of Insecurity

In 2013 the United States held its first high-level talks with Iran since 1979, when Iranian militants in Tehran stormed the U.S. embassy and took its employees hostage. On November 23, Secretary of State John Kerry,

A limited nuclear negotiation with Iran

who succeeded Hillary Clinton in that role that year, reached a multinational agreement with Iran to scale back its nuclear development program for six months as a first step toward a more comprehensive agreement not to develop nuclear weapons that might threaten Israel or Iran's Arab neighbors.

> **Russians avert U.S. intervention in Syria**

At the same time that the United States was trying to reduce Iran's nuclear threat, an increasingly bloody civil war in Syria that had so far claimed 150,000 lives was beginning to have major international repercussions. In 2013, U.S. intelligence analysts confirmed that the Syrian government on August 21 had used chemical weapons to kill 1,400 people, many of them children. President Obama had repeatedly warned that the use of such weapons of mass destruction was a "red line" that would trigger international military intervention. In late August, he (and the French government) hesitantly began preparations for a military strike, although a war-fatigued Congress and most Americans opposed such action. On September 9, Secretary of State John Kerry defused the crisis by signing an agreement with Russia to dispose of Syria's chemical weapons. By the end of October, all the chemical weapon stockpiles at twenty-three locations had been destroyed or dismantled, but the ferocious civil war raged on. Obama's reluctance to use force in Syria illustrated his reluctance to order another U.S. military intervention in the fractious and complex Middle East, especially after twelve years of inconclusive warfare in Iraq and Afghanistan.

As the Syrian civil war continued, a civil uprising occurred in Ukraine, the former Soviet republic of 46 million people that had gained its independence in 1991. For years, Russian president Vladimir Putin, who viewed the humiliating disintegration of the Soviet Union as the "greatest geopolitical catastrophe of the century," had been trying to exert economic and political control over the republics of the former Soviet Union.

Vladimir Putin President of Russia and former Soviet secret service agent.

On February 27, Putin sent troops into the Crimea, a disputed part of the Ukraine. A week later, the Crimean parliament voted to become part of the Russian Federation. Putin, claiming that Crimea had "always been an inseparable part of Russia" even as he lied about the role of Russian troops in Crimea, quickly made the illegal annexation official.

The speed and ruthlessness with which Putin seized control of Crimea, mobilized 40,000 Russian troops on the Ukrainian border, and cut off Ukraine's crucial access to natural gas surprised President Obama and European leaders. It may not have been the start of a new cold war, but it put an end to hope that Russia would become a sincere partner of the Western democracies. The United States and the European Union refused to recognize the legitimacy of Russia's annexation of Crimea, warned Russia not to invade eastern Ukraine, and announced economic sanctions against Russia while pledging financial assistance to struggling Ukraine. "If Russia continues to interfere in Ukraine, we stand ready to impose further sanctions," Obama said. By a vote of 100–11, the UN General Assembly also opposed Russia's annexation of Crimea.

In April 2014, heavily armed pro-Russian separatists, as many as a third of whom were in fact Russian soldiers and agents, seized control of several cities in eastern Ukraine. They declared a "people's republic" and called for secession from Ukraine.

Pressure mounted on the United States and Europe to impose even more sanctions against Russia when a Malaysian passenger jet flying across eastern Ukraine was shot down by a Russian-made rocket in July 2014, killing all 298 on board, most of them Dutch citizens. The missile launcher was quickly spirited back into Russia. The U.S. and its allies slammed Russia with more severe economic sanctions, but the coldly calculating Putin showed no sign of backing away from his adventurism in Ukraine.

> Sanctions over Russian aggression in Ukraine

Events overseas during the summer of 2014 gave Obama the opportunity to take decisive action. In June, the volatile Middle East took a sudden turn for the worse when Sunni jihadists from around the world (including the United States and Great Britain) who had been fighting in the civil war in Syria against the Assad government invaded northern Iraq and announced the creation of their own nation ("caliphate"), called the Islamic State (IS or ISIS). The Islamic State had become the largest, best equipped, and most brutal of the many Islamist terrorist groups, financing its far-flung operations and 40,000 fanatical fighters by selling oil and ransoming hostages.

In the face of the IS advance, many Iraqi government soldiers that the United States had spent billions of dollars training and equipping simply fled, leaving to IS their valuable weapons and vehicles. The blood-thirsty IS fighters seized huge tracts of territory in Syria and Iraq while gleefully enslaving, terrorizing, raping, massacring, crucifying, or beheading thousands who refused to embrace their ruthless version of the Sunni faith. In August 2014, after IS terrorists gruesomely beheaded two captured Americans, President Obama ordered "systematic" airstrikes in Iraq—and later Syria—to prevent genocide as well-armed and financed IS fighters assaulted Christians, Yazidis, and Kurds in the region. The U.S. president scored a diplomatic coup by building a broad coalition of Arab and European partners to avoid "going it alone" against the "cancer" of the Islamic State, but there was no doubt that American warplanes would bear the brunt of the action. Obama assured Americans that he would not "get dragged into another ground war."

Although some criticized Obama's actions, he characterized the effort to stop the mass murder and mayhem by the Islamic State as "American leadership at its best." Preventing genocide is not simply a burden of great power, it is an obligation.

A Fading American Dream?

When Barack Obama won the Democratic nomination for president in 2008, he and his supporters touted him as an uplifting example of the American Dream at work, a biracial man who had defied the odds and won great success. His inspiring story echoed one of the most powerful themes in the nation's history: America as a mythic land of unique opportunities for people from around the world. In 1811, former president John Adams marveled at the growth and prosperity of the young American republic: "There is no people on earth so ambitious as the people of America . . . because the lowest [poorest] can aspire [to wealth] as freely as the highest."

The ideal of equal opportunity has always been the engine of American distinctiveness. By the early twenty-first century, though, that ideal seemed increasingly out of reach to millions of disenchanted Americans. The most striking change in modern life since the 1970s was the *widening* inequality of income and wealth between the powerful groups making up the economic elite and the rest of society. Modern America had become a tale of two very different societies in which "the rich get richer and the poor get poorer," to quote a famous song. America at the end of 2014 had never experienced more income inequality or less social mobility. "Today," reported the Nobel Prize–winning economist Joseph Stiglitz in 2012, "the United States has less equality of opportunity than almost any other advanced industrial country." The American dream of the poor having an equal chance to succeed, he said, had become more of a myth than ever before. America had grown much better at encouraging innovation then spreading opportunity.

By 2014, the richest 1 percent controlled more than 20 percent of total income. The 46 million Americans living *below* the official poverty line in 2014 ($11,702 annual income for an individual, or $23,850 for a family of four) was the highest in history. One out of every five children lives in poverty. And at the other extreme, corporate executives were reaping an ever-higher percentage of national wealth. In 1993 the disparity in pay between corporate leaders and the average U.S. worker was 195 to 1; in 2012, it had almost doubled to 360 to 1. "Increasingly," as journalist Hedrick Smith reported in 2012, America is becoming a society in which "privilege sustains privilege; poverty begets poverty," resulting in the "slow, poisonous polarization and disintegration of our great democracy."

A growing inequality gap

What caused the widening economic inequality, the shrinking of the middle class, and the new culture of poverty? Some argued that capitalism, by its vary nature, produced violent extremes of poverty and wealth. Others suggested that the United States had developed a "high-poverty economy" in which widespread poverty was simply the price to be paid for a highly competitive and largely deregulated high-tech economy in which the undereducated and unskilled were relegated to minimum-wage jobs. The globalization of the economy and the computer/Internet revolution paid huge dividends for the wealthiest and best-educated Americans while undercutting middle-class job opportunities. At the same time, economic inequality over time produces political inequality, as the role of "big money" in determining elections has steadily increased. Candidates have grown dependent on rich donors and corporate contributions, so that once elected, they often reciprocate by cutting taxes on the wealthy and reducing regulations of businesses.

Whatever its causes, what came to be called the "great divide" between the "1 percent" and the "99 percent" had profound social and political consequences as well as problematic moral dimensions. A nation founded on the ideal of equal opportunity ("All men are created equal") had become fabulously richer but less equal and less socially mobile than other advanced industrial nations. The true test of a capitalist democracy is not how wealthy the richest citizens are, but the quality of life of the average citizen. As Theodore Roosevelt had pledged in 1903, he would ensure a "Square Deal" for "every man, great or small, rich or poor."

What the two extremes of the political spectrum—the Tea Party and the Occupy Wall Street movement—agreed upon in the new century was that economic and political elites had come to rule America at the expense of the citizenry. Al Gore's slogan during the 2000 presidential campaign—"the people versus the powerful"—came to define the political dynamics of the twenty-first century.

Unlike many nations in the past, the United States has so far survived its growing economic inequalities and social strife without serious upheavals. For all its growing diversity and deepening divisions, the nation remains united under a common government and political system, something that few societies can claim. For centuries, Americans have also displayed a distinctively self-critical temperament, especially noticeable to foreign visitors. In the early nineteenth century, the English writer Charles Dickens said that the American "always is depressed, and always is stagnated, and always is at an alarming crisis, and never was otherwise."

Perhaps that is why the nation has always overcome its greatest crises: Americans have high expectations and eventually address their urgent problems. The nation has always displayed a remarkable genius for self-renewal, a confident ability to maneuver itself through the most difficult threats and challenges, emerging not only intact but stronger. It needs such innovative resilience today, for unless the entwined ideals of equal opportunity and fair reward are addressed, Americans may lose what has always united the republic and informed the nation's sense of purpose: the widely shared hope, even expectation, of a better future—for all—based on hard work, ingenuity, and sacrifice. As President Obama declared in 2014, growing income inequality had become a "fundamental threat to the American Dream, our way of life, and what we stand for around the globe."

U.S. Foreign Policy Post-Cold War

As the twentieth century came to an end, the United States' relationship with the rest of the world entered a new era. "Containment" of the Soviet Union had become less crucial, but regional conflicts and other issues of national security did not disappear, and American leaders—no longer locked in a fierce nuclear rivalry with the Soviet Union—struggled to define America's role in an unstable post-Cold War era. U.S. military forces would intervene in regions and conflicts unimaginable a few decades earlier and not always successfully or with clear purpose.

Two key issues have shaped post-Cold War policies. On September 11, 2001, the United States suffered its worst attack since the Japanese bombing of Pearl Harbor. Terrorists linked to al Qaeda, a worldwide network of Islamic extremists, crashed hijacked commercial airliners into the World Trade Center in New York City and the Pentagon in Washington, D.C., killing thousands. Then, in 2008, the nation plunged into the Great Recession, the worst economic crisis since the Great Depression of the 1930s. Review the following foreign policy highlights from the first three "post-Cold War" presidents and answer the questions further below.

Foreign Policy Highlights from the Clinton Presidency, 1993–2001

1993 Congress passes the North American Free Trade Agreement (NAFTA).

American negotiators broker an agreement between Israel and the Palestinian Liberation Organization (PLO) that restored Palestinian self-rule in parts of Israeli-occupied territory in the Gaza Strip and West Bank.

1994 President Clinton, with United Nations authorization, intervenes to restore the democratically-elected President of Haiti, Jean-Bertrand Aristide, after a military coup.

1995 American negotiators broker a peace settlement in Bosnia. After declaring its independence from Yugoslavia in 1991, Bosnia quickly became embroiled in an ethnic and religious civil war. The peace plan divided the country into two states and committed 60,000 NATO troops to enforce the agreement.

1998 President Clinton negotiates a deal among leaders of Israel, Jordan, and the PLO, by which Israel agreed to surrender land in return for security guarantees by the Palestinians.

1999 NATO forces, relying heavily on the U.S. military, launch airstrikes against Serbia that end its attempts to assert control over Kosovo by brutalizing its ethnic Albanian population.

Foreign Policy Highlights from the Bush Presidency, 2001–2009

October 2001 U.S. forces lead "Operation Enduring Freedom," an international coalition into Afghanistan, after the Taliban government refused to turn over Osama bin Laden, mastermind of al Qaeda and the 9/11 attacks. After the collapse of the Taliban in December, American-led international forces continued to occupy the country searching for bin Laden and support a new internationally recognized government.

Congress passes the USA Patriot Act.

Bush Presidency, 2001–2009, continued

November 2002 Congress creates the Office of Homeland Security.

Fall of 2002 Bush announces the "Bush Doctrine."

March 2003 The U.S. and its allies invade Iraq and overthrow its dictator, Saddam Hussein, based on the Bush administration's claim that the regime possessed chemical and biological weapons of mass destruction, weapons that were never found by occupying forces.

Fall of 2003 President Bush announces that 150,000 U.S. troops would remain in Iraq and that rebuilding the fracturing country would take years and be very expensive.

Foreign Policy Highlights from the Obama Presidency, 2009–2014

2009 President Obama announces that U.S. troops would be withdrawn from Iraq by the end of 2011. The U.S. intervention in Iraq had cost over 4,500 American lives, 30,000 wounded, over 100,000 Iraqi lives, and $2 trillion.

President Obama transfers 21,000 additional troops to Afghanistan but confines their mission to suppressing terrorists, not nation building.

Late 2010–2011 An "Arab Awakening" emerges as spontaneous democratic uprisings break out in several Arab countries dominated by authoritarian leaders. Demonstrators toppled regimes in Egypt, Libya, and Tunisia, but failed to establish stable democracies in their place. President Obama exercised restraint in responding to these developments.

2011 President Obama announces that the military surge in Afghanistan had worked and American forces would be withdrawn from the country by the end of 2014.

March 2011 President Obama supports a British and French bombing campaign against dictator Colonel Muammar Gaddafi and in support of the rebellion against him. The rebels eventually overthrew Gaddafi and killed him in October.

May 1, 2011 A U.S. Navy Seal Team kills Osama bin Laden in a secret compound in Pakistan.

2013 The United States holds its first high-level talks with Iranian officials since 1979. Iran agrees to scale back its nuclear development program.

August 2013 President Obama and French officials organize a military strike against the Syrian government after it used chemical weapons in its civil war. Before Congress could vote on the measure, Syria agreed to dispose of its remaining chemical weapons, thus diffusing the crisis.

September 2014 President Obama orders U.S. airstrikes against IS forces operating in Iraq and Syria.

QUESTIONS FOR ANALYSIS

1. How did Presidents Clinton and Bush differ in their use of military force to intervene abroad?

2. Out of all three presidents in the new millennia, which president seemed most willing to use military force to promote his objectives and which seemed least? What events and developments shaped their decisions?

3. Why do you think each president focused so much attention on the Middle East?

■ **Changing Demographics** From 1980 to 2010, the U.S. population grew by 25 percent, to 306 million, and was more racially and ethnically diverse. Because of a wave of immigration from Latin America, Hispanics surpassed African Americans as the nation's largest minority. The rate at which the nonwhite population increased had quadrupled since the 1970s. By 2012, the U.S. population included more foreign-born and first-generation residents than ever before.

■ **Divided Government** Just two years into the presidency of "New Democrat" Bill Clinton, Republican Speaker of the House Newt Gingrich crafted his *Contract with America* against the "corrupt liberal welfare state" and achieved, a Republican landslide in the 1994 midterm elections. The *North American Free Trade Act (NAFTA)* (1994) and the *Personal Responsibility and Work Opportunity Act of 1996* were bipartisan successes. The prosperous high-tech *"new economy"* thriving on the *globalization* of commerce helped Clinton balance the federal budget. Yet, Clinton's personal scandals tarnished his presidency even though he was ultimately acquitted. He later intervened in the Balkans to stop *ethnic cleansing* and brokered the Wye River Accords in the Middle East.

■ **Global Terrorism** The 9/11 terrorist attacks led President George W. Bush to declare a *war on terror.* The U.S. invaded Afghanistan (Operation Enduring Freedom) to capture the 9/11 attack's mastermind, Osama bin Laden, destroy his terrorist organization, al Qaeda, and oust the Islamist Taliban government that harbored it. Congress also authorized the Office of Homeland Security and the *USA Patriot Act.* In 2003, the Bush administration invoked the *Bush Doctrine* against Saddam Hussein, the leader of Iraq. The Second Iraq War succeeded in removing Hussein

from power but turned up no weapons of mass destruction. The administration was unprepared to establish order in postwar Iraq, which was soon wracked by sectarian violence. Americans became bitterly divided over the war and whether the Bush Doctrine enhanced U.S. security.

■ **A Historic Election** The 2008 presidential campaigns featured Democrats Senator Hillary Clinton and Senator Barack Obama, the first female and African American candidates, respectively; The Republicans nominated Senator John McCain, the oldest candidate in history. Obama won the popular vote and a landslide victory in the electoral college, becoming the nation's first African American president. His victory resulted from public dismay about the *Great Recession* and weariness with Bush's policies. His Internet- and grassroots-based campaign excelled at fundraising and voter turnout. He won much of the nonwhite vote, a rapidly increasing share of the electorate.

■ **Obama's Priorities** Obama's first priority was shoring up the failing economy through controversial Wall Street bailouts and a huge economic stimulus package: the American Recovery and Reinvestment Act. Economic recovery remained sluggish and unequal, widening the economic divide and spawning the Occupy Wall Street movement. Obama's legacy legislation, the *Affordable Care Act (ACA),* incited bitter opposition from the *Tea Party*, which leveraged its control over the House of Representatives to shut down the federal government for sixteen days. Obama reduced U.S. military abroad, removing all combat troops from Iraq in 2011, downsizing their presence in Afghanistan, refusing to make broad military commitments in the Arab Awakening. Obama also endorsed *same-sex marriage* and a path to citizenship for undocumented residents.

KEY TERMS

North American Free Trade Agreement (NAFTA) (1994) *p. 1132*

Contract with America (1994) *p. 1133*

Personal Responsibility and Work Opportunity Act of 1996 (PRWOA) *p. 1135*

"new economy" *p. 1135*

globalization *p. 1136*

ethnic cleansing *p. 1138*

war on terror *p. 1143*

USA Patriot Act (2001) *p. 1143*

Bush Doctrine *p. 1144*

Great Recession (2007–2009) *p. 1150*

Affordable Care Act (ACA) (2010) *p. 1152*

Tea Party *p. 1156*

same-sex marriage *p. 1158*

CHRONOLOGY

1991	Ethnic conflict explodes in Yugoslavia
1992	Bill Clinton elected president
1993	Congress passes NAFTA
1995	Contract with America
1996	Congress passes welfare reform
1998	President Clinton impeached
2000	Supreme Court issues *Bush v. Gore* decision
September 11, 2001	9/11 Terrorist attacks
October 2001	Operation Enduring Freedom begins
2003–2011	Second Iraq War begins
August 2005	Hurricane Katrina
2007–2009	Great Recession begins
2009	Barack Obama elected president
	Tea Party movement begins
2010	Congress passes the Affordable Care Act
2011	Occupy Wall Street, Arab Awakening
August 2011	Osama bin Laden killed
2013	Defense of Marriage Act overturned
2014	Islamic State of Iraq and Syria (ISIS) established

INQUIZITIVE

Go to InQuizitive to see what you've learned—and learn what you've missed—with personalized feedback along the way.

DEBATING Contemporary Immigration and the Uses of History

One of the reasons that the study of history is so important is that it informs the way we think about society today. Comparisons with the past are an essential part of how policy makers and citizens debate the key issues of the day. For instance, one of the most controversial issues in American society today is immigration, and many arguments hinge on comparisons to past generations of immigrants and how they were perceived at the time. For Part Seven, *The American Age*, the issue of Latino immigration demonstrates how history influences contemporary political debates. For this exercise, you will be taking on the role of historian, and thus you should focus on evaluating the uses of history, not current immigration policy.

For this exercise you have two tasks:

PART 1: Compare the ways that history is used in two secondary sources discussing contemporary Latino immigration.

PART 2: Using primary sources, evaluate how history is used in these secondary sources.

PART I Comparing Secondary Sources

Each of the secondary sources that is included here is written by a scholar of contemporary immigration politics. In these selections, the authors draw comparisons between the issues surrounding past generations of immigrants and the issues surrounding immigrants today. The first is from Dr. Jason Richwine, a contributing writer at the National Review and former Senior Policy Analyst, Heritage Foundation. The second text is from Leo Chavez, a professor of anthropology at the University of California, Irvine. While Richwine is interested in assimilation, immigration, and national culture, Chavez is concerned with how immigrant groups are represented in contemporary discourse.

Compare the views of these two scholars by answering the following questions. Be sure to find specific examples in the selections to support your answers.

■ What issues that surround Latino immigration to America does each author address?

■ What comparisons does each author make to historical immigration groups?

■ In what ways might these authors respond to each other's work?

■ Based on what you have learned, what examples from American history can you think of that would support or refute each author's argument?

Secondary Source 1

Jason Richwine, on Assimilation (2009)

They're not just like the Irish—or the Italians or the Poles, for that matter. The large influx of Hispanic immigrants after 1965 represents a unique assimilation challenge for the United States. Many optimistic observers have assumed—incorrectly, it turns out—that Hispanic immigrants will follow the same economic trajectory European immigrants did in the early part of the last century. Many of those Europeans came to America with no money and few skills, but their status steadily improved. Their children outperformed them, and their children's children were often indistinguishable from the "founding stock." The speed of economic assimilation varied somewhat by ethnic group, but three generations were typically enough to turn "ethnics" into plain old Americans.

This would be the preferred outcome for the tens of millions of Hispanic Americans, who are significantly poorer and less educated on average than native whites. When immigration skeptics question the wisdom of importing so many unskilled people into our nation at one time, the most common response cites the remarkable progress of Europeans a century ago. "People used to say the Irish or the Poles would always be poor, but look at them today!" For Hispanics, we are led to believe, the same thing will happen.

But that claim isn't true. Though about three-quarters of Hispanics living in the U.S. today are either immigrants or the children of immigrants, a significant number have roots here going back many generations. We have several ways to measure their intergenerational progress, and the results leave little room for optimism about their prospects for assimilation . . . .

First, the second generation still does not come close to matching the socioeconomic status of white natives. Even if Hispanics were to keep climbing the ladder each generation, their assimilation would be markedly slower than that of other groups. But even that view is overly optimistic, because of the second, larger problem with Hispanic assimilation: It appears to stall after the second generation. We see little further ladder-climbing from the grandchildren of Hispanic immigrants. They do not rise out of the lower class . . . .

So why do Hispanics, on average, not assimilate? Theories abound. Popular explanations from the left include the legacy of white racism, labor-market discrimination, housing segregation, and poor educational opportunities. Those on the right tend to cite enforced multiculturalism, ethnic enclaves, and a self-perpetuating culture of poverty. . . . [T]he lack of Hispanic assimilation is likely to create ethnic tensions that threaten our cultural core. Human beings are a tribal species, and this makes ethnicity a natural fault line in any society. Intra-European ethnic divisions have been largely overcome through economic assimilation—Irish and Italian immigrants may have looked a bit different from natives, but by the third generation their socioeconomic profiles were similar. Hispanic Americans do not have that benefit.

Persistent ethnic disparities in socioeconomic status add to a sense of "otherness" felt by minorities outside the economic mainstream. Though it is encouraging that Hispanics often profess a belief in the American creed, an undercurrent of this "otherness" is still apparent. For example, a Pew Hispanic Center Survey in 2002 asked American-born Hispanics "which terms they would use first to describe themselves." Less than half (46 percent) said "American," while the majority said they primarily identified either with their ancestral country or as simply Hispanic or Latino. . . .

It is difficult to see how a unifying national culture can be preserved and extended in that environment.

Source: Jason Richwine, "The Congealing Pot," *National Review* 61 no. 15 (August 24, 2009): 37–39.

Secondary Source 2
Leo Chavez, on Illegal Aliens (2008)

This book grew out of my attempt to unpack the meanings of . . . [negative] views about Latinos. Rather than considering them in isolation, I began to see them as connected, as part of a larger set of concerns over immigration, particularly from Mexico and other parts of Latin America; the meaning of citizenship; and the power of media spectacles in contemporary life. The Latino Threat Narrative provides the raw material that weaves these concerns together.

The Latino Threat Narrative posits that Latinos are not like previous immigrant groups, who ultimately became part of the nation. According to the assumptions and taken-for-granted "truths" inherent in this narrative, Latinos are unwilling or incapable of integrating, of becoming part of the national community. Rather, they are part of an invading force from south of the border that is bent on reconquering land that was formerly theirs (the U.S. Southwest) and destroying the American way of life. . . .

The contemporary Latino Threat Narrative has its antecedents in U.S. history: the German language threat, the Catholic threat, the Chinese and Japanese immigration threats, and the southern and eastern European threat. In their day, each discourse of threat targeted particular immigrant groups and their children. Each was pervasive and defined "truths" about the threats posed by immigrants that, in hindsight, were unjustified or never materialized in the long run of history. And each of these discourses generated actions, such as alarmist newspaper stories (the media of the day), anti-immigrant riots, restrictive immigration laws, forced internments, and acrimonious public debates over government policies. In this sense, the Latino Threat Narrative is part of a grand tradition of alarmist discourse about immigrants and their perceived negative impacts on society. . . .

Latinos have been in what is now the United States since the late sixteenth and early seventeenth centuries, actually predating the English colonies. Since the Mexican-American War, immigration from Mexico and other Latin countries has waxed and waned, building in the early twentieth century, diminishing in the 1930s, and building again the post-1965 years. These migrations paralleled those of other immigrant groups. But Mexicans in particular have been represented as the quintessential "illegal aliens," which distinguishes them from other immigrant groups. Their social identity has been plagued by the mark of illegality, which in much public discourse means that they are criminals and thus illegitimate members of society undeserving of social benefits, including citizenship. Latinos are an alleged threat because of this history and social identity, which supposedly make their integration difficult and imbue them, particularly Mexicans, with a desire to remain socially apart as they prepare for a reconquest of the U.S. Southwest.

Source: Leo Chavez, *The Latino Threat: Constructing Immigrants, Citizens, and the Nation* (Redwood City, CA: Stanford University Press, 2008), 3–4.

PART II Using Primary Sources to Evaluate Secondary Sources

When historians are faced with competing interpretations of the past, they often look at primary source material as part of the process of evaluating the different arguments. Below is a selection of primary source materials relating to some of the historical issues relating to immigration and assimilation brought up by the two authors. The first document is excerpted from a short essay, one of the first works on demography, by Benjamin Franklin in 1751. The second document is an 1878 statement from the California State Senate to the U.S. Congress requesting that immigration to the United States from China be restricted. The third document is an article by Republican Senator Henry Cabot Lodge of Massachusetts, a leading immigration restrictionist who was instrumental in the passage of such legislation in the 1920s. The final document is from the 1963 book, *Beyond the Melting Pot: The Negroes, Puerto Ricans, Jews, Italians, and Irish of New York City*, by sociologist Nathan Glazer and future U.S. senator Daniel Patrick Moynihan. This book appeared just prior to the liberalization of U.S. immigration policy in 1965 and explores the assimilation of various ethnic groups in New York City.

Carefully read each of the following primary sources and answer the following questions.

■ How does each document address the issue of assimilation and identity?

■ Based on these documents, what pattern do you see in how Americans historically have responded to the arrival of new immigrant groups?

■ Which of the primary sources do you think Richwine and Chavez would find most useful, and how might they use them to support their arguments?

■ Which of the secondary sources do you think is best supported by the primary source evidence?

Primary Source 1

Benjamin Franklin, on the Germans (1755)

And since detachments of English from Britain sent to America, will have their places at home so soon supply'd and increase so largely here; why should the Palatine Boors [Germans] be suffered to swarm into our settlements, and by herding together establish their languages and manners to the exclusion of ours? Why should Pennsylvania, founded by the English, become a colony of Aliens, who will shortly be so numerous as to Germanize us instead of our Anglifying them, and will never adopt our language or customs, any more than they can acquire our complexion? Which leads me to add one remark: That the number of purely white people in the world is proportionally very small. All Africa is black or tawny. Asia chiefly tawny. America (exclusive of the new comers) wholly so. And in Europe, the Spaniards, Italians, French, Russians, and Swedes are generally of what we call a swarthy complexion; as are the Germans also, the Saxons only excepted, who with the English make the principal body of white people on the face of the earth. I could wish their numbers were increased. And while we are, as I may call it, scouring our planet, by clearing America of woods, and so making this side of our globe reflect a brighter light to the eyes of inhabitants in Mars or Venus, why should we in the sight of superior beings, darken its people? Why increase the sons of Africa, by planting them in America, where we have so fair an opportunity, by excluding all blacks and tawneys, of increasing the lovely white and red? But perhaps I am partial to the complexion of my Country, for such kind of partiality is natural to Mankind.

Source: Benjamin Franklin, *Observations Concerning the Increase of Mankind, Peopling of Countries, etc.* (Boston, MA: Printed and Sold by S. Kneeland in Queen Street, 1755), 224.

Primary Source 2

Senate of California to the Congress, on Chinese Immigration (1878)

The State of California has a population variously estimated at from seven hundred thousand to eight hundred thousand, of which one hundred and twenty-five thousand are Chinese. The additions to this class have been very rapid since the organization of the State, but have been caused almost entirely by immigration, and scarcely at all by natural increase. . . .

The pious anticipations that the influence of Christianity upon the Chinese would be salutary, have proved unsubstantial and vain. Among one hundred and twenty-five thousand of them, with a residence here beneath the elevating influences of Christian precept and example, and with the zealous labors of earnest Christian teachers, and the liberal expenditure of ecclesiastical revenues, we have no evidence of a single genuine conversion to Christianity, or of a single instance of an assimilation with our manners, or habits of thought or life. . . . Neither is there any possibility that in the future education, religion, or the other influences of our civilization can effect any change in this condition of things. . . .

Above and beyond these considerations, however, we believe, and the researches of those who have most attentively studied the Chinese character confirm us in the consideration, that the Chinese are incapable of adaptation to our institutions. The national intellect of China has become decrepit from sheer age. It has long since passed its prime and is waning into senility. . . . Their code of morals, their forms of worship, and their maxims of life are those of the remotest antiquity. In this aspect they stand a barrier against which the elevating tendency of a higher civilization exerts itself in vain. And, in an ethnological point of view, there can be no hope that any contact with our people, however long continued, will ever conform them to our institutions, enable them to comprehend or appreciate our form of government, or to assume the duties or discharge the functions of citizens.

During their entire settlement in California they have never adapted themselves to our habits, modes of dress, or our educational system, have never learned the sanctity of an oath, never desired to become citizens, or to perform the duties of citizenship, never discovered the difference between right and wrong, never ceased the worship of their idol gods, or advanced a step beyond the musty traditions of their native hive. Impregnable to all the influences of our Anglo-Saxon life, they remain the same stolid Asiatics that have floated on the rivers and slaved in the fields of China for thirty centuries of time.

We thus find one-sixth of our entire population composed of Chinese coolies, not involuntary, but, by the unalterable structure of their intellectual being, voluntary slaves. This alien mass, constantly increasing by Immigration, is injected into a republic of' freemen, eating of its substance, expelling free white labor, and contributing nothing to the support of the government. All of the physical conditions of California are in the highest degree favorable to their influx. Our climate is essentially Asiatic in all its aspects. And the Federal Government by its legislation and treaties fosters and promotes the immigration. What is to be the result? Does it require any prophetic power to foretell? Can American statesmen project their vision forward for a quarter of a century and convince themselves that this problem will work out for itself a wise solution? In that brief period, with the same ratio of increase, this fair State will contain a Chinese population outnumbering its free men. White labor will be unknown, because unobtainable, and then how long a period will elapse before California will, nay must, become essentially . . . lesser Asia, with all its deathly lethargy?

Source: "Memorial of the Senate of California to the Congress of the United States," *Chinese Immigration; Its Social, Moral, and Political Effect. Report to the California State Senate of Its Special Committee on Chinese Immigration* (Sacramento: State Office, F. P. Thompson, Supt. State Printing, 1878), 60, 62–4.

Primary Source 3

Henry Cabot Lodge, "The Restriction of Immigration" (1891)

The nations of Europe which chiefly contributed to the upbuilding of the original thirteen colonies were the English, the Scotch-Irish, so called, the Dutch, the Germans, and the Huguenot French. With the exception of the last they were practically all people of the same stock. During this century and until very recent years these same nations, with the addition of Ireland and the Scandinavian countries, have continued to furnish the chief component parts of the immigration which has helped to populate so rapidly the territory of the United States. Among all these people, with few exceptions, community of race or language, or both, has facilitated the work of assimilation. In the last ten years, however, as appears from the figures just given, new and wholly different elements have been introduced into our immigration, and what is more important still the rate of immigration of these new elements has risen with much greater rapidity than that of those which previously had furnished the bulk of the population of the country. The mass of immigration, absolutely speaking, continues, of course, to come from the United Kingdom and from Germany, but relatively the immigration from these two sources is declining rapidly in comparison with the immigration from Italy and from the Slavic countries of Russia, Poland, Hungary, and Bohemia, the last of which appears under the head of Austria. . . .

Thus it is proved, first, that immigration to this country is increasing, and, second, that it is making its greatest relative increase from races most alien to the body of the American people and from the lowest and most illiterate classes among those races. In other words, it is apparent that, while our immigration is increasing, it is showing at the same time a marked tendency to deteriorate in character. . . . As one example of the practical effect of unrestricted immigration the committee [of the Fiftieth Congress to investigate immigration] cite the case of the coal-mining country: "Generally speaking, the class of immigrants who have lately been imported and employed in the coal regions of this country are not such, in the opinion of the committee, as would make desirable inhabitants of the United States. They are of a very low order of intelligence. They do not come here with the intention of becoming citizens; their whole purpose being to accumulate by parsimonious, rigid, and unhealthy economy a sum of money and then return to their native land. They live in miserable sheds like beasts; the food they eat is so meagre, scant, unwholesome, and revolting that it would nauseate and disgust an American workman, and he would find it difficult to sustain life upon it. Their habits are vicious, their customs are disgusting, and the effect of their presence here upon our social condition is to be deplored. . . . [I]n the opinion of the committee, no amount of effort would improve their morals or 'Americanize' this class of immigrants."

Source: Henry Cabot Lodge, "The Restriction of Immigration," *North American Review* 152, no. 410 (Jan. 1891), 28, 30, 32–33.

Primary Source 4

Nathan Glazer and Daniel Patrick Moynihan, on the Nonexistent "American" (1963)

Perhaps the meaning of ethnic labels will yet be erased in America. But it has not yet worked out this way in New York. It is true that immigrants to this country were rapidly transformed, in comparison with immigrants to other countries, that they lost their language and altered their culture. It was reasonable to believe that a new American type would emerge, a new nationality in which it would be a matter of indifference whether a man was of Anglo-Saxon or German or Italian or Jewish origin, and in which indeed, because of the diffusion of populations through all parts of the country and all levels of the social order, and because of the consequent close contact and intermarriage, it would be impossible to make such distinctions. This may still be the most likely result in the long run. After all, in 1960 almost half of New York City's population was still foreign-born or the children of foreign-born. Yet it is also true that it is forty years since the end of mass immigration, and new processes, scarcely visible when our chief concern was with the great masses of immigrants and the problems of their "Americanization," now emerge to surprise us. The initial notion of an American melting pot did not, it seems, quite grasp what would happen in America. At least it did not grasp what would happen in the short run, and since this short run encompasses at least the length of a normal lifetime, it is not something we can ignore.

It is true that language and culture are very largely lost in the first and second generations, and this makes the dream of "cultural pluralism"—of a new Italy or Germany or Ireland in America, a League of Nations established in the New World—as unlikely as the hope of a "melting pot." But as the groups were transformed by influences in American society, stripped of their original attributes, they were recreated as something new, but still as identifiable groups. Concretely, persons think of themselves as members of that group, with that name; they are thought of by others as members of that group, with that name; and most significantly, they are linked to other members of the group by new attributes that the original immigrants would never have recognized as identifying their group, but which nevertheless serve to mark them off, by more than simply name and association, in the third generation and even beyond.

The assimilating power of American society and culture operated on immigrant groups in different ways, to make them, it is true, something they had not been, but still something distinct and identifiable. The impact of assimilating trends on the groups is different in part because the groups are different—Catholic peasants from Southern Italy were affected differently, in the same city and the same time, from urbanized Jewish workers and merchants from Eastern Europe. . . .

Conceivably the fact that one's origins can become only a memory suggests the general direction for ethnic groups in the United States—toward assimilation and absorption into a homogeneous American mass. And yet, as we suggested earlier, it is hard to see in the New York of the 1960s just how this comes about. Time alone does not dissolve the groups if they are not close to the Anglo-Saxon center. Color marks off a group, regardless of time; and perhaps most significantly, the "majority" group, to which assimilation should occur, has taken on the color of an ethnic group, too. To what does one assimilate in modern America? The "American" in abstract does not exist, though some sections of the country, such as the Far West, come closer to realizing him than does New York City.

Source: Nathan Glazer and Daniel Patrick Moynihan, *Beyond the Melting Pot: The Negroes, Puerto Ricans, Jews, Italians, and Irish of New York City* (Cambridge, MA: Massachusetts Institute of Technology Press and Harvard University Press, 1963), 12–14, 20.

Glossary

36°30' According to the Missouri Compromise, any part of the Louisiana Purchase north of this line (Missouri's southern border) was to be excluded from slavery.

54th Massachusetts Regiment After President Abraham Lincoln's Emancipation Proclamation, the Union army organized all black military units, which white officers led. The 54th Massachusetts Regiment was one of the first of such units to be organized.

Abigail Adams (1744–1818) As the wife of John Adams, she endured long periods of separation from him while he served in many political roles. During these times apart, she wrote often to her husband, and their correspondence has provided a detailed portrait of life during the Revolutionary War.

abolition In the early 1830s, the anti-slavery movement shifted its goal from the gradual end of slavery to the immediate end or abolition of slavery.

abolitionism Movement that called for an immediate end to slavery throughout the United States.

John Adams (1735–1826) He was a signer of the Declaration of Independence and a delegate to the First and Second Continental Congresses. A member of the Federalist Party, he served as the first vice president and the second president of the United States. As president, he passed the Alien and Sedition Acts and endured a stormy relationship with France, which included the XYZ affair.

John Quincy Adams (1767–1848) As secretary of state, he urged President Monroe to issue the Monroe Doctrine, which incorporated his belief in an expanded use of federal powers. As the sixth president, Adams's nationalism and praise of European leaders caused a split in his party, causing some Republicans to leave and form the Democrat party.

Samuel Adams (1722–1803) A genius of revolutionary agitation, he believed that English Parliament had no right to legislate for the colonies. He organized the Sons of Liberty as well as protests in Boston against the British.

Jane Addams (1860–1935) She founded and ran of one of the best known settlement houses, the Hull House. Active in the peace and suffragist movements, she established child care for working mothers, health clinics, job training, and other social programs.

affirmative action Programs designed to give preferential treatment to women and minorities as compensation for past injustices.

Affordable Care Act (ACA) (2010) Vast health-care reform initiative signed into law and championed by President Obama, and widely criticized by Republicans, that aims to make health insurance more affordable and make health care accessible to everyone, regardless of income or prior medical conditions.

Agricultural Adjustment Act (1933) Legislation that paid farmers to produce less in order to raise crop prices for all; the AAA was later declared unconstitutional by the U.S. Supreme Court in the case of *United States v. Butler* (1936).

Emilio Aguinaldo (1869?–1964) He was a leader in the Filipino struggle for independence. During the war of 1898, Commodore George Dewey brought Aguinaldo back to the Philippines from exile to help fight the Spanish. However, after the Spanish surrendered to Americans, America annexed the Philippines and Aguinaldo fought against the American military until he was captured in 1901.

Alamo, Battle of the Siege in the Texas War for Independence of 1836, in which the San Antonio mission fell to the Mexicans. Davy Crockett and Jim Bowie were among the courageous defenders.

Albany Plan of Union A failed proposal by the seven northern colonies in anticipation of the French and Indian War, urging the unification of the colonies under one Crown-appointed president.

Alien and Sedition Acts of 1798 Four measures passed during the undeclared war with France that limited the freedoms of speech and press and restricted the liberty of non-citizens.

Allied Powers The nations fighting the Central Powers during the First World War, including France, Great Britain, and Russia; later joined by Italy and, after Russia quit the war in 1917, the United States.

American Anti-Imperialist League Coalition of anti-imperialist groups united in 1899 to protest American territorial expansion, especially in the Philippine Islands; its membership included prominent politicians, industrialists, labor leaders, and social reformers.

American Colonization Society Established in 1817, an organization whose mission was to return freed slaves to Africa.

American Federation of Labor Founded in 1881 as a national federation of trade unions made up of skilled workers.

American Indian Movement (AIM) Fed up with the poor conditions on Indian reservations and the federal government's unwillingness to help, Native Americans founded the American Indian Movement (AIM) in 1963. In 1973, AIM led 200 Sioux in the occupation of Wounded Knee. After a ten-week standoff with the federal authorities, the government agreed to reexamine Indian treaty rights and the occupation ended.

American Recovery and Reinvestment Act Hoping to restart the weak economy, President Obama signed this $787-billion economic stimulus bill in February of 2009. The bill included cash distributions to states, funds for food stamps, unemployment benefits, construction projects to renew the nation's infrastructure, funds for renewable-energy systems, and tax reductions.

American System Economic plan championed by Henry Clay of Kentucky that called for federal tariffs on imports, a strong national bank, and federally-financed internal improvements—roads, bridges, canals—all intended to strengthen the national economy and end American dependence on Great Britain.

American Tobacco Company Business founded in 1890 by North Carolina's James Buchanan Duke, who combined the major tobacco manufacturers of the time, ultimately controlling 90 percent of the country's cigarette production.

Anaconda Plan The Union's primary war strategy calling for a naval blockade of major southern seaports and then dividing the Confederacy by gaining control of the Tennessee, Cumberland, and Mississippi Rivers.

Annapolis Convention In 1786, all thirteen colonies were invited to a convention in Annapolis to discuss commercial problems, but only representatives from five states attended. However, the convention was not a complete failure because the delegates decided to have another convention in order to write the constitution.

Battle of Antietam (1862) Turning-point battle near Sharpsburg, Maryland, leaving over 20,000 soldiers dead or wounded, in which Union forces halted a Confederate invasion of the North.

anti-Federalists Opponents of the Constitution as an infringement on individual and states' rights, whose criticism led to the addition of a Bill of Rights to the document. Many anti-Federalists later joined Thomas Jefferson's Democratic-Republican party.

Anti-Masonic party This party grew out of popular hostility toward the Masonic fraternal order and entered the presidential election of 1832 as a third party. It was the first party to run as a third party in a presidential election as well as the first to hold a nomination convention and announce a party platform.

Appomattox Court House Virginia village where Confederate general Robert E. Lee surrendered to Union general Ulysses S. Grant on April 9, 1865.

Arab Awakening A wave of spontaneous democratic uprisings that spread throughout the Arab world beginning in 2011, in which long-oppressed peoples demanded basic liberties from generations-old authoritarian regimes.

Benedict Arnold (1741–1801) A traitorous American commander who planned to sell out the American garrison at West Point to the British; his plot was discovered before it could be executed and he joined the British army.

Articles of Confederation The first form of government for the United States, ratified by the original thirteen states in 1781; weak in central authority, it was replaced by the U.S. Constitution in 1789.

The Atlanta Compromise A speech by Booker T. Washington that called for the black community to strive for economic prosperity before attempting political and social equality.

Atlantic Charter (1941) Joint statement crafted by Franklin D. Roosevelt and British prime minister Winston Churchill that listed the war goals of the Allied Powers.

Aztec Empire A network of more than 300 city-states and upward of 30 provinces, established in the fourteenth century under the imperialistic Mexica, or Aztecs, in the valley of Mexico.

Crispus Attucks (1723–1770) During the Boston Massacre, he was supposedly at the head of the crowd of hecklers who baited the British troops. He was killed when the British troops fired on the crowd.

Stephen F. Austin (1793–1836) He established the first colony of Americans in Texas, which eventually attracted 2,000 people.

"Axis" alliance Military alliance formed in 1937 by the three major fascist powers: Germany, Italy, and Japan.

Aztec Empire Mesoamerican people who were conquered by the Spanish under Hernando Cortés, 1519–1528.

baby boom Markedly high birth rate in the years following World War II, leading to the biggest demographic "bubble" in U.S. history.

Bacon's Rebellion Unsuccessful 1676 revolt led by planter Nathaniel Bacon against Virginia governor William Berkeley's administration, which, Bacon charged, had failed to protect settlers from Indian raids.

Bank of the United States (1791) National bank responsible for holding and transferring federal government funds, making business loans, and issuing a national currency.

The Bank War Political struggle in the early 1830s between President Jackson and financier Nicholas Biddle over the renewing of the Second Bank's charter.

Barbary pirates North Africans who waged war (1801–1805) on the United States after President Thomas Jefferson refused to pay tribute (a bribe) to protect American ships.

Bay of Pigs Failed CIA operation that, in April 1961, deployed a band of Cuban rebels to overthrow Fidel Castro's Communist regime.

Battle of the Bulge On December 16, 1944, the German army launched a counterattack against the Allied forces, which pushed them back. However, the Allies were eventually able to recover and break through the German lines. This defeat was a great blow to the Nazi's morale and their army's strength. The battle used up the last of Hitler's reserve units and opened a route into Germany's heartland.

Bear Flag Republic On June 14, 1846, a group of Americans in California captured Sonoma from the Mexican army and declared it the Republic of California whose flag featured a grizzly bear. In July, the commodore of the U.S. Pacific Fleet landed troops on California's shores and declared it part of the United States.

Beats Group of bohemian, downtown New York writers, artists, and musicians who flouted convention in favor of liberated forms of self-expression.

beatnik A name referring to almost any young rebel who openly dissented from the middle-class life. The name itself stems from the Beats.

Berlin airlift (1948) Effort by the United States and Great Britain to deliver massive amounts of food and supplies flown to West Berlin in response to the Soviet land blockade of the city.

Berlin Wall Twenty-seven-mile-long concrete wall constructed in 1961 by East German authorities to stop the flow of East Germans fleeing to West Berlin.

Bessemer converter Apparatus that blasts air through molten iron to produce steel in very large quantities.

Nicholas Biddle (1786–1844) He was the president of the second Bank of the United States. In response to President Andrew Jackson's attacks on the bank, Biddle curtailed the bank's loans and exchanged its paper currency for gold and silver. In response, state banks began printing paper without restraint and lent it to speculators, causing a binge in speculating and an enormous increase in debt.

Bill of Rights First ten amendments to the U.S. Constitution, adopted in 1791 to guarantee individual rights and to help secure ratification of the Constitution by the states.

Osama bin Laden (1957–2011) The Saudi-born leader of al Qaeda, whose members attacked America on September 11, 2001. Years before the attack, he had declared *jihad* (holy war) on the United States, Israel, and the Saudi monarchy. In Afghanistan, the Taliban leaders gave bin Laden a safe haven in exchange for aid in fighting the Northern Alliance, who were rebels opposed to the Taliban. Following the Taliban's refusal to turn over bin Laden to the United States, America and a multinational coalition invaded Afghanistan and overthrew the Taliban. In May 2011, bin Laden was shot and killed by American special forces during a covert operation in Pakistan.

birth rate Proportion of births per 1,000 of the total population.

black codes Laws passed in southern states to restrict the rights of former slaves; to combat the codes, Congress passed the Civil Rights Act of 1866 and the Fourteenth Amendment and set up military governments in southern states that refused to ratify the amendment.

black power movement Militant form of civil rights protest focused on urban communities in the North and led by Malcolm X that grew as a response to impatience with the nonviolent tactics of Martin Luther King, Jr.

James Gillepsie Blaine (1830–1893) As a Republican congressman from Maine, he developed close ties with business leaders, which contributed to him losing the presidential election of 1884. He later opposed President Cleveland's efforts to reduce tariffs, which became a significant issue in the 1888 presidential election. Blaine served as secretary of state under President Benjamin Harrison.

Bleeding Kansas (1856) A series of violent conflicts in the Kansas territory between anti-slavery and pro-slavery factions over the status of slavery.

blitzkrieg (1940) The German "lightning war" strategy characterized by swift, well-organized attacks using infantry, tanks, and warplanes.

Bolsheviks Under the leadership of Vladimir Lenin, this Marxist party led the November 1917 revolution against the newly formed provisional government in Russia. After seizing control, the Bolsheviks negotiated a peace treaty with Germany, the Treaty of Brest-Litovsk, and ended their participation in World War I.

Bonus Expeditionary Force (1932) Protest march in Washington, D.C. by thousands of World War I veterans and their families, calling for immediate payment of their service bonuses certificates; violence ensued when President Herbert Hoover ordered their tent villages cleared.

boomtown Town, often in the West, that developed rapidly due to the sudden influx of wealth and work opportunities; often male-dominated with a substantial immigrant population.

Daniel Boone (1734–1820) He found and expanded a trail into Kentucky, which pioneers used to reach and settle the area.

John Wilkes Booth (1838?–1865) He assassinated President Abraham Lincoln at the Ford's Theater on April 14, 1865. He was pursued and killed.

Boston Massacre Violent confrontation between British soldiers and a Boston mob on March 5, 1770, in which five colonists were killed.

Boston Tea Party Demonstration against the Tea Act of 1773 in which the Sons of Liberty, dressed as Indians, dumped hundreds of chests of British-owned tea into Boston Harbor.

Bourbons In post–Civil War southern politics, the opponents of the Redeemers were called Bourbons. They were known for having forgotten nothing and learned nothing from the ordeal of the Civil War.

bracero **program (1942)** System created in 1942 that permitted seasonal farm workers from Mexico to work in the United States on year-long contracts.

Joseph Brant (1742?–1807) Mohawk leader who led the Iroquois against the Americans in the Revolutionary War.

brinksmanship Secretary of State John Foster Dulles believed that communism could be contained by bringing America to the brink of war with an aggressive Communist nation. He believed that the aggressor would back down when confronted with the prospect of receiving a mass retaliation from a country with nuclear weapons.

John Brown (1800–1859) In response to a pro-slavery mob's sacking of the free-state town of Lawrence, Kansas, Brown went to the pro-slavery settlement of Pottawatomie, Kansas, which led to a guerrilla war in the Kansas territory. In 1859, he attempted to raid the federal arsenal at Harpers Ferry, hoping to use the stolen weapons to arm slaves, but he was captured and executed.

Brown v. Board of Education **(1952)** Landmark Supreme Court case that struck down racial segregation in public schools and declared "separate-but-equal" unconstitutional.

William Jennings Bryan (1860–1925) He delivered the pro-silver "cross of gold" speech at the 1896 Democratic Convention and won his party's nomination for president. Disappointed pro-gold Democrats chose to walk out of the convention and nominate their own candidate, which split the Democratic party and cost them the White House. Bryan's loss also crippled the Populist movement that had endorsed him.

"Bull Moose" Progressive party *See* Progressive party

Bull Run, Battles of (First and Second Manassas) First land engagement of the Civil War took place on July 21, 1861, at Manassas Junction, Virginia, at which surprised Union troops quickly retreated; one year later, on August 29–30, Confederates captured the federal supply depot and forced Union troops back to Washington.

Martin Van Buren (1782–1862) During President Jackson's first term, he served as secretary of state and minister to London. In 1836, Van Buren was elected president, and he inherited a financial crisis. He believed that the government should not continue to keep its deposits in state banks and set up an independent Treasury, which was approved by Congress after several years of political maneuvering.

General John Burgoyne (1722–1792) He was the commander of Britain's northern forces during the Revolutionary War. He and most of his troops surrendered to the Americans at the Battle of Saratoga.

burial mounds A funeral tradition, practiced in the Mississippi and Ohio Valleys by the Adena-Hopewell cultures, of erecting massive mounds of earth over graves, often in the designs of serpents and other animals.

burned-over district Area of western New York strongly influenced by the revivalist fervor of the Second Great Awakening; Disciples of Christ and Mormons are among the many sects that trace their roots to the phenomenon.

Aaron Burr (1756–1836) Even though he was Thomas Jefferson's vice president, he lost favor with Jefferson's Republican supporters. He sought to work with the Federalists and run as their candidate for the governor of New York. Alexander Hamilton opposed Burr's candidacy and his stinging remarks on the subject led to Burr challenging him to duel in which Hamilton was killed.

George H. W. Bush (1924–) He served as vice president during the Reagan administration and then won the presidential election of 1988. His presidency was marked by raised taxes in the face of the federal deficit, the creation of the Office of National Drug Control Policy, and military activity abroad, including the invasion of Panama and Operation Desert Storm in Kuwait. He lost the 1992 presidential election to Bill Clinton.

George W. Bush (1946–) In the 2000 presidential election, Texas governor George W. Bush won as the Republican nominee against Democratic nominee Vice President Al Gore. After the September 11 terrorist attacks, he launched his "war on terrorism." President Bush adopted the Bush Doctrine, and United States invaded Afghanistan and Iraq with unclear outcomes leaving the countries divided. In September 2008, the nation's economy nose-dived as a credit crunch spiraled into a global economic meltdown. Bush signed into law the bank bailout fund called Troubled Asset Relief Program (TARP), but the economy did not improve.

Bush v. Gore (2000) The close 2000 presidential election came down to Florida's decisive twenty-five electoral votes. The final tally in Florida gave Bush a slight lead, but it was so small that a recount was required by state law. While the votes were being recounted, a legal battle was being waged to stop the recount. Finally, the case, *Bush v. Gore*, was presented to the Supreme Court who ruled 5–4 to stop the recount and Bush was declared the winner.

Bush Doctrine National security policy launched in 2002 by which the Bush administration claimed the right to launch preemptive military attacks against perceived enemies, particularly outlaw nations or terrorist organizations believed to possess weapons of mass destruction.

buying (stock) on margin The investment practice of making a small down payment (the "margin") on a stock and borrowing the rest of the money needed for the purchase from a broker who held the stock as security against a down market. If the stock's value declined and the buyer failed to meet a margin call for more funds, the broker could sell the stock to cover his loan.

Cahokia The largest chiefdom and city of the Mississippian Indian culture located in present-day Illinois, and the site of a sophisticated farming settlement that supported up to 15,000 inhabitants.

John C. Calhoun (1782–1850) He served in both the House of Representatives and the Senate for South Carolina before becoming secretary of war under President Monroe and then John Quincy Adams's vice president. Though he started his political career as an advocate of a strong national government, he eventually believed that states' rights, limited central government, and the power of nullification were necessary to preserve the Union.

California Gold Rush (1849) A massive migration of gold hunters, mostly men, who transformed the economy of California after gold was discovered in the foothills of northern California.

Camp David Accords (1978) Peace agreement between Prime Minister Menachem Begin of Israel and President Anwar Sadat of Egypt, the first Arab head of state to officially recognize the state of Israel.

"Scarface" Al Capone (1899–1947) The most successful gangster of the Prohibition era whose Chicago-based criminal empire included bootlegging, prostitution, and gambling.

Andrew Carnegie (1835–1919) A steel magnate who believed that the general public benefited from big business even if these companies employed harsh business practices. This philosophy became deeply ingrained in the conventional wisdom of some Americans. After retiring, he devoted himself to philanthropy in hopes of promoting social welfare and world peace.

Carnegie Steel Company Corporation under the leadership of Andrew Carnegie that came to dominate the American steel industry.

Carolina colonies English proprietary colonies comprised of North and South Carolina, whose semitropical climate made them profitable centers of rice, timber, and tar production.

carpetbaggers Northern emigrants who participated in the Republican governments of the reconstructed South.

Jimmy Carter (1924–) Elected president in 1976, Jimmy Carter was an outsider to Washington. He created the departments of Energy and Education and signed into law several environmental initiatives. In 1978, he successfully brokered a peace agreement between Israel and Egypt called the Camp David Accords. However, his unwillingness to make deals with legislators caused other bills to be either gutted or stalled in Congress. His administration was plagued with a series of crises: a recession and increased inflation, a fuel shortage, the Soviet invasion of Afghanistan, and the overthrow of the Shah of Iran, leading to the Iran Hostage Crisis. Carter struggled to get the hostages released and was unable to do so until after he lost the 1980 election to Ronald Reagan. He was awarded the Nobel Peace Prize in 2002 for his efforts to further peace and democratic elections around the world.

Jacques Cartier (1491–1557) He led the first French effort to colonize North America and explored the Gulf of St. Lawrence, reaching as far as present day Montreal on the St. Lawrence River.

Fidel Castro (1926–) In 1959, his Communist regime came to power in Cuba after two years of guerrilla warfare against the dictator Fulgenico Batista. He enacted land redistribution programs and nationalized all foreign-owned property. The latter action as well as his political trials and summary executions damaged relations between Cuba and America. Castro was turned down when he asked for loans from the United States. However, he did receive aid from the Soviet Union.

Central Intelligence Agency (CIA) Intelligence-gathering government agency founded in 1947; under President Eisenhower's orders, secretly undermined elected governments deemed susceptible to communism.

Central Powers One of the two sides during the First World War, including Germany, Austria-Hungary, the Ottoman Empire (Turkey), and Bulgaria.

Carrie Chapman Catt (1859–1947) She was a leader of a new generation of activists in the women's suffrage movement who carried on the work started by Elizabeth Cady Stanton and Susan B. Anthony.

Cesar Chavez (1927–1993) He founded the United Farm Workers (UFW) in 1962 and worked to organize migrant farm workers. In 1965, the UFW joined Filipino farm workers striking against corporate grape farmers in California's San Joaquin Valley. In 1970, the strike and a consumer boycott on grapes compelled the farmers to formally recognize the UFW. As the result of Chavez's efforts, wages and working conditions improved for migrant workers. In 1975, the California state legislature passed a bill that required growers to bargain collectively with representatives of the farm workers.

child labor The practice of sending children to work in mines, mills, and factories, often in unsafe conditions; widespread among poor families in the late nineteenth century.

Chinese Exclusion Act (1882) Federal law that barred Chinese laborers from immigrating to America.

Church of Jesus Christ of Latter-day Saints / Mormons Founded in 1830 by Joseph Smith, the sect was a product of the intense revivalism of the burned-over district of New York; Smith's successor Brigham Young led 15,000 followers to Utah in 1847 to escape persecution.

Winston Churchill (1874–1965) The British prime minister who led the country during the Second World War. Along with Roosevelt and Stalin, he helped shape the post-war world at the Yalta Conference. He also coined the term "iron curtain," which he used in his famous "The Sinews of Peace" speech.

citizen-soldiers Part-time non-professional soldiers, mostly poor farmers or recent immigrants who had been indentured servants, who played an important role in the Revolutionary War.

"city machines" Local political party officials used these organizations to dispense patronage and favoritism amongst voters and businesses to ensure their loyal support to the political party.

Civil Rights Act of 1957 First federal civil rights law since Reconstruction; established the Civil Rights Commission and the Civil Rights Division of the Department of Justice.

Civil Rights Act of 1964 Legislation that outlawed discrimination in public accommodations and employment, passed at the urging of President Lyndon B. Johnson.

civil service reform An extended effort led by political reformers to end the patronage system; led to the Pendleton Act (1883), which called for government positions to be awarded based on merit rather than party loyalty.

Henry Clay (1777–1852) In the first half of the nineteenth century, he was the foremost spokesman for the American system. As Speaker of the House in the 1820s, he promoted economic nationalism, "market revolution," and the rapid development of western states and territories. A broker of compromise, he formulated the "second" Missouri Compromise and the Compromise of 1850. In 1824, Clay supported John Quincy Adams, who won the presidency and appointed Clay to secretary of state. Andrew Jackson claimed that Clay had entered into a "corrupt bargain" with Adams for his own selfish gains.

Clayton Anti-Trust Act (1914) Legislation that served to enhance the Sherman Anti-Trust Act (1890) by clarifying what constituted "monopolistic" activities and declaring that labor unions were not to be viewed as "monopolies in restraint of trade."

Bill Clinton (1946–) The governor of Arkansas won the 1992 presidential election against President George H. W. Bush. In his first term, he pushed through Congress a tax increase, an economic stimulus package, the adoption of the North America Free Trade Agreement, welfare reform, a raise in the minimum wage, and improved public access to health insurance. His administration also negotiated the Oslo Accord and the Dayton Accords. After his re-election in 1996, he was involved in two high-profile scandals: his investment in the fraudulent Whitewater Development Corporation (but no evidence was found of him being involved in any wrongdoing) and his sexual affair with a White House intern. His attempt to cover up the affair led to a vote in Congress on whether or not to begin an impeachment inquiry. The House of Representatives voted to impeach Clinton, but the Senate found him not guilty.

Hillary Rodham Clinton (1947–) In the 2008 presidential election, Senator Hillary Clinton, the spouse of former President Bill Clinton, initially was the front-runner for the Democratic nomination, which made her the first woman with a serious chance to win the presidency. However, Senator Barack Obama's Internet-based and grassroots-orientated campaign garnered him enough delegates to win the nomination. After Obama became president, she was appointed secretary of state.

clipper ships Tall, slender, mid-nineteenth-century sailing ships that were favored over older merchant ships for their speed, but ultimately gave way to steamships because they lacked cargo space.

Coercive Acts Four parliamentary measures of 1774 that required the colonies to pay for the Boston Tea Party's damages, imposed a military government, disallowed colonial trials of British soldiers, and forced the quartering of troops in private homes.

coffin ships Irish immigrants fleeing the potato famine had to endure a six-week journey across the Atlantic to reach America. During these voyages, thousands of passengers died of disease and starvation, which led to the ships being called "coffin ships."

Columbian Exchange The transfer of biological and social elements, such as plants, animals, people, diseases, and cultural practices, among Europe, the Americas, and Africa in the wake of Christopher Columbus's voyages to the "New World."

Christopher Columbus (1451–1506) The Italian sailor who persuaded King Ferdinand and Queen Isabella of Spain to fund his expedition across the Atlantic to discover a new trade route to Asia. Instead of arriving at China or Japan, he reached the Bahamas in 1492.

Committee of Correspondence Group organized by Samuel Adams in retaliation for the *Gaspée* incident to address American grievances, assert American rights, and form a network of rebellion.

Committee on Public Information During the First World War, this committee produced war propaganda that conveyed the Allies' war aims to Americans as well as attempted to weaken the enemy's morale.

Committee to Re-elect the President (CREEP) During Nixon's presidency, his administration engaged in a number of immoral acts, such as attempting to steal information and falsely accusing political appointments of sexual improprieties. These acts were funded by money illegally collected through CREEP.

Common Sense Popular pamphlet written by Thomas Paine attacking British principles of hereditary rule and monarchical government, and advocating a declaration of American independence.

Compromise of 1850 A package of five bills presented to the Congress by Henry Clay intended to avoid secession or civil war by reducing tensions between North and South over the status of slavery.

Compromise of 1877 Deal made by a special congressional commission on March 2, 1877, to resolve the disputed presidential election of 1876; Republican Rutherford B. Hayes, who had lost the popular vote, was declared the winner in exchange for the withdrawal of federal troops from the South, marking the end of Reconstruction.

Comstock Lode Mine in eastern Nevada acquired by Canadian fur trapper Henry Comstock that between 1860 and 1880 yielded almost $1 billion worth of gold and silver.

Conestoga wagons These large horse-drawn wagons were used to carry people or heavy freight long distances, including from the East to the western frontier settlements.

conquistadores Spanish term for "conquerors," applied to Spanish and Portuguese soldiers who conquered lands held by indigenous peoples in central and southern America as well as the current states of Texas, New Mexico, Arizona, and California.

consumer culture A society in which mass production and consumption of nationally advertised products comes to dictate much of social life and status.

containment U.S. cold war strategy that sought to prevent global Soviet expansion and influence through political, economic, and, if necessary, military pressure as a means of combating the spread of communism.

Continental army Army authorized by the Continental Congress, 1775–1784, to fight the British; commanded by General George Washington.

Contract with America (1994) A list of conservative promises in response to the supposed liberalism of the Clinton administration, that was drafted by Speaker of the House Newt Gingrich and other congressional Republicans as the GOP platform for the 1994 midterm elections. More a campaign tactic than a practical program, few of its proposed items ever became law.

contrabands Slaves who sought refuge in Union military camps or who lived in areas of the Confederacy under Union control.

Contras The Reagan administration ordered the CIA to train and supply guerrilla bands of anti-Communist Nicaraguans called Contras. They were fighting the Sandinista government that had recently come to power in Nicaragua. The State Department believed that the Sandinista government was supplying the leftist Salvadoran rebels with Soviet and Cuban arms. A cease-fire agreement between the Contras and Sandinistas was signed in 1988.

Calvin Coolidge (1872–1933) After President Harding's death, his vice president, Calvin Coolidge, assumed the presidency. Coolidge believed that the nation's welfare was tied to the success of Big Business, and he worked to end government regulation of business and industry as well as reduce taxes. In particular, he focused on the nation's industrial development.

Copperhead Democrats Democrats in northern states who opposed the Civil War and argued for an immediate peace settlement with the Confederates; Republicans labeled them "Copperheads," likening them to venomous snakes.

Hernán Cortés (1485–1547) The Spanish conquistador who conquered the Aztec Empire and set the precedent for other plundering conquistadores.

General Charles Cornwallis (1738–1805) He was in charge of British troops in the South during the Revolutionary War. His surrender to George Washington at the Battle of Yorktown ended the Revolutionary War.

Corps of Discovery Meriwether Lewis and William Clark led this group of men on an expedition of the newly purchased Louisiana territory, which took them from Missouri to Oregon. As they traveled, they kept detailed journals and drew maps of the previously unexplored territory. Their reports attracted traders and trappers to the region and gave the United States a claim to the Oregon country by right of discovery and exploration.

"corrupt bargain" Scandal in which presidential candidate and Speaker of the House Henry Clay secured John Quincy Adams's victory over Andrew Jackson in the 1824 election, supposedly in exchange for Clay being named secretary of state.

cotton gin Hand-operated machine invented by Eli Whitney in the late eighteenth century that quickly removed seeds from cotton bolls, enabling the mass production of cotton in nineteenth-century America.

cotton kingdom Cotton-producing region, relying predominantly on slave labor, that spanned from North Carolina west to Louisiana and reached as far north as southern Illinois.

cotton White fibers harvested from cotton plants, spun into yarn, and woven into textiles that made comfortable, easy-to-clean products, especially clothing; the most valuable cash crop driving the economy in the United States and Great Britain during the nineteenth century.

the counterculture "Hippie" youth culture of the 1960s, which rejected the values of the dominant culture in favor of illicit drugs, communes, free sex, and rock music.

counterculture Unorganized youth rebellion against mainstream institutions, values, and behavior that more often focused on cultural rather than political activism.

court-packing plan President Franklin D. Roosevelt's failed 1937 attempt to increase the number of U.S. Supreme Court justices from nine to fifteen in order to save his Second New Deal programs from constitutional challenges.

covenant theory A Puritan concept that believed true Christians could enter a voluntary union for the common worship of God. Taking the idea one step further, the union could also be used for the purposes of establishing governments.

crop-lien system Credit system used by sharecroppers and share tenants who pledged a portion ("share") of their future crop to local merchants or land owners in exchange for farming supplies and food.

"Cross of Gold" Speech In the 1896 election, the Democratic Party split over the issue of whether to use gold or silver to back American currency. Significant to this division was the pro-silver "Cross of Gold" speech that William Jennings Bryan delivered at the Democratic convention, which was so well received that Bryan won the nomination to be their presidential candidate. Disappointed pro-gold Democrats chose to walk out of the convention and nominate their own candidate.

Cuban missile crisis Thirteen-day U.S.-Soviet standoff in October 1962, sparked by the discovery of Soviet missile sites in Cuba; the crisis was the closest the world has come to nuclear war since 1945.

cult of domesticity A pervasive nineteenth-century ideology that urged women to celebrate their role as manager of the household and nurturer of the children.

George A. Custer (1839–1876) He was a reckless and glory-seeking Lieutenant Colonel of the U.S. Army who fought the Sioux Indians in the Great Sioux War. In 1876, he and his detachment of soldiers were entirely wiped out in the Battle of Little Bighorn.

***Dartmouth College v. Woodward* (1819)** Supreme Court ruling that enlarged the definition of *contract* to put corporations beyond the reach of the states that chartered them.

Daughters of Liberty Colonial women who protested the British government's tax policies by boycotting British products, such as clothing, and who wove their own fabric, or "homespun."

Dawes Severalty Act of 1887 Federal legislation that divided ancestral Native American lands among the heads of each Indian family in an attempt to "Americanize" Indians by forcing them to become farmers working individual plots of land.

D-day June 6, 1944, when an Allied amphibious assault landed on the Normandy coast and established a foothold in Europe from which Hitler's defenses could not recover.

Jefferson Davis (1808–1889) He was the president of the Confederacy during the Civil War. When the Confederacy's defeat seemed invitable in early 1865, he refused to surrender. Union forces captured him in May of that year.

Bartolomé de Las Casas (1484–1566) A Catholic missionary who renounced the Spanish practice of coercively converting Indians and advocated their better treatment. In 1552, he wrote *A Brief Relation of the Destruction of the Indies*, which described the Spanish's cruel treatment of the Indians.

death rate Proportion of deaths per 1,000 of the total population; also called *mortality rate.*

Eugene V. Debs (1855–1926) Founder of the American Railway Union, which he organized against the Pullman Palace Car Company during the Pullman strike. Later he organized the Social Democratic party, which eventually became the Socialist Party of America. In the 1912 presidential election, he ran as the Socialist party's candidate and received more than 900,000 votes.

Declaration of Independence Formal statement, principally drafted by Thomas Jefferson and adopted by the Second Continental Congress on July 4, 1776, that officially announced the thirteen colonies' break with Great Britain.

Declaration of Sentiments Document based on the Declaration of Independence that called for gender equality, written primarily by Elizabeth Cady Stanton and signed by Seneca Falls Convention delegates in 1848.

Declaratory Act Following the repeal of the Stamp Act in 1766, Parliament passed this act which asserted Parliament's full power to make laws binding the colonies "in all cases whatsoever."

Deism Enlightenment thought applied to religion, emphasizing reason, morality, and natural law rather than scriptural authority or an ever-present God intervening in human life.

détente Period of improving relations between the United States and Communist nations, particularly China and the Soviet Union, during the Nixon administration.

George Dewey (1837–1917) On April 30, 1898, Commodore George Dewey's small U.S. naval squadron defeated the Spanish warships in Manila Bay in the Philippines. This quick victory aroused expansionist fever in the United States.

John Dewey (1859–1952) He is an important philosopher of pragmatism. However, he preferred to use the term *instrumentalism*, because he saw ideas as instruments of action.

Ngo Dinh Diem (1901–1963) Following the Geneva Accords, the French, with the support of America, forced the Vietnamese emperor to accept Dinh Diem as the new premier of South Vietnam. President Eisenhower sent advisors to train Diem's police and army. In return, the United States expected Diem to enact democratic reforms and distribute land to the peasants. Instead, he suppressed his political opponents, did little or no land distribution, and let corruption grow. In 1956, he refused to participate in elections to reunify Vietnam. Eventually, he ousted the emperor and declared himself president.

Distribution Act (1836) Law requiring the distribution of the federal budget surplus to the states, creating chaos among state banks that had become dependent on such federal funds.

Dorothea Lynde Dix (1802–1887) She was an important figure in increasing the public's awareness of the plight of the mentally ill. After a two-year investigation of the treatment of the mentally ill in Massachusetts, she presented her findings and won the support of leading reformers. She eventually convinced twenty states to reform their treatment of the mentally ill.

Dixiecrats Breakaway faction of southern Democrats who defected from the national Democratic party in 1948 to protest the party's increased support for civil rights and to nominate their own segregationist candidates for elective office.

"dollar diplomacy" practice advocated by President Theodore Roosevelt in which the U.S. government fostered American investments in less developed nations and then used U.S. military force to protect those investments

Donner party Forty-seven surviving members of a group of migrants to California were forced to resort to cannibalism to survive a brutal winter trapped in the Sierra Nevadas, 1846–1847; highest death toll of any group traveling the Overland Trail.

Stephen A. Douglas (1812–1861) As a senator from Illinois, he authored the Kansas-Nebraska Act. Running for senatorial reelection in 1858, he engaged Abraham Lincoln in a series of public debates about slavery in the territories. Even though Douglas won the election, the debates gave Lincoln a national reputation.

Frederick Douglass (1818–1895) He escaped from slavery and become an eloquent speaker and writer against the institution. In 1845, he published his autobiography entitled *Narrative of the Life of Frederick Douglass* and two years later he founded an abolitionist newspaper for blacks called the *North Star*.

dot-coms In the late 1990s, the stock market soared to new heights and defied the predictions of experts that the economy could not sustain such a performance. Much of the economic success was based on dot-com enterprises, which were firms specializing in computers, software, telecommunications, and the internet. However, many of the companies' stock market values were driven higher and higher by speculation instead of financial success. Eventually the stock market bubble burst.

Dred Scott v. Sandford **(1857)** U.S. Supreme Court ruling that slaves were not U.S. citizens and therefore could not sue for their freedom and that Congress could not prohibit slavery in the western territories.

W. E. B. Du Bois (1868–1963) He criticized Booker T. Washington's views on civil rights as being accommodationist. He advocated "ceaseless agitation" for civil rights and the immediate end to segregation and an enforcement of laws to protect civil rights and equality. He promoted an education for African Americans that would nurture bold leaders who were willing to challenge discrimination in politics.

John Foster Dulles (1888–1959) As President Eisenhower's secretary of state, he institutionalized the policy of containment and introduced the strategy of deterrence. He believed in using brinkmanship to halt the spread of communism. He attempted to employ it in Indochina, which led to the United States' involvement in Vietnam.

Dust Bowl Vast area of the Midwest where windstorms blew away millions of tons of topsoil from parched farmland after a long drought in the 1930s, causing great social distress and a massive migration of farm families.

Eastern Woodlands Peoples Various Native American peoples, particularly the Algonquian, Iroquoian, and Muskogean regional groups, who once dominated the Atlantic seaboard from Maine to Louisiana.

Peggy Eaton (1796–1879) The wife of John Eaton, President Jackson's secretary of war, was the daughter of a tavern owner with an unsavory past. Supposedly her first husband had committed suicide after learning that she was having an affair with John Eaton. The wives of members of Jackson's cabinet snubbed her because of her lowly origins and past, resulting in a scandal known as the Eaton Affair.

Economic Opportunity Act Key legislation in President Johnson's "War on Poverty" which created the Office of Economic Opportunity and programs like Head Start and work-study.

Jonathan Edwards (1703–1758) New England Congregationalist minister who began a religious revival in his Northampton church and was an important figure in the Great Awakening.

election of 1800 Presidential election between Thomas Jefferson and John Adams; resulted in the first Democratic-Republican victory after the Federalist administrations of George Washington and John Adams.

1864 Election Abraham Lincoln's successful re-election campaign, capitalizing on Union military successes in Georgia, to defeat Democratic opponent, former general George B. McClellan, who ran on a peace platform.

election of 1912 The presidential election of 1912 featured four candidates: Wilson, Taft, Roosevelt, and Debs. Each candidate believed in the basic assumptions of progressive politics, but each had a different view on how progressive ideals should be implemented through policy. In the end, Taft and Roosevelt split the Republican party votes and Wilson emerged as the winner.

Queen Elizabeth I of England (1533–1603) The protestant daughter of Henry VIII, she was Queen of England from 1558–1603 and played a major role in the Protestant Reformation. During her long reign, the doctrines and services of the Church of England were defined and the Spanish Armada was defeated.

General Dwight D. Eisenhower (1890–1969) During the Second World War, he commanded the Allied Forces landing in Africa and was the supreme Allied commander as well as planner for Operation Overlord. In 1952, he was elected president on his popularity as a war hero and his promises to clean up Washington. His administration sought to cut the nation's domestic programs and budget, ended the fighting in Korea, and institutionalized the policies of containment and deterrence. He established the Eisenhower doctrine, which promised to aid any nation against aggression by a Communist nation.

Ellis Island Reception center in New York Harbor through which most European immigrants to America were processed from 1892 to 1954.

Emancipation Proclamation (1863) Military order issued by President Abraham Lincoln that freed slaves in areas still controlled by the Confederacy

Embargo Act (1807) A law promoted by President Thomas Jefferson prohibiting American ships from leaving for foreign ports, in order to safeguard them from British and French attacks. This ban on American exports proved disastrous to the U.S. economy.

Ralph Waldo Emerson (1803–1882) As a leader of the transcendentalist movement, he wrote poems, essays, and speeches that discussed the sacredness of nature, optimism, self-reliance, and the unlimited potential of the individual. He wanted to transcend the limitations of inherited conventions and rationalism to reach the inner recesses of the self.

encomienda A land-grant system under which Spanish army officers (*conquistadores*) were awarded large parcels of land taken from Native Americans.

Enlightenment A revolution in thought begun in Europe in the seventeenth century that emphasized reason and science over the authority and myths of traditional religion.

enumerated goods According to the Navigation Act, these particular goods, like tobacco or cotton, could only be shipped to England or other English colonies.

Environmental Protection Agency (EPA) (1970) Federal environmental agency created by Nixon to appease the demands of congressional Democrats for a federal environmental watchdog agency.

Erie Canal Most important and profitable of the barge canals of the 1820s and 1830s; stretched from Buffalo to Albany, New York, connecting the Great Lakes to the East Coast and making New York City the nation's largest port.

ethnic cleansing The systematic removal of an ethnic group from a territory through violence or intimidation in order to create a homogenous society; the term was popularized by the Yugoslav policy brutally targeting Albanian Muslims in Kosovo.

exodusters African Americans who migrated west from the South in search of a haven from racism and poverty after the collapse of Radical Republican rule.

The Fair Deal (1949) President Truman's proposals to build upon the New Deal with national health insurance, the repeal of the Taft-Hartley Act, new civil rights legislation, and other initiatives; most were rejected by the Republican-controlled Congress.

Fair Employment Practices Commission Created in 1941 by executive order, the FEPC sought to eliminate racial discrimination in jobs; it possessed little power but represented a step toward civil rights for African Americans.

falling domino theory Theory that if one country fell to communism, its neighboring countries would follow suit.

Farmers' Alliances Like the Granger Movement, these organizations sought to address the issues of small farming communities; however Alliances emphasized more political action and called for the creation of a Third Party to advocate their concerns.

fascism A radical form of totalitarian government that emerged in Italy and Germany in the 1920s in which a dictator uses propaganda and brute force to seize control of all aspects of national life.

field hands Slaves who toiled in the cotton or cane fields in organized work gangs.

Federal-Aid Highway Act (1956) Largest federal project in U.S. history that created a national network of interstate highways and was the largest federal project in history.

Federal Deposit Insurance Corporation (1933) Independent government agency, established to prevent bank panics, that guarantees the safety of deposits in citizens' savings accounts.

Federal Reserve Act (1913) Legislation passed by Congress to create a new national banking system in order to regulate the nation's currency supply and ensure the stability and integrity of member banks who made up the Federal Reserve System across the nation.

Federal Trade Commission (1914) Independent agency created by the Wilson administration that replaced the Bureau of Corporations as an even more powerful tool to combat unfair trade practices and monopolies.

Federal Writers' Project During the Great Depression, this project provided writers, such as Ralph Ellison, Richard Wright, and Saul Bellow, with work, which gave them employment and a chance to develop as artists.

federalism Concept of dividing governmental authority between the national government and the states.

The Federalist Papers Collection of eighty-five essays, published widely in newspapers in 1787 and 1788, written by Alexander Hamilton, James Madison, and John Jay in support of adopting the proposed U.S. Constitution.

Federalists Proponents of a centralized federal system and the ratification of the Constitution. Most Federalists were relatively young, educated men who supported a broad interpretation of the Constitution whenever national interest dictated such flexibility. Notable Federalists included Alexander Hamilton and John Jay.

Geraldine Ferraro (1935–) In the 1984 presidential election, Democratic nominee, Walter Mondale, chose her as his running mate. As a member of the U.S. House of Representatives from New York, she was the first woman to be a vice-presidential nominee for a major political party. However, she was placed on the defensive because of her husband's complicated business dealings.

Fifteenth Amendment This amendment forbids states to deny any person the right to vote on grounds of "race, color or pervious condition of servitude." Former Confederate states were required to ratify this amendment before they could be readmitted to the Union.

"final solution" The Nazi party's systematic murder of some 6 million Jews along with more than a million other people including, but not limited to, gypsies, homosexuals, and handicap individuals.

First New Deal (1933–1935) Franklin D. Roosevelt's ambitious first-term cluster of economic and social programs designed to combat the Great Depression.

First Red Scare Outbreak of anti-Communist hysteria that included the arrest without warrants of thousands of suspected radicals, most of whom (mainly Russian immigrants) were deported.

flappers Young women of the 1920s whose rebellion against prewar standards of femininity included wearing shorter dresses, bobbing their hair, dancing to jazz music, driving cars, smoking cigarettes, and indulging in illegal drinking and gambling.

Food Administration After America's entry into World War I, the economy of the home front needed to be reorganized to provide the most efficient means of conducting the war. The Food Administration was a part of this effort. Under the leadership of Herbert Hoover, the organization sought to increase agricultural production while reducing civilian consumption of foodstuffs.

The "Force Bill" (1833) Legislation, sparked by the Nullification Crisis in South Carolina, that authorized the president's use of the army to compel states to comply with federal law.

Gerald Ford (1913–2006) He was appointed to the vice presidency under President Nixon after the resignation of Spiro Agnew, and assumed the presidency after President Nixon's resignation. He resisted congressional pressure to both reduce taxes and increase federal spending, which sent the American economy into the deepest recession since the Great Depression. Ford retained Kissinger as his secretary of state and continued Nixon's foreign policy goals. He was heavily criticized following the collapse of South Vietnam.

Fort Laramie Treaty (1851) Restricted the Plains Indians from using the Overland Trail and permitted the building of government forts.

Fort Necessity After attacking a group of French soldiers, George Washington constructed and took shelter in this fort from vengeful French troops. Washington eventually surrendered to them after a day-long battle. This conflict was a significant event in igniting the French and Indian War.

Fort Sumter First battle of the Civil War, in which the federal fort in Charleston (South Carolina) Harbor was captured by the Confederates on April 14, 1861, after two days of shelling.

"forty-niners" Speculators who went to northern California following the discovery of gold in 1848; the first of several years of large-scale migration was 1849.

Fourteen Points President Woodrow Wilson's proposed plan for the peace agreement after the First World War that included the creation of a "league of nations" intended to keep the peace.

Fourteenth Amendment (1868) Guaranteed rights of citizenship to former slaves, in words similar to those of the Civil Rights Act of 1866.

alliance with France Critical diplomatic, military, and economic alliance between France and the newly independent United States, codified by the Treaty of Amity and Commerce and the Treaty of Alliance (1778).

Franciscan Missions In 1769, Franciscan missioners accompanied Spanish soldiers to California and over the next fifty years established a chain of missions from San Diego to San Francisco. At these missions, friars sought to convert Indians to Catholicism and make them members of the Spanish empire. The friars stripped the Indians of their native heritage and used soldiers to enforce their will.

Benjamin Franklin (1706–1790) A Boston-born American, who epitomized the Enlightenment for many Americans and Europeans, Franklin's wide range of interests led him to become a publisher, inventor, and statesman. As the latter, he contributed to the writing of the Declaration of Independence, served as the minister to France during the Revolutionary War, and was a delegate to the Constitutional Convention.

Free-Soil Party A political coalition created in 1848 that opposed the expansion of slavery into the new western territories.

Freedmen's Bureau Reconstruction agency established in 1865 to protect the legal rights of former slaves and to assist with their education, jobs, health care, and landowning.

Freedom Riders Activists who, beginning in 1961, traveled by bus through the South to test federal court rulings that banned segregation on buses and trains.

John C. Frémont "the Pathfinder" (1813–1890) He was an explorer and surveyor who helped inspire Americans living in California to rebel against the Mexican government and declare independence.

French and Indian War (Seven Years' War) The last—and most important—of four colonial wars fought between England and France for control of North America east of the Mississippi River.

French Revolution Revolutionary movement beginning in 1789 that overthrew the monarchy and transformed France into an unstable republic before Napoleon Bonaparte assumed power in 1799.

Sigmund Freud (1865–1939) He was the founder of psychoanalysis, which suggested that human behavior was motivated by unconscious and irrational forces. By the 1920s, his ideas were being discussed more openly in America.

frontier revivals Religious revival movement within the Second Great Awakening, that took place in frontier churches in western territories and states in the early nineteenth century.

Fugitive Slave Act (1850) Part of the Compromise of 1850, a provision that authorized federal officials to help capture and then return escaped slaves to their owners without trials.

fundamentalism Anti-modernist Protestant movement started in the early twentieth century that proclaimed the literal truth of the Bible; the name came from *The Fundamentals*, published by conservative leaders.

William Lloyd Garrison (1805–1879) In 1831, he started the anti-slavery newspaper *Liberator* and helped start the New England Anti-Slavery Society. Two years later, he assisted Arthur and Lewis Tappan in the founding of the American Anti-Slavery Society. He and his followers believed that America had been thoroughly corrupted and needed a wide range of reforms, embracing abolition, temperance, pacifism, and women's rights.

Marcus Garvey (1887–1940) He was the leading spokesman for Negro Nationalism, which exalted blackness, black cultural expression, and black exclusiveness. He called upon African Americans to liberate themselves from the surrounding white culture and create their own businesses, cultural centers, and newspapers. He was also the founder of the Universal Negro Improvement Association.

Citizen Genet (1763–1834) As the ambassador to the United States from the new French Republic, he engaged American privateers to attack British ships and conspired with frontiersmen and land speculators to organize an attack on Spanish Florida and Louisiana. His actions and the French radicals excessive actions against their enemies in the new French Republic caused the French Revolution to lose support among Americans.

Geneva Accords In 1954, the Geneva Accords were signed, which ended French colonial rule in Indochina. The agreement created the independent nations of Laos and Cambodia and divided Vietnam along the 17th parallel until an election in 1956 would reunify the country.

Battle of Gettysburg (1863) A monumental three-day battle in southern Pennsylvania, widely considered a turning point in the war, in which Union forces successfully countered a second Confederate invasion of the North.

Ghost Dance movement A spiritual and political movement among Native Americans whose followers performed a ceremonial "ghost dance" intended to connect the living with the dead and make the Indians bulletproof in battles to restore their homelands.

GI Bill of Rights (1944) Provided unemployment, education, and financial benefits for World War II veterans to ease their transition back to the civilian world.

***Gibbons v. Ogden* (1824)** Supreme Court case that gave the federal government the power to regulate interstate commerce.

Newt Gingrich (1943–) He led the Republican insurgency in Congress in the mid 1990s through mobilizing religious and social conservatives. Along with other Republican congressmen, he created the Contract with America, which was a ten-point anti-big government program. However, the program fizzled out after many of its bills were not passed by Congress.

Gilded Age (1860–1896): An era of dramatic industrial and urban growth characterized by widespread political corruption and loose government oversight of corporations.

The Gilded Age Mark Twain and Charles Dudley Warner's 1873 novel, the title of which became the popular name for the period from the end of the Civil War to the turn of the century.

glasnost Russian term for "openness"; applied to the loosening of censorship in the Soviet Union under Mikhail Gorbachev.

globalization An important, and controversial, transformation of the world economy whereby the Internet helped revolutionize global commerce by creating an international marketplace for goods and services. Led by the growing number of multinational companies and the Americanization of many foreign consumer cultures, with companies like McDonald's and Starbucks appearing in all of the major cities of the world.

Glorious Revolution Successful 1688 coup, instigated by a group of English aristocrats, which overthrew King James II and instated William of Orange and Mary, his English wife, to the British throne.

Barry Goldwater (1909–1998) A leader of the Republican right whose book, *The Conscience of a Conservative*, was highly influential to that segment of the party. He proposed eliminating the income tax and overhauling Social Security. In 1964, he ran as the Republican presidential candidate and lost to President Johnson. He campaigned against Johnson's war on poverty, the tradition of New Deal, the nuclear test ban and the Civil Rights Act of 1964 and advocated the wholesale bombing of North Vietnam.

Samuel Gompers (1850–1924) He served as the president of the American Federation of Labor from its inception until his death. He focused on achieving concrete economic gains such as higher wages, shorter hours, and better working conditions.

"good neighbor" policy Proclaimed by President Franklin D. Roosevelt in his first inaugural address in 1933, it sought improved diplomatic relations between the United States and its Latin American neighbors.

Mikhail Gorbachev (1931–) In the late 1980s, Soviet leader Mikhail Gorbachev attempted to reform the Soviet Union through his programs of *perestroika* and *glasnost* and pursued a renewal of détente with America, signing new arms-control agreements with President Reagan. Gorbachev allowed the velvet revolutions of Eastern Europe to occur without outside interference. Eventually the political, social, and economic upheaval he had unleashed would lead to the break-up of the Soviet Union.

Albert Gore Jr. (1948–) He served as a senator of Tennessee and then as President Clinton's vice president. In the 2000 presidential election, he was the Democratic candidate against Governor George W. Bush. The close election came down to Florida's electoral votes. While the votes were being recounted as required by state law, a legal battle was being waged to stop the recount. Finally, the case, *Bush v. Gore*, was presented to the Supreme Court who ruled 5–4 to stop the recount and Bush was declared the winner.

Jay Gould (1836–1892) As one of the biggest railroad robber barons, he was infamous for buying rundown railroads, making cosmetic improvements and then reselling them for a profit. He used corporate funds for personal investments and to bribe politicians and judges.

gradualism This strategy for ending slavery involved promoting the banning of slavery in the new western territories and encouraging the release of slaves from slavery. Supporters of this method believed that it would bring about the gradual end of slavery.

Granger Movement Began by offering social and educational activities for isolated farmers and their families and later started to promote "cooperatives" where farmers could join together to buy, store, and sell their crops to avoid the high fees charged by brokers and other middle-men.

Ulysses S. Grant (1822–1885) After distinguishing himself in the western theater of the Civil War, he was appointed general in chief of the Union army in 1864. Afterward, he defeated General Robert E. Lee through a policy of aggressive attrition. Lee surrendered to Grant on April 9th, 1865 at the Appomattox Court House. His presidential tenure suffered from scandals and fiscal problems, including the debate on whether or not greenbacks, paper money, should be removed from circulation.

Great Awakening Fervent religious revival movement that swept the thirteen colonies from the 1720s through the 1740s.

Great Compromise (Connecticut Compromise) Mediated the differences between the New Jersey and Virginia delegations to the Constitutional Convention by providing for a bicameral legislature, the upper house of which would have equal representation and the lower house of which would be apportioned by population.

Great Depression (1929–1941) Worst economic downturn in American history; it was spurred by the stock market crash in the fall of 1929 and lasted until the Second World War.

Great Migration Mass exodus of African Americans from the rural South to the Northeast and Midwest during and after the First World War.

Great Railroad Strike of 1877 A series of demonstrations, some violent, held nationwide in support of striking railroad workers in Martinsburg, West Virginia, who refused to work due to wage cuts.

Great Recession (2007–2009) Massive, prolonged economic downturn sparked by the collapse of the housing market and the financial institutions holding unpaid mortgages; it lasted from December 2007 to January 2009 and resulted in 9 million Americans losing their jobs.

Great Sioux War Conflict between Sioux and Cheyenne Indians and federal troops over lands in the Dakotas in the mid-1870s.

Great Society Term coined by President Lyndon B. Johnson in his 1965 State of the Union address, in which he proposed legislation to address problems of voting rights, poverty, diseases, education, immigration, and the environment.

Horace Greeley (1811–1872) In reaction to Radical Reconstruction and corruption in President Ulysses S. Grant's administration, a group of Republicans broke from the party to form the Liberal Republicans. In 1872, the Liberal Republicans chose Horace Greeley as their presidential candidate who ran on a platform of favoring civil service reform and condemning the Republican's Reconstruction policy.

greenbacks Paper money issued during the Civil War. After the war ended, a debate emerged on whether or not to remove the paper currency from circulation and revert back to hard-money currency (gold coins). Opponents of hard-money feared that eliminating the greenbacks would shrink the money supply, which would lower crop prices and make it more difficult to repay long-term debts. President Ulysses S. Grant, as well as hard-currency advocates, believed that gold coins were morally preferable to paper currency.

Greenback party Formed in 1876 in reaction to economic depression, the party favored issuance of unsecured paper money to help farmers repay debts; the movement for free coinage of silver took the place of the greenback movement by the 1880s.

General Nathanael Greene (1742–1786) He was appointed by Congress to command the American army fighting in the South during the Revolutionary War. Using his patience and his skills of managing men, saving supplies, and avoiding needless risks, he waged a successful war of attrition against the British.

Sarah Grimké (1792–1873) and **Angelina Grimké (1805–1879)** These two sisters gave anti-slavery speeches to crowds of mixed gender that caused some people to condemn them for engaging in unfeminine activities. In 1840, William Lloyd Garrison convinced the Anti-Slavery Society to allow women equal participation in the organization.

Half-Way Covenant Allowed baptized children of church members to be admitted to a "halfway" membership in the church and secure baptism for their own children in turn, but allowed them neither a vote in the church, nor communion.

Alexander Hamilton (1755–1804) His belief in a strong federal government led him to become a leader of the Federalists. As the first secretary of the Treasury, he laid the foundation for American capitalism through his creation of a federal budget, funded debt, a federal tax system, a national bank, a customs service, and a coast guard. His "Reports on Public Credit" and "Reports on Manufactures" outlined his vision for economic development and government finances. He died in a duel against Aaron Burr.

Alexander Hamilton's economic reforms Various measures designed to strengthen the nation's economy and generate federal revenue through the promotion of new industries, the adoption of new tax policies, the payment of war debts, and the establishment of a national bank.

Warren G. Harding (1865–1923) In the 1920 presidential election, he was the Republican nominee who promised Americans a "return to normalcy." Once in office, Harding's administration dismantled many of the social and economic components of progressivism and pursued a pro-business agenda. Harding appointed four pro-business Supreme Court Justices, cut taxes, increased tariffs, and promoted a lenient attitude towards regulation of corporations. However, he did speak out against racism and ended the exclusion of African Americans from federal positions.

Harlem Renaissance The nation's first self-conscious black literary and artistic movement; it was centered in New York City's Harlem district, which had a largely black population in the wake of the Great Migration from the South.

Hartford Convention A series of secret meetings in December 1814 and January 1815 at which New England Federalists protested American involvement in the War of 1812 and discussed several constitutional amendments, including limiting each president to one term, designed to weaken the dominant Republican Party.

Haymarket Riot (1886) Violent uprising in Haymarket Square, Chicago, where police clashed with labor demonstrators in the aftermath of a bombing.

headright A land-grant policy that promised fifty acres to any colonist who could afford passage to Virginia, as well as fifty more for any accompanying servants. The headright policy was eventually expanded to include any colonists—and was also adopted in other colonies.

Patrick Henry (1736–1799) He inspired the Virginia Resolves, which declared that Englishmen could only be taxed by their elected representatives. In March of 1775, he met with other colonial leaders to discuss the goals of the upcoming

Continental Congress and famously declared "Give me liberty or give me death." During the ratification process of the U.S. Constitution, he became one of the leaders of the anti-federalists.

Hiroshima (1945) Japanese port city that was the first target of the newly developed atomic bomb on August 6, 1945. Most of the city was destroyed.

Alger Hiss (1904–1996) During the second Red Scare he had served in several government departments and was accused of being a spy for the Soviet Union and was convicted of lying about espionage. The case was politically damaging to the Truman administration because the president called the charges against Hiss a "red herring."

Adolph Hitler (1889–1945) The leader of the Nazis who advocated a violent anti-Semitic, anti-Marxist, pan-German ideology. He started World War II in Europe and orchestrated the systematic murder of some 6 million Jews along with more than a million others.

HIV/AIDS Human immunodeficiency virus (HIV) transmitted via the bodily fluids of infected persons to cause acquired immunodeficiency syndrome (AIDS), an often-fatal disease of the immune system when it appeared in the 1980s.

holding company A corporation established to own and manage other companies' stock rather than to produce goods and services itself.

Holocaust Systematic racist attempt by the Nazis to exterminate the Jews of Europe, resulting in the murder of over 6 million Jews and more than a million other "undesirables."

Homestead Act (1862) Legislation granting "homesteads" of 160 acres of government-owned land to settlers who agreed to work the land for at least five years.

Homestead steel strike (1892) Labor conflict at the Homestead steel mill near Pittsburgh, Pennsylvania, culminating in a battle between strikers and private security agents hired by the factory's management.

Herbert Hoover (1874–1964) Prior to becoming president, Hoover served as the secretary of commerce in both the Harding and Coolidge administrations. As president during the Great Depression, he believed that the nation's business structure was sound and sought to revive the economy through boosting the nation's confidence. He also tried to restart the economy with government constructions projects, lower taxes and new federal loan programs, but nothing worked.

horizontal integration The process by which a corporation acquires or merges with its competitors.

horse A tall, four-legged mammal (*Equus caballus*), domesticated and bred since prehistoric times for carrying riders and pulling heavy loads. The Spanish introduced horses to the Americas, eventually transforming many Native American cultures.

House Committee on Un-American Activities (HUAC) Committee of the U.S. House of Representatives formed in 1938; it was originally tasked with investigating Nazi subversion during the Second World War and later shifted its focus to rooting out Communists in the government and the motion-picture industry.

Sam Houston (1793–1863) During Texas's fight for independence from Mexico, Sam Houston was the commander in chief of the Texas forces, and he led the attack that captured General Antonio López de Santa Anna. After Texas gained its independence, he was named its first president.

Jacob Riis' *How the Other Half Lives* Jacob Riis was an early muckraking journalist who exposed the slum conditions in New York City in his book *How the Other Half Lives*.

General William Howe (1729–1814) As the commander of the British army in the Revolutionary War, he seized New York City from Washington's army, but failed to capture it. He missed several more opportunities to quickly end the rebellion, and he resigned his command after the British defeat at Saratoga.

Saddam Hussein (1937–2006) The former dictator of Iraq who became the head of state in 1979. In 1980, he invaded Iran and started the eight-year-long Iran-Iraq War. In 1990, he invaded Kuwait, which caused the Gulf War of 1991. In 2003, he was overthrown and captured when the United States invaded. He was sentenced to death by hanging in 2006.

Anne Hutchinson (1591–1643) The articulate, strong-willed, and intelligent wife of a prominent Boston merchant, who espoused her belief in direct divine revelation. She quarreled with Puritan leaders over her beliefs; and they banished her from the colony.

Immigration Act of 1924 Federal legislation intended to favor northern and western European immigrants over those from southern and eastern Europe by restricting the number of immigrants from any one European country to 2 percent of the total number of immigrants per year, with an overall limit of slightly over 150,000 new arrivals per year.

Immigration and Nationality Services Act of 1965 Legislation that abolished discriminatory quotas based upon immigrants' national origin and treated all nationalities and races equally.

imperialism The use of diplomatic or military force to extend a nation's power and enhance its economic interests, often by acquiring territory or colonies and justifying such behavior with assumptions of racial superiority.

impressment The British navy used press-gangs to kidnap men in British and colonial ports who were then forced to serve in the British navy.

indentured servitude A defined period of labor (often four to seven years) which settlers consented to in exchange for having their passage to the New World paid by their "master."

Independent Treasury Act (1840) System created by President Martin Van Buren and approved by Congress in 1840 whereby the federal government moved its funds from favored state banks to the U.S. Treasury, whose financial transactions could only be in gold or silver coins of paper currency backed by gold or silver.

"Indian New Deal" This phrase refers to the reforms implemented for Native Americans during the New Deal era. John Collier, the commissioner of the Bureau of Indian Affairs (BIA), increased the access Native Americans had to relief programs and employed more Native Americans at the BIA. He worked to pass the Indian Reorganization Act. However, the version of the act passed by Congress was a much-diluted version of Collier's original proposal and did not greatly improve the lives of Native Americans.

Indian Removal Act (1830) Law permitting the forced relocation of Indians to federal lands west of the Mississippi River in exchange for the land they occupied in the East and South.

Indian wars Bloody conflicts between U.S. soldiers and Native Americans that raged in the West from the early 1860s to the late 1870s, sparked by American settlers moving into ancestral Indian lands.

Indochina This area of Southeast Asia consists of Laos, Cambodia, and Vietnam and was once controlled by France as a colony. After the Viet Minh defeated the French, the Geneva Accords were signed, which ended French colonial rule. The agreement created the independent nations of Laos and Cambodia and divided Vietnam along the 17th parallel until an election would reunify the country. Fearing a Communist take over, the United States government began intervening in the region during the Truman administration, which led to President Johnson's full-scale military involvement in Vietnam.

Industrial Revolution Major shift in the nineteenth century from hand-made manufacturing to mass production in mills and factories using water-, coal-, and steam-powered machinery.

industrial war A new concept of war enabled by industrialization that developed from the early 1800s through the Atomic Age. New technologies, including automatic weaponry, forms of transportation like the railroad and airplane, and communication technologies such as the telegraph and telephone, enabled nations to equip large, mass-conscripted armies with chemical and automatic weapons to decimate opposing armies in a "total war."

Industrial Workers of the World (IWW) A radical union organized in Chicago in 1905, nicknamed the Wobblies; its opposition to World War I led to its destruction by the federal government under the Espionage Act.

infectious diseases Also called contagious diseases, illnesses that can pass from one person to another by way of invasive biological organisms able to reproduce in the bodily tissues of their hosts. Europeans unwittingly brought many such diseases to the Americas, devastating the Native American peoples.

Intermediate-Range Nuclear Forces (INF) Treaty (1987) Agreement signed by U.S. president Ronald Reagan and Soviet premier Mikhail Gorbachev to eliminate the deployment of intermediate-range missiles with nuclear warheads.

internal improvements Construction of roads, bridges, canals, harbors, and other infrastructural projects intended to facilitate the flow of goods and people.

internationalists Prior to the United States' entry in World War II, internationalists believed that America's national security depended on aiding Britain in its struggle against Germany.

Interstate Commerce Commission An independent federal agency established in 1887 to oversee businesses engaged in interstate trade, especially railroads, but whose regulatory power was limited when tested in the courts.

interstate highway system In the late 1950s, construction began on a national network of interstate superhighways for the purpose of commerce and defense. The interstate highways would enable the rapid movement of military convoys and the evacuation of cities after a nuclear attack.

Iran-Contra affair (1987) Reagan administration scandal over the secret, unlawful U.S. sale of arms to Iran in partial exchange for the release of hostages in Lebanon; the arms money in turn was used illegally to aid Nicaraguan right-wing insurgents, the Contras.

Iranian hostage crisis (1979) Storming of the U.S. embassy in Tehran by Iranian revolutionaries, who held fifty-two Americans hostage for 444 days, despite President Carter's appeals for their release as well as a botched rescue attempt.

Irish Potato Famine In 1845, an epidemic of potato rot brought a famine to rural Ireland that killed over 1 million peasants and instigated a huge increase in the number of Irish immigrating to America. By 1850, the Irish made up 43 percent of the foreign-born population in the United States; and in the 1850s, they made up over half the population of New York City and Boston.

iron curtain Term coined by Winston Churchill to describe the cold war divide between western Europe and the Soviet Union's Eastern European satellites.

Iroquois League An alliance of the Iroquois tribes, originally formed sometime between 1450 and 1600, that used their combined strength to pressure Europeans to work with them in the fur trade and to wage war across what is today eastern North America.

Andrew Jackson (1767–1837) As a major general in the Tennessee militia, he had a number of military successes. As president, he worked to enable the "common man" to play a greater role in the political arena. He vetoed the re-chartering of the Second National Bank and reduced federal spending. When South Carolina nullified the Tariffs of 1828 and 1832, Jackson requested that Congress pass a "force bill" that would authorize him to use the army to compel the state to comply with the tariffs. He forced eastern Indians to move west of the Mississippi River so their lands could be used by white settlers. Groups of those who opposed Jackson come together to form a new political party called the Whigs.

Thomas "Stonewall" Jackson (1824–1863) A Confederate general who was known for his fearlessness in leading rapid marches, bold flanking movements, and furious assaults. He earned his nickname at the Battle of the First Bull Run for standing courageously against Union fire. During the battle of Chancellorsville, his own men accidentally mortally wounded him.

William James (1842–1910) He was the founder of Pragmatism and one of the fathers of modern psychology. He believed that ideas gained their validity not from their inherent truth, but from their social consequences and practical application.

Jay's Treaty (1794) Agreement between Britain and the United States, negotiated by Chief Justice John Jay, that settled disputes over trade, prewar debts owed to British merchants, British-occupied forts in American territory, and the seizure of American ships and cargo.

Jazz Age Term coined by writer F. Scott Fitzgerald to characterize the spirit of rebellion and spontaneity among young Americans in the 1920s, a spirit epitomized by the hugely popular jazz music of the era.

Thomas Jefferson (1743–1826) He was a plantation owner, author, the drafter of the Declaration Independence, ambassador to France, leader of the Republican party, secretary of state, and the third president of the United States. As president, he purchased the Louisiana territory from France, withheld appointments made by President Adams leading to *Marybury v. Madison*, outlawed foreign slave trade, and was committed to a "wise and frugal" government.

Jeffersonian Republicans Political party founded by Thomas Jefferson in opposition to the Federalist Party led by Alexander Hamilton and John Adams; also known as the Democratic-Republican Party.

Jesuits A religious order founded in 1540 by Ignatius Loyola. They sought to counter the spread of Protestantism during the Protestant Reformation and spread the Catholic faith through work as missionaries. Roughly 3,500 served in New Spain and New France.

"Jim Crow" laws In the New South, these laws mandated the separation of races in various public places that served as a way for the ruling whites to impose their will on all areas of black life.

Andrew Johnson (1808–1875) He was elevated to the presidency after Abraham Lincoln's assassination. In order to restore the Union after the Civil War, he issued an amnesty proclamation and required former Confederate states to ratify the Thirteenth Amendment. After disagreements over the power to restore states rights, the Radical Republicans attempted to impeach Johnson but fell short on the required number of votes needed to remove him from office.

Lyndon B. Johnson (1908–1973) Former member of the House of Representatives and the former Majority Leader of the Senate, Vice President Lyndon B. Johnson assumed the presidency after President Kennedy's assassination. During his presidency, he passed the Civil Rights Act of 1964, declared a "war on poverty" promoting his own social program called the Great Society, and signed the Immigration and Nationality Service Act of 1965. Johnson greatly increased America's role in Vietnam.

joint-stock companies Businesses owned by investors, who purchase shares of companies' stocks and share all the profits and losses.

Kansas-Nebraska Act (1854) Controversial legislation that created two new territories taken from Native Americans, Kansas and Nebraska, where residents would vote to decide whether slavery would be allowed (popular sovereignty).

Florence Kelley (1859–1932) As the head of the National Consumer's League, she led the crusade to promote state laws to regulate the number of working hours imposed on women who were wives and mothers.

George F. Kennan (1904–2005) While working as an American diplomat, he devised the strategy of containment, which called for the halting of Soviet expansion. It became America's choice strategy throughout the cold war.

John F. Kennedy (1917–1963) He was elected president in 1960. Despite the difficulties he had in getting his legislation through Congress, he established the Alliance for Progress programs to help Latin America, the Peace Corps, the Trade Expansion Act of 1962, and funding for urban renewal projects and the space program. His foreign political involvement included the failed Bay of Pigs invasion and the missile crisis in Cuba, as well as support of local governments in Indochina. In 1963, he was assassinated by Lee Harvey Oswald in Dallas, Texas.

Kent State During the spring of 1970, students on college campuses across the country protested the expansion of the Vietnam War into Cambodia. At Kent State University, the National Guard attempted to quell the rioting students. The guardsmen panicked and shot at rock-throwing demonstrators. Four student bystanders were killed.

Kentucky and Virginia Resolutions (1798–1799) Passed in response to the Alien and Sedition Acts, the resolutions advanced the state-compact theory that held states could nullify an act of Congress if they deemed it unconstitutional.

Francis Scott Key (1779–1843) During the War of 1812, he watched British forces bombard Fort McHenry, but fail to take it. Seeing the American flag still flying over the fort at dawn inspired him to write "The Star-Spangled Banner," which became the American national anthem.

Martin Luther King, Jr. (1929–1968) A central leader of the civil rights movement, he urged people to use nonviolent civil disobedience to demand their rights and bring about change. He successfully led the Montgomery Bus Boycott. While in jail for his role in demonstrations, he wrote his famous "Letter from Birmingham City Jail," in which he defended his strategy of nonviolent protest. In 1963, he delivered his famous "I Have a Dream Speech" from the steps of the Lincoln Memorial as a part of the March on Washington. A year later, he was awarded the Nobel Peace Prize. In 1968, he was assassinated.

King Philip's War A bloody, three-year war in New England (1675–1678), resulting from the escalation of tensions between Indians and English settlers; the defeat of the Indians led to broadened freedoms for the settlers and their dispossessing the region's Indians of most of their land.

King William's War (War of the League of Augsburg) First (1689–1697) of four colonial wars between England and France.

Henry Kissinger (1923–) He served as the secretary of state and national security advisor in the Nixon administration. He negotiated with North Vietnam for an end to the Vietnam War, but the cease-fire did not last; South Vietnam fell to North Vietnam. He helped organize Nixon's historic trips to China and the Soviet Union. In the Middle East, he negotiated a cease-fire between Israel and its neighbors following the Yom Kippur War and solidified Israel's promise to return to Egypt most of the land it had taken during the 1967 war.

Knights of Labor A national labor organization with a broad reform platform; reached peak membership in the 1880s.

Know-Nothing party Nativist, anti-Catholic third party organized in 1854 in reaction to large-scale German and Irish immigration.

Ku Klux Klan Organized in Pulaski, Tennessee, in 1866 to terrorize former slaves who voted and held political offices during Reconstruction; a revived organization in the 1910s and 1920s stressed white, Anglo-Saxon, fundamentalist Protestant supremacy; the Klan revived a third time to fight the civil rights movement of the 1950s and 1960s in the South.

Marquis de Lafayette (1757–1834) A wealthy French idealist excited by the American cause, he offered to serve in Washington's army for free in exchange for being named a major general. He overcame Washington's initial skepticism to become one of his most trusted aides.

laissez-faire An economic doctrine holding that businesses and individuals should be able to pursue their economic interests without government interference.

Land Ordinance of 1785 Directed surveying of the Northwest Territory into townships of thirty-six sections (square miles) each, the sale of the sixteenth section of which was to be used to finance public education.

League of Nations Organization of nations formed in the aftermath of the First World War to mediate disputes and maintain international peace; despite President Wilson's intense lobbying for the League of Nations, Congress did not ratify the treaty and the United States failed to join.

Mary Elizabeth Lease (1850–1933) She was a leader of the farm protest movement who advocated violence if change could not be obtained at the ballot box. She believed that the urban-industrial East was the enemy of the working class.

Robert E. Lee (1807–1870) Even though he had served in the United States Army for thirty years, he chose to fight on the side of the Confederacy. Lee was excellent at using his field commanders and his soldiers respected him. However, General Ulysses S. Grant eventually wore down his army, and Lee surrendered to Grant at the Appomattox Court House on April 9, 1865.

Lend-Lease Bill (1941) Legislation that allowed the president to lend or lease military equipment to any country whose own defense was deemed vital to the defense of the United States.

Levittown First low-cost, mass-produced development of suburban tract housing built by William Levitt on Long Island, New York, in 1947.

Lewis and Clark Expedition (1804) Led by Meriwether Lewis and William Clark, a mission to the Pacific coast commissioned for the purposes of scientific and geographical exploration

Lexington and Concord, Battle of The first shots fired in the Revolutionary War, on April 19, 1775, near Boston; approximately 100 Minutemen and 250 British soldiers were killed.

Liberator William Lloyd Garrison started this anti-slavery newspaper in 1831 in which he renounced gradualism and called for abolition.

Queen Liliuokalani (1838–1917) In 1891, she ascended to the throne of the Hawaiian royal family and tried to eliminate white control of the Hawaiian government. Two years later, Hawaii's white population revolted and seized power with the support of American Marines.

Abraham Lincoln (1809–1865) Shortly after he was elected president in 1860, southern states began seceding from the Union, and in April of 1861 he declared war on the seceding states. On January 1, 1863, Lincoln signed the Emancipation Proclamation. At the end of the war, he favored a reconstruction strategy for the former Confederate states that did not radically alter southern social and economic life. He was assassinated by John Wilkes Booth at Ford's Theater on April 14, 1865.

Lincoln-Douglas Debates (1858) In the Illinois race between Republican Abraham Lincoln and Democrat Stephen A. Douglas for a seat in the U.S. Senate, a series of seven dramatic debates focusing on the issue of slavery in the territories.

John Locke (1632–1704) An English philosopher whose ideas were influential during the Enlightenment. He argued in his *Essay on Human Understanding* (1690) that humanity is largely the product of the environment, the mind being a blank tablet, *tabula rasa,* on which experience is written.

Henry Cabot Lodge (1850–1924) He was the chairman of the Senate Foreign Relations Committee who favored limiting America's involvement in the League of Nations' covenant and sought to amend the Treaty of Versailles.

de Lôme letter Private correspondence written in 1898 by the Spanish ambassador to the U.S., Depuy de Lôme, that described President McKinley as "weak"; the letter was stolen by Cuban revolutionaries and published in the *New York Journal*, deepening American resentment of Spain and moving the two countries closer to war in Cuba.

Lone Star Republic After winning independence from Mexico, Texas became its own nation that was called the Lone Star Republic. In 1836, Texans drafted a constitution, legalized slavery, banned free blacks, named Sam Houston president, and voted for the annexation to the United States. However, quarrels over adding a slave state and fears of instigating a war with Mexico delayed Texas's entrance into the Union until December 29, 1845.

Huey P. Long (1893–1935) He began his political career in Louisiana where he developed a reputation for being an unscrupulous reformer. As a U.S. senator, he became a critic of President Roosevelt's New Deal Plan and offered his alternative called the Share-the-Wealth program. He was assassinated in 1935.

Louisiana Purchase (1803) President Thomas Jefferson's purchase of the Louisiana Territory from France for $15 million, doubling the size of U.S. territory.

The Lowell system Model New England factory communities that during the first half of the nineteenth century provided employees, mostly young women, with meals, a boardinghouse, and moral discipline, as well as educational and cultural opportunities.

Loyalists Colonists who remained loyal to Great Britain before and during the Revolutionary War.

Lusitania British ocean liner torpedoed and sunk by a German U-boat; the deaths of nearly 1,200 of its civilian passengers, including many Americans, caused international outrage.

Martin Luther (1483–1546) A German monk who founded the Lutheran church. He protested abuses in the Catholic Church by posting his Ninety-five Theses, which began the Protestant Reformation.

General Douglas MacArthur (1880–1964) During World War II, he and Admiral Chester Nimitz dislodged the Japanese military from the Pacific Islands they had occupied. Following the war, he was in charge of the occupation of Japan. After North Korea invaded South Korea, Truman sent the U.S. military to defend South Korea under the command of MacArthur. Later in the war, Truman expressed his willingness to negotiate the restoration of prewar boundaries which MacArthur attempted to undermine. Truman fired MacArthur for his open insubordination.

James Madison (1751–1836) He participated in the Constitutional Convention during which he proposed the Virginia Plan. He believed in a strong federal government and was a leader of the Federalists. However, he also presented to Congress the Bill of Rights and drafted the Virginia Resolutions. As secretary of state, he withheld a commission for William Marbury, which led to the landmark *Marbury v. Madison* decision. During his presidency, he declared war on Britain in response to violations of American shipping rights, which started the War of 1812.

Alfred Thayer Mahan, *The Influence of Sea Power upon History, 1660–1783* **(1890)** Historical work in which Rear Admiral Alfred Thayer Mahan argues that a nation's greatness and prosperity comes from the power of its navy; the book helped bolster imperialist sentiment in the United States in the late nineteenth century.

U.S. battleship *Maine* American warship that exploded in the Cuban port of Havana on January 25, 1898; though later discovered to be the result of an accident, the destruction of the *Maine* was attributed by war-hungry Americans to Spain, contributing to the onset of the War of 1812.

maize (corn) The primary grain crop in Mesoamerica yielding small kernels often ground into cornmeal. Easy to grow in a broad range of conditions, it enabled a global population explosion after being brought to Europe, Africa, and Asia.

Malcolm X (1925–1964) The most articulate spokesman for black power. Originally the chief disciple of Elijah Muhammad, the black Muslim leader in the United States, Malcolm X broke away and founded his own organization committed to establishing relations between African Americans and the nonwhite peoples of the world. Near the end of his life, he began to preach a biracial message of social change. In 1964, he was assassinated by members of a rival group of black Muslims.

Manchuria incident The northeast region of Manchuria was an area contested between China and Russia. In 1931, the Japanese claimed that they needed to protect their extensive investments in the area and moved their army into Manchuria. They quickly conquered the region and set up their own puppet empire. China asked both the United States and the League of Nations for help and neither responded.

Manifest Destiny The widespread belief that America was "destined" by God to expand westward across the continent into lands claimed by Native Americans as well as European nations.

Horace Mann (1796–1859) He believed the public school system was the best way to achieve social stability and equal opportunity. As a reformer of education, he sponsored a state board of education, the first state-supported "normal" school for training teachers, a state association for teachers, the minimum school year of six months, and led the drive for a statewide school system.

Marbury v. Madison **(1803)** First Supreme Court decision to declare a federal law—the Judiciary Act of 1801—unconstitutional.

March on Washington Civil rights demonstration on August 28, 1963, on the National Mall, where Martin Luther King, Jr. gave his famous "I Have a Dream" speech.

market economy Large-scale manufacturing and commercial agriculture that emerged in America during the first half of the nineteenth century, displacing much of the pre-market subsistence and barter-based economy and producing boom-and-bust cycles while raising the American standard of living.

George C. Marshall (1880–1959) As the chairman of the Joint Chiefs of Staff, he orchestrated the Allied victories over Germany and Japan in the Second World War. In 1947, he became President Truman's secretary of state and proposed the massive reconstruction program for western Europe called the Marshall Plan.

Chief Justice John Marshall (1755–1835) During his long tenure as chief justice of the supreme court (1801–1835), he established the foundations for American jurisprudence, the authority of the Supreme Court, and the constitutional supremacy of the national government over states.

Marshall Plan (1948) Secretary of State George C. Marshall's post–World War II program providing massive U.S. financial and technical assistance to war-torn European countries.

Massachusetts Bay Colony English colony founded by English Puritans in 1630 as a haven for persecuted Congregationalists.

massive resistance White rallying cry disrupting federal efforts to enforce racial integration in the South.

massive retaliation Strategy that used the threat of nuclear warfare as a means of combating the global spread of communism.

Mayflower Compact A formal agreement signed by the Separatist colonists aboard the *Mayflower* in 1620 to abide by laws made by leaders of their own choosing.

Senator Joseph R. McCarthy (1908–1957) In 1950, this senator became the shrewdest and most ruthless exploiter of America's anxiety of communism. He claimed that the United States government was full of Communists and led a witch hunt to find them, but he was never able to uncover a single communist agent.

McCarthyism Anti-Communist hysteria led by Senator Joseph McCarthy's "witch hunts" attacking the loyalty of politicians, federal employees, and public figures, despite a lack of evidence.

George B. McClellan (1826–1885) In 1861, President Abraham Lincoln appointed him head of the Army of the Potomac and, later, general in chief of the U.S. Army. He built his army into well trained and powerful force. After failing to achieve a decisive victory against the Confederacy, he was removed from command in 1862.

Cyrus Hall McCormick (1809–1884) In 1831, he invented a mechanical reaper to harvest wheat, which transformed the scale of agriculture. By hand a farmer could only harvest a half an acre a day, while the McCormick reaper allowed two people to harvest twelve acres of wheat a day.

McCormick reaper Mechanical reaper invented by Cyrus Hall McCormick in 1831 that dramatically increased the production of wheat.

William McKinley (1843–1901) As a congressman, he was responsible for the McKinley Tariff of 1890, which raised the duties on manufactured products to their highest level ever. Voters disliked the tariff and McKinley, as well as other Republicans, lost his seat in Congress the next election. However, he won the presidential election of 1896 and raised the tariffs again. In 1898, he annexed Hawaii and declared war on Spain. The war concluded with the Treaty of Paris, which gave America control over Puerto Rico, Guam, and the Philippines. Soon America was fighting Filipinos, who were seeking independence for their country. In 1901, McKinley was assassinated.

Robert McNamara (1916–) He was the secretary of defense for both President Kennedy and President Johnson and a supporter of America's involvement in Vietnam.

Medicare and Medicaid Health-care programs designed to aid the elderly and disadvantaged, respectively, as part of President Johnson's Great Society initiative.

Andrew W. Mellon (1855–1937) As President Harding's secretary of the Treasury, he sought to generate economic growth through reducing government spending and lowering taxes. However, he insisted that the tax reductions mainly go to the rich because he believed the wealthy would reinvest their money. In order to bring greater efficiency and nonpartisanship to the government's budget process, he persuaded Congress to created a new Bureau of the Budget and a General Accounting Office.

mercantilism Policy of Great Britain and other imperial powers of regulating the economies of colonies to benefit the mother country.

James Meredith (1933–) In 1962, the governor of Mississippi defied a Supreme Court ruling and refused to allow James Meredith, an African American, to enroll at the University of Mississippi. Federal marshals were sent to enforce the law which led to clashes between a white mob and the marshals. Federal troops intervened and two people were killed and many others were injured. A few days later, Meredith was able to register at the university.

Merrimack* (ship renamed the *Virginia*) and the *Monitor First engagement between ironclad ships; fought at Hampton Roads, Virginia, on March 9, 1862.

Metacomet (?–1676) or King Philip The chief of the Wampanoages, who the colonists called King Philip. He resented English efforts to convert Indians to Christianity and waged a war against the English colonists in which he was killed.

Mexica Otherwise known as "Aztecs," a Mesoamerican people of northern Mexico who founded the vast Aztec Empire in the fourteenth century, later conquered by the Spanish under Hernán Cortés in 1521.

microprocessor An electronic circuit printed on a small silicon chip; a major technological breakthrough in 1971, it paved the way for the development of the personal computer.

Middle Passage The hellish and often deadly middle leg of the transatlantic "Triangular Trade" in which European ships carried manufactured goods to Africa, then transported enslaved Africans to the Americas and the Caribbean, and finally conveyed American agricultural products back to Europe; from the late sixteenth to the early nineteenth centuries, some 12 million Africans were transported via the Middle Passage, unknown millions more dying en route.

militant nonviolence After the success of the Montgomery bus boycott, people were inspired by Martin Luther King, Jr.'s use of this nonviolent form of protest. Throughout the civil rights movement, demonstrators used this method of protest to challenge racial segregation in the South.

Militia Act (1862) Congressional measure that permitted freed slaves to serve as laborers or soldiers in the United States Army.

Ho Chi Minh (1890–1969) He was the Vietnamese communist resistance leader who drove the French and the United States out of Vietnam. After the Geneva Accords divided the region into four countries, he controlled North Vietnam, and ultimately became the leader of all of Vietnam at the conclusion of the Vietnam War.

minstrelsy A form of entertainment that was popular from the 1830s to the 1870s. The performances featured white performers who were made up as African Americans or blackface. They performed banjo and fiddle music, "shuffle" dances and lowbrow humor that reinforced racial stereotypes.

Minutemen Special units organized by the militia to be ready for quick mobilization.

***Miranda v. Arizona* (1966)** U.S. Supreme Court decision required police to advise persons in custody of their rights to legal counsel and against self-incrimination.

The Mississippi Plan Series of state constitutional amendments in 1890 which sought to severely disenfranchise black voters and were quickly adopted by other southern states.

Missouri Compromise (1820) Legislative decision to admit Missouri as a slave state and abolish slavery in the area west of the Mississippi River and north of the parallel 36°30′.

Model T Ford Henry Ford developed this model of car so that it was affordable for everyone. Its success led to an increase in the production of automobiles which stimulated other related industries such steel, oil, and rubber. The mass use of automobiles increased the speed goods could be transported, encouraged urban sprawl, and sparked real estate booms in California and Florida.

moderate Republicanism Promise to curb federal government and restore state and local government authority, spearheaded by President Eisenhower.

modernism An early-twentieth-century intellectual and artistic movement that rejected traditional notions of reality and adopted radical new forms of artistic expression.

monopoly A corporation so large that it effectively controls the entire market for its products or services.

the "money question" Late-nineteenth-century national debate over the nature of U.S. currency; supporters of a fixed gold standard were generally money lenders, and thus preferred to keep the value of money high, while supporters of silver (and gold) coinage were debtors, they owed money, so they wanted to keep the value of money low by increasing the currency supply (inflation).

James Monroe (1758–1831) He served as secretary of state and war under President Madison and was elected president. As the latter, he signed the Transcontinental Treaty with Spain which gave the United States Florida and expanded the Louisiana territory's western border to the Pacific coast. In 1823, he established the Monroe Doctrine. This foreign policy proclaimed the American continents were no longer open to colonization and America would be neutral in European affairs.

Monroe Doctrine (1823) U.S. foreign policy that barred further colonization in the Western Hemisphere by European powers and pledged that there would be no American interference with any existing European colonies.

Montgomery bus boycott Boycott of bus system in Montgomery, Alabama, organized by civil rights activists after the arrest of Rosa Parks.

Moral Majority Televangelist Jerry Falwell's political lobbying organization, the name of which became synonymous with the religious right—conservative evangelical Protestants who helped ensure President Ronald Reagan's 1980 victory.

J. Pierpont Morgan (1837–1913) As a powerful investment banker, he would acquire, reorganize, and consolidate companies into giant trusts. His biggest achievement was the consolidation of the steel industry into the United States Steel Corporation, which was the first billion-dollar corporation.

J. Pierpont Morgan and Company An investment bank under the leadership of J. Pierpont Morgan that bought or merged unrelated American companies, often using capital acquired from European investors.

Mormons Members of the Church of Jesus Christ of Latter-day Saints, which dismissed other Christian denominations, emphasizing universal salvation and a modest lifestyle; Mormons were often persecuted for their secrecy and clannishness.

Morrill Land Grant Act (1862) Federal statute that allowed for the creation of land-grant colleges and universities, which were founded to provide technical education in agriculture, mining, and industry.

Samuel F. B. Morse (1791–1872) In 1832, he invented the telegraph and revolutionized the speed of communication.

mountain men Inspired by the fur trade, these men left civilization to work as trappers and reverted to a primitive existence in the wilderness. They were the first white people to find routes through the Rocky Mountains, and they pioneered trails that settlers later used to reach the Oregon country and California in the 1840s.

muckrakers Writers who exposed corruption and abuses in politics, business, consumer safety, working conditions, and more, spurring public interest in progressive reforms.

Mugwumps Reformers who bolted the Republican party in 1884 to support Democratic Grover Cleveland for president over Republican James G. Blaine, whose secret dealings on behalf of railroad companies had brought charges of corruption.

mulattoes Mixed-race people who constituted most of the South's free black population.

Benito Mussolini (1883–1945) The Italian founder of the Fascist party who came to power in Italy in 1922 and allied himself with Adolf Hitler and the Axis powers during the Second World War.

National Association for the Advancement of Colored People (NAACP) Organization founded in 1910 by black activists and white progressives that promoted education as a means of combating social problems and focused on legal action to secure the civil rights supposedly guaranteed by the Fourteenth and Fifteenth Amendments.

North American Free Trade Agreement (NAFTA) (1994) Agreement eliminating trade barriers that was signed in 1994 by the United States, Canada, and Mexico, making North America the largest free-trade zone in the world.

North Atlantic Treaty Organization (NATO) Defensive political and military alliance formed in 1949 by the United States, Canada, and ten Western European nations to deter Soviet expansion in Europe.

National Industrial Recovery Act (1933) Passed on the last of the Hundred Days; it created public-works jobs through the Federal Emergency Relief Administration and established a system of self-regulation for industry through the National Recovery Administration, which was ruled unconstitutional in 1935.

National Labor Union A federation of labor and reform leaders established in 1866 to advocate for new state and local laws to improve working conditions.

National Recovery Administration (1933) Controversial federal agency that brought together business and labor leaders to create "codes of fair competition" and "fair labor" policies, including a national minimum wage.

National Security Act Congressional legislation passed in 1947 that created the Department of Defense, the National Security Council, and the Central Intelligence Agency.

National Socialist German Workers' Party (Nazi) Founded in the 1920s, this party gained control over Germany under the leadership of Adolf Hitler in 1933 and continued in power until Germany's defeat at the end of the Second World War. It advocated a violent anti-Semitic, anti-Marxist, pan-German ideology. The Nazi party perpetrated the Holocaust.

National Trades' Unions Formed in 1834 to organize all local trade unions into a stronger national association, only to be dissolved amid the economic depression during the late 1830s.

nativism Reactionary conservative movement characterized by heightened nationalism, anti-immigrant sentiment, and the enactment of laws setting stricter regulations on immigration.

natural rights An individual's basic rights that should not be violated by any government or community.

Navigation Acts Restrictions passed by the British Parliament between 1650 and 1775 to control colonial trade and bolster the mercantile system.

Negrophobia A violent new wave of racism that spread in the late nineteenth century largely spurred by white resentment for African American financial success and growing political influence.

new conservatism The political philosophy of those who led the conservative insurgency of the early 1980s. This brand of conservatism was personified in Ronald Reagan who believed in less government, supply-side economics, and "family values."

First New Deal Franklin D. Roosevelt's campaign promise, in his speech to the Democratic National Convention of 1932, to combat the Great Depression with a "new deal for the American people;" the phrase became a catchword for his ambitious plan of economic programs.

New Democrats Centrist ("moderate") Democrats led by President Bill Clinton that emerged in the late 1980s and early 1990s to challenge the "liberal" direction of the party.

"new economy" Period of sustained economic prosperity during the nineties marked by budget surpluses, the explosion of dot.com industries, low inflation, and low unemployment.

New France The name used for the area of North America that was colonized by the French. Unlike Spanish or English colonies, New France had a small number of colonists, which forced them to initially seek good relations with the indigenous people they encountered.

New Freedom Program championed in 1912 by the Woodrow Wilson campaign that aimed to restore competition in the economy by eliminating all trusts rather than simply regulating them.

New Frontier Proposed domestic program championed by the incoming Kennedy administration in 1961 that aimed to jump-start the economy and trigger social progress.

"new immigrants" Wave of newcomers from southern and eastern Europe, including many Jews, who became a majority among immigrants to America after 1890.

New Jersey Plan The delegations to the Constitutional Convention were divided between two plans on how to structure the government: New Jersey wanted one legislative body with equal representation for each state.

New Left Term coined by the Students for a Democratic Society to distinguish their efforts at grassroots democracy from those of the 1930s Old Left, which had embraced orthodox Marxism.

New Mexico A U.S. territory and later a state in the American Southwest, originally established by the Spanish, who settled there in the sixteenth century, founded Catholic missions, and exploited the region's indigenous peoples.

New Nationalism Platform of the Progressive party and slogan of former President Theodore Roosevelt in the presidential campaign of 1912; stressed government activism, including regulation of trusts, conservation, and recall of state court decisions that had nullified progressive programs.

"New Negro" In the 1920s, a slow and steady growth of black political influence occurred in northern cities where African Americans were freer to speak and act. This political activity created a spirit of protest that expressed itself culturally in the Harlem Renaissance and politically in "new Negro" nationalism.

New Netherland Dutch colony conquered by the English in 1667 and out of which four new colonies were created—New York, New Jersey, Pennsylvania, and Delaware.

Battle of New Orleans (1815) Final major battle in the War of 1812, in which the Americans under General Andrew Jackson unexpectedly and decisively countered the British attempt to seize the port of New Orleans, Louisiana.

New South *Atlanta Constitution* editor Henry W. Grady's 1886 term for the prosperous post–Civil War South: democratic, industrial, urban, and free of nostalgia for the defeated plantation South.

William Randolph Hearst's *New York Journal* In the late 1890s, the *New York Journal* and its rival, the *New York World*, printed sensationalism on the Cuban revolution as part of their heated competition for readership. The *New York Journal* printed a negative letter from the Spanish ambassador about President McKinley and inflammatory coverage of the sinking of the *Maine* in Havana Harbor. These two events roused the American public's outcry against Spain.

Joseph Pulitzer's *New York World* In the late 1890s, the *New York World* and its rival, *New York Journal*, printed sensationalism on the Cuban revolution as part of their heated competition for readership.

Admiral Chester Nimitz (1885–1966) During the Second World War, he was the commander of central Pacific. Along with General Douglas MacArthur, he dislodged the Japanese military from the Pacific Islands they had occupied.

Nineteenth Amendment Constitutional amendment that granted women the right to vote in 1920.

Richard M. Nixon (1913–1994) He first came to national prominence as a congressman involved in the investigation of Alger Hiss, and later served as vice president during the Eisenhower administration. After being elected president in 1968, he slowed the federal enforcement of civil rights and appointed pro-Southern justices to the Supreme Court. He began a program of Vietnamization of the war. In 1973, America, North and South Vietnam, and the Viet Cong agreed to end the war and the United States withdrew. However, the cease-fire was broken, and the South Vietnam fell to North Vietnam. In 1970, Nixon declared that America was no longer the world's policeman and he would seek some partnerships with Communist countries, historically traveling to China and the Soviet Union. In 1972, he was reelected, but the Watergate scandal erupted shortly after his victory; he resigned the presidency under threat of impeachment.

No Child Left Behind President George W. Bush's education reform plan that required states to set and meet learning standards for students and make sure that all students were "proficient" in reading and writing by 2014. States had to submit annual reports of students' standardized test scores. Teachers were required to be "proficient" in their subject area. Schools who failed to show progress would face sanctions. States criticized the lack of funding for remedial programs and noted that poor school districts would find it very difficult to meet the new guidelines.

nonviolent civil disobedience Tactic of defying unjust laws through peaceful actions championed by Dr. Martin Luther King, Jr.

Lord North (1732–1792) The first minister of King George III's cabinet whose efforts to subdue the colonies only brought them closer to revolution. He helped bring about the Tea Act of 1773, which led to the Boston Tea Party. In an effort to discipline Boston, he wrote, and Parliament passed, four acts that galvanized colonial resistance.

North Atlantic Treaty Organization (NATO) Defensive alliance founded in 1949 by ten western European nations, the United States, and Canada to deter Soviet expansion in Europe.

Northwest Ordinance (1787) Land policy for new western territories in the Ohio valley that established the terms and conditions for self-government and statehood while also banning slavery from the region.

NSC-68 (1950) Top-secret policy paper approved by President Truman that outlined a militaristic approach to combating the spread of global communism.

nullification The right claimed by some states to veto a federal law deemed unconstitutional.

Nuremberg trials At the site of the annual Nazi party rallies, twenty-one major German offenders faced an international military tribunal for Nazi atrocities. After a ten-month trial, the court acquitted three and sentenced eleven to death, three to life imprisonment, and four to shorter terms.

Barack Obama (1961–) In the 2008 presidential election, Senator Barack Obama mounted an innovative Internet based and grassroots orientated campaign. As the nation's economy nose-dived in the fall of 2008, Obama linked the Republican economic philosophy with the country's dismal financial state and promoted a message of "change" and "politics of hope," which resonated with voters. He decisively won the presidency and became America's first person of color to be elected president.

Occupy Wall Street A grassroots movement protesting a capitalist system that fostered social and economic inequality. Begun in Zuccotti Park, New York City, during 2011, the movement spread rapidly across the nation, triggering a national conversation about income inequality and protests of the government's "bailouts" of the banks and corporations allegedly responsible for the Great Recession.

Sandra Day O'Connor (1930–) She was the first woman to serve on the Supreme Court of the United States and was appointed by President Reagan. Reagan's critics charged that her appointment was a token gesture and not a sign of any real commitment to gender equality.

Ohio gang In order to escape the pressures of the White House, President Harding met with a group of people, called the "Ohio gang," in a house on K Street in Washington D.C. Members of this gang were given low-level positions in the American government and they used their White House connection to "line their pockets" by granting government contracts without bidding, which led to a series of scandals, most notably the Teapot Dome Scandal.

The Old Southwest Region covering western Georgia, Alabama, Mississippi, Louisiana, Arkansas, and Texas, where low land prices and fertile soil attracted hundreds of thousands of settlers after the American Revolution.

Frederick Law Olmsted (1822–1903) In 1858, he constructed New York's Central Park, which led to a growth in the movement to create urban parks. He went on to design parks for Boston, Brooklyn, Chicago, Philadelphia, San Francisco, and many other cities.

Open Door policy Official U.S. insistence that Chinese trade would be open to all nations; Secretary of State John Hay unilaterally announced the policy in 1899 in hopes of protecting the Chinese market for U.S. exports.

open shop Business policy of not requiring union membership as a condition of employment; such a policy, where legal, has the effect of weakening unions and diminishing workers' rights.

open range Informal system of governing property on the frontier in which small ranchers could graze their cattle anywhere on unfenced lands; brought to an end by the introduction of barbed wire, a low-cost way to fence off one's land.

Operation Desert Shield After Saddam Hussein invaded Kuwait in 1990, President George H. W. Bush sent American military forces to Saudi Arabia on a strictly defensive mission. They were soon joined by a multinational coalition. When the coalition's mission changed to the retaking of Kuwait, the operation was renamed Desert Storm.

Operation Desert Storm (1991) Assault by American-led multinational forces that quickly defeated Iraqi forces under Saddam Hussein in the First Gulf War, ending the Iraqi occupation of Kuwait.

Operation Overlord The Allies' assault on Hitler's "Atlantic Wall," a seemingly impregnable series of fortifications and minefields along the French coastline that German forces had created using captive Europeans for laborers.

J. Robert Oppenheimer (1904–1967) He led the group of physicists at the laboratory in Los Alamos, New Mexico, who constructed the first atomic bomb.

Oregon Country The Convention of 1818 between Britain and the United States established the Oregon Country as being west of the crest of the Rocky Mountains and the two countries were to jointly occupy it. In 1824, the United States and Russia signed a treaty that established the line of 54°40′ as the southern boundary of Russia's territorial claim in North America. A similar agreement between Britain and Russia finally gave the Oregon Country clearly defined boarders, but it remained under joint British and American control.

"Oregon Fever" The lure of fertile land and economic opportunities in the Oregon Country that drew thousands of settlers westward, beginning in the late 1830s.

Osceola (1804?–1838) He was the leader of the Seminole nation who resisted the federal Indian removal policy through a protracted guerilla war. In 1837, he was treacherously seized under a flag of truce and imprisoned at Fort Moultrie, where he was left to die.

Overland Trails Trail routes followed by wagon trains bearing settlers and trade goods from Missouri to the Oregon Country, California, and New Mexico, beginning in the 1840s.

A. Mitchell Palmer (1872–1936) As the attorney general, he played an active role in the government's response to the Red Scare. After several bombings across America, including one at Palmer's home, he and other Americans became convinced that there was a well-organized Communist terror campaign at work. The federal government launched a campaign of raids, deportations, and collecting files on radical individuals.

Panic of 1819 A financial panic that began a three-year-long economic crisis triggered by a reduced demand of American imports, declining land values, and reckless practices by local and state banks.

Panic of 1837 A financial calamity in the United States brought on by a dramatic slowdown in the British economy and exacerbated by falling cotton prices, failed crops, high inflation, and reckless state banks.

Panic of 1893 A major collapse in the national economy after several major railroad companies declared bankruptcy, leading to a severe depression and several violent clashes between workers and management.

panning A method of mining that used a large metal pan to sift gold dust and nuggets from riverbeds during the California gold rush of 1849.

Rosa Parks (1913–2005) In 1955, she refused to give up her seat to a white man on a city bus in Montgomery, Alabama, which a local ordinance required of blacks. She was arrested for disobeying the ordinance. In response, black community leaders organized the Montgomery bus boycott.

Parliament Legislature of Great Britain, composed of the House of Commons, whose members are elected, and the House of Lords, whose members are either hereditary or appointed.

party "boss" A powerful political leader who controlled a "machine" of associates and operatives to promote both individual and party interests, often using informal tactics such as intimidation or the patronage system.

paternalism A moral position developed during the first half of the nineteenth century which claimed that slaves were deprived of liberty for their own "good." Such a rationalization was adopted by some slave owners to justify slavery.

Patriots Colonists who rebelled against British authority before and during the Revolutionary War.

patronage An informal system (sometimes called the "spoils system") used by politicians to reward their supporters with government appointments or contracts.

Alice Paul (1885–1977) She was a leader of the women's suffrage movement and head of the Congressional Committee of National Women Suffrage Association. She instructed female suffrage activists to use more militant tactics, such as picketing state legislatures, chaining themselves to public buildings, inciting police to arrest them, and undertaking hunger strikes.

Norman Vincent Peale (1898–1993) He was a champion of the upbeat and feel-good theology that was popular in the 1950s religious revival. He advocated getting rid of any depressing or negative thoughts and replacing them with "faith, enthusiasm and joy," which would make an individual popular and well liked.

Pearl Harbor (1941) Surprise Japanese attack on the U.S. fleet at Pearl Harbor on December 7, which prompted the immediate American entry into the war.

"peculiar institution" A phrase used by whites in the antebellum South to refer to slavery without using the word slavery.

Pennsylvania English colony founded by William Penn in 1681 as a Quaker commonwealth, though it welcomed people of all religions.

Pentagon Papers Informal name for the Defense Department's secret history of the Vietnam conflict; leaked to the press by former official Daniel Ellsberg and published in the *New York Times* in 1971.

People's Party (Populists) Political party largely made up of farmers from the South and West that struggled to gain political influence from the East. Populists advocated a variety of reforms, including free coinage of silver, a progressive income tax, postal savings banks, regulation of railroads, and direct election of U.S. senators.

Pequot War Massacre in 1637 and subsequent dissolution of the Pequot Nation by Puritan settlers, who seized the Indians' lands.

perestroika Russian term for "economic restructuring"; applied to Mikhail Gorbachev's series of political and economic reforms that included shifting a centrally planned Commmunist economy to a mixed economy allowing for capitalism.

Commodore Matthew Perry (1794–1858) In 1854, he negotiated the Treaty of Kanagawa, which was the first step in starting a political and commercial relationship between the United States and Japan.

John J. Pershing United States general sent by President Wilson to put down attacks on the Mexican border led by Francisco "Pancho" Villa.

Personal Responsibility and Work Opportunity Act of 1996 (PRWOA) Comprehensive welfare-reform measure, passed by a Republican Congress and signed by President Clinton, that aimed to decrease the size of the "welfare state" by limiting the amount of government aid provided the unemployed so as to encourage recipients to find jobs.

"pet banks" During President Andrew Jackson's fight with the national bank, Jackson resolved to remove all federal deposits from it. To comply with Jackson's demands, Secretary of the Treasury Taney continued to draw on government's accounts in the national bank, but deposit all new federal receipts in state banks. The state banks that received these deposits were called "pet banks."

Pilgrims Puritan Separatists who broke completely with the Church of England and sailed to the New World aboard the *Mayflower*, founding Plymouth Colony on Cape Cod in 1620.

King Philip (?–1676) or Metacomet The chief of the Wampanoages, who the colonists called King Philip. He resented English efforts to convert Indians to Christianity and waged a war against the English colonists in which he was killed.

Dien Bien Phu Cluster of Vietnamese villages and site of a major Vietnamese victory over the French in the First Indochina War.

Gifford Pinchot (1865–1946) As the head of the Division of Forestry, he implemented a conservation policy that entailed the scientific management of natural resources to serve the public interest. His work helped start the conservation movement.

Elizabeth Lucas Pinckney (1722? –1793) One of the most enterprising horticulturists in colonial America, she began managing her family's three plantations in South Carolina at the age of sixteen. She had tremendous success growing indigo, which led to many other plantations growing the crop as well.

Pinckney's Treaty Treaty with Spain negotiated by Thomas Pinckney in 1795; established United States boundaries at the Mississippi River and the 31st parallel and allowed open transportation on the Mississippi.

Francisco Pizarro (1478?–1541) In 1531, he lead his Spanish soldiers to Peru and conquered the Inca Empire.

"plain white folk" Yeoman farmers who lived and worked on their own small farms, growing a food and cash crops to trade for necessities.

plantation mistress Matriarch of a planter's household, responsible for supervising the domestic aspects of the estate.

planters Owners of large farms in the South that were worked by twenty or more slaves and supervised by overseers.

political "machine" A network of political activists and elected officials, usually controlled by a powerful "boss," that attempts to manipulate local politics

James Knox Polk "Young Hickory" (1795–1849) As president, his chief concern was the expansion of the United States. Shortly, after taking office, Mexico broke off relations with the United States over the annexation of Texas. Polk declared war on Mexico and sought to subvert Mexican authority in California. The United States defeated Mexico; and the two nations signed the Treaty of Guadalupe Hidalgo in which Mexico gave up any claims on Texas north of the Rio Grande River and ceded New Mexico and California to the United States.

Pontiac's Rebellion An Indian attack on British forts and settlements after France ceded to the British its territory east of the Mississippi River, as part of the Treaty of Paris in 1763, without consulting France's Indian allies.

"Popular Sovereignty" Legal concept by which the white male settlers in a new U.S. territory would vote to decide whether or not to permit slavery.

Populist/People's party Political success of Farmers' Alliance candidates encouraged the formation in 1892 of the People's party (later renamed the Populist party); active until 1912, it advocated a variety of reform issues, including free coinage of silver, income tax, postal savings, regulation of railroads, and direct election of U.S. senators.

Pottawatomie Massacre In retaliation for the "sack of Lawrence," John Brown and his abolitionist cohorts hacked five men to death in the pro-slavery settlement of Pottawatomie, Kansas, on May 24, 1856, triggering a guerrilla war in the Kansas Territory that cost 200 settler lives.

The Powhatan Confederacy An alliance of several powerful Algonquian tribes under the leadership of Chief Powhatan, organized into thirty chiefdoms along much of the Atlantic coast in the late sixteenth and early seventeenth centuries.

Chief Powhatan Wahunsonacock He was called Powhatan by the English after the name of his tribe, and was the powerful, charismatic chief of numerous Algonquian-speaking towns in eastern Virginia representing over 10,000 Indians.

pragmatism William James founded this philosophy in the early 1900s. Pragmatists believed that ideas gained their validity not from their inherent truth, but from their social consequences and practical application.

Proclamation of 1763 Proclamation drawing a boundary along the Appalachian Mountains from Canada to Georgia in order to minimize occurrences of settler–Indian violence; colonists were forbidden to go west of the line.

professions Occupations requiring specialized knowledge of some field; the Industrial Revolution and its new organization of labor created an array of professions in the nineteenth century.

Progressive party In the 1912 election, Theodore Roosevelt was unable to secure the Republican nomination for president. He left the Republican party and formed his own party of progressive Republicans, called the "Bull Moose" party (later Progressive Party). Roosevelt and Taft split the Republican vote, which allowed Democrat Woodrow Wilson to win.

Prohibition National ban on the manufacture and sale of alcohol that lasted from 1920 to 1933, though the law was widely violated and proved too difficult to enforce effectively.

proprietary colonies A colony owned by an individual, rather than a joint-stock company.

Protestant Reformation Sixteenth-century religious movement initiated by Martin Luther, a German monk whose public criticism of corruption in the Roman Catholic Church, and whose teaching that Christians can communicate directly with God, gained a wide following.

public schools Elementary and secondary schools funded by the state and free of tuition.

pueblos The Spanish term for the adobe cliff dwellings of the indigenous people of the southwestern United States.

Pullman strike (1894) A national strike by the American Railway Union, whose members shut down major railways in sympathy with striking workers in Pullman, Illinois; ended with intervention of federal troops.

Puritans English religious dissenters who sought to "purify" the Church of England of its Catholic practices.

Quakers George Fox founded the Quaker religion in 1647. They rejected the use of formal sacraments and ministry, refused to take oaths and embraced pacifism. Fleeing persecution, they settled and established the colony of Pennsylvania.

race-based slavery Institution that uses racial characteristics and myths to justify enslaving a people.

Radical Republicans Senators and congressmen who, strictly identifying the Civil War with the abolitionist cause, sought swift emancipation of the slaves, punishment of the rebels, and tight controls over the former Confederate states after the war.

railroad Steam-powered vehicles that improved passenger transportation, quickened western settlement, and enabled commercial agriculture in the nineteenth century.

Raleigh's Roanoke Island Colony English expedition of 117 settlers, including Virginia Dare, the first English child born in the New World; colony disappeared from Roanoke Island in the Outer Banks sometime between 1587 and 1590.

A. Philip Randolph (1889–1979) He was the head of the Brotherhood of Sleeping Car Porters who planned a march on Washington D.C. to demand an end to racial discrimination in the defense industries. To stop the march, the Roosevelt administration negotiated an agreement with the Randolph group. The demonstration would be called off and an executive order would be issued that forbid discrimination in defense work and training programs and set up the Fair Employment Practices Committee.

range wars In the late 1800s, conflicting claims over land and water rights triggered violent disputes between farmers and ranchers in parts of the western United States.

Ronald Reagan (1911–2004) In 1980, the former actor and governor of California was elected president. In office, he reduced social spending, cut taxes, and increased defense spending. During his presidency, the federal debt tripled, the federal deficit rose, programs such as housing and school lunches were cut, and the HIV/AIDS crisis grew to prominence in the United States. He signed an arms-control treaty with the Soviet Union in 1987, authorized covert CIA operations in Central America, and in 1986 the Iran-Contra scandal was revealed.

Reaganomics President Reagan's "supply-side" economic philosophy combining tax cuts with the goals of decreased government spending, reduced regulation of business, and a balanced budget.

Reconstruction Finance Corporation (1932) Federal program established under President Hoover to loan money to banks and other corporations to help them avoid bankruptcy.

Red Power Activism by militant Native American groups to protest living conditions on Indian reservations through demonstrations, legal action, and, at times, violence.

First Red Scare Fear among many Americans after the First World War of Communists in particular and noncitizens in general, it was a reaction to the Russian Revolution, mail bombs, strikes, and riots.

Redeemers Post–Civil War Democratic leaders who supposedly saved the South from Yankee domination and preserved the primarily rural economy.

Dr. Walter Reed (1851–1902) His work on yellow fever in Cuba led to the discovery that the fever was carried by mosquitoes. This understanding helped develop more effective controls of the worldwide disease.

Reform Darwinism A social philosophy developed by Lester Frank War that challenged the ruthlessness of Social Darwinism by asserting that humans were not passive pawns of evolutionary forces. Instead, people could actively shape the process of evolutionary social development through cooperation, innovation, and planning.

Reformation European religious movement that challenged the Catholic Church and resulted in the beginnings of Protestant Christianity. During this period, Catholics and Protestants persecuted, imprisoned, tortured, and killed each other in large numbers.

religious right Christian conservatives with a faith-based political agenda that includes prohibition of abortion and allowing prayer in public schools.

reparations As a part of the Treaty of Versailles, Germany was required to confess its responsibility for the First World War and make payments to the victors for the entire expense of the war. These two requirements created a deep bitterness among Germans.

Alexander Hamilton's Report on Manufactures First Secretary of the Treasury Alexander Hamilton's 1791 analysis that accurately foretold the future of American industry and proposed tariffs and subsidies to promote it.

Republican ideology Political belief in representative democracy in which citizens govern themselves by electing representatives, or legislators, to make key decisions on the citizens' behalf.

Republican simplicity Deliberate attitude of humility and frugality, as opposed to monarchical pomp and ceremony, adopted by Thomas Jefferson in his presidency.

Republicans First used during the early nineteenth century to describe supporters of a strict interpretation of the Constitution, which they believed would safeguard individual freedoms and states' rights from the threats posed by a strong central government. The idealist Republican vision of sustaining an agrarian-oriented union was developed largely by Thomas Jefferson.

"return to normalcy" Campaign promise of Republican presidential candidate Warren G. Harding in 1920, meant to contrast with Woodrow Wilson's progressivism and internationalism.

Paul Revere (1735–1818) On the night of April 18, 1775, British soldiers marched toward Concord to arrest American Revolutionary leaders and seize their depot of supplies. Paul Revere famously rode through the night and raised the alarm about the approaching British troops.

Roaring Twenties The 1920s, an era of social and intellectual revolution in which young people experimented with new forms of recreation and sexuality. The Eastern, urban cultural shift clashed with conservative and insular Midwestern America, which increased the tensions between the two regions.

Jackie Robinson (1919–1972) In 1947, he became the first African American to play major league baseball. He won over fans and players and stimulated the integration of other professional sports.

rock-and-roll music Alan Freed, a disc jockey, noticed white teenagers were buying rhythm and blues records that had been only purchased by African Americans and Hispanic Americans. Freed began playing these records, but called them rock-and-roll records as a way to overcome the racial barrier. As the popularity of the music genre increased, it helped bridge the gap between "white" and "black" music.

John D. Rockefeller (1839–1937) In 1870, he founded the Standard Oil Company of Ohio, which was his first step in creating his vast oil empire. He perfected the idea of a holding company.

***Roe v. Wade* (1973)** Landmark Supreme Court decision striking down state laws that banned abortions during the first trimester of pregnancy.

Roman Catholicism The Christian faith and religious practices of the Roman Catholic Church, which exerted great political, economic, and social influence on much of Western Europe and, through the Spanish and Portuguese Empires, on the Americas.

Romanticism Philosophical, literary, and artistic movement of the nineteenth century that was largely a reaction to the rationalism of the previous century; Romantics valued emotion, mysticism, and individualism.

Eleanor Roosevelt (1884–1962) She redefined the role of the presidential spouse and was the first woman to address a national political convention, write a nationally syndicated column and hold regular press conferences. She travelled throughout the nation to promote the New Deal, women's causes, organized labor, and meet with African American leaders.

Franklin Delano Roosevelt (1882–1945) Elected during the Great Depression, Roosevelt sought to help struggling Americans through his New Deal programs that created employment and social programs, such as Social Security. After the bombing of Pearl Harbor, he declared war on Japan and Germany and led the country through most of the Second World War before dying of cerebral hemorrhage.

Theodore Roosevelt (1858–1919) As the assistant secretary of the navy, he supported expansionism, American imperialism, and war with Spain. He led the Rough Riders in Cuba during the war of 1898 and used the notoriety of this military campaign for political gain. As President McKinley's vice president, he succeeded McKinley after his assassination. His forceful foreign policy became known as "big stick diplomacy." Domestically, his policies on natural resources helped start the conservation movement. Unable to win the Republican nomination for president in 1912, he formed his own party of progressive Republicans called the "Bull Moose" party.

Roosevelt Corollary President Theodore Roosevelt's 1904 revision of the Monroe Doctrine (1823) in which he argued that the United States could use military force in Central and South American nations to prevent European nations from intervening in the Western Hemisphere.

Rough Riders The First U.S. Volunteer Cavalry, led in the War of 1898 by Theodore Roosevelt; they were victorious in their only engagement, the Battle of San Juan Hill near Santiago, Cuba, and Roosevelt was celebrated as a national hero, bolstering his political career.

Nicola Sacco (1891–1927) In 1920, he and Bartolomeo Vanzetti were Italian immigrants who were arrested for stealing $16,000 and killing a paymaster and his guard. Their trial took place during a time of numerous bombings by anarchists and their judge was openly prejudicial; many liberals and radicals believe that their conviction was based on their political ideas and ethnic origin rather than the evidence against them.

Sacco and Vanzetti case 1921 trial of two Italian immigrants that occurred at the height of Italian immigration and against the backdrop of numerous terror attacks by anarchists; despite a lack of clear evidence, the two defendants, both self-professed anarchists, were convicted of murder and were executed in 1927.

saloons Bars or taverns where mostly men would gather to drink, eat, relax, play games, and, often, to discuss politics.

salutary neglect Informal British policy during the first half of the eighteenth century that allowed the American colonies considerable freedom to pursue their economic and political interests in exchange for colonial obedience.

same-sex marriage The legal right for gay and lesbian couples to marry; it became the most divisive issue in the culture wars of the early 2010s as more and more court rulings affirmed this right in states and municipalities across the United States.

Sandinista Cuban-sponsored government that came to power in Nicaragua after toppling a corrupt dictator. The State Department believed that the Sandinistas were supplying the leftist Salvadoran rebels with Cuban and Soviet arms. In response, the Reagan administration ordered the CIA to train and supply guerrilla bands of anti-Communist Nicaraguans called Contras. A cease-fire agreement between the Contras and Sandinistas was signed in 1988.

Sandlot Incident Violence occurring during the Great Railroad Strike of 1877, when mobs of frustrated working-class whites in San Francisco attacked Chinese immigrants, blaming them for economic hardship.

General Antonio López de Santa Anna (1794–1876) In 1834, he seized political power in Mexico and became a dictator. In 1835, Texans rebelled against him and he led his army to Texas to crush their rebellion. He captured the mission called the Alamo and killed all of its defenders, which inspired Texans to continue resistance and Americans to volunteer to fight for Texas. The Texans captured Santa Anna during a surprise attack and he bought his freedom by signing a treaty recognizing Texas's independence.

battles of Saratoga Decisive defeat of 5,000 British troops under General John Burgoyne in several battles near Saratoga, New York, in October 1777; the American victory helped convince France to enter the war on the side of the Patriots.

scalawags White southern Republicans—some former Unionists—who served in Reconstruction governments.

Phyllis Schlafly (1924–) A right-wing Republican activist who spearheaded the anti-feminism movement. She believed feminists were "anti-family, anti-children, and pro-abortion." She worked against the equal-rights amendment for women and civil rights protection for gays.

Scopes Trial Highly publicized 1925 trial of a high school teacher in Tennessee for violating a state law that prohibited the teaching of evolution; the trial was seen as the climax of the fundamentalist war on Darwinism.

Winfield Scott (1786–1866) During the Mexican War, he was the American general who captured Mexico City, which ended the war. Using his popularity from his military success, he ran as a Whig party candidate for President.

Sears, Roebuck and Company By the end of the nineteenth century, this company dominated the mail-order industry and helped create a truly national market. Its mail-order catalog and low prices allowed people living in rural areas and small towns to buy products that were previously too expensive or available only to city dwellers.

secession Shortly after President Abraham Lincoln was elected, southern states began dissolving their ties with the United States because they believed Lincoln and the Republican party were a threat to slavery.

Second Bank of the United States Established in 1816 after the first national bank's charter expired; it stabilized the economy by creating a sound national currency, by making loans to farmers, small manufacturers, and entrepreneurs, and by regulating the ability of state banks to issue their own paper currency.

Second Great Awakening Religious revival movement that arose in reaction to the growth of secularism and rationalist religion; spurred the growth of the Baptist and Methodist churches.

Second Industrial Revolution Beginning in the late nineteenth century, a wave of technological innovations, especially in iron and steel production, steam and electrical power, and telegraphic communications, all of which spurred industrial development and urban growth.

Second New Deal (1935–1938) Expansive cluster of legislation proposed by President Roosevelt that established new regulatory agencies, strengthened the rights of workers to organize unions, and laid the foundation of a federal social welfare system through the creation of Social Security.

Securities and Exchange Commission (1934) Federal agency established to regulate the issuance and trading of stocks and bonds in an effort to avoid financial panics and stock market "crashes."

Seneca Falls Convention (1848) Convention organized by feminists Lucretia Mott and Elizabeth Cady Stanton to promote women's rights and issue the pathbreaking Declaration of Sentiments.

"separate but equal" Principle underlying legal racial segregation, which was upheld in *Plessy v. Ferguson* (1896) and struck down in *Brown v. Board of Education* (1954).

separation of powers Strict division of the powers of government among three separate branches (executive, legislative, and judicial) which, in turn, check and balance each other.

September 11 On September 11, 2001, Islamic terrorists, who were members of the al Qaeda terrorist organization, hijacked four commercial airliners. Two were flown into the World Trade Center, a third into the Pentagon, and a fourth plane was brought down in Pennsylvania. In response, President George W. Bush launched his "war on terrorism." His administration assembled an international coalition to fight terrorism, which invaded Afghanistan after the country's government would not turn over Osama bin Laden. Bush and Congress passed the U.S.A. Patriot Act, which allowed government agencies to try suspected terrorists in secret military courts and eavesdrop on confidential conversations.

settlement houses Product of the late nineteenth-century movement to offer a broad array of social services in urban immigrant neighborhoods; Chicago's Hull House was one of hundreds of settlement houses that operated by the early twentieth century.

Seventeenth Amendment (1913) Constitutional amendment that provided for the direct election of senators rather than the traditional practice allowing state legislatures to name them.

Shakers Founded by Mother Ann Lee Stanley in England, the United Society of Believers in Christ's Second Appearing settled in Watervliet, New York, in 1774 and subsequently established eighteen additional communes in the Northeast, Indiana, and Kentucky.

share tenants Poor farmers who rented land to farm in exchange for a substantial share of the crop, though they would often have their own horse or mule, tools, and line of credit with a nearby store.

sharecroppers Poor, mostly black farmers who would work an owner's land in return for shelter, seed, fertilizer, mules, supplies, and food, as well as a substantial share of the crop produced.

Share-the-Wealth program Huey Long offered this program as an alternative to the New Deal. The program proposed to confiscate large personal fortunes, which would be used to guarantee every poor family a cash grant of $5,000 and every worker an annual income of $2,500. This program promised to provide pensions, reduce working hours, pay veterans' bonuses, and ensures a college education to every qualified student.

Shays's Rebellion Storming of the Massachusetts federal arsenal in 1787 by Daniel Shays and 1,200 armed farmers seeking debt relief from the state legislature through issuance of paper currency and lower taxes.

Sherman's "March to the Sea" The Union army's devastating march through Georgia from Atlanta to Savannah led by General William T. Sherman, intended to demoralize civilians and destroy the resources the Confederate army needed to fight.

silent majority Term popularized by President Richard Nixon to describe the great majority of American voters who did not express their political opinions publicly—"the non-demonstrators."

Sixteenth Amendment (1913) Constitutional amendment that authorized the federal income tax.

slave codes Ordinances passed by a colony or state to regulate the behavior of slaves, often including brutal punishments for infractions.

Alfred E. Smith (1873–1944) In the 1928 presidential election, he won the Democratic nomination, but failed to win the presidency. Rural voters distrusted him for being Catholic and the son of Irish immigrants as well as his anti-Prohibition stance.

Captain John Smith (1580–1631) A swashbuckling soldier of fortune with rare powers of leadership and self-promotion, he was appointed to the resident council to manage Jamestown.

Joseph Smith (1805–1844) In 1823, he claimed that the Angel Moroni showed him the location of several gold tablets on which the Book of Mormon was written. Using the Book of Mormon as his gospel, he founded the Church of Jesus Christ of Latter-day Saints, or Mormons. In 1839, they settled in Commerce, Illinois, to avoid persecution. In 1844, Joseph and his brother were arrested and jailed for ordering the destruction of a newspaper that opposed them. While in jail, an anti-Mormon mob stormed the jail and killed both of them.

Social Darwinism The application of Charles Darwin's theory of evolutionary natural selection to human society; Social Darwinists used the concept of "survival of the fittest" to justify class distinctions, explain poverty, and oppose government intervention in the economy.

social gospel Protestant movement that stressed the Christian obligation to address the mounting social problems caused by urbanization and industrialization.

social justice An important part of the Progressive's agenda, social justice sought to solve social problems through reform and regulation. Methods used to bring about social justice ranged from the founding of charities to the legislation of a ban on child labor.

Social Security Act (1935) Legislation enacted to provide federal assistance to retired workers through tax-funded pension payments and benefit payments to the unemployed and disabled.

Sons of Liberty First organized by Samuel Adams in the 1770s, groups of colonists dedicated to militant resistance against British control of the colonies.

Hernando de Soto (1500?–1542) A conquistador who explored the west coast of Florida, western North Carolina, and along the Arkansas river from 1539 till his death in 1542.

Southern Christian Leadership Conference (SCLC) Civil rights organization formed by Dr. Martin Luther King, Jr., that championed nonviolent direct action as a means of ending segregation.

"southern strategy" This strategy was a major reason for Richard Nixon's victory in the 1968 presidential election. To gain support in the South, Nixon assured southern conservatives that he would slow the federal enforcement of civil rights laws and appoint pro-southern justices to the Supreme Court. As president, Nixon fulfilled these promises.

Spanish Armada A massive Spanish fleet of 130 warships that was defeated at Plymouth in 1588 by the English navy during the reign of Queen Elizabeth I.

Spanish flu Unprecedentedly lethal influenza epidemic of 1918 that killed more than 22 million people worldwide.

Herbert Spencer (1820–1903) As the first major proponent of social Darwinism, he argued that human society and institutions are subject to the process of natural selection and that society naturally evolves for the better. He was against any form of government interference with the evolution of society, like business regulations, because it would help the "unfit" to survive.

spirituals Songs with religious messages sung by slaves to help ease the strain of field labor and to voice their suffering at the hands of their masters and overseers.

spoils system The term—meaning the filling of federal government jobs with persons loyal to the party of the president—originated in Andrew Jackson's first term; the system was replaced in the Progressive Era by civil service.

Square Deal Roosevelt's progressive agenda of the "Three C's": control of corporations, conservation of natural resources, and consumer protection.

stagflation Term coined by economists during the Nixon presidency to describe the unprecedented situation of stagnant economic growth and consumer price inflation occurring at the same time.

Joseph Stalin (1879–1953) The Bolshevik leader who succeeded Lenin as the leader of the Soviet Union in 1924 and ruled the country until his death. During his totalitarian rule of the Soviet Union, he used purges and a system of forced labor camps to maintain control over the country, and claimed vast areas of Eastern Europe for Soviet domination.

Stalwarts Conservative Republican party faction during the presidency of Rutherford B. Hayes, 1877–1881; led by Senator Roscoe B. Conkling of New York, Stalwarts opposed civil service reform and favored a third term for President Ulysses S. Grant.

Stamp Act Act of Parliament requiring that all printed materials (e.g., newspapers, bonds, and even playing cards) in the American colonies use paper with an official tax stamp in order to pay for British military protection of the colonies.

Stamp Act Congress Twenty-seven delegates from nine of the colonies met from October 7 to 25, 1765 and wrote a Declaration of the Rights and Grievances of the Colonies, a petition to the King and a petition to Parliament for the repeal of the Stamp Act.

Standard Oil Company Corporation under the leadership of John D. Rockefeller that attempted to dominate the entire oil industry through horizontal and vertical integration.

Elizabeth Cady Stanton (1815–1902) A prominent reformer and advocate for the rights of women, she helped organize the Seneca Falls Convention to discuss women's rights. The convention was the first of its kind and produced the Declaration of Sentiments, which proclaimed the equality of men and women.

staple crop A profitable market crop, such as cotton, tobacco, or rice that predominates in a given region.

state constitutions Charters that define the relationship between the state government and local governments and individuals, and also protects their rights from violation by the national government.

steamboats Ships and boats powered by wood-fired steam engines. First used in the early nineteenth century, they made two-way traffic possible in eastern river systems, creating a transcontinental market and an agricultural empire.

Thaddeus Stevens (1792–1868) As one of the leaders of the Radical Republicans, he argued that the former Confederate states should be viewed as conquered provinces, which were subject to the demands of the conquerors. He believed that all of Southern society needed to be changed, and he supported the abolition of slavery and racial equality.

Adlai E. Stevenson (1900–1965) In the 1952 and 1956 presidential elections, he was the Democratic nominee who lost to Dwight Eisenhower. He was also the U.S. Ambassador to the United Nations and is remembered for his famous speech in 1962 before the UN Security Council that unequivocally demonstrated that the Soviet Union had built nuclear missile bases in Cuba.

Stono Rebellion A 1739 slave uprising in South Carolina that was brutally quashed, leading to executions as well as a severe tightening of the slave code.

Stonewall Riots (1969) Violent clashes between police and gay patrons of New York City's Stonewall Inn, seen as the starting point of the modern gay rights movement.

Strategic Arms Limitation Treaty (SALT I) (1972) Agreement signed by President Nixon and Secretary Brezhnev prohibiting the development of missile defense systems in the United States and Soviet Union and limiting the quantity of nuclear warheads for both.

Strategic Defense Initiative (SDI) (1983) Ronald Reagan's proposed space-based anti-missile defense system, dubbed "Star Wars" by the media, that aroused great controversy and escalated the arms race between the United States and the Soviet Union.

Levi Strauss (1829–1902) A Jewish tailor who followed miners to California during the gold rush and began making durable work pants that were later dubbed blue jeans or Levi's.

Student Nonviolent Coordinating Committee (SNCC) Interracial organization formed in 1960 with the goal of intensifying the effort to end racial segregation.

Students for a Democratic Society (SDS) Major organization of the New Left, founded at the University of Michigan in 1960 by Tom Hayden and Al Haber.

suburbia Communities formed from mass migration of middle-class whites from urban centers.

Suez crisis (1956) British, French, and Israeli attack on Egypt after Nasser's seizure of the Suez Canal; President Eisenhower interceded to demand the withdrawal of the British, French, and Israeli forces from the Sinai peninsula and canal.

Sunbelt The label for an arc that stretched from the Carolinas to California. During the postwar era, much of the urban population growth occurred in this area.

the "surge" In early 2007, President Bush decided he would send a "surge" of new troops to Iraq and implement a new strategy. U.S. forces would shift their focus from offensive operations to the protection of Iraqi civilians from attacks by terrorist insurgents and sectarian militias. While the "surge" reduced the violence in Iraq, Iraqi leaders were still unable to develop a self-sustaining democracy.

Taft-Hartley Labor Act (1947) Congressional legislation that banned "unfair labor practices" by labor unions, required union leaders to sign anti-Communist "loyalty oaths," and prohibited federal employees from going on strike.

Taliban A coalition of ultraconservative Islamists who rose to power in Afghanistan after the Soviets withdrew. The Taliban leaders gave Osama bin Laden a safe haven in their country in exchange for aid in fighting the Northern Alliance, who were rebels opposed to the Taliban. After they refused to turn bin Laden over to the United States, America invaded Afghanistan.

Tammany Hall The "city machine" used by "Boss" Tweed to dominate politics in New York City until his arrest in 1871.

tariff A tax on goods imported from other nations, typically used to protect home industries from foreign competitors and to generate revenue for the federal government.

Tariff of 1816 A cluster of taxes on imports passed by Congress to protect America's emerging iron and textile industries from British competition.

Tariff of 1832 This tariff act reduced the duties on many items, but the tariffs on cloth and iron remained high. South Carolina nullified it along with the tariff of 1828. President Andrew Jackson sent federal troops to the state and asked Congress to grant him the authority to enforce the tariffs. Henry Clay presented a plan of gradually reducing the tariffs until 1842, which Congress passed and ended the crisis.

"Tariff of Abominations" (1828) Tax on imported goods, including British cloth and clothing, that strengthened New England textile companies but hurt southern consumers, who experienced a decrease in British demand for raw cotton grown in the South.

tariff reform Effort led by the Democratic party to reduce taxes on imported goods, which Republicans argued were needed to protect American industries from foreign competition.

Troubled Asset Relief Program (TARP) In 2008 President George W. Bush signed into law the bank bailout fund called Troubled Asset Relief Program (TARP), which required the Treasury Department to spend $700 billion to keep banks and other financial institutions from collapsing.

Zachary Taylor (1784–1850) During the Mexican War, he scored two quick victories against Mexico, which made him very popular in America. He used his popularity from his military victories to be elected president as a member of the Whig party, but died before he could complete his term.

Taylorism Labor system based on detailed study of work tasks, championed by Frederick Winslow Taylor, intended to maximize efficiency and profits for employers.

Tea Party Right-wing populist movement, largely made up of middle-class, white male conservatives, that emerged as a response to the expansion of the federal government under the Obama administration.

Teapot Dome Harding administration scandal in which Secretary of the Interior Albert B. Fall profited from secret leasing of government oil reserves in Wyoming to private oil companies.

Tecumseh (1768–1813) He was a leader of the Shawnee tribe who tried to unite all Indians into a confederation that could defend their hunting grounds. He believed that no land cessions could be made without the consent of all the tribes since they held the land in common. His beliefs and leadership made him seem dangerous to the American government and they waged war on him and his tribe. He was killed at the Battle of the Thames.

Tecumseh's Indian Confederacy A group of Native Americans under leadership of Shawnee leader Tecumseh and his prophet brother Tenskwatawa; its mission of fighting off American expansion was thwarted in the Battle of Tippecanoe (1811), when the confederacy fell apart.

Tejanos Texas settlers of Spanish or Mexican descent.

telegraph system System of electronic communication invented by Samuel F. B. Morse that could be transmitted instantaneously across great distances (first used in the 1840s).

Teller Amendment Addition to the congressional war resolution of April 20, 1898, which marked the U.S. entry into the war with Spain; the amendment declared that the United States' goal in entering the war was to ensure Cuba's independence, not to annex Cuba as a territory.

temperance A widespread reform movement, led by militant Christians, focused on reducing the use of alcoholic beverages.

tenements Shabby, low-cost inner-city apartment buildings that housed the urban poor in cramped, unventilated apartments.

Tenochtitlán The capital city of the Aztec Empire. The city was built on marshy islands on the western side of Lake Tetzcoco, which is the site of present-day Mexico City.

Tet offensive Surprise attack by Viet Cong guerrillas and the North Vietnamese army on U.S. and South Vietnamese forces in 1968 that shocked the American public and led to widespread sentiment against the war.

The Texas Revolution (1835–1836) Conflict between Texas colonists and the Mexican government that resulted in the creation of the separate Republic of Texas in 1836.

textile industry Commercial production of thread, fabric, and clothing from raw cotton in mills in New England during the first half of the nineteenth century, and later in the South in the late nineteenth century.

Thirteenth Amendment (1865) Amendment to the U. S. Constitution that freed all slaves in the United States.

Battle of Tippecanoe (1811) Battle in northern Indiana between U.S. troops and Native American warriors led by Tenskwatawa, the brother of Tecumseh, who had organized an anti-American Indian confederacy to fight American efforts to settle on Indian lands.

tobacco A cash crop grown in the Caribbean as well as the Virginia and Maryland colonies, made increasingly profitable by the rapidly growing popularity of smoking in Europe after the voyages of Columbus.

Gulf of Tonkin incident On August 2 and 4 of 1964, North Vietnamese vessels attacked two American destroyers in the Gulf of Tonkin off the coast of North Vietnam. President Johnson described the attacks as unprovoked. In reality, the U.S. ships were monitoring South Vietnamese attacks on North Vietnamese islands that America advisors had planned. The incident spurred the Tonkin Gulf resolution.

Tonkin Gulf Resolution Congressional action that granted the president unlimited authority to defend U.S. forces abroad, passed in August 1964 after an allegedly unprovoked attack on American warships off the coast of North Vietnam.

Tories Term used by Patriots to refer to Loyalists, or colonists who supported the Crown after the Declaration of Independence.

Townshend Acts Parliamentary measures to extract more revenue from the colonies; the Revenue Act of 1767, which taxed tea, paper, and other colonial imports, was one of the most notorious of these policies.

"Trail of Tears" The Cherokees' eight-hundred mile journey (1838–1839) from the southern Appalachians to Indian Territory (in present-day Oklahoma); four thousand died people along the way.

transcendentalism Philosophy of a small group of New England writers and thinkers who advocated personal spirituality, self-reliance, social reform, and harmony with nature.

Transcontinental railroad First line across the continent from Omaha, Nebraska, to Sacramento, California, established in 1869 with the linkage of the Union Pacific and Central Pacific railroads at Promontory, Utah.

Transcontinental Treaty (1819) (Adams-Onís Treaty) Treaty between Spain and the United States that clarified the boundaries of the Louisiana Purchase and arranged the transfer of Florida to the United States in exchange for cash.

triangular trade A network of trade in which exports from one region were sold to another region, which sent its exports to a third region, which exported its own goods back to the first country or colony.

Treaty of Ghent (1814) Agreement between Great Britain and the United States that ended the War of 1812, signed on December 24, 1814.

The Treaty of Guadeloupe Hidalgo (1848) Treaty between United States and Mexico that ended the Mexican-American War.

Treaty of Paris Settlement between Great Britain and France that ended the French and Indian War.

Treaty of Versailles Peace treaty that ended the First World War, forcing Germany to dismantle its military, pay immense war reparations, and give up its colonies around the world.

trench warfare A form of prolonged combat between the entrenched positions of opposing armies, often with little tactical movement.

Harry S. Truman (1884–1972) As President Roosevelt's vice president, he succeeded him after his death near the end of the Second World War. After the war, Truman wrestled with the inflation of both prices and wages, worked with Congress to pass the National Security Act, and banned racial discrimination in the hiring of federal employees and ended racial segregation in the armed forces. In foreign affairs, he established the Truman Doctrine to contain communism, developed the Marshall Plan to rebuild Europe, and sent the U.S. military to defend South Korea after North Korea invaded.

Truman Doctrine (1947) President Truman's program of "containing" communism in Eastern Europe and providing economic and military aid to any nations at risk of Communist takeover.

trust A business arrangement that gives a person or corporation (the "trustee") the legal power to manage another person's money or another company without owning those entities outright.

Sojourner Truth (1797?–1883) She was born into slavery, but New York State freed her in 1827. She spent the 1840s and 1850s travelling across the country and speaking to audiences about her experiences as slave and asking them to support abolition and women's rights.

Harriet Tubman (1820–1913) She was born a slave, but escaped to the North. She then returned to the South nineteen times and guided 300 slaves to freedom.

Frederick Jackson Turner An influential historian who authored the "Frontier Thesis" in 1893, arguing that the existence of an alluring frontier and the experience of persistent westward expansion informed the nation's democratic politics, unfettered economy, and rugged individualism.

Nat Turner (1800–1831) He was the leader of the only slave revolt to get past the planning stages. In August of 1831, the revolt began with the slaves killing the members of Turner's master's household. Then they attacked other neighboring farmhouses and recruited more slaves until the militia crushed the revolt. At least fifty-five whites were killed during the uprising and seventeen slaves were hanged afterwards.

Nat Turner's Rebellion (1831) Insurrection in rural Virginia led by black overseer Nat Turner, who killed slave owners and their families; in turn, federal troops indiscriminately killed hundreds of slaves in the process of putting down Turner and his rebels.

Tuskegee Airmen U.S. Army Air Corps unit of African American pilots whose combat success spurred military and civilian leaders to desegregate the armed forces after the war.

Mark Twain (1835–1910) Born Samuel Langhorne Clemens in Missouri, he became a popular humorous writer and lecturer and established himself as one of the great American satirists and authors. His two greatest books, *The Adventures of Tom Sawyer* and *The Adventures of Huckleberry Finn*, drew heavily on his childhood in Missouri.

"Boss" Tweed (1823–1878) An infamous political boss in New York City, Tweed used his "city machine," the Tammany Hall ring, to rule, plunder and sometimes improve the city's government. His political domination of New York City ended with his arrest in 1871 and conviction in 1873.

Twenty-first Amendment (1933) Repealed prohibition on the manufacture, sale, and transportation of alcoholic beverages, effectively nullifying the Eighteenth Amendment.

two-party system Domination of national politics by two major political parties, such as the Whigs and Democrats during the 1830s and 1840s.

Underground Railroad A secret system of routes and safe houses through which runaway slaves were led to freedom in the North.

Unitarians Members of the liberal New England Congregationalist offshoot, often well-educated and wealthy, who profess the oneness of God and the goodness of rational man.

United Farm Workers (UFW) Organization formed in 1962 to represent the interests of Mexican American migrant workers.

United Nations Security Council A major agency within the United Nations which remains in permanent session and has the responsibility of maintaining international peace and security. Originally, it consisted of five permanent members, (United States, Soviet Union, Britain, France, and the Republic of China), and six members elected to two-year terms. After 1965, the number of rotating members was increased to ten. In 1971, the Republic of China was replaced with the People's Republic of China and the Soviet Union was replaced by the Russian Federation in 1991.

Universalists Members of a New England religious movement, often from the working class, who believed in a merciful God and universal salvation.

USA Patriot Act (2001) Wide-reaching Congressional legislation, triggered by the War on Terror, which gave government agencies the right to eavesdrop on confidential conversations between prison inmates and their lawyers and permitted suspected terrorists to be tried in secret military courts.

U-boat German military submarine (*Unterseeboot*) used during the First World War to attack enemy naval vessels as well as merchant ships of enemy and neutral nations.

utopian communities Ideal communities that offered innovative social and economic relationships to those who were interested in achieving salvation.

Valley Forge American military encampment near Philadelphia, where more than 3,500 soldiers deserted or died from cold and hunger in the winter of 1777–1778.

Cornelius Vanderbilt (1794–1877) In the 1860s, he consolidated several separate railroad companies into one vast entity, New York Central Railroad.

Bartolomeo Vanzetti (1888–1927) In 1920, he and Nicola Sacco were Italian immigrants who were arrested for stealing $16,000 and killing a paymaster and his guard. Their trial took place during a time of numerous bombings by anarchists and their judge was openly prejudicial. Many liberals and radicals believe that their conviction was based on their political ideas and ethnic origin rather than the evidence against them.

vertical integration The process by which a corporation gains control of all aspects of the resources and processes needed to produce and sell a product.

Amerigo Vespucci (1455–1512) Italian explorer who reached the New World in 1499 and was the first to suggest that South America was a new continent. Afterward, European mapmakers used a variant of his first name, America, to label the New World.

Battle of Vicksburg (1863) A protracted battle in northern Mississippi in which Union forces under Ulysses Grant besieged the last major Confederate fortress on the Mississippi River, forcing the inhabitants into starvation and then submission.

Viet Cong Communist guerrillas in Vietnam who launched attacks on the Diem government.

Vietnamization Nixon-era policy of equipping and training South Vietnamese forces to take over the burden of combat from U.S. troops.

Vikings Norse people from Scandinavia who sailed to Newfoundland about A.D. 1001.

Francisco Pancho Villa (1877–1923) While the leader of one of the competing factions in the Mexican civil war, he provoked the United States into intervening. He hoped attacking the United States would help him build a reputation as an opponent of the United States, which would increase his popularity and discredit Mexican President Carranza.

Virginia Company A joint stock enterprise that King James I chartered in 1606. The company was to spread Christianity in the New World as well as find ways to make a profit in it.

Virginia Plan The delegations to the Constitutional Convention were divided between two plans on how to structure the government: Virginia called for a strong central government and a two-house legislature apportioned by population.

Virginia Statute of Religious Freedom A Virginia law, drafted by Thomas Jefferson in 1777 and enacted in 1786, that guarantees freedom of, and from, religion.

virtual representation The idea that the American colonies, although they had no actual representative in Parliament, were "virtually" represented by all members of Parliament.

Voting Rights Act of 1965 Legislation ensuring that all Americans were able to vote; the law ended literacy tests and other means of restricting voting rights.

Wagner Act (1935) Legislation that guaranteed workers the right to organize unions, granted them direct bargaining power, and barred employers from interfering with union activities.

George Wallace (1919–1998) An outspoken defender of segregation. As the governor of Alabama, he once attempted to block African American students from enrolling at the University of Alabama. He ran as the presidential candidate for the American Independent party in 1968, appealing to voters who were concerned about rioting anti-war protestors, the welfare system, and the growth of the federal government.

war hawks In 1811, congressional members from the southern and western districts who clamored for a war to seize Canada and Florida were dubbed "war hawks."

War of 1812 Conflict fought in North America and at sea between Great Britain and the United States, 1812–1815, over American shipping rights and British efforts to spur Indian attacks on American settlements. Canadians and Native Americans also fought in the war.

war on terror Global crusade to root out anti-American, anti-Western Islamist terrorist cells launched by President George W. Bush as a response to the 9/11 attacks.

War Powers Act (1973) Legislation requiring the president to inform Congress within 48 hours of the deployment of U.S. troops abroad and to withdraw them after 60 days unless Congress approves their continued deployment.

War Production Board Federal agency created by President Roosevelt in 1942 that converted America's industrial output to war production.

"war relocation camps" Detention camps housing thousands of Japanese Americans from the West Coast who were forcibly interned from 1942 until the end of the Second World War.

Warren Court The U.S. Supreme Court under Chief Justice Earl Warren, 1953–1969, decided such landmark cases as *Brown v. Board of Education* (school desegregation), *Baker v. Carr* (legislative redistricting), and *Gideon v. Wainwright* and *Miranda v. Arizona* (rights of criminal defendants).

Booker T. Washington (1856–1915) He founded a leading college for African Americans in Tuskegee, Alabama, and become the foremost black educator in America by the 1890s. He believed that the African American community should establish an economic base for its advancement before striving for social equality. His critics charged that his philosophy sacrificed educational and civil rights for dubious social acceptance and economic opportunities.

George Washington (1732–1799) In 1775, the Continental Congress named him the commander in chief of the Continental Army which defeated the British in the American Revolution. He had previously served as an officer in the French and Indian War. In 1787, he was the presiding officer over the Constitutional Convention, but participated little in the debates. In 1789, the Electoral College chose Washington to be the nation's first president. Washington faced the nation's first foreign and domestic crises, maintaining the United States' neutrality in foreign affairs. After two terms in office, Washington chose to step down; and the power of the presidency was peacefully passed to John Adams.

Watergate (1972–1974) Scandal that exposed the criminality and corruption of the Nixon administration and ultimately led to President Nixon's resignation in 1974.

Daniel Webster (1782–1852) As a representative from New Hampshire, he led the New Federalists in opposition to the moving of the second national bank from Boston to Philadelphia. Later, he served as representative and a senator for Massachusetts and emerged as a champion of a stronger national government. He also switched from opposing to supporting tariffs because New England had built up its manufactures with the understanding tariffs would protect them from foreign competitors.

Webster-Ashburton Treaty Settlement in 1842 of U.S.–Canadian border disputes in Maine, New York, Vermont, and in the Wisconsin Territory (now northern Minnesota).

Webster-Hayne debate U.S. Senate debate of January 1830 between Daniel Webster of Massachusetts and Robert Hayne of South Carolina over nullification and states' rights.

Western Front The contested frontier between the Central and Allied Powers that ran along northern France and across Belgium.

Whig party Political party founded in 1834 in opposition to the Jacksonian Democrats; Whigs supported federal funding for internal improvements, a national bank, and high tariffs on imported goods.

Whigs Another name for revolutionary Patriots.

Whiskey Rebellion (1794) Violent protest by western Pennsylvania farmers against the federal excise tax on corn whiskey, put down by a federal army.

Eli Whitney (1765–1825) He invented the cotton gin which could separate cotton from its seeds. One machine operator could separate fifty times more cotton than worker could by hand, which led to an increase in cotton production and prices. These increases gave planters a new profitable use for slavery and a lucrative slave trade emerged from the coastal South to the Southwest.

Wilderness Road Originally an Indian path through the Cumberland Gap, it was used by over 300,000 settlers who migrated westward to Kentucky in the last quarter of the eighteenth century.

Roger Williams (1603–1683) Puritan who believed that the purity of the church required a complete separation between church and state and freedom from coercion in matters of faith. In 1636, he established the town of Providence, the first permanent settlement in Rhode Island and the first to allow religious freedom in America.

Wendell L. Willkie (1892–1944) In the 1940 presidential election, he was the Republican nominee who ran against President Roosevelt. He supported aid to the Allies and criticized the New Deal programs. Voters looked at the increasingly dangerous world situation and chose to keep President Roosevelt in office for a third term.

Wilmot Proviso (1846) Proposal by Congressman David Wilmot, a Pennsylvania Democrat, to prohibit slavery in any land acquired in the Mexican-American War.

Woodrow Wilson (1856–1924) In the 1912 presidential election, Woodrow Wilson ran under the slogan of New Freedom, which promised to improve of the banking system, lower tariffs, and break up monopolies. At the beginning of the First World War, Wilson kept America neutral, but provided the Allies with credit for purchases of supplies; however, the sinking of U.S. merchant ships and the Zimmerman telegram caused him to ask Congress to declare war on Germany. Wilson supported the entry of America into the League of Nations and the ratification of the Treaty of Versailles, but Congress would not approve the entry or ratification.

John Winthrop Puritan leader and Governor of the Massachusetts Bay Colony who resolved to use the colony as a refuge for persecuted Puritans and as an instrument of building a "wilderness Zion" in America.

woman suffrage Movement to give women the right to vote through a constitutional amendment, spearheaded by Susan B. Anthony and Elizabeth Cady Stanton's National Woman Suffrage Association.

Women Accepted for Voluntary Emergency Services (WAVES) During the Second World War, the increased demand for labor shook up old prejudices about gender roles in the workplace and in the military. Nearly 200,000 women served in the Women's Army Corps or its naval equivalent, Women Accepted for Volunteer Emergency Service (WAVES).

Women's Army Corps Women's branch of the United States Army; by the end of the Second World War nearly 150,000 women had served in the WAC.

women's movement Wave of activism sparked by Betty Friedan's *The Feminine Mystique* (1963); it argued for equal rights for women and fought against the cult of domesticity of the 1950s that limited women's roles to the home as wife, mother, and housewife.

women's work The traditional term referring to routine tasks in the house, garden, and fields performed by women. The sphere of women's occupations expanded in the colonies to include medicine, shopkeeping, upholstering, and the operation of inns and taverns.

Woodstock In 1969, roughly a half a million young people converged on a farm near Bethel, New York, for a three-day music festival that was an expression of the flower children's free spirit.

Works Progress Administration (1935) Government agency established to manage several federal job programs created under the New Deal; it became the largest employer in the nation.

Wounded Knee, Battle of Last incident of the Indians Wars took place in 1890 in the Dakota Territory, where the U.S. Cavalry killed over 200 Sioux men, women, and children who were in the process of surrender.

XYZ affair French foreign minister Tallyrand's three anonymous agents demanded payments to stop French plundering of American ships in 1797; refusal to pay the bribe led to two years of sea war with France (1798–1800).

Yalta Conference (1945) Meeting of the "Big Three" Allied leaders, Franklin D. Roosevelt, Winston Churchill, and Joseph Stalin, to discuss how to divide control of postwar Germany and eastern Europe

yellow journalism A type of news reporting, epitomized in the 1890s by the newspaper empires of William Randolph Hearst and Joseph Pulitzer, that intentionally manipulates public opinion through sensational headlines, illustrations, and articles about both real and invented events.

yeomen Small landowners (the majority of white families in the South) who farmed their own land and usually did not own slaves.

Battle of Yorktown Last major battle of the Revolutionary War; General Cornwallis along with over 7,000 British troops surrendered to George Washington at Yorktown, Virginia, on October 17, 1781.

Brigham Young (1801–1877) Following Joseph Smith's death, he became the leader of the Mormons and promised Illinois officials that the Mormons would leave the state. In 1846, he led the Mormons to Utah and settled near the Salt Lake. After the United States gained Utah as part of the Treaty of Guadalupe Hidalgo, he became the governor of the territory and kept the Mormons virtually independent of federal authority.

youth culture The youth of the 1950s had more money and free time than any previous generation which allowed a distinct youth culture to emerge. A market emerged for products and activities that were specifically for young people such as transistor radios, rock records, *Seventeen* magazine, and Pat Boone movies.

Zimmermann telegram Message sent by a German official to the Mexican government in 1917 urging an invasion of the United States; the telegram was intercepted by British intelligence agents and angered Americans, many of whom called for war against Germany.

Appendix

The Declaration of Independence (1776)

When in the Course of human events, it becomes necessary for one people to dissolve the political bands which have connected them with another, and to assume among the powers of the earth, the separate and equal station to which the Laws of Nature and of Nature's God entitle them, a decent respect to the opinions of mankind requires that they should declare the causes which impel them to the separation.

We hold these truths to be self-evident, that all men are created equal, that they are endowed by their Creator with certain unalienable Rights, that among these are Life, Liberty and the pursuit of Happiness. —That to secure these rights, Governments are instituted among Men, deriving their just powers from the consent of the governed, —That whenever any Form of Government becomes destructive of these ends, it is the Right of the People to alter or to abolish it, and to institute new Government, laying its foundation on such principles and organizing its powers in such form, as to them shall seem most likely to effect their Safety and Happiness. Prudence, indeed, will dictate that Governments long established should not be changed for light and transient causes; and accordingly all experience hath shewn, that mankind are more disposed to suffer, while evils are sufferable, than to right themselves by abolishing the forms to which they are accustomed. But when a long train of abuses and usurpations, pursuing invariably the same Object evinces a design to reduce them under absolute Despotism, it is their right, it is their duty, to throw off such Government, and to provide new Guards for their future security.— Such has been the patient sufferance of these Colonies; and such is now the necessity which constrains them to alter their former Systems of Government. The history of the present King of Great Britain is a history of repeated injuries and usurpations, all having in direct object the establishment of an absolute Tyranny over these States. To prove this, let Facts be submitted to a candid world.

He has refused his Assent to Laws, the most wholesome and necessary for the public good.

He has forbidden his Governors to pass Laws of immediate and pressing importance, unless suspended in their operation till his Assent should be obtained; and when so suspended, he has utterly neglected to attend to them.

He has refused to pass other Laws for the accommodation of large districts of people, unless those people would relinquish the right of Representation in the Legislature, a right inestimable to them and formidable to tyrants only.

He has called together legislative bodies at places unusual, uncomfortable, and distant from the depository of their public Records, for the sole purpose of fatiguing them into compliance with his measures.

He has dissolved Representative Houses repeatedly, for opposing with manly firmness his invasions on the rights of the people.

He has refused for a long time, after such dissolutions, to cause others to be elected; whereby the Legislative powers, incapable of Annihilation, have returned to the People at large for their exercise; the State remaining in the mean time exposed to all the dangers of invasion from without, and convulsions within.

He has endeavoured to prevent the population of these States; for that purpose obstructing the Laws for Naturalization of Foreigners; refusing to pass others to encourage their migrations hither, and raising the conditions of new Appropriations of Lands.

He has obstructed the Administration of Justice, by refusing his Assent to Laws for establishing Judiciary powers.

He has made Judges dependent on his Will alone, for the tenure of their offices, and the amount and payment of their salaries.

He has erected a multitude of New Offices, and sent hither swarms of Officers to harrass our people, and eat out their substance.

He has kept among us, in times of peace, Standing Armies without the Consent of our legislatures.

He has affected to render the Military independent of and superior to the Civil power.

He has combined with others to subject us to a jurisdiction foreign to our constitution, and unacknowledged by our laws; giving his Assent to their Acts of pretended Legislation:

For quartering large bodies of armed troops among us:

For protecting them, by a mock Trial, from punishment for any Murders which they should commit on the Inhabitants of these States:

For cutting off our Trade with all parts of the world:

For imposing Taxes on us without our Consent:

For depriving us in many cases, of the benefits of Trial by Jury:

For transporting us beyond Seas to be tried for pretended offences

For abolishing the free System of English Laws in a neighbouring Province, establishing therein an Arbitrary government, and enlarging its Boundaries so as to render it at once an example and fit instrument for introducing the same absolute rule into these Colonies:

For taking away our Charters, abolishing our most valuable Laws, and altering fundamentally the Forms of our Governments:

For suspending our own Legislatures, and declaring themselves invested with power to legislate for us in all cases whatsoever.

He has abdicated Government here, by declaring us out of his Protection and waging War against us.

He has plundered our seas, ravaged our Coasts, burnt our towns, and destroyed the lives of our people.

He is at this time transporting large Armies of foreign Mercenaries to compleat the works of death, desolation and tyranny, already begun with circumstances of Cruelty & perfidy scarcely paralleled in the most barbarous ages, and totally unworthy the Head of a civilized nation.

He has constrained our fellow Citizens taken Captive on the high Seas to bear Arms against their Country, to become the executioners of their friends and Brethren, or to fall themselves by their Hands.

He has excited domestic insurrections amongst us, and has endeavoured to bring on the inhabitants of our frontiers, the merciless Indian Savages, whose known rule of warfare, is an undistinguished destruction of all ages, sexes and conditions.

In every stage of these Oppressions We have Petitioned for Redress in the most humble terms: Our repeated Petitions have been answered only by repeated injury. A Prince whose character is thus marked by every act which may define a Tyrant, is unfit to be the ruler of a free people.

Nor have We been wanting in attentions to our Brittish brethren. We have warned them from time to time of attempts by their legislature to extend an unwarrantable jurisdiction over us. We have reminded them of the circumstances of our emigration and settlement here. We have appealed to their native justice and magnanimity, and we have conjured them by the ties of our common kindred to disavow these usurpations, which, would inevitably interrupt our connections and correspondence. They too have been deaf to the voice of justice and of consanguinity. We must, therefore, acquiesce in the necessity, which denounces our Separation, and hold them, as we hold the rest of mankind, Enemies in War, in Peace Friends.

We, therefore, the Representatives of the united States of America, in General Congress, Assembled, appealing to the Supreme Judge of the world for the rectitude of our intentions, do, in the Name, and by Authority of the good People of these Colonies, solemnly publish and declare, That these United Colonies are, and of Right ought to be Free and Independent States; that they are Absolved from all Allegiance to the British Crown, and that all political connection between them and the State of Great Britain, is and ought to be totally dissolved; and that as Free and Independent States, they have full Power to levy War, conclude Peace, contract Alliances, establish Commerce, and to do all other Acts and Things which Independent States may of right do. And for the support of this Declaration, with a firm reliance on the protection of divine Providence, we mutually pledge to each other our Lives, our Fortunes and our sacred Honor.

Georgia
Button Gwinnett
Lyman Hall
George Walton

North Carolina
William Hooper
Joseph Hewes
John Penn

South Carolina
Edward Rutledge
Thomas Heyward, Jr.
Thomas Lynch, Jr.
Arthur Middleton

Massachusetts
John Hancock

Maryland
Samuel Chase
William Paca
Thomas Stone
Charles Carroll
    of Carrollton

Virginia
George Wythe
Richard Henry Lee
Thomas Jefferson
Benjamin Harrison
Thomas Nelson, Jr.
Francis Lightfoot Lee
Carter Braxton

Pennsylvania
Robert Morris
Benjamin Rush
Benjamin Franklin
John Morton
George Clymer
James Smith
George Taylor
James Wilson
George Ross

Delaware
Caesar Rodney
George Read
Thomas McKean

New York
William Floyd
Philip Livingston
Francis Lewis
Lewis Morris

New Jersey
Richard Stockton
John Witherspoon
Francis Hopkinson
John Hart
Abraham Clark

New Hampshire
Josiah Bartlett
William Whipple

Massachusetts
Samuel Adams
John Adams
Robert Treat Paine
Elbridge Gerry

Rhode Island
Stephen Hopkins
William Ellery

Connecticut
Roger Sherman
Samuel Huntington
William Williams
Oliver Wolcott

New Hampshire
Matthew Thornton

Articles of Confederation (1787)

To ALL TO WHOM these Presents shall come, we the undersigned Delegates of the States affixed to our Names send greeting.

Whereas the Delegates of the United States of America in Congress assembled did on the fifteenth day of November in the Year of our Lord One Thousand Seven Hundred and Seventy-seven, and in the Second Year of the Independence of America agree to certain articles of Confederation and perpetual Union between the States of Newhampshire, Massachusetts-bay, Rhodeisland and Providence Plantations, Connecticut, New York, New Jersey, Pennsylvania, Delaware, Maryland, Virginia, North-Carolina, South-Carolina and Georgia in the Words following, viz.

Articles of Confederation and perpetual Union between the States of Newhampshire, Massachusetts-bay, Rhodeisland and Providence Plantations, Connecticut, New-York, New-Jersey, Pennsylvania, Delaware, Maryland, Virginia, North-Carolina, South-Carolina and Georgia.

ARTICLE I. The stile of this confederacy shall be "The United States of America."

ARTICLE II. Each State retains its sovereignty, freedom and independence, and every power, jurisdiction and right, which is not by this confederation expressly delegated to the United States, in Congress assembled.

ARTICLE III. The said States hereby severally enter into a firm league of friendship with each other, for their common defence, the security of their liberties, and their mutual and general welfare, binding themselves to assist each other, against all force offered to, or attacks made upon them, or any of them, on account of religion, sovereignty, trade or any other pretence whatever.

ARTICLE IV. The better to secure and perpetuate mutual friendship and intercourse among the people of the different States in this Union, the free inhabitants of each of these States, paupers, vagabonds and fugitives from justice excepted, shall be entitled to all privileges and immunities of free citizens in the several States; and the people of each State shall have free ingress and regress to and from any other State, and shall enjoy therein all the privileges of trade and commerce, subject to the same duties, impositions and restrictions as the inhabitants thereof respectively, provided that such restrictions shall not extend so far as to prevent the removal of property imported into any State, to any other State of which the owner is an inhabitant; provided also that no imposition, duties or restriction shall be laid by any State, on the property of the United States, or either of them.

If any person guilty of, or charged with treason, felony, or other high misdemeanor in any State, shall flee from justice, and be found in any of the United States, he shall upon demand of the Governor or Executive power, of the State from which he fled, be delivered up and removed to the State having jurisdiction of his offence.

Full faith and credit shall be given in each of these States to the records, acts and judicial proceedings of the courts and magistrates of every other State.

ARTICLE V. For the more convenient management of the general interests of the United States, delegates shall be annually appointed in such manner as the legislature of each State shall direct, to meet in Congress on the first Monday in November, in every year, with a power reserved to each State, to recall its delegates, or any of them, at any time within the year, and to send others in their stead, for the remainder of the year.

No State shall be represented in Congress by less than two, nor by more than seven members; and no person shall be capable of being a delegate for more than three years in any term of six years; nor shall any person, being a delegate, be capable of holding any office under the United States, for which he, or another for his benefit receives any salary, fees or emolument of any kind.

Each State shall maintain its own delegates in a meeting of the States, and while they act as members of the committee of the States.

In determining questions in the United States, in Congress assembled, each State shall have one vote.

Freedom of speech and debate in Congress shall not be impeached or questioned in any court, or place out of Congress, and the members of Congress shall be protected in their persons from arrests and imprisonments, during the time of their going to and from, and attendance on Congress, except for treason, felony, or breach of the peace.

ARTICLE VI. No State without the consent of the United States in Congress assembled, shall send any embassy to, or receive any embassy from, or enter into any conference, agreement, alliance or treaty with any king, prince or state; nor shall any person holding any office of profit or trust under the United States, or any of them, accept of any present, emolument, office or title of any kind whatever from any king, prince or foreign state; nor shall the United States in Congress assembled, or any of them, grant any title of nobility.

No two or more States shall enter into any treaty, confederation or alliance whatever between them, without the consent of the United States in Congress assembled, specifying accurately the purposes for which the same is to be entered into, and how long it shall continue.

No State shall lay any imposts or duties, which may interfere with any stipulations in treaties, entered into by the United States in Congress assembled, with any king, prince or state, in pursuance of any treaties already proposed by Congress, to the courts of France and Spain.

No vessels of war shall be kept up in time of peace by any State, except such number only, as shall be deemed necessary by the United States in Congress assembled, for the defence of such State, or its trade; nor shall any body of forces be kept up by any State, in time of peace, except such number only, as in the judgment of the United States, in Congress assembled, shall be deemed requisite to garrison the forts necessary for the defence of such State; but every State shall always keep up a well regulated and disciplined militia, sufficiently armed and accoutred, and shall provide and constantly have ready for use, in public stores, a due number of field pieces and tents, and a proper quantity of arms, ammunition and camp equipage.

No State shall engage in any war without the consent of the United States in Congress assembled, unless such State be actually invaded by enemies, or shall have received certain advice of a resolution being formed by some nation of Indians to invade such State, and the danger is so imminent as not to admit of a delay, till the United States in Congress assembled can be consulted: nor shall any State grant commissions to any ships or vessels of war, nor letters of marque or reprisal, except it be after a declaration of war by the United States in Congress assembled, and then only against the kingdom or state and the subjects thereof, against which war has been so declared, and under such regulations as shall be established by the United States in Congress assembled, unless such State be infested by pirates, in which case vessels of war may be fitted out for that occasion, and kept so long as the danger shall continue, or until the United States in Congress assembled shall determine otherwise.

ARTICLE VII. When land-forces are raised by any State of the common defence, all officers of or under the rank of colonel, shall be appointed by the Legislature of each State respectively by whom such forces shall be raised, or in such manner as such State shall direct, and all vacancies shall be filled up by the State which first made the appointment.

ARTICLE VIII. All charges of war, and all other expenses that shall be incurred for the common defence or general welfare, and allowed by the United States in Congress assembled, shall be defrayed out of a common treasury, which shall be supplied by the several States, in proportion to the value of all land within each State, granted to or surveyed for any person, as such land and the buildings and improvements thereon shall be estimated according to such mode as the United States in Congress assembled, shall from time to time direct and appoint.

The taxes for paying that proportion shall be laid and levied by the authority and direction of the Legislatures of the several States within the time agreed upon by the United States in Congress assembled.

ARTICLE IX. The United States in Congress assembled, shall have the sole and exclusive right and power of determining on peace and war, except in the cases mentioned in the sixth article—of sending and receiving ambassadors—entering into treaties and alliances, provided that no treaty of commerce shall be made whereby the legislative power of the respective States shall be restrained from imposing such imposts and duties on foreigners, as their own people are subjected to, or from prohibiting the exportation or importation of and species of goods or commodities whatsoever—of establishing rules for deciding in all cases, what captures on land or water shall be legal, and in what manner prizes taken by land or naval forces in the service of the United States shall be divided or appropriated—of granting letters of marque and reprisal in times of peace—appointing courts for the trial of piracies and felonies committed on the high seas and establishing courts for receiving and determining finally appeals in all cases of captures, provided that no member of Congress shall be appointed a judge of any of the said courts.

The United States in Congress assembled shall also be the last resort on appeal in all disputes and differences now subsisting or that hereafter may arise between two or more States concerning boundary, jurisdiction or any other cause whatever; which authority shall always be exercised in the manner following. Whenever the legislative or executive authority or lawful agent of any State in controversy with another shall present a petition to Congress, stating the matter in question and praying for a hearing, notice thereof shall be given by order of Congress to the legislative or executive authority of the other State in controversy, and a day assigned for the appearance of the parties by their lawful agents, who shall then be directed to appoint by joint consent, commissioners or judges to constitute a court for hearing and determining the matter in question: but if they cannot agree, Congress shall name three persons out of each of the United States, and from the list of such persons each party shall alternately strike out one, the petitioners beginning, until the number shall be reduced to thirteen; and from that number not less than seven, nor more than nine names as Congress shall direct, shall in the presence of Congress be drawn out by lot, and the persons whose names shall be so drawn or any five of them, shall be commissioners or judges, to hear and finally determine the controversy, so always as a major part of the judges who shall hear the cause shall agree in the determination: and if either party shall neglect to attend at the day appointed, without reasons, which Congress shall judge sufficient, or being present shall refuse to strike, the Congress shall proceed to nominate three persons out of each State, and the Secretary of Congress shall strike in behalf of such party absent or refusing; and the judgment and sentence of the court to be appointed, in the manner before prescribed, shall be final and conclusive; and if any of the parties shall refuse to submit to the authority of such court, or to appear or defend their claim or cause, the court shall nevertheless proceed to pronounce sentence, or judgment, which shall in like manner be final and decisive, the judgment or sentence and other proceedings being in either case transmitted to Congress, and lodged among the acts of Congress for the security of the parties concerned: provided that every commissioner, before he sits in judgment, shall take an oath to be administered by one of the judges of the supreme or superior court of the State where the case shall be tried, "well and truly to hear and determine the matter in question, according to the best of his judgment, without favour, affection or hope of reward:" provided also that no State shall be deprived of territory for the benefit of the United States.

All controversies concerning the private right of soil claimed under different grants of two or more States, whose jurisdiction as they may respect such lands, and the states which passed such grants are adjusted, the said grants or either of them being at the same time claimed to have originated antecedent to such settlement of jurisdiction, shall on the petition of either party to the Congress of the United States, be finally determined as near as may be in the same manner as is before prescribed for deciding disputes respecting territorial jurisdiction between different States.

The United States in Congress assembled shall also have the sole and exclusive right and power of regulating the alloy and value of coin struck by their own authority, or by that of the respective States—fixing the standard of weights and measures throughout the United States—regulating the trade and managing all affairs with the Indians, not members of any of the States, provided that the legislative right of any State within its own limits be not infringed or violated—establishing and regulating post-offices from one State to another, throughout all of the United States, and exacting such postage on the papers passing thro' the same as may be requisite to defray the expenses of the said office—appointing all officers of the land forces, in the service of the United States, excepting regimental officers—appointing all the officers of the naval forces, and commissioning all officers whatever in the service of the United States—making rules for the government and regulation of the said land and naval forces, and directing their operations.

The United States in Congress assembled shall have authority to appoint a committee, to sit in the recess of Congress, to be denominated "a Committee of the States," and to consist of one delegate from each State; and to appoint such other committees and civil officers as may be necessary for managing the general affairs of the United States under their direction—to appoint one of their number to preside, provided that no person be allowed to serve in the office of president more than one year in any term of three years; to ascertain the necessary sums of money to be raised for the service of the United States, and to appropriate and apply the same for defraying the public expenses—to borrow money, or emit bills on the credit of the United States, transmitting every half year to the respective States an account of the sums of money so borrowed or emitted,—to build and equip a navy—to agree upon the number of land forces, and to make requisitions from each State for its quota, in proportion to the number of white inhabitants in such State; which requisition shall be binding, and thereupon the Legislature of each State shall appoint the regimental officers, raise the men and cloath, arm and equip them in a soldier like manner, at the expense of the United States; and the officers and men so cloathed, armed and equipped shall march to the place appointed, and within the time agreed on by the United States in Congress assembled: but if the United States in Congress assembled shall, on consideration of circumstances judge proper that any State should not raise men, or should raise a smaller number of men than the quota thereof, such extra number shall be raised, officered, cloathed, armed and equipped in the same manner as the quota of such State, unless the legislature of such State shall judge that such extra number cannot be safely spared out of the same, in which case they shall raise officer, cloath, arm and equip as many of such extra number as they judge can be safely spared. And the officers and men so cloathed, armed and equipped, shall march to the place appointed, and within the time agreed on by the United States in Congress assembled.

The United States in Congress assembled shall never engage in a war, nor grant letters of marque and reprisal in time of peace, nor enter into any treaties or alliances, nor coin money, nor regulate the value thereof, nor ascertain the sums and expenses necessary for the defence and welfare of the United States, or any of them, nor emit bills, nor borrow money on the credit of the United States, nor appropriate money, nor agree upon the number of vessels to be built or purchased, or the number of land or sea forces to be raised, nor appoint a commander in chief of the army or navy, unless nine States assent to the same: nor shall a question on any other point, except for adjourning from day to day be determined, unless by the votes of a majority of the United States in Congress assembled.

The Congress of the United States shall have power to adjourn to any time within the year, and to any place within the United States, so that no period of adjournment be for a longer duration than the space of six months, and shall publish the journal of their proceedings monthly, except such parts thereof relating to treaties, alliances or military operations, as in their judgment require secrecy; and the yeas and nays of the delegates of each State on any question shall be entered on the Journal, when it is desired by any delegate; and the delegates of a State, or any of them, at his or their request shall be furnished with a transcript of the said journal, except such parts as are above excepted, to lay before the Legislatures of the several States.

Article X. The committee of the States, or any nine of them, shall be authorized to execute, in the recess of Congress, such of the powers of Congress as the United States in Congress assembled, by the consent of nine States, shall from time to time think expedient to vest them with; provided that no power be delegated to the said committee, for the exercise of which, by the articles of confederation, the voice of nine States in the Congress of the United States assembled is requisite.

Article XI. Canada acceding to this confederation, and joining in the measures of the United States, shall be admitted into, and entitled to all the advantages of this Union: but no other colony shall be admitted into the same, unless such admission be agreed to by nine States.

Article XII. All bills of credit emitted, monies borrowed and debts contracted by, or under the authority of Congress, before the assembling of the United States, in pursuance of the present confederation, shall be deemed and considered as a charge against the United States, for payment and satisfaction whereof the said United States, and the public faith are hereby solemnly pledged.

ARTICLE XIII. Every State shall abide by the determinations of the United States in Congress assembled, on all questions which by this confederation are submitted to them. And the articles of this confederation shall be inviolably observed by every State, and the Union shall be perpetual; nor shall any alteration at any time hereafter be made in any of them; unless such alteration be agreed to in a Congress of the United States, and be afterwards confirmed by the Legislatures of every State.

And whereas it has pleased the Great Governor of the world to incline the hearts of the Legislatures we respectively represent in Congress, to approve of, and to authorize us to ratify the said articles of confederation and perpetual union. Know ye that we the undersigned delegates, by virtue of the power and authority to us given for that purpose, do by these presents, in the name and in behalf of our respective constituents, fully and entirely ratify and confirm each and every of the said articles of confederation and perpetual union, and all and singular the matters and things therein contained: and we do further solemnly plight and engage the faith of our respective constituents, that they shall abide by the determinations of the United States in Congress assembled, on all questions, which by the said confederation are submitted to them. And that the articles thereof shall be inviolably observed by the States we respectively represent, and that the Union shall be perpetual.

In witness thereof we have hereunto set our hands in Congress. Done at Philadelphia in the State of Pennsylvania the ninth day of July in the year of our Lord one thousand seven hundred and seventy-eight, and in the third year of the independence of America.

The Constitution of the United States (1787)

We the People of the United States, in Order to form a more perfect Union, establish Justice, insure domestic Tranquility, provide for the common defence, promote the general Welfare, and secure the Blessings of Liberty to ourselves and our Posterity, do ordain and establish this Constitution for the United States of America.

Article. I.

Section. 1. All legislative Powers herein granted shall be vested in a Congress of the United States, which shall consist of a Senate and House of Representatives.

Section. 2. The House of Representatives shall be composed of Members chosen every second Year by the People of the several States, and the Electors in each State shall have the Qualifications requisite for Electors of the most numerous Branch of the State Legislature.

No Person shall be a Representative who shall not have attained to the Age of twenty five Years, and been seven Years a Citizen of the United States, and who shall not, when elected, be an Inhabitant of that State in which he shall be chosen.

Representatives and direct Taxes shall be apportioned among the several States which may be included within this Union, according to their respective Numbers, which shall be determined by adding to the whole Number of free Persons, including those bound to Service for a Term of Years, and excluding Indians not taxed, three fifths of all other Persons. The actual Enumeration shall be made within three Years after the first Meeting of the Congress of the United States, and within every subsequent Term of ten Years, in such Manner as they shall by Law direct. The Number of Representatives shall not exceed one for every thirty Thousand, but each State shall have at Least one Representative; and until such enumeration shall be made, the State of New Hampshire shall be entitled to chuse three, Massachusetts eight, Rhode-Island and Providence Plantations one, Connecticut five, New-York six, New Jersey four, Pennsylvania eight, Delaware one, Maryland six, Virginia ten, North Carolina five, South Carolina five, and Georgia three.

When vacancies happen in the Representation from any State, the Executive Authority thereof shall issue Writs of Election to fill such Vacancies.

The House of Representatives shall chuse their Speaker and other Officers; and shall have the sole Power of Impeachment.

Section. 3. The Senate of the United States shall be composed of two Senators from each State, chosen by the Legislature thereof for six Years; and each Senator shall have one Vote.

Immediately after they shall be assembled in Consequence of the first Election, they shall be divided as equally as may be into three Classes. The Seats of the Senators of the first Class shall be vacated at the Expiration of the second Year, of the second Class at the Expiration of the fourth Year, and of the third Class at the Expiration of the sixth Year, so that one third may be chosen every second Year; and if Vacancies happen by Resignation, or otherwise, during the Recess of the Legislature of any State, the Executive thereof may make temporary Appointments until the next Meeting of the Legislature, which shall then fill such Vacancies.

No Person shall be a Senator who shall not have attained to the Age of thirty Years, and been nine Years a Citizen of the United States, and who shall not, when elected, be an Inhabitant of that State for which he shall be chosen.

The Vice President of the United States shall be President of the Senate, but shall have no Vote, unless they be equally divided.

The Senate shall chuse their other Officers, and also a President pro tempore, in the Absence of the Vice President, or when he shall exercise the Office of President of the United States.

The Senate shall have the sole Power to try all Impeachments. When sitting for that Purpose, they shall be on Oath or Affirmation. When the President of the United States is tried, the Chief Justice shall preside: And no Person shall be convicted without the Concurrence of two thirds of the Members present.

Judgment in Cases of Impeachment shall not extend further than to removal from Office, and disqualification to hold and enjoy any Office of honor, Trust or Profit under the United States: but the Party convicted shall nevertheless be liable and subject to Indictment, Trial, Judgment and Punishment, according to Law.

Section. 4. The Times, Places and Manner of holding Elections for Senators and Representatives, shall be prescribed in each State by the Legislature thereof; but the Congress may at any time by Law make or alter such Regulations, except as to the Places of chusing Senators.

The Congress shall assemble at least once in every Year, and such Meeting shall be on the first Monday in December, unless they shall by Law appoint a different Day.

Section. 5. Each House shall be the Judge of the Elections, Returns and Qualifications of its own Members, and a Majority of each shall constitute a Quorum to do Business; but a smaller Number may adjourn from day to day, and may be authorized to compel the Attendance of absent Members, in such Manner, and under such Penalties as each House may provide.

Each House may determine the Rules of its Proceedings, punish its Members for disorderly Behaviour, and, with the Concurrence of two thirds, expel a Member.

Each House shall keep a Journal of its Proceedings, and from time to time publish the same, excepting such Parts as may in their Judgment require Secrecy; and the Yeas and Nays of the Members of either House on any question shall, at the Desire of one fifth of those Present, be entered on the Journal.

Neither House, during the Session of Congress, shall, without the Consent of the other, adjourn for more than three days, nor to any other Place than that in which the two Houses shall be sitting.

Section. 6. The Senators and Representatives shall receive a Compensation for their Services, to be ascertained by Law, and paid out of the Treasury of the United States. They shall in all Cases, except Treason, Felony and Breach of the Peace, be privileged from Arrest during their Attendance at the Session of their respective Houses, and in going to and returning from the same; and for any Speech or Debate in either House, they shall not be questioned in any other Place.

No Senator or Representative shall, during the Time for which he was elected, be appointed to any civil Office under the Authority of the United States, which shall have been created, or the Emoluments whereof shall have been encreased during such time; and no Person holding any Office under the United States, shall be a Member of either House during his Continuance in Office.

Section. 7. All Bills for raising Revenue shall originate in the House of Representatives; but the Senate may propose or concur with Amendments as on other Bills.

Every Bill which shall have passed the House of Representatives and the Senate shall, before it become a Law, be presented to the President of the United States; If he approve he shall sign it, but if not he shall return it, with his Objections to that House in which it shall have originated, who shall enter the Objections at large on their Journal, and proceed to reconsider it. If after such Reconsideration two thirds of that House shall agree to pass the Bill, it shall be sent, together with the Objections, to the other House, by which it shall likewise be reconsidered, and if approved by two thirds of that House, it shall become a Law. But in all such Cases the Votes of both Houses shall be determined by yeas and Nays, and the Names of the Persons voting for and against the Bill shall be entered on the Journal of each House respectively. If any Bill shall not be returned by the President within ten Days (Sundays excepted) after it shall have been presented to him, the Same shall be a Law, in like Manner as if he had signed it, unless the Congress by their Adjournment prevent its Return, in which Case it shall not be a Law.

Every Order, Resolution, or Vote to which the Concurrence of the Senate and House of Representatives may be necessary (except on a question of Adjournment) shall be presented to the President of the United States; and before the Same shall take Effect, shall be approved by him, or being disapproved by him, shall be repassed by two thirds of the Senate and House of Representatives, according to the Rules and Limitations prescribed in the Case of a Bill.

Section. 8. The Congress shall have Power To lay and collect Taxes, Duties, Imposts and Excises, to pay the Debts and provide for the common Defence and general Welfare of the United States; but all Duties, Imposts and Excises shall be uniform throughout the United States;

To borrow Money on the credit of the United States;

To regulate Commerce with foreign Nations, and among the several States, and with the Indian Tribes;

To establish an uniform Rule of Naturalization, and uniform Laws on the subject of Bankruptcies throughout the United States;

To coin Money, regulate the Value thereof, and of foreign Coin, and fix the Standard of Weights and Measures;

To provide for the Punishment of counterfeiting the Securities and current Coin of the United States;

To establish Post Offices and post Roads;

To promote the Progress of Science and useful Arts, by securing for limited Times to Authors and Inventors the exclusive Right to their respective Writings and Discoveries;

To constitute Tribunals inferior to the supreme Court;

To define and punish Piracies and Felonies committed on the high Seas, and Offences against the Law of Nations;

To declare War, grant Letters of Marque and Reprisal, and make Rules concerning Captures on Land and Water;

To raise and support Armies, but no Appropriation of Money to that Use shall be for a longer Term than two Years;

To provide and maintain a Navy;

To make Rules for the Government and Regulation of the land and naval Forces;

To provide for calling forth the Militia to execute the Laws of the Union, suppress Insurrections and repel Invasions;

To provide for organizing, arming, and disciplining, the Militia, and for governing such Part of them as may be employed in the Service of the United States, reserving to the States respectively, the Appointment of the Officers, and the Authority of training the Militia according to the discipline prescribed by Congress;

To exercise exclusive Legislation in all Cases whatsoever, over such District (not exceeding ten Miles square) as may, by Cession of particular States, and the Acceptance of Congress, become the Seat of the Government of the United States, and to exercise like Authority over all Places purchased by the Consent of the Legislature of the State in which the Same shall be, for the Erection of Forts, Magazines, Arsenals, dock-Yards, and other needful Buildings;—And

To make all Laws which shall be necessary and proper for carrying into Execution the foregoing Powers, and all other Powers vested by this Constitution in the Government of the United States, or in any Department or Officer thereof.

Section. 9. The Migration or Importation of such Persons as any of the States now existing shall think proper to admit, shall not be prohibited by the Congress prior to the Year one thousand eight hundred and eight, but a Tax or duty may be imposed on such Importation, not exceeding ten dollars for each Person.

The Privilege of the Writ of Habeas Corpus shall not be suspended, unless when in Cases of Rebellion or Invasion the public Safety may require it.

No Bill of Attainder or ex post facto Law shall be passed.

No Capitation, or other direct, Tax shall be laid, unless in Proportion to the Census or enumeration herein before directed to be taken.

No Tax or Duty shall be laid on Articles exported from any State.

No Preference shall be given by any Regulation of Commerce or Revenue to the Ports of one State over those of another; nor shall Vessels bound to, or from, one State, be obliged to enter, clear, or pay Duties in another.

No Money shall be drawn from the Treasury, but in Consequence of Appropriations made by Law; and a regular Statement and Account of the Receipts and Expenditures of all public Money shall be published from time to time.

No Title of Nobility shall be granted by the United States: And no Person holding any Office of Profit or Trust under them, shall, without the Consent of the Congress, accept of any present, Emolument, Office, or Title, of any kind whatever, from any King, Prince, or foreign State.

Section. 10. No State shall enter into any Treaty, Alliance, or Confederation; grant Letters of Marque and Reprisal; coin Money; emit Bills of Credit; make any Thing but gold and silver Coin a Tender in Payment of Debts; pass any Bill of Attainder, ex post facto Law, or Law impairing the Obligation of Contracts, or grant any Title of Nobility.

No State shall, without the Consent of the Congress, lay any Imposts or Duties on Imports or Exports, except what may be absolutely necessary for executing it's inspection Laws: and the net Produce of all Duties and Imposts, laid by any State on Imports or Exports, shall be for the Use of the Treasury of the United States; and all such Laws shall be subject to the Revision and Controul of the Congress.

No State shall, without the Consent of Congress, lay any Duty of Tonnage, keep Troops, or Ships of War in time of Peace, enter into any Agreement or Compact with another State, or with a foreign Power, or engage in War, unless actually invaded, or in such imminent Danger as will not admit of delay.

Article. II.

Section. 1. The executive Power shall be vested in a President of the United States of America. He shall hold his Office during the Term of four Years, and, together with the Vice President, chosen for the same Term, be elected, as follows:

Each State shall appoint, in such Manner as the Legislature thereof may direct, a Number of Electors, equal to the whole Number of Senators and Representatives to which the State may be entitled in the Congress: but no Senator or Representative, or Person holding an Office of Trust or Profit under the United States, shall be appointed an Elector.

The Electors shall meet in their respective States, and vote by Ballot for two Persons, of whom one at least shall not be an Inhabitant of the same State with themselves. And they shall make a List of all the Persons voted for, and of the Number of Votes for each; which List they shall sign and certify, and transmit sealed to the Seat of the Government of the United States, directed to the President of the Senate. The President of the Senate shall, in the Presence of the Senate and House of Representatives, open all the Certificates, and the Votes shall then be counted. The Person having the greatest Number of Votes shall be the President, if such Number be a Majority of the whole Number of Electors appointed; and if there be more than one who have such Majority, and have an equal Number of Votes, then the House of Representatives shall immediately chuse by Ballot one of them for President; and if no Person have a Majority, then from the five highest on the List the said House shall in like Manner chuse the President. But in chusing the President, the Votes shall be taken by States, the Representation from each State having one Vote; A quorum for this purpose shall consist of a Member or Members from two thirds of the States, and a Majority of all the States shall be necessary to a Choice. In every Case, after the Choice of the President, the Person having the greatest Number of Votes of the Electors shall be the Vice President. But if there should remain two or more who have equal Votes, the Senate shall chuse from them by Ballot the Vice President.

The Congress may determine the Time of chusing the Electors, and the Day on which they shall give their Votes; which Day shall be the same throughout the United States.

No Person except a natural born Citizen, or a Citizen of the United States, at the time of the Adoption of this Constitution, shall be eligible to the Office of President; neither shall any Person be eligible to that Office who shall not have attained to the Age of thirty five Years, and been fourteen Years a Resident within the United States.

In Case of the Removal of the President from Office, or of his Death, Resignation, or Inability to discharge the Powers and Duties of the said Office, the Same shall devolve on the Vice President, and the Congress may by Law provide for the Case of Removal, Death, Resignation or Inability, both of the President and Vice President, declaring what Officer shall then act as President, and such Officer shall act accordingly, until the Disability be removed, or a President shall be elected.

The President shall, at stated Times, receive for his Services, a Compensation, which shall neither be increased nor diminished during the Period for which he shall have been elected, and he shall not receive within that Period any other Emolument from the United States, or any of them.

Before he enter on the Execution of his Office, he shall take the following Oath or Affirmation:—"I do solemnly swear (or affirm) that I will faithfully execute the Office of President of the United States, and will to the best of my Ability, preserve, protect and defend the Constitution of the United States."

Section. 2. The President shall be Commander in Chief of the Army and Navy of the United States, and of the Militia of the several States, when called into the actual Service of the United States; he may require the Opinion, in writing, of the principal Officer in each of the executive Departments, upon any Subject relating to the Duties of their respective Offices, and he shall have Power to grant Reprieves and Pardons for Offences against the United States, except in Cases of Impeachment.

He shall have Power, by and with the Advice and Consent of the Senate, to make Treaties, provided two thirds of the Senators present concur; and he shall nominate, and by and with the Advice and Consent of the Senate, shall appoint Ambassadors, other public Ministers and Consuls, Judges of the supreme Court, and all other Officers of the United States, whose Appointments are not herein otherwise provided for, and which shall be established by Law: but the Congress may by Law vest the Appointment of such inferior Officers, as they think proper, in the President alone, in the Courts of Law, or in the Heads of Departments.

The President shall have Power to fill up all Vacancies that may happen during the Recess of the Senate, by granting Commissions which shall expire at the End of their next Session.

Section. 3. He shall from time to time give to the Congress Information of the State of the Union, and recommend to their Consideration such Measures as he shall judge necessary and expedient; he may, on extraordinary Occasions, convene both Houses, or either of them, and in Case of Disagreement between them, with Respect to the Time of Adjournment, he may adjourn them to such Time as he shall think proper; he shall receive Ambassadors and other public Ministers; he shall take Care that the Laws be faithfully executed, and shall Commission all the Officers of the United States.

Section. 4. The President, Vice President and all civil Officers of the United States, shall be removed from Office on Impeachment for, and Conviction of, Treason, Bribery, or other high Crimes and Misdemeanors.

Article III.

Section. 1. The judicial Power of the United States shall be vested in one supreme Court, and in such inferior Courts as the Congress may from time to time ordain and establish. The Judges, both of the supreme and inferior Courts, shall hold their Offices during good Behaviour, and shall, at stated Times, receive for their Services a Compensation, which shall not be diminished during their Continuance in Office.

Section. 2. The judicial Power shall extend to all Cases, in Law and Equity, arising under this Constitution, the Laws of the United States, and Treaties made, or which shall be made, under their Authority;—to all Cases affecting Ambassadors, other public Ministers and Consuls;—to all Cases of admiralty and maritime Jurisdiction;—to Controversies to which the United States shall be a Party;—to Controversies between two or more States;— between a State and Citizens of another State,—between Citizens of different States,—between Citizens of the same State claiming Lands under Grants of different States, and between a State, or the Citizens thereof, and foreign States, Citizens or Subjects.

In all Cases affecting Ambassadors, other public Ministers and Consuls, and those in which a State shall be Party, the supreme Court shall have original Jurisdiction. In all the other Cases before mentioned, the supreme Court shall have appellate Jurisdiction, both as to Law and Fact, with such Exceptions, and under such Regulations as the Congress shall make.

The Trial of all Crimes, except in Cases of Impeachment, shall be by Jury; and such Trial shall be held in the State where the said Crimes shall have been committed; but when not committed within any State, the Trial shall be at such Place or Places as the Congress may by Law have directed.

Section. 3. Treason against the United States, shall consist only in levying War against them, or in adhering to their Enemies, giving them Aid and Comfort. No Person shall be convicted of Treason unless on the Testimony of two Witnesses to the same overt Act, or on Confession in open Court.

The Congress shall have Power to declare the Punishment of Treason, but no Attainder of Treason shall work Corruption of Blood, or Forfeiture except during the Life of the Person attainted.

Article. IV.

Section. 1. Full Faith and Credit shall be given in each State to the public Acts, Records, and judicial Proceedings of every other State. And the Congress may by general Laws prescribe the Manner in which such Acts, Records and Proceedings shall be proved, and the Effect thereof.

Section. 2. The Citizens of each State shall be entitled to all Privileges and Immunities of Citizens in the several States.

A Person charged in any State with Treason, Felony, or other Crime, who shall flee from Justice, and be found in another State, shall on Demand of the executive Authority of the State from which he fled, be delivered up, to be removed to the State having Jurisdiction of the Crime.

No Person held to Service or Labour in one State, under the Laws thereof, escaping into another, shall, in Consequence of any Law or Regulation therein, be discharged from such Service or Labour, but shall be delivered up on Claim of the Party to whom such Service or Labour may be due.

Section. 3. New States may be admitted by the Congress into this Union; but no new State shall be formed or erected within the Jurisdiction of any other State; nor any State be formed by the Junction of two or more States, or Parts of States, without the Consent of the Legislatures of the States concerned as well as of the Congress.

The Congress shall have Power to dispose of and make all needful Rules and Regulations respecting the Territory or other Property belonging to the United States; and nothing in this Constitution shall be so construed as to Prejudice any Claims of the United States, or of any particular States.

Section. 4. The United States shall guarantee to every State in this Union a Republican Form of Government, and shall protect each of them against Invasion; and on Application of the Legislature, or of the Executive (when the Legislature cannot be convened), against domestic Violence.

Article. V.

The Congress, whenever two thirds of both Houses shall deem it necessary, shall propose Amendments to this Constitution, or, on the Application of the Legislatures of two thirds of the several States, shall call a Convention for proposing Amendments, which, in either Case, shall be valid to all Intents and Purposes, as Part of this Constitution, when ratified by the Legislatures of three fourths of the several States, or by Conventions in three fourths thereof, as the one or the other Mode of Ratification may be proposed by the Congress; Provided that no Amendment which may be made prior to the Year One thousand eight hundred and eight shall in any Manner affect the first and fourth Clauses in the Ninth Section of the first Article; and that no State, without its Consent, shall be deprived of its equal Suffrage in the Senate.

Article. VI.

All Debts contracted and Engagements entered into, before the Adoption of this Constitution, shall be as valid against the United States under this Constitution, as under the Confederation.

This Constitution, and the Laws of the United States which shall be made in Pursuance thereof; and all Treaties made, or which shall be made, under the Authority of the United States, shall be the supreme Law of the Land; and the Judges in every State shall be bound thereby, any Thing in the Constitution or Laws of any State to the Contrary notwithstanding.

The Senators and Representatives before mentioned, and the Members of the several State Legislatures, and all executive and judicial Officers, both of the United States and of the several States, shall be bound by Oath or Affirmation, to support this Constitution; but no religious Test shall ever be required as a Qualification to any Office or public Trust under the United States.

Article. VII.

The Ratification of the Conventions of nine States, shall be sufficient for the Establishment of this Constitution between the States so ratifying the Same.

The Word, "the," being interlined between the seventh and eighth Lines of the first Page, the Word "Thirty" being partly written on an Erazure in the fifteenth Line of the first Page, The Words "is tried" being interlined between the thirty second and thirty third Lines of the first Page and the Word "the" being interlined between the forty third and forty fourth Lines of the second Page.

Attest William Jackson Secretary

Done in Convention by the Unanimous Consent of the States present the Seventeenth Day of September in the Year of our Lord one thousand seven hundred and Eighty seven and of the Independance of the United States of America the Twelfth In witness whereof We have hereunto subscribed our Names,

G°. Washington
Presidt and deputy from Virginia

Delaware	Geo: Read Gunning Bedford jun John Dickinson Richard Bassett Jaco: Broom
Maryland	James McHenry Dan of St Thos. Jenifer Danl. Carrol
Virginia	John Blair James Madison Jr.
North Carolina	Wm. Blount Richd. Dobbs Spaight Hu Williamson
South Carolina	J. Rutledge Charles Cotesworth Pinckney Charles Pinckney Pierce Butler
Georgia	William Few Abr Baldwin

New Hampshire	John Langdon Nicholas Gilman
Massachusetts	Nathaniel Gorham Rufus King
Connecticut	Wm. Saml. Johnson Roger Sherman
New York	Alexander Hamilton
New Jersey	Wil: Livingston David Brearley Wm. Paterson Jona: Dayton
Pennsylvania	B Franklin Thomas Mifflin Robt. Morris Geo. Clymer Thos. FitzSimons Jared Ingersoll James Wilson Gouv Morris

Amendments to the Constitution

The Bill of Rights: A Transcription

The Preamble to The Bill of Rights

Congress of the United States
begun and held at the City of New-York, on
Wednesday the fourth of March, one thousand seven hundred and eighty nine.

THE Conventions of a number of the States, having at the time of their adopting the Constitution, expressed a desire, in order to prevent misconstruction or abuse of its powers, that further declaratory and restrictive clauses should be added: And as extending the ground of public confidence in the Government, will best ensure the beneficent ends of its institution.

RESOLVED by the Senate and House of Representatives of the United States of America, in Congress assembled, two thirds of both Houses concurring, that the following Articles be proposed to the Legislatures of the several States, as amendments to the Constitution of the United States, all, or any of which Articles, when ratified by three fourths of the said Legislatures, to be valid to all intents and purposes, as part of the said Constitution; viz.

ARTICLES in addition to, and Amendment of the Constitution of the United States of America, proposed by Congress, and ratified by the Legislatures of the several States, pursuant to the fifth Article of the original Constitution.

Note: The first ten amendments to the Constitution were ratified December 15, 1791, and form what is known as the "Bill of Rights."

Amendment I

Congress shall make no law respecting an establishment of religion, or prohibiting the free exercise thereof; or abridging the freedom of speech, or of the press; or the right of the people peaceably to assemble, and to petition the Government for a redress of grievances.

Amendment II

A well regulated Militia, being necessary to the security of a free State, the right of the people to keep and bear Arms, shall not be infringed.

Amendment III

No Soldier shall, in time of peace be quartered in any house, without the consent of the Owner, nor in time of war, but in a manner to be prescribed by law.

Amendment IV

The right of the people to be secure in their persons, houses, papers, and effects, against unreasonable searches and seizures, shall not be violated, and no Warrants shall issue, but upon probable cause, supported by Oath or affirmation, and particularly describing the place to be searched, and the persons or things to be seized.

Amendment V

No person shall be held to answer for a capital, or otherwise infamous crime, unless on a presentment or indictment of a Grand Jury, except in cases arising in the land or naval forces, or in the Militia, when in actual service in time of War or public danger; nor shall any person be subject for the same offence to be twice put in jeopardy of life or limb; nor shall be compelled in any criminal case to be a witness against himself, nor be deprived of life, liberty, or property, without due process of law; nor shall private property be taken for public use, without just compensation.

Amendment VI

In all criminal prosecutions, the accused shall enjoy the right to a speedy and public trial, by an impartial jury of the State and district wherein the crime shall have been committed, which district shall have been previously ascertained by law, and to be informed of the nature and cause of the accusation; to be confronted with the witnesses against him; to have compulsory process for obtaining witnesses in his favor, and to have the Assistance of Counsel for his defence.

Amendment VII

In Suits at common law, where the value in controversy shall exceed twenty dollars, the right of trial by jury shall be preserved, and no fact tried by a jury, shall be otherwise re-examined in any Court of the United States, than according to the rules of the common law.

Amendment VIII

Excessive bail shall not be required, nor excessive fines imposed, nor cruel and unusual punishments inflicted.

Amendment IX

The enumeration in the Constitution, of certain rights, shall not be construed to deny or disparage others retained by the people.

Amendment X

The powers not delegated to the United States by the Constitution, nor prohibited by it to the States, are reserved to the States respectively, or to the people.

Amendment XI

Passed by Congress March 4, 1794. Ratified February 7, 1795.

Note: Article III, section 2, of the Constitution was modified by amendment 11.

The Judicial power of the United States shall not be construed to extend to any suit in law or equity, commenced or prosecuted against one of the United States by Citizens of another State, or by Citizens or Subjects of any Foreign State.

Amendment XII

Passed by Congress December 9, 1803. Ratified June 15, 1804.

Note: A portion of Article II, section 1 of the Constitution was superseded by the 12th amendment.

The Electors shall meet in their respective states and vote by ballot for President and Vice-President, one of whom, at least, shall not be an inhabitant of the same state with themselves; they shall name in their ballots the person voted for as President, and in distinct ballots the person voted for as Vice-President, and they shall make distinct lists of all persons voted for as President, and of all persons voted for as Vice-President, and of the number of votes for each, which lists they shall sign and certify, and transmit sealed to the seat of the government of the United States, directed to the President of the Senate; — the President of the Senate shall, in the presence of the Senate and House of Representatives, open all the certificates and the votes shall then be counted; — The person having the greatest number of votes for President, shall be the President, if such number be a majority of the whole number of Electors appointed; and if no person have such majority, then from the persons having the highest numbers not exceeding three on the list of those voted for as President, the House of Representatives shall choose immediately, by ballot, the President. But in choosing the President, the votes shall be taken by states, the representation from each state having one vote; a quorum for this purpose shall consist of a member or members from two-thirds of the states, and a majority of all the states shall be necessary to a choice. [And if the House of Representatives shall not choose a President whenever the right of choice shall devolve upon them, before the fourth day of March next following, then the Vice-President shall act as President, as in case of the death or other constitutional disability of the President. —]* The person having the greatest number of votes as Vice-President, shall be the Vice-President, if such number be a majority of the whole number of Electors appointed, and if no person have a majority, then from the two highest numbers on the list, the Senate shall choose the Vice-President; a quorum for the purpose shall consist of two-thirds of the whole number of Senators, and a majority of the whole number shall be necessary to a choice. But no person constitutionally ineligible to the office of President shall be eligible to that of Vice-President of the United States.

*Superseded by section 3 of the 20th amendment.

Amendment XIII

Passed by Congress January 31, 1865. Ratified December 6, 1865.

Note: A portion of Article IV, section 2, of the Constitution was superseded by the 13th amendment.

Section 1.
Neither slavery nor involuntary servitude, except as a punishment for crime whereof the party shall have been duly convicted, shall exist within the United States, or any place subject to their jurisdiction.

Section 2.
Congress shall have power to enforce this article by appropriate legislation.

Amendment XIV

Passed by Congress June 13, 1866. Ratified July 9, 1868.

Note: Article I, section 2, of the Constitution was modified by section 2 of the 14th amendment.

Section 1.
All persons born or naturalized in the United States, and subject to the jurisdiction thereof, are citizens of the United States and of the State wherein they reside. No State shall make or enforce any law which shall abridge the privileges or immunities of citizens of the United States; nor shall any State deprive any person of life, liberty, or property, without due process of law; nor deny to any person within its jurisdiction the equal protection of the laws.

Section 2.
Representatives shall be apportioned among the several States according to their respective numbers, counting the whole number of persons in each State, excluding Indians not taxed. But when the right to vote at any election for the choice of electors for President and Vice-President of the United States, Representatives in Congress, the Executive and Judicial officers of a State, or the members of the Legislature thereof, is denied to any of the male inhabitants of such State, being twenty-one years of age,* and citizens of the United States, or in any way abridged, except for participation in rebellion, or other crime, the basis of representation therein shall be reduced in the proportion which the number of such male citizens shall bear to the whole number of male citizens twenty-one years of age in such State.

Section 3.
No person shall be a Senator or Representative in Congress, or elector of President and Vice-President, or hold any office, civil or military, under the United States, or under any State, who, having previously taken an oath, as a member of Congress, or as an officer of the United States, or as a member of any State legislature, or as an executive or judicial officer of any State, to support the Constitution of the United States, shall have engaged in insurrection or rebellion against the same, or given aid or comfort to the enemies thereof. But Congress may by a vote of two-thirds of each House, remove such disability.

Section 4.
The validity of the public debt of the United States, authorized by law, including debts incurred for payment of pensions and bounties for services in suppressing insurrection or rebellion, shall not be questioned. But neither the United States nor any State shall assume or pay any debt or obligation incurred in aid of insurrection or rebellion against the United States, or any claim for the loss or emancipation of any slave; but all such debts, obligations and claims shall be held illegal and void.

Section 5.
The Congress shall have the power to enforce, by appropriate legislation, the provisions of this article.

Changed by section 1 of the 26th amendment.

Amendment XV

Passed by Congress February 26, 1869. Ratified February 3, 1870.

Section 1.
The right of citizens of the United States to vote shall not be denied or abridged by the United States or by any State on account of race, color, or previous condition of servitude—

Section 2.
The Congress shall have the power to enforce this article by appropriate legislation.

Amendment XVI

Passed by Congress July 2, 1909. Ratified February 3, 1913.

Note: Article I, section 9, of the Constitution was modified by amendment 16.

The Congress shall have power to lay and collect taxes on incomes, from whatever source derived, without apportionment among the several States, and without regard to any census or enumeration.

Amendment XVII

Passed by Congress May 13, 1912. Ratified April 8, 1913.

Note: Article I, section 3, of the Constitution was modified by the 17th amendment.

The Senate of the United States shall be composed of two Senators from each State, elected by the people thereof, for six years; and each Senator shall have one vote. The electors in each State shall have the qualifications requisite for electors of the most numerous branch of the State legislatures.

When vacancies happen in the representation of any State in the Senate, the executive authority of such State shall issue writs of election to fill such vacancies: *Provided*, That the legislature of any State may empower the executive thereof to make temporary appointments until the people fill the vacancies by election as the legislature may direct.

This amendment shall not be so construed as to affect the election or term of any Senator chosen before it becomes valid as part of the Constitution.

Amendment XVIII

Passed by Congress December 18, 1917. Ratified January 16, 1919. Repealed by amendment 21.

Section 1.
After one year from the ratification of this article the manufacture, sale, or transportation of intoxicating liquors within, the importation thereof into, or the exportation thereof from the United States and all territory subject to the jurisdiction thereof for beverage purposes is hereby prohibited.

Section 2.
The Congress and the several States shall have concurrent power to enforce this article by appropriate legislation.

Section 3.
This article shall be inoperative unless it shall have been ratified as an amendment to the Constitution by the legislatures of the several States, as provided in the Constitution, within seven years from the date of the submission hereof to the States by the Congress.

Amendment XIX

Passed by Congress June 4, 1919. Ratified August 18, 1920.

The right of citizens of the United States to vote shall not be denied or abridged by the United States or by any State on account of sex.

Congress shall have power to enforce this article by appropriate legislation.

Amendment XX

Passed by Congress March 2, 1932. Ratified January 23, 1933.

Note: Article I, section 4, of the Constitution was modified by section 2 of this amendment. In addition, a portion of the 12th amendment was superseded by section 3.

Section 1.
The terms of the President and the Vice President shall end at noon on the 20th day of January, and the terms of Senators and Representatives at noon on the 3rd day of January, of the years in which such terms would have ended if this article had not been ratified; and the terms of their successors shall then begin.

Section 2.

The Congress shall assemble at least once in every year, and such meeting shall begin at noon on the 3d day of January, unless they shall by law appoint a different day.

Section 3.

If, at the time fixed for the beginning of the term of the President, the President elect shall have died, the Vice President elect shall become President. If a President shall not have been chosen before the time fixed for the beginning of his term, or if the President elect shall have failed to qualify, then the Vice President elect shall act as President until a President shall have qualified; and the Congress may by law provide for the case wherein neither a President elect nor a Vice President shall have qualified, declaring who shall then act as President, or the manner in which one who is to act shall be selected, and such person shall act accordingly until a President or Vice President shall have qualified.

Section 4.

The Congress may by law provide for the case of the death of any of the persons from whom the House of Representatives may choose a President whenever the right of choice shall have devolved upon them, and for the case of the death of any of the persons from whom the Senate may choose a Vice President whenever the right of choice shall have devolved upon them.

Section 5.

Sections 1 and 2 shall take effect on the 15th day of October following the ratification of this article.

Section 6.

This article shall be inoperative unless it shall have been ratified as an amendment to the Constitution by the legislatures of three-fourths of the several States within seven years from the date of its submission.

Amendment XXI

Passed by Congress February 20, 1933. Ratified December 5, 1933.

Section 1.

The eighteenth article of amendment to the Constitution of the United States is hereby repealed.

Section 2.

The transportation or importation into any State, Territory, or Possession of the United States for delivery or use therein of intoxicating liquors, in violation of the laws thereof, is hereby prohibited.

Section 3.

This article shall be inoperative unless it shall have been ratified as an amendment to the Constitution by conventions in the several States, as provided in the Constitution, within seven years from the date of the submission hereof to the States by the Congress.

Amendment XXII

Passed by Congress March 21, 1947. Ratified February 27, 1951.

Section 1.
No person shall be elected to the office of the President more than twice, and no person who has held the office of President, or acted as President, for more than two years of a term to which some other person was elected President shall be elected to the office of President more than once. But this Article shall not apply to any person holding the office of President when this Article was proposed by Congress, and shall not prevent any person who may be holding the office of President, or acting as President, during the term within which this Article becomes operative from holding the office of President or acting as President during the remainder of such term.

Section 2.
This article shall be inoperative unless it shall have been ratified as an amendment to the Constitution by the legislatures of three-fourths of the several States within seven years from the date of its submission to the States by the Congress.

Amendment XXIII

Passed by Congress June 16, 1960. Ratified March 29, 1961.

Section 1.
The District constituting the seat of Government of the United States shall appoint in such manner as Congress may direct:

A number of electors of President and Vice President equal to the whole number of Senators and Representatives in Congress to which the District would be entitled if it were a State, but in no event more than the least populous State; they shall be in addition to those appointed by the States, but they shall be considered, for the purposes of the election of President and Vice President, to be electors appointed by a State; and they shall meet in the District and perform such duties as provided by the twelfth article of amendment.

Section 2.
The Congress shall have power to enforce this article by appropriate legislation.

Amendment XXIV

Passed by Congress August 27, 1962. Ratified January 23, 1964.

Section 1.
The right of citizens of the United States to vote in any primary or other election for President or Vice President, for electors for President or Vice President, or for Senator or Representative in Congress, shall not be denied or abridged by the United States or any State by reason of failure to pay poll tax or other tax.

Section 2.
The Congress shall have power to enforce this article by appropriate legislation.

Amendment XXV

Passed by Congress July 6, 1965. Ratified February 10, 1967.

Note: Article II, section 1, of the Constitution was affected by the 25th amendment.

Section 1.

In case of the removal of the President from office or of his death or resignation, the Vice President shall become President.

Section 2.

Whenever there is a vacancy in the office of the Vice President, the President shall nominate a Vice President who shall take office upon confirmation by a majority vote of both Houses of Congress.

Section 3.

Whenever the President transmits to the President pro tempore of the Senate and the Speaker of the House of Representatives his written declaration that he is unable to discharge the powers and duties of his office, and until he transmits to them a written declaration to the contrary, such powers and duties shall be discharged by the Vice President as Acting President.

Section 4.

Whenever the Vice President and a majority of either the principal officers of the executive departments or of such other body as Congress may by law provide, transmit to the President pro tempore of the Senate and the Speaker of the House of Representatives their written declaration that the President is unable to discharge the powers and duties of his office, the Vice President shall immediately assume the powers and duties of the office as Acting President.

Thereafter, when the President transmits to the President pro tempore of the Senate and the Speaker of the House of Representatives his written declaration that no inability exists, he shall resume the powers and duties of his office unless the Vice President and a majority of either the principal officers of the executive department or of such other body as Congress may by law provide, transmit within four days to the President pro tempore of the Senate and the Speaker of the House of Representatives their written declaration that the President is unable to discharge the powers and duties of his office. Thereupon Congress shall decide the issue, assembling within forty-eight hours for that purpose if not in session. If the Congress, within twenty-one days after receipt of the latter written declaration, or, if Congress is not in session, within twenty-one days after Congress is required to assemble, determines by two-thirds vote of both Houses that the President is unable to discharge the powers and duties of his office, the Vice President shall continue to discharge the same as Acting President; otherwise, the President shall resume the powers and duties of his office.

Amendment XXVI

Passed by Congress March 23, 1971. Ratified July 1, 1971.

Note: Amendment 14, section 2, of the Constitution was modified by section 1 of the 26th amendment.

Section 1.
The right of citizens of the United States, who are eighteen years of age or older, to vote shall not be denied or abridged by the United States or by any State on account of age.

Section 2.
The Congress shall have power to enforce this article by appropriate legislation.

Amendment XXVII

Originally proposed Sept. 25, 1789. Ratified May 7, 1992.

No law, varying the compensation for the services of the Senators and Representatives, shall take effect, until an election of representatives shall have intervened.

PRESIDENTIAL ELECTIONS

Year	Number of States	Candidates	Parties	Popular Vote	% of Popular Vote	Electoral Vote	% Voter Participation
1789	11	**GEORGE WASHINGTON**	No party designations			69	
		John Adams				34	
		Other candidates				35	
1792	15	**GEORGE WASHINGTON**	No party designations			132	
		John Adams				77	
		George Clinton				50	
		Other candidates				5	
1796	16	**JOHN ADAMS**	Federalist			71	
		Thomas Jefferson	Democratic-Republican			68	
		Thomas Pinckney	Federalist			59	
		Aaron Burr	Democratic-Republican			30	
		Other candidates				48	
1800	16	**THOMAS JEFFERSON**	Democratic-Republican			73	
		Aaron Burr	Democratic-Republican			73	
		John Adams	Federalist			65	
		Charles C. Pinckney	Federalist			64	
		John Jay	Federalist			1	
1804	17	**THOMAS JEFFERSON**	Democratic-Republican			162	
		Charles C. Pinckney	Federalist			14	

Year	Number of States	Candidates	Parties	Popular Vote	Percentage of Popular Vote	Electoral Vote	Percentage Voter Participation
1808	17	**JAMES MADISON**	Democratic-Republican			122	
		Charles C. Pinckney	Federalist			47	
		George Clinton	Democratic-Republican			6	
1812	18	**JAMES MADISON**	Democratic-Republican			128	
		DeWitt Clinton	Federalist			89	
1816	19	**JAMES MONROE**	Democratic-Republican			183	
		Rufus King	Federalist			34	
1820	24	**JAMES MONROE**	Democratic-Republican			231	
		John Quincy Adams	Independent			1	
1824	24	**JOHN QUINCY ADAMS**	Democratic-Republican	108,740	30.5	84	26.9
		Andrew Jackson	Democratic-Republican	153,544	43.1	99	
		Henry Clay	Democratic-Republican	47,136	13.2	37	
		William H. Crawford	Democratic-Republican	46,618	13.1	41	
1828	24	**ANDREW JACKSON**	Democratic	647,286	56.0	178	57.6
		John Quincy Adams	National-Republican	508,064	44.0	83	

Year	Number of States	Candidates	Parties	Popular Vote	% of Popular Vote	Electoral Vote	% Voter Participation
1832	24	**ANDREW JACKSON**	Democratic	688,242	54.5	219	55.4
		Henry Clay	National-Republican	473,462	37.5	49	
		William Wirt	Anti-Masonic	101,051	8.0	7	
		John Floyd	Democratic			11	
1836	26	**MARTIN VAN BUREN**	Democratic	765,483	50.9	170	57.8
		William H. Harrison	Whig			73	
		Hugh L. White	Whig	739,795	49.1	26	
		Daniel Webster	Whig			14	
		W. P. Mangum	Whig			11	
1840	26	**WILLIAM H. HARRISON**	Whig	1,274,624	53.1	234	80.2
		Martin Van Buren	Democratic	1,127,781	46.9	60	
1844	26	**JAMES K. POLK**	Democratic	1,338,464	49.6	170	78.9
		Henry Clay	Whig	1,300,097	48.1	105	
		James G. Birney	Liberty	62,300	2.3		
1848	30	**ZACHARY TAYLOR**	Whig	1,360,967	47.4	163	72.7
		Lewis Cass	Democratic	1,222,342	42.5	127	
		Martin Van Buren	Free Soil	291,263	10.1		
1852	31	**FRANKLIN PIERCE**	Democratic	1,601,117	50.9	254	69.6
		Winfield Scott	Whig	1,385,453	44.1	42	
		John P. Hale	Free Soil	155,825	5.0		
1856	31	**JAMES BUCHANAN**	Democratic	1,832,955	45.3	174	78.9
		John C. Frémont	Republican	1,339,932	33.1	114	
		Millard Fillmore	American	871,731	21.6	8	

Year	Number of States	Candidates	Parties	Popular Vote	% of Popular Vote	Electoral Vote	% Voter Participation
1860	33	ABRAHAM LINCOLN	Republican	1,865,593	39.8	180	81.2
		Stephen A. Douglas	Democratic	1,382,713	29.5	12	
		John C. Breckinridge	Democratic	848,356	18.1	72	
		John Bell	Constitutional Union	592,906	12.6	39	
1864	36	ABRAHAM LINCOLN	Republican	2,206,938	55.0	212	73.8
		George B. McClellan	Democratic	1,803,787	45.0	21	
1868	37	ULYSSES S. GRANT	Republican	3,013,421	52.7	214	78.1
		Horatio Seymour	Democratic	2,706,829	47.3	80	
1872	37	ULYSSES S. GRANT	Republican	3,596,745	55.6	286	71.3
		Horace Greeley	Democratic	2,843,446	43.9	66	
1876	38	Rutherford B. Hayes	Republican	4,036,572	48.0	185	81.8
		Samuel J. Tilden	Democratic	4,284,020	51.0	184	
1880	38	JAMES A. GARFIELD	Republican	4,453,295	48.5	214	79.4
		Winfield S. Hancock	Democratic	4,414,082	48.1	155	
		James B. Weaver	Greenback-Labor	308,578	3.4		
1884	38	GROVER CLEVELAND	Democratic	4,879,507	48.5	219	77.5
		James G. Blaine	Republican	4,850,293	48.2	182	
		Benjamin F. Butler	Greenback-Labor	175,370	1.8		
		John P. St. John	Prohibition	150,369	1.5		
1888	38	BENJAMIN HARRISON	Republican	5,477,129	47.9	233	79.3
		Grover Cleveland	Democratic	5,537,857	48.6	168	
		Clinton B. Fisk	Prohibition	249,506	2.2		
		Anson J. Streeter	Union Labor	146,935	1.3		

Year	Number of States	Candidates	Parties	Popular Vote	% of Popular Vote	Electoral Vote	% Voter Participation
1892	44	**GROVER CLEVELAND**	Democratic	5,555,426	46.1	277	74.7
		Benjamin Harrison	Republican	5,182,690	43.0	145	
		James B. Weaver	People's	1,029,846	8.5	22	
		John Bidwell	Prohibition	264,133	2.2		
1896	45	**WILLIAM McKINLEY**	Republican	7,102,246	51.1	271	79.3
		William J. Bryan	Democratic	6,492,559	47.7	176	
1900	45	**WILLIAM McKINLEY**	Republican	7,218,491	51.7	292	73.2
		William J. Bryan	Democratic; Populist	6,356,734	45.5	155	
		John C. Wooley	Prohibition	208,914	1.5		
1904	45	**THEODORE ROOSEVELT**	Republican	7,628,461	57.4	336	65.2
		Alton B. Parker	Democratic	5,084,223	37.6	140	
		Eugene V. Debs	Socialist	402,283	3.0		
		Silas C. Swallow	Prohibition	258,536	1.9		
1908	46	**WILLIAM H. TAFT**	Republican	7,675,320	51.6	321	65.4
		William J. Bryan	Democratic	6,412,294	43.1	162	
		Eugene V. Debs	Socialist	420,793	2.8		
		Eugene W. Chafin	Prohibition	253,840	1.7		
1912	48	**WOODROW WILSON**	Democratic	6,296,547	41.9	435	58.8
		Theodore Roosevelt	Progressive	4,118,571	27.4	88	
		William H. Taft	Republican	3,486,720	23.2	8	
		Eugene V. Debs	Socialist	900,672	6.0		
		Eugene W. Chafin	Prohibition	206,275	1.4		

Year	Number of States	Candidate	Parties	Popular Vote	% of Popular Vote	Electoral Vote	% Voter Participation
1916	48	**WOODROW WILSON**	Democratic	9,127,695	49.4	277	61.6
		Charles E. Hughes	Republican	8,533,507	46.2	254	
		A.L. Benson	Socialist	585,113	3.2		
		J. Frank Hanly	Prohibition	220,506	1.2		
1920	48	**WARREN G. HARDING**	Republican	16,143,407	60.4	404	49.2
		James M. Cox	Democratic	9,130,328	34.2	127	
		Eugene V. Debs	Socialist	919,799	3.4		
		P. P. Christensen	Farmer-Labor	265,411	1.0		
1924	48	**CALVIN COOLIDGE**	Republican	15,718,211	54.0	382	48.9
		John W. Davis	Democratic	8,385,283	28.8	136	
		Robert M. La Follette	Progressive	4,831,289	16.6	13	
1928	48	**HERBERT C. HOOVER**	Republican	21,391,993	58.2	444	56.9
		Alfred E. Smith	Democratic	15,016,169	40.9	87	
1932	48	**FRANKLIN D. ROOSEVELT**	Democratic	22,809,638	57.4	472	56.9
		Herbert C. Hoover	Republican	15,758,901	39.7	59	
		Norman Thomas	Socialist	881,951	2.2		
1936	48	**FRANKLIN D. ROOSEVELT**	Democratic	27,752,869	60.8	523	61.0
		Alfred M. Landon	Republican	16,674,665	36.5	8	
		William Lemke	Union	882,479	1.9		
1940	48	**FRANKLIN D. ROOSEVELT**	Democratic	27,307,819	54.8	449	62.5
		Wendell L. Willkie	Republican	22,321,018	44.8	82	
1944	48	**FRANKLIN D. ROOSEVELT**	Democratic	25,606,585	53.5	432	55.9
		Thomas E. Dewey	Republican	22,014,745	46.0	99	

Year	Number of States	Candidates	Parties	Popular Vote	% of Popular Vote	Electoral Vote	% Voter Participation
1948	48	**HARRY S. TRUMAN**	Democratic	24,179,345	49.6	303	53.0
		Thomas E. Dewey	Republican	21,991,291	45.1	189	
		J. Strom Thurmond	States' Rights	1,176,125	2.4	39	
		Henry A. Wallace	Progressive	1,157,326	2.4		
1952	48	**DWIGHT D. EISENHOWER**	Republican	33,936,234	55.1	442	63.3
		Adlai E. Stevenson	Democratic	27,314,992	44.4	89	
1956	48	**DWIGHT D. EISENHOWER**	Republican	35,590,472	57.6	457	60.6
		Adlai E. Stevenson	Democratic	26,022,752	42.1	73	
1960	50	**JOHN F. KENNEDY**	Democratic	34,226,731	49.7	303	62.8
		Richard M. Nixon	Republican	34,108,157	49.5	219	
1964	50	**LYNDON B. JOHNSON**	Democratic	43,129,566	61.1	486	61.9
		Barry M. Goldwater	Republican	27,178,188	38.5	52	
1968	50	**RICHARD M. NIXON**	Republican	31,785,480	43.4	301	60.9
		Hubert H. Humphrey	Democratic	31,275,166	42.7	191	
		George C. Wallace	American Independent	9,906,473	13.5	46	
1972	50	**RICHARD M. NIXON**	Republican	47,169,911	60.7	520	55.2
		George S. McGovern	Democratic	29,170,383	37.5	17	
		John G. Schmitz	American	1,099,482	1.4		

Year	Number of States	Candidates	Parties	Popular Vote	% of Popular Vote	Electoral Vote	% Voter Participation
1976	50	**JIMMY CARTER**	Democratic	40,830,763	50.1	297	53.5
		Gerald R. Ford	Republican	39,147,793	48.0	240	
1980	50	**RONALD REAGAN**	Republican	43,901,812	50.7	489	52.6
		Jimmy Carter	Democratic	35,483,820	41.0	49	
		John B. Anderson	Independent	5,719,437	6.6		
		Ed Clark	Libertarian	921,188	1.1		
1984	50	**RONALD REAGAN**	Republican	54,451,521	58.8	525	53.1
		Walter F. Mondale	Democratic	37,565,334	40.6	13	
1988	50	**GEORGE H. W. BUSH**	Republican	47,917,341	53.4	426	50.1
		Michael Dukakis	Democratic	41,013,030	45.6	111	
1992	50	**BILL CLINTON**	Democratic	44,908,254	43.0	370	55.0
		George H. W. Bush	Republican	39,102,343	37.4	168	
		H. Ross Perot	Independent	19,741,065	18.9		
1996	50	**BILL CLINTON**	Democratic	47,401,185	49.0	379	49.0
		Bob Dole	Republican	39,197,469	41.0	159	
		H. Ross Perot	Independent	8,085,295	8.0		
2000	50	**GEORGE W. BUSH**	Republican	50,455,156	47.9	271	50.4
		Al Gore	Democrat	50,997,335	48.4	266	
		Ralph Nader	Green	2,882,897	2.7		
2004	50	**GEORGE W. BUSH**	Republican	62,040,610	50.7	286	60.7
		John F. Kerry	Democrat	59,028,444	48.3	251	
2008	50	**BARACK OBAMA**	Democrat	69,456,897	52.92%	365	63.0
		John McCain	Republican	59,934,814	45.66%	173	

Candidates receiving less than 1 percent of the popular vote have been omitted. Thus the percentage of popular vote given for any election year may not total 100 percent.

Before the passage of the Twelfth Amendment in 1804, the electoral college voted for two presidential candidates; the runner-up became vice president.

ADMISSION OF STATES

Order of Admission	State	Date of Admission	Order of Admission	State	Date of Admission
1	Delaware	December 7, 1787	26	Michigan	January 26, 1837
2	Pennsylvania	December 12, 1787	27	Florida	March 3, 1845
3	New Jersey	December 18, 1787	28	Texas	December 29, 1845
4	Georgia	January 2, 1788	29	Iowa	December 28, 1846
5	Connecticut	January 9, 1788	30	Wisconsin	May 29, 1848
6	Massachusetts	February 7, 1788	31	California	September 9, 1850
7	Maryland	April 28, 1788	32	Minnesota	May 11, 1858
8	South Carolina	May 23, 1788	33	Oregon	February 14, 1859
9	New Hampshire	June 21, 1788	34	Kansas	January 29, 1861
10	Virginia	June 25, 1788	35	West Virginia	June 30, 1863
11	New York	July 26, 1788	36	Nevada	October 31, 1864
12	North Carolina	November 21, 1789	37	Nebraska	March 1, 1867
13	Rhode Island	May 29, 1790	38	Colorado	August 1, 1876
14	Vermont	March 4, 1791	39	North Dakota	November 2, 1889
15	Kentucky	June 1, 1792	40	South Dakota	November 2, 1889
16	Tennessee	June 1, 1796	41	Montana	November 8, 1889
17	Ohio	March 1, 1803	42	Washington	November 11, 1889
18	Louisiana	April 30, 1812	43	Idaho	July 3, 1890
19	Indiana	December 11, 1816	44	Wyoming	July 10, 1890
20	Mississippi	December 10, 1817	45	Utah	January 4, 1896
21	Illinois	December 3, 1818	46	Oklahoma	November 16, 1907
22	Alabama	December 14, 1819	47	New Mexico	January 6, 1912
23	Maine	March 15, 1820	48	Arizona	February 14, 1912
24	Missouri	August 10, 1821	49	Alaska	January 3, 1959
25	Arkansas	June 15, 1836	50	Hawaii	August 21, 1959

POPULATION OF THE UNITED STATES

Year	Number of States	Population	% Increase	Population per Square Mile
1790	13	3,929,214		4.5
1800	16	5,308,483	35.1	6.1
1810	17	7,239,881	36.4	4.3
1820	23	9,638,453	33.1	5.5
1830	24	12,866,020	33.5	7.4
1840	26	17,069,453	32.7	9.8
1850	31	23,191,876	35.9	7.9
1860	33	31,443,321	35.6	10.6
1870	37	39,818,449	26.6	13.4
1880	38	50,155,783	26.0	16.9
1890	44	62,947,714	25.5	21.1
1900	45	75,994,575	20.7	25.6
1910	46	91,972,266	21.0	31.0
1920	48	105,710,620	14.9	35.6
1930	48	122,775,046	16.1	41.2
1940	48	131,669,275	7.2	44.2
1950	48	150,697,361	14.5	50.7
1960	50	179,323,175	19.0	50.6
1970	50	203,235,298	13.3	57.5
1980	50	226,504,825	11.4	64.0
1985	50	237,839,000	5.0	67.2
1990	50	250,122,000	5.2	70.6
1995	50	263,411,707	5.3	74.4
2000	50	281,421,906	6.8	77.0
2005	50	296,410,404	5.3	77.9
2010	50	308,745,538	9.7	87.4

IMMIGRATION TO THE UNITED STATES, FISCAL YEARS 1820–2011

Year	Number	Year	Number	Year	Number	Year	Number
1820–1989	55,457,531	1871–80	2,812,191	1921–30	4,107,209	1971–80	4,493,314
1820	8,385	1871	321,350	1921	805,228	1971	370,478
1821–30	143,439	1872	404,806	1922	309,556	1972	384,685
1821	9,127	1873	459,803	1923	522,919	1973	400,063
1822	6,911	1874	313,339	1924	706,896	1974	394,861
1823	6,354	1875	227,498	1925	294,314	1975	386,914
1824	7,912	1876	169,986	1926	304,488	1976	398,613
1825	10,199	1877	141,857	1927	335,175	1976	103,676
1826	10,837	1878	138,469	1928	307,255	1977	462,315
1827	18,875	1879	177,826	1929	279,678	1978	601,442
1828	27,382	1880	457,257	1930	241,700	1979	460,348
1829	22,520	1881–90	5,246,613	1931–40	528,431	1980	530,639
1830	23,322	1881	669,431	1931	97,139	1981–90	7,338,062
1831–40	599,125	1882	788,992	1932	35,576	1981	596,600
1831	22,633	1883	603,322	1933	23,068	1982	594,131
1832	60,482	1884	518,592	1934	29,470	1983	559,763
1833	58,640	1885	395,346	1935	34,956	1984	543,903
1834	65,365	1886	334,203	1936	36,329	1985	570,009
1835	45,374	1887	490,109	1937	50,244	1986	601,708
1836	76,242	1888	546,889	1938	67,895	1987	601,516
1837	79,340	1889	444,427	1939	82,998	1988	643,025
1838	38,914	1890	455,302	1940	70,756	1989	1,090,924
1839	68,069	1891–1900	3,687,564	1941–50	1,035,039	1990	1,536,483
1840	84,066	1891	560,319	1941	51,776	1991–2000	9,090,857
1841–50	1,713,251	1892	579,663	1942	28,781	1991	1,827,167
1841	80,289	1893	439,730	1943	23,725	1992	973,977
1842	104,565	1894	285,631	1944	28,551	1993	904,292
		1895	258,536	1945	38,119	1994	804,416
		1896	343,267	1946	108,721		

Year	Number	Year	Number	Year	Number	Year	Number
1843	52,496	1897	230,832	1947	147,292	1995	720,461
1844	78,615	1898	229,299	1948	170,570	1996	915,900
1845	114,371	1899	311,715	1949	188,317	1997	798,378
1846	154,416	1900	448,572	1950	249,187	1998	660,477
1847	234,968					1999	644,787
1848	226,527					2000	841,002
1849	297,024	**1901–10**	**8,795,386**	**1951–60**	**2,515,479**	**2001–10**	**10,501,053**
1850	369,980	1901	487,918	1951	205,717	2001	1,058,902
		1902	648,743	1952	265,520	2002	1,059,356
1851–60	**2,598,214**	1903	857,046	1953	170,434	2003	705,827
1851	379,466	1904	812,870	1954	208,177	2004	957,883
1852	371,603	1905	1,026,499	1955	237,790	2005	1,122,373
1853	368,645	1906	1,100,735	1956	321,625	2006	1,266,129
1854	427,833	1907	1,285,349	1957	326,867	2007	1,052,415
1855	200,877	1908	782,870	1958	253,265	2008	1,107,126
1856	200,436	1909	751,786	1959	260,686	2009	1,130,818
1857	251,306	1910	1,041,570	1960	265,398	2010	1,042,625
1858	123,126					2011	1,062,040
1859	121,282	**1911–20**	**5,735,811**	**1961–70**	**3,321,677**		
1860	153,640	1911	878,587	1961	271,344		
		1912	838,172	1962	283,763		
1861–70	**2,314,824**	1913	1,197,892	1963	306,260		
1861	91,918	1914	1,218,480	1964	292,248		
1862	91,985	1915	326,700	1965	296,697		
1863	176,282	1916	298,826	1966	323,040		
1864	193,418	1917	295,403	1967	361,972		
1865	248,120	1918	110,618	1968	454,448		
1866	318,568	1919	141,132	1969	358,579		
1867	315,722	1920	430,001	1970	373,326		
1868	138,840						
1869	352,768						
1870	387,203						

Source: U.S. Department of Homeland Security.

IMMIGRATION BY REGION AND SELECTED COUNTRY OF LAST RESIDENCE, FISCAL YEARS 1820–2011

Region and country of last residence	1820 to 1829	1830 to 1839	1840 to 1849	1850 to 1859	1860 to 1869	1870 to 1879	1880 to 1889	1890 to 1899
Total	128,502	538,381	1,427,337	2,814,554	2,081,261	2,742,137	5,248,568	3,694,294
Europe	99,272	422,771	1,369,259	2,619,680	1,877,726	2,251,878	4,638,677	3,576,411
Austria-Hungary	—	—	—	—	3,375	60,127	314,787	534,059
Austria	—	—	—	—	2,700	54,529	204,805	268,218
Hungary	—	—	—	—	483	5,598	109,982	203,350
Belgium	28	20	3,996	5,765	5,785	6,991	18,738	19,642
Bulgaria	—	—	—	—	—	—	—	52
Czechoslovakia	—	—	—	—	—	—	—	—
Denmark	173	927	671	3,227	13,553	29,278	85,342	56,671
Finland	—	—	—	—	—	—	—	—
France	7,694	39,330	75,300	81,778	35,938	71,901	48,193	35,616
Germany	5,753	124,726	385,434	976,072	723,734	751,769	1,445,181	579,072
Greece	17	49	17	32	51	209	1,807	12,732
Ireland	51,617	170,672	656,145	1,029,486	427,419	422,264	674,061	405,710
Italy	430	2,225	1,476	8,643	9,853	46,296	267,660	603,761
Netherlands	1,105	1,377	7,624	11,122	8,387	14,267	52,715	29,349
Norway-Sweden	91	1,149	12,389	22,202	82,937	178,823	586,441	334,058
Norway	—	—	—	—	16,068	88,644	185,111	96,810
Sweden	—	—	—	—	24,224	90,179	401,330	237,248
Poland	19	366	105	1,087	1,886	11,016	42,910	107,793
Portugal	177	820	196	1,299	2,083	13,971	15,186	25,874
Romania	—	—	—	—	—	—	5,842	6,808
Russia	86	280	520	423	1,670	35,177	182,698	450,101
Spain	2,595	2,010	1,916	8,795	6,966	5,540	3,995	9,189
Switzerland	3,148	4,430	4,819	24,423	21,124	25,212	81,151	37,020
United Kingdom	26,336	74,350	218,572	445,322	532,956	578,447	810,900	328,759
Yugoslavia	—	—	—	—	—	—	—	—
Other Europe	3	40	79	4	9	590	1,070	145

Region / Country								
Asia	34	55	121	36,080	54,408	134,128	71,151	61,285
China	3	8	32	35,933	54,028	133,139	65,797	15,268
Hong Kong	—	—	—	—	—	—	—	102
India	9	38	33	42	50	166	247	102
Iran	—	—	—	—	—	—	—	—
Israel	—	—	—	—	—	—	—	—
Japan	—	—	—	—	138	193	1,583	13,998
Jordan	—	—	—	—	—	—	—	—
Korea	—	—	—	—	—	—	—	—
Philippines	—	—	—	—	—	—	—	—
Syria	—	—	—	—	—	—	—	—
Taiwan	19	8	45	94	129	382	2,478	27,510
Turkey	—	—	—	—	—	—	—	—
Vietnam	—	—	—	—	—	—	—	—
Other Asia	3	1	11	11	63	248	1,046	4,407
America	9,655	31,905	50,516	84,145	130,292	345,010	524,826	37,350
Canada and Newfoundland	2,297	11,875	34,285	64,171	117,978	324,310	492,865	3,098
Mexico	3,835	7,187	3,069	3,446	1,957	5,133	2,405	734
Caribbean	3,061	11,792	11,803	12,447	8,751	14,285	27,323	31,480
Cuba	—	—	—	—	—	—	—	—
Dominican Republic	—	—	—	—	—	—	—	—
Haiti	—	—	—	—	—	—	—	—
Jamaica	—	—	—	—	—	—	—	—
Other Caribbean	3,061	11,792	11,803	12,447	8,751	14,285	27,323	31,480
Central America	57	94	297	512	70	173	279	649
Belize	—	—	—	—	—	—	—	—
Costa Rica	—	—	—	—	—	—	—	—
El Salvador	—	—	—	—	—	—	—	—
Guatemala	—	—	—	—	—	—	—	—
Honduras	—	—	—	—	—	—	—	—
Nicaragua	—	—	—	—	—	—	—	—
Panama	—	—	—	—	—	—	—	—
Other Central America	57	94	297	512	70	173	279	649
South America	405	957	1,062	3,569	1,536	1,109	1,954	1,389
Argentina	—	—	—	—	—	—	—	—
Bolivia	—	—	—	—	—	—	—	—

Region and country of last residence	*1820 to 1829*	*1830 to 1839*	*1840 to 1849*	*1850 to 1859*	*1860 to 1869*	*1870 to 1879*	*1880 to 1889*	*1890 to 1899*
Brazil	—	—	—	—	—	—	—	—
Chile	—	—	—	—	—	—	—	—
Colombia	—	—	—	—	—	—	—	—
Ecuador	—	—	—	—	—	—	—	—
Guyana	—	—	—	—	—	—	—	—
Paraguay	—	—	—	—	—	—	—	—
Peru	—	—	—	—	—	—	—	—
Suriname	—	—	—	—	—	—	—	—
Uruguay	—	—	—	—	—	—	—	—
Venezuela	—	—	—	—	—	—	—	—
Other South America	405	957	1,062	3,569	1,536	1,109	1,954	1,389
Other America	—	—	—	—	—	—	—	—
Africa	15	50	61	84	407	371	763	432
Egypt	—	—	—	—	4	29	145	51
Ethiopia	—	—	—	—	—	—	—	—
Liberia	1	8	5	7	43	52	21	9
Morocco	—	—	—	—	—	—	—	—
South Africa	—	—	—	—	35	48	23	9
Other Africa	14	42	56	77	325	242	574	363
Oceania	3	7	14	166	187	9,996	12,361	4,704
Australia	—	—	—	—	—	8,930	7,250	3,098
New Zealand	2	1	2	15	—	39	21	12
Other Oceania	1	6	12	151	187	1,027	5,090	1,594
Not Specified	19,523	83,593	7,366	74,399	18,241	754	790	14,112

Total	8,202,388	6,347,380	4,295,510	699,375	856,608	2,499,268	3,213,749	6,244,379
Europe	7,572,569	4,985,411	2,560,340	444,399	472,524	1,404,973	1,133,443	668,866
Austria-Hungary	2,001,376	1,154,727	60,891	12,531	13,574	113,015	27,590	20,437
Austria	532,416	589,174	31,392	5,307	8,393	81,354	17,571	15,374
Hungary	685,567	565,553	29,499	7,224	5,181	31,661	10,019	5,063
Belgium	37,429	32,574	21,511	4,013	12,473	18,885	9,647	7,028
Bulgaria	34,651	27,180	2,824	1,062	449	97	598	1,124
Czechoslovakia	—	—	101,182	17,757	8,475	1,624	2,758	5,678
Denmark	61,227	45,830	34,406	3,470	4,549	10,918	9,797	4,847
Finland	—	—	16,922	2,438	2,230	4,923	4,310	2,569
France	67,735	60,335	54,842	13,761	36,954	50,113	46,975	32,066
Germany	328,722	174,227	386,634	119,107	119,506	576,905	209,616	85,752
Greece	145,402	198,108	60,774	10,599	8,605	45,153	74,173	37,729
Ireland	344,940	166,445	202,854	28,195	15,701	47,189	37,788	22,210
Italy	1,930,475	1,229,916	528,133	85,053	50,509	184,576	200,111	55,562
Netherlands	42,463	46,065	29,397	7,791	13,877	46,703	37,918	11,234
Norway-Sweden	426,981	192,445	170,329	13,452	17,326	44,224	36,150	13,941
Norway	182,542	79,488	70,327	6,901	8,326	22,806	17,371	3,835
Sweden	244,439	112,957	100,002	6,551	9,000	21,418	18,779	10,106
Poland	—	—	223,316	25,555	7,577	6,465	55,742	63,483
Portugal	65,154	82,489	44,829	3,518	6,765	13,928	70,568	42,685
Romania	57,322	13,566	67,810	5,264	1,254	914	24,753	24,753
Russia	1,501,301	1,106,998	61,604	2,463	605	453	2,329	33,311
Spain	24,818	53,262	47,109	3,669	2,774	6,880	40,793	22,783
Switzerland	32,541	22,839	31,772	5,990	9,904	17,577	19,193	8,316
United Kingdom	469,518	371,878	341,552	61,813	131,794	195,709	220,213	153,644
Yugoslavia	—	—	49,215	6,920	2,039	6,966	17,990	16,267
Other Europe	514	6,527	22,434	9,978	5,584	11,756	6,845	3,447
Asia	299,836	269,736	126,740	19,231	34,532	135,844	358,605	2,391,356
China	19,884	20,916	30,648	5,874	16,072	8,836	14,060	170,897
Hong Kong	—	—	—	—	—	13,781	67,047	112,132
India	3,026	3,478	2,076	554	1,692	1,850	18,638	231,649
Iran	—	—	208	198	1,144	3,195	9,059	98,141
Israel	—	—	—	—	98	21,376	30,911	43,669

Region and country of last residence	1900 to 1909	1910 to 1919	1920 to 1929	1930 to 1939	1940 to 1949	1950 to 1959	1960 to 1969	1980 to 1989
Japan	139,712	77,125	42,057	2,683	1,557	40,651	40,956	44,150
Jordan	—	—	—	—	—	4,899	9,230	28,928
Korea	—	—	—	—	83	4,845	27,048	322,708
Philippines	—	—	—	391	4,099	17,245	70,660	502,056
Syria	—	—	5,307	2,188	1,179	1,091	2,432	14,534
Taiwan	—	—	—	—	—	721	15,657	119,051
Turkey	127,999	160,717	40,450	1,327	754	2,980	9,464	19,208
Vietnam	—	—	—	—	—	290	2,949	200,632
Other Asia	9,215	7,500	5,994	6,016	7,854	14,084	40,494	483,601
America	277,809	1,070,539	1,591,278	230,319	328,435	921,610	1,674,172	2,695,329
Canada and Newfoundland	123,067	708,715	949,286	162,703	160,911	353,169	433,128	156,313
Mexico	31,188	185,334	498,945	32,709	56,158	273,847	441,824	1,009,586
Caribbean	100,960	120,860	83,482	18,052	46,194	115,661	427,235	790,109
Cuba	—	—	12,769	10,641	25,976	73,221	202,030	132,552
Dominican Republic	—	—	—	1,026	4,802	10,219	83,552	221,552
Haiti	—	—	—	156	823	3,787	28,992	121,406
Jamaica	—	—	—	—	—	7,397	62,218	193,874
Other Caribbean	100,960	120,860	70,713	6,229	14,593	21,037	50,443	120,725
Central America	7,341	15,692	16,511	6,840	20,135	40,201	98,560	339,376
Belize	77	40	285	193	433	1,133	4,185	14,964
Costa Rica	—	—	—	431	1,965	4,044	17,975	25,017
El Salvador	—	—	—	597	4,885	5,094	14,405	137,418
Guatemala	—	—	—	423	1,303	4,197	14,357	58,847
Honduras	—	—	—	679	1,874	5,320	15,078	39,071
Nicaragua	—	—	—	405	4,393	7,812	10,383	31,102
Panama	—	—	—	1,452	5,282	12,601	22,177	32,957
Other Central America	7,264	15,652	16,226	2,660	—	—	—	—

South America	15,253	39,938	43,025	9,990	19,662	78,418	250,754	399,862
Argentina	—	—	—	1,067	3,108	16,346	49,384	23,442
Bolivia	—	—	—	50	893	2,759	6,205	9,798
Brazil	—	—	4,627	1,468	3,653	11,547	29,238	22,944
Chile	—	—	—	347	1,320	4,669	12,384	19,749
Colombia	—	—	—	1,027	3,454	15,567	68,371	105,494
Ecuador	—	—	—	244	2,207	8,574	34,107	48,015
Guyana	—	—	—	131	596	1,131	4,546	85,886
Paraguay	—	—	—	33	85	576	1,249	3,518
Peru	—	—	—	321	1,273	5,980	19,783	49,958
Suriname	—	—	—	25	130	299	612	1,357
Uruguay	—	—	—	112	754	1,026	4,089	7,235
Venezuela	—	—	—	1,155	2,182	9,927	20,758	22,405
Other South America	15,253	39,938	38,398	4,010	7	17	28	61
Other America	—	—	29	25	25,375	60,314	22,671	83
Africa	6,326	8,867	6,362	2,120	6,720	13,016	23,780	141,990
Egypt	—	—	1,063	781	1,613	1,996	5,581	26,744
Ethiopia	—	—	—	10	28	302	804	12,927
Liberia	—	—	—	35	37	289	841	6,420
Morocco	—	—	—	73	879	2,703	2,880	3,471
South Africa	—	—	—	312	1,022	2,278	4,360	15,505
Other Africa	6,326	8,867	5,299	909	3,141	5,448	9,314	76,923
Oceania	12,355	12,339	9,860	3,306	14,262	11,353	23,630	41,432
Australia	11,191	11,280	8,404	2,260	11,201	8,275	14,986	16,901
New Zealand	—	—	935	790	2,351	1,799	3,775	6,129
Other Oceania	1,164	1,059	521	256	710	1,279	4,869	18,402
Not Specified	33,493	488	930	—	135	12,472	119	305,406

Region and country of last residence	1990 to 1999	2000 to 2009	2010	2011
Total	9,775,398	10,299,430	1,042,625	1,062,040
Europe	1,348,612	1,349,609	95,429	90,712
Austria-Hungary	27,529	33,929	4,325	4,703
Austria	18,234	21,151	3,319	3,654
Hungary	9,295	12,778	1,006	1,049
Belgium	7,077	8,157	732	700
Bulgaria	16,948	40,003	2,465	2,549
Czechoslovakia	8,970	18,691	1,510	1,374
Denmark	6,189	6,049	545	473
Finland	3,970	3,970	414	398
France	35,945	45,637	4,339	3,967
Germany	92,207	122,373	7,929	7,072
Greece	25,403	16,841	966	1,196
Ireland	65,384	15,642	1,610	1,533
Italy	75,992	28,329	2,956	2,670
Netherlands	13,345	17,351	1,520	1,258
Norway-Sweden	17,825	19,382	1,662	1,530
Norway	5,211	4,599	363	405
Sweden	12,614	14,783	1,299	1,125
Poland	172,249	117,921	7,391	6,634
Portugal	25,497	11,479	759	878
Romania	48,136	52,154	3,735	3,679
Russia	433,427	167,152	7,502	8,548
Spain	18,443	17,695	2,040	2,319
Switzerland	11,768	12,173	868	861
United Kingdom	156,182	171,979	14,781	13,443
Yugoslavia	57,039	131,831	4,772	4,611
Other Europe	29,087	290,871	22,608	20,316

Asia	2,859,899	3,470,835	410,209	438,580
China	342,058	591,711	67,634	83,603
Hong Kong	116,894	57,583	3,263	3,149
India	352,528	590,464	66,185	66,331
Iran	76,899	76,755	9,078	9,015
Israel	41,340	54,081	5,172	4,389
Japan	66,582	84,552	7,100	6,751
Jordan	42,755	53,550	9,327	8,211
Korea	179,770	209,758	22,022	22,748
Philippines	534,338	545,463	56,399	55,251
Syria	22,906	30,807	7,424	7,983
Taiwan	132,647	92,657	6,785	6,206
Turkey	38,687	48,394	7,435	9,040
Vietnam	275,379	289,616	30,065	33,486
Other Asia	637,116	745,444	112,320	122,417
America	5,137,743	4,441,529	426,981	423,277
Canada and Newfoundland	194,788	236,349	19,491	19,506
Mexico	2,757,418	1,704,166	138,717	142,823
Caribbean	1,004,687	1,053,357	139,389	133,012
Cuba	159,037	271,742	33,372	36,261
Dominican Republic	359,818	291,492	53,890	46,036
Haiti	177,446	203,827	22,336	21,802
Jamaica	177,143	172,523	19,439	19,298
Other Caribbean	181,243	113,773	10,352	9,615
Central America	610,189	591,130	43,597	43,249
Belize	12,600	9,682	997	933
Costa Rica	17,054	21,571	2,306	2,230
El Salvador	273,017	251,237	18,547	18,477
Guatemala	126,043	156,992	10,263	10,795
Honduras	72,880	63,513	6,381	6,053

Region and country of last residence	1990 to 1999	2000 to 2009	2010	2011
Nicaragua	80,446	70,015	3,476	3,314
Panama	28,149	18,120	1,627	1,447
Other Central America	—			–
South America	570,624	856,508	85,783	84,687
Argentina	30,065	47,955	4,312	4,335
Bolivia	18,111	21,921	2,211	2,113
Brazil	50,744	115,404	12,057	11,643
Chile	18,200	19,792	1,940	1,854
Colombia	137,985	236,570	21,861	22,130
Ecuador	81,358	107,977	11,463	11,068
Guyana	74,407	70,373	6,441	6,288
Paraguay	6,082	4,623	449	501
Peru	110,117	137,614	14,063	13,836
Suriname	2,285	2,363	202	167
Uruguay	6,062	9,827	1,286	1,521
Venezuela	35,180	82,087	9,497	9,229
Other South America	28	2	1	2
Other America	37	19	4	–
Africa	346,416	759,734	98,246	97,429
Egypt	44,604	81,564	9,822	9,096
Ethiopia	40,097	87,207	13,853	13,985
Liberia	13,587	23,316	2,924	3,117
Morocco	15,768	40,844	4,847	4,249
South Africa	21,964	32,221	2,705	2,754
Other Africa	210,396	494,582	64,095	64,228
Oceania	56,800	65,793	5,946	5,825
Australia	24,288	32,728	3,077	3,062
New Zealand	8,600	12,495	1,046	1,006
Other Oceania	23,912	20,570	1,823	1,757
Not Specified	25,928	211,930	5,814	6,217

— Represents zero or not available.

PRESIDENTS, VICE PRESIDENTS, AND SECRETARIES OF STATE

	President	Vice President	Secretary of State
1.	George Washington, Federalist 1789	John Adams, Federalist 1789	Thomas Jefferson 1789 Edmund Randolph 1794 Timothy Pickering 1795
2.	John Adams, Federalist 1797	Thomas Jefferson, Dem.-Rep. 1797	Timothy Pickering 1797 John Marshall 1800
3.	Thomas Jefferson, Dem.-Rep. 1801	Aaron Burr, Dem.-Rep. 1801 George Clinton, Dem.-Rep. 1805	James Madison 1801
4.	James Madison, Dem.-Rep. 1809	George Clinton, Dem.-Rep. 1809 Elbridge Gerry, Dem.-Rep. 1813	Robert Smith 1809 James Monroe 1811
5.	James Monroe, Dem.-Rep. 1817	Daniel D. Tompkins, Dem.-Rep. 1817	John Q. Adams 1817
6.	John Quincy Adams, Dem.-Rep. 1825	John C. Calhoun, Dem.-Rep. 1825	Henry Clay 1825
7.	Andrew Jackson, Democratic 1829	John C. Calhoun, Democratic 1829 Martin Van Buren, Democratic 1833	Martin Van Buren 1829 Edward Livingston 1831 Louis McLane 1833 John Forsyth 1834
8.	Martin Van Buren, Democratic 1837	Richard M. Johnson, Democratic 1837	John Forsyth 1837
9.	William H. Harrison, Whig 1841	John Tyler, Whig 1841	Daniel Webster 1841

	President	Vice President	Secretary of State
10.	John Tyler, Whig and Democratic 1841	None	Daniel Webster 1841 Hugh S. Legaré 1843 Abel P. Upshur 1843 John C. Calhoun 1844
11.	James K. Polk, Democratic 1845	George M. Dallas, Democratic 1845	James Buchanan 1845
12.	Zachary Taylor, Whig 1849	Millard Fillmore, Whig 1848	John M. Clayton 1849
13.	Millard Fillmore, Whig 1850	None	Daniel Webster 1850 Edward Everett 1852
14.	Franklin Pierce, Democratic 1853	William R. King, Democratic 1853	William L. Marcy 1853
15.	James Buchanan, Democratic 1857	John C. Breckinridge, Democratic 1857	Lewis Cass 1857 Jeremiah S. Black 1860
16.	Abraham Lincoln, Republican 1861	Hannibal Hamlin, Republican 1861 Andrew Johnson, Unionist 1865	William H. Seward 1861
17.	Andrew Johnson, Unionist 1865	None	William H. Seward 1865
18.	Ulysses S. Grant, Republican 1869	Schuyler Colfax, Republican 1869 Henry Wilson, Republican 1873	Elihu B. Washburne 1869 Hamilton Fish 1869
19.	Rutherford B. Hayes, Republican 1877	William A. Wheeler, Republican 1877	William M. Evarts 1877

	President	*Vice President*	*Secretary of State*
20.	James A. Garfield, Republican 1881	Chester A. Arthur, Republican 1881	James G. Blaine 1881
21.	Chester A. Arthur, Republican 1881	None	Frederick T. Frelinghuysen 1881
22.	Grover Cleveland, Democratic 1885	Thomas A. Hendricks, Democratic 1885	Thomas F. Bayard 1885
23.	Benjamin Harrison, Republican 1889	Levi P. Morton, Republican 1889	James G. Blaine 1889 John W. Foster 1892
24.	Grover Cleveland, Democratic 1893	Adlai E. Stevenson, Democratic 1893	Walter Q. Gresham 1893 Richard Olney 1895
25.	William McKinley, Republican 1897	Garret A. Hobart, Republican 1897 Theodore Roosevelt, Republican 1901	John Sherman 1897 William R. Day 1898 John Hay 1898
26.	Theodore Roosevelt, Republican 1901	Charles Fairbanks, Republican 1905	John Hay 1901 Elihu Root 1905 Robert Bacon 1909
27.	William H. Taft, Republican 1909	James S. Sherman, Republican 1909	Philander C. Knox 1909
28.	Woodrow Wilson, Democratic 1913	Thomas R. Marshall, Democratic 1913	William J. Bryan 1913 Robert Lansing 1915 Bainbridge Colby 1920
29.	Warren G. Harding, Republican 1921	Calvin Coolidge, Republican 1921	Charles E. Hughes 1921
30.	Calvin Coolidge, Republican 1923	Charles G. Dawes, Republican 1925	Charles E. Hughes 1923 Frank B. Kellogg 1925

	President	Vice President	Secretary of State
31.	Herbert Hoover, Republican 1929	Charles Curtis, Republican 1929	Henry L. Stimson 1929
32.	Franklin D. Roosevelt, Democratic 1933	John Nance Garner, Democratic 1933 Henry A. Wallace, Democratic 1941 Harry S. Truman, Democratic 1945	Cordell Hull 1933 Edward R. Stettinius, Jr. 1944
33.	Harry S. Truman, Democratic 1945	Alben W. Barkley, Democratic 1949	Edward R. Stettinius, Jr. 1945 James F. Byrnes 1945 George C. Marshall 1947 Dean G. Acheson 1949
34.	Dwight D. Eisenhower, Republican 1953	Richard M. Nixon, Republican 1953	John F. Dulles 1953 Christian A. Herter 1959
35.	John F. Kennedy, Democratic 1961	Lyndon B. Johnson, Democratic 1961	Dean Rusk 1961
36.	Lyndon B. Johnson, Democratic 1963	Hubert H. Humphrey, Democratic 1965	Dean Rusk 1963
37.	Richard M. Nixon, Republican 1969	Spiro T. Agnew, Republican 1969 Gerald R. Ford, Republican 1973	William P. Rogers 1969 Henry Kissinger 1973
38.	Gerald R. Ford, Republican 1974	Nelson Rockefeller, Republican 1974	Henry Kissinger 1974
39.	Jimmy Carter, Democratic 1977	Walter Mondale, Democratic 1977	Cyrus Vance 1977 Edmund Muskie 1980

	President	*Vice President*	*Secretary of State*
40.	Ronald Reagan, Republican 1981	George H. W. Bush, Republican 1981	Alexander Haig 1981 George Schultz 1982
41.	George H. W. Bush, Republican 1989	J. Danforth Quayle, Republican 1989	James A. Baker 1989 Lawrence Eagleburger 1992
42.	William J. Clinton, Democratic 1993	Albert Gore, Jr., Democratic 1993	Warren Christopher 1993 Madeleine Albright 1997
43.	George W. Bush, Republican 2001	Richard B. Cheney, Republican 2001	Colin L. Powell 2001 Condoleezza Rice 2005
44.	Barack Obama, Democratic 2009	Joseph R. Biden, Democratic 2009	Hillary Rodham Clinton 2009 John Kerry 2013

Further Readings

Chapter 15

The most comprehensive treatment of Reconstruction is Eric Foner's *Reconstruction: America's Unfinished Revolution, 1863–1877* (1988). On Andrew Johnson, see Hans L. Trefousse's *Andrew Johnson: A Biography* (1989) and David D. Stewart's *Impeached: The Trial of Andrew Johnson and the Fight for Lincoln's Legacy* (2009). An excellent brief biography of Grant is Josiah Bunting III's *Ulysses S. Grant* (2004).

Scholars have been sympathetic to the aims and motives of the Radical Republicans. See, for instance, Herman Belz's *Reconstructing the Union: Theory and Policy during the Civil War* (1969) and Richard Nelson Current's *Those Terrible Carpetbaggers: A Reinterpretation* (1988). The ideology of the Radicals is explored in Michael Les Benedict's *A Compromise of Principle: Congressional Republicans and Reconstruction, 1863–1869* (1974). On the black political leaders, see Phillip Dray's *Capitol Men: The Epic Story of Reconstruction through the Lives of the First Black Congressmen* (2008).

The intransigence of southern white attitudes is examined in Michael Perman's *Reunion without Compromise: The South and Reconstruction, 1865– 1868* (1973) and Dan T. Carter's *When the War Was Over: The Failure of Self-Reconstruction in the South, 1865–1867* (1985). Allen W. Trelease's *White Terror: The Ku Klux Klan Conspiracy and Southern Reconstruction* (1971) covers the various organizations that practiced vigilante tactics. On the massacre of African Americans, see Charles Lane's *The Day Freedom Died: The Colfax Massacre, the Supreme Court, and the Betrayal of Reconstruction* (2008).

The difficulties former slaves had in adjusting to the new labor system are documented in James L. Roark's *Masters without Slaves: Southern Planters in the Civil War and Reconstruction* (1977). Books on southern politics during Reconstruction include Michael Perman's *The Road to Redemption: Southern Politics, 1869–1879* (1984), Terry L. Seip's *The South Returns to Congress: Men, Economic Measures, and Intersectional Relationships, 1868–1879* (1983), and Mark W. Summers's *Railroads, Reconstruction, and the Gospel of Prosperity: Aid under the Radical Republicans, 1865–1877* (1984).

Numerous works study the freed blacks' experience in the South. Start with Leon F. Litwack's *Been in the Storm So Long: The Aftermath of Slavery* (1979). The Freedmen's Bureau is explored in William S. McFeely's *Yankee Stepfather: General O. O. Howard and the Freedmen* (1968). The situation of freed slave women is discussed in Jacqueline Jones's *Labor of Love, Labor of Sorrow: Black Women, Work and the Family, from Slavery to the Present* (1985).

The politics of corruption outside the South is depicted in William S. McFeely's *Grant: A Biography* (1981). The political maneuvers of the election of 1876 and the resultant crisis and compromise are explained in Michael Holt's *By One Vote: The Disputed Presidential Election of 1876* (2008).

Chapter 16

For masterly syntheses of post–Civil War industrial development, see Walter Licht's *Industrializing America: The Nineteenth Century* (1995) and Maury Klein's *The Genesis of Industrial America, 1870–1920* (2007). On the growth of railroads, see Richard White's *Railroaded: The Transcontinentals and the Making of Modern America* (2011) and Albro Martin's *Railroad Triumphant: The Growth, Rejection, and Rebirth of a Vital American Force* (1992).

On entrepreneurship in the iron and steel sector, and Thomas J. Misa's *A Nation of Steel: The Making of Modern America, 1865–1925* (1995). The best biographies of the leading business tycoons are Ron Chernow's *Titan: The Life of John D. Rockefeller, Sr.* (1998), David Nasaw's *Andrew Carnegie* (2006), and Jean Strouse's *Morgan: American Financier* (1999). Nathan Rosenberg's *Technology and American Economic Growth* (1972) documents the growth of invention during the period.

For an overview of the struggle of workers to organize unions, see Philip Bray's *There Is Power in a Union: The Epic Story of Labor in America* (2010). On the 1877 railroad strike, see David O. Stowell's *Streets, Railroad, and the Great Strike of 1877* (1999). For the role of women in the changing workplace, see Alice Kessler-Harris's *Out to Work: A History of Wage-Earning Women in the United States* (1982) and Susan E. Kennedy's *If All We Did Was to Weep at Home: A History of White Working-Class Women in American* (1979). On Mother Jones, see Elliott J. Gorn's *Mother Jones: The Most Dangerous Woman in America* (2001). To trace the rise of socialism among organized workers, see Nick Salvatore's *Eugene V. Debs: Citizen and Socialist* (1982). The key strikes are discussed in Paul Arvich's *The Haymarket Tragedy* (1984) and Paul Krause's *The Battle for Homestead, 1880–1892: Politics, Culture, and Steel* (1992).

Chapter 17

The classic study of the emergence of the New South remains C. Vann Woodward's *Origins of the New South, 1877–1913* (1951). A more recent treatment of southern society after the end of Reconstruction is Edward L. Ayers's *Southern Crossing: A History of the American South, 1877–1906* (1995). A thorough survey of industrialization in the South is James C. Cobb's *Industrialization and Southern Society, 1877–1984* (1984).

On race relations, see Howard N. Rabinowitz's *Race Relations in the Urban South, 1865–1890* (1978). Leon F. Litwack's *Trouble in Mind: Black Southerners in the Age of Jim Crow* (1998) treats the rise of legal segregation, while Michael Perman's *Struggle for Mastery: Disfranchisement in the South, 1888–1908* (2001) surveys efforts to keep African Americans from voting. An award-winning study of white women and the race issue is Glenda Elizabeth Gilmore's *Gender and Jim Crow: Women and the Politics of White Supremacy in North Carolina, 1896–1920* (1996). On W. E. B. Du Bois, see David Levering Lewis's *W. E. B. Du Bois: Biography of a Race, 1868–1919* (1993). On Booker T. Washington, see Robert J. Norrell's *Up from History: The Life of Booker T. Washington* (2009).

For stimulating reinterpretations of the frontier and the development of the West, see William Cronon's *Nature's Metropolis: Chicago and the Great West* (1991), Patricia Nelson Limerick's *The Legacy of Conquest: The Unbroken Past of the American West* (1987), Richard White's *"It's Your Misfortune and None of My Own": A New History of the American West* (1991), and Walter Nugent's *Into the West: The Story of Its People* (1999). An excellent overview is James M. McPherson's *Into the West: From Reconstruction to the Final Days of the American Frontier* (2006).

The role of African Americans in western settlement is the focus of William Loren Katz's *The Black West: A Documentary and Pictorial History of the African American Role in the Westward Expansion of the United States,* rev. ed. (2005), and Nell Irvin Painter's *Exodusters: Black Migration to Kansas after Reconstruction* (1977).

The best account of the conflicts between Indians and whites is Robert M. Utley's *The Indian Frontier of the American West, 1846–1890* (1984). For the Sand Creek massacre, see Ari Kellman's *A Misplaced Massacre: Struggling over the Memory of Sand Creek* (2013). On the Battle of the Little Bighorn, see Nathaniel Philbrick's *The Last Stand: Custer, Sitting Bull, and the Battle of the Little Bighorn* (2010). On Crazy Horse, see Thomas Powers's *The Killing of Crazy Horse* (2010).

For a presentation of the Native American side of the story, see Peter Nabokov's *Native American Testimony: A Chronicle of Indian-White Relations from Prophecy to the Present, 1492–2000,* rev. ed. (1999). On the demise of the buffalo herds, see Andrew C. Isenberg's *The Destruction of the Bison: An Environmental History, 1750–1920* (2000).

Chapter 18

For a survey of urbanization, see David R. Goldfield's *Urban America: A History* (1989). Gunther Barth discusses the emergence of a new urban culture in *City People: The Rise of Modern City Culture in Nineteenth-Century America* (1980). John Bodnar offers a synthesis of the urban immigrant experience in *The Transplanted: A History of Immigrants in Urban America* (1985). See also Roger Daniels's *Guarding the Golden Door: American Immigration Policy and Immigrants since 1882* (2004). Walter Nugent's *Crossings: The Great Transatlantic Migrations, 1870–1914* (1992) provides a wealth of demographic information and insight. Efforts to stop Chinese immigration are described in Erika Lee's *At America's Gates: Chinese Immigration during the Exclusion Era* (2003).

On urban environments and sanitary reforms, see Martin V. Melosi's *The Sanitary City: Urban Infrastructure in America from Colonial Times to the Present* (2000), Joel A. Tarr's *The Search for the Ultimate Sink: Urban Pollution in Historical Perspective* (1996), and Suellen Hoy's *Chasing Dirt: The American Pursuit of Cleanliness* (1995).

For the growth of urban leisure and sports, see Roy Rosenzweig's *Eight Hours for What We Will: Workers and Leisure in an Industrial City, 1870–1920* (1983) and Steven A. Riess's *City Games: The Evolution of American Urban Society and the Rise of Sports* (1989). Saloon culture is examined in Madelon Powers's *Faces along the Bar: Lore and Order in the Workingman's Saloon, 1870–1920* (1998).

On the impact of Darwin's theory of evolution, see Barry Werth's *Banquet at Delmonico's: Great Minds, the Gilded Age, and the Triumph of Evolution in America* (2009). On the rise of realism in thought and the arts during the second half of the nineteenth century, see David E. Shi's *Facing Facts: Realism in American Thought and Culture, 1850–1920* (1995). The rise of pragmatism is the focus of Louis Menand's *The Metaphysical Club: A Story of Ideas in America* (2001).

Two good overviews of the Gilded Age are Sean Cashman's *America in the Gilded Age: From the Death of Lincoln to the Rise of Theodore Roosevelt* (1984) and Mark Summers's *The Gilded Age or, The Hazard of New Functions* (1996). Nell Irvin Painter's *Standing at Armageddon: The United States, 1877–1919* (1987) focuses on the experience of the working class.

For a stimulating overview of the political, social, and economic trends during the Gilded Age, see Jack Beatty's *Age of Betrayal: The Triumph of Money in America, 1865–1900* (2007). On the development of city rings and bosses, see Kenneth D. Ackerman's *Boss Tweed: The Rise and Fall of the Corrupt Pol Who Conceived the Soul of Modern New York* (2005). Excellent presidential biographies include Hans L. Trefousse's *Rutherford B. Hayes* (2002), Zachary Karabell's *Chester Alan Arthur* (2004), Henry F. Graff's *Grover Cleveland* (2002), and Kevin Phillips's *William McKinley*

(2003). On the political culture of the Gilded Age, see Charles Calhoun's *Minority Victory: Gilded Age Politics and the Front Porch Campaign of 1888* (2008).

A balanced account of Populism is Charles Postel's *The Populist Vision* (2007). The election of 1896 is the focus of R. Hal Williams's *Realigning America: McKinley, Bryan, and the Remarkable Election of 1896* (2010). On the role of religion in the agrarian protest movements, see Joe Creech's *Righteous Indignation: Religion and the Populist Revolution* (2006). The best biography of Bryan is Michael Kazin's *A Godly Hero: The Life of William Jennings Bryan* (2006).

Chapter 19

An excellent survey of the diplomacy of the era is Charles S. Campbell's *The Transformation of American Foreign Relations, 1865–1900* (1976). For background on the events of the 1890s, see David Healy's *U.S. Expansionism: The Imperialist Urge in the 1890s* (1970). The dispute over American policy in Hawaii is covered in Thomas J. Osborne's *"Empire Can Wait": American Opposition to Hawaiian Annexation, 1893–1898* (1981).

Ivan Musicant's *Empire by Default: The Spanish-American War and the Dawn of the American Century* (1998) is the most comprehensive volume on the conflict. A colorful treatment of the powerful men promoting war is Evan Thomas's *The War Lovers: Roosevelt, Lodge, Mahan, and the Rush to Empire, 1898* (2010). For the war's aftermath in the Philippines, see Stuart Creighton Miller's *"Benevolent Assimilation": The American Conquest of the Philippines, 1899–1903* (1982). On the Philippine-American War, see David J. Silbey's *A War of Frontier and Empire: The Philippine-American War, 1899–1902* (2007).

A good introduction to American interest in China is Michael H. Hunt's *The Making of a Special Relationship: The United States and China to 1914* (1983). John Taliaferro's All the Great Prizes: The Life of *John Hay* (2013) examines the role of this key secretary of state in forming policy.

For U.S. policy in the Caribbean and Central America, see Walter LaFeber's *Inevitable Revolutions: The United States in Central America,* 2nd ed. (1993). David McCullough's *The Path between the Seas: The Creation of the Panama Canal, 1870–1914* (1977) presents an admiring account of how the United States secured the Panama Canal. A more sober assessment is Julie Greene's *The Canal Builders: Making America's Empire at the Panama Canal* (2009). For a detailed treatment of TR's diplomacy as president, see James Bradley's *The Imperial Cruise: A Secret History of Empire and War* (2009).

Chapter 20

Splendid analyses of progressivism can be found in John Whiteclay Chambers II's *The Tyranny of Change: America in the Progressive Era, 1890–1920,* rev. ed. (2000), Steven J. Diner's *A Very Different Age: Americans of the Progressive Era* (1997), Maureen A. Flanagan's *America Reformed: Progressives and Progressivisms, 1890-1920* (2006), Michael McGerr's *A Fierce Discontent: The Rise and Fall of the Progressive Movement in America* (2003) and David Traxel's *Crusader Nation: The United States in Peace and the Great War, 1898-19*20 (2006). On Ida Tarbell and the muckrakers, see Steve Weinberg's *Taking on the Trust: The Epic Battle of Ida Tarbell and John D. Rockefeller* (2008).

The evolution of government policy toward business is examined in Martin J. Sklar's *The Corporate Reconstruction of American Capitalism, 1890–1916: The Mar-*

ket, the Law, and Politics (1988). Mina Carson's *Settlement Folk: Social Thought and the American Settlement Movement, 1885–1930* (1990) examines the social problems in the cities. Robert Kanigel's *The One Best Way: Frederick Winslow Taylor and the Enigma of Efficiency* (1997) highlights the role of efficiency and expertise in the Progressive Era.

An excellent study of the role of women in progressivism's emphasis on social justice is Kathryn Kish Sklar's *Florence Kelley and the Nation's Work: The Rise of Women's Political Culture, 1830–1900* (1995). On the tragic fire at the Triangle Shirtwaist Company, see David Von Drehle's *Triangle: The Fire That Changed America* (2003). The best study of the settlement house movement is Jean Bethke Elshtain's *Jane Addams and the Dream of American Democracy: A Life* (2002).

On Theodore Roosevelt and the conservation movement, see Douglas Brinkley's *The Wilderness Warrior: Theodore Roosevelt and the Crusade for America* (2009) The pivotal election of 1912 is covered in James Chace's *1912: Wilson, Roosevelt, Taft, and Debs—The Election That Changed the Country* (2004) and Sidney M. Milkis's *TR, the Progressive Party, and the Transformation of Democracy* (2009). Excellent biographies include Kathleen Dalton's *Theodore Roosevelt: A Strenuous Life* (2002) and A. Scott Berg's *Wilson* (2013). The racial blind spot of Progressivism is assessed in David W. Southern's *The Progressive Era and Race: Reform and Reaction, 1900-1917* (2006).

Chapter 21

A lucid overview of international events in the early twentieth century is Robert H. Ferrell's *Woodrow Wilson and World War I, 1917–1921* (1985). For a vivid account of U.S. intervention in Mexico, see Frederick Katz's *The Life and Times of Pancho Villa* (1999). On Wilson's stance toward war, see Robert W. Tucker's *Woodrow Wilson and the Great War: Reconsidering America's Neutrality, 1914-1917* (2007). An excellent biography is John Milton Cooper, Jr.'s *Woodrow Wilson: A Biography* (2010).

For the European experience in the First World War, see Adam Hochschild's *To End All Wars: A Story of Loyalty and Rebellion, 1914-1918* (2011) and Margaret MacMillan's *The War That Ended Peace* (2013). Edward M. Coffman's *The War to End All Wars: The American Military Experience in World War I* (1968) is a detailed presentation of America's military involvement. See also Gary Mead's *The Doughboys: America and the First World War* (2000).

For a survey of the impact of the war on the home front, see Meirion Harries and Susie Harries's *The Last Days of Innocence: America at War, 1917–1918* (1997). Maurine Weiner Greenwald's *Women, War, and Work: The Impact of World War I on Women Workers in the United States* (1980) discusses the role of women in the war effort while Sara Hunter Graham's *Woman Suffrage and the New Democracy* (1996) traces the movement during the war to give women the vote. Ronald Schaffer's *America in the Great War: The Rise of the War Welfare State* (1991) shows the effect of war mobilization on business organization. Richard Polenberg's *Fighting Faiths: The Abrams Case, the Supreme Court, and Free Speech* (1987) examines the prosecution of a case under the 1918 Sedition Act. See also Ernest Freeberg's *Democracy's Prisoner: Eugene V. Debs, the Great War, and the Right to Dissent* (2009).

How American diplomacy fared in the making of peace has received considerable attention. Thomas J. Knock connects domestic affairs and foreign relations in his explanation of Wilson's peacemaking in *To End All Wars: Woodrow Wilson and the Quest for a New World Order* (1992). See also John Milton Cooper, Jr.'s *Breaking the Heart of the World: Woodrow Wilson and the Fight for the League of Nations* (2002).

The problems of the immediate postwar years are chronicled by a number of historians. The best overview is Ann Hagedorn's *Savage Peace: Hope and Fear in America, 1919* (2007). On the Spanish flu, see John M. Barry's *The Great Influenza: The Epic Story of the Deadliest Plague in History* (2004). Labor tensions are examined in David E. Brody's *Labor in Crisis: The Steel Strike of 1919* (1965) and Francis Russell's *A City in Terror: Calvin Coolidge and the 1919 Boston Police Strike* (1975). On racial strife, see Jan Voogd's *Race Riots and Resistance: The Red Summer of 1919* (2008). The fear of Communists is analyzed in Robert K. Murray's *Red Scare: A Study in National Hysteria, 1919–1920* (1955).

Chapter 22

For a lively survey of the social and cultural changes during the interwar period, start with William E. Leuchtenburg's *The Perils of Prosperity, 1914–32*, 2nd ed. (1993). Even more comprehensive is Michael E. Parrish's *Anxious Decades: America in Prosperity and Depression, 1920-1941* (1992). The best introduction to the culture of the 1920s remains Roderick Nash's *The Nervous Generation: American Thought, 1917-1930* (1990). See also Lynn Dumenil's *The Modern Temper: American Culture and Society in the 1920s* (1995).

John Higham's *Strangers in the Land: Patterns of American Nativism, 1860–1925*, 2nd ed. (2002) details the story of immigration restriction. The controversial Sacco and Vanzetti case is the focus of Moshik Temkin's *The Sacco-Vanzetti Affair: America on Trial* (2009). For analysis of the revival of Klan activity, see Thomas R. Pegram's *One Hundred Percent American: The Rebirth and Decline of the Ku Klux Klan in the 1920s* (2011). The best analysis of the Scopes trial is Edward J. Larson's *Summer for the Gods: The Scopes Trial and America's Continuing Debate over Science and Religion* (1997). On Prohibition, see Daniel Okrent's *Last Call: The Rise and Fall of Prohibition* (2011).

The impact of woman suffrage is treated in Kristi Anderson's *After Suffrage: Women in Partisan and Electoral Politics before the New Deal* (1996). The best study of the birth-control movement is Ellen Chesler's *Woman of Valor: Margaret Sanger and the Birth Control Movement in America* (1992).

On the African American migration from the South, see James N. Gregory's *The Southern Diaspora: How the Great Migrations of Black and White Southerners Transformed America* (2005). See Charles Flint Kellogg's *NAACP: A History of the National Association for the Advancement of Colored People* (1967) for his analysis of the pioneering court cases against racial discrimination. Nathan Irvin Huggins's *Harlem Renaissance* (1971) assesses the cultural impact of the Great Migration on New York City. The emergence of jazz is ably documented in Burton W. Peretti's *The Creation of Jazz: Music, Race, and Culture in Urban America* (1992). Scientific breakthroughs are analyzed in Manjit Kumar's *Quantum: Einstein, Bohr, and the Great Debate about the Nature of Reality* (2010). The best overview of cultural modernism in Europe is Peter Gay's *Modernism: The Lure of Heresy from Baudelaire to Beckett and Beyond* (2009). On southern modernism, see Daniel Joseph Singal's *The War Within: From Victorian to Modernist Thought in the South, 1919–1945* (1982). Stanley Coben's *Rebellion against Victorianism: The Impetus for Cultural Change in 1920s America* (1991) surveys the appeal of modernism among writers, artists, and intellectuals. See also Charles J. Shindo's *1927 and the Rise of Modern America* (2010).

On Harding, see Robert K. Murray's *The Harding Era: Warren G. Harding and His Administration* (1969). On Coolidge, see Amith Shlaes's *Coolidge* (2013). On Hoover, see Martin L. Fausold's *The Presidency of Herbert C. Hoover* (1985). The influential secretary of the Treasury during the 1920s is ably analyzed in David Cannadine's *Mellon: An American Life* (2006).

On the stock market crash in 1929, see Maury Klein's *Rainbow's End: The Crash of 1929* (2000). Overviews of the depressed economy are found in Charles P. Kindleberger's *The World in Depression, 1929–1939,* rev. and enlarged ed. (1986) and Peter Fearon's *War, Prosperity, and Depression: The U.S. Economy, 1917–1945* (1987). On the removal of the Bonus Army, see Paul Dickson and Thomas B. Allen's *The Bonus Army: An American Epic* (2004).

Chapter 23

Two excellent overviews of the New Deal are Ira Katznelson's Fear Itself: The New Deal and the Origins of Our Time (2013) and David M. Kennedy's *Freedom from Fear: The American People in Depression and War, 1929–1945* (1999). A lively biography of Roosevelt is H. W. Brands's *Traitor to His Class: The Privileged Life and Radical Presidency of Franklin Delano Roosevelt* (2009). The Roosevelt marriage is well described in Hazel Rowley's *Franklin and Eleanor: An Extraordinary Marriage* (2011).

The busy first year of the New Deal is ably detailed in Anthony J. Badger's *FDR: The First Hundred Days* (2008). Perhaps the most successful of the early New Deal programs is the focus of Neil M. Maher's *Nature's New Deal: The Civilian Conservation Corps and the Roots of the American Environmental Movement* (2008). On the political opponents of the New Deal, see Alan Brinkley's *Voices of Protest: Huey Long, Father Coughlin, and the Great Depression* (1982). Roosevelt's battle with the Supreme Court is detailed in Jeff Shesol's *Supreme Power: Franklin Roosevelt vs. The Supreme Court* (2010). The actual effects of the New Deal on the economy are detailed in Elliot A. Rosen's *Roosevelt, the Great Depression, and the Economics of Recovery* (2005).

A critical assessment of Roosevelt and the New Deal is Amity Schlaes's *The Forgotten Man* (2007). James N. Gregory's *American Exodus: The Dust Bowl Migration and Okie Culture in California* (1989) describes the migratory movement. The dramatic Scottsboro court case is the focus of James Goodman's *Stories of Scottsboro* (1995). On the environmental and human causes of the dust bowl, see Donald Worster, *Dust Bowl: The Southern Plains in the 1930s* (1979). On cultural life during the 1930s, see Morris Dickstein's *Dancing in the Dark: A Cultural History of the Great Depression* (2009).

The best overview of diplomacy between the world wars remains Selig Adler's *The Uncertain Giant, 1921–1941: American Foreign Policy between the Wars* (1965). Robert Dallek's *Franklin D. Roosevelt and American Foreign Policy, 1932–1945* (1979) provides a judicious assessment of Roosevelt's foreign policy initiatives during the 1930s.

On Roosevelt's war of words with isolationists, see Lynne Olsen's *Those Angry Days: Roosevelt, Lindbergh, and America's Fight over World War II, 1939-1942* (2013), and David Kaiser's *No End Save Victory: How FDR Led the Naiton into War* (2014). See also David Reynolds's *From Munich to Pearl Harbor: Roosevelt's America and the Origins of the Second World War* (2001). For the Japanese perspective, see Eri Hotta's *Japan 1941: Countdown to Infamy* (2014). On the surprise attack on Pearl Harbor, see Gordon W. Prange's *Pearl Harbor: The Verdict of History* (1986). Japan's perspective is described in Akira Iriye's *The Origins of the Second World War in Asia and the Pacific* (1987).

Chapter 24

For a sweeping survey of the Second World War, consult Anthony Roberts's *The Storm of War: A New History of the Second World War* (2011). The best detailed treatment of U.S. involvement is Rick Atkinson's multi-volume Pulitzer-prize winning series, *An Army at Dawn* (2007), *The Day of Battle* (2008), and *The Guns at Last Light* (2013). Roosevelt's wartime leadership is analyzed in Eric Larrabee's *Commander in Chief: Franklin Delano Roosevelt, His Lieutenants, and Their War* (1987).

Books on specific European campaigns include Anthony Beevor's *D-Day: The Battle for Normandy* (2010) and Charles B. MacDonald's *A Time for Trumpets: The Untold Story of the Battle of the Bulge* (1985). On the Allied commander, see Carlo D'Este's *Eisenhower: A Soldier's Life* (2002). Richard Overy assesses the controversial role of air power in *The Bombing War: Europe, 1939-1945* (2013).

For the war in the Far East, see John Costello's *The Pacific War, 1941–1945* (1981), Ronald H. Spector's *Eagle against the Sun: The American War with Japan* (1985), John W. Dower's award-winning *War without Mercy: Race and Power in the Pacific War* (1986), and Dan van der Vat's *The Pacific Campaign: The U.S.-Japanese Naval War, 1941–1945* (1991).

An excellent overview of the war's effects on the home front is Michael C. C. Adams's *The Best War Ever: America and World War II* (1994). On the transformation to the wartime economy, see Arthur Herman's *Freedom's Forge: How American Business Produced Victory in World War II* (2012) and Maury Klein's *A Call to Arms* (2013). Susan M. Hartmann's *The Home Front and Beyond: American Women in the 1940s* (1982) treats the new working environment for women. Kenneth D. Rose tells the story of problems on the home front in *Myth and the Greatest Generation: A Social History of Americans in World War II* (2008). Neil A. Wynn looks at the participation of blacks in *The Afro-American and the Second World War* (1976). The story of the oppression of Japanese Americans is told in Greg Robinson's *A Tragedy for Democracy: Japanese Confinement in North America* (2009). On the development of the atomic bomb, see Jim Baggott's *The First War of Physics: The Secret History of the Atomic Bomb* (2010). For the controversy over America's policies towards the Holocaust, see Richard Breitman and Alan J. Lichtman's *FDR and the Jews* (2013).

A detailed introduction to U.S. diplomacy during the conflict can be found in Gaddis Smith's *American Diplomacy during the Second World War, 1941–1945* (1965). To understand the role that Roosevelt played in policy making, consult Warren F. Kimball's *The Juggler: Franklin Roosevelt as Wartime Statesman* (1991). The most important wartime summit meeting is assessed in S. M. Plokhy's *Yalta: The Price of Peace* (2010). The issues and events that led to the deployment of atomic weapons are addressed in Martin J. Sherwin's *A World Destroyed: The Atomic Bomb and the Grand Alliance* (1975).

Chapter 25

The cold war remains a hotly debated topic. The traditional interpretation is best reflected in John Lewis Gaddis's *The Cold War: A New History (2005)*. Both superpowers, Gaddis argues, were responsible for causing the cold war, but the Soviet Union was more culpable. The revisionist perspective is represented by Gar Alperovitz's *Atomic Diplomacy: Hiroshima and Potsdam: The Use of the Atomic Bomb and the American Confrontation with Soviet Power*, 2nd ed. (1994). Also see H. W. Brands's

The Devil We Knew: Americans and the Cold War (1993) and Melvyn P. Leffler's *For the Soul of Mankind: The United States, the Soviet Union, and the Cold War* (2007). On the architect of the containment strategy, see John L. Gaddis, *George F. Kennan: An American Life* (2011).

Frank Constigliola assesses Franklin Roosevelt's role in the start of the cold war in *Roosevelt's Lost Alliances: How Personal Politics Helped Start the Cold War* (2013). Arnold A. Offner indicts Truman for clumsy statesmanship in *Another Such Victory: President Truman and the Cold War, 1945–1953* (2002). For a positive assessment of Truman's leadership, see Alonzo L. Hamby's *Beyond the New Deal: Harry S. Truman and American Liberalism* (1973) and Robert Dallek's *The Lost Peace: Leadership in a Time of Horror and Hope, 1945-1953* (2010). The domestic policies of the Fair Deal are treated in William C. Berman's *The Politics of Civil Rights in the Truman Administration* (1970), Richard M. Dalfiume's *Desegregation of the U.S. Armed Forces: Fighting on Two Fronts, 1939–1953* (1969), and Maeva Marcus's *Truman and the Steel Seizure Case: The Limits of Presidential Power* (1977). The most comprehensive biography of Truman is David McCullough's *Truman* (1992).

For an introduction to the tensions in Asia, see Akira Iriye's *The Cold War in Asia: A Historical Introduction* (1974). For the Korean conflict, see Callum A. MacDonald's *Korea: The War before Vietnam* (1986) and Max Hasting's *The Korean War* (1987).

The anti-Communist crusade is surveyed in David Caute's *The Great Fear: The Anti-Communist Purge under Truman and Eisenhower* (1978). Arthur Herman's *Joseph McCarthy: Reexamining the Life and Legacy of America's Most Hated Senator* (2000) covers McCarthy himself. For a well-documented account of how the cold war was sustained by superpatriotism, intolerance, and suspicion, see Stephen J. Whitfield's *The Culture of the Cold War*, 2nd ed. (1996).

Chapter 26

Two excellent overviews of social and cultural trends in the postwar era are William H. Chafe's *The Unfinished Journey: America since World War II*, 6th ed. (2006), and William E. Leuchtenburg's *A Troubled Feast: America since 1945,* rev. ed. (1979). For insights into the cultural life of the 1950s, see Jeffrey Hart's *When the Going Was Good! American Life in the Fifties* (1982) and David Halberstam's *The Fifties* (1993).

The baby boom generation and its impact are vividly described in Paul C. Light's *Baby Boomers* (1988). The emergence of the television industry is discussed in Erik Barnouw's *Tube of Plenty: The Evolution of American Television,* 2nd rev. ed. (1990), and Ella Taylor's *Prime-Time Families: Television Culture in Postwar America* (1989).

On the process of suburban development, see Kenneth T. Jackson's *Crabgrass Frontier: The Suburbanization of the United States* (1985). Equally good is Tom Martinson's *American Dreamscape: The Pursuit of Happiness in Postwar Suburbia* (2000).

The middle-class ideal of family life in the 1950s is examined in Elaine Tyler May's *Homeward Bound: American Families in the Cold War Era,* rev. ed. (2008). Thorough accounts of women's issues are found in Wini Breines's *Young, White, and Miserable: Growing Up Female in the Fifties* (1992). For an overview of the resurgence of religion in the 1950s, see George M. Marsden's *Religion and American Culture,* 2nd ed. (2000).

The origins and growth of rock and roll are surveyed in Carl Belz's *The Story of Rock,* 2nd ed. (1972). The colorful Beats are brought to life in Steven Watson's *The Birth of the Beat Generation: Visionaries, Rebels, and Hipsters, 1944–1960* (1995).

Scholarship on the Eisenhower years is extensive. A balanced treatment is Jean Edward Smith's *Eisenhower in War and Peace* (2012). For the manner in which Eisenhower conducted foreign policy, see Evan Thomas's *Ike's Bluff: President Eisenhower's Secret Battle to Save the World* (2012).

The best overview of American foreign policy since 1945 is Stephen E. Ambrose and Douglas G. Brinkley's *Rise to Globalism: American Foreign Policy since 1938* 9th ed. (2011). For the buildup of U.S. involvement in Indochina, consult Fredrik Logevall's *Embers of War: The Fall of an Empire and the Making of America's Vietnam* (2012). The Cold War strategy of the Eisenhower administration is the focus of Chris Tudda's *The Truth Is Our Weapon: The Rhetorical Diplomacy of Dwight D. Eisenhower and John Foster Dulles* (2006). To learn about the CIA's secret activities in Iran, see Ervand Abrahamian's *The Coup: 1953, the CIA, and the Roots of Modern U.S.-Iranian Relations* (2013).

The impact of the Supreme Court during the 1950s is the focus of Archibald Cox's *The Warren Court: Constitutional Decision as an Instrument of Reform* (1968). A masterly study of the important Warren Court decision on school desegregation is James T. Patterson's *Brown v. Board of Education: A Civil Rights Milestone and Its Troubled Legacy* (2001).

For the story of the early years of the civil rights movement, see Taylor Branch's *Parting the Waters: America in the King Years, 1954–1963* (1988) Robert Weisbrot's *Freedom Bound: A History of America's Civil Rights Movement* (1990), and David A. Nicholas's *A Matter of Justice: Eisenhower and the Beginning of the Civil Rights Revolution* (2007). On Rosa Parks, see Jeanne Theoharis's *The Rebellious Life of Mrs. Rosa Parks* (2013). On the testy relationship of Eisenhower and his vice president, Richard Nixon, see Jeffrey Frank's *Ike and Dick: Portrait of a Strange Political Marriage* (2013).

Chapter 27

A superb analysis of John Kennedy's life is Thomas C. Reeves's *A Question of Character: A Life of John F. Kennedy* (1991). The 1960 campaign is detailed in Gary A. Donaldson's *The First Modern Campaign: Kennedy, Nixon, and the Election of 1960* (2007). The best study of the Kennedy administration's domestic policies is Irving Bernstein's *Promises Kept: John F. Kennedy's New Frontier* (1991). See also Robert Dallek's *Camelot's Court: Inside the Kennedy White House* (2013), Thurston Clarke's *JFK's Last Hundred Days* (2013), and Ira Stoll's *JFK, Conservative* (2013). For details on the still swirling conspiracy theories about the assassination, see David W. Belin's *Final Disclosure: The Full Truth about the Assassination of President Kennedy* (1988).

On LBJ, see the magisterial multi-volume biography by Robert Caro's titled *The Years of Lyndon Johnson*. On the Johnson administration, see Vaughn Davis Bornet's *The Presidency of Lyndon B. Johnson* (1984).

Among the works that interpret liberal social policy during the 1960s, John E. Schwarz's *America's Hidden Success: A Reassessment of Twenty Years of Public Policy* (1983) offers a glowing endorsement of Democratic programs. For a contrasting perspective, see Charles Murray's *Losing Ground: American Social Policy, 1950–1980* (1994).

On foreign policy, see *Kennedy's Quest for Victory: American Foreign Policy, 1961–1963* (1989), edited by Thomas G. Paterson. To learn more about Kennedy's problems in Cuba, see Mark J. White's *Missiles in Cuba: Kennedy, Khrushchev, Castro and the 1962 Crisis* (1997). See also Aleksandr Fursenko and Timothy Naftali's *"One Hell of a Gamble": Khrushchev, Castro and Kennedy, 1958–1964* (1997).

American involvement in Vietnam has received voluminous treatment from all political perspectives. For an excellent overview, see Larry Berman's *Planning a Tragedy: The Americanization of the War in Vietnam* (1983) and *Lyndon Johnson's War: The Road to Stalemate in Vietnam* (1989), as well as Stanley Karnow's *Vietnam: A History,* 2nd rev. ed. (1997). An analysis of policy making concerning the Vietnam War is David M. Barrett's *Uncertain Warriors: Lyndon Johnson and His Vietnam Advisors* (1993). A fine account of the military involvement is Robert D. Schulzinger's *A Time for War: The United States and Vietnam, 1941–1975* (1997). On the legacy of the Vietnam War, see Arnold R. Isaacs's *Vietnam Shadows: The War, Its Ghosts, and Its Legacy* (1997).

Many scholars have dealt with various aspects of the civil rights movement and race relations in the 1960s. See especially Carl M. Brauer's *John F. Kennedy and the Second Reconstruction* (1977), David J. Garrow's *Bearing the Cross: Martin Luther King, Jr., and the Southern Christian Leadership Conference* (1986), and Adam Fairclough's *To Redeem the Soul of America: The Southern Christian Leadership Conference and Martin Luther King, Jr.* (1987). William H. Chafe's *Civilities and Civil Rights: Greensboro, North Carolina, and the Black Struggle for Freedom* (1980) details the original sit-ins. An award-winning study of racial and economic inequality in a representative American city is Thomas J. Sugrue's *The Origins of the Urban Crisis: Race and Inequality in Postwar Detroit* (1996).

Chapter 28

An engaging overview of the cultural trends of the 1960s is Maurice Isserman and Michael Kazin's *America Divided: The Civil War of the 1960s,* 3rd ed. (2007). The New Left is assessed in Irwin Unger's *The Movement: A History of the American New Left, 1959–1972* (1974). On the Students for a Democratic Society, see Kirkpatrick Sale's *SDS* (1973) and Allen J. Matusow's *The Unraveling of America: A History of Liberalism in the 1960s* (1984). Also useful is Todd Gitlin's *The Sixties: Years of Hope, Days of Rage,* rev. ed. (1993). For a focused study, see James T. Patterson's *The Eve of Destruction: How 1965 Transformed America* (2013).

For insights into the black power movement, see Peniel E. Joseph's *Stokely: A Life* (2014), and Joshua Bloom and Waldo E. Martin, Jr.'s *Black against Empire: The History and Politics of the Black Panther Party* (2013).

Two influential assessments of the counterculture by sympathetic commentators are Theodore Roszak's *The Making of a Counter-Culture: Reflections on the Technocratic Society and Its Youthful Opposition* (1969) and Charles A. Reich's *The Greening of America: How the Youth Revolution Is Trying to Make America Livable* (1970). A good scholarly analysis that takes the hippies seriously is Timothy Miller's *The Hippies and American Values* (1991).

The best study of the women's liberation movement is Ruth Rosen's *The World Split Open: How the Modern Women's Movement Changed America,* rev. ed. (2006). The organizing efforts of Cesar Chavez are detailed in Ronald B. Taylor's *Chavez and the Farm Workers* (1975). The struggles of Native Americans for recognition and power are sympathetically described in Stan Steiner's *The New Indians* (1968).

The best overview of the 1970s and 1980s is James T. Patterson's *Restless Giant: The United States from Watergate to Bush v. Gore* (2005). On Nixon, see Melvin Small's thorough analysis in *The Presidency of Richard Nixon* (1999). A good slim biography is Elizabeth Drew's *Richard M. Nixon* (2007). For an overview of the Watergate scandal, see Stanley I. Kutler's *The Wars of Watergate: The Last Crisis of Richard Nixon* (1990). For the way the Republicans handled foreign affairs, consult

Tad Szulc's *The Illusion of Peace: Foreign Policy in the Nixon Years* (1978). The Nixon White House tapes make for fascinating reading. See *The Nixon Tapes* (2014), ed. by Douglas Brinkley and Luke Nichter. Rick Perlstein traces the effects of Nixon's career on the Republican party and the conservative movement in two compelling books: *Nixonland: The Rise of a President and the Fracturing of America* (2007) and *The Invisible Bridge: The Fall of Nixon and the Rise of Reagan* (2014).

The Communist takeover of Vietnam and the end of American involvement there are traced in Larry Berman's *No Peace, No Honor: Nixon, Kissinger, and Betrayal in Vietnam* (2001). William Shawcross's *Sideshow: Kissinger, Nixon and the Destruction of Cambodia*, rev. ed. (2002), deals with the broadening of the war, while Larry Berman's *Planning a Tragedy: The Americanization of the War in Vietnam* (1982) assesses the final impact of U.S. involvement. The most comprehensive treatment of the anti-war movement is Tom Wells's *The War Within: America's Battle over Vietnam* (1994).

A comprehensive treatment of the Ford administration is contained in John Robert Greene's *The Presidency of Gerald R. Ford* (1995). The best overview of the Carter administration is Burton I. Kaufman's *The Presidency of James Earl Carter, Jr.,* 2nd rev. ed. (2006). A work more sympathetic to the Carter administration is John Dumbrell's *The Carter Presidency: A Re-evaluation,* 2nd ed. (1995). Gaddis Smith's *Morality, Reason, and Power: American Diplomacy in the Carter Years* (1986) provides an overview. Background on how the Middle East came to dominate much of American policy is found in William B. Quandt's *Decade of Decisions: American Policy toward the Arab-Israeli Conflict, 1967–1976* (1977). For a biography of Carter, see Randall Balmer, *Redeemer: The Life of Jimmy Carter* (2014).

Chapter 29

The rise of modern political conservatism is well told in Patrick Allitt's *The Conservatives: Ideas and Personalities throughout American History* (2009) and Michael Schaller's *Right Turn: American Life in the Reagan-Bush Era, 1980-1992* (2007).

On Reagan, see John Patrick Diggins's *Ronald Reagan: Fate, Freedom, and the Making of History* (2007), Richard Reeves's *President Reagan: The Triumph of Imagination* (2005), and Sean Wilentz's *The Age of Reagan: A History, 1974–2008* (2008). The best political analysis is Robert M. Collins's *Transforming America: Politics and Culture during the Reagan Years* (2007). For insights into the 1980 election, see Andrew E. Busch's *Reagan's Victory: The Presidential Election of 1980 and the Rise of the Right* (2005). On Reaganomics, see David A. Stockman's *The Triumph of Politics: Why the Reagan Revolution Failed* (1986).

For Reagan's foreign policy in Central America, see James Chace's *Endless War: How We Got Involved in Central America—and What Can Be Done* (1984) and Walter LaFeber's *Inevitable Revolutions: The United States in Central America*, 2nd ed. (1993). On Reagan's second term, see Jane Mayer and Doyle McManus's *Landslide: The Unmaking of the President, 1984–1988* (1988). For a masterly work on the Iran-Contra affair, see Theodore Draper's *A Very Thin Line: The Iran Contra Affairs* (1991). Several collections of essays include varying assessments of the Reagan years. Among these are *The Reagan Revolution?* (1988), edited by B. B. Kymlicka and Jean V. Matthews; *The Reagan Presidency: An Incomplete Revolution?* (1990), edited by Dilys M. Hill, Raymond A. Moore, and Phil Williams, and *Looking Back on the Reagan Presidency* (1990), edited by Larry Berman.

The 41st president is the focus of Timothy Naftali's *George H. W. Bush* (2007). On the 1988 campaign, see Sidney Blumenthal's *Pledging Allegiance: The Last Campaign of the Cold War* (1990). For a social history of the decade, see John Ehrman's

The Eighties: America in the Age of Reagan (2005). On the Persian Gulf conflict, see Lester H. Brune's *America and the Iraqi Crisis, 1990–1992: Origins and Aftermath* (1993).

Chapter 30

Analysis of the Clinton years can be found in Joe Klein's *The Natural: The Misunderstood Presidency of Bill Clinton* (2002). Clinton's impeachment is assessed in Richard A. Posner's *An Affair of State: The Investigation, Impeachment, and Trial of President Clinton* (1999). The conflict between Clinton and Gingrich is explained in Elizabeth Drew's *The Struggle between Gingrich and the Clinton White House* (1996).

On changing demographic trends, see Sam Roberts's *Who We Are Now: The Changing Face of America in the Twenty-First Century* (2004). For a textured account of the exploding Latino culture, see Roberto Suro's *Strangers among Us: How Latino Immigration Is Transforming America* (1998). On social and cultural life in the 1990s, see Haynes Johnson's *The Best of Times: America in the Clinton Years* (2001). Economic and technological changes are assessed in Daniel T. Rogers's *Age of Fracture* (2011). The onset and growth of the AIDS epidemic are traced in *And the Band Played On: Politics, People, and the AIDS Epidemic,* 20th anniversary ed. (2007), by Randy Shilts.

On the religious right, see George M. Marsden's *Understanding Fundamentalism and Evangelicalism,* new ed. (2006) and Ralph E. Reed's *Politically Incorrect: The Emerging Faith Factor in American Politics* (1994).

On the invention of the computer and the Internet, see Paul E. Ceruzzi's *A History of Modern Computing,* 2nd ed. (2003), Janet Abbate's *Inventing the Internet* (1999), and Michael Lewis, *The New New Thing: A Silicon Valley Story* (1999). The booming economy of the 1990s is well analyzed in Joseph E. Stiglitz's *The Roaring Nineties: A New History of the World's Most Prosperous Decade* (2003).

For further treatment of the end of the cold war, see Michael R. Beschloss and Strobe Talbott's *At the Highest Levels: The Inside Story of the End of the Cold War* (1993) and Richard Crockatt's *The Fifty Years War: The United States and the Soviet Union in World Politics, 1941–1991* (1995).

On the transformation of American foreign policy, see James Mann's *Rise of the Vulcans: The History of Bush's War Cabinet* (2004), Claes G. Ryn's *America the Virtuous: The Crisis of Democracy and the Quest for Empire* (2003), and Stephen M. Walt's *Taming American Power: The Global Response to U.S. Primacy* (2005).

The disputed 2000 presidential election is the focus of Jeffrey Toobin's *Too Close to Call: The Thirty-Six-Day Battle to Decide the 2000 Election* (2001). On the Bush presidency, see *The Presidency of George W. Bush: A First Historical Assessment,* edited by Julian E. Zelizer (2010). See also Fred H. Israel and Jonathan Mann's *The Election of 2000 and the Administration of George W. Bush* (2003). Also see Dick Cheney's illuminating, if self-serving, account of his service as Bush's vice president in *In My Time: A Personal and Political Memoir* (2011).

On the attacks of September 11, 2001, and their aftermath, see *The Age of Terror: America and the World after September 11,* edited by Strobe Talbott and Nayan Chanda (2001). For a devastating account of the Bush administration by a White House insider, see Scott McClellan's *What Happened: Inside the Bush White House and Washington's Culture of Deception* (2008). On the historic 2008 election, see Michael Nelson's *The Elections of 2008* (2009). The best biography of Obama is David Maraniss's *Barack Obama: The Story* (2012). A conservative critique is provided in Edward Klein's *The Amateur: Barack Obama in the White House* (2012).

The Great Recession is explained in Alan S. Blinder's *After the Music Stopped: The Financial Crisis, the Response, and the Work Ahead* (2013). The Tea Party movement is assessed in Theda Skocpol and Vanessa Williamson's *The Tea Party and the Remaking of Republican Conservatism* (2012) and Elizabeth Price Foley's *The Tea Party: Three Principles* (2012). The partisan gridlock in Congress is the focus of Thomas E. Mann and Norman J. Ornstein's *The Broken Branch: How Congress Is Failing America and How to Get it Back on Track* (2012). The tension between the conservative majority on the U.S. Supreme Court and the Obama administration is examined in Jeffrey Toobin's *The Oath: The Obama White Hosue and the Supreme Court* (2012). On the growing economic inequality in America, see Joseph Stiglitz's *The Price of Inequality: How Today's Divided Society Endangers Our Future* (2013).

Credits

Text Credits

Richard Breitman and Allan J. Lichtman: Excerpts reprinted by permission of the publisher from *FDR and the Jews* by Richard Breitman and Allan J. Lichtman, pp. 2, 6-7, Cambridge, Mass.: Harvard University Press, Copyright © 2013 by Richard Breitman and Allan J. Lichtman.

Leo Chavez: Excerpts from *The Latno Threat: Constructing Immigrants, Citizens, and the Nation, Second Edition,* by Leo Chavez. Copyright © 2008, 2014 By the Board of Trustees of the Leland Stanford Jr. University. All rights reserved. With the permission of Stanford University Press, www.sup.org

Paul Finkelman: Excerpts from "Jefferson and Slavery," in *Jeffersonian Legacies,* edited by Peter S. Onuf. pp. 181-183, 210-211. © 1993 by the Rector and Visitors of the University of Virginia. Reprinted by permission of the University of Virginia Press.

Nathan Glazer & Daniel Moynihan: From *Beyond The Melting Pot,* excerpts from pp. 12 - 14, 20, © 1963 Massachusetts Institute of Technology, used by permission of The MIT Press.

Gary B. Nash: Excerpts from "Social Change and the Growth of Prerevolutionary Urban Radicalism," by Gary B. Nash. From *The American Revolution: Explorations in History of American Radicalism,* by Alfred F. Young (ed.). Copyright © 1976 by Northern Illinois University Press. Used with permission of Northern Illinois University Press.

Jason Richwine: "The Congealing Pot," by Jason Richwine from National Review, August 24, 2009. © 2009 by National Review, Inc. Reprinted by permission.

Douglas L. Wilson: Excerpts from "Thomas Jefferson and the Character Issue," by Douglas L. Wilson. Originally published in *The Atlantic Monthly,* November 1992. Used by permission the author.

Image Credits

Chapter 15: p. 522: Smithsonian American Art Museum, Washington, DC/Art Resource; **p. 525:** The Granger Collection; **p. 527:** Library of Congress; **p. 528:** Bettmann/Corbis; **p. 529:** Library of Congress; **p. 531:** Library of Congress; **p. 533:** Library of Congress; **p. 536:** Library of Congress; **p. 537:** Bettmann/Corbis; **p. 538:** The Granger Collection; **p. 539:** The Granger Collection; **p. 541:** Library of Congress.

Chapter 16: p. 558: Library of Congress; **p. 558:** Wikimedia Commons; **p. 558:** Library of Congress: **p. 558:** Bridgeman Art Library; **p. 558:** Library of Congress; **pp. 560 & 561:** Wikimedia Commons; **p. 560:** Union Pacific Museum; **p. 561 (top):** Corbis; **p. 561 (bottom):** Corbis; **p. 562:** The Granger Collection; **p. 566:** The Granger Collection; **p. 568 (top):** Bettmann/CORBIS; **p. 568 (bottom):** Union Pacific Museum; **p. 571:** Wikimedia Commons;

p. 573: American Petroleum Institute Historical Photo Collection; **p. 574:** Library of Congress; **p. 575:** Library of Congress; **p. 577:** Carnegie Library of Pittsburgh; **p. 578:** Bridgeman Art Library; **p. 580:** Special Collections, Vassar College Libraries; **p. 582:** Wikimedia Commons; **p. 583:** New York Public Library; **p. 584:** Bettmann/Corbis; **p. 586:** Bridgeman Art Library; **p. 588:** T.V. Powderly Photographic Collection, The American Catholic History Research Center University Archives, The Catholic University of America, Washington, D.C.; **p. 589:** Bettmann/Corbis; **p. 593:** Walter **p. 594:** Reuther Library, Wayne State University; **p. 596:** Library of Congress.

Chapter 17: p. 600: The Granger Collection; **p. 604:** New York Public Library; **p. 606:** Library of Congress; **p. 611:** Corbis; **p. 612:** Corbis; **p. 613 (top):** Library of Congress; **p. 613 (bottom):** Library of Congress; **p. 617:** Kansas State Historical Society; **p. 619:** Bettmann/Corbis; **p. 621:** Corbis; **p. 625:** Kansas State Historical Society; **p. 627 (top):** Library of Congress; **p. 627 (bottom):** Corbis; **p. 628:** Library of Congress.

Chapter 18: p. 636: Bridgeman Art Library; **p. 641:** Library of Congress; **p. 643:** William Williams Papers, Manuscripts and Archives Division, The New York Public Library, Astor, Lenox and Tilden Foundations, Art Resource; **p. 645:** The Granger Collection; **p. 646:** Bettmann/CORBIS; **p. 648:** American Museum of Natural History; **p. 651:** Bridgeman Art Library; **p. 653:** Library of Congress; **p. 659:** Bettmann/Corbis; **p. 662:** Bettmann/Corbis; **p. 663:** Library of Congress; **p. 669:** Corbis; **p. 672 (top):** Corbis; **p. 672 (bottom):** Corbis.

Chapter 19: p. 676: Frederic Remington Art Museum; **p. 680:** The Granger Collection; **p. 681:** Corbis; **p. 683:** Wikimedia Commons; **p. 685 (top):** Corbis; **p. 685 (bottom):** Corbis; **p. 688:** The Granger Collection; **p. 691:** Corporal George J. Vennage c/o Ohio State University Rare Books and Manuscripts Library; **p. 694:** Bettmann/Corbis; **p. 699:** The Granger Collection; **p. 701:** Corbis; **p. 704:** The Granger Collection.

Chapter 20: p. 712: Getty Images; **p. 712:** Bettmann/Corbis; **p. 712:** The Granger Collection; **p. 712:** Art Resource; **p. 712:** Corbis; **pp. 714 & 715:** Getty Images; **p. 714:** From the Collections of The Henry Ford Museum; **p. 716:** The Granger Collection; **p. 721:** The Granger Collection; **p. 725:** Library of Congress; **p. 729:** Wikimedia Commons; **p. 731:** Corbis; **p. 732:** Library of Congress; **p. 733:** Library of Congress; **p. 735:** Library of Congress; **p. 737:** NYPL Digital Collection: **p. 739:** Art Resource; **p. 740:** The Granger Collection; **p. 743:** Donald C. & Elizabeth M. Dickinson Research Center, National Cowboy & Western Heritage Museum; **p. 744:** Library of Congress; **p. 750:** Corbis; **p. 751:** The Granger Collection.

Chapter 21: p. 758: Library of Congress; **p. 763:** Getty Images; **p. 765:** The Granger Collection; **p. 770:** Library of Congress; **p. 771:** Corbis; **p. 772:** Library of Congress; **p. 773:** Library of Congress; **p. 774:** Corbis; **p. 775:** Getty Images; **p. 777:** Wikimedia

Index

Page numbers in *italics* refer to illustrations.